Microsoft Visual Basic 5.0
Reference Library

Microsoft®
Visual Basic® 5.0
Language Reference

D1122132

Microsoft Press

PUBLISHED BY
Microsoft Press
A Division of Microsoft Corporation
One Microsoft Way
Redmond, Washington 98052-6399

Library of Congress Cataloging-in-Publication Data
Microsoft Visual Basic 5.0 Language Reference
      p.   cm.
   ISBN 1-57231-507-5
   1. Microsoft Visual Basic.   2. BASIC (Computer program language).
  I. Microsoft Corporation.
  QA76.73.B3M557   1997
  005.26'8--dc21   97-3524
                                               CIP

Printed and bound in the United States of America.

1 2 3 4 5 6 7 8 9 QMQM 2 1 0 9 8 7

Distributed to the book trade in Canada by Macmillan of Canada, a division of Canada Publishing Corporation.

A CIP catalogue record for this book is available from the British Library.

Microsoft Press books are available through booksellers and distributors worldwide. For further information about international editions, contact your local Microsoft Corporation office. Or contact Microsoft Press International directly at fax (206) 936-7329.

Acquisitions Editor: Eric Stroo
Project Editor: Maureen Williams Zimmerman

Contents

Introduction

This guide is an alphabetic reference for the Visual Basic Programming System. The guide includes an A—Z reference listing objects, functions, statements, methods, properties, and events for the Visual Basic language. Several appendixes provide information on the ANSI character set, data types, operators, and derived math functions.

The information in this guide is the best available at the time of publication and is essentially identical to the information contained in the Visual Basic online Help. In some cases, more up-to-date or complete information may be available in online Help.

Document Conventions

Visual Basic documentation uses the following typographic conventions.

Convention	Description
Sub, **If**, **ChDir**, **Print**, **True**, **Debug**	Words in bold with initial letter capitalized indicate language-specific keywords.
setup	Words you are instructed to type appear in bold.
object, *varname*, *arglist*	Italic, lowercase letters indicate placeholders for information you supply.
pathname, ***filenumber***	Bold, italic, and lowercase letters indicate placeholders for arguments where you can use either positional or named-argument syntax.
[*expressionlist*]	In syntax, items inside brackets are optional.
{**While** | **Until**}	In syntax, braces and a vertical bar indicate a mandatory choice between two or more items. You must choose one of the items unless all of the items are also enclosed in brackets. For example:
	[{**This** | **OrThat**}]
ESC, ENTER	Words in small capital letters indicate key names and key sequences.
ALT+F1, CTRL+R	A plus sign (+) between key names indicates a combination of keys. For example, ALT+F1 means hold down the ALT key while pressing the F1 key.

Code Conventions

The following code conventions are used:

Sample Code	Description
`MyString = "Hello, world!"`	This font is used for code, variables, and error message text.
`' This is a comment.`	An apostrophe (') introduces code comments.

`MyVar = "This is an " _`
`& "example" _`
`& " of how to continue code."`
	A space and an underscore (_) continue a line of code.

A-Z Reference

& Operator

Used to force string concatenation of two expressions.

Syntax

result = expression1 **&** *expression2*

The **&** operator syntax has these parts:

Part	Description
result	Required; any **String** or **Variant** variable.
expression1	Required; any expression.
expression2	Required; any expression.

Remarks

If an *expression* is not a string, it is converted to a **String** variant. The data type of *result* is **String** if both expressions are string expressions; otherwise, *result* is a **String** variant. If both expressions are **Null**, *result* is **Null**. However, if only one *expression* is **Null**, that expression is treated as a zero-length string ("") when concatenated with the other expression. Any expression that is **Empty** is also treated as a zero-length string.

See Also

Operator Summary, **Operator** Precedence, **Concatenation** Operators

Example

This example uses the **&** operator to force string concatenation.

```
Dim MyStr
MyStr = "Hello" & " World"          ' Returns "Hello World".
MyStr = "Check " & 123 & " Check"   ' Returns "Check 123 Check".
```

- Operator

Used to find the difference between two numbers or to indicate the negative value of a numeric expression.

Syntax 1

result = number1–number2

Syntax 2

–number

The – operator syntax has these parts:

Part	Description
result	Required; any numeric variable.
number	Required; any numeric expression.
number1	Required; any numeric expression.
number2	Required; any numeric expression.

Remarks

In Syntax 1, the – operator is the arithmetic subtraction operator used to find the difference between two numbers. In Syntax 2, the – operator is used as the unary negation operator to indicate the negative value of an expression.

The data type of *result* is usually the same as that of the most precise expression. The order of precision, from least to most precise, is **Byte**, **Integer**, **Long**, **Single**, **Double**, **Currency**, and **Decimal**. The following are exceptions to this order:

If	Then *result* is
Subtraction involves a **Single** and a **Long**,	converted to a **Double**.
The data type of *result* is a **Long**, **Single**, or **Date** variant that overflows its legal range,	converted to a **Variant** containing a **Double**.
The data type of *result* is a **Byte** variant that overflows its legal range,	converted to an **Integer** variant.
The data type of *result* is an **Integer** variant that overflows its legal range,	converted to a **Long** variant.
Subtraction involves a **Date** and any other data type,	a **Date**.
Subtraction involves two **Date** expressions,	a **Double**.

Note The order of precision used by addition and subtraction is not the same as the order of precision used by multiplication.

One or both expressions are **Null** expressions, *result* is **Null**. If an expression is **Empty**, it is treated as 0.

See Also

Operator Summary, **Operator** Precedence, **Arithmetic** Operators

Example

This example uses the–operator to calculate the difference between two numbers.

```
Dim MyResult
MyResult = 4 - 2            ' Returns 2.
MyResult = 459.35 - 334.90 ' Returns 124.45.
```

* Operator

Used to multiply two numbers.

Syntax

result = *number1**number2

The * operator syntax has these parts:

Part	Description
result	Required; any numeric variable.
number1	Required; any numeric expression.
number2	Required; any numeric expression.

Remarks

The data type of *result* is usually the same as that of the most precise expression. The order of precision, from least to most precise, is **Byte**, **Integer**, **Long**, **Single**, **Currency**, **Double**, and **Decimal**. The following are exceptions to this order:

If	Then *result* is
Multiplication involves a **Single** and a **Long**,	converted to a **Double**.
The data type of *result* is a **Long**, **Single**, or **Date** variant that overflows its legal range,	converted to a **Variant** containing a **Double**.
The data type of *result* is a **Byte** variant that overflows its legal range,	converted to an **Integer** variant.
the data type of *result* is an **Integer** variant that overflows its legal range,	converted to a **Long** variant.

If one or both expressions are **Null** expressions, *result* is **Null**. If an expression is **Empty**, it is treated as 0.

Note The order of precision used by multiplication is not the same as the order of precision used by addition and subtraction.

See Also

Operator Summary, **Operator** Precedence, **Arithmetic** Operators

Example

This example uses the * operator to multiply two numbers.

```
Dim MyValue
MyValue = 2 * 2' Returns 4.
MyValue = 459.35 * 334.90   ' Returns 153836.315.
```

/ Operator

Used to divide two numbers and return a floating-point result.

Syntax

result = number1/number2

The / operator syntax has these parts:

Part	Description
result	Required; any numeric variable.
number1	Required; any numeric expression.
number2	Required; any numeric expression.

Remarks

The data type of *result* is usually a **Double** or a **Double** variant. The following are exceptions to this rule:

If	Then *result* is
Both expressions are **Byte**, **Integer**, or **Single** expressions,	a **Single** unless it overflows its legal range; in which case, an error occurs.
Both expressions are **Byte**, **Integer**, or **Single** variants,	a **Single** variant unless it overflows its legal range; in which case, *result* is a **Variant** containing a **Double**.
Division involves a **Decimal** and any other data type,	a **Decimal** data type.

One or both expressions are **Null** expressions, *result* is **Null**. Any expression that is **Empty** is treated as 0.

See Also

Operator Summary, **Operator** Precedence, **Arithmetic** Operators

Example

This example uses the / operator to perform floating-point division.

```
Dim MyValue
MyValue = 10 / 4   ' Returns 2.5.
MyValue = 10 / 3   ' Returns 3.333333.
```

\ Operator

Used to divide two numbers and return an integer result.

Syntax

result = number1\number2

The \ operator syntax has these parts:

Part	Description
result	Required; any numeric variable.
number1	Required; any numeric expression.
number2	Required; any numeric expression.

Remarks

Before division is performed, the numeric expressions are rounded to **Byte**, **Integer**, or **Long** expressions.

Usually, the data type of *result* is a **Byte**, **Byte** variant, **Integer**, **Integer** variant, **Long**, or **Long** variant, regardless of whether *result* is a whole number. Any fractional portion is truncated. However, if any expression is **Null**, *result* is **Null**. Any expression that is **Empty** is treated as 0.

See Also

Operator Summary, **Operator** Precedence, **Arithmetic** Operators

Example

This example uses the \ operator to perform integer division.

```
Dim MyValue
MyValue = 11 \ 4      ' Returns 2.
MyValue = 9 \ 3       ' Returns 3.
MyValue = 100 \ 3     ' Returns 33.
```

^ Operator

Used to raise a number to the power of an exponent.

Syntax

result = number^exponent

The ^ operator syntax has these parts:

Part	Description
result	Required; any numeric variable.
number	Required; any numeric expression.
exponent	Required; any numeric expression.

Remarks

A *number* can be negative only if *exponent* is an integer value. When more than one exponentiation is performed in a single expression, the ^ operator is evaluated as it is encountered from left to right.

Usually, the data type of *result* is a **Double** or a **Variant** containing a **Double**. However, if either *number* or *exponent* is a **Null** expression, *result* is **Null**.

See Also

Operator Summary, **Operator** Precedence, **Arithmetic** Operators

Example

This example uses the ^ operator to raise a number to the power of an exponent.

```
Dim MyValue
MyValue = 2 ^ 2' Returns 4.
MyValue = 3 ^ 3 ^ 3  ' Returns 19683.
MyValue = (-5) ^ 3' Returns -125.
```

+ Operator

Used to sum two numbers.

Syntax

result = expression1+expression2

The + operator syntax has these parts:

Part	Description
result	Required; any numeric variable.
expression1	Required; any expression.
expression2	Required; any expression.

Remarks

When you use the + operator, you may not be able to determine whether addition or string concatenation will occur. Use the **&** operator for concatenation to eliminate ambiguity and provide self-documenting code.

If at least one expression is not a **Variant**, the following rules apply:

If	Then
Both expressions are numeric data types (**Byte**, **Boolean**, **Integer**, **Long**, **Single**, **Double**, **Date**, **Currency**, or **Decimal**)	Add.
Both expressions are **String**	Concatenate.
One expression is a numeric data type and the other is any **Variant** except **Null**	Add.

(continued)

If	Then
One expression is a **String** and the other is any **Variant** except **Null**	Concatenate.
One expression is an **Empty Variant**	Return the remaining expression unchanged as *result*.
One expression is a numeric data type and the other is a **String**	A `Type mismatch` error occurs.
Either expression is **Null**	*result* is **Null**.

If both expressions are **Variant** expressions, the following rules apply:

If	Then
Both **Variant** expressions are numeric	Add.
Both **Variant** expressions are strings	Concatenate.
One **Variant** expression is numeric and the other is a string	Add.

For simple arithmetic addition involving only expressions of numeric data types, the data type of *result* is usually the same as that of the most precise expression. The order of precision, from least to most precise, is **Byte**, **Integer**, **Long**, **Single**, **Double**, **Currency**, and **Decimal**. The following are exceptions to this order:

If	Then *result* is
A **Single** and a **Long** are added,	a **Double**.
The data type of *result* is a **Long**, **Single**, or **Date** variant that overflows its legal range,	converted to a **Double** variant.
The data type of *result* is a **Byte** variant that overflows its legal range,	converted to an **Integer** variant.
The data type of *result* is an **Integer** variant that overflows its legal range,	converted to a **Long** variant.
A **Date** is added to any data type,	a **Date**.

If one or both expressions are **Null** expressions, *result* is **Null**. If both expressions are **Empty**, *result* is an **Integer**. However, if only one expression is **Empty**, the other expression is returned unchanged as *result*.

Note The order of precision used by addition and subtraction is not the same as the order of precision used by multiplication.

See Also

Operator Summary, **Operator** Precedence, **Arithmetic** Operators, **Concatenation** Operators

Example

This example uses the **+** operator to sum numbers. The **+** operator can also be used to concatenate strings. However, to eliminate ambiguity, you should use the **&** operator instead. If the components of an expression created with the **+** operator include both strings and numerics, the arithmetic result is assigned. If the components are exclusively strings, the strings are concatenated.

```
Dim MyNumber, Var1, Var2
MyNumber = 2 + 2   ' Returns 4.
MyNumber = 4257.04 + 98112 ' Returns 102369.04.

Var1 = "34": Var2 = 6' Initialize mixed variables.
MyNumber = Var1 + Var2   ' Returns 40.

Var1 = "34": Var2 = "6" ' Initialize variables with strings.
MyNumber = Var1 + Var2   ' Returns "346" (string concatenation).
```

AboutBox Method

Displays the **About** box for the control.

Applies To

DBGrid Control, **MSChart** Control

Syntax

object.**AboutBox**

The *object* placeholder represents an object expression that evaluates to an object in the **Applies To** list.

Remarks

This is the same as clicking **About** in the **Properties** window.

Abs Function

Returns a value of the same type that is passed to it specifying the absolute value of a number.

Syntax

Abs(*number*)

The required *number* argument can be any valid numeric expression. If *number* contains **Null**, **Null** is returned; if it is an uninitialized variable, zero is returned.

Remarks

The absolute value of a number is its unsigned magnitude. For example, ABS(-1) and ABS(1) both return 1.

See Also

> **Math** Functions, **Sgn** Function

Example

> This example uses the **Abs** function to compute the absolute value of a number.

```
Dim MyNumber
MyNumber = Abs(50.3) ' Returns 50.3.
MyNumber = Abs(-50.3)' Returns 50.3.
```

AbsolutePosition Property

> Sets or returns the relative record number of a **Recordset** object's current record.

Applies To

> **Dynaset-Type Recordset** Object, **Recordset** Object, **Snapshot-Type Recordset** Object, **Dynamic-Type Recordset** Object

Settings and Return Values

> The setting or return value is a **Long** integer from 0 to one less than the number of records in the **Recordset** object. It corresponds to the ordinal position of the current record in the **Recordset** object specified by the object.

Remarks

> You can use the **AbsolutePosition** property to position the current record pointer to a specific record based on its ordinal position in a dynaset- or snapshot-type **Recordset** object. You can also determine the current record number by checking the **AbsolutePosition** property setting.

> Because the **AbsolutePosition** property value is zero-based (that is, a setting of 0 refers to the first record in the **Recordset** object), you cannot set it to a value greater than or equal to the number of populated records; doing so causes a trappable error. You can determine the number of populated records in the **Recordset** object by checking the **RecordCount** property setting. The maximum allowable setting for the **AbsolutePosition** property is the value of the **RecordCount** property minus 1.

> If there is no current record, as when there are no records in the **Recordset** object, **AbsolutePosition** returns −1. If the current record is deleted, the **AbsolutePosition** property value isn't defined, and a trappable error occurs if it's referenced. New records are added to the end of the sequence.

> You shouldn't use this property as a surrogate record number. Bookmarks are still the recommended way of retaining and returning to a given position and are the only way to position the current record across all types of **Recordset** objects. In particular, the position of a record changes when one or more records preceding it are deleted. There is also no assurance that a record will have the same absolute position if the

Recordset object is re-created again because the order of individual records within a **Recordset** object isn't guaranteed unless it's created with an SQL statement by using an ORDER BY clause.

Notes

- Setting the **AbsolutePosition** property to a value greater than zero on a newly opened but unpopulated **Recordset** object causes a trappable error. Populate the **Recordset** object first with the **MoveLast** method.

- The **AbsolutePosition** property isn't available on forward-only – type **Recordset** objects, or on **Recordset** objects opened from pass-through queries against Microsoft Jet-connected ODBC databases.

See Also

PercentPosition Property, **RecordCount** Property

Example

This example uses the **AbsolutePosition** property to track the progress of a loop that enumerates all the records of a **Recordset**.

```
Sub AbsolutePositionX()

    Dim dbsNorthwind As Database
    Dim rstEmployees As Recordset
    Dim strMessage As String

    Set dbsNorthwind = OpenDatabase("Northwind.mdb")
    ' AbsolutePosition only works with dynasets or snapshots.
    Set rstEmployees = _
        dbsNorthwind.OpenRecordset("Employees", _
        dbOpenSnapshot)

    With rstEmployees
        ' Populate Recordset.
        .MoveLast
        .MoveFirst

        ' Enumerate Recordset.
        Do While Not .EOF
            ' Display current record information. Add 1 to
            ' AbsolutePosition value because it is zero-based.
            strMessage = "Employee: " & !LastName & vbCr & _
                "(record " & (.AbsolutePosition + 1) & _
                " of " & .RecordCount & ")"
            If MsgBox(strMessage, vbOKCancel) = vbCancel _
                Then Exit Do
            .MoveNext
        Loop

        .Close
    End With

    dbsNorthwind.Close

End Sub
```

AbsolutePosition Property (Remote Data)

Returns or sets the absolute row number of an **rdoResultset** object's current row.

Applies To

rdoResultset Object

Syntax

object.**AbsolutePosition** [= *value*]

The **AbsolutePosition** property syntax has these parts:

Part	Description
object	An object expression that evaluates to an object in the **Applies To** list.
value	A **Long Data Type** value from -1 to the maximum number of rows in the **rdoResultset**. Corresponds to the ordinal position of the current row in the **rdoResultset** specified by *object*. Default value is -1.

Remarks

Use the **AbsolutePosition** property to position the current row pointer to a specific row based on its ordinal position in a keyset-, or static-type **rdoResultset**. It is *not* supported for dynamic or forward-only-type **rdoResultset** objects. While a value is returned for a dynamic cursor, the value is not necessarily accurate. Generally, the **rdoResultset** object's **Bookmarkable** property must be **True** before **AbsolutePosition** values are supported.

You can also determine the current row number by checking the **AbsolutePosition** property setting. For example, if you have populated 10 rows of a 50 row **rdoResultset**, the **AbsolutePosition** property returns 10. After you execute a **MoveLast** method against the result set, **AbsolutePosition** returns 50. You can then set the **AbsolutePosition** property to any value between 1 and 50 to position the current row pointer to that row.

The **AbsolutePosition** property value is -1 based thus a setting of 1 refers to the first row in the **rdoResultset**. Setting a value greater than the number of *populated* rows causes RDO to position to the last row in the result set (EOF).

If there is no current row, as when there are no rows in the **rdoResultset**, -1 is returned. If the current row is deleted, the **AbsolutePosition** property value isn't defined and a trappable error occurs if it is referenced. New rows are added to the end of the sequence if the type of cursor includes dynamic membership.

Note This property isn't intended to be used as a surrogate row number. Using bookmarks is still the recommended way of retaining and returning to a given position in a cursor. Also, there is no assurance that a given row will have the same absolute position if the **rdoResultset** is re-created because the order and membership of individual rows within an **rdoResultset** can vary between executions.

See Also

Move Method (Remote Data), **MoveFirst**, **MoveLast**, **MoveNext**, **MovePrevious** Methods (Remote Data), **rdoResultset** Object, **Bookmark** Property (Remote Data), **PercentPosition** Property (Remote Data), **RowCount** Property (Remote Data)

Example

The following example uses the SQL Server Pubs database to illustrate use of the **AbsolutePosition** property as a secondary letter index to a set of rows. The program begins by fetching the name and ID of all publishers into a dropdown **ComboBox** control. Initially, and as a specific publisher is chosen from the **ComboBox**, the set of titles for this publisher is fetched from the Titles table. This is accomplished by creating a query using the concatenation method and setting the **RemoteData** control's SQL property to this query. A **DBGrid** control is bound to the **RemoteData** control, so it reflects the current set of titles based on the publisher chosen. In the process of populating the result set, the first letter of each title is placed in an array along with the **AbsolutePosition** value for the row. When a letter is chosen and the **MoveToRow** button is clicked, the **RemoteData** control's **AbsolutePosition** property is set to the value associated with the letter.

```
Dim cn As rdoConnection
Dim en As rdoEnvironment
Dim rs As rdoResultset
Dim LetterIndex() As Long

Private Sub Form_Load()
Dim Li As Integer
'
'    Open the connection. This is a DSN-less Connection
'
Set en = rdoEnvironments(0)
Set cn = en.OpenConnection(dsName:="", _
    Prompt:=rdDriverNoPrompt, _
    Connect:="uid=;pwd=;driver={SQL Server};" _
       & "server=SEQUEL;database=pubs;")

MsRdc1.Connect = cn.Connect

'
'    Fill Publishers list combo box.
'
Set rs = cn.OpenResultset _
    ("Select distinct Pub_Name, Pub_ID" _
    & " from Publishers", _
    rdOpenStatic, rdConcurReadOnly)
Do Until rs.EOF
    If rs(0) = Null Then
    Else
       PubList.AddItem " " _
          & rs!Pub_ID & ":" & rs!Pub_Name
    End If
```

```
      rs.MoveNext
Loop
PubList.ListIndex = 1
rs.Close

PubList_Click ' Make the first query

End Sub

Sub GetLetterIndexes()
'
'   Build an index array for the first
'   occurance of a letter in the list
'   of titles. Save an AbsolutePosition
'   for each letter.

ReDim LetterIndex(122) As Long
Screen.MousePointer = vbHourglass

Set rs = MsRdc1.Resultset
Do Until rs.EOF
    Li = Convert(Left$(rs!Title, 1))
    If LetterIndex(Li) = 0 Then
        LetterIndex(Li) = rs.AbsolutePosition
    End If
    rs.MoveNext
Loop

Screen.MousePointer = vbDefault
End Sub
'
'   Position the RemoteData control's
'   rdoResultset to the first row of the letter
'   chosen based on the AbsolutePosition
'
Private Sub MoveToRow_Click()
Dim i
i = Convert(LetterWanted)
If LetterIndex(i) > 0 Then
    MsRdc1.Resultset.AbsolutePosition = LetterIndex(i)
Else
    LetterWanted = "(Not Found)"
    Beep
    For i = i + 1 To Asc("z")
        If LetterIndex(i) > 0 Then
            MsRdc1.Resultset.AbsolutePosition = _
↪ LetterIndex(i)
            LetterWanted = Chr(i + 64)
            Exit For
        End If
    Next i
End If
End Sub
```

```
Private Function Convert(Li As String) As Integer
Dim i As Integer
i = Asc(Li) ' Only references first letter
Select Case i
    Case Is < 65: Convert = 0
    Case Is > 122: Convert = 58
    Case Else: Convert = i - 64
End Select
End Function
'
'   Fetch List of Titles for this
'   publisher
'
Private Sub PubList_Click()
Dim PubWanted As String
'   Pick off the PUB_ID
'
'   Build the SQL Query based on
'   publisher chosen
'
PubWanted = Trim(Left(PubList,
    InStr(PubList, ":") - 1))
Screen.MousePointer = vbHourglass

MsRdc1.SQL = "select * from Titles" _
    & " where Pub_ID = '" _
    & PubWanted & "'" _
    & " order by Title"
MsRdc1.Refresh
Screen.MousePointer = vbDefault
If MsRdc1.Resultset.EOF Then
    MoveToRow.Enabled = False
Else
    MoveToRow.Enabled = True
    GetLetterIndexes
    MsRdc1.Resultset.MoveFirst
End If
End Sub
```

AccessKeyPress Event

Occurs when the user of the control presses one of the control's access keys, or when the ENTER key is pressed when the developer has set the **Default** property to **True**, or when the ESCAPE key is pressed when the developer has set the **Cancel** property to **True**. The **Default** property and the **Cancel** property are enabled by the author of the control setting the **DefaultCancel** property to **True**.

Applies To

UserControl Object

Sub *object_***AccessKeyPress**(*KeyAscii* **As Integer**)

The **AccessKeyPress** event syntax has these parts:

Part	Description
object	An object expression that evaluates to an object in the **Applies To** list.
KeyAscii	An integer that contains the Ascii value of the key (without the ALT) that caused the AccessKeyPress event to fire, in the same manner as the standard KeyPress event.

See Also

DefaultCancel Property, **Cancel** Property, **Default** Property

AccessKeys Property

Returns or sets a string that contains the keys that will act as the access keys (or hot keys) for the control.

Applies To

UserControl Object

Syntax

*object.***AccessKeys** [= *AccessKeyString*]

The **AccessKeys** property syntax has these parts:

Part	Description
object	An object expression that evaluates to an object in the **Applies To** list.
AccessKeyString	A string containing the keys that will act as the access keys.

Remarks

The **AccessKeys** property is a string that contains all the access keys for the control. As an example, to set the letters S and Y as the access keys, the **AccessKeys** property would be set to "sy".

When a user presses one of the access keys in conjunction with the ALT key, the control will get the focus (depending on the setting of the **ForwardFocus** property).

Access keys for constituent controls are implicitly included as AccessKeys, although they will not appear in the **AccessKeys** property.

See Also

ForwardFocus Property

Action Property (OLE Container)

Sets a value that determines an action. Not available at design time.

Note The **Action** property is included for compatibility with earlier versions. For current functionality, use the methods listed in Settings.

Applies To

OLE Container Control

Syntax

object.**Action** = *value*

The **Action** property syntax has these parts:

Part	Description
object	An object expression that evaluates to an object in the **Applies To** list.
value	A constant or integer specifying the type of action, as described in Settings.

Settings

The settings for *value* are:

Value	Description	Current method
0	Creates an embedded object.	**CreateEmbed**
1	Creates a linked object from the contents of a file.	**CreateLink**
4	Copies the object to the system Clipboard.	**Copy**
5	Copies data from the system Clipboard to an **OLE** container control.	**Paste**
6	Retrieves the current data from the application that supplied the object and displays that data as a picture in the **OLE** container control.	**Update**
7	Opens an object for an operation, such as editing.	**DoVerb**
9	Closes an object and terminates the connection to the application that provided the object.	**Close**
10	Deletes the specified object and frees the memory associated with it.	**Delete**
11	Saves an object to a data file.	**SaveToFile**
12	Loads an object that was saved to a data file.	**ReadFromFile**
14	Displays the Insert Object dialog box.	**InsertObjDlg**
15	Displays the Paste Special dialog box.	**PasteSpecialDlg**
17	Updates the list of verbs an object supports.	**FetchVerbs**
18	Saves an object to the OLE version 1.0 file format.	**SaveToOle1File**

See Also

> **PasteSpecialDlg** Method, **Copy** Method, **CreateEmbed** Method, **CreateLink** Method, **Delete** Method (OLE Container), **InsertObjDlg** Method, **Paste** Method, **ReadFromFile** Method, **SaveToFile** Method, **DoVerb** Method, **FetchVerbs** Method, **Close** Method (OLE Container), **Update** Method (OLE Container), **SaveToOle1File** Method

Activate Method

> Causes the currently selected component in the project window to be activated as if it were double-clicked.

Applies To

> **VBComponent** Object

Syntax

> *object*.**Activate**

> The *object* placeholder represents an object expression that evaluates to an object in the **Applies To** list.

Activate, Deactivate Events

> The **Activate** event occurs when an object becomes the active window. The **Deactivate** event occurs when an object is no longer the active window.

Applies To

> **Form** Object, **Forms** Collection, **MDIForm** Object, **PropertyPage** Object

Syntax

> **Private Sub** *object*_**Activate**()
> **Private Sub** *object*_**Deactivate**()

> The *object* placeholder represents an object expression that evaluates to an object in the **Applies To** list.

Remarks

> An object can become active by using the **Show** method in code.

> The **Activate** event can occur only when an object is visible. A **UserForm** loaded with **Load** isn't visible unless you use the **Show** method.

> The **Activate** and **Deactivate** events occur only when you move the focus within an application. Moving the focus to or from an object in another application doesn't trigger either event.

> The **Deactivate** event doesn't occur when unloading an object.

See Also

GotFocus Event, **LostFocus** Event, **SetFocus** Method, **Show** Method, **Visible** Property

Example

This example updates the status bar text to display the caption of the active form. To try this example, create a **Form** object (Form1) and a new **MDIForm** object (MDIForm1). On MDIForm1, draw a **PictureBox** control containing a **Label** control. On Form1, set the **MDIChild** property to **True**. Paste the MDIForm_Load event procedure code into the Declarations section of the **MDIForm** object. Paste the Form_Activate event procedure code into the Declarations section of the MDI child form, and then press F5.

```
Private Sub MDIForm_Load ()
    Form1.Caption = "Form #1"          ' Set caption of Form1.
    Dim NewForm As New Form1          ' Create a new child form.
    Load NewForm
    NewForm.Caption = "Form #2"       ' Set caption of new form.
    NewForm.Show                      ' Display the new form.
End Sub

Private Sub Form_Activate ()
    ' Set status bar text.
    MDIForm1.Label1.Caption = "Current form: " & Me.Caption
End Sub
```

ActiveCodePane Property

Returns the active or last active **CodePane** object or sets the active **CodePane** object. Read/write.

Applies to

VBE Object

Remarks

You can set the **ActiveCodePane** property to any valid **CodePane** object, as shown in the following example:

```
Set MyApp.VBE.ActiveCodePane = MyApp.VBE.CodePanes(1)
```

The preceding example sets the first code pane in a collection of code panes to be the active code pane. You can also activate a code pane using the **Set** method.

See Also

CodePane Object, **CodePanes** Collection, **ActiveWindow** Property, **CodePaneView** Property

Example

The following example uses the **ActiveCodePane** property and **TopLine** properties to obtain the number of the top line in the active code pane.

```
Debug.Print Application.VBE.ActiveCodePane.TopLine
```

ActiveConnection Property

Returns or sets an object reference indicating the connection this query should be associated with.

Applies To

rdoResultset Object, **rdoQuery** Object

Syntax

object.**ActiveConnection** [= *value*]

The **ActiveConnection** property syntax has these parts:

Part	Description
object	An object expression that evaluates to an object in the **Applies To** list.
value	An expression that evaluates to a valid **rdoConnection** or derived object. *Value* defaults to the **rdoConnection** used to create the object or **Nothing**.

Remarks

The **ActiveConnection** property holds a reference to the connection associated with the **rdoQuery** or **rdoResultset** object. All database statements executed by the object are executed against this connection.

When working with an **rdoQuery** object, the **ActiveConnection** property can be set to **Nothing** which dissociates the object from a specific connection. You can subsequently re-associate the **rdoQuery** object to another **rdoConnection** object by setting the **ActiveConnection** object. Using this technique, a query can be executed against a set of connections.

When working with the **rdoResultset** object and the Client Batch cursor library, you can set the **ActiveConnection** property to **Nothing**. In this case, if the result set is created with a static cursor and the **rdConcurBatch** concurrency option, the **rdoResultset** data is still available and you are free to make changes or additions to the result set. Once you set the **ActiveConnection** to an open **rdoConnection** object, you can use the **BatchUpdate** method to post these changes to the remote database.

Example

The following examples illustrates use of the **ActiveConnection** property to select an **rdoConnection**. In this case, the application opens two separate connections and uses the same **rdoQuery** against each.

```
Dim rdoCn As New rdoConnection
Dim rdoCn2 As New rdoConnection
Dim rdoQy As New rdoQuery
Dim rdoRs As rdoResultset
Dim rdoCol As rdoColumn
Dim rdoEn As rdoEnvironment
```

```
Private Sub Form_Load()
On Error GoTo CnEh

Set rdoEn = rdoEnvironments(0)

With rdoCn

    .Connect = "UID=;PWD=;Database=WorkDB;" _
        & "Server=Betav486;Driver={SQL Server}" _
        & "DSN='';"
    .LoginTimeout = 5
    .EstablishConnection rdDriverNoPrompt, True
    rdoEn.rdoConnections.Add rdoCn
End With

With rdoCn2
    .Connect = "UID=;PWD=;Database=Pubs;" _
        & "Server=Betav486;Driver={SQL Server}" _
        & "DSN='';"
    .LoginTimeout = 5
    .EstablishConnection rdDriverNoPrompt, True
    rdoEn.rdoConnections.Add rdoCn2
End With

With rdoQy
    Set .ActiveConnection = rdoCn
    .SQL = "Select Name, refDate " _
        & " from Sysobjects where type = 'U' "
    .LockType = rdConcurReadOnly
    .RowsetSize = 1
    .CursorType = rdUseServer
End With

For Each rdoCn In rdoEn.rdoConnections
    Set rdoQy.ActiveConnection = rdoCn
    Set rdoRs = rdoQy.OpenResultset(rdOpenForwardOnly)
    With rdoRs
        For Each rdoCol In rdoRs.rdoColumns
            Debug.Print rdoCol.Name,
        Next
        Debug.Print
        Do Until rdoRs.EOF
                For Each rdoCol In rdoRs.rdoColumns
                    Debug.Print rdoCol
                Next
            rdoRs.MoveNext
        Loop
    End With
Next                            ' Next Connection
```

```
Exit Sub
CnEh:
Dim er As rdoError
   Debug.Print Err, Error
   For Each er In rdoErrors
      Debug.Print er.Description, er.Number
   Next er
   Resume Next
End Sub
```

ActiveControl Property

Returns the control that has the focus. When a form is referenced, as in `ChildForm.ActiveControl`, **ActiveControl** specifies the control that would have the focus if the referenced form were active. Not available at design time; read-only at run time.

Applies To

PropertyPage Object, **UserControl** Object, **UserDocument** Object, **Screen** Object, **Form** Object**, Forms** Collection, **MDIForm** Object t

Syntax

object.**ActiveControl**

The *object* placeholder represents an object expression that evaluates to an object in the **Applies To** list.

Remarks

You can use **ActiveControl** to access a control's properties or to invoke its methods: For example, `Screen.ActiveControl.Tag = "0"`. A run-time error occurs if all controls on the form are invisible or disabled.

Each form can have an active control (`Form.ActiveControl`), regardless of whether or not the form is active. You can write code that manipulates the active control on each form in your application even when the form isn't the active form.

This property is especially useful in a multiple-document interface (MDI) application where a button on a toolbar must initiate an action on a control in an MDI child form. When a user clicks the Copy button on the toolbar, your code can reference the text in the active control on the MDI child form, as in `ActiveForm.ActiveControl.SelText`.

Note If you plan to pass `Screen.ActiveControl` to a procedure, you must declare the argument in that procedure with the clause `As Control` rather than specifying a control type (`As TextBox` or `As ListBox`) even if `ActiveControl` always refers to the same type of control.

See Also

GotFocus Event, **LostFocus** Event, **ActiveForm** Property

Examples

This example displays the text of the active control. To try this example, paste the code into the Declarations section of a form that contains **TextBox**, **Label**, and **CommandButton** controls, and then press F5 and click the form.

```
Private Sub Form_Click ()
    If TypeOf Screen.ActiveControl Is TextBox Then
        Label1.Caption = Screen.ActiveControl.Text
    Else
        Label1.Caption = "Button: " + Screen.ActiveControl.Caption
    End If
End Sub
```

This example shows how you can use the **Clipboard** object in cut, copy, paste, and delete operations using buttons on a toolbar. To try this example, put **TextBox** and **CheckBox** controls on Form1, and then create a new MDI form. On the MDI form, insert a **PictureBox** control, and then insert a **CommandButton** in the **PictureBox**. Set the **Index** property of the **CommandButton** to 0 (creating a control array). Set the **MDIChild** property of Form1 to **True**.

To run the example, copy the code into the Declarations section of the **MDIForm**, and then press F5. Notice that when the **CheckBox** has the focus, the buttons don't work, since the **CheckBox** is now the active control instead of the **TextBox**.

```
Private Sub MDIForm_Load ()
    Dim I ' Declare variable.
    Command1(0).Move 0, 0, 700, 300    ' Position button on toolbar.
    For I = 1 To 3 ' Create other buttons.
        Load Command1(I)   ' Create button.
        Command1(I).Move I * 700, 0, 700, 300  ' Place and size button.
        Command1(I).Visible = True    ' Display button.
    Next I
    Command1(0).Caption = "Cut"        ' Set button captions.
    Command1(1).Caption = "Copy"
    Command1(2).Caption = "Paste"
    Command1(3).Caption = "Del"

End Sub

Private Sub Command1_Click (Index As Integer)
    ' ActiveForm refers to the active form in the MDI form.
    If TypeOf ActiveForm.ActiveControl Is TextBox Then
        Select Case Index
            Case 0 ' Cut.
                ' Copy selected text onto Clipboard.
                Clipboard.SetText ActiveForm.ActiveControl.SelText
                ' Delete selected text.
                ActiveForm.ActiveControl.SelText = ""
            Case 1 ' Copy.
                ' Copy selected text onto Clipboard.

Clipboard.SetText ActiveForm.ActiveControl.SelText
```

```
        Case 2 ' Paste.
           ' Put Clipboard text in text box.
           ActiveForm.ActiveControl.SelText = Clipboard.GetText()
        Case 3 ' Delete.
           ' Delete selected text.
           ActiveForm.ActiveControl.SelText = ""
     End Select
   End If
End Sub
```

ActiveForm Property

Returns the form that is the active window. If an **MDIForm** object is active or is referenced, it specifies the active MDI child form.

Applies To

Screen Object, **Form** Object**, Forms** Collection, **MDIForm** Object

Syntax

object.**ActiveForm**

The *object* placeholder represents an object expression that evaluates to an object in the **Applies To** list.

Remarks

Use the **ActiveForm** property to access a form's properties or to invoke its methods— for example, `Screen.ActiveForm.MousePointer = 4`.

This property is especially useful in a multiple-document interface (MDI) application where a button on a toolbar must initiate an action on a control in an MDI child form. When a user clicks the Copy button on the toolbar, your code can reference the text in the active control on the MDI child form—for example, `ActiveForm.ActiveControl.SelText`.

When a control on a form has the focus, that form is the active form on the screen (`Screen.ActiveForm`). In addition, an **MDIForm** object can contain one child form that is the active form within the context of the MDI parent form (`MDIForm.ActiveForm`). The **ActiveForm** on the screen isn't necessarily the same as the **ActiveForm** in the MDI form, such as when a dialog box is active. For this reason, specify the **MDIForm** with **ActiveForm** when there is a chance of a dialog box being the **ActiveForm** property setting.

Note When an active MDI child form isn't maximized, the title bars of both the parent form and the child form appear active.

If you plan to pass `Screen.ActiveForm` or `MDIForm.ActiveForm` to a procedure, you must declare the argument in that procedure with the generic type (`As Form`) rather than a specific form type (`As MyForm`) even if **ActiveForm** always refers to the same type of form.

The **ActiveForm** property determines the default value for the **ProjectTemplate** object.

See Also

Activate, **Deactivate** Events, **MDIChild** Property

Examples

This example prints the time on the active child form in an **MDIForm** object.
To try this example, create an **MDIForm**, draw a **PictureBox** control on it and a
CommandButton control in the **PictureBox**. In Form1, set the **MDIChild** property
to **True**. (You can also set **AutoRedraw** to **True** to keep text on the form even after
covering it with another form.) Paste the appropriate code into the Declarations
section of each form, and then press F5.

```
' Copy all code into the MDI form.
Private Sub MDIForm_Load ()
   Dim NewForm As New Form1 ' Create new instance of Form1.
   NewForm.Show
End Sub
```

This example shows how you can use the **Clipboard** object in cut, copy, paste,
and delete operations using buttons on a toolbar. To try this example, create a new
project, then put **TextBox** and **CheckBox** controls on Form1, and then create a
new MDI form. On the MDI form, place a **PictureBox** control, and then insert
a **CommandButton** control in the **PictureBox**. Set the **Index** property of the
CommandButton to 0 (creating a control array). Set the **MDIChild** property
of Form1 to **True**.

To run the example, copy the code into the Declarations section of the **MDIForm**,
and then press F5. Notice that when the **CheckBox** has the focus, the buttons don't
work, since the **CheckBox** is now the active control instead of the **TextBox**.

```
Private Sub MDIForm_Load ()
   Dim I        ' Declare variable.
   Command1(0).Move 0, 0, 700, 300    ' Position button on toolbar.
   For I = 1 To 3 ' Create other buttons.
      Load Command1(I)  ' Create button.
      Command1(I).Move I * 700, 0, 700, 300  ' Place and size button.
      Command1(I).Visible = True      ' Display button.
   Next I
   Command1(0).Caption = "Cut"        ' Set button captions.
   Command1(1).Caption = "Copy"
   Command1(2).Caption = "Paste"
   Command1(3).Caption = "Del"

End Sub

Private Sub Command1_Click (Index As Integer)
   ' ActiveForm refers to the active form in the MDI form.
   If TypeOf ActiveForm.ActiveControl Is TextBox Then
      Select Case Index
         Case 0' Cut.
            ' Copy selected text to Clipboard.
            Clipboard.SetText ActiveForm.ActiveControl.SelText
```

```
            ' Delete selected text.
            ActiveForm.ActiveControl.SelText = ""
        Case 1' Copy.
            ' Copy selected text to Clipboard.

Clipboard.SetText ActiveForm.ActiveControl.SelText
        Case 2' Paste.
            ' Put Clipboard text in text box.
            ActiveForm.ActiveControl.SelText = Clipboard.GetText()
        Case 3' Delete.
            ' Delete selected text.
            ActiveForm.ActiveControl.SelText = ""
        End Select
    End If
End Sub
```

ActiveVBProject Property

Returns the active project in the **Project** window. Read-only.

Applies to

VBE Object

Remarks

The **ActiveVBProject** property returns the project that is selected in the **Project** window or the project in which the components are selected. In the latter case, the project itself isn't necessarily selected. Whether or not the project is explicitly selected, there is always an active project .

See Also

VBProject Object, **VBProjects** Collection

Example

The following example uses the **ActiveVBProject** property to return the name of the active project.

```
Debug.Print Application.VBE.ActiveVBProject.Name
```

ActiveWindow Property

Returns the active window in the development environment. Read-only.

Applies to

VBE Object

Remarks

When more than one window is open in the development environment, the **ActiveWindow** property setting is the window with the focus. If the main window has the focus, **ActiveWindow** returns **Nothing**.

SetFocus Method, **Window** Object, **ActiveCodePane** Property, **MainWindow** Property

Example

The following example uses the **ActiveWindow** property to return the caption of the active window.

```
Debug.Print Application.VBE.ActiveWindow.Caption
```

Add-In Toolbar

A toolbar on which to place add-ins and Wizards for quick and easy user access. To start an add-in or Wizard, simply click its icon on the toolbar.

The add-ins and Wizards placed on the Add-In toolbar are not activated until their button is clicked. The Add-In toolbar eliminates the need for activating the add-in through the **Add-In Manager** dialog box.

You can add Wizards and add-ins to the Add-In toolbar through the **Add/Remove Toolbar Items** (+/-) button. When you click this button, you get the following dialog box:

To add an add-in or Wizard to the list of available add-ins, click the **Browse** button. Point to an add-in or Wizard's .Exe or .Dll file in the dialog box, then click **Open**. It should appear in the **Available Add-Ins** list. It will not show up on the Add-In toolbar, however, unless its box is checked in the **Available Add-Ins** list.

The **OK** button closes the **Add/Remove Toolbar Items** dialog box and updates the Add-In toolbar with the checked items.

The **Cancel** button closes the **Add/Remove Toolbar Items** dialog box and ignores any changes made when it was opened.

When you click the **Delete** button, the currently selected add-in or Wizard is removed from the **Available Add-Ins** list. Note that this does not remove the add-in or Wizard from the system, nor its reference in the **Add-In Manager** dialog box. The **Delete** button removes only the entry in the Add-In toolbar **Available Add-Ins** list.

See Also

AddToAddInToolbar Method, **AddToAddInToolbar Method** Example, **RemoveAddInFromToolbar** Method, **RemoveAddInFromToolbar Method** Example

Add Method

Adds a member to a **Collection** object.

Applies to

Collection Object

Syntax

object.**Add** *item, key, before, after*

The **Add** method syntax has the following object qualifier and named arguments:

Part	Description
object	Required. An object expression that evaluates to an object in the **Applies To** list.
item	Required. An expression of any type that specifies the member to add to the collection.
key	Optional. A unique string expression that specifies a key string that can be used, instead of a positional index, to access a member of the collection.
before	Optional. An expression that specifies a relative position in the collection. The member to be added is placed in the collection before the member identified by the *before* argument. If a numeric expression, *before* must be a number from 1 to the value of the collection's **Count** property. If a string expression, *before* must correspond to the *key* specified when the member being referred to was added to the collection. You can specify a *before* position or an *after* position, but not both.
after	Optional. An expression that specifies a relative position in the collection. The member to be added is placed in the collection after the member identified by the *after* argument. If numeric, *after* must be a number from 1 to the value of the collection's **Count** property. If a string, *after* must correspond to the *key* specified when the member referred to was added to the collection. You can specify a *before* position or an *after* position, but not both.

Remarks

Whether the *before* or *after* argument is a string expression or numeric expression, it must refer to an existing member of the collection, or an error occurs.

An error also occurs if a specified *key* duplicates the *key* for an existing member of the collection.

See Also

Item Method, **Remove** Method

Examples

The following example uses the **Add** method to add one standard module to the **VBComponents** collection.

```
Application.VBE.VBProjects(1).VBComponents.Add(vbext_ct_StdModule)
```

This example uses the **Add** method to add `Inst` objects (instances of a class called `Class1` containing a **Public** variable `InstanceName`) to a collection called `MyClasses`. To see how this works, insert a class module and declare a public variable called `InstanceName` at module level of `Class1` (type **Public** `InstanceName`) to hold the names of each instance. Leave the default name as `Class1`. Copy and paste the following code into the **Form_Load** event procedure of a form module.

```
Dim MyClasses As New Collection      ' Create a Collection object.
Dim Num As Integer                   ' Counter for individualizing keys.
Dim Msg
Dim TheName                          ' Holder for names user enters.
Do
    Dim Inst As New Class1           ' Create a new instance of Class1.
    Num = Num + 1                    ' Increment Num, then get a name.
    Msg = "Please enter a name for this object." & Chr(13) _
     & "Press Cancel to see names in collection."
    TheName = InputBox(Msg, "Name the Collection Items")
    Inst.InstanceName = TheName         ' Put name in object instance.
    ' If user entered name, add it to the collection.
    If Inst.InstanceName <> "" Then
        ' Add the named object to the collection.
        MyClasses.Add item := Inst, key := CStr(Num)
    End If
    ' Clear the current reference in preparation for next one.
    Set Inst = Nothing
Loop Until TheName = ""
For Each x In MyClasses
    MsgBox x.instancename, , "Instance Name"
Next
```

Add Method (Columns, SelBookmarks, Splits Collections)

Adds a new column to the **Columns** collection, a new bookmark to the **SelBookmarks** collection, or a new split to the **Splits** collection of the **DBGrid** control. Doesn't support named arguments.

Applies To

Splits Collection, **Columns** Collection, **DBGrid** Control, **SelBookmarks** Collection

Syntax

object.**Add** *colindex*
object.**Add** *bookmark*

The **Add** method syntax has these parts:

Part	Description
object	An object expression that evaluates to an object in the **Applies To** list.
colindex	Required. An integer that specifies where the new **Column** or **Split** object is inserted in the **Columns** collection or **Splits** collection, as described in Settings.
bookmark	The bookmark to be added to the collection.

Settings

The settings for *colindex* are:

Setting	Description
0	Inserts new column as leftmost column.
Count	If the *colindex* argument is the same as the **Count** property setting, the new column is inserted as the rightmost column.
n	Inserts the new column to the left of the nth column in the **Columns** collection. The *n*th column and all subsequent columns are incremented accordingly.

Remarks

The **Add** method inserts a new **Column** object into the **Columns** collection based on the *colindex* argument. New columns are added with their **Visible** property set to **False** and all other properties set to their default values. Initially, new columns are unbound because the **DataField** property is set to a zero-length string (""). The **Count** property of the **Columns** collection is incremented to reflect the new column.

Important   If you have previously deleted a column using the **Remove** method, after adding new columns, you may need to refresh the display with the **Rebind** and **Refresh** methods. This instructs the **DBGrid** control to rebuild its internal column layout matrix to correctly reflect the true status of the control.

Use the **Add** method to add bookmarks to the **SelBookmarks** collection. Once a bookmark is appended to the **SelBookmarks** collection, it appears selected in the **DBGrid** control.

See Also

Data Control, **DBGrid** Control, **Remove** Method (DBGrid), **ColIndex** Property

Add Method (Linked Windows)

Adds an object to a collection.

Applies To

LinkedWindows Collection, **VBComponents** Collection

Syntax

object.**Add**(*component*)

Add syntax has these parts:

Part	Description
object	Required. An object expression that evaluates to an object in the **Applies To** list.
component	Required. For the **LinkedWindows** collection, an object. For the **VBComponents** collection, an enumerated constant representing a class module, a form, or a standard module.

You can use one of the following constants for the *component* argument:

Constant	Description
vbext_ct_ClassModule	Adds a class module to the collection.
vbext_ct_MSForm	Adds a form to the collection.
vbext_ct_StdModule	Adds a standard module to the collection.

Remarks

For the **LinkedWindows** collection, the **Add** method adds a window to the collection of currently linked windows.

Note You can add a window that is a pane in one linked window frame to another linked window frame; the window is simply moved from one pane to the other. If the linked window frame that the window was moved from no longer contains any panes, it's destroyed.

For the **VBComponents** collection, the **Add** method creates a new standard component and adds it to the project.

For the **VBComponents** collection, the **Add** method returns a **VBComponent** object. For the **LinkedWindows** collection, the **Add** method returns **Nothing**.

See Also

AddFromFile Method, **AddFromGuid** Method, **AddFromString** Method, **Remove** Method

Add Method (VBControls, VBProjects)

- **ContainedVBControls** collection: Adds a new **VBControl** object to the **ContainedVBControls** collection.
- **VBControls** collection: Adds a new **VBControl** object to the **VBControls** collection.
- **VBProjects** collection: Adds a new, empty project to the set of projects in the **VBProjects** collection.

Applies To

LinkedWindows Collection, **VBControls** Collection, **VBProjects** Collection

Syntax

object.**Add** (*progid* **As String**, [*relativevbcontrol* **As VBControl**] [*before* **As Boolean**])
  ↳ **As VBControl**
object.**Add** (*projecttype* **As vbext_ProjectType**, [*exclusive* **As Boolean**]) **As VBProject**

The **Add** method syntax has these parts:

Part	Description
object	An object expression that evaluates to an object in the **Applies To** list.
progid	Required. A string expression specifying the **ProgID** of the component to be added.
relativevbcontrol	Optional. An existing **VBControl** object specifying the point where the new component is to be inserted.
before	Optional. Default = **False**. A Boolean expression specifying whether the new **VBControl** is to be placed before or after the *relativevbcontrol*.
projecttype	Required. A **VBProject** object specifying the type of the new project. For a list of kinds of projects, see the **Kind** property.
exclusive	Optional. Default = **False**. A Boolean expression specifying whether a new project is added to an existing set of projects, or added as the only project.

Remarks

If the *exclusive* parameter is specified as **True**, then the existing group project is closed and the new project becomes the only project in the collection.

AddCustom Method

Returns a **VBComponent** object, or creates a new custom component and adds it to the project.

Syntax

object.**AddCustom** (**ByVal** *progid* **As String**) **As VBComponent**

The **AddCustom** method syntax has these parts:

Part	Description
object	An object expression that evaluates to an object in the **Applies To** list.
progid	Required. The **ProgID** of the custom component to be created.

AddFile Method

Returns the newly added component.

Syntax

*object***.AddFile** (**ByVal** *pathname* **As String**, [*relateddocument* **As Boolean**])
↳ **As VBComponent**

The **AddFile** method syntax has these parts:

Part	Description
object	An object expression that evaluates to an object in the **Applies To** list.
pathname	Required. A string expression specifying the path and filename of the file to open as a template.
relateddocument	Optional (for text files only). Default = **False**. A Boolean expression specifying whether the file is to be treated as a standard module or a document. If set to **True**, then the file added is treated as a document file.

Remarks

Files that are normally Visual Basic project components, such as forms, cause an error if the *relateddocument* parameter is set to **True**. The *relateddocument* parameter is required only when adding text files that can be treated as either standard modules or documents.

AddFromFile Method

Adds or opens a project or group project.

Applies To

CodeModule Object, **VBProjects** Collection

Syntax

*object***.AddFromFile** (**ByVal** *pathname* **As String**, [*exclusive* **As Boolean**])
↳ **As VBNewProjects**

The **AddFromFile** method syntax has these parts:

Part	Description
object	An object expression that evaluates to an object in the **Applies To** list.
pathname	Required. A string expression specifying the path to the file to use as the template.
exclusive	Optional. Default = **False**. A Boolean expression. If set to **True**, then the existing group project is closed and the new project is created as the only open project.

Remarks

If the file is a group project file and *exclusive* is set to **False**, then all projects in that group project are added to the current group project. If the file is a group project file and *exclusive* is set to **True**, then the current group project is replaced by the specified one.

AddFromFile Method (Add-Ins)

For the **References** collection, adds a reference to a project from a file. For the **CodeModule** object, adds the contents of a file to a module.

Applies To

CodeModule Object, **References** Collection

Syntax

object.**AddFromFile**(*filename*)

AddFromFile syntax has these parts:

Part	Description
object	Required. An object expression that evaluates to an object in the **Applies To** list.
filename	Required. A string expression specifying the name of the file you want to add to the project or module. If the file name isn't found and a path name isn't specified, the directories searched by the **Windows OpenFile** function are searched.

Remarks

For the **CodeModule** object, the **AddFromFile** method inserts the contents of the file starting on the line preceding the first procedure in the code module. If the module doesn't contain procedures, **AddFromFile** places the contents of the file at the end of the module.

See Also

ItemAdded Event, **ItemRemoved** Event, **Add** Method, **AddFromGuid** Method, **AddFromString** Method, **Remove** Method

Example

The following example uses the **AddFromFile** method to add the contents of a file to a specified code pane.

```
Application.VBE.CodePanes(3).CodeModule.AddFromFile
↳ "c:\Code Files\book2.frm"
```

AddFromGuid Method

Adds a reference to the **References** collection using the globally unique identifier (GUID) of the reference.

Applies To

References Collection

Syntax

object.**AddFromGuid**(*guid*, *major*, *minor*) **As Reference**

AddFromGuid syntax has these parts:

Part	Description
object	Required. An object expression that evaluates to an object in the **Applies To** list.
guid	Required. A string expression representing the GUID of the reference.
major	Required. A **Long** specifying the major version number of the reference.
minor	Required. A **Long** specifying the minor version number of the reference.

Remarks

The **AddFromGuid** method searches the registry to find the reference you want to add. The GUID can be a type library, control, class identifier, and so on.

See Also

ItemAdded Event, **ItemRemoved** Event, **Add** Method, **AddFromString** Method, **Remove** Method

Example

The following example uses the **AddFromGUID** method to add a reference to the current project, identifying the reference using the globally unique ID value of the **Reference** object.

```
Application.VBE.ActiveVBProject.References.AddFromGuid
  ↳ ("{000204EF-0000-0000-C000-000000000046}", 5, 0)
```

AddFromString Method

Adds text to a module.

Applies To

CodeModule Object

Syntax

object.**AddFromString**

The *object* placeholder is an object expression that evaluates to an object in the **Applies To** list.

Remarks

The **AddFromString** method inserts the text starting on the line preceding the first procedure in the module. If the module doesn't contain procedures, **AddFromString** places the text at the end of the module.

See Also

CreateEventProc Method, **DeleteLines** Method, **InsertLines** Method, **Lines** Method, **ProcBodyLine** Method, **ProcCountLines** Method, **ProcOfLine** Method, **ProcStartLine** Method, **ReplaceLine** Method d

Example

The following example uses the **AddFromString** method to add a line, "Dim intJack As Integer," to the specified code pane.

```
Application.VBE.CodePanes(3).CodeModule.AddFromString
↳ "Dim intJack As Integer"
```

AddFromTemplate Method

- **VBComponents** collection: Returns the newly created component, and creates a new component from a template.
- **VBProjects** collection: Returns a collection of all projects added as a result of a call to this method, or creates a new project using an existing project as a template.

Applies To

VBProjects Collection

Syntax

object.**AddFromTemplate** (*filename* **As String**) **As VBComponent**
object.**AddFromTemplate** (**ByVal** *pathname* **As String**, [*exclusive* **As Boolean**])
    ↳ **As VBNewProjects**

The **AddFromTemplate** method syntax has these parts:

Part	Description
object	An object expression that evaluates to an object in the **Applies To** list.
filename	Required. A string expression specifying the path and filename of the file to open as a template.
exclusive	Optional. Default = **False**. A Boolean expression. If set to **True**, then the existing group project is closed and the new project is created as the only open project.
pathname	Required. A string expression specifying the path to the file to use as the template.

Remarks

If the file type referenced is a group project file, and *exclusive* is set to **False**, then all projects in that file are created as templates and added to the current set of open projects. If *exclusive* is set to **True**, however, the current group project is closed and a new group project created, and all projects within the group project template are created as project templates. The object returned by the method is **Nothing**.

New project or projects are given the usual default names.

AddIn Object

The **AddIn** object provides information about an add-in to other add-ins.

Syntax

AddIn

Remarks

An **AddIn** object is created for every add-in that appears in the Vbaddin.Ini file.

Properties

Collection Property, **Connect** Property, **Description** Property, **GUID** Property, **Object** Property, **ProgID** Property, **VBE** Property

See Also

AddIns Collection

AddIns Collection

Returns a collection of add-ins listed in the Vbaddin.Ini file.

Syntax

AddIns

Remarks

The **AddIns** collection is accessed through the **VBE** object. Every add-in listed in the Add-in Manager in an instance of Visual Basic has an object in the **AddIns** collection.

This collection replaces the **ExternalObjects** collection used in Visual Basic version 4.0.

Properties

Count Property, **Parent** Property, **VBE** Property

Methods

Item Method**, Update** Method

See Also

AddIn Object

AddIns Property

Returns a collection which add-ins can use to register their automation components into the extensibility object model.

Syntax

object.**AddIns**

The *object* placeholder represents an object expression that evaluates to an object in the **Applies To** list.

AddItem Method

Adds an item to a **ListBox** or **ComboBox** control or adds a row to a **MS Flex Grid** control. Doesn't support named arguments.

Applies To

ComboBox Control, **ListBox** Control

Syntax

object.**AddItem** *item*, *index*

The **AddItem** method syntax has these parts:

Part	Description
object	Required. An object expression that evaluates to an object in the **Applies To** list.
item	Required. string expression specifying the item to add to the object. For the **MS Flex Grid** control only, use the tab character (character code 09) to separate multiple strings you want to insert into each column of a newly added row.
index	Optional. Integer specifying the position within the object where the new item or row is placed. For the first item in a **ListBox** or **ComboBox** control or for the first row in a **MS Flex Grid** control, *index* is 0.

Remarks

If you supply a valid value for *index*, *item* is placed at that position within the *object*. If *index* is omitted, *item* is added at the proper sorted position (if the **Sorted** property is set to **True**) or to the end of the list (if **Sorted** is set to **False**).

A **ListBox** or **ComboBox** control that is bound to a **Data** control doesn't support the **AddItem** method.

See Also

Clear Method (Clipboard, ComboBox, ListBox), **RemoveItem** Method, **Index** Property (ActiveX Controls), **Key** Property (ActiveX Controls)

Example

This example uses the **AddItem** method to add 100 items to a list box. To try this example, paste the code into the Declarations section of a form with a **ListBox** control named List1, and then press F5 and click the form.

```
Private Sub Form_Click ()
    Dim Entry, I, Msg        ' Declare variables.
    Msg = "Choose OK to add 100 items to your list box."
    MsgBox Msg               ' Display message.
    For I = 1 To 100         ' Count from 1 to 100.
        Entry = "Entry " & I ' Create entry.
        List1.AddItem Entry  ' Add the entry.
    Next I
    Msg = "Choose OK to remove every other entry."
    MsgBox Msg               ' Display message.
    For I = 1 To 50          ' Determine how to
        List1.RemoveItem I   ' remove every other

Next I' item.
    Msg = "Choose OK to remove all items from the list box."
    MsgBox Msg               ' Display message.
    List1.Clear              ' Clear list box.
End Sub
```

AddNew Method

Creates a new record for an updatable **Recordset** object.

Applies To

Dynaset-Type Recordset Object, **Recordset** Object, **Snapshot-Type Recordset** Object, **Table-Type Recordset** Object, **Forward-Only–Type Recordset** Object, **Dynamic-Type Recordset** Object t

Syntax

recordset.**AddNew**

The *recordset* placeholder is an object variable that represents an updatable **Recordset** object to which you want to add a new record.

Remarks

Use the **AddNew** method to create and add a new record in the **Recordset** object named by *recordset*. This method sets the fields to default values, and if no default values are specified, it sets the fields to **Null** (the default values specified for a table-type **Recordset**).

After you modify the new record, use the **Update** method to save the changes and add the record to the **Recordset**. No changes occur in the database until you use the **Update** method.

Caution If you issue an **AddNew** and then perform any operation that moves to another record, but without using **Update**, your changes are lost without warning. In addition, if you close the **Recordset** or end the procedure that declares the **Recordset** or its **Database** object, the new record is discarded without warning.

Note When you use **AddNew** in a Microsoft Jet workspace and the database engine has to create a new page to hold the current record, page locking is pessimistic. If the new record fits in an existing page, page locking is optimistic.

If you haven't moved to the last record of your **Recordset**, records added to base tables by other processes may be included if they are positioned beyond the current record. If you add a record to your own **Recordset**, however, the record is visible in the **Recordset** and included in the underlying table where it becomes visible to any new **Recordset** objects.

The position of the new record depends on the type of **Recordset**:

- In a dynaset-type **Recordset** object, records are inserted at the end of the **Recordset**, regardless of any sorting or ordering rules that were in effect when the **Recordset** was opened.

- In a table-type **Recordset** object whose **Index** property has been set, records are returned in their proper place in the sort order. If you haven't set the **Index** property, new records are returned at the end of the **Recordset**.

The record that was current before you used **AddNew** remains current. If you want to make the new record current, you can set the **Bookmark** property to the bookmark identified by the **LastModified** property setting.

Note To add, edit, or delete a record, there must be a unique index on the record in the underlying data source. If not, a "Permission denied" error will occur on the **AddNew**, **Delete**, or **Edit** method call in a Microsoft Jet workspace, or an "Invalid argument" error will occur on the **Update** call in an ODBCDirect workspace.

See Also

Index Object, **CancelUpdate** Method, **Delete** Method, **Move** Method, **MoveFirst**, **MoveLast**, **MoveNext**, **MovePrevious** Methods, **Seek** Method, **Update** Method, **Bookmark** Property, **EditMode** Property, **LastModified** Property

Example

This example uses the **AddNew** method to create a new record with the specified name. The **AddName** function is required for this procedure to run.

```
Sub AddNewX()

    Dim dbsNorthwind As Database
    Dim rstEmployees As Recordset
    Dim strFirstName As String
    Dim strLastName As String
```

```
        Set dbsNorthwind = OpenDatabase("Northwind.mdb")
        Set rstEmployees = _
            dbsNorthwind.OpenRecordset("Employees", dbOpenDynaset)

        ' Get data from the user.
        strFirstName = Trim(InputBox( _
            "Enter first name:"))
        strLastName = Trim(InputBox( _
            "Enter last name:"))

        ' Proceed only if the user actually entered something
        ' for both the first and last names.
        If strFirstName <> "" and strLastName <> "" Then

            ' Call the function that adds the record.
            AddName rstEmployees, strFirstName, strLastName

            ' Show the newly added data.
            With rstEmployees
                Debug.Print "New record: " & !FirstName & _
                    " " & !LastName
                ' Delete new record because this is a demonstration.
                .Delete
            End With

        Else
            Debug.Print _
                "You must input a string for first and last name!"
        End If

        rstEmployees.Close
        dbsNorthwind.Close

End Sub

Function AddName(rstTemp As Recordset, _
    strFirst As String, strLast As String)

    ' Adds a new record to a Recordset using the data passed
    ' by the calling procedure. The new record is then made
    ' the current record.
    With rstTemp
        .AddNew
        !FirstName = strFirst
        !LastName = strLast
        .Update
        .Bookmark = .LastModified
    End With

End Function
```

AddNew Method (Remote Data)

Creates a new row for an updatable **rdoResultset** object.

Applies To

rdoResultset Object

Syntax

object.**AddNew**

The *object* placeholder represents an object expression that evaluates to an object in the **Applies To** list.

Remarks

The **AddNew** method prepares a new row you can edit and subsequently add to the **rdoResultset** object named by *object* using the **Update** method. This method initializes the columns to SQL_IGNORE to ensure columns not specifically referenced are not included in the update operation.

When the **AddNew** method is executed, the **EditMode** property is set to **rdEditAdd** until you execute the **Update** method.

After you modify the new row, use the **Update** method to save the changes and add the row to the result set. No changes are made to the database until you use the **Update** method—unless you are using the Client Batch cursor library—which does not write to the database until the **BatchUpdate** method is used.

The **AddNew** method does not return an error if the **rdoResultset** is not updatable. A trappable error is triggered when the **Update** method is used against an object that is not updatable. For an object to be updatable, the **rdoColumn**, **rdoResultset**, and **rdoConnection** objects must all be updatable—check the **Updatable** property of each of these objects before performing an update. There are a variety of reasons why an **rdoResultset** is not updatable as discussed in the **Update** method topic.

Caution If you use the **AddNew** method on a row and then perform any operation that moves to another row without using **Update**, your changes are lost without warning. In addition, if you close the *object* or end the procedure which declares the *object* or its **rdoConnection** object, the new row and the changes made to it are discarded without warning.

A newly added row might be visible as a part of the **rdoResultset** if your data source and type of cursor support it. For example, newly added rows are not included in a static-type **rdoResultset**.

When newly added rows are included in the **rdoResultset**, the row that was current *before* you used **AddNew** remains current. When the row is added to the cursor keyset, and you want to make the new row current, you can set the **Bookmark** property to the bookmark identified by the **LastModified** property setting.

If you need to cancel a pending **AddNew** operation, use the **CancelUpdate** method.

When you use the **Update** method after using the **AddNew** method, the **RowCurrencyChange** event is fired.

See Also

BeginTrans, **CommitTrans**, **RollbackTrans** Methods, **CancelUpdate** Method (Remote Data), **Delete** Method (Remote Data), **Edit** Method (Remote Data), **Move** Method (Remote Data), **MoveFirst**, **MoveLast**, **MoveNext**, **MovePrevious** Methods (Remote Data), **Update** Method (Remote Data), **rdoConnection** Object, **Bookmark** Property (Remote Data), **EditMode** Property (Remote Data), **LastModified** Property (Remote Data), **Updatable** Property (Remote Data)

Example

The following example illustrates use of the **AddNew** method to add new rows to a base table. This example assumes that you have read-write access to the table, that the column data provided meets the rules and other constraints associated with the table, and there is a unique index on the table. The data values for the operation are taken from three **TextBox** controls on the form. Note that the unique key for this table is not provided here as it is provided automatically—it is an *identity* column.

```
Option Explicit
Dim er As rdoError
Dim cn As New rdoConnection
Dim qy As New rdoQuery
Dim rs As rdoResultset
Dim col As rdoColumn

Private Sub AddNewJob_Click()
On Error GoTo ANEH

With rs
    .AddNew
    !job_desc = JobDescription
    !min_lvl = MinLevel
    !max_lvl = MaxLevel
    .Update
End With
Exit Sub

UpdateFailed:
MsgBox "Update did not suceed."
rs.CancelUpdate
Exit Sub
A
NEH:
Debug.Print Err, Error
For Each er In rdoErrors
    Debug.Print er
Next
Resume UpdateFailed

End Sub
```

```
Private Sub Form_Load()

cn.CursorDriver = rdUseOdbc
cn.Connect = "uid=;pwd=;server=sequel;" _
    & "driver={SQL Server};database=pubs;dsn='';"
cn.EstablishConnection
With qy
    .Name = "JobsQuery"
    .SQL = "Select * from Jobs"
    .RowsetSize = 1
    Set .ActiveConnection = cn
    Set rs = .OpenResultset(rdOpenKeyset, _
        rdConcurRowver)
    Debug.Print rs.Updatable
End With

Exit Sub
End Sub
```

AddNewMode Property

Returns a value that describes the location of the current cell with respect to the grid's **AddNew** row. Read-only at run time and not available at design time.

Applies To

DBGrid Control

Syntax

object.**AddNewMode**

The **AddNewMode** property syntax has these parts:

Part	Description
object	An object expression that evaluates to an object in the **Applies To** list.

Values

The **AddNewMode** property returns one of the following:

Constant	Value	Description
dbgNoAddNew	0	The current cell is not in the last row, and no **AddNew** operation is pending.
dbgAddNewCurrent	1	The current cell is in the last row, but no **AddNew** operation is pending.
dbgAddNewPending	2	The current cell is in the next to last row as a result of a pending **AddNew** operation initiated by the user through the grid's user interface, or by code as a result of setting the **Value** or **Text** properties of a column.

Remarks

If the **AllowAddNew** property is **True**, the last row displayed in the grid is left blank to permit users to enter new records. If the **AllowAddNew** property is **False**, the blank row is not displayed, and **AddNewMode** always returns 0.

Note This property is valid in both bound and unbound modes.

See Also

Value Property (Column Object), **AllowAddNew** Property, **Text** Property

---

AddressOf Operator

A unary operator that causes the address of the procedure it precedes to be passed to an API procedure that expects a function pointer at that position in the argument list.

Syntax

AddressOf *procedurename*

The required *procedurename* specifies the procedure whose address is to be passed. It must represent a procedure in a standard module module in the project in which the call is made.

Remarks

When a procedure name appears in an argument list, usually the procedure is evaluated, and the address of the procedure's return value is passed. **AddressOf** permits the address of the procedure to be passed to a Windows API function in a dynamic-link library (DLL), rather passing the procedure's return value. The API function can then use the address to call the Basic procedure, a process known as a callback. The **AddressOf** operator appears only in the call to the API procedure. However, in the **Declare** statement that describes the API function to which the pointer is passed, the procedure address argument must be declared **As Any**.

Although you can use **AddressOf** to pass procedure pointers among Basic procedures, you can't call a function through such a pointer from within Basic. This means, for example, that a class written in Basic can't make a callback to its controller using such a pointer. When using **AddressOf** to pass a procedure pointer among procedures within Basic, the parameter of the called procedure must be typed **As Long**.

Warning Using **AddressOf** may cause unpredictable results if you don't completely understand the concept of function callbacks. You must understand how the Basic portion of the callback works, and also the code of the DLL into which you are passing your function address. Debugging such interactions is difficult since the program runs in the same process as the development environment. In some cases, systematic debugging may not be possible.

Note   You can create your own call-back function prototypes in DLLs compiled with Microsoft Visual C++ (or similar tools). To work with **AddressOf**, your prototype must use the __stdcall calling convention. The default calling convention (__cdecl) will not work with **AddressOf**.

Since the caller of a callback is not within your program, it is important that an error in the callback procedure not be propagated back to the caller. You can accomplish this by placing the **On Error Resume Next** statement at the beginning of the callback procedure.

See Also

Declare Statement, **Function** Statement, **Property Get** Statement, **Property Let** Statement, **Property Set** Statement, **Sub** Statement

Example

The following example creates a form with a list box containing an alphabetically sorted list of the fonts in your system.

To run this example, create a form with a list box on it. The code for the form is as follows:

```
Option Explicit

Private Sub Form_Load()
    Module1.FillListWithFonts List1
End Sub
```

Place the following code in a module. The third argument in the definition of the **EnumFontFamilies** function is a **Long** that represents a procedure. The argument must contain the address of the procedure, rather than the value that the procedure returns. In the call to **EnumFontFamilies**, the third argument requires the **AddressOf** operator to return the address of the **EnumFontFamProc** procedure, which is the name of the callback procedure you supply when calling the Windows API function, **EnumFontFamilies**. Windows calls **EnumFontFamProc** once for each of the font families on the system when you pass **AddressOf EnumFontFamProc** to **EnumFontFamilies**. The last argument passed to **EnumFontFamilies** specifies the list box in which the information is displayed.

```
'Font enumeration types
Public Const LF_FACESIZE = 32
Public Const LF_FULLFACESIZE = 64

Type LOGFONT
        lfHeight As Long
        lfWidth As Long
        lfEscapement As Long
        lfOrientation As Long
        lfWeight As Long
        lfItalic As Byte
        lfUnderline As Byte
        lfStrikeOut As Byte
        lfCharSet As Byte
```

```
            lfOutPrecision As Byte
            lfClipPrecision As Byte
            lfQuality As Byte
            lfPitchAndFamily As Byte
            lfFaceName(LF_FACESIZE) As Byte
End Type

Type NEWTEXTMETRIC
            tmHeight As Long
            tmAscent As Long
            tmDescent As Long
            tmInternalLeading As Long
            tmExternalLeading As Long
            tmAveCharWidth As Long
            tmMaxCharWidth As Long
            tmWeight As Long
            tmOverhang As Long
            tmDigitizedAspectX As Long
            tmDigitizedAspectY As Long
            tmFirstChar As Byte
            tmLastChar As Byte
            tmDefaultChar As Byte
            tmBreakChar As Byte
            tmItalic As Byte
            tmUnderlined As Byte
            tmStruckOut As Byte
            tmPitchAndFamily As Byte
            tmCharSet As Byte
            ntmFlags As Long
            ntmSizeEM As Long
            ntmCellHeight As Long
            ntmAveWidth As Long
End Type

' ntmFlags field flags
Public Const NTM_REGULAR = &H40&
Public Const NTM_BOLD = &H20&
Public Const NTM_ITALIC = &H1&

' tmPitchAndFamily flags
Public Const TMPF_FIXED_PITCH = &H1
Public Const TMPF_VECTOR = &H2
Public Const TMPF_DEVICE = &H8
Public Const TMPF_TRUETYPE = &H4

Public Const ELF_VERSION = 0
Public Const ELF_CULTURE_LATIN = 0

' EnumFonts Masks
Public Const RASTER_FONTTYPE = &H1
Public Const DEVICE_FONTTYPE = &H2
Public Const TRUETYPE_FONTTYPE = &H4
```

```
Declare Function EnumFontFamilies Lib "gdi32" Alias _
   "EnumFontFamiliesA" _
   (ByVal hDC As Long, ByVal lpszFamily As String, _
   ByVal lpEnumFontFamProc As Long, LParam As Any) As Long
Declare Function GetDC Lib "user32" (ByVal hWnd As Long) As Long
Declare Function ReleaseDC Lib "user32" (ByVal hWnd As Long, _
   ByVal hDC As Long) As Long

Function EnumFontFamProc(lpNLF As LOGFONT, lpNTM As NEWTEXTMETRIC, _
   ByVal FontType As Long, LParam As ListBox) As Long
Dim FaceName As String
Dim FullName As String
   FaceName = StrConv(lpNLF.lfFaceName, vbUnicode)
   LParam.AddItem Left$(FaceName, InStr(FaceName, vbNullChar) - 1)
   EnumFontFamProc = 1
End Function

Sub FillListWithFonts(LB As ListBox)
Dim hDC As Long
   LB.Clear
   hDC = GetDC(LB.hWnd)
   EnumFontFamilies hDC, vbNullString, AddressOf EnumFontFamProc, LB
   ReleaseDC LB.hWnd, hDC
End Sub
```

AddToAddInToolbar Method

Inserts a button on the Add-In toolbar which references an add-in or Wizard.

Applies To

Add-In Toolbar

Syntax

object.**AddToAddInToolbar** (*sfilename* **As String**, *sprogid* **As String**, *showontoolbar* **As Boolean**, *forceaddintoolbar* **As Boolean**)

Part	Description
object	An object expression that evaluates to an object in the **Applies To** list.
sfilename	Required. A string expression specifying the path to the add-in or Wizard and the name of its .Exe or .Dll file.
sprogid	Required. A string expression specifying the programmatic ID (ProgID) of the add-in or Wizard.
saddinname	Required. A string expression specifying the title of the add-in or Wizard.
showontoolbar	Required. A Boolean expression specifying whether the add-in or Wizard referred to will appear on the Add-In toolbar. **True** = yes, **False** = no.
forceaddintoolbar	Required. A Boolean expression specifying whether the Add-In toolbar is automatically displayed the next time Visual Basic is started. **True** = yes, **False** = no.

See Also

> **RemoveAddInFromToolbar** Method

Example

> This example uses the **AddToAddInToolbar** method to add a button to the Add-In toolbar for a fictitious add-in called MyAdd.Dll. Setting **ForceAddInToolbar** to **True** ensures that the Add-In toolbar is loaded the next time Visual Basic is started.
>
> You could modify the following in a small Visual Basic application to serve as a Setup for your add-in.

```
Sub Main()
    dim x as Object
    Set x=CreateObject("AddInToolbar.Manager")
    x.AddToAddInToolbar sFileName:="C:\VB5\MyAdd.DLL", _
        sProgID:="MyAddIn.Connect", _
        sAddInName:="MyAddIn Title" _
        ShowOnToolBar:=True, _
        ForceAddInToolbar:=True
End Sub
```

AddToolboxProgID Method

> Places the control or embedded component in the toolbox and adds a control reference to the project.

Applies To

> **VBProject** Object

Syntax

> *object*.**AddToolboxProgID** (**ByVal** *progid* **As String**, [*filename* **As String**])
>
> The **AddToolboxProgID** method syntax has these parts:

Part	Description
object	An object expression that evaluates to an object in the **Applies To** list.
progid	Required. A string expression specifying the programmatic identifier (**ProgID**) of the compound document object to add to the Visual Basic toolbox. Either a version-independent or version-dependent **ProgID** can be used. If a version-independent progid is specified, the most recent version is used. If the compound document object has an associated type library, this type library is referenced as well.
filename	Optional. A string expression specifying the filename of the desired type library to be added to Visual Basic. A complete pathname can be used, but if the file isn't found, the directories searched by the Windows **OpenFile** function are searched, even if a complete pathname is specified.

AfterAddFile Event

Occurs after a component is added to the current Visual Basic project with the **Add File** command in the **Project** menu.

Applies To

FileControlEvents Object

Syntax

Sub *object*_**AfterAddFile**(*vbproject* **As VBProject**, *filetype* **As vbext_FileType**,
↳ *filename* **As String**)

The **AfterAddFile** event syntax has these parts:

Part	Description
object	An object expression that evaluates to an object in the **Applies To** list.
vbproject	A **VBProject** object specifying the name of the project in which the file was added.
filetype	An enumerated value (**vbext_FileType**) specifying the type of file that was added, as listed in **Settings**.
filename	A string expression specifying the name of the file that was added.

Settings

The enumerated values for **vbext_FileType** are:

Constant	Value	Description
vbext_ft_Form	0	File type is a form.
vbext_ft_Module	1	File type is a basic module.
vbext_ft_Class	2	File type is a class module
vbext_ft_Project	3	File type is a project.
vbext_ft_Exe	4	File type is an executable file.
vbext_ft_Res	6	File type is a resource file.
vbext_ft_UserControl	7	File type is a **User** control.
vbext_ft_PropertyPage	8	File type is a **Property Page**.
vbext_ft_DocObject	9	File type is a **User Document**.
vbext_ft_Binary	10	File type is a binary file.
vbext_ft_GroupProject	11	File type is a group project.
vbext_ft_Designer	12	File type is a designer object.

Remarks

Visual Basic triggers this event only for files you can add from the **Project** menu. (That is, forms, classes, **User** controls, **Property Pages**, and modules). The **AfterAddFile** event does not occur if you select **Add** *object* from the **Project** menu. It also does not occur when an .Frx file is created for the first time, and doesn't occur twice when a form is added.

This event occurs in all add-ins that are connected to the **FileControl** object. The add-in cannot prevent the file from being written to disk because the operation is complete. However, you can use this event to perform other tasks, such as:

- Log information about the event.
- Update information about the file.
- Backup the file.

AfterChangeFileName Event

Occurs after a file in the current project has been saved for the first time, or saved with a new name. It also occurs when the project is first compiled to an .Exe file, or when compiled to a new .Exe name.

Applies To

FileControlEvents Object

Syntax

Sub *object*_**AfterChangeFileName** (*vbproject* **As VBProject**,
↪ *filetype* **As vbext_FileType**, *newname* **As String**, *oldname* **As String**)

The **AfterChangeFileName** event syntax has these parts:

Part	Description
object	An object expression that evaluates to an object in the **Applies To** list.
vbproject	A **VBProject** object specifying the name of the project in which the file was changed.
filetype	An enumerated value (**vbext_FileType**) specifying the type of file that was changed, as listed in Settings.
newname	A string expression specifying the new name of the file.
oldname	A string expression specifying the old name of the file.

Settings

The enumerated values for **vbext_FileType** are:

Constant	Value	Description
vbext_ft_Form	0	File type is a form.
vbext_ft_Module	1	File type is a basic module.
vbext_ft_Class	2	File type is a class module.
vbext_ft_Project	3	File type is a project.
vbext_ft_Exe	4	File type is an executable file.
vbext_ft_Res	6	File type is a resource file.
vbext_ft_UserControl	7	File type is a **User** control.
vbext_ft_PropertyPage	8	File type is a **Property Page**.
vbext_ft_DocObject	9	File type is a **User Document**.
vbext_ft_Binary	10	File type is a binary file.
vbext_ft_GroupProject	11	File type is a group project.
vbext_ft_Designer	12	File type is a designer object.

AfterCloseFile Event

Occurs after a project has been closed, either directly by the user, or by Visual Basic when the user quits the program.

Applies To

FileControlEvents Object

Syntax

Sub *object*_**AfterCloseFile**(*vbproject* **As VBProject**, *filetype* **As vbext_FileType**,
↪ *filename* **As String**, *wasdirty* **As Boolean**)

The **AfterCloseFile** event syntax has these parts:

Part	Description
object	An object expression that evaluates to an object in the **Applies To** list.
vbproject	A **VBProject** object specifying the name of the project in which the file was closed.
filetype	An enumerated value (**vbext_FileType**) specifying the type of file that was closed, as listed in Settings.
filename	A string expression specifying the name of the file that was closed.
wasdirty	A Boolean expression that specifies whether changes were saved to a file prior to it being closed, as listed in Settings.

Settings

The enumerated values for **vbext_FileType** are:

Constant	Value	Description
vbext_ft_Form	0	File type is a form.
vbext_ft_Module	1	File type is a basic module.
vbext_ft_Class	2	File type is a class module.
vbext_ft_Project	3	File type is a project.
vbext_ft_Exe	4	File type is an executable file.
vbext_ft_Res	6	File type is a resource file.
vbext_ft_UserControl	7	File type is a **User** control.
vbext_ft_PropertyPage	8	File type is a **Property Page**.
vbext_ft_DocObject	9	File type is a **User Document**.
vbext_ft_Binary	10	File type is a binary file.
vbext_ft_GroupProject	11	File type is a group project.
vbext_ft_Designer	12	File type is a designer object.

The settings for *wasdirty* are:

Setting	Description
True	The file was dirty when it was closed. (That is, the user elected to not save changes made to the file prior to closing it.)
False	The file was not dirty when it was closed (That is, the user selected to save changes made to the file prior to closing it.)

Remarks

This event can occur once for each add-in connected to the **FileControl** object in each project; once for each form, module, class, and control file, and once for the project file.

The **AfterCloseFile** event does not occur if the form is dirty and the user selects **No** on the **Save changes to the following files** dialog box. Also, this event does not occur for .Frx files when a project is closed. It occurs when the .Frm file is saved.

This event occurs in all add-ins that are connected to the **FileControl** object. The add-in cannot prevent the file from being written to disk because the operation is complete. However, you can use this event to perform other tasks, such as:

- Log information about the event.
- Update information about the file.
- Back up the file.
- Compare versions of the executable (.EXE) file.

See Also

AfterWriteFile Event

AfterColEdit Event

Occurs after editing is completed in a grid cell.

Applies To

DBGrid Control

Syntax

Private Sub *object*_**AfterColEdit**([*index* **As Integer**,] **ByVal** *colindex* **As Integer**)

The **AfterColEdit** event syntax has these parts:

Part	Description
object	An object expression that evaluates to an object in the **Applies To** list.
Index	An integer that identifies a control if it is in a control array.
colindex	An integer that identifies the column that was edited.

Remarks

When the user completes editing within a grid cell, as when tabbing to another column in the same row, pressing the ENTER key, or clicking on another cell, the **BeforeColUpdate** and **AfterColUpdate** events are executed, and data from the cell is moved to the grid's copy buffer. The **AfterColEdit** event immediately follows the **AfterColUpdate** event.

When editing is completed in a grid cell, this event is always triggered, even if no changes were made to the cell or the **BeforeColUpdate** event was canceled.

The **AfterColEdit** event will not be fired if the **BeforeColEdit** event is canceled.

See Also

BeforeColEdit Event, **AfterColUpdate** Event, **BeforeColUpdate** Event

---

AfterColUpdate Event

Occurs after data is moved from a cell in the **DBGrid** control to the control's copy buffer.

Applies To

DBGrid Control

Syntax

Private Sub *object*_**AfterColUpdate** ([*index* **As Integer**,] *colindex* **As Integer**)

The **AfterColUpdate** event syntax has these parts:

Part	Description
object	An object expression that evaluates to an object in the **Applies To** list.
index	An integer that identifies a control if it is in a control array.
colindex	An integer that identifies the column in the control.

Remarks

When a user completes editing within a **DBGrid** control cell, as when tabbing to another column in the same row, pressing ENTER, or when the control loses focus, the **BeforeColUpdate** event is executed, and unless canceled, data from the cell is moved to the control's copy buffer. Once moved, the **AfterColUpdate** event is executed.

The **AfterColUpdate** event occurs after the **BeforeColUpdate** event, and only if the *cancel* argument in the **BeforeColUpdate** event is not set to **True**.

Once the **AfterColUpdate** event procedure begins, the cell data has already been moved to the control's copy buffer and can't be canceled, but other updates can occur before the data is committed to the **Recordset**.

See Also

DBGrid Control, **BeforeColUpdate** Event, **ColIndex** Property

Example

This example does a lookup when one column is updated and places the result in another column.

```
Private Sub DataGrid1_AfterColUpdate (ColIndex As Integer)
   If ColIndex = 1 Then
      Data1.Recordset.FindFirst "PubId = " _
      & DataGrid1.Columns(1).Value
      If Not Data1.Recordset.NoMatch Then
         DataGrid1.Columns(2).Value = _
          Data1.Recordset.Fields("Publisher")
      Else
         DataGrid1.Columns(2).Value = "No Match"
      End If
   End If
End Sub
```

AfterDelete Event

Occurs after the user deletes a selected record in the **DBGrid** control.

Applies To

DBGrid Control

Syntax

Private Sub *object_***AfterDelete** ([*index* **As Integer**,] *colindex* **As Integer**)

The **AfterDelete** event syntax has these parts:

Part	Description
object	An object expression that evaluates to an object in the **Applies To** list.
index	An integer that identifies a control if it is in a control array.
colindex	An integer that identifies the column.

Remarks

When the user selects a record selector in the **DBGrid** control and presses DEL or CTRL+X, the selected row is deleted. Before the record is deleted, the **BeforeDelete** event is triggered. Once the row is deleted, the **AfterDelete** event is triggered. The row selected for deletion is available in the collection provided by the **SelBookmarks** property.

See Also

BeforeColUpdate Event, **BeforeDelete** Event, **SelBookmarks** Property

Example

This example displays a message confirming that a record has successfully been deleted.

```
Private Sub DataGrid1_AfterDelete ()
    MsgBox "Record has successfully been deleted!"
End Sub
```

AfterInsert Event

Occurs after the user inserts a new record into the **DBGrid** control.

Applies To

DBGrid Control

Syntax

Private Sub *object*_**AfterInsert** (*index* **As Integer**)

The **AfterInsert** event syntax has these parts:

Part	Description
object	An object expression that evaluates to an object in the **Applies To** list.
index	An integer that identifies a control if it is in a control array.

Remarks

When the user selects the new record (at the bottom of the control) and enters a character in one of the cells, the **BeforeInsert** event is triggered, followed by the **BeforeUpdate**, **AfterUpdate** and **AfterInsert** events.

When the **AfterInsert** event is triggered, the record has already been added to the database. The **Bookmark** property can be used to access the new record.

The **AfterInsert** event can't be canceled.

The **AfterInsert** event procedure can be used to update other tables or to perform post-update cleanup of other controls.

See Also

AfterUpdate Event, **BeforeInsert** Event, **BeforeUpdate** Event

Example

This example creates an entry in a related table if the user enters a value in a column in the grid.

```
Private SubDataGrid1_AfterInsert ()
    If DataGrid1.Columns(1).Value <> "" Then
        Data2.Recordset.AddNew
        Data2.Recordset.Fields("PubId") = DataGrid1.Columns(1).Value
        Data2.Recordset.Update
    End If
End Sub
```

AfterRemoveFile Event

Occurs after a file is removed from the active Visual Basic project.

Applies To

FileControlEvents Object

Syntax

Sub *object*_**AfterRemoveFile**(*vbproject* **As VBProject**, *filetype* **As vbext_FileType**, *filename* **As String**)

The **AfterRemoveFile** event syntax has these parts:

Part	Description
object	An object expression that evaluates to an object in the **Applies To** list.
vbproject	A **VBProject** object specifying the name of the project from which the file was removed.
filetype	An enumerated value (**vbext_FileType**) specifying the type of file that was removed, as listed in Settings.
filename	A string expression specifying the name of the file that was removed.

Remarks

The **AfterRemoveFile** event does not occur for components that are removed before they have been saved.

This event occurs in all add-ins that are connected to the **FileControl** object. The add-in cannot prevent the file from being written to disk because the operation is complete. However, you can use this event to perform other tasks, such as:

- Log information about the event.
- Update information about the file.
- Back up the file.

See Also

AfterCloseFile Event

AfterUpdate Event

Occurs after changed data has been written to the database from a **DBGrid** control.

Applies To

DBGrid Control

Syntax

Sub *object*_**AfterUpdate** (*index* **As Integer**)

The **AfterUpdate** event syntax has these parts:

Part	Description
object	An object expression that evaluates to an object in the **Applies To** list.
index	An integer that identifies a control if it is in a control array.

Remarks

When the user moves to another row, or the **Recordset** object's **Update** method is executed, data is moved from the control's copy buffer to the **Data** control's copy buffer and written to the database. Once the write is complete, the **AfterUpdate** event is triggered.

The updated record is available by using the **Bookmark** property of the **DBGrid** control.

The **AfterUpdate** event occurs after the **BeforeUpdate** event, but before the **LostFocus** event for the control (or **GotFocus** for the next control in the tab order). This event occurs in bound and unbound mode and can't be canceled.

Unlike the **Change** event, changing data in a control or record using code doesn't trigger this event.

See Also

BeforeColUpdate Event, **BeforeInsert** Event, **BeforeUpdate** Event

Example

This example updates a label when any change has been made in the grid.

```
Private Sub DataGrid1_AfterUpdate ()
    Label1.Caption = "Last modified: " & Format$(Now, "Long Date")
End Sub
```

AfterWriteFile Event

Occurs after a file is written to disk.

Applies To

FileControlEvents Object

Syntax

Sub *object*_**AfterWriteFile**(*vbproject* As **VBProject**, *filetype* As **vbext_FileType**,
↪ *filename* As **String**, *result* As **Integer**)

The **AfterWriteFile** event syntax has these parts:

Part	Description
object	An object expression that evaluates to an object in the **Applies To** list.
vbproject	A **VBProject** object specifying the name of the project to which the file was written.
filetype	An enumerated value (**vbext_FileType**) specifying the type of file that was written, as listed in Settings.
filename	A string expression specifying the name of the file that was written.
result	A numeric expression that specifies the result of the write operation, as listed in Settings.

Settings

The enumerated values for **vbext_FileType** are:

Constant	Value	Description
vbext_ft_Form	0	File type is a form.
vbext_ft_Module	1	File type is a basic module.
vbext_ft_Class	2	File type is a class module.
vbext_ft_Project	3	File type is a project.
vbext_ft_Exe	4	File type is an executable file.
vbext_ft_Res	6	File type is a resource file.
vbext_ft_UserControl	7	File type is a **User** control.
vbext_ft_PropertyPage	8	File type is a **Property Page**.

(continued)

Constant	Value	Description
vbext_ft_DocObject	9	File type is a **User Document**.
vbext_ft_Binary	10	File type is a binary file.
vbext_ft_GroupProject	11	File type is a group project.
vbext_ft_Designer	12	File type is a designer object.

The settings for *result* are:

Value	Description
0	Write was successful.
1	Write was canceled.
2	Write failed.

Remarks

The **AfterWriteFile** event occurs when the binary data file associated with a component (such as an .Frx file) is saved for the first time, and occurs in all add-ins that are connected to the **FileControl** object. The add-in cannot prevent the file from being written to disk because the operation is complete. However, you can use this event to perform other tasks, such as:

- Log information about the event.
- Update information about the file.
- Back up the file.
- Compare versions of the executable (.EXE) file.

Align Property

Returns or sets a value that determines whether an object is displayed in any size anywhere on a form or whether it's displayed at the top, bottom, left, or right of the form and is automatically sized to fit the form's width.

Applies To

Data Control, **DBGrid** Control, **ProgressBar** Control, **RemoteData** Control, **StatusBar** Control, **Toolbar** Control, **PictureBox** Control

Syntax

object.**Align** [= *number*]

The **Align** property syntax has these parts:

Part	Description
object	An object expression that evaluates to an object in the **Applies To** list.
number	An integer that specifies how an object is displayed, as described in Settings.

Settings

The settings for *number* are:

Constant	Setting	Description
vbAlignNone	0	(Default in a non-MDI form) None—size and location can be set at design time or in code. This setting is ignored if the object is on an MDI form.
vbAlignTop	1	(Default in an MDI form) Top—object is at the top of the form, and its width is equal to the form's **ScaleWidth** property setting.
vbAlignBottom	2	Bottom—object is at the bottom of the form, and its width is equal to the form's **ScaleWidth** property setting.
vbAlignLeft	3	Left—object is at the left of the form, and its width is equal to the form's **ScaleWidth** property setting.
vbAlignRight	4	Right—object is at the right of the form, and its width is equal to the form's **ScaleWidth** property setting.

Remarks

You can use the **Align** property to quickly create a toolbar or status bar at the top or bottom of a form. As a user changes the size of the form, an object with **Align** set to 1 or 2 automatically resizes to fit the width of the form.

PictureBox and **Data** controls are the only standard controls that can be placed on an MDI form. The internal area of an MDI form is defined by the space not covered by controls. When an MDI child form is maximized within the parent MDI form, it won't cover any controls.

Use *number* settings 3 and 4 to align toolbars at the left and right sides of a form or MDI form. If there are two toolbars in a corner of an MDI form, the top- or bottom-aligned one extends to the corner, taking precedence over the left- or right-aligned one. Left- and right-aligned objects occupy the internal area on an MDI form, just like top- and bottom-aligned objects.

See Also

Alignment Property, **ScaleHeight**, **ScaleWidth** Properties

Example

This example uses a **PictureBox** control as a toolbar on an **MDIForm** object, with a **CommandButton** control to move the **PictureBox** from the top to the bottom of the form. To try this example, create a new **MDIForm** and set the **MDIChild** property of Form1 to **True**. Draw a **PictureBox** on the **MDIForm**, and put a **CommandButton** on the **PictureBox**. Paste the code into the Declarations section of the **MDIForm**, and then press F5. Click the **CommandButton** to move the **PictureBox**.

```
Private Sub Command1_Click ()
   If Picture1.Align = vbAlignTop Then
      Picture1.Align = vbAlignBottom
      ' Align to bottom of form.
   Else
      Picture1.Align = vbAlignTop
      ' Align to top of form.
   End If
End Sub
```

Alignable Property

Returns or sets a value determining if a control is alignable, and can use the extender **Align** property. The **Alignable** property is read/write at the control's authoring time, and not available at the control's run time.

Applies To

UserControl Object

Settings

The settings for **Alignable** are:

Setting	Description
True	The control is alignable; the container will add the **Align** property to the extender object.
False	The control is not alignable. This is the default value.

Remarks

The alignment of the control itself will be handled by the container; the author of the control can use the **Align** extender property to decide how to redraw the control and arrange the constituent controls in response to an alignment.

Note Not all containers support alignable controls. Error trapping should be used if you access the **Align** extender property to determine how your control has been aligned.

See Also

Align Property

Alignment Property

Returns or sets a value that determines the alignment of a **CheckBox** or **OptionButton** control, text in a control, or values in a column of a **DBGrid** control. Read-only at run time for **CheckBox**, **OptionButton**, and **TextBox** controls.

Applies To

CheckBox Control, **Label** Control, **OptionButton** Control, **TextBox** Control, **Column** Object

Syntax

object.**Alignment** [= *number*]

The **Alignment** property syntax has these parts:

Part	Description
object	An object expression that evaluates to an object in the **Applies To** list.
Number	An integer that specifies the type of alignment, as described in Settings.

Settings

For **CheckBox** and **OptionButton** controls, the settings for *number* are:

Constant	Setting	Description
vbLeftJustify	0	(Default) Text is left-aligned; control is right-aligned.
vbRightJustify	1	Text is right-aligned; control is left-aligned.

For **Label** and **TextBox** controls, the settings for *number* are:

Constant	Setting	Description
vbLeftJustify	0	(Default) Text is left-aligned.
vbRightJustify	1	Text is right-aligned.
vbCenter	2	Text is centered.

For a **DBGrid** column, the settings for *number* are:

Constant	Setting	Description
dbgLeft	0	Text is left-aligned.
dbgRight	1	Text is right-aligned.
dbgCenter	2	Text is centered.
dbgGeneral	3	(Default) General—Text is left-aligned; numbers are right-aligned.

Remarks

You can display text to the right or left of **OptionButton** and **CheckBox** controls. By default, text is left-aligned.

The **MultiLine** property in a **Textbox** control must be set to **True** for the **Alignment** property to work correctly. If the **MultiLine** property setting of a **TextBox** control is **False**, the **Alignment** property is ignored.

See Also

Align Property, **Add** Method (ColumnHeaders Collection), **ListView Control** Constants, **ColumnHeader** Object, **ColumnHeaders** Collection

---

AllowAddNew Property

Returns or sets a value indicating whether the user can add new records to the **Recordset** object underlying a **DBGrid** control.

Applies To

DBGrid Control

Syntax

object.**AllowAddNew** [= *value*]

The **AllowAddNew** property syntax has these parts:

Part	Description
object	An object expression that evaluates to an object in the **Applies To** list.
value	A Boolean expression that determines whether a user can add new records, as described in Settings.

Settings

The settings for *value* are:

Setting	Description
True	Users can add records to the **Recordset** object underlying the **DBGrid** control.
False	Users can't add records to the **Recordset** underlying the **DBGrid** control.

Remarks

If the **AllowAddnew** property is **True**, the last row displayed in the **DBGrid** control is left blank to permit users to enter new records. If the **AllowAddNew** property is **False**, no blank line is displayed.

The underlying **Recordset** may not enable insertions even if the **AllowAddNew** property is **True**. In this case, an error occurs when the user tries to add a record.

See Also

Data Control, **Recordset** Property, **AllowDelete** Property, **AllowUpdate** Property

Example

This example checks the value of a check box. If it is **False**, the user can't make changes to the grid.

```
Private Sub Form_Load ()
    If Check1.Value = 0 Then
        DBGrid1.AllowDelete = False
        DBGrid1.AllowAddNew = False
        DBGrid1.AllowUpdate = False
    End If
End Sub
```

AllowArrows Property

Sets or returns a value that determines whether the control uses the arrow keys for grid navigation.

Applies To

DBGrid Control

Syntax

object.**AllowArrows** [= *value*]

The **AllowArrows** property syntax has these parts:

Part	Description
object	An object expression that evaluates to an object in the **Applies To** list.
value	A Boolean expression that determines the arrow keys are used for grid navigation, as described in Settings.

Settings

The settings for *value* are:

Setting	Description
True	(Default) The user can use the arrow keys to move from cell to cell within the same row.
False	The left and right arrow keys will move focus from control to control and cannot be used to move between cells.

Remarks

The user cannot use the arrow keys to move out of the **DBGrid** control when this property is set to **True**. If the **WrapCellPointer** property is also set to **True**, then the arrow keys will wrap around rows and the user can navigate the entire grid using the arrow keys.

See Also

WrapCellPointer Property

AllowDelete Property

Returns or sets a value indicating whether the user can delete records from the **Recordset** object underlying a **DBGrid** control.

Applies To

DBGrid Control

Syntax

object.**AllowDelete** [= *value*]

The **AllowDelete** property syntax has these parts:

Part	Description
object	An object expression that evaluates to an object in the **Applies To** list.
value	A Boolean expression that determines whether a user can delete records, as described in **Settings**.

Settings

The settings for *value* are:

Setting	Description
True	Users can delete records from the **Recordset** object underlying the **DBGrid** control.
False	Users can't delete records from the **Recordset** underlying the **DBGrid** control.

Remarks

Use the **AllowDelete** property to prevent the user from deleting records from the **Recordset** through interaction with the **DBGrid** control.

The underlying **Recordset** may not enable deletions even if the **AllowDelete** property is **True** for the **DBGrid** control. In this case, an error occurs when the user tries to delete a record.

See Also

Data Control, **AllowAddNew** Property, **AllowUpdate** Property

AllowFocus Property

Sets or returns a value that determines whether cells within a split can receive focus.

Applies To

Split Object

Syntax

object.**AllowFocus** [= *value*]

The **AllowFocus** property syntax has these parts:

Part	Description
object	An object expression that evaluates to an object in the **Applies To** list.
value	A Boolean expression that determines whether a cell receives focus, as described in Settings.

Settings

The settings for *value* are:

Setting	Description
True	(Default) The user will be able to interactively select the split, giving it focus.
False	The user will not be able to interactively select the split. When clicked on, the split will not receive focus and the control that previously had focus will retain it.

Remarks

Use this property in combination with the **AllowSizing** property to completely prohibit the user from making any changes to a split (by setting both properties to **False**). Unselectable splits are passed over when **TabAcrossSplits** is set to **True**.

See Also

TabAcrossSplits Property, **AllowSizing** Property

AllowRowSizing Property

Returns or sets a value indicating whether a user can resize the rows of the **DBGrid** control or **Split** object at run-time.

Applies To

Split Object, **DBGrid** Control

Syntax

object.**AllowRowSizing** [= *value*]

The **AllowRowSizing** property syntax has these parts:

Part	Description
object	An object expression that evaluates to an object in the **Applies To** list.
value	A Boolean expression that determines whether a user can resize rows, as described in Settings.

Settings

The settings for *value* are:

Setting	Description
True	Rows can be sized by the user.
False	Rows can't be sized by the user.

Remarks

If the **AllowRowSizing** property is **True**, the mouse pointer turns into a double-headed (Size N S) arrow when positioned over the row divider between any record selectors, and the user can resize the rows by dragging. Any change in row size causes a **RowResize** event.

All rows of the **DBGrid** control are always the same height, which is determined by the **RowHeight** property.

Note Even if the **AllowRowSizing** property is **False**, the height of the rows can still be changed programmatically with the **RowHeight** property.

See Also

Data Control, **RowResize** Event, **DefColWidth** Property, **VisibleRows** Property

Example

This example checks the database to see if it has any memo fields; if not, row resizing is disabled.

```
Sub CheckForMemoField()
    Dim Fld As Field
    DBGrid1.AllowRowSizing = False
    For Each Fld in Data1.Recordset.Fields
        If Fld.Type = dbMemo Then
            DBGrid1.AllowRowSizing = True
            DBGrid1.RowHeight = DBGrid1.RowHeight * 2
            Exit For
        End If
    Next
End Sub
```

AllowSizing Property

Returns or sets a value indicating whether a user can resize columns or splits in the **DBGrid** control at run-time.

Applies To

Split Object, **Column** Object

Syntax

object.**AllowSizing** [= *value*]

The **AllowSizing** property syntax has these parts:

Part	Description
object	An object expression that evaluates to an object in the **Applies To** list.
value	A Boolean expression that determines whether a column or split can be resized, as described in Settings.

Settings

The settings for *value* are:

Setting	Description
True	(Default for **Column**) User can resize column or split.
False	(Default for **Split**) User can't resize column or split.

Remarks

If the **AllowSizing** property is **True**, the mouse pointer turns into a double-headed (Size W E) arrow when positioned over the divider of the specified column, and the user can resize the column by dragging. Any change in column size causes a ColResize event.

For the leftmost split with **AllowSizing** set to **True**, the mouse pointer turns into a pair of vertical lines with a downward arrow when positioned over that split's size box (at the lower left corner), and the user can create a new split by dragging. The creation of a new split causes a **SplitChange** event.

If **AllowSizing** is **True** for any other split, the mouse pointer turns into a pair of vertical lines with a double-headed arrow when positioned over that split's size box, and the user can resize the split by dragging. No event is fired in this case (except for the standard mouse events).

See Also

Data Control, **ColResize** Event, **RowResize** Event, **AllowRowSizing** Property, **DefColWidth** Property, **VisibleRows** Property

Example

This example prevents the user from resizing or editing the first three columns of the grid.

```
Private Sub Form_Load ()
    Dim I
    For I = 0 to 2
        DBGrid1.Columns(I).AllowSizing = False
        DBGrid1.Columns(I).Locked = True
    Next I
End Sub
```

AllowUpdate Property

Returns or sets a value indicating whether a user can modify any data in the **DBGrid** control.

Applies To

DBGrid Control

Syntax

object.**AllowUpdate** [= *value*]

The **AllowUpdate** property syntax has these parts:

Part	Description
object	An object expression that evaluates to an object in the **Applies To** list.
value	A Boolean expression that determines whether the user can change data, as described in **Settings**.

Settings

The settings for *value* are:

Setting	Description
True	The user can modify data in the **DBGrid** control
False	The user can't modify data in the **DBGrid** control

Remarks

When the **AllowUpdate** property is **False**, the user can still scroll through the **DBGrid** control and select data, but can't change any of the values; any attempt to change the data in the grid is ignored.

You can also use the **Column** object properties to make individual columns of the **DBGrid** control read-only, but the **AllowUpdate** property setting takes precedence over the column settings (without changing the column settings).

Note The **Recordset** object may not enable updates even if **AllowUpdate** is **True** for the **DBGrid** control; in this case a trappable error occurs when the user tries to change the record.

See Also

Data Control, **AllowAddNew** Property, **AllowDelete** Property

AllowZeroLength Property

Sets or returns a value that indicates whether a zero-length string ("") is a valid setting for the **Value** property of the **Field** object with a **Text** or **Memo** data type.

Applies To

Field Object

Settings and Return Values

The setting or return value is a **Boolean** data type that indicates if a value is valid. The value is **True** if the **Field** object accepts a zero-length string as its **Value** property; the default value is **False**.

Remarks

For an object not yet appended to the **Fields** collection, this property is read/write.

Once appended to a **Fields** collection, the availability of the **AllowZeroLength** property depends on the object that contains the **Fields** collection, as shown in the following table.

If the Fields collection belongs to an	Then AllowZeroLength is
Index object	Not supported
QueryDef object	Read-only
Recordset object	Read-only
Relation object	Not supported
TableDef object	Read/write

You can use this property along with the **Required**, **ValidateOnSet**, or **ValidationRule** property to validate a value in a field.

See Also

TableDef Object, **Required** Property, **ValidateOnSet** Property, **ValidationRule** Property, **ValidationText** Property, **Value** Property

Example

In this example, the **AllowZeroLength** property allows the user to set the value of a **Field** to an empty string. In this situation, the user can distinguish between a record where data is not known and a record where the data does not apply.

```
Sub AllowZeroLengthX()

    Dim dbsNorthwind As Database
    Dim tdfEmployees As TableDef
    Dim fldTemp As Field
    Dim rstEmployees As Recordset
    Dim strMessage As String
    Dim strInput As String

    Set dbsNorthwind = OpenDatabase("Northwind.mdb")
    Set tdfEmployees = dbsNorthwind.TableDefs("Employees")
    ' Create a new Field object and append it to the Fields
    ' collection of the Employees table.
    Set fldTemp = tdfEmployees.CreateField("FaxPhone", _
        dbText, 24)
    fldTemp.AllowZeroLength = True
    tdfEmployees.Fields.Append fldTemp

    Set rstEmployees = _
        dbsNorthwind.OpenRecordset("Employees")

    With rstEmployees
        ' Get user input.
        .Edit
        strMessage = "Enter fax number for " & _
            !FirstName & " " & !LastName & "." & vbCr & _
            "[? - unknown, X - has no fax]"
        strInput = UCase(InputBox(strMessage))
        If strInput <> "" Then
            Select Case strInput
                Case "?"
                    !FaxPhone = Null
                Case "X"
                    !FaxPhone = ""
                Case Else
                    !FaxPhone = strInput
            End Select

            .Update

            ' Print report.
            Debug.Print "Name - Fax number"
            Debug.Print !FirstName & " " & !LastName & " - ";
```

```
            If IsNull(!FaxPhone) Then
                Debug.Print "[Unknown]"
            Else
                If !FaxPhone = "" Then
                    Debug.Print "[Has no fax]"
                Else
                    Debug.Print !FaxPhone
                End If
            End If

        Else
            .CancelUpdate
        End If

        .Close
    End With

    ' Delete new field because this is a demonstration.
    tdfEmployees.Fields.Delete fldTemp.Name
    dbsNorthwind.Close

End Sub
```

AllowZeroLength Property (Remote Data)

Returns a value that indicates whether a zero-length string ("") is a valid setting for the **Value** property of an **rdoColumn** object with a data type of **rdTypeCHAR**, **rdTypeVARCHAR**, or **rdTypeLONGVARCHAR**.

Applies To

rdoColumn Object

Syntax

object.**AllowZeroLength**

The *object* placeholder represents an object expression that evaluates to an object in the **Applies To** list.

Return Values

The **AllowZeroLength** property return values are:

Value	Description
True	A zero-length string is a valid value.
False	A zero-length string isn't a valid value.

Remarks

If **AllowZeroLength** is **False** for a column, you must use **Null** to represent "unknown" states — you cannot use empty strings.

See Also

rdoColumn Object, **rdoPreparedStatement** Object, **rdoResultset** Object, **Required** Property, **Value** Property (Remote Data)

AllPermissions Property

Returns all the permissions that apply to the current **UserName** property of the **Container** or **Document** object, including permissions that are specific to the user as well as the permissions a user inherits from memberships in groups (Microsoft Jet workspaces only).

Applies To

Container Object, **Document** Object

Return Values

For any **Container** or **Document** object, the return value is a **Long** value or constant(s) that may include the following.

Constant	Description
dbSecReadDef	The user can read the table definition, including column and index information.
dbSecWriteDef	The user can modify or delete the table definition, including column and index information.
dbSecRetrieveData	The user can retrieve data from the **Document** object.
dbSecInsertData	The user can add records.
dbSecReplaceData	The user can modify records.
dbSecDeleteData	The user can delete records.

In addition, the Databases container or any **Document** object in a **Documents** collection may include the following:

Constant	Description
dbSecDeleteData	The user can delete records.
dbSecDBAdmin	The user can replicate the database and change the database password.
dbSecDBCreate	The user can create new databases. This setting is valid only on the Databases container in the workgroup information file (System.mdw).
dbSecDBExclusive	The user has exclusive access to the database.
dbSecDBOpen	The user can open the database.

Remarks

This property contrasts with the **Permissions** property, which returns only the permissions that are specific to the user and doesn't include any permissions that the user may also have as a member of groups. If the current value of the **UserName** property is a group, then the **AllPermissions** property returns the same values as the **Permissions** property.

Example

This example uses the **SystemDB**, **AllPermissions**, and **Permissions** properties to show how users can have different levels of permissions depending on the permissions of the group to which they belong.

```
Sub AllPermissionsX()

    ' Ensure that the Microsoft Jet workgroup information
    ' file is available.
    DBEngine.SystemDB = "system.mdw"

    Dim dbsNorthwind As Database
    Dim ctrLoop As Container

    Set dbsNorthwind = OpenDatabase("Northwind.mdb")

    ' Enumerate Containers collection and display the current
    ' user and the permissions set for that user.
    For Each ctrLoop In dbsNorthwind.Containers
        With ctrLoop
            Debug.Print "Container: " & .Name
            Debug.Print "User: " & .UserName
            Debug.Print "    Permissions: " & .Permissions
            Debug.Print "    AllPermissions: " & _
                .AllPermissions
        End With
    Next ctrLoop

    dbsNorthwind.Close

End Sub
```

Ambient Property

Returns an **AmbientProperties** object holding the ambient properties of the container. The **Ambient** property is not available at the control's authoring time, and read-only at the control's run time.

Applies To

UserControl Object

Syntax

object.**Ambient**

The **Ambient** property syntax has this part:

Part	Description
object	An object expression that evaluates to an object in the **Applies To** list.

See Also

AmbientProperties Object

AmbientChanged Event

Occurs when an ambient property's value changes.

Applies To

UserControl Object

Syntax

Sub *object_***AmbientChanged**(*PropertyName* **As String**)

The **AmbientChanged** event syntax has these parts:

Part	Description
object	An object expression that evaluates to an object in the **Applies To** list.
PropertyName	A string that identifies the ambient property that has changed.

Remarks

Using *PropertyName*, the control can access the **AmbientProperties** object in the **Ambient** property to check for the new value of the changed ambient property.

If an instance of the control is placed on a Visual Basic form, and the **FontTransparent** property of the form is changed, the **AmbientChanged** event will not be raised.

See Also

AmbientProperties Object, **FontTransparent** Property

AmbientProperties Object

An **AmbientProperties** object holds ambient information from a container to suggest behavior to controls contained within the container.

Remarks

Containers provide ambient properties in order to suggest behavior to controls. As an example, **BackColor** is one of the standard ambient properties; the container is suggesting what the well-behaved control should set its back color property to.

The **AmbientProperties** object's properties are the ambient properties of the container. These properties are read-only.

Some ambient properties are standard, while others are specific to certain containers. A control may access non-standard ambient properties, but this will make the control container-specific. The control should handle the case where an ambient property is not present in the current container.

When the control is compiled, Visual Basic has no way of knowing what container-specific ambient properties may be available when the control is run; therefore references to container-specific ambient properties will always be late bound.

The **AmbientProperties** object is not available when the **Initialize** event is raised; but is available when the **InitProperties** event or **ReadProperties** event is raised.

The **AmbientProperties** object has several standard properties:

- The **BackColor** property, a Color that contains the suggested interior color of the contained control. The Visual Basic supplied default if the container does not support this property is 0x80000005: the system color for a window background.

- The **DisplayAsDefault** property, a Boolean that specifies if the control is the default control. The Visual Basic supplied default if the container does not support this property is **False**.

- The **DisplayName** property, a String containing the name that the control should display for itself. The Visual Basic supplied default if the container does not support this property is an empty string: "".

- The **Font** property, a **Font** object that contains the suggested font information of the contained control. The Visual Basic supplied default if the container does not support this property is MS Sans Serif 8.

- The **ForeColor** property, a Color that contains the suggested foreground color of the contained control. The Visual Basic supplied default if the container does not support this property is 0x80000008: the system color for window text.

- The **LocaleID** property, a Long that specifies the language and country of the user. The Visual Basic supplied default if the container does not support this property is the current system locale ID.

- The **MessageReflect** property, a Boolean that specifies if the container supports message reflection. The Visual Basic supplied default if the container does not support this property is **False**.

- The **Palette** property, a **Picture** object whose palette specifies the suggested palette for the contained control.

- The **RightToLeft** property, a Boolean that indicates the text display direction and control visual appearance on a bidirectional system. The Visual Basic supplied default if the container does not support this property is **False**.

- The **ScaleUnits** property, a String containing the name of the coordinate units being used by the container. The Visual Basic supplied default if the container does not support this property is an empty string: "".

- The **ShowGrabHandles** property, a Boolean that specifies if the container handles the showing of grab handles. The Visual Basic supplied default if the container does not support this property is **True**.

- The **ShowHatching** property, a Boolean that specifies if the container handles the showing of hatching. The Visual Basic supplied default if the container does not support this property is **True**.

- The **SupportsMnemonics** property, a Boolean that specifies if the container handles access keys for the control. The Visual Basic supplied default if the container does not support this property is **False**.

- The **TextAlign** property, an enumeration that specifies how text is to be aligned. The Visual Basic supplied default if the container does not support this property is **0 - General Align**.

- The **UserMode** property, a Boolean that specifies if the environment is in design mode or end user mode. The Visual Basic supplied default if the container does not support this property is **True**.

- The **UIDead** property, a Boolean that specifies if the User Interface is nonresponsive. The Visual Basic supplied default if the container does not support this property is **False**.

Properties

DisplayAsDefault Property, **DisplayName** Property, **LocaleID** Property, **MessageReflect** Property, **RightToLeft** Property, **ScaleUnits** Property, **ShowGrabHandles** Property, **ShowHatching** Property, **SupportsMnemonics** Property, **TextAlign** Property, **UIDead** Property, **UserMode** Property, **Palette** Property, **BackColor, ForeColor** Properties, **Font** Property

And Operator

Used to perform a logical conjunction on two expressions.

Syntax

result = *expression1* **And** *expression2*

The **And** operator syntax has these parts:

Part	Description
result	Required; any numeric variable.
expression1	Required; any expression.
expression2	Required; any expression.

Remarks

If both expressions evaluate to **True**, *result* is **True**. If either expression evaluates to **False**, *result* is **False.** The following table illustrates how *result* is determined:

If *expression1* is	And *expression2* is	The *result* is
True	True	True
True	False	False
True	Null	Null
False	True	False
False	False	False

(continued)

If *expression1* is	And *expression2* is	The *result* is
False	Null	False
Null	True	Null
Null	False	False
Null	Null	Null

The **And** operator also performs a bitwise comparison of identically positioned bits in two numeric expressions and sets the corresponding bit in *result* according to the following table:

If bit in *expression1* is	And bit in *expression2* is	The *result* is
0	0	0
0	1	0
1	0	0
1	1	1

See Also

Operator Summary, **Operator** Precedence, **Logical** Operators

Example

This example uses the **And** operator to perform a logical conjunction on two expressions.

```
Dim A, B, C, D, MyCheck
A = 10: B = 8: C = 6: D = Null    ' Initialize variables.
MyCheck = A > B And B > C         ' Returns True.
MyCheck = B > A And B > C         ' Returns False.
MyCheck = A > B And B > D         ' Returns Null.
MyCheck = A And B                 ' Returns 8 (bitwise comparison).
```

App Object

The **App** object is a global object accessed with the **App** keyword. It determines or specifies information about the application's title, version information, the path and name of its executable file and Help files, and whether or not a previous instance of the application is running.

Syntax

App

Properties

OLERequestPendingMsgText Property, **OLERequestPendingMsgTitle** Property, **OLERequestPendingTimeout** Property, **OLEServerBusyMsgText** Property, **OLEServerBusyMsgTitle** Property, **OLEServerBusyRaiseError** Property, **OLEServerBusyTimeout** Property, **TaskVisible** Property, **hInstance** Property, **Comments** Property, **CompanyName** Property, **FileDescription** Property,

LegalCopyright Property, LegalTrademarks Property, Major Property, Minor Property, ProductName Property, Revision Property, LogMode Property, LogPath Property, NonModalAllowed Property, ThreadID Property, UnattendedApp Property, HelpFile Property (App, CommonDialog, MenuLine), PrevInstance Property, Title Property, StartMode Property, Path Property, EXEName Property

Methods

LogEvent Method, StartLogging Method

See Also

HelpContextID Property

App Property

Returns the **App** object, a global object accessed with the **App** keyword. It determines or specifies information about the application's title, version information, the path and name of its executable file and Help files, and whether or not a previous instance of the application is running.

Applies To

Global Object

Syntax

App

Remarks

The **App** object has no events or methods.

See Also

Global Object, App Object

AppActivate Statement

Activates an application window.

Syntax

AppActivate *title*[, *wait*]

The **AppActivate** statement syntax has these named arguments:

Part	Description
title	Required. String expression specifying the title in the title bar of the application window you want to activate. The task ID returned by the **Shell** function can be used in place of *title* to activate an application.
wait	Optional. **Boolean** value specifying whether the calling application has the focus before activating another. If **False** (default), the specified application is immediately activated, even if the calling application does not have the focus. If **True**, the calling application waits until it has the focus, then activates the specified application.

Remarks

The **AppActivate** statement changes the focus to the named application or window but does not affect whether it is maximized or minimized. Focus moves from the activated application window when the user takes some action to change the focus or close the window. Use the **Shell** function to start an application and set the window style.

In determining which application to activate, *title* is compared to the title string of each running application. If there is no exact match, any application whose title string begins with *title* is activated. If there is more than one instance of the application named by *title*, one instance is arbitrarily activated.

See Also

Shell Function, **SendKeys** Statement

Example

This example illustrates various uses of the **AppActivate** statement to activate an application window. The **Shell** statements assume the applications are in the paths specified.

```
Dim MyAppID, ReturnValue
AppActivate "Microsoft Word"                    ' Activate Microsoft
                                                ' Word.

' AppActivate can also use the return value of the Shell function.
MyAppID = Shell("C:\WORD\WINWORD.EXE", 1)       ' Run Microsoft Word.
AppActivate MyAppID                             ' Activate Microsoft
                                                ' Word.

' You can also use the return value of the Shell function.
ReturnValue = Shell("c:\EXCEL\EXCEL.EXE",1)     ' Run Microsoft Excel.
AppActivate ReturnValue                         ' Activate Microsoft
                                                ' Excel.
```

Appearance Property

Returns or sets the paint style of controls on an **MDIForm** or **Form** object at run time. Read-only at run time.

Applies To

PropertyPage Object, **UserControl** Object, **UserDocument** Object, **CheckBox** Control, **ComboBox** Control, **CommandButton** Control, **DirListBox** Control, **DriveListBox** Control, **FileListBox** Control, **Form** Object, **Forms** Collection, **Frame** Control, **Image** Control, **Label** Control, **ListBox** Control, **MDIForm** Object, **OptionButton** Control, **PictureBox** Control, **TextBox** Control, **OLE Container** Control, **Data** Control, **DBCombo** Control, **DBGrid** Control, **DBList** Control, **RemoteData** Control

Syntax

object.**Appearance**

The *object* placeholder represents an object expression that evaluates to an object in the **Applies To** list.

Settings

The **Appearance** property settings are:

Setting	Description
0	Flat. Paints controls and forms without visual effects.
1	(Default) 3D. Paints controls with three-dimensional effects.

Remarks

If set to 1at design time, the **Appearance** property draws controls with three-dimensional effects. If the form's **BorderStyle** property is set to Fixed Double (**vbFixedDouble**, or 3), the caption and border of the form are also painted with three-dimensional effects. Setting the **Appearance** property to 1 also causes the form and its controls to have their **BackColor** property set to the color selected for 3D Objects in the Appearance tab of the operating system's Display Properties dialog box.

Setting the **Appearance** property to 1 for an **MDIForm** object affects only the MDI parent form. To have three-dimensional effects on MDI child forms, you must set each child form's **Appearance** property to 1.

See Also

BackColor, **ForeColor** Properties, **BorderStyle** Property

---

Append Method

Adds a new DAO object to a collection.

Applies To

Fields Collection, **Groups** Collection, **Indexes** Collection, **Properties** Collection, **QueryDefs** Collection, **Relations** Collection, **TableDefs** Collection, **Users** Collection, **Workspaces** Collection

Syntax

collection.**Append** *object*

The **Append** method syntax has these parts.

Part	Description
collection	An object variable that represents any collection that can accept new objects (for limitations, see the table at the end of this topic).
object	An object variable that represents the object being appended, which must be of the same type as the elements of *collection*.

Remarks

You can use the **Append** method to add a new table to a database, add a field to a table, and add a field to an index.

The appended object becomes a persistent object, stored on disk, until you delete it by using the **Delete** method. If *collection* is a **Workspaces** collection (which is stored only in memory), the object is active until you remove it by using the **Close** method.

The addition of a new object occurs immediately, but you should use the **Refresh** method on any other collections that may be affected by changes to the database structure.

If the object you're appending isn't complete (such as when you haven't appended any **Field** objects to a **Fields** collection of an **Index** object before it's appended to an **Indexes** collection) or if the properties set in one or more subordinate objects are incorrect, using the **Append** method causes an error. For example, if you haven't specified a field type and then try to append the **Field** object to the **Fields** collection in a **TableDef** object, using the **Append** method triggers a run-time error.

The following table lists some limitations of the **Append** method. The object in the first column is an object containing the collection in the second column. The third column indicates whether you can append an object to that collection (for example, you can never append a **Container** object to the **Containers** collection of a **Database** object).

Object	Collection	Can you append new objects?
DBEngine	**Workspaces**	Yes
DBEngine	**Errors**	No. New Error objects are automatically appended when they occur.
Workspace	**Connections**	No. Using the **OpenConnection** method automatically appends new objects.
Workspace	**Databases**	No. Using the **OpenDatabase** method automatically appends new objects.
Workspace	**Groups**	Yes
Workspace	**Users**	Yes
Connection	**QueryDefs**	No. Using the **CreateQueryDef** method automatically appends new objects.
Connection	**Recordsets**	No. Using the **OpenRecordset** method automatically appends new objects.
Database	**Containers**	No
Database	**QueryDefs**	Only when the **QueryDef** object is a new, unappended object created with no name. See the **CreateQueryDef** method for details.
Database	**Recordsets**	No. Using the **OpenRecordset** method automatically appends new objects.
Database	**Relations**	Yes	*(continued)*

(continued)

Object	Collection	Can you append new objects?
Database	**TableDefs**	Yes
Group	**Users**	Yes
User	**Groups**	Yes
Container	**Documents**	No
QueryDef	**Fields**	No
QueryDef	**Parameters**	No
Recordset	**Fields**	No
Relation	**Fields**	Yes
TableDef	**Fields**	Only when the **Updatable** property of the **TableDef** object is set to **True**, or when the **TableDef** object is unappended.
TableDef	**Indexes**	Only when the **Updatable** property of the **TableDef** is set to **True**, or when the **TableDef** object is unappended.
Index	**Fields**	Only when the **Index** object is a new, unappended object.
Database, Field, Index, QueryDef, TableDef	**Properties**	Only when the **Database**, **Field**, **Index**, **QueryDef**, or **TableDef** object is in a Microsoft Jet workspace.
DBEngine, Parameter, Recordset, Workspace	**Properties**	No

See Also

Delete Method, **GetChunk** Method, **Refresh** Method, **Type** Property

Example

This example uses either the **Append** method or the **Delete** method to modify the **Fields** collection of a **TableDef**. The **AppendDeleteField** procedure is required for this procedure to run.

```
Sub AppendX()

    Dim dbsNorthwind As Database
    Dim tdfEmployees As TableDef
    Dim fldLoop As Field

    Set dbsNorthwind = OpenDatabase("Northwind.mdb")
    Set tdfEmployees = dbsNorthwind.TableDefs!Employees

    ' Add three new fields.
    AppendDeleteField tdfEmployees, "APPEND", _
        "E-mail", dbText, 50
    AppendDeleteField tdfEmployees, "APPEND", _
        "Http", dbText, 80
    AppendDeleteField tdfEmployees, "APPEND", _
        "Quota", dbInteger, 5
```

```
    Debug.Print "Fields after Append"
    Debug.Print , "Type", "Size", "Name"

    ' Enumerate the Fields collection to show the new fields.
    For Each fldLoop In tdfEmployees.Fields
        Debug.Print , fldLoop.Type, fldLoop.Size, fldLoop.Name
    Next fldLoop

    ' Delete the newly added fields.
    AppendDeleteField tdfEmployees, "DELETE", "E-mail"
    AppendDeleteField tdfEmployees, "DELETE", "Http"
    AppendDeleteField tdfEmployees, "DELETE", "Quota"

    Debug.Print "Fields after Delete"
    Debug.Print , "Type", "Size", "Name"

    ' Enumerate the Fields collection to show that the new
    ' fields have been deleted.
    For Each fldLoop In tdfEmployees.Fields
        Debug.Print , fldLoop.Type, fldLoop.Size, fldLoop.Name
    Next fldLoop

    dbsNorthwind.Close

End Sub

Sub AppendDeleteField(tdfTemp As TableDef, _
    strCommand As String, strName As String, _
    Optional varType, Optional varSize)

    With tdfTemp

        ' Check first to see if the TableDef object is
        ' updatable. If it isn't, control is passed back to
        ' the calling procedure.
        If .Updatable = False Then
            MsgBox "TableDef not Updatable! " & _
                "Unable to complete task."
            Exit Sub
        End If

        ' Depending on the passed data, append or delete a
        ' field to the Fields collection of the specified
        ' TableDef object.
        If strCommand = "APPEND" Then
            .Fields.Append .CreateField(strName, _
                varType, varSize)
        Else
            If strCommand = "DELETE" Then .Fields.Delete _
                strName
        End If

    End With

End Sub
```

AppendChunk Method

Appends data from a string expression to a Memo or Long Binary **Field** object in a **Recordset**.

Applies To

Field Object

Syntax

recordset ! *field*.**AppendChunk** *source*

The **AppendChunk** method syntax has these parts.

Part	Description
recordset	An object variable that represents the **Recordset** object containing the **Fields** collection.
field	An object variable that represents the name of a **Field** object whose **Type** property is set to **dbMemo** (Memo), **dbLongBinary** (Long Binary), or the equivalent.
source	A **Variant** (**String** subtype) expression or variable containing the data you want to append to the **Field** object specified by *field*.

Remarks

You can use the **AppendChunk** and **GetChunk** methods to access subsets of data in a Memo or Long Binary field.

You can also use these methods to conserve string space when you work with Memo and Long Binary fields. Certain operations (copying, for example) involve temporary strings. If string space is limited, you may need to work with chunks of a field instead of the entire field.

If there is no current record when you use **AppendChunk**, an error occurs.

Notes

- The initial **AppendChunk** operation (after an **Edit** or **AddNew** call) will simply place the data in the field, overwriting any existing data. Subsequent **AppendChunk** calls within the same **Edit** or **AddNew** session will then add to the existing data.

- In an ODBCDirect workspace, unless you first edit another field in the current record, using **AppendChunk** will fail (though no error occurs) while you are in **Edit** mode.

- In an ODBCDirect workspace, after you use **AppendChunk** on a field, you cannot read or write that field in an assignment statement until you move off the current record and then return to it. You can do this by using the **MoveNext** and **MovePrevious** methods.

See Also

AddNew Method, **Edit** Method, **GetChunk** Method, **Type** Property, **FieldSize** Property

Example

This example uses the **AppendChunk** and **GetChunk** methods to fill an OLE object field with data from another record, 32K at a time. In a real application, one might use a procedure like this to copy an employee record (including the employee's photo) from one table to another. In this example, the record is simply being copied back to same table. Note that all the chunk manipulation takes place within a single **AddNew**-**Update** sequence.

```
Sub AppendChunkX()

    Dim dbsNorthwind As Database
    Dim rstEmployees As Recordset
    Dim rstEmployees2 As Recordset

    Set dbsNorthwind = OpenDatabase("Northwind.mdb")

    ' Open two recordsets from the Employees table.
    Set rstEmployees = _
        dbsNorthwind.OpenRecordset("Employees", _
        dbOpenDynaset)
    Set rstEmployees2 = rstEmployees.Clone

    ' Add a new record to the first Recordset and copy the
    ' data from a record in the second Recordset.
    With rstEmployees
        .AddNew
        !FirstName = rstEmployees2!FirstName
        !LastName = rstEmployees2!LastName
        CopyLargeField rstEmployees2!Photo, !Photo
        .Update

        ' Delete new record because this is a demonstration.
        .Bookmark = .LastModified
        .Delete
        .Close
    End With

    rstEmployees2.Close
    dbsNorthwind.Close

End Sub

Function CopyLargeField(fldSource As Field, _
    fldDestination As Field)

    ' Set size of chunk in bytes.
    Const conChunkSize = 32768

    Dim lngOffset As Long
    Dim lngTotalSize As Long
    Dim strChunk As String
```

```
' Copy the photo from one Recordset to the other in 32K
' chunks until the entire field is copied.
lngTotalSize = fldSource.FieldSize
Do While lngOffset < lngTotalSize
    strChunk = fldSource.GetChunk(lngOffset, conChunkSize)
    fldDestination.AppendChunk strChunk
    lngOffset = lngOffset + conChunkSize
Loop

End Function
```

AppendChunk Method (Remote Data)

Appends data from a **Variant** expression to an **rdoColumn** object with a data type of **rdTypeLONGVARBINARY** or **rdTypeLONGVARCHAR**.

Applies To

rdoColumn Object

Syntax

object ! *column*.**AppendChunk** *source*

The **AppendChunk** method syntax has these parts:

Part	Description
object	An object expression that evaluates to the **rdoResultset** object containing the **rdoColumns** collection.
column	An object expression that evaluates to an **rdoColumn** object whose **ChunkRequired** property is set to **True**.
source	A string expression or variable containing the data you want to append to the **rdoColumn** object specified by *column*.

Remarks

Chunk data columns are designed to store large binary (BLOB) or text values that can range in size from a few characters to over 1.2GB and are stored in the database on successive data pages. In many cases, *chunk* data cannot be managed with a single operation, so you must use the *chunk* methods to save and write data. If the **ChunkRequired** property is **True** for a column, you should use the **AppendChunk** method to manipulate column data. However, if there is sufficient internal memory available, RDO might be able to carry out the operation without use of the **AppendChunk** method. In other words, you might be able to simply assign a value to a BLOB column.

Use the **AppendChunk** method to write successive blocks of data to the database column and **GetChunk** to extract data from the database column. Certain operations (copying, for example) involve temporary strings. If string space is limited, you may need to work with smaller segments of a *chunk* column instead of the entire column.

Use the **BindThreshold** property to specify the largest column size that will be automatically bound.

Use the **ColumnSize** property to determine the number of bytes in a *chunk* column. Note that for variable-sized columns, it is not necessary to write back the same number of bytes as returned by the **ColumnSize** property as **ColumnSize** reflects the size of the column before changes are made.

If there is no current row when you use **AppendChunk**, a trappable error occurs.

Note The initial **AppendChunk** (after the first **Edit** method), even if the row already contains data, replaces existing column data. Subsequent **AppendChunk** calls within a single **Edit** session appends data to existing column data.

See Also

ColumnSize Method (Remote Data), **GetChunk** Method (Remote Data), **rdoColumn** Object, **rdoResultset** Object, **ChunkRequired** Property (Remote Data), **Type** Property (Remote Data)

Example

This example illustrates use of the **AppendChunk** and **GetChunk** methods to write page-based binary large object (BLOB) data to a remote data source. The code expects a table with a char, text, and image field named *Chunks*. To create this table, submit the following as an action query against your test database:

```
CREATE TABLE Chunks (ID integer identity NOT NULL, PName char(10) NULL,
Description TEXT NULL,
Photo IMAGE NULL)
CREATE UNIQUE INDEX ChunkIDIndex on Chunks(ID)
```

Once the table is created, you will need to locate one or more .BMP or other suitable graphics images that can be loaded by the **PictureBox** control.

```
'
Option Explicit
Dim en As rdoEnvironment
Dim Qd As rdoQuery
Dim Cn As rdoConnection
Dim Rs As rdoResultset
Dim SQL As String
Dim DataFile As Integer, Fl As Long, Chunks As Integer
Dim Fragment As Integer, Chunk() As Byte, I As Integer
Const ChunkSize As Integer = 16384

Private Sub Form_Load()
Set en = rdoEnvironments(0)
Set Cn = en.OpenConnection(dsname:="", _
Connect:="UID=;PWD=;DATABASE=WorkDB;" _
& "Driver={SQL Server};SERVER=Betav486", _
prompt:=rdDriverNoPrompt)
Set Qd = Cn.CreateQuery("TestChunk", "Select * from Chunks Where PName = ?")
End Sub
Private Sub LoadFromFile_Click()
```

```
'
'  Locates a file and sets the Filename to this file.
'
With CommonDialog1
.Filter = "Pictures(*.bmp;*.ico)|*.bmp;*.ico"
.ShowOpen
FileName = .FileName
End With
End Sub

Private Sub ReadFromDB_Click()
If Len(NameWanted) = 0 Then _
NameWanted = InputBox("Enter name wanted", "Animal")
Qd(0) = NameWanted
Set Rs = Qd.OpenResultset(rdOpenKeyset, rdConcurRowver)
If Rs Is Nothing Or Rs.Updatable = False Then
MsgBox "Can't open or write to result set"
Exit Sub
End If
If Rs.EOF Then
MsgBox "Can't find picture by that name"
Exit Sub
End If
Description = Rs!Description
DataFile = 1
Open "pictemp" For Binary Access Write As DataFile
Fl = Rs!Photo.ColumnSize
Chunks = Fl \ ChunkSize
Fragment = Fl Mod ChunkSize
ReDim Chunk(Fragment)
Chunk() = Rs!Photo.GetChunk(Fragment)
Put DataFile, , Chunk()
For I = 1 To Chunks
ReDim Buffer(ChunkSize)
Chunk() = Rs!Photo.GetChunk(ChunkSize)
Put DataFile, , Chunk()
Next I
Close DataFile
FileName = "pictemp"
End Sub

Private Sub SaveToDB_Click()
If Len(NameWanted) = 0 Then _
NameWanted = InputBox("Enter name for this" _
& " picture", "Animal")
Qd(0) = NameWanted
Set Rs = Qd.OpenResultset(rdOpenKeyset, _
rdConcurRowver)
If Rs Is Nothing Or Rs.Updatable = False Then
MsgBox "Can't open or write to result set"
Exit Sub
End If
```

```
If Rs.EOF Then
Rs.AddNew
Rs!PName = NameWanted
If Description = "" Then _
Description = InputBox("Describe the picture", _
"Don't care")
'Rs!Description = Description
Else
Rs.Edit
End If
DataFile = 1
Open FileName For Binary Access Read As DataFile
Fl = LOF(DataFile)    ' Length of data in file
If Fl = 0 Then Close DataFile: Exit Sub
Chunks = Fl \ ChunkSize
Fragment = Fl Mod ChunkSize
Rs!Photo.AppendChunk Null
ReDim Chunk(Fragment)
Get DataFile, , Chunk()
Rs!Photo.AppendChunk Chunk()
ReDim Chunk(ChunkSize)
For I = 1 To Chunks
Get DataFile, , Chunk()
Rs!Photo.AppendChunk Chunk()
Next I
Close DataFile
Rs.Update
End Sub

Private Sub FileName_Change()
Picture1.Picture = LoadPicture(FileName)
End Sub
```

AppIsRunning Property

Returns or sets a value that indicates whether the application that created the object in the **OLE** container control is running. Not available at design time.

Applies To

OLE Container Control

Syntax

object.**AppIsRunning** [= *boolean*]

The **AppIsRunning** property syntax has these parts:

Part	Description
object	An object expression that evaluates to an object in the **Applies To** list.
boolean	A Boolean expression specifying whether or not the application that produced the object in the **OLE** container control is running, as described in Settings.

Settings

The settings for *Boolean* are:

Setting	Description
True	The application that produced the object in the **OLE** container control is running.
False	The application that produced the object in the **OLE** container control isn't running.

Remarks

You can set the value of the **AppIsRunning** property to start the application that produces the object in the **OLE** container control. Doing this causes objects to activate more rapidly. You can also set this property to **False** to close the application when the object loses the focus.

See Also

OLEType Property

ApplyChanges Event

Occurs when the user presses the **OK** button or the **Apply** button on the property page, or when property pages are switched by selecting tabs.

Applies To

MSChart Control, **PropertyPage** Object

Syntax

Sub *object*_**ApplyChanges**()

The **ApplyChanges** event syntax has these parts:

Part	Description
object	An object expression that evaluates to an object in the **Applies To** list.

Remarks

When the **ApplyChanges** event is raised, the author of the property page needs to handle the setting of all the new property values to the controls; hopefully the author kept track of which properties were changed, otherwise all properties will have to be set. To know what controls are to be changed, use the **SelectedControls** property.

The **ApplyChanges** event will be raised only if the **Changed** property is set to **True**.

See Also

Changed Property, **SelectedControls** Property

ApproxCount Property

Sets or returns the approximate number of rows in the grid.

Applies To

DBGrid Control

Syntax

object.**ApproxCount** [= *value*]

The **ApproxCount** property syntax has these parts:

Part	Description
object	An object expression that evaluates to an object in the **Applies To** list.
value	An integer that represents the approximate number of rows in the grid.

Remarks

This property sets or returns the approximate row count used by the grid to calibrate the vertical scroll bar.

Typically, the **ApproxCount** property is used in unbound mode to improve the accuracy of the vertical scroll bar. This is particularly useful for situations where the number of rows is known in advance, such as when an unbound grid is used in conjunction with an array.

Note For a bound grid, setting the **ApproxCount** property has no effect. However, getting the **ApproxCount** property will query the underlying data source.

Archive, Hidden, Normal, System Properties

Return or set a value that determines whether a **FileListBox** control displays files with Archive, Hidden, Normal, or System attributes.

Applies To

FileListBox Control, **ListView** Control, **TreeView** Control

Syntax

object.**Archive** [= *boolean*]
object.**Hidden** [= *boolean*]
object.**Normal** [= *boolean*]
object.**System** [= *boolean*]

The **Archive**, **Hidden**, **Normal**, and **System** property syntaxes have these parts:

Part	Description
object	An object expression that evaluates to an object in the **Applies To** list.
boolean	A Boolean expression that specifies the type of files displayed, as described in Settings.

Settings

The settings for *boolean* are:

Setting	Description
True	(Default for Archive and Normal) Displays files with the property's attribute in the **FileListBox** control.
False	(Default for Hidden and System) Displays files without the property's attribute in the **FileListBox** control.

Remarks

Use these properties to specify the type of files to display in a **FileListBox** control, based on standard file attributes used in the operating environment. Setting any of these properties with code at run time resets the **FileListBox** control to display only those files with the specified attributes.

For example, in a find-and-replace operation you could display only system files by setting the **System** property to **True** and the other properties to **False**. Or, as part of a file backup procedure, you could set the **Archive** property to **True** to list only those files modified since the previous backup.

See Also

Pattern Property, **Path** Property

Arithmetic Operators

^ Operator

* Operator

/ Operator

\ Operator

Mod Operator

+ Operator

- Operator

Arrange Method

Arranges the windows or icons within an **MDIForm** object. Doesn't support named arguments.

Applies To

MDIForm Object

Syntax

object.**Arrange** *arrangement*

The **Arrange** method syntax has these parts:

Part	Description
object	Required. An object expression that evaluates to an object in the **Applies To** list.
arrangement	Required. A value or constant that specifies how to arrange windows or icons on an **MDIForm** object, as described in **Settings**.

Settings

The settings for *arrangement* are:

Constant	Value	Description
vbCascade	0	Cascades all non-minimized MDI child forms
vbTileHorizontal	1	Tiles all non-minimized MDI child forms horizontally
vbTileVertical	2	Tiles all non-minimized MDI child forms vertically
vbArrangeIcons	3	Arranges icons for minimized MDI child forms

Remarks

These constants are listed in the Visual Basic (VB) object library in the Object Browser.

Windows or icons are arranged even if the **MDIForm** object is minimized. Results are visible when the **MDIForm** is maximized.

See Also

ZOrder Method

Example

This example uses the **Arrange** method to arrange windows and icons in an MDI form. To try this example, paste the code into the Declarations section of an MDI form named MDIForm1 that has an MDI child form (named Form1, with its **MDIChild** property set to **True**) and a picture box on the MDI Form (named Picture1). Press F5 and click anywhere in the picture box to see the effects of the **Arrange** method.

```
Const FORMCOUNT = 5
Dim F(1 To FORMCOUNT) As New Form1
Private Sub MDIForm_Load ()
   Dim I                              ' Declare local variable.
   Load Form1                         ' Load original Form1.
   For I = 1 To FORMCOUNT
      F(I).Caption = "Form" & I + 1   ' Change caption on copies.
   Next I
End Sub

Private Sub Picture1_Click ()
   Static ClickCount                  ' Declare variables.
   Dim I, PrevWidth, Start
   ClickCount = ClickCount + 1        ' Increment click counter.
   Select Case ClickCount
      Case 1
         MDIForm1.Arrange 1           ' Tile horizontally.
      Case 2
         MDIForm1.Arrange 2           ' Tile vertically.
      Case 3                          ' Minimize each form.
         PrevWidth = MDIForm1.Width   ' Get MDI form width.
         MDIForm1.Width = PrevWidth / 2 ' Divide it in half.
         Form1.WindowState = 1        ' Minimize the original.
         For I = 1 To FORMCOUNT       ' Look at each instance of F.
            F(I).WindowState = 1      ' Minimize each copy of F.
         Next I
         Start = Timer
         Do
         Loop Until Timer = Start + 5
         MDIForm1.Width = PrevWidth   ' Resize to original size.
         MDIForm1.Arrange 3           ' Arrange icons.
   End Select
End Sub
```

Array Function

Returns a **Variant** containing an array.

Syntax

Array(*arglist*)

The required *arglist* argument is a comma-delimited list of values that are assigned to the elements of the array contained within the **Variant**. If no arguments are specified, an array of zero length is created.

Remarks

The notation used to refer to an element of an array consists of the variable name followed by parentheses containing an index number indicating the desired element. In the following example, the first statement creates a variable named A as a **Variant**.

The second statement assigns an array to variable A. The last statement assigns the value contained in the second array element to another variable.

```
Dim A As Variant
A = Array(10,20,30)
B = A(2)
```

The lower bound of an array created using the **Array** function is determined by the lower bound specified with the **Option Base** statement, unless **Array** is qualified with the name of the type library (for example **VBA.Array**). If qualified with the type-library name, **Array** is unaffected by **Option Base**.

Note A **Variant** that is not declared as an array can still contain an array. A **Variant** variable can contain an array of any type, except fixed-length strings and user-defined types. Although a **Variant** containing an array is conceptually different from an array whose elements are of type **Variant**, the array elements are accessed in the same way.

See Also

Variant Data Type, **Deftype** Statements, **Dim** Statement, **Let** Statement, **Option Base** Statement

Example

This example uses the **Array** function to return a **Variant** containing an array.

```
Dim MyWeek, MyDay
MyWeek = Array("Mon", "Tue", "Wed", "Thu", "Fri", "Sat", "Sun")
' Return values assume lower bound set to 1 (using Option Base
' statement).
MyDay = MyWeek(2) ' MyDay contains "Tue".
MyDay = MyWeek(4) ' MyDay contains "Thu".
```

Asc Function

Returns an **Integer** representing the character code corresponding to the first letter in a string.

Syntax

Asc(*string*)

The required *string* argument is any valid string expression. If the *string* contains no characters, a run-time error occurs.

Remarks

The range for returns is 0 –255 on non-DBCS systems, but -32768 –32767 on DBCS systems.

Note The **AscB** function is used with byte data contained in a string. Instead of returning the character code for the first character, **AscB** returns the first byte. The **AscW** function returns the Unicode character code except on platforms where Unicode is not supported, in which case, the behavior is identical to the **Asc** function.

See Also

Conversion Functions, **Type Conversion** Functions, **Chr** Function

Example

This example uses the **Asc** function to return a character code corresponding to the first letter in the string.

```
Dim MyNumber
MyNumber = Asc("A")      ' Returns 65.
MyNumber = Asc("a")      ' Returns 97.
MyNumber = Asc("Apple")  ' Returns 65.
```

Assert Method

Conditionally suspends execution at the line on which the method appears.

Applies To

Debug Object

Syntax

object.**Assert** *booleanexpression*

The **Assert** method syntax has the following object qualifier and argument:

Part	Description
object	Required. Always the **Debug** object.
booleanexpression	Required. An expression that evaluates to either **True** or **False**.

Remarks

Assert invocations work only within the development environment. When the module is compiled into an executable, the method calls on the **Debug** object are omitted.

All of *booleanexpression* is always evaluated. For example, even if the first part of an **And** expression evaluates **False**, the entire expression is evaluated.

See Also

Print Method

Example

The following example shows how to use the **Assert** method. The example requires a form with two button controls on it. The default button names are Command1 and Command2.

When the example runs, clicking the Command1 button toggles the text on the button between 0 and 1. Clicking Command2 either does nothing or causes an assertion, depending on the value displayed on Command1. The assertion stops execution with the last statement executed, the Debug.Assert line, highlighted.

```
Option Explicit
Private blnAssert As Boolean
Private intNumber As Integer
```

```
Private Sub Command1_Click()
    blnAssert = Not blnAssert
    intNumber = IIf(intNumber <> 0, 0, 1)
    Command1.Caption = intNumber
End Sub

Private Sub Command2_Click()
    Debug.Assert blnAssert
End Sub

Private Sub Form_Load()
    Command1.Caption = intNumber
    Command2.Caption = "Assert Tester"
End Sub
```

Associate Event

Fired after a new connection is associated with the object.

Applies To

rdoResultset Object

Syntax

Private Sub *object*.**Associate( )**

The *object* placeholder represents an object expression that evaluates to an object in the **Applies To** list.

Remarks

This event is raised after the result set is associated with a new **rdoConnection** object. You can use this event to initialize the new connection. The **ActiveConnection** property of the associated **rdoResultset** object refers to the new connection.

For example, you can use the Associate event procedure to send a special query each time a connection is established, but before other operations are executed.

See Also

rdoConnection Object, **ActiveConnection** Property

AsyncCheckInterval Property (Remote Data)

Returns or sets a value specifying the number of milliseconds that RDO waits between checks to see if an asynchronous query is complete.

Applies To

rdoConnection Object

Syntax

object.**AsyncCheckInterval** [= *value*]

The **AsyncCheckInterval** property syntax has these parts:

Part	Description
object	An object expression that evaluates to an object in the **Applies To** list.
value	A Long expression as described in Remarks.

Remarks

When you use the **rdAsyncEnable** option to execute a query asynchronously, RDO polls the data source periodically to determine if the query has completed. You can change the duration of time between checks by using the **AsyncCheckInterval** property. RDO also checks the status of an asynchronous query when you examine the **StillExecuting** property.

The **AsyncCheckInterval** property defaults to 1000 milliseconds (once a second).

Polling too often can adversely affect both server and workstation performance. Polling less frequently can improve performance, but may affect how quickly data is made available to the user.

As long as the asynchronous query is executing, the **StillExecuting** property returns **True**. Once the query is completed, the **StillExecuting** property is set to false and the **QueryComplete** event is fired. You can also interrupt and end an asynchronous query by using the **rdoResultset** object's **Cancel** or **Close** method.

See Also

QueryCompleted Event (Remote Data), **Cancel** Method (Remote Data), **Execute** Method (Remote Data), **Options** Property (Remote Data), **StillExecuting** Property (Remote Data)

AsyncProperty Object

The **AsyncProperty** object is passed in to the **AsyncReadComplete** event and contains the results of the **AsyncRead** method.

Properties

AsyncType Property, **PropertyName** Property, **Value** Property

See Also

AsyncRead Method, **AsyncReadComplete** Event

AsyncRead Method

Start the reading in of data by the container from a file or URL asynchronously.

Applies To

UserControl Object, **UserDocument** Object

Syntax

object.**AsyncRead** *Target*, *AsyncType* [, *PropertyName*]

The **AsyncRead** method syntax has these parts:

Part	Description
object	An object expression that evaluates to an object in the **Applies To** list.
Target	A string expression specifying the location of the data. This can be a path or a URL.
AsyncType	An integer expression specifying how the data will be presented, as described in **Settings**.
PropertyName	An optional string expression specifying the name of the property to be loaded.

Settings

The settings for *AsyncType* are:

Setting	Description
vbAsyncTypeFile	The data is provided in a file that is created by Visual Basic.
vbAsyncTypeByteArray	The data is provided as a byte array that contains the retrieved data. It is assumed that the control author will know how to handle the data.
vbAsyncTypePicture	The data is provided in a **Picture** object.

Remarks

Once the data that is requested by the **AsyncRead** method is available the **AsyncReadComplete** event will be raised in the object. The asynchronous read may be canceled before it is completed by calling the **CancelAsyncRead** method.

The *PropertyName* parameter can be any arbitrary name, since it's only function is to act as an identifier for this particular data request. The value in *PropertyName* is used to identify the particular asynchronous read to cancel in the **CancelAsyncRead** method, and the value in *PropertyName* is also used to identify the particular asynchronous read that has completed in the **AsyncReadComplete** event.

See Also

AsyncReadComplete Event, **CancelAsyncRead** Method, **Picture** Object, **Visual Basic** Constants

AsyncReadComplete Event

Occurs when the container has completed an asynchronous read request.

Applies To

UserControl Object, **UserDocument Object**

Syntax

Sub *object*_**AsyncReadComplete**(*PropertyValue* **As AsyncProperty**)

The **AsyncReadComplete** event syntax has these parts:

Part	Description
object	An object expression that evaluates to an object in the **Applies To** list.
PropertyValue	An **AsyncProperty** object that contains the following properties:
Value	A Variant containing the results of the asynchronous read. This is the default property.
PropertyName	A string containing the property name that was passed in the **AsyncRead** method.
AsyncType	An integer specifying the type of the data in the *Value* property, as described in Settings.

Settings

The settings for *AsyncType* are:

Setting	Description
vbAsyncTypeFile	The *Value* property contains a string that is a path to a temporary file that contains the data.
vbAsyncTypeByteArray	The *Value* property contains a byte array that contains the data.
vbAsyncTypePicture	The *Value* property contains a picture object of the correct format.

Remarks

The value in *PropertyName* specifies the particular asynchronous data read request that has completed, and matches the value given in a previous **AsyncRead** method invocation.

Error handling code should be placed in the **AsyncReadComplete** event procedure, because an error condition may have stopped the download. If this was the case, that error will be raised when the **Value** property of the **AsyncProperty** object is accessed.

AsyncType Property

Returns or sets the type of the data returned by the **Value** property. This property is available only as an argument of the **AsyncRead** method.

Applies To

AsyncProperty Object

Syntax

object.**AsyncType** = *dataType*

Part	Description
object	An object expression that evaluates to an object in the **Applies To** list.
dataType	An integer specifying the data type, as shown in Settings below.

Settings

The settings for *dataType* are:

Constant	Value	Description
vbAsyncTypePicture	0	Default. Picture object.
VbAsyncTypeFile	1	The data is provided in a file created by Visual Basic.
VbAsyncTypeByteArray	2	The data is provided as a byte array that contains the retrieved data.

See Also

AsyncRead Method, **AsyncReadComplete** Event

Atn Function

Returns a **Double** specifying the arctangent of a number.

Syntax

Atn(*number*)

The required *number* argument is a **Double** or any valid numeric expression.

Remarks

The **Atn** function takes the ratio of two sides of a right triangle (*number*) and returns the corresponding angle in radians. The ratio is the length of the side opposite the angle divided by the length of the side adjacent to the angle.

The range of the result is -pi/2 to pi/2 radians.

To convert degrees to radians, multiply degrees by pi/180. To convert radians to degrees, multiply radians by 180/pi.

Note   **Atn** is the inverse trigonometric function of **Tan**, which takes an angle as its argument and returns the ratio of two sides of a right triangle. Do not confuse **Atn** with the cotangent, which is the simple inverse of a tangent (1/tangent).

See Also

Math Functions, **Cos** Function, **Sin** Function, **Tan** Function, **Derived Math** Functions

Example

This example uses the **Atn** function to calculate the value of pi.

```
Dim pi
pi = 4 * Atn(1)    ' Calculate the value of pi.
```

Attributes Property

Sets or returns a value that indicates one or more characteristics of a **Field**, **Relation**, or **TableDef** object.

Applies To

Field Object, **Relation** Object, **TableDef** Object

Settings and Return Values

The setting or return value is **Long** data type, and the default value is 0.

For a **Field** object, the value specifies characteristics of the field represented by the **Field** object and can be a combination of these constants.

Constant	Description
dbAutoIncrField	The field value for new records is automatically incremented to a unique **Long** integer that can't be changed (in a Microsoft Jet workspace, supported only for Microsoft Jet database(.mdb) tables).
dbDescending	The field is sorted in descending (Z to A or 100 to 0) order; this option applies only to a **Field** object in a **Fields** collection of an **Index** object. If you omit this constant, the field is sorted in ascending (A to Z or 0 to 100) order. This is the default value for **Index** and **TableDef** fields (Microsoft Jet workspaces only).
dbFixedField	The field size is fixed (default for Numeric fields).
dbHyperlinkField	The field contains hyperlink information (Memo fields only).
dbSystemField	The field stores replication information for replicas; you can't delete this type of field (Microsoft Jet workspaces only).
dbUpdatableField	The field value can be changed.
dbVariableField	The field size is variable (Text fields only).

For a **Relation** object, the value specifies characteristics of the relationship represented by the **Relation** object and can be a combination of these constants.

Constant	Description
dbRelationUnique	The relationship is one-to-one.
dbRelationDontEnforce	The relationship isn't enforced (no referential integrity).
dbRelationInherited	The relationship exists in a non-current database that contains the two linked tables.
dbRelationUpdateCascade	Updates will cascade.
dbRelationDeleteCascade	Deletions will cascade.

Note If you set the **Relation** object's **Attributes** property to activate cascading operations, the Microsoft Jet database engine automatically updates or deletes records in one or more other tables when changes occur in related primary tables.

For example, suppose you establish a cascading delete relationship between a Customers table and an Orders table. When you delete records from the Customers table, records in the Orders table related to that customer are also deleted. In addition, if you establish cascading delete relationships between the Orders table and other tables, records from those tables are automatically deleted when you delete records from the Customers table.

For a **TableDef** object, the value specifies characteristics of the table represented by the **TableDef** object and can be a combination of these **Long** constants.

Constant	Description
dbAttachExclusive	For databases that use the Microsoft Jet database engine, the table is a linked table opened for exclusive use. You can set this constant on an appended **TableDef** object for a local table, but not on a remote table.
dbAttachSavePWD	For databases that use the Microsoft Jet database engine, the user ID and password for the remotely linked table are saved with the connection information. You can set this constant on an appended **TableDef** object for a remote table, but not on a local table.
dbSystemObject	The table is a system table provided by the Microsoft Jet database engine. You can set this constant on an appended **TableDef** object.
dbHiddenObject	The table is a hidden table provided by the Microsoft Jet database engine. You can set this constant on an appended **TableDef** object.
dbAttachedTable	The table is a linked table from a non-ODBC data source such as a Microsoft Jet or Paradox database (read-only).
dbAttachedODBC	The table is a linked table from an ODBC data source, such as Microsoft SQL Server (read-only).

Remarks

For an object not yet appended to a collection, this property is read/write.

For an appended **Field** object, the availability of the **Attributes** property depends on the object that contains the **Fields** collection.

If the Field object belongs to an	Then Attributes is
Index object	Read/write until the **TableDef** object that the **Index** object is appended to is appended to a **Database** object; then the property is read-only.
QueryDef object	Read-only
Recordset object	Read-only
Relation object	Not supported
TableDef object	Read/write

For an appended **Relation** object, the **Attributes** property setting is read-only.

For an appended **TableDef** object, the property is read/write, although you can't set all of the constants if the object is appended, as noted in **Settings** and **Return Values**.

When you set multiple attributes, you can combine them by summing the appropriate constants. Any invalid values are ignored without producing an error.

Example

This example displays the **Attributes** property for **Field**, **Relation**, and **TableDef** objects in the Northwind database.

```
Sub AttributesX()

    Dim dbsNorthwind As Database
    Dim fldLoop As Field
    Dim relLoop As Relation
    Dim tdfloop As TableDef

    Set dbsNorthwind = OpenDatabase("Northwind.mdb")

    With dbsNorthwind

        ' Display the attributes of a TableDef object's
        ' fields.
        Debug.Print "Attributes of fields in " & _
            .TableDefs(0).Name & " table:"
        For Each fldLoop In .TableDefs(0).Fields
            Debug.Print "    " & fldLoop.Name & " = " & _
                fldLoop.Attributes
        Next fldLoop

        ' Display the attributes of the Northwind database's
        ' relations.
        Debug.Print "Attributes of relations in " & _
            .Name & ":"
        For Each relLoop In .Relations
            Debug.Print "    " & relLoop.Name & " = " & _
                relLoop.Attributes
        Next relLoop
```

```
' Display the attributes of the Northwind database's
' tables.
Debug.Print "Attributes of tables in " & .Name & ":"
For Each tdfloop In .TableDefs
   Debug.Print "     " & tdfloop.Name & " = " & _
      tdfloop.Attributes
Next tdfloop

.Close
End With

End Sub
```

Attributes Property (Remote Data)

Returns a value that indicates one or more characteristics of an **rdoColumn** object.

Applies To

rdoColumn Object

Syntax

object.**Attributes**

The *object* placeholder represents an object expression that evaluates to an object in the **Applies To** list.

Return Values

The **Attributes** property return value specifies characteristics of the column represented by the **rdoColumn** object and can be a sum of these constants:

Constant	Value	Description
rdFixedColumn	1	The column size is fixed (default for numeric columns) For example, Char, Binary.
rdVariableColumn	2	The column size is variable. For example, **VarChar** and **LongVarChar**, **VarBinary** and **LongVarBinary** columns.
rdAutoIncrColumn	16	The column value for new rows is automatically incremented to a unique value that can't be changed.
rdUpdatableColumn	32	The column value can be changed.
rdTimeStampColumn	64	The column is a timestamp value. This attribute is set only for **rdClientBatch** cursors.

Remarks

When checking the setting of this property, you should use the **And** operator to test for a specific attribute. Testing for absolute values can jeopardize future compatibility.

For example, to determine whether an **rdoColumn** object is fixed-size, you can use code like the following:

```
If MyResultset![ColumnName].Attributes And rdFixedColumn Then...
```

See Also

rdoColumn Object, **rdoTable** Object, **Type** Property (Remote Data)

AutoActivate Property

Returns or sets a value that enables the user to activate an object by double-clicking the **OLE** container control or by moving the focus to the **OLE** container control.

Applies To

OLE Container Control

Syntax

object.**AutoActivate** [= *value*]

The **AutoActivate** property syntax has these parts:

Part	Description
object	An object expression that evaluates to an object in the **Applies To** list.
value	An integer or constant specifying the technique used to activate the object within the **OLE** container control, as described in Settings.

Settings

The settings for *value* are:

Constant	Value	Description
vbOLEActivateManual	0	Manual. The object isn't automatically activated. You can activate an object programmatically using the **DoVerb** method.
vbOLEActivateGetFocus	1	Focus. If the **OLE** container control contains an object that supports single click activation, the application that provides the object is activated when the **OLE** container control receives the focus.
vbOLEActivateDoubleclick	2	(Default) **Double-Click**. If the **OLE** container control contains an object, the application that provides the object is activated when the user double-clicks the **OLE** container control or presses ENTER when the control has the focus.
vbOLEActivateAuto	3	Automatic. If the **OLE** container control contains an object, the application that provides the object is activated based on the object's normal method of activation—either when the control receives the focus or when the user double-clicks the control.

Remarks

You can determine if the **OLE** container control contains an object by checking the **OLEType** property.

Note When **AutoActivate** is set to 2 (**Double-Click**), the **DblClick** event doesn't occur when the user double-clicks an **OLE** container control.

See Also

OLEType Property, **DoVerb** Method

AutoRedraw Property

Returns or sets the output from a graphics method to a persistent graphic.

Applies To

PropertyPage Object, **UserControl** Object, **UserDocument** Object, **Form** Object, **Forms** Collection, **PictureBox** Control

Syntax

object.**AutoRedraw** [= *boolean*]

The **AutoRedraw** property syntax has these parts:

Part	Description
object	An object expression that evaluates to an object in the **Applies To** list.
boolean	A Boolean expression that specifies how the object is repainted, as described in Settings.

Settings

The settings for *boolean* are:

Setting	Description
True	Enables automatic repainting of a **Form** object or **PictureBox** control. Graphics and text are written to the screen and to an image stored in memory. The object doesn't receive Paint events; it's repainted when necessary, using the image stored in memory.
False	(Default) Disables automatic repainting of an object and writes graphics or text only to the screen. Visual Basic invokes the object's Paint event when necessary to repaint the object.

Remarks

This property is central to working with the following graphics methods: **Circle**, **Cls**, **Line**, **Point**, **Print**, and **PSet**. Setting **AutoRedraw** to **True** automatically redraws the output from these methods in a **Form** object or **PictureBox** control when, for example, the object is resized or redisplayed after being hidden by another object.

You can set **AutoRedraw** in code at run time to alternate between drawing persistent graphics (such as a background or grid) and temporary graphics. If you set **AutoRedraw** to **False**, previous output becomes part of the background screen. When **AutoRedraw** is set to **False**, background graphics aren't deleted if you clear the drawing area with the **Cls** method. Setting **AutoRedraw** back to **True** and then using **Cls** clears the background graphics.

Note If you set the **BackColor** property, all graphics and text, including the persistent graphic, are erased. In general, all graphics should be displayed using the Paint event unless **AutoRedraw** is set to **True**.

To retrieve the persistent graphic created when **AutoRedraw** is set to **True**, use the **Image** property. To pass the persistent graphic to a Windows API when **AutoRedraw** is set to **True**, use the object's **hDC** property.

If you set a form's **AutoRedraw** property to **False** and then minimize the form, the **ScaleHeight** and **ScaleWidth** properties are set to icon size. When **AutoRedraw** is set to **True**, **ScaleHeight** and **ScaleWidth** remain the size of the restored window.

If **AutoRedraw** is set to **False**, the **Print** method will print on top of graphical controls such as the **Image** and **Shape** controls.

See Also

Paint Event, **Cls** Method, **Point** Method, **hDC** Property, **Image** Property, **ScaleHeight**, **ScaleWidth** Properties

Example

This example alternately displays two graphics on a **PictureBox** control: a persistent filled circle and temporary vertical lines. Click the **PictureBox** to draw or redraw the lines. Resizing the form requires the temporary graphic to be redrawn. To try this example, paste the code into the Declarations section of a form that has a **PictureBox** control named Picture1. Press F5 to run the program, and click the graphic each time you resize the form.

```
Private Sub Form_Load ()
    Picture1.ScaleHeight = 100          ' Set scale to 100.
    Picture1.ScaleWidth = 100
    Picture1.AutoRedraw = True          ' Turn on AutoRedraw.
    Picture1.ForeColor = 0  ' Set ForeColor.
    Picture1.FillColor = QBColor(9)     ' Set FillColor.
    Picture1.FillStyle = 0  ' Set FillStyle.
    Picture1.Circle (50, 50), 30        ' Draw a circle.
    Picture1.AutoRedraw = False         ' Turn off AutoRedraw.
End Sub

Private Sub Picture1_Click ()
    Dim I ' Declare variable.
    Picture1.ForeColor = Rgb(Rnd * 255, 0, 0) ' Select random color.
    For I = 5 To 95 Step 10             ' Draw lines.
        Picture1.Line (I, 0)-(I, 100)
    Next
End Sub
```

AutoShowChildren Property

Returns or sets a value that determines whether MDI child forms are displayed when loaded.

Applies To

MDIForm Object

Syntax

object.**AutoShowChildren** [= *boolean*]

The **AutoShowChildren** property syntax has these parts:

Part	Description
object	An object expression that evaluates to an object in the **Applies To** list.
boolean	A Boolean expression that specifies whether MDI child forms are automatically visible, as described in Settings.

Settings

The settings for *boolean* are:

Setting	Description
True	(Default) MDI child forms are automatically displayed when loaded.
False	MDI child forms aren't automatically displayed when loaded.

Remarks

You can use the **AutoShowChildren** property to load MDI child forms and leave them hidden until they're displayed using the **Show** method.

See Also

MDIChild Property, **ActiveForm** Property

Example

This example presents an **MDIForm** object with an MDI child form, uses the **AutoShowChildren** property to create a hidden form as another instance of the MDI child form, and then creates a visible MDI child form. To try this example, set the **MDIChild** property to **True** on Form1, and then create an **MDIForm** with the Add MDI Form command on the Project menu. Copy the code into the Declarations section of the **MDIForm**, and then press F5 to run the program.

```
Private Sub MDIForm_Load()
    MDIForm1.AutoShowChildren = False  ' Set to hide child forms.
    Dim HideForm As New Form1          ' Declare new form.
    HideForm.Caption = "HideForm"      ' Set its caption.
    Load HideForm                      ' Load it; it's hidden.
    MDIForm1.AutoShowChildren = True    ' Set to show child forms.
    Dim ShowForm As New Form1          ' Declare another new form.
    ShowForm.Caption = "ShowForm"      ' Set its caption.
    Load ShowForm                      ' Load it; it's displayed.
End Sub
```

AutoSize Property

Returns or sets a value that determines whether a control is automatically resized to display its entire contents.

Applies To

Label Control, **PictureBox** Control

Syntax

object.**AutoSize** [= *boolean*]

The **AutoSize** property syntax has these parts:

Part	Description
object	An object expression that evaluates to an object in the **Applies To** list.
boolean	A Boolean expression that specifies whether the control is resized, as described in Settings.

Settings

The settings for *boolean* are:

Setting	Description
True	Automatically resizes the control to display its entire contents.
False	(Default) Keeps the size of the control constant. Contents are clipped when they exceed the area of the control.

See Also

Resize Event, **Alignment** Property

AutoVerbMenu Property

Returns or sets a value that determines if a pop-up menu containing the object's verbs is displayed when the user clicks the **OLE** container control with the right mouse button.

Applies To

OLE Container Control, **OLEObject** Object

Syntax

object.**AutoVerbMenu**[= *boolean*]

The **AutoVerbMenu** property syntax has these parts:

Part	Description
object	An object expression that evaluates to an object in the **Applies To** list.
boolean	A Boolean expression specifying whether a pop-up menu is displayed, as described in Settings.

Settings

The settings for *boolean* are:

Setting	Description
True	(Default) When the user clicks the **OLE** container control with the right mouse button, a pop-up menu is displayed, showing the commands the object supports.
False	No pop-up menu is displayed.

Remarks

When this property is set to **True**, **Click** events and **MouseDown** events don't occur when the **OLE** container control is clicked with the right mouse button.

In order to display your own menus, the **AutoVerbMenu** property must be set to **False**.

See Also

ObjectVerbs Property, **ObjectVerbsCount** Property, **Verb** Property

BackColor, ForeColor Properties

- **BackColor**—returns or sets the background color of an object.
- **ForeColor**—returns or sets the foreground color used to display text and graphics in an object.

Applies To

AmbientProperties Object, **PropertyPage** Object, **UserControl** Object, **UserDocument** Object, **Printer** Object, **Printers** Collection, **CheckBox** Control, **ComboBox** Control, **CommandButton** Control, **DirListBox** Control, **DriveListBox** Control, **FileListBox** Control, **Form** Object, **Forms** Collection, **Frame** Control, **Label** Control, **ListBox** Control, **MDIForm** Object, **OptionButton** Control, **PictureBox** Control, **Shape** Control, **TextBox** Control, **OLE Container** Control, **Animation** Control, **Data** Control, **DBCombo** Control, **DBGrid** Control, **DBList** Control, **ImageList** Control, **ListView** Control, **Masked Edit** Control, **MSFlexGrid** Control, **RemoteData** Control, **RichTextBox** Control, **SSTab** Control

Syntax

object.**BackColor** [= *color*]
object.**ForeColor** [= *color*]

The **BackColor** and **ForeColor** property syntaxes have these parts:

Part	Description
object	An object expression that evaluates to an object in the **Applies To** list.
color	A value or constant that determines the background or foreground colors of an object, as described in Settings.

Settings

Visual Basic uses the Microsoft Windows operating environment red-green-blue (RGB) color scheme. The settings for *color* are:

Setting	Description
Normal RGB colors	Colors specified by using the Color palette or by using the **RGB** or **QBColor** functions in code.
System default colors	Colors specified by system color constants listed in the Visual Basic (VB) object library in the Object Browser. The Windows operating environment substitutes the user's choices as specified in the Control Panel settings.

For all forms and controls, the default settings at design time are:

- **BackColor**—set to the system default color specified by the constant **vbWindowBackground**.

- **ForeColor**—set to the system default color specified by the constant **vbWindowText**.

Remarks

In the **Label**, and **Shape**, controls, the **BackColor** property is ignored if the **BackStyle** property setting is 0 (Transparent).

If you set the **BackColor** property on a **Form** object or a **PictureBox** control, all text and graphics, including the persistent graphics, are erased. Setting the **ForeColor** property doesn't affect graphics or print output already drawn. On all other controls, the screen color changes immediately.

The valid range for a normal RGB color is 0 to 16,777,215 (&HFFFFFF). The high byte of a number in this range equals 0; the lower 3 bytes, from least to most significant byte, determine the amount of red, green, and blue, respectively. The red, green, and blue components are each represented by a number between 0 and 255 (&HFF). If the high byte isn't 0, Visual Basic uses the system colors, as defined in the user's Control Panel settings and by constants listed in the Visual Basic (VB) object library in the Object Browser.

To display text in the Windows operating environment, both the text and background colors must be solid. If the text or background colors you've selected aren't displayed, one of the selected colors may be dithered—that is, comprised of up to three different-colored pixels. If you choose a dithered color for either the text or background, the nearest solid color will be substituted.

See Also

FillColor Property, **FillStyle** Property, **TreeView** Control

Example

This example resets foreground and background colors randomly twice each second for a form and **PictureBox** control. To try this example, paste the code into the

Declarations section of a form that contains a **PictureBox** control and a **Timer** control, and then press F5.

```
Private Sub Form_Load ()
   Timer1.Interval = 500
End Sub

Private Sub Timer1_Timer ()
   BackColor = QBColor(Rnd * 15)
   ForeColor = QBColor(Rnd * 10)
   Picture1.BackColor = QBColor(Rnd * 15)
   Picture1.ForeColor = QBColor(Rnd * 10)
End Sub
```

BackStyle Property

Returns or sets a value indicating whether a **Label** control or the background of a **Shape** control is transparent or opaque.

Applies To

UserControl Object, **Label** Control, **Shape** Control, **OLE Container** Control

Syntax

object.**BackStyle** [= *number*]

The **BackStyle** property syntax has these parts:

Part	Description
object	An object expression that evaluates to an object in the **Applies To** list.
number	A numeric expression specifying transparency, as described in Settings.

Settings

The settings for *number* are:

Setting	Description
0	Transparent—background color and any graphics are visible behind the control.
1	(Default) Opaque—the control's **BackColor** property setting fills the control and obscures any color or graphics behind it.

Remarks

You can use the **BackStyle** property to create transparent controls when you're using a background color on a **Form** object or **PictureBox** control or when you want to place a control over a graphic. Use an opaque control when you want it to stand out.

A control's **BackColor** property is ignored if **BackStyle** = 0.

See Also

BackColor, **ForeColor** Properties

BackStyle Property (UserControl Object)

Returns or sets a value indicating the type of the control's background. The **BackStyle** property is read/write at the control's authoring time, and read-only at the control's run time.

Applies To

UserControl Object

Syntax

object.**BackStyle** [= *enum*]

The **BackStyle** property syntax has these parts:

Part	Description
object	An object expression that evaluates to an object in the **Applies To** list.
enum	An enumerated value that determines how the background of the control will be displayed, as described in **Settings**.

Settings

The settings for *enum* are:

Setting	Description
0-Transparent	Transparent background. Controls behind this control and the containing form's background will show through this control's blank areas. The area of the control's display can then be divided into two areas: the portion that is part of a constituent control, and the rest. This latter area of the control display area cannot be drawn on, and the portions of controls that are placed on the control by the developer or end user that fall into this latter area will also be invisible. Mouse events that fall in this latter area will not be given to the control, but rather to the underlying container.
1-Opaque	Opaque background. This is the default.
2-TransparentPaint	Transparent background. The difference between this option and **0-Transparent** is that controls behind this control and the containing form's background will show through this control's blank areas, but the entire area of this control can be drawn upon, controls placed on this control will not be invisible, and all mouse events that fall within this control will be given to this control.

BatchCollisionCount Property (DAO)

Returns the number of records that did not complete the last batch update (**ODBCDirect** workspaces only).

Applies To

Dynaset-Type Recordset Object, **Recordset** Object, **Snapshot-Type Recordset** Object, **Forward-Only–Type Recordset** Object, **Dynamic-Type Recordset** Object

Return Value

The return value is a **Long** that indicates the number of failing records, or 0 if all records were successfully updated.

Remarks

This property indicates how many records encountered collisions or otherwise failed to update during the last batch update attempt. The value of this property corresponds to the number of bookmarks in the **BatchCollisions** property.

If you set the working **Recordset** object's **Bookmark** property to bookmark values in the **BatchCollisions** array, you can move to each record that failed to complete the most recent batch **Update** operation.

After the collision records are corrected, a batch-mode **Update** method can be called again. At this point DAO attempts another batch update, and the **BatchCollisions** property again reflects the set of records that failed the second attempt. Any records that succeeded in the previous attempt are not sent in the current attempt, because they now have a **RecordStatus** property of **dbRecordUnmodified**. This process can continue as long as collisions occur, or until you abandon the updates and close the result set.

Example

This example uses the **BatchCollisionCount** property and the **Update** method to demonstrate batch updating where any collisions are resolved by forcing the batch update.

```
Sub BatchX()

    Dim wrkMain As Workspace
    Dim conMain As Connection
    Dim rstTemp As Recordset
    Dim intLoop As Integer
    Dim strPrompt As String

    Set wrkMain = CreateWorkspace("ODBCWorkspace", _
        "admin", "", dbUseODBC)
    ' This DefaultCursorDriver setting is required for
    ' batch updating.
    wrkMain.DefaultCursorDriver = dbUseClientBatchCursor

    Set conMain = wrkMain.OpenConnection("Publishers", _
        dbDriverNoPrompt, False, _
        "ODBC;DATABASE=pubs;UID=sa;PWD=;DSN=Publishers")
    ' The following locking argument is required for
    ' batch updating.
    Set rstTemp = conMain.OpenRecordset( _
        "SELECT * FROM roysched", dbOpenDynaset, 0, _
        dbOptimisticBatch)
```

```
With rstTemp
   ' Modify data in local recordset.
   Do While Not .EOF
      .Edit
      If !royalty <= 20 Then
         !royalty = !royalty - 4
      Else
         !royalty = !royalty + 2
      End If
      .Update
      .MoveNext
   Loop

   ' Attempt a batch update.
   .Update dbUpdateBatch

   ' If there are collisions, give the user the option
   ' of forcing the changes or resolving them
   ' individually.
   If .BatchCollisionCount > 0 Then
      strPrompt = "There are collisions. " & vbCr & _
         "Do you want the program to force " & _
         vbCr & "an update using the local data?"
      If MsgBox(strPrompt, vbYesNo) = vbYes Then _
         .Update dbUpdateBatch, True
   End If

   .Close
End With

conMain.Close
wrkMain.Close

End Sub
```

BatchCollisionCount Property (Remote Data)

Returns a value that specifies the number of rows that did not complete the last batch-mode update.

Applies To

rdoResultset Object, **RemoteData** Control

Syntax

object.**BatchCollisionCount**

The *object* placeholder represents an object expression that evaluates to an object in the **Applies To** list.

Return Values

The **BatchCollisionCount** property return value is a **Long** expression that specifies the number of failing rows or 0 if all rows were processed.

Remarks

This property indicates how many rows encountered collisions or otherwise failed to update during the last batch update attempt. The value of this property corresponds to the number of bookmarks in the **BatchCollisionRows** array.

By setting the working **rdoResultset** object's **Bookmark** property to bookmark values in the **BatchCollisionRows** array, you can position to each row that failed to complete the most recent **BatchUpdate** operation.

After the collision rows are corrected, the **BatchUpdate** method can be called again. At this point RDO attempts another batch update, and the **BatchCollisionRows** property again reflects the set of rows that failed the second attempt. Any rows that succeeded in the previous attempt are not sent in the current attempt, as they now have a **Status** of **rdRowUnmodified**. This process can continue as long as collisions occur, or until you abandon the updates and close the result set.

See Also

BatchCollisionRows Property, **BatchConflictValue** Property, **BatchSize** Property, **Status** Property, **UpdateCriteria** Property, **UpdateOperation** Property

---

BatchCollisionRows Property

Returns an array of bookmarks indicating the rows that generated collisions in the last batch update operation.

Applies To

rdoResultset Object, **RemoteData** Control

Syntax

object.**BatchCollisionRows**

The *object* placeholder represents an object expression that evaluates to an object in the **Applies To** list.

Return Values

The **BatchCollisionRows** property return value is a **Variant**(string) expression as described in Remarks.

Remarks

This property contains an array of bookmarks to rows that encountered a collision during the last invocation of the **BatchUpdate** method. The number of elements in the array is indicated by the **BatchCollisionCount** property.

By setting the working **rdoResultset** object's **Bookmark** property to bookmark values in the **BatchCollisionRows** array, you can position to each row that failed to complete the most recent **BatchUpdate** operation.

After the collision rows are corrected, the **BatchUpdate** method can be called again. At this point RDO attempts another batch update, and the **BatchCollisionRows** property again reflects the set of rows that failed the second attempt. Any rows that succeeded in the previous attempt are not sent in the current attempt, as they now have a **Status** of **rdRowUnmodified**. This process can continue as long as collisions occur, or until you abandon the updates and close the result set.

This array is re-created each time the **BatchUpdate** method executes.

See Also

BatchCollisionCount Property, **BatchUpdate** Method

BatchCollisions Property

Returns an array of bookmarks indicating the rows that generated collisions in the last batch update operation (**ODBCDirect** workspaces only).

Applies To

Dynaset-Type Recordset Object, **Recordset** Object, **Snapshot-Type Recordset** Object, **Forward-Only–Type Recordset** Object, **Dynamic-Type Recordset** Object

Return Value

The return value is a variant expression containing an array of bookmarks.

Remarks

This property contains an array of bookmarks to rows that encountered a collision during the last attempted batch **Update** call. The **BatchCollisionCount** property indicates the number of elements in the array.

If you set the working **Recordset** object's **Bookmark** property to bookmark values in the **BatchCollisions** array, you can move to each record that failed to complete the most recent batch-mode **Update** operation.

After the collision records are corrected, you can call the batch mode **Update** method again. At this point DAO attempts another batch update, and the **BatchCollisions** property again reflects the set of records that failed the second attempt. Any records that succeeded in the previous attempt are not sent in the current attempt, as they now have a **RecordStatus** property of **dbRecordUnmodified**. This process can continue as long as collisions occur, or until you abandon the updates and close the result set.

This array is re-created each time you execute a batch-mode **Update** method.

BatchConflictValue Property

Returns a value currently in the database that is newer than the **Value** property as determined by an optimistic batch update conflict.

Applies To

rdoColumn Object

Syntax

object.**BatchConflictValue**

The *object* placeholder represents an object expression that evaluates to an object in the **Applies To** list.

Return Values

The **BatchConflictValue** property return value is a **Variant**(String) expression as described in Remarks.

Remarks

This property contains the value of the column that is currently in the database on the server. During an optimistic batch update, a collision may occur where a second client modified the same column and row in between the time the first client fetched the data and the update attempt. When this happens, the value that the second client set will be accessible through this property.

See Also

BatchCollisionCount Property, **BatchSize** Property, **BatchUpdate** Method, **rdoColumn** Object, **rdoResultset** Object, **Status** Property

---

BatchSize Property (DAO)

Sets or returns the number of statements sent back to the server in each batch (**ODBCDirect** workspaces only).

Applies To

Dynaset-Type Recordset Object, **Recordset** Object, **Snapshot-Type Recordset** Object, **Forward-Only–Type Recordset** Object, **Dynamic-Type Recordset** Object

Settings And Return Values

The setting or return value is a **Long** that indicates the number of batched statements sent the server in a single batch update. The default value is 15.

Remarks

The **BatchSize** property determines the batch size used when sending statements to the server in a batch update. The value of the property determines the number of statements sent to the server in one command buffer. By default, 15 statements are sent to the server in each batch. This property can be changed at any time. If a database server doesn't support statement batching, you can set this property to 1, causing each statement to be sent separately.

Example

This example uses the **BatchSize** and **UpdateOptions** properties to control aspects of any batch updating for the specified **Recordset** object.

```
Sub BatchSizeX()

    Dim wrkMain As Workspace
    Dim conMain As Connection
    Dim rstTemp As Recordset

    Set wrkMain = CreateWorkspace("ODBCWorkspace", _
        "admin", "", dbUseODBC)
    ' This DefaultCursorDriver setting is required for
    ' batch updating.
    wrkMain.DefaultCursorDriver = dbUseClientBatchCursor

    Set conMain = wrkMain.OpenConnection("Publishers", _
        dbDriverNoPrompt, False, _
        "ODBC;DATABASE=pubs;UID=sa;PWD=;DSN=Publishers")
    ' The following locking argument is required for
    ' batch updating.
    Set rstTemp = conMain.OpenRecordset( _
        "SELECT * FROM roysched", dbOpenDynaset, 0, _
        dbOptimisticBatch)

    With rstTemp
        ' Increase the number of statements sent to the server
        ' during a single batch update, thereby reducing the
        ' number of times an update would have to access the
        ' server.
        .BatchSize = 25

        ' Change the UpdateOptions property so that the WHERE
        ' clause of any batched statements going to the server
        ' will include any updated columns in addition to the
        ' key column(s). Also, any modifications to records
        ' will be made by deleting the original record
        ' and adding a modified version rather than just
        ' modifying the original record.
        .UpdateOptions = dbCriteriaModValues + _
            dbCriteriaDeleteInsert

        ' Engage in batch updating using the new settings
        ' above.
        ' ...

        .Close
    End With

    conMain.Close
    wrkMain.Close

End Sub
```

BatchSize Property (Remote Data)

Returns or sets a value that specifies the number of statements sent back to the server in each batch.

Applies To

rdoResultset Object, **RemoteData** Control

Syntax

object.**BatchSize** [= *value*]

The **BatchSize** property syntax has these parts:

Part	Description
object	An object expression that evaluates to an object in the **Applies To** list.
value	A **Long** integer representing the number of statements sent back to the server in each batch. The default value is 15.

Remarks

This property determines the batch size used when sending statements to the server during an optimistic batch update. The value of the property determines the number of statements sent to the server in one command buffer. By default, 15 statements are sent to the server in each batch. This property can be changed at any time. If a DBMS doesn't support statement batching, you can set this property to 1, causing each statement to be sent separately.

See Also

BatchCollisionCount Property**, BatchCollisionRows** Property**, BatchConflictValue** Property**, BatchUpdate** Method

---

BatchUpdate Method (Remote Data)

Performs a batched optimistic update.

Applies To

rdoResultset Object

Syntax

object.**BatchUpdate** (*SingleRow*, *Force*)

The **BatchUpdate** method syntax has these parts:

Part	Description
object	An object expression that evaluates to an object in the **Applies To** list.
SingleRow	A **Boolean** value that is **True** if the update is done only for the current row, or **False** if the update **Applies To** all rows in the batch. Default is False.
Force	A **Boolean** value that is **True** if the row or batch of rows will overwrite existing rows in the database regardless if they cause collisions or not. Default is **False**.

Remarks

This method performs a batch optimistic update operation. When using batch optimistic concurrency, it is necessary to call this method to actually send the changes back to the server.

Batch updates are used whenever you open a connection using the **ClientBatch** cursor library (**rdUseClientBatch**). In this case, each time you use the **Update** or **UpdateRow** methods, the local **rdoResultset** is updated, but the base database tables are not changed. The **BatchUpdate** method is used to update the base database table(s) with any information changed since the **rdoResultset** was last created or synchronized with the **BatchUpdate** command.

The **BatchUpdate** method updates the **BatchCollisionRows** property to include a bookmark for each row that failed to update—collided with an existing row that has data more current than the **rdoResultset** object as it existed when first read. The **BatchCollisionCount** property indicates how many collisions occurred during the batch update process.

If you use the **CancelBatch** method, the changes saved to the local **rdoResultset** object are discarded. When you use the **CancelUpdate** method, only the current row's changes are rolled back to the state prior to execution of the last **Update** method.

The *SingleRow* parameter can be used in conjunction with the *Force* parameter to force the client's version of the data back into the database, even if collisions have occurred. The *SingleRow* parameter will tell RDO to only send the current row back to the server and not the entire batch, and the *Force* parameter will tell RDO to force the data in, and not use the normal optimistic concurrency detection.

Setting both the *SingleRow* and *Force* parameters to **True** overlays a single database row with the current updated **rdoResultset** row. This is useful when processing collision rows and you want to force your local version of the data to be saved regardless of the current database row setting.

Setting *SingleRow* to **False** and *Force* to **True** will cause all rows that are dirty to be forced into the database, which is useful as a shorthand way of forcing everything in (the last-one-in-wins scenario).

Setting *SingleRow* to **True** and *Force* to **False** will cause just the current row to go through the optimistic concurrency update, which is useful when you only want to update the current row, not the entire batch.

See Also

QueryCompleted Event (Remote Data), **QueryComplete** Event, **Cancel** Method (Remote Data), **Close** Method (Remote Data), **Execute** Method (Remote Data), **Update** Method (Remote Data), **UpdateControls** Method (Remote Data), **UpdateRow** Method (Remote Data), **CancelBatch** Method (Remote Data), **BatchCollisionCount** Property (DAO), **BatchCollisionRows** Property, **BatchConflictValue** Property, **BatchSize** Property (Remote Data)

Beep Statement

Sounds a tone through the computer's speaker.

Syntax

Beep

Remarks

The frequency and duration of the beep depend on your hardware and system software, and vary among computers.

Example

This example uses the **Beep** statement to sound three consecutive tones through the computer's speaker.

```
Dim I
For I = 1 To 3    ' Loop 3 times.
   Beep           ' Sound a tone.
Next I
```

BeforeColEdit Event

Occurs just before the user enters edit mode by typing a character.

Applies To

DBGrid Control

Syntax

Private Sub *object*_**BeforeColEdit**([*index* **As Integer**,] **ByVal** *colindex* **As Integer**,
↳ **ByVal** *keyascii* **As Integer**, *cancel* **As Integer**)

The **BeforeColEdit** event syntax has these parts:

Part	Description
object	An object expression that evaluates to an object in the **Applies To** list.
Index	An integer that identifies a control if it is in a control array.
colindex	An integer that identifies the column to be edited.
keyascii	An integer representing the ANSI key code of the character typed by the user to initiate editing, or 0 if the user initiated editing by clicking the mouse. **KeyAscii** is passed by value, not by reference; you cannot change its value to initiate editing with a different character.
cancel	An integer that may be set to **True** to prevent the user from editing the cell, as described in Settings.

Settings

The settings for *cancel* are:

Setting	Description
True	The cell will not enter edit mode
False	(Default) The **ColEdit** event is fired immediately, followed by the Change and **KeyUp** events for the **KeyAscii** argument, if non-zero.

Remarks

If a floating editor marquee is not in use, this event also occurs when the user clicks the current cell or double clicks another cell.

Use this event to control the editability of cells on a per-cell basis, or to translate the initial keystroke into a default value.

Note   The *keyascii* argument can only be 0 if a floating editor marquee is not in use.

See Also

AfterColEdit Event, **ColEdit** Event

BeforeColUpdate Event

Occurs after editing is completed in a cell, but before data is moved from the cell to the **DBGrid** control's copy buffer.

Applies To

DBGrid Control

Syntax

Private Sub *object*_**BeforeColUpdate** ([*index* **As Integer**,] *colindex* **As Integer**,
↪ *oldvalue* **As Variant**, *cancel* **As Integer**)

The **BeforeColUpdate** event syntax has these parts:

Part	Description
object	An object expression that evaluates to an object in the **Applies To** list.
index	An integer that identifies a control if it is in a control array.
colindex	An integer that identifies the column.
oldvalue	A value that contains the value contained in the cell prior to the change.
cancel	A Boolean expression expression that specifies whether the change occurs, as described in Settings.

Settings

The settings for *cancel* are:

Setting	Description
True	Cancels the change, restores cell to *oldvalue*, and restores focus to the control.
False	(Default) Continues with change and permits change of focus.

Remarks

The data specified by the *oldvalue* argument moves from the cell to the control's copy buffer when a user completes editing within a cell, as when tabbing to another column in the same row, pressing ENTER, or changing focus away from the cell. Before the data has been moved from the cell into the control's copy buffer, the **BeforeColUpdate** event is triggered. This event gives your application an opportunity to check the individual grid cells before they are committed to the control's copy buffer.

If your event procedures set the *cancel* argument to **True**, the previous value is restored in the cell and focus remains on the control and the **AfterColUpdate** event is not triggered.

To restore *oldvalue* in the cell and permit the user to move focus off of the cell, set *cancel* to **False** and set the cell to *oldvalue* as follows:

```
Cancel = False
DBGrid1.Columns(ColIndex).Value = OldValue
```

The **AfterColUpdate** event occurs after the **BeforeColUpdate** event.

By setting the *cancel* argument to **True**, the user can not move the focus from the control until the application determines that the data can be safely moved back to the control's copy buffer.

See Also

DBGrid Control, **AfterColUpdate** Event, **AfterUpdate** Event, **BeforeInsert** Event, **BeforeUpdate** Event, **ColIndex** Property

Example

This example checks to make sure that the value the user has typed in is within a certain range; otherwise it disables the update.

```
Private Sub DataGrid1.BeforeColUpdate (ColIndex As Long, OldValue As
Variant, Cancel As Integer)
   If ColIndex = 1 Then
      If DataGrid1.Columns(1).Value < Now Then
         Cancel = True
         MsgBox "You must enter a date that is later than today."
      End If
   End If
End Sub
```

BeforeConnect Event

Occurs just before RDO calls the ODBC API **SQLDriverConnect** function to establish a connection to the server.

Applies To

rdoConnection Object

Syntax

Private Sub *object*.**BeforeConnect**(*ConnectString* as **String**, *Prompt* as **Variant**)

The **BeforeConnect** event syntax has these parts:

Part	Description
object	An object expression that evaluates to an object in the **Applies To** list.
ConnectString	A **Variant** expression that evaluates to a connect string used to provide connect parameters for the ODBC **SQLDriverConnect** function.
Prompt	Determines how the user should be prompted.

Remarks

The **BeforeConnect** event is fired just before RDO calls the ODBC API **SQLDriverConnect** function to establish a connection to the server. This event gives your code an opportunity to provide custom prompting, or just provide or capture connection information.

The *ConnectString* parameter is the ODBC connect string RDO will pass to the ODBC API **SQLDriverConnect** function. This string can be changed during this event, and RDO will use the changed value. For example, your code can provide additional parameters, or change existing parameters of the connect string.

The *Prompt* parameter is the ODBC prompting constant (see the **Prompt** property). This parameter will default to the value of the *Prompt* parameter passed in the **OpenConnection** or **EstablishConnection** methods. The developer may change this value, and RDO will use the new value when calling **SQLDriverConnect**.

See Also

Connect Event, **Disconnect** Event, **OpenConnection** Method (Remote Data), **EstablishConnection** Method (Remote Data), **rdoConnection** Object, **Connect** Property (Remote Data), **Prompt** Property (Remote Data)

BeforeDelete Event

Occurs before a selected record is deleted in a **DBGrid** control.

Applies To

DBGrid Control

Syntax

Private Sub *object*_**BeforeDelete** ([*index* **As Integer**,] *cancel* **As Integer**)

The **BeforeDelete** event syntax has these parts:

Part	Description
object	An object expression that evaluates to an object in the **Applies To** list.
index	An integer that identifies a control if it is in a control array.
cancel	A Boolean expression that determines whether a record is deleted, as described in Settings.

Settings

The settings for *cancel* are:

Setting	Description
True	Leaves focus on control and doesn't delete the record.
False	(Default) Continues with delete operation and enables change of focus.

Remarks

When the user selects a record selector in the control and presses DEL or CTL+X, the **BeforeDelete** event is triggered before the selected row is deleted.

Once the row is deleted, the **AfterDelete** event is triggered. The row selected for deletion is available in the collection provided by the **SelBookmarks** property.

If your event procedure sets the *cancel* argument to **True**, the row isn't deleted.

If more than one row is selected, the error message `Multiple rows cannot be deleted` is displayed.

See Also

AfterDelete Event, **AfterUpdate** Event, **BeforeInsert** Event, **BeforeUpdate** Event

Example

This example displays a message that asks the user to confirm a deletion in a grid.

```
Private Sub DataGrid1_BeforeDelete (Cancel As Integer)
   Dim mResult As Integer
   mResult = MsgBox("Are you sure that you want to delete " &
↳ DataGrid1.SelectedRows &  " record?", _
     vbYesNo And vbQuestion, "Delete Confirmation")
   If mResult = vbNo Then Cancel = True
End Sub
```

BeforeInsert Event

Occurs before new records are inserted into a **DBGrid** control.

Applies To

DBGrid Control

Syntax

Private Sub *object*_**BeforeInsert** ([*index* **As Integer**,] *cancel* **As Integer**)

The **BeforeInsert** event syntax has these parts:

Part	Description
object	An object expression that evaluates to an object in the **Applies To** list.
index	An integer that identifies a control if it is in a control array.
cancel	A Boolean expression that determines if a record is added, as described in Settings.

Settings

The settings for *cancel* are:

Setting	Description
True	Leaves focus on control and doesn't add a new record
False	(Default) Continues with copy and enables change of focus

Remarks

When the user selects the new record (at the bottom of the **DBGrid** control) and enters a character in one of the cells, the **BeforeInsert** event is triggered, followed by the **BeforeUpdate**, **AfterUpdate** and **AfterInsert** events.

If your event procedure sets the *cancel* argument to **True**, the row isn't inserted and the cell is cleared.

When the **BeforeInsert** event is triggered, the record has not been added to the database. The new record exists in the **DBGrid** control's copy buffer until this event procedure ends.

After the **AfterInsert** event is finished, the new record row in the **DBGrid** control is reinitialized and the edited record becomes the last row in the **DBGrid** control.

See Also

AfterDelete Event, **AfterInsert** Event, **AfterUpdate** Event, **BeforeUpdate** Event

Example

This example displays a message that asks the user to confirm the addition of a new record.

```
Private Sub DataGrid1_BeforeInsert (Cancel As Integer)
   Dim mResult As Integer
   mResult = MsgBox("Confirm: Add a new record?", _
   vbYesNo And vbQuestion, "Confirmation")
   If mResult = vbNo Then Cancel = True
End Sub
```

BeforeLoadFile Event

Occurs when a component is added (not opened) to a project, or when a component's associated binary file (such as an .Frx file) is accessed.

Applies To

FileControlEvents Object

Syntax

Sub *object*_**BeforeLoadFile**(*vbproject* **As VBProject**, *filenames()* **As String**)

The **BeforeLoadFile** event syntax has these parts:

Part	Description
object	An object expression that evaluates to an object in the **Applies To** list.
vbproject	A **VBProject** object specifying the name of the project in which the file is to be loaded.
filenames	A string expression specifying the names of the files to be loaded.

Remarks

This event occurs in all add-ins that are connected to the **FileControl** object. This event occurs several times for a project: once for the project file; once for all the forms, modules, classes, **User** controls, **Property Pages**, and control files; and once for each of the .Frx files. This event occurs if a form file with an associated .Frx file is saved, because the .Frx is loaded when the .Frm file is saved.

This event occurs in all add-ins that are connected to the **FileControl** object. The add-in cannot prevent the file from being written to disk because the operation is complete. However, you can use this event to perform other tasks, such as:

* Log information about the event.
* Update information about the file.
* Back up the file.

BeforeUpdate Event

Occurs before data is moved from a **DBGrid** control to the control's copy buffer.

Applies To

DBGrid Control

Syntax

Private Sub *object*_**BeforeUpdate** ([*index* **As Integer**,] *cancel* **As Integer**)

The **BeforeUpdate** event syntax has these parts:

Part	Description
object	An object expression that evaluates to an object in the **Applies To** list.
index	An integer that identifies a control if it is in a control array.
cancel	A Boolean expression that determines if data is copied, as described in Settings.

Settings

The settings for *cancel* are:

Setting	Description
True	Leaves focus on control and doesn't copy data.
False	(Default) Continues with copy operation and enables change of focus.

Remarks

When the user moves to another row or the **Recordset** object's **Update** method is executed, data is moved from the **DBGrid** control's copy buffer to the **Data** control's copy buffer and written to the database.

Just before the data is moved from the **DBGrid** control's copy buffer back into the **Data** control's copy buffer, the **BeforeUpdate** event is triggered. Unless the copy operation is canceled, the **AfterUpdate** event is triggered after the data has been moved back into the **Data** control's copy buffer and written to the database. The updated record is available by using the **Bookmark** property of the **DBGrid** control.

If you set the **BeforeUpdate** event *cancel* argument to **True**, focus remains on the control, neither the **AfterUpdate** or **LostFocus** event is triggered, and the record isn't saved to the database.

The **BeforeUpdate** event occurs before the **AfterUpdate** and **LostFocus** events for this control, or before the **GotFocus** event for the next control in the tab order.

This event occurs even if the control isn't bound.

Unlike the **Change** event, changing data in a control or record using code doesn't trigger this event.

You can use this event to validate data in a bound control record before permitting the user to commit the change to the **Data** control's copy buffer. By setting the *cancel* argument to **True**, the user can't move focus from the control until the application determines whether the data can be safely moved back to the **Data** control's copy buffer.

See Also

DBCombo Control, **DBList** Control, **AfterUpdate** Event

Example

This example displays a message that tells the user to enter a value in the first column before the grid can be updated.

```
Private Sub DataGrid1_BeforeUpdate (Cancel As Integer)
   If DataGrid1.Columns(1).Value = "" Then
      MsgBox "You must enter value in the first column!"
      Cancel = True
   End If
End Sub
```

BeginTrans Event

Occurs after the **BeginTrans** method has completed.

Applies To

rdoEnvironment Object

Syntax

Private Sub *object***.BeginTrans**( )

The *object* placeholder represents an object expression that evaluates to an object in the **Applies To** list.

Remarks

The **BeginTrans** event is raised after a **BeginTrans** method has completed. This event procedure can synchronize some other process with the transaction.

See Also

BeginTrans, **CommitTrans**, **RollbackTrans** Methods

BeginTrans, CommitTrans, Rollback Methods

The transaction methods manage transaction processing during a session defined by a **Workspace** object as follows:

- **BeginTrans** begins a new transaction.
- **CommitTrans** ends the current transaction and saves the changes.
- **Rollback** ends the current transaction and restores the databases in the **Workspace** object to the state they were in when the current transaction began.

Applies To

DBEngine Object, **Workspace** Object

Syntax

*workspace***.BeginTrans** | **CommitTrans** [**dbFlushOSCacheWrites**] | **Rollback**

The *workspace* placeholder is an object variable that represents the **Workspace** containing the databases that will use transactions.

Remarks

You use these methods with a **Workspace** object when you want to treat a series of changes made to the databases in a session as one unit.

Typically, you use transactions to maintain the integrity of your data when you must both update records in two or more tables and ensure changes are completed (committed) in all tables or none at all (rolled back). For example, if you transfer money from one account to another, you might subtract an amount from one and add the amount to another. If either update fails, the accounts no longer balance. Use the **BeginTrans** method before updating the first record, and then, if any subsequent update fails, you can use the **Rollback** method to undo all of the updates. Use the **CommitTrans** method after you successfully update the last record.

In a Microsoft Jet workspace, you can include the **dbFlushOSCacheWrites** constant with **CommitTrans**, This forces the database engine to immediately flush all updates to disk, instead of caching them temporarily. Without using this option, a user could get control back immediately after the application program calls **CommitTrans**, turn the computer off, and not have the data written to disk. While using this option may affect your application's performance, it is useful in situations where the computer could be shut off before cached updates are saved to disk.

Caution Within one **Workspace** object, transactions are always global to the **Workspace** and aren't limited to only one **Connection** or **Database** object. If you perform operations on more than one connection or database within a **Workspace** transaction, resolving the transaction (that is, using the **CommitTrans** or **Rollback** method) affects all operations on all connections and databases within that workspace.

After you use **CommitTrans**, you can't undo changes made during that transaction unless the transaction is nested within another transaction that is itself rolled back. If you nest transactions, you must resolve the current transaction before you can resolve a transaction at a higher level of nesting.

If you want to have simultaneous transactions with overlapping, non-nested scopes, you can create additional **Workspace** objects to contain the concurrent transactions.

If you close a **Workspace** object without resolving any pending transactions, the transactions are automatically rolled back.

If you use the **CommitTrans** or **Rollback** method without first using the **BeginTrans** method, an error occurs.

Some ISAM databases used in a Microsoft Jet workspace may not support transactions, in which case the **Transactions** property of the **Database** object or **Recordset** object is **False**. To make sure the database supports transactions, check the value of the **Transactions** property of the **Database** object before using the **BeginTrans** method. If you are using a **Recordset** object based on more than one database, check the **Transactions** property of the **Recordset** object. If a **Recordset** is based entirely on Microsoft Jet tables, you can always use transactions. **Recordset** objects based on tables created by other database products, however, may not support transactions. For example, you can't use transactions in a **Recordset** based on a Paradox table. In this case, the **Transactions** property is **False**. If the **Database** or **Recordset** doesn't support transactions, the methods are ignored and no error occurs.

You can't nest transactions if you are accessing ODBC data sources through the Microsoft Jet database engine.

Notes

- You can often improve the performance of your application by breaking operations that require disk access into transaction blocks. This buffers your operations and may significantly reduce the number of times a disk is accessed.

- In a Microsoft Jet workspace, transactions are logged in a file kept in the directory specified by the TEMP environment variable on the workstation. If the transaction log file exhausts the available storage on your TEMP drive, the database engine triggers a run-time error. At this point, if you use **CommitTrans**, an indeterminate number of operations are committed, but the remaining uncompleted operations are lost, and the operation has to be restarted. Using a **Rollback** method releases the transaction log and rolls back all operations in the transaction.

See Also

Close Method, **CreateWorkspace** Method, **Refresh** Method, **Transactions** Property

Example

This example changes the job title of all sales representatives in the Employees table of the database. After the **BeginTrans** method starts a transaction that isolates all the changes made to the Employees table, the **CommitTrans** method saves the changes. Notice that you can use the **Rollback** method to undo changes that you saved using the **Update** method. Furthermore, the main transaction is nested within another transaction that automatically rolls back any changes made by the user during this example.

One or more table pages remain locked while the user decides whether or not to accept the changes. For this reason, this technique isn't recommended but shown only as an example.

```
Sub BeginTransX()

    Dim strName As String
    Dim strMessage As String
    Dim wrkDefault As Workspace
    Dim dbsNorthwind As Database
    Dim rstEmployees As Recordset

    ' Get default Workspace.
    Set wrkDefault = DBEngine.Workspaces(0)
    Set dbsNorthwind = OpenDatabase("Northwind.mdb")
    Set rstEmployees = _
        dbsNorthwind.OpenRecordset("Employees")

    ' Start of outer transaction.
    wrkDefault.BeginTrans
    ' Start of main transaction.
    wrkDefault.BeginTrans

    With rstEmployees

        ' Loop through recordset and ask user if she wants to
        ' change the title for a specified employee.
        Do Until .EOF
            If !Title = "Sales Representative" Then
                strName = !LastName & ", " & !FirstName
                strMessage = "Employee: " & strName & vbCr & _
                    "Change title to Account Executive?"
```

```
            ' Change the title for the specified employee.
            If MsgBox(strMessage, vbYesNo) = vbYes Then
               .Edit
               !Title = "Account Executive"
               .Update
            End If
         End If

         .MoveNext
      Loop

      ' Ask if the user wants to commit to all the changes
      ' made above.
      If MsgBox("Save all changes?", vbYesNo) = vbYes Then
         wrkDefault.CommitTrans
      Else
         wrkDefault.Rollback
      End If

      ' Print current data in recordset.
      .MoveFirst
      Do While Not .EOF
         Debug.Print !LastName & ", " & !FirstName & _
            " - " & !Title
         .MoveNext
      Loop

      ' Roll back any changes made by the user since this is
      ' a demonstration.
      wrkDefault.Rollback
      .Close
   End With

   dbsNorthwind.Close

End Sub
```

BeginTrans, CommitTrans, RollbackTrans Methods (Remote Data)

The transaction methods manage transaction processing during a session represented by the *object* placeholder as follows:

- **BeginTrans** begins a new transaction.

- **CommitTrans** ends the current transaction and saves the changes.

- **RollbackTrans** ends the current transaction and restores the databases in the **rdoEnvironment** object to the state they were in when the current transaction began.

You can use the transaction methods with an **rdoConnection** object—but in this case, the transaction scope only includes **rdoResultset** and **rdoQuery** objects created under the **rdoConnection**.

Applies To

rdoConnection Object, **rdoEnvironment** Object, **RemoteData** Control

Syntax

object.**BeginTrans** | **CommitTrans** | **RollbackTrans**

The *object* placeholder represents an object expression that evaluates to an object in the **Applies To** list.

Remarks

You use the transaction methods with an **rdoEnvironment** or **rdoConnection** object when you want to treat a series of changes made to the databases in a session as one logical unit. That is, either the set of operations completes as a set, or is rolled back as a set. This way if any operation in the set fails, the entire transaction fails. Transactions also permit you to make *temporary* changes to the database—changes that can be undone with the **RollbackTrans** method.

Typically, ODBC drivers work in one of two modes:

- **Auto-commit Mode:** When you have not explicitly started a transaction using the BeginTrans method, every operation executed is immediately committed to the database upon completion.

- **Manual-commit Mode:** When you explicitly start a transaction using the **BeginTrans** method or use the ODBC **SQLSetStmtOption** function to disable the SQL_AUTO_COMMIT mode, or send an SQL statement to begin a transaction (BEGIN TRANS), operations are part of a transaction and no changes are committed to the database until you use the **CommitTrans** method. If the connection fails before **CommitTrans** is executed, or you use the **RollbackTrans** method, the operations are undone—rolled back.

Note When working with remote servers that support a Distributed Transaction Coordinator (DTC) like Microsoft SQL Server, you can initiate and control transactions that span more than one server. That is, if you invoke a procedure on the remote server that invokes a remote procedure call, the DTC service can ensure that this operation is included in the initial transaction. See *Building Client/Server Applications with Visual Basic* for more information.

Typically, you use transactions to maintain the integrity of your data when you must update rows in two or more tables and ensure that changes made are completed (committed) in all tables or none at all (rolled back). For example, if you transfer money from one account to another, you might subtract an amount from one and add the amount to another. If either update fails, the accounts no longer balance. Use the **BeginTrans** method before updating the first row, and then, if any subsequent update fails, you can use the **RollbackTrans** method to undo all of the updates. Use the **CommitTrans** method after you successfully update the last row.

Caution   Within one **rdoEnvironment** object, transactions are always global to the **rdoEnvironment** and aren't limited to only one database or result set. If you perform operations on more than one database or result set within an **rdoEnvironment** transaction, the **RollbackTrans** method restores all operations on those databases and result sets.

Once you use **CommitTrans**, you can't undo changes made during that transaction unless the transaction is nested within another transaction that is itself rolled back. You cannot nest transactions unless you use an action query to directly execute SQL transaction management statements. If you want to have simultaneous transactions with overlapping, non-nested scopes, you can create additional **rdoEnvironment** objects to contain the concurrent transactions.

Note   You can use SQL action queries that contain transaction statements. For example, with Microsoft SQL Server, you can use SQL statements like BEGIN TRANSACTION, COMMIT TRANSACTION, or ROLLBACK TRANSACTION. This technique supports nested transactions which may not be supported by the ODBC driver.

If you close an **rdoEnvironment** object without saving or rolling back any pending transactions, the transactions are automatically rolled back.

No error occurs If you use the **CommitTrans** or **RollbackTrans** method without first using the **BeginTrans** method.

Some databases may not support transactions, in which case the **Transactions** property of the **rdoConnection** object or **rdoResultset** object is **False**. To make sure that the database supports transactions, check the value of the **Transactions** property of the **rdoConnection** object before using the **BeginTrans** method. If you are using an **rdoResultset** object based on more than one database, check the **Transactions** property of the **rdoResultset** object. If the **rdoConnection** or **rdoResultset** doesn't support transactions, the methods are ignored and no error occurs.

Bindable Property

Returns or sets the **Bindable** property associated with a **Member** object.

Applies To

Member Object

Syntax

object.**Bindable**

The *object* placeholder represents an object expression that evaluates to an object in the **Applies To** list.

BindThreshold Property

Returns or sets a value specifying the largest column that will be automatically bound under ODBC.

Applies To

rdoQuery Object

Syntax

object.**BindThreshold** [= *value*]

The **BindThreshold** property syntax has these parts:

Part	Description
object	An object expression that evaluates to an object in the **Applies To** list.
value	A Long expression as described in Remarks.

Remarks

The default value for **BindThreshold** is 1024 bytes.

Several data types support sizes that are far too large to handle using conventional string or byte array techniques. For these columns, you should use the **GetChunk** and **AppendChunk** methods. However, use of these methods is not required—you can simply address the **Value** property assuming the size of the chunk data does not exhaust your resources.

By setting the **BindThreshold** property, you can set the maximum size of chunk that RDO automatically binds to strings. Columns larger than the **BindThreshold** value require use of the **GetChunk** method to retrieve data. The **ChunkRequired** property indicates if the column requires use of **AppendChunk** and **GetChunk** methods by comparing the column's data size against the **BindThreshold** value.

See Also

AppendChunk Method (Remote Data), **ColumnSize** Method (Remote Data), **GetChunk** Method (Remote Data), **ChunkRequired** Property (Remote Data)

BOF, EOF Properties

- **BOF** — returns a value that indicates whether the current record position is before the first record in a **Recordset** object.

- **EOF**—returns a value that indicates whether the current record position is after the last record in a **Recordset** object.

Applies To

Dynaset-Type Recordset Object, **Recordset** Object, **Snapshot-Type Recordset** Object, **Table-Type Recordset** Object, **Forward-Only–Type Recordset** Object, **Dynamic-Type Recordset** Object

Return Values

The return values for the **BOF** and **EOF** properties are **Boolean** values.

The **BOF** property returns **True** if the current record position is before the first record, and **False** if the current record position is on or after the first record.

The **EOF** property returns **True** if the current record position is after the last record, and **False** if the current record position is on or before the last record.

Remarks

You can use the **BOF** and **EOF** properties to determine whether a **Recordset** object contains records or whether you've gone beyond the limits of a **Recordset** object when you move from record to record.

The location of the current record pointer determines the **BOF** and **EOF** return values.

If either the **BOF** or **EOF** property is **True**, there is no current record.

If you open a **Recordset** object containing no records, the **BOF** and **EOF** properties are set to **True**, and the **Recordset** object's **RecordCount** property setting is 0. When you open a **Recordset** object that contains at least one record, the first record is the current record and the **BOF** and **EOF** properties are **False**; they remain **False** until you move beyond the beginning or end of the **Recordset** object by using the **MovePrevious** or **MoveNext** method, respectively. When you move beyond the beginning or end of the **Recordset**, there is no current record or no record exists.

If you delete the last remaining record in the **Recordset** object, the **BOF** and **EOF** properties may remain **False** until you attempt to reposition the current record.

If you use the **MoveLast** method on a **Recordset** object containing records, the last record becomes the current record; if you then use the **MoveNext** method, the current record becomes invalid and the **EOF** property is set to **True**. Conversely, if you use the **MoveFirst** method on a **Recordset** object containing records, the first record becomes the current record; if you then use the **MovePrevious** method, there is no current record and the **BOF** property is set to **True**.

Typically, when you work with all the records in a **Recordset** object, your code will loop through the records by using the **MoveNext** method until the **EOF** property is set to **True**.

If you use the **MoveNext** method while the **EOF** property is set to **True** or the **MovePrevious** method while the **BOF** property is set to **True**, an error occurs.

This table shows which Move methods are allowed with different combinations of the **BOF** and **EOF** properties.

	MoveFirst, MoveLast	MovePrevious, Move < 0	Move 0	MoveNext, Move > 0
BOF=True, EOF=False	Allowed	Error	Error	Allowed
BOF=False, EOF=True	Allowed	Allowed	Error	Error
Both **True**	Error	Error	Error	Error
Both **False**	Allowed	Allowed	Allowed	Allowed

Allowing a Move method doesn't mean that the method will successfully locate a record. It merely indicates that an attempt to perform the specified Move method is allowed and won't generate an error. The state of the **BOF** and **EOF** properties may change as a result of the attempted Move.

An **OpenRecordset** method internally invokes a **MoveFirst** method. Therefore, using an **OpenRecordset** method on an empty set of records sets the **BOF** and **EOF** properties to **True**. (See the following table for the behavior of a failed **MoveFirst** method.)

All Move methods that successfully locate a record will set both **BOF** and **EOF** to **False**.

In a Microsoft Jet workspace, if you add a record to an empty **Recordset**, **BOF** will become **False**, but **EOF** will remain **True**, indicating that the current position is at the end of **Recordset**. In an ODBCDirect workspace, both **BOF** and **EOF** will become **False**, indicating that the current position is on the new record.

Any **Delete** method, even if it removes the only remaining record from a **Recordset**, won't change the setting of the **BOF** or **EOF** property.

The following table shows how Move methods that don't locate a record affect the **BOF** and **EOF** property settings.

	BOF	EOF
MoveFirst, MoveLast	**True**	**True**
Move 0	No change	No change
MovePrevious, Move < 0	**True**	No change
MoveNext, Move > 0	No change	**True**

See Also

MoveFirst, MoveLast, MoveNext, MovePrevious Methods

Example

This example demonstrates how the **BOF** and **EOF** properties let the user move
forward and backward through a **Recordset**.

```
Sub BOFX()

    Dim dbsNorthwind As Database
    Dim rstCategories As Recordset
    Dim strMessage As String

    Set dbsNorthwind = OpenDatabase("Northwind.mdb")
    Set rstCategories = _
        dbsNorthwind.OpenRecordset("Categories", _
        dbOpenSnapshot)

    With rstCategories
        ' Populate Recordset.
        .MoveLast
        .MoveFirst

        Do While True
            ' Display current record information and get user
            ' input.
            strMessage = "Category: " & !CategoryName & _
                vbCr & "(record " & (.AbsolutePosition + 1) & _
                " of " & .RecordCount & ")" & vbCr & vbCr & _
                "Enter 1 to go forward, 2 to go backward:"

            ' Move forward or backward and trap for BOF or EOF.
            Select Case InputBox(strMessage)
                Case 1
                    .MoveNext
                    If .EOF Then
                        MsgBox _
                            "End of the file!" & vbCr & _
                            "Pointer being moved to last record."
                        .MoveLast
                    End If

                Case 2
                    .MovePrevious
                    If .BOF Then
                        MsgBox _
                            "Beginning of the file!" & vbCr & _
                            "Pointer being moved to first record."
                        .MoveFirst
                    End If

                Case Else
                    Exit Do
            End Select

        Loop

        .Close
    End With

    dbsNorthwind.Close
End Sub
```

BOF, EOF Properties (Remote Data)

- **BOF**—returns a value that indicates whether the current row position is before the first row in an **rdoResultset**.
- **EOF**—returns a value that indicates whether the current row position is after the last row in an **rdoResultset**.

Applies To

rdoResultset Object

Syntax

object.**BOF**
object.**EOF**

The *object* placeholder represents an object expression that evaluates to an object in the **Applies To** list.

Return Values

The **BOF** property return values are:

Value	Description
True	The current row position is before the first row.
False	The current row position is on or after the first row.

The **EOF** property return values are:

Value	Description
True	The current row position is after the last row.
False	The current row position is on or before the last row.

Remarks

The **BOF** and **EOF** return values are determined by the location of the current row pointer—if this pointer is valid. If either **BOF** or **EOF** is **True**, there is no current row, and any attempt to reference **rdoResultset** data results in a trappable error.

You can use the **BOF** and **EOF** properties to determine whether an **rdoResultset** object contains rows or whether you've gone beyond the limits of an **rdoResultset** as you move from row to row.

If you open an **rdoResultset** containing no rows, **BOF** and **EOF** are set to **True**, and the result set's **RowCount** property setting is 0. When you open an **rdoResultset** that contains at least one row, the first row is the current row and **BOF** and **EOF** are **False**; they remain **False** until you move beyond the beginning or end of the **rdoResultset** using the **MovePrevious** or **MoveNext** method, respectively. When you move beyond the beginning or end of the **rdoResultset**, there is no current row.

If you delete the last remaining row in the **rdoResultset** object, **BOF** and **EOF** might remain **False** until you attempt to reposition the current row.

If you use the **MoveLast** method on an **rdoResultset** containing rows, the last row becomes the current row; if you then use the **MoveNext** method, the current row becomes invalid and **EOF** is set to **True**. Conversely, if you use the **MoveFirst** method on an **rdoResultset** containing rows, the first row becomes the current row; if you then use the **MovePrevious** method, there is no current row and **BOF** is set to **True**.

Typically, when you work with all the rows in an **rdoResultset**, your code will loop through the rows using **MoveNext** until the **EOF** property is set to **True**.

If you use **MoveNext** while **EOF** is set to **True** or **MovePrevious** while **BOF** is set to **True**, a trappable error occurs.

This table shows which *Move* methods are allowed with different combinations of **BOF** and **EOF**.

	MoveFirst, MoveLast	MovePrevious, Move < 0	Move 0	MoveNext, Move > 0
BOF = True, EOF = False	Allowed	Error	Error	Allowed
BOF = False, EOF = True	Allowed	Allowed	Error	Error
Both **True**	Error	Error	Error	Error
Both **False**	Allowed	Allowed	Allowed	Allowed

Allowing a *Move* method doesn't mean that the method will successfully locate a row. It merely indicates that an attempt to perform the specified *Move* method is allowed and won't generate an error. The state of the **BOF** and **EOF** properties may change as a result of the attempted Move.

Effect of specific methods on **BOF** and **EOF** settings:

- An **OpenResultset** method internally invokes a **MoveFirst**. Therefore, an **OpenResultset** on an empty set of rows results in **BOF** and **EOF** being set to **True**.

- All *Move* methods that successfully locate a row set both **BOF** and **EOF** to **False**.

- For dynamic-type **rdoResultset** objects, any **Delete** method, even if it removes the only remaining row from an **rdoResultset**, won't change the setting of **BOF** or **EOF**.

- For other types of **rdoResultset** objects, the **BOF** and **EOF** properties are unchanged as add and delete operations are made because result set membership is fixed.

See Also

MoveFirst, MoveLast, MoveNext, MovePrevious Methods (Remote Data), **rdoResultset** Object, **RemoteData** Control, **BOFAction, EOFAction** Properties (Remote Data), **RowCount** Property (Remote Data)

BOFAction, EOFAction Properties

Returns or sets a value indicating what action the **Data** control takes when the **BOF** or **EOF** properties are **True**.

Applies To

Data Control

Syntax

object.**BOFAction** [= *integer*]
object.**EOFAction** [= *integer*]

The **BOFAction** and **EOFAction** property syntax's have these parts:

Part	Description
object	An object expression that evaluates to an object in the **Applies To** list
integer	An integer value that specifies an action, as described in **Settings**

Settings

For the **BOFAction** property, the settings for *integer* are:

Setting	Value	Description
vbBOFActionMoveFirst	0	**MoveFirst** (Default): Keeps the first record as the current record.
vbBOFActionBOF	1	**BOF**: Moving past the beginning of a **Recordset** triggers the **Data** control **Validate** event on the first record, followed by a **Reposition** event on the invalid (**BOF**) record. At this point, the **Move Previous** button on the **Data** control is disabled.

For the **EOFAction** property, the settings for *integer* are:

Setting	Value	Description
vbEOFActionMoveLast	0	**MoveLast** (Default): Keeps the last record as the current record.
vbEOFActionEOF	1	**EOF**: Moving past the end of a **Recordset** triggers the **Data** control's **Validation** event on the last record, followed by a **Reposition** event on the invalid (**EOF**) record. At this point, the **MoveNext** button on the **Data** control is disabled.
vbEOFActionAddNew	2	**AddNew**: Moving past the last record triggers the **Data** control's **Validation** event to occur on the current record, followed by an automatic **AddNew**, followed by a **Reposition** event on the new record.

Remarks

These constants are listed in the Visual Basic (VB) object library in the Object Browser.

If you set the **EOFAction** property to **vbEOFActionAddNew**, once the user moves the current record pointer to **EOF** using the **Data** control, the current record is positioned to a new record in the copy buffer. At this point you can edit the newly added record. If you make changes to the new record and the user subsequently moves the current record pointer using the **Data** control, the record is automatically appended to the **Recordset**. If you don't make changes to this new record, and reposition the current record to another record, the new record is discarded. If you use the **Data** control to position to another record while positioned over this new record, another new record is created.

When you use code to manipulate **Recordsets** created with the **Data** control, the **EOFAction** property has no effect it only takes effect when manipulating the **Data** control with the mouse.

In situations where the **Data** control **Recordset** is returned with no records, or after the last record has been deleted, using the **vbEOFActionAddNew** option for the **EOFAction** property greatly simplifies your code because a new record is always editable as the current record. If this option is not enabled, you are likely to trigger a "No current record" error.

Data Type

Integer

See Also

BOF, EOF Properties, **RecordSet** Object, **RecordSource** Property

---

BOFAction, EOFAction Properties (Remote Data)

Returns or sets a value indicating what action the **RemoteData** control takes when the **BOF** or **EOF** property is **True**.

Applies To

RemoteData Control

Syntax

object.**BOFAction** [= *value*]
object.**EOFAction** [= *value*]

The **BOFAction** and **EOFAction** property syntaxes have these parts:

Part	Description
object	An object expression that evaluates to an object in the **Applies To** list.
value	A constant or value that specifies an action, as described in Settings.

Settings

For the **BOFAction** property, the settings for *value* are:

Constant	Value	Description
rdMoveFirst	0	**MoveFirst** (Default): Keeps the first row as the current row.
rdBOF	1	**BOF**: Moving past the beginning of an **rdoResultset** triggers the **RemoteData** control's Validate event on the first row, followed by a Reposition event on the invalid (**BOF**) row. At this point, the Move Previous button on the **RemoteData** control is disabled.

For the **EOFAction** property, the settings for *value* are:

Constant	Value	Description
rdMoveLast	0	**MoveLast** (Default): Keeps the last row as the current row.
rdEOF	1	**EOF**: Moving past the end of an **rdoResultset** triggers the **RemoteData** control's **Validation** event on the last row, followed by a Reposition event on the invalid (**EOF**) row. At this point, the Move Next button on the **RemoteData** control is disabled.
rdAddNew	2	**AddNew**: Moving past the last row triggers the **RemoteData** control's **Validation** event to occur on the current row, followed by an automatic **AddNew**, followed by a **Reposition** event on the new row.

Remarks

If you set the **EOFAction** property to **rdAddNew**, once the user moves the current row pointer to **EOF** using the **RemoteData** control, the current row is positioned to a new row in the copy buffer. At this point you can edit the newly added row. If you make changes to the new row and the user subsequently moves the current row pointer using the **RemoteData** control, the row is automatically appended to the **rdoResultset**. If you don't make changes to this new row, and reposition the current row to another row, the new row is discarded. If you use the **RemoteData** control to position to another row while it is positioned over this new row, another new row is created.

When you use code to manipulate **rdoResultset** objects created with the **RemoteData** control, the **EOFAction** property has no effect—it only takes effect when manipulating the **RemoteData** control with the mouse.

In situations where the **RemoteData** control **rdoResultset** is returned with no rows, or after the last row has been deleted, using the **rdAddNew** option for the **EOFAction** property greatly simplifies your code because a new row can always be edited as the current row.

See Also

MoveFirst, MoveLast, MoveNext, MovePrevious Methods, **rdoResultset** Object, **RemoteData** Control, **RowCount** Property, **AddNew** Method, **BOF, EOF** Properties, **Edit** Method, **Reposition** Event, **SQL** Property, **Type** Property, **Validate** Event

---

Bold Property

Returns or sets the font style of the **Font** object to either bold or non-bold.

Applies To

Font Object

Syntax

object.**Bold** [= *boolean*]

The **Bold** property syntax has these parts:

Part	Description
object	An object expression that evaluates to an object in the **Applies To** list.
boolean	A Boolean expression specifying the font style, as described in **Settings**.

Settings

The settings for *boolean* are:

Setting	Description
True	Turns on bold formatting.
False	(Default) Turns off bold formatting.

Remarks

The **Font** object isn't directly available at design time. Instead you set the **Bold** property by selecting a control's **Font** property in the Properties window and clicking the Properties button. In the Font Style box of the Font dialog box, select either Bold or Bold Italic. At run-time, however, you set **Bold** directly by specifying its setting for the **Font** object.

See Also

FontTransparent Property, **Italic** Property, **Size** Property (Font), **StrikeThrough** Property, **Underline** Property, **Weight** Property, **Name** Property

Example

This example prints text on a form with each mouse click. To try this example, paste the code into the Declarations section of a form, and then press F5 and click the form twice.

```
Private Sub Form_Click ()
    Font.Bold = Not Font.Bold                         ' Toggle bold.
    Font.StrikeThrough = Not Font.StrikeThrough ' Toggle strikethrough.
    Font.Italic = Not Font.Italic                     ' Toggle italic.
    Font.Underline = Not Font.Underline               ' Toggle underline.
    Font.Size = 16                                    ' Set Size property.
    If Font.Bold Then
        Print "Font weight is " & Font.Weight & " (bold)."
    Else
        Print "Font weight is " & Font.Weight & " (not bold)."

    End If
End Sub
```

Bookmark Property

Sets or returns a bookmark that uniquely identifies the current record in a **Recordset** object.

Applies To

Dynaset-Type Recordset Object, **Recordset** Object, **Snapshot-Type Recordset** Object, **Table-Type Recordset** Object, **Dynamic-Type Recordset** Object

Settings and Return Values

The setting or return value is a string expression or variant expression that evaluates to a valid bookmark. The data type is a **Variant** array of **Byte** data.

Remarks

For a **Recordset** object based entirely on Microsoft Jet tables, the value of the **Bookmarkable** property is **True**, and you can use the **Bookmark** property with that **Recordset**. Other database products may not support bookmarks, however. For example, you can't use bookmarks in any **Recordset** object based on a linked Paradox table that has no primary key.

When you create or open a **Recordset** object, each of its records already has a unique bookmark. You can save the bookmark for the current record by assigning the value of the **Bookmark** property to a variable. To quickly return to that record at any time after moving to a different record, set the **Recordset** object's **Bookmark** property to the value of that variable.

There is no limit to the number of bookmarks you can establish. To create a bookmark for a record other than the current record, move to the desired record and assign the value of the **Bookmark** property to a **String** variable that identifies the record.

To make sure the **Recordset** object supports bookmarks, check the value of its **Bookmarkable** property before you use the **Bookmark** property. If the **Bookmarkable** property is **False**, the **Recordset** object doesn't support bookmarks, and using the **Bookmark** property results in a trappable error.

If you use the **Clone** method to create a copy of a **Recordset** object, the **Bookmark** property settings for the original and the duplicate **Recordset** objects are identical and can be used interchangeably. However, you can't use bookmarks from different **Recordset** objects interchangeably, even if they were created by using the same object or the same SQL statement.

If you set the **Bookmark** property to a value that represents a deleted record, a trappable error occurs.

The value of the **Bookmark** property isn't the same as a record number.

See Also

Bookmarkable Property, **RecordCount** Property

Example

This example uses the **Bookmark** and **Bookmarkable** properties to let the user flag a record in a **Recordset** and return to it later.

```
Sub BookmarkX()

    Dim dbsNorthwind As Database
    Dim rstCategories As Recordset
    Dim strMessage As String
    Dim intCommand As Integer
    Dim varBookmark As Variant

    Set dbsNorthwind = OpenDatabase("Northwind.mdb")
    Set rstCategories = _
        dbsNorthwind.OpenRecordset("Categories", _
        dbOpenSnapshot)

    With rstCategories

        If .Bookmarkable = False Then
            Debug.Print "Recordset is not Bookmarkable!"
        Else
            ' Populate Recordset.
            .MoveLast
            .MoveFirst

            Do While True
                ' Show information about current record and get
                ' user input.
                strMessage = "Category: " & !CategoryName & _
                    " (record " & (.AbsolutePosition + 1) & _
                    " of " & .RecordCount & ")" & vbCr & _
                    "Enter command:" & vbCr & _
                    "[1 - next / 2 - previous /" & vbCr & _
                    "3 - set bookmark / 4 - go to bookmark]"
                intCommand = Val(InputBox(strMessage))
```

```
        Select Case intCommand
           ' Move forward or backward, trapping for BOF
           ' or EOF.
           Case 1
              .MoveNext
              If .EOF Then .MoveLast
           Case 2
              .MovePrevious
              If .BOF Then .MoveFirst

           ' Store the bookmark of the current record.
           Case 3
              varBookmark = .Bookmark

           ' Go to the record indicated by the stored
           ' bookmark.
           Case 4
              If IsEmpty(varBookmark) Then
                 MsgBox "No Bookmark set!"
              Else
                 .Bookmark = varBookmark
              End If

           Case Else
              Exit Do
        End Select

     Loop

   End If

   .Close
  End With

  dbsNorthwind.Close

End Sub
```

Bookmark Property (DBGrid)

Returns or sets a bookmark for the specified row within a **RowBuffer** object in an unbound **DBGrid** control.

Applies To

    RowBuffer Object, **DBGrid** Control

Syntax

    object.**Bookmark** (*row*) [= *value*]

The **Bookmark** property syntax has these parts:

Part	Description
object	An object expression that evaluates to an object in the **Applies To** list.
row	An integer specifying the row where the bookmark is placed. The range of this value can be from 0 to **RowCount**–1.
value	A variant representing the bookmark for the specified *row*.

Remarks

Use the value returned by the **Bookmark** property to save a reference to the current row that remains valid even after another row becomes current.

When you set the **Bookmark** property to a valid value in code, the row associated with that value becomes the current row, and the grid adjusts its display to bring the new current row into view if necessary.

The **Bookmark** property is defined as a Variant to accommodate user-defined bookmarks in unbound mode.

In the **UnboundReadData** event there may be multiple rows, so you must provide a bookmark for each row.

The **UnboundWriteData** event passes a bookmark to you to identify the row of data to be updated.

The **UnboundAddData** event passes a bookmark to you to identify the row of data to be added.

Note   In unbound mode, setting the **Bookmark** property to itself will force the current row to be updated via the **UnboundWriteData** event.

See Also

UnboundAddData Event, **UnboundReadData** Event, **UnboundWriteData** Event, **RowCount** Property

Example

In this example, when the user deletes a row in the unbound **DBGrid** control, the **UnboundDeleteRow** event is triggered, allowing you to manually delete the row from your data set, in this case, a simple array. The following code fragment shows how a bookmark is passed as an argument in the **UnboundDeleteRow** event to identify the row to be deleted.

```
Private Sub DBGrid1_UnboundDeleteRow(Bookmark As Variant)
   For i% = Bookmark + 1 To RowCount - 1
      For j% = 0 to MAXCOLS - 1
         UserData(j%, I% - 1) = UserData(j%, I%)
      Next j%
   Next I%
End Sub
```

Refer to the **UnboundReadData** event example for an example of assigning data to the **Bookmark** property.

Bookmark Property (Remote Data)

Returns or sets a bookmark that uniquely identifies the current row in an **rdoResultset** object. If you have a valid bookmark, you can use it to reposition the current row in an **rdoResultset**.

Applies To

rdoResultset Object

Syntax

object.**Bookmark** [= *value*]

The **Bookmark** property syntax has these parts:

Part	Description
object	An object expression that evaluates to an object in the **Applies To** list.
value	A Variant(string) expression that evaluates to a valid bookmark.

Remarks

When a non-forward-only-type **rdoResultset** object is created or opened, each of its rows already has a unique bookmark. You can save the bookmark for the current row by assigning the value of the **Bookmark** property to a variable declared as **Variant**. To quickly return to that row at any time after moving to a different row, set the **rdoResultset** object's **Bookmark** property to the value of that variable.

There is no limit to the number of bookmarks you can establish. To create a bookmark for a row other than the current row, move to the desired row and assign the value of the **Bookmark** property to a **Variant** variable that identifies the row.

To make sure the **rdoResultset** supports bookmarks, inspect the value of its **Bookmarkable** property before you use the **Bookmark** property. If **Bookmarkable** is **False**, the **rdoResultset** doesn't support bookmarks, and using the **Bookmark** property results in a trappable error. While a bookmark value might be returned when using a dynamic cursor, this value cannot always be trusted.

The value of the **Bookmark** property isn't guaranteed to be the same as a row number.

Note The **Bookmark** property doesn't apply to forward-only type **rdoResultset** objects.

See Also

AddNew Method (Remote Data), **Edit** Method (Remote Data), **rdoResultset** Object, **Bookmarkable** Property (Remote Data)

Example

This example illustrates use of the **LastModified** property to reposition the current row pointer to the row most recently modified by RDO. The code opens a connection against SQL Server and creates a keyset cursor-based query on the Authors table.

The query expects a single parameter to pass in the name of the Author to edit. Once selected, edited and updated, the row pointer is repositioned to the last row modified by setting the bookmark property of the **rdoResultset** to the **LastModified** property.

```
Option Explicit
Dim er As rdoError
Dim cn As New rdoConnection
Dim qy As New rdoQuery
Dim rs As rdoResultset
Dim col As rdoColumn

Private Sub TestLM_Click()
qy(0) = LookFor.Text

rs.Edit
rs!City = NewCity.Text    ' a TextBox control
rs.Update

rs.Bookmark = rs.LastModified

'Simply show data in picture control
Pic.Cls   'Clear the picture control.

For Each col In rs.rdoColumns
    Pic.Print col.Name,
Next
Pic.Print String(80, "-")
For Each col In rs.rdoColumns

    Pic.Print col,
Next

End Sub

Private Sub Form_Load()
cn.CursorDriver = rdUseOdbc
cn.Connect = "uid=;pwd=;server=sequel;" _
    & "driver={SQL Server};database=pubs;dsn='';"
cn.EstablishConnection

With qy
    .Name = "ShowWhite"
    .SQL = "Select * from Authors " _
      & " where Au_LName like ?"
    .LockType = rdConcurReadOnly
    .CursorType = rdOpenForwardOnly
    .RowsetSize = 1
    Set .ActiveConnection = cn
End With

qy(0) = LookFor.Text     ' a textbox control

Set rs = qy.OpenResultset(rdOpenKeyset, rdConcurRowver)

Exit Sub
End Sub
```

Bookmarkable Property

Returns a value that indicates whether a **Recordset** object supports bookmarks, which you can set by using the **Bookmark** property.

Applies To

Dynaset-Type Recordset Object, **Recordset** Object, **Snapshot-Type Recordset** Object, **Table-Type Recordset** Object, **Dynamic-Type Recordset** Object

Return Values

The return value is a **Boolean** data type that returns **True** if the object supports bookmarks.

Remarks

Check the **Bookmarkable** property setting of a **Recordset** object before you attempt to set or check the **Bookmark** property.

For **Recordset** objects based entirely on Microsoft Jet tables, the value of the **Bookmarkable** property is **True**, and you can use bookmarks. Other database products may not support bookmarks, however. For example, you can't use bookmarks in any **Recordset** object based on a linked Paradox table that has no primary key.

See Also

Bookmark Property, **RecordCount** Property

Example

This example uses the **Bookmark** and **Bookmarkable** properties to let the user flag a record in a **Recordset** and return to it later.

```
Sub BookmarkX()

    Dim dbsNorthwind As Database
    Dim rstCategories As Recordset
    Dim strMessage As String
    Dim intCommand As Integer
    Dim varBookmark As Variant

    Set dbsNorthwind = OpenDatabase("Northwind.mdb")
    Set rstCategories = _
        dbsNorthwind.OpenRecordset("Categories", _
        dbOpenSnapshot)

    With rstCategories

        If .Bookmarkable = False Then
            Debug.Print "Recordset is not Bookmarkable!"
        Else
            ' Populate Recordset.
            .MoveLast
            .MoveFirst
```

```
            Do While True
               ' Show information about current record and get
               ' user input.
               strMessage = "Category: " & !CategoryName & _
                  " (record " & (.AbsolutePosition + 1) & _
                  " of " & .RecordCount & ")" & vbCr & _
                  "Enter command:" & vbCr & _
                  "[1 - next / 2 - previous /" & vbCr & _
                  "3 - set bookmark / 4 - go to bookmark]"
               intCommand = Val(InputBox(strMessage))

               Select Case intCommand
                  ' Move forward or backward, trapping for BOF
                  ' or EOF.
                  Case 1
                     .MoveNext
                     If .EOF Then .MoveLast
                  Case 2
                     .MovePrevious
                     If .BOF Then .MoveFirst

                  ' Store the bookmark of the current record.
                  Case 3
                     varBookmark = .Bookmark

                  ' Go to the record indicated by the stored
                  ' bookmark.
                  Case 4
                     If IsEmpty(varBookmark) Then
                        MsgBox "No Bookmark set!"
                     Else
                        .Bookmark = varBookmark
                     End If

                  Case Else
                     Exit Do
               End Select

            Loop

         End If

         .Close
      End With

      dbsNorthwind.Close

   End Sub
```

Bookmarkable Property (Remote Data)

Returns a value that indicates whether an **rdoResultset** object supports bookmarks, which you can set using the **Bookmark** property.

Applies To

rdoResultset Object

Syntax

object.**Bookmarkable**

The *object* placeholder represents an object expression that evaluates to an object in the **Applies To** list.

Return Values

The **Bookmarkable** property return values are:

Value	Description
True	The **rdoResultset** supports bookmarks.
False	The **rdoResultset** doesn't support bookmarks.

Remarks

To make sure an **rdoResultset** supports bookmarks, check the **Bookmarkable** property setting before you attempt to set or check the **Bookmark** property.

See Also

rdoResultset Object, **Bookmarkable** Property (Remote Data)

Boolean Data Type

Boolean variables are stored as 16-bit (2-byte) numbers, but they can only be **True** or **False**. **Boolean** variables display as either True or False (when **Print** is used) or #TRUE# or #FALSE# (when **Write #** is used). Use the keywords **True** and **False** to assign one of the two states to **Boolean** variables.

When other numeric types are converted to **Boolean** values, 0 becomes **False** and all other values become **True**. When **Boolean** values are converted to other data types, **False** becomes 0 and **True** becomes -1.

See Also

Data Type Summary, **Integer Data** Type, **Deftype** Statements

BorderColor Property

Returns or sets the color of an object's border.

Applies To

Line Control, **Shape** Control

Syntax

object.**BorderColor** [= *color*]

The **BorderColor** property syntax has these parts:

Part	Description
object	An object expression that evaluates to an object in the **Applies To** list.
color	A value or constant that determines the border color, as described in Settings.

Settings

Visual Basic uses the Microsoft Windows operating environment red-green-blue (RGB) color scheme. The settings for *color* are:

Setting	Description
Normal RGB colors	Colors specified using the Color palette or by using the **RGB** or **QBColor** functions in code.
System default colors	Colors specified by system color constants listed in the Visual Basic (VB) object library in the Object Browser . The system default color is specified by the **vbWindowText** constant. The Windows operating environment substitutes the user's choices as specified in the Control Panel settings.

Remarks

The valid range for a normal RGB color is 0 to 16,777,215 (&HFFFFFF). The high byte of a number in this range equals 0; the lower 3 bytes, from least to most significant byte, determine the amount of red, green, and blue, respectively. The red, green, and blue components are each represented by a number between 0 and 255 (&HFF). If the high byte isn't 0, Visual Basic uses the system colors, as defined in the user's Control Panel settings and by constants listed in the Visual Basic (VB) object library in the Object Browser.

See Also

BackColor, **ForeColor** Properties, **DrawWidth** Property

BorderStyle Property

Returns or sets the border style for an object. For the **Form** object and the **TextBox** control, read-only at run time.

Applies To

UserControl Object, **Form** Object, **Forms** Collection, **Frame** Control, **Image** Control, **Label** Control, **Line** Control, **PictureBox** Control, **Shape** Control, **TextBox** Control, **OLE Container** Control, **MSChart** Control, **Slider** Control

Syntax

object.**BorderStyle** = [*value*]

The **BorderStyle** property syntax has these parts:

Part	Description
object	An object expression that evaluates to an object in the **Applies To** list.
value	A value or constant that determines the border style, as described in Settings.

Settings

The **BorderStyle** property settings for a **Form** object are:

Constant	Setting	Description
vbBSNone	0	None (no border or border-related elements).
vbFixedSingle	1	Fixed Single. Can include Control-menu box, title bar, Maximize button, and Minimize button. Resizable only using Maximize and Minimize buttons.
vbSizable	2	(Default) Sizable. Resizable using any of the optional border elements listed for setting 1.
vbFixedDouble	3	Fixed Dialog. Can include Control-menu box and title bar; can't include Maximize or Minimize buttons. Not resizable.
vbFixedToolWindow	4	Fixed ToolWindow. Displays a non-sizable window with a Close button and title bar text in a reduced font size. The form does not appear in the Windows 95 task bar.
vbSizableToolWindow	5	Sizable ToolWindow. Displays a sizable window with a Close button and title bar text in a reduced font size. The form does not appear in the Windows 95 task bar.

The **BorderStyle** property settings for **MS Flex Grid**, **Image**, **Label**, **OLE** container, **PictureBox**, **Frame**, and **TextBox** controls are:

Setting	Description
0	(Default for **Image** and **Label** controls) None.
1	(Default for **MS Flex Grid**, **PictureBox**, **TextBox**, and **OLE** container controls) Fixed Single.

The **BorderStyle** property settings for **Line** and **Shape** controls are:

Constant	Setting	Description
vbTransparent	0	Transparent
vbBSSolid	1	(Default) Solid. The border is centered on the edge of the shape.
vbBSDash	2	Dash
vbBSDot	3	Dot
vbBSDashDot	4	Dash-dot
vbBSDashDotDot	5	Dash-dot-dot
vbBSInsideSolid	6	Inside solid. The outer edge of the border is the outer edge of the shape.

Remarks

For a form, the **BorderStyle** property determines key characteristics that visually identify a form as either a general-purpose window or a dialog box. Setting 3 (Fixed Dialog) is useful for standard dialog boxes. Settings 4 (Fixed ToolWindow) and 5 (Sizable ToolWindow) are useful for creating toolbox-style windows.

MDI child forms set to 2 (Sizable) are displayed within the MDI form in a default size defined by the Windows operating environment at run time. For any other setting, the form is displayed in the size specified at design time.

Changing the setting of the **BorderStyle** property of a **Form** object may change the settings of the **MinButton**, **MaxButton**, and **ShowInTaskbar** properties. When **BorderStyle** is set to 1 (Fixed Single) or 2 (Sizable), the **MinButton**, **MaxButton**, and **ShowInTaskbar** properties are automatically set to **True**. When **BorderStyle** is set to 0 (None), 3 (Fixed Dialog), 4 (Fixed ToolWindow), or 5 (Sizable ToolWindow), the **MinButton**, **MaxButton**, and **ShowInTaskbar** properties are automatically set to **False**.

Note If a form with a menu is set to 3 (Fixed Dialog), it is displayed with a setting 1 (Fixed Single) border instead.

At run time, a form is either modal or modeless, which you specify using the **Show** method.

See Also

ControlBox Property, **MaxButton** Property, **MinButton** Property, **DrawStyle** Property, **Caption** Property, **ShowInTaskbar** Property, **BorderStyle** Constants (MSChart)

BorderWidth Property

Returns or sets the width of a control's border.

Applies To

Line Control, **Shape** Control

Syntax

object.**BorderWidth** [= *number*]

The **BorderWidth** property syntax has these parts:

Part	Description
object	An object expression that evaluates to an object in the **Applies To** list.
number	A numeric expression from 1 to 8192, inclusive.

Remarks

Use the **BorderWidth** and **BorderStyle** properties to specify the kind of border you want for a **Line** or **Shape** control. The following table shows the effect of **BorderStyle** settings on the **BorderWidth** property:

BorderStyle	Effect on BorderWidth
0	**BorderWidth** setting is ignored.
1–5	The border width expands from the center of the border; the height and width of the control are measured from the center of the border.
6	The border width expands inward on the control from the outside of the border; the height and width of the control are measured from the outside of the border.

If the **BorderWidth** property setting is greater than 1, the only effective settings of **BorderStyle** are 1 (Solid) and 6 (Inside Solid).

See Also

BorderStyle Property, **DrawWidth** Property, **Height**, **Width** Properties

Example

This example uses two **ComboBox** controls to select different widths and styles for the borders of a **Shape** control. To try this example, paste the code into the Declarations section of a form that contains a **Shape** control and one **ComboBox** control. For the **ComboBox**, set **Style** = 2 and **Index** = 0 (to create a control array), and then press F5 and click the form.

```
Private Sub Form_Load ()
   Combo1(0).Width = 1440 * 1.5
   Load Combo1(1)
   Combo1(1).Top = Combo1(0).Top + Combo1(0).Height * 1.5
   Combo1(1).Visible = True
   For I = 0 To 6
      Combo1(0).AddItem "BorderStyle = " & I
   Next I
```

```
        For I = 1 To 10
            Combo1(1).AddItem "BorderWidth = " & I
        Next I
        Combo1(0).ListIndex = 1
        Combo1(1).ListIndex = 0
    End Sub

    Private Sub Combo1_Click (Index As Integer)
        If Index = 0 Then
            Shape1.BorderStyle = Combo1(0).ListIndex
        Else
            Shape1.BorderWidth = Combo1(1).ListIndex + 1
        End If
    End Sub
```

BoundColumn Property

Returns or sets the name of the source field in a **Recordset** object that is used to supply a data value to another **Recordset**.

Applies To

DBCombo Control, **DBList** Control

Syntax

object.**BoundColumn** [= *value*]

The **BoundColumn** property syntax has these parts:

Part	Description
object	An object expression that evaluates to an object in the **Applies To** list.
value	A string expression that specifies the name of a field in the **Recordset** created by the **Data** control specified by the **RowSource** property.

Remarks

Generally, when working with the **DBList** and **DBCombo** controls, you use two **Data** controls; one to fill the list as designated by the **Listfield** and **RowSource** properties and one to update a field in a database specified by the **DataSource** and **DataField** properties.

The **ListField** property designates the field used to fill the list. The second **Data** control, as designated by the **DataSource** property, manages a **Recordset** containing a field to be updated. Once the user chooses one of the items in the list, the field specified by the **BoundColumn** property is passed to the field in the second **Data** control, as designated by the **DataSource** and **DataField** properties. This way you can designate one field to fill the list, and another field (from the same **Recordset**) to pass as data to the **Recordset** designated by the **DataSource** and **DataField** properties when an item is selected.

If the field specified by the **BoundColumn** property can't be found in the **Recordset**, a trappable error occurs.

Data Type

 String

See Also

 Data Control, **DataField** Property, **DataSource** Property, **ListField** Property,
 Recordset Object, **RecordSource** Property

BoundText Property

 Returns or sets the value of the field specified by the **BoundColumn** property.

Applies To

 DBCombo Control, **DBList** Control

Syntax

 object.**BoundText** [= *value*]

 The **BoundText** property syntax has these parts:

Part	Description
object	An object expression that evaluates to an object in the **Applies To** list.
value	A string expression that specifies a data value.

Remarks

 After a user makes a selection with a **DBList** or **DBCombo** control, the **BoundText** property contains the field value of the **BoundColumn** property. When an item in the list is selected, the item becomes available to the **Data** control specified by the **DataSource** property. The selection also appears in the text box portion of the **DBCombo** control where it can be edited. If the user enters a value in the text box portion, the list portion attempts to position to a matching item. If a match is found, the **BoundText** property value is set, based on the field value of the **BoundColumn** property. If no match is found, the **BoundText** property is set to Null.

 Positioning the **Data** control, specified by the **DataSource** property, to a new record sets the **BoundText** property to the value specified by **DataField**. The **DBList** or **DBCombo** control then searches the records in the list to see if the **BoundText** value matches the value of the field in the **BoundColumn** property. If a match is found, the record is highlighted in the list or placed in the text box portion of the **DBCombo** control.

Data Type

 String

See Also

 Data Control, **DataSource** Property, **RecordSource** Property, **BoundColumn** Property, **ListField** Property

Browsable Property

Returns or sets the **Browsable** attribute associated with a **Member** object.

Applies To

Member Object

Syntax

object.**Browsable**

The *object* placeholder represents an object expression that evaluates to an object in the **Applies To** list.

BuildFileName Property

Returns the executable or DLL name that will be used when the project is built.

Applies To

VBProject Object

Syntax

object.**BuildFileName**

The *object* placeholder represents an object expression that evaluates to an object in the **Applies To** list.

BuiltIn Property

Returns a **Boolean** value indicating whether or not the reference is a default reference that can't be removed. Read-only.

Applies to

Reference Object

Return Values

The **BuiltIn** property returns these values:

Value	Description
True	The reference is a default reference that can't be removed.
False	The reference isn't a default reference; it can be removed.

See Also

Remove Method, **References** Collection, **Description** Property, **GUID** Property, **IsBroken** Property, **FullPath** Property

Example

The following example uses the **BuiltIn** property to return a **Boolean** indicating whether or not a particular reference in the active project is built-in.

```
Debug.Print Application.VBE.ActiveVBProject.References(1).BuiltIn
```

Button Property (Column Object)

Sets or returns a value that determines whether a button is displayed within the current cell.

Applies To

Column Object

Syntax

object.**Button** [= *value*]

The **Button** property syntax has these parts:

Part	Description
object	An object expression that evaluates to an object in the **Applies To** list.
value	A Boolean expression that determines if a button is displayed within the current cell, as described in Settings.

Settings

The settings for *value* are:

Setting	Description
True	A button will be displayed in the upper right corner of the current cell at run time.
False	(Default) No button will be displayed.

Remarks

Typically, you enable the column button when you want to drop down a control (such as the built-in combo box, a bound list box, or even another **DBGrid** control) for editing or data entry. When the button in the current cell is clicked, the **ButtonClick** event will be fired. You can then write code to drop down the desired control from the cell.

See Also

ButtonClick Event (DBGrid Control)

ButtonClick Event (DBGrid Control)

Occurs when the current cell's built-in button is clicked.

Applies To

DBGrid Control

Syntax

Private Sub *object*_**ButtonClick**([*index* **As Integer**,] **ByVal** *colindex* **As Integer**)

The **ButtonClick** event syntax has these parts:

Part	Description
object	An object expression that evaluates to an object in the **Applies To** list.
Index	An integer that identifies a control if it is in a control array.
colindex	An integer that identifies the column whose button was clicked.

Remarks

The built-in button is enabled for a column when its **Button** property is set to **True**.

Typically, you enable the column button when you want to drop down a Visual Basic control (such as the built-in combo box, a bound list box, or even another **DBGrid** control) for editing or data entry. When the button in the current cell is clicked, the **ButtonClick** event will be fired. You can then write code to drop down the desired control from the cell.

See Also

Button Property (Column Object)

Byte Data Type

Byte variables are stored as single, unsigned, 8-bit (1-byte) numbers ranging in value from 0–255.

The **Byte** data type is useful for containing binary data.

See Also

Data Type Summary, **Integer Data** Type, **Deftype** Statements

CacheSize Property

Sets or returns the number of records retrieved from an ODBC data source that will be cached locally.

Applies To

Dynaset-Type Recordset Object, **QueryDef** Object, **Recordset** Object, **Snapshot-Type Recordset** Object, **Dynamic-Type Recordset** Object

Settings and Return Values

The setting or return value is a **Long** value and must be between 5 and 1200, but not greater than available memory will allow. A typical value is 100. A setting of 0 turns off caching.

Remarks

Data caching improves performance if you use **Recordset** objects to retrieve data from a remote server. A cache is a space in local memory that holds the data most recently retrieved from the server; this is useful if users request the data again while the application is running. When users request data, the Microsoft Jet database engine checks the cache for the requested data first rather than retrieving it from the server, which takes more time. The cache only saves data that comes from an ODBC data source.

Any Microsoft Jet-connected ODBC data source, such as a linked table, can have a local cache. To create the cache, open a **Recordset** object from the remote data source, set the **CacheSize** and **CacheStart** properties, and then use the **FillCache** method, or step through the records by using the Move methods.

An ODBCDirect workspace can use a local cache. To create the cache, set the **CacheSize** property on a **QueryDef** object. On a **Relation** object, **CacheSize** is read-only and depends on the value of the **QueryDef** object's **CacheSize** property. You can't use the **CacheStart** property on **FillCache** method in an ODBCDirect workspace.

You can base the **CacheSize** property setting on the number of records your application can handle at one time. For example, if you're using a **Recordset** object as the source of the data to be displayed on screen, you could set its **CacheSize** property to 20 to display 20 records at one time.

The Microsoft Jet database engine requests records within the cache range from the cache, and it requests records outside the cache range from the server.

Records retrieved from the cache don't reflect concurrent changes that other users made to the source data.

To force an update of all the cached data, set the **CacheSize** property of the **Recordset** object to 0, re-set it to the size of the cache you originally requested, and then use the **FillCache** method.

See Also

FillCache Method, **Bookmark** Property, **Bookmarkable** Property

Example

This example uses the **CreateTableDef** and **FillCache** methods and the **CacheSize**, **CacheStart** and **SourceTableName** properties to enumerate the records in a linked table twice. Then it enumerates the records twice with a 50-record cache. The example then displays the performance statistics for the uncached and cached runs through the linked table.

```
Sub ClientServerX3()

    Dim dbsCurrent As Database
    Dim tdfRoyalties As TableDef
    Dim rstRemote As Recordset
    Dim sngStart As Single
    Dim sngEnd As Single
```

```
         Dim sngNoCache As Single
         Dim sngCache As Single
         Dim intLoop As Integer
         Dim strTemp As String
         Dim intRecords As Integer

         ' Open a database to which a linked table can be
         ' appended.
         Set dbsCurrent = OpenDatabase("DB1.mdb")

         ' Create a linked table that connects to a Microsoft SQL
         ' Server database.
         Set tdfRoyalties = _
            dbsCurrent.CreateTableDef("Royalties")
         tdfRoyalties.Connect = _
            "ODBC;DATABASE=pubs;UID=sa;PWD=;DSN=Publishers"
         tdfRoyalties.SourceTableName = "roysched"
         dbsCurrent.TableDefs.Append tdfRoyalties
         Set rstRemote = _
            dbsCurrent.OpenRecordset("Royalties")

      With rstRemote
         ' Enumerate the Recordset object twice and record
         ' the elapsed time.
         sngStart = Timer

         For intLoop = 1 To 2
            .MoveFirst
            Do While Not .EOF
               ' Execute a simple operation for the
               ' performance test.
               strTemp = !title_id
               .MoveNext
            Loop
         Next intLoop

         sngEnd = Timer
         sngNoCache = sngEnd - sngStart

         ' Cache the first 50 records.
         .MoveFirst
         .CacheSize = 50
         .FillCache
         sngStart = Timer

         ' Enumerate the Recordset object twice and record
         ' the elapsed time.
         For intLoop = 1 To 2
            intRecords = 0
            .MoveFirst
            Do While Not .EOF
               ' Execute a simple operation for the
               ' performance test.
```

```
            strTemp = !title_id
            ' Count the records. If the end of the
            ' cache is reached, reset the cache to the
            ' next 50 records.
            intRecords = intRecords + 1
            .MoveNext
            If intRecords Mod 50 = 0 Then
                .CacheStart = .Bookmark
                .FillCache
            End If
        Loop
    Next intLoop

    sngEnd = Timer
    sngCache = sngEnd - sngStart

    ' Display performance results.
    MsgBox "Caching Performance Results:" & vbCr & _
        "    No cache: " & Format(sngNoCache, _
        "#0.000") & " seconds" & vbCr & _
        "    50-record cache: " & Format(sngCache, _
        "#0.000") & " seconds"
    .Close
End With

' Delete linked table because this is a demonstration.
dbsCurrent.TableDefs.Delete tdfRoyalties.Name
dbsCurrent.Close

End Sub
```

CacheStart Property

Sets or returns a value that specifies the bookmark of the first record in a dynaset-type **Recordset** object containing data to be locally cached from an ODBC data source (Microsoft Jet workspaces only).

Applies To
Dynaset-Type Recordset Object, **Recordset** Object

Settings And Return Values
The setting or return value is a **String** that specifies a bookmark.

Remarks
Data caching improves the performance of an application that retrieves data from a remote server through dynaset-type **Recordset** objects. A cache is a space in local memory that holds the data most recently retrieved from the server in the event that the data will be requested again while the application is running. When data is requested, the Microsoft Jet database engine checks the cache for the requested data first rather than retrieving it from the server, which takes more time. Only data from an ODBC data source can be saved in the cache.

Any Microsoft Jet-connected ODBC data source, such as a linked table, can have a local cache. To create the cache, open a **Recordset** object from the remote data source, set the **CacheSize** and **CacheStart** properties, and then use the **FillCache** method or step through the records using the **Move** methods.

The **CacheStart** property setting is the bookmark of the first record in the **Recordset** object to be cached. You can use the bookmark of any record to set the **CacheStart** property. Make the record you want to start the cache the current record, and set the **CacheStart** property equal to the **Bookmark** property.

The Microsoft Jet database engine requests records within the cache range from the cache, and it requests records outside the cache range from the server.

Records retrieved from the cache don't reflect changes made concurrently to the source data by other users.

To force an update of all the cached data, set the **CacheSize** property of the **Recordset** object to 0, set it to the size of the cache you originally requested, and then use the **FillCache** method.

See Also

CacheSize Property

Calendar Property

Returns or sets a value specifying the type of calendar to use with your project.

You can use one of two settings for **Calendar**:

Setting	Value	Description
vbCalGreg	0	Use Gregorian calendar (default).
vbCalHijri	1	Use Hijri calendar.

Remarks

You can only set the **Calendar** property programmatically. For example, to use the Hijri calendar, use:

```
Calendar = vbCalHijri
```

Call Statement

Transfers control to a **Sub** procedure, **Function** procedure, or dynamic-link library (DLL) procedure.

Syntax

[**Call**] *name* [*argumentlist*]

The **Call** statement syntax has these parts:

Part	Description
Call	Optional; keyword. If specified, you must enclose *argumentlist* in parentheses. For example: `Call MyProc(0)`
name	Required. Name of the procedure to call.
argumentlist	Optional. Comma-delimited list of variables, arrays, or expressions to pass to the procedure. Components of *argumentlist* may include the keywords **ByVal** or **ByRef** to describe how the arguments are treated by the called procedure. However, **ByVal** and **ByRef** can be used with **Call** only when calling a DLL procedure.

Remarks

You are not required to use the **Call** keyword when calling a procedure. However, if you use the **Call** keyword to call a procedure that requires arguments, *argumentlist* must be enclosed in parentheses. If you omit the **Call** keyword, you also must omit the parentheses around *argumentlist*. If you use either **Call** syntax to call any intrinsic or user-defined function, the function's return value is discarded.

To pass a whole array to a procedure, use the array name followed by empty parentheses.

See Also

Declare Statement, **Function** Statement, **Sub** Statement

Example

This example illustrates how the **Call** statement is used to transfer control to a **Sub** procedure, an intrinsic function, and a dynamic-link library (DLL) procedure.

```
' Call a Sub procedure.
Call PrintToDebugWindow("Hello World")
' The above statement causes control to be passed to the following
' Sub procedure.
Sub PrintToDebugWindow(AnyString)
    Debug.Print AnyString    ' Print to Debug window.
End Sub


' Call an intrinsic function. The return value of the function is
' discarded.
Call Shell(AppName, 1)        ' AppName contains the path of the
                              ' executable file.


' Call a Microsoft Windows DLL procedure. The Declare statement must be
' Private in a Class Module, but not in a standard Module.
Private Declare Sub MessageBeep Lib "User" (ByVal N As Integer)
Sub CallMyDll()
    Call MessageBeep(0)       ' Call Windows DLL procedure.
    MessageBeep 0             ' Call again without Call keyword.
End Sub
```

Cancel Method

Cancels execution of a pending asynchronous method call (ODBCDirect workspaces only).

Applies To

Dynaset-Type Recordset Object, **QueryDef** Object, **Recordset** Object, **Snapshot-Type Recordset** Object, **Connection** Object, **Forward-Only–Type Recordset** Object, **Dynamic-Type Recordset** Object

Syntax

object.**Cancel**

The **Cancel** method syntax has these parts.

Part	Description
object	A string expression that evaluates to one of the objects in the **Applies To** list.

Remarks

Use the **Cancel** method to terminate execution of an asynchronous **Execute**, **MoveLast**, **OpenConnection,** or **OpenRecordset** method call (that is, the method was invoked with the **dbRunAsync** option). **Cancel** will return a run-time error if **dbRunAsync** was not used in the method you're trying to terminate.

The following table shows what task is terminated when you use the **Cancel** method on a particular type of object.

If *object* is a	This asynchronous method is terminated
Connection	**Execute** or **OpenConnection**
QueryDef	**Execute**
Recordset	**MoveLast** or **OpenRecordset**

An error will occur if, following a **Cancel** method call, you try to reference the object that would have been created by an asynchronous **OpenConnection** or **OpenRecordset** call (that is, the **Connection** or **Recordset** object from which you called the **Cancel** method).

See Also

Execute Method, **MoveFirst**, **MoveLast**, **MoveNext**, **MovePrevious** Methods, **OpenRecordset** Method, **OpenConnection** Method, **StillExecuting** Property

Example

This example uses the **StillExecuting** property and the **Cancel** method to asynchronously open a **Connection** object.

```
Sub CancelConnectionX()

    Dim wrkMain As Workspace
    Dim conMain As Connection
    Dim sngTime As Single
```

```
   Set wrkMain = CreateWorkspace("ODBCWorkspace", _
      "admin", "", dbUseODBC)
   ' Open the connection asynchronously.
   Set conMain = wrkMain.OpenConnection("Publishers", _
      dbDriverNoPrompt + dbRunAsync, False, _
      "ODBC;DATABASE=pubs;UID=sa;PWD=;DSN=Publishers")

   sngTime = Timer

   ' Wait five seconds.
   Do While Timer - sngTime < 5
   Loop

   ' If the connection has not been made, ask the user
   ' if she wants to keep waiting. If she does not, cancel
   ' the connection and exit the procedure.
   Do While conMain.StillExecuting

      If MsgBox("No connection yet--keep waiting?", _
            vbYesNo) = vbNo Then
         conMain.Cancel
         MsgBox "Connection cancelled!"
         wrkMain.Close
         Exit Sub
      End If

   Loop

   With conMain
      ' Use the Connection object conMain.
      .Close
   End With

   wrkMain.Close

End Sub
```

This example uses the **StillExecuting** property and the **Cancel** method to asynchronously execute a **QueryDef** object.

```
Sub CancelQueryDefX()

   Dim wrkMain As Workspace
   Dim conMain As Connection
   Dim qdfTemp As QueryDef
   Dim sngTime As Single

   Set wrkMain = CreateWorkspace("ODBCWorkspace", _
      "admin", "", dbUseODBC)
   Set conMain = wrkMain.OpenConnection("Publishers", _
      dbDriverNoPrompt, False, _
      "ODBC;DATABASE=pubs;UID=sa;PWD=;DSN=Publishers")
```

```
        Set qdfTemp = conMain.CreateQueryDef("")

    With qdfTemp
        .SQL = "UPDATE roysched " & _
            "SET royalty = royalty * 2 " & _
            "WHERE title_id LIKE 'BU____' OR " & _
            "title_id LIKE 'PC____'"

        ' Execute the query asynchronously.
        .Execute dbRunAsync

        sngTime = Timer

        ' Wait five seconds.
        Do While Timer - sngTime < 5
        Loop

        ' If the query has not completed, ask the user if
        ' she wants to keep waiting. If she does not, cancel
        ' the query and exit the procedure.
        Do While .StillExecuting

            If MsgBox( _
                "Query still running--keep waiting?", _
                vbYesNo) = vbNo Then
                .Cancel
                MsgBox "Query cancelled!"
                Exit Do
            End If

        Loop

    End With

    conMain.Close
    wrkMain.Close

End Sub
```

This example uses the **StillExecuting** property and the **Cancel** method to asynchronously move to the last record of a **Recordset** object.

```
Sub CancelRecordsetX()

    Dim wrkMain As Workspace
    Dim conMain As Connection
    Dim rstTemp As Recordset
    Dim sngTime As Single

    Set wrkMain = CreateWorkspace("ODBCWorkspace", _
        "admin", "", dbUseODBC)
    Set conMain = wrkMain.OpenConnection("Publishers", _
        dbDriverNoPrompt, False, _
        "ODBC;DATABASE=pubs;UID=sa;PWD=;DSN=Publishers")
    Set rstTemp = conMain.OpenRecordset( _
        "SELECT * FROM roysched", dbOpenDynaset)
```

```
With rstTemp

    ' Call the MoveLast method asynchronously.
    .MoveLast dbRunAsync

    sngTime = Timer

    ' Wait five seconds.
    Do While Timer - sngTime < 5
    Loop

    ' If the MoveLast has not completed, ask the user if
    ' she wants to keep waiting. If she does not, cancel
    ' the MoveLast and exit the procedure.
    Do While .StillExecuting

        If MsgBox( _
            "Not at last record yet--keep waiting?", _
            vbYesNo) = vbNo Then
          .Cancel
          MsgBox "MoveLast cancelled!"
          conMain.Close
          wrkMain.Close
          Exit Sub
        End If

    Loop

    ' Use recordset.

    .Close

    End With

    conMain.Close
    wrkMain.Close

End Sub
```

Cancel Method (Remote Data)

Cancels the processing of a query running in asynchronous mode, or cancels any
pending results against the specified RDO object.

Applies To

rdoConnection Object, **rdoPreparedStatement** Object, **rdoQuery** Object,
rdoResultset Object, **RemoteData** Control

Syntax

object.**Cancel**

The *object* placeholder represents an object expression that evaluates to an object in
the **Applies To** list.

Remarks

The **Cancel** method *requests* that the remote data source stop work on a pending asynchronous query or cancels any pending results. In some cases, it might not be possible to cancel an operation once it is started, and in other cases it might be possible to cancel the operation, but part of its steps might have already been completed.

In situations where you need to create a result set, but do not want to wait until the query engine completes the operation, you can use the **rdAsyncEnable** option with the **OpenResultset** or **Execute** method. This option returns control to your application as soon as the operation is initiated, but before the first row is ready for processing. This gives you an opportunity to execute other code while the query is executed. If you need to stop this operation before it is completed, use the **Cancel** method against the object being created.

The **Cancel** method can also be used against an **rdoConnection** object when you use the **rdAsyncEnable** option to request an asynchronous connection. In this case the attempt to connect to the remote server is abandoned.

You can also use the **Cancel** method against a synchronous **rdoResultset** or **rdoQuery** object to flush remaining result set rows and release resources committed to the query and **rdoResultset**.

If you use the **Cancel** method against **rdoResultset** objects that have multiple result sets pending, *all* result sets are flushed. To simply cancel the *current* set of results and begin processing the next set, use the **MoreResults** method.

Note Using the **Cancel** method against an executing action query might have unpredictable results. If the query is performing an operation that affects a number of rows, some of the rows might be changed, while others are not. For example, if you execute an action query containing an SQL UPDATE statement and use the **Cancel** method before the operation is complete, an indeterminate number of rows are updated—leaving others unchanged. If you intend to use the **Cancel** method against this type of action query, it is recommended that you use transaction methods to rollback or commit partially completed operations.

See Also

CancelUpdate Method (Remote Data), **Execute** Method (Remote Data), **MoreResults** Method (Remote Data), **OpenResultset** Method (Remote Data)

Cancel Property

Returns or sets a value indicating whether a command button is the Cancel button on a form. This command button can be the **CommandButton** control or any object within an **OLE** container control that behaves as a command button.

Applies To

Extender Object, **CommandButton** Control

Syntax

object.**Cancel** [= *boolean*]

The **Cancel** property syntax has these parts:

Part	Description
object	An object expression that evaluates to an object in the **Applies To** list.
boolean	A Boolean expression specifying whether the object is the Cancel button, as described in Settings.

Settings

The settings for *boolean* are:

Setting	Description
True	The **CommandButton** control is the Cancel button.
False	(Default) The **CommandButton** control isn't the Cancel button.

Remarks

Use the **Cancel** property to give the user the option of canceling uncommitted changes and returning the form to its previous state.

Only one **CommandButton** control on a form can be the Cancel button. When the **Cancel** property is set to **True** for one **CommandButton**, it's automatically set to **False** for all other **CommandButton** controls on the form. When a **CommandButton** control's **Cancel** property setting is **True** and the form is the active form, the user can choose the **CommandButton** by clicking it, pressing the ESC key, or pressing ENTER when the button has the focus.

For **OLE** container controls, the **Cancel** property is provided only for those objects that specifically behave as command buttons.

Tip   For a form that supports irreversible operations, such as deletions, it's a good idea to make the Cancel button the default button. To do this, set both the **Cancel** property and the **Default** property to **True**.

See Also

KeyDown, KeyUp Events, **KeyPress** Event, **Default** Property

CancelAsyncRead Method

Cancel an asynchronous data request.

Applies To

UserControl Object, **UserDocument** Object

Syntax

object.**CancelAsyncRead** [*PropertyName*]

The **CancelAsyncRead** method syntax has these parts:

Part	Description
object	An object expression that evaluates to an object in the **Applies To** list.
PropertyName	An optional string expression specifying the name of the asynchronous data request to cancel.

Remarks

Only the asynchronous data read request specified by *PropertyName* is canceled; all others continue normally.

The value in *PropertyName* specifies the particular asynchronous data read request to cancel, and should match the value given in a previous **AsyncRead** method invocation. If *PropertyName* is not given, then the last **AsyncRead** method invocation that did not give a *PropertyName* will be canceled.

See Also

AsyncRead Method

CancelBatch Method (Remote Data)

Cancels all uncommitted changes in the local cursor (used in batch mode)

Applies To

rdoResultset Object

Syntax

object.**CancelBatch**

The *object* placeholder represents an object expression that evaluates to an object in the **Applies To** list.

Remarks

The **CancelBatch** method cancels all uncommitted changes in the local cursor, and reverts the data back to the state it was when originally fetched from the database. Note that this method does not refresh the data by re-querying the server like the **Refresh** method does—instead it just discards changes made in the local cursor that have not already been sent in a batch update operation.

When you use the **CancelUpdate** method, only the current row's changes are rolled back to the state prior to execution of the last **Update** method.

Batch updates are used whenever you open a connection using the **ClientBatch** cursor library (**rdUseClientBatch**). In this case, each time you use the **Update** or **UpdateRow** methods, the local **rdoResultset** is updated, but the base database tables are not changed. The **BatchUpdate** method is used to update the base database table(s) with any information changed since the **rdoResultset** was last created or synchronized with the **BatchUpdate** command.

The **BatchUpdate** method updates the **BatchCollisionRows** property to include a bookmark for each row that failed to update—collided with an existing row that has data more current than the **rdoResultset** object as it existed when first read. The **BatchCollisionCount** property indicates how many collisions occurred during the batch update process.

See Also

Cancel Method (Remote Data), **CancelUpdate** Method (Remote Data), **Close** Method (Remote Data)

CancelUpdate Method

Cancels any pending updates for a **Recordset** object.

Applies To

Dynaset-Type Recordset Object, **Recordset** Object, **Snapshot-Type Recordset** Object, **Table-Type Recordset** Object, **Forward-Only–Type Recordset** Object, **Dynamic-Type Recordset** Object

Syntax

recordset.**CancelUpdate** *type*

The **AppendChunk** method syntax has these parts.

Part	Description
recordset	An object variable that represents the **Recordset** object for which you are canceling pending updates.
Type	Optional. A constant indicating the type of update, as specified in Settings (ODBCDirect workspaces only).

Settings

You can use the following values for the *type* argument only if batch updating is enabled.

Constant	Description
dbUpdateRegular	Default. Cancels pending changes that aren't cached.
DbUpdateBatch	Cancels pending changes in the update cache.

Remarks

You can use the **CancelUpdate** method to cancel any pending updates resulting from an **Edit** or **AddNew** operation. For example, if a user invokes the **Edit** or **AddNew** method and hasn't yet invoked the **Update** method, **CancelUpdate** cancels any changes made after **Edit** or **AddNew** was invoked.

Check the **EditMode** property of the **Recordset** to determine if there is a pending operation that can be canceled.

Note Using the **CancelUpdate** method has the same effect as moving to another record without using the **Update** method, except that the current record doesn't change, and various properties, such as **BOF** and **EOF**, aren't updated.

See Also

> **AddNew** Method, **Update** Method, **BOF**, **EOF** Properties, **EditMode** Property

Example

> This example shows how the **CancelUpdate** method is used with the **AddNew** method.

```
Sub CancelUpdateX()

    Dim dbsNorthwind As Database
    Dim rstEmployees As Recordset
    Dim intCommand As Integer

    Set dbsNorthwind = OpenDatabase("Northwind.mdb")
    Set rstEmployees = dbsNorthwind.OpenRecordset( _
        "Employees", dbOpenDynaset)

    With rstEmployees
        .AddNew
        !FirstName = "Kimberly"
        !LastName = "Bowen"
        intCommand = MsgBox("Add new record for " & _
            !FirstName & " " & !LastName & "?", vbYesNo)
        If intCommand = vbYes Then
            .Update
            MsgBox "Record added."
            ' Delete new record because this is a
            ' demonstration.
            .Bookmark = .LastModified
            .Delete
        Else
            .CancelUpdate
            MsgBox "Record not added."
        End If
    End With

    dbsNorthwind.Close

End Sub
```

CancelUpdate Method (Remote Data)

> Cancels any pending updates to an **rdoResultset** object.

Applies To

> **rdoResultset** Object

Syntax

> *object*.**CancelUpdate**

> The *object* placeholder represents an object expression that evaluates to an object in the **Applies To** list.

Remarks

The **CancelUpdate** method flushes the copy buffer and cancels any pending updates from an **Edit** or **AddNew** operation. For example, if a user invokes the **Edit** or **AddNew** method and hasn't yet invoked the **Update** method, **CancelUpdate** cancels any changes made after **Edit** or **AddNew** was invoked. Any information in the copy buffer is lost—that is, any changes made to the row after the **Edit** or **AddNew** methods are invoked, are flushed.

Use the **EditMode** property to determine if there is a pending operation that can be canceled.

If the **CancelUpdate** method is used before using the **Edit** or **AddNew** methods or when the **EditMode** property is set to **rdEditNone**, the method is ignored.

Note Using the **CancelUpdate** method has the same effect as moving to another row without using the **Update** method, except that the current row doesn't change, and various properties, such as **BOF** and **EOF**, aren't updated.

See Also

AddNew Method (Remote Data), **Cancel** Method (Remote Data), **Edit** Method (Remote Data), **Update** Method (Remote Data), **rdoResultset** Object, **BOF**, **EOF** Properties (Remote Data), **EditMode** Property (Remote Data)

Example

The following example illustrates use of the AddNew method to add new rows to a base table. This example assumes that you have read-write access to the table, that the column data provided meets the rules and other constraints associated with the table, and there is a unique index on the table. The data values for the operation are taken from three TextBox controls on the form. Note that the unique key for this table is not provided here as it is provided automatically – it is an identity column.

```
Option Explicit
Dim er As rdoError
Dim cn As New rdoConnection
Dim qy As New rdoQuery
Dim rs As rdoResultset
Dim col As rdoColumn

Private Sub AddNewJob_Click()
On Error GoTo ANEH

With rs
   .AddNew
   !job_desc = JobDescription
   !min_lvl = MinLevel
   !max_lvl = MaxLevel
   .Update
End With
Exit Sub

UpdateFailed:
MsgBox "Update did not suceed."
rs.CancelUpdate
Exit Sub
```

```
A
NEH:
Debug.Print Err, Error
For Each er In rdoErrors

Debug.Print er
Next
Resume UpdateFailed

End Sub

Private Sub Form_Load()

cn.CursorDriver = rdUseOdbc
cn.Connect = "uid=;pwd=;server=sequel;" _
    & "driver={SQL Server};database=pubs;dsn='';"
cn.EstablishConnection
With qy
    .Name = "JobsQuery"
    .SQL = "Select * from Jobs"
    .RowsetSize = 1
    Set .ActiveConnection = cn
    Set rs = .OpenResultset(rdOpenKeyset, _
        rdConcurRowver)
    Debug.Print rs.Updatable
End With

Exit Sub
End Sub
```

CanGetFocus Property

Returns or sets a value determining if a control can receive focus. The **CanGetFocus** property is read/write at the control's authoring time, and not available at the control's run time.

Applies To

UserControl Object

Settings

The settings for **CanGetFocus** are:

Setting	Description
True	The control can receive focus. If the control contains constituent controls, the control itself will be unable to receive the focus unless none of its constituent controls can receive the focus. It is up to the author of the control to write the code that draws a focus rectangle on the control when it does receive focus. This is the default value.
False	The control cannot receive focus.

Remarks

As long as the control contains at least one constituent control that has been set to receive the focus, **CanGetFocus** cannot be set to **False**. If **CanGetFocus** is **False**, then no constituent control can be set to receive the focus.

CanPaste Property

Returns a Boolean value indicating whether or not the Clipboard contains appropriate information (that is, controls) for pasting to the form.

Applies To

VBForm Object

Syntax

object.**CanPaste**

The *object* placeholder represents an object expression that evaluates to an object in the **Applies To** list.

CanPropertyChange Method

Asks the container if a property bound to a data source can have its value changed. The **CanPropertyChange** method is most useful if the property specified in *PropertyName* is bound to a data source.

Applies To

UserControl Object

Syntax

object.**CanPropertyChange** *PropertyName*

The **CanPropertyChange** method syntax has these parts:

Part	Description
object	An object expression that evaluates to an object in the **Applies To** list.
PropertyName	A string expression that represents a name of the property that the control is requesting to change.

Return values

The possible return values for **CanPropertyChange** are:

Setting	Description
True	The property specified in *PropertyName* can be changed at this time.
False	The property specified in *PropertyName* cannot be changed at this time; the container has the bound data table open as read only. Do not set the property value; doing so may cause errors in some control containers.

Remarks

The control should always call **CanPropertyChange** before changing the value of a property that can be data-bound.

Note At present, **CanPropertyChange** always returns **True** in Visual Basic, even if the bound field is read-only in the data source. Visual Basic doesn't raise an error when the control attempts to change a read-only field; it just doesn't update the data source.

As an example, the following code shows how the **CanPropertyChange** method is used:

```
Public Property Let Address(ByVal cValue As String)
    If CanPropertyChange("Address") Then
        m_Address = cValue
        PropertyChanged "Address"
    End If
End Property
```

Caption Property

- Form—determines the text displayed in the **Form** or **MDIForm** object's title bar . When the form is minimized, this text is displayed below the form's icon.
- Control—determines the text displayed in or next to a control.
- **MenuLine** object—determines the text displayed for a **Menu** control or an object in the **MenuItems** collection.

For a **Menu** control, **Caption** is normally read/write at run time. But **Caption** is read-only for menus that are exposed or supplied by Visual Basic to add-ins, such as the **MenuLine** object.

Applies To

PropertyPage Object, **CheckBox** Control, **CommandButton** Control, **Form** Object, **Forms** Collection, **Frame** Control, **Label** Control, **MDIForm** Object, **Menu** Control, **OptionButton** Control, **Data** Control, **DBGrid** Control, **Frame** Control, **RemoteData** Control

Syntax

object.**Caption** [= *string*]

The **Caption** property syntax has these parts:

Part	Description
object	An object expression that evaluates to an object in the **Applies To** list. If *object* is omitted, the form associated with the active form module is assumed to be *object*.
string	A string expression that evaluates to the text displayed as the caption.

Remarks

When you create a new object, its default caption is the default **Name** property setting. This default caption includes the object name and an integer, such as Command1 or Form1. For a more descriptive label, set the **Caption** property.

You can use the **Caption** property to assign an access key to a control. In the caption, include an ampersand (&) immediately preceding the character you want to designate as an access key. The character is underlined. Press the ALT key plus the underlined character to move the focus to that control. To include an ampersand in a caption without creating an access key, include two ampersands (&&). A single ampersand is displayed in the caption and no characters are underlined.

A **Label** control's caption size is unlimited. For forms and all other controls that have captions, the limit is 255 characters.

To display the caption for a form, set the **BorderStyle** property to either Fixed Single (1 or **vbFixedSingle**), Sizable (2 or **vbSizable**), or Fixed Dialog (3 or **vbFixedDialog**). A caption too long for the form's title bar is clipped. When an MDI child form is maximized within an **MDIForm** object, the child form's caption is included in the parent form's caption.

Tip For a label, set the **AutoSize** property to **True** to automatically resize the control to fit its caption.

See Also

BorderStyle Property, **AutoSize** Property, **Name** Property

Example

This example changes the **Caption** property of a **CommandButton** control each time the user clicks the button. To try this example, paste the code into the Declarations section of a form containing a **CommandButton** named Command1, and then press F5 and click the button.

```
Private Sub Command1_Click ()
   ' Check caption, then change it.
   If Command1.Caption = "Clicked" Then
      Command1.Caption = "OK"
   Else
      Command1.Caption = "Clicked"
   End If
End Sub
```

Caption Property (DBGrid Control, Column Object)

For a **DBGrid** control, this property determines the text displayed in the caption bar at the top of the grid.

For a **Column** object, this property determines the text displayed in the column's heading area.

Applies To

Column Object, **DBGrid** Control

Syntax

object.**Caption** [= *value*]

The **Caption** property syntax has these parts:

Part	Description
object	An object expression that evaluates to an object in the **Applies To** list.
value	A string expression that determines what is displayed, as described below.

Remarks

Setting the **Caption** property to an empty string for a **DBGrid** control hides its caption bar.

Setting the **Caption** property to an empty string for a **Column** object clears the text in the column's heading area but does not hide the heading. Column captions are only displayed if the **DBGrid** control's **ColumnHeaders** property is set to **True** and the **HeadLines** property is not set to 0.

See Also

ColumnHeaders Property, **HeadLines** Property

CaptureImage Method

Returns a captured image of the grid's display in its current state.

Applies To

DBGrid Control

Syntax

object.**CaptureImage**

The *object* placeholder represents an object expression that evaluates to an object in the **Applies To** list.

Remarks

Use the **CaptureImage** method to retrieve a snapshot of the grid.

The following code uses the **CaptureImage** method to assign a snapshot of a **DBGrid** control to a **PictureBox** control.

```
Picture1.Picture = DBGrid1.CaptureImage
```

Note   The **CaptureImage** method retrieves the image as a metafile typed image. Therefore, the image will resize to the size of its container.

See Also

PictureBox Control

Category Property

Returns or sets the Category attribute associated with a **Member** object.

Applies To

Member Object

Syntax

object.**Category**

The *object* placeholder represents an object expression that evaluates to an object in the **Applies To** list.

CellText Method

Returns a formatted text value from a **DBGrid** control cell. Doesn't support named arguments.

Applies To

Column Object

Syntax

object.**CellText** *bookmark*

The **CellText** method syntax has these parts:

Part	Description
object	An object expression that evaluates to an object in the **Applies To** list.
bookmark	Required. A string expression that represents a row in the **DBGrid** control.

Remarks

The **CellText** method returns a formatted string representation of the data in the current column for the row specified by the *bookmark* value. Using the **CellText** method is similar to accessing the **Text** property, except you can select a specific row from which to retrieve the value.

The value returned by the **CellText** method is derived from the **Text** property by applying the formatting as specified by the **NumberFormat** property of the **Column** object.

When using the **CellText** method, use the **Columns** collection to specify the specific column of the **DBGrid** control and set the *bookmark* argument to a specific row.

Using the **CellText** method to extract information from a cell doesn't affect the current selection.

See Also

Data Control, **Column** Object, **DBGrid** Control, **CellValue** Method, **Add** Method (Columns, SelBookmarks, Splits Collections), **ColIndex** Property, **NumberFormat** Property

Example

This examples gets information from the top and bottom rows and displays it in a label.

```
Sub DBGrid1_Scroll (Cancel As Integer)
    Dim TopRow, BottomRow
    TopRow = DBGrid1.Columns(1).CellText(DBGrid1.FirstRow)
    BottomRow = DBGrid1.Columns(1).CellText(DBGrid1.RowBookmark _
      (DBGrid1.VisibleRows - 1))
    Label1.Caption = "Records " & TopRow & " to " & _
      BottomRow & " are currently displayed."
End Sub
```

CellValue Method

Returns a raw data value in a column for a specified row in a **DBGrid** control. Doesn't support named arguments.

Applies To

Column Object

Syntax

object.**CellValue** *bookmark*

The **CellValue** method syntax has these parts:

Part	Description
object	An object expression that evaluates to an object in the **Applies To** list.
bookmark	Required. A string expression that contains the unformatted data stored in a selected **DBGrid** control cell.

Remarks

When using the **CellValue** method, use the **Columns** collection to specify the specific column of the **DBGrid** control and set the *bookmark* argument to a specific row.

Using the **CellValue** method returns the same value as the **Value** property setting of the current **Column** object, except that you can specify a specific row in the **DBGrid** control to reference.

Using the **CellValue** method to extract information from a cell doesn't affect the current selection.

See Also

Data Control, **DBGrid** Control, **ColIndex** Property, **NumberFormat** Property

Example

This example retrieves all the values in a given column from the selected range of rows and loads them into an array for later use.

```
Sub Command1_Click ()
    Dim I
    ReDim CalcArray (0 to DBGrid1.SelBookmarks.Count - 1)
    For I = 0 to DBGrid1.SelBookmarks.Count -1
    ' Puts the value of the current row in the selected row
    ' array into corresponding CalcArray cell.
        CalcArray(I) = _
        DBGrid1.Columns(1).CellValue(DBGrid1.SelBookmarks(I))
    Next I
End Sub
```

Change Event

Indicates the contents of a control have changed. How and when this event occurs varies with the control:

- **ComboBox**—changes the text in the text box portion of the control. Occurs only if the **Style** property is set to 0 (Dropdown Combo) or 1 (Simple Combo) and the user changes the text or you change the **Text** property setting through code.

- **DirListBox**—changes the selected directory. Occurs when the user double-clicks a new directory or when you change the **Path** property setting through code.

- **DriveListBox**—changes the selected drive. Occurs when the user selects a new drive or when you change the **Drive** property setting through code.

- **HScrollBar** and **VScrollBar** (horizontal and vertical scroll bars)—move the scroll box portion of the scroll bar. Occurs when the user scrolls or when you change the **Value** property setting through code.

- **Label**—changes the contents of the **Label**. Occurs when a DDE link updates data or when you change the **Caption** property setting through code.

- **PictureBox**—changes the contents of the **PictureBox**. Occurs when a DDE link updates data or when you change the **Picture** property setting through code.

- **TextBox**—changes the contents of the text box. Occurs when a DDE link updates data, when a user changes the text, or when you change the **Text** property setting through code.

Applies To

ComboBox Control, **DirListBox** Control, **DriveListBox** Control, **HScrollBar**, **VScrollBar** Controls, **Label** Control, **PictureBox** Control, **TextBox** Control, **DBCombo** Control, **DBGrid** Control

Syntax

Private Sub *object*_**Change(**[*index* **As Integer**]**)**

The **Change** event syntax has these parts:

Part	Description
object	An object expression that evaluates to an object in the **Applies To** list.
index	An integer that uniquely identifies a control if it's in a control array

Remarks

The Change event procedure can synchronize or coordinate data display among controls. For example, you can use a scroll bar's Change event procedure to update the scroll bar's **Value** property setting in a **TextBox** control. Or you can use a Change event procedure to display data and formulas in a work area and results in another area.

Change event procedures are also useful for updating properties in file-system controls (**DirListBox**, **DriveListBox**, and **FileListBox**). For example, you can update the **Path** property setting for a **DirListBox** control to reflect a change in a **DriveListBox** control's **Drive** property setting.

Note A Change event procedure can sometimes cause a cascading event. This occurs when the control's Change event alters the control's contents, for example, by setting a property in code that determines the control's value, such as the **Text** property setting for a **TextBox** control. To prevent a cascading event:

- If possible, avoid writing a Change event procedure for a control that alters that control's contents. If you do write such a procedure, be sure to set a flag that prevents further changes while the current change is in progress.

- Avoid creating two or more controls whose Change event procedures affect each other, for example, two **TextBox** controls that update each other during their **Change** events.

- Avoid using a **MsgBox** function or statement in this event for **HScrollBar** and **VScrollBar** controls.

See Also

KeyDown, **KeyUp** Events, **KeyPress** Event, **LostFocus** Event, **PathChange** Event, **PatternChange** Event, **Picture** Property, **Text** Property, **Value** Property, **Drive** Property, **LinkTopic** Property, **Style** Property, **Caption** Property, **Path** Property, **AllowCustomize** Property, **Customize** Method, **RestoreToolbar** Method, **SaveToolbar** Method

Example

This example displays the numeric setting of a horizontal scroll bar's **Value** property in a **TextBox** control. To try this example, create a form with a **TextBox** control and an **HScrollBar** control and then paste the code into the Declarations section of a form that contains a horizontal scroll bar (**HScrollBar** control) and a **TextBox** control. Press F5 and click the horizontal scroll bar.

```
Private Sub Form_Load ()
   HScroll1.Min = 0              ' Set Minimum.
   HScroll1.Max = 1000           ' Set Maximum.
```

```
    HScroll1.LargeChange = 100 ' Set LargeChange.
    HScroll1.SmallChange = 1   ' Set SmallChange.
End Sub

Private Sub HScroll1_Change ()
    Text1.Text = HScroll1.Value
End Sub
```

Changed Property

Returns or sets a value indicating that a value of a property on a property page has changed. The **Changed** property is not available at the property page's authoring time, and read/write at the property page's run time.

Applies To

PropertyPage Object

Syntax

object.**Changed** [= *boolean*]

The **Changed** property syntax has these parts:

Part	Description
object	An object expression that evaluates to an object in the **Applies To** list.
boolean	A Boolean value that determines if a property on the property page has been changed, making the property page dirty.

Settings

The settings for *boolean* are:

Setting	Description
True	The property page is now dirty, since the value of a property on the page has been changed.
False	The property page is not dirty, and no properties on the page have had their value changed.

Remarks

When the user changes the value of properties on a property page, these changes should not take effect immediately; instead, the changes should be applied only if the user presses the **Apply** button, the **OK** button, or changes property pages by selecting tabs. This allows the user to easily back out of any changes that have been made to a property page.

The **Changed** property should be set to **True**, for example, when a user changes a property value on a property page. Setting the **Changed** property to **True** would notify the property page to make available the **Apply** button.

Character Set (0 – 127)

0	•	32	[space]	64	@	96	`
1	•	33	!	65	A	97	a
2	•	34	"	66	B	98	b
3	•	35	#	67	C	99	c
4	•	36	$	68	D	100	d
5	•	37	%	69	E	101	e
6	•	38	&	70	F	102	f
7	•	39	'	71	G	103	g
8	* *	40	(	72	H	104	h
9	* *	41	)	73	I	105	i
10	* *	42	*	74	J	106	j
11	•	43	+	75	K	107	k
12	•	44	,	76	L	108	l
13	* *	45	-	77	M	109	m
14	•	46	.	78	N	110	n
15	•	47	/	79	O	111	o
16	•	48	0	80	P	112	p
17	•	49	1	81	Q	113	q
18	•	50	2	82	R	114	r
19	•	51	3	83	S	115	s
20	•	52	4	84	T	116	t
21	•	53	5	85	U	117	u
22	•	54	6	86	V	118	v
23	•	55	7	87	W	119	w
24	•	56	8	88	X	120	x
25	•	57	9	89	Y	121	y
26	•	58	:	90	Z	122	z
27	•	59	;	91	[	123	{
28	•	60	<	92	\	124	|
29	•	61	=	93	]	125	}
30	•	62	>	94	^	126	~
31	•	63	?	95	_	127	•

• These characters aren't supported by Microsoft Windows.

** Values 8, 9, 10, and 13 convert to backspace, tab, linefeed, and carriage return characters, respectively. They have no graphical representation but, depending on the application, can affect the visual display of text.

See Also

Character Set (128-255)

Character Set (128 – 255)

128	•	160	[space]	192	À	224	à
129	•	161	¡	193	Á	225	á
130	•	162	¢	194	Â	226	â
131	•	163	£	195	Ã	227	ã
132	•	164	¤	196	Ä	228	ä
133	•	165	¥	197	Å	229	å
134	•	166	¦	198	Æ	230	æ
135	•	167	§	199	Ç	231	ç
136	•	168	¨	200	È	232	è
137	•	169	©	201	É	233	é
138	•	170	ª	202	Ê	234	ê
139	•	171	«	203	Ë	235	ë
140	•	172	¬	204	Ì	236	ì
141	•	173	-	205	Í	237	í
142	•	174	®	206	Î	238	î
143	•	175	¯	207	Ï	239	ï
144	•	176	°	208	Ð	240	ð
145	'	177	±	209	Ñ	241	ñ
146	'	178	²	210	Ò	242	ò
147	•	179	³	211	Ó	243	ó
148	•	180	´	212	Ô	244	ô
149	•	181	µ	213	Õ	245	õ
150	•	182	¶	214	Ö	246	ö
151	•	183	·	215	×	247	÷
152	•	184	¸	216	Ø	248	ø
153	•	185	¹	217	Ù	249	ù
154	•	186	º	218	Ú	250	ú
155	•	187	»	219	Û	251	û
156	•	188	¼	220	Ü	252	ü
157	•	189	½	221	Ý	253	ý
158	•	190	¾	222	Þ	254	þ
159	•	191	¿	223	ß	255	ÿ

• These characters aren't supported by Microsoft Windows.

See Also

Character Set (0 – 127)

Charset Property

Sets or returns the character set used in the font.

Syntax

object.**Charset** [= *value*]

The **Charset** property syntax has these parts:

Part	Description
object	An object expression that evaluates to an object in the **Applies To** list.
value	A integer value that specifies the character set used by the font, as described in **Settings**.

Settings

The following are some common settings for *value*:

Value	Description
0	Standard Windows characters
2	The symbol character set.
128	Double-byte character set (DBCS) unique to the Japanese version of Windows
255	Extended characters normally displayed by DOS applications.

Remarks

Setting the **Charset** property to one of its available values selects the character set only if it is available in the current font.

ChDir Statement

Changes the current directory or folder.

Syntax

ChDir *path*

The required *path* argument is a string expression that identifies which directory or folder becomes the new default directory or folder. The *path* may include the drive. If no drive is specified, **ChDir** changes the default directory or folder on the current drive.

Remarks

The **ChDir** statement changes the default directory but not the default drive. For example, if the default drive is C, the following statement changes the default directory on drive D, but C remains the default drive:

```
ChDir "D:\TMP"
```

See Also

ChDrive Statement, **CurDir** Function, **Dir** Function, **MkDir** Statement, **RmDir** Statement

Example

This example uses the **ChDir** statement to change the current directory or folder.

```
' Change current directory or folder to "MYDIR".
ChDir "MYDIR"

' Assume "C:" is the current drive. The following statement changes
' the default directory on drive "D:". "C:" remains the current drive.
ChDir "D:\WINDOWS\SYSTEM"
```

ChDrive Statement

Changes the current drive.

Syntax

ChDrive *drive*

The required *drive* argument is a string expression that specifies an existing drive. If you supply a zero-length string (""), the current drive doesn't change. If the *drive* argument is a multiple-character string, **ChDrive** uses only the first letter.

See Also

ChDir Statement, **CurDir** Function, **MkDir** Statement, **RmDir** Statement

Example

This example uses the **ChDrive** statement to change the current drive.

```
ChDrive "D" ' Make "D" the current drive.
```

CheckBox Control

A **CheckBox** control displays an X when selected; the X disappears when the **CheckBox** is cleared. Use this control to give the user a True/False or Yes/No option. You can use **CheckBox** controls in groups to display multiple choices from which the user can select one or more. You can also set the value of a **CheckBox** programmatically with the Value property.

Syntax

CheckBox

Remarks

CheckBox and **OptionButton** controls function similarly but with an important difference: Any number of **CheckBox** controls on a form can be selected at the same time. In contrast, only one **OptionButton** in a group can be selected at any given time.

To display text next to the **CheckBox**, set the **Caption** property. Use the **Value** property to determine the state of the control—selected, cleared, or unavailable.

Properties

OLEDropMode Property, **BackColor, ForeColor** Properties, **FontBold, FontItalic, FontStrikethru, FontUnderline** Properties, **FontName** Property, **FontSize** Property, **Height, Width** Properties, **Left, Top** Properties, **Picture** Property, **TabIndex** Property, **Tag** Property, **Value** Property, **Visible** Property, **Alignment** Property, **DragIcon** Property, **DragMode** Property, **hWnd** Property, **MouseIcon** Property, **MousePointer** Property, **Style** Property, **TabStop** Property, **Appearance** Property, **Caption** Property, **Enabled** Property, **HelpContextID** Property, **Index** Property (Control Array), **Name** Property, **Parent** Property, **Font** Property, **Container** Property, **ToolTipText** Property, **DisabledPicture** Property, **DownPicture** Property, **MaskColor** Property, **UseMaskColor** Property, **WhatsThisHelpID** Property, **DataField** Property, **DateChanged** Property

Methods

Refresh Method, **SetFocus** Method, **Drag** Method, **Move** Method, **ZOrder** Method, **OLEDrag** Method, **ShowWhatsThis** Method

See Also

Value Property, **Caption** Property

Checked Property

Returns or sets a value that determines whether a check mark is displayed next to a menu item.

Applies To

Menu Control

Syntax

object.**Checked** [= *boolean*]

The **Checked** property syntax has these parts:

Part	Description
object	An object expression that evaluates to an object in the **Applies To** list.
boolean	A Boolean expression that specifies whether a check mark is displayed next to a menu item.

Settings

The settings for *boolean* are:

Setting	Description
True	Places a check mark next to a menu item.
False	(Default) Doesn't place a check mark next to a menu item.

Remarks

At design time, you can use the Menu Editor to set **Checked** to **True**. At run time, you can toggle **Checked** on and off as part of a Click event procedure attached to a **Menu** control. You can also set the value of **Checked** in a startup procedure or in a form's Load event procedure.

For a **Menu** control, **Checked** is normally read/write at run time. But **Checked** is read-only for menu items that are exposed or supplied by Visual Basic to add-ins, such as the Add-In Manager command on the Add-Ins menu.

See Also

Load Event, **Visible** Property, **Enabled** Property

Example

This example displays and removes a check mark next to a menu item. To try this example, create a form with a **Menu** control that has one menu item (set both the **Caption** and **Name** properties to MyMenuItem), and then press F5 and choose the menu item.

```
Private Sub MyMenuItem_Click ()
   ' Turn check mark on menu item on and off.
   MyMenuItem.Checked = Not MyMenuItem.Checked
End Sub
```

Choose Function

Selects and returns a value from a list of arguments.

Syntax

Choose(*index*, *choice-1*[, *choice-2*, ... [, *choice-n*]])

The **Choose** function syntax has these parts:

Part	Description
index	Required. Numeric expression or field that results in a value between 1 and the number of available choices.
choice	Required. **Variant** expression containing one of the possible choices.

Remarks

Choose returns a value from the list of choices based on the value of *index*. If *index* is 1, **Choose** returns the first choice in the list; if *index* is 2, it returns the second choice, and so on.

You can use **Choose** to look up a value in a list of possibilities. For example, if *index* evaluates to 3 and *choice-1* = "one", *choice-2* = "two", and *choice-3* = "three", **Choose** returns "three". This capability is particularly useful if *index* represents the value in an option group.

Choose evaluates every choice in the list, even though it returns only one. For this reason, you should watch for undesirable side effects. For example, if you use the

MsgBox function as part of an expression in all the choices, a message box will be displayed for each choice as it is evaluated, even though **Choose** returns the value of only one of them.

The **Choose** function returns a **Null** if *index* is less than 1 or greater than the number of choices listed.

If *index* is not a whole number, it is rounded to the nearest whole number before being evaluated.

See Also

IIf Function, **Select Case** Statement, **Switch** Function

Example

This example uses the **Choose** function to display a name in response to an index passed into the procedure in the Ind parameter.

```
Function GetChoice(Ind As Integer)
    GetChoice = Choose(Ind, "Speedy", "United", "Federal")
End Function
```

Chr Function

Returns a **String** containing the character associated with the specified character code.

Syntax

Chr(*charcode*)

The required *charcode* argument is a **Long** that identifies a character.

Remarks

Numbers from 0 – 31 are the same as standard, nonprintable ASCII codes. For example, **Chr**(10) returns a linefeed character. The normal range for *charcode* is 0—255. However, on DBCS systems, the actual range for *charcode* is -32768 to 65536.

Note   The **ChrB** function is used with byte data contained in a **String**. Instead of returning a character, which may be one or two bytes, **ChrB** always returns a single byte. The **ChrW** function returns a **String** containing the Unicode character except on platforms where Unicode is not supported, in which case, the behavior is identical to the **Chr** function.

See Also

Asc Function, **Str** Function

Example

This example uses the **Chr** function to return the character associated with the specified character code.

```
Dim MyChar
MyChar = Chr(65)   ' Returns A.
MyChar = Chr(97)   ' Returns a.
MyChar = Chr(62)   ' Returns >.
MyChar = Chr(37)   ' Returns %.
```

ChunkRequired Property (Remote Data)

Returns a Boolean value that indicates if data must be accessed using the **GetChunk** method.

Applies To

rdoColumn Object

Syntax

object.**ChunkRequired**

The *object* placeholder represents an object expression that evaluates to an object in the **Applies To** list.

Return Values

The **ChunkRequired** property return values are:

Value	Description
True	The data should be accessed using the **GetChunk** method.
False	The data need not be accessed using the **GetChunk** method.

Remarks

Use the **ChunkRequired** property to determine if the column in question should be manipulated using the **AppendChunk** and **GetChunk** methods. Accessing the **Value** property of a column whose **ChunkRequired** property is **True**, will *only* result in a trappable error when RDO is unable to fetch the data without use of the **AppendChunk** or **GetChunk** methods. In other words, when the data column does not contain more data than can be handled by conventional string handling, you are *not* required to use the **GetChunk** and **AppendChunk** methods.

By setting the **BindThreshold** property, you can adjust the number of bytes that will force the use of the **AppendChunk** and **GetChunk** methods. You can also determine the length of a *chunk* column by using the **ColumnSize** method.

See Also

AppendChunk Method (Remote Data), **ColumnSize** Method (Remote Data), **GetChunk** Method (Remote Data), **Type** Property (Remote Data)

Circle Method

Draws a circle, ellipse, or arc on an object.

Applies To

PropertyPage Object, **UserControl** Object, **UserDocument** Object, **Printer** Object, **Printers** Collection, **Form** Object, **Forms** Collection, **PictureBox** Control

Syntax

object.**Circle** [**Step**] (*x, y*), *radius,* [*color, start, end, aspect*]

The **Circle** method syntax has the following object qualifier and parts.

Part	Description
object	Optional. Object expression that evaluates to an object in the **Applies To** list. If *object* is omitted, the **Form** with the focus is assumed to be *object*.
Step	Optional. Keyword specifying that the center of the circle, ellipse, or arc is relative to the current coordinates given by the **CurrentX** and **CurrentY** properties of *object*.
(x, y)	Required. **Single** values indicating the coordinates for the center point of the circle, ellipse, or arc. The **ScaleMode** property of *object* determines the units of measure used.
radius	Required. **Single** value indicating the radius of the circle, ellipse, or arc. The **ScaleMode** property of *object* determines the unit of measure used.
color	Optional. **Long** integer value indicating the RGB color of the circle's outline. If omitted, the value of the **ForeColor** property is used. You can use the **RGB** function or **QBColor** function to specify the color.
start, end	Optional. Single-precision values. When an arc or a partial circle or ellipse is drawn, *start* and *end* specify (in radians) the beginning and end positions of the arc. The range for both is -2 pi radians to 2 pi radians. The default value for *start* is 0 radians; the default for *end* is 2 * pi radians.
aspect	Optional. Single-precision value indicating the aspect ratio of the circle. The default value is 1.0, which yields a perfect (non-elliptical) circle on any screen.

Remarks

To fill a circle, set the **FillColor** and **FillStyle** properties of the object on which the circle or ellipse is drawn. Only a closed figure can be filled. Closed figures include circles, ellipses, or pie slices (arcs with radius lines drawn at both ends).

When drawing a partial circle or ellipse, if *start* is negative, **Circle** draws a radius to *start*, and treats the angle as positive; if *end* is negative, **Circle** draws a radius to *end* and treats the angle as positive. The **Circle** method always draws in a counter-clockwise (positive) direction.

The width of the line used to draw the circle, ellipse, or arc depends on the setting of the **DrawWidth** property. The way the circle is drawn on the background depends on the setting of the **DrawMode** and **DrawStyle** properties.

When drawing pie slices, to draw a radius to angle 0 (giving a horizontal line segment to the right), specify a very small negative value for *start*, rather than zero.

You can omit an argument in the middle of the syntax, but you must include the argument's comma before including the next argument. If you omit an optional argument, omit the comma following the last argument you specify.

When **Circle** executes, the **CurrentX** and **CurrentY** properties are set to the center point specified by the arguments.

This method cannot be used in an **With…End With** block.

See Also

Line Method

Example

This example uses the **Circle** method to draw a number of concentric circles in the center of a form. To try this example, paste the code into the General section of a form. Then press F5 and click the form.

```
Sub Form_Click ()
    Dim CX, CY, Radius, Limit        ' Declare variable.
    ScaleMode = 3                    ' Set scale to pixels.
    CX = ScaleWidth / 2              ' Set X position.
    CY = ScaleHeight / 2             ' Set Y position.
    If CX > CY Then Limit = CY Else Limit = CX
    For Radius = 0 To Limit          ' Set radius.
        Circle (CX, CY), Radius,RGB(Rnd * 255, Rnd * 255, Rnd * 255)
    Next Radius
End Sub
```

Class Property

Returns or sets the class name of an embedded object.

Applies To

OLE Container Control

Syntax

object.**Class** [= *string*]

The **Class** property syntax has these parts:

Part	Description
object	An object expression that evaluates to an object in the **Applies To** list.
string	A string expression specifying the class name.

Remarks

A class name defines the type of an object. Applications that support ActiveX components fully qualify the class names of their objects using either of the following syntaxes:

application.objecttype.version
objecttype.version

The syntax for ActiveX component class names has the following parts:

Part	Description
application	The name of the application that supplies the object.
objecttype	The object's name as defined in the object library.
version	The version number of the object or application that supplies the object.

For example, Microsoft Excel version 5.0 supports a number of objects, including worksheets and charts. Their class names are **Excel.Sheet.5** and **Excel.Chart.5**. Microsoft WordArt version 2.0 supports a single object with the class name **MSWordArt.2**.

Note Some ActiveX component programming documentation refers to the class name syntax as a programmatic ID.

To view a list of class names available on your system, select the **OLE** container control, select the **Class** property in the Properties window, and then click the builder button.

Copying an object from the system Clipboard updates the control's **Class** property. For example, if you paste a Microsoft Excel chart from the system Clipboard into an **OLE** container control that previously contained a Microsoft Excel worksheet, its **Class** property setting changes from **Excel.Sheet.5** to **Excel.Chart.5**. You can paste an object from the system Clipboard at run time with the **Paste** method or the **PasteSpecialDlg** method.

See Also

Paste Method, **PasteOK** Property, **PasteSpecialDlg** Method

Clear Method

Clears all property settings of the **Err** object.

Applies To

Err Object

Syntax

object.**Clear**

The *object* is always the **Err** object.

Remarks

Use **Clear** to explicitly clear the **Err** object after an error has been handled, for example, when you use deferred error handling with **On Error Resume Next**. The **Clear** method is called automatically whenever any of the following statements is executed:

- Any type of **Resume** statement
- **Exit Sub**, **Exit Function**, **Exit Property**
- Any **On Error** statement

Note The **On Error Resume Next** construct may be preferable to **On Error GoTo** when handling errors generated during access to other objects. Checking **Err** after each interaction with an object removes ambiguity about which object was accessed by the code. You can be sure which object placed the error code in **Err.Number**, as well as which object originally generated the error (the object specified in **Err.Source**).

See Also

On Error Statement, **Raise** Method, **Err** Object, **Description** Property, **HelpContext** Property, **HelpFile** Property, **LastDLLError** Property, **Number** Property, **Source** Property, **HelpContextID** Property

Example

This example uses the **Err** object's **Clear** method to reset the numeric properties of the **Err** object to zero and its string properties to zero-length strings. If **Clear** were omitted from the following code, the error message dialog box would be displayed on every iteration of the loop (after an error occurs) whether or not a successive calculation generated an error. You can single-step through the code to see the effect.

```
Dim Result(10) As Integer   ' Declare array whose elements
                            ' will overflow easily.
Dim indx
On Error Resume Next        ' Defer error trapping.
Do Until indx = 10
   ' Generate an occasional error or store result if no error.
   Result(indx) = Rnd * indx * 20000
   If Err.Number <> 0 Then
      MsgBox Err, , "Error Generated: ", Err.HelpFile, Err.HelpContext
      Err.Clear               ' Clear Err object properties.
   End If
   indx = indx + 1
Loop
```

Clear Method (Clipboard, ComboBox, ListBox)

Clears the contents of a **ListBox**, **ComboBox**, or the system **Clipboard**.

Applies To

Clipboard Object, **ComboBox** Control, **ListBox** Control

Syntax

object.**Clear**

The *object* placeholder represents an object expression that evaluates to an object in the **Applies To** list.

Remarks

A **ListBox** or **ComboBox** control bound to a **Data** control doesn't support the **Clear** method.

See Also

AddItem Method, **Cls** Method, **RemoveItem** Method

Example

This example uses the **Clear** method to clear all items from a list box. To try this example, paste the code into the Declarations section of a form with a **ListBox** control named List1, and then press F5 and click the form.

```
Private Sub Form_Click ()
   Dim Entry, I, Msg                          ' Declare variables.
   Msg = "Choose OK to add 100 items to your list box."
   MsgBox Msg                                 ' Display message.
   For I = 1 To 100                           ' Count from 1 to 100.
      Entry = "Entry " & I                    ' Create entry.
      List1.AddItem Entry                     ' Add the entry.
   Next I
   Msg = "Choose OK to remove every other entry."
   MsgBox Msg                                 ' Display message.
   For I = 1 To 50                            ' Determine how to
      List1.RemoveItem I                      ' remove every other
   Next I                                     ' item.

Msg = "Choose OK to remove all items from the list box."
   MsgBox Msg                                 ' Display message.
   List1.Clear                                ' Clear list box.
End Sub
```

This example uses the **Clear** method to clear the **Clipboard** object. To try this example, paste the code into the Declarations section of a form, and then press F5 and click the form.

```
Private Sub Form_Click ()
   Const CF_BITMAP = 2                        ' Define bitmap format.
   Dim Msg   ' Declare variable.
   On Error Resume Next                       ' Set up error handling.
   Msg = "Choose OK to load a bitmap onto the Clipboard."
   MsgBox Msg                                 ' Display message.
   Clipboard.Clear                            ' Clear Clipboard.
   Clipboard.SetData LoadPicture("PAPER.BMP") ' Get bitmap.
   If Err Then
      Msg = "Can't find the .BMP file."
      MsgBox Msg                              ' Display error message.
      Exit Sub
   End If

Msg = "A bitmap is now on the Clipboard. Choose OK to copy "
   Msg = Msg & "the bitmap from the Clipboard to the form."
   MsgBox Msg                                 ' Display message.
   Picture = Clipboard.GetData()              ' Copy from Clipboard.
   Msg = "Choose OK to clear the picture."
   MsgBox Msg                                 ' Display message.
   Picture = LoadPicture()                    ' Clear picture.
End Sub
```

Clear Method (DataObject Object)

Deletes the contents of the **DataObject** object.

Applies To

DataObject Object

Syntax

object.**Clear**

The *object* placeholder represents an object expression that evaluates to an object in the **Applies To** list.

Remarks

This method is available only for component drag sources. If **Clear** is called from a component drop target, an error is generated.

Most components support manual OLE drag and drop events, and some support automatic OLE drag and drop events.

Clear Method (Remote Data)

Clears all members from the **rdoErrors** collection.

Applies To

rdoError Object

Syntax

object.**Clear**

The *object* placeholder represents an object expression that evaluates to an object in the **Applies To** list.

Remarks

Use this method to remove all **rdoError** objects from the **rdoErrors** collection.

Generally, it is unnecessary to clear the **rdoErrors** collection because it is automatically cleared when the first error occurs after initiating a new operation. Use the **Clear** method in cases where you need to clear the **rdoErrors** collection manually, for example if you wish to clear errors that have already been processed.

See Also

rdoError Object

ClearFields Method

Restores the default grid layout.

Applies To

DBGrid Control

Syntax

object.**ClearFields**

The *object* placeholder represents an object expression that evaluates to an object in the **Applies To** list.

Remarks

The **ClearFields** method restores the default grid layout (with two blank columns) so that subsequent **ReBind** operations will automatically derive new column bindings from the (possibly changed) data source. You can cancel the grid's automatic layout behavior by invoking the **HoldFields** method.

See Also

HoldFields Method, **Rebind** Method

ClearSelCols Method

Deselects all columns in a split. If no columns are selected, then this method does nothing.

Applies To

Split Object, **DBGrid** Control

Syntax

object.**ClearSelCols**

The *object* placeholder represents an object expression that evaluates to an object in the **Applies To** list.

Remarks

If a grid contains multiple splits, then invoking its **ClearSelCols** method has the same effect as invoking the **ClearSelCols** method for the current split. The index of the current split is available through the **DBGrid** control's **Split** property.

Use the **SelStartCol** and **SelEndCol** properties to determine the current column selection range for a split.

See Also

Split Property, **SelEndCol**, **SelStartCol**, **SelEndRow**, **SelStartRow** Properties

Click Event

Occurs when the user presses and then releases a mouse button over an object. It can also occur when the value of a control is changed.

For a **Form** object, this event occurs when the user clicks either a blank area or a disabled control. For a control, this event occurs when the user:

- Clicks a control with the left or right mouse button. With a **CheckBox**, **CommandButton**, **Listbox**, or **OptionButton** control, the Click event occurs only when the user clicks the left mouse button.

- Selects an item in a **ComboBox** or **ListBox** control, either by pressing the arrow keys or by clicking the mouse button.

- Presses the SPACEBAR when a **CommandButton**, **OptionButton**, or **CheckBox** control has the focus.

- Presses ENTER when a form has a **CommandButton** control with its **Default** property set to **True**.

- Presses ESC when a form has a Cancel button—a **CommandButton** control with its **Cancel** property set to **True**.

- Presses an access key for a control. For example, if the caption of a **CommandButton** control is "&G", pressing ALT+G triggers the event.

You can also trigger the Click event in code by:

- Setting a **CommandButton** control's **Value** property to **True**.

- Setting an **OptionButton** control's **Value** property to **True**.

- Changing a **CheckBox** control's **Value** property setting.

Applies To

PropertyPage Object, **UserControl** Object, **UserDocument** Object, **CheckBox** Control, **ComboBox** Control, **CommandButton** Control, **DirListBox** Control, **FileListBox** Control, **Form** Object, **Forms** Collection, **Frame** Control, **Image** Control, **Label** Control, **ListBox** Control, **MDIForm** Object, **Menu** Control, **OptionButton** Control, **PictureBox** Control, **TextBox** Control, **OLE Container** Control, **Animation** Control, **DBCombo** Control, **DBGrid** Control, **DBList** Control, **ListView** Control, **ProgressBar** Control, **Rich TextBox** Control, **Slider** Control, **StatusBar** Control, **TapStrip** Control, **Toolbar** Control, **TreeView** Control

Syntax

Private Sub Form_Click( )
Private Sub *object*_**Click([***index* **As Integer])**

The **Click** event syntax has these parts:

Part	Description
object	An object expression that evaluates to an object in the **Applies To** list.
index	An integer that uniquely identifies a control if it's in a control array.

Remarks

Typically, you attach a Click event procedure to a **CommandButton** control, **Menu** object, or **PictureBox** control to carry out commands and command-like actions. For the other applicable controls, use this event to trigger actions in response to a change in the control.

You can use a control's **Value** property to test the state of the control from code. Clicking a control generates **MouseDown** and **MouseUp** events in addition to the **Click** event. The order in which these three events occur varies from control to control. For example, for **ListBox** and **CommandButton** controls, the events occur in this order: **MouseDown**, Click, **MouseUp**. But for **FileListBox**, **Label**, or **PictureBox** controls, the events occur in this order: **MouseDown**, **MouseUp**, and Click. When you're attaching event procedures for these related events, be sure that their actions don't conflict. If the order of events is important in your application, test the control to determine the event order.

Note To distinguish between the left, right, and middle mouse buttons, use the **MouseDown** and **MouseUp** events.

If there is code in the **Click** event, the **DlbClick** event will never trigger, because the **Click** event is the first event to trigger between the two. As a result, the mouse click is intercepted by the **Click** event, so the **DblClick** event doesn't occur.

See Also

MouseDown, **MouseUp** Events, **DblClick** Event, **Cancel** Property, **Value** Property, **Default** Property

Example

In this example, each time a **PictureBox** control is clicked it moves diagonally across a form. To try this example, paste the code into the Declarations section of a form that contains a **PictureBox** control positioned at the lower-left corner of the form, and then press F5 and click the **PictureBox**.

```
Private Sub Picture1_Click ()
   Picture1.Move Picture1.Left + 750, Picture1.Top - 550
End Sub
```

Click Event (Add-Ins)

Occurs when the **OnAction** property of a corresponding command bar control is set.

Applies To

PropertyPage Object, **UserControl** Object, **UserDocument** Object, **CheckBox** Control, **ComboBox** Control, **CommandButton** Control, **DirListBox** Control, **FileListBox** Control, **Form** Object, **Forms** Collection, **Frame** Control, **Image** Control, **Label** Control, **ListBox** Control, **MDIForm** Object, **Menu** Control, **OptionButton** Control, **PictureBox** Control, **TextBox** Control, **OLE Container** Control, **Animation** Control, **DBCombo** Control, **DBGrid** Control, **DBList** Control, **ListView** Control, **ProgressBar** Control, **Rich TextBox** Control, **Slider** Control, **StatusBar** Control, **TapStrip** Control, **Toolbar** Control, **TreeView** Control

Syntax

Sub *object*_**Click (ByVal** *ctrl* **As Object, ByRef** *handled* **As Boolean,**
  ↳ ByRef *canceldefault* **As Boolean)**

The **Click** event syntax has these *named arguments*:

Part	Description
ctrl	Required; **Object**. Specifies the object that is the source of the **Click** event.
handled	Required; **Boolean**. If **True**, other add-ins should handle the event. If **False**, the action of the command bar item has not been handled.
canceldefault	Required; **Boolean**. If **True**, default behavior is performed unless canceled by a downstream add-in. If **False**, default behavior is not performed unless restored by a downstream add-in.

Remarks

The **Click** event is specific to the **CommandBarEvents** object. Use a variable declared using the **WithEvents** keyword to receive the **Click** event for a **CommandBar** control. This variable should be set to the return value of the **CommandBarEvents** property of the **Events** object. The **CommandBarEvents** property takes the **CommandBar** control as an argument. When the **CommandBar** control is clicked (for the variable you declared using the **WithEvents** keyword), the code is executed.

See Also

MouseDown, **MouseUp** Events, **DblClick** Event, **Cancel** Property, **Value** Property, **Default** Property

Example

The following example illustrates how you can set up code for a **Click** event procedure using **WithEvents** and **Set**. Note that the object reference ce is used in place of the menu name **Tools** in the name of the **Click** event.

```
Private WithEvents ce As CommandBarEvents

Sub Test()
    Dim c As CommandBarControl
    Set c = Application.VBE.CommandBars("Tools").Controls(1)
    Set ce = Application.VBE.Events.CommandBarEvents(c)
End Sub

Private Sub ce_Click(ByVal CommandBarControl As Object,
    Handled As Boolean, CancelDefault As Boolean)
    ' Put event-handling code here
End Sub
```

Click Event (DBCombo Control)

Occurs when the user presses and then releases a mouse button over the **DBCombo** control. This event also occurs by pressing the up or down arrow keys on the keyboard to select an item.

Applies To

DBCombo Control

Syntax

Private Sub *object*_**Click**([*index* **As Integer** ,] *Area* **As Integer**)

The **Click** event syntax has these parts:

Part	Description
object	An object expression that evaluates to an object in the **Applies To** list.
index	An integer that uniquely identifies a control if it's in a control array.
Area	An integer expression that specifies where the control was clicked, as described below.

The *Area* parameter can contain the following values:

Constant	Value	Description
dbcAreaButton	0	The user clicked the button on the **DBCombo** control.
dbcAreaEdit	1	The user click in the text box part of the **DBCombo** control.
dbcAreaList	2	The user clicked in the drop-down list part of the **DBCombo** control.

Remarks

The **DBCombo** control does not have a **DropDown** event like the standard combo box to signal when the user drops down the list portion of the **DBCombo** control. Instead the user can use the *Area* parameter in the Click event to tell the user which area in the **DBCombo** control the user clicked.

Typically, you attach a Click event procedure to a control to carry out commands and command-like actions.

Clicking a control generates **MouseDown** and **MouseUp** events in addition to the Click event. When you're attaching event procedures for these related events, be sure that their actions don't conflict. If the order of events is important in your application, test the control to determine the event order.

Note To distinguish between the left, right, and middle mouse buttons, use the **MouseDown** and **MouseUp** events.

See Also

Data Control, **DblClick** Event (DBCombo Control), **DropDown** Event, **MouseDown, MouseUp** Events

---

Clipboard Object

Provides access to the system Clipboard.

Syntax

Clipboard

Remarks

The **Clipboard** object is used to manipulate text and graphics on the Clipboard. You can use this object to enable a user to copy, cut, and paste text or graphics in your application. Before copying any material to the **Clipboard** object, you should clear its contents by as performing a **Clear** method, such as `Clipboard.Clear`.

Note that the **Clipboard** object is shared by all Windows applications, and thus, the contents are subject to change whenever you switch to another application.

The **Clipboard** object can contain several pieces of data as long as each piece is in a different format. For example, you can use the **SetData** method to put a bitmap on the **Clipboard** with the **vbCFDIB** format, and then use the **SetText** method with the **vbCFText** format to put text on the **Clipboard**. You can then use the **GetText** method to retrieve the text or the **GetData** method to retrieve the graphic. Data on the **Clipboard** is lost when another set of data of the same format is placed on the **Clipboard** either through code or a menu command.

Methods

Clear Method (Clipboard, ComboBox, ListBox), **GetData** Method, **GetFormat** Method, **GetText** Method, **SetData** Method, **SetText** Method

Clipboard Property

Returns a **Clipboard** object, which provides access to the system Clipboard.

Applies To

Global Object

Syntax

Clipboard

Remarks

The **Clipboard** object is used to manipulate text and graphics on the Clipboard. You can use this object to enable a user to copy, cut, and paste text or graphics in your application. Before copying any material to the **Clipboard** object, you should clear its contents by performing a **Clear** method, such as `Clipboard.Clear`.

Note that the **Clipboard** object is shared by all Windows applications, and thus, the contents are subject to change whenever you switch to another application.

The **Clipboard** object can contain several pieces of data as long as each piece is in a different format. For example, you can use the **SetData** method to put a bitmap on the Clipboard with the **vbCFDIB** format, and then use the **SetText** method with the **vbCFText** format to put text on the Clipboard. You can then use the **GetText** method to retrieve the text or the **GetData** method to retrieve the graphic. Data on the Clipboard is lost when another set of data of the same format is placed on the Clipboard either through code or a menu command.

See Also

Global Object, **Clipboard** Object

ClipControls Property

Returns or sets a value that determines whether graphics methods in Paint events repaint the entire object or only newly exposed areas. Also determines whether the Microsoft Windows operating environment creates a clipping region that excludes nongraphical controls contained by the object. Read-only at run time.

Applies To

PropertyPage Object, **UserControl** Object, **UserDocument** Object, **Form** Object, **Forms** Collection, **Frame** Control, **PictureBox** Control

Syntax

object.**ClipControls**

The **ClipControls** property syntax has these parts:

Part	Description
object	An object expression that evaluates to an object in the **Applies To** list.
boolean	A Boolean expression that specifies how objects are repainted, as described in Settings.

Settings

The settings for *boolean* are:

Setting	Description
True	(Default) Graphics methods in Paint events repaint the entire object. A clipping region is created around nongraphical controls on the form before a Paint event.
False	Graphics methods in Paint events repaint only newly exposed areas. A clipping region isn't created around nongraphical controls before a Paint event. Complex forms usually load and repaint faster when **ClipControls** is set to **False**.

Remarks

Clipping is the process of determining which parts of a form or container, such as a **Frame** or **PictureBox** control, are painted when the form is displayed. An outline of the form and controls is created in memory. The Windows operating environment uses this outline to paint some parts, such as the background, without affecting other parts, such as the contents of a **TextBox** control. Because the clipping region is created in memory, setting this property to **False** can reduce the time needed to paint or repaint a form.

The clipping region includes most controls, but doesn't clip around the **Image**, **Label**, **Line**, or **Shape** controls.

Avoid nesting intrinsic controls with **ClipControls** set to **True** inside a control with **ClipControls** set to **False** (for instance, a command button inside a picture box). This kind of control nesting causes the controls to repaint incorrectly. To fix this problem, set the **ClipControls** property for both the container control and the nested controls to **True**.

See Also

Paint Event, **AutoRedraw** Property

Example

This example shows how the **ClipControls** property affects the repainting of a form. To try this example, paste the code into the Declarations section of a form, and then press F5. Notice that the color of the entire form changes each time you resize it or cover part of it with another form or application. End the program and set **ClipControls** to **False**, and then run the program again. Notice that only newly exposed parts of the form are repainted.

```
Private Sub Form_Paint ()
   ' Select a random color for the background.
   BackColor = &HFFFFFF * Rnd
End Sub
```

Clone Method

Creates a duplicate **Recordset** object that refers to the original **Recordset** object.

Applies To

Dynaset-Type Recordset Object, **Recordset** Object, **Snapshot-Type Recordset** Object, **Table-Type Recordset** Object

Syntax

Set *duplicate* = *original*.**Clone**

The **Clone** method syntax has these parts.

Part	Description
duplicate	An object variable identifying the duplicate **Recordset** object you're creating.
Original	An object variable identifying the **Recordset** object you want to duplicate.

Remarks

Use the **Clone** method to create multiple, duplicate **Recordset** objects. Each **Recordset** can have its own current record. Using **Clone** by itself doesn't change the data in the objects or in their underlying structures. When you use the **Clone** method, you can share bookmarks between two or more **Recordset** objects because their bookmarks are interchangeable.

You can use the **Clone** method when you want to perform an operation on a **Recordset** that requires multiple current records. This is faster and more efficient than opening a second **Recordset**. When you create a **Recordset** with the **Clone** method, it initially lacks a current record. To make a record current before you use the **Recordset** clone, you must set the **Bookmark** property or use one of the Move methods, one of the Find methods, or the **Seek** method.

Using the **Close** method on either the original or duplicate object doesn't affect the other object. For example, using **Close** on the original **Recordset** doesn't close the clone.

Notes

- Closing a clone **Recordset** within a pending transaction will cause an implicit **Rollback** operation.
- When you clone a table-type **Recordset** object in a Microsoft Jet workspace, the **Index** property setting is not cloned on the new copy of the **Recordset**. You must copy the **Index** property setting manually.
- You can use the **Clone** method with forward-only–type **Recordset** objects only in an ODBCDirect workspace.

See Also

Bookmark Property

Example

This example uses the **Clone** method to create copies of a **Recordset** and then lets the user position the record pointer of each copy independently.

```
Sub CloneX()

    Dim dbsNorthwind As Database
    Dim arstProducts(1 To 3) As Recordset
    Dim intLoop As Integer
    Dim strMessage As String
    Dim strFind As String

    Set dbsNorthwind = OpenDatabase("Northwind.mdb")

    ' If the following SQL statement will be used often,
    ' creating a permanent QueryDef will result in better
    ' performance.
    Set arstProducts(1) = dbsNorthwind.OpenRecordset( _
        "SELECT ProductName FROM Products " & _
        "ORDER BY ProductName", dbOpenSnapshot)

    ' Create two clones of the original Recordset.
    Set arstProducts(2) = arstProducts(1).Clone
    Set arstProducts(3) = arstProducts(1).Clone

    Do While True

        ' Loop through the array so that on each pass, the
        ' user is searching a different copy of the same
        ' Recordset.
        For intLoop = 1 To 3

            ' Ask for search string while showing where the
            ' current record pointer is for each Recordset.
            strMessage = _
                "Recordsets from Products table:" & vbCr & _
                " 1 - Original - Record pointer at " & _
                arstProducts(1)!ProductName & vbCr & _
                " 2 - Clone - Record pointer at " & _
                arstProducts(2)!ProductName & vbCr & _
                " 3 - Clone - Record pointer at " & _
                arstProducts(3)!ProductName & vbCr & _
                "Enter search string for #" & intLoop & ":"
            strFind = Trim(InputBox(strMessage))
            If strFind = "" Then Exit Do

            ' Find the search string; if there's no match, jump
            ' to the last record.
            With arstProducts(intLoop)
                .FindFirst "ProductName >= '" & strFind & "'"
                If .NoMatch Then .MoveLast
            End With
        Next intLoop

    Loop

    arstProducts(1).Close
    arstProducts(2).Close
    arstProducts(3).Close
    dbsNorthwind.Close

End Sub
```

Close Method

Closes and destroys a window.

Applies To

Window Object

Syntax

object.**Close**

The *object* placeholder is an object expression that evaluates to an object in the **Applies To** list.

Remarks

The following types of windows respond to the **Close** method in different ways:

- For a window that is a code pane, **Close** destroys the code pane.
- For a window that is a designer, **Close** destroys the contained designer.
- For windows that are always available on the **View** menu, **Close** hides the window.

See Also

Add Method, **Remove** Method

Example

The following example uses the **Close** method to close a specified member of the **Windows** collection.

```
Application.VBE.Windows(9).Close
```

Close Method (DAO)

Closes an open DAO object.

Applies To

Database Object, **Dynaset-Type Recordset** Object, **QueryDef** Object, **Recordset** Object, **Snapshot-Type Recordset** Object, **Table-Type Recordset** Object, **Workspace** Object, **Connection** Object, **Forward-Only–Type Recordset** Object, **Dynamic-Type Recordset** Object

Syntax

object.**Close**

The *object* placeholder is an object variable that represents an open **Connection**, **Database**, **Recordset**, or **Workspace** object.

Remarks

Closing an open object removes it from the collection to which it's appended. Any attempt to close the default workspace is ignored.

If the **Connection**, **Database**, **Recordset**, or **Workspace** object named by *object* is already closed when you use **Close**, a run-time error occurs.

Caution If you exit a procedure that declares **Connection**, **Database**, or **Recordset** objects, those objects are closed, all pending transactions are rolled back, and any pending edits to your data are lost.

If you try to close a **Connection** or **Database** object while it has any open **Recordset** objects, the **Recordset** objects will be closed and any pending updates or edits will be canceled. Similarly, if you try to close a **Workspace** object while it has any open **Connection** or **Database** objects, those **Connection** and **Database** objects will be closed, which will close their **Recordset** objects.

Using the **Close** method on either an original or cloned **Recordset** object doesn't affect the other **Recordset** object.

To remove objects from updatable collections other than the **Connections**, **Databases**, **Recordsets**, and **Workspaces** collections, use the **Delete** method on those collections. You can't add a new member to the **Containers**, **Documents**, and **Errors** collections.

An alternative to the **Close** method is to set the value of an object variable to **Nothing** (Set dbsTemp = Nothing).

See Also

Clone Method, **Delete** Method, **OpenDatabase** Method, **OpenRecordset** Method

Example

This example uses the **Close** method on both **Recordset** and **Database** objects that have been opened. It also demonstrates how closing a **Recordset** will cause unsaved changes to be lost.

```
Sub CloseX()

    Dim dbsNorthwind As Database
    Dim rstEmployees As Recordset

    Set dbsNorthwind = OpenDatabase("Northwind.mdb")
    Set rstEmployees = _
        dbsNorthwind.OpenRecordset("Employees")

    ' Make changes to a record but close the recordset before
    ' saving the changes.
    With rstEmployees
        Debug.Print "Original data"
        Debug.Print "   Name - Extension"
        Debug.Print "   " & !FirstName & " " & _
            !LastName & " - " & !Extension
        .Edit
        !Extension = "9999"
        .Close
    End With
```

```
' Reopen Recordset to show that the data hasn't
' changed.
Set rstEmployees = _
   dbsNorthwind.OpenRecordset("Employees")

With rstEmployees
   Debug.Print "Data after Close"
   Debug.Print "    Name - Extension"
   Debug.Print "    " & !FirstName & " " & _
      !LastName & " - " & !Extension
   .Close
End With

dbsNorthwind.Close

End Sub
```

Close Method (OLE Container)

Closes an object and terminates the connection to the application that provided the object.

Applies To

OLE Container Control

Syntax

object.**Close**

The *object* is an object expression that evaluates to an object in the **Applies To** list.

Remarks

This method applies only to embedded objects and is equivalent to closing the object. It has no effect on linked objects.

Close Method (Remote Data)

Closes an open remote data object.

Applies To

rdoConnection Object, **rdoEnvironment** Object, **rdoPreparedStatement** Object, **rdoQuery** Object, **rdoResultset** Object

Syntax

object.**Close**

The *object* placeholder represents an object expression that evaluates to an object in the **Applies To** list.

Remarks

Closing an open object removes it from the collection of like objects—except for the **rdoConnection** object. For example, using the **Close** method on an **rdoResultset** removes it from the **rdoResultsets** collection. However, using the **Close** method on the **rdoConnection** object, simply closes and discards any subordinate objects (like **rdoResultset** or **rdoQuery** objects) but does not remove it from the **rdoConnections** collection.

Closing the **rdoConnection** object also releases its parent **rdoEnvironment** object. Any attempt to close the default environment **rdoEnvironments**(0) is ignored. Unlike DAO, RDO collection members cannot be removed with the **Delete** method.

If you try to close an **rdoConnection** object while any **rdoResultset** objects are open, or if you try to close an **rdoEnvironment** object while any **rdoConnection** objects belonging to that specific **rdoEnvironment** are open, those **rdoResultset** objects are closed and any pending updates or edits are rolled back.

If the **rdoConnection** object is defined outside the scope of the procedure, and you exit the procedure without closing it, the **rdoConnection** object remains open until it is explicitly closed or the module in which it is defined is out of scope. Any **rdoResultset** or **rdoQuery** objects that are opened against the **rdoConnection** remain open until explicitly closed. Once all result sets are closed on an **rdoConnection** that is no longer in scope, the **rdoConnection** is closed.

If *object* is already closed when you use **Close**, a trappable error is triggered.

Note Using the **Close** method against an executing action query might have unpredictable results. If the query is performing an operation that affects a number of rows, some of the rows might be changed, while others are not. For example, if you execute an action query containing an SQL UPDATE statement and use the **Close** method before the operation is complete, an indeterminate number of rows are updated—leaving others unchanged. If you intend to use the **Close** method against this type of action query, it is recommended that you use transaction methods to roll back or commit partially completed operations.

See Also

Delete Method (Remote Data), **OpenResultset** Method (Remote Data), **Update** Method (Remote Data)

Close Statement

Concludes input/output (I/O) to a file opened using the **Open** statement.

Syntax

Close [*filenumberlist*]

The optional *filenumberlist* argument can be one or more file numbers using the following syntax, where *filenumber* is any valid file number:

[[#]*filenumber*] [, [#]*filenumber*] . . .

Remarks

If you omit *filenumberlist*, all active files opened by the **Open** statement are closed.

When you close files that were opened for **Output** or **Append**, the final buffer of output is written to the operating system buffer for that file. All buffer space associated with the closed file is released.

When the **Close** statement is executed, the association of a file with its file number ends.

See Also

End Statement, **Stop** Statement, **Open** Statement, **Reset** Statement

Example

This example uses the **Close** statement to close all three files opened for **Output**.

```
Dim I, FileName
For I = 1 To 3 ' Loop 3 times.
   FileName = "TEST" & I' Create file name.
   Open FileName For Output As #I      ' Open file.
   Print #I, "This is a test."         ' Write string to file.
Next I
Close ' Close all 3 open files.
```

Cls Method

Clears graphics and text generated at run time from a **Form** or **PictureBox**.

Applies To

PropertyPage Object, **UserControl** Object, **UserDocument** Object, **Form** Object, **Forms** Collection, **PictureBox** Control

Syntax

object.**Cls**

The *object* placeholder represents an object expression that evaluates to an object in the **Applies To** list. If *object* is omitted, the **Form** with the focus is assumed to be *object*.

Remarks

Cls clears text and graphics generated at run time by graphics and printing statements. Background bitmaps set using the **Picture** property and controls placed on a **Form** at design time aren't affected by **Cls**. Graphics and text placed on a **Form** or **PictureBox** while the **AutoRedraw** property is set to **True** aren't affected if **AutoRedraw** is set to **False** before **Cls** is invoked. That is, you can maintain text and graphics on a **Form** or **PictureBox** by manipulating the **AutoRedraw** property of the object you're working with.

After **Cls** is invoked, the **CurrentX** and **CurrentY** properties of *object* are reset to 0.

See Also

Clear Method (Clipboard, ComboBox, ListBox), **AutoRedraw** Property, **CurrentX**, **CurrentY** Properties

Example

This example uses the **Cls** method to delete printed information from a form. To try this example, paste the code into the Declarations section of a form, and then press F5 and click the form.

```
Private Sub Form_Click ()
    Dim Msg                             ' Declare variable.
    AutoRedraw = -                      ' Turn on AutoRedraw.
    ForeColor = QBColor(15)             ' Set foreground to white.
    BackColor = QBColor(1)              ' Set background to blue.
    FillStyle = 7                       ' Set diagonal crosshatch.
    Line (0, 0)-(ScaleWidth, ScaleHeight), , B  ' Put box on form.
    Msg = "This is information printed on the form background."
    CurrentX = ScaleWidth / 2 - TextWidth(Msg) / 2  ' Set X position.
    CurrentY = 2 * TextHeight(Msg)      ' Set Y position.

    Print Msg                           ' Print message to form.
    Msg = "Choose OK to clear the information and background "
    Msg = Msg & "pattern just displayed on the form."
    MsgBox Msg                          ' Display message.
    Cls                                 ' Clear form background.
End Sub
```

Clustered Property

Sets or returns a value that indicates whether an **Index** object represents a clustered index for a table (Microsoft Jet workspaces only).

Applies To

Index Object

Settings and Return Values

The setting or return value is a **Boolean** data type that is **True** if the **Index** object represents a clustered index.

Remarks

Some IISAM desktop database formats use clustered indexes. A clustered index consists of one or more nonkey fields that, taken together, arrange all records in a table in a predefined order. A clustered index provides efficient access to records in a table in which the index values may not be unique.

The **Clustered** property is read/write for a new **Index** object not yet appended to a collection and read-only for an existing **Index** object in an **Indexes** collection.

Notes

- Microsoft Jet databases ignore the **Clustered** property because the Microsoft Jet database engine doesn't support clustered indexes.

- For ODBC data sources the **Clustered** property always returns **False**; it does not detect whether or not the ODBC data source has a clustered index.

See Also

Attributes Property, **Primary** Property, **Unique** Property

CodeLocation Property

Returns the line location in the code module where the member is defined.

Applies To

Member Object

Syntax

object.**CodeLocation** [= *propkind*]

The **CodeLocation** property syntax has these parts:

Part	Description
object	An object expression that evaluates to an object in the **Applies To** list.
propkind	An enumerated value of **vbext_PropertyKind**, as described in Settings.

Settings

The settings for **vbext_PropertyKind** are:

Constant	Value	Description
vbext_PropertyGet	1	(Default) Returns the code location for the Get element of the property.
vbext_PropertyLet	2	Returns the code location for the Let element of the property.
vbext_PropertySet	3	Returns the code location for the Set element of the property.

CodeModule Object

Represents the code behind a component, such as a form, class, or document.

Remarks

You use the **CodeModule** object to modify (add, delete, or edit) the code associated with a component.

Each component is associated with one **CodeModule** object. However, a **CodeModule** object can be associated with multiple code panes.

The methods associated with the **CodeModule** object enable you to manipulate and return information about the code text on a line-by-line basis. For example, you can use the **AddFromString** method to add text to the module. **AddFromString** places the text just above the first procedure in the module or places the text at the end of the module if there are no procedures.

Use the **Parent** property to return the **VBComponent** object associated with a code module.

Properties

CountOfLines Property, **CountOfDeclarationLines** Property, **Parent** Property, **VBE** Property, **Lines** Property, **Members** Property

Methods

AddFromFile Method, **AddFromString** Method, **CreateEventProc** Method, **DeleteLines** Method, **Find** Method, **InsertLines** Method, **Lines** Method, **ProcBodyLine** Method, **ProcCountLines** Method, **ProcOfLine** Method, **ProcStartLine** Method, **ReplaceLine** Method

See Also

VBComponent Object, **VBComponents** Collection, **CodePane** Object, **CodePanes** Collection

---

CodeModule Property

Returns an object representing the code behind the component. Read-only.

Applies To

VBComponent Object, **CodePane** Object

Remarks

The **CodeModule** property returns **Nothing** if the component doesn't have a code module associated with it.

Note   The **CodePane** object represents a visible code window. A given component can have several **CodePane** objects. The **CodeModule** object represents the code within a component. A component can only have one **CodeModule** object.

See Also

CodeModule Object

Example

The following example uses the **CodeModule** and **CountOfLines** properties to return the number of lines in a particular code module.

```
Debug.Print Application.VBE.ActiveVBProject.VBComponents(6)
↳ .CodeModule.CountOfLines
```

CodePane Object

Represents a code pane.

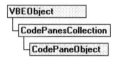

Remarks

Use the **CodePane** object to manipulate the position of visible text or the text selection displayed in the code pane.

You can use the **Show** method to make the code pane you specify visible. Use the **SetSelection** method to set the selection in a code pane and the **GetSelection** method to return the location of the selection in a code pane.

Specifics

CodePanes Collection

Properties

CodeModule Property, **CodePaneView** Property, **Collection** Property, **CountOfVisibleLines** Property, **TopLine** Property, **VBE** Property, **Window** Property

Methods

GetSelection Method, **SetSelection** Method, **Show** Method

See Also

CodeModule Object, **CodePanes** Collection

CodePane Property

Returns a **CodePane** object. Read-only.

Applies To

CodeModule Object

Remarks

If a code pane exists, it becomes the active code pane, and the window that contains it becomes the active window. If a code pane doesn't exist for the module, the **CodePane** property creates one.

Specifics

CodePanes Property

See Also

CodePane Object, **CodePanes** Collection, **ActiveCodePane** Property, **CodePanes** Property

Example

The following example uses the **ActiveCodePane** property and **TopLine** properties to obtain the number of the top line in the active code pane.

```
Debug.Print Application.VBE.ActiveCodePane.TopLine
```

CodePanes Collection

Contains the active code panes in the **VBE** object.

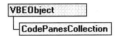

Remarks

Use the **CodePanes** collection to access the open code panes in a project.

You can use the **Count** property to return the number of active code panes in a collection.

Properties

Count Property, **Parent** Property, **VBE** Property

Methods

Item Method

See Also

CodeModule Object, **CodePane** Object, **VBE** Object

CodePanes Property

Returns the collection of active **CodePane** objects. Read-only.

Applies To

VBE Object

See Also

CodePanes Collection, **ActiveCodePane** Property

Example

The following example uses the **CodePanes** and **TopLine** properties to display the line number of the top line in the specified code pane.

```
Debug.Print Application.VBE.CodePanes(3).TopLine
```

CodePaneView Property

Returns a value indicating whether the code pane is in Procedure view or Full Module view. Read-only.

Applies To

CodePane Object

Return Values

The **CodePaneView** property return values are:

Constant	Description
vbext_cv_ProcedureView	The specified code pane is in Procedure view.
vbext_cv_FullModuleView	The specified project is in Full Module view.

Example

The following example uses the **CodePaneView** property to return a value indicating whether the specified code pane is in procedure view or full module view.

```
Debug.Print Application.VBE.CodePanes(3).CodePaneView
```

Col, Row Properties

Return or set the active cell in a **DBGrid** control. Not available at design time.

Applies To

DBGrid Control

Syntax

object.**Col** [= *number*]
object.**Row** [= *number*]

The **Col** and **Row** property syntaxes have these parts:

Part	Description
object	An object expression that evaluates to an object in the **Applies To** list.
number	The number of the column or row containing the active cell.

Remarks

Use these properties to specify a cell in a **DBGrid** control or to find out which column or row contains the active cell in a selected region. Columns and rows are numbered from zero, beginning at the top for rows and at the left for columns. Setting these properties at run time doesn't change which cells are selected. Use the **SelEndCol**, **SelStartCol**, **SelEndRow**, and **SelStartRow** properties to specify a selected region.

Note The **Col** and **Row** properties aren't the same as the **Cols** and **Rows** properties.

Specifics

Col, Row Properties

See Also

Cols, Rows Properties, **Text** Property, **SelEndCol**, **SelStartCol**, **SelEndRow**, **SelStartRow** Properties

Example

This example puts "Here" into the current cell and then changes the active cell to the third cell in the third row and puts "There" into that cell. To try this example, use the

Components dialog box to add an **MS Flex Grid** control to the toolbox (from the Project menu, choose Components, and then check Microsoft Flex Grid Control), and then draw a grid on a new form. To run the program, press F5, and then click the grid.

```
Private Sub Form_Load ()
   MSFlexGrid1.Rows = 8 ' Set rows and columns.
   MSFlexGrid1.Cols = 5
End Sub

Private Sub MSFlexGrid1_Click ()
   ' Put text in current cell.
   MSFlexGrid1.Text = "Here"
   ' Put text in third row, third column.
   MSFlexGrid1.Col = 2
   MSFlexGrid1.Row = 2
   MSFlexGrid1.Text = "There"
End Sub
```

The next example displays the location of the active cell and the range of the selection as a user selects a cell or range of cells. Notice that when selecting a range, the active cell doesn't change. Select a range, and then click the form to move the active cell around the perimeter of the selection. Notice that the selected range doesn't change.

To try this example, create a new project, add an **MS Flex Grid** control using the Components dialog box (from the Project menu, choose Components, and then check Microsoft Flex Grid Control), and then draw an **MS Flex Grid** and two labels. Copy the code into the Declarations section, and then press F5 to run the program.

```
Private Sub Form_Load ()
   MSFlexGrid1.Cols = 6 ' Set columns and rows.
   MSFlexGrid1.Rows = 7
End Sub

Private Sub MSFlexGrid1_RowColChange ()
   Msg = "Active Cell: " & Chr(64 + MSFlexGrid1.Col)
   Mst = Msg & MSFlexGrid1.Row
   Label1.Caption = Msg
End Sub

Private Sub MSFlexGrid1_SelChange ()
   Msg = "Selection: " & Chr(64 + MSFlexGrid1.SelStartCol)
   Msg = Msg & MSFlexGrid1.SelStartRow
   Msg = Msg & ":" & Chr(64 + MSFlexGrid1.SelEndCol)
   Msg = Msg & MSFlexGrid1.SelEndRow
   Label2.Caption = Msg
End Sub

Private Sub Form_Click ()
   ' This procedure moves the active cell around
   ' the perimeter of the selected range
   ' of cells with each click on the form.
   Dim GR, GC As Integer
```

```
        If MSFlexGrid1.Row = MSFlexGrid1.SelStartRow Then
            If MSFlexGrid1.Col = MSFlexGrid1.SelEndCol Then
                GR = 1: GC = 0
            Else
                GR = 0: GC = 1
            End If
        ElseIf MSFlexGrid1.Row = MSFlexGrid1.SelEndRow Then
            If MSFlexGrid1.Col = MSFlexGrid1.SelStartCol Then

GR = -1: GC = 0
            Else
                GR = 0: GC = -1
            End If
        Else
            If MSFlexGrid1.Col = MSFlexGrid1.SelStartCol Then
                GR = -1: GC = 0
            Else
                GR = 1: GC = 0
            End If
        End If
        MSFlexGrid1.Row = MSFlexGrid1.Row + GR
        MSFlexGrid1.Col = MSFlexGrid1.Col + GC
End Sub
```

ColContaining Method

Returns the **ColIndex** value of the **DBGrid** control column containing the specified coordinate (X) value. Doesn't support named arguments.

Applies To

DBGrid Control

Syntax

object.**ColContaining** *coordinate*

The **ColContaining** method syntax has these parts:

Part	Description
object	An object expression that evaluates to an object in the **Applies To** list.
coordinate	Required. A single numeric expression that defines a horizontal coordinate (X value) based on the coordinate system of the container.

Remarks

The **ColContaining** method returns a number that corresponds to one of the column indexes of the control specified by *object*. This number ranges from 0 to 1 less than the setting of the **Count** property of the **Columns** collection (0 to **Columns.Count**-1). This method is useful when working with mouse and drag events when you are trying to determine where the user clicked or dropped another control in terms of a column of the **DBGrid** control.

If *coordinate* is outside of the coordinate system of the container, a trappable error occurs.

Note The **ColContaining** method returns the **ColIndex** of the column indicated, not the visible column. If *coordinate* falls in the first visible column, but two columns have been scrolled off the left side of the control, the **ColContaining** method returns 2.

See Also

Data Control, **Column** Object, **RowContaining** Method, **ColIndex** Property

Example

This example saves the value of the cell where the user began a drag method.

```
Dim SaveValue
Sub DBGrid1_MouseDown (Button As Integer, Shift As Integer, _
 X As Single, Y As Single)
    Dim RowValue, ColValue
    ' Get the value of the row and column that the mouse is over
    RowValue = DBGrid1.RowContaining(Y)
    ColValue = DBGrid1.ColContaining(X)
    ' If the values are both valid, save the text of the cell and
    ' begin dragging.
    If RowValue > 0 And RowValue < DBGrid1.VisibleRows And _
     ColValue > 0 And ColValue < DBGrid1.VisibleCols Then

SaveValue = DBGrid1.Columns(ColValue). _
    CellValue(DBGrid1.RowBookmark(RowValue))
        DBGrid1.Drag 1
    End If
End Sub
```

ColEdit Event

Occurs when a cell first enters edit mode by typing a character.

Applies To

DBGrid Control

Syntax

Private Sub *object*_**ColEdit**([*index* **As Integer**,] **ByVal** *colindex* **As Integer**)

The **ColEdit** event syntax has these parts:

Part	Description
object	An object expression that evaluates to an object in the **Applies To** list.
Index	An integer that identifies a control if it is in a control array.
colindex	An integer that identifies the column being edited.

Remarks

If a floating editor marquee is not in use, this event also occurs when the user clicks the current cell or double clicks another cell.

The **ColEdit** event immediately follows the **BeforeColEdit** event only when the latter is not canceled.

When the user completes editing within a grid cell, as when tabbing to another column in the same row, pressing the ENTER key, or clicking on another cell, the **BeforeColUpdate** and **AfterColUpdate** events are executed if the data has been changed. The **AfterColEdit** event is then fired to indicate that editing is completed.

See Also

AfterColEdit Event, **BeforeColEdit** Event, **AfterColUpdate** Event

ColIndex Property

Returns a value indicating the position of the column in the **Columns** collection of the **DBGrid** control and the visible position (left-to-right) of the column in the **DBGrid** control. This property is read-only at run time and not available at design time.

Applies To

Column Object

Syntax

object.**ColIndex** [= *value*]

The **ColIndex** property syntax has these parts:

Part	Description
object	An object expression that evaluates to an object in the **Applies To** list.
value	An integer ranging from 0 (the column furthest to the left) to the setting of the **Count** property.

Remarks

This property returns the zero-based index of a column within the **Columns** collection.

See Also

Data Control, **Column** Object, **DBGrid** Control

CollatingOrder Property

Returns a value that specifies the sequence of the sort order in text for string comparison or sorting (Microsoft Jet workspaces only).

Applies To

Database Object, **Field** Object

Return Values

The return value is a **Long** value or constant that can be one of the following values.

Constant	Sort order
dbSortGeneral	General (English, French, German, Portuguese, Italian, and Modern Spanish)
dbSortArabic	Arabic
dbSortChineseSimplified	Simplified Chinese
dbSortChineseTraditional	Traditional Chinese
dbSortCyrillic	Russian
dbSortCzech	Czech
dbSortDutch	Dutch
dbSortGreek	Greek
dbSortHebrew	Hebrew
dbSortHungarian	Hungarian
dbSortIcelandic	Icelandic
dbSortJapanese	Japanese
dbSortKorean	Korean
dbSortNeutral	Neutral
dbSortNorwDan	Norwegian or Danish
dbSortPDXIntl	Paradox International
dbSortPDXNor	Paradox Norwegian or Danish
dbSortPDXSwe	Paradox Swedish or Finnish
dbSortPolish	Polish
dbSortSlovenian	Slovenian
dbSortSpanish	Spanish
dbSortSwedFin	Swedish or Finnish
dbSortThai	Thai
dbSortTurkish	Turkish
dbSortUndefined	Undefined or unknown

Remarks

The availability of the **CollatingOrder** property depends on the object that contains the **Fields** collection, as shown in the following table.

If the Fields collection belongs to an	Then CollatingOrder is
Index object	Not supported
QueryDef object	Read-only
Recordset object	Read-only
Relation object	Not supported
TableDef object	Read-only

The **CollatingOrder** property setting corresponds to the *locale* argument of the **CreateDatabase** method when the database was created or the **CompactDatabase** method when the database was most recently compacted.

Check the **CollatingOrder** property setting of a **Database** or **Field** object to determine the string comparison method for the database or field. You can set the **CollatingOrder** property of a new, unappended **Field** object if you want the setting
of the **Field** object to differ from that of the **Database** object that contains it.

The **CollatingOrder** and **Attributes** property settings of a **Field** object in a **Fields** collection of an **Index** object together determine the sequence and direction of the sort order in an index. However, you can't set a collating order for an individual index—youcan only set it for an entire table.

See Also

Attributes Property

Example

This example displays the **CollatingOrder** property for the Northwind database and for individual fields in a table.

```
Sub CollatingOrderX()

    Dim dbsNorthwind As Database
    Dim fldLoop As Field

    Set dbsNorthwind = OpenDatabase("Northwind.mdb")

    With dbsNorthwind
        ' Show collating order of Northwind database.
        Debug.Print "Collating order of " & .Name & " = " & _
            .CollatingOrder

        ' Show collating order of a TableDef object's fields.
        Debug.Print "Collating order of fields in " & _
            .TableDefs(0).Name & " table:"
        For Each fldLoop In .TableDefs(0).Fields
            Debug.Print "    " & fldLoop.Name & " = " & _
                fldLoop.CollatingOrder
        Next fldLoop

        .Close
    End With

End Sub
```

Collection Object

A **Collection** object is an ordered set of items that can be referred to as a unit.

Remarks

The **Collection** object provides a convenient way to refer to a related group of items as a single object. The items, or members, in a collection need only be related by the fact that they exist in the collection. Members of a collection don't have to share the same data type.

A collection can be created the same way other objects are created. For example:

```
Dim X As New Collection
```

Once a collection is created, members can be added using the **Add** method and removed using the **Remove** method. Specific members can be returned from the collection using the **Item** method, while the entire collection can be iterated using the **For Each...Next** statement.

Properties

Count Property

Methods

Add Method, **Item** Method, **Remove** Method

See Also

For Each...Next Statement, **Add** Method, **Item** Method, **Remove** Method

Example

This example creates a **Collection** object (MyClasses), and then creates a dialog box in which users can add objects to the collection. To see how this works, choose the **Class Module** command from the **Insert** menu and declare a public variable called InstanceName at module level of Class1 (type **Public** InstanceName) to hold the names of each instance. Leave the default name as Class1. Copy and paste the following code into the General section of another module, and then start it with the statement ClassNamer in another procedure. (This example only works with host applications that support classes.)

```
Sub ClassNamer()
    Dim MyClasses As New Collection      ' Create a Collection object.
    Dim Num                              ' Counter for individualizing keys.
    Dim Msg As String ' Variable to hold prompt string.
    Dim TheName, MyObject, NameList      ' Variants to hold information.
    Do
        Dim Inst As New Class1           ' Create a new instance of Class1.
        Num = Num + 1                    ' Increment Num, then get a name.
```

```
          Msg = "Please enter a name for this object." & Chr(13) _
            & "Press Cancel to see names in collection."
          TheName = InputBox(Msg, "Name the Collection Items")
          Inst.InstanceName = TheName      ' Put name in object instance.
          ' If user entered name, add it to the collection.
          If Inst.InstanceName <> "" Then
          ' Add the named object to the collection.
             MyClasses.Add item := Inst, key := CStr(Num)
          End If
          ' Clear the current reference in preparation for next one.
          Set Inst = Nothing
       Loop Until TheName = ""
       For Each MyObject In MyClasses      ' Create list of names.
          NameList = NameList & MyObject.InstanceName & Chr(13)
       Next MyObject
       ' Display the list of names in a message box.
       MsgBox NameList, , "Instance Names In MyClasses Collection"

       For Num = 1 To MyClasses.Count      ' Remove name from the collection.
          MyClasses.Remove 1               ' Since collections are reindexed
                                           ' automatically, remove the first
       Next                                ' member on each iteration.
    End Sub
```

Collection Property

Returns the collection that contains the object you are working with.
Read-only.

Applies To

AddIn Object, **VBComponent** Object, **CodePane** Object, **Property** Object,
Reference Object, **VBProject** Object, **Window** Object

Remarks

Most objects in this object model have either a **Parent** property or a **Collection**
property that points to the object's parent object.

Use the **Collection** property to access the properties, methods, and controls of
the collection to which the object belongs.

See Also

Parent Property

Example

The following example uses the **Collection** and **Count** properties to return
the number of objects the active project contains, when viewed as a collection
of objects.

```
Debug.Print Application.VBE.ActiveVBProject.Collection.Count
```

ColorMode Property

Returns or sets a value that determines whether a color printer prints output in color or monochrome. Not available at design time.

Applies To

Printer Object, Printers Collection

Syntax

object.**ColorMode** [= *value*]

The **ColorMode** property syntax has these parts:

Part	Description
object	An object expression that evaluates to an object in the **Applies To** list.
value	A constant or integer that specifies the print mode, as described in Settings.

Settings

The settings for *value* are:

Setting	Value	Description
vbPRCMMonochrome	1	Print output in monochrome (usually shades of black and white).
vbPRCMColor	2	Print output in color.

Remarks

The default value depends on the printer driver and the current printer settings. Monochrome printers ignore this property.

Note The effect of the properties of the **Printer** object depends on the driver supplied by the printer manufacturer. Some property settings may have no effect, or several different property settings may all have the same effect. If you set the **ColorMode** property for a printer which doesn't support color, the setting is ignored. If you attempt to reference the **ColorMode** property, however, you will get an error message. Settings outside the accepted range may also produce an error. For more information, see the manufacturer's documentation for the specific driver.

See Also

Printer Object**, Printers** Collection

ColResize Event

Occurs when a user resizes a column of a **DBGrid** control.

Applies To

DBGrid Control

Syntax

Private Sub *object*_**ColResize** ([*index* **As Integer**,] *colindex* **As Integer**, *cancel* **As Integer**)

The **ColResize** event syntax has these parts:

Part	Description
object	An object expression that evaluates to an object in the **Applies To** list.
index	An integer that identifies a control if it is in a control array.
colindex	An integer that identifies the column.
cancel	A Boolean expression that determines whether a column is resized, as described in Settings.

Settings

The settings for *cancel* are:

Setting	Description
True	Cancels the change, restores column to its original width.
False	(Default) Continues with width change.

Remarks

When the user resizes a column, the **ColResize** event is triggered. Your event procedure can accept the change, alter the degree of change, or cancel the change completely.

If you set the *cancel* argument to **True**, the column width is restored. To alter the degree of change, set the **Width** property of the **Column** object to the desired value.

Executing the **Refresh** method within the procedure causes the control to be repainted even if the *cancel* argument is **True**.

See Also

RowResize Event, **ColIndex** Property

Example

This example resizes all the columns to the size of the first column if the user sizes the first column.

```
Private Sub DataGrid1_ColResize (ColIndex As Integer, Cancel As Integer)
    Dim nCol As Column
    If ColIndex = 1 Then
        For Each nCol In DataGrid1.Columns
            nCol.Width = DataGrid.Columns(1).Width
        Next
    End If
End Sub
```

Cols, Rows Properties

Return or set the total number of columns or rows in a **DBGrid** control.

Syntax

object.**Cols** [= *number*]
object.**Rows** [= *number*]

The **Cols** and **Rows** property syntaxes have these parts:

Part	Description
object	An object expression that evaluates to an object in the **Applies To** list.
number	The number of columns or rows in a **DBGrid** control. The minimum number of columns is 1, the maximum is 400; the minimum number of rows is 1, the maximum is 2000.

Remarks

Use these properties to expand a **DBGrid** control dynamically at run time. A **DBGrid** control must have at least one non-fixed column and one non-fixed row.

Note   The **Cols** and **Rows** properties aren't the same as the **Col** and **Row** properties.

See Also

Col, **Row** Properties

Example

This example puts "Here" into the current cell and then changes the active cell to the third cell in the third row and puts "There" into that cell. To try this example, use the Components dialog box to add an **MS Flex Grid** control to the toolbox (from the Project menu, choose Components, and then check Microsoft Flex Grid Control), and then draw a grid on a new form. To run the program, press F5, and then click the grid.

```
Private Sub Form_Load ()
   MSFlexGrid1.Rows = 8 ' Set rows and columns.
   MSFlexGrid1.Cols = 5
End Sub

Private Sub MSFlexGrid1_Click ()
   ' Put text in current cell.
   MSFlexGrid1.Text = "Here"
   ' Put text in third row, third column.
   MSFlexGrid1.Col = 2
   MSFlexGrid1.Row = 2
   MSFlexGrid1.Text = "There"
End Sub
```

The next example displays the location of the active cell and the range of the selection as a user selects a cell or range of cells. Notice that when selecting a range, the active cell doesn't change. Select a range, and then click the form to move the active cell around the perimeter of the selection. Notice that the selected range doesn't change.

To try this example, create a new project, add an **MS Flex Grid** control using the Components dialog box (from the Project menu, choose Components, and then check Microsoft Flex Grid Control), and then draw an **MS Flex Grid** and two labels. Copy the code into the Declarations section, and then press F5 to run the program.

```
Private Sub Form_Load ()
    MSFlexGrid1.Cols = 6 ' Set columns and rows.
    MSFlexGrid1.Rows = 7
End Sub

Private Sub MSFlexGrid1_RowColChange ()
    Msg = "Active Cell: " & Chr(64 + MSFlexGrid1.Col)
    Mst = Msg & MSFlexGrid1.Row
    Label1.Caption = Msg
End Sub

Private Sub MSFlexGrid1_SelChange ()
    Msg = "Selection: " & Chr(64 + MSFlexGrid1.SelStartCol)
    Msg = Msg & MSFlexGrid1.SelStartRow
    Msg = Msg & ":" & Chr(64 + MSFlexGrid1.SelEndCol)
    Msg = Msg & MSFlexGrid1.SelEndRow
    Label2.Caption = Msg
End Sub

Private Sub Form_Click ()
    ' This procedure moves the active cell around
    ' the perimeter of the selected range
    ' of cells with each click on the form.
    Dim GR, GC As Integer
    If MSFlexGrid1.Row = MSFlexGrid1.SelStartRow Then
        If MSFlexGrid1.Col = MSFlexGrid1.SelEndCol Then
            GR = 1: GC = 0
        Else
            GR = 0: GC = 1
        End If
    ElseIf MSFlexGrid1.Row = MSFlexGrid1.SelEndRow Then
        If MSFlexGrid1.Col = MSFlexGrid1.SelStartCol Then

GR = -1: GC = 0
        Else
            GR = 0: GC = -1
        End If
    Else
        If MSFlexGrid1.Col = MSFlexGrid1.SelStartCol Then
            GR = -1: GC = 0
        Else
            GR = 1: GC = 0
        End If
    End If
    MSFlexGrid1.Row = MSFlexGrid1.Row + GR
    MSFlexGrid1.Col = MSFlexGrid1.Col + GC
End Sub
```

Column Object

A **Column** object represents a column within a **DBGrid** control.

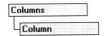

Remarks

You manipulate a column in a **DBGrid** control by using a **Column** object's methods and properties. With a **Column** object, you can modify attributes of the column header as well as the column itself.

To use a **Column** object, you can either use the **Columns** property of the **DBGrid** control directly or assign each column to a separate variable dimensioned as a **Column** object. The following demonstrates the latter:

```
Dim Col1, Col2 as Column
Set Col1 = DBGrid1.Columns(0)
Set Col2 = DBGrid1.Columns(1)
Col1.Caption = "Column 1"
Col2.Caption = "Column 2"
```

If often referring to the columns in a **DBGrid** control, you will increase performance by using the above method to assign values to columns rather than using the **Columns** property as in:

```
DBGrid1.Columns(0).Caption = "Column 1"
```

Properties

Alignment Property, **Button** Property (Column Object), **Caption** Property, **Height, Width** Properties, **Left, Top** Properties, **Left, Top** Properties (ActiveX Controls), **WrapText** Property (Column Object), **DataChanged** Property, **DataField** Property, **AllowSizing** Property, **ColIndex** Property, **DividerStyle** Property, **NumberFormat** Property, **DefaultValue** Property (DBGrid Control), **Locked** Property, **NumberFormat** Property, **Object** Property (ActiveX Controls), **Text Property** (ActiveX Controls), **Visible** Property (ActiveX Controls)

Methods

CellText Method, **CellValue** Method

See Also

Columns Collection, **DBGrid** Control

ColumnCount Property

Returns the number of columns present in a **RowBuffer** object in an unbound **DBGrid** control.

Applies To

RowBuffer Object

Syntax

object.**ColumnCount**

The *object* placeholder represents an object expression that evaluates to an object in the **Applies To** list.

See Also

ColumnName Property, **RowCount** Property, **DBGrid** Control

---

ColumnHeaders Property

Returns or sets a value indicating whether the column headers are displayed in a **DBGrid** control.

Applies To

DBGrid Control

Syntax

object.**ColumnHeaders** [= *value*]

The **ColumnHeaders** property syntax has these parts:

Part	Description
object	An object expression that evaluates to an object in the **Applies To** list.
value	A Boolean expression that determines whether column headers are displayed, as described in **Settings**.

Settings

The settings for *value* are:

Setting	Description
True	**DBGrid** control's column headers are displayed
False	**DBGrid** control's column headers aren't displayed

See Also

Data Control, **Column** Object, **Columns** Property (DBGrid)

ColumnName Property

Returns the name of the specified column within a **RowBuffer** object in an unbound **DBGrid** control.

Applies To

RowBuffer Object, **DBGrid** Control

Syntax

object.**ColumnName** (*column*)

The **ColumnName** property syntax has these parts:

Part	Description
object	An object expression that evaluates to an object in the **Applies To** list.
column	A string specifying the column for which you want the name.

Remarks

Enables you to obtain the name of a specified column.

See Also

UnboundAddData Event, **UnboundReadData** Event, **UnboundWriteData** Event, **Bookmark** Property (DBGrid), **RowCount** Property

---

Columns Collection

The **Columns** collection contains all stored **Column** objects of a **DBGrid** control.

```
Columns
  └─Column
```

Syntax

Columns(*index*)
Columns.Item(*index*)

Remarks

You can use the properties and methods of the **Columns** collection to add and remove **Column** objects, count the number of columns in the **Columns** collection, and address individual columns of the **Columns** collection.

The **Columns** collection can be accessed through the **Columns** property of the **DBGrid** control.

Properties

Count Property (Visual Basic for Applications)

Methods

> **Add** Method (Columns, SelBookmarks, Splits Collections), **Item** Method, **Remove** Method (DBGrid)

See Also

> **Column** Object, **DBGrid** Control

Columns Property (DBGrid)

> Returns a collection of **Column** objects.

Applies To

> **Split** Object, **DBGrid** Control

Syntax

> *object*.**Columns**
>
> The *object* placeholder represents an object expression that evaluates to an object in the **Applies To** list.

Remarks

> The **Columns** property returns a collection of **Column** objects in a **Variant**.
>
> You can manipulate most of a **DBGrid** control's attributes by changing the properties of **Column** objects. Choose a specific **Column** object with the **Col** property.

See Also

> **Data** Control, **Column** Object, **Add** Method (Columns, SelBookmarks, Splits Collections)

Columns Property (ListBox)

> Returns or sets a value that determines whether a **ListBox** control scrolls vertically or horizontally and how the items in the columns are displayed. If it scrolls horizontally, the **Columns** property determines how many columns are displayed.

Applies To

> **ListBox** Control

Syntax

> *object*.**Columns** [= *number*]
>
> The **Columns** property syntax has these parts:

Part	Description
object	An object expression that evaluates to an object in the **Applies To** list.
number	An integer that specifies how a control scrolls and how items are arranged in columns, as described in Settings.

Settings

The settings for *number* are:

Setting	Description
0	(Default) Items are arranged in a single column and the **ListBox** scrolls vertically.
1 to *n*	Items are arranged in snaking columns, filling the first column, then the second column, and so on. The **ListBox** scrolls horizontally and displays the specified number of columns.

Remarks

For horizontal-scrolling **ListBox** controls, the column width is equal to the width of the **ListBox** divided by the number of columns.

This property can't be set to 0 or changed from 0 at run time—that is, you can't change a multiple-column **ListBox** to a single-column **ListBox** or a single-column **ListBox** to a multiple-column **ListBox** at run time. However, you can change the number of columns in a multiple-column **ListBox** at run time.

See Also

AddItem Method, **RemoveItem** Method, **List** Property, **ListCount** Property, **ListIndex** Property, **TopIndex** Property

Example

This example illustrates how the two different kinds of **ListBox** controls work when they contain the same data. To try this example, paste the code into the Declarations section of a form that contains two **ListBox** controls. Set the **Columns** property to 2 for List2, and then press F5 and click the form.

```
Private Sub Form_Load ()
   Dim I ' Declare variable.
   List1.Move 50, 50, 2000, 1750      ' Arrange list boxes.
   List2.Move 2500, 50, 3000, 1750
   For I = 0 To Screen.FontCount -1   ' Fill both boxes with
      List1.AddItem Screen.Fonts(I)   ' names of screen fonts.
      List2.AddItem Screen.Fonts(I)
   Next I
End Sub
```

ColumnSize Method (Remote Data)

Returns the number of bytes in an **rdoColumn** object with a data type of **rdTypeLONGVARBINARY** or **rdTypeLONGVARCHAR**.

Applies To

rdoColumn Object

Syntax

varname = *object* **!** *column*.**ColumnSize( )**

The **ColumnSize** method syntax has these parts:

Part	Description
varname	The name of a **Long** or **Variant** variable.
object	An object expression that evaluates to the **rdoResultset** object containing the **rdoColumns** collection.
column	The name of an **rdoColumn** object whose **ChunkRequired** property is set to **True**.

Remarks

Depending on the driver being used, the **ColumnSize** method either returns the size of a binary large object (BLOB) column, or -1 if the size is not available. If the BLOB column size is not available, you can still use the **GetChunk** method to read chunks of data from your BLOB column. The last block has been fetched when the value returned by **GetChunk** is smaller than the size requested (for binary data), at least two bytes smaller than your buffer (for character data), or returns a NULL value.

When working with data types that span multiple database pages, you should use the *chunk* methods to manage the data—but this is not an absolute requirement. You should also use the **GetChunk** and **AppendChunk** methods to manage *chunk* data when the **ChunkRequired** property is **True**. Note that when the size of BLOB data columns is smaller than the **BindThreshold**, it is not necessary to use the chunk methods.

Use the **ColumnSize** method to determine the size of *chunk* columns.

Because the size of a *chunk* data column can exceed 64K, you should assign the value returned by the **GetChunk** method to a variable large enough to store the data returned based on the size returned by the **ColumnSize** method.

Note To determine the size of a non-*chunk* **rdoColumn** object, use the **Size** property.

See Also

AppendChunk Method (Remote Data), **AppendChunk**, **GetChunk Method** Example, **GetChunk** Method (Remote Data), **rdoColumn** Object, **rdoResultset** Object, **BindThreshold** Property, **ChunkRequired** Property (Remote Data), **Size** Property (Remote Data), **Type** Property (Remote Data)

Example

This example illustrates use of the **AppendChunk** and **GetChunk** methods to write page-based binary large object (BLOB) data to a remote data source. The code expects a table with a char, text, and image field named *Chunks*. To create this table, submit the following as an action query against your test database:

```
CREATE TABLE Chunks (ID integer identity NOT NULL, PName char(10) NULL,
Description TEXT NULL,
Photo IMAGE NULL)
CREATE UNIQUE INDEX ChunkIDIndex on Chunks(ID)
```

Once the table is created, you will need to locate one or more .BMP or other suitable graphics images that can be loaded by the **PictureBox** control.

```
'
Option Explicit
Dim en As rdoEnvironment
Dim Qd As rdoQuery
Dim Cn As rdoConnection
Dim Rs As rdoResultset
Dim SQL As String
Dim DataFile As Integer, Fl As Long, Chunks As Integer
Dim Fragment As Integer, Chunk() As Byte, I As Integer
Const ChunkSize As Integer = 16384

Private Sub Form_Load()
Set en = rdoEnvironments(0)
Set Cn = en.OpenConnection(dsname:="", _
Connect:="UID=;PWD=;DATABASE=WorkDB;" _
& "Driver={SQL Server};SERVER=Betav486", _
prompt:=rdDriverNoPrompt)

Set Qd = Cn.CreateQuery("TestChunk", "Select * from Chunks Where PName = ?")
End Sub
Private Sub LoadFromFile_Click()
'
'   Locates a file and sets the Filename to this file.
'
With CommonDialog1
.Filter = "Pictures(*.bmp;*.ico)|*.bmp;*.ico"
.ShowOpen
FileName = .FileName
End With
End Sub

Private Sub ReadFromDB_Click()
If Len(NameWanted) = 0 Then _
NameWanted = InputBox("Enter name wanted", "Animal")
Qd(0) = NameWanted
Set Rs = Qd.OpenResultset(rdOpenKeyset, rdConcurRowver)

If Rs Is Nothing Or Rs.Updatable = False Then
MsgBox "Can't open or write to result set"
Exit Sub
End If
If Rs.EOF Then
MsgBox "Can't find picture by that name"
Exit Sub
End If
Description = Rs!Description
DataFile = 1
Open "pictemp" For Binary Access Write As DataFile
Fl = Rs!Photo.ColumnSize
Chunks = Fl \ ChunkSize
Fragment = Fl Mod ChunkSize
ReDim Chunk(Fragment)
Chunk() = Rs!Photo.GetChunk(Fragment)
```

```
            Put DataFile, , Chunk()
            For I = 1 To Chunks

            ReDim Buffer(ChunkSize)
            Chunk() = Rs!Photo.GetChunk(ChunkSize)
            Put DataFile, , Chunk()
            Next I
            Close DataFile
            FileName = "pictemp"
            End Sub

            Private Sub SaveToDB_Click()
            If Len(NameWanted) = 0 Then _
            NameWanted = InputBox("Enter name for this" _
            & " picture", "Animal")
            Qd(0) = NameWanted
            Set Rs = Qd.OpenResultset(rdOpenKeyset, _
            rdConcurRowver)
            If Rs Is Nothing Or Rs.Updatable = False Then
            MsgBox "Can't open or write to result set"
            Exit Sub
            End If

            If Rs.EOF Then
            Rs.AddNew
            Rs!PName = NameWanted
            If Description = "" Then _
            Description = InputBox("Describe the picture", _
            "Don't care")
            'Rs!Description = Description
            Else
            Rs.Edit
            End If
            DataFile = 1
            Open FileName For Binary Access Read As DataFile
            Fl = LOF(DataFile)    ' Length of data in file
            If Fl = 0 Then Close DataFile: Exit Sub
            Chunks = Fl \ ChunkSize
            Fragment = Fl Mod ChunkSize
            Rs!Photo.AppendChunk Null
            ReDim Chunk(Fragment)
            Get DataFile, , Chunk()

            Rs!Photo.AppendChunk Chunk()
            ReDim Chunk(ChunkSize)
            For I = 1 To Chunks
            Get DataFile, , Chunk()
            Rs!Photo.AppendChunk Chunk()
            Next I
            Close DataFile
            Rs.Update
            End Sub

            Private Sub FileName_Change()
            Picture1.Picture = LoadPicture(FileName)
            End Sub
```

ComboBox Control

A **ComboBox** control combines the features of a **TextBox** control and a **ListBox** control—users can enter information in the text box portion or select an item from the list box portion of the control.

Syntax

ComboBox

Remarks

To add or delete items in a **ComboBox** control, use the **AddItem** or **RemoveItem** method. Set the **List**, **ListCount**, and **ListIndex** properties to enable a user to access items in the **ComboBox**. Alternatively, you can add items to the list by using the **List** property at design time.

Note A Scroll event will occur in a **ComboBox** control only when the contents of the dropdown portion of the **ComboBox** are scrolled, not each time the contents of the **ComboBox** change. For example, if the dropdown portion of a **ComboBox** contains five items and the top item is highlighted, a Scroll event will not occur until you press the down arrow six times (or the PGDN key once). After that, a Scroll event occurs for each press of the down arrow key. However, if you then press the up arrow key, a Scroll event will not occur until you press the up arrow key six times (or the PGUP key once). After that, each up arrow key press will result in a Scroll event.

Properties

OLEDragMode Property, **OLEDropMode** Property, **BackColor, ForeColor** Properties, **FontBold, FontItalic, FontStrikethru, FontUnderline** Properties, **FontName** Property, **FontSize** Property, **Height, Width** Properties, **Left, Top** Properties, **List** Property, **ListCount** Property, **ListIndex** Property, **Sorted** Property, **TabIndex** Property, **Tag** Property, **Text** Property, **Visible** Property, **DragIcon** Property, **DragMode** Property, **hWnd** Property, **ItemData** Property, **Locked** Property, **MouseIcon** Property, **MousePointer** Property, **NewIndex** Property, **SelLength, SelStart, SelText** Properties, **Style** Property, **TabStop** Property, **TopIndex** Property, **Appearance** Property, **Enabled** Property, **HelpContextID** Property, **Index** Property (Control Array), **Name** Property, **Parent** Property, **Font** Property, **Container** Property, **ToolTipText** Property, **WhatsThisHelpID** Property, **DataChanged** Property, **DataField** Property, **IntegralHeight** Property, **ItemData** Property, **Sorted** Property

Methods

Refresh Method, **SetFocus** Method, **AddItem** Method, **Clear** Method (Clipboard, ComboBox, ListBox), **Drag** Method, **Move** Method, **RemoveItem** Method, **ZOrder** Method, **OLEDrag** Method, **ShowWhatsThis** Method

See Also

ListBox Control, **TextBox** Control

Command Function

Returns the argument portion of the command line used to launch Microsoft Visual Basic or an executable program developed with Visual Basic.

Syntax

Command

Remarks

When Visual Basic is launched from the command line, any portion of the command line that follows /cmd is passed to the program as the command-line argument. In the following example, cmdlineargs represents the argument information returned by the **Command** function.

```
VB /cmd cmdlineargs
```

For applications developed with Visual Basic and compiled to an .exe file, **Command** returns any arguments that appear after the name of the application on the command line. For example:

```
MyApp cmdlineargs
```

To find how command line arguments can be changed in the user interface of the application you're using, search Help for "command line arguments."

Example

This example uses the **Command** function to get the command line arguments in a function that returns them in a **Variant** containing an array.

```
Function GetCommandLine(Optional MaxArgs)
    'Declare variables.
    Dim C, CmdLine, CmdLnLen, InArg, I, NumArgs
    'See if MaxArgs was provided.
    If IsMissing(MaxArgs) Then MaxArgs = 10
    'Make array of the correct size.
    ReDim ArgArray(MaxArgs)
    NumArgs = 0: InArg = False
    'Get command line arguments.
    CmdLine = Command()
    CmdLnLen = Len(CmdLine)
    'Go thru command line one character
    'at a time.
    For I = 1 To CmdLnLen
        C = Mid(CmdLine, I, 1)
        'Test for space or tab.
        If (C <> " " And C <> vbTab) Then
            'Neither space nor tab.
            'Test if already in argument.
            If Not InArg Then
            'New argument begins.
            'Test for too many arguments.
```

```
            If NumArgs = MaxArgs Then Exit For
            NumArgs = NumArgs + 1
            InArg = True
        End If
        'Concatenate character to current argument.
        ArgArray(NumArgs) = ArgArray(NumArgs) & C
    Else
        'Found a space or tab.
        'Set InArg flag to False.
        InArg = False
    End If
Next I
'Resize array just enough to hold arguments.
ReDim Preserve ArgArray(NumArgs)
'Return Array in Function name.
GetCommandLine = ArgArray()
End Function
```

CommandBar Object

The **CommandBar** object contains other **CommandBar** objects which can act as either buttons or menu commands.

Syntax

CommandBar

CommandBarEvents Object

Returned by the **CommandBarEvents** property. The **CommandBarEvents** object triggers an event when a control on the command bar is clicked.

Remarks

The **CommandBarEvents** object is returned by the **CommandBarEvents** property of the **Events** object. The object that is returned has one event in its interface, the **Click** event. You can handle this event using the **WithEvents** object declaration.

Events

Click Event

See Also

CommandBars Collection, **Events** Object

CommandBarEvents Property

Returns the **CommandBarEvents** object. Read-only.

Applies To

Events Object

Settings

The setting for the argument you pass to the **CommandBarEvents** property is:

Argument	Description
vbcontrol	Must be an object of type **CommandBarControl**.

Remarks

Use the **CommandBarEvents** property to return an event source object that triggers an event when a command bar button is clicked. The argument passed to the **CommandBarEvents** property is the command bar control for which the **Click** event will be triggered.

See Also

Click Event, **CommandBarEvents** Object, **CommandBars** Collection, **ReferencesEvents** Property

Example

The following example uses code including the **CommandBarEvents** property to support any code to handle a mouse click on a command bar.

```
Private WithEvents ce As CommandBarEvents

Sub Test()
    Dim c As CommandBarControl
    Set c = Application.VBE.CommandBars("Tools").Controls(1)
    Set ce = Application.VBE.Events.CommandBarEvents(c)
End Sub

Private Sub ce_Click(ByVal CommandBarControl As Object,
Handled As Boolean, CancelDefault As Boolean)
    ' Put event-handling code here
End Sub
```

CommandBars Collection

Contains all of the command bars in a project, including command bars that support shortcut menus.

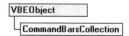

Remarks

Use the **CommandBars** collection to enable add-ins to add command bars and controls or to add controls to existing, built-in, command bars.

See Also

CommandBarEvents Object, **Events** Object, **CommandBarEvents** Property

CommandButton Control

Use a **CommandButton** control to begin, interrupt, or end a process. When chosen, a **CommandButton** appears pushed in and so is sometimes called a push button.

Syntax

CommandButton

Remarks

To display text on a **CommandButton** control, set its **Caption** property. A user can always choose a **CommandButton** by clicking it. To allow the user to choose it by pressing ENTER, set the **Default** property to **True**. To allow the user to choose the button by pressing ESC, set the **Cancel** property of the **CommandButton** to **True**.

Properties

OLEDropMode Property, **BackColor, ForeColor** Properties, **Cancel** Property, **FontBold, FontItalic, FontStrikethru, FontUnderline** Properties, **FontName** Property, **FontSize** Property, **Height, Width** Properties, **Left, Top** Properties, **Picture** Property, **TabIndex** Property, **Tag** Property, **Value** Property, **Visible** Property, **Default** Property, **DragIcon** Property, **DragMode** Property, **hWnd** Property, **MouseIcon** Property, **MousePointer** Property, **Style** Property, **TabStop** Property, **Appearance** Property, **Caption** Property, **Enabled** Property, **HelpContextID** Property, **Index** Property (Control Array), **Name** Property, **Parent** Property, **Font** Property, **Container** Property, **ToolTipText** Property, **DisabledPicture** Property, **DownPicture** Property, **MaskColor** Property, **UseMaskColor** Property, **WhatsThisHelpID** Property

Events

Click Event, **DragDrop** Event, **DragOver** Event, **GotFocus** Event, **KeyDown, KeyUp** Events, **KeyPress** Event, **LostFocus** Event, **MouseDown, MouseUp** Events, **MouseMove** Event, **OLECompleteDrag** Event, **OLEDragDrop** Event, **OLEDragOver** Event, **OLEGiveFeedback** Event, **OLESetData** Event, **OLEStartDrag** Event

Methods

Refresh Method, **SetFocus** Method, **Drag** Method, **Move** Method, **ZOrder** Method, **OLEDrag** Method, **ShowWhatsThis** Method

See Also

Cancel Property, **Default** Property, **Caption** Property

Comments Property

Returns or sets a string containing comments about the running application. Read-only at run time.

Applies To

App Object

Syntax

object.**Comments**

The *object* placeholder represents an object expression that evaluates to an object in the **Applies To** list.

Remarks

You can set this property at design time in the **Type** box in the **Make** tab of the **Project Properties** dialog box.

See Also

CompanyName Property, **FileDescription** Property, **LegalCopyright** Property, **LegalTrademarks** Property, **ProductName** Property

---

CommitTrans Event

Occurs after the **CommitTrans** method has completed.

Applies To

rdoEnvironment Object

Syntax

Private Sub *object*.**CommitTrans( )**

The *object* placeholder represents an object expression that evaluates to an object in the **Applies To** list.

Remarks

This event is raised after a **CommitTrans** method has been executed. The developer can respond to this event to synchronize some other process with the transaction.

See Also

BeginTrans Event, **RollbackTrans** Event, **BeginTrans**, **CommitTrans**, **RollbackTrans** Methods

CompactDatabase Method

Copies and compacts a closed database, and gives you the option of changing its version, collating order, and encryption. (Microsoft Jet workspaces only).

Applies To

DBEngine Object

Syntax

DBEngine.CompactDatabase *olddb*, *newdb*, *locale*, *options*, *password*

The **CompactDatabase** method syntax has these parts.

Part	Description
olddb	A **String** that identifies an existing, closed database. It can be a full path and file name, such as `"C:\db1.mdb"`. If the file name has an extension, you must specify it. If your network supports it, you can also specify a network path, such as `"\\server1\share1\dir1\db1.mdb"`.
newdb	A **String** that is the file name (and path) of the compacted database that you're creating. You can also specify a network path. You can't use the *newdb* argument to specify the same database file as *olddb*.

Locale	Optional. A **Variant** that is a string expression that specifies a collating order for creating *newdb*, as specified in Settings. If you omit this argument, the locale of *newdb* is the same as *olddb*.
	
	You can also create a password for *newdb* by concatenating the password string (starting with `";pwd="`) with a constant in the *locale* argument, like this:
	
	`dbLangSpanish & ";pwd=NewPassword"`
	
	If you want to use the same *locale* as *olddb* (the default value), but specify a new password, simply enter a password string for *locale*:
	
	`";pwd=NewPassword"`

options	Optional. A constant or combination of constants that indicates one or more options, as specified in Settings. You can combine options by summing the corresponding constants.
password	Optional. A **Variant** that is a string expression containing a password, if the database is password protected. The string `";pwd="` must precede the actual password. If you include a password setting in *locale*, this setting is ignored.

Settings

You can use one of the following constants for the *locale* argument to specify the **CollatingOrder** property for string comparisons of text.

Constant	Collating order
dbLangGeneral	English, German, French, Portuguese, Italian, and Modern Spanish
dbLangArabic	Arabic
dbLangChineseSimplified	Simplified Chinese
dbLangChineseTraditional	Traditional Chinese
dbLangCyrillic	Russian
dbLangCzech	Czech
dbLangDutch	Dutch
dbLangGreek	Greek
dbLangHebrew	Hebrew
dbLangHungarian	Hungarian
dbLangIcelandic	Icelandic
dbLangJapanese	Japanese
dbLangKorean	Korean
dbLangNordic	Nordic languages (Microsoft Jet database engine version 1.0 only)
dbLangNorwDan	Norwegian and Danish
dbLangPolish	Polish
dbLangSlovenian	Slovenian
dbLangSpanish	Traditional Spanish
dbLangSwedFin	Swedish and Finnish
dbLangThai	Thai
dbLangTurkish	Turkish

You can use one of the following constants in the *options* argument to specify whether to encrypt or to decrypt the database while it's compacted.

Constant	Description
dbEncrypt	Encrypt the database while compacting.
dbDecrypt	Decrypt the database while compacting.

If you omit an encryption constant or if you include both **dbDecrypt** and **dbEncrypt**, *newdb* will have the same encryption as *olddb*.

You can use one of the following constants in the *options* argument to specify the version of the data format for the compacted database. This constant affects only the version of the data format of *newdb* and doesn't affect the version of any Microsoft Access-defined objects, such as forms and reports.

Constant	Description
dbVersion10	Creates a database that uses the Microsoft Jet database engine version 1.0 file format while compacting.
dbVersion11	Creates a database that uses the Microsoft Jet database engine version 1.1 file format while compacting.
dbVersion20	Creates a database that uses the Microsoft Jet database engine version 2.0 file format while compacting.
dbVersion30	Creates a database that uses the Microsoft Jet database engine version 3.0 file format (compatible with version 3.5) while compacting.

You can specify only one version constant. If you omit a version constant, *newdb* will have the same version as *olddb*. You can compact *newdb* only to a version that is the same or later than that of *olddb*.

Remarks

As you change data in a database, the database file can become fragmented and use more disk space than is necessary. Periodically, you can use the **CompactDatabase** method to compact your database to defragment the database file. The compacted database is usually smaller and often runs faster. You can also change the collating order, the encryption, or the version of the data format while you copy and compact the database.

You must close *olddb* before you compact it. In a multiuser environment, other users can't have *olddb* open while you're compacting it. If *olddb* isn't closed or isn't available for exclusive use, an error occurs.

Because **CompactDatabase** creates a copy of the database, you must have enough disk space for both the original and the duplicate databases. The compact operation fails if there isn't enough disk space available. The *newdb* duplicate database doesn't have to be on the same disk as *olddb*. After successfully compacting a database, you can delete the *olddb* file and rename the compacted *newdb* file to the original file name.

The **CompactDatabase** method copies all the data and the security permission settings from the database specified by *olddb* to the database specified by *newdb*.

If you use **CompactDatabase** to convert a version 1.*x* database to version 2.5 or 3.*x*, only applications using version Microsoft Jet 2.5 or 3.*x* can open the converted database.

Note In an ODBCDirect workspace, using the **CompactDatabase** method doesn't return an error, but instead loads the Microsoft Jet database engine into memory.

Caution Because the **CompactDatabase** method doesn't convert Microsoft Access objects, you shouldn't use **CompactDatabase** to convert a database containing such objects. To convert a database containing Microsoft Access objects, on the **Tools** menu, point to **Database Utilities**, and then click **Convert Database**.

See Also

Database Object, **CreateDatabase** Method, **RepairDatabase** Method, **CollatingOrder** Property

Example

This example uses the **CompactDatabase** method to change the collating order of a database. You cannot use this code in a module belonging to Northwind.mdb.

```
Sub CompactDatabaseX()

    Dim dbsNorthwind As Database

    Set dbsNorthwind = OpenDatabase("Northwind.mdb")

    ' Show the properties of the original database.
    With dbsNorthwind
        Debug.Print .Name & ", version " & .Version
        Debug.Print "    CollatingOrder = " & .CollatingOrder
        .Close
    End With

    ' Make sure there isn't already a file with the
    ' name of the compacted database.
    If Dir("NwindKorean.mdb") <> "" Then _
        Kill "NwindKorean.mdb"

    ' This statement creates a compact version of the
    ' Northwind database that uses a Korean language
    ' collating order.
    DBEngine.CompactDatabase "Northwind.mdb", _
        "NwindKorean.mdb", dbLangKorean

    Set dbsNorthwind = OpenDatabase("NwindKorean.mdb")

    ' Show the properties of the compacted database.
    With dbsNorthwind
        Debug.Print .Name & ", version " & .Version
        Debug.Print "    CollatingOrder = " & .CollatingOrder
        .Close
    End With

End Sub
```

CompanyName Property

Returns or sets a string value containing the name of the company or creator of the running application. Read-only at run time.

Applies To

App Object

Syntax

object.**CompanyName**

The *object* placeholder represents an object expression that evaluates to an object in the **Applies To** list.

Remarks

You can set this property at design time in the Type box in the Make tab of the Project **Properties** dialog box.

See Also

Comments Property, **FileDescription** Property, **LegalCopyright** Property, **LegalTrademarks** Property, **ProductName** Property

---

Comparison Operators

Used to compare expressions.

Syntax

result = expression1 comparisonoperator expression2
result = object1 **Is** *object2*
result = string **Like** *pattern*

Comparison operators have these parts:

Part	Description
result	Required; any numeric variable.
expression	Required; any expression.
comparisonoperator	Required; any comparison operator.
object	Required; any object name.
string	Required; any string expression.
pattern	Required; any string expression or range of characters.

Remarks

The following table contains a list of the comparison operators and the conditions that determine whether *result* is **True**, **False**, or **Null**:

Operator	True if	False if	Null if
< (Less than)	*expression1 < expression2*	*expression1 >= expression2*	*expression1* or *expression2* = **Null**
<= (Less than or equal to)	*expression1 <= expression2*	*expression1 > expression2*	*expression1* or *expression2* = **Null**
> (Greater than)	*expression1 > expression2*	*expression1 <= expression2*	*expression1* or *expression2* = **Null**
>= (Greater than or equal to)	*expression1 >= expression2*	*expression1 < expression2*	*expression1* or *expression2* = **Null**
= (Equal to)	*expression1 = expression2*	*expression1 <> expression2*	*expression1* or *expression2* = **Null**
<> (Not equal to)	*expression1 <> expression2*	*expression1 = expression2*	*expression1* or *expression2* = **Null**

Note   The **Is** and **Like** operators have specific comparison functionality that differs from the operators in the table.

When comparing two expressions, you may not be able to easily determine whether the expressions are being compared as numbers or as strings. The following table shows how the expressions are compared or the result when either expression is not a **Variant**:

If	Then
Both expressions are numeric data types (**Byte**, **Boolean**, **Integer**, **Long**, **Single**, **Double**, **Date**, **Currency**, or **Decimal**)	Perform a numeric comparison.
Both expressions are **String**	Perform a string comparison.
One expression is a numeric data type and the other is a **Variant** that is, or can be, a number	Perform a numeric comparison.
One expression is a numeric data type and the other is a string **Variant** that can't be converted to a number	A `Type Mismatch` error occurs.
One expression is a **String** and the other is any **Variant** except a **Null**	Perform a string comparison.
One expression is **Empty** and the other is a numeric data type	Perform a numeric comparison, using 0 as the **Empty** expression.
One expression is **Empty** and the other is a **String**	Perform a string comparison, using a zero-length string ("") as the **Empty** expression.

If *expression1* and *expression2* are both **Variant** expressions, their underlying type determines how they are compared. The following table shows how the expressions are compared or the result from the comparison, depending on the underlying type of the **Variant**:

If	Then
Both **Variant** expressions are numeric	Perform a numeric comparison.
Both **Variant** expressions are strings	Perform a string comparison.
One **Variant** expression is numeric and the other is a string	The numeric expression is less than the string expression.
One **Variant** expression is **Empty** and the other is numeric	Perform a numeric comparison, using 0 as the **Empty** expression.
One **Variant** expression is **Empty** and the other is a string	Perform a string comparison, using a zero-length string ("") as the **Empty** expression.
Both **Variant** expressions are **Empty**	The expressions are equal.

When a **Single** is compared to a **Double**, the **Double** is rounded to the precision of the **Single**.

If a **Currency** is compared with a **Single** or **Double**, the **Single** or **Double** is converted to a **Currency**. Similarly, when a **Decimal** is compared with a **Single** or **Double**, the **Single** or **Double** is converted to a **Decimal**. For **Currency**, any fractional value less than .0001 may be lost; for **Decimal**, any fractional value less than 1E-28 may be lost, or an overflow error can occur. Such fractional value loss may cause two values to compare as equal when they are not.

See Also

Option Compare Statement, **Operator** Summary, **Operator** Precedence, **Is** Operator, **Like** Operator

Example

This example shows various uses of comparison operators, which you use to compare expressions.

```
Dim MyResult, Var1, Var2
MyResult = (45 < 35) ' Returns False.
MyResult = (45 = 45) ' Returns True.
MyResult = (4 <> 3)  ' Returns True.
MyResult = ("5" > "4")  ' Returns True.

Var1 = "5": Var2 = 4 ' Initialize variables.
MyResult = (Var1 > Var2)' Returns True.

Var1 = 5: Var2 = Empty
MyResult = (Var1 > Var2)' Returns True.

Var1 = 0: Var2 = Empty
MyResult = (Var1 = Var2)' Returns True.
```

CompatibleOLEServer Property

Returns or sets the compatible **ActiveX** component of this project.

Applies To

VBProject Object

Syntax

object.**CompatibleOLEServer**

The *object* placeholder represents an object expression that evaluates to an object in the **Applies To** list.

Concatenation Operators

& Operator

+ Operator

ConflictTable Property

Returns the name of a conflict table containing the database records that conflicted during the synchronization of two replicas (Microsoft Jet workspaces only).

Applies To

TableDef Object

Return Values

The return value is a **String** data type that is a zero-length string if there is no conflict table or the database isn't a replica.

Remarks

If two users at two separate replicas each make a change to the same record in the database, the changes made by one user will fail to be applied to the other replica. Consequently, the user with the failed change must resolve the conflicts.

Conflicts occur at the record level, not between fields. For example, if one user changes the Address field and another updates the Phone field in the same record, then one change is rejected. Because conflicts occur at the record level, the rejection occurs even though the successful change and the rejected change are unlikely to result in a true conflict of information.

The synchronization mechanism handles the record conflicts by creating conflict tables, which contain the information that would have been placed in the table, if the change had been successful. You can examine these conflict tables and work through them row by row, fixing whatever is appropriate.

All conflict tables are named *table*_conflict, where *table* is the original name of the table, truncated to the maximum table name length.

See Also

Synchronize Method

Example

This example uses the **ConflictTable** property to report the table names that had conflicts during synchronization.

```
Sub ConflictTableX()

    Dim dbsNorthwind As Database
    Dim tdfTest As TableDef

    Set dbsNorthwind = OpenDatabase("Northwind.mdb")

    ' Enumerate TableDefs collection and check ConflictTable
    ' property of each.
    For Each tdfTest In dbsNorthwind.TableDefs
        If tdfTest.ConflictTable <> "" Then _
            Debug.Print tdfTest.Name & " had a conflict."
    Next tdfTest

    dbsNorthwind.Close

End Sub
```

This example opens a **Recordset** from the conflict table and one from the table that caused the conflict. It then processes the records in these tables, using the RequiredDate field to copy information from one table to the other depending on which record was more recently updated.

```
Sub ConflictTableX2(dbsResolve As Database)

    Dim tdfTest As TableDef
    Dim rstSource As Recordset
    Dim rstConflict As Recordset
    Dim fldLoop As Field

    Set tdfTest = dbsResolve.TableDefs("Orders")

    If tdfTest.ConflictTable <> "" Then

        Set rstSource = dbsResolve.OpenRecordset( _
            tdfTest.Name, dbOpenTable)
        Set rstConflict = dbsResolve.OpenRecordset( _
            tdfTest.ConflictTable, dbOpenTable)
        rstSource.Index = "[d_Guid]"
        rstConflict.MoveFirst

        Do Until rstConflict.EOF
            rstSource.Seek "=", rstConflict![s_Guid]
            If Not rstSource.NoMatch Then
                If rstSource!RequiredDate < _
                        rstConflict!RequiredDate Then
                    On Error Resume Next
                    For Each fldLoop in rstConflict.Fields
                        fldLoop = rstSource(fldLoop.Name)
                    Next fldLoop
                    On Error Goto 0
                End If
            End If
            rstConflict.Delete
            rstConflict.MoveNext
        Loop

        rstConflict.Close
        rstSource.Close
    End If

End Sub
```

Connect Event

Occurs after a connection is established to the server.

Applies To

    rdoConnection Object

Syntax

    Private Sub *object*.**Connect**(*ErrorOccurred* **As Boolean**)

Part	Description
object	An object expression that evaluates to an object in the **Applies To** list.
ErrorOccurred	A **Boolean** expression that determines whether the connection was successful, as described in Settings.

Settings

The *ErrorOccurred* argument will be set to one of the following values:

Value	Description
True	The connection failed.
False	The connection succeeded.

Remarks

You can catch the Connect event and do any kind of initial queries required on a new connection, such as verifying the version of the database against the version of the client or setting a default database not established in the connect string. You can also check for errors or messages returned during the process of opening the connection—or perhaps simply clear the **rdoErrors** collection of informational messages.

See Also

BeforeConnect Event, **Disconnect** Event, **Dissociate** Event, **OpenConnection** Method (Remote Data), **EstablishConnection** Method (Remote Data), **rdoConnection** Object, **rdoEnvironment** Object, **StillConnecting** Property

Connect Property (DAO)

Sets or returns a value that provides information about the source of an open connection, an open database, a database used in a pass-through query, or a linked table. For **Database** objects, new **Connection** objects, linked tables, and **TableDef** objects not yet appended to a collection, this property setting is read/write. For **QueryDef** objects and base tables, this property is read-only.

Applies To

Database Object, **QueryDef** Object, **TableDef** Object, **Connection** Object, **Data** Control

Syntax

object.**Connect** = *databasetype*;*parameters*;

The **Connect** property syntax has these parts.

Part	Description
object	An object expression that evaluates to an object in the **Applies To** list.
databasetype	Optional. A **String** that specifies a database type. For Microsoft Jet databases, exclude this argument; if you specify *parameters*, use a semicolon (;) as a placeholder.
parameters	Optional. A **String** that specifies additional parameters to pass to ODBC or installable ISAM drivers. Use semicolons to separate parameters.

Settings

The **Connect** property setting is a **String** composed of a database type specifier and zero or more parameters separated by semicolons. The **Connect** property passes additional information to ODBC and certain ISAM drivers as needed.

To perform an SQL pass-through query on a table linked to your Microsoft Jet database (.mdb) file, you must first set the **Connect** property of the linked table's database to a valid ODBC connection string.

For a **TableDef** object that represents a linked table, the **Connect** property setting consists of one or two parts (a database type specifier and a path to the database), each of which ends with a semicolon.

The path as shown in the following table is the full path for the directory containing the database files and must be preceded by the identifier DATABASE=. In some cases (as with Microsoft Excel and Microsoft Jet databases), you should include a specific file name in the database path argument.

The following table shows possible database types and their corresponding database specifiers and paths for the **Connect** property setting. You can also specify "FTP://*path/etc.*" or "HTTP://*path/etc.*" For the path. In an ODBCDirect workspace, only the "ODBC" specifier can be used.

Database type	Specifier	Example
Microsoft Jet Database	[*database*];	*drive:\path\filename.mdb*
dBASE III	dBASE III;	*drive:\path*
dBASE IV	dBASE IV;	*drive:\path*
dBASE 5	dBASE 5.0;	*drive:\path*
Paradox 3.x	Paradox 3.x;	*drive:\path*
Paradox 4.x	Paradox 4.x;	*drive:\path*
Paradox 5.x	Paradox 5.x;	*drive:\path*
FoxPro 2.0	FoxPro 2.0;	*drive:\path*
FoxPro 2.5	FoxPro 2.5;	*drive:\path*
FoxPro 2.6	FoxPro 2.6;	*drive:\path*
Excel 3.0	Excel 3.0;	*drive:\path\filename.xls*
Excel 4.0	Excel 4.0;	*drive:\path\filename.xls*
Excel 5.0 or Excel 95	Excel 5.0;	*drive:\path\filename.xls*
Excel 97	Excel 97;	*drive:\path\filename.xls*
HTML Import	HTML Import;	*drive:\path\filename*
HTML Export	HTML Export;	*drive:\path*
Text	Text;	*drive:\path*

(continued)

Database type	Specifier	Example
ODBC	ODBC; DATABASE=*database*; UID=*user*; PWD=*password*; DSN= *datasourcename*; [LOGINTIMEOUT=*seconds*;]	None
Exchange	Exchange; MAPILEVEL=*folderpath*; [TABLETYPE={ 0 1 1 }]; [PROFILE=*profile*;] [PWD=*password*;] [DATABASE=*database*;]	*drive*:*path**filename.mdb*

Remarks

If the specifier is only "ODBC;", the ODBC driver displays a dialog box listing all registered ODBC data source names so that the user can select a database.

If a password is required but not provided in the **Connect** property setting, a login dialog box is displayed the first time a table is accessed by the ODBC driver and again if the connection is closed and reopened.

For data in Microsoft Exchange, the required MAPILEVEL key should be set to a fully-resolved folder path (for example, "Mailbox - Pat SmithIAlpha/Today"). The path does not include the name of the folder that will be opened as a table; that folder's name should instead be specified as the *name* argument to the **CreateTable** method. The TABLETYPE key should be set to "0" to open a folder (default) or "1" to open an address book. The PROFILE key defaults to the profile currently in use.

For base tables in a Microsoft Jet database (.mdb), the **Connect** property setting is a zero-length string ("").

You can set the **Connect** property for a **Database** object by providing a *source* argument to the **OpenDatabase** method. You can check the setting to determine the type, path, user ID, password, or ODBC data source of the database.

On a **QueryDef** object in a Microsoft Jet workspace, you can use the **Connect** property with the **ReturnsRecords** property to create an ODBC SQL pass-through query. The *databasetype* of the connection string is "ODBC;", and the remainder of the string contains information specific to the ODBC driver used to access the remote data. For more information, see the documentation for the specific driver.

Notes

- You must set the **Connect** property before you set the **ReturnsRecords** property.
- You must have access permissions to the computer that contains the database server you're trying to access.

See Also

OpenDatabase Method, **ReturnsRecords** Property

Example

This example uses the **Connect** and **SourceTableName** properties to link various external tables to a Microsoft Jet database. The **ConnectOutput** procedure is required for this procedure to run.

```
Sub ConnectX()

    Dim dbsTemp As Database
    Dim strMenu As String
    Dim strInput As String

    ' Open a Microsoft Jet database to which you will link
    ' a table.
    Set dbsTemp = OpenDatabase("DB1.mdb")

    ' Build menu text.
    strMenu = "Enter number for data source:" & vbCr
    strMenu = strMenu & _
        "   1. Microsoft Jet database" & vbCr
    strMenu = strMenu & _
        "   2. Microsoft FoxPro 3.0 table" & vbCr
    strMenu = strMenu & _
        "   3. dBASE table" & vbCr
    strMenu = strMenu & _
        "   4. Paradox table" & vbCr
    strMenu = strMenu & _
        "   M. (see choices 5-9)"

    ' Get user's choice.
    strInput = InputBox(strMenu)

    If UCase(strInput) = "M" Then

        ' Build menu text.
        strMenu = "Enter number for data source:" & vbCr
        strMenu = strMenu & _
            "   5. Microsoft Excel spreadsheet" & vbCr
        strMenu = strMenu & _
            "   6. Lotus spreadsheet" & vbCr
        strMenu = strMenu & _
            "   7. Comma-delimited text (CSV)" & vbCr
        strMenu = strMenu & _
            "   8. HTML table" & vbCr
        strMenu = strMenu & _
            "   9. Microsoft Exchange folder"

        ' Get user's choice.
        strInput = InputBox(strMenu)

    End If

    ' Call the ConnectOutput procedure. The third argument
    ' will be used as the Connect string, and the fourth
    ' argument will be used as the SourceTableName.
    Select Case Val(strInput)
```

```
            Case 1
                ConnectOutput dbsTemp, _
                    "JetTable", _
                    ";DATABASE=C:\My Documents\Northwind.mdb", _
                    "Employees"
            Case 2
                ConnectOutput dbsTemp, _
                    "FoxProTable", _
                    "FoxPro 3.0;DATABASE=C:\FoxPro30\Samples", _
                    "Q1Sales"
            Case 3
                ConnectOutput dbsTemp, _
                    "dBASETable", _
                    "dBase IV;DATABASE=C:\dBASE\Samples", _
                    "Accounts"
            Case 4
                ConnectOutput dbsTemp, _
                    "ParadoxTable", _
                    "Paradox 3.X;DATABASE=C:\Paradox\Samples", _
                    "Accounts"
            Case 5
                ConnectOutput dbsTemp, _
                    "ExcelTable", _
                    "Excel 5.0;" & _
                        "DATABASE=C:\Excel\Samples\Q1Sales.xls", _
                    "January Sales"
            Case 6
                ConnectOutput dbsTemp, _
                    "LotusTable", _
                    "Lotus WK3;" & _
                        "DATABASE=C:\Lotus\Samples\Sales.xls", _
                    "THIRDQTR"
            Case 7
                ConnectOutput dbsTemp, _
                    "CSVTable", _
                    "Text;DATABASE=C:\Samples", _
                    "Sample.txt"
            Case 8
                ConnectOutput dbsTemp, _
                    "HTMLTable", _
                    "HTML Import;DATABASE=http://" & _
                        "www.server1.com/samples/page1.html", _
                    "Q1SalesData"
            Case 9
                ConnectOutput dbsTemp, _
                    "ExchangeTable", _
                    "Exchange 4.0;MAPILEVEL=" & _
                        "Mailbox - Michelle Wortman (Exchange)" & _
                        "|People\Important;", _
                    "Jerry Wheeler"
        End Select

        dbsTemp.Close

    End Sub
```

```
Sub ConnectOutput(dbsTemp As Database, _
    strTable As String, strConnect As String, _
    strSourceTable As String)

    Dim tdfLinked As TableDef
    Dim rstLinked As Recordset
    Dim intTemp As Integer

    ' Create a new TableDef, set its Connect and
    ' SourceTableName properties based on the passed
    ' arguments, and append it to the TableDefs collection.
    Set tdfLinked = dbsTemp.CreateTableDef(strTable)

    tdfLinked.Connect = strConnect
    tdfLinked.SourceTableName = strSourceTable
    dbsTemp.TableDefs.Append tdfLinked

    Set rstLinked = dbsTemp.OpenRecordset(strTable)

    Debug.Print "Data from linked table:"

    ' Display the first three records of the linked table.
    intTemp = 1
    With rstLinked
        Do While Not .EOF And intTemp <= 3
            Debug.Print , .Fields(0), .Fields(1)
            intTemp = intTemp + 1
            .MoveNext
        Loop
        If Not .EOF Then Debug.Print , "[additional records]"
        .Close
    End With

    ' Delete the linked table because this is a demonstration.
    dbsTemp.TableDefs.Delete strTable

End Sub
```

Connect Property (Add-Ins)

Returns or sets the connected state of an add-in.

Applies To

AddIn Object

Syntax

object.**Connect**

The *object* placeholder represents an object expression that evaluates to an object in the **Applies To** list.

Remarks

Returns True if the add-in is registered and currently connected (active).

Returns False if the add-in is registered, but not connected (inactive).

Connect Property (Remote Data)

Returns or sets a value that provides information about the source of an open **rdoConnection**. The **Connect** property contains the ODBC connect string. This property is always readable, but cannot be changed after the connection is established.

Applies To

rdoConnection Object, **rdoPreparedStatement** Object, **RemoteData** Control

Syntax

object.**Connect** [= *value*]

The **Connect** property syntax has these parts:

Part	Description
object	An object expression that evaluates to an object in the **Applies To** list.
value	A string expression as described in Remarks. (Data type is String)

Settings

The **Connect** property return value is a **String** expression composed of zero or more parameters separated by semicolons, as described in Remarks.

Remarks

When used with the **rdoQuery** or **rdoConnection** objects, this property is read-only unless created as a stand-alone object when it is read-write until the connection is established. The **Connect** property becomes read-write when the **rdoConnection** object is closed. When used with the **RemoteData control**, this property is read-write.

The **Connect** property is used to pass additional information to and from the ODBC driver manager to establish a connection with a data source. The **Connect** property holds the ODBC connect string which is also used as an argument to the **OpenConnection** method. When used with a stand-alone **rdoConnection** or **rdoQuery** objects, the **Connect** property is used by the **EstablishConnection** method.

Except when associated with the **RemoteData** control, once a connection is made, the **Connect** property is completed with the values optionally supplied by the user and the ODBC driver manager. The **Connect** property of the **rdoQuery** contains this amended connect string.

The **RemoteData** control's **Connect** property is not changed after the connection is established. However, the completed connect string can be extracted from the **RemoteData** control's **Connection** property. For example:

```
FullConnect = MSRDC1.Connection.Connect
```

The following table details valid ODBC connect string arguments and typical usage. Note that each parameter is delineated with a semi-colon (;).

Parameter	Specifies	Example
DSN	Registered ODBC data source by name.	DSN=MyDataSource; (If specified when establishing a DSN-less connection, DSN must be the *last* argument)
UID	User name of a recognized user of the database	UID=Victoria;
PWD	Password associated with user name	PWD=ChemMajor;
DRIVER	Description of driver. (Note brackets for driver names that include spaces.)	DRIVER={SQL Server};
DATABASE	Default database to use once connected	DATABASE=Pubs;
SERVER	Name of remote server	SERVER=SEQUEL;
WSID	Workstation ID (your system's Net name)	WSID=MYP5
APP	Application name. At design time this is set to your project name. At runtime this is your .exe name.	APP=Accounting

Note Some ODBC drivers require different parameters not shown in this list.

For example, to set the **Connect** property of a **RemoteData** control you could use code like the following:

```
Dim Cnct As String
Cnct = "DSN=WorkData;UID=Chrissy;" _
↳ & "PWD=MIDFLD;DATABASE=WorkDB;"
RemoteData1.Connect = Cnct
RemoteData1.SQL = "Select Name, City " _
    & " From Teams Where Type = 12"
RemoteData1.Refresh
```

You can use this same connect string to establish a new connection:

```
Dim Cn As rdoConnection
Set Cn = rdoEnvironments(0).OpenConnection("", _
↳ rdDriverNoPrompt,True,Cnct$)
```

Note Valid parameters are determined by the ODBC driver. The parameters shown in the preceding example are supported by the Microsoft SQL Server ODBC driver. ODBC, LOGINTIMEOUT and DBQ are not valid parameters of the **RemoteData** control or the **rdoConnection** object's **Connect** property. These parameters are supported by the Microsoft Jet database engine, and not by the ODBC driver. To set login timeout delay, you must use the **LoginTimeout** property of the **rdoEnvironment** object.

Capturing Missing Arguments

If the connect string is null, the information provided by the DSN is incomplete, or invalid arguments are provided, the connection cannot be established. If your code sets the *prompt* argument of the **OpenConnection** method or the **RemoteData** control's **Prompt** property to prohibit user completion of missing ODBC connect arguments, a trappable error is triggered. Otherwise the ODBC driver manager displays a dialog box to gather missing information from the user. Depending on the setting of the **Prompt** argument of the **OpenConnection** or **EstablishConnection** methods, these dialogs capture the DSN from a list of registered ODBC data sources. Names presented to the user, and optionally, the user ID and password. If the connection fails to succeed using these user-provided values, the dialogs are presented again until the connection succeeds or the user cancels the operation. In some cases, the user can create their own DSN using these dialogs.

If a password is required, but not provided in the **Connect** property setting, a login dialog box is displayed the first time a table is accessed by the ODBC driver and each time the connection is closed and reopened.

Connecting with Domain-Managed Security

When connecting to ODBC data sources that support domain-managed security, set the UID and PWD parameters to "". In this case, the Windows NT user name and password are passed to the data source for validation. This strategy permits access to the data source by users with access to the NT domain through authenticated workstation logons.

You can set the **Connect** property for an **rdoConnection** object by providing a *connect* argument to the **OpenConnection** method. Once the connection is established, you can check the **Connect** property setting to determine the DSN, database, user name, password, or ODBC data source of the database.

Registering Data Source Names

Before you can establish a connection using a Data Source Name (DSN), you must either manually register the DSN using the Windows control panel application or use the **rdoRegisterDataSource** method. This process establishes the server name, driver name and other options used when referencing this data source.

Establishing DSN-Less Connections

Under the right circumstances you might not need to pre-register a DSN before connecting. If the following conditions are met, RDO can establish a DSN-less connection using the **RemoteData** control, or the **OpenConnection** or **EstablishConnection** methods with a fully-populated **Connect** property or connect string:

- The connection uses the default named-pipes networking protocol.

- The connection does not set the OEMTOANSI option.

- You specify the name of the server using the SERVER argument in the connect string.

- You specify the name of the ODBC driver using the DRIVER argument in the connect string.

- You set the DSN argument in the connect string (or wherever it appears—as in the **DataSourceName** property of the **RemoteData** control) to an empty string. The empty DSN argument must be specified as the *last* parameter of the connect string.

See Also

OpenConnection Method (Remote Data), **EstablishConnection** Method (Remote Data), **rdoConnection** Object, **rdoPreparedStatement** Object, **rdoTable** Object, **Connection** Property (Remote Data)

Example

The following example establishes a DSN-less ODBC connection using the **OpenConnection** method against the default **rdoEnvironment**. In this case the example prints the resulting **Connect** property to the Immediate window.

```
Dim en as rdoEnvironment
Dim cn as rdoConnection

Set en = rdoEnvironments(0)
Set cn = en.OpenConnection(dsName:="", _
    Prompt:=rdDriverNoPrompt, _
    Connect:="uid=;pwd=;driver={SQL Server};" _
        & "server=SEQUEL;database=pubs;")
debug.print cn.Connect
```

The following example establishes an ODBC connection using the **OpenConnection** method but requires the user to provide all connection information. In this case the example prints the resulting **Connect** property to the Immediate window.

```
Dim cn As rdoConnection
Dim en As rdoEnvironment

Set en = rdoEnvironments(0)
Set cn = en.OpenConnection(dsName:="WorkDB", _
    Prompt:=rdDriverCompleteRequired)
debug.print cn.Connect
```

The following example establishes a DSN-less ODBC connection by creating a stand-alone **rdoConnection** object and uses the **EstablishConnection** method to open the connection. Note that the DSN='';; argument is positioned at the end of the connect string. The example prints the resulting **Connect** property to the Immediate window.

```
' Create a DSN-less connection
'   using a stand-alone rdoConnection object and
'   the EstablishConnection method
'
Dim cn As New rdoConnection
Dim qd As New rdoQuery

cn.Connect = "uid=;pwd=;server=SEQUEL;" _
    & "driver={SQL Server};database=pubs;" _
    & "DSN='';"
cn.cursordriver = rdUseOdbc
cn.EstablishConnection rdDriverNoprompt
debug.print cn.Connect

Set qd.ActiveConnection = cn
```

The following example establishes an ODBC connection using a registered DSN to provide most of the required arguments. The User ID and Password are to be provided by domain-managed security. In this case the example prints the resulting **Connect** property to the Immediate window.

```
Dim cn As New rdoConnection
Dim qd As New rdoQuery

cn.Connect = "uid=;pwd=;"DSN=WorkDB;"
cn.cursordriver = rdUseOdbc
cn.EstablishConnection rdDriverNoprompt
debug.print cn.Connect
```

Connection Object

A **Connection** object represents a connection to an ODBC database (ODBCDirect workspaces only).

Remarks

A **Connection** is a non-persistent object that represents a connection to a remote database. The **Connection** object is only available in ODBCDirect workspaces (that is, a **Workspace** object created with the type option set to **dbUseODBC**).

Note   Code written for earlier versions of DAO can continue to use the **Database** object for backward compatibility, but if the new features of a **Connection** are desired, you should revise code to use the **Connection** object. To help with code conversion, you can obtain a **Connection** object reference from a **Database** by reading the **Connection** property of the **Database** object. Conversely, you can obtain a **Database** object reference from the **Connection** object's **Database** property.

Properties

Connect Property, **Name** Property, **QueryTimeout** Property, **RecordsAffected** Property, **Transactions** Property, **Updatable** Property, **Database** Property, **StillExecuting** Property

Methods

Close Method, **CreateQueryDef** Method, **Execute** Method, **OpenRecordset** Method, **Cancel** Method

See Also

Database Object, **Connection** Property

Example

This example demonstrates the **Connection** object and **Connections** collection by opening a Microsoft Jet **Database** object and two ODBCDirect **Connection** objects and listing the properties available to each object.

```
Sub ConnectionObjectX()

    Dim wrkJet as Workspace
    Dim dbsNorthwind As Database
    Dim wrkODBC As Workspace
    Dim conPubs As Connection
    Dim conPubs2 As Connection
    Dim conLoop As Connection
    Dim prpLoop As Property

    ' Open Microsoft Jet Database object.
    Set wrkJet = CreateWorkspace("NewJetWorkspace", _
        "admin", "", dbUseJet)
    Set dbsNorthwind = wrkJet.OpenDatabase("Northwind.mdb")

    ' Create ODBCDirect Workspace object and open Connection
    ' objects.
    Set wrkODBC = CreateWorkspace("NewODBCWorkspace", _
        "admin", "", dbUseODBC)
    Set conPubs = wrkODBC.OpenConnection("Connection1", , , _
        "ODBC;DATABASE=pubs;UID=sa;PWD=;DSN=Publishers")
    Set conPubs2 = wrkODBC.OpenConnection("Connection2", , _
        True, "ODBC;DATABASE=pubs;UID=sa;PWD=;DSN=Publishers")

    Debug.Print "Database properties:"

    With dbsNorthwind
        ' Enumerate Properties collection of Database object.
        For Each prpLoop In .Properties
            On Error Resume Next
            Debug.Print "    " & prpLoop.Name & " = " & _
                prpLoop.Value
            On Error GoTo 0
        Next prpLoop
    End With

    ' Enumerate the Connections collection.
    For Each conLoop In wrkODBC.Connections
        Debug.Print "Connection properties for " & _
            conLoop.Name & ":"

        With conLoop
            ' Print property values by explicitly calling each
            ' Property object; the Connection object does not
            ' support a Properties collection.
            Debug.Print "    Connect = " & .Connect
            ' Property actually returns a Database object.
            Debug.Print "    Database[.Name] = " & _
                .Database.Name
```

```
            Debug.Print "    Name = " & .Name
            Debug.Print "    QueryTimeout = " & .QueryTimeout
            Debug.Print "    RecordsAffected = " & _
                .RecordsAffected
            Debug.Print "    StillExecuting = " & _
                .StillExecuting
            Debug.Print "    Transactions = " & .Transactions
            Debug.Print "    Updatable = " & .Updatable
        End With

    Next conLoop

    dbsNorthwind.Close
    conPubs.Close
    conPubs2.Close
    wrkJet.Close
    wrkODBC.Close

End Sub
```

Connection Property

On a **Database** object, returns the **Connection** object that corresponds to the database (**ODBCDirect** workspaces only).

On a **Recordset** object, returns the **Connection** object that owns the **Recordset** (**ODBCDirect** workspaces only).

Applies To

Database Object, **Dynaset-Type Recordset** Object, **Recordset** Object, **Snapshot-Type Recordset** Object, **Forward-Only–Type Recordset** Object, **Dynamic-Type Recordset** Object

Settings And Return Values

The return value is an object variable that represents the **Connection**. On a **Database** object, the **Connection** property is read-only, while on a **Recordset** object the property is read/write.

Remarks

On a **Database** object, use the **Connection** property to obtain a reference to a **Connection** object that corresponds to the **Database**. In DAO, a **Connection** object and its corresponding **Database** object are simply two different object variable references to the same object. The **Database** property of a **Connection** object and the **Connection** property of a **Database** object make it easier to change connections to an ODBC data source through the Microsoft Jet database engine to use **ODBCDirect**.

See Also

Database Property

Connection Property (Remote Data)

Returns a reference to a **RemoteData** control's underlying **rdoConnection** object.

Applies To

RemoteData Control

Syntax

object.**Connection**
Set *connection* = *object*.**Connection**

The **Connection** property syntax has these parts:

Part	Description
connection	An object expression that evaluates to a valid **rdoConnection** object.
object	An object expression that evaluates to an object in the **Applies To** list.

Remarks

When a **RemoteData** control is initialized, **RemoteData** opens a connection to the data source specified in the control's **Connect** property. The **rdoConnection** object created by RDO is exposed by the **Connection** property.

rdoConnection objects have properties and methods you can use to manage data. You can use any method of an **rdoConnection** object, such as **Close** and **Execute**, with the **Connection** property of a **RemoteData** control.

Except when associated with the **RemoteData** control, once a connection is made, the **Connect** property is completed with the values optionally supplied by the user and the ODBC driver manager. The **Connect** property of the **rdoQuery** contains this amended connect string.

The **RemoteData** control's **Connect** property is not changed after the connection is established. However, the completed connect string can be extracted from the **RemoteData** control's **Connection** property. For example:

```
FullConnect = MSRDC1.Connection.Connect
```

See Also

Close Method (Remote Data), **Execute** Method (Remote Data), **rdoColumn** Object, **rdoConnection** Object, **rdoResultset** Object, **RemoteData** Control, **Connect** Property (Remote Data), **DataSourceName** Property (Remote Data), **Name** Property (Remote Data)

Connections Collection

A **Connections** collection contains the current **Connection** objects of a **Workspace** object. (ODBCDirect workspaces only).

Remarks

When you open a **Connection** object, it is automatically appended to the **Connections** collection of the **Workspace**. When you close a **Connection** object with the **Close** method, it is removed from the **Connections** collection. You should close all open **Recordset** objects within the **Connection** before closing it.

At the same time you open a **Connection** object, a corresponding **Database** object is created and appended to the **Databases** collection in the same **Workspace**, and vice versa. Similarly, when you close the **Connection**, the corresponding **Database** is deleted from the **Databases** collection, and so on.

The **Name** property setting of a **Connection** is a string that specifies the path of the database file. To refer to a **Connection** object in a collection by its ordinal number or by its **Name** property setting, use any of the following syntax forms:

Connections(0)
Connections("*name*")
Connections![*name*]

Note   You can open the same data source more than once, creating duplicate names in the **Connections** collection. You should assign **Connection** objects to object variables and refer to them by variable name.

Example

This example demonstrates the **Connection** object and **Connections** collection by opening a Microsoft Jet **Database** object and two ODBCDirect **Connection** objects and listing the properties available to each object.

```
Sub ConnectionObjectX()

    Dim wrkJet as Workspace
    Dim dbsNorthwind As Database
    Dim wrkODBC As Workspace
    Dim conPubs As Connection
    Dim conPubs2 As Connection
    Dim conLoop As Connection
    Dim prpLoop As Property
```

```
' Open Microsoft Jet Database object.
Set wrkJet = CreateWorkspace("NewJetWorkspace", _
   "admin", "", dbUseJet)
Set dbsNorthwind = wrkJet.OpenDatabase("Northwind.mdb")

' Create ODBCDirect Workspace object and open Connection
' objects.
Set wrkODBC = CreateWorkspace("NewODBCWorkspace", _
   "admin", "", dbUseODBC)
Set conPubs = wrkODBC.OpenConnection("Connection1", , , _
   "ODBC;DATABASE=pubs;UID=sa;PWD=;DSN=Publishers")
Set conPubs2 = wrkODBC.OpenConnection("Connection2", , _
   True, "ODBC;DATABASE=pubs;UID=sa;PWD=;DSN=Publishers")

Debug.Print "Database properties:"

With dbsNorthwind
   ' Enumerate Properties collection of Database object.
   For Each prpLoop In .Properties
      On Error Resume Next
      Debug.Print "   " & prpLoop.Name & " = " & _
         prpLoop.Value
      On Error GoTo 0
   Next prpLoop
End With

' Enumerate the Connections collection.
For Each conLoop In wrkODBC.Connections
   Debug.Print "Connection properties for " & _
      conLoop.Name & ":"

   With conLoop
      ' Print property values by explicitly calling each
      ' Property object; the Connection object does not
      ' support a Properties collection.
      Debug.Print "   Connect = " & .Connect
      ' Property actually returns a Database object.
      Debug.Print "   Database[.Name] = " & _
         .Database.Name
      Debug.Print "   Name = " & .Name
      Debug.Print "   QueryTimeout = " & .QueryTimeout
      Debug.Print "   RecordsAffected = " & _
         .RecordsAffected
      Debug.Print "   StillExecuting = " & _
         .StillExecuting
      Debug.Print "   Transactions = " & .Transactions
      Debug.Print "   Updatable = " & .Updatable
   End With

Next conLoop

dbsNorthwind.Close
conPubs.Close
conPubs2.Close
wrkJet.Close
wrkODBC.Close

End Sub
```

Const Statement

Declares constants for use in place of literal values.

Syntax

[**Public** | **Private**] **Const** *constname* [**As** *type*] = *expression*

The **Const** statement syntax has these parts:

Part	Description
Public	Optional. Keyword used at module level to declare constants that are available to all procedures in all modules. Not allowed in procedures.
Private	Optional. Keyword used at module level to declare constants that are available only within the module where the declaration is made. Not allowed in procedures.
constname	Required. Name of the constant; follows standard variable naming conventions.
type	Optional. Data type of the constant; may be **Byte**, **Boolean**, **Integer**, **Long**, **Currency**, **Single**, **Double**, **Decimal** (not currently supported), **Date**, **String**, or **Variant**. Use a separate **As** *type* clause for each constant being declared.
expression	Required. Literal, other constant, or any combination that includes all arithmetic or logical operators except **Is**.

Remarks

Constants are private by default. Within procedures, constants are always private; their visibility can't be changed. In standard modules, the default visibility of module-level constants can be changed using the **Public** keyword. In class modules, however, constants can only be private and their visibility can't be changed using the **Public** keyword.

To combine several constant declarations on the same line, separate each constant assignment with a comma. When constant declarations are combined in this way, the **Public** or **Private** keyword, if used, applies to all of them.

You can't use variables, user-defined functions, or intrinsic Visual Basic functions (such as **Chr**) in expressions assigned to constants.

Note Constants can make your programs self-documenting and easy to modify. Unlike variables, constants can't be inadvertently changed while your program is running.

If you don't explicitly declare the constant type using **As** *type*, the constant has the data type that is most appropriate for *expression*.

Constants declared in a **Sub**, **Function**, or **Property** procedure are local to that procedure. A constant declared outside a procedure is defined throughout the module in which it is declared. You can use constants anywhere you can use an expression.

See Also

#Const Directive, **Deftype** Statements, **Function** Statement, **Let** Statement, **Property Get** Statement, **Property Let** Statement, **Property Set** Statement, **Sub** Statement

Example

This example uses the **Const** statement to declare constants for use in place of literal values. **Public** constants are declared in the General section of a standard module, rather than a class module. **Private** constants are declared in the General section of any type of module.

```
' Constants are Private by default.
Const MyVar = 459

' Declare Public constant.
Public Const MyString = "HELP"

' Declare Private Integer constant.
Private Const MyInt As Integer = 5

' Declare multiple constants on same line.
Const MyStr = "Hello", MyDouble As Double = 3.4567
```

ContainedControls Property

Returns a collection of the controls that were added to the control by the developer or the end user at the control's run-time. The **ContainedControls** property is not available at the control's authoring time, and read-only at the control's run time.

Applies To

UserControl Object

Syntax

object.**ContainedControls**

The **ContainedControls** property syntax has this part:

Part	Description
object	An object expression that evaluates to an object in the **Applies To** list.

Remarks

The **ContainedControls** collection is filled with all the controls that were added to the control by the developer or the end-user. The control can use the **ContainedControls** collection to perform operations on any of these contained controls.

This collection functions in a similar manner to the **Controls** collection on a form.

In order to allow contained controls to be placed on the control, the **ControlContainer** property must be **True**.

Contained controls cannot be added or removed through this **ContainedControls** collection; the contained controls must be changed in whatever manner the container allows.

The **ContainedControls** property may not be supported by all containers, even though the container may support the control having contained controls; Visual Basic forms do support this property. If this property is not supported, then calls to the **ContainedControls** collection will cause errors; use error handling when accessing the collection. Note, however, that if error handling is done while in an event procedure such as the **InitProperties** event procedure or the **ReadProperties** event procedure, the error handler should not raise an error event; doing this may be fatal to the container.

The **ContainedControls** collection is not available when the Initialize event is raised; but is available when the **InitProperties** event or **ReadProperties** event is raised.

Once the **ContainedControls** collection is present, it may not immediately contain references to the controls a developer has placed on the control. For example, if the control is on a Visual Basic form, the **Count** property of the **ContainedControls** collection will be zero until after the **ReadProperties** event procedure has executed.

See Also

InitProperties Event, **ReadProperties** Event, **Controls** Collection, **Initialize** Event, **Item** Property (ActiveX Controls)

ContainedVBControls Collection

The **ContainedVBControls** collection represents a collection of **VBControl** objects.

Properties

VBE Property

Methods

Add Method, **Item** Method, **Remove Method** (Visual Basic Extensibility)

See Also

ContainedControls Property, **VBControl** Object

Container Object

A **Container** object groups similar types of **Document** objects together.

Remarks

Each **Database** object has a **Containers** collection consisting of built-in **Container** objects. Applications can define their own document types and corresponding containers (Microsoft Jet databases only); however, these objects may not always be supported through DAO.

Some of these **Container** objects are defined by the Microsoft Jet database engine while others may be defined by other applications. The following table lists the name of each **Container** object defined by the Microsoft Jet database engine and what type of information it contains.

Container name	Contains information about
Databases	Saved databases
Tables	Saved tables and queries
Relations	Saved relationships

Note Don't confuse the **Container** objects listed in the preceding table with the collections of the same name. The Databases **Container** object refers to all saved database objects, but the **Databases** collection refers only to database objects that are open in a particular workspace.

Each **Container** object has a **Documents** collection containing **Document** objects that describe instances of built-in objects of the type specified by the **Container**. You typically use a **Container** object as an intermediate link to the information in the **Document** object. You can also use the **Containers** collection to set security for all **Document** objects of a given type.

With an existing **Container** object, you can:

- Use the **Name** property to return the predefined name of the **Container** object.

- Use the **Owner** property to set or return the owner of the **Container** object. To set the **Owner** property, you must have write permission for the **Container** object, and you must set the property to the name of an existing **User** or **Group** object.

- Use the **Permissions** and **UserName** properties to set access permissions for the **Container** object; any **Document** object created in the **Documents** collection of a **Container** object inherits these access permission settings.

Because **Container** objects are built-in, you can't create new **Container** objects or delete existing ones.

To refer to a **Container** object in a collection by its ordinal number or by its **Name** property setting, use any of the following syntax forms:

Containers(0)
Containers("*name*")
Containers![*name*]

Properties

AllPermissions Property, **Inherit** Property, **Name** Property, **Owner** Property, **Permissions** Property, **UserName** Property

See Also

User Object

Example

This example enumerates the **Containers** collection of the Northwind database and the **Properties** collection of each **Container** object in the collection.

```
Sub ContainerObjectX()

    Dim dbsNorthwind As Database
    Dim ctrLoop As Container
    Dim prpLoop As Property

    Set dbsNorthwind = OpenDatabase("Northwind.mdb")

    With dbsNorthwind

        ' Enumerate Containers collection.
        For Each ctrLoop In .Containers
            Debug.Print "Properties of " & ctrLoop.Name _
                & " container"

            ' Enumerate Properties collection of each
            ' Container object.
            For Each prpLoop In ctrLoop.Properties
                Debug.Print "    " & prpLoop.Name _
                    & " = " prpLoop
            Next prpLoop

        Next ctrLoop

        .Close
    End With

End Sub
```

Container Property

Returns or sets the container of a control on a **Form**. Not available at design time.

Applies To

Animation Control, **CheckBox** Control, **ComboBox** Control, **CommandButton** Control, **DBCombo** Control, **DBGrid** Control, **DBList** Control, **DirListBox** Control, **DriveListBox** Control, **FileListBox** Control, **Frame** Control, **HscrollBar**, **VScrollBar** Controls, **Image** Control, **Label** Control, **Line** Control, **ListBox** Control, **ListView** Control, **Masked Edit** Control, **MSChart** Control, **MSFlexGrid** Control, **Multimedia MCI** Control, **OLE Container** Control, **OptionButton** Control, **PictureBox** Control, **ProgressBar** Control, **RemoteData** Control, **RichTextBox** Control, **Shape** Control, **Slider** Control, **SSTab** Control, **StatusBar** Control, **TabStrip** Control, **TextBox** Control, **Toolbar** Control, **TreeView** Control, **UpDown** Control

Syntax

Set *object*.**Container** [= *container*]

The **Container** property syntax has these parts:

Part	Description
object	An object expression that evaluates to an object in the **Applies To** list.
container	An object expression that evaluates to an object that can serve as a container for other controls, as described in Remarks.

Remarks

The following controls can contain other controls:

- **Frame** control
- **PictureBox** control.

See Also

Frame Control, **PictureBox** Control, **Parent** Property

Example

This example demonstrates moving a **CommandButton** control from container to container on a **Form** object. To try this example, paste the code into the Declarations section of a form that contains a **Frame** control, a **PictureBox** control and a **CommandButton**, and then press F5.

```
Private Sub Form_Click()
    Static intX As Integer
    Select Case intX
        Case 0
            Set Command1.Container = Picture1
            Command1.Top= 0
            Command1.Left= 0
        Case 1
            Set Command1.Container = Frame1
            Command1.Top= 0
            Command1.Left= 0
        Case 2
            Set Command1.Container = Form1
            Command1.Top= 0
            Command1.Left= 0
    End Select
    intX = intX + 1
End Sub
```

Container Property (DAO)

Returns the name of the **Container** object to which a **Document** object belongs (Microsoft Jet workspaces only).

Applies To
Document Object

Return Values

The return value is a **String** data type.

See Also

Container Object

Example

This example displays the **Container** property for a variety of **Document** objects.

```
Sub ContainerPropertyX()

    Dim dbsNorthwind As Database
    Dim ctrLoop As Container

    Set dbsNorthwind = OpenDatabase("Northwind.mdb")

    ' Display the container name for the first Document
    ' object in each Container object's Documents collection.
    For Each ctrLoop In dbsNorthwind.Containers
        Debug.Print "Document: " & ctrLoop.Documents(0).Name
        Debug.Print "    Container = " & _
            ctrLoop.Documents(0).Container
    Next ctrLoop

    dbsNorthwind.Close

End Sub
```

Containers Collection

A **Containers** collection contains all of the **Container** objects that are defined in a database (Microsoft Jet databases only).

Remarks

Each **Database** object has a **Containers** collection consisting of built-in **Container** objects. Some of these **Container** objects are defined by the Microsoft Jet database engine while others may be defined by other applications.

Properties

Count Property

Methods

Refresh Method

Example

This example enumerates the **Containers** collection of the Northwind database and the **Properties** collection of each **Container** object in the collection.

```
Sub ContainerObjectX()

    Dim dbsNorthwind As Database
    Dim ctrLoop As Container
    Dim prpLoop As Property

    Set dbsNorthwind = OpenDatabase("Northwind.mdb")

    With dbsNorthwind

        ' Enumerate Containers collection.
        For Each ctrLoop In .Containers
            Debug.Print "Properties of " & ctrLoop.Name _
                & " container"

            ' Enumerate Properties collection of each
            ' Container object.
            For Each prpLoop In ctrLoop.Properties
                Debug.Print "    " & prpLoop.Name _
                    & " = " prpLoop
            Next prpLoop

        Next ctrLoop

        .Close
    End With

End Sub
```

ContinuousScroll Property

Returns or sets a value that determines if scrolling is continuous, or if the **UserDocument** only redraws when the scroll thumb is released.

Applies To

UserDocument Object

Syntax

object.**ContinuousScroll** = *boolean*

Part	Description
object	An object expression that evaluates to an object in the **Applies To** list.
boolean	A Boolean expression that specifies whether scrolling is continuous or not.

Settings

The settings for Boolean are:

Setting	Description
True	Default. Scrolling is continuous.
False	The **UserDocument** redraws only when the thumb is released.

Control Object

The class name of all Visual Basic internal controls.

Syntax

Control

Remarks

You can dimension a variable as a **Control** object and reference it as you would a control on a form. The following demonstrates this:

```
Dim C as Control
Set C = Command1
```

ControlBox Property

Returns or sets a value indicating whether a Control-menu box is displayed on a form at run time. Read-only at run time.

Applies To

Form Object, **Forms** Collection

Syntax

object.**ControlBox**

The *object* placeholder represents an object expression that evaluates to an object in the **Applies To** list.

Settings

The **ControlBox** property settings are:

Setting	Description
True	(Default) Displays the Control-menu box.
False	Removes the Control-menu box.

Remarks

To display a Control-menu box, you must also set the form's **BorderStyle** property to 1 (Fixed Single), 2 (Sizable), or 3 (Fixed Dialog).

Both modal and modeless windows can include a Control-menu box.

The commands available at run time depend on the settings for related properties—for example, setting **MaxButton** and **MinButton** to **False** disables the Maximize and Minimize commands on the Control menu, but the Move and Close commands remain available.

Note Settings you specify for the **ControlBox**, **BorderStyle**, **MaxButton**, and **MinButton** properties aren't reflected in the form's appearance until run time.

See Also

BorderStyle Property, **MaxButton** Property, **MinButton** Property

ControlContainer Property

Returns or sets a value determining if a control can contain controls placed on it by the developer or the end user at the control's run time; in the same way the **PictureBox** control can contain other controls. The **ControlContainer** property is read/write at the control's authoring time, and not available at the control's run time.

Applies To

UserControl Object

Settings

The settings for **ControlContainer** are:

Setting	Description
True	The control can contain controls placed on it. If an instance of this control is placed on a container that is not aware of **ISimpleFrame**, support of contained controls will be disabled. The control will continue to work correctly in all other ways, but developers or end users will be unable to place controls on an instance of this control.
False	The control cannot contain controls placed on it. This is the default value.

Remarks

Contained control support does work on a Visual Basic form.

Contained controls placed on a control with a transparent background are only visible where their location overlaps any constituent controls. Mouse events will be passed to the contained control only if they occur where the contained control is visible.

See Also

PictureBox Control

ControlObject Property

Returns a reference to an instance of the design-time **IDispatch** pointer provided by the control. If there isn't one, this property returns **Nothing**.

Applies To

VBControl Object

Syntax

object.**ControlObject**

The *object* placeholder represents an object expression that evaluates to an object in the **Applies To** list.

Remarks

For example, the **Toolbar** control provides an object through a **Property Page's ControlObject** property to set the number of buttons.

Controls Collection

A collection whose elements represent each control on a form, including elements of control array. The **Controls** collection has a single property, **Count**, that specifies the number of elements in an array.

Syntax

object.**Controls**(*index*)

The **Controls** collection syntax has these parts:

Part	Description
object	An object expression that evaluates to a **Form** object.
Index	An integer with a range from 0 to `Controls.Count - 1`.

Remarks

The **Controls** collection enumerates loaded controls on a form and is useful for iterating through them. The **Controls** collection identifies an intrinsic form-level variable named **Controls**. If you omit the optional *object* placeholder, you must include the **Controls** keyword. However, if you include *object*, you can omit the **Controls** keyword. For example, the following two lines of code have the same effect:

```
MyForm.Controls(6).Top = MyForm.Controls(5).Top + increment
MyForm(6).Top = MyForm(5).Top + increment
```

You can pass **Controls**(*index*) to a function whose argument is specified as a **Controls** class. You can also access members using their name. For example:

```
Controls("Command1").Top
```

Properties

Count Property, **Item** Method

Methods

Clear Method, **Remove** Method

See Also

Form Object, **Forms** Collection

Example

This example enables all currently loaded controls on a form (except menus).

```
Sub EnableControlsOn (Frm As Form, State As Integer)
    Dim I      ' Declare variable.
    For I = 0 To Frm.Controls.Count - 1
        If Not TypeOf Frm.Controls(I) Is Menu Then
            Frm.Controls(I).Enabled = State
        End If
    Next I
End Sub
```

Controls Property

Returns a reference to a collection of **Control** objects.

Applies To

PropertyPage Object, **UserControl** Object, **UserDocument** Object, **Form** Object, **Forms** Collection, **MDIForm** Object

Syntax

object.**Controls**

The *object* placeholder represents an object expression that evaluates to an object in the **Applies To** list.

Remarks

You can manipulate **Control** objects using the reference returned by the **Controls** property.

See Also

PropertyPage Object, **UserDocument** Object, **Form** Object, **Forms** Collection, **MDIForm** Object

ControlType Property

Returns the type of run-time window that a control creates.

Applies To

VBControl Object

Syntax

object.**ControlType As vbext_ControlType**

The *object* placeholder represents an object expression that evaluates to an object in the **Applies To** list.

Settings

The settings for **vbext_ControlType** are:

Constant	Value	Description
vbext_ct_Light	1	(Default) No hWnd at run-time.
vbext_ct_Standard	2	hWnd at run-time.
vbext_ct_Container	3	hWnd at run-time, and can contain other controls.

Conversion Functions

Asc Function

CBool Function

CByte Function

CCur Function

CDate Function

CDec Function

CDbl Function

Chr Function

CInt Function

CLng Function

CSng Function

CStr Function

CVar Function

CVErr Function

Format Function

Hex Function

Oct Function

Str Function

Val Function

Copies Property

Returns or sets a value that determines the number of copies to be printed. For the **Printer** object, not available at design time.

Applies To

Printer Object, **Printers** Collection, **CommonDialog** Control

Syntax

object.**Copies** [= *number*]

The **Copies** property syntax has these parts:

Part	Description
object	An object expression that evaluates to an object in the **Applies To** list.
number	A numeric expression that specifies the number of copies to print. This value must be an integer.

Remarks

For the Print dialog box, this property returns the number of copies entered by the user in the Copies box. If the **cdlPDUseDevModeCopies** flag is set for the **CommonDialog** control, this property always returns 1.

For the **Printer** object, multiple copies may or may not be collated, depending on the printer driver. Multiple copies of the entire document or multiple copies of each page may be printed. For printers that don't support collating, set **Copies** = 1, and then use a loop in code to print multiple copies of the entire document.

Note   The effect of the properties of the **Printer** object depends on the driver supplied by the printer manufacturer. Some property settings may have no effect, or several different property settings may all have the same effect. Settings outside the accepted range may produce an error. For more information, see the manufacturer's documentation for the specific driver.

See Also

Duplex Property, **PaperBin** Property

Copy Method

Copies the object within an **OLE** container control to the system Clipboard.

Applies To

OLE Container Control

Syntax

object.**Copy**

The *object* is an object expression that evaluates to an object in the **Applies To** list.

Remarks

When you copy an object onto the system Clipboard, all the data and link information associated with the object is placed on the system Clipboard. You can copy both linked and embedded objects onto the system Clipboard.

You can use this method to support an Edit Copy command on a menu.

See Also

Paste Method

CopyQueryDef Method

Returns a **QueryDef** object that is a copy of the **QueryDef** used to create the **Recordset** object represented by the *recordset* placeholder (Microsoft Jet workspaces only).

Applies To

Dynaset-Type Recordset Object, **Recordset** Object, **Snapshot-Type Recordset** Object, **Forward-Only–Type Recordset** Object

Syntax

Set *querydef* = *recordset*.**CopyQueryDef**

The **CopyQueryDef** method syntax has these parts.

Part	Description
querydef	An object variable that represents the copy of a **QueryDef** object you want to create.
recordset	An object variable that represents the **Recordset** object created with the original **QueryDef** object.

Remarks

You can use the **CopyQueryDef** method to create a new **QueryDef** that is a duplicate of the **QueryDef** used to create the **Recordset**.

If a **QueryDef** wasn't used to create this **Recordset**, an error occurs. You must first open a **Recordset** with the **OpenRecordset** method before using the **CopyQueryDef** method.

This method is useful when you create a **Recordset** object from a **QueryDef**, and pass the **Recordset** to a function, and the function must re-create the SQL equivalent of the query, for example, to modify it in some way.

See Also

QueryDef Object

Example

This example uses the **CopyQueryDef** method to create a copy of a **QueryDef** from an existing **Recordset** and modifies the copy by adding a clause to the **SQL** property. When you create a permanent **QueryDef,** spaces, semicolons, or linefeeds may be added to the **SQL** property; these extra characters must be stripped before any new clauses can be attached to the SQL statement.

```
Function CopyQueryNew(rstTemp As Recordset, _
    strAdd As String) As QueryDef

    Dim strSQL As String
    Dim strRightSQL As String
```

```
    Set CopyQueryNew = rstTemp.CopyQueryDef
    With CopyQueryNew
        ' Strip extra characters.
        strSQL = .SQL
        strRightSQL = Right(strSQL, 1)
        Do While strRightSQL = " " Or strRightSQL = ";" Or _
                strRightSQL = Chr(10) Or strRightSQL = vbCr
            strSQL = Left(strSQL, Len(strSQL) - 1)
            strRightSQL = Right(strSQL, 1)
        Loop
        .SQL = strSQL & strAdd
    End With

End Function
```

This example shows a possible use of **CopyQueryNew()**.

```
Sub CopyQueryDefX()

    Dim dbsNorthwind As Database
    Dim qdfEmployees As QueryDef
    Dim rstEmployees As Recordset
    Dim intCommand As Integer
    Dim strOrderBy As String
    Dim qdfCopy As QueryDef
    Dim rstCopy As Recordset

    Set dbsNorthwind = OpenDatabase("Northwind.mdb")
    Set qdfEmployees = dbsNorthwind.CreateQueryDef( _
        "NewQueryDef", "SELECT FirstName, LastName, " & _
        "BirthDate FROM Employees")
    Set rstEmployees = qdfEmployees.OpenRecordset( _
        dbOpenForwardOnly)

    Do While True
        intCommand = Val(InputBox( _
            "Choose field on which to order a new " & _
            "Recordset:" & vbCr & "1 - FirstName" & vbCr & _
            "2 - LastName" & vbCr & "3 - BirthDate" & vbCr & _
            "[Cancel - exit]"))
        Select Case intCommand
            Case 1
                strOrderBy = " ORDER BY FirstName"
            Case 2
                strOrderBy = " ORDER BY LastName"
            Case 3
                strOrderBy = " ORDER BY BirthDate"
            Case Else
                Exit Do
        End Select
```

```
            Set qdfCopy = CopyQueryNew(rstEmployees, strOrderBy)
            Set rstCopy = qdfCopy.OpenRecordset(dbOpenSnapshot, _
               dbForwardOnly)
            With rstCopy
               Do While Not .EOF
                  Debug.Print !LastName & ", " & !FirstName & _
                     " - " & !BirthDate
                  .MoveNext
               Loop
               .Close
            End With
            Exit Do
         Loop

      rstEmployees.Close
      ' Delete new QueryDef because this is a demonstration.
      dbsNorthwind.QueryDefs.Delete qdfEmployees.Name
      dbsNorthwind.Close

   End Sub
```

Cos Function

Returns a **Double** specifying the cosine of an angle.

Syntax

Cos(*number*)

The required *number* argument is a **Double** or any valid numeric expression that expresses an angle in radians.

Remarks

The **Cos** function takes an angle and returns the ratio of two sides of a right triangle. The ratio is the length of the side adjacent to the angle divided by the length of the hypotenuse.

The result lies in the range -1 to 1.

To convert degrees to radians, multiply degrees by pi/180. To convert radians to degrees, multiply radians by 180/pi.

See Also

Math Functions, **Atn** Function, **Sin** Function, **Tan** Function, **Derived Math** Functions

Example

This example uses the **Cos** function to return the cosine of an angle.

```
Dim MyAngle, MySecant
MyAngle = 1.3   ' Define angle in radians.
MySecant = 1 / Cos(MyAngle)' Calculate secant.
```

Count Property

Returns the number of objects in a collection.

Applies To

ColumnHeader Object, **ColumnHeaders** Collection, **Columns** Collect, **Controls** Collection, **DataObjectFiles** Collection, **DBGrid** Control, **Form** Object, **Forms** Collection, **ListImage** Object, **ListImages** Collection, **ListItem** Object, **ListItems** Collection, **MDIForm** Object, **Node** Object, **Nodes** Collection, **OLEObject** Object, **Printer** Object, **Printers** Collection, **PropertyPage** Object, **Splits** Collection, **SSTabControl**, **Tab** Object, **UserControl** Object, **UserDocument** Object

Syntax

object.**Count**

The *object* placeholder is an object expression that evaluates to an object in the **Applies To** list.

Remarks

You can use this property with a **For...Next** statement to carry out an operation on the forms or controls in a collection. For example, the following code moves all controls on a form 0.5 inches to the right (**ScaleMode** property setting is 1 or **vbTwips**):

```
For I = 0 To Form1.Controls.Count - 1
    Form1.Controls(I).Left = Form1.Controls(I).Left + 720
Next I
```

You can also use this kind of structure to quickly enable or disable all controls on a form.

When used with the **If TypeOf** statement, you can cycle through all controls and change, for example, the **Enabled** property setting of only the text boxes or the **BackColor** property setting of only the option buttons.

See Also

Count Property (VB Collections)

CountOfDeclarationLines Property

Returns a **Long** containing the number of lines of code in the Declarations section of a code module. Read-only.

Applies To

CodeModule Object

See Also

DeleteLines Method, **InsertLines** Method, **Lines** Method, **ReplaceLine** Method, **CountOfLines** Property, **CountOfVisibleLines** Property

Example

The following example uses the **CountOfDeclarationLines** property to return the number of declaration lines in a particular code pane.

```
Debug.Print Application.VBE.CodePanes(2).CodeModule.CountOfDeclarationLines
```

CountOfLines Property

Returns a **Long** containing the number of lines of code in a code module. Read-only.

Applies To

CodeModule Object

See Also

DeleteLines Method, **InsertLines** Method, **Lines** Method, **ReplaceLine** Method, **CountOfDeclarationLines** Property, **CountOfVisibleLines** Property

Example

The following example uses the **CountOfLines** property to return the total number of lines in a particular code pane.

```
Application.VBE.CodePanes(2).CodeModule.CountOfLines
```

CountOfVisibleLines Property

Returns a **Long** containing the number of lines visible in a code pane. Read-only.

Applies To

CodePane Object

See Also

DeleteLines Method, **InsertLines** Method, **Lines** Method, **ReplaceLine** Method, **CountOfLines** Property, **CountOfDeclarationLines** Property

Example

The following example uses the **CountOfVisibleLines** property to return the number of lines visible at one time in a particular code pane, based on the height of the pane.

```
Debug.Print Application.VBE.Codepanes(3).CountOfVisibleLines
```

CreateDatabase Method

Creates a new **Database** object, saves the database to disk, and returns an opened **Database** object (Microsoft Jet workspaces only).

Applies To

DBEngine Object, **Workspace** Object

Syntax

Set *database* = *workspace*.**CreateDatabase** (*name*, *locale*, *options*)

The **CreateDatabase** method syntax has these parts.

Part	Description
database	An object variable that represents the **Database** object you want to create.
Workspace	An object variable that represents the existing **Workspace** object that will contain the database. If you omit *workspace*, **CreateDatabase** uses the default **Workspace**.
Name	A **String** up to 255 characters long that is the name of the database file that you're creating. It can be the full path and file name, such as `"C:\db1.mdb"`. If you don't supply a file name extension, .mdb is appended. If your network supports it, you can also specify a network path, such as `"\\server1\share1\dir1\db1"`. You can only create .mdb database files with this method.

Locale	A string expression that specifies a collating order for creating the database, as specified in Settings. You must supply this argument or an error occurs.
	
	You can also create a password for the new **Database** object by concatenating the password string (starting with `";pwd="`) with a constant in the *locale* argument, like this:
	`dbLangSpanish & ";pwd=NewPassword"`
	If you want to use the default *locale*, but specify a password, simply enter a password string for the *locale* argument:
	`";pwd=NewPassword"`

options	Optional. A constant or combination of constants that indicates one or more options, as specified in Settings. You can combine options by summing the corresponding constants.

Settings

You can use one of the following constants for the *locale* argument to specify the **CollatingOrder** property of text for string comparisons.

Constant	Collating order
dbLangGeneral	English, German, French, Portuguese, Italian, and Modern Spanish
dbLangArabic	Arabic
dbLangChineseSimplified	Simplified Chinese
dbLangChineseTraditional	Traditional Chinese
dbLangCyrillic	Russian
dbLangCzech	Czech
dbLangDutch	Dutch
dbLangGreek	Greek
dbLangHebrew	Hebrew

(continued)

(continued)

Constant	Collating order
dbLangHungarian	Hungarian
dbLangIcelandic	Icelandic
dbLangJapanese	Japanese
dbLangKorean	Korean
dbLangNordic	Nordic languages (Microsoft Jet database engine version 1.0 only)
dbLangNorwDan	Norwegian and Danish
dbLangPolish	Polish
dbLangSlovenian	Slovenian
dbLangSpanish	Traditional Spanish
dbLangSwedFin	Swedish and Finnish
dbLangThai	Thai
dbLangTurkish	Turkish

You can use one or more of the following constants in the *options* argument to specify which version the data format should have and whether or not to encrypt the database.

Constant	Description
dbEncrypt	Creates an encrypted database.
dbVersion10	Creates a database that uses the Microsoft Jet database engine version 1.0 file format.
dbVersion11	Creates a database that uses the Microsoft Jet database engine version 1.1 file format.
dbVersion20	Creates a database that uses the Microsoft Jet database engine version 2.0 file format.
dbVersion30	(Default) Creates a database that uses the Microsoft Jet database engine version 3.0 file format (compatible with version 3.5).

If you omit the encryption constant, **CreateDatabase** creates an un-encrypted database. You can specify only one version constant. If you omit a version constant, **CreateDatabase** creates a database that uses the Microsoft Jet database engine version 3.0 file format.

Remarks

Use the **CreateDatabase** method to create and open a new, empty database, and return the **Database** object. You must complete its structure and content by using additional DAO objects. If you want to make a partial or complete copy of an existing database, you can use the **CompactDatabase** method to make a copy that you can customize.

e Also

Database Object, **CompactDatabase** Method, **OpenDatabase** Method, **CollatingOrder** Property

Example

This example uses **CreateDatabase** to create a new, encrypted **Database** object.

```
Sub CreateDatabaseX()

    Dim wrkDefault As Workspace
    Dim dbsNew As DATABASE
    Dim prpLoop As Property

    ' Get default Workspace.
    Set wrkDefault = DBEngine.Workspaces(0)

    ' Make sure there isn't already a file with the name of
    ' the new database.
    If Dir("NewDB.mdb") <> "" Then Kill "NewDB.mdb"

    ' Create a new encrypted database with the specified
    ' collating order.
    Set dbsNew = wrkDefault.CreateDatabase("NewDB.mdb", _
        dbLangGeneral, dbEncrypt)

    With dbsNew
        Debug.Print "Properties of " & .Name
        ' Enumerate the Properties collection of the new
        ' Database object.
        For Each prpLoop In .Properties
            If prpLoop <> "" Then Debug.Print "    " & _
                prpLoop.Name & " = " & prpLoop
        Next prpLoop
    End With

    dbsNew.Close

End Sub
```

CreateEmbed Method

Creates an embedded object. Doesn't support named arguments.

Applies To

OLE Container Control

Syntax

object.**CreateEmbed** *sourcedoc, class*

The **CreateEmbed** method syntax has these parts:

Part	Description
object	An object expression that evaluates to an object in the **Applies To** list.
sourcedoc	Required. The filename of a document used as a template for the embedded object. Must be a zero-length string ("") if you don't specify a source document.
class	Optional. The name of the class of the embedded object. Ignored if you specify a filename for *sourcedoc*.

Remarks

To view a list of valid class names available on your system, select a control, such as the **OLE** container control, select the **Class** property in the Properties window, and then click the builder button.

Note   You don't need to set the **Class** and **SourceDoc** properties when using the **CreateEmbed** method to create an embedded object.

When you create a new object, the application associated with the class name (for example, Excel.exe) must be correctly registered with the operating system. (The application setup program should register the application correctly.)

See Also

Class Property, **OLETypeAllowed** Property

CreateEventProc Method

Creates an event procedure.

Applies To

CodeModule Object

Syntax

object.**CreateEventProc**(*eventname*, *objectname*) **As Long**

CreateEventProc syntax has these parts:

Part	Description
object	Required. An object expression that evaluates to an object in the **Applies To** list.
eventname	Required. A string expression specifying the name of the event you want to add to the module.
objectname	Required. A string expression specifying the name of the object that is the source of the event.

Remarks

Use the **CreateEventProc** method to create an event procedure. For example, to create an event procedure for the **Click** event of a **Command Button** control named Command1 you would use the following code, where CM represents a object of type **CodeModule**:

```
TextLocation = CM.CreateEventProc("Click", "Command1")
```

The **CreateEventProc** method returns the line at which the body of the event procedure starts. **CreateEventProc** fails if the arguments refer to a nonexistent event.

AddFromString Method, **DeleteLines** Method, **InsertLines** Method, **ProcBodyLine** Method, **ProcCountLines** Method, **ProcOfLine** Method, **ProcStartLine** Method, **ReplaceLine** Method

Example

The following example uses the **CreateEventProc** method to create the Button_Click procedure.

```
Debug.Print Application.VBE.SelectVBComponents.CodeModule.
↳ CreateEventProc("Click", "Button")
```

CreateField Method

Creates a new **Field** object (Microsoft Jet workspaces only).

Applies To

Index Object, **Relation** Object, **TableDef** Object

Syntax

Set *field* = *object*.**CreateField** (*name*, *type*, *size*)

The **CreateField** method syntax has these parts.

Part	Description
field	An object variable that represents the **Field** object you want to create.
object	An object variable that represents the **Index**, **Relation**, or **TableDef** object for which you want to create the new **Field** object.
name	Optional. A **Variant** (**String** subtype) that uniquely names the new **Field** object. See the **Name** property for details on valid **Field** names.
type	Optional. A constant that determines the data type of the new **Field** object. See the **Type** property for valid data types.
size	Optional. A **Variant** (**Integer** subtype) that indicates the maximum size, in bytes, of a **Field** object that contains text. See the **Size** property for valid *size* values. This argument is ignored for numeric and fixed-width fields.

Remarks

You can use the **CreateField** method to create a new field, as well as specify the name, data type, and size of the field. If you omit one or more of the optional parts when you use **CreateField**, you can use an appropriate assignment statement to set or reset the corresponding property before you append the new object to a collection. After you append the new object, you can alter some but not all of its property settings. See the individual property topics for more details.

The *type* and *size* arguments apply only to **Field** objects in a **TableDef** object. These arguments are ignored when a **Field** object is associated with an **Index** or **Relation** object.

If *name* refers to an object that is already a member of the collection, a run-time error occurs when you use the **Append** method.

To remove a **Field** object from a **Fields** collection, use the **Delete** method on the collection. You can't delete a **Field** object from a **TableDef** object's **Fields** collection after you create an index that references the field.

See Also

Field Object, **Append** Method, **Delete** Method, **Name** Property, **Size** Property, **Type** Property

Example

This example uses the **CreateField** method to create three **Fields** for a new **TableDef**. It then displays the properties of those **Field** objects that are automatically set by the **CreateField** method. (Properties whose values are empty at the time of **Field** creation are not shown.)

```
Sub CreateFieldX()

    Dim dbsNorthwind As Database
    Dim tdfNew As TableDef
    Dim fldLoop As Field
    Dim prpLoop As Property

    Set dbsNorthwind = OpenDatabase("Northwind.mdb")

    Set tdfNew = dbsNorthwind.CreateTableDef("NewTableDef")

    ' Create and append new Field objects for the new
    ' TableDef object.
    With tdfNew
        ' The CreateField method will set a default Size
        ' for a new Field object if one is not specified.
        .Fields.Append .CreateField("TextField", dbText)
        .Fields.Append .CreateField("IntegerField", dbInteger)
        .Fields.Append .CreateField("DateField", dbDate)
    End With

    dbsNorthwind.TableDefs.Append tdfNew

    Debug.Print "Properties of new Fields in " & tdfNew.Name

    ' Enumerate Fields collection to show the properties of
    ' the new Field objects.
    For Each fldLoop In tdfNew.Fields
        Debug.Print "    " & fldLoop.Name

        For Each prpLoop In fldLoop.Properties
            ' Properties that are invalid in the context of
            ' TableDefs will trigger an error if an attempt
            ' is made to read their values.
            On Error Resume Next
            Debug.Print "        " & prpLoop.Name & " - " & _
                IIf(prpLoop = "", "[empty]", prpLoop)
            On Error GoTo 0
        Next prpLoop
```

```
    Next fldLoop

    ' Delete new TableDef because this is a demonstration.
    dbsNorthwind.TableDefs.Delete tdfNew.Name
    dbsNorthwind.Close

End Sub
```

CreateGroup Method

Creates a new **Group** object (Microsoft Jet workspaces only).

Applies To

User Object, **Workspace** Object

Syntax

Set *group* = *object*.**CreateGroup** (*name*, *pid*)

The **CreateGroup** method syntax has these parts.

Part	Description
group	An object variable that represents the **Group** you want to create.
Object	An object variable that represents the **User** or **Workspace** object for which you want to create the new **Group** object.
Name	Optional. A **Variant** (**String** subtype) that uniquely names the new **Group** object. See the **Name** property for details on valid **Group** names.
Pid	Optional. A **Variant** (**String** subtype) containing the PID of a group account. The identifier must contain from 4 to 20 alphanumeric characters. See the **PID** property for more information on valid personal identifiers.

Remarks

You can use the **CreateGroup** method to create a new **Group** object for a **User** or **Workspace**. If you omit one or both of the optional parts when you use **CreateGroup**, you can use an appropriate assignment statement to set or reset the corresponding property before you append the new object to a collection. After you append the object, you can alter some but not all of its property settings. See the individual property topics for more details.

If *name* refers to an object that is already a member of the collection, a run-time error occurs when you use the **Append** method.

To remove a **Group** object from a collection, use the **Delete** method on the **Groups** collection.

See Also

Group Object, **Append** Method, **Delete** Method, **Name** Property, **PID** Property

Example

This example uses the **CreateGroup** method to create a new **Group** object; it then makes the "admin" user a member of the new **Group** object and lists its properties and users.

```
Sub CreateGroupX()

    Dim wrkDefault As Workspace
    Dim grpNew As Group
    Dim grpTemp As Group
    Dim prpLoop As Property
    Dim usrLoop As User

    Set wrkDefault = DBEngine.Workspaces(0)

    With wrkDefault

        ' Create and append new group.
        Set grpNew = .CreateGroup("NewGroup", _
            "AAA123456789")
        .Groups.Append grpNew

        ' Make the user "admin" a member of the
        ' group NewGroup by creating and adding the
        ' appropriate Group object to the user's Groups
        ' collection.
        Set grpTemp = .Users("admin").CreateGroup("NewGroup")
        .Users("admin").Groups.Append grpTemp

        Debug.Print "Properties of " & grpNew.Name

        ' Enumerate the Properties collection of NewGroup. The
        ' PID property is not readable.
        For Each prpLoop In grpNew.Properties
            On Error Resume Next
            If prpLoop <> "" Then Debug.Print "    " & _
                prpLoop.Name & " = " & prpLoop
            On Error GoTo 0
        Next prpLoop

        Debug.Print "Users collection of " & grpNew.Name

        ' Enumerate the Users collection of NewGroup.
        For Each usrLoop In grpNew.Users
            Debug.Print "    " & _
                usrLoop.Name
        Next usrLoop

        ' Delete the new Group object because this
        ' is a demonstration.
        .Groups.Delete "NewGroup"

    End With

End Sub
```

CreateIndex Method

Creates a new **Index** object (Microsoft Jet workspaces only).

Applies To

TableDef Object

Syntax

Set *index* = *tabledef*.**CreateIndex** (*name*)

The **CreateIndex** method syntax has these parts.

Part	Description
index	An object variable that represents the index you want to create.
Tabledef	An object variable that represents the **TableDef** object you want to use to create the new **Index** object.
Name	Optional. A **Variant** (**String** subtype) that uniquely names the new **Index** object. See the **Name** property for details on valid **Index** names.

Remarks

You can use the **CreateIndex** method to create a new **Index** object for a **TableDef** object. If you omit the optional *name* part when you use **CreateIndex**, you can use an appropriate assignment statement to set or reset the **Name** property before you append the new object to a collection. After you append the object, you may or may not be able to set its **Name** property, depending on the type of object that contains the **Indexes** collection. See the **Name** property topic for more details.

If *name* refers to an object that is already a member of the collection, a run-time error occurs when you use the **Append** method.

To remove an **Index** object from a collection, use the **Delete** method on the collection.

See Also

Index Object, **Append** Method, **Delete** Method, **Name** Property

Example

This example uses the **CreateIndex** method to create two new **Index** objects and then appends them to the **Indexes** collection of the Employees **TableDef** object. It then enumerates the **Indexes** collection of the **TableDef** object, the **Fields** collection of the new **Index** objects, and the **Properties** collection of the new **Index** objects. The **CreateIndexOutput** function is required for this procedure to run.

```
Sub CreateIndexX()

    Dim dbsNorthwind As Database
    Dim tdfEmployees As TableDef
    Dim idxCountry As Index
    Dim idxFirstName As Index
    Dim idxLoop As Index
```

```
        Set dbsNorthwind = OpenDatabase("Northwind.mdb")
        Set tdfEmployees = dbsNorthwind!Employees

    With tdfEmployees
        ' Create first Index object, create and append Field
        ' objects to the Index object, and then append the
        ' Index object to the Indexes collection of the
        ' TableDef.
        Set idxCountry = .CreateIndex("CountryIndex")
        With idxCountry
            .Fields.Append .CreateField("Country")
            .Fields.Append .CreateField("LastName")
            .Fields.Append .CreateField("FirstName")
        End With
        .Indexes.Append idxCountry

        ' Create second Index object, create and append Field
        ' objects to the Index object, and then append the
        ' Index object to the Indexes collection of the
        ' TableDef.
        Set idxFirstName = .CreateIndex
        With idxFirstName
            .Name = "FirstNameIndex"
            .Fields.Append .CreateField("FirstName")
            .Fields.Append .CreateField("LastName")
        End With
        .Indexes.Append idxFirstName

        ' Refresh collection so that you can access new Index
        ' objects.
        .Indexes.Refresh

        Debug.Print .Indexes.Count & " Indexes in " & _
            .Name & " TableDef"

        ' Enumerate Indexes collection.
        For Each idxLoop In .Indexes
            Debug.Print "    " & idxLoop.Name
        Next idxLoop

        ' Print report.
        CreateIndexOutput idxCountry
        CreateIndexOutput idxFirstName

        ' Delete new Index objects because this is a
        ' demonstration.
        .Indexes.Delete idxCountry.Name
        .Indexes.Delete idxFirstName.Name
    End With

    dbsNorthwind.Close

End Sub
```

```
Function CreateIndexOutput(idxTemp As Index)

    Dim fldLoop As Field
    Dim prpLoop As Property

    With idxTemp
        ' Enumerate Fields collection of Index object.
        Debug.Print "Fields in " & .Name
        For Each fldLoop In .Fields
            Debug.Print "    " & fldLoop.Name
        Next fldLoop

        ' Enumerate Properties collection of Index object.
        Debug.Print "Properties of " & .Name
        For Each prpLoop In .Properties
            Debug.Print "    " & prpLoop.Name & " - " & _
                IIf(prpLoop = "", "[empty]", prpLoop)
        Next prpLoop
    End With

End Function
```

CreateLink Method

Creates a linked object from the contents of a file. Doesn't support named arguments.

Applies To

OLE Container Control

Syntax

object.**CreateLink** *sourcedoc*, *sourceitem*

The **CreateLink** method syntax has these parts:

Part	Description
object	An object expression that evaluates to an object in the **Applies To** list.
sourcedoc	Required. The file from which the object is created.
sourceitem	Optional. The data within the file to be linked in the linked object.

Remarks

If you specify values for the arguments of this method, those values override the settings of the **SourceDoc** and **SourceItem** properties. Those properties are updated to reflect the argument values when the method is invoked.

When an object is created with this method, the **OLE** container control displays an image of the file specified by the **SourceDoc** property. If the object is saved, only the link references are saved because the **OLE** container control contains only a metafile image of the data and no actual source data.

When you create a new object, the application associated with the class name (for example, Excel.exe) must be correctly registered with the operating system. (The application setup program should register the application correctly.)

See Also

SourceDoc Property, **SourceItem** Property, **OLETypeAllowed** Property, **CreateEmbed** Method

---

CreateObject Function

Creates and returns a reference to an **ActiveX** object.

Syntax

CreateObject(*class*)

The *class* argument uses the syntax *appname.objecttype* and has these parts:

Part	Description
appname	Required; **Variant** (**String**). The name of the application providing the object.
objecttype	Required; **Variant** (**String**). The type or class of object to create.

Remarks

Every application that supports Automation provides at least one type of object. For example, a word processing application may provide an **Application** object, a **Document** object, and a **Toolbar** object.

To create an **ActiveX** object, assign the object returned by **CreateObject** to an object variable:

```
' Declare an object variable to hold the object
' reference. Dim as Object causes late binding.
Dim ExcelSheet As Object
Set ExcelSheet = CreateObject("Excel.Sheet")
```

This code starts the application creating the object, in this case, a Microsoft Excel spreadsheet. Once an object is created, you reference it in code using the object variable you defined. In the following example, you access properties and methods of the new object using the object variable, ExcelSheet, and other Microsoft Excel objects, including the Application object and the Cells collection.

```
' Make Excel visible through the Application object
ExcelSheet.Application.Visible = True
' Place some text in the first cell of the sheet
ExcelSheet.Cells(1, 1).Value = "This is column A, row 1"
' Save the sheet to C:\test.doc directory
ExcelSheet.SaveAs "C:\ TEST.DOC"
' Close Excel with the Quit method on the Application object
ExcelSheet.Application.Quit
' Release the object variable
Set ExcelSheet = Nothing
```

Declaring an object variable with the `As Object` clause creates a variable that can contain a reference to any type of object. However, access to the object through that variable is late bound; that is, the binding occurs when your program is run. To create an object variable that results in early binding; that is, binding when the program is compiled, declare the object variable with a specific class ID. For example, you can declare and create the following Microsoft Excel references:

```
Dim xlApp As Excel.Application
Dim xlBook As Excel.Workbook
Dim xlSheet As Excel.WorkSheet
Set xlApp = CreateObject("Excel.Application")
Set xlBook = xlApp.Workbooks.Add
Set xlSheet = xlBook.Worksheets(1)
```

The reference through an early-bound variable can give better performance, but can only contain a reference to the class specified in the declaration.

You can pass an object returned by the **CreateObject** function to a function expecting an object as an argument. For example, the following code creates and passes a reference to an **Excel.Application** object:

```
Call MySub (CreateObject("Excel.Application"))
```

Note Use **CreateObject** when there is no current instance of the object. If an instance of the object is already running, a new instance is started, and an object of the specified type is created. To use the current instance, or to start the application and have it load a file, use the **GetObject** function.

If an object has registered itself as a single-instance object, only one instance of the object is created, no matter how many times **CreateObject** is executed.

See Also

    GetObject Function, **Set** Statement

Example

This example uses the **CreateObject** function to set a reference (xlApp) to Microsoft Excel. It uses the reference to access the **Visible** property of Microsoft Excel, and then uses the Microsoft Excel **Quit** method to close it. Finally, the reference itself is released.

```
Dim xlApp As Object   ' Declare variable to hold the reference.

Set xlApp = CreateObject("excel.application")
                      ' You may have to set Visible property to True
                      ' if you want to see the application.
xlApp.Visible = True
                      ' Use xlApp to access Microsoft Excel's
                      ' other objects.
xlApp.Quit            ' When you finish, use the Quit method to close
Set xlApp = Nothing   ' the application, then release the reference.
```

CreatePreparedStatement Method (Remote Data)

Creates a new **rdoPreparedStatement** object.

Applies To

rdoConnection Object

Syntax

Set *prepstmt* = *connection*.**CreatePreparedStatement**(*name*, *sqlstring*)

The **CreatePreparedStatement** method syntax has these parts:

Part	Description
prepstmt	An object expression that evaluates to the **rdoPreparedStatement** object you want to create.
connection	An object expression that represents the open **rdoConnection** object.
name	A **String** that is the name of the new **rdoPreparedStatement**. This part is required, but may be an empty string ("").
sqlstring	A **Variant** expression (a valid SQL statement) that defines the **rdoPreparedStatement**. This part is required, but you can provide an empty string—if you do, you must define the **rdoPreparedStatement** by setting its **SQL** property before executing the new **rdoPreparedStatement**.

Remarks

Note   Support for the **rdoPreparedStatement** object is provided in this version of Visual Basic to provide compatibility with previous versions. The **rdoQuery** object should be used as a direct replacement for this object. Because of this, it is also recommended that use of the **CreatePreparedStatement** method be discontinued in favor of the **CreateQuery** method.

See Also

Close Method (Remote Data), **Execute** Method (Remote Data), **OpenResultset** Method (Remote Data), **CreateQuery** Method (Remote Data), **rdoConnection** Object, **rdoPreparedStatement** Object, **rdoQuery** Object, **rdoResultset** Object, **Name** Property (Remote Data), **SQL** Property, **Type** Property (Remote Data)

CreateProperty Method

Creates a new user-defined **Property** object (Microsoft Jet workspaces only).

Applies To

Database Object, **Document** Object, **Field** Object, **Index** Object, **QueryDef** Object, **TableDef** Object

Syntax

Set *property* = *object*.**CreateProperty** (*name*, *type*, *value*, *DDL*)

The **CreateProperty** method syntax has these parts.

Part	Description
property	An object variable that represents the **Property** object you want to create.
object	An object variable that represents the **Database**, **Field**, **Index**, **QueryDef**, **Document**, or **TableDef** object you want to use to create the new **Property** object.
name	Optional. A **Variant** (**String** subtype) that uniquely names the new **Property** object. See the **Name** property for details on valid **Property** names.
type	Optional. A constant that defines the data type of the new **Property** object. See the **Type** property for valid data types.
value	Optional. A **Variant** containing the initial property value. See the **Value** property for details.
DDL	Optional. A **Variant** (**Boolean** subtype) that indicates whether or not the **Property** is a DDL object. The default is **False**. If *DDL* is **True**, users can't change or delete this **Property** object unless they have **dbSecWriteDef** permission.

Remarks

You can create a user-defined **Property** object only in the **Properties** collection of an object that is persistent.

If you omit one or more of the optional parts when you use **CreateProperty**, you can use an appropriate assignment statement to set or reset the corresponding property before you append the new object to a collection. After you append the object, you can alter some but not all of its property settings. See the **Name**, **Type**, and **Value** property topics for more details.

If *name* refers to an object that is already a member of the collection, a run-time error occurs when you use the **Append** method.

To remove a user-defined **Property** object from the collection, use the **Delete** method on the **Properties** collection. You can't delete built-in properties.

Note   If you omit the *DDL* argument, it defaults to **False** (non-DDL). Because no corresponding DDL property is exposed, you must delete and re-create a **Property** object you want to change from DDL to non-DDL.

See Also

Append Method, **Delete** Method, **Name** Property, **Type** Property, **Value** Property

Example

This example tries to set the value of a user-defined property. If the property doesn't exist, it uses the **CreateProperty** method to create and set the value of the new property. The **SetProperty** procedure is required for this procedure to run.

```
Sub CreatePropertyX()

    Dim dbsNorthwind As Database
    Dim prpLoop As Property

    Set dbsNorthwind = OpenDatabase("Northwind.mdb")

    ' Set the Archive property to True.
    SetProperty dbsNorthwind, "Archive", True

    With dbsNorthwind
        Debug.Print "Properties of " & .Name

        ' Enumerate Properties collection of the Northwind
        ' database.
        For Each prpLoop In .Properties
            If prpLoop <> "" Then Debug.Print "     " & _
                prpLoop.Name & " = " & prpLoop
        Next prpLoop

        ' Delete the new property since this is a
        ' demonstration.
        .Properties.Delete "Archive"

        .Close
    End With

End Sub

Sub SetProperty(dbsTemp As Database, strName As String, _
    booTemp As Boolean)

    Dim prpNew As Property
    Dim errLoop As Error

    ' Attempt to set the specified property.
    On Error GoTo Err_Property
    dbsTemp.Properties("strName") = booTemp
    On Error GoTo 0

    Exit Sub

Err_Property:

    ' Error 3270 means that the property was not found.
    If DBEngine.Errors(0).Number = 3270 Then
        ' Create property, set its value, and append it to the
        ' Properties collection.
        Set prpNew = dbsTemp.CreateProperty(strName, _
            dbBoolean, booTemp)
        dbsTemp.Properties.Append prpNew
        Resume Next
    Else
```

```
        ' If different error has occurred, display message.
        For Each errLoop In DBEngine.Errors
            MsgBox "Error number: " & errLoop.Number & vbCr & _
                errLoop.Description
        Next errLoop
        End
    End If

End Sub
```

CreateQuery Method (Remote Data)

Creates a new query object and adds it to the **rdoQueries** collection.

Applies To

rdoConnection Object

Syntax

object.**CreateQuery** *Name*, *SQLString*

The **CreateQuery** method syntax has these parts:

Part	Description
object	An object expression that evaluates to an **rdoConnection** object
Name	Required. A string expression that evaluates to the name for the new object
SQLString	Optional. SQL query for the new prepared statement

Remarks

The **CreateQuery** method creates a new **rdoQuery** object for this connection and adds it to the **rdoQueries** collection. You can also declare stand-alone **rdoQuery** objects using the **Dim** statement as follows:

```
Dim myQuery as New rdoQuery
```

Stand-alone **rdoQuery** objects are not associated with a connection until you set the **ActiveConnection** property.

The **rdoQuery** corresponds to the ODBC prepared statement used to define a reusable SQL query that can contain parameters. You can execute the **rdoQuery** any number of times, and pass parameters that are substituted into the SQL statement before it is executed. Parameters are maintained in the **rdoParameters** collection. Generally, if you intend to execute a query more than once in your code, it is more efficient to use **rdoQuery** objects than to use the **Execute** or **OpenResultset** method on objects other than the **rdoQuery**.

The value passed for the *Name* parameter can be used with the **Item** method to locate the new object in its collection. If *Name* is not provided, the **rdoQuery** is appended to the **rdoQueries** collection, and the **rdoQuery** can be used by referencing the query variable or the **rdoQuery** object's ordinal value. If the object specified by name is already a member of the **rdoQueries** collection (including an empty string), a trappable error occurs. All **rdoQuery** objects are temporary—they are discarded when the **rdoConnection** object is closed.

To remove an **rdoQuery** object from an **rdoQueries** collection, use the **Close** method on the **rdoQuery**.

The *SQLString* parameter is optional, but if not provided, you must set the **SQL** property of the resulting **rdoQuery** object before executing it.

Use the **Execute** method to run an SQL statement in an **rdoQuery** object that does not return rows (an action query). Use the **OpenResultset** method to run an **rdoQuery** that returns rows.

If there is an unpopulated **rdoResultset** pending on a data source that can only support a single operation on an **rdoConnection** object, you cannot create additional **rdoQuery** or **rdoResultset** objects, or use the **Refresh** method on the **rdoTable** object until the **rdoResultset** is flushed, closed, or fully populated. For example, when using SQL Server 4.2 as a data source, you cannot create an additional **rdoResultset** object until you move to the last row of the current **rdoResultset** object. To populate the result set, use the **MoreResults** method to move through all pending result sets, or use the **Cancel** or **Close** method on the **rdoResultset** to flush all pending result sets.

See Also

QueryCompleted Event (Remote Data), **QueryComplete** Event, **QueryTimeout** Event, **Execute** Method (Remote Data), **OpenResultset** Method (Remote Data), **rdoConnection** Object, **rdoParameters** Collection, **rdoQuery** Object, **rdoQueries** Collection, **rdoResultset** Object, **QueryTimeout** Property (Remote Data), **QueryTimeout** Property, **QueryTimeout** Event Example, **SQL** Property, **ActiveConnection** Property, **RemoteData** Control, **Type** Property, **rdoQuery** Object Constants

CreateQueryDef Method

Creates a new **QueryDef** object in a specified **Connection** or **Database** object.

Applies To

Database Object, **Connection** Object

Syntax

Set *querydef* = *object*.**CreateQueryDef** (*name*, *sqltext*)

The **CreateQueryDef** method syntax has these parts.

Part	Description
querydef	An object variable that represents the **QueryDef** object you want to create.
Object	An object variable that represents an open **Connection** or **Database** object that will contain the new **QueryDef**.
Name	Optional. A **Variant** (**String** subtype) that uniquely names the new **QueryDef**.
Sqltext	Optional. A **Variant** (**String** subtype) that is an SQL statement defining the **QueryDef**. If you omit this argument, you can define the **QueryDef** by setting its **SQL** property before or after you append it to a collection.

Remarks

In a Microsoft Jet workspace, if you provide anything other than a zero-length string for the name when you create a **QueryDef**, the resulting **QueryDef** object is automatically appended to the **QueryDefs** collection. In an ODBCDirect workspace, **QueryDef** objects are always temporary.

In an ODBCDirect workspace, the *sqltext* argument can specify an SQL statement or a Microsoft SQL Server stored procedure and its parameters.

If the object specified by *name* is already a member of the **QueryDefs** collection, a run-time error occurs. You can create a temporary **QueryDef** by using a zero-length string for the *name* argument when you execute the **CreateQueryDef** method. You can also accomplish this by setting the **Name** property of a newly created **QueryDef** to a zero-length string (""). Temporary **QueryDef** objects are useful if you want to repeatedly use dynamic SQL statements without having to create any new permanent objects in the **QueryDefs** collection. You can't append a temporary **QueryDef** to any collection because a zero-length string isn't a valid name for a permanent **QueryDef** object. You can always set the **Name** and **SQL** properties of the newly created **QueryDef** object and subsequently append the **QueryDef** to the **QueryDefs** collection.

To run the SQL statement in a **QueryDef** object, use the **Execute** or **OpenRecordset** method.

Using a **QueryDef** object is the preferred way to perform SQL pass-through queries with ODBC databases.

To remove a **QueryDef** object from a **QueryDefs** collection in a Microsoft Jet database, use the **Delete** method on the collection. For an ODBCDirect database, use the **Close** method on the **QueryDef** object.

See Also

QueryDef Object, **Append** Method, **CreateProperty** Method, **Delete** Method, **OpenRecordset** Method, **Connect** Property, **LogMessages** Property, **Name** Property, **ReturnsRecords** Property, **SQL** Property, **Type** Property, **Value** Property

Example

This example uses the **CreateQueryDef** method to create and execute both a temporary and a permanent **QueryDef**. The **GetrstTemp** function is required for this procedure to run.

```
Sub CreateQueryDefX()

    Dim dbsNorthwind As Database
    Dim qdfTemp As QueryDef
    Dim qdfNew As QueryDef

    Set dbsNorthwind = OpenDatabase("Northwind.mdb")

    With dbsNorthwind
        ' Create temporary QueryDef.
        Set qdfTemp = .CreateQueryDef("", _
            "SELECT * FROM Employees")
        ' Open Recordset and print report.
        GetrstTemp qdfTemp
        ' Create permanent QueryDef.
        Set qdfNew = .CreateQueryDef("NewQueryDef", _
            "SELECT * FROM Categories")
        ' Open Recordset and print report.
        GetrstTemp qdfNew
        ' Delete new QueryDef because this is a demonstration.
        .QueryDefs.Delete qdfNew.Name
        .Close
    End With

End Sub

Function GetrstTemp(qdfTemp As QueryDef)

    Dim rstTemp As Recordset

    With qdfTemp
        Debug.Print .Name
        Debug.Print "    " & .SQL
        ' Open Recordset from QueryDef.
        Set rstTemp = .OpenRecordset(dbOpenSnapshot)

        With rstTemp
            ' Populate Recordset and print number of records.
            .MoveLast
            Debug.Print "    Number of records = " & _
                .RecordCount
            Debug.Print
            .Close
        End With

    End With

End Function
```

CreateRelation Method

Creates a new **Relation** object (Microsoft Jet workspaces only).

Applies To

Database Object

Syntax

Set *relation* = *database*.**CreateRelation** (*name*, *table*, *foreigntable*, *attributes*)

The **CreateRelation** method syntax uses these parts.

Part	Description
relation	An object variable that represents the **Relation** object you want to create.
database	An object variable that represents the **Database** object for which you want to create the new **Relation** object.
name	Optional. A **Variant** (**String** subtype) that uniquely names the new **Relation** object. See the **Name** property for details on valid **Relation** names.
table	Optional. A **Variant** (**String** subtype) that names the primary table in the relation. If the table doesn't exist before you append the **Relation** object, a run-time error occurs.
foreigntable	Optional. A **Variant** (**String** subtype) that names the foreign table in the relation. If the table doesn't exist before you append the **Relation** object, a run-time error occurs.
attributes	Optional. A constant or combination of constants that contains information about the relationship type. See the **Attributes** property for details.

Remarks

The **Relation** object provides information to the Microsoft Jet database engine about the relationship between fields in two **TableDef** or **QueryDef** objects. You can implement referential integrity by using the **Attributes** property.

If you omit one or more of the optional parts when you use the **CreateRelation** method, you can use an appropriate assignment statement to set or reset the corresponding property before you append the new object to a collection. After you append the object, you can't alter any of its property settings. See the individual property topics for more details.

Before you can use the **Append** method on a **Relation** object, you must append the appropriate **Field** objects to define the primary and foreign key relationship tables.

If *name* refers to an object that is already a member of the collection or if the **Field** object names provided in the subordinate **Fields** collection are invalid, a run-time error occurs when you use the **Append** method.

You can't establish or maintain a relationship between a replicated table and a local table.

To remove a **Relation** object from the **Relations** collection, use the **Delete** method on the collection.

See Also

>   **TableDef** Object, **Append** Method, **Delete** Method, **Attributes** Property, **Name** Property

Example

>   This example uses the **CreateRelation** method to create a **Relation** between the Employees **TableDef** and a new **TableDef** called Departments. This example also demonstrates how creating a new **Relation** will also create any necessary **Indexes** in the foreign table (the DepartmentsEmployees **Index** in the Employees table).

```
Sub CreateRelationX()

    Dim dbsNorthwind As Database
    Dim tdfEmployees As TableDef
    Dim tdfNew As TableDef
    Dim idxNew As Index
    Dim relNew As Relation
    Dim idxLoop As Index

    Set dbsNorthwind = OpenDatabase("Northwind.mdb")

    With dbsNorthwind
        ' Add new field to Employees table.
        Set tdfEmployees = .TableDefs!Employees
        tdfEmployees.Fields.Append _
            tdfEmployees.CreateField("DeptID", dbInteger, 2)

        ' Create new Departments table.
        Set tdfNew = .CreateTableDef("Departments")

        With tdfNew
            ' Create and append Field objects to Fields
            ' collection of the new TableDef object.
            .Fields.Append .CreateField("DeptID", dbInteger, 2)
            .Fields.Append .CreateField("DeptName", dbText, 20)

            ' Create Index object for Departments table.
            Set idxNew = .CreateIndex("DeptIDIndex")
            ' Create and append Field object to Fields
            ' collection of the new Index object.
            idxNew.Fields.Append idxNew.CreateField("DeptID")
            ' The index in the primary table must be Unique in
            ' order to be part of a Relation.
            idxNew.Unique = True
            .Indexes.Append idxNew
        End With

        .TableDefs.Append tdfNew

        ' Create EmployeesDepartments Relation object, using
        ' the names of the two tables in the relation.
        Set relNew = .CreateRelation("EmployeesDepartments", _
            tdfNew.Name, tdfEmployees.Name, _
            dbRelationUpdateCascade)
```

```
        ' Create Field object for the Fields collection of the
        ' new Relation object. Set the Name and ForeignName
        ' properties based on the fields to be used for the
        ' relation.
        relNew.Fields.Append relNew.CreateField("DeptID")
        relNew.Fields!DeptID.ForeignName = "DeptID"
        .Relations.Append relNew

        ' Print report.
        Debug.Print "Properties of " & relNew.Name & _
            " Relation"
        Debug.Print "    Table = " & relNew.Table
        Debug.Print "    ForeignTable = " & _
            relNew.ForeignTable
        Debug.Print "Fields of " & relNew.Name & " Relation"

        With relNew.Fields!DeptID
            Debug.Print "    " & .Name
            Debug.Print "        Name = " & .Name
            Debug.Print "        ForeignName = " & .ForeignName
        End With

        Debug.Print "Indexes in " & tdfEmployees.Name & _
            " TableDef"
        For Each idxLoop In tdfEmployees.Indexes
            Debug.Print "    " & idxLoop.Name & _
                ", Foreign = " & idxLoop.Foreign
        Next idxLoop

        ' Delete new objects because this is a demonstration.
        .Relations.Delete relNew.Name
        .TableDefs.Delete tdfNew.Name
        tdfEmployees.Fields.Delete "DeptID"
        .Close
    End With

End Sub
```

CreateTableDef Method

Creates a new **TableDef** object (Microsoft Jet workspaces only).

Applies To

Database Object

Syntax

Set *tabledef* = *database*.**CreateTableDef** (*name*, *attributes*, *source*, *connect*)

The **CreateTableDef** method syntax has these parts.

Part	Description
tabledef	An object variable that represents the **TableDef** object you want to create.
Database	An object variable that represents the **Database** object you want to use to create the new **TableDef** object.
Name	Optional. A **Variant** (**String** subtype) that uniquely names the new **TableDef** object. See the **Name** property for details on valid **TableDef** names.
Attributes	Optional. A constant or combination of constants that indicates one or more characteristics of the new **TableDef** object. See the **Attributes** property for more information.
Source	Optional. A **Variant** (**String** subtype) containing the name of a table in an external database that is the original source of the data. The *source* string becomes the **SourceTableName** property setting of the new **TableDef** object.
Connect	Optional. A **Variant** (**String** subtype) containing information about the source of an open database, a database used in a pass-through query, or a linked table. See the **Connect** property for more information about valid connection strings.

Remarks

If you omit one or more of the optional parts when you use the **CreateTableDef** method, you can use an appropriate assignment statement to set or reset the corresponding property before you append the new object to a collection. After you append the object, you can alter some but not all of its properties. See the individual property topics for more details.

If *name* refers to an object that is already a member of the collection, or you specify an invalid property in the **TableDef** or **Field** object you're appending, a run-time error occurs when you use the **Append** method. Also, you can't append a **TableDef** object to the **TableDefs** collection until you define at least one **Field** for the **TableDef** object.

To remove a **TableDef** object from the **TableDefs** collection, use the **Delete** method on the collection.

See Also

TableDef Object, **Append** Method, **Delete** Method, **Attributes** Property, **Connect** Property, **Name** Property

Example

This example creates a new **TableDef** object in the Northwind database.

```
Sub CreateTableDefX()

    Dim dbsNorthwind As Database
    Dim tdfNew As TableDef
    Dim prpLoop As Property
```

```
    Set dbsNorthwind = OpenDatabase("Northwind.mdb")

    ' Create a new TableDef object.
    Set tdfNew = dbsNorthwind.CreateTableDef("Contacts")
    With tdfNew
        ' Create fields and append them to the new TableDef
        ' object. This must be done before appending the
        ' TableDef object to the TableDefs collection of the
        ' Northwind database.
        .Fields.Append .CreateField("FirstName", dbText)
        .Fields.Append .CreateField("LastName", dbText)
        .Fields.Append .CreateField("Phone", dbText)
        .Fields.Append .CreateField("Notes", dbMemo)

        Debug.Print "Properties of new TableDef object " & _
            "before appending to collection:"

        ' Enumerate Properties collection of new TableDef
        ' object.
        For Each prpLoop In .Properties
            On Error Resume Next
            If prpLoop <> "" Then Debug.Print "    " & _
                prpLoop.Name & " = " & prpLoop
            On Error GoTo 0
        Next prpLoop

        ' Append the new TableDef object to the Northwind
        ' database.
        dbsNorthwind.TableDefs.Append tdfNew

        Debug.Print "Properties of new TableDef object " & _
            "after appending to collection:"

        ' Enumerate Properties collection of new TableDef
        ' object.
        For Each prpLoop In .Properties
            On Error Resume Next
            If prpLoop <> "" Then Debug.Print "    " & _
                prpLoop.Name & " = " & prpLoop
            On Error GoTo 0
        Next prpLoop

    End With

    ' Delete new TableDef object since this is a
    ' demonstration.
    dbsNorthwind.TableDefs.Delete "Contacts"

    dbsNorthwind.Close

End Sub
```

CreateUser Method

Creates a new **User** object (Microsoft Jet workspaces only).

Applies To

Group Object, **Workspace** Object

Syntax

Set *user* = *object*.**CreateUser** (*name*, *pid*, *password*)

The **CreateUser** method syntax has these parts.

Part	Description
user	An object variable that represents the **User** object you want to create.
object	An object variable that represents the **Group** or **Workspace** object for which you want to create the new **User** object.
name	Optional. A **Variant** (**String** subtype) that uniquely names the new **User** object. See the **Name** property for details on valid **User** names.
pid	Optional. A **Variant** (**String** subtype) containing the PID of a user account. The identifier must contain from 4 to 20 alphanumeric characters. See the **PID** property for more information on valid personal identifiers.
password	Optional. A **Variant** (**String** subtype) containing the password for the new **User** object. The password can be up to 14 characters long and can include any characters except the ASCII character 0 (null). See the **Password** property for more information on valid passwords.

Remarks

If you omit one or more of the optional parts when you use the **CreateUser** method, you can use an appropriate assignment statement to set or reset the corresponding property before you append the new object to a collection. After you append the object, you can alter some but not all of its property settings. See the **PID**, **Name**, and **Password** property topics for more details.

If *name* refers to an object that is already a member of the collection, a run-time error occurs when you use the **Append** method.

To remove a **User** object from the **Users** collection, use the **Delete** method on the collection.

See Also

User Object, **Append** Method, **Delete** Method, **Name** Property, **Password** Property, **PID** Property

Example

This example illustrates the use of the **Group** and **User** objects and the **Groups** and **Users** collections. First, it creates a new **User** object and appends the object to the **Users** collection of the default **Workspace** object. Next, it creates a new **Group** object and appends the object to the **Groups** collection of the default **Workspace** object. Then the example adds user Pat Smith to the Accounting group. Finally, it enumerates the **Users** and **Groups** collections of the default **Workspace** object. See the methods and properties listed in the **Group** and **User** summary topics for additional examples.

```
Sub GroupX()

    Dim wrkDefault As Workspace
    Dim usrNew As User
    Dim usrLoop As User
    Dim grpNew As Group
    Dim grpLoop As Group
    Dim grpMember As Group

    Set wrkDefault = DBEngine.Workspaces(0)

    With wrkDefault

        ' Create and append new user.
        Set usrNew = .CreateUser("Pat Smith", _
            "abc123DEF456", "Password1")
        .Users.Append usrNew

        ' Create and append new group.
        Set grpNew = .CreateGroup("Accounting", _
            "UVW987xyz654")
        .Groups.Append grpNew

        ' Make the user Pat Smith a member of the
        ' Accounting group by creating and adding the
        ' appropriate Group object to the user's Groups
        ' collection. The same is accomplished if a User
        ' object representing Pat Smith is created and
        ' appended to the Accounting group's Users
        ' collection.
        Set grpMember = usrNew.CreateGroup("Accounting")
        usrNew.Groups.Append grpMember

        Debug.Print "Users collection:"

        ' Enumerate all User objects in the default
        ' workspace's Users collection.
        For Each usrLoop In .Users
            Debug.Print "    " & usrLoop.Name
            Debug.Print "        Belongs to these groups:"

            ' Enumerate all Group objects in each User
            ' object's Groups collection.
            If usrLoop.Groups.Count <> 0 Then
```

```
                        For Each grpLoop In usrLoop.Groups
                           Debug.Print "                " & _
                              grpLoop.Name
                        Next grpLoop
                     Else
                        Debug.Print "                [None]"
                     End If

             Next usrLoop

             Debug.Print "Groups collection:"

             ' Enumerate all Group objects in the default
             ' workspace's Groups collection.
             For Each grpLoop In .Groups
                Debug.Print "     " & grpLoop.Name
                Debug.Print "        Has as its members:"

                ' Enumerate all User objects in each Group
                ' object's Users collection.
                If grpLoop.Users.Count <> 0 Then
                   For Each usrLoop In grpLoop.Users
                      Debug.Print "             " & _
                         usrLoop.Name
                   Next usrLoop
                Else
                   Debug.Print "             [None]"
                End If

             Next grpLoop

             ' Delete new User and Group objects because this
             ' is only a demonstration.
             .Users.Delete "Pat Smith"
             .Groups.Delete "Accounting"

          End With

       End Sub
```

CreateWorkspace Method

Creates a new **Workspace** object.

Applies To

> **DBEngine** Object

Syntax

> **Set** *workspace* = **CreateWorkspace**(*name*, *user*, *password*, *type*)

> The **CreateWorkspace** method syntax has these parts.

Part	Description
workspace	An object variable that represents the **Workspace** object you want to create.
Name	A **String** that uniquely names the new **Workspace** object. See the **Name** property for details on valid **Workspace** names.
User	A **String** that identifies the owner of the new **Workspace** object. See the **UserName** property for more information.
Password	A **String** containing the password for the new **Workspace** object. The password can be up to 14 characters long and can include any characters except ASCII character 0 (null). See the **Password** property for more information on valid passwords.
Type	Optional. A constant that indicates the type of workspace, as described in Settings.

Settings

You can use the following constants for *type*.

Constant	Description
dbUseJet	Creates a Microsoft Jet workspace.
DbUseODBC	Creates an ODBCDirect workspace.

Remarks

Once you use the **CreateWorkspace** method to create a new **Workspace** object, a **Workspace** session is started, and you can refer to the **Workspace** object in your application.

Workspace objects aren't permanent, and you can't save them to disk. Once you create a **Workspace** object, you can't alter any of its property settings, except for the **Name** property, which you can modify before appending the **Workspace** object to the **Workspaces** collection.

You don't have to append the new **Workspace** object to a collection before you can use it. You append a newly created **Workspace** object only if you need to refer to it through the **Workspaces** collection.

The *type* option determines whether the new **Workspace** is a Microsoft Jet or ODBCDirect workspace. If you set *type* to **dbUseODBC** and you haven't already created any Microsoft Jet workspaces, then the Microsoft Jet database engine will not be loaded into memory, and all activity will occur with the ODBC data source subsequently identified in a **Connection** object. If you omit *type*, the **DefaultType** property of **DBEngine** will determine which type of data source the **Workspace** is connected to. You can have both Microsoft Jet and ODBCDirect workspaces open at the same time.

To remove a **Workspace** object from the **Workspaces** collection, close all open databases and connections and then use the **Close** method on the **Workspace** object.

See Also

> **Workspace** Object, **Close** Method, **Name** Property, **Password** Property, **UserName** Property

Example

> This example uses the **CreateWorkspace** method to create both a Microsoft Jet workspace and an ODBCDirect workspace. It then lists the properties of both types of workspace.

```
Sub CreateWorkspaceX()

    Dim wrkODBC As Workspace
    Dim wrkJet As Workspace
    Dim wrkLoop As Workspace
    Dim prpLoop As Property

    ' Create an ODBCDirect workspace. Until you create
    ' Microsoft Jet workspace, the Microsoft Jet database
    ' engine will not be loaded into memory.
    Set wrkODBC = CreateWorkspace("ODBCWorkspace", "admin", _
        "", dbUseODBC)
    Workspaces.Append wrkODBC

    DefaultType = dbUseJet
    ' Create an unnamed Workspace object of the type
    ' specified by the DefaultType property of DBEngine
    ' (dbUseJet).
    Set wrkJet = CreateWorkspace("", "admin", "")

    ' Enumerate Workspaces collection.
    Debug.Print "Workspace objects in Workspaces collection:"
    For Each wrkLoop In Workspaces
        Debug.Print "    " & wrkLoop.Name
    Next wrkLoop

    With wrkODBC
        ' Enumerate Properties collection of ODBCDirect
        ' workspace.
        Debug.Print "Properties of " & .Name
        On Error Resume Next
        For Each prpLoop In .Properties
            Debug.Print "    " & prpLoop.Name & " = " & prpLoop
        Next prpLoop
        On Error GoTo 0
    End With

    With wrkJet
        ' Enumerate Properties collection of Microsoft Jet
        ' workspace.
        Debug.Print _
            "Properties of unnamed Microsoft Jet workspace"
        On Error Resume Next
        For Each prpLoop In .Properties
```

```
        Debug.Print "      " & prpLoop.Name & " = " & prpLoop
      Next prpLoop
      On Error GoTo 0
   End With

   wrkODBC.Close
   wrkJet.Close

End Sub
```

CurDir Function

Returns a **Variant** (**String**) representing the current path.

Syntax

CurDir[(*drive*)]

The optional *drive* argument is a string expression that specifies an existing drive. If no drive is specified or if *drive* is a zero-length string (""), **CurDir** returns the path for the current drive.

See Also

ChDir Statement, **ChDrive** Statement, **MkDir** Statement, **RmDir** Statement

Example

This example uses the **CurDir** function to return the current path.

```
' Assume current path on C drive is "C:\WINDOWS\SYSTEM".
' Assume current path on D drive is "D:\EXCEL".
' Assume C is the current drive.
Dim MyPath
MyPath = CurDir            ' Returns "C:\WINDOWS\SYSTEM".
MyPath = CurDir("C")       ' Returns "C:\WINDOWS\SYSTEM".
MyPath = CurDir("D")       ' Returns "D:\EXCEL".
```

Currency Data Type

Currency variables are stored as 64-bit (8-byte) numbers in an integer format, scaled by 10,000 to give a fixed-point number with 15 digits to the left of the decimal point and 4 digits to the right. This representation provides a range of -922,337,203,685,477.5808 to 922,337,203,685,477.5807. The type-declaration character for **Currency** is the at sign (@).

The **Currency** data type is useful for calculations involving money and for fixed-point calculations in which accuracy is particularly important.

See Also

Data Type Summary, **Long Data** Type, **Deftype** Statements

CurrentCellModified Property

Sets or returns modification status of the current cell. Not available at design time.

Applies To

DBGrid Control

Syntax

object.**CurrentCellModified** [= *value*]

The **CurrentCellModified** property syntax has these parts:

Part	Description
object	An object expression that evaluates to an object in the **Applies To** list.
value	A Boolean expression that determines the modification status of the current cell, as described in Settings.

Settings

The settings for *value* are:

Setting	Description
True	Editing is in progress and the current cell (indicated by the **Bookmark** and **Col** properties) has been modified by the user.
False	The cell has not been modified or editing is not in progress.

Remarks

You can use this property to cancel any changes the user has made to the current text. For example, to program a function key to discard the user's changes (like the ESC key), trap the key code in the grid's **KeyDown** event and set **CurrentCellModified** to **False**. This will revert the current cell to its original contents.

See Also

Bookmark Property (DBGrid), **Col, Row** Properties

CurrentCellVisible Property

Sets or returns the visibility of the current cell. Not available at design time.

Applies To

Split Object, **DBGrid** Control

Syntax

object.**CurrentCellVisible** [= *value*]

The **CurrentCellVisible** property syntax has these parts:

Part	Description
object	An object expression that evaluates to an object in the **Applies To** list.
value	A Boolean expression that determines the visibility of the current cell, as described in Settings.

Settings

The settings for *value* are:

Setting	Description
True	The current cell (indicated by the **Bookmark** and **Col** properties) is visible within the displayed area of a grid or split.
False	The cell is not visible.

Remarks

For a **DBGrid** control, setting the **CurrentCellVisible** property to **True** causes the grid to scroll so that the current cell is brought into view. If a grid contains multiple splits, then the current cell becomes visible in each split.

For a **Split** object, setting the **CurrentCellVisible** property to **True** makes the current cell visible in that split only.

In all cases, setting this property to **False** is meaningless and is ignored.

See Also

Bookmark Property (DBGrid)), **Col, Row** Properties

CurrentX, CurrentY Properties

Return or set the horizontal (**CurrentX**) or vertical (**CurrentY**) coordinates for the next printing or drawing method. Not available at design time.

Applies To

PropertyPage Object, **UserControl** Object, **UserDocument** Object, **Printer Object, Printers** Collection, **Form Object, Forms** Collection, **PictureBox** Control

Syntax

object.**CurrentX** [= *x*]
   object.**CurrentY** [= *y*]

The **CurrentX** and **CurrentY** properties syntax have these parts:

Part	Description
object	An object expression that evaluates to an object in the **Applies To** list.
x	A number that specifies the horizontal coordinate.
y	A number that specifies the vertical coordinate.

Remarks

Coordinates are measured from the upper-left corner of an object. The **CurrentX** property setting is 0 at an object's left edge, and the **CurrentY** property setting is 0 at its top edge. Coordinates are expressed in twips, or the current unit of measurement defined by the **ScaleHeight**, **ScaleWidth**, **ScaleLeft**, **ScaleTop**, and **ScaleMode** properties.

When you use the following graphics methods, the **CurrentX** and **CurrentY** settings are changed as indicated:

This method	Sets CurrentX, CurrentY to
Circle	The center of the object.
Cls	0, 0.
EndDoc	0, 0.
Line	The end point of the line.
NewPage	0, 0.
Print	The next print position.
PSet	The point drawn.

See Also

Cls Method, **EndDoc** Method, **NewPage** Method, **Left**, **Top** Properties, **DrawMode** Property, **DrawStyle** Property, **ScaleHeight**, **ScaleWidth** Properties, **ScaleLeft**, **ScaleTop** Properties

CursorDriver Property (Remote Data)

Returns or sets a value that specifies the type of cursor to be created.

Applies To

rdoEnvironment Object, **RemoteData** Control

Syntax

object.**CursorDriver** [= *value*]

The **CursorDriver** property syntax has these parts:

Part	Description
object	An object expression that evaluates to an object in the **Applies To** list.
value	An **Integer** or constant as described in Settings.

Settings

Constant	Value	Description
rdUseIfNeeded	0	The ODBC driver will choose the appropriate style of cursors. Server-side cursors are used if they are available.
rdUseOdbc	1	**RemoteData** will use the ODBC cursor library.
rdUseServer	2	Use server-side cursors.
rdUseClientBatch	3	RDO will use the optimistic batch cursor library.
rdUseNone	4	Result set is not returned as a cursor.

Remarks

The **CursorDriver** property only affects connections established *after* the **CursorDriver** property has been set—the property is read-only on existing connections.

When the initial (default), and each subsequent **rdoEnvironment** object is created, the **CursorDriver** property is set from the **rdoEngine** object's **rdoDefaultCursorDriver** property which is set using the same constants.

Choosing a Cursor Driver

Choosing the right cursor driver can have a significant impact on the overall performance of your application, what resources are consumed by the cursor, and limit the type or complexity of the cursors you create. Each type of cursor has its own benefits and limitations. In many cases, the best choice is no cursor at all because your application often does not need to scroll through the data or perform update operations against a keyset.

The following paragraphs outline the functionality and suggested purposes for each of the cursor types.

- Server-Side Cursors

  This cursor library maintains the cursor keyset on the server (in *TempDB*) which eliminates the need to transmit the keyset to the workstation where it consumes needed resources. However, this cursor driver consumes *TempDB* space on the remote server so this database must be expanded to meet this requirement. Cursors created with the server-side driver cannot contain more than one SELECT statement—if they do, a trappable error is fired. You can still use the server-side cursor driver with multiple result set queries if you disable the cursor by creating a forward-only, read-only cursor with a rowset size of one. Not all remote servers support server-side cursors. Note that server-side cursors are enabled when using either **rdUseIfNeeded** or **rdUseServer** against Microsoft SQL Server databases.

- ODBC Client-Side Cursors

  This cursor library builds keysets on the workstation in local RAM overflowing to disk if necessary. Because of this design considerably more network operations must be performed to initially create the keyset, but with small cursors this should not impose a significant load on the workstation or network. ODBC client-side cursors do not impose any type of restriction on the type of query executed. This option gives better performance for small result sets, but degrades quickly for larger result sets.

- Client-Batch Cursors

  This cursor library is designed to deal with the special requirements of optimistic batch updates and several other more complex cursor features. Client-batch cursors are required for dissociate connections, batch mode, and multi-table updates. This cursor also supports delayed BLOB column fetch, buffered cursors, and additional control over updates. This library is somewhat larger than the others, but also performs better in many situations.

- The No-Cursor Option

  In cases where you need to fetch rows quickly, or perform action queries against the database without the overhead of a cursor, you can choose to instruct RDO to bypass creation of a cursor. Basically, this option creates a forward-only, read-only result set with a **RowsetSize** set to 1. This option can improve performance in many operations. While you cannot update rows or scroll between rows with this cursor, you can submit independent action queries to manipulate data. This option is especially useful when accessing data through stored procedures.

See Also

rdoConnection Object, **rdoEngine** Object, **rdoEnvironment** Object

CursorType Property

Returns or sets a value that specifies the default type of cursor to use when opening a result set from the specified query.

Applies To

rdoQuery Object

Syntax

object.**CursorType** [= *value*]

The **CursorType** property syntax has these parts:

Part	Description
object	An object expression that evaluates to an object in the **Applies To** list.
value	A **Long** integer representing the type of cursor as described by one of the following constants:

Constant	Value	rdoResultset type
rdOpenForwardOnly	0	(Default) Fixed set, non-scrolling.
rdOpenKeyset	1	Updatable, fixed set, scrollable query result set cursor.
rdOpenDynamic	2	Updatable, dynamic set, scrollable query result set cursor.
rdOpenStatic	3	Read-only, fixed set.

Remarks

Determines the cursor type to use when opening an **rdoResultset** object from this query.

When creating a stand-alone **rdoQuery** object whose query is to be used as a method, you should set the **CursorType** before the query is executed because there is no option to do so when the query is executed.

The value of the **CursorType** property is used as the **Type** argument of the **OpenResultset** method.

Not all cursor libraries support all types of cursors. For example, the ODBC client-side driver can only support **rdOpenStatic** and **rdOpenForwardOnly** cursor types, while the SQL Server server-side driver supports all four types. Generally, most drivers support forward-only and static cursors.

See Also

Move Method, **MoveFirst**, **MoveLast**, **MoveNext**, **MovePrevious** Methods, **OpenResultset** Method, **rdoResultset** Object, **Updatable** Property

Example

```
Option Explicit
Dim er As rdoError
Dim cn As New rdoConnection
Dim qy As New rdoQuery
Dim rs As rdoResultset
Dim col As rdoColumn

Private Sub Form_Load()

cn.CursorDriver = rdUseClientBatch
cn.Connect = "uid=;pwd=;server=sequel;" _
    & "driver={SQL Server};database=pubs;dsn='';"
cn.EstablishConnection

'
'  Setup the query
'
With qy
    .Name = "ShowAuthor"
    .SQL = "Select * from Authors " _
        & "where Au_LName = ? "
    .LockType = rdConcurReadOnly
    .CursorType = rdOpenForwardOnly
    .RowsetSize = 1
    Set .ActiveConnection = cn
End With
```

```
'
'  Execute the Query by Name
'  Pass in a parameter to the query
'
cn.ShowAuthor "White"
'
'  Process the resulting rows
'
If cn.LastQueryResults is Nothing then
Else
    Set rs = cn.LastQueryResult
    For Each col In rs.rdoColumns
        Print col.Name,
    Next
    Print String(80, "-")

    Do Until rs.EOF
        For Each col In rs.rdoColumns
            Print col,
        Next
        Print
        rs.MoveNext
    Loop
End if

End Sub
```

CVErr Function

Returns a **Variant** of subtype **Error** containing an error number specified by the user.

Syntax

CVErr(*errornumber*)

The required *errornumber* argument is any valid error number.

Remarks

Use the **CVErr** function to create user-defined errors in user-created procedures. For example, if you create a function that accepts several arguments and normally returns a string, you can have your function evaluate the input arguments to ensure they are within acceptable range. If they are not, it is likely your function will not return what you expect. In this event, **CVErr** allows you to return an error number that tells you what action to take.

Note that implicit conversion of an **Error** is not allowed. For example, you can't directly assign the return value of **CVErr** to a variable that is not a **Variant**. However, you can perform an explicit conversion (using **CInt**, **CDbl**, and so on) of the value returned by **CVErr** and assign that to a variable of the appropriate data type.

See Also

Conversion Functions, **Data Type** Summary, **IsError** Function

Example

This example uses the **CVErr** function to return a **Variant** whose **VarType** is **vbError** (10). The user-defined function CalculateDouble returns an error if the argument passed to it isn't a number. You can use **CVErr** to return user-defined errors from user-defined procedures or to defer handling of a run-time error. Use the **IsError** function to test if the value represents an error.

```
' Call CalculateDouble with an error-producing argument.
Sub Test()
   Debug.Print CalculateDouble("345.45robert")
End Sub
   ' Define CalculateDouble Function procedure.
Function CalculateDouble(Number)
   If IsNumeric(Number) Then
      CalculateDouble = Number * 2    ' Return result.
   Else
      CalculateDouble = CVErr(2001)   ' Return a user-defined error
   End If                             ' number.
End Function
```

Data Control

Provides access to data stored in databases using any one of three types of **Recordset** objects. The **Data** control enables you to move from record to record and to display and manipulate data from the records in bound controls. Without a **Data** control or an equivalent data source control like the **RemoteData** control, data-aware (bound) controls on a form can't automatically access data.

Syntax

Data

Properties

Align Property, **Appearance** Property, **BackColor, ForeColor** Properties, **BOFAction, EOFAction** Properties, **Caption** Property, **Connect** Property (DAO), **Database** Property, **DatabaseName** Property, **DefaultCursorType** Property (Data Control), **DefaultType** Property (Data Control), **DragIcon** Property, **DragMode** Property, **EditMode** Property (DAO), **Enabled** Property, **Exclusive** Property, **Font** Property, **FontBold, FontItalic, FontStrikethru, FontUnderline** Properties, **FontName** Property, **FontSize** Property, **Height, Width** Properties, **Index** Property (Control Array), **Left, Top** Properties, **MouseIcon** Property, **MousePointer** Property, **Name** Property, **OLEDropMode** Property, **Options** Property, **Parent** Property, **ReadOnly** Property (Data Access), **Recordset** Property, **RecordSource** Property, **Tag** Property, **ToolTipText** Property, **Visible** Property, **WhatsThisHelpID** Property

Events

DragDrop Event, **DragOver** Event, **Error** Event, **MouseDown, MouseUp** Events, **MouseMove** Event, **OLECompleteDrag** Event, **OLEDragDrop** Event, **OLEDragOver** Event, **OLEGiveFeedback** Event, **OLESetData** Event, **OLEStartDrag** Event, **Reposition** Event, **Resize** Event, **Validate** Event

Remarks

You can perform most data access operations using the **Data** control without writing any code at all. Data-aware controls bound to a **Data** control automatically display data from one or more fields for the current record or, in some cases, for a set of records on either side of the current record. The **Data** control performs all operations on the current record.

If the **Data** control is instructed to move to a different record, all bound controls automatically pass any changes to the **Data** control to be saved in the database. The **Data** control then moves to the requested record and passes back data from the current record to the bound controls where it's displayed.

The **Data** control automatically handles a number of contingencies including empty recordsets, adding new records, editing and updating existing records, and handling some types of errors. However, in more sophisticated applications, you need to trap some error conditions that the **Data** control can't handle. For example, if the Microsoft Jet database engine has a problem accessing the database file, doesn't have permission, or can't execute the query as coded, a trappable error results. If the error occurs before your application procedures start or due to some internal errors, the Error event is triggered.

Bound Controls

The **DBList**, **DBCombo**, **DBGrid**, and **MSFlexGrid** controls are all capable of managing sets of records when bound to a **Data** control. All of these controls permit several records to be displayed or manipulated at once.

The intrinsic **Picture**, **Label**, **TextBox**, **CheckBox**, **Image**, **OLE**, **ListBox** and **ComboBox** controls are also data-aware and can be bound to a single field of a **Recordset** managed by the **Data** control. Additional data-aware controls like the **MaskedEdit** and **RichTextBox** controls are available in the Professional and Enterprise Editions and from third-party vendors.

Operation

Once the application begins, Visual Basic uses **Data** control properties to open the selected database, create a **Database** object and create a **Recordset** object. The **Data** control's **Database** and **Recordset** properties refer to the newly created **Database** and **Recordset** objects which may be manipulated independently of the **Data** control with or without bound controls. The **Data** control is initialized *before* the initial **Form_Load** event for the form on which it is placed. If any errors occur during this initialization step a non-trappable error results.

When Visual Basic uses the Jet database engine to create a **Recordset**, no other Visual Basic operations or events can occur until the operation is complete. However, other Windows-based applications are permitted to continue executing while the **Recordset** is being created. If the user presses CTRL+BREAK while the Jet engine is building a **Recordset**, the operation is terminated, a trappable error results, and the **Recordset** property of the **Data** control is set to **Nothing**. In design time, a second CTRL+BREAK causes Visual Basic to display the Debug window.

When you use a **Data** control to create a **Recordset** object or when you create a **Recordset** object in code and assign it to the **Data** control, the Microsoft Jet database engine automatically populates the **Recordset** object. As a result, bookmarks (and for snapshot-type **Recordset** objects, recordset data) are saved in local memory; the user doesn't need to manipulate the **Data** control, and you don't need to invoke the **MoveLast** method in code. Page locks used to create the **Recordset** are released more quickly, making it possible for other **Recordset** objects to access the same data. **Recordset** objects created in code but not assigned to the **Data** control aren't automatically populated by the Jet engine. Populate these objects through code. Because of the way that the **Data** control populates its **Recordset** in the background, an additional cloned **Recordset** might be created.

You can manipulate the **Data** control with the mouse, moving from record to record or to the beginning or end of the **Recordset**. The **EOFAction** and **BOFAction** properties determine what happens when the user moves to the beginning or end of a **Recordset** with the mouse. You can't set focus to the **Data** control.

Validation

Use the Validate event and the **DataChanged** property to perform last minute checks on the records being written to the database.

Data Access Objects

You can use the **Database** and **Recordset** data access objects created by the **Data** control in your procedures. The **Database** and **Recordset** objects each have properties and methods of their own, and you can write procedures that use these properties and methods to manipulate your data.

For example, the **MoveNext** method of a **Recordset** object moves the current record to the next record in the **Recordset**. To invoke this method, you could use this code:

```
Data1.Recordset.MoveNext
```

The **Data** control is capable of accessing any of the three types of Jet engine Version 3.0 **Recordset** objects. If you don't select a recordset type, a dynaset-type **Recordset** is created.

In many cases, the default type and configuration of the **Recordset** object created is extremely inefficient. That is, you might not need an updatable, fully-scrollable, keyset-type cursor to access your data. For example, a read-only, forward-only, snapshot-type **Recordset** might be far faster to create than the default cursor. Be sure to choose the most efficient **Type, Exclusive, Options** and **ReadOnly** properties possible for your situation.

Note The constants used to request a specific **Recordset** type when using the **Data** control are different than the constants used to determine the type of **Recordset** created or to create a **Recordset** using the **OpenRecordset** method.

To select a specific type of **Recordset**, set the **Data** control's **RecordsetType** property to:

Recordset Type	Value	Constant
Table	0	**vbRSTypeTable**
Dynaset	1	(Default) **vbRSTypeDynaset**
Snapshot	2	**vbRSTypeSnapshot**

Important The **Data** control cannot be used to access **Recordset** objects created with the **dbForwardOnly** option bit set.

Professional and Enterprise Editions

As far as data access is concerned, the primary difference between the Learning Edition, Professional and Enterprise Editions of Visual Basic is the ability to create new data access objects. In the Standard Edition, you can't declare (with the **Dim** keyword) variables as data access objects in code. This means that only the **Data** control can create **Database** and **Recordset** objects.

In Visual Basic Version 5.0 Professional and Enterprise Editions, you can create a new **Recordset** object and assign it to the **Data** control's **Recordset** property. Any bound controls connected to the **Data** control permit manipulation of the records in the **Recordset** you created. Make sure that your bound controls' **DataField** properties are set to field names that are valid in the new **Recordset**.

Stored Queries

Another important option when using the **Data** control is the ability to execute stored queries. If you create a **QueryDef** object beforehand, the **Data** control can execute it and create a **Recordset** using the **QueryDef** object's stored **SQL, Connect** and other properties. To execute a **QueryDef**, set the **Data** control's **RecordSource** property to the **QueryDef** name and use the **Refresh** method.

If the stored **QueryDef** contains parameters, you need to create the **Recordset** and pass it to the **Data** control.

BOF/EOF Handling

The **Data** control can also manage what happens when you encounter a **Recordset** with no records. By changing the **EOFAction** property, you can program the **Data** control to enter **AddNew** mode automatically.

You can program the **Data** control to automatically snap to the top or bottom of its parent form by using the **Align** property. In either case, the **Data** control is resized horizontally to fill the width of its parent form whenever the parent form is resized. This property allows a **Data** control to be placed on an MDI form without requiring an enclosing **Picture** control.

Methods

Drag Method, **OLEDrag** Method, **Refresh** Method, **ShowWhatsThis** Method, **Zorder** Method, **UpdateControls** Method, **UpdateRecord** Method, **Move** Method

Error Event Constants

Constant	Value	Description
vbDataErrContinue	0	Continue
vbDataErrDisplay	1	(Default) Display the error message

Validate Event Action Constants

Constant	Value	Description
vbDataActionCancel	0	Cancel the operation when the **Sub** exits
vbDataActionMoveFirst	1	**MoveFirst** method
vbDataActionMovePrevious	2	**MovePrevious** method
vbDataActionMoveNext	3	**MoveNext** method
vbDataActionMoveLast	4	**MoveLast** method
vbDataActionAddNew	5	**AddNew** method
vbDataActionUpdate	6	Update operation (not **UpdateRecord**)
vbDataActionDelete	7	**Delete** method
vbDataActionFind	8	**Find** method
vbDataActionBookmark	9	The **Bookmark** property is set
vbDataActionClose	10	**Close** method
vbDataActionUnload	11	The form is being unloaded

Beginning-Of-File Action Constants

Constant	Value	Description
vbMoveFirst	0	Move to first record
vbBOF	1	Move to beginning of file

End-Of-File Action Constants

Constant	Value	Description
vbMoveLast	0	Move to last record
vbEOF	1	Move to end of file
vbAddNew	2	Add new record to end of file

Recordset-Type Constants

Constant	Value	Description
vbRSTypeTable	0	Table-type recordset
vbRSTypeDynaset	1	Dynaset-type recordset
vbRSTypeSnapShot	2	Snapshot-type recordset

See Also

Connect Property (DAO)**, Data Control** Constants, **Database** Object (DAO)
DBCombo Control, **DBGrid** Control, **DBList** Control, **Recordset** Object (DAO),
RemoteData Control

Data Property

Returns or sets a handle to a memory object or graphical device interface (GDI) object containing data in a specified format. Not available at design time.

Applies To

OLE Container Control

Syntax

object.**Data** [= *number*]

The **Data** property syntax has these parts:

Part	Description
object	An object expression that evaluates to an object in the **Applies To** list.
number	A Long integer specifying the handle.

Remarks

Set this property to send data to an application that created an object. Before using the **Data** property, set the **Format** property to specify the type of data contained in the memory object or GDI object.

You can get a list of acceptable formats for an object using the **ObjectAcceptFormats** and **ObjectGetFormats** properties.

Setting this property to 0 frees the memory associated with the handle.

Tip Automation provides an easier and more reliable solution for sending data and commands to and from an object. If an object supports Automation, you can access the object through the **Object** property or using the **CreateObject** and **GetObject** functions

Specifics

CheckBox Control, **ComboBox** Control, **Image** Control, **Label** Control, **ListBox** Control, **PictureBox** Control

See Also

DataText Property, **ObjectAcceptFormatsCount** Property, **ObjectGetFormats**
Property, **ObjectGetFormatsCount** Property, **Object** Property (OLE Container),
Format Property

Data Type Summary

The following table shows the supported data types, including storage sizes and
ranges.

Data type	Storage size	Range
Byte	1 byte	0 to 255
Boolean	2 bytes	**True** or **False**
Integer	2 bytes	-32,768 to 32,767
Long (long integer)	4 bytes	-2,147,483,648 to 2,147,483,647
Single (single-precision floating-point)	4 bytes	-3.402823E38 to -1.401298E-45 for negative values; 1.401298E-45 to 3.402823E38 for positive values
Double (double-precision floating-point)	8 bytes	-1.79769313486232E308 to -4.94065645841247E-324 for negative values; 4.94065645841247E-324 to 1.79769313486232E308 for positive values
Currency (scaled integer)	8 bytes	-922,337,203,685,477.5808 to 922,337,203,685,477.5807
Decimal	14 bytes	+/-79,228,162,514,264,337,593,543,950,335 with no decimal point; +/-7.9228162514264337593543950335 with 28 places to the right of the decimal; smallest non-zero number is +/-0.0000000000000000000000000001
Date	8 bytes	January 1, 100 to December 31, 9999
Object	4 bytes	Any **Object** reference
String (variable-length)	10 bytes + string length	0 to approximately 2 billion
String (fixed-length)	Length of string	1 to approximately 65,400
Variant (with numbers)	16 bytes	Any numeric value up to the range of a **Double**
Variant (with characters)	22 bytes + string length	Same range as for variable-length **String**
User-defined (using **Type**)	Number required by elements	The range of each element is the same as the range of its data type.

Note Arrays of any data type require 20 bytes of memory plus 4 bytes for each array dimension plus the number of bytes occupied by the data itself. The memory occupied by the data can be calculated by multiplying the number of data elements by the size of each element. For example, the data in a single-dimension array consisting of 4 **Integer** data elements of 2 bytes each occupies 8 bytes. The 8 bytes required for the data plus the 24 bytes of overhead brings the total memory requirement for the array to 32 bytes.

A **Variant** containing an array requires 12 bytes more than the array alone.

See Also

Boolean Data Type, **Byte Data** Type, **Currency Data** Type, **Date Data** Type, **Decimal Data** Type, **Double Data** Type, **Integer Data** Type, **Long Data** Type, **Object Data** Type, **Single Data** Type, **String Data** Type, **User-Defined Data** Type, **Variant Data** Type, **Deftype** Statements, **Type** Statement, **Int**, **Fix** Functions

Database Object

A **Database** object represents an open database.

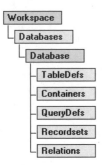

Remarks

You use the **Database** object and its methods and properties to manipulate an open database. In any type of database, you can:

- Use the **Execute** method to run an action query.
- Set the **Connect** property to establish a connection to an ODBC data source.
- Set the **QueryTimeout** property to limit the length of time to wait for a query to execute against an ODBC data source.
- Use the **RecordsAffected** property to determine how many records were changed by an action query.
- Use the **OpenRecordset** method to execute a select query and create a **Recordset** object.
- Use the **Version** property to determine which version of a database engine created the database.

With a Microsoft Jet database (.mdb file), you can also use other methods, properties, and collections to manipulate a **Database** object, as well as create, modify, or get information about its tables, queries, and relationships. For example, you can:

- Use the **CreateTableDef** and **CreateRelation** methods to create tables and relations, respectively.

- Use the **CreateProperty** method to define new **Database** properties.

- Use the **CreateQueryDef** method to create a persistent or temporary query definition.

- Use **MakeReplica**, **Synchronize**, and **PopulatePartial** methods to create and synchronize full or partial replicas of your database.

- Set the **CollatingOrder** property to establish the alphabetic sorting order for character-based fields in different languages.

In an ODBCDirect workspace, you can:

- Use the **Connection** property to obtain a reference to the **Connection** object that corresponds to the **Database** object.

Note For a complete list of all methods, properties, and collections available on a **Database** object in either a Microsoft Jet workspace or ODBCDirect workspace, see the **Summary** topic.

You use the **CreateDatabase** method to create a persistent **Database** object that is automatically appended to the **Databases** collection, thereby saving it to disk.

You don't need to specify the **DBEngine** object when you use the **OpenDatabase** method.

Opening a database with linked tables doesn't automatically establish links to the specified external files or Microsoft Jet-connected ODBC data sources. You must either reference the table's **TableDef** or **Field** objects or open a **Recordset** object. If you can't establish links to these tables, a trappable error occurs. You may also need permission to access the database, or another user might have the database opened exclusively. In these cases, trappable errors occur.

You can also use the **OpenDatabase** method to open an external database (such as FoxPro, dBASE, and Paradox) directly instead of opening a Microsoft Jet database that has links to its tables.

Note Opening a **Database** object directly on a Microsoft Jet-connected ODBC data source, such as Microsoft SQL Server, is not recommended because query performance is much slower than when using linked tables. However, performance is not a problem with opening a **Database** object directly on an external ISAM database file, such as FoxPro, Paradox, and so forth.

When a procedure that declares a **Database** object has executed, local **Database** objects are closed along with any open **Recordset** objects. Any pending updates are lost and any pending transactions are rolled back, but no trappable error occurs. You should explicitly complete any pending transactions or edits and close **Recordset** objects and **Database** objects before exiting procedures that declare these object variables locally.

When you use one of the transaction methods (**BeginTrans**, **CommitTrans**, or **Rollback**) on the **Workspace** object, these transactions apply to all databases opened on the **Workspace** from which the **Database** object was opened. If you want to use independent transactions, you must first open an additional **Workspace** object, and then open another **Database** object in that **Workspace** object.

Note   You can open the same data source or database more than once, creating duplicate names in the **Databases** collection. You should assign **Database** objects to object variables and refer to them by variable name.

Properties

CollatingOrder Property, **Connect** Property, **Name** Property, **QueryTimeout** Property, **RecordsAffected** Property, **Transactions** Property, **Updatable** Property, **V1xNullBehavior** Property, **Version** Property, **Replicable** Property, **ReplicaID** Property, **Connection** Property

Methods

Close Method, **CreateProperty** Method, **CreateQueryDef** Method, **CreateRelation** Method, **CreateTableDef** Method, **Execute** Method, **MakeReplica** Method, **NewPassword** Method, **OpenRecordset** Method, **Synchronize** Method, **PopulatePartial** Method

See Also

OpenDatabase Method, **Database** Property

Example

This example creates a new **Database** object and opens an existing **Database** object in the default **Workspace** object. Then it enumerates the **Database** collection and the **Properties** collection of each **Database** object. See the methods and properties listed in the **Database** summary topic for additional examples.

```
Sub DatabaseObjectX()

    Dim wrkJet As Workspace
    Dim dbsNorthwind As Database
    Dim dbsNew As Database
    Dim dbsLoop As Database
    Dim prpLoop As Property

    Set wrkJet = CreateWorkspace("JetWorkspace", "admin", _
        "", dbUseJet)
```

```
' Make sure there isn't already a file with the name of
' the new database.
If Dir("NewDB.mdb") <> "" Then Kill "NewDB.mdb"

' Create a new database with the specified
' collating order.
Set dbsNew = wrkJet.CreateDatabase("NewDB.mdb", _
    dbLangGeneral)
Set dbsNorthwind = wrkJet.OpenDatabase("Northwind.mdb")

' Enumerate the Databases collection.
For Each dbsLoop In wrkJet.Databases
    With dbsLoop
        Debug.Print "Properties of " & .Name
        ' Enumerate the Properties collection of each
        ' Database object.
        For Each prpLoop In .Properties
            If prpLoop <> "" Then Debug.Print "     " & _
                prpLoop.Name & " = " & prpLoop
        Next prpLoop
    End With
Next dbsLoop

dbsNew.Close
dbsNorthwind.Close
wrkJet.Close

End Sub
```

Database Property (DAO)

Returns the **Database** object that corresponds to this connection (**ODBCDirect** workspaces only).

Applies To

Connection Object, **Data** Control

Return Values

The return value is an object variable that represents a **Database** object.

Remarks

On a **Connection** object, use the **Database** property to obtain a reference to a **Database** object that corresponds to the **Connection**. In DAO, a **Connection** object and its corresponding **Database** object are simply two different object variable references to the same object. The **Database** property of a **Connection** object and the **Connection** property of a **Database** object make it easier to change connections to an ODBC data source through the Microsoft Jet database engine to use **ODBCDirect**.

Database Property (DAO)

See Also

Connection Property, **Data** Control, **DatabaseName** Property, **Exclusive** Property, **ReadOnly** Property (Data Access), **Recordset** Property

Example

This example uses the **Database** property to show how code that used to access ODBC data through the Microsoft Jet database engine can be converted to use **ODBCDirect Connection** objects.

The **OldDatabaseCode** procedure uses a Microsoft Jet-connected data source to access an ODBC database.

```
Sub OldDatabaseCode()

    Dim wrkMain As Workspace
    Dim dbsPubs As Database
    Dim prpLoop As Property

    ' Create Microsoft Jet Workspace object.
    Set wrkMain = CreateWorkspace("", "admin", "", dbUseJet)

    ' Open a Database object based on information in
    ' the connect string.
    Set dbsPubs = wrkMain.OpenDatabase("Publishers", _
        dbDriverNoPrompt, False, _
        "ODBC;DATABASE=pubs;UID=sa;PWD=;DSN=Publishers")

    ' Enumerate the Properties collection of the Database
    ' object.
    With dbsPubs
        Debug.Print "Database properties for " & _
            .Name & ":"

        On Error Resume Next
        For Each prpLoop In .Properties
            If prpLoop.Name = "Connection" Then
                ' Property actually returns a Connection object.
                Debug.Print "   Connection[.Name] = " & _
                    .Connection.Name
            Else
                Debug.Print "   " & prpLoop.Name & " = " & _
                    prpLoop
            End If
        Next prpLoop
        On Error GoTo 0

    End With

    dbsPubs.Close
    wrkMain.Close

End Sub
```

The **NewDatabaseCode** example opens a **Connection** object in an **ODBCDirect** workspace. It then assigns the **Database** property of the **Connection** object to an object variable with the same name as the data source in the old procedure. None of the subsequent code has to be changed as long as it doesn't use any features specific to Microsoft Jet workspaces.

```
Sub NewDatabaseCode()

    Dim wrkMain As Workspace
    Dim conPubs As Connection
    Dim dbsPubs As Database
    Dim prpLoop As Property

    ' Create ODBCDirect Workspace object instead of Microsoft
    ' Jet Workspace object.
    Set wrkMain = CreateWorkspace("", "admin", "", dbUseODBC)

    ' Open Connection object based on information in
    ' the connect string.
    Set conPubs = wrkMain.OpenConnection("Publishers", _
        dbDriverNoPrompt, False, _
        "ODBC;DATABASE=pubs;UID=sa;PWD=;DSN=Publishers")
    ' Assign the Database property to the same object
    ' variable as in the old code.
    Set dbsPubs = conPubs.Database

    ' Enumerate the Properties collection of the Database
    ' object. From this point on, the code is the same as the
    ' old example.
    With dbsPubs
        Debug.Print "Database properties for " & _
            .Name & ":"

        On Error Resume Next
        For Each prpLoop In .Properties
            If prpLoop.Name = "Connection" Then
                ' Property actually returns a Connection object.
                Debug.Print "    Connection[.Name] = " & _
                    .Connection.Name
            Else
                Debug.Print "    " & prpLoop.Name & " = " & _
                    prpLoop
            End If
        Next prpLoop
        On Error GoTo 0

    End With

    dbsPubs.Close
    wrkMain.Close

End Sub
```

Database Property (Data Control)

Returns a reference to a **Data** control's underlying **Database** object.

Applies To

Connection Object (DAO), **Data** Control

Syntax

object.**Database**
Set *databaseobject* = *object*.**Database** (Professional and Enterprise Editions only)

The **Database** property syntax has these parts:

Part	Description
databaseobject	An object expression that evaluates to an valid **Database** object created by the **Data** control.
object	An object expression that evaluates to an object in the **Applies To** list.

Remarks

The **Database** object created by the **Data** control is based on the control's **DatabaseName**, **Exclusive**, **ReadOnly**, and **Connect** properties.

Database objects have properties and methods you can use to manage your data. You can use any method of a **Database** object with the **Database** property of a **Data** control, such as **Close** and **Execute**. You can also examine the internal structure of the **Database** by using its **TableDefs** collection, and in turn, the **Fields** and **Indexes** collections of individual **TableDef** objects.

Although you can create a **Recordset** object and pass it to a **Data** control's **Recordset** property, you can't open a database and pass the newly created **Database** object to the **Data** control's **Database** property.

Data Type

Database

See Also

Connect Property (DAO)**, Connection** Property, **Data** Control, **Database** Object, **DatabaseName** Property, **Exclusive** Property, **Indexes** Collection, **ReadOnly** Property (Data Access), **Recordset** Property

Example

This example examines the Database property of a data control and prints the name of each Table in the Debug window.

```
Sub PrintTableNames ()
    Dim Td As TableDef
    ' Set database file.
    Data1.DatabaseName = "BIBLIO.MDB"
    Data1.Refresh   ' Open the Database.
    ' Read and print the name of each table in the database.
```

```
   For Each Td in Data1.Database.TableDefs
      Debug.Print Td.Name
   Next
End Sub
```

DatabaseName Property

Returns or sets the name and location of the source of data for a **Data** control.

Applies To

Data Control

Syntax

object.**DatabaseName** [= *pathname*]

The **DatabaseName** property syntax has these parts:

Part	Description
object	An object expression that evaluates to an object in the **Applies To** list.
pathname	A string expression that indicates the location of the database file(s) or the Data Source name for ODBC data sources.

Remarks

If your network system supports it, the *pathname* argument can be a fully qualified network path name such as \\Myserver\Myshare\Database.mdb.

The database type is indicated by the file or directory that *pathname* points to, as follows:

pathname **Points To...**	**Database Type**
.mdb file	Microsoft Access database
Directory containing .dbf file(s)	dBASE database
Directory containing .xls file	Microsoft Excel database
Directory containing .dbf files(s)	FoxPro database
Directory containing .wk1, .wk3, .wk4, or .wks file(s)	Lotus Database
Directory containing .pdx file(s)	Paradox database
Directory containing text format database files	Text format database

For ODBC databases, such as SQL Server and Oracle, this property can be left blank if the control's **Connect** property identifies a data source name (DSN) that identifies an ODBC data source entry in the registry.

If you change the **DatabaseName** property after the control's **Database** object is open, you must use the **Refresh** method to open the new database.

Note For better performance when accessing external databases, it's recommended that you attach external database tables to a Microsoft Jet engine database (.mdb) and use the name of the Jet .mdb database in the **DatabaseName** property.

Data Type

> **String**

See Also

> **Connect** Property (DAO), **Data** Control, **Database** Object, **Refresh** Method

Example

> This example examines the Database property of a data control and prints the name of each Table in the Debug window.

```
Sub PrintTableNames ()
    Dim Td As TableDef
    ' Set database file.
    Data1.DatabaseName = "BIBLIO.MDB"
    Data1.Refresh   ' Open the Database.
    ' Read and print the name of each table in the database.
    For Each Td in Data1.Database.TableDefs
        Debug.Print Td.Name
    Next
End Sub
```

Databases Collection

> A **Databases** collection contains all open **Database** objects opened or created in a **Workspace** object.

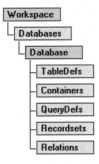

Remarks

> When you open an existing **Database** object or create a new one from a **Workspace**, it is automatically appended to the **Databases** collection. When you close a **Database** object with the **Close** method, it is removed from the **Databases** collection but not deleted from disk. You should close all open **Recordset** objects before closing a **Database** object.

> In a Microsoft Jet workspace, the **Name** property setting of a database is a string that specifies the path of the database file. In an ODBCDirect workspace, the **Name** property is the name of the corresponding **Connection** object.

To refer to a **Database** object in a collection by its ordinal number or by its **Name** property setting, use any of the following syntax forms:

Databases(0)
Databases("*name*")
Databases![*name*]

Note   You can open the same data source or database more than once, creating duplicate names in the **Databases** collection. You should assign **Database** objects to object variables and refer to them by variable name.

Properties

Count Property (DAO)

Methods

Refresh Method (DAO)

Example

This example creates a new **Database** object and opens an existing **Database** object in the default **Workspace** object. Then it enumerates the **Database** collection and the **Properties** collection of each **Database** object. See the methods and properties listed in the **Database** summary topic for additional examples.

```
Sub DatabaseObjectX()

    Dim wrkJet As Workspace
    Dim dbsNorthwind As Database
    Dim dbsNew As Database
    Dim dbsLoop As Database
    Dim prpLoop As Property

    Set wrkJet = CreateWorkspace("JetWorkspace", "admin", _
        "", dbUseJet)

    ' Make sure there isn't already a file with the name of
    ' the new database.
    If Dir("NewDB.mdb") <> "" Then Kill "NewDB.mdb"

    ' Create a new database with the specified
    ' collating order.
    Set dbsNew = wrkJet.CreateDatabase("NewDB.mdb", _
        dbLangGeneral)
    Set dbsNorthwind = wrkJet.OpenDatabase("Northwind.mdb")

    ' Enumerate the Databases collection.
    For Each dbsLoop In wrkJet.Databases
        With dbsLoop
            Debug.Print "Properties of " & .Name
            ' Enumerate the Properties collection of each
            ' Database object.
            For Each prpLoop In .Properties
```

```
            If prpLoop <> "" Then Debug.Print "    " & _
                prpLoop.Name & " = " & prpLoop
        Next prpLoop
    End With
Next dbsLoop

dbsNew.Close
dbsNorthwind.Close
wrkJet.Close

End Sub
```

DataBinding Object

The **DataBinding** object represents a bindable property of a component.

Syntax

DataBinding

Remarks

There is one **DataBinding** object for each property of a component marked as Bindable in the **Procedure Attributes** dialog box.

Visual Basic version 4.0 supported binding only one property of a control to a database at a time. Visual Basic 5.0, however, gives you the ability to bind multiple properties of a control to a database. This is used most commonly with **User** controls. For more information on this, see Chapter 9 in "Creating ActiveX Components" in the *Component Tools Guide*.

Properties

DataChanged Property, **DataField** Property, **DataSource** Property, **IsBindable** Property, **IsDataSource** Property, **PropertyName** Property

DataBindings Collection

The **DataBindings** collection is an extender property that collects the bindable properties that are available to the developer and end-user.

Remarks

All bindable properties appear in the **DataBindings** collection at end user run time. At developer design time (control run time), only properties marked "show in **DataBindings** collection at design time" will appear when the **DataBindings** property is accessed in the Properties window.

Properties

Count Property, **Item** Method

DataBindings Property

Returns the **DataBindings** collection object containing the bindable properties available to the developer.

Applies To

DBCombo Control, **DBGrid** Control, **DBList** Control, **Masked Edit** Control, **MSChart** Control, **MSFlexGrid** Control, **Multimedia MCI** Control, **RichTextBox** Control, **Slider** Control, **SSTab** Control, **TabStrip** Control, **Toolbar** Control

Syntax

object.**DataBindings**

The *object* placeholder represents an object expression that evaluates to an object in the **Applies To** list.

DataChanged Event

Occurs when the value of the column has changed.

Applies To

rdoColumn Object

Syntax

Private Sub *object*.**DataChanged**( )

The *object* placeholder represents an object expression that evaluates to an object in the **Applies To** list.

Remarks

This event is raised after the data in a column has been changed. The new data can be accessed through the **rdoColumn** object's **Value** property. You can also use the **WillChange** event to prevent or modify the change about to be made on a column-by-column basis. However, once the **DataChanged** event fires, the change has already been committed to the database.

See Also

WillChangeData Event, **WillUpdateRows** Event, **AddNew** Method (Remote Data), **Edit** Method (Remote Data), **GetChunk** Method (Remote Data), **Refresh** Method (Remote Data), **Requery** Method (Remote Data), **Update** Method (Remote Data), **UpdateRow** Method (Remote Data)

DataChanged Property

Returns or sets a value indicating that the data in the bound control has been changed by some process other than that of retrieving data from the current record. Not available at design time.

Applies To

CheckBox Control, **Image** Control, **Label** Control, **ListBox** Control, **Masked Edit** Control, **OLE Container** Control, **PictureBox** Control, **Rich TextBox** Control, **TextBox** Control, **DBCombo** Control, **DBList** Control, **Column** Object, **DBGrid** Control, **ComboBox** Control

Syntax

object.**DataChanged** [= *value*]

The **DataChanged** property syntax has these parts:

Part	Description
object	An object expression that evaluates to an object in the **Applies To** list.
Value	A Boolean expression that indicates whether data has changed, as described in Settings.

Settings

The settings for *value* are:

Setting	Description
True	The data currently in the control isn't the same as in the current record.
False	(Default) The data currently in the control, if any, is the same as the data in the current record.

Remarks

When a **Data** control moves from record to record, it passes data from fields in the current record to controls bound to the specific field or the entire record. As data is displayed in the bound controls, the **DataChanged** property is set to **False**. If the user or any other operation changes the value in the bound control, the **DataChanged** property is set to **True**. Simply moving to another record doesn't affect the **DataChanged** property.

When the **Data** control starts to move to a different record, the **Validate** event occurs. If **DataChanged** is **True** for any bound control, the **Data** control automatically invokes the **Edit** and **Update** methods to post the changes to the database.

If you don't wish to save changes from a bound control to the database, you can set the **DataChanged** property to **False** in the **Validate** event.

Inspect the value of the **DataChanged** property in your code for a control's **Change** event to avoid a cascading event. This applies to both bound and unbound controls.

Data Type

       Integer (Boolean)

See Also

       Data Control, **Validate** Event, **UpdateRecord** Method

DataChanged Property (DBGrid)

Returns or sets a value indicating that the data in the bound control has been changed by some process other than that of retrieving data from the current record. Not available at design time.

Applies To

       DBGrid Control

Syntax

       object.**DataChanged** [= *value*]

The **DataChanged** property syntax has these parts:

Part	Description
object	An object expression that evaluates to an object in the **Applies To** list.
Value	A Boolean expression that indicates whether data has changed, as described in **Settings**.

Settings

The settings for *value* are:

Setting	Description
True	The data currently in the control isn't the same as in the current record.
False	(Default) The data currently in the control, if any, is the same as the data in the current record.

Remarks

When a **Data** control moves from record to record, it passes data from fields in the current record to controls bound to the specific field or the entire record. As data is displayed in the bound controls, the **DataChanged** property is set to **False**. If the user or any other operation changes the value in the bound control, the **DataChanged** property is set to **True**. Simply moving to another record doesn't affect the **DataChanged** property.

When the **Data** control starts to move to a different record, the **Validate** event occurs. If **DataChanged** is **True** for any bound control, the **Data** control automatically invokes the **Edit** and **Update** methods to post the changes to the database.

If you don't wish to save changes from a bound control to the database, you can set the **DataChanged** property to **False** in the **Validate** event.

Inspect the value of the **DataChanged** property in your code for a control's **Change** event to avoid a cascading event. This applies to both bound and unbound controls.

Data Type

Integer (Boolean)

See Also

DBGrid Control Constants

DataField Property

Returns or sets a value that binds a control to a field in the current record

Applies To

CheckBox Control, **ComboBox** Control, **Image** Control, **Label** Control, **ListBox** Control, **Masked Edit** Control, **OLE Container** Control, **PictureBox** Control, **ProgressBar** Control, **Rich TextBox** Control, **TextBox** Control, **DBCombo** Control, **DBList** Control, **Column** Object, **DBGrid** Control

Syntax

object.**DataField** [= *value*]

The **DataField** property syntax has these parts:

Part	Description
object	An object expression that evaluates to an object in the **Applies To** list.
Value	A string expression that evaluates to the name of one of the fields in the **Recordset** object specified by a **Data** control's **RecordSource** and **DatabaseName** properties.

Remarks

Bound controls provide access to specific data in your database. Bound controls that manage a single field typically display the value of a specific field in the current record. The **DataSource** property of a bound control specifies a valid **Data** control name, and the **DataField** property specifies a valid field name in the **Recordset** object created by the **Data** control. Together, these properties specify what data appears in the bound control.

When you use a **QueryDef** object or SQL statement that returns the results of an expression, the field name is automatically generated by the Microsoft Jet database engine. For example, when you code an SQL aggregate function or an expression in your SQL query, unless you alias the aggregate fields using an AS clause, the field names are automatically generated. Generally, the expression field name is Expr1 followed by a three-character number starting with 000. The first expression returned would be named Expr1000.

It's recommended that you code your SQL queries to alias expression columns as shown below:

```
Data1.RecordSource = "Select AVG(Sales)   " _
    & " AS AverageSales From SalesTable"
Text1.DataField = "AverageSales"
Data1.Refresh
```

Note   Make sure the **DataField** property setting is valid for each bound control. If you change the setting of a **Data** control's **RecordSource** property and then use **Refresh**, the **Recordset** identifies the new object. This may invalidate the **DataField** settings of bound controls and produce a trappable error.

Data Type

String

See Also

Data Control, **DBCombo** Control, **DBList** Control, **DBGrid** Control, **DataSource** Property, **Recordset** Property

DataField Property (DBGrid Control, Column Object)

Returns or sets a value that binds a control to a field in the current record

Applies To

Column Object, **DBGrid** Control

Syntax

object.**DataField** [= *value*]

The **DataField** property syntax has these parts:

Part	Description
object	An object expression that evaluates to an object in the **Applies To** list.
Value	A string expression that evaluates to the name of one of the fields in the **Recordset** object specified by a **Data** control's **RecordSource** and **DatabaseName** properties.

Remarks

Bound controls provide access to specific data in your database. Bound controls that manage a single field typically display the value of a specific field in the current record. The **DataSource** property of a bound control specifies a valid **Data** control name, and the **DataField** property specifies a valid field name in the **Recordset** object created by the **Data** control. Together, these properties specify what data appears in the bound control.

When you use a **QueryDef** object or SQL statement that returns the results of an expression, the field name is automatically generated by the Microsoft Jet database engine. For example, when you code an SQL aggregate function or an expression in your SQL query, unless you alias the aggregate fields using an AS clause, the field names are automatically generated. Generally, the expression field name is Expr1 followed by a three-character number starting with 000. The first expression returned would be named Expr1000.

It's recommended that you code your SQL queries to alias expression columns as shown below:

```
Data1.RecordSource = "Select AVG(Sales)  " _
    & " AS AverageSales From SalesTable"
Text1.DataField = "AverageSales"
Data1.Refresh
```

Note Make sure the **DataField** property setting is valid for each bound control. If you change the setting of a **Data** control's **RecordSource** property and then use **Refresh**, the **Recordset** identifies the new object. This may invalidate the **DataField** settings of bound controls and produce a trappable error.

Data Type

String

See Also

DBGrid Control Constants

DataMode Property

Sets a value specifying whether the **DBGrid** operates in bound or unbound mode. This property is not available at run time.

Applies To

DBGrid Control

Remarks

The **DataMode** property may be set to one of the following values:

Constant	Value	Description
dbgBound	0	The **DBGrid** displays data available from the bound data source.
dbgUnbound	1	The **DBGrid** uses the unbound control events to retrieve and update displayed data.

Note The above constants may only be used for comparisons because the property is not available at run time.

The **DataMode** property controls how the data is handled for the **DBGrid** control. In unbound mode, you are responsible for maintaining data and supplying the **DBGrid** control with the appropriate data when requested through the unbound events. In bound mode, the data is retrieved and updated automatically using the **Data** control's **Recordset**.

Normally, the unbound mode of the **DBGrid** control is used when displaying data that is not stored in a database accessible by the Microsoft Jet Database Engine. You can use the unbound mode for whatever type of data you have available. For example, you can use the unbound mode of the **DBGrid** control to display data from a proprietary database format or use it to manage data that you keep track of in a text file.

Note   When the **DBGrid** is bound to a data source, setting the **DataMode** to 1 results in an error.

See Also

UnboundAddData Event, **UnboundDeleteRow** Event, **UnboundReadData** Event, **UnboundWriteData** Event, **RowBuffer** Object, **DBGrid Control** Constants, **Data** Control

DataObject Object

The **DataObject** object is a container for data being transferred from an component source to an component target. The data is stored in the format defined by the method using the **DataObject** object.

Syntax

DataObject

Remarks

The **DataObject**, which mirrors the **IDataObject** interface, allows OLE drag and drop and clipboard operations to be implemented.

Most components support manual OLE drag and drop events, and some support automatic OLE drag and drop events.

Properties

Files Property

Methods

SetData Method, **Clear** Method (DataObject Object), **GetData** Method (DataObject Object), **GetFormat** Method (DataObject Object), **SetData** Method (DataObject Object)

DataObjectFiles Collection

A collection of strings which is the type of the **Files** property on the **DataObject** object.

Syntax

object.**DataObjectFiles**

The *object* placeholder represents an object expression that evaluates to an object in the **Applies To** list.

Remarks

The **DataObjectFiles** collection is a collection of strings which represent a set of files which have been selected either through the **GetData** method, or through selection in an application such as the Windows Explorer.

Although the **DataObjectFiles** collection has methods and properties of its own, you should use the **Files** property of the **DataObject** object to view and manipulate the contents of the **DataObjectFiles** collection.

Here are some code examples showing the use of the **Files** property to view and manipulate data contained in the **DataObjectFiles** collection (where "Data" represents an object of type **DataObject**):

```
Debug.Print Data.Files(index)
For Each v in Data.Files
    Debug.Print v
Next v
Data.Files.Add "autoexec.bat"
Data.Files.Remove index
Data.Files.Clear
For i = 0 to Data.Files.Count - 1
    Debug.print Data.Files(i)
Next i
```

Note   This collection is used by the **Files** property only when the data in the **DataObject** object is in the **vbCFFiles** format.

Properties

Item Method

Methods

Clear Method, **Remove** Method

DataSource Property

Sets a value that specifies the **Data** control through which the current control is bound to a database. Not available at run time.

Applies To

CheckBox Control, **ComboBox** Control, **Image** Control, **Label** Control, **ListBox** Control, **Masked Edit** Control, **PictureBox** Control, **Rich TextBox** Control, **DBCombo** Control, **DBList** Control, **DBGrid** Control

Remarks

To bind a control to a field in a database at run time, you must specify a **Data** control in the **DataSource** property at design time using the Properties window.

To complete the connection with a field in the **Recordset** managed by the **Data** control, you must also provide the name of a **Field** object in the **DataField** property.

Unlike the **DataField** property, the **DataSource** property setting isn't available at run time.

Data Type

String

See Also

Data Control, **DataField** Property, **RecordSource** Property, **Recordset** Property

---

DataSourceName Property (Remote Data)

Returns or sets the data source name for a **RemoteData** control.

Applies To

RemoteData Control

Syntax

object.**DataSourceName** [= *datasourcename*]

The **DataSourceName** property syntax has these parts:

Part	Description
object	An object expression that evaluates to an object in the **Applies To** list.
Datasourcename	A string expression that indicates a registered data source name.

Remarks

This property can be left blank if the **RemoteData** control's **Connect** property identifies a data source name (DSN) registered in the Windows Registry (32-bit) or if you create a DSN-less connection that provides all required information in the **Connect** property.

Once the **rdoConnection** is opened by the **RemoteData** control, the **DataSourceName** property contains the DSN used to establish the connection— it may be different from the value set before the connection is opened, because a user might select a data source from a list of valid DSN entries during the connection process.

If you change this property after the control's **rdoConnection** object is open, you must use the **RemoteData** control's **Refresh** method to open a new connection to the data source.

See Also

OpenConnection Method (Remote Data), **rdoRegisterDataSource** Method (Remote Data), **Refresh** Method (Remote Data), **rdoEngine** Object, **RemoteData** Control, **Connect** Property (Remote Data)

DataText Property

Returns a string from or sets a string for the specified object.

Applies To

OLE Container Control

Syntax

object.**DataText** [= *string*]

The **DataText** property syntax has these parts:

Part	Description
object	An object expression that evaluates to an object in the **Applies To** list.
String	A string expression specifying the string.

Remarks

To send a string to an object, first set the **Format** property to a format the object supports. Use the **ObjectGetFormats** and **ObjectAcceptFormats** properties to get a list of formats supported by an object.

When getting data from an object, the **DataText** property returns the string sent from the object, ending at the first null character.

The **DataText** string can be as large as available memory permits.

Tip Automation provides an easier and more reliable solution for sending data and commands to and from an object. If an object supports Automation, you can access the object through the **Object** property or using the **CreateObject** and **GetObject** functions.

See Also

Data Property, **ObjectAcceptFormatsCount** Property, **ObjectGetFormats** Property, **ObjectGetFormatsCount** Property, **Object** Property (OLE Container), **Format** Property

Example

This example sends data to the Microsoft Graph application, so you must have **MS Graph** installed on your system to run the example. (This is installed by most Microsoft Office components.) Create a form about one-half the size of the screen with a **CommandButton** control (Command1) in the upper-left corner of the form and an **OLE** container control (OLE1) placed below the **CommandButton**.

When you place the **OLE** container control on the form, the Insert Object dialog box is displayed. Choose Cancel and press F5 to run the example.

```
Private Sub Command1_Click ()
Dim Msg, NL, TB' Declare variables.
   TB = Chr(9) ' Tab character.
   NL = Chr(10)' Newline character.
```

```
                  ' Create data to replace default Graph data.
                  Msg = TB + "Drew" & TB & "Teresa" & TB & "Bob"
                  Msg = Msg + NL & "Eric" & TB & "1" & TB & "2" & TB & "3"
                  Msg = Msg + NL & "Ted" & TB & "11" & TB & "22" & TB & "33"
                  Msg = Msg + NL & "Arthur" & TB & "21" & TB & "32" & TB & "23"
                  ' Send the data using the DataText property.
                  ' Activate MSGRAPH as hidden.

          Ole1.DoVerb - 3
              If Ole1.AppIsRunning Then
                  Ole1.DataText = Msg
                  ' Update the object.
                  Ole1.Update
              Else
                  MsgBox "Graph isn't active."
              End If
          End Sub
          Sub Form_Load ()
              Ole1.Format = "CF_TEXT" ' Set the file format to text.
              Ole1.SizeMode = 2 ' Autosize.
              Ole1.CreateEmbed "", "MSGRAPH"
          End Sub
              List3.Clear
              ' Fill the verbs list box. Because ObjectVerbs(0) is
              ' the default verb and is repeated in the ObjectVerbs()
              ' array, start the count at 1.
              For I = 1 To Ole1.ObjectVerbsCount - 1
                  List1.AddItem Ole1.ObjectVerbs(I)
              Next I
              'Fill the Accept Formats list box.
              For I = 0 To Ole1.ObjectAcceptFormatsCount - 1
                  List2.AddItem Ole1.ObjectAcceptFormats(I)
              Next I
              ' Fill the Get Formats list box.
              For I = 0 To Ole1.ObjectGetFormatsCount - 1
                  List3.AddItem Ole1.ObjectGetFormats(I)
              Next I
          End Sub
```

DataUpdatable Property

Returns a value that indicates whether the data in the field represented by a Field object is updatable.

Applies To

Field Object

Return Values

The return value is a **Boolean** data type that returns **True** if the data in the field is updatable.

Remarks

Use this property to determine whether you can change the **Value** property setting of a **Field** object. This property is always **False** on a **Field** object whose **Attributes** property is **dbAutoIncrField**.

You can use the **DataUpdatable** property on **Field** objects that are appended to the **Fields** collection of **QueryDef**, **Recordset**, and **Relation** objects, but not the **Fields** collection of **Index** or **TableDef** objects.

See Also

Attributes Property, **Updatable** Property, **Value** Property

Example

This example demonstrates the **DataUpdatable** property using the first field from six different **Recordsets**. The **DataOutput** function is required for this procedure to run.

```
Sub DataUpdatableX()

    Dim dbsNorthwind As Database
    Dim rstNorthwind As Recordset

    Set dbsNorthwind = OpenDatabase("Northwind.mdb")

    With dbsNorthwind
        ' Open and print report about a table-type Recordset.
        Set rstNorthwind = .OpenRecordset("Employees")
        DataOutput rstNorthwind

        ' Open and print report about a dynaset-type Recordset.
        Set rstNorthwind = .OpenRecordset("Employees", _
            dbOpenDynaset)
        DataOutput rstNorthwind

        ' Open and print report about a snapshot-type Recordset.
        Set rstNorthwind = .OpenRecordset("Employees", _
            dbOpenSnapshot)
        DataOutput rstNorthwind

        ' Open and print report about a forward-only-type Recordset.
        Set rstNorthwind = .OpenRecordset("Employees", _
            dbOpenForwardOnly)
        DataOutput rstNorthwind

        ' Open and print report about a Recordset based on
        ' a select query.
        Set rstNorthwind = _
            .OpenRecordset("Current Product List")
        DataOutput rstNorthwind

        ' Open and print report about a Recordset based on a
        ' select query that calculates totals.
        Set rstNorthwind = .OpenRecordset("Order Subtotals")
        DataOutput rstNorthwind
```

```
            .Close
        End With

    End Sub

    Function DataOutput(rstTemp As Recordset)

        With rstTemp
            Debug.Print "Recordset: " & .Name & ", ";
            Select Case .Type
                Case dbOpenTable
                    Debug.Print "dbOpenTable"
                Case dbOpenDynaset
                    Debug.Print "dbOpenDynaset"
                Case dbOpenSnapshot
                    Debug.Print "dbOpenSnapshot"
                Case dbOpenForwardOnly
                    Debug.Print "dbOpenForwardOnly"
            End Select
            Debug.Print "    Field: " & .Fields(0).Name & ", " & _
                "DataUpdatable = " & .Fields(0).DataUpdatable
            Debug.Print
            .Close
        End With

    End Function
```

Date Data Type

Date variables are stored as IEEE 64-bit (8-byte) floating-point numbers that represent dates ranging from 1 January 100 to 31 December 9999 and times from 0:00:00 to 23:59:59. Any recognizable literal date values can be assigned to **Date** variables. Date literals must be enclosed within number signs (#), for example, #January 1, 1993# or #1 Jan 93#.

Date variables display dates according to the short date format recognized by your computer. Times display according to the time format (either 12-hour or 24-hour) recognized by your computer.

When other numeric types are converted to **Date**, values to the left of the decimal represent date information while values to the right of the decimal represent time. Midnight is 0 and midday is 0.5. Negative whole numbers represent dates before 30 December 1899.

See Also

Data Type Summary, **Double Data** Type, **Variant Data** Type, **Deftype** Statements

Date Function

Returns a **Variant** (**Date**) containing the current system date.

Syntax

> **Date**

Remarks

To set the system date, use the **Date** statement.

See Also

Date Statement, **Now** Function, **Time** Function, **Time** Statement, **Format** Function

Example

This example uses the **Date** function to return the current system date.

```
Dim MyDate
MyDate = Date   ' MyDate contains the current system date.
```

Date Statement

Sets the current system date.

Syntax

> **Date** = *date*

For systems running Microsoft Windows 95, the required *date* specification must be a date from January 1, 1980 through December 31, 2099. For systems running Microsoft Windows NT, *date* must be a date from January 1, 1980 through December 31, 2079.

See Also

Date Function, **Time** Function, **Time** Statement

Example

This example uses the **Date** statement to set the computer system date. In the development environment, the date literal is displayed in short date format using the locale settings of your code.

```
Dim MyDate
MyDate = #February 12, 1985#  ' Assign a date.
Date = MyDate                 ' Change system date.
```

DateAdd Function

Returns a **Variant** (**Date**) containing a date to which a specified time interval has been added.

Syntax

> **DateAdd**(*interval, number, date*)

The **DateAdd** function syntax has these named arguments:

Part	Description
interval	Required. String expression that is the interval of time you want to add.
number	Required. Numeric expression that is the number of intervals you want to add. It can be positive (to get dates in the future) or negative (to get dates in the past).
date	Required. **Variant** (**Date**) or literal representing date to which the interval is added.

Settings

The *interval* argument has these settings:

Setting	Description
yyyy	Year
q	Quarter
m	Month
y	Day of year
d	Day
w	Weekday
ww	Week
h	Hour
n	Minute
s	Second

Remarks

You can use the **DateAdd** function to add or subtract a specified time interval from a date. For example, you can use **DateAdd** to calculate a date 30 days from today or a time 45 minutes from now.

To add days to *date*, you can use Day of Year ("y"), Day ("d"), or Weekday ("w").

The **DateAdd** function won't return an invalid date. The following example adds one month to January 31:

```
DateAdd("m", 1, "31-Jan-95")
```

In this case, **DateAdd** returns 28-Feb-95, not 31-Feb-95. If *date* is 31-Jan-96, it returns 29-Feb-96 because 1996 is a leap year.

If the calculated date would precede the year 100 (that is, you subtract more years than are in *date*), an error occurs.

If *number* isn't a **Long** value, it is rounded to the nearest whole number before being evaluated.

See Also

DateDiff Function, **DatePart** Function, **Day** Function, **Now** Function, **Weekday** Function, **Year** Function, **Format** Function

Example

This example takes a date and, using the **DateAdd** function, displays a corresponding date a specified number of months in the future.

```
Dim FirstDate As Date    ' Declare variables.
Dim IntervalType As String
Dim Number As Integer
Dim Msg
IntervalType = "m"       ' "m" specifies months as interval.
FirstDate = InputBox("Enter a date")
Number = InputBox("Enter number of months to add")
Msg = "New date: " & DateAdd(IntervalType, Number, FirstDate)
MsgBox Msg
```

DateCreated, LastUpdated Properties

- **DateCreated** — returns the date and time that an object was created, or the date and time a base table was created if the object is a table-type **Recordset** object (Microsoft Jet workspaces only).

- **LastUpdated** — returns the date and time of the most recent change made to an object, or to a base table if the object is a table-type **Recordset** object (Microsoft Jet workspaces only).

Applies To

Document Object, **QueryDef** Object, **Recordset** Object, **Table-Type Recordset** Object, **TableDef** Object

Return Values

The return value is a **Variant** (**Date/Time** subtype).

Remarks

For table-type **Recordset** objects, the date and time settings are derived from the computer on which the base table was created or last updated. For other objects, **DateCreated** and **LastUpdated** return the date and time that the object was created or last updated. In a multiuser environment, users should get these settings directly from the file server to avoid discrepancies in the **DateCreated** and **LastUpdated** property settings.

Example

This example demonstrates the **DateCreated** and **LastUpdated** properties by adding a new **Field** to an existing **TableDef** and by creating a new **TableDef**. The DateOutput function is required for this procedure to run.

```
Sub DateCreatedX()

    Dim dbsNorthwind As Database
    Dim tdfEmployees As TableDef
    Dim tdfNewTable As TableDef

    Set dbsNorthwind = OpenDatabase("Northwind.mdb")
```

```
    With dbsNorthwind
        Set tdfEmployees = .TableDefs!Employees

        With tdfEmployees
            ' Print current information about the Employees
            ' table.
            DateOutput "Current properties", tdfEmployees

            ' Create and append a field to the Employees table.
            .Fields.Append .CreateField("NewField", dbDate)

            ' Print new information about the Employees
            ' table.
            DateOutput "After creating a new field", _
                tdfEmployees

            ' Delete new Field because this is a demonstration.
            .Fields.Delete "NewField"
        End With

        ' Create and append a new TableDef object to the
        ' Northwind database.
        Set tdfNewTable = .CreateTableDef("NewTableDef")
        With tdfNewTable
            .Fields.Append .CreateField("NewField", dbDate)
        End With
        .TableDefs.Append tdfNewTable

        ' Print information about the new TableDef object.
        DateOutput "After creating a new table", tdfNewTable

        ' Delete new TableDef object because this is a
        ' demonstration.
        .TableDefs.Delete tdfNewTable.Name
        .Close
    End With

End Sub

Function DateOutput(strTemp As String, _
    tdfTemp As TableDef)

    ' Print DateCreated and LastUpdated information about
    ' specified TableDef object.
    Debug.Print strTemp
    Debug.Print "    TableDef: " & tdfTemp.Name
    Debug.Print "        DateCreated = " & _
        tdfTemp.DateCreated
    Debug.Print "        LastUpdated = " & _
        tdfTemp.LastUpdated
    Debug.Print

End Function
```

DateDiff Function

Returns a **Variant** (**Long**) specifying the number of time intervals between two specified dates.

Syntax

DateDiff(*interval, date1, date2*[, *firstdayofweek*[, *firstweekofyear*]])

The **DateDiff** function syntax has these named arguments:

Part	Description
interval	Required. String expression that is the interval of time you use to calculate the difference between *date1* and *date2*.
date1, *date2*	Required; **Variant** (**Date**). Two dates you want to use in the calculation.
firstdayofweek	Optional. A constant that specifies the first day of the week. If not specified, Sunday is assumed.
firstweekofyear	Optional. A constant that specifies the first week of the year. If not specified, the first week is assumed to be the week in which January 1 occurs.

Settings

The *interval* argument has these settings:

Setting	Description
yyyy	Year
q	Quarter
m	Month
y	Day of year
d	Day
w	Weekday
ww	Week
h	Hour
n	Minute
s	Second

The *firstdayofweek* argument has these settings:

Constant	Value	Description
vbUseSystem	0	Use the NLS API setting.
vbSunday	1	Sunday (default)
vbMonday	2	Monday
vbTuesday	3	Tuesday
vbWednesday	4	Wednesday
vbThursday	5	Thursday
vbFriday	6	Friday
vbSaturday	7	Saturday

The *firstweekofyear* argument has these settings:

Constant	Value	Description
vbUseSystem	0	Use the NLS API setting.
vbFirstJan1	1	Start with week in which January 1 occurs (default).
vbFirstFourDays	2	Start with the first week that has at least four days in the new year.
vbFirstFullWeek	3	Start with first full week of the year.

Remarks

You can use the **DateDiff** function to determine how many specified time intervals exist between two dates. For example, you might use **DateDiff** to calculate the number of days between two dates, or the number of weeks between today and the end of the year.

To calculate the number of days between *date1* and *date2*, you can use either Day of year ("y") or Day ("d"). When *interval* is Weekday ("w"), **DateDiff** returns the number of weeks between the two dates. If *date1* falls on a Monday, **DateDiff** counts the number of Mondays until *date2*. It counts *date2* but not *date1*. If *interval* is Week ("ww"), however, the **DateDiff** function returns the number of calendar weeks between the two dates. It counts the number of Sundays between *date1* and *date2*. **DateDiff** counts *date2* if it falls on a Sunday; but it doesn't count *date1*, even if it does fall on a Sunday.

If *date1* refers to a later point in time than *date2*, the **DateDiff** function returns a negative number.

The *firstdayofweek* argument affects calculations that use the "w" and "ww" interval symbols.

If *date1* or *date2* is a date literal, the specified year becomes a permanent part of that date. However, if *date1* or *date2* is enclosed in double quotation marks (" "), and you omit the year, the current year is inserted in your code each time the *date1* or *date2* expression is evaluated. This makes it possible to write code that can be used in different years.

When comparing December 31 to January 1 of the immediately succeeding year, **DateDiff** for Year ("yyyy") returns 1 even though only a day has elapsed.

See Also

DateAdd Function, **DatePart** Function, **Day** Function, **Now** Function, **Weekday** Function, **Year** Function, **Format** Function

Example

This example uses the **DateDiff** function to display the number of days between a given date and today.

```
Dim TheDate As Date   ' Declare variables.
Dim Msg
TheDate = InputBox("Enter a date")
Msg = "Days from today: " & DateDiff("d", Now, TheDate)
MsgBox Msg
```

DatePart Function

Returns a **Variant** (**Integer**) containing the specified part of a given date.

Syntax

DatePart(*interval, date*[,*firstdayofweek*[, *firstweekofyear*]])

The **DatePart** function syntax has these named arguments:

Part	Description
interval	Required. String expression that is the interval of time you want to return.
date	Required. **Variant** (**Date**) value that you want to evaluate.
firstdayofweek	Optional. A constant that specifies the first day of the week. If not specified, Sunday is assumed.
firstweekofyear	Optional. A constant that specifies the first week of the year. If not specified, the first week is assumed to be the week in which January 1 occurs.

Settings

The *interval* argument has these settings:

Setting	Description
yyyy	Year
q	Quarter
m	Month
y	Day of year
d	Day
w	Weekday
ww	Week
h	Hour
n	Minute
s	Second

The *firstdayofweek* argument has these settings:

Constant	Value	Description
vbUseSystem	0	Use the NLS API setting.
vbSunday	1	Sunday (default)
vbMonday	2	Monday
vbTuesday	3	Tuesday
vbWednesday	4	Wednesday
vbThursday	5	Thursday
vbFriday	6	Friday
vbSaturday	7	Saturday

The *firstweekofyear* argument has these settings:

Constant	Value	Description
vbUseSystem	0	Use the NLS API setting.
vbFirstJan1	1	Start with week in which January 1 occurs (default).
vbFirstFourDays	2	Start with the first week that has at least four days in the new year.
vbFirstFullWeek	3	Start with first full week of the year.

Remarks

You can use the **DatePart** function to evaluate a date and return a specific interval of time. For example, you might use **DatePart** to calculate the day of the week or the current hour.

The *firstdayofweek* argument affects calculations that use the "w" and "ww" interval symbols.

If *date* is a date literal, the specified year becomes a permanent part of that date. However, if *date* is enclosed in double quotation marks (" "), and you omit the year, the current year is inserted in your code each time the *date* expression is evaluated. This makes it possible to write code that can be used in different years.

See Also

DateAdd Function, **DateDiff** Function, **Day** Function, **Now** Function, **Weekday** Function, **Year** Function, **Format** Function

Example

This example takes a date and, using the **DatePart** function, displays the quarter of the year in which it occurs.

```
Dim TheDate As Date   ' Declare variables.
Dim Msg
TheDate = InputBox("Enter a date:")
Msg = "Quarter: " & DatePart("q", TheDate)
MsgBox Msg
```

DateSerial Function

Returns a **Variant** (**Date**) for a specified year, month, and day.

Syntax

DateSerial(*year, month, day*)

The **DateSerial** function syntax has these named arguments:

Part	Description
year	Required; **Integer**. Number between 100 and 9999, inclusive, or a numeric expression.
month	Required; **Integer**. Any numeric expression.
day	Required; **Integer**. Any numeric expression.

Remarks

To specify a date, such as December 31, 1991, the range of numbers for each **DateSerial** argument should be in the accepted range for the unit; that is, 1–31 for days and 1–12 for months. However, you can also specify relative dates for each argument using any numeric expression that represents some number of days, months, or years before or after a certain date.

The following example uses numeric expressions instead of absolute date numbers. Here the **DateSerial** function returns a date that is the day before the first day (1 - 1), two months before August (8 - 2), 10 years before 1990 (1990 - 10); in other words, May 31, 1980.

```
DateSerial(1990 - 10, 8 - 2, 1 - 1)
```

For the *year* argument, values between 0 and 99, inclusive, are interpreted as the years 1900–1999. For all other *year* arguments, use a four-digit year (for example, 1800).

When any argument exceeds the accepted range for that argument, it increments to the next larger unit as appropriate. For example, if you specify 35 days, it is evaluated as one month and some number of days, depending on where in the year it is applied. If any single argument is outside the range -32,768 to 32,767, an error occurs. If the date specified by the three arguments falls outside the acceptable range of dates, an error occurs.

See Also

Date Function, **Date** Statement, **DateValue** Function, **Day** Function, **Month** Function, **Now** Function, **TimeSerial** Function, **TimeValue** Function, **Weekday** Function, **Year** Function

Example

This example uses the **DateSerial** function to return the date for the specified year, month, and day.

```
Dim MyDate
' MyDate contains the date for February 12, 1969.
MyDate = DateSerial(1969, 2, 12)     ' Return a date.
```

DateValue Function

Returns a **Variant** (**Date**).

Syntax

DateValue(*date*)

The required *date* argument is normally a string expression representing a date from January 1, 100 through December 31, 9999. However, *date* can also be any expression that can represent a date, a time, or both a date and time, in that range.

Remarks

If *date* is a string that includes only numbers separated by valid date separators, **DateValue** recognizes the order for month, day, and year according to the Short Date format you specified for your system. **DateValue** also recognizes unambiguous dates that contain month names, either in long or abbreviated form. For example, in addition to recognizing 12/30/1991 and 12/30/91, **DateValue** also recognizes December 30, 1991 and Dec 30, 1991.

If the year part of *date* is omitted, **DateValue** uses the current year from your computer's system date.

If the *date* argument includes time information, **DateValue** doesn't return it. However, if *date* includes invalid time information (such as "89:98"), an error occurs.

See Also

Date Function, **Date** Statement, **DateSerial** Function, **Day** Function, **Month** Function, **Now** Function, **TimeSerial** Function, **TimeValue** Function, **Weekday** Function, **Year** Function

Example

This example uses the **DateValue** function to convert a string to a date. You can also use date literals to directly assign a date to a **Variant** or **Date** variable, for example, MyDate = #2/12/69#.

```
Dim MyDate
MyDate = DateValue("February 12, 1969")      ' Return a date.
```

Day Function

Returns a **Variant** (**Integer**) specifying a whole number between 1 and 31, inclusive, representing the day of the month.

Syntax

Day(*date*)

The required *date* argument is any **Variant**, numeric expression, string expression, or any combination, that can represent a date. If *date* contains **Null**, **Null** is returned.

See Also

Date Function, **Date** Statement, **Hour** Function, **Minute** Function, **Month** Function, **Now** Function, **Second** Function, **Weekday** Function, **Year** Function

Example

This example uses the **Day** function to obtain the day of the month from a specified date. In the development environment, the date literal is displayed in short format using the locale settings of your code.

```
Dim MyDate, MyDay
MyDate = #February 12, 1969#  ' Assign a date.
MyDay = Day(MyDate)           ' MyDay contains 12.
```

DBCombo Control

The **DBCombo** control is a data bound combo box with a drop-down list box which is automatically populated from a field in an attached **Data** control, and optionally updates a field in a related table of another **Data** control. The text box portion of **DBCombo** can be used to edit the selected field.

Syntax

DBCombo

Remarks

The **DBCombo** control differs from the standard **ComboBox** control. While the **ComboBox** control list is filled using the **AddItem** method, the **DBCombo** control is automatically filled with data from a field in the **Recordset** object of a **Data** control to which it is attached. The standard **ComboBox** control must be populated manually by using the **AddItem** method. In addition, the **DBCombo** control has the ability to update a field within a related **Recordset** object which may reside in a different **Data** control.

The **DBCombo** control also supports an automated search mode that can quickly locate items in the list without additional code.

Shown below is a list of the properties used to fill and manage the **DBCombo** control, and bind the selected data to a **Data** control.

Property	Specifies
DataSource	Name of **Data** control that is updated once a selection is made.
DataField	Name of a field that is updated in the **Recordset** specified by the **DataSource** property.
RowSource	Name of **Data** control used as a source of items for the list portion of the control.
ListField	Name of a field in the **Recordset** specified by **RowSource** that is used to fill the drop-down list. **DBCombo** does not support fields of **LongBinary** type for the **Listfield** property.
BoundColumn	Name of a **Field** in the **Recordset** specified by **RowSource** to be passed back to the **DataField** once a selection is made. **DBCombo** does not support fields of **LongBinary** type for the **BoundColumn**.
BoundText	Text value of **BoundColumn** field. Once a selection is made, this value is passed back to update the **Recordset** object specified by the **DataSource** and **DataField** properties.
Text	Text value of the selected item in the list.
MatchEntry	How the list is searched as the user types in characters at run time.
SelectedItem	The bookmark of the selected item in the **Recordset** specified by the **RowSource** property.
VisibleCount	The number of items visible in the list (fully or partially).
VisibleItems	An array of bookmarks with a maximum number of items equal to the **VisibleCount** property.

Users can search the **DBCombo** control by typing a value into the text box portion of the control. Once entered, this value is located in the list and the current list item is set to that item. If the item is not found, the **BoundText** property is set to null.

Note If you do not make the boundary of the control large enough for at least one row of the dropdown list, the list will not appear at run time.

Properties

Appearance Property, **BackColor, Forecolor** Properties, **Container** Property, **DataBindings** Property, **DragIcon** Property, **DragMode** Property, **Enabled** Property, **Font** Property, **Height, Width** Properties, **Height, Width** Properties (ActiveX Controls), **Help ContextID** Property, **hWnd** Property, **Index** Property (ActiveX Controls), **Index** Property (Control Array), **IntegralHeight** Property, **Left, Top** Properties, **Left, Top** Properties (ActiveX Controls), **Locked** Property, **MouseIcon** Property, **MousePointer** Property (ActiveX Controls), **Name** Property, **Object** Property, **Object** Property (ActiveX Controls), **OLEDragMode** Property, **OLEDropMode** Property, **Parent** Property, **RightToLeft** Property (ActiveX Controls), **SelLength, SelStart, SelText** Properties, **SelLength, SelStart, SelText** Properties (ActiveX Controls), **Style** Property, **TabIndex** Property, **TabStop** Property, **Tag** Property (ActiveX Controls), **Text** Property (ActiveX Controls), **ToolTipText** Property, **Visible** Property (ActiveX Controls), **DataChanged** Property, **DataField** Property, **DataSource** Property, **IntegralHeight** Property, **BoundColumn** Property, **ListField** Property, **RowSource** Property, **SelectedItem** Property, **VisibleItems** Property, **VisibleCount** Property, **MatchedWithList** Property, **MatchEntry** Property, **BoundText** Property

Events

Change Event, **Click** Event (DBCombo Control), **DblClick** Event (DBCombo Control), **DragDrop** Event, **DragOver** Event, **GotFocus** Event, **KeyDown, KeyUp** Events, **KeyDown, KeyUp** Events (ActiveX Controls), **KeyPress** Event, **KeyPress** Event (ActiveX Controls), **LostFocus** Event, **MouseDown, MouseUp** Events, **MouseMove** Event, **OLECompleteDrag** Event, **OLEDragDrop** Event, **OLEDragOver** Event, **OLEGiveFeedback** Event, **OLESetData** Event, **OLEStartDrag** Event

Methods

ReFill Method, **AboutBox** Method, **Drag** Method, **Move** Method, **OLEDrag** Method, **Refresh** Method (ActiveX Controls), **SelFocus** Method, **ShowWhatsThis** Method, **Zorder** Method

See Also

Data Control, **DBList** Control, **DBList and DBCombo Controls** Constants, **DBGrid** Control, **UpdateRecord** Method, **ComboBox** Control

DBEngine Object

The **DBEngine** object is the top level object in the DAO object model.

Remarks

The **DBEngine** object contains and controls all other objects in the hierarchy of DAO objects. You can't create additional **DBEngine** objects, and the **DBEngine** object isn't an element of any collection.

Note When you reference an ODBC data source directly through DAO, it is called an "ODBCDirect workspace." This is to distinguish it from an ODBC data source that you reference indirectly through the Microsoft Jet database engine, using a "Microsoft Jet workspace." Each method of accessing ODBC data requires one of two types of **Workspace** object; you can set the **DefaultType** property to choose the default type of **Workspace** object that you will create from the **DBEngine** object. The **Workspace** type and associated data source determines which DAO objects, methods, and properties you can use.

With any type of database or connection, you can:

- Use the **Version** property to obtain the DAO version number.

- Use the **LoginTimeout** property to obtain or set the ODBC login timeout, and the **RegisterDatabase** method to provide ODBC information to the Microsoft Jet database engine. You can use these features the same way, regardless of whether you connect to the ODBC data source through Microsoft Jet or through an ODBCDirect workspace.

- Use the **DefaultType** property to set the default type of database connection that subsequently created **Workspace** objects will use — either Microsoft Jet or ODBCDirect.

- Use the **DefaultPassword** and **DefaultUser** properties to set the user identification and password for the default **Workspace** object.

- Use the **CreateWorkspace** method to create a new **Workspace** object. You can use optional arguments to override the settings of the **DefaultType**, **DefaultPassword**, and **DefaultUser** properties.

- Use the **OpenDatabase** method to open a database in the default **Workspace**, and use the **BeginTrans**, **Commit**, and **Rollback** methods to control transactions on the default **Workspace**.

- Use the **Workspaces** collection to reference specific **Workspace** objects.

- Use the **Errors** collection to examine data access error details.

Other properties and methods are only available when you use DAO with the Microsoft Jet database engine. You can use them to control the Microsoft Jet database engine, manipulate its properties, and perform tasks on temporary objects that aren't elements of collections. For example, you can:

- Use the **CreateDatabase** method to create a new Microsoft Jet **Database** object.

- Use the **Idle** method to enable the Microsoft Jet database engine to complete any pending tasks.

- Use the **CompactDatabase** and **RepairDatabase** methods to maintain database files.

- Use the **IniPath** and **SystemDB** properties to specify the location of Microsoft Jet Windows Registry information and the Microsoft Jet workgroup information file, respectively. The **SetOption** method allows you override windows registry settings for the Microsoft Jet database engine.

After you change the **DefaultType** and **IniPath** property settings, only subsequent **Workspace** objects will reflect these changes.

Note For a complete list of all methods, properties, and collections available on the **DBEngine** object, see the **Summary** topic.

To refer to a collection that belongs to the **DBEngine** object, or to refer to a method or property that applies to this object, use this syntax:

[**DBEngine.**][*collection* | *method* | *property*]

Properties

DefaultUser, DefaultPassword Properties, **IniPath** Property, **LoginTimeout** Property, **Version** Property, **SystemDB** Property, **DefaultType** Property

Methods

BeginTrans, CommitTrans, Rollback Methods, **CompactDatabase** Method, **CreateDatabase** Method, **CreateWorkspace** Method, **Idle** Method, **OpenDatabase** Method, **RegisterDatabase** Method, **RepairDatabase** Method, **OpenConnection** Method, **SetOption** Method

Example

This example enumerates the collections of the **DBEngine** object. See the methods and properties of **DBEngine** for additional examples.

```
Sub DBEngineX()

    Dim wrkLoop As Workspace
    Dim prpLoop As Property

    With DBEngine
        Debug.Print "DBEngine Properties"
```

```
' Enumerate Properties collection of DBEngine,
' trapping for properties whose values are
' invalid in this context.
For Each prpLoop In .Properties
   On Error Resume Next
   Debug.Print "    " & prpLoop.Name & " = " _
       & prpLoop
   On Error GoTo 0
Next prpLoop

Debug.Print "Workspaces collection of DBEngine"

' Enumerate Workspaces collection of DBEngine.
For Each wrkLoop In .Workspaces
   Debug.Print "    " & wrkLoop.Name

   ' Enumerate Properties collection of each
   ' Workspace object, trapping for properties
   ' whose values are invalid in this context.
   For Each prpLoop In wrkLoop.Properties
      On Error Resume Next
      Debug.Print "        " & prpLoop.Name & _
         " = " & prpLoop
      On Error GoTo 0
   Next prpLoop

Next wrkLoop

End With

End Sub
```

DBGrid Control

Displays and enables data manipulation of a series of rows and columns representing records and fields from a **Recordset** object.

Syntax

DBGrid

Remarks

The data-aware **DBGrid** control appears similar to the **Grid** control; however, you can set the **DBGrid** control's **DataSource** property to a **Data** control so that the control is automatically filled and its column headers set automatically from a **Data** control's **Recordset** object. The **DBGrid** control is really a fixed collection of columns, each with an indeterminate number of rows.

Each cell of a **DBGrid** control can hold text values, but not linked or embedded objects. You can specify the current cell in code, or the user can change it at run time using the mouse or the arrow keys. Cells can be edited interactively, by typing into the cell, or programmatically. Cells can be selected individually or by row.

If a cell's text is too long to be displayed in the cell, the text wraps to the next line within the same cell. To display the wrapped text, you must increase the cell's **Column** object's **Width** property and/or the **DBGrid** control's **RowHeight** property. At design time, you can change the column width interactively by resizing the column or by changing the column's width in the **Column** object's property page.

Use the **DBGrid** control's **Columns** collection's **Count** property and the **Recordset** object's **RecordCount** property to determine the number of columns and rows in the control. A **DBGrid** control can have as many rows as the system resources can support and about 1700 columns.

When you select a cell, the **ColIndex** property is set, thus selecting one of the **Column** objects in the **DBGrid** object's **Columns** collection. The **Text** and **Value** properties of the **Column** object reference the contents of the current cell. The data in the current row can be accessed using the **Bookmark** property, which provides access to the underlying **Recordset** object's record. Each column of the **DBGrid** control has its own font, border, word wrap, color and other attributes that can be set without regard to other columns. At design time, you can set the column width and row height and establish columns that are not visible to the user. You can also prevent users from changing the formatting at run time.

Note If you set any of the **DBGrid** column properties at design time, you will need to set all of them in order to maintain the current settings.

Note If you use the **Move** method to position the **DBGrid** control, you may need to use the **Refresh** method to force it to repaint.

Properties

DataMode Property, **Bookmark** Property (DB Grid), **AddNewMode** Property, **AllowArrows** Property, **ApproxCount** Property, **CurrentCellModified** Property, **CurrentCellVisible** Property, **EditActive** Property, **ErrorText** Property, **hWndEditor** Property, **MarqueeStyle** Property, **MarqueeUnique** Property, **Split** Property, **Splits** Property, **TabAcrossSplits** Property, **TabAction** Property, **WrapCellPointer** Property, **DataChanged** Property, **DataSource** Property, **AllowAddNew** Property, **AllowDelete** Property, **AllowRowSizing** Property, **AllowUpdate** Property, **ColumnHeaders** Property, **Columns** Property (DBGrid), **DefColWidth** Property, **FirstRow** Property, **HeadFont** Property, **HeadLines** Property, **RecordSelectors** Property, **RowDividerStyle** Property, **SelBookmarks** Property, **VisibleCols** Property, **VisibleRows** Property, **Align** Property, **Appearance** Property, **BackColor, ForeColor** Properties, **BorderStyle** Property, **Caption** Property, **Col, Row** Properties, **Container** Property, **DataBinding** Object, **DragIcon** Property, **DragMode** Property, **Enabled** Property, **Font** Property, **Height, Width**

Properties (ActiveX Controls), **HelpContextID** Property, **hWnd** Property, **Index** Property (ActiveX Controls), **Index** Property (Control Array), **Left, Top** Properties (ActiveX Controls), **Name** Property, **Object** Property, **Object** Property (ActiveX Controls), **Parent** Property, **RowHeight** Property, **ScrollBars** Property, **SelEndCol**, **SelStartCol**, **SelEndRow**, **SelStartRow** Properties, **SelLength, SelStart, SelText** Properties, **SelLength, SelStart, SelText** Properties (ActiveX Controls), **TabIndex** Property, **TabStop** Property, **Tag** Property (ActiveX Controls), **Text** Property (ActiveX Controls), **ToolTipText** Property, **Visible** Property (ActiveX Controls), **WhatsThisHelpID** Property

Events

AfterColEdit Event, **AfterColUpdate** Event, **AfterDelete** Event, **AfterInsert** Event, **AfterUpdate** Event, **BeforeColEdit** Event, **BeforeColUpdate** Event, **BeforeDelete** Event, **BeforeInsert** Event, **BeforeUpdate** Event, **ButtonClick** Event (DBGrid Control), **Change** Event, **Click** Event, **ColEdit** Event, **ColResize** Event, **DblClick** Event, **DragDrop** Event, **DragOver** Event, **Error** Event, **GotFocus** Event, **HeadClick** Event, **KeyDown, KeyUp** Events, **KeyDown, KeyUp** Events (ActiveX Controls), **LostFocus** Event, **MouseDown, MouseUp** Events, **MouseMove** Event, **OnAddNew** Event, **RowColChange** Event, **RowResize** Event, **Scroll** Event, **SelChange** Event, **SplitChange** Event, **UnboundAddData** Event, **UnboundDeleteRow** Event, **UnboundGetRelativeBookmark** Event, **UnboundReadData** Event, **UnboundWriteData** Event

Methods

ClearFields Method, **ClearSelCols** Method, **HoldFields** Method, **SplitContaining** Method, **ColContaining** Method, **GetBookmark** Method, **Rebind** Method, **RowBookmark** Method, **RowContaining** Method, **RowTop** Method, **Scroll** Method, **Drag** Method, **Move** Method, **Refresh** Method (ActiveX Controls), **SetFocus** Method, **ShowWhatsThis** Method, **Zorder** Method

See Also

DBGrid Control Constants, **Data** Control, **Column** Object, **SelBookmarks** Collection, **RowSource** Property

---

DblClick Event

Occurs when the user presses and releases a mouse button and then presses and releases it again over an object.

For a form, the **DblClick** event occurs when the user double-clicks a disabled control or a blank area of a form. For a control, it occurs when the user:

- Double-clicks a control with the left mouse button.

- Double-clicks an item in a **ComboBox** control whose **Style** property is set to 1 (Simple) or in a **FileListBox**, **ListBox**, **DBCombo**, or **DBList** control.

Applies To

PropertyPage Object, **UserControl** Object, **UserDocument** Object, **ComboBox** Control, **FileListBox** Control, **Form** Object, **Forms** Collection, **Frame** Control, **Image** Control, **Label** Control, **ListBox** Control, **MDIForm** Object, **OptionButton** Control, **PictureBox** Control, **TextBox** Control, **OLE Container** Control, **Animation** Control, **DBCombo** Control, **DBList** Control

Syntax

Private Sub Form_DblClick ( )
Private Sub *object*_**DblClick** (*index* **As Integer**)

Part	Description
object	An object expression that evaluates to an object in the **Applies To** list.
index	Identifies the control if it's in a control array.

Remarks

The argument *Index* uniquely identifies a control if it's in a control array. You can use a **DblClick** event procedure for an implied action, such as double-clicking an icon to open a window or document. You can also use this type of procedure to carry out multiple steps with a single action, such as double-clicking to select an item in a list box and to close the dialog box.

To produce such shortcut effects in Visual Basic, you can use a **DblClick** event procedure for a list box or file list box in tandem with a default button—a **CommandButton** control with its **Default** property set to **True**. As part of the **DblClick** event procedure for the list box, you simply call the default button's **Click** event.

For those objects that receive Mouse events, the events occur in this order: **MouseDown**, **MouseUp**, Click, **DblClick**, and **MouseUp**.

If **DblClick** doesn't occur within the system's double-click time limit, the object recognizes another Click event. The double-click time limit may vary because the user can set the double-click speed in the Control Panel. When you're attaching procedures for these related events, be sure that their actions don't conflict. Controls that don't receive **DblClick** events may receive two clicks instead of a **DblClick**.

Note To distinguish between the left, right, and middle mouse buttons, use the **MouseDown** and **MouseUp** events.

If there is code in the **Click** event, the **DlbClick** event will never trigger.

See Also

Click Event, **MouseDown**, **MouseUp** Events

Example

This example displays a selected list item in a **TextBox** control when either a **CommandButton** control is clicked or a list item is double-clicked. To try this example, paste the code into the Declarations section of a **Form** object that contains a **ListBox** control, a **TextBox** control, and a **CommandButton** control. Then run the example and click the **CommandButton** control or double-click an item in the **ListBox** control.

```
Private Sub Form_Load ()
    List1.AddItem "John"        ' Add list box entries.
    List1.AddItem "Paul"
    List1.AddItem "George"
    List1.AddItem "Ringo"
End Sub

Private Sub List1_DblClick ()
    Command1.Value = True       ' Trigger Click event.
End Sub

Private Sub Command1_Click ()
    Text1.Text = List1.Text     ' Display selection.
End Sub
```

DblClick Event (DBCombo Control)

Occurs when the user double-clicks the **DBCombo** control with the mouse button.

Applies To

DBCombo Control

Syntax

Private Sub *object*_**DblClick** ([*index* **As Integer**,] *Area* **As Integer**)

Part	Description
object	An object expression that evaluates to an object in the **Applies To** list.
index	An integer that uniquely identifies a control if it's in a control array.
Area	An integer expression that specifies where the control was double clicked, as described below.

The *Area* parameter can contain the following values:

Constant	Value	Description
dbcAreaButton	0	The user double-clicked the button on the **DBCombo** control.
dbcAreaEdit	1	The user double-clicked in the text box part of the **DBCombo** control.
dbcAreaList	2	The user double-clicked in the list part of the **DBCombo** control. (This only occurs when the **Style** property is set to 1)

Remarks

You can use a **DblClick** event procedure for an implied action or use it to carry out multiple steps with a single action.

If **DblClick** doesn't occur within the system's double-click time limit, the object recognizes another **Click** event. The double-click time limit may vary because the user can set the double-click speed in the Control Panel.

Note To distinguish between the left, right, and middle mouse buttons, use the **MouseDown** and **MouseUp** events.

DBList Control

The **DBList** control is a data bound list box which is automatically populated from a field in an attached **Data** control, and optionally updates a field in a related table of another **Data** control.

Syntax

    DBList

Remarks

The **DBList** control differs from the standard **ListBox** control. While the **ListBox** control list is filled using the **AddItem** method, the **DBList** control is automatically filled with data from a field in the **Recordset** object of a **Data** control to which it is attached. The standard **ListBox** control must be populated manually by using the **AddItem** method. In addition, the **DBList** control has the ability to update a field within a related **Recordset** object which may reside in a different **Data** control.

The **DBList** control also supports an automated search mode that can quickly locate items in the list without additional code.

Shown below is a list of the properties you use to fill and manage the list, and bind the selected data to a **Data** control.

Property	Specifies
DataSource	Name of **Data** control that is updated once a selection is made.
DataField	Name of a field that is updated in the **Recordset** specified by the **DataSource** property.
RowSource	Name of **Data** control used as a source of items for the list portion of the control.
ListField	Name of a field in the **Recordset** specified by **RowSource** that is used to fill the list. **DBList** does not support fields of **LongBinary** type for the **ListField** property.
BoundColumn	Name of a field in the **Recordset** specified by **RowSource** that is passed back to the **DataField** once a selection is made. **DBList** does not support fields of **LongBinary** type for the **BoundColumn**.
BoundText	Text value of the **BoundColumn** field. Once a selection is made, this value is passed back to update the **Recordset** object specified by the **DataSource** and **DataField** properties.

(continued)

(continued)

Property	Specifies
Text	Text value of the selected item in the list.
MatchEntry	How the list is searched as the user types characters at run time.
SelectedItem	The bookmark of the selected item in the **Recordset** specified by the **RowSource** property.
VisibleCount	The number of items visible in the list (fully or partially).
VisibleItems	An array of bookmarks with a maximum number of items equal to the **VisibleCount** property.

The **DBList** control will automatically highlight an item in the list if the **BoundText** property becomes equal to the value of the field specified by the **DataSource** and **DataField** properties, such as when using a **Data** control to change the current record.

Properties

DataChanged Property, **DataField** Property, **DataSource** Property, **IntegralHeight** Property, **BoundColumn** Property, **ListField** Property, **RowSource** Property, **SelectedItem** Property, **VisibleItems** Property, **VisibleCount** Property, **MatchedWithList** Property, **MatchEntry** Property, **BoundText** Property, **BoundColumn** Property, **Container** Property, **DataBindings** Property, **DragIcon** Property, **DragMode** Property, **Enabled** Property, **Font** Property, **Height, Width** Properties (ActiveX Controls), **HelpContextID** Property, **hWnd** Property, **Index** Property (ActiveX Controls), **Index** Property (Control Array), **Left, Top** Properties (ActiveX Controls), **Locked** Property, **MouseIcon** Property, **MousePointer** Property (ActiveX Controls), **Name** Property, **Object** Property, **Object** Property (ActiveX Controls), **OLEDragMode** Property, **OLEDropMode** Property, **Parent** Property, **RightToLeft** Property (ActiveX Controls), **SelectedItem** Property, **TabIndex** Property, **TabStop** Property, **Tag** Property (ActiveX Controls), **Text** Property (ActiveX Controls), **ToolTipText** Property, **Visible** Property (ActiveX Controls), **WhatsThisHelpID** Property

Events

Click Event, **Click** Event (ActiveX Controls), **DblClick** Event, **DragDrop** Event, **DragOver** Event, **GotFocus** Event, **KeyDown, KeyUp** Events, **KeyDown KeyUp** Events (ActiveX Controls), **KeyPress** Event, **KeyPress** Event (ActiveX Controls), **LostFocus** Event, **MouseDown, MouseUp** Event, **MouseMove** Event, **OLECompleteDrag** Event, **OLEDragDrop** Event, **OLEDragOver** Event, **OLEGiveFeedback** Event, **OLESetData** Event, **OLEStartDrag** Event

Methods

ReFill Method, **AboutBox** Method, **Drag** Method, **Move** Method, **OLEDrag** Method, **Refresh** Method (ActiveX Controls), **SetFocus** Method, **ShowWhatsThis** Method, **Zorder** Method

See Also

Data Control, **DBCombo** Control, **DBList** and **DBCombo Controls** Constants, **DBGrid** Control, **UpdateRecord** Method

DDB Function

Returns a **Double** specifying the depreciation of an asset for a specific time period using the double-declining balance method or some other method you specify.

Syntax

DDB(*cost, salvage, life, period*[, *factor*])

The **DDB** function has these named arguments:

Part	Description
cost	Required. **Double** specifying initial cost of the asset.
salvage	Required. **Double** specifying value of the asset at the end of its useful life.
life	Required. **Double** specifying length of useful life of the asset.
period	Required. **Double** specifying period for which asset depreciation is calculated.
factor	Optional. **Variant** specifying rate at which the balance declines. If omitted, 2 (double-declining method) is assumed.

Remarks

The double-declining balance method computes depreciation at an accelerated rate. Depreciation is highest in the first period and decreases in successive periods.

The *life* and *period* arguments must be expressed in the same units. For example, if *life* is given in months, *period* must also be given in months. All arguments must be positive numbers.

The **DDB** function uses the following formula to calculate depreciation for a given period:

Depreciation / *period* = ((*cost*−*salvage*) * *factor*) / *life*

See Also

FV Function, **IPmt** Function, **IRR** Function, **MIRR** Function, **NPer** Function, **NPV** Function, **Pmt** Function, **PPmt** Function, **PV** Function, **Rate** Function, **SLN** Function, **SYD** Function

Example

This example uses the **DDB** function to return the depreciation of an asset for a specified period given the initial cost (InitCost), the salvage value at the end of the asset's useful life (SalvageVal), the total life of the asset in years (LifeTime), and the period in years for which the depreciation is calculated (Depr).

```
Dim Fmt, InitCost, SalvageVal, MonthLife, LifeTime, DepYear, Depr
Const YRMOS = 12                        ' Number of months in a year.
Fmt = "###,##0.00"
InitCost = InputBox("What's the initial cost of the asset?")
```

```
SalvageVal = InputBox("Enter the asset's value at end of its life.")
MonthLife = InputBox("What's the asset's useful life in months?")
Do While MonthLife < YRMOS          ' Ensure period is >= 1 year.
   MsgBox "Asset life must be a year or more."
   MonthLife = InputBox("What's the asset's useful life in months?")
Loop
LifeTime = MonthLife / YRMOS          ' Convert months to years.
If LifeTime <> Int(MonthLife / YRMOS) Then
   LifeTime = Int(LifeTime + 1)      ' Round up to nearest year.
End If
DepYear = CInt(InputBox("Enter year for depreciation calculation."))
Do While DepYear < 1 Or DepYear > LifeTime
   MsgBox "You must enter at least 1 but not more than " & LifeTime
   DepYear = InputBox("Enter year for depreciation calculation.")
Loop
Depr = DDB(InitCost, SalvageVal, LifeTime, DepYear)
MsgBox "The depreciation for year " & DepYear & " is " & _
Format(Depr, Fmt) & "."
```

Debug Object

The **Debug** object sends output to the **Immediate** window at run time.

Methods

Print Method, **Assert** Method

Decimal Data Type

Decimal variables are stored as 96-bit (12-byte) unsigned integers scaled by a variable power of 10. The power of 10 scaling factor specifies the number of digits to the right of the decimal point, and ranges from 0 to 28. With a scale of 0 (no decimal places), the largest possible value is +/-79,228,162,514,264,337,593,543,950,335.

With a 28 decimal places, the largest value is +/-7.9228162514264337593543950335 and the smallest, non-zero value is +/-0.0000000000000000000000000001.

Note   At this time the **Decimal** data type can only be used within a Variant, that is, you cannot declare a variable to be of type **Decimal**. You can, however, create a **Variant** whose subtype is **Decimal** using the **CDec** function.

See Also

Data Type Summary

Declare Statement

Used at module level to declare references to external procedures in a dynamic-link library (DLL).

Syntax 1

[**Public** | **Private**] **Declare Sub** *name* **Lib** "*libname*" [**Alias** "*aliasname*"] [([*arglist*])]

Syntax 2

[**Public** | **Private**] **Declare Function** *name* **Lib** "*libname*" [**Alias** "*aliasname*"]
↪ [([*arglist*])] [**As** *type*]

The **Declare** statement syntax has these parts:

Part	Description
Public	Optional. Used to declare procedures that are available to all other procedures in all modules.
Private	Optional. Used to declare procedures that are available only within the module where the declaration is made.
Sub	Optional (either **Sub** or **Function** must appear). Indicates that the procedure doesn't return a value.
Function	Optional (either **Sub** or **Function** must appear). Indicates that the procedure returns a value that can be used in an expression.
name	Required. Any valid procedure name. Note that DLL entry points are case sensitive.
Lib	Required. Indicates that a DLL or code resource contains the procedure being declared. The **Lib** clause is required for all declarations.
libname	Required. Name of the DLL or code resource that contains the declared procedure.
Alias	Optional. Indicates that the procedure being called has another name in the DLL. This is useful when the external procedure name is the same as a keyword. You can also use **Alias** when a DLL procedure has the same name as a public variable, constant, or any other procedure in the same scope. **Alias** is also useful if any characters in the DLL procedure name aren't allowed by the DLL naming convention.
aliasname	Optional. Name of the procedure in the DLL or code resource. If the first character is not a number sign (#), *aliasname* is the name of the procedure's entry point in the DLL. If (#) is the first character, all characters that follow must indicate the ordinal number of the procedure's entry point.
arglist	Optional. List of variables representing arguments that are passed to the procedure when it is called.
type	Optional. Data type of the value returned by a **Function** procedure; may be **Byte**, **Boolean**, **Integer**, **Long**, **Currency**, **Single**, **Double**, **Decimal** (not currently supported), **Date**, **String** (variable length only), or **Variant**, a user-defined type, or an object type.

The *arglist* argument has the following syntax and parts:

[**Optional**] [**ByVal** I **ByRef**] [**ParamArray**] *varname*[( )] [**As** *type*]

Part	Description
Optional	Optional. Indicates that an argument is not required. If used, all subsequent arguments in *arglist* must also be optional and declared using the **Optional** keyword. **Optional** can't be used for any argument if **ParamArray** is used.
ByVal	Optional. Indicates that the argument is passed by value.
ByRef	Indicates that the argument is passed by reference. **ByRef** is the default in Visual Basic.
ParamArray	Optional. Used only as the last argument in *arglist* to indicate that the final argument is an **Optional** array of **Variant** elements. The **ParamArray** keyword allows you to provide an arbitrary number of arguments. The **ParamArray** keyword can't be used with **ByVal**, **ByRef**, or **Optional**.
varname	Required. Name of the variable representing the argument being passed to the procedure; follows standard variable naming conventions.
( )	Required for array variables. Indicates that *varname* is an array.
type	Optional. Data type of the argument passed to the procedure; may be **Byte**, **Boolean**, **Integer**, **Long**, **Currency**, **Single**, **Double**, **Decimal** (not currently supported), **Date**, **String** (variable length only), **Object**, **Variant**, a user-defined type, or an object type.

Remarks

For **Function** procedures, the data type of the procedure determines the data type it returns. You can use an **As** clause following *arglist* to specify the return type of the function. Within *arglist*, you can use an **As** clause to specify the data type of any of the arguments passed to the procedure. In addition to specifying any of the standard data types, you can specify **As Any** in *arglist* to inhibit type checking and allow any data type to be passed to the procedure.

Empty parentheses indicate that the **Sub** or **Function** procedure has no arguments and that Visual Basic should ensure that none are passed. In the following example, First takes no arguments. If you use arguments in a call to First, an error occurs:

```
Declare Sub First Lib "MyLib" ()
```

If you include an argument list, the number and type of arguments are checked each time the procedure is called. In the following example, First takes one **Long** argument:

```
Declare Sub First Lib "MyLib" (X As Long)
```

Note   You can't have fixed-length strings in the argument list of a **Declare** statement; only variable-length strings can be passed to procedures. Fixed-length strings can appear as procedure arguments, but they are converted to variable-length strings before being passed.

Note   The **vbNullString** constant is used when calling external procedures, where the external procedure requires a string whose value is zero. This is not the same thing as a zero-length string ("").

See Also

Call Statement, **Function** Statement, **Sub** Statement, **LastDLLError** Property, **AddressOf** Operator

Example

This example shows how the **Declare** statement is used at the module level of a standard module to declare a reference to an external procedure in a dynamic-link library (DLL). You can place the **Declare** statements in class modules if the **Declare** statements are **Private**.

```
' In Microsoft Windows (16-bit):
Declare Sub MessageBeep Lib "User" (ByVal N As Integer)
' Assume SomeBeep is an alias for the procedure name.
Declare Sub MessageBeep Lib "User" Alias "SomeBeep"(ByVal N As Integer)
' Use an ordinal in the Alias clause to call GetWinFlags.
Declare Function GetWinFlags Lib "Kernel" Alias "#132"() As Long

' In 32-bit Microsoft Windows systems, specify the library USER32.DLL,
' rather than USER.DLL. You can use conditional compilation to write
' code that can run on either Win32 or Win16.
#If Win32 Then
    Declare Sub MessageBeep Lib "User32" (ByVal N As Long)
#Else
    Declare Sub MessageBeep Lib "User" (ByVal N As Integer)
#End If
```

Default Property

Returns or sets a value that determines which **CommandButton** control is the default command button on a form.

Applies To

Extender Object, **CommandButton** Control, **OLE Container** Control

Syntax

object.**Default** [= *boolean*]

The **Default** property syntax has these parts:

Part	Description
object	An object expression that evaluates to an object in the **Applies To** list.
boolean	A Boolean expression that specifies whether the command button is the default, as described in Settings.

Settings

The settings for *boolean* are:

Setting	Description
True	The **CommandButton** is the default command button.
False	(Default) The **CommandButton** isn't the default command button.

Remarks

Only one command button on a form can be the default command button. When **Default** is set to **True** for one command button, it's automatically set to **False** for all other command buttons on the form. When the command button's **Default** property setting is **True** and its parent form is active, the user can choose the command button (invoking its **Click** event) by pressing ENTER. Any other control with the focus doesn't receive a keyboard event (**KeyDown**, **KeyPress**, or **KeyUp**) for the ENTER key unless the user has moved the focus to another command button on the same form. In this case, pressing ENTER chooses the command button that has the focus instead of the default command button.

For a form or dialog box that supports an irreversible action such as a delete operation, make the Cancel button the default command button by setting its **Default** property to **True**.

For **OLE** container controls, the **Default** property is provided only for those objects that specifically behave like **CommandButton** controls.

See Also

Cancel Property

DefaultBind Property

Returns or sets the **DefaultBind** attribute of a **Member** object.

Applies To

Member Object

Syntax

object.**DefaultBind**

The *object* placeholder represents an object expression that evaluates to an object in the **Applies To** list.

DefaultCancel Property

Returns or sets a value determining if a control can act as a standard command button. The **DefaultCancel** property is read/write at the control's authoring time, and not available at the control's run time.

Applies To

UserControl Object

Settings

The settings for DefaultCancel are:

Setting	Description
True	The control can act as a default or cancel command button. The container will add the **Default** and **Cancel** properties to the extender object. The presence of the **Default** and **Cancel** properties allow the control to act as a standard command button. The control can then set these added extender properties.
False	The control cannot act as a default or cancel command button. No constituent control can have its **Default** or **Cancel** property set to **True**. This is the default value.

Remarks

Setting the **Default** property to **True** and also having a constituent control with its **Default** property set to **True** will cause the constituent control to be pressed when the ENTER key is pressed, otherwise the control's **AccessKeyPress** event will be raised when the ENTER key is pressed.

Setting the **Cancel** property to **True** and also having a constituent control with its **Cancel** property set to **True** will cause the constituent control to be pressed when the ESCAPE key is pressed, otherwise the control's **AccessKeyPress** event will be raised when the ESCAPE key is pressed.

Important The status of a default or cancel button can change at any time. Code must be placed in the control's **AmbientChanged** event procedure to detect changes in the **DisplayAsDefault** property, and the control's appearance adjusted accordingly.

See Also

AccessKeyPress Event, **AmbientChanged** Event, **Cancel** Property, **Default** Property

DefaultCursorDriver Property

Sets or returns the type of cursor driver used on the connection created by the **OpenConnection** or **OpenDatabase** methods (**ODBCDirect** workspaces only).

Applies To

Workspace Object

Settings And Return Values

The setting or return value is a **Long** that can be set to one of the following constants:

Constant	Description
dbUseDefaultCursor	(Default) Uses server-side cursors if the server supports them; otherwise use the ODBC Cursor Library.
dbUseODBCCursor	Always uses the ODBC Cursor Library. This option provides better performance for small result sets, but degrades quickly for larger result sets.

(continued)

(continued)

Constant	Description
dbUseServerCursor	Always uses server-side cursors. For most large operations this option provides better performance, but might cause more network traffic.
dbUseClientBatchCursor	Always uses the client batch cursor library. This option is required for batch updates.
dbUseNoCursor	Opens all cursors (that is, **Recordset** objects) as forward-only type, read-only, with a rowset size of 1. Also known as "cursorless queries."

Remarks

This property setting only affects connections established after the property has been set. Changing the **DefaultCursorDriver** property has no effect on existing connections.

Example

This example uses the **NextRecordset** method to view the data from a compound SELECT query. The **DefaultCursorDriver** property must be set to **dbUseODBCCursor** when executing such queries. The **NextRecordset** method will return **True** even if some or all of the SELECT statements return zero records—it will return **False** only after all the individual SQL clauses have been checked.

```
Sub NextRecordsetX()

    Dim wrkODBC As Workspace
    Dim conPubs As Connection
    Dim rstTemp As Recordset
    Dim intCount As Integer
    Dim booNext As Boolean

    ' Create ODBCDirect Workspace object and open Connection
    ' object. The DefaultCursorDriver setting is required
    ' when using compound SQL statements.
    Set wrkODBC = CreateWorkspace("", _
        "admin", "", dbUseODBC)
    wrkODBC.DefaultCursorDriver = dbUseODBCCursor
    Set conPubs = wrkODBC.OpenConnection("Publishers", , , _
        "ODBC;DATABASE=pubs;UID=sa;PWD=;DSN=Publishers")

    ' Construct compound SELECT statement.
    Set rstTemp = conPubs.OpenRecordset("SELECT * " & _
        "FROM authors; " & _
        "SELECT * FROM stores; " & _
        "SELECT * FROM jobs")

    ' Try printing results from each of the three SELECT
    ' statements.
    booNext = True
    intCount = 1
```

```
    With rstTemp
       Do While booNext
          Debug.Print "Contents of recordset #" & intCount
          Do While Not .EOF
             Debug.Print , .Fields(0), .Fields(1)
             .MoveNext
          Loop
          booNext = .NextRecordset
          Debug.Print "    rstTemp.NextRecordset = " & _
             booNext
          intCount = intCount + 1
       Loop
    End With

    rstTemp.Close
    conPubs.Close
    wrkODBC.Close

End Sub
```

Another way to accomplish the same task would be to create a prepared statement containing the compound SQL statement. The **CacheSize** property of the **QueryDef** object must be set to 1, and the **Recordset** object must be forward-only and read-only.

```
Sub NextRecordsetX2()

    Dim wrkODBC As Workspace
    Dim conPubs As Connection
    Dim qdfTemp As QueryDef
    Dim rstTemp As Recordset
    Dim intCount As Integer
    Dim booNext As Boolean

    ' Create ODBCDirect Workspace object and open Connection
    ' object. The DefaultCursorDriver setting is required
    ' when using compound SQL statements.
    Set wrkODBC = CreateWorkspace("", _
       "admin", "", dbUseODBC)
    wrkODBC.DefaultCursorDriver = dbUseODBCCursor
    Set conPubs = wrkODBC.OpenConnection("Publishers", , , _
       "ODBC;DATABASE=pubs;UID=sa;PWD=;DSN=Publishers")

    ' Create a temporary stored procedure with a compound
    ' SELECT statement.
    Set qdfTemp = conPubs.CreateQueryDef("", _
       "SELECT * FROM authors; " & _
       "SELECT * FROM stores; " & _
       "SELECT * FROM jobs")
    ' Set CacheSize and open Recordset object with arguments
    ' that will allow access to multiple recordsets.
```

```
            qdfTemp.CacheSize = 1
            Set rstTemp = qdfTemp.OpenRecordset(dbOpenForwardOnly, _
               dbReadOnly)

            ' Try printing results from each of the three SELECT
            ' statements.
            booNext = True
            intCount = 1
            With rstTemp
               Do While booNext
                  Debug.Print "Contents of recordset #" & intCount
                  Do While Not .EOF
                     Debug.Print , .Fields(0), .Fields(1)
                     .MoveNext
                  Loop
                  booNext = .NextRecordset
                  Debug.Print "    rstTemp.NextRecordset = " & _
                     booNext
                  intCount = intCount + 1
               Loop
            End With

            rstTemp.Close
            qdfTemp.Close
            conPubs.Close
            wrkODBC.Close

         End Sub
```

DefaultCursorType Property (Data Control)

Controls what type of cursor driver is used on the connection (ODBCDirect only) created by the **Data** control.

Applies To

Data Control

Syntax

object.**DefaultCursorType** [= *value*]

The **DefaultCursorType** property syntax has these parts:

Part	Description
object	An object expression that evaluates to an object in the **Applies To** list.
Value	An integer constant or value that specifies a type of cursor driver, as described in **Settings**.

Settings

The settings for *value* are:

Setting	Value	Description
vbUseDefaultCursor	0	Let the ODBC driver determine which type of cursors to use.
VbUseODBCCursor	1	Use the ODBC cursor library. This option gives better performance for small result sets, but degrades quickly for larger result sets.
VbUseServerSideCursor	2	Use server-side cursors. For most large operations this gives better performance, but might cause more network traffic.

Remarks

Use this property when the **DefaultType** property of the **Data** control is set to **dbUseODBC**. Refer to the **DefaultCursorDriver** property of the **Workspace** object for more information.

Data Type

Integer

See Also

DefaultType Property, **DefaultCursorType** Property Constants, **OpenConnection** Method, **Workspace** Object

---

DefaultType Property

Sets or returns a value that indicates what type of workspace (Microsoft Jet or **ODBCDirect**) will be used by the next **Workspace** object created.

Applies To

DBEngine Object

Settings And Return Values

The setting or return value is a **Long** that can be set to either of the following constants:

Constant	Description
dbUseJet	Creates **Workspace** objects connected to the Microsoft Jet database engine
dbUseODBC	Creates **Workspace** objects connected to an ODBC data source

Remarks

The setting can be overridden for a single **Workspace** by setting the *type* argument to the **CreateWorkspace** method.

Example

This example uses the **DefaultType** property to predetermine what type of **Workspace** object will be created when you call the **CreateWorkspace** method. The **TypeOutput** function is required for this procedure to run.

```
Sub DefaultTypeX()

    Dim wrkODBC As Workspace
    Dim wrkJet As Workspace
    Dim prpLoop As Property

    ' Set DefaultType property and create Workspace object
    ' without specifying a type.
    DBEngine.DefaultType = dbUseODBC
    Set wrkODBC = CreateWorkspace("ODBCWorkspace", _
        "admin", "")

    Debug.Print "DBEngine.DefaultType = " & _
        TypeOutput(DBEngine.DefaultType)
    With wrkODBC
        ' Enumerate Properties collection of Workspace object.
        Debug.Print "Properties of " & .Name
        On Error Resume Next
        For Each prpLoop In .Properties
            Debug.Print "    " & prpLoop.Name & " = " & prpLoop
            If prpLoop.Name = "Type" Then Debug.Print _
                "        (" & TypeOutput(prpLoop.Value) & ")"
        Next prpLoop
        On Error GoTo 0
    End With

    ' Set DefaultType property and create Workspace object
    ' without specifying a type.
    DBEngine.DefaultType = dbUseJet
    Set wrkJet = CreateWorkspace("JetWorkspace", "admin", "")

    Debug.Print "DBEngine.DefaultType = " & _
        TypeOutput(DBEngine.DefaultType)
    With wrkJet
        ' Enumerate Properties collection of Workspace object.
        Debug.Print "Properties of " & .Name
        On Error Resume Next
        For Each prpLoop In .Properties
            Debug.Print "    " & prpLoop.Name & " = " & prpLoop
            If prpLoop.Name = "Type" Then Debug.Print _
                "        (" & TypeOutput(prpLoop.Value) & ")"
        Next prpLoop
        On Error GoTo 0
    End With

    wrkODBC.Close
    wrkJet.Close

End Sub

Function TypeOutput(intTemp As Integer) As String
```

```
        If intTemp = dbUseJet Then
            TypeOutput = "dbUseJet"
        Else
            TypeOutput = "dbUseODBC"
        End If

    End Function
```

DefaultType Property (Data Control)

Returns or sets a value which determines the type of data source (Jet or ODBCDirect) that is used by the **Data** control.

Applies To

Data Control

Syntax

object.**DefaultType** [= *value*]

The **DefaultType** property syntax has these parts:

Part	Description
object	An object expression that evaluates to an object in the **Applies To** list.
value	An integer constant or value that specifies the type of data source, as described in **Settings**.

Settings

The settings for *value* are:

Setting	Value	Description
dbUseODBC	1	Use ODBCDirect to access your data.
dbUseJet	2	(Default) Use the Microsoft Jet database engine to access your data.

Remarks

Setting the **DefaultType** property tells the **Data** control what type of data source (Jet or ODBCDirect) to use when creating a **Recordset**. The **DefaultType** property also determines the type of the underlying **Workspace** object used with the **Data** control. The Jet database engine will not be loaded unless this property is set to **dbUseJet**.

When setting the **DefaultType** property to **dbUseODBC**, Visual Basic creates a new **Workspace** object and adds it to the **Workspaces** collection. The **DefaultType** property of the **Data** control is similar to the *type* parameter of the **CreateWorkspace** method. When using **dbUseJet**, the default **Workspace** object is used.

Note When you select **dbUseODBC** for the **DefaultType** property, DAO routes all data access operations through a Remote Data Objects (RDO) DLL. Also, if you select "1 - UseODBC" in the **DefaultType** property in the property sheet, you must also specify an ODBC connect string in the **Connect** property box. To do this, select Text, then enter the ODBC connect string. For more information on ODBC connect strings, see the Visual Basic *Guide to Data Access Objects*.

Choosing a Data Source

Data Access Objects (DAO) can be programmed to connect to remote ODBC data sources in one of two ways: through the Jet database engine or through Remote Data Objects (RDO) which bypasses Jet completely. Depending on the features and performance you need, either approach might make sense for your particular application.

Using ODBCDirect: This approach permits you to use the **Data** control against remote ODBC data sources by routing all DAO operations through the RDO interface. That is, when you establish a connection and create a **Recordset** object using the **Data** control, the Jet database engine is not loaded or used in any way. This also means that many of the DAO features provided by the Jet engine are not available on this **Workspace**. For example, you cannot perform heterogeneous joins, or access ISAM on .mdb databases without use of additional ODBC drivers. However, when you choose ODBCDirect, many RDO features not ordinarily supported by Jet are enabled.

Using The Jet Database Engine: Unless you enable ODBCDirect, the Jet database engine is loaded and performs all local and remote database operations. Once a Jet **Workspace** is created, it cannot be used to pass data to an ODBCDirect **Workspace**.

Data Type

Integer

See Also

DefaultCursorType Property, **CreateWorkspace** Method, **Workspace** Object

---

DefaultUser, DefaultPassword Properties

- **DefaultUser** — sets the user name used to create the default **Workspace** when it is initialized.

- **DefaultPassword** — sets the password used to create the default **Workspace** when it is initialized.

Applies To

DBEngine Object

Settings

The setting for **DefaultUser** is a **String** data type. It can be 1–20 characters long in Microsoft Jet workspaces and any length in ODBCDirect workspaces, and it can include alphabetic characters, accented characters, numbers, spaces, and symbols except for: " (quotation marks), / (forward slash), \ (backslash), [ ] (brackets), : (colon), | (pipe), < (less-than sign), > (greater-than sign), + (plus sign), = (equal sign), ; (semicolon), , (comma), ? (question mark), * (asterisk), leading spaces, and control characters (ASCII 00 to ASCII 31).

The setting for **DefaultPassword** is a **String** data type that can be up to 14 characters long in Microsoft Jet databases and any length in ODBCDirect connections. It can contain any character except ASCII 0.

By default, the **DefaultUser** property is set to "admin" and the **DefaultPassword** property is set to a zero-length string ("").

Remarks

User names aren't usually case-sensitive; however, if you're re-creating a user account that was deleted or created in a different workgroup, the user name must be an exact case-sensitive match of the original name. Passwords are case-sensitive.

Typically, you use the **CreateWorkspace** method to create a **Workspace** object with a given user name and password. However, for backward compatibility with earlier versions and for convenience when you don't implement a secured database, the Microsoft Jet database engine automatically creates a default **Workspace** object when needed if one isn't already open. In this case, the **DefaultUser** and **DefaultPassword** property values define the user and password for the default **Workspace** object.

For this property to take effect, you should set it before calling any DAO methods.

Example

This example sets the **DefaultUser** and **DefaultPassword** properties which will determine the settings for the default **Workspace** object.

```
Sub DefaultUserX()

    ' Set the DefaultUser and DefaultPassword properties for
    ' the DBEngine object.
    DBEngine.DefaultUser = "NewUser"
    DBEngine.DefaultPassword = ""

    Debug.Print _
        "Setting DBEngine.DefaultUser to 'NewUser'..."
    Debug.Print _
        "Setting DBEngine.DefaultPassword to " & _
            "[zero-length string]..."

    Dim wrkJet As Workspace
    Dim wrkLoop As Workspace
    Dim prpLoop As Property

    Set wrkJet = CreateWorkspace("JetWorkspace", "admin", _
        "", dbUseJet)

    ' Enumerate Workspaces collection.
    On Error Resume Next
    For Each wrkLoop In Workspaces
        Debug.Print "Workspace: " & wrkLoop.Name
        ' Enumerate Properties collection of each Workspace
        ' object.
```

```
        For Each prpLoop In wrkLoop.Properties
            Debug.Print "    " & prpLoop.Name & " = " & prpLoop
        Next prpLoop
    Next wrkLoop
    On Error GoTo 0

    wrkJet.Close

End Sub
```

DefaultValue Property (DBGrid Control)

Sets the default value for a **Column** object in an unbound **DBGrid** control.

Applies To

Column Object

Syntax

object.**DefaultValue** [= *value*]

The **DefaultValue** property syntax has these parts:

Part	Description
object	An object expression that evaluates to an object in the **Applies To** list.
value	A Variant expression containing the default value for the specified column.

Remarks

The **DBGrid** control does not use this property itself, but provides it as a placeholder for you to associate default values with columns in an unbound grid. In the **UnboundAddData** event, you can use this property to retrieve default values for columns that were not supplied by the end-user. Such columns will contain a **Null** variant in the corresponding **RowBuffer.Value** property array. This property can also be used as a tag for a column (whether it is bound or unbound). Arbitrary values can be stored and retrieved later

See Also

Column Object

DefColWidth Property

Returns or sets a value indicating the default column width for all columns in the **DBGrid** control.

Applies To

DBGrid Control

Syntax

object.**DefColWidth** [= *value*]

The **DefColWidth** property syntax has these parts:

Part	Description
object	An object expression that evaluates to an object in the **Applies To** list.
value	An integer based on the scale mode of the control.

Remarks

If you set the **DefColWidth** property to 0, the control automatically sizes all columns based on either the width of the column heading or the **Size** property setting of the underlying field, whichever is larger. For example, to set the default column width of all columns to the width of the first column:

```
DBGrid1.DefColWidth = DBGrid1.Columns(0).Width
```

See Also

Data Control, **Column** Object, **AllowRowSizing** Property

Deftype Statements

Used at module level to set the default data type for variables, arguments passed to procedures, and the return type for **Function** and **Property Get** procedures whose names start with the specified characters.

Syntax

DefBool *letterrange*[, *letterrange*] . . .
DefByte *letterrange*[, *letterrange*] . . .
DefInt *letterrange*[, *letterrange*] . . .
DefLng *letterrange*[, *letterrange*] . . .
DefCur *letterrange*[, *letterrange*] . . .
DefSng *letterrange*[, *letterrange*] . . .
DefDbl *letterrange*[, *letterrange*] . . .
DefDec *letterrange*[, *letterrange*] . . .
DefDate *letterrange*[, *letterrange*] . . .
DefStr *letterrange*[, *letterrange*] . . .
DefObj *letterrange*[, *letterrange*] . . .
DefVar *letterrange*[, *letterrange*] . . .

The required *letterrange* argument has the following syntax:

letter1[-*letter2*]

The *letter1* and *letter2* arguments specify the name range for which you can set a default data type. Each argument represents the first letter of the variable, argument, **Function** procedure, or **Property Get** procedure name and can be any letter of the alphabet. The case of letters in *letterrange* isn't significant.

Remarks

The statement name determines the data type:

Statement	Data Type
DefBool	**Boolean**
DefByte	**Byte**
DefInt	**Integer**
DefLng	**Long**
DefCur	**Currency**
DefSng	**Single**
DefDbl	**Double**
DefDec	**Decimal** (not currently supported)
DefDate	**Date**
DefStr	**String**
DefObj	**Object**
DefVar	**Variant**

For example, in the following program fragment, `Message` is a string variable:

```
DefStr A-Q
. . .
Message = "Out of stack space."
```

A **Def***type* statement affects only the module where it is used. For example, a **DefInt** statement in one module affects only the default data type of variables, arguments passed to procedures, and the return type for **Function** and **Property Get** procedures declared in that module; the default data type of variables, arguments, and return types in other modules is unaffected. If not explicitly declared with a **Def***type* statement, the default data type for all variables, all arguments, all **Function** procedures, and all **Property Get** procedures is **Variant**.

When you specify a letter range, it usually defines the data type for variables that begin with letters in the first 128 characters of the character set. However, when you specify the letter range A – Z, you set the default to the specified data type for all variables, including variables that begin with international characters from the extended part of the character set (128 – 255).

Once the range A – Z has been specified, you can't further redefine any subranges of variables using **Def***type* statements. Once a range has been specified, if you include a previously defined letter in another **Def***type* statement, an error occurs. However, you can explicitly specify the data type of any variable, defined or not, using a **Dim** statement with an **As** *type* clause. For example, you can use the following code at module level to define a variable as a **Double** even though the default data type is **Integer**:

```
DefInt A-Z
Dim TaxRate As Double
```

Def*type* statements don't affect elements of user-defined types because the elements must be explicitly declared.

See Also

Function Statement, **Let** Statement, **Property Get** Statement

Example

This example shows various uses of the **Def***type* statements to set default data types of variables and function procedures whose names start with specified characters. The default data type can be overridden only by explicit assignment using the **Dim** statement. **Def***type* statements can only be used at the module level (that is, not within procedures).

```
' Variable names beginning with A through K default to Integer.
DefInt A-K
' Variable names beginning with L through Z default to String.
DefStr L-Z
CalcVar = 4                      ' Initialize Integer.
StringVar = "Hello there"        ' Initialize String.
AnyVar = "Hello"                 ' Causes "Type mismatch" error.
Dim Calc As Double               ' Explicitly set the type to Double.
Calc = 2.3455                    ' Assign a Double.

' Deftype statements also apply to function procedures.
CalcNum = ATestFunction(4)       ' Call user-defined function.
' ATestFunction function procedure definition.
Function ATestFunction(INumber)
   ATestFunction = INumber * 2   ' Return value is an integer.
End Function
```

Delete Method

- **Recordset** objects—deletes the current record in an updatable **Recordset** object. For ODBCDirect workspaces, the type of driver determines whether **Recordset** objects are updatable and therefore support the **Delete** method.

- Collections—deletes a persistent object from a collection.

Applies To

Dynaset-Type Recordset Object, **Fields** Collection, **Groups** Collection, **Indexes** Collection, **Properties** Collection, **QueryDefs** Collection, **Recordset** Object, **Relations** Collection, **Snapshot-Type Recordset** Object, **Table-Type Recordset** Object, **TableDefs** Collection, **Users** Collection, **Workspaces** Collection, **Forward-Only–Type Recordset** Object, **Dynamic-Type Recordset** Object

Syntax

recordset.**Delete**
collection.**Delete** *objectname*

The **Delete** method syntax has these parts.

Part	Description
recordset	An object variable that represents an updatable **Recordset** object containing the record you want to delete.
Collection	An object variable that represents a collection from which you are deleting *objectname*.
Objectname	A **String** that is the **Name** property setting of an object in *collection*.

Remarks

You can use the **Delete** method to delete a current record from a **Recordset** or a member from a collection, such as a stored table from a database, a stored field from a table, or a stored index from a table.

Recordsets

A **Recordset** must contain a current record before you use **Delete**; otherwise, a run-time error occurs.

In an updatable **Recordset** object, **Delete** removes the current record and makes it inaccessible. Although you can't edit or use the deleted record, it remains current. Once you move to another record, however, you can't make the deleted record current again. Subsequent references to a deleted record in a **Recordset** are invalid and produce an error.

You can undo a record deletion if you use transactions and the **Rollback** method.

If the base table is the primary table in a cascading delete relationship, deleting the current record may also delete one or more records in a foreign table.

Note   To add, edit, or delete a record, there must be a unique index on the record in the underlying data source. If not, a "Permission denied" error will occur on the **AddNew**, **Delete**, or **Edit** method call in a Microsoft Jet workspace, or an "Invalid argument" error will occur on the **Update** method call in an ODBCDirect workspace.

Collections

You can use the **Delete** method to delete a persistent object. However, if the collection is a **Databases**, **Recordsets**, or **Workspaces** collection (each of which is stored only in memory), you can remove an open or active object only by closing that object with the **Close** method.

The deletion of a stored object occurs immediately, but you should use the **Refresh** method on any other collections that may be affected by changes to the database structure.

When you delete a **TableDef** object from the **TableDefs** collection, you delete the table definition and the data in the table.

The following table lists some limitations of the **Delete** method. The object in the first column contains the collection in the second column. The third column indicates if you can delete an object from that collection (for example, you can never delete a **Container** object from the **Containers** collection of a **Database** object).

Object	Collection	Can you use the Delete method?
DBEngine	**Workspaces**	No. Closing the objects deletes them.
DBEngine	**Errors**	No
Workspace	**Connections**	No. Closing the objects deletes them.
Workspace	**Databases**	No. Closing the objects deletes them.
Workspace	**Groups**	Yes
Workspace	**Users**	Yes
Connection	**QueryDefs**	No
Connection	**Recordsets**	No. Closing the objects deletes them.
Database	**Containers**	No
Database	**QueryDefs**	Yes
Database	**Recordsets**	No. Closing the objects deletes them.
Database	**Relations**	Yes
Database	**TableDefs**	Yes
Group	**Users**	Yes
User	**Groups**	Yes
Container	**Documents**	No
QueryDef	**Fields**	No
QueryDef	**Parameters**	No
Recordset	**Fields**	No
Relation	**Fields**	Only when the **Relation** object is a new, unappended object.
TableDef	**Fields**	Only when the **TableDef** object is new and hasn't been appended to the database, or when the **Updatable** property of the **TableDef** is set to **True**.
TableDef	**Indexes**	Only when the **TableDef** object is new and hasn't been appended to the database, or when the **Updatable** property of the **TableDef** is set to **True**.
Index	**Fields**	Only when the **Index** object is new and hasn't been appended to the database.
Database, Field, Index, QueryDef, TableDef	**Properties**	Only when the property is user-defined.
DBEngine, Parameter, Recordset, Workspace	**Properties**	No

Delete Method

Example

This example uses the **Delete** method to remove a specified record from a **Recordset**. The **DeleteRecord** procedure is required for this procedure to run

```
Sub DeleteX()

    Dim dbsNorthwind As Database
    Dim rstEmployees As Recordset
    Dim lngID As Long

    Set dbsNorthwind = OpenDatabase("Northwind.mdb")
    Set rstEmployees = _
        dbsNorthwind.OpenRecordset("Employees")

    ' Add temporary record to be deleted.
    With rstEmployees
        .Index = "PrimaryKey"
        .AddNew
        !FirstName = "Janelle"
        !LastName = "Tebbs"
        .Update
        .Bookmark = .LastModified
        lngID = !EmployeeID
    End With

    ' Delete the employee record with the specified ID
    ' number.
    DeleteRecord rstEmployees, lngID

    rstEmployees.Close
    dbsNorthwind.Close

End Sub

Sub DeleteRecord(rstTemp As Recordset, _
    lngSeek As Long)

    With rstTemp
        .Seek "=", lngSeek
        If .NoMatch Then
            MsgBox "No employee #" & lngSeek & " in file!"
        Else
            .Delete
            MsgBox "Record for employee #" & lngSeek & _
                " deleted!"
        End If
    End With

End Sub
```

Delete Method (OLE Container)

Deletes the specified object and frees the memory associated with it.

Applies To

OLE Container Control

Syntax

object.**Delete**

The *object* is an object expression that evaluates to an object in the **Applies To** list.

Remarks

This method enables you to explicitly delete an object. Objects are automatically deleted when a form is closed or when the object is replaced with a new object.

Delete Method (Remote Data)

Deletes the current row in an updatable **rdoResultset** object.

Applies To

rdoResultset Object

Syntax

object.**Delete**

The *object* placeholder represents an object expression that evaluates to an object in the **Applies To** list.

Remarks

Delete removes the current row and makes it inaccessible. The deleted row is removed from the **rdoResultset** cursor and the database. When you delete rows from an **rdoResultset**, there must be a current row in the **rdoResultset** before you use **Delete**; otherwise, a trappable error is triggered.

Once you delete a row in an **rdoResultset**, you must reposition the current row pointer to another row in the **rdoResultset** before performing an operation that accesses the current row. Although you can't edit or use the deleted row, it remains current until you reposition to another row. Once you move to another row, however, you can't make the deleted row current again.

When you position to a row in your **rdoResultset** that has been deleted by another user, or if you delete a common row in another **rdoResultset**, a trappable error occurs indicating that the row has been deleted. At this point, the current row is invalid and you must reposition to another valid row. For example, if you use a bookmark to position to a deleted row, a trappable error occurs.

You can undo a row deletion if you use transactions and the **RollbackTrans** method—assuming you use **BeginTrans** before using the **Delete** method.

Using **Delete** produces an error under any of the following conditions:

- There is no current row.
- The connection or **rdoResultset** is read-only.
- No columns in the row are updatable.
- The row has already been deleted.
- Another user has locked the data page containing your row.
- The user does not have permission to perform the operation.

See Also

AddNew Method (Remote Data), **BeginTrans**, **CommitTrans**, **RollbackTrans** Methods, **Refresh** Method (Remote Data), **rdoConnection** Object, **rdoEnvironment** Object, **rdoResultset** Object, **rdoTable** Object, **Bookmark** Property (Remote Data), **LastModified** Property (Remote Data), **Name** Property (Remote Data), **Updatable** Property (Remote Data)

DeleteLines Method

Applies To

CodeModule Object

Deletes a single line or a specified range of lines.

Syntax

object.**DeleteLines** (*startline* [, *count*])

The**DeleteLines** syntax has these parts:

Part	Description
object	Required. An object expression that evaluates to an object in the **Applies To** list.
startline	Required. A **Long** specifying the first line you want to delete.
count	Optional. A **Long** specifying the number of lines you want to delete.

Remarks

If you don't specify how many lines you want to delete, **DeleteLines** deletes one line.

See Also

InsertLines Method, **Lines** Method

Example

The following example has two steps. The first **For...Next** loop uses the **InsertLines** method to insert into CodePanes(1) 26 ever-longer initial segments of the alphabet, starting with "a." The last line inserted is the entire alphabet.

The second **For...Next** loop uses the **DeleteLines** method to delete the odd-numbered lines. Although it seems that the second loop should simply delete every other line, note that after each deletion the lines get renumbered. Therefore the deletion is advancing by two lines at each step, one line because I is increasing by one and another line because the larger line numbers are each decreasing by one.

```
For I = 1 to 26
   Application.VBE.SelectedVBComponent.CodeModule.InsertLines i, Mid$
↪ ("abcdefghijklmnopqrstuvwxyz", 1, I)
Next
For I = 1 to 13
   Application.VBE.SelectedVBComponent.CodeModule.DeleteLines I
Next
```

DeleteSetting Statement

Deletes a section or key setting from an application's entry in the Windows registry.

Syntax

DeleteSetting *appname*, *section*[, *key*]

The **DeleteSetting** statement syntax has these named arguments:

Part	Description
appname	Required. String expression containing the name of the application or project to which the section or key setting applies.
section	Required. String expression containing the name of the section where the key setting is being deleted. If only *appname* and *section* are provided, the specified section is deleted along with all related key settings.
key	Optional. String expression containing the name of the key setting being deleted.

Remarks

If all arguments are provided, the specified key setting is deleted. However, the **DeleteSetting** statement does nothing if the specified section or key setting does not exist.

See Also

GetAllSettings Function, **GetSetting** Function, **SaveSetting** Statement

Example

The following example first uses the **SaveSetting** statement to make entries in the Windows registry (or .ini file on 16-bit Windows platforms) for the MyApp application, and then uses the **DeleteSetting** statement to remove them. Because no *key* argument is specified, the whole section is deleted, including the section name and all its keys.

```
' Place some settings in the registry.
SaveSetting appname := "MyApp", section := "Startup", _
         key := "Top", setting := 75
SaveSetting "MyApp","Startup", "Left", 50
' Remove section and all its settings from registry.
DeleteSetting "MyApp", "Startup"
```

Description Property

Returns or sets a string expression containing a descriptive string associated with an object. Read/write.

For the **Err** object, returns or sets a descriptive string associated with an error.

Applies To

Reference Object, **Err** Object

Remarks

The **Description** property setting consists of a short description of the error. Use this property to alert the user to an error that you either can't or don't want to handle. When generating a user-defined error, assign a short description of your error to the **Description** property. If **Description** isn't filled in, and the value of **Number** corresponds to a Visual Basic run-time error, the string returned by the **Error** function is placed in **Description** when the error is generated.

See Also

Error Function, **Err** Object, **HelpContext** Property, **HelpFile** Property, **LastDLLError** Property, **Number** Property, **Source** Property

Example

This example assigns a user-defined message to the **Description** property of the **Err** object.

```
Err.Description = "It was not possible to access an object necessary " _
& "for this operation."
```

Description Property (Remote Data)

Returns a descriptive string associated with an error.

Applies To

rdoError Object

Syntax

object.**Description**

The *object* placeholder represents an object expression that evaluates to an object in the **Applies To** list.

Return Values

The **Description** property return value is a string expression containing a description of the error.

Remarks

When an error occurs either on the remote server, or in the ODBC interface while processing your query, an **rdoError** object is created and appended to the **rdoErrors** collection. The **rdoError** object's **Description** property returns a short description and context information about where the error occurred. This can be used to alert the user to an error that you cannot, or do not want to handle. The **SQLState** code is appended to the front of message, followed by a colon and a space. For example "S0021: Cannot find XXX".

See Also

rdoError Object, **HelpContext**, **HelpFile** Properties (Remote Data), **Number** Property (Remote Data), **Source** Property (Remote Data), **SQLRetCode** Property (Remote Data), **SQLState** Property (Remote Data)

Example

The following code opens a read-only ODBC cursor connection against the SQL Server "SEQUEL" and includes a simple error handler that displays the error description and number.

```
Sub MakeConnection()
Dim rdoCn As New rdoConnection
On Error GoTo CnEh
With rdoCn
    .Connect = "UID=;PWD=;Database=WorkDB;" _
        & "Server=SEQUEL;Driver={SQL Server}" _
        & "DSN='';"
    .LoginTimeout = 5
    .CursorDriver = rdUseODBC
    .EstablishConnection rdDriverNoPrompt, True
End With
AbandonCn:
Exit Sub

CnEh:
Dim er As rdoError
Dim msg as string
    Msg = "An error occured " _
    & "while opening the connection:" _
    & Err & " - " & Error & VbCr

    For Each er In rdoErrors
        Msg = Msg & er.Description _
            & ":" & er.Number & VbCr
    Next er
    Resume AbandonCn
End Sub
```

Designer Property

Returns the object that enables you to access the design characteristics of a component.

Applies to

VBComponent Object

Remarks

If the object has an open designer, the **Designer** property returns the open designer; otherwise a new designer is created. The designer is a characteristic of certain **VBComponent** objects. For example, when you create certain types of **VBComponent** object, a designer is created along with the object. A component can have only one designer, and it's always the same designer. The **Designer** property enables you to access a component-specific object. In some cases, such as in standard modules and class modules, a designer isn't created because that type of **VBComponent** object doesn't support a designer.

The **Designer** property returns **Nothing** if the **VBComponent** object doesn't have a designer.

See Also

DesignerWindow Property, **HasOpenDesigner** Property

Example

The following example uses the **Designer** and **Count** properties to return the number of controls on a form. Note that the window containing the form must be selected. The **Designer** object is the form itself.

```
Debug.Print Application.VBE.SelectVBComponent.Designer.Controls.Count
```

DesignerWindow Property

Returns the **Window** object that represents the component's designer.

Applies to

VBComponent Object

Remarks

If the component supports a designer but doesn't have an open designer, accessing the **DesignerWindow** property creates the designer, but it isn't visible. To make the window visible, set the **Window** object's **Visible** property to **True**.

See Also

Window Object, **Designer** Property, **HasOpenDesigner** Property, **Visible** Property

Example

The following example uses the **DesignerWindow** and **Visibile** properties to find out whether or not a particular designer is visible. Note that the **VBComponent** object must be a form.

```
Debug.Print Application.VBE.VBProjects(1).VBComponents(1).
↪ DesignerWindow.Visible
```

DesignMasterID Property

Sets or returns a 16-byte value that uniquely identifies the Design Master in a replica set (Microsoft Jet workspaces only).

Applies To

Database Object

Settings and Return Values

The setting or return value is a **GUID** that uniquely identifies the Design Master.

Remarks

You should set the **DesignMasterID** property only if you need to move the current Design Master. Setting this property makes a specific replica in the replica set the Design Master.

Caution Never create a second Design Master in a replica set. The existence of a second Design Master can result in the loss of data.

Under extreme circumstances—for example, if the Design Master is erased or corrupted—you can set this property at the current replica. However, setting this property at a replica when there is already another Design Master in the set might partition your replica set into two irreconcilable sets and prevent any further synchronization of data.

If you decide to make a replica the new Design Master for the set, synchronize it with all the replicas in the replica set before setting the **DesignMasterID** property in the replica. The replica must be open in exclusive mode in order to make it the Design Master.

If you make a replica that is designated read-only into the Design Master, the target replica is made read/write; the old Design Master also remains read/write.

The **DesignMasterID** property setting is stored in the **MSysRepInfo** system table.

See Also

ReplicaID Property

Example

This example sets the **DesignMasterID** property to the **ReplicaID** property setting of another database, making that database the Design Master in the replica set. The old and new Design Masters are synchronized to update the design change. For this code to work, you must create a Design Master and replica, include their names and paths as appropriate, and run this code from a database other than the old or new Design Master.

```
Sub SetNewDesignMaster(strOldDM as String, _
    strNewDM as String)

    Dim dbsOld As Database
    Dim dbsNew As Database

    ' Open the current Design Master in exclusive mode.
    Set dbsOld = OpenDatabase(strOldDM, True)

    ' Open the database that will become the new
    ' Design Master.
    Set dbsNew = OpenDatabase(strNewDM)

    ' Make the new database the Design Master.
    dbsOld.DesignMasterID = dbsNew.ReplicaID

    ' Synchronize the old Design Master with the new
    ' Design Master, and allow two-way exchanges.
    dbsOld.Synchronize strNewDM, dbRepImpExpChanges
    dbsOld.Close
    dbsNew.Close

End Sub
```

DeviceName Property

Returns the name of the device a driver supports.

Applies To

Printer Object, **Printers** Collection

Syntax

object.**DeviceName**

The *object* placeholder represents an object expression that evaluates to an object in the **Applies To** list.

Remarks

Each printer driver supports one or more devices—for example, HP LaserJet IIISi is a device name.

Note The effect of properties of the **Printer** object depends on the driver supplied by the printer manufacturer. Some property settings may have no effect, or several different property settings may all have the same effect. Settings outside the accepted range may produce an error. For more information, see the manufacturer's documentation for the specific driver.

See Also

hDC Property

Dim Statement

Declares variables and allocates storage space.

Syntax

Dim [**WithEvents**] *varname*[([*subscripts*])] [**As** [**New**] *type*] [**,** [**WithEvents**]
↪ *varname*[([*subscripts*])] [**As** [**New**] *type*]] . . .

The **Dim** statement syntax has these parts:

Part	Description
WithEvents	Optional. Keyword that specifies that *varname* is an object variable used to respond to events triggered by an **ActiveX** object. **WithEvents** is valid only in class modules. You can declare as many individual variables as you like using **WithEvents**, but you can't create arrays with **WithEvents**. You can't use **New** with **WithEvents**.
varname	Required. Name of the variable; follows standard variable naming conventions.
subscripts	Optional. Dimensions of an array variable; up to 60 multiple dimensions may be declared. The *subscripts* argument uses the following syntax: [*lower* **To**] *upper* [**,** [*lower* **To**] *upper*] . . . When not explicitly stated in *lower*, the lower bound of an array is controlled by the **Option Base** statement. The lower bound is zero if no **Option Base** statement is present.
New	Optional. Keyword that enables implicit creation of an object. If you use **New** when declaring the object variable, a new instance of the object is created on first reference to it, so you don't have to use the **Set** statement to assign the object reference. The **New** keyword can't be used to declare variables of any intrinsic data type, can't be used to declare instances of dependent objects, and can't be used with **WithEvents**.
type	Optional. Data type of the variable; may be **Byte**, **Boolean**, **Integer**, **Long**, **Currency**, **Single**, **Double**, **Decimal** (not currently supported), **Date**, **String** (for variable-length strings), **String** * *length* (for fixed-length strings), **Object**, **Variant**, a user-defined type, or an object type. Use a separate **As** *type* clause for each variable you declare.

Remarks

Variables declared with **Dim** at the module level are available to all procedures within the module. At the procedure level, variables are available only within the procedure.

Use the **Dim** statement at module or procedure level to declare the data type of a variable. For example, the following statement declares a variable as an **Integer**.

```
Dim NumberOfEmployees As Integer
```

Also use a **Dim** statement to declare the object type of a variable. The following declares a variable for a new instance of a worksheet.

```
Dim X As New Worksheet
```

If the **New** keyword is not used when declaring an object variable, the variable that refers to the object must be assigned an existing object using the **Set** statement before it can be used. Until it is assigned an object, the declared object variable has the special value **Nothing**, which indicates that it doesn't refer to any particular instance of an object.

You can also use the **Dim** statement with empty parentheses to declare a dynamic array. After declaring a dynamic array, use the **ReDim** statement within a procedure to define the number of dimensions and elements in the array. If you try to redeclare a dimension for an array variable whose size was explicitly specified in a **Private**, **Public**, or **Dim** statement, an error occurs.

If you don't specify a data type or object type, and there is no **Def***type* statement in the module, the variable is **Variant** by default.

When variables are initialized, a numeric variable is initialized to 0, a variable-length string is initialized to a zero-length string (""), and a fixed-length string is filled with zeros. **Variant** variables are initialized to **Empty**. Each element of a user-defined type variable is initialized as if it were a separate variable.

Note   When you use the **Dim** statement in a procedure, you generally put the **Dim** statement at the beginning of the procedure.

See Also

Array Function, **Option Base** Statement, **Private** Statement, **Public** Statement, **ReDim** Statement, **Set** Statement, **Static** Statement, **Type** Statement

Example

This example shows the **Dim** statement used to declare variables. It also shows the **Dim** statement used to declare arrays. The default lower bound for array subscripts is 0 and can be overridden at the module level using the **Option Base** statement.

```
' AnyValue and MyValue are declared as Variant by default with values
' set to Empty.
Dim AnyValue, MyValue

' Explicitly declare a variable of type Integer.
Dim Number As Integer

' Multiple declarations on a single line. AnotherVar is of type Variant
' because its type is omitted.
Dim AnotherVar, Choice As Boolean, BirthDate As Date
```

```
' DayArray is an array of Variants with 51 elements indexed, from
' 0 thru 50, assuming Option Base is set to 0 (default) for
' the current module.
Dim DayArray(50)

' Matrix is a two-dimensional array of integers.
Dim Matrix(3, 4) As Integer

' MyMatrix is a three-dimensional array of doubles with explicit
' bounds.
Dim MyMatrix(1 To 5,  4 To 9,  3 To 5) As Double

' BirthDay is an array of dates with indexes from 1 to 10.
Dim BirthDay(1 To 10) As Date

' MyArray is a dynamic array of variants.
Dim MyArray()
```

Dir Function

Returns a **String** representing the name of a file, directory, or folder that matches a specified pattern or file attribute, or the volume label of a drive.

Syntax

Dir[(*pathname*[, *attributes*])]

The **Dir** function syntax has these parts:

Part	Description
pathname	Optional. String expression that specifies a file name—may include directory or folder, and drive. A zero-length string ("") is returned if *pathname* is not found.
attributes	Optional. Constant or numeric expression, whose sum specifies file attributes. If omitted, all files are returned that match *pathname*.

Settings

The *attributes* argument settings are:

Constant	Value	Description
vbNormal	0	Normal
vbHidden	2	Hidden
vbSystem	4	System file
vbVolume	8	Volume label; if specified, all other attributes are ignored
vbDirectory	16	Directory or folder

Note These constants are specified by Visual Basic for Applications and can be used anywhere in your code in place of the actual values.

Remarks

Dir supports the use of multiple-character (*) and single-character (?) wildcards to specify multiple files.

You must specify *pathname* the first time you call the **Dir** function, or an error occurs. If you also specify file attributes, *pathname* must be included.

Dir returns the first file name that matches *pathname*. To get any additional file names that match *pathname*, call **Dir** again with no arguments. When no more file names match, **Dir** returns a zero-length string (""). Once a zero-length string is returned, you must specify *pathname* in subsequent calls or an error occurs. You can change to a new *pathname* without retrieving all of the file names that match the current *pathname*. However, you can't call the **Dir** function recursively. Calling **Dir** with the **vbDirectory** attribute does not continually return subdirectories.

Tip Because file names are retrieved in no particular order, you may want to store returned file names in an array, and then sort the array.

See Also

ChDir Statement, **CurDir** Function

Example

This example uses the Dir function to check if certain files and directories exist.

```
Dim MyFile, MyPath, MyName
' Returns "WIN.INI" if it exists.
MyFile = Dir("C:\WINDOWS\WIN.INI")

' Returns filename with specified extension. If more than one *.ini
' file exists, the first file found is returned.
MyFile = Dir("C:\WINDOWS\*.INI")

' Call Dir again without arguments to return the next *.INI file in
' the same directory.
MyFile = Dir

' Return first *.TXT file with a set hidden attribute.
MyFile = Dir("*.TXT", vbHidden)

' Display the names in C:\ that represent directories.
MyPath = "c:\" ' Set the path.
MyName = Dir(MyPath, vbDirectory)    ' Retrieve the first entry.
Do While MyName <> ""' Start the loop.
   ' Ignore the current directory and the encompassing directory.
   If MyName <> "." And MyName <> ".." Then
      ' Use bitwise comparison to make sure MyName is a directory.

If (GetAttr(MyPath & MyName) And vbDirectory) = vbDirectory Then
         Debug.Print MyName' Display entry only if it
      End If' it represents a directory.
   End If
   MyName = Dir' Get next entry.
Loop
```

Direction Property

Sets or returns a value that indicates whether a **Parameter** object represents an input parameter, an output parameter, both, or the return value from the procedure (**ODBCDirect** workspaces only).

Applies To

Parameter Object

Settings And Return Values

The setting or return value is a **Long** that can be set to one of the following constants:

Constant	Description
dbParamInput	(Default) Passes information to the procedure.
dbParamInputOutput	Passes information both to and from the procedure.
dbParamOutput	Returns information from the procedure as in an output parameter in SQL.
dbParamReturnValue	Passes the return value from a procedure.

Remarks

Use the **Direction** property to determine whether the parameter is an input parameter, output parameter, both, or the return value from the procedure. Some ODBC drivers do not provide information on the direction of parameters to a SELECT statement or procedure call. In these cases, it is necessary to set the direction prior to executing the query.

For example, the following procedure returns a value from a stored procedure named "get_employees":

```
{? = call get_employees}
```

This call produces one parameter—the return value. You need to set the direction of this parameter to **dbParamOutput** or **dbParamReturnValue** before executing the **QueryDef**.

You need to set all parameter directions except **dbParamInput** before accessing or setting the values of the parameters and before executing the **QueryDef**.

You should use **dbParamReturnValue** for return values, but in cases where that option is not supported by the driver or the server, you can use **dbParamOutput** instead.

Note The Microsoft SQL Server 6.0 driver automatically sets the **Direction** property for all procedure parameters. Not all ODBC drivers can determine the direction of a query parameter. In these cases, it is necessary to set the direction prior to executing the query.

Example

This example uses the **Direction** property to configure the parameters of a query to an ODBC data source.

```
Sub DirectionX()

    Dim wrkMain As Workspace
    Dim conMain As Connection
    Dim qdfTemp As QueryDef
    Dim rstTemp As Recordset
    Dim strSQL As String
    Dim intLoop As Integer

    ' Create ODBC workspace and open a connection to a
    ' Microsoft SQL Server database.
    Set wrkMain = CreateWorkspace("ODBCWorkspace", _
        "admin", "", dbUseODBC)
    Set conMain = wrkMain.OpenConnection("Publishers", _
        dbDriverNoPrompt, False, _
        "ODBC;DATABASE=pubs;UID=sa;PWD=;DSN=Publishers")

    ' Set SQL string to call the stored procedure
    ' getempsperjob.
    strSQL = "{ call getempsperjob (?, ?) }"

    Set qdfTemp = conMain.CreateQueryDef("", strSQL)

    With qdfTemp
        ' Indicate that the two query parameters will only
        ' pass information to the stored procedure.
        .Parameters(0).Direction = dbParamInput
        .Parameters(1).Direction = dbParamInput

        ' Assign initial parameter values.
        .Parameters(0) = "0877"
        .Parameters(1) = 0

        Set rstTemp = .OpenRecordset()

        With rstTemp
            ' Loop through all valid values for the second
            ' parameter. For each value, requery the recordset
            ' to obtain the correct results and then print out
            ' the contents of the recordset.
            For intLoop = 1 To 14
                qdfTemp.Parameters(1) = intLoop
                .Requery
                Debug.Print "Publisher = " & _
                    qdfTemp.Parameters(0) & _
                    ", job = " & intLoop
                Do While Not .EOF
                    Debug.Print , .Fields(0), .Fields(1)
                    .MoveNext
```

```
        Loop
      Next intLoop
      .Close
    End With

  End With

  conMain.Close
  wrkMain.Close

End Sub
```

Direction Property (Remote Data)

Returns or sets a value indicating how a parameter is passed to or from a procedure.

Applies To

rdoParameter Object

Syntax

object.**Direction** [= *value*]

The **Direction** property syntax has these parts:

Part	Description
object	An object expression that evaluates to an object in the **Applies To** list.
value	A constant or **Integer** as described in Settings.

Settings

The settings for *value* are one of the following values:

Constant	Value	Description
rdParamInput	0	(Default) The parameter is used to pass information to the procedure.
rdParamInputOutput	1	The parameter is used to pass information both to and from the procedure.
rdParamOutput	2	The parameter is used to return information from the procedure as in an output parameter in SQL.
rdParamReturnValue	3	The parameter is used to return the return status value from a procedure.

Remarks

When working with stored procedures, and parameter queries you should identify those parameters that are to be managed by RDO on your behalf — but only when using drivers that do not automatically detect parameter direction. A parameterized query can take virtually any number of input arguments — each of these need to be marked when you create your query.

Generally, your query returns a set of rows that meet the requirements established in the query based on the parameters you provide at runtime. However, when working with stored procedures, another aspect is exposed. Stored procedures return information using row sets, return status, and output parameters. Because of this, each parameter returned by your stored procedure must be marked when creating your query.

The **Direction** property determines whether the parameter is an input parameter, output parameter, or both—or if the parameter is the return value from the procedure.

Note When first addressing the **rdoParameter** object to set the Direction property you might trip a trappable error if the **rdoParameters** collection could not be created. Generally this is due to syntax errors in the query or other problems that prevented RDO from creating the collection.

Some ODBC drivers do not provide information on the direction of parameters to a SELECT statement or procedure call so all parameter directions default to **rdParamInput.** In these cases, it is necessary to set the direction in code prior to executing the query.

Note The Microsoft SQL Server 6.x driver automatically sets the **Direction** property for all procedure parameters so you should not have to set the **Direction** property for any of your queries' parameters.

The **Direction** property is associated with the **rdoParameter** object but it is generally unnecessary to address the **rdoParameter** object itself as it is the default collection of the **rdoQuery** object as shown in the examples below.

For example, the following procedure returns a value from a stored procedure:

```
{? = call sp_test}
```

This call produces one parameter—the return value. It is necessary to set the direction of this parameter to **rdParamOutput** or **rdParamReturnValue** before executing the prepared statement. For example:

```
Dim my_statement As rdoQuery
Set my_statement = someRdoConnection.CreateQuery _
    ("MyPs", "{? = call sp_testprocedure }", ...)
my_statement.rdoParameters(0).Direction = _
    rdParamReturnValue
my_statement.Execute
Print my_statement.rdoParameters(0)
```

You need to set all parameter directions except **rdParamInput** before accessing or setting the values of the parameters and before executing the **rdoQuery**.

You should use **rdParamReturnValue** for return values, but you can use **rdParamOutput** where **rdParamReturnValue** is not supported.

See Also

    Execute Method (Remote Data), **rdoParameter** Object, **rdoQuery** Object

DirListBox Control

A **DirListBox** control displays directories and paths at run time. Use this control to display a hierarchical list of directories. You can create dialog boxes that, for example, enable a user to open a file from a list of files in all available directories.

Syntax

DirListBox

Remarks

Set the **List**, **ListCount**, and **ListIndex** properties to enable a user to access items in a list. If you also display the **DriveListBox** and **FileListBox** controls, you can write code to synchronize them with the **DirListBox** control and with each other.

Properties

OLEDragMode Property, **OLEDropMode** Property, **BackColor, ForeColor** Properties, **FontBold, FontItalic, FontStrikethru, FontUnderline** Properties, **FontName** Property, **FontSize** Property, **Height, Width** Properties, **Left, Top** Properties, **List** Property, **ListCount** Property, **ListIndex** Property, **TabIndex** Property, **Tag** Property, **Visible** Property, **DragIcon** Property, **DragMode** Property, **hWnd** Property, **MouseIcon** Property, **MousePointer** Property, **TabStop** Property, **TopIndex** Property, **Appearance** Property, **Enabled** Property, **HelpContextID** Property, **Index** Property (Control Array), **Name** Property, **Parent** Property, **Path** Property, **Font** Property, **Container** Property, **ToolTipText** Property, **WhatsThisHelpID** Property

Methods

Refresh Method, **SetFocus** Method, **Drag** Method, **Move** Method, **ZOrder** Method, **OLEDrag** Method, **ShowWhatsThis** Method

See Also

DriveListBox Control, **FileListBox** Control, **List** Property, **ListCount** Property, **ListIndex** Property

---

DisabledPicture Property

Returns or sets a reference to a picture to display in a control when it is disabled. (That is, when its **Enabled** property is set to **False**.)

Applies To

CheckBox Control, **CommandButton** Control, **OptionButton** Control

Syntax

object.**DisabledPicture** [= *picture*]

The **DisabledPicture** property syntax has these parts:

Part	Description
object	An object expression that evaluates to an object in the **Applies To** list.
picture	A **Picture** object containing a graphic, as described in **Settings**.

Settings

The settings for *picture* are:

Setting	Description
(None)	(Default) No picture.
(Bitmap, icon, metafile)	Specifies a graphic. You can load the graphic from the **Properties** window at design time. At run time, you can also set this property by using the **LoadPicture** function on a bitmap, icon, or metafile, or by setting it to the **Picture** property of another control.

Remarks

The **DisabledPicture** property specifies a picture object to display when the control (such as a **CommandButton**) is disabled. The **DisabledPicture** property is ignored unless the **Style** property of the control is set to 1 (graphical).

The picture is centered horizontally and vertically on the control. If there is a caption as well as a picture, the picture is centered above the caption. If the picture object is too large to fit on the control, then it is clipped.

If no picture is assigned to the **DisabledPicture** property, but one is assigned to the **Picture** property, then a grayed version of that picture is displayed when the control is disabled.

Disconnect Event

Occurs after a connection has been closed.

Applies To

rdoConnection Object

Syntax

Private Sub *object*.**Disconnect**( )

The *object* placeholder represents an object expression that evaluates to an object in the **Applies To** list.

Remarks

Fired after a physical connection is closed. The developer can catch this event to do any clean-up work necessary.

Applies to **rdoConnection** object.

See Also

BeforeConnect Event, **Connect** Event, **OpenConnection** Method (Remote Data), **EstablishConnection** Method (Remote Data), **rdoConnection** Object, **rdoEnvironment** Object

DisplayAsDefault Property

Returns a boolean value to determine if the control is the default button for the container, and therefore should display itself as the default control.

Applies To

AmbientProperties Object

Syntax

object.**DisplayAsDefault**

The **DisplayAsDefault** property syntax has this part:

Part	Description
object	An object expression that evaluates to an object in the **Applies To** list.

Settings

The possible Boolean return values from the **DisplayAsDefault** property are:

Setting	Description
True	The control is the default button.
False	The control is not the default button. If the container does not implement this ambient property, this will be the default value.

Remarks

Only one control in a container may be the default control; the container of the control will determine which control is currently the default control and notify that control through the **DisplayAsDefault** ambient property. The notified control should draw itself to show it is the default control. All other controls will have their **DisplayAsDefault** ambient property value be **False**.

Only button type controls may be default controls.

DisplayBind Property

Returns or sets the **DisplayBind** attribute of a **Member** object.

Applies To

Member Object

Syntax

object.**DisplayBind**

The *object* placeholder represents an object expression that evaluates to an object in the **Applies To** list.

DisplayModel Property

Returns or sets the display model used by the system.

Applies To

VBE Object

Syntax

object.**DisplayModel As vbext_VBADisplayModel**

The *object* placeholder represents an object expression that evaluates to an object in the **Applies To** list.

Settings

The settings for **vbext_VBADisplayModel** are:

Constant	Value	Description
vbext_dm_SDI	0	(Default) Display model is SDI (Single Document Interface).
vbext_dm_MDI	1	Display model is MDI (Multiple Document Interface).

DisplayName Property

Returns a string value that contains the name the control should display to identify itself in error messages.

Syntax

object.**DisplayName**

The **DisplayName** property syntax has this part:

Part	Description
object	An object expression that evaluates to an object in the **Applies To** list.

Remarks

This ambient property is the way the control finds out what the container (such as Visual Basic) is calling this instance of the control. This string should be used in error messages as the name for the instance of the control.

If the container does not implement this ambient property, the default value will be an empty string.

DisplayType Property

Returns or sets a value indicating whether an object displays its contents or an icon.

Applies To

OLE Container Control, **OLEObject** Object

Syntax

object.**DisplayType** [= *value*]

The **DisplayType** property syntax has these parts:

Part	Description
object	An object expression that evaluates to an object in the **Applies To** list.
value	An integer or constant specifying whether an object displays its contents or an icon, as described in Settings.

Settings

The settings for *value* are:

Constant	Value	Descriptioni
vbOLEDisplayContent	0	(Default) Content. When the **OLE** container control contains an object, the object's data is displayed in the control.
vbOLEDisplayIcon	1	Icon. When the **OLE** container control contains an object, the object's icon is displayed in the control.

Remarks

This property determines the default setting of the Display As Icon check box in the Insert Object and Paste Special dialog boxes. When you display these dialog boxes either at run time (with the **InsertObjDlg** or **PasteSpecialDlg** methods) or design time, the Display As Icon check box is automatically selected if this property is set to 1 (Icon).

When creating an object at run time using the **CreateEmbed** or **CreateLink** methods, use the **DisplayType** property to determine if the object is displayed as an icon (set **DisplayType** = 1) or if the object's data is displayed in the control (set **DisplayType** = 0).

Once you create an object, you can't change its display type.

See Also

PasteSpecialDlg Method, **CreateEmbed** Method, **CreateLink** Method, **InsertObjDlg** Method

Dissociate Event

Occurs after an **rdoResultset** object has been dissociated from a connection.

Applies To

rdoResultset Object

Syntax

Private Sub *object*.**Dissociate( )**

The *object* placeholder represents an object expression that evaluates to an object in the **Applies To** list.

This event is raised after the **ActiveConnection** property has been set to **Nothing** and the result set has been dissociated from its connection.

See Also

BeforeConnect Event, **Associate** Event, **Connect** Event, **Disconnect** Event, **WillAssociate** Event, **WillDissociate** Event, **OpenConnection** Method (Remote Data), **EstablishConnection** Method (Remote Data), **rdoConnection** Object

DistinctCount Property

Returns a value that indicates the number of unique values for the **Index** object that are included in the associated table (Microsoft Jet workspaces only).

Applies To

Index Object

Return Values

The return value is a **Long** data type.

Remarks

Check the **DistinctCount** property to determine the number of unique values, or keys, in an index. Any key is counted only once, even though there may be multiple occurrences of that value if the index permits duplicate values. This information is useful in applications that attempt to optimize data access by evaluating index information. The number of unique values is also known as the *cardinality* of an **Index** object.

The **DistinctCount** property won't always reflect the actual number of keys at a particular time. For example, a change caused by a rolled back transaction won't be reflected immediately in the **DistinctCount** property. The **DistinctCount** property value also may not reflect the deletion of records with unique keys. The number will be accurate immediately after you use the **CreateIndex** method.

Example

This example uses the **DistinctCount** property to show how you can determine the number of unique values in an **Index** object. However, this value is only accurate immediately after creating the **Index**. It will remain accurate if no keys change, or if new keys are added and no old keys are deleted; otherwise, it will not be reliable. (If this procedure is run several times, you can see the effect on the **DistinctCount** property values of the existing **Index** objects.)

```
Sub DistinctCountX()

    Dim dbsNorthwind As Database
    Dim tdfEmployees As TableDef
    Dim idxCountry As Index
    Dim idxLoop As Index
    Dim rstEmployees As Recordset

    Set dbsNorthwind = OpenDatabase("Northwind.mdb")
    Set tdfEmployees = dbsNorthwind!Employees

    With tdfEmployees
        ' Create and append new Index object to the Employees
        ' table.
        Set idxCountry = .CreateIndex("CountryIndex")
        idxCountry.Fields.Append _
            idxCountry.CreateField("Country")
        .Indexes.Append idxCountry

        ' The collection must be refreshed for the new
        ' DistinctCount data to be available.
        .Indexes.Refresh

        ' Enumerate Indexes collection to show the current
        ' DistinctCount values.
        Debug.Print "Indexes before adding new record"
        For Each idxLoop In .Indexes
            Debug.Print "    DistinctCount = " & _
                idxLoop.DistinctCount & ", Name = " & _
                idxLoop.Name
        Next idxLoop

        Set rstEmployees = _
            dbsNorthwind.OpenRecordset("Employees")
```

```
                ' Add a new record to the Employees table.
                With rstEmployees
                   .AddNew
                   !FirstName = "April"
                   !LastName = "LaMonte"
                   !Country = "Canada"
                   .Update
                End With

                ' Enumerate Indexes collection to show the modified
                ' DistinctCount values.
                Debug.Print "Indexes after adding new record and " & _
                   "refreshing Indexes"
                .Indexes.Refresh
                For Each idxLoop In .Indexes
                   Debug.Print "     DistinctCount = " & _
                      idxLoop.DistinctCount & ", Name = " & _
                      idxLoop.Name
                Next idxLoop

                ' Delete new record because this is a demonstration.
                With rstEmployees
                   .Bookmark = .LastModified
                   .Delete
                   .Close
                End With

                ' Delete new Indexes because this is a demonstration.
                .Indexes.Delete idxCountry.Name
             End With

             dbsNorthwind.Close

          End Sub
```

DividerStyle Property

Returns or sets a value specifying the style of border drawn on the right edge of the specified column of a **DBGrid** control.

Applies To

Column Object

Syntax

object.**DividerStyle** [= *value*]

The **DividerStyle** property syntax has these parts:

Part	Description
object	An object expression that evaluates to an object in the **Applies To** list.
value	An integer that specifies the border style, as described in Settings.

Settings

The settings for *value* are:

Constant	Value	Description
dbgNoDividers	0	No divider
dbgBlackLine	1	Black line
dbgDarkGrayLine	2	(Default) Dark gray line
dbgRaised	3	Raised
dbgInset	4	Inset
dbgUserForeColor	5	Divider is drawn using the color set by the **ForeColor** property
dbgLightGrayLine	6	Light gray line

Remarks

The **DividerStyle** property doesn't affect whether the column can be resized by dragging it or not. When the border is either raised or inset, the colors used are set by Microsoft Windows.

See Also

Data Control, **RowDividerStyle** Property

Example

This example changes the column divider style when the user clicks a heading.

```
Private Sub DBGrid1_HeadClick (ColIndex As Long)
   If DBGrid1.Columns(ColIndex).DividerStyle <> 5 Then
      DBGrid1.Columns(ColIndex).DividerStyle = _
       DBGrid1.Columns(ColIndex).DividerStyle + 1
   Else
      DBGrid1.Columns(ColIndex).DividerStyle = 0
   End If
End Sub
```

Do...Loop Statement

Repeats a block of statements while a condition is **True** or until a condition becomes **True**.

Syntax

Do [{**While** | **Until**} *condition*]
   [*statements*]
   [**Exit Do**]
   [*statements*]
Loop

Or, you can use this syntax:

Do

    [*statements*]

    [Exit Do]

    [*statements*]

Loop [{**While** | **Until**} *condition*]

The **Do Loop** statement syntax has these parts:

Part	Description
condition	Optional. Numeric expression or string expression that is **True** or **False**. If *condition* is **Null**, *condition* is treated as **False**.
statements	One or more statements that are repeated while, or until, *condition* is **True**.

Remarks

Any number of **Exit Do** statements may be placed anywhere in the **Do...Loop** as an alternate way to exit a **Do...Loop**. **Exit Do** is often used after evaluating some condition, for example, **If...Then**, in which case the **Exit Do** statement transfers control to the statement immediately following the **Loop**.

When used within nested **Do...Loop** statements, **Exit Do** transfers control to the loop that is one nested level above the loop where **Exit Do** occurs.

See Also

Exit Statement, **For...Next** Statement, **While...Wend** Statement

Example

This example shows how **Do...Loop** statements can be used. The inner **Do...Loop** statement loops 10 times, sets the value of the flag to **False**, and exits prematurely using the **Exit Do** statement. The outer loop exits immediately upon checking the value of the flag.

```
Dim Check, Counter
Check = True: Counter = 0     ' Initialize variables.
Do                            ' Outer loop.
   Do While Counter < 20      ' Inner loop.
      Counter = Counter + 1'  Increment Counter.
      If Counter = 10 Then    ' If condition is True.
         Check = False        ' Set value of flag to False.
         Exit Do              ' Exit inner loop.
      End If
   Loop
Loop Until Check = False      ' Exit outer loop immediately.
```

Document Object

A **Document** object includes information about one instance of an object. The object can be a database, saved table, query, or relationship (Microsoft Jet databases only).

Remarks

Each **Container** object has a **Documents** collection containing **Document** objects that describe instances of built-in objects of the type specified by the **Container**. The following table lists the type of object each **Document** describes, the name of its **Container** object, and what type of information **Document** contains.

Document	Container	Contains information about
Database	Databases	Saved database
Table or query	Tables	Saved table or query
Relationship	Relations	Saved relationship

Note Don't confuse the **Container** objects listed in the preceding table with the collections of the same name. The Databases **Container** object refers to all saved database objects, but the **Databases** collection refers only to database objects that are open in a particular workspace.

With a **Document** object, you can:

- Use the **Name** property to return the name that a user or the Microsoft Jet database engine gave to the object when it was created.

- Use the **Container** property to return the name of the **Container** object that contains the **Document** object.

- Use the **Owner** property to set or return the owner of the object. To set the **Owner** property, you must have write permission for the **Document** object, and you must set the property to the name of an existing **User** or **Group** object.

- Use the **UserName** or **Permissions** properties to set or return the access permissions of a user or group for the object. To set these properties, you must have write permission for the **Document** object, and you must set the **UserName** property to the name of an existing **User** or **Group** object.

- Use the **DateCreated** and **LastUpdated** properties to return the date and time when the **Document** object was created and last modified.

Because a **Document** object corresponds to an existing object, you can't create new **Document** objects or delete existing ones. To refer to a **Document** object in a collection by its ordinal number or by its **Name** property setting, use any of the following syntax forms:

Documents(0)
Documents("*name*")
Documents![*name*]

See Also

User Object

Properties

AllPermissions Property, **Container** Property, **DateCreated, LastUpdated** Properties, **Name** Property, **Owner** Property, **Permissions** Property, **UserName** Property, **KeepLocal** Property, **Replicable** Property

Methods

CreateProperty Method

Example

This example enumerates the **Documents** collection of the Tables container, and then enumerates the **Properties** collection of the first **Document** object in the collection.

```
Sub DocumentX()

    Dim dbsNorthwind As Database
    Dim docLoop As Document
    Dim prpLoop As Property

    Set dbsNorthwind = OpenDatabase("Northwind.mdb")

    With dbsNorthwind.Containers!Tables
        Debug.Print "Documents in " & .Name & " container"
        ' Enumerate the Documents collection of the Tables
        ' container.
        For Each docLoop In .Documents
            Debug.Print "    " & docLoop.Name
        Next docLoop
        With .Documents(0)
            ' Enumerate the Properties collection of the first.
            ' Document object of the Tables container.
            Debug.Print "Properties of " & .Name & " document"
            On Error Resume Next
            For Each prpLoop In .Properties
                Debug.Print "    " & prpLoop.Name & " = " & _
                    prpLoop
            Next prpLoop
            On Error GoTo 0
        End With
    End With

    dbsNorthwind.Close

End Sub
```

Documents Collection

A **Documents** collection contains all of the **Document** objects for a specific type of object (Microsoft Jet databases only).

Remarks

Each **Container** object has a **Documents** collection containing **Document** objects that describe instances of built-in objects of the type specified by the **Container**.

To refer to a **Document** object in a collection by its ordinal number or by its **Name** property setting, use any of the following syntax forms:

Documents(0)
Documents("*name*")
Documents![*name*]

Properties

Count Property

Methods

Refresh Method

Example

This example enumerates the **Documents** collection of the Tables container, and then enumerates the **Properties** collection of the first **Document** object in the collection.

```
Sub DocumentX()

    Dim dbsNorthwind As Database
    Dim docLoop As Document
    Dim prpLoop As Property

    Set dbsNorthwind = OpenDatabase("Northwind.mdb")

    With dbsNorthwind.Containers!Tables
        Debug.Print "Documents in " & .Name & " container"
        ' Enumerate the Documents collection of the Tables
        ' container.
        For Each docLoop In .Documents
            Debug.Print "    " & docLoop.Name
        Next docLoop
        With .Documents(0)
            ' Enumerate the Properties collection of the first.
            ' Document object of the Tables container.
            Debug.Print "Properties of " & .Name & " document"
            On Error Resume Next
```

```
            For Each prpLoop In .Properties
                Debug.Print "     " & prpLoop.Name & " = " & _
                    prpLoop
            Next prpLoop
            On Error GoTo 0
        End With
    End With

    dbsNorthwind.Close


    End Sub
```

DoEvents Function

Yields execution so that the operating system can process other events.

Syntax

DoEvents( )

Remarks

The **DoEvents** function returns an **Integer** representing the number of open forms in stand-alone versions of Visual Basic, such as Visual Basic, Professional Edition. **DoEvents** returns zero in all other applications.

DoEvents passes control to the operating system. Control is returned after the operating system has finished processing the events in its queue and all keys in the **SendKeys** queue have been sent.

DoEvents is most useful for simple things like allowing a user to cancel a process after it has started, for example a search for a file. For long-running processes, yielding the processor is better accomplished by using a Timer or delegating the task to an ActiveX EXE component. In the latter case, the task can continue completely independent of your application, and the operating system takes case of multitasking and time slicing.

Caution Any time you temporarily yield the processor within an event procedure, make sure the procedure is not executed again from a different part of your code before the first call returns; this could cause unpredictable results. In addition, do not use **DoEvents** if other applications could possibly interact with your procedure in unforeseen ways during the time you have yielded control.

See Also

SendKeys Statement

Example

This example uses the **DoEvents** function to cause execution to yield to the operating system once every 1000 iterations of the loop. **DoEvents** returns the number of open Visual Basic forms, but only when the host application is Visual Basic.

```
' Create a variable to hold number of Visual Basic forms loaded
' and visible.
Dim I, OpenForms
For I = 1 To 150000          ' Start loop.
   If I Mod 1000 = 0 Then    ' If loop has repeated 1000 times.
      OpenForms = DoEvents   ' Yield to operating system.
   End If
Next I                       ' Increment loop counter.
```

DoGetNewFileName Event

Occurs whenever a **Save As** operation is performed on any component or project, whether manually performed from the **File** menu, or programmatically performed.

Applies To

FileControlEvents Object

Syntax

Sub DoGetNewFileName(*vbproject* **As VBProject**, *filetype* **As vbext_FileType**,
→ *newname* **As String**, *oldname* **As String**, *canceldefault* **As Boolean**)

The **DoGetNewFileName** event syntax has these parts:

Part	Description
vbproject	A **VBProject** object specifying the name of the project which will be written.
filetype	An enumerated value (**vbext_FileType**) specifying the type of file to be written, as listed in Settings.
newname	A string expression specifying the name of the new file. The file specification must be relative to the current **LastUsedPath** property or a fully qualified filename.
oldname	A string expression specifying the old name of the file.
canceldefault	A Boolean expression that determines the default Visual Basic action, as described in Settings.

Settings

The enumerated values for **vbext_FileType** are:

Constant	Value	Description
vbext_ft_Form	0	File type is a form.
vbext_ft_Module	1	File type is a basic module.
vbext_ft_Class	2	File type is a class module.

(continued)

(continued)

Constant	Value	Description
vbext_ft_Project	3	File type is a project.
vbext_ft_Exe	4	File type is an executable file.
vbext_ft_Res	6	File type is a resource file.
vbext_ft_UserControl	7	File type is a **User** control.
vbext_ft_PropertyPage	8	File type is a **Property Page**.
vbext_ft_DocObject	9	File type is a **User Document**.
vbext_ft_Binary	10	File type is a binary file.
vbext_ft_GroupProject	11	File type is a group project.
vbext_ft_Designer	12	File type is a designer object.

The settings for *canceldefault* are:

Setting	Description
True	Stops triggering this event for any subsequent add-ins connected to the **FileControl** object. If *newname* is a zero-length string ("") when *canceldefault* is set to **True**, the event is canceled; otherwise, the name entered in *newname* is used as the new filename.
False	Continues triggering this event for subsequent add-ins connected to the **FileControl** object. If no add-in sets *canceldefault* to **True**, the **Save File As** or **Make .Exe** dialog box is displayed with the string you entered in *newname* selected.

Remarks

If the *canceldefault* parameter is set to **True**, the **Save File As** dialog box is not displayed. If *canceldefault* is set to **False**, the **Save File As** dialog box displays. If more than one add-ins is connected, and *canceldefault* is set to **True** at any time during a Save As operation, the **Save File As** dialog box will not display for any of the add-ins until the next Save As operation is performed.

The *newname* argument is initially set to the same value as *oldname*, but any add-in that receives this event can change it. One way to do this is through a custom user interface where you obtain the new name of the file and set *newname* to the user's selection. However, if *canceldefault* is **True** (meaning that a previous add-in has set it to **True**), you shouldn't set *newname* again.

This event occurs in all add-ins that are connected to the **FileControl** object. The add-in cannot prevent the file from being written to disk because the operation is complete. However, you can use this event to perform other tasks, such as:

- Log information about the event.
- Update information about the file.
- Back up the file.

Double Data Type

Double (double-precision floating-point) variables are stored as IEEE 64-bit (8-byte) floating-point numbers ranging in value from -1.79769313486232E308 to -4.94065645841247E-324 for negative values and from 4.94065645841247E-324 to 1.79769313486232E308 for positive values. The type-declaration character for **Double** is the number sign (#).

See Also

Data Type Summary, **Single Data** Type, **Deftype** Statements

---

DoVerb Method

Opens an object for an operation, such as editing. Doesn't support named arguments.

Applies To

OLE Container Control, **OLEObject** Object

Syntax

object.**DoVerb** (*verb*)

The **DoVerb** method syntax has these parts:

Part	Description
object	An object expression that evaluates to an object in the **Applies To** list.
verb	Optional. The verb to execute of the object within the **OLE** container control. If not specified, the default verb is executed. The value of this argument can be one of the standard verbs supported by all objects or an index of the **ObjectVerbs** property array.

Remarks

If you set the **AutoActivate** property to 2 (**Double-Click**), the **OLE** container control automatically activates the current object when the user double-clicks the control.

Each object can support its own set of verbs. The following values represent standard verbs every object should support:

Constant	Value	Description
vbOLEPrimary	0	The default action for the object.
vbOLEShow	-1	Activates the object for editing. If the application that created the object supports in-place activation, the object is activated within the **OLE** container control.
vbOLEOpen	-2	Opens the object in a separate application window. If the application that created the object supports in-place activation, the object is activated in its own window.

(continued)

(continued)

Constant	Value	Description
vbOLEHide	–3	For embedded objects, hides the application that created the object.
vbOLEUIActivate	–4	If the object supports in-place activation, activates the object for in-place activation and shows any user interface tools. If the object doesn't support in-place activation, the object doesn't activate, and an error occurs.
VbOLEInPlaceActivate	–5	If the user moves the focus to the **OLE** container control, creates a window for the object and prepares the object to be edited. An error occurs if the object doesn't support activation on a single mouse click.
VbOLEDiscardUndoState	–6	Used when the object is activated for editing to discard all record of changes that the object's application can undo.

Note   These verbs may not be listed in the **ObjectVerbs** property array.

See Also

ObjectVerbs Property, **Verb** Property, **AutoActivate** Property

---

DownPicture Property

Returns or sets a reference to a picture to display in a control when it is clicked and in the down (depressed) position.

Applies To

CheckBox Control, **CommandButton** Control, **OptionButton** Control

Syntax

object.**DownPicture** [= *picture*]

The **DownPicture** property syntax has these parts:

Part	Description
object	An object expression that evaluates to an object in the **Applies To** list.
picture	A **Picture** object containing a graphic, as described in **Settings**.

Settings

The settings for *picture* are:

Setting	Description
(None)	(Default) No picture.
(Bitmap, icon, metafile)	Specifies a graphic. You can load the graphic from the **Properties** window at design time. At run time, you can also set this property by using the **LoadPicture** function on a bitmap, icon, or metafile, or by setting it to the **Picture** property of another control.

Remarks

The **DownPicture** property refers to a picture object that displays when the button is in the down state. The **DownPicture** property is ignored unless the **Style** property is set to 1 (graphical). Note that when an **OptionButton** or **CheckBox** control's **Style** property is set to graphical and its button depressed, the background of the button is dithered, but the picture on the button is not.

The picture is centered both horizontally and vertically on the button. If there is a caption included with the picture, the picture will be centered above the caption. If no picture is assigned to this property when the button is depressed, then the picture currently assigned to the **Picture** property is used. If no picture is assigned to either the **Picture** or **DownPicture** properties, then only the caption is displayed. If the picture object is too large to fit on the button, then it is clipped.

Drag Method

Begins, ends, or cancels a drag operation of any control except the **Line**, **Menu**, **Shape**, **Timer**, or **CommonDialog** controls. Doesn't support named arguments.

Applies To

Animation Control, **CheckBox** Control, **ComboBox** Control, **CommandButton** Control, **Data** Control, **DBCombo** Control, **DBGrid** Control, **DBList** Control, **DirListBox** Control, **DriveListBox** Control, **FileListBox** Control, **Frame** Control, **HScrollBar, VScrollBar** Controls, **Image** Control, **Label** Control, **ListBox** Control, **ListView** Control, **Masked Edit** Control, **MSFlexGrid** Control, **OLE Container** Control, **OptionButton** Control, **PictureBox** Control, **ProgressBar** Control, **RemoteData** Control, **RichTextBox** Control, **Slider** Control, **StatusBar** Control, **TabStrip** Control, **TextBox** Control, **Toolbar** Control, **TreeView** Control, **UpDown** Control

Syntax

object.**Drag** *action*

The **Drag** method syntax has these parts:

Part	Description
object	Required. An object expression that evaluates to an object in the **Applies To** list. If *object* is omitted, the object whose event procedure contains the **Drag** method is assumed.
action	Optional. A constant or value that specifies the action to perform, as described in **Settings**. If *action* is omitted, the default is to begin dragging the object.

Settings

The settings for *action* are:

Constant	Value	Description
vbCancel	0	Cancels drag operation
vbBeginDrag	1	Begins dragging *object*
vbEndDrag	2	Ends dragging and drop *object*

Remarks

These constants are listed in the Visual Basic (VB) object library in the Object Browser.

Using the **Drag** method to control a drag-and-drop operation is required only when the **DragMode** property of the object is set to Manual (0). However, you can use **Drag** on an object whose **DragMode** property is set to Automatic (1 or **vbAutomatic**).

If you want the mouse pointer to change shape while the object is being dragged, use either the **DragIcon** or **MousePointer** property. The **MousePointer** property is only used if no **DragIcon** is specified.

In earlier versions of Visual Basic, **Drag** was an asynchronous method where subsequent statements were invoked even though the Drag action wasn't finished.

See Also

DragDrop Event, **DragOver** Event, **DragIcon** Property, **DragMode** Property, **MousePointer** Property

Example

This example uses the **Drag** method to drag the filename of a bitmap (.bmp) file to a picture box where the bitmap is displayed. To try this example, paste all of the code into the Declarations section of a form that contains **DriveListBox**, **DirListBox**, **FileListBox**, **PictureBox**, and **Label** controls. Use the default names for all of the controls. Size and position all controls so they can be easily seen and used. The size and position of the label is unimportant because it's changed at run time. When the program begins, you can browse your file system and load any bitmaps. Once you''ve located a bitmap that you want to display, click the filename of that bitmap, and drag it to the picture box.

```
Private Sub Form_Load ()
    Picture1.AutoSize = -1   ' Turn on AutoSize.
    Label1.Visible = 0' Make the label invisible.
    File1.Pattern = "*.BMP; *.ICO; *.WMF"     ' Set file patterns.
End Sub

Private Sub Dir1_Change () ' Any change in Dir1
    File1.Path = Dir1.Path   ' is reflected in File1.
End Sub
```

```
Private Sub Drive1_Change ()   ' Any change in Drive1
   Dir1.Path = Drive1.Drive' is reflected in Dir1.
End Sub

Private Sub File1_MouseDown (Button As Integer, Shift As Integer,
X As Single, Y As Single)

Dim DY' Declare variable.
   DY = TextHeight("A") ' Get height of one line.
   Label1.Move File1.Left, File1.Top + Y - DY /2, File1.Width, DY
   Label1.Drag ' Drag label outline.
End Sub

Private Sub Dir1_DragOver (Source As Control, X As Single, Y As Single,
State As Integer)
   ' Change pointer to no drop.
   If State = 0 Then Source.MousePointer = 12
   ' Use default mouse pointer.
   If State = 1 Then Source.MousePointer = 0
End Sub

Private Sub Drive1_DragOver (Source As Control, X As Single, Y As Single,
State As Integer)

' Change pointer to no drop.
   If State = 0 Then Source.MousePointer = 12
   ' Use default mouse pointer.
   If State = 1 Then Source.MousePointer = 0
End Sub

Private Sub Form_DragOver (Source As Control, X As Single, Y As Single,
State As Integer)
   ' Change pointer to no drop.
   If State = 0 Then Source.MousePointer = 12
   ' Use default mouse pointer.
   If State = 1 Then Source.MousePointer = 0
End Sub

Private Sub File1_DragOver (Source As Control, X As Single, Y As Single,
State As Integer)

On Error Resume Next
   If State = 0 And Right$(File1.Filename,4) = ".ICO" Then
      Label1.DragIcon = LoadPicture(File1.Path + "\" + File1.Filename)
   If Err Then MsgBox "The icon file can't be loaded."
   ElseIf State = 1 Then
      Label1.DragIcon = LoadPicture ()         ' Use no drag icon.
   End If
End Sub

Private Sub Picture1_DragDrop (Source As Control, X As Single, Y As Single)
   On Error Resume Next
   Picture1.Picture = LoadPicture(File1.Path + "\" + File1.Filename)

If Err Then MsgBox "The picture file can't be loaded."
End Sub
```

DragDrop Event

Occurs when a drag-and-drop operation is completed as a result of dragging a control over an object and releasing the mouse button or using the **Drag** method with its *action* argument set to 2 (Drop).

Applies To

PropertyPage Object, **UserControl** Object, **UserDocument** Object, **CheckBox** Control, **ComboBox** Control, **CommandButton** Control, **DirListBox** Control, **DriveListBox** Control, **FileListBox** Control, **Form** Object, **Forms** Collection, **Frame** Control, **HScrollBar**, **VScrollBar** Controls, **Image** Control, **Label** Control, **ListBox** Control, **MDIForm** Object, **OptionButton** Control, **PictureBox** Control, **TextBox** Control, **OLE Container** Control, **Animation** Control, **Data** Control, **DBCombo** Control, **DBGrid** Control, **DBList** Control, **DirListBox** Control, **ListView** Control, **Masked Edit** Control, **MSFlexGrid** Control, **ProgressBar** Control, **RemoteData** Control, **RichTextBox** Control, **Slider** Control, **StatusBar** Control, **TabStrip** Control, **Toolbar** Control, **TreeView** Control, **UpDown** Control

Syntax

Private Sub Form_DragDrop(*source* **As Control**, *x* **As Single**, *y* **As Single**)
Private Sub MDIForm_DragDrop(*source* **As Control**, *x* **As Single**, *y* **As Single**)
Private Sub *object*_**DragDrop**([*index* **As Integer**,]*source* **As Control**,
↪ *x* **As Single**, *y* **As Single**)

The **DragDrop** event syntax has these parts:

Part	Description
object	An object expression that evaluates to an object in the **Applies To** list.
index	An integer that uniquely identifies a control if it's in a control array.
source	The control being dragged. You can include properties and methods in the event procedure with this argument—for example, `Source.Visible = 0`.
x, y	A number that specifies the current horizontal (*x*) and vertical (*y*) position of the mouse pointer within the target form or control. These coordinates are always expressed in terms of the target's coordinate system as set by the **ScaleHeight**, **ScaleWidth**, **ScaleLeft**, and **ScaleTop** properties.

Remarks

Use a **DragDrop** event procedure to control what happens after a drag operation is completed. For example, you can move the source control to a new location or copy a file from one location to another.

When multiple controls can potentially be used in a *source* argument:

- Use the **TypeOf** keyword with the **If** statement to determine the type of control used with *source*.

- Use the control's **Tag** property to identify a control, and then use a **DragDrop** event procedure.

Note   Use the **DragMode** property and **Drag** method to specify the way dragging is initiated. Once dragging has been initiated, you can handle events that precede a **DragDrop** event with a **DragOver** event procedure.

See Also

DragOver Event, **MouseDown**, **MouseUp** Events, **MouseMove** Event, Drag Method, **DragIcon** Property, **DragMode** Property

Example

This example demonstrates the visual effect of dropping a **PictureBox** control onto another **PictureBox** control. To try this example, paste the code into the **Declarations** section of a form that contains three **PictureBox** controls. Set the **DragMode** property for Picture1 and Picture2 to 1 (Automatic). Use the **Picture** property to assign bitmaps to Picture1 and Picture2, and then press F5 and drag Picture1 or Picture2 over Picture3.

```
Private Sub Picture3_DragDrop (Source As Control, X as Single, Y As Single)
   If TypeOf Source Is PictureBox Then
      ' Set Picture3 bitmap to same as source control.
      Picture3.Picture = Source.Picture
   End If
End Sub
```

DragIcon Property

Returns or sets the icon to be displayed as the pointer in a drag-and-drop operation.

Applies To

CheckBox Control, **ComboBox** Control, **CommandButton** Control, **DirListBox** Control, **DriveListBox** Control, **FileListBox** Control, **Frame** Control, **HScrollBar, VScrollBar** Controls, **Image** Control, **Label** Control, **ListBox** Control, **OptionButton** Control, **PictureBox** Control, **TextBox** Control, **OLE Container** Control, **Data** Control, **DBCombo** Control, **DBGrid** Control, **DBList** Control, **ListView** Control, **Masked Edit** Control, **MSChart** Control, **MSFlexGrid** Control, **ProgressBar** Control, **RemoteData** Control, **RichTextBox** Control, **Slider** Control, **SSTab** Control, **StatusBar** Control, **TabStrip** Control, **Toolbar** Control, **TreeView** Control, **UpDown** Control

Syntax

object.**DragIcon** [= *icon*]

The **DragIcon** property syntax has these parts:

Part	Description
object	An object expression that evaluates to an object in the **Applies To** list.
icon	Any code reference that returns a valid icon, such as a reference to a form's icon (Form1.Icon), a reference to another control's **DragIcon** property (Text1.DragIcon), or the **LoadPicture** function.

Settings

The settings for *icon* are:

Setting	Description
(none)	(Default) An arrow pointer inside a rectangle.
Icon	A custom mouse pointer. You specify the icon by setting it using the Properties window at design time. You can also use the **LoadPicture** function at run time. The file you load must have the .ico filename extension and format.

Remarks

You can use the **DragIcon** property to provide visual feedback during a drag-and-drop operation—for example, to indicate that the source control is over an appropriate target. **DragIcon** takes effect when the user initiates a drag-and-drop operation. Typically, you set **DragIcon** as part of a MouseDown or DragOver event procedure.

Note At run time, the **DragIcon** property can be set to any object's **DragIcon** or **Icon** property, or you can assign it an icon returned by the **LoadPicture** function.

When you set the **DragIcon** property at run time by assigning the **Picture** property of one control to the **DragIcon** property of another control, the **Picture** property must contain an .ico file, not a .bmp file.

See Also

DragDrop Event, **LoadPicture** Function, **Drag** Method, **DragMode** Property, **MousePointer** Property

Example

This example changes the **DragIcon** property setting each time you drag a **PictureBox** control. To try this example, paste the code into the **Declarations** section of a form that contains a **PictureBox** control. Set the **DragMode** property = 1, and then press F5 and click and drag the **PictureBox** control.

```
Private Sub Form_DragDrop (Source As Control, X As Single, Y As Single)
   Dim Pic   ' Declare variable.
   Source.Move X, Y   ' Set position of control.
   Pic = "ICONS\OFFICE\CRDFLE01.ICO" ' Get name of icon file.
   If Source.DragIcon = False Then   ' If no picture loaded,
      Source.DragIcon = LoadPicture(Pic)    ' load picture.
   Else
      Source.DragIcon = LoadPicture() ' Unload picture.
   End If
End Sub
```

DragMode Property

Returns or sets a value that determines whether manual or automatic drag mode is used for a drag-and-drop operation.

Applies To

CheckBox Control, **ComboBox** Control, **CommandButton** Control, **DirListBox** Control, **DriveListBox** Control, **FileListBox** Control, **Frame** Control, **HScrollBar, VScrollBar** Controls, **Image** Control, **Label** Control, **ListBox** Control, **OptionButton** Control, **PictureBox** Control, **TextBox** Control, **OLE Container** Control, **Data** Control, **DBCombo** Control, **DBGrid** Control, **DBList** Control, **ListView** Control, **Masked Edit** Control, **MSChart** Control, **MSFlexGrid** Control, **ProgressBar** Control, **RemoteData** Control, **RichTextBox** Control, **Slider** Control, **SSTab** Control, **StatusBar** Control, **TabStrip** Control, **Toolbar** Control, **TreeView** Control, **UpDown** Control

Syntax

object.**DragMode** [= *number*]

The **DragMode** property syntax has these parts:

Part	Description
object	An object expression that evaluates to an object in the **Applies To** list.
number	An integer that specifies the drag mode, as described in Settings.

Settings

The settings for *number* are:

Constant	Setting	Description
vbManual	0	(Default) Manual—requires using the **Drag** method to initiate a drag-and-drop operation on the source control.
vbAutomatic	1	Automatic—clicking the source control automatically initiates a drag-and-drop operation. **OLE** container controls are automatically dragged only when they don't have the focus.

Remarks

When **DragMode** is set to 1 (Automatic), the control doesn't respond as usual to mouse events. Use the 0 (Manual) setting to determine when a drag-and-drop operation begins or ends; you can use this setting to initiate a drag-and-drop operation in response to a keyboard or menu command or to enable a source control to recognize a **MouseDown** event prior to a drag-and-drop operation.

Clicking while the mouse pointer is over a target object or form during a drag-and-drop operation generates a **DragDrop** event for the target object. This ends the drag-and-drop operation. A drag-and-drop operation may also generate a **DragOver** event.

Note While a control is being dragged, it can't recognize other user-initiated mouse or keyboard events (**KeyDown**, **KeyPress** or **KeyUp**, **MouseDown**, **MouseMove**, or **MouseUp**). However, the control can receive events initiated by code or by a DDE link.

See Also

DragDrop Event, **DragOver** Event, **DragIcon** Property

Example

This example enables and disables the ability to drag a **CommandButton** control each time a form is clicked. To try this example, paste the code into the **Declarations** section of a form that contains a **CommandButton**, and then press F5 and click the form.

```
Private Sub Form_Click ()
    ' Check DragMode.
    If Command1.DragMode = vbManual Then
        ' Turn it on.
        Command1.DragMode = vbAutomatic
    Else
        ' Or turn it off.
        Command1.DragMode = vbManual
    End If
End Sub
```

DragOver Event

Occurs when a drag-and-drop operation is in progress. You can use this event to monitor the mouse pointer as it enters, leaves, or rests directly over a valid target. The mouse pointer position determines the target object that receives this event.

Applies To

CheckBox Control, **ComboBox** Control, **CommandButton** Control, **DirListBox** Control, **DriveListBox** Control, **FileListBox** Control, **Frame** Control, **HScrollBar**, **VScrollBar** Controls, **Image** Control, **Label** Control, **ListBox** Control, **OptionButton** Control, **PictureBox** Control, **TextBox** Control, **OLE Container** Control, **Data** Control, **DBCombo** Control, **DBGrid** Control, **DBList** Control, **ListView** Control, **Masked Edit** Control, **MSChart** Control, **MSFlexGrid** Control, **ProgressBar** Control, **RemoteData** Control, **RichTextBox** Control, **Slider** Control, **SSTab** Control, **StatusBar** Control, **TabStrip** Control, **Toolbar** Control, **TreeView** Control, **UpDown** Control, **UserControl** Object, **UserDocument** Object

Syntax

Private Sub Form_DragOver(*source* **As Control**, *x* **As Single**, *y* **As Single**, *state* **As Integer)**
Private Sub MDIForm_DragOver(*source* **As Control**, *x* **As Single**, *y* **As Single**, *state* **As Integer)**

Private Sub *object*_**DragOver**([*index* **As Integer**,]*source* **As Control**, *x* **As Single**,
↳ *y* **As Single**, *state* **As Integer**)

The **DragOver** event syntax has these parts:

Part	Description
object	An object expression that evaluates to an object in the **Applies To** list.
index	An integer that uniquely identifies a control if it's in a control array.
source	The control being dragged. You can refer to properties and methods in the event procedure with this argument—for example, `Source.Visible = False`.
x, y	A number that specifies the current horizontal (*x*) and vertical (*y*) position of the mouse pointer within the target form or control. These coordinates are always expressed in terms of the target's coordinate system as set by the **ScaleHeight**, **ScaleWidth**, **ScaleLeft**, and **ScaleTop** properties.
state	An integer that corresponds to the transition state of the control being dragged in relation to a target form or control: 0 = Enter (source control is being dragged within the range of a target). 1 = Leave (source control is being dragged out of the range of a target). 2 = Over (source control has moved from one position in the target to another).

Remarks

Use a **DragOver** event procedure to determine what happens after dragging is initiated and before a control drops onto a target. For example, you can verify a valid target range by highlighting the target (set the **BackColor** or **ForeColor** property from code) or by displaying a special drag pointer (set the **DragIcon** or **MousePointer** property from code).

Use the *state* argument to determine actions at key transition points. For example, you might highlight a possible target when *state* is set to 0 (Enter) and restore the object's previous appearance when *state* is set to 1 (Leave).

When an object receives a **DragOver** event while *state* is set to 0 (Enter):

- If the source control is dropped on the object, that object receives a **DragDrop** event.

- If the source control isn't dropped on the object, that object receives another DragOver event when *state* is set to 1 (Leave).

Note Use the **DragMode** property and **Drag** method to specify the way dragging is initiated. For suggested techniques with the *source* argument, see Remarks for the **DragDrop** event topic.

See Also

DragDrop Event, **MouseDown**, **MouseUp** Events, **MouseMove** Event, **Drag** Method, **DragIcon** Property, **DragMode** Property

Example

This example demonstrates one way to indicate a valid drop target. The pointer changes from the default arrow to a special icon when a **TextBox** control is dragged over a **PictureBox** control. The pointer returns to the default when the source is dragged elsewhere. To try this example, paste the code into the **Declarations** section of a form that contains a small **TextBox** and a **PictureBox**. Set the **TextBox** control's **DragMode** property to 1, and then press F5 and drag the **TextBox** over the **PictureBox**.

```
Private Sub Picture1_DragOver (Source As Control, X As Single,
Y As Single, State As Integer)
   Select Case State
     Case vbEnter
   ' Load icon.
        Source.DragIcon = LoadPicture("ICONS\ARROWS\POINT03.ICO")
     Case vbLeave
        Source.DragIcon = LoadPicture()       ' Unload icon.
   End Select
End Sub

Private Sub Picture1_DragDrop (Source As Control, X As Single,
Y As Single)
   Source.DragIcon = LoadPicture()    ' Unload icon.
End Sub
```

DrawMode Property

Returns or sets a value that determines the appearance of output from graphics method or the appearance of a **Shape** or **Line** control.

Applies To

PropertyPage Object, **UserControl** Object, **UserDocument** Object, **Printer** Object, **Printers** Collection, **Form** Object, **Forms** Collection, **Line** Control, **PictureBox** Control, **Shape** Control

Syntax

object.**DrawMode** [= *number*]

The **DrawMode** property syntax has these parts:

Part	Description
object	An object expression that evaluates to an object in the **Applies To** list.
number	An integer that specifies appearance, as described in Settings.

Settings

The settings for *number* are:

Constant	Setting	Description
vbBlackness	1	Blackness.
vbNotMergePen	2	Not Merge Pen—Inverse of setting 15 (Merge Pen).
vbMaskNotPen	3	Mask Not Pen—Combination of the colors common to the background color and the inverse of the pen.
vbNotCopyPen	4	Not Copy Pen—Inverse of setting 13 (Copy Pen).
vbMaskPenNot	5	Mask Pen Not—Combination of the colors common to both the pen and the inverse of the display.
vbInvert	6	Invert—Inverse of the display color.
vbXorPen	7	Xor Pen—Combination of the colors in the pen and in the display color, but not in both.
vbNotMaskPen	8	Not Mask Pen—Inverse of setting 9 (Mask Pen).
vbMaskPen	9	Mask Pen—Combination of the colors common to both the pen and the display.
vbNotXorPen	10	Not Xor Pen—Inverse of setting 7 (Xor Pen).
vbNop	11	Nop—No operation—output remains unchanged. In effect, this setting turns drawing off.
vbMergeNotPen	12	Merge Not Pen—Combination of the display color and the inverse of the pen color.
vbCopyPen	13	Copy Pen (Default)—Color specified by the **ForeColor** property.
vbMergePenNot	14	Merge Pen Not—Combination of the pen color and the inverse of the display color.
vbMergePen	15	Merge Pen—Combination of the pen color and the display color.
vbWhiteness	16	Whiteness.

Remarks

Use this property to produce visual effects with **Shape** or **Line** controls or when drawing with the graphics methods. Visual Basic compares each pixel in the draw pattern to the corresponding pixel in the existing background and then applies bit-wise operations. For example, setting 7 (Xor Pen) uses the **Xor** operator to combine a draw pattern pixel with a background pixel.

The exact effect of a **DrawMode** setting depends on the way the color of a line drawn at run time combines with colors already on the screen. Settings 1, 6, 7, 11, 13, and 16 yield the most predictable results.

See Also

BackColor, **ForeColor** Properties, **DrawWidth** Property, **DrawStyle** Property, **FillColor** Property, **FillStyle** Property

Example

This example enables drawing on a form by dragging the mouse pointer. Each mouse click sets a different value for the **DrawMode** property. To try this example, paste the code into the **Declarations** section of a form, and then press F5 and click the form.

```
Private Sub Form_Load
    DrawWidth = 10 ' Set DrawWidth.
End Sub
Private Sub Form_Click ()
    Static M As Integer  ' Current DrawMode setting.
    ForeColor = QBColor(Int(Rnd * 15))' Choose a color.
    M = ((M + 1) Mod 16) + 1' Keep DrawMode 16 or less.
    DrawMode = M' Set DrawMode.
End Sub
Private Sub Form_MouseMove (Button As Integer, Shift As Integer,
X As Single, Y As Single)
    If Button Then ' While button is pressed,
        PSet (X, Y) ' draw a big point.
    End If
End Sub
```

DrawStyle Property

Returns or sets a value that determines the line style for output from graphics methods.

Applies To

PropertyPage Object, **UserControl** Object, **UserDocument** Object, **Printer** Object, **Printers** Collection, **Form** Object, **Forms** Collection, **PictureBox** Control

Syntax

object.**DrawStyle** [= *number*]

The **DrawStyle** property syntax has these parts:

Part	Description
object	An object expression that evaluates to an object in the **Applies To** list.
number	An integer that specifies line style, as described in Settings.

Settings

The settings for *number* are:

Constant	Setting	Description
vbSolid	0	(Default) Solid
vbDash	1	Dash
vbDot	2	Dot
vbDashDot	3	Dash-Dot
vbDashDotDot	4	Dash-Dot-Dot
vbInvisible	5	Transparent
vbInsideSolid	6	Inside Solid

Remarks

If **DrawWidth** is set to a value greater than 1, **DrawStyle** settings 1 through 4 produce a solid line (the **DrawStyle** property value isn't changed). If **DrawWidth** is set to 1, **DrawStyle** produces the effect described in the preceding table for each setting.

See Also

BackColor, **ForeColor** Properties, **DrawWidth** Property, **DrawMode** Property, **FillColor** Property, **FillStyle** Property

Example

This example draws seven lines across a form, with each line displaying a different **DrawStyle** property. (If you set **AutoRedraw** = True, the form accumulates a new set of lines each time you resize it and then click it.) To try this example, paste the code into the **Declarations** section of a form, and then press F5 and click the form.

```
Private Sub Form_Click ()
    Dim I             ' Declare variable.
    ScaleHeight = 8   ' Divide height by 8.
    For I = 0 To 6
        DrawStyle = I ' Change style.
        Line (0, I + 1) - (ScaleWidth, I + 1)  ' Draw new line.
    Next I
End Sub
```

DrawWidth Property

Returns or sets the line width for output from graphics methods.

Applies To

PropertyPage Object, **UserControl** Object, **UserDocument** Object, **Printer** Object, **Printers** Collection, **Form** Object, **Forms** Collection, **PictureBox** Control

Syntax

object.**DrawWidth** [= *size*]

The **DrawWidth** property syntax has these parts:

Part	Description
object	An object expression that evaluates to an object in the **Applies To** list.
size	A numeric expression from 1 through 32,767. This value represents the width of the line in pixels. The default is 1; that is, 1 pixel wide.

Remarks

Increase the value of this property to increase the width of the line. If the **DrawWidth** property setting is greater than 1, **DrawStyle** property settings 1 through 4 produce a solid line (the **DrawStyle** property value isn't changed). Setting **DrawWidth** to 1 allows **DrawStyle** to produce the results shown in the **DrawStyle** property table.

See Also

BackColor, **ForeColor** Properties, **DrawMode** Property, **DrawStyle** Property, **FillColor** Property, **FillStyle** Property

Example

This example draws a gradually thickening line across a form. To try this example, paste the code into the **Declarations** section of a form, and then press F5 and click the form.

```
Private Sub Form_Click ()
   Dim I ' Declare variable.
   DrawWidth = 1  ' Set starting pen width.
   PSet (0, ScaleHeight / 2)  ' Set starting point.
   ForeColor = QBColor(5)   ' Set pen color.
   For I = 1 To 100 Step 10' Set up loop.
      DrawWidth = I  ' Reset pen width.
      Line - Step(ScaleWidth / 10, 0)' Draw a line.
   Next I
End Sub
```

Drive Property

Returns or sets the selected drive at run time. Not available at design time.

Applies To

DriveListBox Control

Syntax

object.**Drive** [= *drive*]

The **Drive** property syntax has these parts:

Part	Description
object	An object expression that evaluates to an object in the **Applies To** list.
drive	A string expression that specifies the selected drive.

Remarks

The valid drives for the **Drive** property include all drives present in or connected to the system when the control is created or refreshed at run time. The default setting of the **Drive** property is the current drive.

When reading this property setting, the selected drive is returned in one of the following formats:

- Floppy disks—"a:" or "b:", and so on

- Fixed media—"c: [*volume id*]"

- Network connections—"x: \\server\share"

When setting this property:

- Only the first character of the string is significant (the string isn't case-sensitive).
- Changing the setting for the **Drive** property invokes a Change event.
- Selecting a drive that isn't present causes an error.
- Setting this property also regenerates the drive list, providing a way in code to track network connections added since the control was created.

If the **FileName** property is set to a qualified network path without a drive designation, the value of the **Drive** property is a zero-length string (""), no drive is selected, and the **ListIndex** property setting is −1.

Note The **Drive** property returns a different value from the **ListIndex** property, which returns the list box selection.

See Also

PathChange Event, **PatternChange** Event, **ListIndex** Property, **FileName** Property, **Pattern** Property, **Path** Property

Example

This example displays a list of files for the current drive and directory. To try this example, paste the code into the **Declarations** section of a form that contains a **DriveListBox** control, a **DirListBox** control, and a **FileListBox** control, and then press F5. Use the mouse to change the drive or directory.

```
Private Sub Drive1_Change ()
    Dir1.Path = Drive1.Drive' When drive changes, set directory path.
End Sub
Private Sub Dir1_Change ()
    File1.Path = Dir1.Path  ' When directory changes, set file path.
End Sub
```

DriveListBox Control

A **DriveListBox** control enables a user to select a valid disk drive at run time. Use this control to display a list of all the valid drives in a user's system. You can create dialog boxes that enable the user to open a file from a list of files on a disk in any available drive.

Syntax

DriveListBox

Remarks

Set the **List**, **ListCount**, and **ListIndex** properties to enable a user to access items in the list. If you also display the **DirListBox** and **FileListBox** controls, you can write code to synchronize them with the **DriveListBox** control and with each other.

Properties

OLEDropMode Property, **BackColor, ForeColor** Properties, **FontBold, FontItalic, FontStrikethru, FontUnderline** Properties, **FontName** Property, **FontSize** Property, **Height, Width** Properties, **Left, Top** Properties, **List** Property, **ListCount** Property, **ListIndex** Property, **TabIndex** Property, **Tag** Property, **Visible** Property, **DragIcon** Property, **DragMode** Property, **Drive** Property, **hWnd** Property, **MouseIcon** Property, **MousePointer** Property, **TabStop** Property, **TopIndex** Property, **Appearance** Property, **Enabled** Property, **HelpContextID** Property, **Index** Property (Control Array), **Name** Property, **Parent** Property, **Font** Property, **Container** Property, **ToolTipText** Property, **WhatsThisHelpID** Property

Methods

Refresh Method, **SetFocus** Method, **Drag** Method, **Move** Method, **ZOrder** Method, **OLEDrag** Method, **ShowWhatsThis** Method

See Also

DirListBox Control, **FileListBox** Control, **List** Property, **ListCount** Property, **ListIndex** Property

---

DriverName Property

Returns the name of the driver for a **Printer** object.

Applies To

Printer Object, **Printers** Collection

Syntax

object.**DriverName**

The *object* placeholder represents an object expression that evaluates to an object in the **Applies To** list.

Remarks

Each driver has a unique name. For example, the **DriverName** for several of the Hewlett-Packard printers is HPPCL5MS. The **DriverName** is typically the driver's filename without an extension.

Note The effect of the properties of the **Printer** object depends on the driver supplied by the printer manufacturer. Some property settings may have no effect, or several different property settings may all have the same effect. Settings outside the accepted range may produce an error. For more information, see the manufacturer's documentation for the specific driver.

See Also

DeviceName Property

DropDown Event

Occurs when the list portion of a **ComboBox** control is about to drop down; this event doesn't occur if a **ComboBox** control's **Style** property is set to 1 (Simple Combo).

Applies To

ComboBox Control

Syntax

Private Sub *object*_**DropDown**([*index* **As Integer**])

The **DropDown** event syntax has these parts:

Part	Description
object	An object expression that evaluates to an object in the **Applies To** list.
index	An integer that uniquely identifies a control if it's in a control array.

Remarks

Use a **DropDown** event procedure to make final updates to a **ComboBox** list before the user makes a selection. This enables you to add or remove items from the list using the **AddItem** or **RemoveItem** methods. This flexibility is useful when you want some interplay between controls—for example, if what you want to load into a **ComboBox** list depends on what the user selects in an **OptionButton** group.

See Also

Style Property

Example

This example updates a **ComboBox** control based on the user's selection in an option button group. To try this example, paste the code into the **Declarations** section of a form that contains a **ComboBox** control and two **OptionButton** controls. Set the **Name** property of both **OptionButton** controls to **OptionGroup**, and then press F5 and click the **OptionButton** controls. The **ComboBox** control reflects different carriers depending on the **OptionButton** selected.

```
Private Sub Form_Load ()
   Combo1.Text = ""  ' Clear combo box.
End Sub

Private Sub Combo1_DropDown ()
   Combo1.Clear          ' Delete existing items.
   If OptionGroup(0).Value = True Then
      Combo1.AddItem "Gray Goose Express", 0
      Combo1.AddItem "Wild Fargo Carriers", 1
   Else
      Combo1.AddItem "Summit Technologies Overnight"
   End If
End Sub
```

Duplex Property

Returns or sets a value that determines whether a page is printed on both sides (if the printer supports this feature). Not available at design time.

Applies To

Printer Object, **Printers** Collection

Syntax

object.**Duplex** [= *value*]

The **Duplex** property syntax has these parts:

Part	Description
object	An object expression that evaluates to an object in the **Applies To** list.
value	A value or constant that specifies the type of printing, as described in Settings.

Settings

The settings for *value* are:

Constant	Value	Description
vbPRDPSimplex	1	Single-sided printing with the current orientation setting.
vbPRDPHorizontal	2	Double-sided printing using a horizontal page turn.
vbPRDPVertical	3	Double-sided printing using a vertical page turn.

Remarks

With horizontal duplex printing, the top of both sides of the page are at the same end of the sheet. With vertical duplex printing, the bottom of one page is at the same end of the sheet as the top of the next page. The following diagram illustrates horizontal and vertical duplex printing:

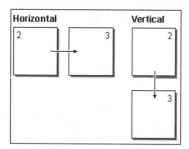

Note The effect of the properties of the **Printer** object depends on the driver supplied by the printer manufacturer. Some property settings may have no effect, or several different property settings may all have the same effect. Settings outside the accepted range may produce an error. For more information, see the manufacturer's documentation for the specific driver.

Dynamic-Type Recordset Object

This **Recordset** type represents a query result set from one or more base tables in which you can add, change, or delete records from a row-returning query. Further, records that other users add, delete, or edit in the base tables also appear in your **Recordset**.

This type is only available in ODBCDirect workspaces, and corresponds to an ODBC dynamic cursor.

Properties

AbsolutePosition Property, **BOF, EOF** Properties, **Bookmark** Property, **Bookmarkable** Property, **CacheSize** Property, **EditMode** Property, **LastModified** Property, **LockEdits** Property, **Name** Property, **PercentPosition** Property, **RecordCount** Property, **Restartable** Property, **Type** Property, **Updatable** Property, **BatchCollisionCount** Property, **BatchCollisions** Property, **BatchSize** Property, **Connection** Property, **RecordStatus** Property, **StillExecuting** Property, **UpdateOptions** Property

Methods

AddNew Method, **CancelUpdate** Method, **Close** Method, **Delete** Method, **Edit** Method, **GetRows** Method, **Move** Method, **MoveFirst**, **MoveLast**, **MoveNext**, **MovePrevious** Method, **Requery** Method, **Update** Method, **Cancel** Method, **NextRecordset** Method

See Also

Dynaset-Type Recordset Object, **Recordset** Object, **Snapshot-Type Recordset** Object, **Table-Type Recordset** Object, **Forward-Only – Type Recordset** Object

Example

This example opens a dynamic-type **Recordset** object and enumerates its records.

```
Sub dbOpenDynamicX()

    Dim wrkMain As Workspace
    Dim conMain As Connection
    Dim qdfTemp As QueryDef
    Dim rstTemp As Recordset
    Dim strSQL As String
    Dim intLoop As Integer

    ' Create ODBC workspace and open connection to
    ' SQL Server database.
    Set wrkMain = CreateWorkspace("ODBCWorkspace", _
        "admin", "", dbUseODBC)
    Set conMain = wrkMain.OpenConnection("Publishers", _
        dbDriverNoPrompt, False, _
        "ODBC;DATABASE=pubs;UID=sa;PWD=;DSN=Publishers")
    ' Open dynamic-type recordset.
    Set rstTemp = _
```

```
              conMain.OpenRecordset("authors", _
              dbOpenDynamic)

     With rstTemp
        Debug.Print "Dynamic-type recordset: " & .Name

        ' Enumerate records.
        Do While Not .EOF
           Debug.Print "          " & !au_lname & ", " & _
               !au_fname
           .MoveNext
        Loop

        .Close
     End With

     conMain.Close
     wrkMain.Close


  End Sub
```

Dynaset-Type Recordset Object

A dynaset-type **Recordset** object is a dynamic set of records that can contain fields from one or more tables or queries in a database and may be updatable. In an ODBCDirect database, a dynaset-type **Recordset** object corresponds to an ODBC keyset cursor.

Remarks

A dynaset-type **Recordset** object is a type of **Recordset** object you can use to manipulate data in an underlying database table or tables.

It differs from a snapshot-type **Recordset** object because the dynaset stores only the primary key for each record, instead of actual data. As a result, a dynaset is updated with changes made to the source data, while the snapshot is not. Like the table-type **Recordset** object, a dynaset retrieves the full record only when it's needed for editing or display purposes.

To create a dynaset-type **Recordset** object, use the **OpenRecordset** method on an open database, against another dynaset- or snapshot-type **Recordset** object, on a **QueryDef** object, or on a **TableDef** object. (Opening **Recordset** objects on other **Recordset** objects or **TableDef** objects is available only in Microsoft Jet workspaces.)

If you request a dynaset-type **Recordset** object and the Microsoft Jet database engine can't gain read/write access to the records, the Microsoft Jet database engine may create a read-only, dynaset-type **Recordset** object.

As users update data, the base tables reflects these changes. Therefore, current data is available to your application when you reposition the current record. In a multiuser database, more than one user can open a dynaset-type **Recordset** object referring to the same records. Because a dynaset-type **Recordset** object is dynamic, when one user changes a record, other users have immediate access to the changed data. However, if one user adds a record, other users won't see the new record until they use the **Requery** method on the **Recordset** object. If a user deletes a record, other users are notified when they try to access it.

Records added to the database don't become a part of your dynaset-type **Recordset** object unless you add them by using the **AddNew** and **Update** methods. For example, if you use an action query containing an INSERT INTO SQL statement to add records, the new records aren't included in your dynaset-type **Recordset** object until you either use the **Requery** method or you rebuild your **Recordset** object using the **OpenRecordset** method.

To maintain data integrity, the Microsoft Jet database engine can lock dynaset- and table-type **Recordset** objects during **Edit** (pessimistic locking) or **Update** operations (optimistic locking) so that only one user can update a particular record at a time. When the Microsoft Jet database engine locks a record, it locks the entire 2K page containing the record.

You can also use optimistic and pessimistic locking with non-ODBC tables. When you access external tables using ODBC through a Microsoft Jet workspace, you should always use optimistic locking. The **LockEdits** property and the *lockedits* parameter of the **OpenRecordset** method determine the locking conditions during editing.

Not all fields can be updated in all dynaset-type **Recordset** objects. To determine whether you can update a particular field, check the **DataUpdatable** property setting of the **Field** object.

A dynaset-type **Recordset** object may not be updatable if:

- There isn't a unique index on the ODBC or Paradox table or tables.

- The data page is locked by another user.

- The record has changed since you last read it.

- The user doesn't have permission.

- One or more of the tables or fields are read-only.

- The database is opened as read-only.

- The **Recordset** object was either created from multiple tables without a JOIN statement or the query was too complex.

The order of a dynaset-type **Recordset** object or **Recordset** data doesn't necessarily follow any specific sequence. If you need to order your data, use an SQL statement with an ORDER BY clause to create the **Recordset** object. You can also use a WHERE clause to filter the records so that only certain records are added to the

Recordset object. Using SQL statements in this way to select a subset of records and order them usually results in faster access to your data than using the **Filter** and **Sort** properties.

Properties

AbsolutePosition Property, **BOF, EOF** Properties, **Bookmark** Property, **Bookmarkable** Property, **CacheSize** Property, **EditMode** Property, **Filter** Property, **LastModified** Property, **LockEdits** Property, **Name** Property, **NoMatch** Property, **PercentPosition** Property, **RecordCount** Property, **Restartable** Property, **Sort** Property, **Transactions** Property, **Type** Property, **Updatable** Property, **ValidationRule** Property, **ValidationText** Property, **BatchCollisionCount** Property, **BatchCollisions** Property, **BatchSize** Property, **CacheStart** Property, **Connection** Property, **RecordStatus** Property, **StillExecuting** Property, **UpdateOptions** Property

Methods

AddNew Method, **CancelUpdate** Method, **Clone** Method, **Close** Method, **CopyQueryDef** Method, **Delete** Method, **Edit** Method, **FillCache** Method, **FindFirst, FindLast, FindNext, FindPrevious** Method, **GetRows** Method, **Move** Method, **MoveFirst, MoveLast, MoveNext, MovePrevious** Methods, **OpenRecordset** Method, **Requery** Method, **Update** Method, **Cancel** Method, **NextRecordset** Method

See Also

Recordset Object, **Snapshot-Type Recordset** Object, **Table-Type Recordset** Object, **Forward-Only–Type Recordset** Object

Example

This example opens a dynaset-type **Recordset** and shows the extent to which its fields are updatable.

```
Sub dbOpenDynasetX()

    Dim dbsNorthwind As Database
    Dim rstInvoices As Recordset
    Dim fldLoop As Field

    Set dbsNorthwind = OpenDatabase("Northwind.mdb")
    Set rstInvoices = _
        dbsNorthwind.OpenRecordset("Invoices", dbOpenDynaset)

    With rstInvoices
        Debug.Print "Dynaset-type recordset: " & .Name

        If .Updatable Then
            Debug.Print "   Updatable fields:"

            ' Enumerate Fields collection of dynaset-type
            ' Recordset object, print only updatable
            ' fields.
            For Each fldLoop In .Fields
```

```
            If fldLoop.DataUpdatable Then
                Debug.Print "          " & fldLoop.Name
            End If
        Next fldLoop

    End If

    .Close
End With

dbsNorthwind.Close

End Sub
```

Edit Method

Copies the current record from an updatable **Recordset** object to the copy buffer for subsequent editing.

Applies To

Dynaset-Type Recordset Object, **Recordset** Object, **Snapshot-Type Recordset** Object, **Table-Type Recordset** Object, **Forward-Only–Type Recordset** Object, **Dynamic-Type Recordset** Object

Syntax

recordset.**Edit**

The *recordset* placeholder represents an open, updatable **Recordset** object that contains the record you want to edit.

Remarks

Once you use the **Edit** method, changes made to the current record's fields are copied to the copy buffer. After you make the desired changes to the record, use the **Update** method to save your changes.

The current record remains current after you use **Edit**.

Caution   If you edit a record and then perform any operation that moves to another record, but without first using **Update**, your changes are lost without warning. In addition, if you close *recordset* or end the procedure which declares the **Recordset** or the parent **Database** or **Connection** object, your edited record is discarded without warning.

Using **Edit** produces an error if:

- There is no current record.
- The **Connection**, **Database**, or **Recordset** object was opened as read-only.
- No fields in the record are updatable.

- The **Database** or **Recordset** was opened for exclusive use by another user (Microsoft Jet workspace).

- Another user has locked the page containing your record (Microsoft Jet workspace).

In a Microsoft Jet workspace, when the **Recordset** object's **LockEdits** property setting is **True** (pessimistically locked) in a multiuser environment, the record remains locked from the time **Edit** is used until the update is complete. If the **LockEdits** property setting is **False** (optimistically locked), the record is locked and compared with the pre-edited record just before it's updated in the database. If the record has changed since you used the **Edit** method, the **Update** operation fails with a run-time error if you use **OpenRecordset** without specifying **dbSeeChanges**. By default, Microsoft Jet-connected ODBC and installable ISAM databases always use optimistic locking.

In an ODBCDirect workspace, once you edit (and use **Update** to update) a record's primary key field, you can no longer edit fields in that record until you close the **Recordset**, and then retrieve the record again in a subsequent query.

Note   To add, edit, or delete a record, there must be a unique index on the record in the underlying data source. If not, a "Permission denied" error will occur on the **AddNew**, **Delete**, or **Edit** method call in a Microsoft Jet workspace, or an "Invalid argument" error will occur on the **Update** call in an ODBCDirect workspace.

See Also

AddNew Method, **Delete** Method, **LockEdits** Property

Example

This example uses the **Edit** method to replace the current data with the specified name. The **EditName** procedure is required for this procedure to run.

```
Sub EditX()

    Dim dbsNorthwind As Database
    Dim rstEmployees As Recordset
    Dim strOldFirst As String
    Dim strOldLast As String
    Dim strFirstName As String
    Dim strLastName As String

    Set dbsNorthwind = OpenDatabase("Northwind.mdb")
    Set rstEmployees = _
        dbsNorthwind.OpenRecordset("Employees", _
        dbOpenDynaset)

    ' Store original data.
    strOldFirst = rstEmployees!FirstName
    strOldLast = rstEmployees!LastName
```

```
    ' Get new data for record.
    strFirstName = Trim(InputBox( _
        "Enter first name:"))
    strLastName = Trim(InputBox( _
        "Enter last name:"))

    ' Proceed if the user entered something for both fields.
    If strFirstName <> "" and strLastName <> "" Then
        ' Update record with new data.
        EditName rstEmployees, strFirstName, strLastName

        With rstEmployees
            ' Show old and new data.
            Debug.Print "Old data: " & strOldFirst & _
                " " & strOldLast
            Debug.Print "New data: " & !FirstName & _
                " " & !LastName
            ' Restore original data because this is a
            ' demonstration.
            .Edit
            !FirstName = strOldFirst
            !LastName = strOldLast
            .Update
        End With

    Else
        Debug.Print _
            "You must input a string for first and last name!"
    End If

    rstEmployees.Close
    dbsNorthwind.Close

End Sub

Sub EditName(rstTemp As Recordset, _
    strFirst As String, strLast As String)

    ' Make changes to record and set the bookmark to keep
    ' the same record current.
    With rstTemp
        .Edit
        !FirstName = strFirst
        !LastName = strLast
        .Update
        .Bookmark = .LastModified
    End With

End Sub
```

Edit Method (Remote Data)

Enables changes to data values in the current row of an updatable **rdoResultset** object.

Applies To

rdoResultset Object

Syntax

object.**Edit**

The *object* placeholder represents an object expression that evaluates to an object in the **Applies To** list.

Remarks

Before you use the Edit method, the data columns of an **rdoResultset** are read-only. Executing the **Edit** method copies the current row from an updatable **rdoResultset** object to the copy buffer for subsequent editing. Changes made to the current row's columns are copied to the copy buffer. After you make the desired changes to the row, use the **Update** method to save your changes or the **CancelUpdate** method to discard them. The current row remains current after you use **Edit**.

Caution If you edit a row, and then perform any operation that repositions the current row pointer to another row without first using **Update**, your changes to the edited row are lost without warning. In addition, if you close *object*, or end the procedure which declares the result set or the parent **rdoConnection** object, your edited row might be discarded without warning.

You cannot use the **Edit** method if the **EditMode** property of the **rdoResultset** object indicates that an **Edit** or **AddNew** operation is in progress.

When the **rdoResultset** object's **LockEdits** property setting is **True** (pessimistically locked), all rows in the **rdoResultset** object's rowset are locked as soon as the cursor is opened and remain locked until the cursor is closed. The number of rows in the rowset is determined by the **RowsetSize** property. Since many remote data sources use page locking schemes, pessimistic locking also locks all data pages of the table(s) containing a row fetched by the **rdoResultset**.

If the **LockEdits** property setting is **False** (optimistically locked), the individual row or the data page containing the row is locked and the new row is compared with the pre-edited row just before it's updated in the database. If the row has changed since you last used the **Edit** method, the **Update** operation fails with a trappable error.

Note Not all data sources use page locking schemes to manage data concurrency. In some cases, data is locked on a row-by-row basis, therefore locks only affect the specific rowset being edited.

Using **Edit** produces an error under any of the following conditions:

- There is no current row.

- The connection or **rdoResultset** is read-only.

- No columns in the row are updatable.

- The **EditMode** property indicates that an **AddNew** or **Edit** is already in progress.

- Another user has locked the row or data page containing your row and the **LockEdits** property is **True**.

See Also

AddNew Method (Remote Data), **BeginTrans**, **CommitTrans**, **RollbackTrans** Methods, **Delete** Method (Remote Data), **Update** Method (Remote Data), **rdoResultset** Object, **EditMode** Property (Remote Data), **LockEdits** Property (Remote Data)

EditActive Property

Sets or returns the editing status of the current cell. Not available at design time.

Applies To

DBGrid Control

Syntax

object.**EditActive** [= *value*]

The **EditActive** property syntax has these parts:

Part	Description
object	An object expression that evaluates to an object in the **Applies To** list.
value	A Boolean expression that determines the editing status, as described in Settings.

Settings

The settings for *value* are:

Setting	Description
True	The current cell is currently being edited by the user.
False	No editing is in progress.

Remarks

If the grid is not already in edit mode, setting **EditActive** to **True** will initiate editing on the current cell. The caret will be positioned at the end of the cell and the **ColEdit** event will be triggered.

If the grid is already in edit mode, setting **EditActive** to **False** will exit edit mode. If the cell has been modified, this will trigger the following events: **BeforeColUpdate**, **AfterColUpdate**, and **AfterColEdit**.

Note To cancel editing completely, set the **CurrentCellModified** property to **False**, then set **EditActive** to **False**.

See Also

AfterColEdit Event, **ColEdit** Event, **CurrentCellModified** Property, **AfterColUpdate** Event, **BeforeColUpdate** Event

---

EditAtDesignTime Property

Returns or sets a value determining if a control can become active during the developer design time. The **EditAtDesignTime** property is read/write at the control's authoring time, and not available at the control's run time.

Applies To

UserControl Object

Settings

The settings for **EditAtDesignTime** are:

Setting	Description
True	Allows the control to become active at the developer design time. An **Edit** verb will appear on the control's context menu. When the developer who uses the control chooses **Edit**, the control will become active and behave as it does at end user run time.
False	The control cannot become active at developer design time. This is the default value.

Remarks

The control will only remain active while it is selected. When the developer selects another control, this control will no longer be active, even if the developer clicks back on this control. The developer must select **Edit** again from the context menu to make the control active.

Note When the control is activated in this fashion, the events of the **UserControl** object will occur, so that the control can operate normally, but the control will be unable to raise any events. The **RaiseEvent** method will simply be ignored; it will not cause an error.

EditMode Property

Returns a value that indicates the state of editing for the current record.

Applies To

Dynaset-Type Recordset Object, **Recordset** Object, **Snapshot-Type Recordset** Object, **Table-Type Recordset** Object, **Forward-Only–Type Recordset** Object, **Dynamic-Type Recordset** Object

Return Values

The return value is a **Long** that indicates the state of editing, as listed in the following table.

Constant	Description
dbEditNone	No editing operation is in progress.
DbEditInProgress	The **Edit** method has been invoked, and the current record is in the copy buffer.
dbEditAdd	The **AddNew** method has been invoked, and the current record in the copy buffer is a new record that hasn't been saved in the database.

Remarks

The **EditMode** property is useful when an editing process is interrupted, for example, by an error during validation. You can use the value of the **EditMode** property to determine whether you should use the **Update** or **CancelUpdate** method.

You can also check to see if the **LockEdits** property setting is **True** and the **EditMode** property setting is **dbEditInProgress** to determine whether the current page is locked.

See Also

AddNew Method, **CancelUpdate** Method, **LockEdits** Property

Example

This example shows the value of the **EditMode** property under various conditions. The **EditModeOutput** function is required for this procedure to run.

```
Sub EditModeX()

   Dim dbsNorthwind As Database
   Dim rstEmployees As Recordset

   Set dbsNorthwind = OpenDatabase("Northwind.mdb")
   Set rstEmployees = _
      dbsNorthwind.OpenRecordset("Employees", _
      dbOpenDynaset)

   ' Show the EditMode property under different editing
   ' states.
   With rstEmployees
      EditModeOutput "Before any Edit or AddNew:", .EditMode
      .Edit
      EditModeOutput "After Edit:", .EditMode
      .Update
      EditModeOutput "After Update:", .EditMode
      .AddNew
      EditModeOutput "After AddNew:", .EditMode
      .CancelUpdate
      EditModeOutput "After CancelUpdate:", .EditMode
      .Close
   End With

   dbsNorthwind.Close

End Sub
```

```
Function EditModeOutput(strTemp As String, _
   intEditMode As Integer)

   ' Print report based on the value of the EditMode
   ' property.
   Debug.Print strTemp
   Debug.Print "    EditMode = ";

   Select Case intEditMode
      Case dbEditNone
         Debug.Print "dbEditNone"
      Case dbEditInProgress
         Debug.Print "dbEditInProgress"
      Case dbEditAdd
         Debug.Print "dbEditAdd"
   End Select

End Function
```

EditMode Property (Remote Data)

Returns a value that indicates the state of editing for the current row.

Applies To

rdoResultset Object, **RemoteData** Control

Syntax

object.**EditMode**

The *object* placeholder represents an object expression that evaluates to an object in the **Applies To** list.

Return Values

The **EditMode** property returns an Integer or constant as described in the following table:

Constant	Value	Description
rdEditNone	0	No editing operation is in progress.
rdEditInProgress	1	The **Edit** method has been invoked, and the current row is in the copy buffer.
rdEditAdd	2	The **AddNew** method has been invoked, and the current row in the copy buffer is a new row that hasn't been saved in the database.

Remarks

The **EditMode** property is most useful when you want to depart from the default functionality of a **RemoteData** control. You can check the value of the **EditMode** property and the value of the *action* parameter in the Validate event procedure to determine whether to invoke the **UpdateRow** method.

You can also check to see if the **LockEdits** property of the **rdoResultset** is **True** and the **EditMode** property setting is **rdEditInProgress** to determine whether the current data page is locked.

See Also

rdoResultset Object, **RemoteData** Control

EditProperty Event

Occurs when a property page is opened because of the developer pressing the ellipsis button to display a particular property for editing.

Applies To

PropertyPage Object

Syntax

Sub *object*_**EditProperty**(*PropertyName* **As String**)

The EditProperty event syntax has these parts:

Part	Description
object	An object expression that evaluates to an object in the **Applies To** list.
PropertyName	A string that identifies the property that is to be displayed and edited by the property page.

Remarks

This event happens when a property is assigned a property page via the **Attributes** dialog box. Assigning a property page through the **Attributes** dialog box means that the property is displayed in the property window with an ellipsis (…) next to it, and the developer can press the ellipsis button and the property page is automatically opened; the **EditProperty** event is then raised, so that the property page author can put the cursor on the correct field.

Empty

The **Empty** keyword is used as a **Variant** subtype. It indicates an uninitialized variable value.

See Also

Variant Data Type, **VarType** Function

Enabled Property

Returns or sets a value that determines whether a form or control can respond to user-generated events.

Applies To

UserControl Object, **CheckBox** Control, **ComboBox** Control, **CommandButton** Control, **DirListBox** Control, **DriveListBox** Control, **FileListBox** Control, **Form** Object, **Forms** Collection, **Frame** Control, **HScrollBar**, **VScrollBar** Controls, **Image** Control, **Label** Control, **ListBox** Control, **MDIForm** Object, **Menu** Control, **OptionButton** Control, **PictureBox** Control, **TextBox** Control, **Timer** Control, **OLE Container** Control, **Data** Control

Syntax

object.**Enabled** [= *boolean*]

The **Enabled** property syntax has these parts:

Part	Description
object	An object expression that evaluates to an object in the **Applies To** list. If *object* is omitted, the form associated with the active form module is assumed to be *object*.
boolean	A Boolean expression that specifies whether *object* can respond to user-generated events.

Settings

The settings for *boolean* are:

Setting	Description
True	(Default) Allows *object* to respond to events.
False	Prevents *object* from responding to events.

Remarks

The **Enabled** property allows forms and controls to be enabled or disabled at run time. For example, you can disable objects that don't apply to the current state of the application. You can also disable a control used purely for display purposes, such as a text box that provides read-only information.

Disabling a **Timer** control by setting **Enabled** to **False** cancels the countdown set up by the control's **Interval** property.

For a **Menu** control, **Enabled** is normally read/write at run time. But **Enabled** is read-only for menu items that are exposed or supplied by Visual Basic to add-ins, such as the Add-In Manager command on the Add-Ins menu.

See Also

Interval Property, **Visible** Property

Example

This example enables a **CommandButton** control whenever a **TextBox** control contains text. To try this example, paste the code into the Declarations section of a form with **CommandButton** and **TextBox** controls, and then press F5 and enter something into the text box.

```
Private Sub Form_Load ()
    Text1.Text = ""' Clear the text box.
    Command1.Caption = "Save"   ' Put caption on button.
End Sub

Private Sub Text1_Change ()
    If Text1.Text = "" Then ' See if text box is empty.
        Command1.Enabled = False      ' Disable button.
    Else
        Command1.Enabled = True ' Enable button.
    End If
End Sub
```

End Statement

Ends a procedure or block.

Syntax

End
End Function
End If
End Property
End Select
End Sub
End Type
End With

The **End** statement syntax has these forms:

Statement	Description
End	Terminates execution immediately. Never required by itself but may be placed anywhere in a procedure to end code execution, close files opened with the **Open** statement and to clear variables.
End Function	Required to end a **Function** statement.
End If	Required to end a block **If...Then...Else** statement.
End Property	Required to end a **Property Let**, **Property Get**, or **Property Set** procedure.
End Select	Required to end a **Select Case** statement.
End Sub	Required to end a **Sub** statement.
End Type	Required to end a user-defined type definition (**Type** statement).
End With	Required to end a **With** statement.

Remarks

When executed, the **End** statement resets all module-level variables and all static local variables in all modules. To preserve the value of these variables, use the **Stop** statement instead. You can then resume execution while preserving the value of those variables.

Note The **End** statement stops code execution abruptly, without invoking the **Unload**, **QueryUnload**, or Terminate event, or any other Visual Basic code. Code you have placed in the **Unload**, **QueryUnload**, and Terminate events of forms and class modules is not executed. Objects created from class modules are destroyed, files opened using the **Open** statement are closed, and memory used by your program is freed. Object references held by other programs are invalidated.

The **End** statement provides a way to force your program to halt. For normal termination of a Visual Basic program, you should unload all forms. Your program closes as soon as there are no other programs holding references to objects created from your public class modules and no code executing.

See Also

Exit Statement, **If...Then...Else** Statement, **Select Case** Statement, **Stop** Statement, **With** Statement, **Function** Statement, **Property Get** Statement, **Property Let** Statement, **Property Set** Statement, **Sub** Statement, **Type** Statementt

Example

This example uses the **End** Statement to end code execution if the user enters an invalid password.

```
Sub Form_Load
    Dim Password, Pword
    PassWord = "Swordfish"
    Pword = InputBox("Type in your password")
    If Pword <> PassWord Then
        MsgBox "Sorry, incorrect password"
        End
    End If
End Sub
```

EndDoc Method

Terminates a print operation sent to the **Printer** object, releasing the document to the print device or spooler.

Applies To

Printer Object, **Printers** Collection

Syntax

object.**EndDoc**

The *object* placeholder represents an object expression that evaluates to an object in the **Applies To** list.

Remarks

If **EndDoc** is invoked immediately after the **NewPage** method, no additional blank page is printed.

See Also

KillDoc Method, **NewPage** Method

Example

This example uses the **EndDoc** method to end a document after printing two pages, each with a centered line of text indicating the page number. To try this example, paste the code into the Declarations section of a form, and then press F5 and click the form.

```
Private Sub Form_Click ()
    Dim HWidth, HHeight, I, Msg        ' Declare variables.
    On Error GoTo ErrorHandler ' Set up error handler.
    Msg = "This is printed on page"
    For I = 1 To 2 ' Set up two iterations.
        HWidth = Printer.TextWidth(Msg) / 2     ' Get half width.
        HHeight = Printer.TextHeight(Msg) /2    ' Get half height.
        Printer.CurrentX = Printer.ScaleWidth / 2 - HWidth
        Printer.CurrentY = Printer.ScaleHeight / 2 - HHeight
        Printer.Print Msg & Printer.Page & "." ' Print.

Printer.NewPage' Send new page.
    Next I
    Printer.EndDoc ' Printing is finished.
    Msg = "Two pages, each with a single, centered line of text, "
    Msg = Msg & "have been sent to your printer."
    MsgBox Msg   ' Display message.
    Exit Sub
ErrorHandler:
    MsgBox "There was a problem printing to your printer."
    Exit Sub
End Sub
```

EnterFocus Event

Occurs when focus enters the object. The object itself could be receiving focus, or a constituent control could be receiving focus.

Applies To

UserControl Object, **UserDocument** Object

Syntax

Sub *object*_**EnterFocus**()

The **EnterFocus** event syntax has these parts:

Part	Description
object	An object expression that evaluates to an object in the **Applies To** list.

Remarks

This event is useful if *object* needs to know that the focus is now inside of it.

The **EnterFocus** event is raised before any **GotFocus** event; the **GotFocus** event will only be raised in *object* or constituent control of *object* that actually got the focus.

See Also

ExitFocus Event, **GotFocus** Event (UserControl Object and UserDocument Object)

Enum Statement

Declares a type for an enumeration.

Syntax

[**Public** | **Private**] **Enum** *name*
    membername [= *constantexpression*]
    membername [= *constantexpression*]
    . . .
End Enum

The **Enum** statement has these parts:

Part	Description
Public	Optional. Specifies that the **Enum** type is visible throughout the project. **Enum** types are **Public** by default.
Private	Optional. Specifies that the **Enum** type is visible only within the module in which it appears.
name	Required. The name of the **Enum** type. The *name* must be a valid Visual Basic identifier and is specified as the type when declaring variables or parameters of the **Enum** type.
membername	Required. A valid Visual Basic identifier specifying the name by which a constituent element of the **Enum** type will be known.
constantexpression	Optional. Value of the element (evaluates to a **Long**). Can be another **Enum** type. If no *constantexpression* is specified, the value assigned is either zero (if it is the first *membername*), or 1 greater than the value of the immediately preceding *membername*.

Remarks

Enumeration variables are variables declared with an **Enum** type. Both variables and parameters can be declared with an **Enum** type. The elements of the **Enum** type are initialized to constant values within the **Enum** statement. The assigned values can't be modified at run time and can include both positive and negative numbers. For example:

```
Enum SecurityLevel
    IllegalEntry = -1
    SecurityLevel1 = 0
    SecurityLevel2 = 1
End Enum
```

An **Enum** statement can appear only at module level. Once the **Enum** type is defined, it can be used to declare variables, parameters, or procedures returning its type. You can't qualify an **Enum** type name with a module name. **Public Enum** types in a class module are not members of the class; however, they are written to the type library. **Enum** types defined in standard modules aren't written to type libraries. **Public Enum** types of the same name can't be defined in both standard modules and class modules, since they share the same name space. When two **Enum** types in different type libraries have the same name, but different elements, a reference to a variable of the type depends on which type library has higher priority in the **References**.

You can't use an **Enum** type as the target in a **With** block.

See Also

Type Statement

Example

The following example shows the **Enum** statement used to define a collection of named constants. In this case, the constants are colors you might choose to design data entry forms for a database.

```
Public Enum InterfaceColors
    icMistyRose = &HE1E4FF&
    icSlateGray = &H908070&
    icDodgerBlue = &HFF901E&
    icDeepSkyBlue = &HFFBF00&
    icSpringGreen = &H7FFF00&
    icForestGreen = &H228B22&
    icGoldenrod = &H20A5DA&
    icFirebrick = &H2222B2&
End Enum
```

Environ Function

Returns the **String** associated with an operating system environment variable.

Syntax

Environ({*envstring* | *number*})

The **Environ** function syntax has these named arguments:

Part	Description
envstring	Optional. String expression containing the name of an environment variable.
number	Optional. Numeric expression corresponding to the numeric order of the environment string in the environment-string table. The ***number*** argument can be any numeric expression, but is rounded to a whole number before it is evaluated.

Remarks

If *envstring* can't be found in the environment-string table, a zero-length string ("") is returned. Otherwise, **Environ** returns the text assigned to the specified *envstring*; that is, the text following the equal sign (=) in the environment-string table for that environment variable.

If you specify *number*, the string occupying that numeric position in the environment-string table is returned. In this case, **Environ** returns all of the text, including *envstring*. If there is no environment string in the specified position, **Environ** returns a zero-length string.

Example

This example uses the **Environ** function to supply the entry number and length of the PATH statement from the environment-string table.

```
Dim EnvString, Indx, Msg, PathLen       ' Declare variables.
Indx = 1                                ' Initialize index to 1.
Do
    EnvString = Environ(Indx)           ' Get environment variable.
    If Left(EnvString, 5) = "PATH=" Then    ' Check PAT
    If Left(EnvString, 5) = "PATH=" Then    ' Check PATH entry.
        PathLen = Len(Environ("PATH"))      ' Get length.
        Msg = "PATH entry = " & Indx & " and length = " & PathLen
        Exit Do
    Else
        Indx = Indx + 1                 ' Not PATH entry,
    End If                              ' so increment.
Loop Until EnvString = ""
If PathLen > 0 Then
    MsgBox Msg                          ' Display message.
Else
    MsgBox "No PATH environment variable exists."
End If
```

Environment Property (Remote Data)

Returns a reference to a **RemoteData** control's underlying **rdoEnvironment** object.

Applies To

RemoteData Control

Syntax

object.**Environment**
Set *environment* = *object*.**Environment**

The **Environment** property syntax has these parts:

Part	Description
environment	An object expression that evaluates to a valid **rdoEnvironment** object.
object	An object expression that evaluates to an object in the **Applies To** list.

Remarks

When a **RemoteData** control is initialized, **RemoteData** uses the default **rdoEnvironments**(0)—the **Environment** property is initially set to this object.

If you assign another **rdoResultset** to the **RemoteData** control's **Resultset** property, the **Environment** property is set to the **rdoEnvironment** object used to create the result set.

rdoEnvironment objects have properties and methods you can use to manage data. For example, you can use any method of an **rdoEnvironment** object, such as **OpenConnection**, **BeginTrans**, **CommitTrans**, or **RollbackTrans**, with the **Environment** property.

See Also

BeginTrans, **CommitTrans**, **RollbackTrans** Methods (Remote Data), **OpenConnection** Method (Remote Data), **rdoConnection** Object, **rdoEnvironment** Object, **rdoResultset** Object, **RemoteData** Control, **Connect** Property (Remote Data), **hEnv** Property (Remote Data)

EOF Function

Returns an **Integer** containing the **Boolean** value **True** when the end of a file opened for **Random** or sequential **Input** has been reached.

Syntax

EOF(*filenumber*)

The required *filenumber* argument is an **Integer** containing any valid file number.

Remarks

Use **EOF** to avoid the error generated by attempting to get input past the end of a file.

The **EOF** function returns **False** until the end of the file has been reached. With files opened for **Random** or **Binary** access, **EOF** returns **False** until the last executed **Get** statement is unable to read an entire record.

With files opened for **Binary** access, an attempt to read through the file using the **Input** function until **EOF** returns **True** generates an error. Use the **LOF** and **Loc** functions instead of **EOF** when reading binary files with **Input**, or use **Get** when using the **EOF** function. With files opened for **Output**, **EOF** always returns **True**.

See Also

Get Statement, **Loc** Function, **LOF** Function, **Open** Statement

Example

This example uses the **EOF** function to detect the end of a file. This example assumes that MYFILE is a text file with a few lines of text.

```
Dim InputData
Open "MYFILE" For Input As #1  ' Open file for input.
Do While Not EOF(1)            ' Check for end of file.
    Line Input #1, InputData   ' Read line of data.
    Debug.Print InputData      ' Print to Debug window.
Loop
Close #1                       ' Close file.
```

Eqv Operator

Used to perform a logical equivalence on two expressions.

Syntax

result = *expression1* **Eqv** *expression2*

The **Eqv** operator syntax has these parts:

Part	Description
result	Required; any numeric variable.
expression1	Required; any expression.
expression2	Required; any expression.

Remarks

If either expression is **Null**, *result* is also **Null**. When neither expression is **Null**, *result* is determined according to the following table:

If *expression1* is	And *expression2* is	The *result* is
True	True	True
True	False	False
False	True	False
False	False	True

The **Eqv** operator performs a bitwise comparison of identically positioned bits in two numeric expressions and sets the corresponding bit in *result* according to the following table:

If bit in *expression1* is	And bit in *expression2* is	The *result* is
0	0	1
0	1	0
1	0	0
1	1	1

See Also

Operator Summary, **Operator** Precedence, **Logical** Operators

Example

This example uses the **Eqv** operator to perform logical equivalence on two expressions.

```
Dim A, B, C, D, MyCheck
A = 10: B = 8: C = 6: D = Null        ' Initialize variables.
MyCheck = A > B Eqv B > C  ' Returns True.
MyCheck = B > A Eqv B > C  ' Returns False.
MyCheck = A > B Eqv B > D  ' Returns Null.
MyCheck = A Eqv B ' Returns -3 (bitwise comparison).
```

Erase Statement

Reinitializes the elements of fixed-size arrays and releases dynamic-array storage space.

Syntax

Erase *arraylist*

The required *arraylist* argument is one or more comma-delimited array variables to be erased.

Remarks

Erase behaves differently depending on whether an array is fixed-size (ordinary) or dynamic. **Erase** recovers no memory for fixed-size arrays. **Erase** sets the elements of a fixed array as follows:

Type of Array	Effect of Erase on Fixed-Array Elements
Fixed numeric array	Sets each element to zero.
Fixed string array (variable length)	Sets each element to a zero-length string ("").
Fixed string array (fixed length)	Sets each element to zero.
Fixed **Variant** array	Sets each element to **Empty**.
Array of user-defined types	Sets each element as if it were a separate variable.
Array of objects	Sets each element to the special value **Nothing**.

Erase frees the memory used by dynamic arrays. Before your program can refer to the dynamic array again, it must redeclare the array variable's dimensions using a **ReDim** statement.

See Also

Array Function, **Dim** Statement, **Private** Statement, **Public** Statement, **ReDim** Statement, **Static** Statement, **Nothing**

Example

This example uses the **Erase** statement to reinitialize the elements of fixed-size arrays and deallocate dynamic-array storage space.

```
' Declare array variables.
Dim NumArray(10) As Integer          ' Integer array.
Dim StrVarArray(10) As String        ' Variable-string array.
Dim StrFixArray(10) As String * 10   ' Fixed-string array.
Dim VarArray(10) As Variant          ' Variant array.
Dim DynamicArray() As Integer        ' Dynamic array.
ReDim DynamicArray(10)               ' Allocate storage space.
Erase NumArray                       ' Each element set to 0.
Erase StrVarArray                    ' Each element set to zero-length
                                     ' string ("").
Erase StrFixArray                    ' Each element set to 0.
Erase VarArray                       ' Each element set to Empty.
Erase DynamicArray                   ' Free memory used by array.
```

Err Object

Contains information about run-time errors.

Remarks

The properties of the **Err** object are set by the generator of an error—Visual Basic, an object, or the Visual Basic programmer.

The default property of the **Err** object is **Number**. Because the default property can be represented by the object name **Err**, earlier code written using the **Err** function or **Err** statement doesn't have to be modified.

When a run-time error occurs, the properties of the **Err** object are filled with information that uniquely identifies the error and information that can be used to handle it. To generate a run-time error in your code, use the **Raise** method.

The **Err** object's properties are reset to zero or zero-length strings ("") after any form of the **Resume** or **On Error** statement and after an **Exit Sub**, **Exit Function**, or **Exit Property** statement within an error-handling routine. The **Clear** method can be used to explicitly reset **Err**.

Use the **Raise** method, rather than the **Error** statement, to generate run-time errors for a class module. Using the **Raise** method in other code depends on the richness of the information you want to return. In code that uses **Error** statements instead of the **Raise** method to generate errors, the properties of the **Err** object are assigned the following default values when **Error** is executed:

Property	Value
Number	Value specified as argument to **Error** statement. Can be any valid error number.
Source	Name of the current Visual Basic project.
Description	A string corresponding to the return of the **Error** function for the specified **Number**, if this string exists. If the string doesn't exist, **Description** contains "Application-defined or object-defined error".
HelpFile	The fully qualified drive, path, and file name of the Visual Basic Help file.
HelpContext	The Visual Basic Help file context ID for the error corresponding to the **Number** property.
LastDLLError	On 32-bit Microsoft Windows operating systems only, contains the system error code for the last call to a dynamic-link library (DLL). The **LastDLLError** property is read-only.

You don't have to change existing code that uses the **Err** object and the **Error** statement. However, using both the **Err** object and the **Error** statement can result in unintended consequences. For example, even if you fill in properties for the **Err** object, they are reset to the default values indicated in the preceding table as soon as the **Error** statement is executed. Although you can still use the **Error** statement to generate Visual Basic run-time errors, it is retained principally for compatibility with existing code. Use the **Err** object, the **Raise** method, and the **Clear** method for system errors and in new code, especially for class modules.

The **Err** object is an intrinsic object with global scope. There is no need to create an instance of it in your code.

Properties
Description Property, **HelpContext** Property, **HelpFile** Property, **LastDLLError** Property, **Number** Property, **Source** Property, **HelpContextID** Property

Methods
Clear Method, **Raise** Method

See Also
Error Function, **Error** Statement, **On Error** Statement, **Resume** Statement

Example
This example uses the properties of the **Err** object in constructing an error-message dialog box. Note that if you use the **Clear** method first, when you generate a Visual Basic error with the **Raise** method, Visual Basic's default values become the properties of the **Err** object.

```
Dim Msg
                      ' If an error occurs, construct an error message
On Error Resume Next ' Defer error handling.
Err.Clear
Err.Raise 6          ' Generate an "Overflow" error.
                     ' Check for error, then show message.
```

```
If Err.Number <> 0 Then
   Msg = "Error # " & Str(Err.Number) & " was generated by " _
         & Err.Source & Chr(13) & Err.Description
   MsgBox Msg, , "Error", Err.Helpfile, Err.HelpContext
End If
```

Error Event

Occurs only as the result of a data access error that takes place when no Visual Basic code is being executed.

Applies To

Data Control, **DBGrid** Control

Syntax

Private Sub *object*_**Error** ([*index* **As Integer**,] *dataerr* **As Integer**, *response* **As Integer**)

The **Error** event syntax has these parts:

Part	Description
object	An object expression that evaluates to an object in the **Applies To** list.
index	Identifies the control if it's in a control array.
dataerr	The error number.
response	A number corresponding to the response you want to take, as described in Settings.

Settings

The settings for *response* are:

Constant	Value	Description
vbDataErrContinue	0	Continue
vbDataErrDisplay	1	(Default) Display the error message

Remarks

These constants are listed in the Visual Basic (VB) object library in the **Object Browser**.

You usually provide error-handling functionality for run-time errors in your code. However, run-time errors can occur when none of your code is running, as when:

- A user clicks a **Data** control button.
- The **Data** control automatically opens a database and loads a **Recordset** object after the **Form_Load** event.
- A custom control performs an operation such as the **MoveNext** method, the **AddNew** method, or the **Delete** method.

If an error results from one of these actions, the **Error** event occurs.

If you don't code an event procedure for the **Error** event, Visual Basic displays the message associated with the error.

Errors that occur *before* the **Form_Load** event, are not trappable and do not trigger the Error event. For example, if at design time you set the properties of the **Data** control to point to an unknown database table an untrappable error results.

Example

This example displays an Open dialog box if the database specified in the **Data** control's **DatabaseName** property isn't found *after* the **Form_Load** event is complete.

```
Private Sub Data1_Error (DataError As Integer, Response As Integer)
   Select Case DataError
      ' If database file not found.
      Case 3024
         ' Display an Open dialog box.
         CommonDialog1.ShowOpen
      ...
   End Select
End Sub
```

Error Event (DBGrid Control)

Occurs only as the result of a data access error that takes place when no Visual Basic code is being executed.

Applies To

DBGrid Control

Syntax

Private Sub *object*_**Error**([*index* **As Integer**,] **ByVal** *dataerror* **As Integer**, *response* **As Integer**)

The **Error** event syntax has these parts:

Part	Description
object	An object expression that evaluates to an object in the **Applies To** list.
Index	An integer that identifies a control if it is in a control array.
dataerror	An integer that identifies the error that occurred.
response	An integer that may be set to 0 to suppress error message display, as described in Settings.

Settings

The settings for *response* are:

Setting	Description
0	No error message will be displayed.
1	(Default) The message associated with the error will be displayed.

Remarks

Even if your application handles run time errors in code, errors can still occur when none of your code is executing, as when the user clicks a **Data** control button or changes the current record by interacting with a bound control. If a data access error results from such an action, the **Error** event is fired.

Not adding code to this event is equivalent to setting the *response* argument to 0.

Note   Use the **ErrorText** property to retrieve the error string that will be displayed.

See Also

ErrorText Property

Error Event (Remote Data)

Occurs only as the result of a data access error that takes place when no Visual Basic code is being executed.

Applies To

RemoteData Control

Syntax

Private Sub *object* **_Error(**[*index* **As Integer,**]*Number* **As Long,** *Description* **As String,**
  ↪ *Scode* **As Long,** *Source* **As String,** *HelpFile* **As String,** *HelpContext* **As Long,**
  ↪ *CancelDisplay* **As Boolean)**

The Error event syntax has these parts:

Part	Description
object	An object expression that evaluates to an object in the **Applies To** list.
index	Identifies the control if it's in a control array.
Number	The native error number.
Description	Describes the error.
Scode	ODBC error return code.
Source	Source of the error.
HelpFile	The path to a Help file containing more information on the error.
HelpContext	The Help file context number.
CancelDisplay	A number corresponding to the action you want to take, as described in Settings.

Settings

The settings for *CancelDisplay* are:

Constant	Value	Description
rdDataErrContinue	0	Continue.
rdDataErrDisplay	1	(Default) Display the error message.

Remarks

Generally, the Error event arguments correspond to the properties of the **rdoError** object.

You usually provide error-handling functionality for run-time errors in your code. However, run-time errors can occur when none of your code is running, as when:

- A user clicks a **RemoteData control** button.
- The **RemoteData** control attempts to open an **rdoConnection** and creates **rdoResultset** objects after the **Form_Load** event.
- A custom control performs an operation, such as the **MoveNext** method, the **AddNew** method, or the **Delete** method.

If an error results from one of these actions, the Error event occurs.

If you don't code an event procedure for the Error event, Visual Basic displays the message associated with the error.

See Also

AddNew Method (Remote Data), **Delete** Method (Remote Data), **MoveFirst**, **MoveLast**, **MoveNext**, **MovePrevious** Methods, **rdoError** Object, **rdoResultset** Object, **RemoteData** Control

Error Function

Returns the error message that corresponds to a given error number.

Syntax

Error[(*errornumber*)]

The optional *errornumber* argument can be any valid error number. If *errornumber* is a valid error number, but is not defined, **Error** returns the string "Application-defined or object-defined error." If *errornumber* is not valid, an error occurs. If *errornumber* is omitted, the message corresponding to the most recent run-time error is returned. If no run-time error has occurred, or *errornumber* is 0, **Error** returns a zero-length string ("").

Remarks

Examine the property settings of the **Err** object to identify the most recent run-time error. The return value of the **Error** function corresponds to the **Description** property of the **Err** object.

See Also

Err Object, **Trappable Errors**

Example

This example uses the **Error** function to print error messages that correspond to the specified error numbers.

```
Dim ErrorNumber
For ErrorNumber = 61 To 64          ' Loop through values 61 - 64.
    Debug.Print Error(ErrorNumber)  ' Print error to Debug window.
Next ErrorNumber
```

Error Object

An **Error** object contains details about data access errors, each of which pertains to a single operation involving DAO.

Remarks

Any operation involving DAO can generate one or more errors. For example, a call to an ODBC server might result in an error from the database server, an error from ODBC, and a DAO error. As each such error occurs, an **Error** object is placed in the **Errors** collection of the **DBEngine** object. A single event can therefore result in several **Error** objects appearing in the **Errors** collection.

When a subsequent DAO operation generates an error, the **Errors** collection is cleared, and one or more new **Error** objects are placed in the **Errors** collection. DAO operations that don't generate an error have no effect on the **Errors** collection.

The set of **Error** objects in the **Errors** collection describes one error. The first **Error** object is the lowest level error (the originating error), the second the next higher level error, and so forth. For example, if an ODBC error occurs while trying to open a **Recordset** object, the first **Error** object—**Errors**(0)—contains the lowest level ODBC error; subsequent errors contain the ODBC errors returned by the various layers of ODBC. In this case, the ODBC driver manager, and possibly the driver itself, return separate **Error** objects. The last **Error** object—**Errors.Count**-1—contains the DAO error indicating that the object couldn't be opened.

Enumerating the specific errors in the **Errors** collection enables your error-handling routines to more precisely determine the cause and origin of an error, and take appropriate steps to recover. On both Microsoft Jet and ODBCDirect workspaces, you can read the **Error** object's properties to obtain specific details about each error, including:

- The **Description** property, which contains the text of the error alert that will be displayed on the screen if the error is not trapped.

- The **Number** property, which contains the **Long** integer value of the error constant.

- The **Source** property, which identifies the object that raised the error. This is particularly useful when you have several **Error** objects in the **Errors** collection following a request to an ODBC data source.

- The **HelpFile** and **HelpContext** properties, which indicate the appropriate Microsoft Windows Help file and Help topic, respectively, (if any exist) for the error.

Note When programming in Microsoft Visual Basic for Applications (VBA), if you use the **New** keyword to create an object that subsequently causes an error before that object has been appended to a collection, the **DBEngine** object's **Errors** collection won't contain an entry for that object's error, because the new object is not associated with the **DBEngine** object. However, the error information is available in the VBA **Err** object.

Your VBA error-handling code should examine the **Errors** collection whenever you anticipate a data access error. If you are writing a centralized error handler, test the VBA **Err** object to determine if the error information in the **Errors** collection is valid. If the **Number** property of the last element of the **Errors** collection (DBEngine.Errors.Count - 1) and the value of the **Err** object match, you can then use a series of **Select Case** statements to identify the particular DAO error or errors that occurred. If they do not match, use the **Refresh** method on the **Errors** collection.

Properties

Description Property, **HelpContext, HelpFile** Properties, **Number** Property, **Source** Property

Example

This example forces an error, traps it, and displays the **Description, Number, Source, HelpContext**, and **HelpFile** properties of the resulting **Error** object.

```
Sub DescriptionX()

    Dim dbsTest As Database

    On Error GoTo ErrorHandler

    ' Intentionally trigger an error.
    Set dbsTest = OpenDatabase("NoDatabase")

    Exit Sub

ErrorHandler:
    Dim strError As String
    Dim errLoop As Error

    ' Enumerate Errors collection and display properties of
    ' each Error object.
```

```
        For Each errLoop In Errors
            With errLoop
                strError = _
                    "Error #" & .Number & vbCr
                strError = strError & _
                    "     " & .Description & vbCr
                strError = strError & _
                    "     (Source: " & .Source & ")" & vbCr
                strError = strError & _
                    "Press F1 to see topic " & .HelpContext & vbCr
                strError = strError & _
                    "     in the file " & .HelpFile & "."
            End With
            MsgBox strError
        Next

        Resume Next

    End Sub
```

Error Statement

Simulates the occurrence of an error.

Syntax

Error *errornumber*

The required *errornumber* can be any valid error number.

Remarks

The **Error** statement is supported for backward compatibility. In new code, especially when creating objects, use the **Err** object's **Raise** method to generate run-time errors.

If *errornumber* is defined, the **Error** statement calls the error handler after the properties of **Err** object are assigned the following default values:

Property	Value
Number	Value specified as argument to **Error** statement. Can be any valid error number.
Source	Name of the current Visual Basic project.
Description	String expression corresponding to the return value of the **Error** function for the specified **Number**, if this string exists. If the string doesn't exist, **Description** contains a zero-length string ("").
HelpFile	The fully qualified drive, path, and file name of the appropriate Visual Basic Help file.
HelpContext	The appropriate Visual Basic Help file context ID for the error corresponding to the **Number** property.
LastDLLError	Zero.

If no error handler exists or if none is enabled, an error message is created and displayed from the **Err** object properties.

Note Not all Visual Basic host applications can create objects. See your host application's documentation to determine whether it can create classes and objects.

See Also

Error Function, **On Error** Statement, **Resume** Statement, **Clear** Method, **Raise** Method, **Err** Object, **Trappable Errors**

Example

This example uses the **Error** statement to simulate error number 11.

```
On Error Resume Next  ' Defer error handling.
Error 11              ' Simulate the "Division by zero" error.
```

Errors Collection

An **Errors** collection contains all stored **Error** objects, each of which pertains to a single operation involving DAO.

Remarks

Any operation involving DAO objects can generate one or more errors. As each error occurs, one or more **Error** objects are placed in the **Errors** collection of the **DBEngine** object. When another DAO operation generates an error, the **Errors** collection is cleared, and the new set of **Error** objects is placed in the **Errors** collection. The highest-numbered object in the **Errors** collection (DBEngine.Errors.Count - 1) corresponds to the error reported by the Microsoft Visual Basic for Applications (VBA) **Err** object.

DAO operations that don't generate an error have no effect on the **Errors** collection.

Elements of the **Errors** collection aren't appended as they typically are with other collections, so the **Errors** collection doesn't support the **Append** and **Delete** methods.

The set of **Error** objects in the **Errors** collection describes one error. The first **Error** object is the lowest level error, the second the next higher level, and so forth. For example, if an ODBC error occurs while trying to open a **Recordset** object, the first error object contains the lowest level ODBC error; subsequent errors contain the ODBC errors returned by the various layers of ODBC. In this case, the ODBC driver manager, and possibly the driver itself, return separate **Error** objects. The last **Error** object contains the DAO error indicating that the object couldn't be opened.

Enumerating the specific errors in the **Errors** collection enables your error-handling routines to more precisely determine the cause and origin of an error, and take appropriate steps to recover.

Note If you use the **New** keyword to create an object that causes an error either before or while being placed into the **Errors** collection, the collection doesn't contain error information about that object, because the new object is not associated with the **DBEngine** object. However, the error information is available in the VBA **Err** object.

Properties
Count Property

Methods
Refresh Method

Example
This example forces an error, traps it, and displays the **Description**, **Number**, **Source**, **HelpContext**, and **HelpFile** properties of the resulting **Error** object.

```
Sub DescriptionX()

    Dim dbsTest As Database

    On Error GoTo ErrorHandler

    ' Intentionally trigger an error.
    Set dbsTest = OpenDatabase("NoDatabase")

    Exit Sub

ErrorHandler:
    Dim strError As String
    Dim errLoop As Error

    ' Enumerate Errors collection and display properties of
    ' each Error object.
    For Each errLoop In Errors
        With errLoop
            strError = _
                "Error #" & .Number & vbCr
            strError = strError & _
                "    " & .Description & vbCr
            strError = strError & _
                "    (Source: " & .Source & ")" & vbCr
            strError = strError & _
                "Press F1 to see topic " & .HelpContext & vbCr
            strError = strError & _
                "    in the file " & .HelpFile & "."
        End With
        MsgBox strError
    Next

    Resume Next

End Sub
```

ErrorText Property

Returns the error message string from the underlying data source. Not available at design time.

Applies To

DBGrid Control

Syntax

object.**ErrorText**

The **ErrorText** property syntax has these parts:

Part	Description
object	An object expression that evaluates to an object in the **Applies To** list.

Remarks

When a database error occurs as a result of user interaction with the grid, such as when the user enters text into a numeric field and then attempts to update the current record by moving to another row, the grid's Error event will fire. However, the error code passed to the event handler in the *DataError* parameter may not identify the specific error that occurred, or may even differ across operating environments. For these reasons, the **ErrorText** property is provided so that your application can parse the actual error message to determine the nature of the error.

Note The **ErrorText** property is only valid within a **DBGrid** control's Error event handler. A trappable error will occur if you attempt to access it in any other context.

See Also

Error Event (DBGrid Control)

ErrorThreshold Property (Remote Data)

Returns or sets a value that determines the severity level that constitutes a fatal error.

Note This property is provided for backward compatibility with RDO version 1.0 code. It should be replaced with code that implements the **rdoEngine** object's **InfoMessage** event which provides equivalent functionality.

Applies To

rdoPreparedStatement Object, **RemoteData** Control

Remarks

In version 4.x of Microsoft SQL Server, it is not possible to set the severity of errors using the RAISERROR statement. As a result, the **ErrorThreshold** property was needed to permit your code to filter those messages beyond a threshold of severity.

Version 6.x of Microsoft SQL Server now supports the inclusion of a severity level in the RAISERROR statement so it is no longer necessary to use the **ErrorThreshold** property.

All errors that are returned with a severity of less than 10 are trapped by the ODBC layers and set the SQL_SUCCESS_WITH_INFO result code. This causes RDO to raise the **InfoMessage** event but not stop query processing.

See Also

QueryTimeout Property (Remote Data), **rdoDefaultErrorThreshold** Property

EstablishConnection Method (Remote Data)

Establishes a physical connection to an ODBC server.

Applies To

rdoConnection Object

Syntax

object.**EstablishConnection** *prompt*, *readonly*, *options*

The **EstablishConnection** method syntax has these parts:

Part	Description
object	An object expression that evaluates to an **rdoConnection** object.
Prompt	Optional. Integer value indicating ODBC prompting characteristic (see the **OpenConnection** method on the **rdoEnvironment** object).
Readonly	Optional. Boolean value which is **True** if intending to use connection as read-only.
Options	Optional. Integer value indicating connection options. This parameter has the same rules, restrictions and possible values that it does in the **OpenConnection** method of the **rdoEnvironment** object.

Remarks

This method causes the **rdoConnection** object to physically connect to the server, if it is not so already. This method is used when creating stand-alone **rdoConnection** objects or when re-connecting **rdoConnection** objects that have been disconnected using the **Close** method.

Unlike the **OpenConnection** method, the **EstablishConnection** method does *not* automatically append the **rdoConnection** object to the **rdoConnections** collection. If you want to add the newly established connection into the **rdoConnections** collection, you must use the **Add** method. You can use the **Remove** method to remove a member from the **rdoConnections** collection.

When using the Client Batch cursor library, the **EstablishConnection** method can be used to establish a connection once the **ActiveConnection** of an **rdoResultset** or **rdoQuery** object has been set to **Nothing**.

Just as with the **OpenConnection** method, the *prompt* argument dictates how the ODBC driver manager prompts the user for missing arguments needed to establish the connection. You can also request that the connection be made asynchronously by using the **rdAsyncEnable** option.

In general, you must set the **Connect** property and other appropriate properties of the **rdoConnection** object prior to making an attempt at connecting to a remote server.

See the **OpenConnection** method for details on how the **rdoConnection** properties should be set prior to attempting to use the **EstablishConnection** method.

See Also

Connect Event, **OpenConnection** Method (Remote Data), **rdoConnection** Object, **rdoEnvironment** Object, **Prompt** Property (Remote Data), **ActiveConnection** Property

Event Statement

Declares a user-defined event.

Syntax

[**Public**] **Event** *procedurename* [(*arglist*)]

The **Event** statement has these parts:

Part	Description
Public	Optional. Specifies that the **Event** visible throughout the project. **Events** types are **Public** by default. Note that events can only be raised in the module in which they are declared.
procedurename	Required. Name of the event; follows standard variable naming conventions.

The *arglist* argument has the following syntax and parts:

[**ByVal** | **ByRef**] *varname*[( )] [**As** *type*]

Part	Description
ByVal	Optional. Indicates that the argument is passed by value.
ByRef	Optional. Indicates that the argument is passed by reference. **ByRef** is the default in Visual Basic.
varname	Required. Name of the variable representing the argument being passed to the procedure; follows standard variable naming conventions.
type	Optional. Data type of the argument passed to the procedure; may be **Byte**, **Boolean**, **Integer**, **Long**, **Currency**, **Single**, **Double**, **Decimal** (not currently supported), **Date**, **String** (variable length only), **Object**, **Variant**, a user-defined type, or an object type.

Remarks

Once the event has been declared, use the **RaiseEvent** statement to fire the event. A syntax error occurs if an **Event** declaration appears in a standard module. An event can't be declared to return a value. A typical event might be declared and raised as shown in the following fragments:

```
' Declare an event at module level of a class module

Event LogonCompleted (UserName as String)

Sub
    RaiseEvent LogonCompleted("AntoineJan")
End Sub
```

Note You can declare event arguments just as you do arguments of procedures, with the following exceptions: events cannot have named arguments, **Optional** arguments, or **ParamArray** arguments. Events do not have return values.

See Also

RaiseEvent Statement

Example

The following example uses events to count off seconds during a demonstration of the fastest 100 meter race. The code illustrates all of the event-related methods, properties, and statements, including the **Event** statement.

The class that raises an event is the event source, and the classes that implement the event are the sinks. An event source can have multiple sinks for the events it generates. When the class raises the event, that event is fired on every class that has elected to sink events for that instance of the object.

The example also uses a form (Form1) with a button (Command1), a label (Label1), and two text boxes (Text1 and Text2). When you click the button, the first text box displays "From Now" and the second starts to count seconds. When the full time (9.84 seconds) has elapsed, the first text box displays "Until Now" and the second displays "9.84".

The code for Form1 specifies the initial and terminal states of the form. It also contains the code executed when events are raised.

```
Option Explicit

Private WithEvents mText As TimerState

Private Sub Command1_Click()
Text1.Text = "From Now"
    Text1.Refresh
    Text2.Text = "0"
    Text2.Refresh
Call mText.TimerTask(9.84)
End Sub
```

```
Private Sub Form_Load()
   Command1.Caption = "Click to Start Timer"
   Text1.Text = ""
   Text2.Text = ""
   Label1.Caption = "The fastest 100 meter run took this long:"
   Set mText = New TimerState
   End Sub

Private Sub mText_ChangeText()
   Text1.Text = "Until Now"
   Text2.Text = "9.84"
End Sub

Private Sub mText_UpdateTime(ByVal dblJump As Double)
   Text2.Text = Str(Format(dblJump, "0"))
   DoEvents
End Sub
```

The remaining code is in a class module named TimerState. The **Event** statements
declare the procedures initiated when events are raised.

```
Option Explicit
Public Event UpdateTime(ByVal dblJump As Double)
Public Event ChangeText()

Public Sub TimerTask(ByVal Duration As Double)
   Dim dblStart As Double
   Dim dblSecond As Double
   Dim dblSoFar As Double
   dblStart = Timer
   dblSoFar = dblStart

   Do While Timer < dblStart + Duration
      If Timer - dblSoFar >= 1 Then
         dblSoFar = dblSoFar + 1
         RaiseEvent UpdateTime(Timer - dblStart)
      End If
   Loop

   RaiseEvent ChangeText

End Sub
```

Events Object

Supplies properties that enable add-ins to connect to all events in Visual Basic for
Applications.

Remarks

The **Events** object provides properties that return event source objects. Use the
properties to return event source objects that notify you of changes in the Visual Basic
for Applications environment.

The properties of the **Events** object return objects of the same type as the property name. For example, the **CommandBarEvents** property returns the **CommandBarEvents** object.

Properties

CommandBarEvents Property, **ReferencesEvents** Property, **FileControlEvents** Property, **SelectedVBControlsEvent** Property, **VBComponentsEvent** Property, **VBControlsEvent** Property, **VBProjectsEvents** Property

See Also

Click Event, **CommandBarEvents** Object, **ReferencesEvents** Object

Events Property

Supplies properties that enable add-ins to connect to all events in Visual Basic for Applications.

Applies To

VBE Object

Syntax

object.**Events**

The *object* placeholder represents an object expression that evaluates to an object in the **Applies To** list.

EventsFrozen Property

Returns a value indicating if the container is currently ignoring events being raised by the control. The **EventsFrozen** property is not available at the control's authoring time, and read-only at the control's run time.

Applies To

UserControl Object

Syntax

object.**EventsFrozen**

The **EventsFrozen** property syntax has this part:

Part	Description
object	An object expression that evaluates to an object in the **Applies To** list.

Remarks

When the **EventsFrozen** property is **True**, the container is ignoring any events that are being raised by the control. If the control wants to raise an event that cannot be lost, it must queue them up until **EventsFrozen** is **False**.

Exclusive Property

Returns or sets a value that indicates whether the underlying database for a **Data** control is opened for single-user or multi-user access.

Applies To

Data Control

Syntax

object.**Exclusive** [= *value*]

The **Exclusive** property syntax has these parts:

Part	Description
object	An object expression that evaluates to an object in the Applies To list.
value	A Boolean expression that determines user access, as described in Settings.

Settings

The settings for *value* are:

Setting	Description
True	The database is open for single-user access. No one else can open the database until it's closed.
False	(Default) The database is open for multi-user access. Other users can open the database and have access to the data while it's open.

Remarks

The *value* of this property, along with the **DatabaseName**, **ReadOnly**, and **Connect** properties, is used to open a database. In the Professional and Enterprise Editions, this property corresponds to the *exclusive* argument in the **OpenDatabase** method.

The **Exclusive** property is used only when opening the **Database**. If you change the value of this property at run time, you must use the **Refresh** method for the change to take effect. If someone else already has the database open, you can't open it for exclusive use and a trappable error results.

Database operations are faster if the database is opened for exclusive use.

After you open a database for exclusive use, your application can have as many instances open as necessary. However, other applications running on your system are not permitted to open the database.

The **Exclusive** property is ignored for databases accessed through ODBC.

Data Type

Boolean

Execute Method

Runs an action query or executes an SQL statement on a specified **Connection** or **Database** object.

Applies To

Database Object, **QueryDef** Object, **Connection** Object

Syntax

object.**Execute** *source, options*
querydef.**Execute** *options*

The **Execute** method syntax has these parts.

Part	Description
object	A **Connection** or **Database** object variable on which the query will run.
Querydef	An object variable that represents the **QueryDef** object whose **SQL** property setting specifies the SQL statement to execute.
Source	A **String** that is an SQL statement or the **Name** property value of a **QueryDef** object.
Options	**Optional.** A constant or combination of constants that determines the data integrity characteristics of the query, as specified in Settings.

Settings

You can use the following constants for *options*.

Constant	Description
dbDenyWrite	Denies write permission to other users (Microsoft Jet workspaces only).
DbInconsistent	(Default) Executes inconsistent updates (Microsoft Jet workspaces only).
DbConsistent	Executes consistent updates (Microsoft Jet workspaces only).
DbSQLPassThrough	Executes an SQL pass-through query. Setting this option passes the SQL statement to an ODBC database for processing (Microsoft Jet workspaces only).
DbFailOnError	Rolls back updates if an error occurs (Microsoft Jet workspaces only).
DbSeeChanges	Generates a run-time error if another user is changing data you are editing (Microsoft Jet workspaces only).
DbRunAsync	Executes the query asynchronously (ODBCDirect **Connection** and **QueryDef** objects only).
DbExecDirect	Executes the statement without first calling **SQLPrepare** ODBC API function (ODBCDirect **Connection** and **QueryDef** objects only).

Note The constants **dbConsistent** and **dbInconsistent** are mutually exclusive. You can use one or the other, but not both in a given instance of **OpenRecordset**. Using both **dbConsistent** and **dbInconsistent** causes an error.

Remarks

The **Execute** method is valid only for action queries. If you use **Execute** with another type of query, an error occurs. Because an action query doesn't return any records, **Execute** doesn't return a **Recordset**. (Executing an SQL pass-through query in an ODBCDirect workspace will not return an error if a **Recordset** isn't returned.)

Use the **RecordsAffected** property of the **Connection**, **Database**, or **QueryDef** object to determine the number of records affected by the most recent **Execute** method. For example, **RecordsAffected** contains the number of records deleted, updated, or inserted when executing an action query. When you use the **Execute** method to run a query, the **RecordsAffected** property of the **QueryDef** object is set to the number of records affected.

In a Microsoft Jet workspace, if you provide a syntactically correct SQL statement and have the appropriate permissions, the **Execute** method won't fail—even if not a single row can be modified or deleted. Therefore, always use the **dbFailOnError** option when using the **Execute** method to run an update or delete query. This option generates a run-time error and rolls back all successful changes if any of the records affected are locked and can't be updated or deleted.

For best performance in a Microsoft Jet workspace, especially in a multiuser environment, nest the **Execute** method inside a transaction. Use the **BeginTrans** method on the current **Workspace** object, then use the **Execute** method, and complete the transaction by using the **CommitTrans** method on the **Workspace**. This saves changes on disk and frees any locks placed while the query is running.

In an ODBCDirect workspace, if you include the optional **dbRunAsync** constant, the query runs asynchronously. To determine whether an asynchronous query is still executing, check the value of the **StillExecuting** property on the object from which the **Execute** method was called. To terminate execution of an asynchronous **Execute** method call, use the **Cancel** method.

See Also

Cancel Method, **RecordsAffected** Property, **StillExecuting** Property

Example

This example demonstrates the **Execute** method when run from both a **QueryDef** object and a **Database** object. The **ExecuteQueryDef** and **PrintOutput** procedures are required for this procedure to run.

```
Sub ExecuteX()

    Dim dbsNorthwind As Database
    Dim strSQLChange As String
    Dim strSQLRestore As String
    Dim qdfChange As QueryDef
```

```
        Dim rstEmployees As Recordset
        Dim errLoop As Error

        ' Define two SQL statements for action queries.
        strSQLChange = "UPDATE Employees SET Country = " & _
            "'United States' WHERE Country = 'USA'"
        strSQLRestore = "UPDATE Employees SET Country = " & _
            "'USA' WHERE Country = 'United States'"

        Set dbsNorthwind = OpenDatabase("Northwind.mdb")
        ' Create temporary QueryDef object.
        Set qdfChange = dbsNorthwind.CreateQueryDef("", _
            strSQLChange)
        Set rstEmployees = dbsNorthwind.OpenRecordset( _
            "SELECT LastName, Country FROM Employees", _
            dbOpenForwardOnly)

        ' Print report of original data.
        Debug.Print _
            "Data in Employees table before executing the query"
        PrintOutput rstEmployees

        ' Run temporary QueryDef.
        ExecuteQueryDef qdfChange, rstEmployees

        ' Print report of new data.
        Debug.Print _
            "Data in Employees table after executing the query"
        PrintOutput rstEmployees

        ' Run action query to restore data. Trap for errors,
        ' checking the Errors collection if necessary.
        On Error GoTo Err_Execute
        dbsNorthwind.Execute strSQLRestore, dbFailOnError
        On Error GoTo 0

        ' Retrieve the current data by requerying the recordset.
        rstEmployees.Requery

        ' Print report of restored data.
        Debug.Print "Data after executing the query " & _
            "to restore the original information"
        PrintOutput rstEmployees

        rstEmployees.Close

        Exit Sub

Err_Execute:

        ' Notify user of any errors that result from
        ' executing the query.
```

```
   If DBEngine.Errors.Count > 0 Then
      For Each errLoop In DBEngine.Errors
         MsgBox "Error number: " & errLoop.Number & vbCr & _
            errLoop.Description
      Next errLoop
   End If

   Resume Next

End Sub

Sub ExecuteQueryDef(qdfTemp As QueryDef, _
   rstTemp As Recordset)

   Dim errLoop As Error

   ' Run the specified QueryDef object. Trap for errors,
   ' checking the Errors collection if necessary.
   On Error GoTo Err_Execute
   qdfTemp.Execute dbFailOnError
   On Error GoTo 0

   ' Retrieve the current data by requerying the recordset.
   rstTemp.Requery

   Exit Sub

Err_Execute:

   ' Notify user of any errors that result from
   ' executing the query.
   If DBEngine.Errors.Count > 0 Then
      For Each errLoop In DBEngine.Errors
         MsgBox "Error number: " & errLoop.Number & vbCr & _
            errLoop.Description
      Next errLoop
   End If

   Resume Next

End Sub

Sub PrintOutput(rstTemp As Recordset)

   ' Enumerate Recordset.
   Do While Not rstTemp.EOF
      Debug.Print "    " & rstTemp!LastName & _
         ", " & rstTemp!Country
      rstTemp.MoveNext
   Loop

End Sub
```

Execute Method (Remote Data)

Runs an action query or executes an SQL statement that does not return rows.

Applies To

rdoConnection Object, **rdoPreparedStatement** Object

Syntax

connection.**Execute** *source*[, *options*]
query.**Execute** [*options*]

The **Execute** method syntax has these parts:

Part	Description
connection	An object expression that evaluates to the **rdoConnection** object on which the query will run.
Query	An object expression that evaluates to the **rdoQuery** object whose **SQL** property setting specifies the SQL statement to execute.
Source	A string expression that contains the action query to execute or the name of an **rdoQuery**.
Options	A **Variant** or constant that determines how the query is run, as specified in Settings.

Settings

You can use the following constants for the *options* argument:

Constant	Value	Description
rdAsyncEnable	32	Execute operation asynchronously.
RdExecDirect	64	Bypass creation of a stored procedure to execute the query. Uses SQLExecDirect instead of SQLPrepare and SQLExecute.

Remarks

It is recommended that you use the **Execute** method only for action queries. Because an action query doesn't return any rows, Execute doesn't return an **rdoResultset**. You can use the **Execute** method on queries that execute multiple statements, but none of these batched statements should return rows. To execute multiple result set queries that are a combination of action and SELECT queries, use the **OpenResultset** method.

Use the **RowsAffected** property of the **rdoConnection** or **rdoQuery** object to determine the number of rows affected by the most recent **Execute** method. **RowsAffected** contains the number of rows deleted, updated, or inserted when executing an action query. When you use the **Execute** method to run an **rdoQuery**, the **RowsAffected** property of the **rdoQuery** object is set to the number of rows affected.

Options

To execute the query asynchronously, use the **rdAsyncEnable** option. If set, the data source query processor immediately begins to process the query and returns to your application before the query is complete. Use the **StillExecuting** property to determine when the query processor is ready to return the results from the query. Use the **Cancel** method to terminate processing of an asynchronous query.

To bypass creation of a temporary stored procedure to execute the query, use the **rdExecDirect** option. This option is required when the query contains references to transactions or temporary tables that only exist in the context of a single operation. For example, if you include a Begin Transaction TSQL statement in your query or reference a temporary table, you must use **rdExecDirect** to ensure that the remote engine is not confused when these objects are left pending at the end of the query.

While it is possible to execute stored procedures using the **Execute** method, it is not recommended because the procedure's return value and output parameters are discarded and the procedure cannot return rows. Use the **OpenResultset** method against an **rdoQuery** to execute stored procedures.

Note When executing stored procedures that do not require parameters, do not include the parenthesis in the SQL statement. For example, to execute the "MySP" procedure use the following syntax: `{Call MySP }`.

See Also

BeginTrans, **CommitTrans**, **RollbackTrans** Methods, **Cancel** Method (Remote Data), **rdoConnection** Object, **rdoPreparedStatement** Object, **Prepared** Property, **RowsAffected** Property (Remote Data), **SQL** Property (Remote Data), **StillExecuting** Property (Remote Data)

Example

This example illustrates use of the **Execute** method to execute SQL queries against a remote data source. These action queries do not return rows, but in some cases do return the number of rows affected in the **RowsAffected** property. The example creates a work table called "TestData," inserts a few rows of data in the table and proceeds to run a DELETE query against the table. Notice that the delete queries have their own embedded transaction management. Because of this, you must use the **rdExecDirect** option to prevent the creation of stored procedures which negate the use of query-provided transactions.

```
Option Explicit
Dim er As rdoError
Dim cn As New rdoConnection
Dim qy As New rdoQuery
Dim rs As rdoResultset
Dim col As rdoColumn
Dim SQL As String
```

```
Private Sub DropRows_Click()
Dim SQL As String, Ans As Integer

SQL = "Begin Transaction Delete TestData " _
    & " Where State = '" & StateWanted & "'"
cn.Execute SQL, rdExecDirect
Ans = MsgBox("Ok to delete these " _
    & cn.RowsAffected & " rows?", vbOKCancel)
If Ans = vbOK Then
    cn.Execute "Commit Transaction", rdExecDirect
Else
    cn.Execute "Rollback Transaction", rdExecDirect
End If
Exit Sub
End Sub

Private Sub Form_Load()
cn.CursorDriver = rdUseOdbc
cn.Connect = "uid=;pwd=;server=sequel;" _
    & "driver={SQL Server};" _
    & "database=pubs;dsn='';"
cn.EstablishConnection
With qy
    .Name = "TestList"
    .SQL = "Select * from TestData Where State = ?"
    .RowsetSize = 1
    Set .ActiveConnection = cn
End With
SQL = "Drop Table TestData"
cn.Execute SQL

SQL = " CREATE TABLE TestData " _
    & " (ID integer identity NOT NULL, " _
    & " PName char(10) NULL," _
    & " State Char(2) NULL) " _
    & " CREATE UNIQUE INDEX " _
    &  "TestDataIndex on TestData(ID)"

cn.Execute SQL
SQL = "Insert TestData (PName,State)  " _
    & "Values('Bob', 'CA')" _
    & " Insert TestData (PName,State) " _
    & " Values('Bill', 'WA')" _
    & " Insert TestData (PName,State) " _
    & " Values('Fred', 'WA')" _
    & " Insert TestData (PName,State) " _
    & " Values('George', 'CA')" _
    & " Insert TestData (PName,State) " _
    & " Values('Sam', 'TX')" _
    & " Insert TestData (PName,State) " _
    & " Values('Marilyn', 'TX')"
cn.Execute SQL
```

```
Debug.Print cn.RowsAffected
' This returns 1
'(The last INSERT statement affected 1 row)
End Sub

Private Sub SeekRows_Click()
qy(0) = StateWanted
Set rs = qy.OpenResultset(rdOpenForwardOnly, _
rdConcurReadOnly)
List1.Clear
If rs.EOF Then
    MsgBox "No hits for that state"
Exit Sub
End If
Do Until rs.EOF
    List1.AddItem rs!PName & " - " & rs!state
    rs.MoveNext
Loop
End Sub
```

EXEName Property

Returns the root name of the executable file (without the extension) that is currently running. If running in the development environment, returns the name of the project.

Applies To

App Object

Syntax

object.**EXEName**

The *object* placeholder represents an object expression that evaluates to an object in the **Applies To** list.

Exit Statement

Exits a block of **Do...Loop**, **For...Next**, **Function**, **Sub**, or **Property** code.

Syntax

Exit Do
Exit For
Exit Function
Exit Property
Exit Sub

The **Exit** statement syntax has these forms:

Statement	Description
Exit Do	Provides a way to exit a **Do...Loop** statement. It can be used only inside a **Do...Loop** statement. **Exit Do** transfers control to the statement following the **Loop** statement. When used within nested **Do...Loop** statements, **Exit Do** transfers control to the loop that is one nested level above the loop where **Exit Do** occurs.
Exit For	Provides a way to exit a **For** loop. It can be used only in a **For...Next** or **For Each...Next** loop. **Exit For** transfers control to the statement following the **Next** statement. When used within nested **For** loops, **Exit For** transfers control to the loop that is one nested level above the loop where **Exit For** occurs.
Exit Function	Immediately exits the **Function** procedure in which it appears. Execution continues with the statement following the statement that called the **Function**.
Exit Property	Immediately exits the **Property** procedure in which it appears. Execution continues with the statement following the statement that called the **Property** procedure.
Exit Sub	Immediately exits the **Sub** procedure in which it appears. Execution continues with the statement following the statement that called the **Sub** procedure.

Remarks

Do not confuse **Exit** statements with **End** statements. **Exit** does not define the end of a structure.

See Also

Do...Loop Statement, **End** Statement, **For Each...Next** Statement, **For...Next** Statement, **Stop** Statement, **Function** Statement, **Property Get** Statement, **Property Let** Statement, **Property Set** Statement, **Sub** Statement

Example

This example uses the **Exit** statement to exit a **For...Next** loop, a **Do...Loop**, and a **Sub** procedure.

```
Sub ExitStatementDemo()
Dim I, MyNum
   Do                              ' Set up infinite loop.
      For I = 1 To 1000            ' Loop 1000 times.
         MyNum = Int(Rnd * 1000)   ' Generate random numbers.
         Select Case MyNum         ' Evaluate random number.
            Case 7: Exit For       ' If 7, exit For...Next.
            Case 29: Exit Do       ' If 29, exit Do...Loop.
            Case 54: Exit Sub      ' If 54, exit Sub procedure.
         End Select
      Next I
   Loop
End Sub
```

ExitFocus Event

Occurs when focus leaves the object. The object itself could be losing focus, or a constituent control could be losing focus.

Applies To

UserControl Object, **UserDocument** Object

Syntax

Sub *object_***ExitFocus**()

The **ExitFocus** event syntax has these parts:

Part	Description
object	An object expression that evaluates to an object in the **Applies To** list.

Remarks

This event is useful if *object* needs to know that the focus is now leaving it.

The **ExitFocus** event is raised after any **LostFocus** event; the **LostFocus** event will only be raised in *object* or constituent control of *object* that actually loses the focus.

See Also

EnterFocus Event, **LostFocus** Event (UserControl Object and UserDocument Object)

Exp Function

Returns a **Double** specifying *e* (the base of natural logarithms) raised to a power.

Syntax

Exp(*number*)

The required *number* argument is a **Double** or any valid numeric expression.

Remarks

If the value of *number* exceeds 709.782712893, an error occurs. The constant *e* is approximately 2.718282.

Note The **Exp** function complements the action of the **Log** function and is sometimes referred to as the antilogarithm.

See Also

Math Functions, **Log** Function, **Derived Math** Functions

Example

This example uses the **Exp** function to return *e* raised to a power.

```
Dim MyAngle, MyHSin
' Define angle in radians.
MyAngle = 1.3
' Calculate hyperbolic sine.
MyHSin = (Exp(MyAngle) - Exp(-1 * MyAngle)) / 2
```

Export Method

Saves a component as a separate file or files.

Applies To

VBComponent Object

Syntax

object.**Export**(*filename*)

Export syntax has these parts:

Part	Description
object	Required. An object expression that evaluates to an object in the **Applies To** list.
filename	Required. A **String** specifying the name of the file that you want to export the component to.

Remarks

When you use the **Export** method to save a component as a separate file or files, use a file name that doesn't already exist; otherwise, an error occurs.

See Also

Import Method

Example

The following example creates a file named `test.bas` and uses the **Export** method to copy the contents of the `VBComponents(1)` code module into the file.

```
Application.VBE.ActiveVBProject.VBComponents(1).Export("test.bas")
```

Extender Object

An **Extender** object holds properties of the control that are actually controlled by the container of the control rather than by the control itself.

Remarks

Some properties of a control are provided by the container rather than the control; these are extender properties. Examples of extender properties are: **Name**, **Tag** and **Left**. The control still needs to know what the value of these extender properties are, and sometimes needs to be able to change an extender property; the **Extender** object gives the control access to these properties.

Some extender properties are standard, while others are specific to certain containers. A control may access non-standard extender properties, but this will make the control container-specific. If the control makes use of an extender property, the control should handle the case where the extender property is not supported by the current container.

When the control is compiled, Visual Basic has no way of knowing what extender properties may be available when the control is run; therefore references to extender properties will always be late bound.

The **Extender** object is not available when the Initialize event is raised; but is available when the **InitProperties** event or **ReadProperties** event is raised.

The **Extender** object has several standard properties:

- The **Name** property, a read only String that contains the user-defined name of the control.

- The **Visible** property, a read/write Boolean that specifies if the control is visible or not.

- The **Parent** property, a read only object that represents the container of the control, such as a form in Visual Basic.

- The **Cancel** property, a read only Boolean that indicates that the control is the default **Cancel** button for the container.

- The **Default** property, a read only Boolean that indicates that the control is the default button for the container.

Visual Basic provides several more extender methods, properties and events; other containers are not guaranteed to provide these extender methods, properties and events. These Visual Basic specific extender methods, properties and events are:

- The **Container** property, a read only object that represents the visual container of the control.

- The **DragIcon** property, a read/write Picture that specifies the icon to use when the control is dragged.

- The **DragMode** property, a read/write Integer that specifies if the control will automatically drag, or if the user of the control must call the **Drag** method.

- The **Enabled** property, a read only Boolean that specifies if the control is enabled. This extender property is not present unless the control also has an **Enabled** property with the correct procedure ID. For additional information, refer to the topic "Allowing Your Controls to be Enabled and Disabled" in Chapter 9: Building ActiveX Controls.

- The **Height** property, a read/write Integer that specifies the height of the control in the container's scale units.

- The **HelpContextID** property, a read/write Integer that specifies the context ID to use when the F1 key is pressed when the control has the focus.

- The **Index** property, a read only Integer that specifies the position in a control array this instance of the control occupies.

- The **Left** property, a read/write Integer that specifies the position of the left edge of the control to the left edge of the container, specified in the container's scale units.

- The **TabIndex** property, a read/write Integer that specifies the position of the control in the tab order of the controls in the container.

- The **TabStop** property, a read/write Boolean that specifies if Tab will stop on the control.

- The **Tag** property, a read/write String that contains a user-defined value.

- The **ToolTipText** property, a read/write String that contains the text to be displayed when the cursor hovers over the control for more than a second.

- The **Top** property, a read/write Integer that specifies the position of the top edge of the control to the top edge of the container, specified in the container's scale units.

- The **WhatThisHelpID** property, a read/write Integer that specifies the context ID to use when the **What's This** pop-up is used on the control.

- The **Width** property, a read/write Integer that specifies the width of the control in the container's scale units.

- The **Drag** method, a method to begin, end, or cancel a drag operation of the control.

- The **Move** method, a method to move the position of the control.

- The **SetFocus** method, a method to set the focus to the control.

- The **ShowWhatsThis** method, a method to display a selected topic in a Help file using the **What's This** popup provided by Help.

- The **ZOrder** method, a method to place the control at the front or back of the z-order within its graphical level.

- The **DragDrop** event, an event that is raised when another control on the form is dropped on this control.

- The **DragOver** event, an event that is raised when another control on the form is dragged over this control.

- The **GotFocus** event, an event that is raised when this control gets the focus.

- The **LostFocus** event, an event that is raised when this control loses the focus.

Properties

Cancel Property, **Height, Width** Properties, **Left, Top** Properties, **TabIndex** Property, **Tag** Property, **Visible** Property, **Default** Property, **DragIcon** Property, **TabStop** Property, **WhatsThisHelpID** Property

Events

> **DragDrop** Event, **DragOver** Event, **GotFocus** Event, **LostFocus** Event

Methods

> **SetFocus** Method, **Drag** Method, **Move** Method, **ZOrder** Method, **ShowWhatsThis** Method

See Also

> **InitProperties** Event, **ReadProperties** Event, **Initialize** Event

---

Extender Property

Returns the **Extender** object for this control that holds the properties of the control that are kept track of by the container. The **Extender** property is not available at the control's authoring time, and read-only at the control's run time.

Applies To

> **UserControl** Object

Syntax

> *object*.**Extender**

The **Extender** property syntax has this part:

Part	Description
object	An object expression that evaluates to an object in the **Applies To** list.

See Also

> **Extender** Object

FetchVerbs Method

Updates the list of verbs an object supports.

Applies To

> **OLE Container** Control, **OLEObject** Object

Syntax

> *object*.**FetchVerbs**

The *object* is an object expression that evaluates to an object in the **Applies To** list.

Remarks

You can read the updated list of verbs using the **ObjectVerbs** property.

See Also

> **ObjectVerbs** Property, **ObjectVerbsCount** Property, **AutoVerbMenu** Property, **DoVerb** Method

Field Object

A **Field** object represents a column of data with a common data type and a common set of properties.

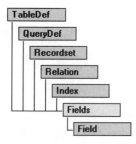

Remarks

The **Fields** collections of **Index**, **QueryDef**, **Relation**, and **TableDef** objects contain the specifications for the fields those objects represent. The **Fields** collection of a **Recordset** object represents the **Field** objects in a row of data, or in a record. You use the **Field** objects in a **Recordset** object to read and set values for the fields in the current record of the **Recordset** object.

In both Microsoft Jet and ODBCDirect workspaces, you manipulate a field using a **Field** object and its methods and properties. For example, you can:

- Use the **OrdinalPosition** property to set or return the presentation order of the **Field** object in a **Fields** collection. (This property is read-only for ODBCDirect databases.)

- Use the **Value** property of a field in a **Recordset** object to set or return stored data.

- Use the **AppendChunk** and **GetChunk** methods and the **FieldSize** property to get or set a value in an OLE Object or Memo field of a **Recordset** object.

- Use the **Type**, **Size**, and **Attributes** properties to determine the type of data that can be stored in the field.

- Use the **SourceField** and **SourceTable** properties to determine the original source of the data.

In Microsoft Jet workspaces, you can:

- Use the **ForeignName** property to set or return information about a foreign field in a **Relation** object.

- Use the **AllowZeroLength**, **DefaultValue**, **Required**, **ValidateOnSet**, **ValidationRule**, or **ValidationText** properties to set or return validation conditions.

- Use the **DefaultValue** property of a field on a **TableDef** object to set the default value for this field when new records are added.

In ODBCDirect workspaces, you can:

- Use the **Value**, **VisibleValue**, and **OriginalValue** properties to verify successful completion of a batch update.

Note For a complete list of all methods, properties, and collections available on a **Field** object in any database or connection, see the Summary topic.

To create a new **Field** object in an **Index**, **TableDef**, or **Relation** object, use the **CreateField** method.

When you access a **Field** object as part of a **Recordset** object, data from the current record is visible in the **Field** object's **Value** property. To manipulate data in the **Recordset** object, you don't usually reference the **Fields** collection directly; instead, you indirectly reference the **Value** property of the **Field** object in the **Fields** collection of the **Recordset** object.

To refer to a **Field** object in a collection by its ordinal number or by its **Name** property setting, use any of the following syntax forms:

Fields(0)
Fields("*name*")
Fields![*name*]

With the same syntax forms, you can also refer to the **Value** property of a **Field** object that you create and append to a **Fields** collection. The context of the field reference will determine whether you are referring to the **Field** object or the **Value** property of the **Field** object.

Summary

Field Object, Fields Collection Summary

Properties

AllowZeroLength Property, **Attributes** Property, **CollatingOrder** Property, **DataUpdatable** Property, **DefaultValue** Property, **ForeignName** Property, **Name** Property, **OrdinalPosition** Property, **Required** Property, **Size** Property, **SourceField, SourceTable** Properties, **Type** Property, **ValidateOnSet** Property, **ValidationRule** Property, **ValidationText** Property, **Value** Property, **FieldSize** Property, **OriginalValue** Property, **VisibleValue** Property

Methods

AppendChunk Method**, CreateProperty** Method**, GetChunk** Method

See Also

CreateField Method

Example

This example shows what properties are valid for a **Field** object depending on where the **Field** resides (for example, the **Fields** collection of a **TableDef**, the **Fields** collection of a **QueryDef**, and so forth). The **FieldOutput** procedure is required for this procedure to run.

```
Sub FieldX()

    Dim dbsNorthwind As Database
    Dim rstEmployees As Recordset
    Dim fldTableDef As Field
    Dim fldQueryDef As Field
    Dim fldRecordset As Field
    Dim fldRelation As Field
    Dim fldIndex As Field
    Dim prpLoop As Property

    Set dbsNorthwind = OpenDatabase("Northwind.mdb")
    Set rstEmployees = _
        dbsNorthwind.OpenRecordset("Employees")

    ' Assign a Field object from different Fields
    ' collections to object variables.
    Set fldTableDef = _
        dbsNorthwind.TableDefs(0).Fields(0)
    Set fldQueryDef =dbsNorthwind.QueryDefs(0).Fields(0)
    Set fldRecordset = rstEmployees.Fields(0)
    Set fldRelation =dbsNorthwind.Relations(0).Fields(0)
    Set fldIndex = _
        dbsNorthwind.TableDefs(0).Indexes(0).Fields(0)

    ' Print report.
    FieldOutput "TableDef", fldTableDef
    FieldOutput "QueryDef", fldQueryDef
    FieldOutput "Recordset", fldRecordset
    FieldOutput "Relation", fldRelation
    FieldOutput "Index", fldIndex

    rstEmployees.Close
    dbsNorthwind.Close

End Sub

Sub FieldOutput(strTemp As String, fldTemp As Field)
    ' Report function for FieldX.

    Dim prpLoop As Property

    Debug.Print "Valid Field properties in " & strTemp

    ' Enumerate Properties collection of passed Field
    ' object.
    For Each prpLoop In fldTemp.Properties
```

```
    ' Some properties are invalid in certain
    ' contexts (the Value property in the Fields
    ' collection of a TableDef for example). Any
    ' attempt to use an invalid property will
    ' trigger an error.
    On Error Resume Next
    Debug.Print "    " & prpLoop.Name & " = " & _
        prpLoop.Value
    On Error GoTo 0
  Next prpLoop

End Sub
```

Fields Collection

A **Fields** collection contains all stored **Field** objects of an **Index**, **QueryDef**, **Recordset**, **Relation**, or **TableDef** object.

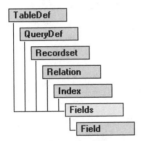

Remarks

The **Fields** collections of the **Index**, **QueryDef**, **Relation**, and **TableDef** objects contain the specifications for the fields those objects represent. The **Fields** collection of a **Recordset** object represents the **Field** objects in a row of data, or in a record. You use the **Field** objects in a **Recordset** object to read and to set values for the fields in the current record of the **Recordset** object.

To refer to a **Field** object in a collection by its ordinal number or by its **Name** property setting, use any of the following syntax forms:

Fields(0)
Fields("*name*")
Fields![*name*]

With the same syntax forms, you can also refer to the **Value** property of a **Field** object that you create and append to a **Fields** collection. The context of the field reference will determine whether you are referring to the **Field** object or the **Value** property of the **Field** object.

Summary

Field Object, Fields Collection Summary

Properties

Count Property

Methods

Append Method, **Delete** Method, **Refresh** Method

Example

This example shows what properties are valid for a **Field** object depending on where the **Field** resides (for example, the **Fields** collection of a **TableDef**, the **Fields** collection of a **QueryDef**, and so forth). The FieldOutput procedure is required for this procedure to run.

```
Sub FieldX()

    Dim dbsNorthwind As Database
    Dim rstEmployees As Recordset
    Dim fldTableDef As Field
    Dim fldQueryDef As Field
    Dim fldRecordset As Field
    Dim fldRelation As Field
    Dim fldIndex As Field
    Dim prpLoop As Property

    Set dbsNorthwind = OpenDatabase("Northwind.mdb")
    Set rstEmployees = _
        dbsNorthwind.OpenRecordset("Employees")

    ' Assign a Field object from different Fields
    ' collections to object variables.
    Set fldTableDef = _
        dbsNorthwind.TableDefs(0).Fields(0)
    Set fldQueryDef =dbsNorthwind.QueryDefs(0).Fields(0)
    Set fldRecordset = rstEmployees.Fields(0)
    Set fldRelation =dbsNorthwind.Relations(0).Fields(0)
    Set fldIndex = _
        dbsNorthwind.TableDefs(0).Indexes(0).Fields(0)

    ' Print report.
    FieldOutput "TableDef", fldTableDef
    FieldOutput "QueryDef", fldQueryDef
    FieldOutput "Recordset", fldRecordset
    FieldOutput "Relation", fldRelation
    FieldOutput "Index", fldIndex

    rstEmployees.Close
    dbsNorthwind.Close

End Sub
```

```
Sub FieldOutput(strTemp As String, fldTemp As Field)
    ' Report function for FieldX.

    Dim prpLoop As Property

    Debug.Print "Valid Field properties in " & strTemp

    ' Enumerate Properties collection of passed Field
    ' object.
    For Each prpLoop In fldTemp.Properties
        ' Some properties are invalid in certain
        ' contexts (the Value property in the Fields
        ' collection of a TableDef for example). Any
        ' attempt to use an invalid property will
        ' trigger an error.
        On Error Resume Next
        Debug.Print "     " & prpLoop.Name & " = " & _
            prpLoop.Value
        On Error GoTo 0
    Next prpLoop

End Sub
```

FieldSize Property

Returns the number of bytes used in the database (rather than in memory) of a Memo or Long Binary **Field** object in the **Fields** collection of a **Recordset** object.

Applies To

Field Object

Return Values

The return value is a **Long** that indicates the number of characters (for a Memo field) or the number of bytes (for a Long Binary field).

Remarks

You can use **FieldSize** with the **AppendChunk** and **GetChunk** methods to manipulate large fields.

Because the size of a Long Binary or Memo field can exceed 64K, you should assign the value returned by **FieldSize** to a variable large enough to store a **Long** variable.

To determine the size of a **Field** object other than Memo and Long Binary types, use the **Size** property.

Note In an **ODBCDirect** workspace, the **FieldSize** property is not available in the following situations:

- If the database server or ODBC driver does not support server-side cursors.

- If you are using the ODBC cursor library (that is, the **DefaultCursorDriver** property is set to **dbUseODBC**, or to **dbUseDefault** when the server does not support server-side cursors).

- If you are using a cursorless query (that is, the **DefaultCursorDriver** property is set to **dbUseNoCursor**).

For example, Microsoft SQL Server version 4.21 does not support server-side cursors, so the **FieldSize** property is not available.

See Also

AppendChunk Method, **GetChunk** Method, **Size** Property, **Type** Property

Example

This example uses the **FieldSize** property to list the number of bytes used by the Memo and Long Binary **Field** objects in two different tables.

```
Sub FieldSizeX()

    Dim dbsNorthwind As Database
    Dim rstCategories As Recordset
    Dim rstEmployees As Recordset

    Set dbsNorthwind = OpenDatabase("Northwind.mdb")
    Set rstCategories = _
        dbsNorthwind.OpenRecordset("Categories", _
        dbOpenDynaset)
    Set rstEmployees = _
        dbsNorthwind.OpenRecordset("Employees", _
        dbOpenDynaset)

    Debug.Print _
        "Field sizes from records in Categories table"

    With rstCategories
        Debug.Print "    CategoryName - " & _
            "Description (bytes) - Picture (bytes)"

    ' Enumerate the Categories Recordset and print the size
    ' in bytes of the picture field for each record.
        Do While Not .EOF
            Debug.Print "        " & !CategoryName & " - " & _
                !Description.FieldSize & " - " & _
                !Picture.FieldSize
            .MoveNext
        Loop

        .Close
    End With

    Debug.Print "Field sizes from records in Employees table"

    With rstEmployees
        Debug.Print "    LastName - Notes (bytes) - " & _
            "Photo (bytes)"
```

```
' Enumerate the Employees Recordset and print the size
' in bytes of the picture field for each record.
   Do While Not .EOF
      Debug.Print "            " & !LastName & " - " & _
         !Notes.FieldSize & " - " & !Photo.FieldSize
      .MoveNext
   Loop

   .Close
End With

dbsNorthwind.Close

End Sub
```

FileAttr Function

Returns a **Long** representing the file mode for files opened using the **Open** statement.

Syntax

FileAttr(*filenumber***,** *returntype***)**

The **FileAttr** function syntax has these named arguments:

Part	Description
filenumber	Required; **Integer**. Any valid file number.
returntype	Required; **Integer**. Number indicating the type of information to return. Specify 1 to return a value indicating the file mode. On 16-bit systems only, specify 2 to retrieve an operating system file handle. *Returntype* 2 is not supported in 32-bit systems and causes an error.

Return Values

When the *returntype* argument is 1, the following return values indicate the file access mode:

Mode	Value
Input	1
Output	2
Random	4
Append	8
Binary	32

See Also

GetAttr Function, **SetAttr** Statement, **Open** Statement

Example

This example uses the **FileAttr** function to return the file mode and file handle of an open file.

```
Dim FileNum, Mode, Handle
FileNum = 1                             ' Assign file number.
Open "TESTFILE" For Append As FileNum   ' Open file.
Mode = FileAttr(FileNum, 1)             ' Returns 8 (Append file mode).
Handle = FileAttr(FileNum, 2)           ' Returns file handle.
Close FileNum                           ' Close file.
```

FileControlEvents Object

Represents all events supplied by Visual Basic which support file control.

Syntax

FileControlEvents

Remarks

The **FileControlEvents** object replaces the **FileControl** object in Visual Basic version 4.0. It works the same as before, only its events have been changed to allow multiple project support.

Events

AfterAddFile Event, **AfterChangeFileName** Event, **AfterCloseFile** Event, **AfterRemoveFile** Event, **AfterWriteFile** Event, **BeforeLoadFile** Event, **DoGetNewFileName** Event, **RequestChangeFileName** Event, **RequestWriteFile** Event

See Also

FileControlEvents Property

FileControlEvents Property

Returns an event object of type **FileControlEvents**.

Applies To

Events Object

Syntax

object.**FileControlEvents**

The *object* placeholder represents an object expression that evaluates to an object in the **Applies To** list.

See Also

FileControlEvents Object

FileCopy Statement

Copies a file.

Syntax

FileCopy *source*, *destination*

The **FileCopy** statement syntax has these named arguments:

Part	Description
source	Required. String expression that specifies the name of the file to be copied. The *source* may include directory or folder, and drive.
destination	Required. String expression that specifies the target file name. The *destination* may include directory or folder, and drive.

Remarks

If you try to use the **FileCopy** statement on a currently open file, an error occurs.

See Also

Kill Statement, **Name** Statement

Example

This example uses the **FileCopy** statement to copy one file to another. For purposes of this example, assume that SRCFILE is a file containing some data.

```
Dim SourceFile, DestinationFile
SourceFile = "SRCFILE"                   ' Define source file name.
DestinationFile = "DESTFILE"             ' Define target file name.
FileCopy SourceFile, DestinationFile     ' Copy source to target.
```

FileCount Property

Returns the number of files associated with a given component.

Applies To

VBComponent Object

Syntax

object.**FileCount**

The *object* placeholder represents an object expression that evaluates to an object in the **Applies To** list.

Remarks

The primary use for **FileCount** is to alert you to whether a component has an associated .Frx file.

For most components, this property setting is 1, but it can be greater. For example, if an .FRX file is associated with a form file, the **FileCount** property setting is 2.

See Also

FileNames Property

FileDateTime Function

Returns a **Variant** (**Date**) that indicates the date and time when a file was created or last modified.

Syntax

FileDateTime(*pathname*)

The required *pathname* argument is a string expression that specifies a file name. The *pathname* may include the directory or folder, and the drive.

See Also

FileLen Function, **GetAttr** Function, **VarType** Function

Example

This example uses the **FileDateTime** function to determine the date and time a file was created or last modified. The format of the date and time displayed is based on the locale settings of your system.

```
Dim MyStamp
' Assume TESTFILE was last modified on February 12, 1993 at 4:35:47 PM.
' Assume English/U.S. locale settings.
MyStamp = FileDateTime("TESTFILE")    ' Returns "2/12/93 4:35:47 PM".
```

FileDescription Property

Returns or sets a string value containing file description information about the running application. Read only at run time.

Applies To

App Object

Syntax

object.**FileDescription**

The *object* placeholder represents an object expression that evaluates to an object in the **Applies To** list.

Remarks

You can set this property at design time in the **Type** box in the **Make** tab of the Project **Properties** dialog box.

See Also

Comments Property, **CompanyName** Property, **LegalCopyright** Property, **LegalTrademarks** Property, **ProductName** Property

FileLen Function

Returns a **Long** specifying the length of a file in bytes.

Syntax

FileLen(*pathname*)

The required *pathname* argument is a string expression that specifies a file. The *pathname* may include the directory or folder, and the drive.

Remarks

If the specified file is open when the **FileLen** function is called, the value returned represents the size of the file immediately before it was opened.

Note   To obtain the length of an open file, use the **LOF** function.

See Also

FileDateTime Function, **GetAttr** Function, **LOF** Function

Example

This example uses the **FileLen** function to return the length of a file in bytes. For purposes of this example, assume that TESTFILE is a file containing some data.

```
Dim MySize
MySize = FileLen("TESTFILE")    ' Returns file length (bytes).
```

FileListBox Control

A **FileListBox** control locates and lists files in the directory specified by the **Path** property at run time. Use this control to display a list of files selected by file type. You can create dialog boxes in your application that, for example, enable the user to select a file or group of files.

Syntax

FileListBox

Remarks

Set the **List**, **ListCount**, and **ListIndex** properties to enable a user to access items in the list. If you also display the **DirListBox** and **DriveListBox** controls, you can write code to synchronize them with the **FileListBox** control and with each other.

Properties

OLEDragMode Property, **OLEDropMode** Property, **BackColor, ForeColor** Properties, **FontBold, FontItalic, FontStrikethru, FontUnderline** Properties, **FontName** Property, **FontSize** Property, **Height, Width** Properties, **Left, Top** Properties, **List** Property, **ListCount** Property, **ListIndex** Property, **TabIndex**

Property, **Tag** Property, **Visible** Property, **Archive, Hidden, Normal, System** Properties, **DragIcon** Property, **DragMode** Property, **FileName** Property, **hWnd** Property, **Locked** Property, **ReadOnly** Property, **MouseIcon** Property, **MousePointer** Property, **MultiSelect** Property, **Pattern** Property, **Selected** Property, **TabStop** Property, **TopIndex** Property, **Appearance** Property, **Enabled** Property, **HelpContextID** Property, **Index** Property (Control Array), **Name** Property, **Parent** Property, **Path** Property, **Font** Property, **Container** Property, **ToolTipText** Property, **WhatsThisHelpID** Property

Events

Click Event, **DblClick** Event, **DragDrop** Event, **DragOver** Event, **GotFocus** Event, **KeyDown, KeyUp** Events, **KeyPress** Event, **LostFocus** Event, **MouseDown, MouseUp** Events, **MouseMove** Event, **OLECompleteDrag** Event, **OLEDragDrop** Event, **OLEDragOver** Event, **OLEGiveFeedback** Event, **OLESetData** Event, **OLEStartDrag** Event, **PathChange** Event, **PatternChange** Event, **Scroll** Event

Methods

Refresh Method, **SetFocus** Method, **Drag** Method, **Move** Method, **ZOrder** Method, **OLEDrag** Method, **ShowWhatsThis** Method

See Also

DirListBox Control, **DriveListBox** Control, **List** Property, **ListCount** Property, **ListIndex** Property, **Path** Property

---

FileName Property

Returns or sets the path and filename of a selected file. Not available at design time for the **FileListBox** control.

Applies To

CommonDialog Control, **FileListBox** Control

Syntax

object.**FileName** [= *pathname*]

The **FileName** property syntax has these parts:

Part	Description
object	An object expression that evaluates to an object in the **Applies To** list.
pathname	A string expression that specifies the path and filename.

Remarks

When you create the control at run time, the **FileName** property is set to a zero-length string (""), meaning no file is currently selected.

In the **CommonDialog** control, you can set the **FileName** property before opening a dialog box to set an initial filename.

Reading this property returns the currently selected filename from the list. The path is retrieved separately, using the **Path** property. The value is functionally equivalent to **List**(*ListIndex*). If no file is selected, **FileName** returns a zero-length string.

When setting this property:

- Including a drive, path, or pattern in the string changes the settings of the **Drive**, **Path**, and **Pattern** properties accordingly.

- Including the name of an existing file (without wildcard characters) in the string selects the file.

- Changing the value of this property may also cause one or more of these events: **PathChange** (if you change the path), **PatternChange** (if you change the pattern), or **DblClick** (if you assign an existing filename).

- This property setting can be a qualified network path and filename using the following syntax:

    ```
    \\servername\sharename\pathname
    ```

Specifics

FileNames Property

See Also

PathChange Event, **PatternChange** Event, **List** Property, **ListIndex** Property, **Drive** Property, **Pattern** Property, **Path** Property, **LoadFile** Method, **RichTextBox** Control, **SaveFile** Method, **Supported RTF Codes**

FileNames Property

Returns the current path name(s) in which the component will be stored.

Applies To

VBComponent Object

Syntax

object.**FileNames**(*index*)

The **FileNames** property syntax has these parts:

Part	Description
object	An object expression that evaluates to an object in the **Applies To** list.
index	A long integer specifying the location of the filename in the indexed string to return.

Remarks

The path name returned will always be provided as an absolute path (for example, "c:\projects\myproject.vbp"), even if it is shown as a relative path in Visual Basic (such as "..\projects").

The number of entries in the indexed string is determined by the **FileCount** property setting. The indexed string for classes and modules contains only one filename, while the indexed string for forms contains both the .Frm and .Frx filename for the form. The values of the filenames are updated when the **SaveAs** method is invoked on the *object*.

See Also

FileCount Property

FileNumber Property

Returns or sets the file number to be used when saving or loading an object, or returns the last file number used. Not available at design time.

Note   The **FileNumber** property is included for compatibility with the **Action** property in earlier versions. For current functionality, use the **SaveToFile** and **ReadFromFile** methods.

Applies To

OLE Container Control

Syntax

object.**FileNumber** [= *number*]

The **FileNumber** property syntax has these parts:

Part	Description
object	An object expression that evaluates to an object in the **Applies To** list.
number	A numeric expression specifying the file number.

Remarks

The file number must correspond to an open, binary file.

You can use this property to specify the number of the file to be opened with the **ReadFromFile** method or saved with the **SaveToFile** or **SaveToOle1File** methods.

See Also

ReadFromFile Method, **SaveToFile** Method, **SaveToOle1File** Method

Files Method

Returns a collection of filenames used by the vbCFFiles format (a **DataObjectFiles** collection) which in turn contains a list of all filenames used by a **DataObject** object; for example, the names of files that a user drags to or from the Windows File Explorer.

Applies To

DataObject Object

Syntax

object.**Files**(*index*)

The **Files** collection syntax has these parts:

Part	Description
object	An object expression that evaluates to a **DataObject** object.
index	An integer which is an index to an array of filenames.

Remarks

The **Files** collection is filled with filenames only when the **DataObject** object contains data of type **vbCFFiles**. The **DataObject** object can contain several different types of data. You can iterate through the collection to retrieve the list of file names.

The **Files** collection can be filled to allow Visual Basic applications to act as a drag source for a list of files.

See Also

DataObject Object, **DataObjectFiles** Collection

Files Property

Returns a **DataObjectFiles** collection, which in turn contains a list of all filenames used by a **DataObject** object (such as the names of files that a user drags to or from the Windows File Explorer.)

Syntax

object.**Files**(*index*)

The **Files** collection syntax has these parts:

Part	Description
object	An object expression that evaluates to a **DataObject** object.
index	An integer which is an index to an array of filenames.

Remarks

The **Files** collection is filled with filenames only when the **DataObject** object contains data of type **vbCFFiles**. (The **DataObject** object can contain several different types of data.) You can iterate through the collection to retrieve the list of file names.

The **Files** collection can be filled to allow Visual Basic applications to act as a drag source for a list of files.

FillCache Method

Fills all or a part of a local cache for a **Recordset** object that contains data from a Microsoft Jet-connected ODBC data source (Microsoft Jet-connected ODBC databases only).

Applies To

Dynaset-Type Recordset Object

Syntax

recordset.**FillCache** *rows*, *startbookmark*

The **FillCache** method syntax has these parts.

Part	Description
recordset	An object variable that represents a **Recordset** object created from an ODBC data source, such as a **TableDef** representing a linked table or a **QueryDef** object derived from such a **TableDef**.
rows	Optional. A **Variant** (**Integer** subtype) that specifies the number of rows to store in the cache. If you omit this argument, the value is determined by the **CacheSize** property setting.
startbookmark	Optional. A **Variant** (**String** subtype) that specifies a bookmark. The cache is filled starting from the record indicated by this bookmark. If you omit this argument, the cache is filled starting from the record indicated by the **CacheStart** property.

Remarks

Caching improves the performance of an application that retrieves data from a remote server. A cache is space in local memory that holds the data most recently retrieved from the server; this assumes that the data will probably be requested again while the application is running. When a user requests data, the Microsoft Jet database engine checks the cache for the data first rather than retrieving it from the server, which takes more time. The cache doesn't save data that doesn't come from an ODBC data source.

Rather than waiting for the cache to be filled with records as they are retrieved, you can use the **FillCache** method to explicitly fill the cache at any time. This is a faster way to fill the cache because **FillCache** retrieves several records at once instead of one at a time. For example, while you view each screenful of records, your application uses **FillCache** to retrieve the next screenful of records for viewing.

Any Microsoft Jet-connected ODBC data source that you access with **Recordset** objects can have a local cache. To create the cache, open a **Recordset** object from the remote data source, and then set the **CacheSize** and **CacheStart** properties of the **Recordset**.

If *rows* and *startbookmark* create a range of records that is partially or entirely outside the range of records specified by the **CacheSize** and **CacheStart** properties, the portion of the *recordset* outside this range is ignored and will not be loaded into the cache.

If **FillCache** requests more records than the number remaining in the remote data source, Microsoft Jet retrieves only the remaining records, and no error occurs.

Notes

- Records retrieved from the cache don't reflect concurrent changes that other users made to the source data.

- **FillCache** only retrieves records not already cached. To force an update of all the cached data, set the **CacheSize** property of the **Recordset** to 0, reset it to the size of the cache you originally requested, and then use **FillCache**.

See Also

Bookmark Property, **Bookmarkable** Property, **CacheSize** Property

Example

This example uses the **CreateTableDef** and **FillCache** methods and the **CacheSize**, **CacheStart** and **SourceTableName** properties to enumerate the records in a linked table twice. Then it enumerates the records twice with a 50-record cache. The example then displays the performance statistics for the uncached and cached runs through the linked table.

```
Sub ClientServerX3()

    Dim dbsCurrent As Database
    Dim tdfRoyalties As TableDef
    Dim rstRemote As Recordset
    Dim sngStart As Single
    Dim sngEnd As Single
    Dim sngNoCache As Single
    Dim sngCache As Single
    Dim intLoop As Integer
    Dim strTemp As String
    Dim intRecords As Integer

    ' Open a database to which a linked table can be
    ' appended.
    Set dbsCurrent = OpenDatabase("DB1.mdb")

    ' Create a linked table that connects to a Microsoft SQL
    ' Server database.
    Set tdfRoyalties = _
        dbsCurrent.CreateTableDef("Royalties")
    tdfRoyalties.Connect = _
        "ODBC;DATABASE=pubs;UID=sa;PWD=;DSN=Publishers"
    tdfRoyalties.SourceTableName = "roysched"
    dbsCurrent.TableDefs.Append tdfRoyalties
    Set rstRemote = _
        dbsCurrent.OpenRecordset("Royalties")
```

```
With rstRemote
    ' Enumerate the Recordset object twice and record
    ' the elapsed time.
    sngStart = Timer

    For intLoop = 1 To 2
        .MoveFirst
        Do While Not .EOF
            ' Execute a simple operation for the
            ' performance test.
            strTemp = !title_id
            .MoveNext
        Loop
    Next intLoop

    sngEnd = Timer
    sngNoCache = sngEnd - sngStart

    ' Cache the first 50 records.
    .MoveFirst
    .CacheSize = 50
    .FillCache
    sngStart = Timer

    ' Enumerate the Recordset object twice and record
    ' the elapsed time.
    For intLoop = 1 To 2
        intRecords = 0
        .MoveFirst
        Do While Not .EOF
            ' Execute a simple operation for the
            ' performance test.
            strTemp = !title_id
            ' Count the records. If the end of the
            ' cache is reached, reset the cache to the
            ' next 50 records.
            intRecords = intRecords + 1
            .MoveNext
            If intRecords Mod 50 = 0 Then
                .CacheStart = .Bookmark
                .FillCache
            End If
        Loop
    Next intLoop

    sngEnd = Timer
    sngCache = sngEnd - sngStart

    ' Display performance results.
    MsgBox "Caching Performance Results:" & vbCr & _
        "    No cache: " & Format(sngNoCache, _
    "##0.000") & " seconds" & vbCr & _
        "    50-record cache: " & Format(sngCache, _
```

```
      "##0.000") & " seconds"
   .Close
End With

' Delete linked table because this is a demonstration.
dbsCurrent.TableDefs.Delete tdfRoyalties.Name
dbsCurrent.Close

End Sub
```

FillColor Property

Returns or sets the color used to fill in shapes; **FillColor** is also used to fill in circles and boxes created with the **Circle** and **Line** graphics methods.

Applies To

PropertyPage Object, **UserControl** Object, **UserDocument** Object, **Printer** Object, **Printers** Collection, **Form** Object, **Forms** Collection, **PictureBox** Control, **Shape** Control

Syntax

object.**FillColor** [= *value*]

The **FillColor** property syntax has these parts:

Part	Description
object	An object expression that evaluates to an object in the **Applies To** list.
value	A value or constant that determines the fill color, as described in Settings.

Settings

The settings for *value* are:

Setting	Description
Normal RGB colors	Colors set with the **RGB** or **QBColor** functions in code.
System default colors	Colors specified with the system color constants in the Visual Basic (VB) object library in the Object Browser. The Microsoft Windows operating environment substitutes the user's choices, as specified by the user's Control Panel settings.

By default, **FillColor** is set to 0 (Black).

Remarks

Except for the **Form** object, when the **FillStyle** property is set to its default, 1 (Transparent), the **FillColor** setting is ignored.

See Also

BackColor, **ForeColor** Properties, **FillStyle** Property, **Color Constants**

Example

This example constructs a circle on your form with random **FillColor** and **FillStyle** property settings as you click the mouse. To try this example, paste the code into the Declarations section of a form, and then press F5 and click the form.

```
Private Sub Form_MouseDown (Button As Integer, Shift As Integer,
X As Single, Y As Single)
    FillColor = QBColor(Int(Rnd * 15))    ' Choose random FillColor.
    FillStyle = Int(Rnd * 8)              ' Choose random FillStyle.
    Circle (X, Y), 250                    ' Draw a circle.
End Sub
```

FillStyle Property

Returns or sets the pattern used to fill **Shape** controls as well as circles and boxes created with the **Circle** and **Line** graphics methods.

Applies To

PropertyPage Object, **UserControl** Object, **UserDocument** Object, **Printer** Object, **Printers** Collection, **Form** Object, **Forms** Collection, **PictureBox** Control, **Shape** Control

Syntax

object.**FillStyle** [= *number*]

The **FillStyle** property syntax has these parts:

Part	Description
object	An object expression that evaluates to an object in the **Applies To** list.
number	An integer that specifies the fill style, as described in Settings.

Settings

The *number* settings are:

Constant	Setting	Description
vbFSSolid	0	Solid
vbFSTransparent	1	(Default) Transparent
vbHorizontalLine	2	Horizontal Line
vbVerticalLine	3	Vertical Line
vbUpwardDiagonal	4	Upward Diagonal
vbDownwardDiagonal	5	Downward Diagonal
vbCross	6	Cross
vbDiagonalCross	7	Diagonal Cross

Remarks

When **FillStyle** is set to 1 (Transparent), the **FillColor** property is ignored, except for the **Form** object.

See Also

Paint Event, **BorderStyle** Property, **FillColor** Property

Example

This example displays a circle on a form with random **FillColor** and **FillStyle** property settings as you click the mouse. To try this example, paste the code into the Declarations section, and then press F5 to run the program.

```
Private Sub Form_MouseDown (Button As Integer, Shift As Integer,
X As Single, Y As Single)
    FillColor = QBColor(Rnd * 15)      ' Choose random FillColor.
    FillStyle = Int(Rnd * 8)           ' Choose random FillStyle.
    Circle (X, Y), 250                 ' Draw a circle.
End Sub
```

Filter Property

Sets or returns a value that determines the records included in a subsequently opened **Recordset** object (Microsoft Jet workspaces only).

Applies To

Dynaset-Type Recordset Object, **Recordset** Object, **Snapshot-Type Recordset** Object, **Forward-Only–Type Recordset** Object

Settings and Return Values

The setting or return value is a **String** data type that contains the WHERE clause of an SQL statement without the reserved word WHERE.

Remarks

Use the **Filter** property to apply a filter to a dynaset-, snapshot-, or forward-only–type **Recordset** object.

You can use the **Filter** property to restrict the records returned from an existing object when a new **Recordset** object is opened based on an existing **Recordset** object.

In many cases, it's faster to open a new **Recordset** object by using an SQL statement that includes a WHERE clause.

Use the U.S. date format (month-day-year) when you filter fields containing dates, even if you're not using the U.S. version of the Microsoft Jet database engine (in which case you must assemble any dates by concatenating strings, for example, strMonth & "-" & strDay & "-" & strYear). Otherwise, the data may not be filtered as you expect.

If you set the property to a string concatenated with a non-integer value, and the system parameters specify a non-U.S. decimal character such as a comma (for example, `strFilter = "PRICE > " & lngPrice`, and `lngPrice = 125,50`), an error occurs when you try to open the next **Recordset**. This is because during concatenation, the number will be converted to a string using your system's default decimal character, and Microsoft Jet SQL only accepts U.S. decimal characters.

See Also

OpenRecordset Method, **Sort** Property, WHERE Clause

Example

This example uses the **Filter** property to create a new **Recordset** from an existing **Recordset** based on a specified condition. The **FilterField** function is required for this procedure to run.

```
Sub FilterX()

    Dim dbsNorthwind As Database
    Dim rstOrders As Recordset
    Dim intOrders As Integer
    Dim strCountry As String
    Dim rstOrdersCountry As Recordset
    Dim strMessage As String

    Set dbsNorthwind = OpenDatabase("Northwind.mdb")
    Set rstOrders = dbsNorthwind.OpenRecordset("Orders", _
        dbOpenSnapshot)

    ' Populate the Recordset.
    rstOrders.MoveLast
    intOrders = rstOrders.RecordCount

    ' Get user input.
    strCountry = Trim(InputBox( _
        "Enter a country to filter on:"))

    If strCountry <> "" Then
        ' Open a filtered Recordset object.
        Set rstOrdersCountry = _
            FilterField(rstOrders, "ShipCountry", strCountry)

        With rstOrdersCountry
            ' Check RecordCount before populating Recordset;
            ' otherwise, error may result.
            If .RecordCount <> 0 Then .MoveLast
            ' Print number of records for the original
            ' Recordset object and the filtered Recordset
            ' object.
            strMessage = "Orders in original recordset: " & _
```

```
                vbCr & intOrders & vbCr & _
                "Orders in filtered recordset (Country = '" & _
                strCountry & "'): " & vbCr & .RecordCount
            MsgBox strMessage
            .Close
        End With

    End If

    rstOrders.Close

    dbsNorthwind.Close

End Sub

Function FilterField(rstTemp As Recordset, _
    strField As String, strFilter As String) As Recordset

    ' Set a filter on the specified Recordset object and then
    ' open a new Recordset object.
    rstTemp.Filter = strField & " = '" & strFilter & "'"
    Set FilterField = rstTemp.OpenRecordset

End Function
```

Note To see the effects of filtering rstOrders, you must set its **Filter** property, and then open a second **Recordset** object based on rstOrders.

Note When you know the data you want to select, it's usually more efficient to create a **Recordset** with an SQL statement. This example shows how you can create just one **Recordset** and obtain records from a particular country.

```
Sub FilterX2()

    Dim dbsNorthwind As Database
    Dim rstOrders As Recordset

    Set dbsNorthwind = OpenDatabase("Northwind.mdb")

    ' Open a Recordset object that selects records from a
    ' table based on the shipping country.
    Set rstOrders = _
        dbsNorthwind.OpenRecordset("SELECT * " & _
        "FROM Orders WHERE ShipCountry = 'USA'", _
        dbOpenSnapshot)

    rstOrders.Close
    dbsNorthwind.Close

End Sub
```

Find Method

Searches the active module for a specified string.

Applies To

CodeModule Object

Syntax

object.**Find**(*target*, *startline*, *startcol*, *endline*, *endcol* [, *wholeword*] [, *matchcase*]
↪ [, *patternsearch*]) **As Boolean**

Find syntax has these parts:

Part	Description
object	Required. An object expression that evaluates to an object in the **Applies To** list.
target	Required. A **String** containing the text or pattern you want to find.
startline	Required. A **Long** specifying the line at which you want to start the search; will be set to the line of the match if one is found.
startcol	Required. A **Long** specifying the column at which you want to start the search; will be set to the column containing the match if one is found.
endline	Required. A **Long** specifying the last line of the match if one is found.
endcol	Required. A **Long** specifying the last line of the match if one is found.
wholeword	Optional. A **Boolean** value specifying whether to only match whole words. If **True**, only matches whole words. **False** is the default.
matchcase	Optional. A **Boolean** value specifying whether to match case. If **True**, the search is case sensitive. **False** is the default.
patternsearch	Optional. A **Boolean** value specifying whether or not the target string is a regular expression pattern. If **True**, the target string is a regular expression pattern. **False** is the default.

Remarks

Find returns **True** if a match is found and **False** if a match isn't found.

The *matchcase* and *patternmatch* arguments are mutually exclusive; if both arguments are passed as **True**, an error occurs.

The content of the **Find** dialog box isn't affected by the **Find** method.

See Also

GetSelection Method, **Lines** Method, **ProcBodyLine** Method, **ProcCountLines** Method, **ProcOfLine** Method, **ProcStartLine** Method, **CodePane** Object

Example

The following example uses the **Find** method to verify that the specified block of lines, lines 1261 through 1279, of a particular code pane does contain the string "Tabs.Clear."

```
Application.VBE.CodePanes(2).CodeModule.Find ("Tabs.Clear",
1261, 1, 1280, 1, False, False)
```

FindFirst, FindLast, FindNext, FindPrevious Methods

Locates the first, last, next, or previous record in a dynaset- or snapshot-type **Recordset** object that satisfies the specified criteria and makes that record the current record (Microsoft Jet workspaces only).

Applies To

Dynaset-Type Recordset Object, **Recordset** Object, **Snapshot-Type Recordset** Object

Syntax

recordset.{**FindFirst** | **FindLast** | **FindNext** | **FindPrevious**} *criteria*

The **Find** methods have these parts.

Part	Description
recordset	An object variable that represents an existing dynaset- or snapshot-type **Recordset** object.
criteria	A **String** used to locate the record. It is like the **WHERE** clause in an SQL statement, but without the word WHERE.

Remarks

If you want to include all the records in your search—not just those that meet a specific condition—use the **Move** methods to move from record to record. To locate a record in a table-type **Recordset**, use the **Seek** method.

If a record matching the criteria isn't located, the current record pointer is unknown, and the **NoMatch** property is set to **True**. If *recordset* contains more than one record that satisfies the criteria, **FindFirst** locates the first occurrence, **FindNext** locates the next occurrence, and so on.

Each of the **Find** methods begins its search from the location and in the direction specified in the following table.

Find method	Begins searching at	Search direction
FindFirst	Beginning of recordset	End of recordset
FindLast	End of recordset	Beginning of recordset
FindNext	Current record	End of recordset
FindPrevious	Current record	Beginning of recordset

When you use the **FindLast** method, the Microsoft Jet database engine fully populates your **Recordset** before beginning the search, if this hasn't already happened.

Using one of the **Find** methods isn't the same as using a **Move** method, however, which simply makes the first, last, next, or previous record current without specifying a condition. You can follow a Find operation with a Move operation.

Always check the value of the **NoMatch** property to determine whether the Find operation has succeeded. If the search succeeds, **NoMatch** is **False**. If it fails, **NoMatch** is **True** and the current record isn't defined. In this case, you must position the current record pointer back to a valid record.

Using the **Find** methods with Microsoft Jet-connected ODBC-accessed recordsets can be inefficient. You may find that rephrasing your *criteria* to locate a specific record is faster, especially when working with large recordsets.

In an ODBCDirect workspace, the **Find** and **Seek** methods are not available on any type of **Recordset** object, because executing a **Find** or **Seek** through an ODBC connection is not very efficient over the network. Instead, you should design the query (that is, using the *source* argument to the **OpenRecordset** method) with an appropriate WHERE clause that restricts the returned records to only those that meet the criteria you would otherwise use in a **Find** or **Seek** method.

When working with Microsoft Jet-connected ODBC databases and large dynaset-type **Recordset** objects, you might discover that using the **Find** methods or using the **Sort** or **Filter** property is slow. To improve performance, use SQL queries with customized ORDER BY or WHERE clauses, parameter queries, or **QueryDef** objects that retrieve specific indexed records.

You should use the U.S. date format (month-day-year) when you search for fields containing dates, even if you're not using the U.S. version of the Microsoft Jet database engine; otherwise, the data may not be found. Use the Visual Basic **Format** function to convert the date. For example:

```
rstEmployees.FindFirst "HireDate > #" _
   & Format(mydate, 'm-d-yy' ) & "#"
```

If *criteria* is composed of a string concatenated with a non-integer value, and the system parameters specify a non-U.S. decimal character such as a comma (for example, strSQL = "PRICE > " & lngPrice, and lngPrice = 125,50), an error occurs when you try to call the method. This is because during concatenation, the number will be converted to a string using your system's default decimal character, and Microsoft Jet SQL only accepts U.S. decimal characters.

Notes

- For best performance, the *criteria* should be in either the form "*field* = *value*" where *field* is an indexed field in the underlying base table, or "*field* LIKE *prefix*" where *field* is an indexed field in the underlying base table and *prefix* is a prefix search string (for example, "ART*").

- In general, for equivalent types of searches, the **Seek** method provides better performance than the **Find** methods. This assumes that table-type **Recordset** objects alone can satisfy your needs.

See Also

Move Method, **MoveFirst, MoveLast, MoveNext, MovePrevious** Methods, **Seek** Method, **AbsolutePosition** Property, **NoMatch** Property

Example

This example uses the **FindFirst**, **FindLast**, **FindNext**, and **FindPrevious** methods to move the record pointer of a **Recordset** based on the supplied search string and command. The **FindAny** function is required for this procedure to run.

```
Sub FindFirstX()

    Dim dbsNorthwind As Database
    Dim rstCustomers As Recordset
    Dim strCountry As String
    Dim varBookmark As Variant
    Dim strMessage As String
    Dim intCommand As Integer

    Set dbsNorthwind = OpenDatabase("Northwind.mdb")
    Set rstCustomers = dbsNorthwind.OpenRecordset( _
        "SELECT CompanyName, City, Country " & _
        "FROM Customers ORDER BY CompanyName", _
        dbOpenSnapshot)

    Do While True
        ' Get user input and build search string.
        strCountry = _
            Trim(InputBox("Enter country for search."))
        If strCountry = "" Then Exit Do
        strCountry = "Country = '" & strCountry & "'"

        With rstCustomers
            ' Populate recordset.
            .MoveLast
            ' Find first record satisfying search string. Exit
            ' loop if no such record exists.
            .FindFirst strCountry
            If .NoMatch Then
                MsgBox "No records found with " & _
                    strCountry & "."
                Exit Do
            End If

            Do While True
                ' Store bookmark of current record.
                varBookmark = .Bookmark
                ' Get user choice of which method to use.
                strMessage = "Company: " & !CompanyName & _
                    vbCr & "Location: " & !City & ", " & _
                    !Country & vbCr & vbCr & _
```

```
                            strCountry & vbCr & vbCr & _
                            "[1 - FindFirst, 2 - FindLast, " & _
                            vbCr & "3 - FindNext, " & _
                            "4 - FindPrevious]"
                    intCommand = Val(Left(InputBox(strMessage), 1))
                    If intCommand < 1 Or intCommand > 4 Then Exit Do

                    ' Use selected Find method. If the Find fails,
                    ' return to the last current record.
                    If FindAny(intCommand, rstCustomers, _
                            strCountry) = False Then
                        .Bookmark = varBookmark
                        MsgBox "No match--returning to " & _
                            "current record."
                    End If

                Loop

            End With

            Exit Do
        Loop

        rstCustomers.Close
        dbsNorthwind.Close

    End Sub

    Function FindAny(intChoice As Integer, _
        rstTemp As Recordset, _
        strFind As String) As Boolean

        ' Use Find method based on user input.
        Select Case intChoice
            Case 1
                rstTemp.FindFirst strFind
            Case 2
                rstTemp.FindLast strFind
            Case 3
                rstTemp.FindNext strFind
            Case 4
                rstTemp.FindPrevious strFind
        End Select

        ' Set return value based on NoMatch property.
        FindAny = IIf(rstTemp.NoMatch, False, True)

    End Function
```

FirstRow Property

Returns or sets a value containing the bookmark for the first visible row in the **DBGrid** control or **Split** object. Not available at design time.

Applies To

Split Object, **DBGrid** Control

Syntax

object.**FirstRow** [= *value*]

The **FirstRow** property syntax has these parts:

Part	Description
object	An object expression that evaluates to an object in the **Applies To** list.
value	A string expression containing a bookmark corresponding to the first visible row in the **DBGrid** control.

Remarks

For a **DBGrid** control, setting the **FirstRow** property causes the grid to scroll so that the specified row becomes the topmost row. If a grid contains multiple splits, then the topmost row changes in each split, even if the splits have different **ScrollGroup** property settings.

For a **Split** object, setting the **FirstRow** property causes the specified row to become the topmost row for that split only.

See Also

RowBookmark Method

Font Object

The **Font** object contains information needed to format text for display in the interface of an application or for printed output.

Syntax

Font

Remarks

You frequently identify a **Font** object using the **Font** property of an object that displays text (such as a **Form** object or the **Printer** object).

You cannot create a **Font** object using code like `Dim X As New Font`. If you want to create a **Font** object, you must use the **StdFont** object like this:

```
Dim X As New StdFont
```

If you put a **TextBox** control named Text1 on a form, you can dynamically change it's font **Font** object to another using the **Set** statement, as in the following example:

```
Dim X As New StdFont
X.Bold = True
X.Name = "Arial"
Set Text1.Font = X
```

Properties

Bold Property, **Italic** Property, **Size** Property (Font), **StrikeThrough** Property, **Underline** Property, **Weight** Property, **Name** Property

See Also

TextHeight Method, **TextWidth** Method, **Fonts** Property, **Font** Property

---

Font Property

Returns a **Font** object.

Applies To

CheckBox Control, **ComboBox** Control, **CommandButton** Control, **Data** Control, **DBCombo** Control, **DBGrid** Control, **DBList** Control, **DirListBox** Control, **DriveListBox** Control, **FileListBox** Control, **Form** Object, **Forms** Collection, **Frame** Control, **Label** Control, **ListBox** Control, **ListView** Control, **Masked Edit** Control, **MSFlexGrid** Control, **OptionButton** Control, **PictureBox** Control, **Printer** Object, **Printers** Collection, **PropertyPage** Object, **RemoteData** Control, **RichTextBox** Control, **SSTab** Control, **StatusBar** Control, **TabStrip** Control, **TextBox** Control, **TreeView** Control, **UserControl** Object, **UserDocument** Object

Syntax

object.**Font**

The *object* placeholder represents an object expression that evaluates to an object in the **Applies To** list.

Remarks

Use the **Font** property of an object to identify a specific **Font** object whose properties you want to use. For example, the following code changes the **Bold** property setting of a **Font** object identified by the **Font** property of a **TextBox** object:

```
txtFirstName.Font.Bold = True
```

Specifics

Fonts Property

See Also

Font Object

FontBold, FontItalic, FontStrikethru, FontUnderline Properties

Return or set font styles in the following formats: **Bold**, *Italic*, ~~Strikethru~~, and Underline.

Note The **FontBold, FontItalic, FontStrikethru,** and **FontUnderline** properties are included for use with the **CommonDialog** control and for compatibility with earlier versions of Visual Basic. For additional functionality, use the new **Font** object properties (not available for the **CommonDialog** control).

Applies To

AmbientProperties Object, **PropertyPage** Object, **UserControl** Object, **UserDocument** Object, **Printer** Object, **Printers** Collection, **CheckBox** Control, **ComboBox** Control, **CommandButton** Control, **DirListBox** Control, **DriveListBox** Control, **FileListBox** Control, **Form** Object, **Forms** Collection, **Frame** Control, **Label** Control, **ListBox** Control, **OptionButton** Control, **PictureBox** Control, **TextBox** Control, **AxisTitle** Object, **CommonDialog** Control, **Data** Control

Syntax

*object***.FontBold** [= *boolean*]
*object***.FontItalic** [= *boolean*]
*object***.FontStrikethru** [= *boolean*]
*object***.FontUnderline** [= *boolean*]

The **FontBold, FontItalic, FontStrikethru,** and **FontUnderline** property syntaxes have these parts:

Part	Description
object	An object expression that evaluates to an object in the **Applies To** list.
boolean	A Boolean expression specifying the font style as described in Settings.

Settings

The settings for *boolean* are:

Setting	Description
True	(Default for **FontBold**, except with the **CommonDialog** control) Turns on the formatting in that style.
False	(Default for **FontItalic, FontStrikethru,** and **FontUnderline,** and **FontBold** with the **CommonDialog** control) Turns off the formatting in that style.

Remarks

Use these font properties to format text, either at design time using the Properties window or at run time using code. For **PictureBox** controls and **Form** and **Printer** objects, setting these properties doesn't affect graphics or text already drawn on the

547

control or object. For all other controls, font changes take effect on screen immediately.

To use these properties with the **CommonDialog** control, the **Effects** flag must be set.

Note Fonts available in Visual Basic vary depending on your system configuration, display devices, and printing devices. Font-related properties can be set only to values for which actual fonts exist.

In general, you should change the **FontName** property before you set size and style attributes with the **FontSize**, **FontBold**, **FontItalic**, **FontStrikethru**, and **FontUnderline** properties. However, when you set TrueType fonts to smaller than 8 points, you should set the point size with the **FontSize** property, then set the **FontName** property, and then set the size again with the **FontSize** property. The Microsoft Windows operating environment uses a different font for TrueType fonts that are smaller than 8 points.

See Also

Font Object, **TextHeight** Method, **TextWidth** Method, **FontName** Property, **FontSize** Property

Example

This example puts text on a form in one of two combinations of styles with each mouse click. To try this example, paste the code into the Declarations section of a form, and then press F5 and click the form.

```
Private Sub Form_Click ()
    FontStrikethru = Not FontStrikethru   ' Toggle strikethrough.
    FontItalic = Not FontItalic           ' Toggle font style.
    Print "Now is the time!"              ' Print some text.
End Sub
```

FontCount Property

Returns the number of fonts available for the current display device or active printer.

Applies To

Screen Object, **Printer** Object, **Printers** Collection

Syntax

object.**FontCount**

The *object* placeholder represents an object expression that evaluates to an object in the **Applies To** list.

Remarks

Use this property with the **Fonts** property to see a list of available screen or printer fonts. Fonts available in Visual Basic vary according to your system configuration, display devices, and printing devices.

See Also

> **FontName** Property, **Fonts** Property

Example

> This example prints a list of the printer fonts in a **ListBox** control. To try this example, paste the code into the Declarations section of a form that has a **ListBox** control named List1. Press F5 to run the program, and then click the form.

```
Private Sub Form_Click ()
    Dim I                                  ' Declare variable.
    For I = 0 To Printer.FontCount -1   ' Determine number of fonts.
        List1.AddItem Printer.Fonts (I) ' Put each font into list box.
    Next I
End Sub
```

FontName Property

> Returns or sets the font used to display text in a control or in a run-time drawing or printing operation.

> **Note**   The **FontName** property is included for use with the **CommonDialog** control and for compatibility with earlier versions of Visual Basic. For additional functionality, use the new **Font** object properties (not available for the **CommonDialog** control).

Applies To

> **PropertyPage** Object, **UserControl** Object, **UserDocument** Object, **Printer** Object, **Printers** Collection, **CheckBox** Control, **ComboBox** Control, **CommandButton** Control, **DirListBox** Control, **DriveListBox** Control, **FileListBox** Control, **Form** Object, **Forms** Collection, **Frame** Control, **Label** Control, **ListBox** Control, **OptionButton** Control, **PictureBox** Control, **TextBox** Control, **CommonDialog** Control (Font Dialog)

Syntax

> *object*.**FontName** [= *font*]

> The **FontName** property syntax has these parts:

Part	Description
object	An object expression that evaluates to an object in the **Applies To** list.
font	A string expression specifying the font name to use.

Remarks

> The default for this property is determined by the system. Fonts available with Visual Basic vary depending on your system configuration, display devices, and printing devices. Font-related properties can be set only to values for which fonts exist.

In general, you should change **FontName** before setting size and style attributes with the **FontSize**, **FontBold**, **FontItalic**, **FontStrikethru**, and **FontUnderline** properties.

Note At run time, you can get information on fonts available to the system through the **FontCount** and **Fonts** properties.

See Also

TextHeight Method, **TextWidth** Method, **FontBold**, **FontItalic**, **FontStrikethru**, **FontUnderline** Properties, **FontSize** Property, **FontCount** Property, **Fonts** Property

Example

This example prints the name of each font using the particular font. To try this example, paste the code into the Declarations section of a form. Press F5 to run the program, and then click the form. Each time you click the form, the font name is printed.

```
Private Sub Form_Click ()
    Static I                        ' Declare variables.
    Dim OldFont
    OldFont = FontName              ' Preserve original font.
    FontName = Screen.Fonts(I)      ' Change to new font.
    Print Screen.Fonts(I)           ' Print name of font.
    I = I + 1                       ' Increment counter.
    If I = FontCount Then I = 0     ' Start over.
    FontName = OldFont              ' Restore original font.
End Sub
```

Fonts Property

Returns all font names available for the current display device or active printer.

Applies To

Screen Object, **Printer** Object, **Printers** Collection

Syntax

object.**Fonts**(*index*)

The **Fonts** property syntax has these parts:

Part	Description
object	An object expression that evaluates to an object in the **Applies To** list.
index	An integer from 0 to **FontCount** −1.

Remarks

The **Fonts** property works in conjunction with the **FontCount** property, which returns the number of font names available for the object. Fonts available in Visual Basic vary according to your system configuration, display devices, and printing devices. Use both the **Fonts** and the **FontCount** properties to get information about available screen or printer fonts.

See Also

TextHeight Method, **TextWidth** Method, **FontBold**, **FontItalic**, **FontStrikethru**, **FontUnderline** Properties, **FontName** Property, **FontSize** Property

Example

This example prints a list of the printer fonts in a **ListBox** control. To try this example, paste the code into the Declarations section of a form that has a **ListBox** control named List1. Press F5 to run the program, and then click the form.

```
Private Sub Form_Click ()
    Dim I                                ' Declare variable.
    For I = 0 To Printer.FontCount -1    ' Determine number of fonts.
        List1.AddItem Printer.Fonts (I)  ' Put each font into list box.
    Next I
End Sub
```

FontSize Property

Returns or sets the size of the font to be used for text displayed in a control or in a run-time drawing or printing operation.

Note The **FontSize** property is included for use with the **CommonDialog** control and for compatibility with earlier versions of Visual Basic. For additional functionality, use the new **Font** object properties (not available for the **CommonDialog** control).

Applies To

PropertyPage Object, **UserControl** Object, **UserDocument** Object, **Printer** Object, **Printers** Collection, **CheckBox** Control, **ComboBox** Control, **CommandButton** Control, **DirListBox** Control, **DriveListBox** Control, **FileListBox** Control, **Form** Object, **Forms** Collection, **Frame** Control, **Label** Control, **ListBox** Control, **OptionButton** Control, **PictureBox** Control, **TextBox** Control, **MSFlexGrid** Control, **CommonDialog** Control (Font Dialog), **Data** Control

Syntax

object.**FontSize** [= *points*]

The **FontSize** property syntax has these parts:

Part	Description
object	An object expression that evaluates to an object in the **Applies To** list.
points	A numeric expression specifying the font size to use, in points.

Remarks

Use this property to format text in the font size you want. The default is determined by the system. To change the default, specify the size of the font in points.

The maximum value for **FontSize** is 2160 points.

Note Fonts available with Visual Basic vary depending on your system configuration, display devices, and printing devices. Font-related properties can be set only to values for which fonts exist.

In general, you should change the **FontName** property before you set size and style attributes with the **FontSize**, **FontBold**, **FontItalic**, **FontStrikethru**, and **FontUnderline** properties. However, when you set TrueType fonts to smaller than 8 points, you should set the point size with the **FontSize** property, then set the **FontName** property, and then set the size again with the **FontSize** property. The Microsoft Windows operating environment uses a different font for TrueType fonts that are smaller than 8 points.

See Also

FontBold, **FontItalic**, **FontStrikethru**, **FontUnderline** Properties, **FontName** Property, **FontCount** Property, **Fonts** Property

Example

This example prints text on your form in two different point sizes with each click of the mouse. To try this example, paste the code into the Declarations section of a form. Press F5 to run the program, and then click the form.

```
Private Sub Form_Click ()
    FontSize = 24                        ' Set FontSize.
    Print "This is 24-point type."       ' Print large type.
    FontSize = 8                         ' Set FontSize.
    Print "This is 8-point type."        ' Print small type.
End Sub
```

FontTransparent Property

Returns or sets a value that determines whether background text and graphics on a **Form** or **Printer** object or a **PictureBox** control are displayed in the spaces around characters.

Applies To

PropertyPage Object, **UserControl** Object, **UserDocument** Object, **Printer** Object, **Printers** Collection, **Form** Object, **Forms** Collection, **PictureBox** Control

Syntax

object.**FontTransparent** [= *boolean*]

The **FontTransparent** property syntax has these parts:

Part	Description
object	An object expression that evaluates to an object in the **Applies To** list.
boolean	A Boolean expression specifying the state of background text and graphics, as described in **Settings**.

Settings

The settings for *boolean* are:

Setting	Description
True	(Default) Permits background graphics and text to show around the spaces of the characters in a font.
False	Masks existing background graphics and text around the characters of a font.

Remarks

Set **FontTransparent** at design time using the Properties window or at run time using code. Changing **FontTransparent** at run time doesn't affect graphics and text already drawn to **Form**, **Printer**, or **PictureBox**.

See Also

Bold Property, **Italic** Property, **Size** Property (Font), **StrikeThrough** Property, **Underline** Property, **Weight** Property, **Name** Property

Example

This example prints text on top of a graphic in a **PictureBox** control. Put a **PictureBox** on a form, set its **AutoSize** property to **True**, and load its **Picture** property with a bitmap (.bmp) file. To try this example, paste the code into the Declarations section of a form, and then press F5 and click the form twice.

```
Private Sub Form_Click ()
   ' Toggle property.
   Picture1.FontTransparent = Not Picture1.FontTransparent
   Picture1.Print "Demo of FontTransparent property."
End Sub
```

For Each...Next Statement

Repeats a group of statements for each element in an array or collection.

Syntax

For Each *element* **In** *group*
    [*statements*]
    [**Exit For**]
    [*statements*]
Next [*element*]

The **For...Each...Next** statement syntax has these parts:

Part	Description
element	Required. Variable used to iterate through the elements of the collection or array. For collections, *element* can only be a **Variant** variable, a generic object variable, or any specific object variable. For arrays, *element* can only be a **Variant** variable.
group	Required. Name of an object collection or array (except an array of user-defined types).
statements	Optional. One or more statements that are executed on each item in *group*.

Remarks

The **For...Each** block is entered if there is at least one element in *group*. Once the loop has been entered, all the statements in the loop are executed for the first element in *group*. If there are more elements in *group*, the statements in the loop continue to execute for each element. When there are no more elements in *group*, the loop is exited and execution continues with the statement following the **Next** statement.

Any number of **Exit For** statements may be placed anywhere in the loop as an alternative way to exit. **Exit For** is often used after evaluating some condition, for example **If...Then**, and transfers control to the statement immediately following **Next**.

You can nest **For...Each...Next** loops by placing one **For...Each...Next** loop within another. However, each loop *element* must be unique.

Note If you omit *element* in a **Next** statement, execution continues as if *element* is included. If a **Next** statement is encountered before its corresponding **For** statement, an error occurs.

You can't use the **For...Each...Next** statement with an array of user-defined types because a **Variant** can't contain a user-defined type.

See Also

Do...Loop Statement, **Exit** Statement, **For...Next** Statement, **While...Wend** Statement

Example

This example uses the **For Each...Next** statement to search the **Text** property of all elements in a collection for the existence of the string "Hello". In the example, MyObject is a text-related object and is an element of the collection MyCollection. Both are generic names used for illustration purposes only.

```
Dim Found, MyObject, MyCollection
Found = False                          ' Initialize variable.
For Each MyObject In MyCollection       ' Iterate through each element.
    If MyObject.Text = "Hello" Then     ' If Text equals "Hello".
        Found = True                    ' Set Found to True.
        Exit For                        ' Exit loop.
    End If
Next
```

For...Next Statement

Repeats a group of statements a specified number of times.

Syntax

For *counter* = *start* **To** *end* [**Step** *step*]
    [*statements*]
    [**Exit For**]
    [*statements*]
Next [*counter*]

The **For...Next** statement syntax has these parts:

Part	Description
counter	Required. Numeric variable used as a loop counter. The variable can't be a **Boolean** or an array element.
start	Required. Initial value of *counter*.
end	Required. Final value of *counter*.
step	Optional. Amount *counter* is changed each time through the loop. If not specified, *step* defaults to one.
statements	Optional. One or more statements between **For** and **Next** that are executed the specified number of times.

Remarks

The *step* argument can be either positive or negative. The value of the *step* argument determines loop processing as follows:

Value	Loop executes if
Positive or 0	*counter* <= *end*
Negative	*counter* >= *end*

After all statements in the loop have executed, *step* is added to *counter*. At this point, either the statements in the loop execute again (based on the same test that caused the loop to execute initially), or the loop is exited and execution continues with the statement following the **Next** statement.

Tip Changing the value of *counter* while inside a loop can make it more difficult to read and debug your code.

Any number of **Exit For** statements may be placed anywhere in the loop as an alternate way to exit. **Exit For** is often used after evaluating of some condition, for example **If...Then**, and transfers control to the statement immediately following **Next**.

You can nest **For...Next** loops by placing one **For...Next** loop within another. Give each loop a unique variable name as its *counter*. The following construction is correct:

```
For I = 1 To 10
   For J = 1 To 10
      For K = 1 To 10
         . . .
      Next K
   Next J
Next I
```

Note If you omit *counter* in a **Next** statement, execution continues as if *counter* is included. If a **Next** statement is encountered before its corresponding **For** statement, an error occurs.

See Also

Do...Loop Statement, **Exit** Statement, **For Each...Next** Statement, **While...Wend** Statement

Example

This example uses the **For...Next** statement to create a string that contains 10 instances of the numbers 0 through 9, each string separated from the other by a single space. The outer loop uses a loop counter variable that is decremented each time through the loop.

```
Dim Words, Chars, MyString
For Words = 10 To 1 Step -1      ' Set up 10 repetitions.
   For Chars = 0 To 9            ' Set up 10 repetitions.
      MyString = MyString & Chars  ' Append number to string.
   Next Chars                    ' Increment counter.
   MyString = MyString & " "     ' Append a space.
Next Words
```

Foreign Property

Returns a value that indicates whether an **Index** object represents a foreign key in a table (Microsoft Jet workspaces only).

Applies To

Index Object

Return Values

The return value is a **Boolean** data type that returns **True** if the **Index** object represents a foreign key.

Remarks

A foreign key consists of one or more fields in a foreign table that uniquely identify all rows in a primary table.

The Microsoft Jet database engine creates an **Index** object for the foreign table and sets the **Foreign** property when you create a relationship that enforces referential integrity.

See Also

TableDef Object, **Primary** Property

Example

This example shows how the **Foreign** property can indicate which **Index** objects in a **TableDef** are foreign key indexes. Such indexes are created by the Microsoft Jet database engine when a **Relation** is created. The default name for the foreign key indexes is the name of the primary table plus the name of the foreign table. The **ForeignOutput** function is required for this procedure to run.

```
Sub ForeignX()

    Dim dbsNorthwind As Database

    Set dbsNorthwind = OpenDatabase("Northwind.mdb")

    With dbsNorthwind
        ' Print report on foreign key indexes from two
        ' TableDef objects and a QueryDef object.
        ForeignOutput .TableDefs!Products
        ForeignOutput .TableDefs!Orders
        ForeignOutput .TableDefs![Order Details]

        .Close
    End With

End Sub

Function ForeignOutput(tdfTemp As TableDef)

    Dim idxLoop As Index

    With tdfTemp
        Debug.Print "Indexes in " & .Name & " TableDef"
        ' Enumerate the Indexes collection of the specified
        ' TableDef object.
        For Each idxLoop In .Indexes
            Debug.Print "    " & idxLoop.Name
            Debug.Print "        Foreign = " & idxLoop.Foreign
        Next idxLoop
    End With

End Function
```

ForeignName Property

Sets or returns a value that specifies the name of the **Field** object in a foreign table that corresponds to a field in a primary table for a relationship (Microsoft Jet workspaces only).

Applies To

Field Object

Settings and Return Values

The setting or return value is a **String** data type that evaluates to the name of a **Field** in the associated **TableDef** object's **Fields** collection.

If the **Relation** object isn't appended to the **Database**, but the **Field** is appended to the **Relation** object, the **ForeignName** property is read/write. Once the **Relation** object is appended to the database, the **ForeignName** property is read-only.

Remarks

Only a **Field** object that belongs to the **Fields** collection of a **Relation** object can support the **ForeignName** property.

The **Name** and **ForeignName** property settings for a **Field** object specify the names of the corresponding fields in the primary and foreign tables of a relationship. The **Table** and **ForeignTable** property settings for a **Relation** object determine the primary and foreign tables of a relationship.

For example, if you had a list of valid part codes (in a field named PartNo) stored in a ValidParts table, you could establish a relationship with an OrderItem table such that if a part code were entered into the OrderItem table, it would have to already exist in the ValidParts table. If the part code didn't exist in the ValidParts table and you had not set the **Attributes** property of the **Relation** object to **dbRelationDontEnforce**, a trappable error would occur.

In this case, the ValidParts table is the foreign table, so the **ForeignTable** property of the **Relation** object would be set to ValidParts and the **Table** property of the **Relation** object would be set to OrderItem. The **Name** and **ForeignName** properties of the **Field** object in the **Relation** object's **Fields** collection would be set to PartNo.

The following illustration depicts the relation described above.

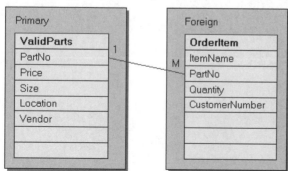

ForeignTable Property, **Name** Property, **Table** Property

Example

This example shows how the **Table**, **ForeignTable**, and **ForeignName** properties
define the terms of a **Relation** between two tables.

```
Sub ForeignNameX()

    Dim dbsNorthwind As Database
    Dim relLoop As Relation

    Set dbsNorthwind = OpenDatabase("Northwind.mdb")

    Debug.Print "Relation"
    Debug.Print "    Table - Field"
    Debug.Print "    Primary (One)   ";
    Debug.Print ".Table - .Fields(0).Name"
    Debug.Print "    Foreign (Many)  ";
    Debug.Print ".ForeignTable - .Fields(0).ForeignName"

    ' Enumerate the Relations collection of the Northwind
    ' database to report on the property values of
    ' the Relation objects and their Field objects.
    For Each relLoop In dbsNorthwind.Relations
        With relLoop
            Debug.Print
            Debug.Print .Name & " Relation"
            Debug.Print "    Table - Field"
            Debug.Print "    Primary (One)   ";
            Debug.Print .Table & " - " & .Fields(0).Name
            Debug.Print "    Foreign (Many)  ";
            Debug.Print .ForeignTable & " - " & _
                .Fields(0).ForeignName
        End With
    Next relLoop

    dbsNorthwind.Close

End Sub
```

ForeignTable Property

Sets or returns the name of the foreign table in a relationship (Microsoft Jet
workspaces only).

Applies To

Relation Object

Settings and Return Values

The setting or return value is a **String** data type that evaluates to the name of a table
in the **Database** object's **TableDefs** collection. This property is read/write for a new

Relation object not yet appended to a collection and read-only for an existing **Relation** object in the **Relations** collection.

Remarks

The **ForeignTable** property setting of a **Relation** object is the **Name** property setting of the **TableDef** or **QueryDef** object that represents the foreign table or query; the **Table** property setting is the **Name** property setting of the **TableDef** or **QueryDef** object that represents the primary table or query.

For example, if you had a list of valid part codes (in a field named PartNo) stored in a ValidParts table, you could establish a relationship with an OrderItem table such that if a part code were entered into the OrderItem table, it would have to already be in the ValidParts table. If the part code didn't exist in the ValidParts table and you had not set the **Attributes** property of the **Relation** object to **dbRelationDontEnforce**, a trappable error would occur.

In this case, the ValidParts table is the primary table, so the **Table** property of the **Relation** object would be set to ValidParts and the **ForeignTable** property of the **Relation** object would be set to OrderItem. The **Name** and **ForeignName** properties of the **Field** object in the **Relation** object's **Fields** collection would be set to PartNo.

The following illustration depicts the relation described above.

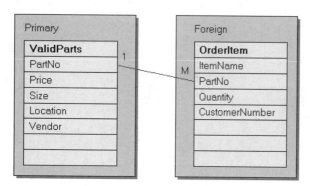

See Also

TableDef Object, **ForeignName** Property, **Name** Property, **Table** Property

Example

This example shows how the **Table**, **ForeignTable**, and **ForeignName** properties define the terms of a **Relation** between two tables.

```
Sub ForeignNameX()

    Dim dbsNorthwind As Database
    Dim relLoop As Relation

    Set dbsNorthwind = OpenDatabase("Northwind.mdb")
```

```
Debug.Print "Relation"
Debug.Print "    Table - Field"
Debug.Print "    Primary (One)   ";
Debug.Print ".Table - .Fields(0).Name"
Debug.Print "    Foreign (Many)  ";
Debug.Print ".ForeignTable - .Fields(0).ForeignName"

' Enumerate the Relations collection of the Northwind
' database to report on the property values of
' the Relation objects and their Field objects.
For Each relLoop In dbsNorthwind.Relations
    With relLoop
        Debug.Print
        Debug.Print .Name & " Relation"
        Debug.Print "    Table - Field"
        Debug.Print "    Primary (One)   ";
        Debug.Print .Table & " - " & .Fields(0).Name
        Debug.Print "    Foreign (Many)  ";
        Debug.Print .ForeignTable & " - " & _
            .Fields(0).ForeignName
    End With
Next relLoop

dbsNorthwind.Close

End Sub
```

Form Object, Forms Collection

A **Form** object is a window or dialog box that makes up part of an application's user interface.

A **Forms** collection is a collection whose elements represent each loaded form in an application. The collection includes the application's MDI form, MDI child forms, and non-MDI forms. The **Forms** collection has a single property, **Count**, that specifies the number of elements in the collection.

Syntax

Form

Forms(*index*)

The placeholder *index* represents an integer with a range from 0 to
`Forms.Count  - 1`.

Remarks

You can use the **Forms** collection to iterate through all loaded forms in an application. It identifies an intrinsic global variable named **Forms**. You can pass **Forms**(*index*) to a function. whose argument is specified as a **Forms** class.

Forms have properties that determine aspects of their appearance, such as position, size, and color; and aspects of their behavior, such as whether or not they are resizable.

Forms can also respond to events initiated by a user or triggered by the system. For example, you could write code in a form's Click event procedure that would enable the user to change the color of a form by clicking it.

In addition to properties and events, you can use methods to manipulate forms using code. For example, you can use the **Move** method to change a form's location and size.

A special kind of form, the MDI form, can contain other forms called MDI child forms. An MDI form is created with the MDI Form command on the Insert menu; an MDI child form is created by choosing New Form from the File menu and then setting the **MDIChild** property to **True**.

You can create multiple instances of forms in code by using the **New** keyword in **Dim**, **Set**, and **Static** statements.

When designing forms, set the **BorderStyle** property to define a form's border, and set the **Caption** property to put text in the title bar. In code, you can use the **Hide** and **Show** methods to make forms invisible or visible at run time.

Note   Setting **BorderStyle** to 0 removes the border. If you want your form to have a border without the title bar, Control-menu box, Maximize button, and Minimize button, delete any text from the form's **Caption** property, and set the form's **ControlBox**, **MaxButton**, and **MinButton** properties to **False**.

Form is an Object data type. You can declare variables as type **Form** before setting them to an instance of a type of form that was declared at design time. Similarly, you can pass an argument to a procedure as type **Form**.

Forms also can act as sources in a DDEconversation, with a **Label**, **PictureBox**, or **TextBox** control furnishing the data.

You can access the collection of controls on a **Form** using the **Controls** collection. For example, to hide all the controls on an **Form** you can use code similar to the following:

```
For Each Control in Form1.Controls
    Control.Visible = False
Next Control
```

Properties

ActiveControl Property, **ActiveForm** Property, **Appearance** Property, **AutoRedraw** Property, **BackColor**, **ForeColor** Properties, **BorderStyle** Property, **Caption** Property, **ClipControls** Property, **ControlBox** Property, **Controls** Property, **Count** Property, **CurrentX**, **CurrentY** Properties, **DrawMode** Property, **DrawStyle** Property, **DrawWidth** Property, **Enabled** Property, **FillColor** Property, **FillStyle** Property, **Font** Property, **FontBold**, **FontItalic**, **FontStrikethru**, **FontUnderline**

Properties, **FontName** Property, **FontSize** Property, **FontTransparent** Property, **hDC**
Property, **Height**, **Width** Properties, **HelpContextID** Property, **hWnd** Property, **Icon**
Property, **Image** Property, **KeyPreview** Property, **Left**, **Top** Properties, **LinkMode**
Property, **LinkTopic** Property, **MaxButton** Property, **MDIChild** Property,
MinButton Property, **MouseIcon** Property, **MousePointer** Property, **Moveable**
Property, **Name** Property, **NegotiateMenus** Property, **OLEDropMode** Property,
Palette Property, **PaletteMode** Property, **Picture** Property, **ScaleHeight**, **ScaleWidth**
Properties, **ScaleLeft**, **ScaleTop** Properties, **ScaleMode** Property, **ShownInTaskbar**
Property, **StartUpObject** Property, **Tag** Property, **Visible** Property,
WhatsThisButton Property, **WhatsThisHelp** Property, **WindowState** Property

Events

Activate, **Deactivate** Events, **Click** Event, **DblClick** Event, **DragDrop** Event,
DragOver Event, **GotFocus** Event, **Initialize** Event, **KeyDown**, **KeyUp** Events,
KeyPress Event, **LinkClose** Event, **LinkError** Event, **LinkExecute** Event,
LinkOpen Event, **Load** Event, **LostFocus** Event, **MouseDown**, **MouseUp** Events,
MouseMove Event, **OLECompleteDrag** Event, **OLEDragDrop** Event,
OLEGiveFeedback Event, **OLESetData** Event, **OLEStartDrag** Event, **Paint** Event,
QueryUnload Event, **Resize** Event, **Terminate** Event, **Unload** Event

Methods

Add Method, **Circle** Method, **Cls** Method, **Hide** Method, **Line** Method, **Move**
Method, **OLEDrag** Method, **PaintPicture** Method, **Point** Method, **PopupMenu**
Method, **PrintForm** Method, **Pset** Method, **Refresh** Method, **Scale** Method, **ScaleX**,
ScaleY Methods, **SetFocus** Method, **Show** Method, **TextHeight,** Method, **TextWidth**
Method, **WhatsThis Mode** Method, **Zorder** Method

See Also

UserDocument Object, **Hide** Method, **Move** Method, **Controls** Collection, **Label**
Control, **MDIForm** Object, **PictureBox** Control, **TextBox** Control, **MDIChild**
Property, **Count** Property (VB Collections)

Example

This example fills a list box with the captions of all the currently loaded forms.

```
Private Sub Form_Activate ()
    Dim I            ' Declare variable.
    ' Refill list (in case an instance was added or removed).
    lstForms.Clear    ' Clear list box.
    For I = 0 To Forms.Count - 1
        lstForms.AddItem Forms(I).Caption
    Next I
End Sub
```

Format Function

Returns a **Variant** (**String**) containing an expression formatted according to instructions contained in a format expression.

Syntax

Format(*expression*[, *format*[, *firstdayofweek*[, *firstweekofyear*]]])

The **Format** function syntax has these parts:

Part	Description
expression	Required. Any valid expression.
format	Optional. A valid named or user-defined format expression.
firstdayofweek	Optional. A constant that specifies the first day of the week.
firstweekofyear	Optional. A constant that specifies the first week of the year.

Settings

The *firstdayofweek* argument has these settings:

Constant	Value	Description
vbUseSystem	0	Use NLS API setting.
VbSunday	1	Sunday (default)
vbMonday	2	Monday
vbTuesday	3	Tuesday
vbWednesday	4	Wednesday
vbThursday	5	Thursday
vbFriday	6	Friday
vbSaturday	7	Saturday

The *firstweekofyear* argument has these settings:

Constant	Value	Description
vbUseSystem	0	Use NLS API setting.
vbFirstJan1	1	Start with week in which January 1 occurs (default).
vbFirstFourDays	2	Start with the first week that has at least four days in the year.
vbFirstFullWeek	3	Start with the first full week of the year.

Remarks

To Format	Do This
Numbers	Use predefined named numeric formats or create user-defined numeric formats.
Dates and times	Use predefined named date/time formats or create user-defined date/time formats.
Date and time serial numbers	Use date and time formats or numeric formats.
Strings	Create your own user-defined string formats.

If you try to format a number without specifying *format*, **Format** provides functionality similar to the **Str** function, although it is internationally aware. However, positive numbers formatted as strings using **Format** don't include a leading space reserved for the sign of the value; those converted using **Str** retain the leading space.

See Also

Named Numeric Formats (Format Function), **User-Defined Numeric** Formats (Format Function), Different Formats for Different Numeric Values (Format Function), **Named Date/Time** Formats (Format Function), **User-Defined Date/Time** Formats (Format Function), **User-Defined String** Formats (Format Function), Different Formats for Different String Values (Format Function), **Str** Function

Example

This example shows various uses of the **Format** function to format values using both named formats and user-defined formats. For the date separator (/), time separator (:), and AM/ PM literal, the actual formatted output displayed by your system depends on the locale settings on which the code is running. When times and dates are displayed in the development environment, the short time format and short date format of the code locale are used. When displayed by running code, the short time format and short date format of the system locale are used, which may differ from the code locale. For this example, English/U.S. is assumed.

MyTime and MyDate are displayed in the development environment using current system short time setting and short date setting.

```
Dim MyTime, MyDate, MyStr
MyTime = #17:04:23#
MyDate = #January 27, 1993#

' Returns current system time in the system-defined long time format.
MyStr = Format(Time, "Long Time")

' Returns current system date in the system-defined long date format.
MyStr = Format(Date, "Long Date")

MyStr = Format(MyTime, "h:m:s")              ' Returns "17:4:23".
MyStr = Format(MyTime, "hh:mm:ss AMPM")      ' Returns "05:04:23 PM".
MyStr = Format(MyDate, "dddd, mmm d yyyy")   ' Returns "Wednesday,
                                             ' Jan 27 1993".
' If format is not supplied, a string is returned.
MyStr = Format(23)' Returns "23".

' User-defined formats.
MyStr = Format(5459.4, "##,##0.00")          ' Returns "5,459.40".
MyStr = Format(334.9, "###0.00")             ' Returns "334.90".
MyStr = Format(5, "0.00%")                   ' Returns "500.00%".
MyStr = Format("HELLO", "<")                 ' Returns "hello".
MyStr = Format("This is it", ">")            ' Returns "THIS IS IT".
```

Format Property

Returns or sets the format when sending data to and getting data from an application that created an object. Not available at design time.

Applies To

OLE Container Control

Syntax

object.**Format** [= *format*]

The **Format** property syntax has these parts:

Part	Description
object	An object expression that evaluates to an object in the **Applies To** list.
format	A string expression specifying the format used with the **Data** and **DataText** properties.

Remarks

Use the **ObjectAcceptFormats**, **ObjectAcceptFormatsCount**, **ObjectGetFormats**, and **ObjectGetFormatsCount** properties to get a list of the acceptable data formats for a specific class of object.

Many applications that provide objects support only one or two formats. For example, Microsoft Draw accepts only the CF_METAFILEPICT format. Although CF_METAFILEPICT resembles the intrinsic constant **vbCFMetafile** (numeric value 3) defined in the Visual Basic (VB) object library in the Object Browser, it's actually a string literal and is assigned as:

```
Ole1.Format = "CF_METAFILEPICT"
```

In many cases, the list of formats an object can accept (**ObjectAcceptFormats**) is different from the list of formats an object can provide (**ObjectGetFormats**).

See Also

Data Property, **DataText** Property, **ObjectAcceptFormatsCount** Property, **ObjectGetFormats** Property, **ObjectGetFormatsCount** Property

---

Forms Property

Returns a **Forms** collection, which is a collection whose elements represent each loaded form in an application. The collection includes the application's MDI form, MDI child forms, and non-MDI forms. The **Forms** collection has a single property, **Count**, that specifies the number of elements in the collection.

Applies To

Global Object

Syntax

Forms(*index*)

The placeholder *index* represents an integer with a range from 0 to
`Forms.Count  - 1`.

Remarks

You can use the **Forms** collection to iterate through all loaded forms in an application.
It identifies an intrinsic global variable named **Forms**. You can pass **Forms**(*index*) to
a function whose argument is specified as a **Forms** class.

See Also

Global Object, **Form** Object**, Forms** Collection

Forward-Only – Type Recordset Object

This **Recordset** type is identical to a snapshot except that you can only scroll forward
through its records. This improves performance in situations where you only need to
make a single pass through a result set.

In an ODBCDirect workspace, this type corresponds to an ODBC forward-only
cursor.

Summary

Forward-Only–Type Recordset Object Summary

Properties

BOF, EOF Properties, **EditMode** Property, **Filter** Property, **Name** Property,
RecordCount Property, **Restartable** Property, **Transactions** Property, **Updatable**
Property, **ValidationRule** Property, **ValidationText** Property, **BatchCollisionCount**
Property, **BatchCollisions** Property, **BatchSize** Property, **Connection** Property,
RecordStatus Property, **StillExecuting** Property, **UpdateOptions** Property

Methods

AddNew Method, **CancelUpdate** Method, **Close** Method, **CopyQueryDef** Method,
Delete Method, **Edit** Method, **GetRows** Method, **Move** Method, **MoveFirst**,
MoveLast, **MoveNext**, **MovePrevious** Methods, **Requery** Method, **Update** Method,
Cancel Method, **NextRecordset** Method

See Also

Dynaset-Type Recordset Object, **Recordset** Object, **Snapshot-Type Recordset**
Object, **Table-Type Recordset** Object

Example

This example opens a forward-only–type **Recordset**, demonstrates its read-only characteristics, and steps through the **Recordset** with the **MoveNext** method.

```
Sub dbOpenForwardOnlyX()

    Dim dbsNorthwind As Database
    Dim rstEmployees As Recordset
    Dim fldLoop As Field

    Set dbsNorthwind = OpenDatabase("Northwind.mdb")
    ' Open a forward-only-type Recordset object. Only the
    ' MoveNext and Move methods may be used to navigate
    ' through the recordset.
    Set rstEmployees = _
        dbsNorthwind.OpenRecordset("Employees", _
        dbOpenForwardOnly)

    With rstEmployees
        Debug.Print "Forward-only-type recordset: " & _
            .Name & ", Updatable = " & .Updatable

        Debug.Print "    Field - DataUpdatable"
        ' Enumerate Fields collection, printing the Name and
        ' DataUpdatable properties of each Field object.
        For Each fldLoop In .Fields
            Debug.Print "        " & _
                fldLoop.Name & " - " & fldLoop.DataUpdatable
        Next fldLoop

        Debug.Print "    Data"
        ' Enumerate the recordset.
        Do While Not .EOF
            Debug.Print "        " & !FirstName & " " & _
                !LastName
            .MoveNext
        Loop

        .Close
    End With

    dbsNorthwind.Close

End Sub
```

ForwardFocus Property

Returns or sets a value determining which control receives focus when one of the access keys for the control is pressed. The **ForwardFocus** property is read/write at the control's authoring time, and not available at the control's run time.

Applies To

UserControl Object

Settings

The settings for **ForwardFocus** are:

Setting	Description
True	The next control in tab order will receive focus when one of the access keys for the control is pressed.
False	If the **CanGetFocus** property is true, the control itself will receive focus when one of the access keys for the control is pressed. This is the default value.

Remarks

The **ForwardFocus** property allows the control to implement the behavior of a **Label** control that has an access key.

Access keys are set through the **AccessKeys** property. When an access key in conjunction with the ALT key is pressed, the control's **AccessKeyPress** event is raised.

See Also

AccessKeys Property, **CanGetFocus** Property

Frame Control

A **Frame** control provides an identifiable grouping for controls. You can also use a **Frame** to subdivide a form functionally—for example, to separate groups of **OptionButton** controls.

Syntax

Frame

Remarks

To group controls, first draw the **Frame** control, and then draw the controls inside the **Frame**. This enables you to move the **Frame** and the controls it contains together. If you draw a control outside the **Frame** and then try to move it inside, the control will be on top of the **Frame** and you'll have to move the **Frame** and controls separately.

To select multiple controls in a **Frame**, hold down the CTRL key while using the mouse to draw a box around the controls.

Properties

Appearance Property, **BackColor, ForeColor** Properties, **BorderStyle** Property, **Caption** Property, **ClipControls** Property, **Container** Property, **DragIcon** Property, **DragMode** Property, **Enabled** Property, **Font** Property, **FontBold, FontItalic, FontStrikethru, FontUnderline** Properties, **FontName** Property, **FontSize** Property, **Height, Width** Properties, **HelpContextID** Property, **hWnd** Property, **Index** Property, **Left, Top** Properties, **MouseIcon** Property, **MousePointer** Property, **Name** Property, **OLEDropMode** Property, **Parent** Property, **TabIndex** Property, **Tag** Property, **ToolTipText** Property, **Visible** Property, **WhatsThisHelpID** Property

Events

Click Event, **DblClick** Event, **DragDrop** Event, **DragOver** Event, **MouseDown**, **MouseUp** Events, **MouseMove** Event, **OLECompleteDrag** Event, **OLEDragDrop** Event, **OLEDragOver** Event, **OLEGiveFeedback** Event, **OLESetData** Event, **OLEStartDrag** Event

Methods

Refresh Method, **Drag** Method, **Move** Method, **ZOrder** Method, **OLEDrag** Method, **ShowWhatsThis** Method

See Also

OptionButton Control

FreeFile Function

Returns an **Integer** representing the next file number available for use by the **Open** statement.

Syntax

FreeFile[(*rangenumber*)]

The optional *rangenumber* argument is a **Variant** that specifies the range from which the next free file number is to be returned. Specify a 0 (default) to return a file number in the range 1–255, inclusive. Specify a 1 to return a file number in the range 256–511.

Remarks

Use **FreeFile** to supply a file number that is not already in use.

See Also

Open Statement

Example

This example uses the **FreeFile** function to return the next available file number. Five files are opened for output within the loop, and some sample data is written to each.

```
Dim MyIndex, FileNumber
For MyIndex = 1 To 5   ' Loop 5 times.
    FileNumber = FreeFile  ' Get unused file number.
    Open "TEST" & MyIndex For Output As #FileNumber  ' Create filename.
    Write #FileNumber, "This is a sample."  ' Output text.
    Close #FileNumber  ' Close file.
Next MyIndex
```

Friend

Modifies the definition of a procedure in a class module to make the procedure callable from modules that are outside the class, but part of the project within which the class is defined.

Syntax

[**Private** | **Friend** | **Public**] [**Static**] [**Sub** | **Function** | **Property**] *procedurename*

The required *procedurename* is the name of the procedure to be made visible throughout the project, but not visible to controllers of the class.

Remarks

Public procedures in a class can be called from anywhere, even by controllers of instances of the class. Declaring a procedure **Private** prevents controllers of the object from calling the procedure, but also prevents the procedure from being called from within the project in which the class itself is defined. **Friend** makes the procedure visible throughout the project, but not to a controller of an instance of the object. **Friend** can appear only in class modules, and can only modify procedure names, not variables or types. Procedures in a class can access the **Friend** procedures of all other classes in a project. **Friend** procedures don't appear in the type library of their class. A **Friend** procedure can't be late bound.

See Also

Function Statement, **Property Get** Statement, **Property Let** Statement, **Property Set** Statement, **Sub** Statement

Example

When placed in a class module, the following code makes the member variable dblBalance accessible to all users of the class within the project. Any user of the class can get the value; only code within the project can assign a value to that variable.

```
Private dblBalance As Double

Public Property Get Balance() As Double
    Balance = dblBalance
End Property

Friend Property Let Balance(dblNewBalance As Double)
    dblBalance = dblNewBalance
End Property
```

FullName Property

Returns the full path name of the Visual Basic IDE. (That is, the path where vb5.exe was run.)

Applies To

VBE Object

Syntax

object.**FullName**

The *object* placeholder represents an object expression that evaluates to an object in the **Applies To** list.

Remarks

The path name returned is always provided as an absolute path (for example, "c:\projects\myproject.vbp"), even if it is shown as a relative path in Visual Basic (such as "..\projects").

FullPath Property

Returns a **String** containing the path and file name of the referenced type library. Read-only.

Applies to

Reference Object

See Also

AddFromFile Method, **AddFromGuid** Method, **GUID** Property, **IsBroken** Property, **BuiltIn** Property

Example

The following example uses the **FullPath** property to return the full path of the object library for the specified reference.

```
Debug.Print Application.VBE.ActiveVBProject.References(1).FullPath
```

Function Statement

Declares the name, arguments, and code that form the body of a **Function** procedure.

Syntax

[**Public** | **Private** | **Friend**] [**Static**] **Function** *name* [(*arglist*)] [**As** *type*]
    [*statements*]
    [*name* = *expression*]
    [**Exit Function**]
    [*statements*]
    [*name* = *expression*]
End Function

The **Function** statement syntax has these parts:

Part	Description
Public	Optional. Indicates that the **Function** procedure is accessible to all other procedures in all modules. If used in a module that contains an **Option Private**, the procedure is not available outside the project.
Private	Optional. Indicates that the **Function** procedure is accessible only to other procedures in the module where it is declared.
Friend	Optional. Used only in a class module. Indicates that the **Function** procedure is visible throughout the project, but not visible to a controller of an instance of an object.
Static	Optional. Indicates that the **Function** procedure's local variables are preserved between calls. The **Static** attribute doesn't affect variables that are declared outside the **Function**, even if they are used in the procedure.
name	Required. Name of the **Function**; follows standard variable naming conventions.
arglist	Optional. List of variables representing arguments that are passed to the **Function** procedure when it is called. Multiple variables are separated by commas.
type	Optional. Data type of the value returned by the **Function** procedure; may be **Byte**, **Boolean**, **Integer**, **Long**, **Currency**, **Single**, **Double**, **Decimal** (not currently supported), **Date**, **String**, or (except fixed length), **Object**, **Variant**, or any user-defined type. Arrays of any type can't be returned, but a **Variant** containing an array can.
statements	Optional. Any group of statements to be executed within the **Function** procedure.
expression	Optional. Return value of the **Function**.

The *arglist* argument has the following syntax and parts:

[**Optional**] [**ByVal** | **ByRef**] [**ParamArray**] *varname*[( )] [**As** *type*] [= *defaultvalue*]

Part	Description
Optional	Optional. Indicates that an argument is not required. If used, all subsequent arguments in *arglist* must also be optional and declared using the **Optional** keyword. **Optional** can't be used for any argument if **ParamArray** is used.
ByVal	Optional. Indicates that the argument is passed by value.
ByRef	Optional. Indicates that the argument is passed by reference. **ByRef** is the default in Visual Basic.
ParamArray	Optional. Used only as the last argument in *arglist* to indicate that the final argument is an **Optional** array of **Variant** elements. The **ParamArray** keyword allows you to provide an arbitrary number of arguments. It may not be used with **ByVal**, **ByRef**, or **Optional**.
varname	Required. Name of the variable representing the argument; follows standard variable naming conventions.

(continued)

(continued)

Part	Description
type	Optional. Data type of the argument passed to the procedure; may be **Byte**, **Boolean**, **Integer**, **Long**, **Currency**, **Single**, **Double**, **Decimal** (not currently supported) **Date**, **String** (variable length only), **Object**, **Variant**. If the parameter is not **Optional**, a user-defined type or an object type may also be specified.
defaultvalue	Optional. Any constant or constant expression. Valid for **Optional** parameters only. If the type is an **Object**, an explicit default value can only be **Nothing**.

Remarks

If not explicitly specified using **Public**, **Private**, or **Friend**, **Function** procedures are public by default. If **Static** isn't used, the value of local variables is not preserved between calls. The **Friend** keyword can only be used in class modules. However, **Friend** procedures can be accessed by procedures in any module of a project. A **Friend** procedure doesn't appear in the type library of its parent class, nor can a **Friend** procedure be late bound.

Caution **Function** procedures can be recursive; that is, they can call themselves to perform a given task. However, recursion can lead to stack overflow. The **Static** keyword usually isn't used with recursive **Function** procedures.

All executable code must be in procedures. You can't define a **Function** procedure inside another **Function**, **Sub**, or **Property** procedure.

The **Exit Function** statement causes an immediate exit from a **Function** procedure. Program execution continues with the statement following the statement that called the **Function** procedure. Any number of **Exit Function** statements can appear anywhere in a **Function** procedure.

Like a **Sub** procedure, a **Function** procedure is a separate procedure that can take arguments, perform a series of statements, and change the values of its arguments. However, unlike a **Sub** procedure, you can use a **Function** procedure on the right side of an expression in the same way you use any intrinsic function, such as **Sqr**, **Cos**, or **Chr**, when you want to use the value returned by the function.

You call a **Function** procedure using the function name, followed by the argument list in parentheses, in an expression. See the **Call** statement for specific information on how to call **Function** procedures.

To return a value from a function, assign the value to the function name. Any number of such assignments can appear anywhere within the procedure. If no value is assigned to *name*, the procedure returns a default value: a numeric function returns 0, a string function returns a zero-length string (""), and a **Variant** function returns **Empty**. A function that returns an object reference returns **Nothing** if no object reference is assigned to *name* (using **Set**) within the **Function**.

The following example shows how to assign a return value to a function named
`BinarySearch`. In this case, **False** is assigned to the name to indicate that some value
was not found.

```
Function BinarySearch(. . .) As Boolean
. . .
    ' Value not found. Return a value of False.
    If lower > upper Then
        BinarySearch = False
        Exit Function
    End If
. . .
End Function
```

Variables used in **Function** procedures fall into two categories: those that are explicitly
declared within the procedure and those that are not. Variables that are explicitly declared
in a procedure (using **Dim** or the equivalent) are always local to the procedure. Variables
that are used but not explicitly declared in a procedure are also local unless they are
explicitly declared at some higher level outside the procedure.

Caution A procedure can use a variable that is not explicitly declared in the procedure, but a
naming conflict can occur if anything you defined at the module level has the same name. If
your procedure refers to an undeclared variable that has the same name as another procedure,
constant, or variable, it is assumed that your procedure refers to that module-level name.
Explicitly declare variables to avoid this kind of conflict. You can use an **Option Explicit**
statement to force explicit declaration of variables.

Caution Visual Basic may rearrange arithmetic expressions to increase internal efficiency.
Avoid using a **Function** procedure in an arithmetic expression when the function changes the
value of variables in the same expression.

See Also

Call Statement, **Dim** Statement, **Option Explicit** Statement, **Property Get** Statement,
Property Let Statement, **Property Set** Statement, **Sub** Statement, **AddressOf**
Operator, **Friend**

Example

This example uses the **Function** statement to declare the name, arguments, and code
that form the body of a **Function** procedure. The last example uses hard-typed,
initialized **Optional** arguments.

```
' The following user-defined function returns the square root of the
' argument passed to it.
Function CalculateSquareRoot(NumberArg As Double) As Double
    If NumberArg < 0 Then                    ' Evaluate argument.
        Exit Function                        ' Exit to calling procedure.
    Else
        CalculateSquareRoot = Sqr(NumberArg) ' Return square root.
    End If
End Function
```

Using the **ParamArray** keyword enables a function to accept a variable number of arguments. In the following definition, FirstArg is passed by value.

```
Function CalcSum(ByVal FirstArg As Integer, ParamArray OtherArgs())
Dim ReturnValue
' If the function is invoked as follows:
ReturnValue = CalcSum(4, 3 ,2 ,1)
' Local variables are assigned the following values: FirstArg = 4,
' OtherArgs(1) = 3, OtherArgs(2) = 2, and so on, assuming default
' lower bound for arrays = 1.
```

Optional arguments can have default values and types other than **Variant**.

```
' If a function's arguments are defined as follows:
Function MyFunc(MyStr As String, Optional MyArg1 As _
    Integer = 5, Optional MyArg2 = "Dolly")
Dim RetVal
' The function can be invoked as follows:
RetVal = MyFunc("Hello", 2, "World")  ' All 3 arguments supplied.
RetVal = MyFunc("Test", , 5)          ' Second argument omitted.
' Arguments one and three using named-arguments.
RetVal = MyFunc(MyStr:="Hello ", MyArg1:=7)
```

FV Function

Returns a **Double** specifying the future value of an annuity based on periodic, fixed payments and a fixed interest rate.

Syntax

FV(*rate*, *nper*, *pmt*[, *pv*[, *type*]])

The **FV** function has these named arguments:

Part	Description
rate	Required. **Double** specifying interest rate per period. For example, if you get a car loan at an annual percentage rate (APR) of 10 percent and make monthly payments, the rate per period is 0.1/12, or 0.0083.
nper	Required. **Integer** specifying total number of payment periods in the annuity. For example, if you make monthly payments on a four-year car loan, your loan has a total of 4 * 12 (or 48) payment periods.
pmt	Required. **Double** specifying payment to be made each period. Payments usually contain principal and interest that doesn't change over the life of the annuity.
pv	Optional. **Variant** specifying present value (or lump sum) of a series of future payments. For example, when you borrow money to buy a car, the loan amount is the present value to the lender of the monthly car payments you will make. If omitted, 0 is assumed.

(continued)

Part	Description
type	Optional. **Variant** specifying when payments are due. Use 0 if payments are due at the end of the payment period, or use 1 if payments are due at the beginning of the period. If omitted, 0 is assumed.

Remarks

An annuity is a series of fixed cash payments made over a period of time. An annuity can be a loan (such as a home mortgage) or an investment (such as a monthly savings plan).

The *rate* and *nper* arguments must be calculated using payment periods expressed in the same units. For example, if *rate* is calculated using months, *nper* must also be calculated using months.

For all arguments, cash paid out (such as deposits to savings) is represented by negative numbers; cash received (such as dividend checks) is represented by positive numbers.

See Also

DDB Function, **IPmt** Function, **IRR** Function, **MIRR** Function, **NPer** Function, **NPV** Function, **Pmt** Function, **PPmt** Function, **PV** Function, **Rate** Function, **SLN** Function, **SYD** Function

Example

This example uses the **FV** function to return the future value of an investment given the percentage rate that accrues per period (APR / 12), the total number of payments (TotPmts), the payment (Payment), the current value of the investment (PVal), and a number that indicates whether the payment is made at the beginning or end of the payment period (PayType). Note that because Payment represents cash paid out, it's a negative number.

```
Dim Fmt, Payment, APR, TotPmts, PayType, PVal, FVal
Const ENDPERIOD = 0, BEGINPERIOD = 1        ' When payments are made.
Fmt = "###,###,##0.00"                      ' Define money format.
Payment = InputBox("How much do you plan to save each month?")
APR = InputBox("Enter the expected interest annual percentage rate.")
If APR > 1 Then APR = APR / 100             ' Ensure proper form.
TotPmts = InputBox("For how many months do you expect to save?")
PayType = MsgBox("Do you make payments at the end of month?", vbYesNo)
If PayType = vbNo Then PayType = BEGINPERIOD Else PayType = ENDPERIOD
PVal = InputBox("How much is in this savings account now?")
FVal = FV(APR / 12, TotPmts, -Payment, -PVal, PayType)
MsgBox "Your savings will be worth " & Format(FVal, Fmt) & "."
```

Get Statement

Reads data from an open disk file into a variable.

Syntax

Get [**#**]*filenumber,* [*recnumber*], *varname*

The **Get** statement syntax has these parts:

Part	Description
filenumber	Required. Any valid file number.
recnumber	Optional. **Variant** (**Long**). Record number (**Random** mode files) or byte number (**Binary** mode files) at which reading begins.
varname	Required. Valid variable name into which data is read.

Remarks

Data read with **Get** is usually written to a file with **Put**.

The first record or byte in a file is at position 1, the second record or byte is at position 2, and so on. If you omit *recnumber*, the next record or byte following the last **Get** or **Put** statement (or pointed to by the last **Seek** function) is read. You must include delimiting commas, for example:

```
Get #4,,FileBuffer
```

For files opened in **Random** mode, the following rules apply:

- If the length of the data being read is less than the length specified in the **Len** clause of the **Open** statement, **Get** reads subsequent records on record-length boundaries. The space between the end of one record and the beginning of the next record is padded with the existing contents of the file buffer. Because the amount of padding data can't be determined with any certainty, it is generally a good idea to have the record length match the length of the data being read.

- If the variable being read into is a variable-length string, **Get** reads a 2-byte descriptor containing the string length and then reads the data that goes into the variable. Therefore, the record length specified by the **Len** clause in the **Open** statement must be at least 2 bytes greater than the actual length of the string.

- If the variable being read into is a **Variant** of numeric type, **Get** reads 2 bytes identifying the **VarType** of the **Variant** and then the data that goes into the variable. For example, when reading a **Variant** of **VarType** 3, **Get** reads 6 bytes: 2 bytes identifying the **Variant** as **VarType** 3 (**Long**) and 4 bytes containing the **Long** data. The record length specified by the **Len** clause in the **Open** statement must be at least 2 bytes greater than the actual number of bytes required to store the variable.

Note You can use the **Get** statement to read a **Variant** array from disk, but you can't use **Get** to read a scalar **Variant** containing an array. You also can't use **Get** to read objects from disk.

- If the variable being read into is a **Variant** of **VarType** 8 (**String**), **Get** reads 2 bytes identifying the **VarType**, 2 bytes indicating the length of the string, and then reads the string data. The record length specified by the **Len** clause in the **Open** statement must be at least 4 bytes greater than the actual length of the string.

- If the variable being read into is a dynamic array, **Get** reads a descriptor whose length equals 2 plus 8 times the number of dimensions, that is, 2 + 8 * *NumberOfDimensions*. The record length specified by the **Len** clause in the **Open** statement must be greater than or equal to the sum of all the bytes required to read the array data and the array descriptor. For example, the following array declaration requires 118 bytes when the array is written to disk.

```
Dim MyArray(1 To 5,1 To 10) As Integer
```

The 118 bytes are distributed as follows: 18 bytes for the descriptor (2 + 8 * 2), and 100 bytes for the data (5 * 10 * 2).

- If the variable being read into is a fixed-size array, **Get** reads only the data. No descriptor is read.

- If the variable being read into is any other type of variable (not a variable-length string or a **Variant**), **Get** reads only the variable data. The record length specified by the **Len** clause in the **Open** statement must be greater than or equal to the length of the data being read.

- **Get** reads elements of user-defined types as if each were being read individually, except that there is no padding between elements. On disk, a dynamic array in a user-defined type (written with **Put**) is prefixed by a descriptor whose length equals 2 plus 8 times the number of dimensions, that is, 2 + 8 * *NumberOfDimensions*. The record length specified by the **Len** clause in the **Open** statement must be greater than or equal to the sum of all the bytes required to read the individual elements, including any arrays and their descriptors.

For files opened in **Binary** mode, all of the **Random** rules apply, except:

- The **Len** clause in the **Open** statement has no effect. **Get** reads all variables from disk contiguously; that is, with no padding between records.

- For any array other than an array in a user-defined type, **Get** reads only the data. No descriptor is read.

- **Get** reads variable-length strings that aren't elements of user-defined types without expecting the 2-byte length descriptor. The number of bytes read equals the number of characters already in the string. For example, the following statements read 10 bytes from file number 1:

```
VarString = String(10," ")
Get #1,,VarString
```

See Also

Type Statement, **Open** Statement, **Put** Statement, **Seek** Function, **VarType** Function

Example

This example uses the **Get** statement to read data from a file into a variable. This example assumes that TESTFILE is a file containing five records of the user-defined type Record.

```
Type Record                          ' Define user-defined type.
   ID As Integer
   Name As String * 20
End Type

Dim MyRecord As Record, Position     ' Declare variables.
' Open sample file for random access.
Open "TESTFILE" For Random As #1 Len = Len(MyRecord)
' Read the sample file using the Get statement.
Position = 3                         ' Define record number.
Get #1, Position, MyRecord           ' Read third record.
Close #1                             ' Close file.
```

GetAllSettings Function

Returns a list of key settings and their respective values (originally created with **SaveSetting**) from an application's entry in the Windows registry.

Syntax

GetAllSettings(*appname, section*)

The **GetAllSettings** function syntax has these named arguments:

Part	Description
appname	Required. String expression containing the name of the application or project whose key settings are requested.
section	Required. String expression containing the name of the section whose key settings are requested. **GetAllSettings** returns a **Variant** whose contents is a two-dimensional array of strings containing all the key settings in the specified section and their corresponding values.

Remarks

GetAllSettings returns an uninitialized **Variant** if either *appname* or *section* does not exist.

See Also

DeleteSetting Statement, **GetSetting** Function, **SaveSetting** Statement

Example

This example first uses the **SaveSetting** statement to make entries in the Windows registry (or .ini file on 16-bit Windows platforms) for the application specified as *appname*, then uses the **GetAllSettings** function to display the settings. Note that application names and *section* names can't be retrieved with **GetAllSettings**. Finally, the **DeleteSetting** statement removes the application's entries.

```
' Variant to hold 2-dimensional array returned by GetAllSettings
' Integer to hold counter.
Dim MySettings As Variant, intSettings As Integer
' Place some settings in the registry.
SaveSetting appname := "MyApp", section := "Startup", _
key := "Top", setting := 75
SaveSetting "MyApp","Startup", "Left", 50
' Retrieve the settings.
MySettings = GetAllSettings(appname := "MyApp", section := "Startup")
    For intSettings = LBound(MySettings, 1) To UBound(MySettings, 1)
        Debug.Print MySettings(intSettings, 0), MySettings(intSettings, 1)
    Next intSettings
DeleteSetting "MyApp", "Startup"
```

GetAttr Function

Returns an **Integer** representing the attributes of a file, directory, or folder.

Syntax

GetAttr(*pathname*)

The required *pathname* argument is a string expression that specifies a file name. The *pathname* may include the directory or folder, and the drive.

Return Values

The value returned by **GetAttr** is the sum of the following attribute values:

Constant	Value	Description
vbNormal	0	Normal
vbReadOnly	1	Read-only
vbHidden	2	Hidden
vbSystem	4	System
vbDirectory	16	Directory or folder
vbArchive	32	File has changed since last backup

Note These constants are specified by Visual Basic for Applications. The names can be used anywhere in your code in place of the actual values.

Remarks

To determine which attributes are set, use the **And** operator to perform a bitwise comparison of the value returned by the **GetAttr** function and the value of the individual file attribute you want. If the result is not zero, that attribute is set for the named file. For example, the return value of the following **And** expression is zero if the Archive attribute is not set:

```
Result = GetAttr(FName) And vbArchive
```

A nonzero value is returned if the Archive attribute is set.

See Also

SetAttr Statement, **FileAttr** Function, **And** Operator

Example

This example uses the **GetAttr** function to determine the attributes of a file and directory or folder.

```
Dim MyAttr
' Assume file TESTFILE has hidden attribute set.
MyAttr = GetAttr("TESTFILE")  ' Returns 2.

' Returns nonzero if hidden attribute is set on TESTFILE.
Debug.Print MyAttr And vbHidden

' Assume file TESTFILE has hidden and read-only attributes set.
MyAttr = GetAttr("TESTFILE")  ' Returns 3.

' Returns nonzero if hidden attribute is set on TESTFILE.
Debug.Print MyAttr And (vbHidden + vbReadOnly)

' Assume MYDIR is a directory or folder.
MyAttr = GetAttr("MYDIR")     ' Returns 16.
```

GetAutoServerSettings Function

Returns information about the state of an ActiveX component's registration.

Syntax

object.**GetAutoServerSettings**([*progid*], [*clsid*])

The **GetAutoServerSettings** function syntax has these parts:

Part	Description
object	Required. An object expression that evaluates to an object in the **Applies To** list.
progid	Optional. A variant expression specifying the ProgID for the component.
clsid	Optional. A variant expression specifying the CLSID for the component.

Return Values

The **GetAutoServerSettings** function returns a Variant that contains an array of values about the given ActiveX component. The index values and descriptions are:

Value	Description
1	True if the ActiveX component is registered remotely.
2	Remote machine name.
3	RPC network protocol name.
4	RPC authentication level.

Remarks

If a value is missing or not available, the value will be an empty string. If there is an error during the method, then the return value will be a Variant of type Empty.

Example

This example retrieves information about a remotely registered object named "Hello":

```
Sub ViewHello()
   Dim oRegClass As New RegClass
   Dim vRC As Variant
   vRC = oRegClass.GetAutoServerSettings _
   ("HelloProj.HelloClass")
   If Not(IsEmpty(vRC)) Then
      If vRC(1) Then
         MsgBox "Hello is registered remotely on a " _
         & "server named: " & vRC(1)
      Else
         MsgBox "Hello is registered locally."
      End If
   End if
End Sub
```

GetBookmark Method

Returns a value containing a bookmark for a row relative to the current row in a **DBGrid** control. Doesn't support named arguments.

Applies To

DBGrid Control

Syntax

object.**GetBookmark** *value*

The **GetBookmark** method syntax has these parts:

Part	Description
object	An object expression that evaluates to an object in the **Applies To** list.
value	Required. A long numeric expression that addresses rows of the **DBGrid** control relative to the current row, as described in Settings.

Settings

The settings for *value* are:

Setting	Description
0	Returns bookmark of the current row—the same as `DBGrid1.Bookmark`.
1	Returns bookmark of the row following current row.
-1	Returns bookmark of the row preceding current row.
n	Returns bookmark of the row relative to current row based on `(DBGrid1.Row + n)`

Remarks

The **GetBookmark** method may return values that are very different from the **RowBookmark** method because the current row may not be visible.

See Also

Data Control, **DBGrid** Control, **RowBookmark** Method

Example

This example checks the updated value of a particular column to make sure that the new value lies between the values of the previous and the next rows.

```
Sub DBGrid1_BeforeColUpdate (ColIndex As Integer, _
  OldValue as Variant, PrevVal, NextVal, CurVal, Cancel As Integer)
    If ColIndex = 1 Then
        PrevVal = DBGrid1.Columns(1).CellValue(_
        DBGrid1.GetBookmark(-1))
        NextVal = DBGrid1.Columns(1).CellValue(_
        DBGrid1.GetBookmark(1))
        CurVal = DBGrid1.Columns(1).Value
        If CurVal > PrevVal Or CurVal < NextVal  Then
            Cancel = True
            MsgBox "Value must be between" & PrevVal _
             & " and " & NextVal
        End If
    End If
End Sub
```

GetChunk Method

Returns all or a portion of the contents of a Memo or Long Binary **Field** object in the **Fields** collection of a **Recordset** object.

Applies To

Field Object

Syntax

Set *variable* = *recordset* ! *field*.**GetChunk** (*offset, numbytes*)

The **GetChunk** method syntax has these parts.

Part	Description
variable	A **Variant** (**String** subtype) that receives the data from the **Field** object named by *field*.
recordset	An object variable that represents the **Recordset** object containing the **Fields** collection.
field	An object variable that represents a **Field** object whose **Type** property is set to **dbMemo** (Memo) or **dbLongBinary** (Long Binary).
offset	A **Long** value equal to the number of bytes to skip before copying begins.
numbytes	A **Long** value equal to the number of bytes you want to return.

Remarks

The bytes returned by **GetChunk** are assigned to *variable*. Use **GetChunk** to return a portion of the total data value at a time. You can use the **AppendChunk** method to reassemble the pieces.

If *offset* is 0, **GetChunk** begins copying from the first byte of the field.

If *numbytes* is greater than the number of bytes in the field, **GetChunk** returns the actual number of remaining bytes in the field.

Caution Use a Memo field for text, and put binary data only in Long Binary fields. Doing otherwise will cause undesirable results.

See Also

AppendChunk Method (Remote Data), **ColumnSize** Method (Remote Data), **rdoColumn** Object, **rdoResultset** Object, **ChunkRequired** Property (Remote Data), **Type** Property (Remote Data)

Example

This example uses the **AppendChunk** and **GetChunk** methods to fill an OLE object field with data from another record, 32K at a time. In a real application, one might use a procedure like this to copy an employee record (including the employee's photo) from one table to another. In this example, the record is simply being copied back to same table. Note that all the chunk manipulation takes place within a single **AddNew-Update** sequence.

```
Sub AppendChunkX()

    Dim dbsNorthwind As Database
    Dim rstEmployees As Recordset
    Dim rstEmployees2 As Recordset

    Set dbsNorthwind = OpenDatabase("Northwind.mdb")

    ' Open two recordsets from the Employees table.
    Set rstEmployees = _
        dbsNorthwind.OpenRecordset("Employees", _
        dbOpenDynaset)
    Set rstEmployees2 = rstEmployees.Clone

    ' Add a new record to the first Recordset and copy the
    ' data from a record in the second Recordset.
    With rstEmployees
        .AddNew
        !FirstName = rstEmployees2!FirstName
        !LastName = rstEmployees2!LastName
        CopyLargeField rstEmployees2!Photo, !Photo
        .Update

        ' Delete new record because this is a demonstration.
        .Bookmark = .LastModified
```

```
            .Delete
            .Close
      End With

      rstEmployees2.Close
      dbsNorthwind.Close

End Sub

Function CopyLargeField(fldSource As Field, _
   fldDestination As Field)

   ' Set size of chunk in bytes.
   Const conChunkSize = 32768

   Dim lngOffset As Long
   Dim lngTotalSize As Long
   Dim strChunk As String

   ' Copy the photo from one Recordset to the other in 32K
   ' chunks until the entire field is copied.
   lngTotalSize = fldSource.FieldSize
   Do While lngOffset < lngTotalSize
      strChunk = fldSource.GetChunk(lngOffset, conChunkSize)
      fldDestination.AppendChunk strChunk
      lngOffset = lngOffset + conChunkSize
   Loop

End Function
```

GetChunk Method (Remote Data)

Returns all or a portion of the contents of an **rdoColumn** object with a data type of **rdTypeLONGVARBINARY** or **rdTypeLONGVARCHAR**.

Applies To

rdoColumn Object

Syntax

varname = object ! column.**GetChunk**(*numbytes*)

The **GetChunk** method syntax has these parts:

Part	Description
varname	The name of a **Variant** that receives the data from the **rdoColumn** object named by *column*.
object	An object expression that evaluates to an **rdoResultset** object containing the **rdoColumns** collection.
column	An object expression that evaluates to an **rdoColumn** object whose **ChunkRequired** property is **True**.
numbytes	A numeric expression that is the number of bytes you want to return.

Remarks

Chunk data columns are designed to store binary or text values that can range in size from a few characters to over 1.2GB and are stored in the database on successive data pages. In most cases, chunk data cannot be managed with a single operation so you must use the chunk methods to save and write data a piece at a time. If the **ChunkRequired** property is **True** for a column, you should use the **GetChunk** and **AppendChunk** methods to manipulate column data. The **BindThreshold** property determines the largest size block that is automatically bound and precludes the need to use the chunk methods.

If the **ChunkRequired** property is **True** for a column, you must use the **GetChunk** method to retrieve the data. The **GetChunk** method moves a portion of the data from a chunk column to a variable. The total number of bytes in the column is determined by executing the **ColumnSize** method.

The **GetChunk** method is used iteratively, copying column data to a variable, one segment or chunk at a time. The chunk size is set by *numbytes*. The starting point of the copy operation is initially 0, which causes data to be copied from the first byte of the column being read. Subsequent calls to **GetChunk** get data from the first position after the previously read chunk.

The bytes returned by **GetChunk** are assigned to *varname*. Due to memory requirements for the returned data and temporary storage, *numbytes* might be limited, but with 32-bit systems this limitation is over 1.2GB, or more practically the memory and disk capacity of your virtual memory system.

If *numbytes* is greater than the number of bytes in the column, the actual number of bytes in the column is returned. After assigning the results of **GetChunk** to a **Variant** variable, you can use the **Len** function to determine the number of bytes returned.

Use the **AppendChunk** method to write successive blocks of data to the column and **GetChunk** to extract data from the column. Certain operations (copying, for example) involve temporary strings. If string space is limited, you may need to work with smaller segments of a *chunk* column instead of the entire column.

Use the **BindThreshold** property to specify the largest column size that will be automatically bound.

Note Because the size of a chunk data column can exceed 1.2GB, you should assign the value returned by the **GetChunk** method to a variable large enough to store the data returned based on the size returned by the **ColumnSize** method.

See Also

AppendChunk Method, **Type** Property, **FieldSize** Property

GetClipString Method

The **GetClipString** method returns a delimited string for '*n*' rows in a result set.

Applies To

rdoResultset Object

Syntax

ResulsetString = *object*.**GetClipString** (*NumRows*, [*ColumnDelimiter*],[*RowDelimiter*], *NullExpr*])

The **GetClipString** method syntax has these parts:

Part	Description
ResultsetString	A variable used to reference the entire result set as a delimited string.
Object	An object expression that evaluates to an **rdoResultset** object.
NumRows	Required: **Long** value. Number of rows to copy into the clip string.
ColumnDelimiter	Optional: **Variant(String)** expression used to separate data columns as described in Settings. Default is Tab (**VbTab**).
RowDelimiter	Optional: **Variant(String)**expression used to separate data rows as described in Settings. Default is carriage return (**VbCr**).
NullExpr	Optional: **Variant(String)**expression used when NULL values are encountered as described in Settings. Default is an empty string.

Settings

The row and column delimiters can be any length, but are generally one or two bytes long. Generally, the *ResultsetString* delimiters are determined by the **Clip** property of the target object. For example, if the string is applied to a grid control, columns are separated by tabs and the rows are separated by carriage returns (the default settings).

The *NullExpr* is used to substitute a suitable value in place of NULL values returned from the query. Generally, an empty string or "<null>" is used.

Result Set

The results of a query. Result sets might contain rows when a query contains a SELECT statement. Action queries do not return rows but do return result sets that contain information about the operation, such as rows affected.

Remarks

The **GetClipString** method returns a delimited string for '*n*' rows in a result set based on the *NumRows* argument. If more rows are requested than are available, only the available rows are returned. Use the **RowCount** property to determine how many rows are actually fetched. The number of rows that can be fetched is constrained by available memory and should be chosen to suit your application. Don't expect to use **GetClipString** to bring your entire table or result set into memory if it is a large table.

Generally, **GetClipString** works just like the **GetRows** method except that the data is returned as a string instead of a 2-dimensional variant array. **GetClipString** can be used fill a grid control, or any control that has a **Clip** property. It can also be used to format export data from a result set to a sequential file.

After a call to **GetClipString**, the current row is positioned at the next unread row. That is, **GetClipString** is equivalent to using the **Move** (rows) method.

If you are trying to fetch all the rows using multiple **GetClipString** calls, use the **EOF** property to determine if there are rows available. **GetClipString** returns less than the number requested either at the end of the **rdoResultset**, or if it cannot fetch a row in the range requested. For example, if a fifth row cannot be retrieved in a group of ten rows that you're trying to fetch, **GetClipString** returns four rows and leaves currency on the row that caused the problem. It will not generate a run-time error.

The *ColumnDelimiter* optional parameter can be used to substitute a different column delimiter than the default tab (**Chr**$(9)) character, and the *RowDelimiter* optional parameter can be used to substitute a different row delimiter. This is useful when working with a control that accepts a clip format, but requires different characters for the column and row delimiters (some grids have been known to require both a carriage return and a line feed character for a row delimiter).

See Also

GetRows Method (Remote Data), **rdoResultset** Object

Example

The following example creates a clip string from a result set containing a selected set of rows from the Publishers table and fills a **Grid** control from the string by applying it to the **Clip** property.

```
Dim rs As rdoResultset
Set rs = MyConnection.OpenResultset( _
"Select * from Publishers Where State = 'WA'", _
    rdOpenNone)
MyGrid.Rows = rs.RowCount
MyGrid.Cols = rs.rdoColumns.Count
MyGrid.SelStartRow = 1
MyGrid.SelEndRow = MyGrid.Rows
MyGrid.SelStartCol = 0
MyGrid.SelEndCol = MyGrid.Cols - 1
MyGrid.Clip = rs.GetClipString(rs.RowCount)
```

GetData Method

Returns a graphic from the **Clipboard** object. Doesn't support named arguments.

Applies To

Clipboard Object

Syntax

object.**GetData** (*format*)

The **GetData** method syntax has these parts:

Part	Description
object	Required. An object expression that evaluates to an object in the **Applies To** list.
format	Optional. A constant or value that specifies the **Clipboard** graphics format, as described in Settings. Parentheses must enclose the constant or value. If *format* is 0 or omitted, **GetData** automatically uses the appropriate format.

Settings

The settings for *format* are:

Constant	Value	Description
vbCFBitmap	2	Bitmap (.bmp files)
vbCFMetafile	3	metafile (.wmf files)
vbCFDIB	8	Device-independent bitmap (DIB)
vbCFPalette	9	Color palette

Remarks

These constants are listed in the Visual Basic (VB) object library in the Object Browser.

If no graphic on the **Clipboard** object matches the expected format, nothing is returned. If only a color palette is present on the **Clipboard** object, a minimum size (1 x 1) DIB is created.

See Also

GetFormat Method, **GetText** Method, **SetData** Method, **SetText** Method

Example

This example uses the **GetData** method to copy a bitmap from the **Clipboard** object to a form. To try this example, paste the code into the Declarations section of a form, and then press F5 and click the form.

```
Private Sub Form_Click ()
    Const CF_BITMAP = 2   ' Define bitmap format.
    Dim Msg  ' Declare variable.
    On Error Resume Next ' Set up error handling.
    Msg = "Choose OK to load a bitmap onto the Clipboard."
    MsgBox Msg  ' Display message.
    Clipboard.Clear' Clear Clipboard.
    Clipboard.SetData LoadPicture("PAPER.BMP")  ' Get bitmap.
    If Err Then
        Msg = "Can't find the .bmp file."
        MsgBox Msg  ' Display error message.
        Exit Sub
    End If
    Msg = "A bitmap is now on the Clipboard. Choose OK to copy "
```

```
Msg = Msg & "the bitmap from the Clipboard to the form "
   MsgBox Msg  ' Display message.
   Picture = Clipboard.GetData()      ' Copy from Clipboard.
   Msg = "Choose OK to clear the form."
   MsgBox Msg  ' Display message.
   Picture = LoadPicture() ' Clear form.
End Sub
```

GetData Method (DataObject Object)

Returns data from a **DataObject** object in the form of a variant.

Applies To

DataObject Object

Syntax

object.**GetData** (*format*)

The **GetData** method syntax has these parts:

Part	Description
object	Required. An object expression that evaluates to an object in the **Applies To** list.
format	A constant or value that specifies the data format, as described in Settings. Parentheses must enclose the constant or value. If *format* is 0 or omitted, **GetData** automatically uses the appropriate format.

Settings

The settings for *format* are:

Constant	Value	Description
vbCFText	1	Text (.txt files)
vbCFBitmap	2	Bitmap (.bmp files)
vbCFMetafile	3	metafile (.wmf files)
vbCFEMetafile	14	Enhanced metafile (.emf files)
vbCFDIB	8	Device-independent bitmap (DIB)
vbCFPalette	9	Color palette
vbCFFiles	15	List of files
vbCFRTF	−16639	Rich text format (.rtf files)

Remarks

These constants are listed in the Visual Basic (VB) object library in the Object Browser.

It's possible for the **GetData** and **SetData** methods to use data formats other than those listed in Settings, including user-defined formats registered with Windows via the `RegisterClipboardFormat()` API function. However, there are a few caveats:

- The **SetData** method requires the data to be in the form of a byte array when it does not recognize the data format specified.

- The **GetData** method always returns data in a byte array when it is in a format that it doesn't recognize, although Visual Basic can transparently convert this returned byte array into other data types, such as strings.

- The byte array returned by **GetData** will be larger than the actual data when running on some operating systems, with arbitrary bytes at the end of the array. The reason for this is that Visual Basic does not know the data's format, and knows only the amount of memory that the operating system has allocated for the data. This allocation of memory is often larger than is actually required for the data. Therefore, there may be extraneous bytes near the end of the allocated memory segment. As a result, you must use appropriate functions to interpret the returned data in a meaningful way (such as truncating a string at a particular length with the **Left** function if the data is in a text format).

Note Not all applications support **vbcfBitmap** or **vbCFPalette**, so it is recommended that you use **vbCFDIB** whenever possible.

GetFormat Method

Returns an integer indicating whether an item on the **Clipboard** object matches a specified format. Doesn't support named argument.

Applies To

Clipboard Object

Syntax

object.**GetFormat** (*format*)

The **GetFormat** method syntax has these parts:

Part	Description
object	Required. An object expression that evaluates to an object in the **Applies To** list.
format	Required. A value or constant that specifies the **Clipboard** object format, as described in **Settings**. Parentheses must enclose the constant or value.

Settings

The settings for *format* are:

Constant	Value	Description
vbCFLink	&HBF00	DDE conversation information
vbCFText	1	Text
vbCFBitmap	2	Bitmap (.bmp files)
vbCFMetafile	3	Metafile (.wmf files)
vbCFDIB	8	Device-independent bitmap (DIB)
vbCFPalette	9	Color palette

Remarks

These constants are listed in the Visual Basic (VB) object library in the Object Browser.

The **GetFormat** method returns **True** if an item on the **Clipboard** object matches the specified format. Otherwise, it returns **False**.

For **vbCFDIB** and **vbCFBitmap** formats, whatever color palette is on the **Clipboard** is used when the graphic is displayed.

See Also

GetData Method, **GetText** Method, **SetData** Method, **SetText** Method

Example

This example uses the **GetFormat** method to determine the format of the data on the **Clipboard** object. To try this example, paste the code into the Declarations section of a form, and then press F5 and click the form.

```
Private Sub Form_Click ()
   ' Define bitmap formats.
   Dim ClpFmt, Msg' Declare variables.
   On Error Resume Next ' Set up error handling.
   If Clipboard.GetFormat(vbCFText) Then ClpFmt = ClpFmt + 1
   If Clipboard.GetFormat(vbCFBitmap) Then ClpFmt = ClpFmt + 2
   If Clipboard.GetFormat(vbCFDIB) Then ClpFmt = ClpFmt + 4
   If Clipboard.GetFormat(vbCFRTF) Then ClpFmt = ClpFmt + 8
   Select Case ClpFmt
      Case 1

Msg = "The Clipboard contains only text."
      Case 2, 4, 6
         Msg = "The Clipboard contains only a bitmap."
      Case 3, 5, 7
         Msg = "The Clipboard contains text and a bitmap."
      Case 8, 9
         Msg = "The Clipboard contains only rich text."
      Case Else
         Msg = "There is nothing on the Clipboard."
   End Select
   MsgBox Msg   ' Display message.
End Sub
```

GetFormat Method (DataObject Object)

Returns an Boolean value indicating whether an item in the **DataObject** object matches a specified format. Doesn't support named arguments.

Syntax

object.**GetFormat** *format*

The **GetFormat** method syntax has these parts:

Part	Description
object	Required. An object expression that evaluates to an object in the **Applies To** list.
format	A constant or value that specifies the data format, as described in Settings.

Settings

The settings for *format* are:

Constant	Value	Description
vbCFText	1	Text (.txt files)
vbCFBitmap	2	Bitmap (.bmp files)
vbCFMetafile	3	metafile (.wmf files)
vbCFEMetafile	14	Enhanced metafile (.emf files)
vbCFDIB	8	Device-independent bitmap (DIB)
vbCFPalette	9	Color palette
vbCFFiles	15	List of files
vbCFRTF	−16639	Rich text format (.rtf files)

Remarks

These constants are listed in the Visual Basic (VB) object library in the Object Browser.

The **GetFormat** method returns **True** if an item in the **DataObject** object matches the specified format. Otherwise, it returns **False**.

GetObject Function

Returns a reference to an **ActiveX** object from a file.

Syntax

GetObject([*pathname*] [, *class*])

The **GetObject** function syntax has these named arguments:

Part	Description
pathname	Optional; **Variant** (**String**). The full path and name of the file containing the object to retrieve. If *pathname* is omitted, *class* is required.
class	Optional; **Variant** (**String**). A string representing the class of the object.

The *class* argument uses the syntax *appname.objecttype* and has these parts:

Part	Description
appname	Required; **Variant** (**String**). The name of the application providing the object.
objecttype	Required; **Variant** (**String**). The type or class of object to create.

Remarks

Use the **GetObject** function to access an **ActiveX** object from a file and assign the object to an object variable. Use the **Set** statement to assign the object returned by **GetObject** to the object variable. For example:

```
Dim CADObject As Object
Set CADObject = GetObject("C:\CAD\SCHEMA.CAD")
```

When this code is executed, the application associated with the specified *pathname* is started and the object in the specified file is activated.

If *pathname* is a zero-length string (""), **GetObject** returns a new object instance of the specified type. If the *pathname* argument is omitted, **GetObject** returns a currently active object of the specified type. If no object of the specified type exists, an error occurs.

Some applications allow you to activate part of a file. Add an exclamation point (!) to the end of the file name and follow it with a string that identifies the part of the file you want to activate. For information on how to create this string, see the documentation for the application that created the object.

For example, in a drawing application you might have multiple layers to a drawing stored in a file. You could use the following code to activate a layer within a drawing called SCHEMA.CAD:

```
Set LayerObject = GetObject("C:\CAD\SCHEMA.CAD!Layer3")
```

If you don't specify the object's *class*, Automation determines the application to start and the object to activate, based on the file name you provide. Some files, however, may support more than one class of object. For example, a drawing might support three different types of objects: an **Application** object, a **Drawing** object, and a **Toolbar** object, all of which are part of the same file. To specify which object in a file you want to activate, use the optional *class* argument. For example:

```
Dim MyObject As Object
Set MyObject = GetObject("C:\DRAWINGS\SAMPLE.DRW", "FIGMENT.DRAWING")
```

In the above example, FIGMENT is the name of a drawing application and DRAWING is one of the object types it supports.

Once an object is activated, you reference it in code using the object variable you defined. In the preceding example, you access properties and methods of the new object using the object variable MyObject. For example:

```
MyObject.Line 9, 90
MyObject.InsertText 9, 100, "Hello, world."
MyObject.SaveAs "C:\DRAWINGS\SAMPLE.DRW"
```

Note   Use the **GetObject** function when there is a current instance of the object or if you want to create the object with a file already loaded. If there is no current instance, and you don't want the object started with a file loaded, use the **CreateObject** function.

If an object has registered itself as a single-instance object, only one instance of the object is created, no matter how many times **CreateObject** is executed. With a single-instance object, **GetObject** always returns the same instance when called with the zero-length string ("") syntax, and it causes an error if the *pathname* argument is omitted. You can't use **GetObject** to obtain a reference to a class created with Visual Basic.

See Also

CreateObject Function, **Set** Statement

Example

This example uses the **GetObject** function to get a reference to a specific Microsoft Excel worksheet (MyXL). It uses the worksheet's **Application** property to make Microsoft Excel visible, to close it, and so on. Using two API calls, the DetectExcel **Sub** procedure looks for Microsoft Excel, and if it is running, enters it in the Running Object Table. The first call to **GetObject** causes an error if Microsoft Excel isn't already running. In the example, the error causes the ExcelWasNotRunning flag to be set to True. The second call to **GetObject** specifies a file to open. If Microsoft Excel isn't already running, the second call starts it and returns a reference to the worksheet represented by the specified file, mytest.xls. The file must exist in the specified location; otherwise, the Visual Basic error Automation error is generated. Next the example code makes both Microsoft Excel and the window containing the specified worksheet visible. Finally, if there was no previous version of Microsoft Excel running, the code uses the **Application** object's **Quit** method to close Microsoft Excel. If the application was already running, no attempt is made to close it. The reference itself is released by setting it to **Nothing**.

```
' Declare necessary API routines:
Declare Function FindWindow Lib "user32" Alias _
"FindWindowA" (ByVal lpClassName as String, _
            ByVal lpWindowName As Long) As Long

Declare Function SendMessage Lib "user32" Alias _
"SendMessageA" (ByVal hWnd as Long,ByVal wMsg as Long _
            ByVal wParam as Long _
            ByVal lParam As Long) As Long
```

```
Sub GetExcel()
    Dim MyXL As Object                  ' Variable to hold reference
                                        ' to Microsoft Excel.
    Dim ExcelWasNotRunning As Boolean   ' Flag for final release.

' Test to see if there is a copy of Microsoft Excel already running.
    On Error Resume Next                ' Defer error trapping.
' Getobject function called without the first argument returns a
' reference to an instance of the application. If the application isn't
' running, an error occurs.
    Set MyXL = Getobject(, "Excel.Application")
    If Err.Number <> 0 Then ExcelWasNotRunning = True
    Err.Clear' Clear Err object in case error occurred.

' Check for Microsoft Excel. If Microsoft Excel is running,
' enter it into the Running Object table.
    DetectExcel

Set the object variable to reference the file you want to see.
    Set MyXL = Getobject("c:\vb4\MYTEST.XLS")

' Show Microsoft Excel through its Application property. Then
' show the actual window containing the file using the Windows
' collection of the MyXL object reference.
    MyXL.Application.Visible = True
    MyXL.Parent.Windows(1).Visible = True
                                        ' Do manipulations of your
                                        ' file here.
                                        ' ...
' If this copy of Microsoft Excel was not running when you
' started, close it using the Application property's Quit method.
' Note that when you try to quit Microsoft Excel, the
' title bar blinks and a message is displayed asking if you
' want to save any loaded files.
    If ExcelWasNotRunning = True Then
        MyXL.Application.Quit
    End IF

    Set MyXL = Nothing                  ' Release reference to the
                                        ' application and spreadsheet.
End Sub

Sub DetectExcel()
' Procedure dectects a running Excel and registers it.
    Const WM_USER = 1024
    Dim hWnd As Long
' If Excel is running this API call returns its handle.
    hWnd = FindWindow("XLMAIN", 0)
    If hWnd = 0 Then                    ' 0 means Excel not running.
        Exit Sub
    Else
    ' Excel is running so use the SendMessage API
    ' function to enter it in the Running Object Table.
        SendMessage hWnd, WM_USER + 18, 0, 0
    End If
End Sub
```

GetRows Method

Retrieves multiple rows from a **Recordset** object.

Applies To

Dynaset-Type Recordset Object, **Recordset** Object, **Snapshot-Type Recordset** Object, **Table-Type Recordset** Object, **Forward-Only–Type Recordset** Object, **Dynamic-Type Recordset** Object t

Syntax

Set *varArray* = *recordset*.**GetRows** (*numrows*)

The **GetRows** method syntax has the following parts.

Part	Description
varArray	A **Variant** that stores the returned data.
recordset	An object variable that represents a **Recordset** object.
numrows	A **Variant** that is equal to the number of rows to retrieve.

Remarks

Use the **GetRows** method to copy records from a **Recordset**. **GetRows** returns a two-dimensional array. The first subscript identifies the field and the second identifies the row number. For example, `intField` represents the field, and `intRecord` identifies the row number:

```
avarRecords(intField, intRecord)
```

To get the first field value in the second row returned, use code like the following:

```
field1 = avarRecords(0,1)
```

To get the second field value in the first row, use code like the following:

```
field2 = avarRecords(1,0)
```

The `avarRecords` variable automatically becomes a two-dimensional array when **GetRows** returns data.

If you request more rows than are available, then **GetRows** returns only the number of available rows. You can use the Visual Basic for Applications **UBound** function to determine how many rows **GetRows** actually retrieved, because the array is sized to fit the number of returned rows. For example, if you returned the results into a **Variant** called `varA`, you could use the following code to determine how many rows were actually returned:

```
numReturned = UBound(varA,2) + 1
```

You need to use "+ 1" because the first row returned is in the 0 element of the array. The number of rows that you can retrieve is constrained by the amount of available memory. You shouldn't use **GetRows** to retrieve an entire table into an array if it is large.

Because **GetRows** returns all fields of the **Recordset** into the array, including Memo and Long Binary fields, you might want to use a query that restricts the fields returned.

After you call **GetRows**, the current record is positioned at the next unread row. That is, **GetRows** has the same effect on the current record as **Move** *numrows*.

If you are trying to retrieve all the rows by using multiple **GetRows** calls, use the **EOF** property to be sure that you're at the end of the **Recordset**. **GetRows** returns less than the number requested if it's at the end of the **Recordset**, or if it can't retrieve a row in the range requested. For example, if you're trying to retrieve 10 records, but you can't retrieve the fifth record, **GetRows** returns four records and makes the fifth record the current record. This will not generate a run-time error. This might occur if another user deletes a record in a dynaset-type **Recordset**. See the example for a demonstration of how to handle this.

See Also

Move Method (Remote Data), **rdoResultset** Object, **ChunkRequired** Property (Remote Data), **UBound** Property

Example

This example uses the **GetRows** method to retrieve a specified number of rows from a **Recordset** and to fill an array with the resulting data. The **GetRows** method will return fewer than the desired number of rows in two cases: either if **EOF** has been reached, or if **GetRows** tried to retrieve a record that was deleted by another user. The function returns **False** only if the second case occurs. The **GetRowsOK** function is required for this procedure to run.

```
Sub GetRowsX()

    Dim dbsNorthwind As Database
    Dim rstEmployees As Recordset
    Dim strMessage As String
    Dim intRows As Integer
    Dim avarRecords As Variant
    Dim intRecord As Integer

    Set dbsNorthwind = OpenDatabase("Northwind.mdb")
    Set rstEmployees = dbsNorthwind.OpenRecordset( _
        "SELECT FirstName, LastName, Title " & _
        "FROM Employees ORDER BY LastName", dbOpenSnapshot)

    With rstEmployees
        Do While True
            ' Get user input for number of rows.
            strMessage = "Enter number of rows to retrieve."
            intRows = Val(InputBox(strMessage))

            If intRows <= 0 Then Exit Do
```

```
                    ' If GetRowsOK is successful, print the results,
                    ' noting if the end of the file was reached.
                    If GetRowsOK(rstEmployees, intRows, _
                        avarRecords) Then
                        If intRows > UBound(avarRecords, 2) + 1 Then
                            Debug.Print "(Not enough records in " & _
                                "Recordset to retrieve " & intRows & _
                                " rows.)"
                        End If
                        Debug.Print UBound(avarRecords, 2) + 1 & _
                            " records found."

                        ' Print the retrieved data.
                        For intRecord = 0 To UBound(avarRecords, 2)
                            Debug.Print "      " & _
                                avarRecords(0, intRecord) & " " & _
                                avarRecords(1, intRecord) & ", " & _
                                avarRecords(2, intRecord)
                        Next intRecord
                    Else
                        ' Assuming the GetRows error was due to data
                        ' changes by another user, use Requery to
                        ' refresh the Recordset and start over.
                        If .Restartable Then
                            If MsgBox("GetRows failed--retry?", _
                                    vbYesNo) = vbYes Then
                                .Requery
                            Else
                                Debug.Print "GetRows failed!"
                                Exit Do
                            End If
                        Else
                            Debug.Print "GetRows failed! " & _
                                "Recordset not Restartable!"
                            Exit Do
                        End If
                    End If

                    ' Because using GetRows leaves the current record
                    ' pointer at the last record accessed, move the
                    ' pointer back to the beginning of the Recordset
                    ' before looping back for another search.
                    .MoveFirst
                Loop
            End With

            rstEmployees.Close
            dbsNorthwind.Close

        End Sub

        Function GetRowsOK(rstTemp As Recordset, _
            intNumber As Integer, avarData As Variant) As Boolean
```

```
' Store results of GetRows method in array.
avarData = rstTemp.GetRows(intNumber)
' Return False only if fewer than the desired number of
' rows were returned, but not because the end of the
' Recordset was reached.
If intNumber > UBound(avarData, 2) + 1 And _
      Not rstTemp.EOF Then
   GetRowsOK = False
Else
   GetRowsOK = True
End If

End Function
```

GetRows Method (Remote Data)

Retrieves multiple rows of an **rdoResultset** into an array.

Applies To

rdoResultset Object

Syntax

array = *object*.**GetRows** (*rows*)

The **GetRows** method syntax has these parts:

Part	Description
array	The name of a **Variant** type variable to store the returned data.
object	An object expression that evaluates to an object in the **Applies To** list.
rows	A **Long** value indicating the number of rows to retrieve.

Remarks

Use the **GetRows** method to copy one or more entire rows from an **rdoResultset** into a two-dimensional array. The first array subscript identifies the column and the second identifies the row number, as follows:

```
avarRows(intColumn)(intRow)
```

To get the first column value in the second row returned, use the following:

```
col1 = avarRows(0,1)
```

To get the second column value in the first row, use the following:

```
col2 = avarRows(1,0)
```

If more rows are requested than are available, only the available rows are returned. Use **Ubound** to determine how many rows are actually fetched, as the array is resized based on the number of rows returned. For example, if you return the results into a **Variant** called varA, you could determine how many rows were actually returned by using:

```
numReturned = Ubound(varA,2) + 1
```

The "+ 1" is used because the first data returned is in the 0th element of the array. The number of rows that can be fetched is constrained by available memory and should be chosen to suit your application—don't expect to use **GetRows** to bring your entire table or result set into an array if it is a large table.

GetRows does not return data from columns whose **ChunkRequired** property is **True**—a variant value containing an ODBC S-code is returned in these columns instead.

After a call to **GetRows**, the current row is positioned at the next unread row. That is, **GetRows** is equivalent to using the **Move** (*rows*) method.

If you are trying to fetch all the rows using multiple **GetRows** calls, use the **EOF** property to determine if there are rows available. **GetRows** returns less than the number requested either at the end of the **rdoResultset**, or if it cannot fetch a row in the range requested. For example, if a fifth row cannot be retrieved in a group of ten rows that you're trying to fetch, **GetRows** returns four rows and leaves currency on the row that caused the problem. It will not generate a run-time error.

The **GetRows** method fetches data from the ODBC buffers based on the **RowsetSize** property. RDO proceeds to fetch from the current row toward the end of the result set—returning as many rows as you requested. As the current rowset is exhausted, RDO issues another **SQLExtendedFetch** function call to fetch subsequent rowsets from the database. This technique **Applies To** all types of cursors.

See Also

Move Method (Remote Data), **rdoResultset** Object, **ChunkRequired** Property (Remote Data), **UBound** Property

Example

This example illustrates use of the **GetRows** method to fetch rows from an **rdoResultset** into a variant array. The code opens a connection to a remote data source and creates an **rdoQuery** object that requires a single parameter. The GetRowsNow procedure executes the query with a user-supplied parameter and uses **GetRows** to fetch the rows from the result set.

```
Option Explicit
Dim er As rdoError
Dim cn As New rdoConnection
Dim qy As New rdoQuery
Dim rs As rdoResultset
Dim RowBuf As Variant
Dim RowsReturned As Integer
Dim i As Integer
Dim Ans As Integer

Private Sub GetRowsNow_Click()
qy(0) = StateWanted
rs.Requery

Do Until rs.EOF
   List1.Clear
   RowBuf = rs.GetRows(5)       'Get the next 5 rows
```

```
      RowsReturned = UBound(RowBuf, 2) + 1
      For i = 0 To RowsReturned - 1
          List1.AddItem RowBuf(0, i) & ":" & RowBuf(1, i)
      Next i
      Ans = MsgBox("Press Ok to see next 5 rows " _
          &" or Cancel to quit", vbOKCancel)
      If Ans = vbOK Then Else Exit Sub
  Loop
  End Sub

  Private Sub Form_Load()
  cn.CursorDriver = rdUseOdbc
  cn.Connect = "uid=;pwd=;server=SEQUEL;" _
      driver={SQL Server};database=pubs;dsn='';"
  cn.EstablishConnection
  With qy
      .Name = "GetRowsQuery"
      .SQL = "Select * from Titles T, Publishers P " _
      & " Where T.Pub_ID = P.Pub_ID " _
      & " and P.State = ?"
      .RowsetSize = 1
      Set .ActiveConnection = cn
      .rdoParameters(0) = "CA"
      Set rs = .OpenResultset(rdOpenKeyset, _
          rdConcurRowver)
  End With
  End Sub
```

GetSelection Method

Returns the selection in a code pane.

Applies To

CodePane Object

Syntax

object.**GetSelection**(*startline*, *startcol*, *endline*, *endcol*)

GetSelection syntax has these parts:

Part	Description
object	Required. An object expression that evaluates to an object in the **Applies To** list.
startline	Required. A **Long** that returns a value specifying the first line of the selection in the code pane.
startcol	Required. A **Long** that returns a value specifying the first column of the selection in the code pane.
endline	Required. A **Long** that returns a value specifying the last line of the selection in the code pane.
endcol	Required. A **Long** that returns a value specifying the last column of the selection in the code pane.

Remarks

When you use the **GetSelection** method, information is returned in output arguments. As a result, you must pass in variables because the variables will be modified to contain the information when returned.

See Also

DeleteLines Method, **Find** Method, **InsertLines** Method, **Lines** Method, **ProcBodyLine** Method, **ProcCountLines** Method, **ProcOfLine** Method, **ProcStartLine** Method, **CodeModule** Objec

Example

The following example returns the locations of the starting and ending points of the current selection in `CodePanes(1)`. The last line in the example uses the **GetSelection** method to place the four values in the four variables.

```
Dim m As Long
Dim n As Long
Dim x As Long
Dim y As Long
Application.VBE.CodePanes(1).GetSelection m, n, x, y
```

GetSetting Function

Returns a key setting value from an application's entry in the Windows registry.

Syntax

GetSetting(*appname*, *section*, *key*[, *default*])

The **GetSetting** function syntax has these named arguments:

Part	Description
appname	Required. String expression containing the name of the application or project whose key setting is requested.
section	Required. String expression containing the name of the section where the key setting is found.
key	Required. String expression containing the name of the key setting to return.
default	Optional. Expression containing the value to return if no value is set in the key setting. If omitted, *default* is assumed to be a zero-length string ("").

Remarks

If any of the items named in the **GetSetting** arguments do not exist, **GetSetting** returns the value of *default*.

See Also

DeleteSetting Statement, **GetAllSettings** Function, **SaveSetting** Statement

Example

This example first uses the **SaveSetting** statement to make entries in the Windows registry (or .ini file on 16-bit Windows platforms) for the application specified as *appname*, and then uses the **GetSetting** function to display one of the settings. Because the *default* argument is specified, some value is guaranteed to be returned. Note that *section* names can't be retrieved with **GetSetting**. Finally, the **DeleteSetting** statement removes all the application's entries.

```
' Variant to hold 2-dimensional array returned by GetSetting.
Dim MySettings As Variant
' Place some settings in the registry.
SaveSetting "MyApp","Startup", "Top", 75
SaveSetting "MyApp","Startup", "Left", 50

Debug.Print GetSetting(appname := "MyApp", section := "Startup", _
                       key := "Left", default := "25")

DeleteSetting "MyApp", "Startup"
```

GetText Method

Returns a text string from the **Clipboard** object. Doesn't support named arguments.

Applies To

Clipboard Object

Syntax

object.**GetText** (*format*)

The **GetText** method syntax has these parts:

Part	Description
object	Required. An object expression that evaluates to an object in the **Applies To** list.
format	Optional. A value or constant that specifies the **Clipboard** object format, as described in Settings. Parentheses must enclose the constant or value.

Settings

The settings for *format* are:

Constant	Value	Description
vbCFLink	&HBF00	DDE conversation information
vbCFText	1	(Default) Text
vbCFRTF	&HBF01	Rich Text Format (.rtf file)

Remarks

These constants are listed in the Visual Basic (VB) object library in the Object Browser.

If no text string on the **Clipboard** object matches the expected format, a zero-length string ("") is returned.

See Also

GetData Method, **GetFormat** Method, **SetData** Method, **SetText** Method

Example

This example uses the **GetText** method to copy a text string from the **Clipboard** object to a string variable. To try this example, paste the code into the Declarations section of a form with a **TextBox** control named Text1, and then press F5 and click the form.

```
Private Sub Form_Click ()
    Dim I, Msg, Temp   ' Declare variables.
    On Error Resume Next ' Set up error handling.
    Msg = "Type anything you like into the text box below."
    Text1.Text = InputBox(Msg)  ' Get text from user.
    Msg = "Choose OK to copy the contents of the text box "
    Msg = Msg & "to the Clipboard."
    MsgBox Msg  ' Display message.
    Clipboard.Clear' Clear Clipboard.
    Clipboard.SetText Text1.Text  ' Put text on Clipboard.
    If Clipboard.GetFormat(vbCFText) Then

Text1.Text = ""' Clear the text box.
        Msg = "The text is now on the Clipboard. Choose OK "
        Msg = Msg & "to copy the text from the Clipboard back "
        Msg = Msg & "to the text box."
        MsgBox Msg  ' Display message.
        Temp = Clipboard.GetText(vbCFText)     ' Get Clipboard text.
        For I = Len(Temp) To 1 Step -1 ' Reverse the text.
           Text1.Text = Text1.Text & Mid(Temp, I, 1)
        Next I
    Else
        Msg = "There is no text on the Clipboard."

MsgBox Msg  ' Display error message.
    End If
End Sub
```

Global Object

A **Global** object is an application object that enables you to access application-level properties and methods.

Syntax

Global

Remarks

Global is an Object data type. Because the **Global** object is an application object that is referenced automatically, it is not necessary to code a specific reference to this object.

Properties

App Property, **Clipboard** Property, **Forms** Property, **Printer** Property, **Printers** Property, **Screen** Property

Methods

> **Load** Statement, **Unload** Statement, **LoadPicture** Function, **SavePicture** Statement, **LoadResData** Function, **LoadResPicture** Function, **LoadResString** Function

See Also

> **App** Object

GoBack Method

Execute a hyperlink jump back in the history list.

Applies To

> **Hyperlink** Object

Syntax

object.**GoBack**

The **GoBack** method syntax has these parts:

Part	Description
object	An object expression that evaluates to an object in the **Applies To** list.

Remarks

If the object is in a container that supports OLE hyperlinking, then the container will jump to the location that is back in the history list. If the object is in a container that does not support OLE hyperlinking, then this method will raise an error.

See Also

> **GoForward** Method

GoForward Method

Execute a hyperlink jump forward in the history list.

Applies To

> **Hyperlink** Object

Syntax

object.**GoForward**

The **GoForward** method syntax has these parts:

Part	Description
object	An object expression that evaluates to an object in the **Applies To** list.

Remarks

If the object is in a container that supports OLE hyperlinking, then the container will jump to the location that is forward in the history list. If the object is in a container that does not support OLE hyperlinking, then this method will raise an error.

See Also

GoBack Method

GoSub...Return Statement

Branches to and returns from a subroutine within a procedure.

Syntax

GoSub *line*

   . . .

  line

   . . .

Return

The *line* argument can be any line label or line number.

Remarks

You can use **GoSub** and **Return** anywhere in a procedure, but **GoSub** and the corresponding **Return** statement must be in the same procedure. A subroutine can contain more than one **Return** statement, but the first **Return** statement encountered causes the flow of execution to branch back to the statement immediately following the most recently executed **GoSub** statement.

Note   You can't enter or exit **Sub** procedures with **GoSub...Return**.

Tip   Creating separate procedures that you can call may provide a more structured alternative to using **GoSub...Return**.

See Also

GoTo Statement, **On...GoSub, On...GoTo** Statements, **Sub** Statement

Example

This example uses **GoSub** to call a subroutine within a **Sub** procedure. The **Return** statement causes the execution to resume at the statement immediately following the **GoSub** statement. The **Exit Sub** statement is used to prevent control from accidentally flowing into the subroutine.

```
Sub GosubDemo()
Dim Num
' Solicit a number from the user.
    Num = InputBox("Enter a positive number to be divided by 2.")
' Only use routine if user enters a positive number.
    If Num > 0 Then GoSub MyRoutine
```

```
    Debug.Print Num
    Exit Sub      ' Use Exit to prevent an error.
MyRoutine:
    Num = Num/2   ' Perform the division.
    Return        ' Return control to statement.
End Sub           ' following the GoSub statement.
```

GotFocus Event

Occurs when an object receives the focus, either by user action, such as tabbing to or clicking the object, or by changing the focus in code using the **SetFocus** method. A form receives the focus only when all visible controls are disabled.

Applies To

Animation Control, **CheckBox** Control, **ComboBox** Control, **CommandButton** Control, **DBCombo** Control, **DBGrid** Control, **DBList** Control, **DirListBox** Control, **DriveListBox** Control, **FileListBox** Control, **Form** Object, **Forms** Collection, **HScrollBar**, **VScrollBar** Controls, **ListBox** Control, **ListView** Control, **Masked Edit** Control, **MSFlexGrid** Control, **OLE Container** Control, **Option Button** Control, **PictureBox** Control, **PropertyPage** Object, **RichTextBox** Control, **Slider** Control, **TabStrip** Control, **TextBox** Control, **TreeView** Control, **UpDown** Control, **UserControl** Object, **UserDocument** Object

Syntax

Private Sub Form_GotFocus( )
Private Sub *object*_**GotFocus**([*index* **As Integer**])

The **GotFocus** event syntax has these parts:

Part	Description
object	An object expression that evaluates to an object in the **Applies To** list.
index	An integer that uniquely identifies a control if it's in a control array.

Remarks

Typically, you use a **GotFocus** event procedure to specify the actions that occur when a control or form first receives the focus. For example, by attaching a **GotFocus** event procedure to each control on a form, you can guide the user by displaying brief instructions or status bar messages. You can also provide visual cues by enabling, disabling, or showing other controls that depend on the control that has the focus.

Note An object can receive the focus only if its **Enabled** and **Visible** properties are set to **True**. To customize the keyboard interface in Visual Basic for moving the focus, set the tab order or specify access keys for controls on a form.

See Also

LostFocus Event, **SetFocus** Method, **TabIndex** Property, **TabStop** Property, **ActiveControl** Property, **ActiveForm** Property

Example

This example displays a status bar message when a button in an **OptionButton** group gets the focus. To try this example, paste the code into the Declarations section of a form that contains two **OptionButton** controls and a **Label** control. Set the **Name** property for both **OptionButton** controls to OptionGroup, and then press F5 and click the **OptionButton** controls.

```
Private Sub Form_Load ()
    Label1.AutoSize = True
End Sub

Private Sub OptionGroup_GotFocus (Index As Integer)
    Select Case Index
        Case 0
            Label1.Caption = "Option 1 has the focus."
        Case 1
            Label1.Caption = "Option 2 has the focus."
    End Select
End Sub

Private Sub OptionGroup_LostFocus (Index As Integer)
    Label1.Caption = ""
End Sub
```

GotFocus Event (UserControl Object and UserDocument Object)

Occurs in the object or constituent control when focus enters it.

Applies To

UserControl Object, **UserDocument** Object

Syntax

Sub *object*_**GotFocus**()

The **GotFocus** event syntax has these parts:

Part	Description
object	An object expression that evaluates to an object in the **Applies To** list.

Remarks

This **GotFocus** event is not the same **GotFocus** extender event that the developer who uses *object* handles. This **GotFocus** event is for the author of *object*, and is internal to *object*.

This event is useful if *object* needs to know that the focus is now on it.

Object itself can get focus only when the **CanGetFocus** property is **True** and there are no constituent controls that can receive the focus.

The **EnterFocus** event is raised before the **GotFocus** event.

Do not raise the **GotFocus** extender event from this event.

See Also

CanGetFocus Property, **EnterFocus** Event, **LostFocus** Event

---

GoTo Statement

Branches unconditionally to a specified line within a procedure.

Syntax

GoTo *line*

The required *line* argument can be any line label or line number.

Remarks

GoTo can branch only to lines within the procedure where it appears.

Note   Too many **GoTo** statements can make code difficult to read and debug. Use structured control statements (**Do...Loop**, **For...Next**, **If...Then...Else**, **Select Case**) whenever possible.

See Also

Do...Loop Statement, **For...Next** Statement, **GoSub...Return** Statement, **If...Then...Else** Statement, **Select Case** Statement

Example

This example uses the **GoTo** statement to branch to line labels within a procedure.

```
Sub GotoStatementDemo()
Dim Number, MyString
    Number = 1      ' Initialize variable.
                    ' Evaluate Number and branch to appropriate label.
    If Number = 1 Then GoTo Line1 Else GoTo Line2

Line1:
    MyString = "Number equals 1"
    GoTo LastLine   ' Go to LastLine.
Line2:
    ' The following statement never gets executed.
    MyString = "Number equals 2"
LastLine:
    Debug.Print MyString ' Print "Number equals 1" in
                         ' Debug window.
End Sub
```

GridLineWidth Property

Returns or sets the width in pixels of the gridlines for an **MSFlexGrid** control.

Applies To

MSFlexGrid Control

Syntax

object.**GridLineWidth** [= *value*]

The **GridLineWidth** property syntax has these parts:

Part	Description
object	An object expression that evaluates to an object in the **Applies To** list.
value	An integer specifying the gridline width. The minimum setting is 1 (default); the maximum setting is 10.

Group Object

A **Group** object represents a group of user accounts that have common access permissions when a **Workspace** object operates as a secure workgroup. (Microsoft Jet workspaces only).

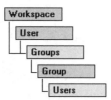

Remarks

You create **Group** objects and then use their names to establish and enforce access permissions for your databases, tables, and queries using the **Document** objects that represent the **Database**, **TableDef**, and **QueryDef** objects with which you're working.

With the properties of a **Group** object, you can:

- Use the **Name** property of an existing **Group** object to return its name. You can't return the **PID** property setting of an existing **Group** object.
- Use the **Name** and **PID** properties of a newly created, unappended **Group** object to set the identity of that **Group** object.

You can append an existing **Group** object to the **Groups** collection in a **User** object to establish membership of a user account in that **Group** object. Alternatively, you can append a **User** object to the **Users** collection in a **Group** object to give a user account the global permissions of that group. If you use a **Groups** or **Users** collection other than the one to which you just appended an object, you may need to use the **Refresh** method to refresh the collection with current information from the database. The Microsoft Jet database engine predefines three **Group** objects named Admins, Users, and Guests. To create a new **Group** object, use the **CreateGroup** method on a **User** or **Workspace** object.

To refer to a **Group** object in a collection by its ordinal number or by its **Name** property setting, use any of the following syntax forms:

Groups(0)
Groups("*name*")
Groups![*name*]

Properties

Name Property, **PID** Property

Methods

CreateUser Method

See Also

CreateGroup Method

Example

This example illustrates the use of the **Group** and **User** objects and the **Groups** and **Users** collections. First, it creates a new **User** object and appends the object to the **Users** collection of the default **Workspace** object. Next, it creates a new **Group** object and appends the object to the **Groups** collection of the default **Workspace** object. Then the example adds user Pat Smith to the Accounting group. Finally, it enumerates the **Users** and **Groups** collections of the default **Workspace** object. See the methods and properties listed in the **Group** and **User** summary topics for additional examples.

```
Sub GroupX()

    Dim wrkDefault As Workspace
    Dim usrNew As User
    Dim usrLoop As User
    Dim grpNew As Group
    Dim grpLoop As Group
    Dim grpMember As Group

    Set wrkDefault = DBEngine.Workspaces(0)

    With wrkDefault

        ' Create and append new user.
        Set usrNew = .CreateUser("Pat Smith", _
            "abc123DEF456", "Password1")
        .Users.Append usrNew

        ' Create and append new group.
        Set grpNew = .CreateGroup("Accounting", _
            "UVW987xyz654")
        .Groups.Append grpNew

        ' Make the user Pat Smith a member of the
        ' Accounting group by creating and adding the
```

```
         ' appropriate Group object to the user's Groups
         ' collection. The same is accomplished if a User
         ' object representing Pat Smith is created and
         ' appended to the Accounting group's Users
         ' collection.
         Set grpMember = usrNew.CreateGroup("Accounting")
         usrNew.Groups.Append grpMember

         Debug.Print "Users collection:"

         ' Enumerate all User objects in the default
         ' workspace's Users collection.
         For Each usrLoop In .Users
            Debug.Print "    " & usrLoop.Name
            Debug.Print "        Belongs to these groups:"

            ' Enumerate all Group objects in each User
            ' object's Groups collection.
            If usrLoop.Groups.Count <> 0 Then
               For Each grpLoop In usrLoop.Groups
                  Debug.Print "            " & _
                     grpLoop.Name
               Next grpLoop
            Else
               Debug.Print "            [None]"
            End If

         Next usrLoop

         Debug.Print "Groups collection:"

         ' Enumerate all Group objects in the default
         ' workspace's Groups collection.
         For Each grpLoop In .Groups
            Debug.Print "    " & grpLoop.Name
            Debug.Print "        Has as its members:"

            ' Enumerate all User objects in each Group
            ' object's Users collection.
            If grpLoop.Users.Count <> 0 Then
               For Each usrLoop In grpLoop.Users
                  Debug.Print "            " & _
                     usrLoop.Name
               Next usrLoop
            Else
               Debug.Print "            [None]"
            End If

         Next grpLoop

         ' Delete new User and Group objects because this
         ' is only a demonstration.
         .Users.Delete "Pat Smith"
         .Groups.Delete "Accounting"

      End With

   End Sub
```

Groups Collection

A **Groups** collection contains all stored **Group** objects of a **Workspace** or user account (Microsoft Jet workspaces only).

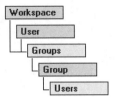

Remarks

You can append an existing **Group** object to the **Groups** collection in a **User** object to establish membership of a user account in that **Group** object. Alternatively, you can append a **User** object to the **Users** collection in a **Group** object to give a user account the global permissions of that group. In either case, the existing **Group** object must already be a member of the **Groups** collection of the current **Workspace** object. If you use a **Groups** or **Users** collection other than the one to which you just appended an object, you may need to use the **Refresh** method to refresh the collection with current information from the database.

To refer to a **Group** object in a collection by its ordinal number or by its **Name** property setting, use any of the following syntax forms:

Groups(0)
Groups("*name*")
Groups![*name*]

Properties

Count Property

Methods

Append Method, **Delete** Method, **Refresh** Method

Example

This example illustrates the use of the **Group** and **User** objects and the **Groups** and **Users** collections. First, it creates a new **User** object and appends the object to the **Users** collection of the default **Workspace** object. Next, it creates a new **Group** object and appends the object to the **Groups** collection of the default **Workspace** object. Then the example adds user Pat Smith to the Accounting group. Finally, it enumerates the **Users** and **Groups** collections of the default **Workspace** object. See the methods and properties listed in the **Group** and **User** summary topics for additional examples.

```
Sub GroupX()

    Dim wrkDefault As Workspace
    Dim usrNew As User
    Dim usrLoop As User
    Dim grpNew As Group
    Dim grpLoop As Group
    Dim grpMember As Group

    Set wrkDefault = DBEngine.Workspaces(0)

    With wrkDefault

        ' Create and append new user.
        Set usrNew = .CreateUser("Pat Smith", _
            "abc123DEF456", "Password1")
        .Users.Append usrNew

        ' Create and append new group.
        Set grpNew = .CreateGroup("Accounting", _
            "UVW987xyz654")
        .Groups.Append grpNew

        ' Make the user Pat Smith a member of the
        ' Accounting group by creating and adding the
        ' appropriate Group object to the user's Groups
        ' collection. The same is accomplished if a User
        ' object representing Pat Smith is created and
        ' appended to the Accounting group's Users
        ' collection.
        Set grpMember = usrNew.CreateGroup("Accounting")
        usrNew.Groups.Append grpMember

        Debug.Print "Users collection:"

        ' Enumerate all User objects in the default
        ' workspace's Users collection.
        For Each usrLoop In .Users
            Debug.Print "    " & usrLoop.Name
            Debug.Print "Belongs to these groups:"

            ' Enumerate all Group objects in each User
            ' object's Groups collection.
            If usrLoop.Groups.Count <> 0 Then
                For Each grpLoop In usrLoop.Groups
                    Debug.Print "            " & _
                        grpLoop.Name
                Next grpLoop
            Else
                Debug.Print "[None]"
            End If
```

```
        Next usrLoop

        Debug.Print "Groups collection:"

        ' Enumerate all Group objects in the default
        ' workspace's Groups collection.
        For Each grpLoop In .Groups
            Debug.Print "    " & grpLoop.Name
            Debug.Print "        Has as its members:"

            ' Enumerate all User objects in each Group
            ' object's Users collection.
            If grpLoop.Users.Count <> 0 Then
                For Each usrLoop In grpLoop.Users
                    Debug.Print "" & _
                        usrLoop.Name
                Next usrLoop
            Else
                Debug.Print "[None]"
            End If

        Next grpLoop

        ' Delete new User and Group objects because this
        ' is only a demonstration.
        .Users.Delete "Pat Smith"
        .Groups.Delete "Accounting"

    End With

End Sub
```

GUID Property

Returns a **String** containing the class identifier of an object. Read-only.

Applies to

Reference Object

See Also

AddFromGuid Method, **FullPath** Property

Example

The following example uses the **GUID** property to return the globally unique ID number for the specified **Reference** object in the specified project.

```
Debug.Print Application.VBE.VBProjects(1).References(1).GUID
```

Handle Property

Returns a handle to the graphic contained within a **Picture** object.

Applies To

Picture Object

Syntax

object.**Handle**

The *object* placeholder represents an object expression that evaluates to an object in the **Applies To** list.

Return Value

The value returned by the **Handle** property depends on the current setting of the **Type** property as shown in the following table:

Type Property	Return Value
1 (Bitmap)	An HBITMAP handle.
2 (Metafile)	An HMETAFILE handle.
3 (Icon)	An HICON or an HCURSOR handle.
4 (Enhanced Metafile)	An HENHMETAFILE handle.

Remarks

The **Handle** property is useful when you need to pass a handle to a graphic as part of a call to a function in a dynamic-link library (DLL) or the Windows API.

See Also

Type Property (Picture)

HasOpenDesigner Property

Returns a **Boolean** value indicating whether or not the **VBComponent** object has an open designer. Read-only.

Applies To

VBComponent Object

Return Values

The **HasOpenDesigner** property returns these values:

Value	Description
True	The **VBComponent** object has an open **Design** window.
False	The **VBComponent** object doesn't have an open **Design** window.

See Also

Designer Property, **DesignerWindow** Property

Example

The following example uses the **HasOpenDesigner** property to return whether or not the specified component, in this case a form, of a particular project has an open designer.

```
Debug.Print Application.VBE.VBProjects(1).VBComponents(1).HasOpenDesigner
```

---

hDC Property

Returns a handle provided by the Microsoft Windows operating environment to the device context of an object.

Applies To

CommonDialog Control, **PropertyPage** Object, **UserControl** Object, **UserDocument** Object, **Printer** Object, **Printers** Collection, **Form** Object, **Forms** Collection, **PictureBox** Control

Syntax

object.**hDC**

The *object* placeholder represents an object expression that evaluates to an object in the **Applies To** list.

Remarks

This property is a Windows operating environment device context handle. The Windows operating environment manages the system display by assigning a device context for the **Printer** object and for each form and **PictureBox** control in your application. You can use the **hDC** property to refer to the handle for an object's device context. This provides a value to pass to Windows API calls.

With a **CommonDialog** control, this property returns a device context for the printer selected in the Print dialog box when the **cdlReturnDC** flag is set or an information context when the **cdlReturnIC** flag is set.

Note The value of the **hDC** property can change while a program is running, so don't store the value in a variable; instead, use the **hDC** property each time you need it.

The **AutoRedraw** property can cause the **hDC** property setting to change. If **AutoRedraw** is set to **True** for a form or **PictureBox** container, **hDC** acts as a handle to the device context of the persistent graphic (equivalent to the **Image** property). When **AutoRedraw** is **False**, **hDC** is the actual **hDC** value of the Form window or the **PictureBox** container. The **hDC** property setting may change while the program is running regardless of the **AutoRedraw** setting.

See Also

Icon Property, **AutoRedraw** Property, **hWnd** Property

Example

This example draws a triangle and then uses a Microsoft Windows function to fill it with color. To try this example, create a new module using the Add Module command on the Project menu. Paste the **Declare** statement into the Declarations section of the new module, being sure that the statement is on one line with no break or wordwrap. Then paste the **Sub** procedure into the Declarations section of a form. Press F5 and click the form.

```
' Declaration of a Windows routine. This statement is
' for the module.
Declare Sub FloodFill Lib "GDI32" Alias "FloodFill" _
 (ByVal hDC As Long, ByVal X As Long, ByVal Y As _
 Long, ByVal crColor As Long) As Long
' Place the following code in the form.
Private Sub Form_Click ()
    ScaleMode = vbPixels      ' Windows draws in pixels.
    ForeColor = vbBlack       ' Set draw line to black.
    Line (100, 50)-(300, 50)  ' Draw a triangle.
    Line -(200, 200)
    Line -(100, 50)

FillStyle = vbFSSolid     ' Set FillStyle to solid.
    FillColor = RGB(128, 128, 255)      ' Set FillColor.
    ' Call Windows API to fill.
    FloodFill hDC, 200, 100, ForeColor
End Sub
```

hDbc Property (Remote Data)

Returns a value corresponding to the ODBC connection handle.

Applies To

rdoConnection Object

Syntax

object.**hDbc**

The *object* placeholder represents an object expression that evaluates to an object in the **Applies To** list.

Return Values

The **hDbc** property returns a **Long** value containing the ODBC connection handle created by the ODBC driver manager corresponding to the specified **rdoConnection** object.

Remarks

This handle can be used to execute ODBC functions that require an ODBC **hDbc** connection handle.

Note   While it is possible to execute ODBC API functions using the ODBC **hEnv, hDbc**, and **hStmt** handles, it is recommended that you do so with caution. Improper use of arbitrary ODBC API functions using these handles can result in unpredictable behavior. You should not attempt to save this handle in a variable for use at a later time as the value is subject to change.

If your application requires access to special ODBC connection option settings, these should be set or retrieved using the **hDbc** property *before* the connection is established. Resetting ODBC settings of any kind after the connection is established can result in unpredictable behavior.

Example

The following example illustrates use of the hDbc property when executing an ODBC API function. In this case, the application sets a connection option that changes how transactions are isolated.

```
Option Explicit
Dim en As rdoEnvironment
Dim cn As rdoConnection
Dim rc As Integer

'Declare Function SQLSetConnectOption Lib "odbc32.dll" (ByVal hdbc&, ByVal fOption%,
ByVal vParam As Any) As Integer
'
'Transaction isolation option masks
'
 Const SQL_TXN_ISOLATION As Long = 108
 Const SQL_TXN_READ_UNCOMMITTED As Long = &H1&
 Const SQL_TXN_READ_COMMITTED As Long = &H2&
 Const SQL_TXN_REPEATABLE_READ As Long = &H4&
 Const SQL_TXN_SERIALIZABLE As Long = &H8&
 Const SQL_TXN_VERSIONING As Long = &H10&

Private Sub Form_Load()
Set en = rdoEngine.rdoEnvironments(0)

Set cn = en.OpenConnection(dsName:="WorkDB", _
    Prompt:=rdDriverNoPrompt, _
    Connect:="Uid=;pwd=;database=workdb")

rc = SQLSetConnectOption(cn.hDbc, SQL_TXN_ISOLATION, SQL_TXN_READ_UNCOMMITTED)

Debug.Print rc

End Sub
```

See Also

hEnv Property (Remote Data), **hStmt** Property (Remote Data)

HeadClick Event

Occurs when the user clicks on the header for a particular column of a **DBGrid** control.

Applies To

DBGrid Control

Syntax

Private Sub *object*_**HeadClick** ([*index* **As Integer**,] *colindex* **As Integer**)

The **HeadClick** event syntax has these parts:

Part	Description
object	An object expression that evaluates to an object in the **Applies To** list.
index	An integer that identifies a control if it is in a control array.
colindex	An integer that identifies the column.

Remarks

One possible use for this event is to resort the **Recordset** object based on the selected column.

See Also

Recordset Property, **ColIndex** Property

Example

This example sorts the record source of the **Data** control based on which column the user clicked.

```
Private Sub DataGrid1_HeadClick (ColIndex As Integer)
    Data1.RecordSource = "Select * From Publishers Order By " & _
      DataGrid1.Columns(ColIndex).DataField
    Data1.Refresh
End Sub
```

HeadFont Property

Returns or sets a value indicating the font used in column headers in a **DBGrid** control.

Applies To

DBGrid Control

Syntax

object.**Type** [= *value*]

The **Type** property syntax has these parts:

Part	Description
object	An object expression that evaluates to an object in the **Applies To** list.
value	An object expression that evaluates to a **Font** object. The default value is the column's current font set to bold.

Remarks

Changing the **HeadFont** property may resize the headers to accommodate the new font.

See Also

Data Control, **Column** Object, **DefColWidth** Property, **Font** Object

HeadLines Property

Returns or sets a value indicating the number of lines of text displayed in the column headers of a **DBGrid** control.

Applies To

DBGrid Control

Syntax

*object***.HeadLines** [= *value*]

The **HeadLines** property syntax has these parts:

Part	Description
object	An object expression that evaluates to an object in the **Applies To** list.
value	A single from 0 to 10. The default value is 1, which causes the control to display the names of underlying fields for each column in the header. A setting of 0 removes the headings.

Remarks

The **HeadLines** property can be used to display more than one line of text in the column headers of the **DBGrid** control.

See Also

Data Control, **Column** Object, **Columns** Property (DBGrid), **DefColWidth** Property

Example

This example checks the value of a check box to determine whether or not to display headings in the grid.

```
Private Sub Check1_Click ()
   If Check1.Value = vbChecked Then
      DBGrid1.HeadLines = 2' If checked,two lines in
                          ' column headings.
   Else
      DBGrid1.HeadLines = 0' No headings.
   End If
End Sub
```

Height Property (Add-Ins)

Returns or sets a **Single** containing the height of the window in twips. Read/write.

Applies To

Window Object

Remarks

Changing the **Height** property setting of a linked window or docked window has no effect as long as the window remains linked or docked.

See Also

Left Property, **Top** Property, **Width** Property

Example

The following example uses the **Height** and **Width** properties to return the height and width of the specified window, in twips. These property settings change after a window is linked or docked because then they refer to the **Window** object to which the original window is linked or docked.

```
Debug.Print Application.VBE.Windows(9).Height
Debug.Print Application.VBE.Windows(9).Width
```

Height, Width Properties

Return or set the dimensions of an object or the width of the **Columns** object of a **DBGrid** control. For the **Printer** and **Screen** objects, not available at design time.

Applies To

CheckBox Control, **Column** Control, **ComboBox** Control, **CommandButton** Control, **Data** Control, **DirListBox** Control, **FileListBox** Control, **Form** Object, **Forms** Collection, **Frame** Control, **HScrollBar, VScrollBar** Controls, **Image** Control, **Label** Control, **ListBox** Control, **MDIForm** Object, **OLE Container** Control, **OptionButton** Control, **Picture** Object, **PictureBox** Control, **Printer** Object, **Printers** Collection, **Property Page** Object, **RemoteData** Control, **Screen** Object, **Shape** Control, **TextBox** Control, **UserControl** Object, **UserDocument** Object

Syntax

object.**Height** [= *number*]
object.**Width** [= *number*]

The **Height** and **Width** property syntaxes have these parts:

Part	Description
object	An object expression that evaluates to an object in the **Applies To** list.
number	A numeric expression specifying the dimensions of an object, as described in Settings.

Settings

Measurements are calculated as follows:

- **Form**—the external height and width of the form, including the borders and title bar.

- **Control**—measured from the center of the control's border so that controls with different border widths align correctly. These properties use the scale units of a control's container.

- **Printer** object—the physical dimensions of the paper set up for the printing device; not available at design time. If set at run time, values in these properties are used instead of the setting of the **PaperSize** property.

- **Screen** object—the height and width of the screen; not available at design time and read-only at run time.

- **Picture** object—the height and width of the picture in HiMetric units.

Remarks

For **Form**, **Printer**, and **Screen** objects, these properties are always measured in twips. For a form or control, the values for these properties change as the object is sized by the user or by your code. Maximum limits of these properties for all objects are system-dependent.

If you set the **Height** and **Width** properties for a printer driver that doesn't allow these properties to be set, no error occurs and the size of the paper remains as it was. If you set **Height** and **Width** for a printer driver that allows only certain values to be specified, no error occurs and the property is set to whatever the driver allows. For example, you could set **Height** to 150 and the driver would set it to 144.

Use the **Height**, **Width**, **Left**, and **Top** properties for operations or calculations based on an object's total area, such as sizing or moving the object. Use the **ScaleLeft**, **ScaleTop**, **ScaleHeight**, and **ScaleWidth** properties for operations or calculations based on an object's internal area, such as drawing or moving objects within another object.

Note The **Height** property can't be changed for the **DriveListBox** control or for the **ComboBox** control, whose **Style** property setting is 0 (Dropdown Combo) or 2 (Dropdown List).

For the **Columns** object of the **DBGrid** control, **Width** is specified in the unit of measure of the object that contains the **DBGrid**. The default value for **Width** is the value of the **DefColWidth** property of **DBGrid**.

For the **Picture** object, use the **ScaleX** and **ScaleY** methods to convert **HiMetric** units into the scale you need.

See Also

Move Method, **ScaleX**, **ScaleY** Methods, **Left**, **Top** Properties, **PaperSize** Property, **ScaleHeight**, **ScaleWidth** Properties, **ScaleLeft**, **ScaleTop** Properties

Example

This example sets the size of a form to 75 percent of screen size and centers the form when it is loaded. To try this example, paste the code into the Declarations section of a form. Then press F5 and click the form.

```
Private Sub Form_Click ()
   Width = Screen.Width * .75 ' Set width of form.
   Height = Screen.Height * .75     ' Set height of form.
   Left = (Screen.Width - Width) / 2 ' Center form horizontally.
   Top = (Screen.Height - Height) / 2 ' Center form vertically.
End Sub
```

HelpContext Property

Returns or sets a string expression containing the context ID for a topic in a Microsoft Windows Help file. Read/write.

Applies To

Err Object

Remarks

The **HelpContext** property is used to automatically display the Help topic specified in the **HelpFile** property. If both **HelpFile** and **HelpContext** are empty, the value of **Number** is checked. If **Number** corresponds to a Visual Basic run-time error value, then the Visual Basic Help context ID for the error is used. If the **Number** value doesn't correspond to a Visual Basic error, the contents screen for the Visual Basic Help file is displayed.

Note You should write routines in your application to handle typical errors. When programming with an object, you can use the object's Help file to improve the quality of your error handling, or to display a meaningful message to your user if the error isn't recoverable.

See Also

Err Object, **Description** Property, **HelpFile** Property, **LastDLLError** Property, **Number** Property, **Source** Property

Example

This example uses the **HelpContext** property of the **Err** object to show the Visual Basic Help topic for the Overflow error.

```
Dim Msg
Err.Clear
On Error Resume Next
Err.Raise 6                     ' Generate "Overflow" error.
If Err.Number <> 0 Then
   Msg = "Press F1 or Help to see " & Err.HelpFile & " topic for" & _
   " the following HelpContext: " & Err.HelpContext
   MsgBox Msg, , "Error: " & Err.Description, Err.HelpFile, _
Err.HelpContext
End If
```

HelpContext, HelpFile Properties

- **HelpContext** — returns a context ID, as a **Long** variable, for a topic in a Microsoft Windows Help file.

- **HelpFile** — returns a **String** that is a fully qualified path to the Help file.

Applies To

Error Object

Remarks

If you specify a Microsoft Windows Help file in **HelpFile**, you can use the **HelpContext** property to automatically display the Help topic it identifies.

Note   You should write procedures in your application to handle typical errors. When programming with an object, you can use the Help supplied by the object's Help file to improve the quality of your error handling, or to display a meaningful message to your user if the error is not recoverable.

See Also

Description Property, **Number** Property, **Source** Property

Example

This example forces an error, traps it, and displays the **Description**, **Number**, **Source**, **HelpContext**, and **HelpFile** properties of the resulting **Error** object.

```
Sub DescriptionX()

    Dim dbsTest As Database

    On Error GoTo ErrorHandler

    ' Intentionally trigger an error.
    Set dbsTest = OpenDatabase("NoDatabase")

    Exit Sub

ErrorHandler:
    Dim strError As String
    Dim errLoop As Error

    ' Enumerate Errors collection and display properties of
    ' each Error object.
    For Each errLoop In Errors
        With errLoop
            strError = _
                "Error #" & .Number & vbCr
            strError = strError & _
                "    " & .Description & vbCr
            strError = strError & _
                "    (Source: " & .Source & ")" & vbCr
            strError = strError & _
                "Press F1 to see topic " & .HelpContext & vbCr
            strError = strError & _
                "    in the file " & .HelpFile & "."
        End With
        MsgBox strError
    Next

    Resume Next

End Sub
```

HelpContext, HelpFile Properties (Remote Data)

- **HelpContext**—returns a context ID for a topic in a Microsoft Windows Help file.
- **HelpFile**—returns a fully qualified path to the Help file as a variable.

Applies To

rdoError Object

Syntax

object.**HelpContext**
object.**HelpFile**

The *object* placeholder represents an object expression that evaluates to an object in the **Applies To** list.

Return Values

The **HelpContext** property returns a **Long** value.

The **HelpFile** property returns a **String** value.

Remarks

If a Microsoft Windows Help file is specified in **HelpFile**, the **HelpContext** property is used to automatically display the Help topic it identifies.

Note You should write routines in your application to handle typical errors. When programming with an object, you can use the Help supplied by the object's Help file to improve the quality of your error handling, or to display a meaningful message to your user if the error is not recoverable.

See Also

rdoError Object, **Description** Property (Remote Data), **Number** Property (Remote Data), **Source** Property (Remote Data), **SQLRetCode** Property (Remote Data), **SQLState** Property (Remote Data)

HelpContextID Property

Returns or sets an associated context number for an object. Used to provide context-sensitive Help for your application.

Applies To

Animation Control, **CheckBox** Control, **ComboBox** Control, **CommandButton** Control, **DBCombo** Control, **DBGrid** Control, **DBList** Control, **DirListBox** Control, **DriveListBox** Control, **FileListBox** Control, **Form Object, Forms** Collection, **Frame** Control, **HScrollBar, VScrollBar** Controls, **ListBox** Control, **ListView**

Control, **Masked Edit** Control, **MDIForm** Object, **Menu** Control, **MSChart** Control, **MSFlexGrid** Control, **OLE Container** Control, **OptionButton** Control, **PictureBox** Control, **PropertyPage** Control, **RichTextBox** Control, **Slider** Control, **SSTab** Control, **TabStrip** Control, **TextBox** Control, **TreeView** Control, **UpDown** Control

Syntax

object.**HelpContextID** [= *number*]

The **HelpContextID** property syntax has these parts:

Part	Description
object	An object expression that evaluates to an object in the **Applies To** list. If *object* is omitted, the form associated with the active form module is assumed to be *object*.
number	A numeric expression that specifies the context number of the Help topic associated with *object*.

Settings

The settings for *number* are:

Setting	Description
0	(Default) No context number specified.
> 0	An integer specifying a valid context number.

Remarks

For context-sensitive Help on an object in your application, you must assign the same context number to both *object* and to the associated Help topic when you compile your Help file.

If you've created a Microsoft Windows operating environment Help file for your application and set the application's **HelpFile** property, when a user presses the F1 key, Visual Basic automatically calls Help and searches for the topic identified by the current context number.

The current context number is the value of **HelpContextID** for the object that has the focus. If **HelpContextID** is set to 0, then Visual Basic looks in the **HelpContextID** of the object's container, and then that object's container, and so on. If a nonzero current context number can't be found, the F1 key is ignored.

For a **Menu** control, **HelpContextID** is normally read/write at run time. But **HelpContextID** is read-only for menu items that are exposed or supplied by Visual Basic to add-ins, such as the Add-In Manager command on the Add-Ins menu.

Note Building a Help file requires the Microsoft Windows Help Compiler, which is included with the Visual Basic Professional Edition.

See Also

HelpFile Property (App, CommonDialog, MenuLine)

Example

This example uses topics in the Visual Basic Help file to demonstrate how to specify context numbers for Help topics. To try this example, paste the code into the Declarations section of a form that contains a **TextBox** control and a **Frame** control with an **OptionButton** control inside of it. Press F5. Once the program is running, move the focus to one of the controls, and press F1.

```
' Actual context numbers from the Visual Basic Help file.
Const winColorPalette = 21004 ' Define constants.
Const winToolbox = 21001
Const winCodeWindow = 21005

Private Sub Form_Load ()
    App.HelpFile = "VB.HLP"
    Frame1.HelpContextID = winColorPalette
    Text1.HelpContextID = winToolbox
    Form1.HelpContextID = winCodeWindow
End Sub
```

HelpFile Property

Returns or sets a string expression for the fully qualified path to a Microsoft Windows Help file. Read/write.

Applies To

Err Object

Remarks

If a Help file is specified in **HelpFile**, it is automatically called when the user presses the **Help** button (or the F1 key) in the error message dialog box. If the **HelpContext** property contains a valid context ID for the specified file, that topic is automatically displayed. If no **HelpFile** is specified, the Visual Basic Help file is displayed.

Note You should write routines in your application to handle typical errors. When programming with an object, you can use the object's Help file to improve the quality of your error handling, or to display a meaningful message to your user if the error isn't recoverable.

See Also

Err Object, **Description** Property, **HelpContext** Property, **LastDLLError** Property, **Number** Property, **Source** Property

Example

This example uses the **HelpFile** property of the **Err** object to start the Microsoft Windows Help system. By default, the **HelpFile** property contains the name of the Visual Basic Help file.

```
Dim Msg
Err.Clear
On Error Resume Next      ' Suppress errors for demonstration purposes.
Err.Raise 6               ' Generate "Overflow" error.
Msg = "Press F1 or Help to see " & Err.HelpFile & _
" topic for this error"
MsgBox Msg, , "Error: " & Err.Description,Err.HelpFile, Err.HelpContext
```

HelpFile Property (App, CommonDialog, MenuLine)

Specifies the path and filename of a Microsoft Windows Help file used by your application to display Help or online documentation.

Applies To

App Object, **CommonDialog** Control

Syntax

object.**HelpFile**[= *filename*]

The **HelpFile** property syntax has these parts:

Part	Description
object	An object expression that evaluates to an object in the **Applies To** list.
filename	A string expression specifying the path and filename of the Windows Help file for your application.

Remarks

If you've created a Windows Help file for your application and set the application's **HelpFile** property, Visual Basic automatically calls Help when a user presses the F1 key. If there is a context number in the **HelpContextID** property for either the active control or the active form, Help displays a topic corresponding to the current Help context; otherwise it displays the main contents screen.

You can also use the **HelpFile** property to determine which Help file is displayed when a user requests Help from the Object Browser for an ActiveX component.

Note   Building a Help file requires the Microsoft Windows Help Compiler, which is available with Visual Basic, Professional Edition.

See Also

HelpContextID Property

Example

This example uses topics in the Visual Basic Help file and demonstrates how to specify context numbers for Help topics. To try this example, paste the code into the

Declarations section of a **Form** object that contains a **TextBox** control and a **Frame** control with an **OptionButton** control inside of it. Run the example. Once the program is running, move the focus to one of the components, and press F1.

```
' Actual context numbers from the Visual Basic Help file.
' Define constants.
Const winPictureBox = 2016002
Const winCommandButton = 2007557

Private Sub Form_Load ()
    App.HelpFile = "VB5.HLP"
    Text1.HelpContextID = winPictureBox
    Form1.HelpContextID = winCommandButton
End Sub
```

hEnv Property (Remote Data)

Returns a value corresponding to the ODBC environment handle.

Applies To

rdoEnvironment Object

Syntax

object.**hEnv**

The *object* placeholder represents an object expression that evaluates to an object in the **Applies To** list.

Return Values

The **hEnv** property returns a **Long** value containing the ODBC environment handle created by the ODBC driver manager corresponding to the specified **rdoEnvironment** object.

Remarks

This handle can be used to execute ODBC functions that require an ODBC **hEnv** environment handle.

Note While it is possible to execute ODBC API functions using the ODBC **hEnv, hDbc,** and **hStmt** handles, it is recommended that you do so with caution. Improper use of arbitrary ODBC API functions using these handles can result in unpredictable behavior. You should not attempt to save this handle in a variable for use at a later time as the value is subject to change.

See Also

hDbc Property (Remote Data), **hStmt** Property (Remote Data)

Example

The following example illustrates use of the **hEnv** property when accessing an ODBC API function. This code displays all registered data source names (DSNs) in a **ListBox** control.

```
Private Sub ShowDSNs_Click()
Dim fDirection As Integer
Dim szDSN As String * 1024
Dim cbDSNMax As Integer
Dim pcbDSN As Integer
Dim szDescription As String * 1024
Dim cbDescriptionMax As Integer
Dim pcbDescription As Integer
Dim Item As String
Set En = rdoEnvironments(0)
fDirection = SQL_FETCH_NEXT
cbDSNMax = 1023
cbDescriptionMax = 1023
List1.Clear
I = SQL_SUCCESS
  While I = SQL_SUCCESS
    szDSN = String(1024, " ")
    szDescription = String(1024, " ")
    I = SQLDataSources(En.hEnv, fDirection, szDSN, _
    cbDSNMax, pcbDSN, szDescription, _
    cbDescriptionMax, pcbDescription)
    Item = Left(szDSN, pcbDSN) & " - " _
       & Left(szDescription, pcbDescription)
    Debug.Print Item
    List1.AddItem Item
Wend

End Sub
```

Hex Function

Returns a **String** representing the hexadecimal value of a number.

Syntax

Hex(*number*)

The required *number* argument is any valid numeric expression or string expression.

Remarks

If *number* is not already a whole number, it is rounded to the nearest whole number before being evaluated.

If *number* is	Hex returns
Null	Null
Empty	Zero (0)
Any other number	Up to eight hexadecimal characters

You can represent hexadecimal numbers directly by preceding numbers in the proper range with &H. For example, &H10 represents decimal 16 in hexadecimal notation.

See Also

See Also

Oct Function

Example

This example uses the **Hex** function to return the hexadecimal value of a number.

```
Dim MyHex
MyHex = Hex(5)        ' Returns 5.
MyHex = Hex(10)       ' Returns A.
MyHex = Hex(459)      ' Returns 1CB.
```

Hidden Property

Returns or sets the Hidden attribute of a **Member** object.

Applies To

SeriesPosition Object

Syntax

object.**Hidden**

The *object* placeholder represents an object expression that evaluates to an object in the **Applies To** list.

Hide Event (UserControl Object)

Occurs when the object's **Visible** property changes to **False**.

Applies To

UserControl Object

Syntax

Sub *object*_**Hide**()

The Hide event syntax has these parts:

Part	Description
object	An object expression that evaluates to an object in the **Applies To** list.

Remarks

In order to draw to the screen in Windows, any object must have a window, temporarily or permanently; Visual Basic ActiveX controls have permanent windows. Before a control has been sited on a form, its window is not on the container. The control receives Hide events when the window is removed.

While the control's window is on the form, the object receives a Hide event when the control's **Visible** property changes to **False**.

The control does *not* receive Hide events if the form is hidden and then shown again, or if the form is minimized and then restored. The control's window remains on the form during these operations, and its **Visible** property doesn't change.

If the control is being shown in an Internet browser, a Hide event occurs when the page is moved to the history list.

Note If the control is used with earlier versions of Visual Basic than 5.0, the control will not receive Hide events at design time. This is because earlier versions of Visual Basic did not put any visible windows on a form at design time.

See Also

Visible Property

Hide Event (UserDocument Object)

Occurs when the object's **Visible** property changes to **False**.

Applies To

UserDocument Object

Syntax

Sub *object*_**Hide**()

The Hide event syntax has these parts:

Part	Description
object	An object expression that evaluates to an object in the **Applies To** list.

Remarks

In order to draw to the screen in Windows, any object must have a window, temporarily or permanently. Visual Basic ActiveX documents have permanent windows. The **UserDocument** object receives **Hide** events when the window is removed.

While *object*'s window is on the container, *object* receives a **Hide** event when *object's* **Visible** property changes to **False**.

Object does *not* receive Hide events if the container is hidden and then shown again, or if the container is minimized and then restored. *Object's* window remains on the container during these operations, and its **Visible** property doesn't change.

If *object* is being shown in an Internet browser, a Hide event occurs when the page is moved to the history list by navigating off *object* to another document, or when Internet Explorer 3.0 is terminated while *object* is being viewed or is still within the cache of active documents. Use the event to destroy any global object references before navigating to another document.

Note If *object* is used with earlier versions of Visual Basic than 5.0, *object* will not receive Hide events at design time. This is because earlier versions of Visual Basic did not put any visible windows on a form at design time.

See Also

Visible Property

Hide Method

Hides an **MDIForm** or **Form** object but doesn't unload it.

Applies To

Form Object**, Forms** Collection, **MDIForm** Object

Syntax

object.**Hide**

The *object* placeholder represents an object expression that evaluates to an object in the **Applies To** list. If *object* is omitted, the form with the focus is assumed to be *object*.

Remarks

When a form is hidden, it's removed from the screen and its **Visible** property is set to **False**. A hidden form's controls aren't accessible to the user, but they are available to the running Visual Basic application, to other processes that may be communicating with the application through DDE, and to **Timer** control events.

When a form is hidden, the user can't interact with the application until all code in the event procedure that caused the form to be hidden has finished executing.

If the form isn't loaded when the **Hide** method is invoked, the **Hide** method loads the form but doesn't display it.

See Also

Load Statement, **Unload** Statement, **Show** Method, **Visible** Property

Example

This example uses the **Hide** method to hide a form. To try this example, paste the code into the **Declarations** section of a **non-MDI** form, and then press F5 and click the form.

```
Private Sub Form_Click ()
   Dim Msg       ' Declare variable.
   Hide          ' Hide form.
   Msg = "Choose OK to make the form reappear."
   MsgBox Msg    ' Display message.
   Show          ' Show form again.
End Sub
```

HideSelection Property

Returns a value that determines whether selected text appears highlighted when a control loses the focus.

Applies To

TextBox Control

Syntax

object.**HideSelection**

The *object* placeholder represents an object expression that evaluates to an object in the **Applies To** list.

Return Values

The **HideSelection** property return values are:

Value	Description
True	(Default) Selected text doesn't appear highlighted when the control loses the focus.
False	Selected text appears highlighted when the control loses the focus.

Remarks

You can use this property to indicate which text is highlighted while another form or a dialog box has the focus—for example, in a spell-checking routine.

Example

This example enables you to select text in each form and switch the focus between forms by clicking each form's title bar. The selection remains visible even when the form isn't active. To try the example, create two forms and draw a **TextBox** control on each. Set the **MultiLine** property to True for both **TextBox** controls, and set the **HideSelection** property to False for one of the **TextBox** controls. Paste the code into the **Declarations** section of both form modules, and then press F5.

```
Private Sub Form_Load ()
   Open "README.TXT" For Input As 1    ' Load file into text box.
   Text1.Text = Input$(LOF(1), 1)
   Close 1
   Form2.Visible = True                ' Load Form2, if not already loaded.
   ' Position forms side by side.
   Form1.Move 0, 1050, Screen.Width / 2, Screen.Height
   Form2.Move Screen.Width / 2, 1050, Screen.Width / 2, Screen.Height
   ' Enlarge text box to fill form.
   Text1.Move 0, 0, ScaleWidth, ScaleHeight
End Sub
```

hInstance Property

Returns a handle to the instance of the application.

Applies To

App Object

Syntax

object.**hInstance**

The *object* placeholder represents an object expression that evaluates to an object in the **Applies To** list.

Remarks

The **hInstance** property returns a Long data type.

When working with a project in the Visual Basic development environment, the **hInstance** property returns the instance handle of the Visual Basic instance.

See Also

hDC Property, **hWnd** Property

HoldFields Method

Sets the current column/field layout as the customized layout.

Applies To

DBGrid Control

Syntax

object.**HoldFields**

The *object* placeholder represents an object expression that evaluates to an object in the **Applies To** list.

Remarks

The **HoldFields** method sets the current column/field layout as the customized layout so that subsequent **ReBind** operations will use the current layout for display. You can resume the grid's automatic layout behavior by invoking the **ClearFields** method.

See Also

ClearFields Method, **Rebind** Method

HostName Property

Returns or sets the user-readable host name of your Visual Basic application.

Applies To

OLE Container Control

Syntax

object.**HostName** [= *name*]

The **HostName** property syntax has these parts:

Part	Description
object	An object expression that evaluates to an object in the **Applies To** list.
name	A string expression specifying the host name.

Remarks

When editing an object, the **HostName** property setting may be displayed in the object's window title. However, some applications that provide objects don't display **HostName**.

Hour Function

Returns a **Variant** (**Integer**) specifying a whole number between 0 and 23, inclusive, representing the hour of the day.

Syntax

Hour(*time*)

The required *time* argument is any **Variant**, numeric expression, string expression, or any combination, that can represent a time. If *time* contains **Null**, **Null** is returned.

See Also

Day Function, **Minute** Function, **Now** Function, **Second** Function, **Time** Function, **Time** Statement

Example

This example uses the **Hour** function to obtain the hour from a specified time. In the development environment, the time literal is displayed in short time format using the locale settings of your code.

```
Dim MyTime, MyHour
MyTime = #4:35:17 PM#     ' Assign a time.
MyHour = Hour(MyTime)     ' MyHour contains 16.
```

hPal Property

Returns or sets a handle to the palette of a picture in a **Picture** object.

Applies To

Picture Object

Syntax

object.**hPal** [= *value*]

The **hPal** property syntax has these parts:

Part	Description
object	An object expression that evaluates to an object in the **Applies To** list.
value	The handle to the palette for the picture (HPAL).

Remarks

The **hPal** property is useful when you need to pass a handle to a palette as part of a call to a function in a dynamic-link library (DLL) or the Windows API.

HScrollBar, VScrollBar Controls

Scroll bars provide easy navigation through a long list of items or a large amount of information. They can also provide an analog representation of current position. You can use a scroll bar as an input device or indicator of speed or quantity—for example, to control the volume of a computer game or to view the time elapsed in a timed process.

Syntax

HScrollBar
VScrollBar

Remarks

When you're using a scroll bar as an indicator of quantity or speed or as an input device, use the **Max** and **Min** properties to set the appropriate range for the control.

To specify the amount of change to report in a scroll bar, use the **LargeChange** property for clicking in the scroll bar, and the **SmallChange** property for clicking the arrows at the ends of the scroll bar. The scroll bar's **Value** property increases or decreases by the values set for the **LargeChange** and **SmallChange** properties. You can position the scroll box at run time by setting **Value** between 0 and 32,767, inclusive.

Properties

Container Property, **DragIcon** Property, **DragMode** Property, **Enabled** Property, **Height, Width** Properties, **HelpContextID** Property, **hWnd** Property, **Index** Property, **LargeChange, SmallChange** Properties, **Left, Top** Properties, **Max, Min** Properties, **MouseIcon** Property, **MousePointer** Property, **Name** Property, **Parent** Property, **TabIndex** Property, **TabStop** Property, **Tag** Property, **Value** Property, **Visible** Property, **WhatsThisHelpID** Property

Methods

Refresh Method, **SetFocus** Method, **Drag** Method, **Move** Method, **ZOrder** Method, **ShowWhatsThis** Method

See Also

Value Property, **LargeChange, SmallChange** Properties, **Max, Min** Properties (Scroll Bar)

HScrollSmallChange, VScrollSmallChange Properties

Returns or sets the distance the **UserDocument** will scroll when the user clicks a scroll arrow.

Applies To

UserDocument Object

Syntax

object.**HScrollSmallChange** = *single*
object.**VScrollSmallChange** = *single*

Part	Description
object	An object expression that evaluates to an object in the **Applies To** list.
single	The distance in twips the **UserDocument** will scroll when the user clicks the scroll arrow.

Remarks

There is no "LargeChange" property counterpart to the **HScrollSmallChange** and **VScrollSmallChange** properties. The "LargeChange" is determined by the **ViewPort** object's **ViewPortHeight** and **ViewPortWidth** properties.

---

hStmt Property (Remote Data)

Returns a value corresponding to the ODBC statement handle.

Applies To

rdoPreparedStatement Object, **rdoQuery** Object, **rdoResultset** Object

Syntax

object.**hStmt**

The *object* placeholder represents an object expression that evaluates to an object in the **Applies To** list.

Return Values

The **hStmt** property returns a **Long** value containing the ODBC statement handle created by the ODBC driver manager corresponding to the specified **rdoResultset** object.

Remarks

This handle can be used to execute ODBC functions that require an ODBC **hStmt** statement handle.

Note While it is possible to execute ODBC API functions using the ODBC **hEnv, hDbc**, and **hStmt** handles, it is recommended that you do so with caution. Improper use of arbitrary ODBC API functions using these handles can result in unpredictable behavior. You should not attempt to save this handle in a variable for use at a later time as the value is subject to change.

Example

This example illustrates use of the **hStmt** property to return a configuration option for a specific statement handle. The example uses the **SQLGetStmtOption** function to determine the type of cursor created by the **OpenResultset** method. Note that this value is also supplied by the **rdoResultset Type** property.

```
Option Explicit
Dim en As rdoEnvironment
Dim cn As rdoConnection
Dim rs As rdoResultset
Dim rc As Integer
Dim CursorType As Long
Dim T As String

Declare Function SQLGetStmtOption Lib "odbc32.dll" (ByVal
hstmt&, ByVal fOption%, ByRef pvParam As Any) As Integer

Private Sub Form_Load()
Set en = rdoEngine.rdoEnvironments(0)

en.CursorDriver = rdUseOdbc

Set cn = en.OpenConnection(dsName:="WorkDB", _
    prompt:=rdDriverNoPrompt, _
    Connect:="Uid=;pwd=;database=Pubs")

Set rs = cn.OpenResultset("Select * from Publishers", _
 rdOpenKeyset, rdConcurRowVer)

Select Case rs.Type
    Case rdOpenForwardOnly: T = "Forward-only"
    Case rdOpenStatic: T = "Static"
    Case rdOpenKeyset: T = "Keyset"
    Case rdOpenDynamic: T = "Dynamic"
End Select
MsgBox "RDO indicates that a " & T _
    & " Cursor was created"
CursorType = 0
rc = SQLGetStmtOption(rs.hStmt, _
    SQL_CURSOR_TYPE, CursorType)

Select Case CursorType
    Case SQL_CURSOR_FORWARD_ONLY: T = "Forward-only"
    Case SQL_CURSOR_STATIC: T = "Static"
    Case SQL_CURSOR_KEYSET_DRIVEN: T = "Keyset"
    Case SQL_CURSOR_DYNAMIC: T = "Dynamic"
End Select
MsgBox "ODBC indicates that a " & T _
    & " Cursor was created"
End Sub
```

hWnd Property

Returns a handle to a form or control.

Note This property is not supported for the **OLE** container control.

Applies To

Animation Control, **CheckBox** Control, **ComboBox** Control, **CommandButton** Control, **DBCombo** Control, **DBGrid** Control, **DBList** Control, **DirListBox** Control, **DriveListBox** Control, **FileListBox** Control, **Form Object, Forms** Collection, **Frame** Control, **HScrollBar, VScrollBar** Controls, **ListBox** Control, **ListView** Control, **Masked Edit** Control, **MDIForm** Object, **MSFlexGrid** Control, **OLE Container** Control, **OptionButton** Control, **PictureBox** Control, **PictureClip** Control, **ProgressBar** Control, **PropertyPage** Object, **RichTextBox** Control, **Slider** Control, **SSTab** Control, **TabStrip** Control, **TextBox** Control, **Toolbar** Control, **TreeView** Control, **UpDown** Control, **UserControl** Object, **UserDocument** Object

Syntax

object.**hWnd**

The *object* placeholder represents an object expression that evaluates to an object in the **Applies To** list.

Remarks

The Microsoft Windows operating environment identifies each form and control in an application by assigning it a handle, or **hWnd**. The **hWnd** property is used with Windows API calls. Many Windows operating environment functions require the **hWnd** of the active window as an argument.

Note Because the value of this property can change while a program is running, never store the **hWnd** value in a variable.

See Also

Icon Property, **hDC** Property

Example

This example forces a form to always remain on top. To try this example, create a form (not an MDI child form), and then create a menu for the form called Main. Insert a submenu in it called Always On Top, and set its Name to mnuTopmost. Create a new module using the Add Module command on the Project menu. Paste the **Declare** statement into the **Declarations** section of the new module, being sure that the statement is on one line with no break or wordwrap. Then paste the **Sub** procedure into the Declarations section of the form and press F5.

```
' Declaration of a Windows routine.
' This statement should be placed in the module.
Declare Function SetWindowPos Lib "user32" Alias_ "SetWindowPos"
(ByVal hwnd As Long, ByVal_ hWndInsertAfter As Long, ByVal x As Long,
ByVal y As_ Long, ByVal cx As Long, ByVal cy As Long, ByVal wFlags_
As Long) As Long
```

```
' Set some constant values (from WIN32API.TXT).
Const conHwndTopmost = -1
Const conHwndNoTopmost = -2
Const conSwpNoActivate = &H10
Const conSwpShowWindow = &H40

Private Sub mnuTopmost_Click ()
   ' Add or remove the check mark from the menu.
   mnuTopmost.Checked = Not mnuTopmost.Checked
   If mnuTopmost.Checked Then
      ' Turn on the TopMost attribute.
      SetWindowPos hWnd, conHwndTopmost, 0, 0, 0, 0,_
      conSwpNoActivate Or conSwpShowWindow
   Else
      ' Turn off the TopMost attribute.
      SetWindowPos hWnd, conHwndNoTopmost, 0, 0, 0,_
      0, conSwpNoActivate Or conSwpShowWindow
   End If
End Sub
```

This example automatically drops down the list portion of a **ComboBox** control
whenever the **ComboBox** receives the focus. To try this example, create a new form
containing a **ComboBox** control and an **OptionButton** control (used only to receive
the focus). Create a new module using the **Add Module** command on the **Project**
menu. Paste the Declare statement into the Declarations section of the new module,
being sure that the statement is on one line with no break or wordwrap. Then paste the
Sub procedure into the Declarations section of the form, and press F5. Use the TAB
key to move the focus to and from the **ComboBox**.

```
Declare Function SendMessage Lib "user32" Alias "SendMessageA" (ByVal hwnd As Long,
ByVal wMsg As Long, ByVal wParam As Long, lParam As Long) As Long

Private Sub Combo1_GotFocus ()
   Const CB_SHOWDROPDOWN = &H14F
   Dim Tmp
   Tmp = SendMessage(Combo1.hWnd, CB_SHOWDROPDOWN, 1, ByVal 0&)
End Sub
```

hWndEditor Property

Returns the unique window handle assigned to a **DBGrid** control's editing window by
the Microsoft Windows operating environment. Not available at design time.

Applies To

DBGrid Control

Syntax

object.**hWndEditor**

The **hWndEditor** property syntax has these parts:

Part	Description
object	An object expression that evaluates to an object in the **Applies To** list.

Remarks

Experienced users can pass the value of this property to Windows API calls that require a valid window handle.

When editing is not in progress, this property returns 0.

Note Since the value of this property can change while a program is running, never store the **hWndEditor** value in a variable. Also, do not use the **hWndEditor** property to test whether editing is in progress. The **EditActive** property is provided for this purpose.

See Also

EditActive Property

Hyperlink Object

Using the properties and methods of the **Hyperlink** object, your ActiveX document or ActiveX control can request a hyperlink-aware container, such as Microsoft Internet Explorer, to jump to a given URL.

Remarks

Use the **NavigateTo** method to jump to a URL. For example, the following code presumes an ActiveX document named "axdMyDoc" exists:

```
UserDocument.Hyperlink.NavigateTo _
"c:\mydocs\axdmydoc.vbd"
```

If your ActiveX document is contained by a hyperlink-aware container (such as Internet Explorer), and if the container maintains a history of documents, use the **GoBack** or **GoForward** methods to go backwards or forwards through the list. However, be sure to use error-checking, as shown in the example below:

```
Private Sub cmdGoForward_Click()
   On Error GoTo noDocInHistory
   UserDocument.Hyperlink.GoForward
   Exit Sub
noDocInHistory:
   Resume Next
End Sub
```

Methods

GoBack Method, **GoForward** Method, **NavigateTo** Method

See Also

UserDocument Object

Hyperlink Property

Returns a reference to the **Hyperlink** object.

Applies To

UserControl Object, **UserDocument** Object

Syntax

object.**Hyperlink**

The *object* placeholder represents an object expression that evaluates to an object in the **Applies To** list.

See Also

Hyperlink Object

Icon Property

Returns the icon displayed when a form is minimized at run time.

Applies To

Form Object, **Forms** Collection, **MDIForm** Object

Syntax

object.**Icon**

The *object* placeholder represents an object expression that evaluates to an object in the **Applies To** list.

Remarks

Use this property to specify an icon for any form that the user can minimize at run time.

For example, you can assign a unique icon to a form to indicate the form's function. Specify the icon by loading it using the Properties window at design time. The file you load must have the .ico filename extension and format. If you don't specify an icon, the Visual Basic default icon for forms is used.

You can use the Visual Basic Icon Library (in the Icons subdirectory) as a source for icons. When you create an executable file, you can assign an icon to the application by using the **Icon** property of any form in that application.

Note You can see a form's icon in Windows 95 in the upper left corner of the form, or when the form is minimized in both Windows 95 and Windows NT. If the form is minimized, the **BorderStyle** property must be set to either 1 (Fixed Single) or 2 (Sizable) and the **MinButton** property must be set to **True** for the icon to be visible.

At run time, you can assign an object's **Icon** property to another object's **DragIcon** or **Icon** property. You can also assign an icon returned by the **LoadPicture** function. Using **LoadPicture** without an argument assigns an empty (null) icon to the form, which enables you to draw on the icon at run time.

See Also

> **LoadPicture** Function, **BorderStyle** Property (ActiveX Controls)

Example

> This example creates a blank icon for a form and draws colored dots on the icon as long as the form is minimized. To try this example, paste the code into the Declarations section of a form, and then press F5 and minimize the form.
>
> **Note**   This example works only with Windows NT 3.5x.

```
Private Sub Form_Resize ()
    Dim X, Y                            ' Declare variables.
    If Form1.WindowState = vbMinimized Then
        Form1.Icon = LoadPicture()      ' Load a blank icon.
        Do While Form1.WindowState = vbMinimized
            ' While form is minimized,
            Form1.DrawWidth = 10         ' set size of dot.
            ' Choose random color for dot.
            Form1.ForeColor = QBColor(Int(Rnd * 15))
            ' Set random location on icon.
            X = Form1.Width * Rnd
            Y = Form1.Height * Rnd

PSet (X, Y)                             ' Draw dot on icon.
            DoEvents                     ' Allow other events.
        Loop
    End If
End Sub
```

> This is the same example, except that it uses the **LoadPicture** method to set the **Icon** property. This example works with all versions of Windows:

```
Private Sub Form_Resize ()
    Dim X, Y ' Declare variables.
    If Form1.WindowState = vbMinimized Then
        Form1.Icon = LoadPicture("c:\myicon.ico")
        ' An icon named "myicon.ico" must be in the
        ' c:\ directory for this example to work
        ' correctly.
    End If
End Sub
```

IconState Property

> Returns or sets the source code control icon (or "glyph") for the project in the project window, indicating its status.

Applies To

> **VBComponent** Object, **VBProject** Object, **VBProjects** Collection

Syntax

> *object*.**IconState** [= *value*]

The **IconState** property syntax has these parts:

Part	Description
object	An object expression that evaluates to an object in the **Applies To** list.
value	A long integer or constant that determines the file status, as described in Settings.

Settings

The settings for *value* are:

Constant	Value	Description
vbextSCCStatusNotControlled	0	File is not under source code control.
vbextSCCStatusControlled	1	File is under source code control.
vbextSCCStatusCheckedOut	2	File is checked out to current user.
vbextSCCStatusOutOther	4	File is checked out to another user.
vbextSCCStatusOutOfDate	32	The file is not the most recent.
vbextSCCStatusShared	512	File is shared between projects.

Remarks

The **IconState** property can be logically **OR**'ed together to form combined states.

See Also

Reload Method, **FileCount** Property, **FileNames** Property

Idle Method

Suspends data processing, enabling the Microsoft Jet database engine to complete any pending tasks, such as memory optimization or page timeouts (Microsoft Jet workspaces only).

Applies To

DBEngine Object

Syntax

DBEngine.Idle [**dbRefreshCache**]

Remarks

The **Idle** method allows the Microsoft Jet database engine to perform background tasks that may not be up-to-date because of intense data processing. This is often true in multiuser, multitasking environments that don't have enough background processing time to keep all records in a **Recordset** current.

Usually, read locks are removed and data in local dynaset-type **Recordset** objects are updated only when no other actions (including mouse movements) occur. If you periodically use the **Idle** method, Microsoft Jet can catch up on background processing tasks by releasing unneeded read locks.

Specifying the optional **dbRefreshCache** argument forces any pending writes to .mdb files, and refreshes memory with the most current data from the .mdb file.

You don't need to use this method in single-user environments unless multiple instances of an application are running. The **Idle** method may increase performance in a multiuser environment because it forces the database engine to write data to disk, releasing locks on memory.

Note You can also release read locks by making operations part of a transaction.

Example

This example uses the **Idle** method to ensure that an output procedure is accessing the most current data available from the database. The **IdleOutput** procedure is required for this procedure to run.

```
Sub IdleX()

    Dim dbsNorthwind As Database
    Dim strCountry As String
    Dim strSQL As String
    Dim rstOrders As Recordset

    Set dbsNorthwind = OpenDatabase("Northwind.mdb")

    ' Get name of country from user and build SQL statement
    ' with it.
    strCountry = Trim(InputBox("Enter country:"))
    strSQL = "SELECT * FROM Orders WHERE ShipCountry = '" & _
        strCountry & "' ORDER BY OrderID"

    ' Open Recordset object with SQL statement.
    Set rstOrders = dbsNorthwind.OpenRecordset(strSQL)

    ' Display contents of Recordset object.
    IdleOutput rstOrders, strCountry

    rstOrders.Close
    dbsNorthwind.Close

End Sub

Sub IdleOutput(rstTemp As Recordset, strTemp As String)

    ' Call the Idle method to release unneeded locks, force
    ' pending writes, and refresh the memory with the current
    ' data in the .mdb file.
    DBEngine.Idle dbRefreshCache

    ' Enumerate the Recordset object.
    With rstTemp
        Debug.Print "Orders from " & strTemp & ":"
        Debug.Print , "OrderID", "CustomerID", "OrderDate"
        Do While Not .EOF
            Debug.Print , !OrderID, !CustomerID, !OrderDate
            .MoveNext
        Loop
    End With

End Sub
```

IDTExtensibility Interface

The **IDTExtensibility** interface contains methods that Visual Basic calls when an add-in is connected to it, whether through the Add-In Manager, or some other manner.

Applies To

OnAddinsUpdate Method, **OnConnection** Method, **OnDisconnection** Method, **OnStartupComplete** Method

Syntax

Implements IDTExtensiblity

Remarks

The usage of interfaces is new to Visual Basic 5.0. Interfaces enable you to choose a pre-configured procedure template from a module's **Procedure** drop down list, eliminating parameter list entry errors and allowing you to program your applications a bit faster.

An interface's methods are exposed through the **Implements** statement. When the above syntax is entered in the Declarations section of the Class module that handles an add-in's events, the interface's methods become available for your use through the module's **Procedure** and **Object** drop down boxes. To add the code to the module, simply select it from the drop down box.

The **IDTExtensiblity** interface currently contains four methods:

- **OnAddinsUpdate** Method
- **OnConnection** Method
- **OnDisconnection** Method
- **OnStartupComplete** Method

While these are methods to the **IDTExtensibility** interface, to you as a Visual Basic programmer, though, they act and behave like events. In other words, when an add-in is connected to Visual Basic, the **OnConnection** method is called automatically, similar to an event firing. When it is disconnected, the **OnDisconnection** method is called automatically, and so forth.

Important   Since an interface is a contract between an object and Visual Basic, you must be sure to implement *all* of the methods in the interface. This means that all four **IDTExtensibility** interface methods are present in your Class module, each containing at least one executable statement. This can consist of as little as a single remark statement, but they must each contain at least one executable statement to prevent the compiler from removing them as empty procedures.

Methods

OnAddinsUpdate Method, **OnConnection** Method, **OnDisconnection** Method, **OnStartupComplete** Method

See Also

OnAddinsUpdate Method, **OnConnection** Method, **OnDisconnection** Method, **OnStartupComplete** Method

If...Then...Else Statement

Conditionally executes a group of statements, depending on the value of an expression.

Syntax

If *condition* **Then** [*statements*] [**Else** *elsestatements*]

Or, you can use the block form syntax:

If *condition* **Then**
   [*statements*]
[**ElseIf** *condition-n* **Then**
   [*elseifstatements*] . . .
[**Else**
   [*elsestatements*]]
End If

The **If...Then...Else** statement syntax has these parts:

Part	Description
condition	Required. One or more of the following two types of expressions:
	A numeric expression or string expression that evaluates to **True** or **False**. If *condition* is **Null**, *condition* is treated as **False**.
	An expression of the form **TypeOf** *objectname* **Is** *objecttype*. The *objectname* is any object reference and *objecttype* is any valid object type. The expression is **True** if *objectname* is of the object type specified by *objecttype*; otherwise it is **False**.
statements	Optional in block form; required in single-line form that has no **Else** clause. One or more statements separated by colons; executed if *condition* is **True**.
condition-n	Optional. Same as *condition*.
elseifstatements	Optional. One or more statements executed if associated *condition-n* is **True**.
elsestatements	Optional. One or more statements executed if no previous *condition* or *condition-n* expression is **True**.

Remarks

You can use the single-line form (first syntax) for short, simple tests. However, the block form (second syntax) provides more structure and flexibility than the single-line form and is usually easier to read, maintain, and debug.

Note With the single-line form, it is possible to have multiple statements executed as the result of an **If...Then** decision. All statements must be on the same line and separated by colons, as in the following statement:

```
If A > 10 Then A = A + 1 : B = B + A : C = C + B
```

A block form **If** statement must be the first statement on a line. The **Else**, **ElseIf**, and **End If** parts of the statement can have only a line number or line label preceding them. The block **If** must end with an **End If** statement.

To determine whether or not a statement is a block **If**, examine what follows the **Then** keyword. If anything other than a comment appears after **Then** on the same line, the statement is treated as a single-line **If** statement.

The **Else** and **ElseIf** clauses are both optional. You can have as many **ElseIf** clauses as you want in a block **If**, but none can appear after an **Else** clause. Block **If** statements can be nested; that is, contained within one another.

When executing a block **If** (second syntax), *condition* is tested. If *condition* is **True**, the statements following **Then** are executed. If *condition* is **False**, each **ElseIf** condition (if any) is evaluated in turn. When a **True** condition is found, the statements immediately following the associated **Then** are executed. If none of the **ElseIf** conditions are **True** (or if there are no **ElseIf** clauses), the statements following **Else** are executed. After executing the statements following **Then** or **Else**, execution continues with the statement following **End If**.

Tip **Select Case** may be more useful when evaluating a single expression that has several possible actions. However, the **TypeOf** *objectname* **Is** *objecttype* clause can't be used with the **Select Case** statement.

See Also

#If...Then...#Else Directive, **Choose** Function, **Select Case** Statement, **Switch** Function

Example

This example shows both the block and single-line forms of the **If...Then...Else** statement. It also illustrates the use of **If TypeOf...Then...Else**.

```
Dim Number, Digits, MyString
Number = 53 ' Initialize variable.
If Number < 10 Then
    Digits = 1
ElseIf Number < 100 Then
' Condition evaluates to True so the next statement is executed.
    Digits = 2
Else
    Digits = 3
End If

' Assign a value using the single-line form of syntax.
If Digits = 1 Then MyString = "One" Else MyString = "More than one"
```

Use **If TypeOf** construct to determine whether the Control passed into a procedure is a text box.

```
Sub ControlProcessor(MyControl As Control)
    If TypeOf MyControl Is CommandButton Then
        Debug.Print "You passed in a " & TypeName(MyControl)
    ElseIf TypeOf MyControl Is CheckBox Then
        Debug.Print "You passed in a " & TypeName(MyControl)
    ElseIf TypeOf MyControl Is TextBox Then
        Debug.Print "You passed in a " & TypeName(MyControl)
    End If
End Sub
```

IgnoreNulls Property

Sets or returns a value that indicates whether records that have **Null** values in their index fields have index entries (Microsoft Jet workspaces only).

Applies To

Index Object

Settings and Return Values

The setting or return value is a **Boolean** that is **True** if the fields with **Null** values don't have an index entry. This property is read/write for a new **Index** object not yet appended to a collection and read-only for an existing **Index** object in an **Indexes** collection.

Remarks

To speed up the process of searching for records, you can define an index for a field. If you allow **Null** entries in an indexed field and expect many of the entries to be **Null**, you can set the **IgnoreNulls** property for the **Index** object to **True** to reduce the amount of storage space that the index uses.

The **IgnoreNulls** property setting and the **Required** property setting together determine whether a record with a **Null** index value has an index entry.

If IgnoreNulls is	And Required is	Then
True	**False**	A **Null** value is allowed in the index field; no index entry added.
False	**False**	A **Null** value is allowed in the index field; index entry added.
True or **False**	**True**	A **Null** value isn't allowed in the index field; no index entry added.

See Also

Required Property

Example

This example sets the **IgnoreNulls** property of a new **Index** to **True** or **False** based on user input, and then demonstrates the effect on a **Recordset** with a record whose key field contains a **Null** value.

```
Sub IgnoreNullsX()

    Dim dbsNorthwind As Database
    Dim tdfEmployees As TableDef
    Dim idxNew As Index
    Dim rstEmployees As Recordset

    Set dbsNorthwind = OpenDatabase("Northwind.mdb")
    Set tdfEmployees = dbsNorthwind!Employees

    With tdfEmployees
        ' Create a new Index object.
        Set idxNew = .CreateIndex("NewIndex")
        idxNew.Fields.Append idxNew.CreateField("Country")

        ' Set the IgnoreNulls property of the new Index object
        ' based on the user's input.
        Select Case MsgBox("Set IgnoreNulls to True?", _
            vbYesNoCancel)
            Case vbYes
                idxNew.IgnoreNulls = True
            Case vbNo
                idxNew.IgnoreNulls = False
            Case Else
                dbsNorthwind.Close
                End
        End Select

        ' Append the new Index object to the Indexes
        ' collection of the Employees table.
        .Indexes.Append idxNew
        .Indexes.Refresh
    End With

    Set rstEmployees = _
        dbsNorthwind.OpenRecordset("Employees")

    With rstEmployees
        ' Add a new record to the Employees table.
        .AddNew
        !FirstName = "Gary"
        !LastName = "Haarsager"
        .Update

        ' Use the new index to set the order of the records.
        .Index = idxNew.Name
        .MoveFirst
```

```
        Debug.Print "Index = " & .Index & _
            ", IgnoreNulls = " & idxNew.IgnoreNulls
        Debug.Print "Country - Name"

        ' Enumerate the Recordset. The value of the
        ' IgnoreNulls property will determine if the newly
        ' added record appears in the output.
        Do While Not .EOF
            Debug.Print "          " & _
                IIf(IsNull(!Country), "[Null]", !Country) & _
                " - " & !FirstName & " " & !LastName
            .MoveNext
        Loop

        ' Delete new record because this is a demonstration.
        .Index = ""
        .Bookmark = .LastModified
        .Delete
        .Close
    End With

    ' Delete new Index because this is a demonstration.
    tdfEmployees.Indexes.Delete idxNew.Name
    dbsNorthwind.Close

End Sub
```

IIf Function

Returns one of two parts, depending on the evaluation of an expression.

Syntax

IIf(*expr*, *truepart*, *falsepart*)

The **IIf** function syntax has these named arguments:

Part	Description
expr	Required. Expression you want to evaluate.
truepart	Required. Value or expression returned if *expr* is **True**.
falsepart	Required. Value or expression returned if *expr* is **False**.

Remarks

IIf always evaluates both *truepart* and *falsepart*, even though it returns only one of them. Because of this, you should watch for undesirable side effects. For example, if evaluating *falsepart* results in a division by zero error, an error occurs even if *expr* is **True**.

See Also

Choose Function, **If...Then...Else** Statement, **Select Case** Statement, **Switch** Function

Example

This example uses the **IIf** function to evaluate the `TestMe` parameter of the `CheckIt` procedure and returns the word "Large" if the amount is greater than 1000; otherwise, it returns the word "Small".

```
Function CheckIt (TestMe As Integer)
   CheckIt = IIf(TestMe > 1000, "Large", "Small")
End Function
```

Image Control

Use the **Image** control to display a graphic. An **Image** control can display a graphic from a bitmap, icon, or metafile, as well as enhanced metafile, JPEG, or GIF files.

Syntax

Image

Remarks

The **Image** control uses fewer system resources and repaints faster than a **PictureBox** control, but it supports only a subset of the **PictureBox** properties, events, and methods. Use the **Stretch** property to determine whether the graphic is scaled to fit the control or vice versa. Although you can place an **Image** control within a container, an **Image** control can't act as a container.

Properties

Appearance Property, **BorderStyle** Property, **DataChanged** Property, **DataField** Property, **DataSource** Property, **DragIcon** Property, **DragMode Height, Width** Properties, **Left, Top** Properties, **MouseIcon** Property, **MousePointer** Property, **OLEDragMode** Property, **OLEDropMode** Property, **Picture** Property, **Stretch** Property, **Tag** Property, **Visible** Property, **WhatsThisHelpId** Property

Methods

Refresh Method, **Drag** Method, **Move** Method, **ZOrder** Method, **OLEDrag** Method, **ShowWhatsThis** Method

See Also

PictureBox Control

Image Property

Returns a handle to a persistent graphic; the handle is provided by the Microsoft Windows operating environment.

Applies To

PropertyPage Object, **UserControl** Object, **UserDocument** Object, **Form** Object, **Forms** Collection, **PictureBox** Control

Syntax

object.**Image**

The *object* placeholder represents an object expression that evaluates to an object in the **Applies To** list.

Remarks

An object's **AutoRedraw** property determines whether the repainting of an object occurs with a persistent graphics or through Paint events. The Windows operating environment identifies an object's persistent graphic by assigning a handle to it; you can use the **Image** property to get this handle.

An **Image** value exists regardless of the setting for the **AutoRedraw** property. If **AutoRedraw** is **True** and nothing has been drawn, the image displays only the color set by the **BackColor** property and the picture.

You can assign the value of **Image** to the **Picture** property. The **Image** property also provides a value to pass to Windows API calls.

The **Image**, **DragIcon**, and **Picture** properties are normally used when assigning values to other properties, when saving with the **SavePicture** statement, or when placing something on the Clipboard. You can't assign these to a temporary variable, other than the Picture data type.

The **AutoRedraw** property can cause **Image**, which is a handle to a bitmap, to change. When **AutoRedraw** is **True**, an object's **hDC** property becomes a handle to a device context that contains the bitmap returned by **Image**.

See Also

Paint Event, **SavePicture** Statement, **BackColor**, **ForeColor** Properties, **Picture** Property, **AutoRedraw** Property, **DragIcon** Property

Example

This example draws a circle in the first **PictureBox** control each time you click it. When you click the second **PictureBox**, the graphic from the first **PictureBox** is copied into it. To try this example, paste the code into the Declarations section of a form that has two large, equal-sized **PictureBox** controls. Press F5 to run the program, and then click the **PictureBox** controls.

```
Private Sub Form_Load ()
   ' Set AutoRedraw to True.
   Picture1.AutoReDraw = True
End Sub

Private Sub Picture1_Click ()
   ' Declare variables.
   Dim PW, PH
   ' Set FillStyle to Solid.
   Picture1.FillStyle = vbFSSolid
   ' Choose random color.
   Picture1.FillColor = QBColor(Int(Rnd * 15))
   PW = Picture1.ScaleWidth' Set ScaleWidth.
   PH = Picture1.ScaleHeight  ' Set ScaleHeight.
   ' Draw a circle in random location.
   Picture1.Circle (Int(Rnd * PW), Int(Rnd * PH)), 250
```

```
    End Sub

    Private Sub Picture2_Click ()
       ' Copy Image to Picture2.
       Picture2.Picture = Picture1.Image
    End Sub
```

IMEStatus Function

Returns an **Integer** specifying the current Input Method Editor (IME) mode of Microsoft Windows; available in Far East versions only.

Syntax

IMEStatus

Return Values

The return values for the Japanese locale are as follows:

Constant	Value	Description
vbIMENoOP	0	No IME installed
vbIMEOn	1	IME on
vbIMEOff	2	IME off
vbIMEDisable	3	IME disabled
vbIMEHiragana	4	Hiragana double-byte characters (DBC)
vbIMEKatakanaDbl	5	Katakana DBC
vbIMEKatakanaSng	6	Katakana single-byte characters (SBC)
vbIMEAlphaDbl	7	Alphanumeric DBC
vbIMEAlphaSng	8	Alphanumeric SBC

The return values for the Chinese (traditional and simplified) locale are as follows:

Constant	Value	Description
vbIMENoOP	0	No IME installed
vbIMEOn	1	IME on
vbIMEOff	2	IME off

For the Korean locale, the first five bits of the return are set as follows:

Bit	Value	Description	Value	Description
0	0	No IME installed	1	IME installed
1	0	IME disabled	1	IME enabled
2	0	IME English mode	1	Hangeul mode
3	0	Banja mode (SB)	1	Junja mode (DB)
4	0	Normal mode	1	Hanja conversion mode

Imp Operator

Used to perform a logical implication on two expressions.

Syntax

result = *expression1* **Imp** *expression2*

The **Imp** operator syntax has these parts:

Part	Description
result	Required; any numeric variable.
expression1	Required; any expression.
expression2	Required; any expression.

Remarks

The following table illustrates how *result* is determined:

If *expression1* is	And *expression2* is	The *result* is
True	True	True
True	False	False
True	Null	Null
False	True	True
False	False	True
False	Null	True
Null	True	True
Null	False	Null
Null	Null	Null

The **Imp** operator performs a bitwise comparison of identically positioned bits in two numeric expressions and sets the corresponding bit in *result* according to the following table:

If bit in *expression1* is	And bit in *expression2* is	The *result* is
0	0	1
0	1	1
1	0	0
1	1	1

See Also

Operator Summary, **Operator** Precedence, **Logical** Operators

Example

This example uses the **Imp** Operator to perform logical implication on two expressions.

```
Dim A, B, C, D, MyCheck
A = 10: B = 8: C = 6: D = Null   ' Initialize variables.
MyCheck = A > B Imp B > C        ' Returns True.
MyCheck = A > B Imp C > B        ' Returns False.
MyCheck = B > A Imp C > B        ' Returns True.
MyCheck = B > A Imp C > D        ' Returns True.
MyCheck = C > D Imp B > A        ' Returns Null.
MyCheck = B Imp A                ' Returns -1 (bitwise comparison).
```

Implements Statement

Specifies an interface or class that will be implemented in the class module in which it appears.

Syntax

Implements [*InterfaceName* | *Class*]

The required *InterfaceName* or *Class* is the name of an interface or class in a type library whose methods will be implemented by the corresponding methods in the Visual Basic class.

Remarks

An interface is a collection of prototypes representing the members (methods and properties) the interface encapsulates; that is, it contains only the declarations for the member procedures. A class provides an implementation of all of the methods and properties of one or more interfaces. Classes provide the code used when each function is called by a controller of the class. All classes implement at least one interface, which is considered the default interface of the class. In Visual Basic, any member that isn't explicitly a member of an implemented interface is implicitly a member of the default interface.

When a Visual Basic class implements an interface, the Visual Basic class provides its own versions of all the **Public** procedures specified in the type library of the Interface. In addition to providing a mapping between the interface prototypes and your procedures, the **Implements** statement causes the class to accept COM QueryInterface calls for the specified interface ID.

When you implement an interface or class, you must include all the **Public** procedures involved. A missing member in an implementation of an interface or class causes an error. If you don't place code in one of the procedures in a class you are implementing, you can raise the appropriate error (**Const** E_NOTIMPL = &H80004001) so a user of the implementation understands that a member is not implemented.

The **Implements** statement can't appear in a standard module.

Example

The following example shows how to use the **Implements** statement to make a set of declarations available to multiple classes. By sharing the declarations through the **Implements** statement, neither class has to make any declarations itself.

Assume there are two forms. The Selector form has two buttons, Customer Data and Supplier Data. To enter name and address information for a customer or a supplier, the user clicks the Customer button or the Supplier button on the Selector form, and then enters the name and address using the Data Entry form. The Data Entry form has two text fields, Name and Address.

The following code for the shared declarations is in a class called PersonalData:

```
Public Name As String
Public Address As String
```

The code supporting the customer data is in a class module called Customer:

```
Implements PersonalData
Private Property Get PersonalData_Address() As String
PersonalData_Address = "CustomerAddress"
End Property

Private Property Let PersonalData_Address(ByVal RHS As String)
'
End Property

Private Property Let PersonalData_Name(ByVal RHS As String)
'
End Property

Private Property Get PersonalData_Name() As String
PersonalData_Name = "CustomerName"
End Property
```

The code supporting the supplier data is in a class module called Supplier:

```
Implements PersonalData

Private Property Get PersonalData_Address() As String
PersonalData_Address = "SupplierAddress"
End Property

Private Property Let PersonalData_Address(ByVal RHS As String)
'
End Property

Private Property Let PersonalData_Name(ByVal RHS As String)
'
End Property

Private Property Get PersonalData_Name() As String
PersonalData_Name = "SupplierName"
End Property
```

The following code supports the Selector form:

```
Private cust As New Customer
Private sup As New Supplier

Private Sub Command1_Click()
Dim frm2 As New Form2
   Set frm2.PD = cust
   frm2.Show 1
End Sub

Private Sub Command2_Click()
Dim frm2 As New Form2
   Set frm2.PD = sup
   frm2.Show 1
End Sub
```

The following code supports the Data Entry form:

```
Private m_pd As PersonalData
Private Sub Form_Load()
   With m_pd
      Text1 = .Name
      Text2 = .Address
   End With
End Sub
Public Property Set PD(Data As PersonalData)
   Set m_pd = Data
End Property
```

Import Method

Adds a component to a project from a file; returns the newly added component.

Applies To

VBComponents Collection

Syntax

object.**Import**(*filename*) **As VBComponent**

Import syntax has these parts:

Part	Description
object	Required. An object expression that evaluates to an object in the **Applies To** list.
filename	Required. A **String** specifying path and file name of the component that you want to import the component from.

Remarks

You can use the **Import** method to add a component, form, module, class, and so on, to your project.

See Also

Export Method

The following example uses the **Import** method on the **VBComponents** collection to copy the contents of the test.bas file into the a code module.

```
Application.VBE.ActiveVBProject.VBComponents.Import("test.bas")
```

Index Object

Index objects specify the order of records accessed from database tables and whether or not duplicate records are accepted, providing efficient access to data. For external databases, **Index** objects describe the indexes established for external tables (Microsoft Jet workspaces only).

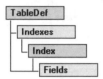

Remarks

The Microsoft Jet database engine uses indexes when it joins tables and creates **Recordset** objects. Indexes determine the order in which table-type **Recordset** objects return records, but they don't determine the order in which the Microsoft Jet database engine stores records in the base table or the order in which any other type of **Recordset** object returns records.

With an **Index** object, you can:

- Use the **Required** property to determine whether the **Field** objects in the index require values that are not **Null**, and then use the **IgnoreNulls** property to determine whether the **Null** values have index entries.

- Use the **Primary** and **Unique** properties to determine the ordering and uniqueness of the **Index** object.

The Microsoft Jet database engine maintains all base table indexes automatically. It updates indexes whenever you add, change, or delete records from the base table. Once you create the database, use the **CompactDatabase** method periodically to bring index statistics up-to-date.

When accessing a table-type **Recordset** object, you specify the order of records using the object's **Index** property. Set this property to the **Name** property setting of an existing **Index** object in the **Indexes** collection. This collection is contained by the **TableDef** object underlying the **Recordset** object that you're populating.

Note You don't have to create indexes for a table, but for large, unindexed tables, accessing a specific record or processing joins can take a long time. Conversely, having too many indexes can slow down updates to the database as each of the table indexes is amended.

The **Attributes** property of each **Field** object in the index determines the order of records returned and consequently determines which access techniques to use for that index.

Each **Field** object in the **Fields** collection of an **Index** object is a component of the index. To define a new **Index** object, set its properties before you append it to a collection, making the **Index** object available for subsequent use.

Note   You can modify the **Name** property setting of an existing **Index** object only if the **Updatable** property setting of the containing **TableDef** object is **True**.

When you set a primary key for a table, the Microsoft Jet database engine automatically defines it as the primary index. A primary index consists of one or more fields that uniquely identify all records in a table in a predefined order. Because the primary index field must be unique, the Microsoft Jet database engine automatically sets the **Unique** property of the primary **Index** object to **True**. If the primary index consists of more than one field, each field can contain duplicate values, but the combination of values from all the indexed fields must be unique. A primary index consists of a key for the table and is always made up of the same fields as the primary key.

Important   Make sure your data complies with the attributes of your new index. If your index requires unique values, make sure that there are no duplicates in existing data records. If duplicates exist, the Microsoft Jet database engine can't create the index; a trappable error results when you attempt to use the **Append** method on the new index.

When you create a relationship that enforces referential integrity, the Microsoft Jet database engine automatically creates an index with the **Foreign** property, set as the foreign key in the referencing table. After you've established a table relationship, the Microsoft Jet database engine prevents additions or changes to the database that violate that relationship. If you set the **Attributes** property of the **Relation** object to allow cascading updates and cascading deletes, the Microsoft Jet database engine updates or deletes records in related tables automatically.

▶ **To create a new Index object:**

1   Use the **CreateIndex** method on a **TableDef** object.

2   Use the **CreateField** method on the **Index** object to create a **Field** object for each field (column) to be included in the **Index** object.

3   Set **Index** properties as needed.

4   Append the **Field** object to the **Fields** collection.

5   Append the **Index** object to the **Indexes** collection.

Note   The **Clustered** property is ignored for databases that use the Microsoft Jet database engine, which doesn't support clustered indexes.

Properties

Clustered Property, **DistinctCount** Property, **Foreign** Property, **IgnoreNulls** Property, **Name** Property, **Primary** Property, **Required** Property, **Unique** Property

Methods

CreateField Method**, CreateProperty** Method

See Also

CreateIndex Method, **Attributes** Property, **Index** Property, **OrdinalPosition** Property

Example

This example creates a new **Index** object, appends it to the **Indexes** collection of the Employees **TableDef**, and then enumerates the **Indexes** collection of the **TableDef**. Finally, it enumerates a **Recordset**, first using the primary **Index**, and then using the new **Index**. The **IndexOutput** procedure is required for this procedure to run.

```
Sub IndexObjectX()

    Dim dbsNorthwind As Database
    Dim tdfEmployees As TableDef
    Dim idxNew As Index
    Dim idxLoop As Index
    Dim rstEmployees As Recordset

    Set dbsNorthwind = OpenDatabase("Northwind.mdb")
    Set tdfEmployees = dbsNorthwind!Employees

    With tdfEmployees
        ' Create new index, create and append Field
        ' objects to its Fields collection.
        Set idxNew = .CreateIndex("NewIndex")

        With idxNew
            .Fields.Append .CreateField("Country")
            .Fields.Append .CreateField("LastName")
            .Fields.Append .CreateField("FirstName")
        End With

        ' Add new Index object to the Indexes collection
        ' of the Employees table collection.
        .Indexes.Append idxNew
        .Indexes.Refresh

        Debug.Print .Indexes.Count & " Indexes in " & _
            .Name & " TableDef"

        ' Enumerate Indexes collection of Employees
        ' table.
        For Each idxLoop In .Indexes
            Debug.Print "    " & idxLoop.Name
        Next idxLoop
```

```
          Set rstEmployees = _
             dbsNorthwind.OpenRecordset("Employees")

          ' Print report using old and new indexes.
          IndexOutput rstEmployees, "PrimaryKey"
          IndexOutput rstEmployees, idxNew.Name
          rstEmployees.Close

          ' Delete new Index because this is a
          ' demonstration.
          .Indexes.Delete idxNew.Name
       End With

       dbsNorthwind.Close

    End Sub

    Sub IndexOutput(rstTemp As Recordset, _
       strIndex As String)
       ' Report function for FieldX.

       With rstTemp
          ' Set the index.
          .Index = strIndex
          .MoveFirst
          Debug.Print "Recordset = " & .Name & _
             ", Index = " & .Index
          Debug.Print "EmployeeID - Country - Name"

          ' Enumerate the recordset using the specified
          ' index.
          Do While Not .EOF
             Debug.Print "     " & !EmployeeID & " - " & _
                !Country & " - " & !LastName & ", " & !FirstName
             .MoveNext
          Loop

       End With

    End Sub
```

Index Property

Sets or returns a value that indicates the name of the current **Index** object in a table-type **Recordset** object (Microsoft Jet workspaces only).

Applies To

Recordset Object, **Table-Type Recordset** Object

Settings and Return Values

The setting or return value is a **String** data type that evaluates to the name of an **Index** object in the **Indexes** collection of the **Tabledef** or table-type **Recordset** object's **TableDef** object.

Remarks

Records in base tables aren't stored in any particular order. Setting the **Index** property changes the order of records returned from the database; it doesn't affect the order in which the records are stored.

The specified **Index** object must already be defined. If you set the **Index** property to an **Index** object that doesn't exist or if the **Index** property isn't set when you use the **Seek** method, a trappable error occurs.

Examine the **Indexes** collection of a **TableDef** object to determine what **Index** objects are available to table-type **Recordset** objects created from that **TableDef** object.

You can create a new index for the table by creating a new **Index** object, setting its properties, appending it to the **Indexes** collection of the underlying **TableDef** object, and then reopening the **Recordset** object.

Records returned from a table-type **Recordset** object can be ordered only by the indexes defined for the underlying **TableDef** object. To sort records in some other order, you can open a dynaset-, snapshot-, or forward-only–type **Recordset** object by using an SQL statement with an ORDER BY clause.

Notes

- You don't have to create indexes for tables. With large, unindexed tables, accessing a specific record or creating a **Recordset** object can take a long time. On the other hand, creating too many indexes slows down update, append, and delete operations because all indexes are automatically updated.

- Records read from tables without indexes are returned in no particular sequence.

- The **Attributes** property of each **Field** object in the **Index** object determines the order of records and consequently determines the access techniques to use for that index.

- A unique index helps optimize finding records.

- Indexes don't affect the physical order of a base table¾indexes affect only how the records are accessed by the table-type **Recordset** object when a particular index is chosen or when **Recordset** is opened.

See Also

Index Object, **TableDef** Object, **Append** Method, **Seek** Method, **Primary** Property, **Sort** Property

Example

This example uses the **Index** property to set different record orders for a table-type **Recordset**.

```
Sub IndexPropertyX()

    Dim dbsNorthwind As Database
    Dim tdfEmployees As TableDef
    Dim rstEmployees As Recordset
    Dim idxLoop As Index
```

```
        Set dbsNorthwind = OpenDatabase("Northwind.mdb")
        Set rstEmployees = _
           dbsNorthwind.OpenRecordset("Employees")
        Set tdfEmployees = dbsNorthwind.TableDefs!Employees

        With rstEmployees

           ' Enumerate Indexes collection of Employees table.
           For Each idxLoop In tdfEmployees.Indexes
              .Index = idxLoop.Name
              Debug.Print "Index = " & .Index
              Debug.Print "EmployeeID - PostalCode - Name"
              .MoveFirst

              ' Enumerate Recordset to show the order of records.
              Do While Not .EOF
                 Debug.Print "          " & !EmployeeID & " - " & _
                    !PostalCode & " - " & !FirstName & " " & _
                    !LastName
                 .MoveNext
              Loop

           Next idxLoop

           .Close
        End With

        dbsNorthwind.Close

     End Sub
```

Index Property (Control Array)

Returns or sets the number that uniquely identifies a control in a control array.
Available only if the control is part of a control array.

Applies To

CheckBox Control, **ComboBox** Control, **CommandButton** Control,
CommonDialog Control, **Data** Control, **DirListBox** Control, **DriveListBox** Control,
FileListBox Control, **Frame** Control, **HScrollBar**, **VScrollBar** Controls, **Image**
Control, **Label** Control, **Line** Control, **ListBox** Control, **Menu** Control, **OLE**
Container Control, **OptionButton** Control, **PictureBox** Control, **RemoteData**
Control, **Shape** Control, **Split** Control, **TextBox** Control, **Timer** Control

Syntax

object[(*number*)].**Index**

The **Index** property syntax has these parts:

Part	Description
object	An object expression that evaluates to an object in the **Applies To** list.
number	A numeric expression that evaluates to an integer that identifies an individual control within a control array.

Settings

The settings for *number* are:

Setting	Description
No value	(Default) Not part of a control array.
0 to 32,767	Part of an array. Specifies an integer greater than or equal to 0 that identifies a control within a control array. All controls in a control array have the same **Name** property. Visual Basic automatically assigns the next integer available within the control array.

Remarks

Because control array elements share the same **Name** property setting, you must use the **Index** property in code to specify a particular control in the array. **Index** must appear as an integer (or a numeric expression evaluating to an integer) in parentheses next to the control array name—for example, MyButtons(3). You can also use the **Tag** property setting to distinguish one control from another within a control array.

When a control in the array recognizes that an event has occurred, Visual Basic calls the control array's event procedure and passes the applicable **Index** setting as an additional argument. This property is also used when you create controls dynamically at run time with the **Load** statement or remove them with the **Unload** statement.

Although Visual Basic assigns, by default, the next integer available as the value of **Index** for a new control in a control array, you can override this assigned value and skip integers. You can also set **Index** to an integer other than 0 for the first control in the array. If you reference an **Index** value in code that doesn't identify one of the controls in a control array, a Visual Basic run-time error occurs.

Note   To remove a control from a control array, change the control's **Name** property setting, and delete the control's **Index** property setting.

See Also

Load Statement, **Unload** Statement, **Tag** Property, **Name** Property

Example

This example starts with two **OptionButton** controls and adds a new **OptionButton** to the form each time you click a **CommandButton** control. When you click an **OptionButton**, the **FillStyle** property is set and a new circle is drawn. To try this example, paste the code into the Declarations section of a form that has two **OptionButton** controls, a **CommandButton**, and a large **PictureBox** control.

Set the **Name** property of both **OptionButton** controls to **optButton** to create a control array.

```
Private Sub OptButton_Click (Index As Integer)
    Dim H, W ' Declare variables.
    Picture1.Cls' Clear picture.
    Picture1.FillStyle = Index ' Set FillStyle.
    W = Picture1.ScaleWidth / 2        ' Get size of circle.
    H = Picture1.ScaleHeight / 2
    Picture1.Circle (W, H), W / 2       ' Draw circle.
End Sub

Private Sub Command1_Click ()
    Static MaxIdx   ' Largest index in array.
    If MaxIdx = 0 Then MaxIdx = 1        ' Preset MaxIdx.
    MaxIdx = MaxIdx + 1   ' Increment index.

If MaxIdx > 7 Then Exit Sub' Put eight buttons on form.
    Load OptButton(MaxIdx)   ' Create new item in array.
    ' Set location of new option button under previous button.
    OptButton(MaxIdx).Top = OptButton(MaxIdx - 1).Top + 360
    OptButton(MaxIdx).Visible = True   ' Make new button visible.
End Sub
```

IndexedValue Property

Returns or sets a value in an indexed list or an array.

Applies To

Property Object

Syntax

object.**IndexedValue** [*index1*, *index2*,][*index3*,] [*index4*]][= *value*]

The **IndexedValue** property syntax has these parts:

Part	Description
object	An object expression that evaluates to an object in the **Applies To** list.
indexn	A numeric expression specifying index position. **IndexedValue** accepts up to four indices. The number of indices accepted by **IndexedValue** is the value for the same property returned by the **NumIndices** property.
value	An expression that evaluates to a type acceptable to the control.

Remarks

If the property is a list (as indicated by **NumIndices**), then **IndexedValue** returns the element of the list specified by the index parameters.

IndexedValue is used only if the value of the **NumIndices** property is greater than zero. Values in indexed lists, as in the **List** property of a **ListBox** control, are set or returned with a single index.

Indexes Collection

An **Indexes** collection contains all the stored **Index** objects of a **TableDef** object (Microsoft Jet workspaces only).

Remarks

When you access a table-type **Recordset** object, use the object's **Index** property to specify the order of records. Set this property to the **Name** property setting of an existing **Index** object in the **Indexes** collection of the **TableDef** object underlying the **Recordset** object.

Note   You can use the **Append** or **Delete** method on an **Indexes** collection only if the **Updatable** property setting of the containing **TableDef** object is **True**.

After you create a new **Index** object, you should use the **Append** method to add it to the **TableDef** object's **Indexes** collection.

Important   Make sure your data complies with the attributes of your new index. If your index requires unique values, make sure that there are no duplicates in existing data records. If duplicates exist, the Microsoft Jet database engine can't create the index; a trappable error results when you attempt to use the **Append** method on the new index.

Properties

Count Property

Methods

Append Method**, Delete** Method**, Refresh** Method

Example

This example creates a new **Index** object, appends it to the **Indexes** collection of the Employees **TableDef**, and then enumerates the **Indexes** collection of the **TableDef**. Finally, it enumerates a **Recordset**, first using the primary **Index**, and then using the new **Index**. The **IndexOutput** procedure is required for this procedure to run.

```
Sub IndexObjectX()

    Dim dbsNorthwind As Database
    Dim tdfEmployees As TableDef
    Dim idxNew As Index
    Dim idxLoop As Index
    Dim rstEmployees As Recordset
```

```
        Set dbsNorthwind = OpenDatabase("Northwind.mdb")
        Set tdfEmployees = dbsNorthwind!Employees

    With tdfEmployees
        ' Create new index, create and append Field
        ' objects to its Fields collection.
        Set idxNew = .CreateIndex("NewIndex")

        With idxNew
            .Fields.Append.CreateField("Country")
            .Fields.Append.CreateField("LastName")
            .Fields.Append.CreateField("FirstName")
        End With

        ' Add new Index object to the Indexes collection
        ' of the Employees table collection.
        .Indexes.Append idxNew
        .Indexes.Refresh

        Debug.Print .Indexes.Count & " Indexes in " & _
            .Name & " TableDef"

        ' Enumerate Indexes collection of Employees
        ' table.
        For Each idxLoop In .Indexes
            Debug.Print "    " & idxLoop.Name
        Next idxLoop

        Set rstEmployees = _
            dbsNorthwind.OpenRecordset("Employees")

        ' Print report using old and new indexes.
        IndexOutput rstEmployees, "PrimaryKey"
        IndexOutput rstEmployees, idxNew.Name
        rstEmployees.Close

        ' Delete new Index because this is a
        ' demonstration.
        .Indexes.Delete idxNew.Name
    End With

    dbsNorthwind.Close

End Sub

Sub IndexOutput(rstTemp As Recordset, _
    strIndex As String)
    ' Report function for FieldX.

    With rstTemp
        ' Set the index.
        .Index = strIndex
        .MoveFirst
```

```
      Debug.Print "Recordset = " & .Name & _
         ", Index = " & .Index
      Debug.Print "EmployeeID - Country - Name"

      ' Enumerate the recordset using the specified
      ' index.
      Do While Not .EOF
         Debug.Print "     " & !EmployeeID & " - " & _
            !Country & " - " & !LastName & ", " & !FirstName
         .MoveNext
      Loop

   End With


   End Sub
```

InfoMessage Event

Occurs when informational messages are added to the **rdoErrors** collection.

Applies To

rdoEngine Object

Syntax

Private Sub *object*.**InfoMessage( )**

The *object* placeholder represents an object expression that evaluates to an object in the **Applies To** list.

Remarks

This event is raised after RDO receives a SQL_SUCCESS_WITH_INFO return code from the ODBC Driver Manager, and populates the **rdoErrors** collection with the informational messages.

The **InfoMessage** event is raised once for each *set* of informational messages. Thus, if an RDO method generates several informational messages, this event is raised only once—after the last message has been added to the collection. You can trap this event and examine the contents of the **rdoErrors** collection and decide what action is appropriate.

See Also

rdoEngine Object, **rdoError** Object

Inherit Property

Sets or returns a value that indicates whether new **Document** objects will inherit a default **Permissions** property setting (Microsoft Jet workspaces only).

Applies To

Container Object

Settings and Return Values

The setting or return value is a **Boolean** data type. If you set the property to **True**, **Document** objects inherit a default **Permissions** property setting.

Remarks

Use the **Inherit** property in conjunction with the **Permissions** property to define what permissions new documents will automatically have when they're created. If you set the **Inherit** property to **True**, and then set a permission on a container, then whenever a new document is created in that container, that permission will be set on the new document. This is a very convenient way of presetting permissions on an object.

Setting the **Inherit** property will not affect existing documents in the container—you can't modify all the permissions on all existing documents in a container by setting the **Inherit** property and a new permission. It will affect only new documents that are created after the **Inherit** property is set.

See Also

Document Object, **Permissions** Property

Example

This example sets the Tables container's **Inherit** property to True so that any subsequently created **Document** objects in the Tables container will have the same security settings as the Tables container.

```
Sub InheritX()

    Dim dbsNorthwind As Database
    Dim conTables As Container

    Set dbsNorthwind = OpenDatabase("Northwind.mdb")
    Set conTables = dbsNorthwind.Containers("Tables")

    ' By setting the Inherit property of the Tables container
    ' to true and setting its permissions, any new Document
    ' object in this container will inherit the same
    ' permissions setting.
    conTables.Inherit = True
    conTables.Permissions = dbSecWriteSec

    dbsNorthwind.Close

End Sub
```

Inherited Property

Returns a value that indicates whether a **Property** object is inherited from an underlying object.

Applies To

Property Object

Return Values

The return value is a **Boolean** data type that is **True** if the **Property** object is inherited. For built-in **Property** objects that represent predefined properties, the only possible return value is **False**. This property is always **False** in an ODBCDirect workspace.

Remarks

You can use the **Inherited** property to determine whether a user-defined **Property** was created for the object it Applies To, or whether the **Property** was inherited from another object. For example, suppose you create a new **Property** for a **QueryDef** object and then open a **Recordset** object from the **QueryDef** object. This new **Property** will be part of the **Recordset** object's **Properties** collection, and its **Inherited** property will be set to **True** because the property was created for the **QueryDef** object, not the **Recordset** object.

See Also

CreateProperty Method

Example

This example use the **Inherited** property to determine if a user-defined **Property** object was created for a **Recordset** object or for some underlying object.

```
Sub InheritedX()

    Dim dbsNorthwind As Database
    Dim tdfTest As TableDef
    Dim rstTest As Recordset
    Dim prpNew As Property
    Dim prpLoop As Property

    ' Create a new property for a saved TableDef object, then
    ' open a recordset from that TableDef object.
    Set dbsNorthwind = OpenDatabase("Northwind.mdb")
    Set tdfTest = dbsNorthwind.TableDefs(0)
    Set prpNew = tdfTest.CreateProperty("NewProperty", _
        dbBoolean, True)
    tdfTest.Properties.Append prpNew
    Set rstTest = tdfTest.OpenRecordset(dbOpenForwardOnly)

    ' Show Name and Inherited property of the new Property
    ' object in the TableDef.
```

```
         Debug.Print "NewProperty of " & tdfTest.Name & _
            " TableDef:"
         Debug.Print "Inherited = " & _
            tdfTest.Properties("NewProperty").Inherited

         ' Show Name and Inherited property of the new Property
         ' object in the Recordset.
         Debug.Print "NewProperty of " & rstTest.Name & _
            " Recordset:"
         Debug.Print "Inherited = " & _
            rstTest.Properties("NewProperty").Inherited

         ' Delete new TableDef because this is a demonstration.
         tdfTest.Properties.Delete prpNew.Name
         dbsNorthwind.Close

      End Sub
```

IniPath Property

Sets or returns information about the Windows Registry key that contains values for the Microsoft Jet database engine (Microsoft Jet workspaces only).

Applies To

DBEngine Object

Settings and Return Values

The setting or return value is a **String** data type that points to a user-supplied portion of the Windows Registry key containing Microsoft Jet database engine settings or parameters needed for installable ISAM databases.

Remarks

You can configure the Microsoft Jet engine with the Windows Registry. You can use the Registry to set options, such as installable ISAM DLLs.

For this option to have any effect, you must set the **IniPath** property before your application invokes any other DAO code. The scope of this setting is limited to your application and can't be changed without restarting your application.

You also use the Registry to provide initialization parameters for some installable ISAM database drivers. For example, to use Paradox version 4.0, set the **IniPath** property to a part of the Registry containing the appropriate parameters.

This property recognizes either HKEY_LOCAL_MACHINE or HKEY_LOCAL_USER. If no root key is supplied, the default is HKEY_LOCAL_MACHINE.

Microsoft Jet versions 2.5 or earlier kept initialization information in .ini files.

See Also

SystemDB Property

Example

This example sets the path in the **IniPath** property to an application's key in the Windows Registry.

```
Sub IniPathX()

    ' Change the IniPath property to point to a different
    ' section of the Windows Registry for settings
    ' information.
    Debug.Print "Original IniPath setting = " & _
        IIf(DBEngine.IniPath = "", "[Empty]", _
        DBEngine.IniPath)
    DBEngine.IniPath = _
        "HKEY_LOCAL_MACHINE\SOFTWARE\Microsoft\" & _
        "Jet\3.5\ISAM Formats\FoxPro 3.0"
    Debug.Print "New IniPath setting = " & _
        IIf(DBEngine.IniPath = "", "[Empty]", _
        DBEngine.IniPath)

End Sub
```

Initialize Event

Occurs when an application creates an instance of a **Form**, **MDIForm**, **User** control, **Property Page**, or class.

Applies To

PropertyPage Object, **UserControl** Object, **UserDocument** Object, **Form Object, Forms** Collection, **MDIForm** Object

Syntax

Private Sub *object*_**Initialize( )**

The *object* placeholder represents an object expression that evaluates to an object in the **Applies To** list.

Remarks

You trigger the Initialize event when you:

- Use the **CreateObject** function to create an instance of a class. For example:

```
Set X = CreateObject("Project1.MyClass")
```

- Refer to a property or event of an automatically created instance of a form or class in your code. For example:

```
MyForm.Caption = "Example"
```

Use this event to initialize any data used by the instance of the **Form**, **MDIForm**, or class. For a **Form** or **MDIForm**, the Initialize event occurs before the Load event.

See Also

Load Event, **Terminate** Event

InitProperties Event

Occurs when a new instance of an object is created.

Applies To

UserControl Object, **UserDocument** Object

Syntax

Sub *object*_**InitProperties**()

The **InitProperties** event syntax has this part:

Part	Description
object	An object expression that evaluates to an object in the **Applies To** list.

Remarks

This event allows the author of the object to initialize a new instance of the object. This event occurs only when a new instance of an object is being created; this is to allow the author of the object to distinguish between creating a new instance of the object and loading an old instance of the object.

By putting in code to initialize new instances in the **InitProperties** event rather than the Initialize event, the author can avoid cases where loading data through a **ReadProperties** event into an old instance of the object will undo the initialization of the object.

See Also

ReadProperties Event, **Initialize** Event

Input # Statement

Reads data from an open sequential file and assigns the data to variables.

Syntax

Input #filenumber, varlist

The **Input #** statement syntax has these parts:

Part	Description
filenumber	Required. Any valid file number.
varlist	Required. Comma-delimited list of variables that are assigned values read from the file — can't be an array or object variable. However, variables that describe an element of an array or user-defined type may be used.

Remarks

Data read with **Input #** is usually written to a file with **Write #**. Use this statement only with files opened in **Input** or **Binary** mode.

When read, standard string or numeric data is assigned to variables without modification. The following table illustrates how other input data is treated:

Data	Value assigned to variable
Delimiting comma or blank line	**Empty**
#NULL#	**Null**
#TRUE# or #FALSE#	**True** or **False**
#yyyy-mm-dd hh:mm:ss#	The date and/or time represented by the expression
#ERROR *errornumber*#	*errornumber* (variable is a **Variant** tagged as an error)

Double quotation marks (" ") within input data are ignored.

Data items in a file must appear in the same order as the variables in *varlist* and match variables of the same data type. If a variable is numeric and the data is not numeric, a value of zero is assigned to the variable.

If you reach the end of the file while you are inputting a data item, the input is terminated and an error occurs.

Note To be able to correctly read data from a file into variables using **Input #**, use the **Write #** statement instead of the **Print #** statement to write the data to the files. Using **Write #** ensures each separate data field is properly delimited.

See Also

Input Function, **Open** Statement, **Print #** Statement, **Write #** Statement

Example

This example uses the **Input #** statement to read data from a file into two variables. This example assumes that TESTFILE is a file with a few lines of data written to it using the **Write #** statement; that is, each line contains a string in quotations and a number separated by a comma, for example, ("Hello", 234).

```
Dim MyString, MyNumber
Open "TESTFILE" For Input As #1      ' Open file for input.
Do While Not EOF(1)                  ' Loop until end of file.
    Input #1, MyString, MyNumber     ' Read data into two variables.
    Debug.Print MyString, MyNumber   ' Print data to Debug window.
Loop
Close #1                             ' Close file.
```

Input Function

Returns **String** containing characters from a file opened in **Input** or **Binary** mode.

Syntax

Input(*number*, [#]*filenumber*)

The **Input** function syntax has these parts:

Part	Description
number	Required. Any valid numeric expression specifying the number of characters to return.
filenumber	Required. Any valid file number.

Remarks

Data read with the **Input** function is usually written to a file with **Print #** or **Put**. Use this function only with files opened in **Input** or **Binary** mode.

Unlike the **Input #** statement, the **Input** function returns all of the characters it reads, including commas, carriage returns, linefeeds, quotation marks, and leading spaces.

With files opened for **Binary** access, an attempt to read through the file using the **Input** function until **EOF** returns **True** generates an error. Use the **LOF** and **Loc** functions instead of **EOF** when reading binary files with **Input**, or use **Get** when using the **EOF** function.

Note Use the **InputB** function for byte data contained within text files. With **InputB**, *number* specifies the number of bytes to return rather than the number of characters to return.

See Also

Input # Statement

Example

This example uses the **Input** function to read one character at a time from a file and print it to the **Debug** window. This example assumes that TESTFILE is a text file with a few lines of sample data.

```
Dim MyChar
Open "TESTFILE" For Input As #1      ' Open file.
Do While Not EOF(1)                  ' Loop until end of file.
    MyChar = Input(1, #1)            ' Get one character.
    Debug.Print MyChar               ' Print to Debug window.
Loop
Close #1                             ' Close file.
```

InputBox Function

Displays a prompt in a dialog box, waits for the user to input text or click a button, and returns a **String** containing the contents of the text box.

Syntax

InputBox(*prompt*[, *title*] [, *default*] [, *xpos*] [, *ypos*] [, *helpfile*, *context*])

The **InputBox** function syntax has these named arguments:

Part	Description
prompt	Required. String expression displayed as the message in the dialog box. The maximum length of *prompt* is approximately 1024 characters, depending on the width of the characters used. If *prompt* consists of more than one line, you can separate the lines using a carriage return character (**Chr**(13)), a linefeed character (**Chr**(10)), or carriage return–linefeed character combination (**Chr**(13) & **Chr**(10)) between each line.
title	Optional. String expression displayed in the title bar of the dialog box. If you omit *title*, the application name is placed in the title bar.
default	Optional. String expression displayed in the text box as the default response if no other input is provided. If you omit *default*, the text box is displayed empty.
xpos	Optional. Numeric expression that specifies, in twips, the horizontal distance of the left edge of the dialog box from the left edge of the screen. If *xpos* is omitted, the dialog box is horizontally centered.
ypos	Optional. Numeric expression that specifies, in twips, the vertical distance of the upper edge of the dialog box from the top of the screen. If *ypos* is omitted, the dialog box is vertically positioned approximately one-third of the way down the screen.
helpfile	Optional. String expression that identifies the Help file to use to provide context-sensitive Help for the dialog box. If *helpfile* is provided, *context* must also be provided.
context	Optional. Numeric expression that is the Help context number assigned to the appropriate Help topic by the Help author. If *context* is provided, *helpfile* must also be provided.

Remarks

When both *helpfile* and *context* are provided, the user can press F1 to view the Help topic corresponding to the **context**. Some host applications, for example, Microsoft Excel, also automatically add a **Help** button to the dialog box. If the user clicks **OK** or presses ENTER, the **InputBox** function returns whatever is in the text box. If the user clicks **Cancel**, the function returns a zero-length string ("").

Note To specify more than the first named argument, you must use **InputBox** in an expression. To omit some positional arguments, you must include the corresponding comma delimiter.

See Also

MsgBox Function

Example

This example shows various ways to use the **InputBox** function to prompt the user to enter a value. If the x and y positions are omitted, the dialog box is automatically centered for the respective axes. The variable MyValue contains the value entered by the user if the user clicks **OK** or presses the ENTER key. If the user clicks **Cancel**, a zero-length string is returned.

```
Dim Message, Title, Default, MyValue
Message = "Enter a value between 1 and 3"     ' Set prompt.
Title = "InputBox Demo" ' Set title.
Default = "1"  ' Set default.
' Display message, title, and default value.
MyValue = InputBox(Message, Title, Default)

' Use Helpfile and context. The Help button is added automatically.
MyValue = InputBox(Message, Title, , , , "DEMO.HLP", 10)

' Display dialog box at position 100, 100.
MyValue = InputBox(Message, Title, Default, 100, 100)
```

InSelection Property

Returns or assigns a control's selection state.

Applies To

VBControl Object

Syntax

object.**InSelection**

The *object* placeholder represents an object expression that evaluates to an object in the **Applies To** list.

Remarks

If the **InSelection** property of a control contained within another control is set to **True**, then any controls not within that control (or any controls within other controls) will be unselected.

InsertLines Method

Inserts a line or lines of code at a specified location in a block of code.

Applies To

CodeModule Object

Syntax

object.**InsertLines**(*line*, *code*)

InsertLines syntax has these parts:

Part	Description
object	Required. An object expression that evaluates to an object in the **Applies To** list.
line	Required. A **Long** specifying the location at which you want to insert the code.
code	Required. A **String** containing the code you want to insert.

Remarks

If the text you insert using the **InsertLines** method is carriage return/line feed delimited, it will be inserted as consecutive lines.

See Also

DeleteLines Method, **Lines** Method

Example

The following example uses the **InsertLines** method to insert a line, "Option Explicit," in the specified code pane.

```
Application.VBE.CodePanes(1).CodeModule.InsertLines 1, "Option Explicit"
```

InsertObjDlg Method

Displays the Insert Object dialog box.

Applies To

OLE Container Control

Syntax

object.**InsertObjDlg**

The *object* is an object expression that evaluates to an object in the **Applies To** list.

Remarks

At run time, you display this dialog box to enable the user to create a linked or embedded object by choosing the type of object (linked or embedded) and the application provides the object.

Use the **OLETypeAllowed** property to determine the type of object that can be created (linked, embedded, or either) using this dialog box.

When you create a new object, the application associated with the class name (for example, Excel.exe) must be correctly registered with the operating system. (The application setup program should register the application correctly.)

See Also

OLETypeAllowed Property

Instancing Property

Sets a value that specifies whether you can create instances of a public class outside a project, and if so, how it will behave. Not available at run time.

Settings

The **Instancing** property has these settings:

Setting	Description
1	(Default) Private. Other applications aren't allowed access to type library information about the class, and cannot create instances of it. Private objects are only for use within your component.
2	PublicNotCreatable. Other applications can use objects of this class only if your component creates the objects first. Other applications cannot use the **CreateObject** function or the **New** operator to create objects from the class.
3	SingleUse. Allows other applications to create objects from the class, but every object of this class that a client creates starts a new instance of your component. Not allowed in ActiveX DLL projects.
4	GlobalSingleUse. Similar to SingleUse, except that properties and methods of the class can be invoked as if they were simply global functions. Not allowed in ActiveX DLL projects.
5	MultiUse. Allows other applications to create objects from the class. One instance of your component can provide any number of objects created in this fashion.
6	GlobalMultiUse. Similar to MultiUse, with one addition: properties and methods of the class can be invoked as if they were simply global functions. It's not necessary to explicitly create an instance of the class first, because one will automatically be created.

Setting	Applies To Project Type			
	ActiveX Exe	ActiveX DLL	ActiveX Control	Standard Exe
Private	X	X	X	X
PublicNotCreatable	X	X	X	
SingleUse	X			
GlobalSingleUse	X			
MultiUse	X	X		
GlobalMultiUse	X	X		

Remarks

The **Instancing** property has been expanded in Visual Basic 5.0 to incorporate the functionality of the Visual Basic 4.0 **Public** property.

When a class is creatable, you can use any of the following techniques to create instances of the class from other applications:

- Use the **CreateObject** function, as in:
  ```
  Set MyInstance = CreateObject("MyProject.MyClass")
  ```
- Use the **Dim** statement within the same project (or outside the project if the **Public** property is also set to **True**), as in:
  ```
  Dim MyInstance As New MyClass
  ```

The **New** keyword indicates that MyInstance is to be declared as a new instance of MyClass.

If the **Public** property is **False**, the setting of the **Instancing** property is ignored. You can always create instances of the class within the project that defines the class. If the **Public** property is **True**, the class is visible and therefore can be controlled by other applications once an instance of the class exists.

Note The properties and methods of a **GlobalMultiUse** object are not part of the global name space of the component that provides the object. For example, within the project that contains the **GlobalUtility** class module, you must explicitly create an instance of **GlobalUtility** in order to use the object's properties and methods. Other limitations of global objects are listed in "Global Objects and Code Libraries," in "Building Code Components" in Books Online.

InStr Function

Returns a **Variant** (**Long**) specifying the position of the first occurrence of one string within another.

Syntax

InStr([*start*,]*string1*, *string2*[, *compare*])

The **InStr** function syntax has these arguments:

Part	Description
start	Optional. Numeric expression that sets the starting position for each search. If omitted, search begins at the first character position. If *start* contains **Null**, an error occurs. The *start* argument is required if *compare* is specified.
string1	Required. String expression being searched.
string2	Required. String expression sought.
compare	Optional. Specifies the type of string comparison. The *compare* argument can be omitted, or it can be 0, 1or 2. Specify **0** (default) to perform a binary comparison. Specify **1** to perform a textual, noncase-sensitive comparison. For Microsoft Access only, specify **2** to perform a comparison based on information contained in your database. If *compare* is Null, an error occurs. If *compare* is omitted, the **Option Compare** setting determines the type of comparison.

Return Values

If	InStr returns
string1 is zero-length	0
string1 is **Null**	Null
string2 is zero-length	*start*
string2 is **Null**	Null
string2 is not found	0
string2 is found within *string1*	Position at which match is found
start > *string2*	0

Remarks

The **InStrB** function is used with byte data contained in a string. Instead of returning the character position of the first occurrence of one string within another, **InStrB** returns the byte position.

See Also

Option Compare Statement, **StrComp** Function

Example

This example uses the **InStr** function to return the position of the first occurrence of one string within another.

```
Dim SearchString, SearchChar, MyPos
SearchString ="XXpXXpXXPXXP"                 ' String to search in.
SearchChar = "P"                             ' Search for "P".

' A textual comparison starting at position 4. Returns 6.
MyPos = Instr(4, SearchString, SearchChar, 1)

' A binary comparison starting at position 1. Returns 9.
MyPos = Instr(1, SearchString, SearchChar, 0)

' Comparison is binary by default (last argument is omitted).
MyPos = Instr(SearchString, SearchChar)      ' Returns 9.

MyPos = Instr(1, SearchString, "W")          ' Returns 0.
```

Int, Fix Functions

Returns a value of the type passed to it containing the integer portion of a number.

Syntax

Int(*number*)
Fix(*number*)

The required *number* argument is a **Double** or any valid numeric expression. If *number* contains **Null**, **Null** is returned.

Remarks

Both **Int** and **Fix** remove the fractional part of *number* and return the resulting integer value.

The difference between **Int** and **Fix** is that if *number* is negative, **Int** returns the first negative integer less than or equal to *number,* whereas **Fix** returns the first negative integer greater than or equal to *number.* For example, **Int** converts −8.4 to −9, and **Fix** converts -8.4 to -8.

Fix(*number*) is equivalent to:

```
Sgn(number) * Int(Abs(number))
```

See Also

Integer Data Type, **Math** Functions

Example

This example illustrates how the **Int** and **Fix** functions return integer portions of numbers. In the case of a negative number argument, the **Int** function returns the first negative integer less than or equal to the number; the **Fix** function returns the first negative integer greater than or equal to the number.

```
Dim MyNumber
MyNumber = Int(99.8) ' Returns 99.
MyNumber = Fix(99.2) ' Returns 99.

MyNumber = Int(-99.8)' Returns -100.
MyNumber = Fix(-99.8)' Returns -99.

MyNumber = Int(-99.2)' Returns -100.
MyNumber = Fix(-99.2)' Returns -99.
```

Integer Data Type

Integer variables are stored as 16-bit (2-byte) numbers ranging in value from -32,768 to 32,767. The type-declaration character for **Integer** is the percent sign (%).

You can also use **Integer** variables to represent enumerated values. An enumerated value can contain a finite set of unique whole numbers, each of which has special meaning in the context in which it is used. Enumerated values provide a convenient way to select among a known number of choices, for example, black = 0, white = 1, and so on. It is good programming practice to define constants using the **Const** statement for each enumerated value.

See Also

Data Type Summary, **Long Data** Type, **Variant Data** Type, **Deftype** Statements

IntegralHeight Property

Returns or sets a value indicating if the control displays partial items. Read-only at run time.

Applies To

DBCombo Control, **DBList** Control, **ComboBox** Control, **ListBox** Control

Syntax

object.**IntegralHeight** [= *value*]

The **IntegralHeight** property syntax has these parts:

Part	Description
object	An object expression that evaluates to an object in the **Applies To** list.
value	A Boolean expression that determines whether the list is resized, as described in **Settings**.

Settings

The settings for *value* are:

Setting	Description
True	(Default) The list resizes itself to display only complete items.
False	The list doesn't resize itself even if the item is too tall to display completely.

Data Type

Boolean

See Also

Data Control

Interval Property

Returns or sets the number of milliseconds between calls to a **Timer** control's Timer event.

Applies To

Timer Control

Syntax

object.**Interval** [= *milliseconds*]

The **Interval** property syntax has these parts:

Part	Description
object	An object expression that evaluates to an object in the **Applies To** list.
milliseconds	A numeric expression specifying the number of milliseconds, as described in Settings.

Settings

The settings for *milliseconds* are:

Setting	Description
0	(Default) Disables a **Timer** control.
1 to 65,535	Sets an interval (in milliseconds) that takes effect when a **Timer** control's **Enabled** property is set to **True**. For example, a value of 10,000 milliseconds equals 10 seconds. The maximum, 65,535 milliseconds, is equivalent to just over 1 minute.

Remarks

You can set a **Timer** control's **Interval** property at design time or run time. When using the **Interval** property, remember:

- The **Timer** control's **Enabled** property determines whether the control responds to the passage of time. Set **Enabled** to **False** to turn a **Timer** control off, and to **True** to turn it on. When a **Timer** control is enabled, its countdown always starts from the value of its **Interval** property setting.

- Create a Timer event procedure to tell Visual Basic what to do each time the **Interval** has passed.

See Also

Enabled Property

Example

This example enables you to adjust the speed at which a form switches colors. To try this example, paste the code into the Declarations section of a form that contains a Timer control, an **HScrollBar** control (horizontal scroll bar), and a **PictureBox** control, and then press F5 and click the scroll bar.

```
Private Sub Form_Load ()
   Timer1.Interval = 900    ' Set interval.
   HScroll1.Min = 100       ' Set minimum.
   HScroll1.Max = 900       ' Set maximum.
End Sub
Private Sub HScroll1_Change ()
   ' Set interval according to scroll bar value.
   Timer1.Interval = 1000 - HScroll1.Value
End Sub
Private Sub Timer1_Timer ()
   ' Switch BackColor between red and blue.
   If Picture1.BackColor = RGB(255, 0, 0) Then
      Picture1.BackColor = RGB(0, 0, 255)
   Else
      Picture1.BackColor = RGB(255, 0, 0)

   End If
End Sub
```

InvisibleAtRuntime Property

Returns or sets a value determining if a control should not have a visible window at run time. The **InvisibleAtRuntime** property is read/write at the control's authoring time, and not available at the control's run time.

Applies To

UserControl Object

Settings

The settings for **InvisibleAtRuntime** are:

Setting	Description
True	Allows the control to not have a visible window at run time. The container of the control may keep the control invisible during run time, like the **Timer** control. The control is still active, and therefore the developer who uses the control can still write programs that can interact with the control. There will be no **Visible** property in the extender object.
False	The control acts as a normal control at run time, where the state of the **Visible** extender property determines the visibility of the control. This is the default value.

Remarks

Important Don't use the **Visible** extender property to make the control invisible at run time. If you do, the control will still have all the overhead of a visible control at run time. Furthermore, the extender properties are available to the developer and end user, who may make the control visible.

Some containers may not support the **InvisibleAtRuntime** property; in this case the control will be visible at run time.

Before creating a control that is invisible at run time, consider creating an ordinary object provided by an in-process code component (ActiveX DLL) instead. Objects provided by in-process code components require fewer resources than controls, even invisible controls. The only reason to implement an invisible control is to take advantage of a feature that is only available to ActiveX controls.

See Also

Visible Property

IPmt Function

Returns a **Double** specifying the interest payment for a given period of an annuity based on periodic, fixed payments and a fixed interest rate.

Syntax

IPmt(*rate*, *per*, *nper*, *pv*[, *fv*[, *type*]])

The **IPmt** function has these named arguments:

Part	Description
rate	Required. **Double** specifying interest rate per period. For example, if you get a car loan at an annual percentage rate (APR) of 10 percent and make monthly payments, the rate per period is 0.1/12, or 0.0083.
per	Required. **Double** specifying payment period in the range 1 through *nper*.
nper	Required. **Double** specifying total number of payment periods in the annuity. For example, if you make monthly payments on a four-year car loan, your loan has a total of 4 * 12 (or 48) payment periods.
pv	Required. **Double** specifying present value, or value today, of a series of future payments or receipts. For example, when you borrow money to buy a car, the loan amount is the present value to the lender of the monthly car payments you will make.
fv	Optional. **Variant** specifying future value or cash balance you want after you've made the final payment. For example, the future value of a loan is $0 because that's its value after the final payment. However, if you want to save $50,000 over 18 years for your child's education, then $50,000 is the future value. If omitted, 0 is assumed.
type	Optional. **Variant** specifying when payments are due. Use 0 if payments are due at the end of the payment period, or use 1 if payments are due at the beginning of the period. If omitted, 0 is assumed.

Remarks

An annuity is a series of fixed cash payments made over a period of time. An annuity can be a loan (such as a home mortgage) or an investment (such as a monthly savings plan).

The *rate* and *nper* arguments must be calculated using payment periods expressed in the same units. For example, if *rate* is calculated using months, *nper* must also be calculated using months.

For all arguments, cash paid out (such as deposits to savings) is represented by negative numbers; cash received (such as dividend checks) is represented by positive numbers.

See Also

DDB Function, **IRR** Function, **MIRR** Function, **NPer** Function, **NPV** Function, **Pmt** Function, **PPmt** Function, **PV** Function, **Rate** Function, **SLN** Function, **SYD** Function

Example

This example uses the **IPmt** function to calculate how much of a payment is interest when all the payments are of equal value. Given are the interest percentage rate per period (APR / 12), the payment period for which the interest portion is desired (Period), the total number of payments (TotPmts), the present value or principal of the loan (PVal), the future value of the loan (FVal), and a number that indicates whether the payment is due at the beginning or end of the payment period (PayType).

```
Dim FVal, Fmt, PVal, APR, TotPmts, PayType, Period, IntPmt, TotInt, Msg
Const ENDPERIOD = 0, BEGINPERIOD = 1          ' When payments are made.
FVal = 0                                       ' Usually 0 for a loan.
Fmt = "###,###,##0.00"                          ' Define money format.
PVal = InputBox("How much do you want to borrow?")
APR = InputBox("What is the annual percentage rate of your loan?")
If APR > 1 Then APR = APR / 100                 ' Ensure proper form.
TotPmts = InputBox("How many monthly payments?")
PayType = MsgBox("Do you make payments at end of the month?", vbYesNo)
If PayType = vbNo Then PayType = BEGINPERIOD Else PayType = ENDPERIOD
For Period = 1 To TotPmts                        ' Total all interest.
   IntPmt = IPmt(APR / 12, Period, TotPmts, -PVal, FVal, PayType)
   TotInt = TotInt + IntPmt
Next Period
Msg = "You'll pay a total of " & Format(TotInt, Fmt)
Msg = Msg & " in interest for this loan."
MsgBox Msg                                       ' Display results.
```

IRR Function

Returns a **Double** specifying the internal rate of return for a series of periodic cash flows (payments and receipts).

Syntax

IRR(*values*()[, *guess*])

The **IRR** function has these named arguments:

Part	Description
values()	Required. Array of **Double** specifying cash flow values. The array must contain at least one negative value (a payment) and one positive value (a receipt).
guess	Optional. **Variant** specifying value you estimate will be returned by **IRR**. If omitted, *guess* is 0.1 (10 percent).

Remarks

The internal rate of return is the interest rate received for an investment consisting of payments and receipts that occur at regular intervals.

The **IRR** function uses the order of values within the array to interpret the order of payments and receipts. Be sure to enter your payment and receipt values in the correct sequence. The cash flow for each period doesn't have to be fixed, as it is for an annuity.

IRR is calculated by iteration. Starting with the value of *guess*, **IRR** cycles through the calculation until the result is accurate to within 0.00001 percent. If **IRR** can't find a result after 20 tries, it fails.

See Also

DDB Function, **FV** Function, **IPmt** Function, **MIRR** Function, **NPer** Function, **NPV** Function, **Pmt** Function, **PPmt** Function, **PV** Function, **Rate** Function, **SLN** Function, **SYD** Function

Example

In this example, the **IRR** function returns the internal rate of return for a series of 5 cash flows contained in the array Values(). The first array element is a negative cash flow representing business start-up costs. The remaining 4 cash flows represent positive cash flows for the subsequent 4 years. Guess is the estimated internal rate of return.

```
Dim Guess, Fmt, RetRate, Msg
Static Values(5) As Double          ' Set up array.
Guess = .1                          ' Guess starts at 10 percent.
Fmt = "#0.00"                       ' Define percentage format.
Values(0) = -70000                  ' Business start-up costs.
' Positive cash flows reflecting income for four successive years.
Values(1) = 22000 : Values(2) = 25000
Values(3) = 28000 : Values(4) = 31000
RetRate = IRR(Values(), Guess) * 100 ' Calculate internal rate.
Msg = "The internal rate of return for these five cash flows is "
Msg = Msg & Format(RetRate, Fmt) & " percent."
MsgBox Msg                          ' Display internal return rate.
```

Is Operator

Used to compare two object reference variables.

Syntax

result = object1 **Is** *object2*

The **Is** operator syntax has these parts:

Part	Description
result	Required; any numeric variable.
object1	Required; any object name.
object2	Required; any object name.

Remarks

If *object1* and *object2* both refer to the same object, *result* is **True**; if they do not, *result* is **False**. Two variables can be made to refer to the same object in several ways.

In the following example, A has been set to refer to the same object as B:

```
Set A = B
```

The following example makes A and B refer to the same object as C:

```
Set A = C
Set B = C
```

See Also

Operator Summary, **Operator** Precedence, **Comparison** Operators

Example

This example uses the **Is** operator to compare two object references. The object variable names are generic and used for illustration purposes only.

```
Dim MyObject, YourObject, ThisObject, OtherObject, ThatObject, MyCheck
Set YourObject = MyObject           ' Assign object references.
Set ThisObject = MyObject
Set ThatObject = OtherObject
MyCheck = YourObject Is ThisObject  ' Returns True.
MyCheck = ThatObject Is ThisObject  ' Returns False.
                                    ' Assume MyObject <> OtherObject
MyCheck = MyObject Is ThatObject    ' Returns False.
```

IsArray Function

Returns a **Boolean** value indicating whether a variable is an array.

Syntax

IsArray(*varname*)

The required *varname* argument is an identifier specifying a variable.

Remarks

IsArray returns **True** if the variable is an array; otherwise, it returns **False**. **IsArray** is especially useful with variants containing arrays.

See Also

Array Function, **IsDate** Function, **IsEmpty** Function, **IsError** Function, **IsMissing** Function, **IsNull** Function, **IsNumeric** Function, **IsObject** Function, **TypeName** Function, **Variant Data** Type, **VarType** Function

Example

This example uses the **IsArray** function to check if a variable is an array.

```
Dim MyArray(1 To 5) As Integer, YourArray, MyCheck
                                ' Declare array variables.
YourArray = Array(1, 2, 3)      ' Use Array function.
MyCheck = IsArray(MyArray)      ' Returns True.
MyCheck = IsArray(YourArray)    ' Returns True.
```

IsBindable Property

Returns a Boolean value indicating whether the property is bindable. This property is read-only.

Applies To

DataBinding Object

Syntax

object.**IsBindable**

The *object* placeholder represents an object expression that evaluates to an object in the **Applies To** list.

Remarks

Use this property to determine if the property is bindable.

Note   This property is usually used in a Wizard to check whether a property is bindable.

IsBroken Property

Returns a **Boolean** value indicating whether or not the **Reference** object points to a valid reference in the registry. Read-only.

Applies to

Reference Object

Return Values

The **IsBroken** property returns these values:

Value	Description
True	The **Reference** object no longer points to a valid reference in the registry.
False	The **Reference** object points to a valid reference in the registry.

See Also

BuiltIn Property, **FullPath** Property

Example

The following example uses the **IsBroken** property to return a value indicating whether or not the specified **Reference** object in a particular project is broken.

```
Debug.Print Application.VBE.vbprojects(1).References(1).IsBroken
```

IsDataSource Property

Returns a Boolean value indicating whether the property is a data source. This property is read-only.

Applies To

DataBinding Object

Syntax

object.**IsDataSource**

The *object* placeholder represents an object expression that evaluates to an object in the **Applies To** list.

Remarks

Use this property to determine if the property is a data source and can be attached to a data control.

Note This property is usually used in a Wizard to check whether a property is a data source.

IsDate Function

Returns a **Boolean** value indicating whether an expression can be converted to a date.

Syntax

IsDate(*expression*)

The required *expression* argument is a **Variant** containing a date expression or string expression recognizable as a date or time.

Remarks

IsDate returns **True** if the expression is a date or can be converted to a valid date; otherwise, it returns **False**. In Microsoft Windows, the range of valid dates is January 1, 100 A.D. through December 31, 9999 A.D.; the ranges vary among operating systems.

See Also

Date Data Type, **IsArray** Function, **IsEmpty** Function, **IsError** Function, **IsMissing** Function, **IsNull** Function, **IsNumeric** Function, **IsObject** Function, **TypeName** Function, **Variant Data** Type, **VarType** Function

Example

This example uses the **IsDate** function to determine if an expression can be converted to a date.

```
Dim MyDate, YourDate, NoDate, MyCheck
MyDate = "February 12, 1969": YourDate = #2/12/69#: NoDate = "Hello"
MyCheck = IsDate(MyDate)          ' Returns True.
MyCheck = IsDate(YourDate)        ' Returns True.
MyCheck = IsDate(NoDate)          ' Returns False.
```

IsDirty Property

Returns a value indicating whether this component was edited since the last time it was saved.

Applies To

VBComponent Object, **VBProject** Object

Syntax

object.**IsDirty**

The *object* placeholder represents an object expression that evaluates to an object in the **Applies To** list.

IsEmpty Function

Returns a **Boolean** value indicating whether a variable has been initialized.

Syntax

IsEmpty(*expression*)

The required *expression* argument is a **Variant** containing a numeric or string expression. However, because **IsEmpty** is used to determine if individual variables are initialized, the *expression* argument is most often a single variable name.

Remarks

IsEmpty returns **True** if the variable is uninitialized, or is explicitly set to **Empty**; otherwise, it returns **False**. **False** is always returned if *expression* contains more than one variable. **IsEmpty** only returns meaningful information for variants.

See Also

IsArray Function, **IsDate** Function, **IsError** Function, **IsMissing** Function, **IsNull** Function, **IsNumeric** Function, **IsObject** Function, **TypeName** Function, **Variant Data** Type, **VarType** Function

Example

This example uses the **IsEmpty** function to determine whether a variable has been initialized.

```
Dim MyVar, MyCheck
MyCheck = IsEmpty(MyVar)        ' Returns True.

MyVar = Null                    ' Assign Null.
MyCheck = IsEmpty(MyVar)        ' Returns False.

MyVar = Empty                   ' Assign Empty.
MyCheck = IsEmpty(MyVar)        ' Returns True.
```

IsError Function

Returns a **Boolean** value indicating whether an expression is an error value.

Syntax

IsError(*expression*)

The required *expression* argument must be a **Variant** of **VarType vbError**.

Remarks

Error values are created by converting real numbers to error values using the **CVErr** function. The **IsError** function is used to determine if a numeric expression represents an error. **IsError** returns **True** if the *expression* argument indicates an error; otherwise, it returns **False**. **IsError** only returns meaningful information for variants of **VarType vbError**.

See Also

CVErr Function, **IsArray** Function, **IsDate** Function, **IsEmpty** Function, **IsMissing** Function, **IsNull** Function, **IsNumeric** Function, **IsObject** Function, **TypeName** Function, **Variant Data** Type, **VarType** Function

Example

This example uses the **IsError** function to check if a numeric expression is an error value. The **CVErr** function is used to return an **Error Variant** from a user-defined function. Assume UserFunction is a user-defined function procedure that returns an error value; for example, a return value assigned with the statement UserFunction = CVErr(32767), where 32767 is a user-defined number.

```
Dim ReturnVal, MyCheck
ReturnVal = UserFunction()
MyCheck = IsError(ReturnVal)   ' Returns True.
```

IsMissing Function

Returns a **Boolean** value indicating whether an optional **Variant** argument has been passed to a procedure.

Syntax

IsMissing(*argname*)

The required *argname* argument contains the name of an optional **Variant** procedure argument.

Remarks

Use the **IsMissing** function to detect whether or not optional **Variant** arguments have been provided in calling a procedure. **IsMissing** returns **True** if no value has been passed for the specified argument; otherwise, it returns **False**. If **IsMissing** returns **True** for an argument, use of the missing argument in other code may cause a user-defined error. If **IsMissing** is used on a **ParamArray** argument, it always returns **False**. To detect an empty **ParamArray**, test to see if the array's upper bound is less than its lower bound.

See Also

Function Statement, **IsArray** Function, **IsDate** Function, **IsEmpty** Function, **IsError** Function, **IsNull** Function, **IsNumeric** Function, **IsObject** Function, **Optional**, **ParamArray**, **Property Get** Statement, **Property Let** Statement, **Property Set** Statement, **Sub** Statement, **TypeName** Function, **Variant Data** Type, **VarType** Function

Example

This example uses the **IsMissing** function to check if an optional argument has been passed to a user-defined procedure. Note that **Optional** arguments can now have default values and types other than **Variant**.

```
Dim ReturnValue
' The following statements call the user-defined function procedure.
ReturnValue = ReturnTwice()          ' Returns Null.
ReturnValue = ReturnTwice(2)         ' Returns 4.

' Function procedure definition.
Function ReturnTwice(Optional A)
   If IsMissing(A) Then
        ' If argument is missing, return a Null.
      ReturnTwice = Null
   Else
        ' If argument is present, return twice the value.
      ReturnTwice = A * 2
   End If
End Function
```

IsNull Function

Returns a **Boolean** value that indicates whether an expression contains no valid data (**Null**).

Syntax

IsNull(*expression*)

The required *expression* argument is a **Variant** containing a numeric expression or string expression.

Remarks

IsNull returns **True** if *expression* is **Null**; otherwise, **IsNull** returns **False**. If *expression* consists of more than one variable, **Null** in any constituent variable causes **True** to be returned for the entire expression.

The **Null** value indicates that the **Variant** contains no valid data. **Null** is not the same as **Empty**, which indicates that a variable has not yet been initialized. It is also not the same as a zero-length string (""), which is sometimes referred to as a null string.

Important Use the **IsNull** function to determine whether an expression contains a **Null** value. Expressions that you might expect to evaluate to **True** under some circumstances, such as If Var = Null and If Var <> Null, are always **False**. This is because any expression containing a **Null** is itself **Null** and, therefore, **False**.

See Also

IsArray Function, **IsDate** Function, **IsEmpty** Function, **IsError** Function, **IsMissing** Function, **IsNumeric** Function, **IsObject** Function, **TypeName** Function, **Variant Data** Type, **VarType** Function

Example

This example uses the **IsNull** function to determine if a variable contains a **Null**.

```
Dim MyVar, MyCheck
MyCheck = IsNull(MyVar) ' Returns False.

MyVar = ""
MyCheck = IsNull(MyVar) ' Returns False.

MyVar = Null
MyCheck = IsNull(MyVar) ' Returns True.
```

IsNumeric Function

Returns a **Boolean** value indicating whether an expression can be evaluated as a number.

Syntax

IsNumeric(*expression*)

The required *expression* argument is a **Variant** containing a numeric expression or string expression.

Remarks

IsNumeric returns **True** if the entire *expression* is recognized as a number; otherwise, it returns **False**.

IsNumeric returns **False** if *expression* is a date expression.

See Also

IsArray Function, **IsDate** Function, **IsEmpty** Function, **IsError** Function, **IsMissing** Function, **IsNull** Function, **IsObject** Function, **TypeName** Function, **Variant Data** Type, **VarType** Function

Example

This example uses the **IsNumeric** function to determine if a variable can be evaluated as a number.

```
Dim MyVar, MyCheck
MyVar = "53"                    ' Assign value.
MyCheck = IsNumeric(MyVar)      ' Returns True.

MyVar = "459.95"                ' Assign value.
MyCheck = IsNumeric(MyVar)      ' Returns True.

MyVar = "45 Help"               ' Assign value.
MyCheck = IsNumeric(MyVar)      ' Returns False.
```

IsObject Function

Returns a **Boolean** value indicating whether an identifier represents an object variable.

Syntax

IsObject(*identifier*)

The required *identifier* argument is a variable name.

Remarks

IsObject is useful only in determining whether a **Variant** is of **VarType vbObject**. This could occur if the **Variant** actually references (or once referenced) an object, or if it contains **Nothing**.

IsObject returns **True** if *identifier* is a variable declared with **Object** type or any valid class type, or if *identifier* is a **Variant** of **VarType vbObject**, or a user-defined object; otherwise, it returns **False**. **IsObject** returns **True** even if the variable has been set to **Nothing**.

Use error trapping to be sure that an object reference is valid.

See Also

IsArray Function, **IsDate** Function, **IsEmpty** Function, **IsError** Function, **IsMissing** Function, **IsNull** Function, **IsNumeric** Function, **Object Data** Type, **Set** Statement, **TypeName** Function, **Variant Data** Type, **VarType** Function

Example

This example uses the **IsObject** function to determine if an identifier represents an object variable. MyObject and YourObject are object variables of the same type. They are generic names used for illustration purposes only.

```
Dim MyInt As Integer, YourObject, MyCheck ' Declare variables.
Dim MyObject As Object
Set YourObject = MyObject              ' Assign an object reference.
MyCheck = IsObject(YourObject)         ' Returns True.
MyCheck = IsObject(MyInt)              ' Returns False.
```

IsolateODBCTrans Property

Sets or returns a value that indicates whether multiple transactions that involve the same Microsoft Jet-connected ODBC data source are isolated (Microsoft Jet workspaces only).

Applies To

Workspace Object

Settings and Return Values

The setting or return value is a **Boolean** data type that is **True** if you want to isolate transactions involving the same ODBC (Open Database Connectivity) connection. **False** (the default) will allow multiple transactions involving the same ODBC connection.

Remarks

In some situations, you need to have multiple simultaneous transactions pending on the same ODBC connection. To do this, you need to open a separate **Workspace** for each transaction. Although each **Workspace** can have its own ODBC connection to the database, this slows system performance. Because transaction isolation isn't usually required, ODBC connections from multiple **Workspace** objects opened by the same user are shared by default.

Some ODBC servers, such as Microsoft SQL Server, don't allow simultaneous transactions on a single connection. If you need to have more than one transaction at a time pending against such a database, set the **IsolateODBCTrans** property to **True** on each **Workspace** as soon as you open it. This forces a separate ODBC connection for each **Workspace**.

Example

This example opens three ODBCDirect workspaces and sets their **IsolateODBCTrans** properties to True so that multiple transactions to the same data source will be isolated from each other.

```
Sub IsolateODBCTransX()

    DBEngine.DefaultType = dbUseJet

    Dim wrkJet1 As Workspace
    Dim wrkJet2 As Workspace
    Dim wrkJet3 As Workspace

    ' Open three ODBCDirect workspaces to separate
    ' transactions involving the same ODBC data source.
    Set wrkJet1 = CreateWorkspace("", "admin", "")
    wrkJet1.IsolateODBCTrans = True

    Set wrkJet2 = CreateWorkspace("", "admin", "")
    wrkJet2.IsolateODBCTrans = True

    Set wrkJet3 = CreateWorkspace("", "admin", "")
    wrkJet3.IsolateODBCTrans = True

    wrkJet1.Close
    wrkJet2.Close
    wrkJet3.Close

End Sub
```

Italic Property

Returns or sets the font style of the **Font** object to either italic or nonitalic.

Applies To

Font Object

Syntax

object.**Italic** [= *boolean*]

The **Italic** property syntax has these parts:

Part	Description
object	An object expression that evaluates to an object in the **Applies To** list.
boolean	A Boolean expression specifying the font style as described in Settings.

Settings

The settings for *boolean* are:

Setting	Description
True	Turns on italic formatting.
False	(Default) Turns off italic formatting.

Remarks

The **Font** object isn't directly available at design time. Instead you set the **Italic** property by selecting a control's **Font** property in the Properties window and clicking the Properties button. In the Font Style box of the Font dialog box, select either Italic or Bold Italic. At run time, however, you set **Italic** directly by specifying its setting for the **Font** object.

See Also

Bold Property, **FontTransparent** Property, **Size** Property (Font), **StrikeThrough** Property, **Underline** Property, **Weight** Property, **Name** Property

Example

This example prints text on a form with each mouse click. To try this example, paste the code into the Declarations section of a form, and then press F5 and click the form twice.

```
Private Sub Form_Click ()
   Font.Bold = Not Font.Bold                    ' Toggle bold.
   Font.StrikeThrough = Not Font.StrikeThrough  ' Toggle strikethrough.
   Font.Italic = Not Font.Italic                ' Toggle italic.
   Font.Underline = Not Font.Underline          ' Toggle underline.
   Font.Size = 16                               ' Set Size property.
```

```
        If Font.Bold Then
            Print "Font weight is " & Font.Weight & " (bold)."
        Else
            Print "Font weight is " & Font.Weight & " (not bold)."

    End If
End Sub
```

Item Method

Returns the indexed member of a collection.

Applies To

Collection Object, **Controls** Collection, **ListItem Object, ListItem** Collection, **OLEObject** Object, **SelBookmarks** Collection, **Splits**Collection

Syntax

object.**Item**(*index*)

The **Item** method syntax has these parts:

Part	Description
object	Required. An object expression that evaluates to an object in the **Applies To** list.
index	Required. An expression that specifies the position of a member of the collection. If a numeric expression, *index* must be a number from 1 to the value of the collection's **Count** property. If a string expression, *index* must correspond to the *key* argument specified when the member was added to the collection.

The following table lists the collections and their corresponding *key* arguments for use with the **Item** method. The string you pass to the **Item** method must match the collection's *key* argument.

Collection	Key argument
Windows	**Caption** property setting
LinkedWindows	**Caption** property setting
CodePanes	No unique string is associated with this collection.
VBProjects	**Name** property setting
VBComponents	**Name** property setting
References	**Name** property setting
Properties	**Name** property setting

Remarks

The *index* argument can be a numeric value or a string containing the title of the object.

Item Method (VB5 Add-ins)

Returns an item from the specified collection by either name or index.

Applies To

Collection Object, **Controls** Collection, **ListItem** Object, **ListItem** Collection, **OLEObject** Object, **SelBookmarks** Collection, **Splits**Collection

Syntax

object.**Item** (*index*)
object.**Item** (*collectionindex,* [*controlindex*]) **As VBControl**
object.**Item** (*var*) **As Member**

The **Item** method syntax has these parts:

Part	Description
object	An object expression that evaluates to an object in the **Applies To** list.
index	Required. A variant expression specifying the name or index in the collection of the object to be accessed.
collectionindex	Required. A numeric expression specifying the index
controlindex	Optional.
var	Required.

Remarks

There is no guarantee that a given index number for a collection will always point to the same item, because items may be added or deleted from the collection. Using index numbers for the collection is useful only when iterating through the whole collection and no items are added or deleted during the iteration.

See Also

Count Property (VB Collections)

Item Property

Returns a specific member of a **Collection** object either by position or by key.

Applies To

DataBindings Collection, **DataObjectFiles** Collection

Syntax

object.**Item**(*index*)

The **Item** property syntax has the following object qualifier and part:

Part	Description
object	Required. An object expression that evaluates to an object in the **Applies To** list.
index	Required. An expression that specifies the position of a member of the collection. If a numeric expression, index must be a number from 1 to the value of the collection's Count property. If a string expression, index must correspond to the key argument specified when the member referred to was added to the collection.

Remarks

If the value provided as index doesn't match any existing member of the collection, an error occurs.

Item is the default property for a collection. Therefore, the following lines of code are equivalent:

```
Print MyCollection(1)
Print MyCollection.Item(1)
```

Item Property (RDO)

Returns a specific member of an Remote Data Objects (RDO) collection object either by position or by key.

Applies To

rdoColumns Collection, **rdoConnections** Collection, **rdoEnvironments** Collection, **rdoErrors** Collection, **rdoParameters** Collection, **rdoPreparedStatements** Collection, **rdoQueries** Collection, **rdoResultsets** Collection, **rdoTables** Collection

Syntax

object.**Item**(*index*)

The **Item** property syntax has these parts:

Part	Description
object	An object expression that evaluates to an object in the **Applies To** list.
index	Required. An expression that specifies the position of a member of the collection. If a numeric expression, index must be a number from 1 to the value of the collection's **Count** property. If a String expression, index must correspond to the key argument specified when the member referred to was added to the collection.

Remarks

Basically, the **Item** property is used to choose a member of the collection either by ordinal number or by a key value.

If the value provided as *index* doesn't match any existing member of the collection, an error occurs.

The **Item** property is the default method for a collection and is rarely used to reference collection members. Therefore, the following lines of code are equivalent:

```
Print MyCollection(1)
Print MyCollection.Item(1)
```

See Also

Name Property (Remote Data)

ItemActivated Event

Occurs when a component is double-clicked in the Project window, and when a project is single-clicked in a project window when there are multiple projects loaded in the IDE.

Applies To

VBComponentsEvents Object, **VBProjectsEvents** Object, **VBProjectsEvents** Property, **VBProjects** Collection

Syntax

Sub *object*_**ItemActivated**(*vbcomponent* **As VBComponent**)
Sub *object*_**ItemActivated**(*vbproject* **As VBProject**)

The **ItemActivated** event syntax has these parts:

Part	Description
object	An object expression that evaluates to an object in the **Applies To** list.
vbcomponent	A **VBComponent** object specifying the name of the component that was double-clicked.
vbproject	A **VBProject** object specifying the name of the project which was double-clicked.

Remarks

The **ItemActivated** event does not occur when a component is double-clicked in the Project window.

ItemAdded Event (Projects, Controls, Components)

Occurs after a project, control, or component is added to the current project.

Applies To

ReferencesEvents Object, **SelectedVBControls** Collection, **SelectedVBControlsEvents** Object, **VBComponentsEvents** Object, **VBControls** Collection, **VBControlsEvents** Object, **VBProjects** Collection, **VBProjectsEvents** Object

Syntax

Sub *object*_**ItemAdded** (*vbproject* **As VBProject**)
Sub *object*_**ItemAdded** (*vbcomponent* **As VBComponent**)
Sub *object*_**ItemAdded** (*vbcontrol* **As VBControl**)

The **ItemAdded** event syntax has these parts:

Part	Description
object	An object expression that evaluates to an object in the **Applies To** list.
vbproject	A **VBProject** object specifying the name of the project that was loaded.
vbcomponent	A **VBComponent** object specifying the name of the component that was loaded.
vbcontrol	A **VBControl** object specifying the name of the control that was loaded.

ItemAdded Event (References)

Occurs after a reference is added.

Applies To

ReferencesEvents Object, **SelectedVBControls** Collection, **SelectedVBControlsEvents** Object, **VBComponentsEvents** Object, **VBControls** Collection, **VBControlsEvents** Object, **VBProjects** Collection, **VBProjectsEvents** Object

Syntax

Sub *object*_**ItemAdded(ByVal** *item* **As Reference)**

The required *item* argument specifies the item that was added.

Remarks

The **ItemAdded** event occurs when a **Reference** is added to the **References** collection.

ItemCheck Event

Occurs when a **ListBox** control **Style** property is set to 1 (checkboxes) and an item's checkbox in the **ListBox** control is selected or cleared.

Applies to

ListBox Control

Syntax

Private Sub *object*_**ItemCheck([***index* **As Integer])**

The **ItemCheck** event syntax has these parts:

Part	Description
object	An object expression that evaluates to an object in the **Applies To** list.
index	An integer that uniquely identifies the item in the listbox which was clicked.

Remarks

Note The **ItemCheck** event does not occur when a list item is only highlighted; rather, it occurs when the check box of the list item is selected or cleared.

The **ItemCheck** event can also occur programmatically whenever an element in Selected array of the **ListBox** is changed (and its **Style** property is set to 1.)

The **ItemCheck** event occurs before the **Click** event.

ItemData Property

Returns or sets a specific number for each item in a **ComboBox** or **ListBox** control.

Applies To

ComboBox Control, **ListBox** Control

Syntax

object.**ItemData**(*index*) [= *number*]

The **ItemData** property syntax has these parts:

Part	Description
object	An object expression that evaluates to an object in the **Applies To** list.
index	The number of a specific item in the object.
number	The number to be associated with the specified item.

Remarks

The **ItemData** property is an array of long integer values with the same number of items as a control's **List** property. You can use the numbers associated with each item to identify the items. For example, you can use an employee's identification number to identify each employee name in a **ListBox** control. When you fill the **ListBox**, also fill the corresponding elements in the **ItemData** array with the employee numbers.

The **ItemData** property is often used as an index for an array of data structures associated with items in a **ListBox** control.

Note When you insert an item into a list with the **AddItem** method, an item is automatically inserted in the **ItemData** array as well. However, the value isn't reinitialized to zero; it retains the value that was in that position before you added the item to the list. When you use the **ItemData** property, be sure to set its value when adding new items to a list.

See Also

AddItem Method, **RemoveItem** Method, **List** Property, **ListIndex** Property, **NewIndex** Property, **Selected** Property, **TopIndex** Property

Example

This example fills a **ListBox** control with employee names and fills the **ItemData** property array with employee numbers using the **NewIndex** property to keep the numbers synchronized with the sorted list. A **Label** control displays the name and number of an item when the user makes a selection. To try this example, paste the code into the Declarations section of a form that contains a **ListBox** and a **Label**. Set the **Sorted** property for the **ListBox** to **True**, and then press F5 and click the **ListBox**.

```
Private Sub Form_Load ()
    ' Fill List1 and ItemData array with
    ' corresponding items in sorted order.
    List1.AddItem "Judy Phelps"
    List1.ItemData(List1.NewIndex) = 42310
    List1.AddItem "Chien Lieu"
    List1.ItemData(List1.NewIndex) = 52855
    List1.AddItem "Mauro Sorrento"
    List1.ItemData(List1.NewIndex) = 64932
    List1.AddItem "Cynthia Bennet"
    List1.ItemData(List1.NewIndex) = 39227
End Sub

Private Sub List1_Click ()
    ' Append the employee number and the employee name.

Msg = List1.ItemData(List1.ListIndex) & " "
    Msg = Msg & List1.List(List1.ListIndex)
    Label1.Caption = Msg
End Sub
```

ItemReloaded Event

Occurs after a component is reloaded.

Applies To

VBComponentsEvents Object

Syntax

Private Sub *object*_**ItemReloaded**(*vbcomponent* **As VBComponent**)

The **ItemReloaded** event syntax has these parts:

Part	Description
object	An object expression that evaluates to an object in the **Applies To** list.
vbcomponent	A **VBComponent** object representing the component that was reloaded.

ItemRemoved Event (Projects, Controls, Components)

Occurs after a project, control, or component is removed from the current project.

Applies To

SelectedVBControls Collection, **SelectedVBControlsEvents** Object, **VBComponentsEvents** Object, **VBControls** Collection, **VBControlsEvents** Object, **VBProjectsEvents** Object, **VBProjects** Collection, **ReferencesEvents** Object

Syntax

Sub *object*_**ItemRemoved** (*vbcontrol* **As VBControl**)
Sub *object*_**ItemRemoved** (*vbproject* **As VBProject**)
Sub *object*_**ItemRemoved** (*vbcomponent* **As VBComponent**)

The **ItemRemoved** event syntax has these parts:

Part	Description
object	An object expression that evaluates to an object in the **Applies To** list.
vbproject	A **VBProject** object specifying the name of the project that was removed.
vbcomponent	A **VBComponent** object specifying the name of the component that was removed.
vbcontrol	A **VBControl** or **SelectedVBControl** object specifying the name of the component that was removed.

ItemRemoved Event (References)

Occurs after a reference is removed from a project.

Applies To

SelectedVBControls Collection, **SelectedVBControlsEvents** Object, **VBComponentsEvents** Object, **VBControls** Collection, **VBControlsEvents** Object, **VBProjectsEvents** Object, **VBProjects** Collection, **ReferencesEvents** Object

Syntax

Sub *object*_**ItemRemoved(ByVal** *item* **As Reference)**

The required *item* argument specifies the **Reference** that was removed.

ItemRenamed Event

Occurs after a project, control, or component is renamed in the current project.

Applies To

VBComponentsEvents Object, **VBControls** Collection, **VBEvents** Object, **VBProjects** Collection, **VBProjectsEvents** Object

Syntax

Sub *object*_**ItemRenamed** (*vbproject* **As VBProject**)
Sub *object*_**ItemRenamed** (*vbcomponent* **As VBComponent**)
Sub *object*_**ItemRenamed** (*vbcontrol* **As VBControl**)

The **ItemRenamed** event syntax has these parts:

Part	Description
object	An object expression that evaluates to an object in the **Applies To** list.
vbproject	A **VBProject** object specifying the name of the project that was renamed.
vbcomponent	A **VBComponent** object specifying the name of the component that was renamed.
vbcontrol	A **VBControl** object specifying the name of the control that was renamed.

ItemSelected Event

Occurs when a component in the Project window or an open designer-window is clicked.

Applies To

VBComponentsEvents Object

Syntax

Sub *object*_**ItemSelected** (*vbcomponent* **As VBComponent**)

The **ItemSelected** event syntax has these parts:

Part	Description
object	An object expression that evaluates to an object in the **Applies To** list.
vbcomponent	A **VBComponent** object specifying the name of the component that was selected.

KeepLocal Property

Sets or returns a value on a table, query, form, report, macro, or module that you do not want to replicate when the database is replicated (Microsoft Jet workspaces only).

Note   Before getting or setting the **KeepLocal** property on a **TableDef**, or **QueryDef** object, you must create it by using the **CreateProperty** method and append it to the **Properties** collection for the object.

Applies To

Document Object, **QueryDef** Object, **TableDef** Object

Settings and Return Values

The setting or return value is a **Text** data type. If you set this property to **"T"**, the object will remain local when the database is replicated. You can't use the **KeepLocal** property on objects after they have been replicated.

Remarks

Once you set the **KeepLocal** property, it will appear in the **Properties** collection for the **Document** object representing the host object.

Before setting the **KeepLocal** property, you should check the value of the **Replicable** property.

After you make a database replicable, all new objects created within the Design Master, or in any other replicas in the set, are local objects. Local objects remain in the replica in which they're created and aren't copied throughout the replica set. Each time you make a new replica in the set, the new replica contains all the replicable objects from the source replica, but none of the local objects from the source replica.

If you create a new object in a replica and want to change it from local to replicable so that all users can use it, you can either create the object in or import it into the Design Master. Be sure to delete the local object from any replicas; otherwise, you will encounter a design error. After the object is part of the Design Master, set the object's **Replicable** property to **True**.

The object on which you are setting the **KeepLocal** property might have already inherited that property from another object. However, the value set by the other object has no effect on the behavior of the object you want to keep local. You must explicitly set the property for each object.

See Also

CreateProperty Method, **Replicable** Property

Example

The following example appends the **KeepLocal** property to the properties collection of a document object for the Utilities module in the Northwind database. You set this property on an object (such as a table) before a database is made replicable. When the database is converted to a Design Master, the object you specified to remain local will not be dispersed to other members of the replica set. Adjust the path to Northwind.mdb as appropriate to its location on your computer.

```
Sub KeepLocalNWObjectX()

    Dim dbsNorthwind As Database
    Dim docTemp As Document
    Dim prpTemp As Property

    Set dbsNorthwind = OpenDatabase("Northwind.mdb")
    Set docTemp = dbsNorthwind.Containers("Modules"). _
        Documents("Utility Functions")
    Set prpTemp = doc.CreateProperty("KeepLocal", _
        dbText, "T")
    docTemp.Properties.Append prpTemp
    dbsNorthwind.Close

End Sub
```

The following code sets the **KeepLocal** property on the specified **TableDef** object to "T". If the **KeepLocal** property doesn't exist, it is created and appended to the table's **Properties** collection, and given a value of "T".

```
Sub SetKeepLocal(tdfTemp As TableDef)

    On Error GoTo ErrHandler

    tdfTemp.Properties("KeepLocal") = "T"

    On Error GoTo 0

    Exit Sub

ErrHandler:

    Dim prpNew As Property

    If Err.Number = 3270 Then
        Set prpNew = tdfTemp.CreateProperty("KeepLocal", _
            dbText, "T")
        tdfTemp.Properties.Append prpNew
    Else
        MsgBox "Error " & Err & ": " & Error
    End If

End Sub
```

KeyColumn Property

Returns or sets a value that specifies if this column is part of the primary key.

Applies To

rdoColumn Object

Syntax

object.**KeyColumn** [= *value*]

The **KeyColumn** property syntax has these parts:

Part	Description
object	An object expression that evaluates to an object in the **Applies To** list.
value	A Boolean expression as described in Settings.

Settings

The **KeyColumn** property has these settings:

Setting	Description
True	If the column is part of the primary key.
False	(Default) If the column is not part of the primary key.

Remarks

This property indicates if the column is part of the primary key for the result set. This property will be read/write when using the client batch cursor library (**CursorDriver** property set to **rdUseClientBatch**) and generates a trappable error when accessed using server-side cursors or ODBC cursor library.

When using the client batch cursor library, you can set this property to indicate which columns make up the primary key of the result set. This assists the cursor library when it builds the WHERE clauses for the update or delete/insert statements during an optimistic batch update.

See Also

BatchUpdate Method, **rdoColumn** Object, **rdoResultset** Object

---

KeyDown, KeyUp Events

Occur when the user presses (**KeyDown**) or releases (**KeyUp**) a key while an object has the focus. (To interpret ANSI characters, use the **KeyPress** event.)

Applies To

CheckBox Control, **ComboBox** Control, **CommandButton** Control, **DBCombo** Control, **DBGrid** Control, **DBList** Control, **DirListBox** Control, **DriveListBox** Control, **FileListBox** Control, **Forms** Object, **Forms** Collection, **HScrollBar**, **VScrollBar** Controls, **ListBox** Control, **ListView** Control, **Masked Edit** Control,

MSFlexGrid Control, **OLE Container** Control, **OptionButton** Control, **PictureBox** Control, **PropertyPage** Object, **RichTextBox** Control, **Slider** Control, **TabStrip** Control, **TextBox** Control, **TreeView** Control, **UserControl** Object, **UserDocument** Object

Syntax

Private Sub Form_KeyDown(*keycode* **As Integer**, *shift* **As Integer**)
Private Sub *object*_**KeyDown**([*index* **As Integer**,]*keycode* **As Integer**, *shift* **As Integer**)
Private Sub Form_KeyUp(*keycode* **As Integer**, *shift* **As Integer**)
Private Sub *object*_**KeyUp**([*index* **As Integer**,]*keycode* **As Integer**, *shift* **As Integer**)

The **KeyDown** and **KeyUp** event syntaxes have these parts:

Part	Description
object	An object expression that evaluates to an object in the **Applies To** list.
index	An integer that uniquely identifies a control if it's in a control array.
keycode	A key code, such as **vbKeyF1** (the F1 key) or **vbKeyHome** (the HOME key). To specify key codes, use the constants in the Visual Basic (VB) object library in the Object Browser.
shift	An integer that corresponds to the state of the SHIFT, CTRL, and ALT keys at the time of the event. The *shift* argument is a bit field with the least-significant bits corresponding to the SHIFT key (bit 0), the CTRL key (bit 1), and the ALT key (bit 2). These bits correspond to the values 1, 2, and 4, respectively. Some, all, or none of the bits can be set, indicating that some, all, or none of the keys are pressed. For example, if both CTRL and ALT are pressed, the value of *shift* is 6.

Remarks

For both events, the object with the focus receives all keystrokes. A form can have the focus only if it has no visible and enabled controls. Although the **KeyDown** and **KeyUp** events can apply to most keys, they're most often used for:

- Extended character keys such as function keys.

- Navigation keys.

- Combinations of keys with standard keyboard modifiers.

- Distinguishing between the numeric keypad and regular number keys.

Use **KeyDown** and **KeyUp** event procedures if you need to respond to both the pressing and releasing of a key.

KeyDown and **KeyUp** aren't invoked for:

- The ENTER key if the form has a **CommandButton** control with the **Default** property set to **True**.

- The ESC key if the form has a **CommandButton** control with the **Cancel** property set to **True**.

- The TAB key.

KeyDown and **KeyUp** interpret the uppercase and lowercase of each character by means of two arguments: *keycode*, which indicates the physical key (thus returning A and a as the same key) and *shift*, which indicates the state of SHIFT+KEY and therefore returns either A or a.

If you need to test for the *shift* argument, you can use the *shift* constants which define the bits within the argument. The constants have the following values:

Constant	Value	Description
vbShiftMask	1	SHIFT key bit mask.
VbCtrlMask	2	CTRL key bit mask.
VbAltMask	4	ALT key bit mask.

The constants act as bit masks that you can use to test for any combination of keys.

You test for a condition by first assigning each result to a temporary integer variable and then comparing *shift* to a bit mask. Use the **And** operator with the *shift* argument to test whether the condition is greater than 0, indicating that the modifier was pressed, as in this example:

```
ShiftDown = (Shift And vbShiftMask) > 0
```

In a procedure, you can test for any combination of conditions, as in this example:

```
If ShiftDown And CtrlDown Then
```

Note If the **KeyPreview** property is set to **True**, a form receives these events before controls on the form receive the events. Use the **KeyPreview** property to create global keyboard-handling routines.

See Also

KeyPreview Property

Example

This example demonstrates a generic keyboard handler that responds to the F2 key and to all the associated ALT, SHIFT, and CTRL key combinations. The key constants are listed in the Visual Basic (VB) object library in the Object Browser. To try this example, paste the code into the **Declarations** section of a form that contains a **TextBox** control, and then press F5 and press F2 with various combinations of the ALT, SHIFT, and CTRL keys.

```
Private Sub Text1_KeyDown (KeyCode As Integer, Shift As Integer)
    Dim ShiftDown, AltDown, CtrlDown, Txt
    ShiftDown = (Shift And vbShiftMask) > 0
    AltDown = (Shift And vbAltMask) > 0
    CtrlDown = (Shift And vbCtrlMask) > 0
    If KeyCode = vbKeyF2 Then   ' Display key combinations.
```

```
    If ShiftDown And CtrlDown And AltDown Then
        Txt = "SHIFT+CTRL+ALT+F2."
    ElseIf ShiftDown And AltDown Then
        Txt = "SHIFT+ALT+F2."
    ElseIf ShiftDown And CtrlDown Then
        Txt = "SHIFT+CTRL+F2."
    ElseIf CtrlDown And AltDown Then
        Txt = "CTRL+ALT+F2."
    ElseIf ShiftDown Then
        Txt = "SHIFT+F2."
    ElseIf CtrlDown Then
    Txt = "CTRL+F2."
    ElseIf AltDown Then
        Txt = "ALT+F2."
    ElseIf SHIFT = 0 Then
        Txt = "F2."
    End If

Text1.Text = "You pressed " & Txt
    End If
End Sub
```

KeyPress Event

Occurs when the user presses and releases an ANSI key.

Applies To

CheckBox Control, **ComboBox** Control, **CommandButton** Control, **DBCombo** Control, **DBGrid** Control, **DBList** Control, **DirListBox** Control, **DriveListBox** Control, **FileListBox** Control, **Form** Object, **Forms** Collection, **HScrollBar**, **VScrollBar** Controls, **ListBox** Control, **ListView** Control, **Masked Edit** Control, **MSFlexGrid** Control, **OLE Container** Control, **OptionButton** Control, **PictureBox** Control, **PropertyPage** Control, **RichTextBox** Control, **Slider** Control, **TabStrip** Control, **TextBox** Control, **TreeView** Control, **UserControl** Object, **UserDocument** Object

Syntax

Private Sub Form_KeyPress(*keyascii* **As Integer**)
Private Sub *object*_**KeyPress**([*index* **As Integer**,]*keyascii* **As Integer**)

The **KeyPress** event syntax has these parts:

Part	Description
object	An object expression that evaluates to an object in the **Applies To** list.
index	An integer that uniquely identifies a control if it's in a control array.
keyascii	An integer that returns a standard numeric ANSI keycode. *Keyascii* is passed by reference; changing it sends a different character to the object. Changing *keyascii* to 0 cancels the keystroke so the object receives no character.

Remarks

The object with the focus receives the event. A form can receive the event only if it has no visible and enabled controls or if the **KeyPreview** property is set to **True**. A KeyPress event can involve any printable keyboard character, the CTRL key combined with a character from the standard alphabet or one of a few special characters, and the ENTER or BACKSPACE key. A **KeyPress** event procedure is useful for intercepting keystrokes entered in a **TextBox** or **ComboBox** control. It enables you to immediately test keystrokes for validity or to format characters as they're typed. Changing the value of the *keyascii* argument changes the character displayed.

You can convert the *keyascii* argument into a character by using the expression:

```
Chr(KeyAscii)
```

You can then perform string operations and translate the character back to an ANSI number that the control can interpret by using the expression:

```
KeyAscii = Asc(char)
```

Use **KeyDown** and **KeyUp** event procedures to handle any keystroke not recognized by **KeyPress**, such as function keys, editing keys, navigation keys, and any combinations of these with keyboard modifiers. Unlike the **KeyDown** and **KeyUp** events, **KeyPress** doesn't indicate the physical state of the keyboard; instead, it passes a character.

KeyPress interprets the uppercase and lowercase of each character as separate key codes and, therefore, as two separate characters. **KeyDown** and **KeyUp** interpret the uppercase and lowercase of each character by means of two arguments: *keycode*, which indicates the physical key (thus returning A and a as the same key), and *shift*, which indicates the state of *shift+key* and therefore returns either A or a.

If the **KeyPreview** property is set to **True**, a form receives the event before controls on the form receive the event. Use the **KeyPreview** property to create global keyboard-handling routines.

Note The ANSI number for the keyboard combination of CTRL+@ is 0. Because Visual Basic recognizes a *keyascii* value of 0 as a zero-length string (""), avoid using CTRL+@ in your applications.

See Also

Change Event, **KeyDown**, **KeyUp** Events, **KeyPreview** Property

Example

This example converts text entered into a **TextBox** control to uppercase. To try this example, paste the code into the **Declarations** section of a form that contains a **TextBox**, and then press F5 and enter something into the **TextBox**.

```
Private Sub Text1_KeyPress (KeyAscii As Integer)
    Char = Chr(KeyAscii)
    KeyAscii = Asc(UCase(Char))
End Sub
```

KeyPreview Property

Returns or sets a value that determines whether keyboard events for forms are invoked before keyboard events for controls. The keyboard events are **KeyDown**, **KeyUp**, and **KeyPress**.

Applies To

PropertyPage Object, **UserControl** Object, **UserDocument** Object, **Form Object**, **Forms** Collection

Syntax

object.**KeyPreview** [= *boolean*]

The **KeyPreview** property syntax has these parts:

Part	Description
object	An object expression that evaluates to an object in the **Applies To** list.
boolean	A Boolean expression that specifies how events are received, as described in Settings.

Settings

The settings for *boolean* are:

Setting	Description
True	The form receives keyboard events first and then the active control.
False	(Default) The active control receives keyboard events; the form doesn't.

Remarks

You can use this property to create a keyboard-handling procedure for a form. For example, when an application uses function keys, you'll want to process the keystrokes at the form level rather than writing code for each control that might receive keystroke events.

If a form has no visible and enabled controls, it automatically receives all keyboard events.

To handle keyboard events only at the form level and not allow controls to receive keyboard events, set *KeyAscii* to 0 in the form's **KeyPress** event, and set *KeyCode* to 0 in the form's **KeyDown** event.

Note   Some controls intercept keyboard events so that the form can't receive them. Examples include the ENTER key when focus is on a **CommandButton** control and arrow keys when focus is on a **ListBox** control.

See Also

KeyDown, **KeyUp** Events, **KeyPress** Event

Example

This example creates a form keyboard handler in the **KeyDown** event. Each of the first four function keys displays a different message. To try this example, paste the code into the **Declarations** section of a form, and then press F5. Once the program is running, press any one of the first four (F1 – F4) function keys.

```
Private Sub Form_Load ()
    KeyPreview = True
End Sub

Private Sub Form_KeyDown (KeyCode As Integer, Shift As Integer)
    Select Case KeyCode
        Case vbKeyF1: MsgBox "F1 is your friend."
        Case vbKeyF2: MsgBox "F2 could copy text."
        Case vbKeyF3: MsgBox "F3 could paste text."
        Case vbKeyF4: MsgBox "F4 could format text."
    End Select
End Sub
```

KeysetSize Property (Remote Data)

Returns or sets a value indicating the number of rows in the keyset buffer.

Applies To

rdoPreparedStatement Object, **rdoQuery** Object**, RemoteData** Control

Syntax

object.**KeysetSize** [= *value*]

The **KeysetSize** property syntax has these parts:

Part	Description
object	An object expression that evaluates to an object in the **Applies To** list.
value	A **Long** expression as described in Settings.

Settings

The settings for *value* must be greater than or equal to the **RowsetSize** property.

Remarks

The **KeysetSize** property is a value that specifies the number of rows in the keyset for a keyset- or dynamic-type **rdoResultset** cursor. If the keyset size is 0 (the default), the cursor is fully keyset-driven. If the keyset size is greater than 0, the cursor is mixed (keyset-driven within the keyset and dynamic outside the keyset).

If **KeysetSize** is a value greater than **RowsetSize**, the value defines the number of rows in the keyset that are to be buffered by the driver.

Not all ODBC data sources support keyset cursors.

> **Note** Because version 2.5 of the Microsoft SQL Server ODBC driver does not support mixed-style cursors, if you set a *value*, **KeysetSize** is reset to 0 and the driver returns error 01S02: `"Option value changed."`

> **Warning** When using **rdConcurLock** concurrency (pessimistic), the **KeysetSize** determines the number of rows locked when the cursor is first opened. The entire keyset remains locked as long as the cursor remains open.

See Also

MaxRows Property (Remote Data), **RowsetSize** Property (Remote Data)

Kill Statement

Deletes files from a disk.

Syntax

Kill *pathname*

The required *pathname* argument is a string expression that specifies one or more file names to be deleted. The *pathname* may include the directory or folder, and the drive.

Remarks

Kill supports the use of multiple-character (*) and single-character (**?**) wildcards to specify multiple files.

An error occurs if you try to use **Kill** to delete an open file.

Note To delete directories, use the **RmDir** statement.

See Also

RmDir Statement

Example

This example uses the **Kill** statement to delete a file from a disk.

```
' Assume TESTFILE is a file containing some data.
Kill "TestFile"    ' Delete file.

' Delete all *.TXT files in current directory.
Kill "*.TXT"
```

KillDoc Method

Immediately terminates the current print job.

Applies To

Printer Object**, Printers** Collection

Syntax

object.**KillDoc**

The *object* placeholder represents an object expression that evaluates to an object in the **Applies To** list.

If the operating system's Print Manager is handling the print job (the Print Manager is running and has background printing enabled), **KillDoc** deletes the current print job and the printer receives nothing.

If Print Manager isn't handling the print job (background printing isn't enabled), some or all of the data may be sent to the printer before **KillDoc** can take effect. In this case, the printer driver resets the printer when possible and terminates the print job.

See Also

EndDoc Method

Example

This example uses the **KillDoc** method to terminate the current print job. To try this example, paste the code into the Declarations section of a form, and then press F5 and click the form.

```
Private Sub Form_Click()
   For i = 1 To 40
      Printer.CurrentX = 1440        ' Set left margin.
      Printer.CurrentY = (i * 300)   ' Advance page to next line.
      Printer.Print "This is line" & Str$(i) & " of text."
      On Error Resume Next           ' Catch any printer error.
      If i = 26 Then
         Printer.KillDoc             ' Terminate print job abruptly.
         Printer.EndDoc
         End
      End If
   Next i
End Sub
```

Label Control

A **Label** control is a graphical control you can use to display text that a user can't change directly.

Syntax

Label

Remarks

You can write code that changes the text displayed by a **Label** control in response to events at run time. For example, if your application takes a few minutes to commit a change, you can display a processing-status message in a **Label**. You can also use a **Label** to identify a control, such as a **TextBox** control, that doesn't have its own **Caption** property.

Set the **AutoSize** and **WordWrap** properties if you want the **Label** to properly display variable-length lines or varying numbers of lines.

A **Label** control can also act as a destination in a DDEconversation. Set the **LinkTopic** property to establish a link, set the **LinkItem** property to specify an item for the conversation, and set the **LinkMode** property to activate the link. When these properties have been set, Visual Basic attempts to initiate the conversation and displays a message if it's unable to do so.

Set the **UseMnemonic** property to **True** if you want to define a character in the **Caption** property of the **Label** as an access key. When you define an access key in a **Label** control, the user can press and hold down ALT+ the character you designate to move the focus to the next control in the tab order.

Properties

Alignment Property, **Appearance** Property, **AutoSize** Property, **BackColor, ForeColor** Properties, **BackStyle** Property, **BorderStyle** Property, **Caption** Property, **Container** Property, **DataChanged** Property, **DataField** Property, **DataSource** Property, **DragIcon** Property, **DragMode** Property, **Enabled** Property, **Font** Property, **FontBold, FontItalic, FontStrikethru, FontUnderline** Properties, **FontName** Property, **Height, Width** Properties, **Index** Property, **Left, Top** Properties, **LinkItem** Property, **LinkMode** Property, **LinkTimeout** Property, **LinkTopic** Property, **MouseIcon** Property, **MousePointer** Property, **Name** Property, **OLEDrag** Method, **OLEDropMode** Property, **Parent** Property, **TabIndex** Property, **Tag** Property, **ToolTipText** Property, **UseMnemonic** Property, **Visible** Property, **WhatsThisHelpID** Property, **WordWrap** Property

Events

Click Event, **DblClick** Event, **DragDrop** Event, **DragOver** Event, **LinkClose** Event, **LinkError** Event, **LinkNotify** Event, **LinkOpen** Event, **MouseDown, MouseUp** Events, **MouseMove** Event

Methods

Refresh Method, **Drag** Method, **LinkExecute** Method, **LinkPoke** Method, **LinkRequest** Method, **LinkSend** Method, **Move** Method, **ZOrder** Method, **OLEDrag** Method, **ShowWhatsThis** Method

See Also

TextBox Control, **TabIndex** Property, **AutoSize** Property, **LinkItem** Property, **LinkMode** Property, **LinkTopic** Property, **WordWrap** Property, **Caption** Property

LargeChange, SmallChange Properties

- **LargeChange**—Returns or sets the amount of change to the **Value** property setting in a scroll bar control (**HScrollBar** or **VScrollBar**) when the user clicks the area between the scroll box and scroll arrow.

- **SmallChange**—Returns or sets the amount of change to the **Value** property setting in a scroll bar control when the user clicks a scroll arrow.

Applies To

UserDocument Object, **HScrollBar, VScrollBar** Controls

Syntax

object.**LargeChange** [= *number*]
   object.**SmallChange** [= *number*]

The **LargeChange** and **SmallChange** property syntaxes have these parts:

Part	Description
object	An object expression that evaluates to an object in the **Applies To** list.
number	An integer that specifies the amount of change to the **Value** property.

Remarks

For both properties, you can specify an integer between 1 and 32,767, inclusive. By default, each property is set to 1.

The Microsoft Windows operating environment automatically sets proportional scrolling increments for scroll bars on **MDI Form** objects, **ComboBox** controls, and **ListBox** controls based on the amount of data in the object. For the **HScrollBar** and **VScrollBar** controls, however, you must specify these increments. Use **LargeChange** and **SmallChange** to set scrolling increments appropriate to how the scroll bar is being used.

Typically, you set **LargeChange** and **SmallChange** at design time. You can also reset them in code at run time when the scrolling increment must change dynamically.

Note You set the maximum and minimum ranges of the **HScrollBar** and **VScrollBar** controls with the **Max** and **Min** properties.

See Also

Change Event, **Value** Property, **Max**, **Min** Properties (Scroll Bar)

Example

This example uses a scroll bar to move a **PictureBox** control across the form. To try this example, paste the code into the Declarations section of a form that contains a small **PictureBox** control and an **HScrollBar** control, and then press F5 and click the scroll bar.

```
Private Sub Form_Load ()
   HScroll1.Max = 100' Set maximum value.
   HScroll1.LargeChange = 20  ' Cross in 5 clicks.
   HScroll1.SmallChange = 5' Cross in 20 clicks.
   Picture1.Left = 0 ' Start picture at left.
   Picture1.BackColor = QBColor(3)   ' Set color of picture box.
End Sub
Private Sub HScroll1_Change ()
   ' Move picture according to scroll bar.
   Picture1.Left = (HScroll1.Value / 100) * ScaleWidth
End Sub
```

LastDLLError Property

Returns a system error code produced by a call to a dynamic-link library (DLL). Read-only.

Applies To

Err Object

Remarks

The **LastDLLError** property applies only to DLL calls made from Visual Basic code. When such a call is made, the called function usually returns a code indicating success or failure, and the **LastDLLError** property is filled. Check the documentation for the DLL's functions to determine the return values that indicate success or failure. Whenever the failure code is returned, the Visual Basic application should immediately check the **LastDLLError** property. No exception is raised when the **LastDLLError** property is set.

See Also

Declare Statement, **Err** Object, **Description** Property, **HelpContext** Property, **HelpFile** Property, **Number** Property, **Source** Property, **HelpContextID** Property

Example

When pasted into a **UserForm** module, the following code causes an attempt to call a DLL function. The call fails because the argument that is passed in (a null pointer) generates an error, and in any event, SQL can't be cancelled if it isn't running. The code following the call checks the return of the call, and then prints at the **LastDLLError** property of the **Err** object to reveal the error code.

```
Private Declare Function SQLCancel Lib "ODBC32.dll" _
(ByVal hstmt As Long) As Integer

Private Sub UserForm_Click()
    Dim RetVal
    ' Call with invalid argument.
    RetVal = SQLCancel(myhandle&)
    ' Check for SQL error code.
    If RetVal = -2 Then
       'Display the information code.
       MsgBox "Error code is :" & Err.LastDllError
    End If
End Sub
```

LastModified Property

Returns a bookmark indicating the most recently added or changed record.

Applies To

Dynaset-Type Recordset Object, **Recordset** Object, **Snapshot-Type Recordset** Object, **Table-Type Recordset** Object, **Dynamic-Type Recordset** Object

Return Values

The return value is a **Variant** array of Byte data.

Remarks

You can use the **LastModified** property to move to the most recently added or updated record. Use the **LastModified** property with table- and dynaset-type **Recordset** objects. A record must be added or modified in the **Recordset** object itself in order for the **LastModified** property to have a value.

See Also

Bookmark Property, **Bookmarkable** Property, **DateCreated**, **LastUpdated** Properties

Example

This example uses the **LastModified** property to move the current record pointer to both a record that has been modified and a newly created record.

```
Sub LastModifiedX()

    Dim dbsNorthwind As Database
    Dim rstEmployees As Recordset
    Dim strFirst As String
    Dim strLast As String

    Set dbsNorthwind = OpenDatabase("Northwind.mdb")
    Set rstEmployees = _
        dbsNorthwind.OpenRecordset("Employees", _
        dbOpenDynaset)

    With rstEmployees
        ' Store current data.
        strFirst = !FirstName
        strLast = !LastName
        ' Change data in current record.
        .Edit
        !FirstName = "Julie"
        !LastName = "Warren"
        .Update
```

```
            ' Move current record pointer to the most recently
            ' changed or added record.
            .Bookmark = .LastModified
            Debug.Print _
               "Data in LastModified record after Edit: " & _
               !FirstName & " " & !LastName

            ' Restore original data because this is a demonstration.
            .Edit
            !FirstName = strFirst
            !LastName = strLast
            .Update

            ' Add new record.
            .AddNew
            !FirstName = "Roger"
            !LastName = "Harui"
            .Update
            ' Move current record pointer to the most recently
            ' changed or added record.
            .Bookmark = .LastModified
            Debug.Print _
               "Data in LastModified record after AddNew: " & _
               !FirstName & " " & !LastName

            ' Delete new record because this is a demonstration.
            .Delete
            .Close
        End With

        dbsNorthwind.Close

    End Sub
```

LastModified Property (Remote Data)

Returns a bookmark indicating the most recently added or changed row.

Applies To

rdoResultset Object

Syntax

object.**LastModified**

The *object* placeholder represents an object expression that evaluates to an object in the **Applies To** list.

Return Values

The return value for this property is a **Variant**(string) data type, as described in Remarks.

Remarks

After you use the **AddNew** method to add a new row, or edit an existing row using the **Update** method, the **LastModified** property returns a bookmark as a pointer to the row most recently modified—providing the keyset supports additions. That is, if new rows are added to the keyset as well as the underlying database table(s), the **LastModified** property will point to this new row in the keyset.

To position the current row pointer to this row, set the **Bookmark** property of the (same) **rdoResultset** object to the **LastModified** property.

If there have been no modifications against this **rdoResultset**, then the **LastModified** property returns 0.

Not all types of **rdoResultsets** support additions to their keysets so the **LastModified** property might return 0 after a row has just been added. For example, while a ODBC cursor static keyset can be updated, its rowset cannot be added to. Inserts are performed on the database, but not to the keyset, so the **LastModified** property always returns 0 in this case.

Server-side keyset cursors support additions to the keyset so the **AddNew** method sets the **LastModified** property—as does the **Update** method.

Client-side static cursors do not add new rows to the cursor's membership, thus the **LastModified** property value is undefined when using the **AddNew** method. However, it is defined after the **Update** method is used. Server-side static cursors are read-only, so the **LastModified** property is not relevant in this case.

Dynamic and forward-only cursors do not support bookmarks (as indicated by the **Bookmarkable** property returning False), so the **LastModified** property is not relevant in these cursors.

The client batch cursor library also supports the **LastModified** property. For static cursors, new rows are added to the cursor membership so the **AddNew** method sets the **LastModified** property—as does the **Update** method.

See Also

rdoResultset Object, **Bookmark** Property (Remote Data), **Bookmarkable** Property (Remote Data)

Example

This example illustrates use of the **LastModified** property to reposition the current row pointer to the row most recently modified by RDO. The code opens a connection against SQL Server and creates a keyset cursor-based query on the Authors table. The query expects a single parameter to pass in the name of the Author to edit. Once selected, edited and updated, the row pointer is repositioned to the last row modified by setting the bookmark property of the **rdoResultset** to the **LastModified** property.

```
Option Explicit
Dim er As rdoError
Dim cn As New rdoConnection
Dim qy As New rdoQuery
Dim rs As rdoResultset
Dim col As rdoColumn

Private Sub TestLM_Click()
qy(0) = LookFor.Text

rs.Edit
rs!City = NewCity.Text   ' a TextBox control
rs.Update

rs.Bookmark = rs.LastModified

'Simply show data in picture control
Pic.Cls   'Clear the picture control.

For Each col In rs.rdoColumns
    Pic.Print col.Name,
Next
Pic.Print String(80, "-")
For Each col In rs.rdoColumns
    Pic.Print col,
Next

End Sub

Private Sub Form_Load()
cn.CursorDriver = rdUseOdbc
cn.Connect = "uid=;pwd=;server=sequel;" _
    & "driver={SQL Server};database=pubs;dsn='';"
cn.EstablishConnection

With qy
    .Name = "ShowWhite"
    .SQL = "Select * from Authors " _
        & " where Au_LName like ?"
    .LockType = rdConcurReadOnly
    .CursorType = rdOpenForwardOnly
    .RowsetSize = 1
    Set .ActiveConnection = cn
End With

qy(0) = LookFor.Text      ' a textbox control
Set rs = qy.OpenResultset(rdOpenKeyset, rdConcurRowver)

Exit Sub
End Sub
```

LastQueryResults Property

Returns a reference to the **rdoResultset** object generated by the last query – if any.

Applies To

rdoConnection Object

Syntax

object.**LastQueryResults**

The *object* placeholder represents an object expression that evaluates to an object in the **Applies To** list.

Return Values

The **LastQueryResults** property return value is an object expression that specifies a valid **rdoResultset** or Nothing if there is no result set available.

Remarks

This new property will contain a reference to the **rdoResultset** object generated by the last query executed on this connection, if any. The necessity of this property comes from the Queries as Methods feature, allowing the developer to call their queries and stored procedures as methods of the parent connection object. Since stored procedures can pass back a return value as well as resultsets, the developer needs this property in order to get a reference to the result set created during the last query as method call. The developer would use this property as shown below:

```
Dim RetCode As Long
Dim rs as rdoResultset
RetCode = MyConnection.MyQuery(x,y,z)
Set rs = MyConnection.LastQueryResults
```

This property is set back to "Nothing" on the next query execution on the connection. This property will be set for any query executed on the connection, even if the developer used the **OpenResultset** or **Execute** methods instead of calling the query as a method of the connection object.

See Also

rdoConnection Object, **rdoQuery** Object, **rdoResultset** Object

LastUsedPath Property

Returns or sets the last path used for the file dialog boxes used in Visual Basic, such as the **Open Project** dialog box.

Applies To

VBE Object

Syntax

object.**LastUsedPath** ([*pathname* **As String**])

The *object* placeholder represents an object expression that evaluates to an object in the **Applies To** list.

The **LastUsedPath** property syntax has these parts:

Part	Description
object	An object expression that evaluates to an object in the **Applies To** list.
pathname	(Optional) A string containing the last path name used for a file dialog box.

LBound Function

Returns a **Long** containing the smallest available subscript for the indicated dimension of an array.

Syntax

LBound(*arrayname*[, *dimension*])

The **LBound** function syntax has these parts:

Part	Description
arrayname	Required. Name of the array variable; follows standard variable naming conventions.
dimension	Optional; **Variant** (**Long**). Whole number indicating which dimension's lower bound is returned. Use 1 for the first dimension, 2 for the second, and so on. If *dimension* is omitted, 1 is assumed.

Remarks

The **LBound** function is used with the **UBound** function to determine the size of an array. Use the **UBound** function to find the upper limit of an array dimension.

LBound returns the values in the following table for an array with the following dimensions:

```
Dim A(1 To 100, 0 To 3, -3 To 4)
```

Statement	Return Value
`LBound(A, 1)`	1
`LBound(A, 2)`	0
`LBound(A, 3)`	-3

The default lower bound for any dimension is either 0 or 1, depending on the setting of the **Option Base** statement. The base of an array created with the **Array** function is zero; it is unaffected by **Option Base**.

Arrays for which dimensions are set using the **To** clause in a **Dim**, **Private**, **Public**, **ReDim**, or **Static** statement can have any integer value as a lower bound.

See Also

Dim Statement, **Option Base** Statement, **Private** Statement, **Public** Statement, **ReDim** Statement, **Static** Statement, **UBound** Function

Example

This example uses the **LBound** function to determine the smallest available subscript for the indicated dimension of an array. Use the **Option Base** statement to override the default base array subscript value of 0.

```
Dim Lower
Dim MyArray(1 To 10, 5 To 15, 10 To 20) ' Declare array variables.
Dim AnyArray(10)
Lower = Lbound(MyArray, 1)              ' Returns 1.
Lower = Lbound(MyArray, 3)              ' Returns 10.
Lower = Lbound(AnyArray)               ' Returns 0 or 1, depending on
                                       ' setting of Option Base.
```

LBound Property

Returns the lowest ordinal value of a control in a control array.

Syntax

object.**LBound**

The *object* placeholder represents an object expression that evaluates to an object in the **Applies To** list.

Remarks

The **LBound** property setting is equal to the **Index** property value of the first control in the array. Typically this value is 0 because Visual Basic automatically assigns an **Index** value of 0 to the first control in a control array. If you manually change the **Index** value for the first control in an array to some other value (for example, 1), **LBound** returns the value you manually assigned to **Index** (in this example, 1).

See Also

UBound Property, **Count** Property (VB Collections), **Index** Property (Control Array)

Example

This example prints the values of these two properties for a control array. Put an **OptionButton** control on a form, and set its **Index** property to 0 (to create a control array). To try this example, paste the code into the Declarations section of a form, and then press F5 and click the form.

```
Private Sub Form_Paint ()
   Static FlagFormPainted As Integer
   If FlagFormPainted <> True Then ' When form is painting for first time,
      For i = 1 To 3
         Load Option1(i)' add three option buttons to array.
         Option1(i).Top = Option1(i - 1).Top + 350
         Option1(i).Visible = True
      Next I
      For I =  0 to 3' Put captions on the option buttons.
         Option1(i).Caption = "Option #" & CStr(i)
      Next I
      Option1(0).Value = True ' Select first option button.

FlagFormPainted = True   ' Form is done painting.
   End If
End Sub
Private Sub Form_Click ()
   Print "Control array's Count property is " & Option1().Count
   Print "Control array's LBound property is " & Option1().LBound
   Print "Control array's UBound property is " & Option1().UBound
End Sub
```

LCase Function

Returns a **String** that has been converted to lowercase.

Syntax

LCase(*string*)

The required *string* argument is any valid string expression. If *string* contains **Null**, Null is returned.

Remarks

Only uppercase letters are converted to lowercase; all lowercase letters and non-letter characters remain unchanged.

See Also

UCase Function

Example

This example uses the **LCase** function to return a lowercase version of a string.

```
Dim UpperCase, LowerCase
Uppercase = "Hello World 1234"        ' String to convert.
Lowercase = Lcase(UpperCase)          ' Returns "hello world 1234".
```

Left Function

Returns a **Variant** (**String**) containing a specified number of characters from the left side of a string.

Syntax

Left(*string*, *length*)

The **Left** function syntax has these named arguments:

Part	Description
string	Required. String expression from which the leftmost characters are returned. If *string* contains **Null**, Null is returned.
length	Required; **Variant** (**Long**). Numeric expression indicating how many characters to return. If 0, a zero-length string ("") is returned. If greater than or equal to the number of characters in *string*, the entire string is returned.

Remarks

To determine the number of characters in *string*, use the **Len** function.

Note Use the **LeftB** function with byte data contained in a string. Instead of specifying the number of characters to return, *length* specifies the number of bytes.

See Also

Len Function, **Mid** Function, **Right** Function

Example

This example uses the **Left** function to return a specified number of characters from the left side of a string.

```
Dim AnyString, MyStr
AnyString = "Hello World"    ' Define string.
MyStr = Left(AnyString, 1)   ' Returns "H".
MyStr = Left(AnyString, 7)   ' Returns "Hello W".
MyStr = Left(AnyString, 20)  ' Returns "Hello World".
```

Left, Top Properties

- **Left**—returns or sets the distance between the internal left edge of an object and the left edge of its container.

- **Top**—returns or sets the distance between the internal top edge of an object and the top edge of its container.

Applies To

CheckBox Control, **Column** Control, **ComboBox** Control, **CommandButton** Control, **CommonDialog** Control, **Data** Control, **DBCombo** Control, **DBGrid**

Control, **DBList** Control, **DirListBox** Control, **DriveListBox** Control, **FileListBox** Control, **Form** Object**, Forms** Collection, **Frame** Control, **HScrollBar, VScrollBar** Controls, **Image** Control, **Label** Control, **ListBox** Control, **MDIForm** Object, **OLE Container** Control, **OptionButton** Control, **PictureBox** Control, **RemoteData** Control, **Shape** Control, **TextBox** Control, **Timer** Control

Syntax

object.**Left** [= *value*]
object.**Top** [= *value*]

The **Left** and **Top** property syntaxes have these parts:

Part	Description
object	An object expression that evaluates to an object in the **Applies To** list.
value	A numeric expression specifying distance.

Remarks

For a form, the **Left** and **Top** properties are always expressed in twips; for a control, they are measured in units depending on the coordinate system of its container. The values for these properties change as the object is moved by the user or by code. For the **CommonDialog** and **Timer** controls, these properties aren't available at run time.

For either property, you can specify a single-precision number.

Use the **Left**, **Top**, **Height**, and **Width** properties for operations based on an object's external dimensions, such as moving or resizing. Use the **ScaleLeft**, **ScaleTop**, **ScaleHeight**, and **ScaleWidth** properties for operations based on an object's internal dimensions, such as drawing or moving objects that are contained within the object. The scale-related properties apply only to **PictureBox** controls and **Form** and **Printer** objects.

See Also

Move Method, **ScaleHeight**, **ScaleWidth** Properties, **ScaleLeft**, **ScaleTop** Properties, **ScaleMode** Property

Example

This example sets the size of a form to 75 percent of screen size and centers the form when it's loaded. To try this example, paste the code into the Declarations section of a form, and then press F5 and click the form.

```
Private Sub Form_Click ()
    Width = Screen.Width * .75 ' Set width of form.
    Height = Screen.Height * .75      ' Set height of form.
    Left = (Screen.Width - Width) / 2 ' Center form horizontally.
    Top = (Screen.Height - Height) / 2 ' Center form vertically.
End Sub
```

LegalCopyright Property

Returns or sets a string value containing legal copyright information about the running application. Read-only at run time.

Applies To

App Object

Syntax

object.**LegalCopyright**

The *object* placeholder represents an object expression that evaluates to an object in the **Applies To** list.

Remarks

You can set this property at design time in the **Type** box in the **Make** tab of the **Project Properties** dialog box.

See Also

Comments Property, **CompanyName** Property, **FileDescription** Property, **LegalTrademarks** Property, **ProductName** Property

---

LegalTrademarks Property

Returns or sets a string value containing legal trademark information about the running application. Read-only at run time.

Applies To

App Object

Syntax

object.**LegalTrademarks**

The *object* placeholder represents an object expression that evaluates to an object in the **Applies To** list.

Remarks

You can set this property at design time in the **Type** box in the **Make** tab of the **Project Properties** dialog box.

See Also

Comments Property, **CompanyName** Property, **FileDescription** Property, **LegalCopyright** Property, **ProductName** Property

Len Function

Returns a **Long** containing the number of characters in a string or the number of bytes required to store a variable.

Syntax

Len(*string* | *varname*)

The **Len** function syntax has these parts:

Part	Description
string	Any valid string expression. If *string* contains **Null**, Null is returned.
Varname	Any valid variable name. If *varname* contains **Null**, **Null** is returned. If *varname* is a **Variant**, **Len** treats it the same as a **String** and always returns the number of characters it contains.

Remarks

One (and only one) of the two possible arguments must be specified. With user-defined types, **Len** returns the size as it will be written to the file.

Note Use the **LenB** function with byte data contained in a string. Instead of returning the number of characters in a string, **LenB** returns the number of bytes used to represent that string. With user-defined types, **LenB** returns the in-memory size, including any padding between elements.

Note **Len** may not be able to determine the actual number of storage bytes required when used with variable-length strings in user-defined data types.

See Also

Data Type Summary, **InStr** Function

Example

This example uses the **Len** function to return the number of characters in a string or the number of bytes required to store a variable. The **Type...End Type** block defining CustomerRecord must be preceded by the keyword **Private** if it appears in a class module. In a standard module, a **Type** statement can be **Public**.

```
Type CustomerRecord              ' Define user-defined type.
    ID As Integer                ' Place this definition in a
    Name As String * 10          ' standard module.
    Address As String * 30
End Type

Dim Customer As CustomerRecord   ' Declare variables.
Dim MyInt As Integer, MyCur As Currency
Dim MyString, MyLen
MyString = "Hello World"         ' Initialize variable.
MyLen = Len(MyInt)               ' Returns 2.
MyLen = Len(Customer)            ' Returns 42.
MyLen = Len(MyString)            ' Returns 11.
MyLen = Len(MyCur)               ' Returns 8.
```

Let Statement

Assigns the value of an expression to a variable or property.

Syntax

[**Let**] *varname* = *expression*

The **Let** statement syntax has these parts:

Part	Description
Let	Optional. Explicit use of the **Let** keyword is a matter of style, but it is usually omitted.
varname	Required. Name of the variable or property; follows standard variable naming conventions.
expression	Required. Value assigned to the variable or property.

Remarks

A value expression can be assigned to a variable or property only if it is of a data type that is compatible with the variable. You can't assign string expressions to numeric variables, and you can't assign numeric expressions to string variables. If you do, an error occurs at compile time.

Variant variables can be assigned either string or numeric expressions. However, the reverse is not always true. Any **Variant** except a **Null** can be assigned to a string variable, but only a **Variant** whose value can be interpreted as a number can be assigned to a numeric variable. Use the **IsNumeric** function to determine if the **Variant** can be converted to a number.

Caution   Assigning an expression of one numeric type to a variable of a different numeric type coerces the value of the expression into the numeric type of the resulting variable.

Let statements can be used to assign one record variable to another only when both variables are of the same user-defined type. Use the **LSet** statement to assign record variables of different user-defined types. Use the **Set** statement to assign object references to variables.

See Also

Data Type Summary, **Variant Data** Type, **Const** Statement, **Set** Statement, **IsNumeric** Function, **LSet** Statement

Example

This example assigns the values of expressions to variables using the explicit **Let** statement.

```
Dim MyStr, MyInt
' The following variable assignments use the Let statement.
Let MyStr = "Hello World"
Let MyInt = 5
```

The following are the same assignments without the **Let** statement.

```
Dim MyStr, MyInt
MyStr = "Hello World"
MyInt = 5
```

Like Operator

Used to compare two strings.

result = *string* **Like** *pattern*

The **Like** operator syntax has these parts:

Part	Description
result	Required; any numeric variable.
string	Required; any string expression.
pattern	Required; any string expression conforming to the pattern-matching conventions described in Remarks.

If *string* matches *pattern*, *result* is **True**; if there is no match, *result* is **False**. If either *string* or *pattern* is **Null**, *result* is **Null**.

The behavior of the **Like** operator depends on the **Option Compare** statement. The default string-comparison method for each module is **Option Compare Binary**.

Option Compare Binary results in string comparisons based on a sort order derived from the internal binary representations of the characters. In Microsoft Windows, sort order is determined by the code page. In the following example, a typical binary sort order is shown:

$A < B < E < Z < a < b < e < z < À < Ê < Ø < à < ê < ø$

Option Compare Text results in string comparisons based on a case-insensitive, textual sort order determined by your system's locale. When you sort The same characters using **Option Compare Text**, the following text sort order is produced:

$(A=a) < (À=à) < (B=b) < (E=e) < (Ê=ê) < (Z=z) < (Ø=ø)$

Built-in pattern matching provides a versatile tool for string comparisons. The pattern-matching features allow you to use wildcard characters, character lists, or character ranges, in any combination, to match strings. The following table shows the characters allowed in *pattern* and what they match:

Characters in *pattern*	Matches in *string*
?	Any single character.
*	Zero or more characters.
#	Any single digit (0–9).
[*charlist*]	Any single character in *charlist*.
[!*charlist*]	Any single character not in *charlist*.

A group of one or more characters (*charlist*) enclosed in brackets ([ ]) can be used to match any single character in *string* and can include almost any character code, including digits.

Note To match the special characters left bracket ([), question mark (**?**), number sign (**#**), and asterisk (*****), enclose them in brackets. The right bracket (]) can't be used within a group to match itself, but it can be used outside a group as an individual character.

By using a hyphen (–) to separate the upper and lower bounds of the range, *charlist* can specify a range of characters. For example, [A-Z] results in a match if the corresponding character position in *string* contains any uppercase letters in the range A–Z. Multiple ranges are included within the brackets without delimiters.

The meaning of a specified range depends on the character ordering valid at run time (as determined by **Option Compare** and the locale setting of the system the code is running on). Using the **Option Compare Binary** example, the range [A-E] matches A, B and E. With **Option Compare Text**, [A-E] matches A, a, À, à, B, b, E, e. The range does not match Ê or ê because accented characters fall after unaccented characters in the sort order.

Other important rules for pattern matching include the following:

- An exclamation point (!) at the beginning of *charlist* means that a match is made if any character except the characters in *charlist* is found in *string*. When used outside brackets, the exclamation point matches itself.

- A hyphen (–) can appear either at the beginning (after an exclamation point if one is used) or at the end of *charlist* to match itself. In any other location, the hyphen is used to identify a range of characters.

- When a range of characters is specified, they must appear in ascending sort order (from lowest to highest). [A-Z] is a valid pattern, but [Z-A] is not.

- The character sequence [] is considered a zero-length string ("").

In some languages, there are special characters in the alphabet that represent two separate characters. For example, several languages use the character "æ" to represent the characters "a" and "e" when they appear together. The **Like** operator recognizes that the single special character and the two individual characters are equivalent.

When a language that uses a special character is specified in the system locale settings, an occurrence of the single special character in either *pattern* or *string* matches the equivalent 2-character sequence in the other string. Similarly, a single special character in *pattern* enclosed in brackets (by itself, in a list, or in a range) matches the equivalent 2-character sequence in *string*.

See Also

Option Compare Statement, **Operator** Summary, **Operator** Precedence, **Comparison** Operators, **InStr** Function, **StrComp** Function

Example

This example uses the **Like** operator to compare a string to a pattern.

```
Dim MyCheck
MyCheck = "aBBBa" Like "a*a"              ' Returns True.
MyCheck = "F" Like "[A-Z]"               ' Returns True.
MyCheck = "F" Like "[!A-Z]"              ' Returns False.
MyCheck = "a2a" Like "a#a"               ' Returns True.
MyCheck = "aM5b" Like "a[L-P]#[!c-e]"    ' Returns True.
MyCheck = "BAT123khg" Like "B?T*"        ' Returns True.
MyCheck = "CAT123khg" Like "B?T*"        ' Returns False.
```

Line Control

A **Line** control is a graphical control displayed as a horizontal, vertical, or diagonal line.

Syntax

Line

Remarks

You can use a **Line** control at design time to draw lines on forms. At run time, you can use a **Line** control instead of, or in addition to, the **Line** method. Lines drawn with the **Line** control remain on the form even if the **AutoRedraw** property setting is **False**. **Line** controls can be displayed on forms, in picture boxes, and in frames. You can't use the **Move** method to move a **Line** control at run time, but you can move or resize it by altering its **X1**, **X2**, **Y1**, and **Y2** properties. The effect of setting the **BorderStyle** property depends on the setting of the **BorderWidth** property. If **BorderWidth** isn't 1 and **BorderStyle** isn't 0 or 6, **BorderStyle** is set to 1.

Properties

BorderColor Property, **BorderStyle** Property, **BorderWidth** Property, **Container** Property, **DrawMode** Property, **Index** Property, **Name** Property, **Parent** Property, **Tag** Property, **Visible** Property, **X1, Y1, X2, Y2** Properties

Methods

Refresh Method**, ZOrder** Method

See Also

Move Method, **Frame** Control, **PictureBox** Control, **BorderStyle** Property, **BorderWidth** Property

Line Input # Statement

Reads a single line from an open sequential file and assigns it to a **String** variable.

Syntax

Line Input #*filenumber*, *varname*

The **Line Input #** statement syntax has these parts:

Part	Description
filenumber	Required. Any valid file number.
varname	Required. Valid **Variant** or **String** variable name.

Remarks

Data read with **Line Input #** is usually written from a file with **Print #**.

The **Line Input #** statement reads from a file one character at a time until it encounters a carriage return (**Chr**(13)) or carriage return–linefeed (**Chr**(13) + **Chr**(10)) sequence. Carriage return–linefeed sequences are skipped rather than appended to the character string.

See Also

Input # Statement, **Chr** Function

Example

This example uses the **Line Input #** statement to read a line from a sequential file and assign it to a variable. This example assumes that TESTFILE is a text file with a few lines of sample data.

```
Dim TextLine
Open "TESTFILE" For Input As #1      ' Open file.
Do While Not EOF(1)                  ' Loop until end of file.
    Line Input #1, TextLine          ' Read line into variable.
    Debug.Print TextLine             ' Print to Debug window.
Loop
Close #1                             ' Close file.
```

Line Method

Draws lines and rectangles on an object.

Applies To

PropertyPage Object, **UserControl** Object, **UserDocument** Object, **Form Object, Forms** Collection

Syntax

object.**Line** [**Step**] (*x1, 1*) [**Step**] (*x2, y2*), [*color*], [**B**][**F**]

The **Line** method syntax has the following object qualifier and parts:

Part	Description
object	Optional. Object expression that evaluates to an object in the Applies To list. If object is omitted, the **Form** with the focus is assumed to be *object*.
Step	Optional. Keyword specifying that the starting point coordinates are relative to the current graphics position given by the **CurrentX** and **CurrentY** properties.
(x1, y1)	Optional. **Single** values indicating the coordinates of the starting point for the line or rectangle. The **ScaleMode** property determines the unit of measure used. If omitted, the line begins at the position indicated by **CurrentX** and **CurrentY**.
Step	Optional. Keyword specifying that the end point coordinates are relative to the line starting point.
(x2, y2)	Required. **Single** values indicating the coordinates of the end point for the line being drawn.
color	Optional. **Long** integer value indicating the RGB color used to draw the line. If omitted, the **ForeColor** property setting is used. You can use the **RGB** function or **QBColor** function to specify the color.
B	Optional. If included, causes a box to be drawn using the coordinates to specify opposite corners of the box.
F	Optional. If the **B** option is used, the **F** option specifies that the box is filled with the same color used to draw the box. You cannot use **F** without **B**. If **B** is used without **F**, the box is filled with the current **FillColor** and **FillStyle**. The default value for **FillStyle** is transparent.

Remarks

To draw connected lines, begin a subsequent line at the end point of the previous line.

The width of the line drawn depends on the setting of the **DrawWidth** property. The way a line or box is drawn on the background depends on the setting of the **DrawMode** and **DrawStyle** properties.

When **Line** executes, the **CurrentX** and **CurrentY** properties are set to the end point specified by the arguments.

This method cannot be used in an **With**...**End With** block.

Specifics

Lines Method

See Also

Circle Method

Example

This example uses the **Line** method to draw concentric boxes on a form. To try this example, paste the code into the General section of a form. Then press F5 and click the form.

```
Sub Form_Click ()
   Dim CX, CY, F, F1, F2, I            ' Declare variables
   ScaleMode = 3                       ' Set ScaleMode to pixels.
   CX = ScaleWidth / 2                 ' Get horizontal center.
   CY = ScaleHeight / 2                ' Get vertical center.
   DrawWidth = 8                       ' Set DrawWidth.
   For I = 50 To 0 Step -2
      F = I / 50                       ' Perform interim
      F1 = 1 - F: F2 = 1 + F           ' calculations.
      Forecolor = QBColor(I Mod 15)    ' Set foreground color.
      Line (CX * F1, CY * F1)-(CX * F2, CY * F2), , BF
   Next I
   DoEvents                            ' Yield for other processing.
   If CY > CX Then' Set DrawWidth.
      DrawWidth = ScaleWidth / 25
   Else
      DrawWidth = ScaleHeight / 25
   End If
   For I = 0 To 50 Step 2              ' Set up loop.
      F = I / 50   ' Perform interim
      F1 = 1 - F: F2 = 1 + F           ' calculations.
      Line (CX * F1, CY)-(CX, CY * F1) ' Draw upper-left.
      Line -(CX * F2, CY)              ' Draw upper-right.
      Line -(CX, CY * F2)              ' Draw lower-right.
      Line -(CX * F1, CY)              ' Draw lower-left.
      Forecolor = QBColor(I Mod 15)    ' Change color each time.
   Next I
   DoEvents                            ' Yield for other processing.
End Sub
```

Lines Method

Returns a specified line of code.

Applies To

CodeModule Object

Syntax

object.**Lines**(*startline*, *count*) **As String**

Lines syntax has these parts:

Part	Description
object	Required. An object expression that evaluates to an object in the **Applies To** list.
startline	Required. A **Long** specifying the first line of the code you want to return.
count	Required. A **Long** specifying the number of lines you want to return.

Remarks

The line numbers in a code module begin at 1.

See Also

DeleteLines Method, **Find** Method, **GetSelection** Method, **InsertLines** Method, **ProcBodyLine** Method, **ProcLines** Method, **ProcOfLine** Method, **ProcStartLine** Method, **CodePane** Object

Example

The following example uses the **Lines** method to return a specific block of code, lines 1 through 4, in a particular code pane.

```
Debug.Print Application.VBE.CodePanes(1).CodeModule.Lines( 1, 4)
```

Lines Property

Returns a string containing the specified block of lines.

Applies To

CodeModule Object

Syntax

object.**Lines**(*startline* **As Long**, *count* **As Long**)

Part	Description
object	An object expression that evaluates to an object in the **Applies To** list.
startline	A Long data type specifying the line number to start at.
count	A Long data type specifying the number of lines to highlight.

LinkClose Event

Occurs when a DDE conversation terminates. Either application in a DDE conversation may terminate a conversation at any time.

Applies To

Form Object, **Forms** Collection, **Label** Control, **MDIForm** Object, **PictureBox** Control, **TextBox** Control

Syntax

Private Sub Form_LinkClose( )
Private Sub MDIForm_LinkClose( )
Private Sub *object*_**LinkClose**([*index* **As Integer**])

The **LinkClose** event syntax has these parts:

Part	Description
object	An object expression that evaluates to an object in the **Applies To** list.
Index	An integer that uniquely identifies a control if it's in a control array.

Remarks

Typically, you use a **LinkClose** event procedure to notify the user that a DDE conversation has been terminated. You can also include troubleshooting information on reestablishing a connection or where to go for assistance. For brief messages, use the **MsgBox** function.

See Also

LinkError Event, **LinkExecute** Event, **LinkNotify** Event, **LinkOpen** Event, **LinkExecute** Method, **LinkMode** Property, **LinkTopic** Property

LinkedWindowFrame Property

Returns the **Window** object representing the frame that contains the window. Read-only.

Applies to

Window Object

Remarks

The **LinkedWindowFrame** property enables you to access the object representing the linked window frame, which has properties distinct from the window or windows it contains. If the window isn't linked, the **LinkedWindowFrame** property returns **Nothing**.

See Also

Add Method, **Remove** Method, **SetFocus** Method, **LinkedWindows** Collection, **DesignerWindow** Property, **Visible** Property, **WindowState** Property

LinkedWindows Collection

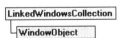

Contains all linked windows in a linked window frame.

Remarks

Use the **LinkedWindows** collection to modify the docked and linked state of windows in the development environment.

The **LinkedWindowFrame** property of the **Window** object returns a **Window** object that has a valid **LinkedWindows** collection.

Linked window frames contain all windows that can be linked or docked. This includes all windows except code windows, designers, the **Object Browser** window, and the **Search and Replace** window.

If all the panes from one linked window frame are moved to another window, the linked window frame with no panes is destroyed. However, if all the panes are removed from the main window, it isn't destroyed.

Use the **Visible** property to check or set the visibility of a window.

You can use the **Add** method to add a window to the collection of currently linked windows. A window that is a pane in one linked window frame can be added to another linked window frame. Use the **Remove** method to remove a window from the collection of currently linked windows; this results in the window being unlinked or undocked.

The **LinkedWindows** collection is used to dock and undock windows from the main window frame.

Properties

Count Property, **Parent** Property, **VBE** Property

Methods

Add Method, **Item** Method, **Remove** Method

See Also

Window Object, **Windows** Collection, **LinkedWindowFrame** Property, **Visible** Property

---

LinkError Event

Occurs when there is an error during a DDE conversation. This event is recognized only as the result of a DDE-related error that occurs when no Visual Basic code is being executed. The error number is passed as an argument.

Applies To

Form Object, **Forms** Collection, **Label** Control, **MDIForm** Object, **PictureBox** Control, **TextBox** Control

Syntax

Private Sub Form_LinkError(*linkerr* **As Integer**)
Private Sub MDIForm_LinkError(*linkerr* **As Integer**)
Private Sub *object*_**LinkError**([*index* **As Integer**,]*linkerr* **As Integer**)

The **LinkError** event syntax has these parts:

Part	Description
object	An object expression that evaluates to an object in the **Applies To** list.
linkerr	Error number of the DDE-related error, as described in Return Values.
index	An integer that uniquely identifies a control if it's in a control array.

Return Values

The following table lists all error numbers returned for the *linkerr* argument and a brief explanation of each error:

Value	Description
1	The other application has requested data in the wrong format. This error may occur several times in succession as Visual Basic tries to find a format the other application recognizes.
6	The destination application attempted to continue a DDE conversation after you set the **LinkMode** property on your source form to 0 (None).
7	All the source links are in use (there is a limit of 128 links per source).
8	For destination controls: An automatic link or **LinkRequest** method failed to update the data in the control.
	For source forms: The destination attempted to poke data to a control and the attempt failed.
11	Not enough memory for DDE.

Remarks

Use a **LinkError** event procedure to notify the user of the particular error that has occurred. You can also include code to fix the problem or troubleshooting information on reestablishing a connection or on where to go for assistance. For brief messages, use the **MsgBox** function.

See Also

LinkClose Event, **LinkExecute** Event, **LinkNotify** Event, **LinkOpen** Event, **LinkExecute** Method, **LinkItem** Property, **LinkMode** Property, **LinkTopic** Property

Example

This example is attached to a **TextBox** control, MyTextBox, that handles selected errors. The procedure displays a message (adapted from the error list in the LinkError event topic) based on the error number passed as the argument LinkErr. You can adapt this code to a source form by substituting Form_LinkError for MyTextBox_LinkError. This example is for illustration only.

```
Private Sub MyTextBox_LinkError (LinkErr As Integer)
Dim Msg
Select Case LinkErr
    Case 1
        Msg = "Data in wrong format."
    Case 11
        Msg = "Out of memory for DDE."
End Select
MsgBox Msg, vbExclamation, "MyTextBox"
End Sub
```

LinkExecute Event

Occurs when a command string is sent by a destination application in a DDE conversation. The destination application expects the source application to perform the operation described by the string.

Applies To

Form Object, **Forms** Collection, **MDIForm** Object

Syntax

Private Sub *object*_**LinkExecute**(*cmdstr* **As String**, *cancel* **As Integer**)

The **LinkExecute** event syntax has these parts:

Part	Description
object	An object expression that evaluates to an object in the **Applies To** list.
cmdstr	The command string expression sent by the destination application.
cancel	An integer that tells the destination whether the command string was accepted or refused. Setting *cancel* to 0 informs the destination that the command string was accepted. Setting *cancel* to any nonzero value informs the destination that the command string was rejected. (The default is set to -1, indicating *cancel*.)

Remarks

There is no required syntax for *cmdstr*. How your application responds to different strings is completely up to you.

If you haven't created a **LinkExecute** event procedure, Visual Basic rejects command strings from destination applications.

See Also

LinkClose Event, **LinkError** Event, **LinkNotify** Event, **LinkOpen** Event, **LinkExecute** Method, **LinkMode** Property, **LinkTopic** Property

Example

This example defines a set of commands for destinations to use in DDE conversations to which your application will respond. This example is for illustration only.

```
Private Sub Form_LinkExecute (CmdStr As String, Cancel As Integer)
   Cancel = False
   Select Case LCase(CmdStr)
   Case "{big}"
      WindowState = 2' Maximize window.
   Case "{little}"
      WindowState = 1' Minimize window.
   Case "{hide}"
      Visible = False' Hide form.
   Case "{view}"
      Visible = True    ' Display form.
   Case Else
      Cancel = True     ' Execute not allowed.
   End Select
End Sub
```

LinkExecute Method

Sends a command string to the source application in a DDE conversation. Doesn't support named arguments.

Applies To

Label Control, **PictureBox** Control, **TextBox** Control

Syntax

object.**LinkExecute** *string*

The **LinkExecute** method syntax has these parts:

Part	Description
object	Required. An object expression that evaluates to an object in the **Applies To** list.
string	Required. String expression containing a command recognized by the source application.

Remarks

The actual value of *string* varies depending on the source application. For example, Microsoft Excel and Microsoft Word for Windows accept command strings that consist of their macro commands enclosed in square brackets ([]). To see command strings that a source application accepts, consult documentation for that application.

See Also

LinkExecute Event, **LinkPoke** Method, **LinkRequest** Method, **LinkSend** Method

Example

This example establishes a DDE link with Microsoft Excel, places some values into cells in the first row of a new worksheet, and charts the values. **LinkPoke** sends the values to be charted to the Microsoft Excel worksheet. To try this example, Microsoft Excel must be installed and in the path statement of your Autoexec.bat file. Paste the code into the Declarations section of a form that has a **TextBox** control with the default name Text1, and then press F5 and click the form.

```
Private Sub Form_Click ()
   Dim Cmd, I, Q, Row, Z                  ' Declare variables.
   Q = Chr(34)                            ' Define quotation marks.
   ' Create a string containing Microsoft Excel macro commands.
   Cmd = "[ACTIVATE(" & Q &"SHEET1" & Q & ")]"
   Cmd = Cmd & "[SELECT(" & Q & "R1C1:R5C2" & Q & ")]"
   Cmd = Cmd & "[NEW(2,1)][ARRANGE.ALL()]"
   If Text1.LinkMode = vbNone Then
      Z = Shell("Excel", 4)               ' Start Microsoft Excel.
      Text1.LinkTopic = "Excel|Sheet1"    ' Set link topic.
      Text1.LinkItem = "R1C1"             ' Set link item.
      Text1.LinkMode = vbLinkManual       ' Set link mode.
   End If
```

```
        For I = 1 To 5
          Row = I                               ' Define row number.
          Text1.LinkItem = "R" & Row & "C1"     ' Set link item.
          Text1.Text = Chr(64 + I)              ' Put value in Text.
          Text1.LinkPoke                        ' Poke value to cell.
          Text1.LinkItem = "R" & Row & "C2"     ' Set link item.
          Text1.Text = Row                      ' Put value in Text.
          Text1.LinkPoke                        ' Poke value to cell.
        Next I
        Text1.LinkExecute Cmd    ' Carry out Microsoft Excel commands.
        On Error Resume Next
        MsgBox "LinkPoke DDE demo with Microsoft Excel finished.", 64
        End
      End Sub
```

LinkItem Property

Returns or sets the data passed to a destination control in a DDE conversation with another application.

Applies To

Label Control, **PictureBox** Control, **TextBox** Control

Syntax

object.**LinkItem** [= *string*]

The **LinkItem** property syntax has these parts:

Part	Description
object	An object expression that evaluates to an object in the **Applies To** list.
string	A string expression that specifies the data to be passed to the destination control.

Remarks

This property corresponds to the *item* argument in the standard DDE syntax, with *application*, *topic*, and *item* as arguments. To set this property, specify a recognizable unit of data in an application as a reference—for example, a cell reference such as "R1C1" in Microsoft Excel.

Use **LinkItem** in combination with the **LinkTopic** property to specify the complete data link for a destination control to a source application. To activate this link, set the **LinkMode** property.

You set **LinkItem** only for a control used as a destination. When a Visual Basic form is a source in a DDE conversation, the name of any **Label**, **PictureBox**, or **TextBox** control on the form can be the *item* argument in the *application*ltopic*!item* string used by the destination. For example, the following syntax represents a valid reference from Microsoft Excel to a Visual Basic application:

=*VizBasicApplication*l*MyForm*!*TextBox1*

You could enter the preceding syntax for a destination cell in the Microsoft Excel formula bar.

A DDE control can potentially act as destination and source simultaneously, causing an infinite loop if a destination-source pair is also a source-destination pair with itself. For instance, a **TextBox** control may be both a source (through its parent form) and destination of the same cell in Microsoft Excel. When data in a Visual Basic **TextBox** changes, sending data to Microsoft Excel, the cell in Microsoft Excel changes, sending the change to the **TextBox**, and so on, causing the loop.

To avoid such loops, use related but not identical items for destination-source and source-destination links in both directions between applications. For example, in Microsoft Excel, use related cells (precedents or dependents) to link a worksheet with a Visual Basic control, avoiding use of a single item as both destination and source. Document any *application|topic* pairs you establish if you include a Paste Link command for run-time use.

Note Setting a permanent data link at design time with the Paste Link command from the Edit menu also sets the **LinkMode**, **LinkTopic**, and **LinkItem** properties. This creates a link that is saved with the form. Each time the form is loaded, Visual Basic attempts to re-establish the conversation.

See Also

LinkMode Property, **LinkTopic** Property

Example

In the example, each mouse click causes a cell in a Microsoft Excel worksheet to update the contents of a Visual Basic **TextBox** control. To try this example, start Microsoft Excel, open a new worksheet named Sheet1, and put some data in the first column. In Visual Basic, create a form with a **TextBox** control. Paste the code into the Declarations section, and then press F5 to run the program.

```
Private Sub Form_Click ()
   Dim CurRow As String
   Static Row                        ' Worksheet row number.
   Row = Row + 1                     ' Increment Row.
   If Row = 1 Then                   ' First time only.
      ' Make sure the link isn't active.
      Text1.LinkMode = 0
      ' Set the application name and topic name.
      Text1.LinkTopic = "Excel|Sheet1"
      Text1.LinkItem = "R1C1"        ' Set LinkItem.
      Text1.LinkMode = 1            ' Set LinkMode to Automatic.
   Else
      ' Update the row in the data item.

CurRow = "R" & Row & "C1"
      Text1.LinkItem = CurRow        ' Set LinkItem.
   End If
End Sub
```

LinkMode Property

Applies To

Form Object, **Forms** Collection, **Label** Control, **MDIForm** Object, **PictureBox** Control, **TextBox** Control

Returns or sets the type of link used for a **DDEconversation** and activates the connection as follows:

- Control—Allows a destination control on a Visual Basic form to initiate a conversation, as specified by the control's **LinkTopic** and **LinkItem** properties.

- Form—Allows a destination application to initiate a conversation with a Visual Basic source form, as specified by the destination application's *application|topic!item* expression.

Syntax

object.**LinkMode** [= *number*]

The **LinkMode** property syntax has these parts:

Part	Description
object	An object expression that evaluates to an object in the **Applies To** list.
number	An integer that specifies the type of connection, as described in Settings.

Settings

For controls used as destinations in DDE conversations, the settings for *number* are:

Constant	Setting	Description
vbLinkNone	0	(Default) None—No DDE interaction.
vbLinkAutomatic	1	Automatic—Destination control is updated each time the linked data changes.
vbLinkManual	2	Manual— Destination control is updated only when the **LinkRequest** method is invoked.
vbLinkNotify	3	Notify—A **LinkNotify** event occurs whenever the linked data changes, but the destination control is updated only when the **LinkRequest** method is invoked.

For forms used as sources in DDE conversations, the settings for *number* are:

Constant	Setting	Description
vbLinkNone	0	(Default) None—No DDE interaction. No destination application can initiate a conversation with the source form as the topic, and no application can poke data to the form. If **LinkMode** is 0 (None) at design time, you can't change it to 1 (Source) at run time.

(continued)

Constant	Setting	Description
vbLinkSource	1	Source—Allows any **Label**, **PictureBox**, or **TextBox** control on a form to supply data to any destination application that establishes a DDE conversation with the form. If such a link exists, Visual Basic automatically notifies the destination whenever the contents of a control are changed. In addition, a destination application can poke data to any **Label**, **PictureBox**, or **TextBox** control on the form. If **LinkMode** is 1 (Source) at design time, you can change it to 0 (None) and back at run time.

Remarks

The following conditions also apply to the **LinkMode** property:

- Setting **LinkMode** to a nonzero value for a destination control causes Visual Basic to attempt to initiate the conversation specified in the **LinkTopic** and **LinkItem** properties. The source updates the destination control according to the type of link specified (automatic, manual, or notify).

- If a source application terminates a conversation with a Visual Basic destination control, the value for that control's **LinkMode** setting changes to 0 (None).

- If you leave **LinkMode** for a form set to the default 0 (None) at design time, you can't change **LinkMode** at run time. If you want a form to act as a source, you must set **LinkMode** to 1 (Source) at design time. You can then change the value of **LinkMode** at run time.

Note Setting a permanent data link at design time with the Paste Link command from the Edit menu also sets the **LinkMode**, **LinkTopic**, and **LinkItem** properties. This creates a link that is saved with the form. Each time the form is loaded, Visual Basic attempts to re-establish the conversation.

See Also

LinkClose Event, **LinkError** Event, **LinkExecute** Event, **LinkNotify** Event, **LinkOpen** Event, **LinkExecute** Method, **LinkRequest** Method, **LinkSend** Method, **LinkItem** Property, **LinkTimeout** Property, **LinkTopic** Property

Example

In the example, each mouse click causes a cell in a Microsoft Excel worksheet to update the contents of a Visual Basic **TextBox** control. To try this example, start Microsoft Excel, open a new worksheet named Sheet1, and put some data in the first column. In Visual Basic, create a form with a **TextBox** control. Paste the code into the Declarations section, and then press F5 to run the program.

```
Private Sub Form_Click ()
   Dim CurRow As String
   Static Row                        ' Worksheet row number.
   Row = Row + 1                     ' Increment Row.
```

```
        If Row = 1 Then                        ' First time only.
            ' Make sure the link isn't active.
            Text1.LinkMode = 0
            ' Set the application name and topic name.
            Text1.LinkTopic = "Excel|Sheet1"
            Text1.LinkItem = "R1C1"            ' Set LinkItem.
            Text1.LinkMode = 1                 ' Set LinkMode to Automatic.
        Else
            ' Update the row in the data item.

    CurRow = "R" & Row & "C1"
            Text1.LinkItem = CurRow            ' Set LinkItem.
        End If
End Sub
```

LinkNotify Event

Occurs when the source has changed the data defined by the DDE link if the **LinkMode** property of the destination control is set to 3 (Notify).

Applies To

Label Control, **PictureBox** Control, **TextBox** Control

Syntax

Private Sub *object*_**LinkNotify**([*index* **As Integer**])

The **LinkNotify** event syntax has these parts:

Part	Description
object	An object expression that evaluates to an object in the **Applies To** list.
index	An integer that uniquely identifies a control if it's in a control array.

Remarks

Typically, in the **LinkNotify** event your code notifies the user, gets the new data immediately, or defers getting the data until later. You can use the **LinkRequest** method to obtain the new data from the source.

See Also

LinkClose Event, **LinkError** Event, **LinkOpen** Event, **LinkExecute** Method, **LinkRequest** Method, **LinkMode** Property, **LinkTopic** Property

Example

This example is attached to a **PictureBox** control, Picture1, that has its **LinkTopic** and **LinkItem** properties set to specify a graphic in the source, and its **LinkMode** property set to 3 (Notify). When the source changes this data, the procedure updates the **PictureBox** control immediately only if the **PictureBox** is on the active form; otherwise, it sets a flag variable. This example is for illustration only.

```
Private Sub Picture1_LinkNotify ()
   If Screen.ActiveForm Is Me Then
   Picture1.LinkRequest   ' Picture is on active form, so update.
   Else
      NewDataFlag = True   ' Assumed to be a module-level variable.
   End If
End Sub
```

LinkOpen Event

Occurs when a DDE conversation is being initiated.

Applies To

Form Object, **Forms** Collection, **Label** Control, **MDIForm** Object, **PictureBox** Control, **TextBox** Control

Syntax

Private Sub Form_LinkOpen(*cancel* **As Integer**)
Private Sub MDIForm_LinkOpen(*cancel* **As Integer**)
Private Sub *object*_**LinkOpen**([*index* **As Integer**,]*cancel* **As Integer**)

The **LinkOpen** event syntax has these parts:

Part	Description
object	An object expression that evaluates to an object in the **Applies To** list.
cancel	An integer that determines whether the DDE conversation is established or not. Leaving *cancel* set to 0 (the default) establishes the conversation. Setting *cancel* to any nonzero value refuses the conversation.
index	An integer that uniquely identifies a control if it's in a control array.

Remarks

This event occurs for forms when a destination application is initiating a DDE conversation with the form. It occurs for controls when a control is initiating a DDE conversation with a source application.

See Also

LinkClose Event, **LinkError** Event, **LinkExecute** Event, **LinkNotify** Event, **LinkExecute** Method, **LinkMode** Property, **LinkTopic** Property

LinkPoke Method

Transfers the contents of a **Label**, **PictureBox**, or **TextBox** control to the source application in a DDE conversation.

Applies To

Label Control, **PictureBox** Control, **TextBox** Control

Syntax

object.**LinkPoke**

The *object* placeholder represents an object expression that evaluates to an object in the **Applies To** list.

Remarks

The *object* is the name of a **Label**, **PictureBox**, or **TextBox** involved in a DDE conversation as a destination. If *object* is a **Label**, **LinkPoke** transfers the contents of the **Caption** property to the source. If *object* is a **PictureBox**, **LinkPoke** transfers the contents of the **Picture** property to the source. If *object* is a **TextBox**, **LinkPoke** transfers the contents of the **Text** property to the source.

Typically, information in a DDE conversation flows from source to destination. However, **LinkPoke** allows a destination object to supply data to the source. Not all source applications accept information supplied this way; if the source application doesn't accept the data, an error occurs.

See Also

LinkExecute Method, **LinkRequest** Method, **LinkSend** Method

Example

This example establishes a DDE link with Microsoft Excel, places some values into cells in the first row of a new worksheet, and charts the values. **LinkPoke** sends the values to be charted to the Microsoft Excel worksheet. To try this example, Microsoft Excel must be installed and in the path statement of your Autoexec.bat file. Paste the code into the Declarations section of a form that has a **TextBox** control with the default name Text1, and then press F5 and click the form.

```
Private Sub Form_Click ()
    Dim Cmd, I, Q, Row, Z            ' Declare variables.
    Q = Chr(34)                      ' Define quotation marks.
    ' Create a string containing Microsoft Excel macro commands.
    Cmd = "[ACTIVATE(" & Q &"SHEET1" & Q & ")]"
    Cmd = Cmd & "[SELECT(" & Q & "R1C1:R5C2" & Q & ")]"
    Cmd = Cmd & "[NEW(2,1)][ARRANGE.ALL()]"
    If Text1.LinkMode = vbNone Then
        Z = Shell("Excel", 4)              ' Start Microsoft Excel.
        Text1.LinkTopic = "Excel|Sheet1"   ' Set link topic.
        Text1.LinkItem = "R1C1"            ' Set link item.
```

```
Text1.LinkMode = vbLinkManual              ' Set link mode.
   End If
   For I = 1 To 5
      Row = I                              ' Define row number.
      Text1.LinkItem = "R" & Row & "C1"    ' Set link item.
      Text1.Text = Chr(64 + I)             ' Put value in Text.
      Text1.LinkPoke                       ' Poke value to cell.
      Text1.LinkItem = "R" & Row & "C2"    ' Set link item.
      Text1.Text = Row                     ' Put value in Text.
      Text1.LinkPoke                       ' Poke value to cell.
   Next I
   Text1.LinkExecute Cmd   ' Carry out Microsoft Excel commands.

On Error Resume Next
   MsgBox "LinkPoke DDE demo with Microsoft Excel finished.", 64
   End
End Sub
```

LinkRequest Method

Asks the source application in a DDE conversation to update the contents of a **Label**, **PictureBox**, or **TextBox** control.

Applies To

Label Control, **PictureBox** Control, **TextBox** Control

Syntax

object.**LinkRequest**

The *object* placeholder represents an object expression that evaluates to an object in the **Applies To** list.

Remarks

The *object* is the name of a **Label**, **PictureBox**, or **TextBox** involved in a DDE conversation as a destination. **LinkRequest** causes the source application to send the most current data to *object*, updating the **Caption** property setting if *object* is a **Label**, the **Picture** property setting if *object* is a **PictureBox**, or the **Text** property setting if *object* is a **TextBox**.

If the **LinkMode** property of *object* is set to Automatic (1 or **vbLinkAutomatic**), the source application automatically updates *object* and **LinkRequest** isn't needed. If the **LinkMode** property of *object* is set to Manual (2 or **vbLinkManual**), the source application updates *object* only when **LinkRequest** is used. If the **LinkMode** property of *object* is set to Notify (3 or **vbLinkNotify**), the source notifies the destination that data has changed by invoking the **LinkNotify** event. The destination must then use **LinkRequest** to update the data.

See Also

LinkNotify Event, **LinkExecute** Method, **LinkPoke** Method, **LinkSend** Method, **LinkMode** Property

Example

This example uses **LinkRequest** to update the contents of a text box with the values in a Microsoft Excel worksheet. To try this example, you must have Microsoft Excel running on your computer. Place some data in the first cells in the first column in the default worksheet (Sheet1.xls). Paste the code into the Declarations section of a form that has a **TextBox** control called Text1, and then press F5 and click the form.

```
Private Sub Form_Click ()
    If Text1.LinkMode = vbNone Then         ' Test link mode.
        Text1.LinkTopic = "Excel|Sheet1"    ' Set link topic.
        Text1.LinkItem = "R1C1"             ' Set link item.
        Text1.LinkMode = vbLinkManual       ' Set link mode.
        Text1.LinkRequest                   ' Update text box.
    Else
        If Text1.LinkItem = "R1C1" Then
            Text1.LinkItem = "R2C1"
            Text1.LinkRequest               ' Update text box.
        Else
            Text1.LinkItem = "R1C1"
            Text1.LinkRequest               ' Update text box.

    End If
        End If
End Sub
```

LinkSend Method

Transfers the contents of a **PictureBox** control to the destination application in a DDE conversation.

Applies To

Label Control, **PictureBox** Control, **TextBox** Control

Syntax

object.**LinkSend**

The *object* placeholder represents an object expression that evaluates to an object in the **Applies To** list.

Remarks

The *object* must be a **PictureBox** on a **Form** object that is a source in a DDE conversation.

When other applications establish automatic links with a **Form** in your application, Visual Basic notifies them when the contents of a **TextBox** or a **Label** on the **Form** change. However, Visual Basic doesn't automatically notify a DDE destination application when the **Picture** property setting of a **PictureBox** on a source **Form** changes. Because the amount of data in a graphic can be very large and because it seldom makes sense to update a destination application as each pixel in the picture changes, Visual Basic requires that you use the **LinkSend** method to explicitly notify DDE destination applications when the contents of a **PictureBox** changes.

See Also

LinkExecute Method, **LinkPoke** Method, **LinkRequest** Method, **Picture** Property

LinkTimeout Property

Applies To

Label Control, **PictureBox** Control, **TextBox** Control

Returns or sets the amount of time a control waits for a response to a DDE message.

Syntax

object.**LinkTimeout** [= *number*]

The **LinkTimeout** property syntax has these parts:

Part	Description
object	An object expression that evaluates to an object in the **Applies To** list.
number	A numeric expression that specifies the wait time.

Remarks

By default, the **LinkTimeout** property is set to 50 (equivalent to 5 seconds). You can specify other settings in tenths of a second.

DDE response time from source applications varies. Use this property to adjust the time a destination control waits for a response from a source application. If you use **LinkTimeout**, you can avoid generating a Visual Basic error if a given source application takes too long to respond.

Note The maximum length of time that a control can wait is 65,535 tenths of a second, or about 1 hour 49 minutes. Setting **LinkTimeout** to −1 tells the control to wait the maximum length of time for a response in a DDE conversation. The user can force the control to stop waiting by pressing the ESC key.

See Also

LinkClose Event, **LinkOpen** Event, **LinkSend** Method, **LinkItem** Property, **LinkMode** Property, **LinkTopic** Property

LinkTopic Property

For a destination control—returns or sets the source application and the topic (the fundamental data grouping used in that application). Use **LinkTopic** with the **LinkItem** property to specify the complete data link.

For a source form—returns or sets the topic that the source form responds to in a DDE conversation.

Applies To

Form Object, **Forms** Collection, **Label** Control, **MDIForm** Object, **PictureBox** Control, **TextBox** Control

Syntax

object.**LinkTopic** [= *value*]

The **LinkTopic** property syntax has these parts:

Part	Description
object	An object expression that evaluates to an object in the **Applies To** list.
value	A string expression specifying a DDE syntax element.

Remarks

The **LinkTopic** property consists of a string that supplies part of the information necessary to set up either a destination link or source link. The string you use depends on whether you're working with a destination control or a source form. Each string corresponds to one or more elements of standard DDE syntax, which include *application*, *topic*, and *item*.

Note While the standard definition for a DDE link includes the *application*, *topic*, and *item* elements, the actual syntax used within applications for a destination link to a source application may vary slightly. For example, within Microsoft Excel, you use the syntax:

application\topic!*item*

Within Microsoft Word for Windows, you use:

application topic item

(Don't use the pipe character [|] or exclamation mark [!].)

Within a Visual Basic application, you use:

application\topic

The exclamation mark for *topic* is implicit.

Destination Control To set **LinkTopic** for a destination control, use a string with the syntax *application*\topic as follows:

- *application* is the name of the application from which data is requested, usually the executable filename without an extension—for example, Excel (for Microsoft Excel).

- The pipe character (l, or character code 124) separates the application from the topic.

- *topic* is the fundamental data grouping used in the source application—for example, a worksheet in Microsoft Excel.

In addition, for a destination control only, you must set the related **LinkItem** property to specify the *item* element for the link. A cell reference, such as R1C1, corresponds to an item in a Microsoft Excel worksheet.

Source Form   To set **LinkTopic** for a source form, set *value* to an appropriate identifier for the form. A destination application uses this string as the *topic* argument when establishing a DDE link with the form. Although this string is all you need to set **LinkTopic** within Visual Basic for a source form, the destination application also needs to specify:

- The *application* element that the destination application uses, which is either the Visual Basic project filename without the .vbp extension (if you're running your application in the Visual Basic development environment) or the Visual Basic application filename without the .exe extension (if you're running your application as a stand-alone executable file). The **EXEName** property of the **App** object provides this string in your Visual Basic code unless the filename was changed by the user. (**EXEName** always returns the actual filename of the application on disk; DDE always uses the original name that was specified in the Project Properties dialog box.)

- The *item* element that the destination application uses, which corresponds to the **Name** property setting for the **Label**, **PictureBox**, or **TextBox** control on the source form.

The following syntax is an example of a valid reference from Microsoft Excel to a Visual Basic application acting as a source:

=*VizBasicApplication|FormN!TextBox1*

You could enter this reference for a destination cell in the Microsoft Excel formula bar.

To activate the data link set with **LinkTopic**, set the **LinkMode** property to the appropriate nonzero value to specify the type of link you want. As a general rule, set **LinkMode** after you set **LinkTopic**. For a destination control, changing **LinkTopic** breaks an existing link and terminates the DDE conversation. For a source form, changing **LinkTopic** breaks all destination links that are using that topic. For these reasons, always set the **LinkMode** property to 0 before changing **LinkTopic**. After changing **LinkTopic** for a destination control, you must set **LinkMode** to 1 (Automatic), 2 (Manual), or 3 (Notify) to establish a conversation with the new topic.

Note Setting a permanent data link at design time with the Paste Link command on the Edit menu also sets the **LinkMode**, **LinkTopic**, and **LinkItem** properties. This creates a link that is saved with the form. Each time the form is loaded, Visual Basic attempts to reestablish the conversation.

See Also

LinkClose Event, **LinkError** Event, **LinkOpen** Event, **LinkSend** Method, **LinkItem** Property, **LinkMode** Property

Example

In the example, each mouse click causes a cell in a Microsoft Excel worksheet to update the contents of a Visual Basic **TextBox** control. To try this example, start Microsoft Excel, open a new worksheet named Sheet1, and put some data in the first column. In Visual Basic, create a form with a **TextBox** control. Paste the code into the Declarations section, and then press F5 to run the program.

```
Private Sub Form_Click ()
   Dim CurRow As String
   Static Row                    ' Worksheet row number.
   Row = Row + 1                 ' Increment Row.
   If Row = 1 Then               ' First time only.
      ' Make sure the link isn't active.
      Text1.LinkMode = 0
      ' Set the application name and topic name.
      Text1.LinkTopic = "Excel|Sheet1"
      Text1.LinkItem = "R1C1"    ' Set LinkItem.
      Text1.LinkMode = 1         ' Set LinkMode to Automatic.
   Else
      ' Update the row in the data item.

CurRow = "R" & Row & "C1"
      Text1.LinkItem = CurRow    ' Set LinkItem.
   End If
End Sub
```

List Property

Returns or sets the items contained in a control's list portion. The list is a string array in which each element is a list item. Available at design time for **ListBox** and **ComboBox** controls through the property browser; read-only at run time for **DirListBox**, **DriveListBox**, and **FileListBox** controls; read/write at run time for **ComboBox** and **ListBox** controls.

Applies To

ComboBox Control, **DirListBox** Control, **DriveListBox** Control, **FileListBox** Control, **ListBox** Control

Syntax

object.**List**(*index*) [= *string*]

The **List** property syntax has these parts:

Part	Description
object	An object expression that evaluates to an object in the **Applies To** list.
index	The number of a specific item in the list.
string	A string expression specifying the list item.

Remarks

Use this property to access list items.

For all controls except the **DirListBox**, the index of the first item is 0 and the index of the last item is **ListCount**–1.

For a **DirListBox** control, the index number sequence is based on the current directories and subdirectories when the control is created at run time. The directory that is currently expanded is represented using the index–1. Directories above the currently expanded directory are represented by negative indexes with higher absolute values. For example,–2 is the parent directory of the directory that is currently expanded and–3 is the directory above that. Directories below the directory that is currently expanded range from 0 to **ListCount**–1.

Initially, **ComboBox** and **ListBox** controls contain an empty list. For the file-system controls, the list is based on conditions that exist when the control is created at run time:

- **DirListBox**—contains a list of all directories, using the range *-n* to **ListCount**–*1*.

- **DriveListBox**—contains the list of drive connections in effect.

- **FileListBox**—contains the list of files in the directory that is currently expanded that match the **Pattern** property. The path isn't included.

The **List** property works in conjunction with the **ListCount** and **ListIndex** properties.

For all applicable controls except a **DirListBox**, enumerating a list from 0 to **ListCount** –1 returns all items in the list. For a **DirListBox** control, enumerating the list from–*n* to **ListCount**–1 returns a list containing all directories and subdirectories visible from the directory that is currently expanded. In this case *n* is the number of directory levels above the directory that is currently expanded.

Note To specify items you want to display in a **ComboBox** or **ListBox** control, use the **AddItem** method. To remove items, use the **RemoveItem** method. To keep items in alphabetic order, set the control's **Sorted** property to **True** before adding items to the list.

Using an `Option Base = 1` statement in the Declarations section doesn't affect the enumeration of elements in Visual Basic controls. The first element is always 0.

When the List index is outside the range of actual entries in the list box, a zero-length string ("") is returned. For example, `List(-1)` returns a zero-length string for a **ComboBox** or **ListBox** control.

See Also

AddItem Method, **RemoveItem** Method, **ComboBox** Control, **DirListBox** Control, **DriveListBox** Control, **FileListBox** Control, **ListBox** Control, **ListCount** Property, **ListIndex** Property, **Sorted** Property, **Pattern** Property

Example

This example loads a list of your printer fonts into a **ComboBox** control, displays the first item in the list, and prints the total number of fonts. Each click of the command button changes all items in the list to uppercase or lowercase. To try this example, paste the code into the Declarations section of a form that contains a **ComboBox** control (**Style** = 2) and a **CommandButton** control, and then press F5 and click the **CommandButton**.

```
Private Sub Form_Load ()
    Dim I                              ' Declare variable.
    AutoRedraw = True                  ' Set AutoRedraw.
    For I = 0 To Printer.FontCount - 1 ' Put font names in list.
        Combo1.AddItem Printer.Fonts(I)
    Next I
    Combo1.ListIndex = 0               ' Set text to first item.
    ' Print ListCount information on form.
    Print "Number of printer fonts: "; Combo1.ListCount
End Sub
Private Sub Command1_Click ()
    Static UpperCase
    Dim I                              ' Declare variable.
    For I = 0 To Combo1.ListCount - 1  ' Loop through list.
        If UpperCase Then
            Combo1.List(I) = UCase(Combo1.List(I))
        Else
            Combo1.List(I) = LCase(Combo1.List(I))
        End If
    Next I
    UpperCase = Not UpperCase          ' Change case.
End Sub
```

ListBox Control

A **ListBox** control displays a list of items from which the user can select one or more. If the number of items exceeds the number that can be displayed, a scroll bar is automatically added to the **ListBox** control.

If no item is selected, the **ListIndex** property value is –1. The first item in the list is **ListIndex** 0, and the value of the **ListCount** property is always one more than the largest **ListIndex** value.

Syntax

ListBox

Remarks

To add or delete items in a **ListBox** control, use the **AddItem** or **RemoveItem** method. Set the **List**, **ListCount**, and **ListIndex** properties to enable a user to access items in the **ListBox**. Alternatively, you can add items to the list by using the **List** property at design time.

Properties

OLEDragMode Property, **OLEDropMode** Property, **BackColor, ForeColor** Properties, **FontBold, FontItalic, FontStrikethru, FontUnderline** Properties, **FontName** Property, **FontSize** Property, **Height, Width** Properties, **Left, Top** Properties, **List** Property, **ListCount** Property, **ListIndex** Property, **Sorted** Property, **TabIndex** Property, **Tag** Property, **Text** Property, **Visible** Property, **DataChanged** Property, **DataField** Property, **DataSource** Property, **Index** Property, **IntegralHeight** Property, **Sorted** Property, **Visible** Property, **Columns** Property (ListBox), **DragIcon** Property, **DragMode** Property, **hWnd** Property, **ItemData** Property, **MouseIcon** Property, **MousePointer** Property, **MultiSelect** Property, **NewIndex** Property, **SelCount** Property, **Selected** Property, **Style** Property, **TabStop** Property, **TopIndex** Property, **Appearance** Property, **Enabled** Property, **HelpContextID** Property, **Index** Property (Control Array), **Name** Property, **Parent** Property, **Font** Property, **Container** Property, **ToolTipText** Property, **WhatsThisHelpID** Property

Methods

Refresh Method, **SetFocus** Method, **AddItem** Method, **Clear** Method (Clipboard, ComboBox, ListBox), **Drag** Method, **Move** Method, **RemoveItem** Method, **ZOrder** Method, **OLEDrag** Method, **ShowWhatsThis** Method

See Also

AddItem Method, **RemoveItem** Method, **List** Property, **ListCount** Property, **ListIndex** Property

---

ListCount Property

Returns the number of items in the list portion of a control.

Applies To

ComboBox Control, **DirListBox** Control, **DriveListBox** Control, **FileListBox** Control, **ListBox** Control

Syntax

object.**ListCount**

The *object* placeholder represents an object expression that evaluates to an object in the **Applies To** list.

Remarks

ListCount provides specific information for each control:

- **ComboBox** and **ListBox** controls—the number of items in the list.
- **DirListBox** control—the number of subdirectories in the current directory.
- **DriveListBox** control—the number of drive connections.
- **FileListBox** control—the number of files in the current directory that match the **Pattern** property setting.

If no item is selected, the **ListIndex** property value is –1. The first item in the list is **ListIndex** = 0, and **ListCount** is always one more than the largest **ListIndex** value.

See Also

AddItem Method, **RemoveItem** Method, **List** Property, **ListIndex** Property, **Pattern** Property

Example

This example loads a list of your printer fonts into a **ComboBox** control, displays the first item in the list, and prints the total number of fonts. Each click of the command button changes all items in the list to uppercase or lowercase. To try this example, paste the code into the Declarations section of a form that contains a **ComboBox** control (**Style** = 2) and a **CommandButton** control, and then press F5 and click the **CommandButton**.

```
Private Sub Form_Load ()
   Dim I                              ' Declare variable.
   AutoRedraw = True                  ' Set AutoRedraw.
   For I = 0 To Printer.FontCount - 1 ' Put font names in list.
      Combo1.AddItem Printer.Fonts(I)
   Next I
   Combo1.ListIndex = 0               ' Set text to first item.
   ' Print ListCount information on form.
   Print "Number of printer fonts: "; Combo1.ListCount
End Sub
Private Sub Command1_Click ()
   Static UpperCase
   Dim I                              ' Declare variable.
   For I = 0 To Combo1.ListCount - 1  ' Loop through list.

If UpperCase Then
         Combo1.List(I) = UCase(Combo1.List(I))

      Else
         Combo1.List(I) = LCase(Combo1.List(I))
      End If
   Next I
   UpperCase = Not UpperCase          ' Change case.
End Sub
```

ListField Property

Returns or sets the name of the field in the **Recordset** object, specified by the **RowSource** property, used to fill the **DBCombo** or **DBList** control's list portion.

Applies To

DBCombo Control, **DBList** Control

Syntax

object.**ListField** [= *value*]

The **ListField** property syntax has these parts:

Part	Description
object	An object expression that evaluates to an object in the **Applies To** list.
value	A string expression that specifies the name of a field in the **Recordset** specified by the **RowSource** property.

Remarks

The **ListField** property enables you to select which field in the **Recordset** is used to fill the list portion of the control. This property is used in conjunction with the **RowSource** property that specifies which **Data** control is used to create the **Recordset** used to fill the list.

Generally, you use two **Recordset** objects with the data-aware list controls. One **Recordset** contains a read-only list of valid selections, while the other **Recordset** is updated with selections from the list. For example, the **DBList** control could be generated from a query that returned a list of valid part numbers and their descriptions. The **ListField** property would point to the description field of the **Recordset**, so that the user doesn't see the actual part numbers. The **BoundColumn** property would point to the part number field, as this is what needs to be updated in the **Recordset**.

If the field specified by the **ListField** property can't be found in the **Recordset**, a trappable error occurs.

Data Type

String

ListIndex Property

Returns or sets the index of the currently selected item in the control. Not available at design time.

Applies To

ComboBox Control, **DirListBox** Control, **DriveListBox** Control, **FileListBox** Control, **ListBox** Control

Syntax

object.**ListIndex** [= *index*]

The **ListIndex** property syntax has these parts:

Part	Description
object	An object expression that evaluates to an object in the **Applies To** list.
index	A numeric expression specifying the index of the current item, as described in Settings.

Settings

The settings for *index* are:

Setting	Description
−1	(Default for **ComboBox**, **DirListBox**, and **DriveListBox** controls) Indicates no item is currently selected. For a **ComboBox** control, indicates the user has entered new text into the text box portion. For a **DirListBox** control, indicates the index of the current path. For a **DriveListBox** control, indicates the index of the current drive when the control is created at run time.
n	(Default for **FileListBox** and **ListBox** controls) A number indicating the index of the currently selected item.

Remarks

The expression `List(List1.ListIndex)` returns the string for the currently selected item.

The first item in the list is **ListIndex** = 0, and **ListCount** is always one more than the largest **ListIndex** value.

For a control in which users can make multiple selections, this property's behavior depends on the number of items selected. If only one item is selected, **ListIndex** returns the index of that item. In a multiple selection, **ListIndex** returns the index of the item contained within the focus rectangle, whether or not that item is actually selected.

See Also

AddItem Method, **RemoveItem** Method, **List** Property, **ListCount** Property, **Drive** Property, **Path** Property

Example

This example displays the names of three players in a **ListBox** control and the corresponding salary of the selected player in a **Label** control. To try this example, paste the code into the Declarations section of a form that contains a **ComboBox** control and a **Label** control, and then press F5 and choose a name from the **ComboBox**.

```
Dim Player(0 To 2)                ' Dimension two arrays.
Dim Salary(0 To 2)
Private Sub Form_Load ()
    Dim I                         ' Declare variable.
    AutoSize = True
    Player(0) = "Miggey McMoo"    ' Enter data into arrays.
    Player(1) = "Alf Hinshaw"
    Player(2) = "Woofer Dean"
    Salary(0) = "$234,500"
    Salary(1) = "$158,900"
    Salary(2) = "$1,030,500"
    For I = 0 To 2                ' Add names to list.
        Combo1.AddItem Player(I)
    Next I
    Combo1.ListIndex = 0          ' Display first item in list.

End Sub

Private Sub Combo1_Click ()
    ' Display corresponding salary for name.
    Label1.Caption = Salary(Combo1.ListIndex)
End Sub
```

Load Event

Occurs when a form is loaded. For a startup form, occurs when an application starts as the result of a **Load** statement or as the result of a reference to an unloaded form's properties or controls.

Applies To

PropertyPage Object, **Form** Object, **Forms** Collection, **MDIForm** Object

Syntax

Private Sub Form_Load( )
Private Sub MDIForm_Load( )

Remarks

Typically, you use a Load event procedure to include initialization code for a form—for example, code that specifies default settings for controls, indicates contents to be loaded into **ComboBox** or **ListBox** controls, and initializes form-level variables.

The Load event occurs after the Initialize event.

When you reference a property of an unloaded form in code, the form is automatically loaded but isn't automatically made visible unless the **MDIChild** property is set to **True**. If an **MDIForm** object isn't loaded and an MDI child form is loaded, both the **MDIForm** and the child form are automatically loaded and both become visible. Other forms aren't shown until you either use the **Show** method or set the **Visible** property to **True**.

The following code in an **MDIForm** Load event automatically loads an MDI child form (assuming Form1 has its **MDIChild** property set to **True**):

```
Dim NewForm As New Form1
NewForm.Caption = "New Form"  ' Loads form by reference.
```

Because all child forms become visible when loaded, the reference to the **Caption** property loads the form and makes it visible.

Note When you create procedures for related events, such as **Activate**, **GotFocus**, **Paint**, and **Resize**, be sure that their actions don't conflict and that they don't cause recursive events.

See Also

Activate, **Deactivate** Events, **QueryUnload** Event, **Unload** Event, **Load** Statement, **Unload** Statement

Example

This example loads items into a **ComboBox** control when a form is loaded. To try this example, paste the code into the Declarations section of a form that contains a **ComboBox**, and then press F5.

```
Private Sub Form_Load ()
    Combo1.AddItem "Mozart"     ' Add items to list.
    Combo1.AddItem "Beethoven"
    Combo1.AddItem "Rock 'n Roll"
    Combo1.AddItem "Reggae"
    Combo1.ListIndex = 2        ' Set default selection.
End Sub
```

Load Statement

Loads a form or control into memory.

Syntax

Load *object*

The *object* placeholder is the name of a **Form** object, **MDIForm** object, or control array element to load.

Remarks

You don't need to use the **Load** statement with forms unless you want to load a form without displaying it. Any reference to a form (except in a **Set** or **If...TypeOf** statement) automatically loads it if it's not already loaded. For example, the **Show** method loads a form before displaying it. Once the form is loaded, its properties and controls can be altered by the application, whether or not the form is actually visible. Under some circumstances, you may want to load all your forms during initialization and display them later as they're needed.

When Visual Basic loads a **Form** object, it sets form properties to their initial values and then performs the Load event procedure. When an application starts, Visual Basic automatically loads and displays the application's startup form.

If you load a **Form** whose **MDIChild** property is set to **True** (in other words, the child form) before loading an **MDIForm**, the **MDIForm** is automatically loaded before the child form. MDI child forms cannot be hidden, and thus are immediately visible after the **Form_Load** event procedure ends.

The standard dialog boxes produced by Visual Basic functions such as **MsgBox** and **InputBox** do not need to be loaded, shown, or unloaded, but can simply be invoked directly.

See Also

Unload Statement, **Hide** Method, **Show** Method

Example

This example uses the **Load** statement to load a **Form** object. To try this example, paste the code into the Declarations section of a **Form** object, and then run the example and click the **Form** object.

```
Private Sub Form_Click ()
   Dim Answer, Msg as String        ' Declare variable.
   Unload Form1                     ' Unload form.
   Msg = "Form1 has been unloaded. Choose Yes to load and "
   Msg = Msg & "display the form. Choose No to load the form "
   Msg = Msg & "and leave it invisible."
   Answer = MsgBox(Msg, vbYesNo)    ' Get user response.
   If Answer = vbYes Then           ' Evaluate answer.
      Show                          ' If Yes, show form.
   Else
      Load Form1                    ' If No, just load it.
      Msg = "Form1 is now loaded. Choose OK to display it."
      MsgBox Msg                    ' Display message.
      Show                          ' Show form.
   End If
End Sub
```

LoadPicture Function

Loads a graphic into a form's **Picture** property, a **PictureBox** control, or **Image** control.

Syntax

LoadPicture([*stringexpression*])

The *stringexpression* argument is the name of a graphics file to be loaded.

Remarks

Graphics formats recognized by Visual Basic include bitmap (.bmp) files, icon (.ico) files, run-length encoded (.rle) files, metafile (.wmf) files, enhanced metafiles (.emf), GIF files, and JPEG (.jpg) files.

Graphics are cleared from forms, picture boxes, and image controls by assigning **LoadPicture** with no argument.

To load graphics for display in a **PictureBox** control, **Image** control, or as the background of a form, the return value of **LoadPicture** must be assigned to the **Picture** property of the object on which the picture is displayed. For example:

```
Set Picture = LoadPicture("PARTY.BMP")
Set Picture1.Picture = LoadPicture("PARTY.BMP")
```

To assign an icon to a form, set the return value of the **LoadPicture** function to the **Icon** property of the **Form** object:

```
Set Form1.Icon = LoadPicture("MYICON.ICO")
```

Icons can also be assigned to the **DragIcon** property of all controls except **Timer** controls and **Menu** controls. For example:

```
Set Command1.DragIcon = LoadPicture("MYICON.ICO")
```

Load a graphics file into the system Clipboard using **LoadPicture** as follows:

```
Clipboard.SetData LoadPicture("PARTY.BMP")
```

See Also

SavePicture Statement, **SetData** Method, **Icon** Property, **Picture** Property, **DragIcon** Property

Example

This example uses the **LoadPicture** function to load a picture into a form's **Picture** property and to clear the picture from the **Form** object. To try this example, paste the code into the Declarations section of a **Form** object, and then run the example and click the **Form** object.

```
Private Sub Form_Click ()
   Dim Msg as String                 ' Declare variables.
   On Error Resume Next              ' Set up error handling.
   Height = 3990
   Width = 4890                      ' Set height and width.
   Set Picture = LoadPicture("PAPER.BMP")
                                     ' Load bitmap.
   If Err Then
      Msg = "Couldn't find the .BMP file."
      MsgBox Msg                     ' Display error message.
      Exit Sub                       ' Quit if error occurs.
   End If
   Msg = "Choose OK to clear the bitmap from the form."
   MsgBox Msg
   Set Picture = LoadPicture()       ' Clear form.
End Sub
```

LoadResData Function

Loads data of several possible types from a resource (.res) file and returns a **Byte** array.

Syntax

LoadResData(*index*, *format*)

The **LoadResData** function syntax has these parts:

Part	Description
index	Required. Integer or string specifying the identifier (ID) of the data in the resource file. The resource whose ID is 1 is reserved for the application icon.
format	Required. Value that specifies the original format of the data being returned, as described in Settings. Value can also be the string name of a user-defined resource.

Settings

The settings for *format* are:

Setting	Description
1	Cursor resource
2	Bitmap resource
3	Icon resource
4	Menu resource
5	Dialog box
6	String resource
7	Font directory resource
8	Font resource
9	Accelerator table
10	User-defined resource
12	Group cursor
14	Group icon

Remarks

The data that **LoadResData** loads from the resource file can be up to 64K.

Using **LoadResData** with a bitmap, icon, or cursor resource type returns a string containing the actual bits in the resource. If you want to use the actual bitmap, icon, or resource, use the **LoadResPicture** function.

Using **LoadResData** is useful for localizing a Visual Basic application because the resources that need to be translated are isolated in one resource file and there is no need to access the source code or recompile the application.

See Also

LoadResPicture Function, **LoadResString** Function

LoadResPicture Function

Loads a bitmap, icon, or cursor from a resource (.res) file.

Syntax

LoadResPicture(*index, format*)

The **LoadResPicture** function syntax has these parts:

Part	Description
index	Required. Integer or string specifying the identifier (ID) of the data in the resource file. The resource whose ID is 1 is reserved for the application icon.
format	Required. Value or constant that specifies the format of the data being returned, as described in **Settings**.

Settings

The settings for *format* are:

Constant	Value	Description
vbResBitmap	0	Bitmap resource
vbResIcon	1	Icon resource
vbResCursor	2	Cursor resource

Remarks

You can use the **LoadResPicture** function instead of referring to graphics stored in the **Picture** property of a **Form** or controls.

Storing bitmaps, icons, or cursors in and accessing them from resource files improves load time because you can load them individually as needed from the resource file, rather than all at once when a **Form** is loaded.

Using **LoadResPicture** is useful for localizing a Visual Basic application because the resources that need to be translated are isolated in one resource file and there is no need to access the source code or recompile the application.

See Also

LoadResData Function, **LoadResString** Function

LoadResString Function

Loads a string from a resource (.res) file.

Syntax

LoadResString(*index*)

The **LoadResString** function syntax has these parts:

Part	Description
index	Required. Integer specifying the identifier (ID) of the data in the resource file. The resource whose ID is 1 is reserved for the application icon.

Remarks

You can use the **LoadResString** function instead of string literals in your code. Storing long strings of data in and accessing them from resource files improves load time because you can load them individually as needed from the resource file, rather than all at once when a form is loaded.

Using **LoadResString** is useful for localizing a Visual Basic application because the resources that need to be translated are isolated in one resource file and there is no need to access the source code or recompile the application.

See Also

LoadResData Function, **LoadResPicture** Function

Loc Function

Returns a **Long** specifying the current read/write position within an open file.

Syntax

Loc(*filenumber*)

The required *filenumber* argument is any valid **Integer** file number.

Remarks

The following describes the return value for each file access mode:

Mode	Return Value
Random	Number of the last record read from or written to the file.
Sequential	Current byte position in the file divided by 128. However, information returned by **Loc** for sequential files is neither used nor required.
Binary	Position of the last byte read or written.

See Also

EOF Function, **LOF** Function, **Seek** Function, **Seek** Statement

Example

This example uses the **Loc** function to return the current read/write position within an open file. This example assumes that TESTFILE is a text file with a few lines of sample data.

```
Dim MyLocation, MyLine
Open "TESTFILE" For Binary As #1      ' Open file just created.
Do While MyLocation < LOF(1)          ' Loop until end of file.
   MyLine = MyLine & Input(1, #1)      ' Read character into variable.
   MyLocation = Loc(1)                 ' Get current position within file.
' Print to Debug window.
   Debug.Print MyLine; Tab; MyLocation
Loop
Close #1                              ' Close file.
```

LocaleID Property

Returns a long value that contains the Locale identification (language and country) of the user.

Applies To

AmbientProperties Object

Syntax

object.**LocaleID**

The **LocaleID** property syntax has this part:

Part	Description
object	An object expression that evaluates to an object in the **Applies To** list.

Remarks

The **LocaleID** ambient property contains identification of the language and country of the current user. Using this identification, the control can modify its behavior and appearance to fit the language and country. This could be as simple as having error notifications in the language of the user, to more complex modifications of property, method, and event names in the language of the user.

If the container does not implement this ambient property, the default value will be the current System **LocaleID**.

Lock, Unlock Statements

Controls access by other processes to all or part of a file opened using the **Open** statement.

Syntax

Lock [#]*filenumber*[, *recordrange*]

. . .

Unlock [#]*filenumber*[, *recordrange*]

The **Lock** and **Unlock** statement syntax has these parts:

Part	Description
filenumber	Required. Any valid file number.
recordrange	Optional. The range of records to lock or unlock.

Settings

The *recordrange* argument settings are:

recnumber | [*start*] **To** *end*

Setting	Description
recnumber	Record number (**Random** mode files) or byte number (**Binary** mode files) at which locking or unlocking begins.
start	Number of the first record or byte to lock or unlock.
end	Number of the last record or byte to lock or unlock.

Remarks

The **Lock** and **Unlock** statements are used in environments where several processes might need access to the same file.

Lock and **Unlock** statements are always used in pairs. The arguments to **Lock** and **Unlock** must match exactly.

The first record or byte in a file is at position 1, the second record or byte is at position 2, and so on. If you specify just one record, then only that record is locked or unlocked. If you specify a range of records and omit a starting record (*start*), all records from the first record to the end of the range (*end*) are locked or unlocked. Using **Lock** without *recnumber* locks the entire file; using **Unlock** without *recnumber* unlocks the entire file.

If the file has been opened for sequential input or output, **Lock** and **Unlock** affect the entire file, regardless of the range specified by *start* and *end*.

Caution Be sure to remove all locks with an **Unlock** statement before closing a file or quitting your program. Failure to remove locks produces unpredictable results.

See Also

Open Statement

Example

This example illustrates the use of the **Lock** and **Unlock** statements. While a record is being modified, access by other processes to the record is denied. This example assumes that TESTFILE is a file containing five records of the user-defined type Record.

```
Type Record                          ' Define user-defined type.
   ID As Integer
   Name As String * 20
End Type

Dim MyRecord As Record, RecordNumber ' Declare variables.
' Open sample file for random access.
Open "TESTFILE" For Random Shared As #1 Len = Len(MyRecord)
RecordNumber = 4                     ' Define record number.
Lock #1, RecordNumber                ' Lock record.
Get #1, RecordNumber, MyRecord       ' Read record.
MyRecord.ID = 234                    ' Modify record.
MyRecord.Name = "John Smith"
Put #1, RecordNumber, MyRecord       ' Write modified record.
Unlock #1, RecordNumber              ' Unlock current record.
Close #1                             ' Close file.
```

Locked Property

Applies To

Column Object, **DBCombo** Control, **DBList** Control, **Split** Object, **TextBox** Control

Returns or sets a value indicating whether a control can be edited.

Syntax

object.**Locked** [= *boolean*]

The **Locked** property syntax has these parts:

Part	Description
object	An object expression that evaluates to an object in the **Applies To** list.
boolean	A Boolean expression that specifies whether the control can be edited, as described in Settings.

Settings

The settings for *boolean* are:

Setting	Description
True	**TextBox** control—you can scroll and highlight the text in the control, but you can't edit it. The program can still modify the text by changing the **Text** property.
	Column object—you can't edit the values in the column.
	ComboBox object—you can't type in the textbox.
False	**TextBox** control—you can edit the text in the control.
	Column object—you can edit the values in the column.
	ComboBox object—you can type in the textbox and drop down its list.

Remarks

For the **Column** object, the default setting of **Locked** is the value of the **DataUpdatable** property for the underlying field; however, if **Column** is unbound or the data source doesn't support **DataUpdatable**, the default is **True**. If **DataUpdatable** in the underlying field is **False**, you do not create an error by setting this property to **True**. However, an error will occur when the control attempts to write the changed data to the database.

For the **ComboBox** control, when **Locked** is set to **True**, the user cannot change any data, but can highlight data in the text box and copy it. This property does not affect programmatic access to the **ComboBox**.

LockEdits Property

Sets or returns a value indicating the type of locking that is in effect while editing.

Applies To

Dynaset-Type Recordset Object, **Recordset** Object, **Snapshot-Type Recordset** Object, **Table-Type Recordset** Object, **Dynamic-Type Recordset** Object

Settings and Return Values

The setting or return value is a **Boolean** that indicates the type of locking, as specified in the following table.

Value	Description
True	Default. Pessimistic locking is in effect. The 2K page containing the record you're editing is locked as soon as you call the **Edit** method.
False	Optimistic locking is in effect for editing. The 2K page containing the record is not locked until the **Update** method is executed.

Remarks

You can use the **LockEdits** property with updatable **Recordset** objects.

If a page is locked, no other user can edit records on the same page. If you set **LockEdits** to **True** and another user already has the page locked, an error occurs when you use the **Edit** method. Other users can read data from locked pages.

If you set the **LockEdits** property to **False** and later use the **Update** method while another user has the page locked, an error occurs. To see the changes made to your record by another user, use the **Move** method with 0 as the argument; however, if you do this, you will lose your changes.

When working with Microsoft Jet-connected ODBC data sources, the **LockEdits** property is always set to **False**, or optimistic locking. The Microsoft Jet database engine has no control over the locking mechanisms used in external database servers.

Note You can preset the value of **LockEdits** when you first open the **Recordset** by setting the *lockedits* argument of the **OpenRecordset** method. Setting the *lockedits* argument to **dbPessimistic** will set the **LockEdits** property to **True**, and setting *lockedits* to any other value will set the **LockEdits** property to **False.**

See Also

Close Method, **FindFirst, FindLast, FindNext, FindPrevious** Methods, **MoveFirst, MoveLast, MoveNext, MovePrevious** Methods, **Bookmark** Property, **IsolateODBCTrans** Property

Example

This example demonstrates pessimistic locking by setting the **LockEdits** property to **True**, and then demonstrates optimistic locking by setting the **LockEdits** property to **False**. It also demonstrates what kind of error handling is required in a multiuser database environment in order to modify a field. The **PessimisticLock** and **OptimisticLock** functions are required for this procedure to run.

```
Sub LockEditsX()

    Dim dbsNorthwind As Database
    Dim rstCustomers As Recordset
    Dim strOldName As String

    Set dbsNorthwind = OpenDatabase("Northwind.mdb")
    Set rstCustomers = _
        dbsNorthwind.OpenRecordset("Customers", _
        dbOpenDynaset)

    With rstCustomers
        ' Store original data.
        strOldName = !CompanyName

        If MsgBox("Pessimistic locking demonstration...", _
                vbOKCancel) = vbOK Then

            ' Attempt to modify data with pessimistic locking
            ' in effect.
            If PessimisticLock(rstCustomers, !CompanyName, _
                    "Acme Foods") Then
                MsgBox "Record successfully edited."

                ' Restore original data...
                .Edit
                !CompanyName = strOldName
                .Update
            End If

        End If

        If MsgBox("Optimistic locking demonstration...", _
                vbOKCancel) = vbOK Then

            ' Attempt to modify data with optimistic locking
            ' in effect.
            If OptimisticLock(rstCustomers, !CompanyName, _
                    "Acme Foods") Then
                MsgBox "Record successfully edited."

                ' Restore original data...
                .Edit
                !CompanyName = strOldName
                .Update
            End If

        End If

        .Close
```

```
    End With

    dbsNorthwind.Close

End Sub

Function PessimisticLock(rstTemp As Recordset, _
    fldTemp As Field, strNew As String) As Boolean

    dim ErrLoop as Error

    PessimisticLock = True

    With rstTemp
        .LockEdits = True

        ' When you set LockEdits to True, you trap for errors
        ' when you call the Edit method.
        On Error GoTo Err_Lock
        .Edit
        On Error GoTo 0

        ' If the Edit is still in progress, then no errors
        ' were triggered; you may modify the data.
        If .EditMode = dbEditInProgress Then
            fldTemp = strNew
            .Update
            .Bookmark = .LastModified
        Else
            ' Retrieve current record to see changes made by
            ' other user.
            .Move 0
        End If

    End With

    Exit Function

Err_Lock:

    If DBEngine.Errors.Count > 0 Then
        ' Enumerate the Errors collection.
        For Each errLoop In DBEngine.Errors
            MsgBox "Error number: " & errLoop.Number & _
                vbCr & errLoop.Description
        Next errLoop
        PessimisticLock = False
    End If

    Resume Next

End Function

Function OptimisticLock(rstTemp As Recordset, _
    fldTemp As Field, strNew As String) As Boolean

    dim ErrLoop as Error

    OptimisticLock = True
```

```
        With rstTemp
           .LockEdits = False
           .Edit
           fldTemp = strNew

           ' When you set LockEdits to False, you trap for errors
           ' when you call the Update method.
           On Error GoTo Err_Lock
           .Update
           On Error GoTo 0

           ' If there is no Edit in progress, then no errors were
           ' triggered; you may modify the data.
           If .EditMode = dbEditNone Then
              ' Move current record pointer to the most recently
              ' modified record.
              .Bookmark = .LastModified
           Else
              .CancelUpdate
              ' Retrieve current record to see changes made by
              ' other user.
              .Move 0
           End If

        End With

        Exit Function

    Err_Lock:

        If DBEngine.Errors.Count > 0 Then
           ' Enumerate the Errors collection.
           For Each errLoop In DBEngine.Errors
              MsgBox "Error number: " & errLoop.Number & _
                  vbCr & errLoop.Description
           Next errLoop
           OptimisticLock = False
        End If

        Resume Next

    End Function
```

LockEdits Property (Remote Data)

Returns a **Boolean** value indicating the type of locking that is in effect.

Applies To

    rdoResultset Object

Syntax

    object.**LockEdits**

The *object* placeholder represents an object expression that evaluates to an object in the **Applies To** list.

Return Values

The return values for **LockEdits** are:

Setting	Description
True	Pessimistic locking is in effect.
False	(Default) Optimistic locking is in effect.

Remarks

If a page is locked and the data source uses page locking, no other user can edit rows on the same page. If row-level locking is used, the row being edited and all other rows in the rowset are locked. The rowset is defined as the number of rows specified by the **RowsetSize** property. If **LockEdits** is **True** and another user already has the page locked, an error occurs when you use the **OpenResultset** method. Generally, other users can read data from locked pages.

If **LockEdits** is **False** (the default) and you later use **Update** while the page is locked by another user, an error occurs. To see the changes made to your row by another user (and lose your changes), set the **Bookmark** property of your **rdoResultset** object to itself.

Note Data page size is determined by the data source. Microsoft SQL Server uses 2K data pages.

See Also

CancelUpdate Method (Remote Data), **Close** Method (Remote Data), **Edit** Method (Remote Data), **Update** Method (Remote Data), **rdoResultset** Object, **Bookmark** Property (Remote Data)

LockType Property (Remote Data)

Returns or sets a **Long** integer value indicating the type of concurrency handling.

Applies To

rdoPreparedStatement Object, **RemoteData** Control

Syntax

object.**LockType** [= *value*]

The **LockType** property syntax has these parts:

Part	Description
object	An object expression that evaluates to an object in the **Applies To** list.
value	A constant or **Long** value as described in Settings.

Settings

The settings for *value* are:

Constant	Value	Description
rdConcurReadOnly	1	(Default) Cursor is read-only. No updates are allowed.
rdConcurLock	2	Pessimistic concurrency.
rdConcurRowVer	3	Optimistic concurrency based on row ID.
rdConcurValues	4	Optimistic concurrency based on row values.
rdConcurBatch	5	Optimistic concurrency using batch mode updates. **Status** values returned for each row successfully updated.

Remarks

In order to maintain adequate control over the data being updated, RDO provides a number of concurrency options that control how other users are granted, or refused access to the data being updated. In many cases, when you lock a particular row using one of the **LockType** settings, the remote engine might also lock the entire page containing the row. If too many pages are locked, the remote engine might also escalate the page lock to a table lock to improve overall system performance.

Not all lock types are supported on all data sources. For example, for SQL Server and Oracle servers using the **rdUseODBC** cursor library, static-type **rdoResultset** objects can only support **rdConcurValues** or **rdConcurReadOnly**.

If the concurrency option is not supported by the data source, the driver substitutes a different concurrency option at execution time if one is available. If the driver cannot substitute a suitable alternative concurrency option, a trappable error is fired (SQLState Code 01S02 "Option Value Changed"). For **rdConcurValues**, the driver substitutes **rdConcurRowVer** and vice versa. For **rdConcurLock**, the driver substitutes, in order: **rdConcurRowVer** or **rdConcurValues**.

Choosing a Concurrency Option

Note RDO concurrency does not function as it does with Data Access Objects (DAO). Be sure to review the following sections to determine the best type of concurrency control for your application.

- **Read-Only Concurrency:** This option does not impose any exclusive locks on the rows fetched. In most cases, however, you must be granted a share lock to gain access to the rows. In other words, other users cannot have exclusive locks (read-write or intend to write locks) on the pages being accessed. Choosing this option makes the cursor read-only. This does not preclude use of action queries to update the data independent of the cursor. This is the default **LockType**.

- **Pessimistic Concurrency:** This option requests an *immediate* exclusive lock on the cursor rows which implements the lowest level of locking sufficient to ensure the row can be updated. Unlike DAO, which defers locking until the **Edit** method is used, RDO locks the first **RowsetSize** rows of the result set when the cursor is first opened with the **OpenResultset** method. That is, if your **RowsetSize** is 100 rows, the remote engine is instructed to lock each page that contains one of these selected rows. This means up to 100 pages can be locked—which can lock hundreds of rows. As the current row pointer is moved through the result set, additional pages are locked, and those no longer referenced are released. This technique assures your application that no other application is granted exclusive (read/write) access to any rows being processed by the cursor.

- **Optimistic Concurrency:** This type of concurrency management does not lock any rows or pages—it simply compares the row being posted to the database with the row as it currently exists on the server. Depending on the type of optimistic concurrency chosen, RDO and the ODBC layers compare either the row ID, the row data values, TimeStamp columns or combinations of these options with existing data to determine if a row has changed since last fetched. If no changes have taken place since the last fetch, the update is made. Otherwise, your application triggers a trappable error.

The **LockType** property supports three types of optimistic concurrency as described below. When using the Optimistic Batch Concurrency option (**rdConcurBatch**), you should also set the **UpdateCriteria** property to choose an appropriate update concurrency option.

- **Optimistic Concurrency — Row Version:** By comparing the row identifier (usually a TimeStamp column), RDO can determine if the row has changed since last fetched. If it has, a trappable error results.

- **Optimistic Concurrency — Row Values:** By comparing row values on a column-by-column basis, RDO can determine if the row has changed since last fetched. If it has, a trappable error results.

- **Optimistic Batch:** This type of concurrency uses the **UpdateCriteria** property to determine how to test if rows have changed when using the **UpdateBatch** method.

See Also

CreatePreparedStatement Method (Remote Data), **OpenResultset** Method (Remote Data), **rdoPreparedStatement** Object

LOF Function

Returns a **Long** representing the size, in bytes, of a file opened using the **Open** statement.

Syntax

LOF(*filenumber*)

The required *filenumber* argument is an **Integer** containing a valid file number.

Note Use the **FileLen** function to obtain the length of a file that is not open.

FileLen Function, **EOF** Function, **Loc** Function, **Open** Statement

Example

This example uses the **LOF** function to determine the size of an open file. This example assumes that TESTFILE is a text file containing sample data.

```
Dim FileLength
Open "TESTFILE" For Input As #1     ' Open file.
FileLength = LOF(1)                 ' Get length of file.
Close #1                            ' Close file.
```

Log Function

Returns a **Double** specifying the natural logarithm of a number.

Syntax

Log(*number*)

The required *number* argument is a **Double** or any valid numeric expression greater than zero.

Remarks

The natural logarithm is the logarithm to the base *e*. The constant *e* is approximately 2.718282.

You can calculate base-*n* logarithms for any number *x* by dividing the natural logarithm of *x* by the natural logarithm of *n* as follows:

$$\text{Log}n(x) = \textbf{Log}(x) / \textbf{Log}(n)$$

The following example illustrates a custom **Function** that calculates base-10 logarithms:

```
Static Function Log10(X)
    Log10 = Log(X) / Log(10#)
End Function
```

See Also

Math Functions, **Exp** Function, **Derived Math** Functions

Example

This example uses the **Log** function to return the natural logarithm of a number.

```
Dim MyAngle, MyLog
' Define angle in radians.
MyAngle = 1.3
' Calculate inverse hyperbolic sine.
MyLog = Log(MyAngle + Sqr(MyAngle * MyAngle + 1))
```

LogEvent Method

Logs an event in the application's log target. On Windows NT platforms, the method writes to the NT Event log. On Windows 95 platforms, the method writes to the file specified in the **LogPath** property; by default, if no file is specified, events will be written to a file named vbevents.

Applies To

App Object

Syntax

object.**LogEvent** (*logBuffer, eventType*)

Part	Description
object	An object expression that evaluates to an object in the **Applies To** list.
logBuffer	Required. String to be written to the log.
eventType	Optional. A Long integer that specifies the type of event, as shown in Settings.

Settings

The settings for *eventType* are:

Constant	Value	Description
vbLogEventTypeError	1	Error.
vbLogEventTypeWarning	2	Warning.
vbLogEventTypeInformation	4	Information.

Remarks

Guidelines for logging are available in the Win32 SDK, and those guidelines should be followed when logging either to the NT Event log or the file specified in the **LogPath** property (on Windows 95 platforms).

See Also

LogMode Property, **LogPath** Property

LoginTimeout Property

Sets or returns the number of seconds before an error occurs when you attempt to log on to an ODBC database.

Applies To

DBEngine Object, **Workspace** Object

Settings and Return Values

The setting or return value is an **Integer** representing the number of seconds before a login timeout error occurs. The default **LoginTimeout** property setting is 20 seconds. When the **LoginTimeout** property is set to 0, no timeout occurs.

Remarks

When you're attempting to log on to an ODBC database, such as Microsoft SQL Server, the connection can fail as a result of network errors or because the server isn't running. Rather than waiting for the default 20 seconds to connect, you can specify how long to wait before raising an error. Logging on to the server happens implicitly as part of a number of different events, such as running a query on an external server database.

You can use **LoginTimeout** on the **DBEngine** object in both Microsoft Jet and ODBCDirect workspaces. You can use **LoginTimeout** on the **Workspace** object only in ODBCDirect workspaces. Setting the property to–1 on a **Workspace** will default to the current setting of **DBEngine.LoginTimeout**. You can change this property in a **Workspace** at any time, and the new setting will take effect with the next **Connection** or **Database** object opened.

The default value is determined by the ODBC driver. In a Microsoft Jet workspace, you can override the driver's default value by creating a new "ODBC" key in the Registry path **\HKEY_LOCAL_MACHINE\SOFTWARE\Jet\3.5**, creating a **LoginTimeout** parameter in this key, and setting the value as desired.

See Also

QueryDef Object, **ODBCTimeout** Property, **QueryTimeout** Property

Example

This example sets the **LoginTimeout** property of the **DBEngine** object to 120 seconds. It then opens three ODBCDirect workspaces and modifies their **LoginTimeout** properties from the default inherited from the **DBEngine** object.

```
Sub LoginTimeoutX()

    ' Change the default LoginTimeout value.
    DBEngine.LoginTimeout = 120

    Dim wrkODBC1 As Workspace
    Dim wrkODBC2 As Workspace
    Dim wrkODBC3 As Workspace

    Set wrkODBC1 = CreateWorkspace("", "admin", "", _
        dbUseODBC)
    Set wrkODBC2 = CreateWorkspace("", "admin", "", _
        dbUseODBC)
    Set wrkODBC3 = CreateWorkspace("", "admin", "", _
        dbUseODBC)

    ' Change the LoginTimeout of the individual ODBCDirect
    ' workspaces for 60 seconds, the default time (120
    ' seconds), and no timeout.
    wrkODBC1.LoginTimeout = 60
    wrkODBC2.LoginTimeout = -1
    wrkODBC2.LoginTimeout = 0

    wrkODBC1.Close
    wrkODBC2.Close
    wrkODBC3.Close

End Sub
```

LoginTimeout Property (Remote Data)

Returns or sets a value that specifies the number of seconds the ODBC driver manager waits before a timeout error occurs when a connection is opened.

Applies To

rdoEnvironment Object, **RemoteData** Control

Syntax

object.**LoginTimeout** [= *value*]

The **LoginTimeout** property syntax has these parts:

Part	Description
object	An object expression that evaluates to an object in the **Applies To** list.
value	A **Long** integer representing the number of seconds the driver manager waits before timing out and returning an error.

Remarks

If *value* is 0, no timeout occurs and an error does not occur if a connection cannot be established. If you are not using asynchronous connections, this might cause your application to block indefinitely.

When you're attempting to connect to an ODBC database, such as SQL Server, there may be delays due to network traffic or heavy use of the ODBC data source. Rather than waiting indefinitely, you can specify how long to wait before the ODBC driver manager produces an error.

The default timeout value is either 15 seconds or a value set by the **rdoDefaultLoginTimeout** property. When used with an **rdoEnvironment** object, the **LoginTimeout** property specifies a global value for all login operations associated with the **rdoEnvironment**. The **LoginTimeout** setting of on an **rdoConnection** object overrides the default value.

If the specified timeout exceeds the maximum timeout in the data source, or is smaller than the minimum timeout, the driver substitutes that value and the following error is logged in the **rdoErrors** collection: SQLState 01S02 `"Option value changed."`

Typically, a connection to a remote server on a Local Area Network (LAN) takes under eight seconds to complete. Remote Access Service (RAS) or Internet connections can take far longer depending on Wide Area Network bandwidth, load and other factors.

See Also

rdoEngine Object, **QueryTimeout** Property (Remote Data), **rdoDefaultLoginTimeout** Property (Remote Data)

LogMessages Property

Sets or returns a value that specifies if the messages returned from a Microsoft Jet-connected ODBC data source are recorded (Microsoft Jet workspaces only).

Note Before you can set or get the value of the **LogMessages** property, you must create the **LogMessages** property with the **CreateProperty** method, and append it to the **Properties** collection of a **QueryDef** object.

Applies To

QueryDef Object

Settings and Return Values

The setting or return value is a **Boolean** that is **True** if ODBC-generated messages are recorded.

Remarks

Some pass-through queries can return messages in addition to data. If you set the **LogMessages** property to **True**, the Microsoft Jet database engine creates a table that contains returned messages. The table name is the user name concatenated with a hyphen (-) and a sequential number starting at 00. For example, because the default user name is Admin, the tables returned would be named Admin-00, Admin-01, and so on.

If you expect the query to return messages, create and append a user-defined **LogMessages** property for the **QueryDef** object, and set its type to **Boolean** and its value to **True**.

Once you've processed the results from these tables, you may want to delete them from the database along with the temporary query used to create them.

Example

This example uses the **LogMessages** and **ReturnsRecords** properties to create a pass-through query that will return data and any messages generated by the remote server.

```
Sub LogMessagesX()

    Dim wrkJet As Workspace
    Dim dbsCurrent As Database
    Dim qdfTemp As QueryDef
    Dim prpNew As Property
    Dim rstTemp As Recordset

    ' Create Microsoft Jet Workspace object.
    Set wrkJet = CreateWorkspace("", "admin", "", dbUseJet)

    Set dbsCurrent = wrkJet.OpenDatabase("DB1.mdb")
```

```
' Create a QueryDef that will log any messages from the
' server in temporary tables.
Set qdfTemp = dbsCurrent.CreateQueryDef("NewQueryDef")
qdfTemp.Connect = _
    "ODBC;DATABASE=pubs;UID=sa;PWD=;DSN=Publishers"
qdfTemp.SQL = "SELECT * FROM stores"
qdfTemp.ReturnsRecords = True
Set prpNew = qdfTemp.CreateProperty("LogMessages", _
    dbBoolean, True)
qdfTemp.Properties.Append prpNew

' Execute query and display results.
Set rstTemp = qdfTemp.OpenRecordset()

Debug.Print "Contents of recordset:"
With rstTemp
    Do While Not .EOF
        Debug.Print , .Fields(0), .Fields(1)
        .MoveNext
    Loop
    .Close
End With

' Delete new QueryDef because this is a demonstration.
dbsCurrent.QueryDefs.Delete qdfTemp.Name
dbsCurrent.Close
wrkJet.Close

End Sub
```

LogMessages Property (Remote Data)

Applies To

rdoPreparedStatement Object, **rdoQuery** Object, **RemoteData** Control

Enables ODBC trace logging and returns or sets a value indicating the path of the ODBC trace file created by the ODBC driver manager to record all ODBC operations.

Syntax

object.**LogMessages** [= *value*]

The **LogMessages** property syntax has these parts:

Part	Description
object	An object expression that evaluates to an object in the **Applies To** list.
value	A **String** expression as described in Settings.

Settings

V*alue* contains the path of an ASCII file used to log ODBC operations. If the **LogMessages** property is an empty string, no logging takes place.

Remarks

When the **LogMessages** property is **True**, all ODBC commands are sent to an ASCII log file that can be used to debug or tune queries or other operations.

On Windows NT or Windows 95, tracing should *only* be used for a single application or each application should specify a different trace file. Otherwise, two or more applications might attempt to open the same trace file at the same time, causing an error.

Note   ODBC performance is adversely affected when the log is enabled.

See Also

rdoResultset Object

LogMode Property

Returns a value which determines how logging (through the **LogEvent** method) will be carried out. Read-only at run time.

Applies To

App Object

Syntax

object.**LogMode** = *mode*

Part	Description
object	An object expression that evaluates to an object in the **Applies To** list.
mode	Long. Determines the method of logging, as shown in Settings below.

Settings

The settings for *mode* are:

Constant	Value	Description
vbLogAuto	0	If running on Windows 95, this option logs messages to the file specified in the **LogFile** property. If running on Windows NT, messages are logged to the NT Application Event Log, with the App.Title string used as the application source.
VbLogOff	1	Turns all logging off. Messages from UI shunts as well as from the **LogEvent** method are ignored and discarded.
VbLogToFile	2	Forces logging to a file. If no valid filename is present in **LogPath**, logging is ignored, and the property is set to **vbLogOff**.

(continued)

Constant	Value	Description
VbLogToNT	3	Forces logging to the NT Event log. If not running on Windows NT, or the event log is unavailable, logging is ignored and the property is set to **vbLogOff**.
VbLogOverwrite	0x10	Indicates that the logfile should be recreated each time the application starts. This value can be combined with other mode options using the OR operator. The default action for logging is to append to the existing file. In the case of NT event logging, this flag has no meaning.
VbLogThreadID	0x20	Indicates that the current thread ID be prepended to the message, in the form "[T:0nnn]". This value can be combined with other mode options using the OR operator. The default action is to show the thread ID only when the application is multi-threaded (either explicitly marked as thread-safe, or implemented as an implicit multithreaded app, such as a local server with the instancing property set to Single-Use, multithreaded).

Return Type

Long

See Also

LogEvent Method, **LogPath** Property

LogPath Property

Returns the path and filename of the file used to capture output from the **LogEvent** method. Not available at design-time; read-only at run time.

Applies To

App Object

Syntax

object.**LogPath** = *path*

Part	Description
object	An object expression that evaluates to an object in the **Applies To** list.
path	String. The path and filename of a log file.

Remarks

The **LogMode** property determines how logging will be carried out. If no **LogPath** is set, the **LogEvent** method writes to the **NT LogEvent** file.

See Also

LogEvent Method, **LogMode** Property

Long Data Type

Long (long integer) variables are stored as signed 32-bit (4-byte) numbers ranging in value from -2,147,483,648 to 2,147,483,647. The type-declaration character for **Long** is the ampersand (**&**).

See Also

Data Type Summary, **Integer Data** Type, **Deftype** Statements

---

LostFocus Event

Occurs when an object loses the focus, either by user action, such as tabbing to or clicking another object, or by changing the focus in code using the **SetFocus** method.

Applies To

PropertyPage Object, **Animation** Control, **DBCombo** Control, **DBGrid** Control, **DBList** Control, **UserControl** Object, **UserDocument** Object, **CheckBox** Control, **ComboBox** Control, **CommandButton** Control, **DirListBox** Control, **DriveListBox** Control, **FileListBox** Control, **Form** Object, **Forms** Collection, **HscrollBar**, **VscrollBar** Controls, **ListView** Control, **Masked Edit** Control, **MSFlexGrid** Control, **RichTextBox** Control, **Slider** Control, **TabStrip** Control, **TreeView** Control, **UpDown** Control, **ListBox** Control, **OptionButton** Control, **PictureBox** Control, **TextBox** Control, **OLE Container** Control

Syntax

Private Sub Form_LostFocus( )
Private Sub *object*_**LostFocus**([*index* **As Integer**])

The **LostFocus** event syntax has these parts:

Part	Description
object	An object expression that evaluates to an object in the **Applies To** list.
index	An integer that uniquely identifies a control if it's in a control array.

Remarks

A **LostFocus** event procedure is primarily useful for verification and validation updates. Using **LostFocus** can cause validation to take place as the user moves the focus from the control. Another use for this type of event procedure is enabling, disabling, hiding, and displaying other objects as in a **GotFocus** event procedure. You can also reverse or change conditions that you set up in the object's **GotFocus** event procedure.

If an .exe file built by Visual Basic displays a dialog box created by a .dll file also built in Visual Basic, the .exe file's form will get Deactivate and **LostFocus** events. This may be unexpected, because you should not get the Deactivate event:

- If the object is an out-of-process component.
- If the object isn't written in Visual Basic.
- In the development environment when calling a DLL built in Visual Basic.

See Also

CanGetFocus Property, **ExitFocus** Event

Example

This example changes the color of a **TextBox** control when it receives or loses the focus (selected with the mouse or TAB key) and displays the appropriate text in the **Label** control. To try this example, paste the code into the Declarations section of a form that contains two **TextBox** controls and a **Label** control, and then press F5 and move the focus between Text1 and Text2.

```
Private Sub Text1_GotFocus ()
   ' Show focus with red.
   Text1.BackColor = RGB(255, 0, 0)
   Label1.Caption = "Text1 has the focus."
End Sub

Private Sub Text1_LostFocus ()
   ' Show loss of focus with blue.
   Text1.BackColor = RGB(0, 0, 255)
   Label1.Caption = "Text1 doesn't have the focus."
End Sub
```

LostFocus Event (UserControl Object and UserDocument Object)

Occurs in the object or constituent control when focus leaves it.

Applies To

UserControl Object, **UserDocument** Object

Syntax

Sub *object*_**LostFocus**()

The **LostFocus** event syntax has these parts:

Part	Description
object	An object expression that evaluates to an object in the **Applies To** list.

Remarks

This **LostFocus** event is not the same **LostFocus** extender event that the developer who uses *object* handles. This **LostFocus** event is for the author of *object*, and is internal to *object*.

This event is useful if *object* needs to know that the focus is now on it.

Object itself can get focus only when the **CanGetFocus** property is **True** and there are no constituent controls that can receive focus.

The **LostFocus** event is raised before the **ExitFocus** event.

See Also

CanGetFocus Property, **ExitFocus** Event

lpOleObject Property

Returns the address of the object.

Applies To

OLE Container Control

Syntax

object.**lpOleObject**

The *object* placeholder represents an object expression that evaluates to an object in the **Applies To** list.

Remarks

Many function calls in the ActiveX DLLs require the address of an object as an argument. Pass the value specified in the **lpOleObject** property when making API calls to the ActiveX DLLs. The value is 0 if no object is currently displayed. If a call is made to an API that makes a callback to the **OLE** container control, the result is unpredictable.

The address returned by this property is a pointer to the **lpOleObject** interface for the active object.

LSet Statement

Left aligns a string within a string variable, or copies a variable of one user-defined type to another variable of a different user-defined type.

Syntax

LSet *stringvar* = *string*
LSet *varname1* = *varname2*

The **LSet** statement syntax has these parts:

Part	Description
stringvar	Required. Name of string variable.
string	Required. String expression to be left-aligned within *stringvar*.
varname1	Required. Variable name of the user-defined type being copied to.
varname2	Required. Variable name of the user-defined type being copied from.

Remarks

LSet replaces any leftover characters in *stringvar* with spaces.

If *string* is longer than *stringvar*, **LSet** places only the leftmost characters, up to the length of the *stringvar,* in *stringvar*.

Warning   Using **LSet** to copy a variable of one user-defined type into a variable of a different user-defined type is not recommended. Copying data of one data type into space reserved for a different data type can cause unpredictable results.

When you copy a variable from one user-defined type to another, the binary data from one variable is copied into the memory space of the other, without regard for the data types specified for the elements.

See Also

Data Type Summary, **RSet** Statement

Example

This example uses the **LSet** statement to left align a string within a string variable. Although **LSet** can also be used to copy a variable of one user-defined type to another variable of a different, but compatible, user-defined type, this practice is not recommended. Due to the varying implementations of data structures among platforms, such a use of **LSet** can't be guaranteed to be portable.

```
Dim MyString
MyString = "0123456789" ' Initialize string.
Lset MyString = "<-Left"' MyString contains "<-Left    ".
```

LTrim, RTrim, and Trim Functions

Returns a **Variant** (**String**) containing a copy of a specified string without leading spaces (**LTrim**), trailing spaces (**RTrim**), or both leading and trailing spaces (**Trim**).

Syntax

LTrim(*string*)
RTrim(*string*)
Trim(*string*)

The required *string* argument is any valid string expression. If *string* contains **Null**, **Null** is returned.

See Also

Left Function, **Right** Function

Example

This example uses the **LTrim** function to strip leading spaces and the **RTrim** function to strip trailing spaces from a string variable. It uses the **Trim** function to strip both types of spaces.

```
Dim MyString, TrimString
MyString = "  <-Trim->  "               ' Initialize string.
TrimString = LTrim(MyString)            ' TrimString = "<-Trim->  ".
TrimString = RTrim(MyString)            ' TrimString = "  <-Trim->".
TrimString = LTrim(RTrim(MyString))     ' TrimString = "<-Trim->".
' Using the Trim function alone achieves the same result.
TrimString = Trim(MyString)             ' TrimString = "<-Trim->".
```

MainWindow Property

Returns a **Window** object representing the main window of the Visual Basic development environment. Read-only.

Applies To

VBE Object

Remarks

You can use the **Window** object returned by the **MainWindow** property to add or remove docked windows. You can also use the **Window** object returned by the **MainWindow** property to maximize, minimize, hide, or restore the main window of the Visual Basic development environment.

See Also

Add Method, **Close** Method, **Remove** Method, **SetFocus** Method, **Window** Object, **Windows** Collection, **ActiveWindow** Property, **Caption** Property, **Visible** Property

Example

The following example uses the **MainWindow** property to return the **Window** object representing the main window, and then prints the caption of the main window.

```
Debug.Print Application.VBE.MainWindow.Caption
```

Major Property (Projects)

Returns or sets the major release number of the project. Read-only at run time.

Applies To

App Object

Syntax

object.**Major**

The *object* placeholder represents an object expression that evaluates to an object in the **Applies To** list.

Remarks

The value of the **Major** property is in the range from 0 to 9999.

This property provides version information about the running application.

You can set this property at design time in the **Major** box in the **Make** tab of the **Project Properties** dialog box.

See Also

Minor Property, **Revision** Property

Major Property (Type Libraries)

Returns a **Long** containing the major version number of the referenced type library. Read-only.

Applies To

Reference Object

Remarks

The number returned by the **Major** property corresponds to the major version number stored in the type library to which you have set the reference.

See Also

Minor Property, **Version** Property

Example

The following example uses the **Major** property to return the major version number of the specified **Reference** object in a particular project.

```
Debug.Print Application.VBE.VBProjects(1).References(1).Major
```

MakeCompiledFile Method

Causes the current project to be written as an Exe, Dll, or control, depending on project type.

Applies To

VBProject Object

Syntax

object.**MakeCompiledFile**

The *object* placeholder represents an object expression that evaluates to an object in the **Applies To** list.

MakeReplica Method

Makes a new replica from another database replica (Microsoft Jet workspaces only).

Applies To

Database Object

Syntax

database.**MakeReplica** *replica*, *description*, *options*

The **MakeReplica** method syntax has the following parts.

Part	Description
database	An object variable that represents an existing **Database** that is a replica.
Replica	A **String** that is the path and file name of the new replica. If *replica* is an existing file name, then an error occurs.
Description	A **String** that describes the replica that you are creating.
Options	Optional. A constant or combination of constants that specifies characteristics of the replica you are creating, as specified in Settings.

Settings

You can use one or more of the following constants in the *options* argument.

Constant	Description
dbRepMakePartial	Creates a partial replica.
DbRepMakeReadOnly	Prevents users from modifying the replicable objects of the new replica; however, when you synchronize the new replica with another member of the replica set, design and data changes will be propagated to the new replica.

Remarks

A newly created partial replica will have all **ReplicaFilter** properties set to **False**, meaning that no data will be in the tables.

Example

This function uses the **MakeReplica** method to create an additional replica of an existing Design Master. The intOptions argument can be a combination of the constants **dbRepMakeReadOnly** and **dbRepMakePartial**, or it can be 0. For example, to create a read-only partial replica, you should pass the value dbRepMakeReadOnly + dbRepMakePartial as the value of intOptions.

```
Function MakeAdditionalReplica(strReplicableDB As _
    String, strNewReplica As String, intOptions As _
    Integer) As Integer

    Dim dbsTemp As Database
    On Error GoTo ErrorHandler
```

```
      Set dbsTemp = OpenDatabase(strReplicableDB)

      ' If no options are passed to
      ' MakeAdditionalReplica, omit the
      ' options argument, which defaults to
      ' a full, read/write replica. Otherwise,
      ' use the value of intOptions.

      If intOptions = 0 Then
         dbsTemp.MakeReplica strNewReplica, _
            "Replica of " & strReplicableDB
      Else
         dbsTemp.MakeReplica strNewReplica, _
            "Replica of " & strReplicableDB, _
            intOptions
      End If

      dbsTemp.Close

ErrorHandler:
   Select Case Err
      Case 0:
         MakeAdditionalReplica = 0
         Exit Function
      Case Else:
         MsgBox "Error " & Err & " : " & Error
         MakeAdditionalReplica = Err
         Exit Function
   End Select

End Function
```

MarqueeStyle Property

Sets or returns the Marquee style for the **DBGrid** control or **Split** object.

Applies To

Split Object, **DBGrid** Control

Syntax

object.**MarqueeStyle** [= *value*]

The **MarqueeStyle** property syntax has these parts:

Part	Description
object	An object expression that evaluates to an object in the **Applies To** list.
value	A number or constant that specifies the Marquee style, as described in Settings.

Settings

The settings for *value* are:

Constant	Value	Description
dbgDottedCellBorder	0	The current cell within the current row will be highlighted by drawing a dotted border around the cell. In Microsoft Windows terminology, this is usually called a focus rectangle.
dbgSolidCellBorder	1	The current cell within the current row will be highlighted by drawing a solid box around the current cell. This is more visible than the dotted cell border, especially when 3-D divider properties are used for the grid.
dbgHighlightCell	2	The entire current cell will be highlighted by inverting the colors within the cell. This provides a very distinctive block-style highlight for the current cell.
dbgHighlightRow	3	The entire row containing the current cell will be highlighted by inverting the colors within the row. In this mode, it is not possible to visually determine which cell is the current cell, only the current row. When the grid or split is not editable, this setting is often preferred, since cell position is then irrelevant.
dbgHighlightRowRaiseCell	4	The entire row will be highlighted. The current cell within the row will be "raised" so that it appears distinctive. This setting doesn't appear clearly with all background color and divider settings. The best effect is achieved by using 3-D dividers and a light gray background.
dbgNoMarquee	5	The marquee will not be shown. This setting is useful for cases where the current row is irrelevant, or where you don't want to draw the user's attention to the grid until necessary.
dbgFloatingEditor	6	The current cell will be highlighted by a floating text editor window with a blinking caret (as in Microsoft Access). This is the default setting.

Remarks

If a grid contains multiple splits, then setting its **MarqueeStyle** property has the same effect as setting the **MarqueeStyle** property of each split individually.

Note If the floating editor marquee setting is in effect and the current cell contains radio buttons or graphics, then a dotted focus rectangle will be displayed.

See Also

MarqueeUnique Property

MarqueeUnique Property

Sets or returns a value that determines whether the marquee is displayed only in the current split.

Applies To

DBGrid Control

Syntax

object.**MarqueeUnique** [= *value*]

The **MarqueeUnique** property syntax has these parts:

Part	Description
object	An object expression that evaluates to an object in the **Applies To** list.
value	A Boolean expression that determines whether the marquee is displayed only in the current split, as described in Settings.

Settings

The settings for *value* are:

Setting	Description
True	(Default) The current cell marquee is only displayed within the current split.
False	All splits with a **MarqueeStyle** setting as described in Remarks will display a marquee at the current cell, provided that the current cell is visible.

Remarks

The current cell marquee is only displayed when the **MarqueeStyle** property for a grid or split has a value of 0, 1, 2, or 4.

In most cases, a single current cell marquee is preferable, and you will not need to change this property.

If this property is set to **False**, you may then see several different current cell marquees. The actual current cell is determined by the setting of the **Split** property.

Note Although the floating editor **MarqueeStyle** (6) is technically a current cell marquee, only one floating editor will be displayed, even if **MarqueeUnique** is set to **False**.

See Also

MarqueeStyle Property

MaskColor Property

Returns or sets a color in a button's picture to be a "mask" (that is, transparent).

Applies To

CheckBox Control, **CommandButton** Control, **OptionButton** Control

Syntax

object.**MaskColor** [= *color*]

The **MaskColor** property syntax has these parts:

Part	Description
object	An object expression that evaluates to an object in the **Applies To** list.
color	A value or constant that determines the color to be used as a mask, as described in **Settings**.

Settings

Visual Basic uses the Microsoft Windows operating environment red-green-blue (RGB) color scheme. The settings for *color* are:

Setting	Description
Normal RGB colors	Colors specified using the Color palette or by using the **RGB** or **QBColor** functions in code.
&H00C0C0C0	(Default) Light gray.

Remarks

If the system colors change, then the color which is transparent will change, making the look of your picture unpredictable. It is good programming practice to use non-system colors.

This property is used only when the **UseMask** property is set to **True** and the button has a bitmap-style picture assigned to its **Picture** property. (Icons and metafiles already contain tranparency information.)

If the **MaskColor** property is changed at run time, the button will redraw itself with the new color acting as a mask.

MatchedWithList Property

Returns **True** if the current content of the **BoundText** property matches one of the records in the list portion of the control.

Applies To

DBCombo Control, **DBList** Control

Syntax

object.**MatchedWithList**

The *object* placeholder represents an object expression that evaluates to an object in the **Applies To** list.

Return Values

The **MatchedWithList** property return values are:

Value	Description
True	The content of the **BoundText** property matches one of the records in the list.
False	The contents of the **BoundText** property does not match any of the records in the list.

Remarks

When you enter a value in the text portion of the **DBCombo** control, the **MatchedWithList** property is set to **True** if the value entered is one of the items shown in the list. Moving the **Data** control specified by the **DataSource** property of the **DBCombo** or **DBList** control also sets the **MatchedWithList** property to **True** if the **BoundText** value matches one of the records in the list. In this case, the record is highlighted.

Data Type

Boolean

See Also

Data Control, **DataSource** Property, **BoundText** Property

MatchEntry Property

Returns or sets a value indicating how the **DBCombo** or **DBList** control performs searches based on user input.

Applies To

DBCombo Control, **DBList** Control

Syntax

object.**MatchEntry** [= *value*]

The **MatchEntry** property syntax has these parts:

Part	Description
object	An object expression that evaluates to an object in the **Applies To** list.
value	A constant or value that defines the behavior of a control when it has focus and the user enters one or more characters, as described in **Settings**.

Settings

The settings for *value* are:

Setting	Value	Description
dblBasicMatching	0	Basic Matching: (Default) The control searches for the next match for the character entered using the first letter of entries in the list. Repeatedly typing the same letter cycles through all of the entries in the list beginning with that letter.
dblExtendedMatching	1	Extended Matching: The control searches for an entry matching all characters entered. The search is done as characters are being typed, further refining the search.

Remarks

When the **MatchEntry** property is set to **dblExtendedMatching** and the user enters a backspace or waits more than a few seconds, the matching string is reset.

Data Type

Integer

See Also

Data Control, **MatchedWithList** Property

Max, Min Properties (Scroll Bar)

- **Max**—returns or sets a scroll bar position's maximum **Value** property setting when the scroll box is in its bottom or rightmost position. For the **ProgressBar** control, it returns or sets its maximum value.

- **Min**—returns or sets a scroll bar position's minimum **Value** property setting when the scroll box is in its top or leftmost position. For the **ProgressBar** control, it returns or sets its minimum value.

Applies To

HScrollBar, VScrollBar Controls

Syntax

object.**Max** [= *value*]
object.**Min** [= *value*]

The **Max** and **Min** property syntaxes have these parts:

Part	Description
object	An object expression that evaluates to an object in the **Applies To** list.
value	A numeric expression specifying the maximum or minimum **Value** property setting, as described in Settings.

Settings

For each property, you can specify an integer between –32,768 and 32,767, inclusive. The default settings are:

- **Max**—32,767.
- **Min**—0.

Remarks

The Microsoft Windows operating environment automatically sets ranges for scroll bars proportional to the contents of forms, **ComboBox** controls, and **ListBox** controls. For a scroll bar (**HScrollBar** or **VScrollBar**) control, however, you must specify these ranges. Use **Max** and **Min** to set a range appropriate to how the scroll bar control is used—for example, as an input device or as an indicator of speed or quantity.

Typically, you set **Max** and **Min** at design time. You can also set them in code at run time if the scrolling range must change dynamically—for example, when adding records to a database that can be scrolled through. You set the maximum and minimum scrolling increments for a scroll bar control with the **LargeChange** and **SmallChange** properties.

Note If **Max** is set to less than **Min**, the maximum value is set at the leftmost or topmost position of a horizontal or vertical scroll bar, respectively. The **Max** property of a **ProgressBar** control must always be greater than its **Min** property, and its **Min** property must always be greater than or equal to 0.

The **Max** and **Min** properties define the range of the control. The **ProgressBar** control's **Min** property is 0 and its **Max** property is 100 by default, representing the percentage duration of the operation.

See Also

LargeChange, **SmallChange** Properties

MaxButton Property

Returns a value indicating whether a form has a Maximize button.

Applies To

Form Object, **Forms** Collection

Syntax

object.**MaxButton**

The *object* placeholder represents an object expression that evaluates to an object in the **Applies To** list.

Settings

The **MaxButton** property settings are:

Setting	Description
True	(Default) The form has a Maximize button.
False	The form doesn't have a Maximize button.

Remarks

A Maximize button enables users to enlarge a form window to full-screen size. To display a Maximize button, you must also set the form's **BorderStyle** property to either 1 (Fixed Single), 2 (Sizable), or 3 (Fixed Double).

A Maximize button automatically becomes a Restore button when a window is maximized. Minimizing or restoring a window automatically changes the Restore button back to a Maximize button.

The settings you specify for the **MaxButton**, **MinButton**, **BorderStyle**, and **ControlBox** properties aren't reflected in the form's appearance until run time.

Note Maximizing a form at run time generates a Resize event. The **WindowState** property reflects the current state of the window. If you set the **WindowState** property to 2 (Maximized), the form is maximized independently of whatever settings are in effect for the **MaxButton** and **BorderStyle** properties.

See Also

ControlBox Property, **MinButton** Property

MaxLength Property

Returns or sets a value indicating whether there is a maximum number of characters that can be entered in the **TextBox** control and, if so, specifies the maximum number of characters that can be entered.

Note In DBCS (double-byte character set) systems, each character can take up to two bytes instead of only one, which limits the number of characters you can enter.

Applies To

TextBox Control

Syntax

object.**MaxLength** [= *value*]

The **MaxLength** property syntax has these parts:

Part	Description
object	An object expression that evaluates to an object in the **Applies To** list.

Part	Description
value	An integer specifying the maximum number of characters a user can enter in a **TextBox** control. The default for the **MaxLength** property is 0, indicating no maximum other than that created by memory constraints on the user's system for single-line **TextBox** controls and a maximum of approximately 32K for multiple-line **TextBox** controls. Any number greater than 0 indicates the maximum number of characters.

Remarks

Use the **MaxLength** property to limit the number of characters a user can enter in a **TextBox**.

If text that exceeds the **MaxLength** property setting is assigned to a **TextBox** from code, no error occurs; however, only the maximum number of characters is assigned to the **Text** property, and extra characters are truncated. Changing this property doesn't affect the current contents of a **TextBox** but will affect any subsequent changes to the contents.

Example

This example uses a numeric value in one **TextBox** control to limit the length of text in another **TextBox** control. To try this example, paste the code into the Declarations section of a form that contains two **TextBox** controls. Make Text1 fairly large, and then press F5. Enter a number into Text2 and text into Text1.

```
Private Sub Text1_Change ()
    Text1.MaxLength = Text2.Text
End Sub
```

MaxRecords Property

Sets or returns the maximum number of records to return from a query.

Applies To

QueryDef Object

Settings And Return Values

The setting or return value is a **Long** that represents the number of records to be returned. The default value is 0, indicating no limit on the number of records returned.

Remarks

Once the number of rows specified by **MaxRecords** is returned to your application in a **Recordset**, the query processor will stop returning additional records even if more records would qualify for inclusion in the **Recordset**. This property is useful in situations where limited client resources prohibit management of large numbers of records.

Example

This example uses the **MaxRecords** property to set a limit on how many records are returned by a query on an ODBC data source.

```
Sub MaxRecordsX()

    Dim dbsCurrent As Database
    Dim qdfPassThrough As QueryDef
    Dim qdfLocal As QueryDef
    Dim rstTemp As Recordset

    ' Open a database from which QueryDef objects can be
    ' created.
    Set dbsCurrent = OpenDatabase("DB1.mdb")

    ' Create a pass-through query to retrieve data from
    ' a Microsoft SQL Server database.
    Set qdfPassThrough = _
        dbsCurrent.CreateQueryDef("")

    ' Set the properties of the new query, limiting the
    ' number of returnable records to 20.
    qdfPassThrough.Connect = _
        "ODBC;DATABASE=pubs;UID=sa;PWD=;DSN=Publishers"
    qdfPassThrough.SQL = "SELECT * FROM titles"
    qdfPassThrough.ReturnsRecords = True
    qdfPassThrough.MaxRecords = 20

    Set rstTemp = qdfPassThrough.OpenRecordset()

    ' Display results of query.
    Debug.Print "Query results:"
    With rstTemp
        Do While Not .EOF
            Debug.Print , .Fields(0), .Fields(1)
            .MoveNext
        Loop
        .Close
    End With

    dbsCurrent.Close

End Sub
```

MaxRows Property (Remote Data)

Returns or sets a value indicating the maximum number of rows to be returned from a query or processed in an action query.

Applies To

rdoPreparedStatement Object, **rdoQuery** Object, **RemoteData** Control

Syntax

object.**MaxRows** [= *value*]

The **MaxRows** property syntax has these parts:

Part	Description
object	An object expression that evaluates to an object in the **Applies To** list.
value	A **Long** expression as described in Settings.

Settings

The setting for *value* ranges from 0 to any number. If *value* is set to 0, no limit is placed on the number of rows returned (default). Setting *value* to a negative number is invalid and is automatically reset to 0.

Remarks

The **MaxRows** property limits the number of rows processed by the remote server. When **MaxRows** is set to a value greater than 0, only '*n*' rows are processed. When executing a query that returns rows, it means that only the first '*n*' rows are returned. When executing an action query, it means that only the first '*n*' rows are updated, inserted or deleted.

This property is useful in situations where limited resources prohibit management of large numbers of result set rows. By setting **MaxRows** to 1 on an action query, you can be assured that no more than one row will be affected by the operation.

See Also

RowsAffected Property

MDIChild Property

Returns or sets a value indicating whether a form is displayed as an MDI child form inside an MDI form. Read only at run time.

Applies To

Form Object, **Forms** Collection

Syntax

object.**MDIChild**

The *object* placeholder represents an object expression that evaluates to an object in the **Applies To** list.

Settings

The **MDIChild** property settings are:

Setting	Description
True	The form is an MDI child form and is displayed inside the parent MDI form.
False	(Default) The form isn't an MDI child form.

Remarks

Use this property when creating a multiple-document interface (MDI) application. At run time, forms with this property set to **True** are displayed inside an MDI form.

An MDI child form can be maximized, minimized, and moved, all inside the parent MDI form.

When working with MDI child forms, keep the following in mind:

- At run time, when an MDI child form is maximized, its caption is combined with that of the parent MDI form.

- At design time, an MDI child form is displayed like any other form because the form is displayed inside the parent form only at run time. An MDI child form's icon in the Project window is different from icons for other kinds of forms.

- MDI child forms can't be modal.

- The initial size and placement of MDI child forms are controlled by the Microsoft Windows operating environment unless you specifically set them in the Load event procedure.

- If an MDI child form is referenced before the parent is loaded, the parent MDI form is automatically loaded. However, if the parent MDI form is referenced before loading an MDI child form, the child form isn't loaded.

Note   All MDI child forms have sizable borders, a Control-menu box, and Minimize and Maximize buttons, regardless of the settings of the **BorderStyle**, **ControlBox**, **MinButton**, and **MaxButton** properties.

Any reference to an **MDIForm** object, including reading or setting properties, causes the form to load and become visible.

See Also

BorderStyle Property, **ControlBox** Property, **MaxButton** Property, **MinButton** Property, **WindowList** Property, **ActiveControl** Property, **ActiveForm** Property

Example

This example creates a second instance of an MDI child form within an **MDIForm** object. To try this example, set the **MDIChild** property to **True** on Form1, and then create an **MDIForm** object with the Add MDI Form command on the Project menu. Paste the code into the Declarations section of the **MDIForm**, and then press F5 to run the program.

```
Private Sub MDIForm_Load ()
   Dim NewForm As New Form1' Declare new form.
   NewForm.Show' Show new form.
End Sub
```

MDIForm Object

An MDI (multiple-document interface) form is a window that acts as the background of an application and is the container for forms that have their **MDIChild** property set to **True**.

Syntax

MDIForm

Remarks

You create an **MDIForm** object by choosing MDI Form from the Insert menu.

An application can have only one **MDIForm** object but many MDI child forms. If an MDI child form has menus, the child form's menu bar automatically replaces the **MDIForm** object's menu bar when the MDI child form is active. A minimized MDI child form is displayed as an icon within the **MDIForm**.

An **MDIForm** object can contain only **Menu** and **PictureBox** controls and custom controls that have an **Align** property. To place other controls on an **MDIForm**, you can draw a picture box on the form, and then draw other controls inside the picture box. You can use the **Print** method to display text in a picture box on an **MDIForm**, but you can't use this method to display text on the **MDIForm** itself.

An **MDIForm** object can't be modal.

MDI child forms are designed independently of the **MDIForm**, but are always contained within the **MDIForm** at run time.

You can access the collection of controls on an **MDIForm** using the **Controls** collection. For example, to hide all the controls on an **MDIForm** you can use code similar to the following:

```
For Each Control in MDIForm1.Controls
    Control.Visible = False
Next Control
```

The **Count** property of the **MDIForm** tells you the number of controls in the **Controls** collection.

Properties

Controls Property, **Moveable** Property, **StartUpPosition** Property, **NegotiateToolbars** Property, **OLEDropMode** Property, **BackColor, ForeColor** Properties, **Height, Width** Properties, **Icon** Property, **Left, Top** Properties, **Name** Property, **Picture** Property, **Tag** Property, **Visible** Property, **AutoShowChildren** Property, **hWnd** Property, **LinkMode** Property, **LinkTopic** Property, **MouseIcon** Property, **MousePointer** Property, **ScaleHeight, ScaleWidth** Properties, **ScrollBars** Property, **WindowState** Property, **ActiveControl** Property, **Appearance** Property, **ActiveForm** Property, **Caption** Property, **Enabled** Property, **HelpContextID** Property, **Name** Property, **Visible** Property, **WindowsState** Property, **WhatsThisHelp** Property

Methods

SetFocus Method, **Arrange** Method, **Hide** Method, **Move** Method, **PopupMenu** Method, **Show** Method, **ZOrder** Method, **OLEDrag** Method, **WhatsThisMode** Method

See Also

MDIChild Property

Me

The **Me** keyword behaves like an implicitly declared variable. It is automatically available to every procedure in a class module. When a class can have more than one instance, **Me** provides a way to refer to the specific instance of the class where the code is executing. Using **Me** is particularly useful for passing information about the currently executing instance of a class to a procedure in another module. For example, suppose you have the following procedure in a module:

```
Sub ChangeFormColor(FormName As Form)
    FormName.BackColor = RGB(Rnd * 256, Rnd * 256, Rnd * 256)
End Sub
```

You can call this procedure and pass the current instance of the Form class as an argument using the following statement:

```
ChangeFormColor Me
```

See Also

Set Statement

Member Object

The **Member** object represents a mixture of code-based properties and type library-based attributes of members.

Syntax

Member

Remarks

Code-based properties like **Name** are read-only, so the add-in must modify the code to change these properties.

Properties

Bindable Property, **Browsable** Property, **Category** Property, **CodeLocation** Property, **Collection** Property, **DefaultBind** Property, **Description** Property, **DisplayBind** Property, **Hidden** Property, **PropertyPage** Property, **RequestEdit** Property, **Scope** Property, **StandardMethod** Property, **Static** Property, **Type** Property, **UIDefault** Property, **VBE** Property

Members Collection

Returns a collection of code module-level members.

Syntax

Members

Remarks

A member of a code module is an identifier that has module-level scope and which can be considered a property, method, or event of that code module.

Properties

VBE Property

Methods

Item Method

Members Property

Contains identifiers that have module-level scope and can be considered properties, methods, or events of the specified **CodeModule** object.

Applies To

CodeModule Object

Syntax

object.**Members**

The *object* placeholder represents an object expression that evaluates to an object in the **Applies To** list.

Menu Control

A **Menu** control displays a custom menu for your application. A menu can include commands, submenus, and separator bars. Each menu you create can have up to four levels of submenus.

Syntax

Menu

Remarks

To create a **Menu** control, use the Menu Editor. Enter the name of the **Menu** control in the Caption box. To create a separator bar, enter a single hyphen (-) in the Caption box. To display a check mark to the left of a menu item, select the Checked box.

While you can set some **Menu** control properties using the Menu Editor, all **Menu** control properties are displayed in the **Properties** window. To display the properties of a **Menu** control, select the menu name in the Objects list at the top of the Properties window.

When you create an MDI application, the menu bar on the MDI child form replaces the menu bar on the **MDIForm** object when the child form is active.

Properties

NegotiatePosition Property, **Tag** Property, **Visible** Property, **Shortcut** Property, **WindowList** Property, **Caption** Property, **Checked** Property, **Enabled** Property, **HelpContextID** Property, **Index** Property (Control Array), **Name** Property, **Parent** Property

See Also

MDIForm Object, **Menu Editor Dialog Box**

MessageReflect Property

Returns a Boolean value stating whether the control container handles message reflection automatically.

Applies To

AmbientProperties Object

Syntax

object.**MessageReflect**

The **MessageReflect** property syntax has this part:

Part	Description
object	An object expression that evaluates to an object in the **Applies To** list.

Settings

The possible Boolean return values from the **MessageReflect** property are:

Setting	Description
True	The container for the control will reflect messages.
False	The container for the control cannot reflect messages. If the container does not implement this ambient property, this will be the default value.

Remarks

When a control is subclassed, there are certain messages that are normally sent to the parent control. Under normal conditions, these messages are actually reflected back to the sending control, so that the control can handle its own message. This message reflection can be handled by the container, which will reflect the messages back as events. The **MessageReflect** property tells if the container for the control does message reflection.

If the control is ever placed in a container that does not reflect messages, the operation of the control will be severely compromised; much of the operation of a control depends on reflected messages.

Mid Function

Returns a **Variant** (**String**) containing a specified number of characters from a string.

Syntax

Mid(*string*, *start*[, *length*])

The **Mid** function syntax has these named arguments:

Part	Description
string	Required. String expression from which characters are returned. If *string* contains **Null**, **Null** is returned.
start	Required; **Long**. Character position in *string* at which the part to be taken begins. If *start* is greater than the number of characters in *string*, **Mid** returns a zero-length string ("").
length	Optional; **Variant** (**Long**). Number of characters to return. If omitted or if there are fewer than *length* characters in the text (including the character at *start*), all characters from the *start* position to the end of the string are returned.

Remarks

To determine the number of characters in *string*, use the **Len** function.

Note Use the **MidB** function with byte data contained in a string. Instead of specifying the number of characters, the arguments specify numbers of bytes.

See Also

Left Function, **Len** Function, **LTrim**, **RTrim**, **and Trim** Functions, **Mid** Statement, **Right** Function

Example

This example uses the **Mid** function to return a specified number of characters from a string.

```
Dim MyString, FirstWord, LastWord, MidWords
MyString = "Mid Function Demo"      ' Create text string.
FirstWord = Mid(MyString, 1, 3)     ' Returns "Mid".
LastWord = Mid(MyString, 14, 4)     ' Returns "Demo".
MidWords = Mid(MyString, 5)         ' Returns "Function Demo".
```

Mid Statement

Replaces a specified number of characters in a **Variant** (**String**) variable with characters from another string.

Syntax

Mid(*stringvar*, *start*[, *length*]) = *string*

The **Mid** statement syntax has these parts:

Part	Description
stringvar	Required. Name of string variable to modify.
start	Required; **Variant** (**Long**). Character position in *stringvar* where the replacement of text begins.
length	Optional; **Variant** (**Long**). Number of characters to replace. If omitted, all of *string* is used.
string	Required. String expression that replaces part of *stringvar*.

Remarks

The number of characters replaced is always less than or equal to the number of characters in *stringvar*.

Note   Use the **MidB** statement with byte data contained in a string. In the **MidB** statement, *start* specifies the byte position within *stringvar* where replacement begins and *length* specifies the numbers of bytes to replace.

See Also

Mid Function

Example

This example uses the **Mid** statement to replace a specified number of characters in a string variable with characters from another string.

```
Dim MyString
MyString = "The dog jumps"              ' Initialize string.
Mid(MyString, 5, 3) = "fox"             ' MyString = "The fox jumps".
Mid(MyString, 5) = "cow"                ' MyString = "The cow jumps".
Mid(MyString, 5) = "cow jumped over"    ' MyString = "The cow jumpe".
Mid(MyString, 5, 3) = "duck"            ' MyString = "The duc jumpe".
```

MinButton Property

Returns a value indicating whether a form has a Minimize button.

Applies To

Form Object, **Forms** Collection

Syntax

object.**MinButton**

The *object* placeholder represents an object expression that evaluates to an object in the **Applies To** list.

Return Values

The **MinButton** return values are:

Setting	Description
True	(Default) The form has a Minimize button.
False	The form doesn't have a Minimize button.

Remarks

A Minimize button enables users to minimize a form window to an icon. To display a Minimize button, you must also set the form's **BorderStyle** property to either 1 (Fixed Single), 2 (Sizable), or 3 (Fixed Double).

The settings you specify for the **MaxButton**, **MinButton**, **BorderStyle**, and **ControlBox** properties aren't reflected in the form's appearance until run time.

Note Minimizing a form to an icon at run time generates a Resize event. The **WindowState** property reflects the current state of the window. If you set the **WindowState** property to 2 (Maximized), the form is maximized independently of whatever settings are in effect for the **MaxButton** and **BorderStyle** properties.

See Also

ControlBox Property, **MaxButton** Property

MinHeight, MinWidth Properties

Returns or sets the minimum height or width of the Viewport at which scrollbars will appear on the container.

Applies To

UserDocument Object

Syntax

object.**MinHeight** = *single*
object.**MinWidth** = *single*

Part	Description
object	An object expression that evaluates to an object in the **Applies To** list.
single	The height or width of a **UserDocument** at which scrollbars will appear on a container.

Remarks

The default values of the **MinHeight** and **MinWidth** properties are set by the **Height** and **Width** properties of the **UserDocument**.

The **MinWidth** and **MinHeight** have no effect if the **ScrollBars** property is set to **False**.

See Also

SetViewport Method, **ViewportHeight**, **ViewportLeft**, **ViewportTop**, **ViewportWidth** Properties

Minor Property (Projects)

Returns or sets the minor release number of the project. Read only at run time.

Applies To

App Object

Syntax

object.**Minor**

The *object* placeholder represents an object expression that evaluates to an object in the **Applies To** list.

Remarks

The value of the **Minor** property is in the range from 0 to 9999.

This property provides version information about the running application.

You can set this property at design time in the **Minor** box in the **Make** tab of the **Project Properties** dialog box.

See Also

Major Property, **Revision** Property

Minor Property (Type Libraries)

Returns a **Long** indicating the minor version number of the referenced type library. Read-only.

Applies To

Reference Object

Remarks

The number returned by the **Minor** property corresponds to the minor version number stored in the type library to which you have set the reference.

See Also

Major Property, **Version** Property

Example

The following example uses the **Minor** property to return the minor version number of the specified **Reference** object in a particular project.

```
Debug.Print Application.VBE.VBProjects(1).References(1).Minor
```

Minute Function

Returns a **Variant** (**Integer**) specifying a whole number between 0 and 59, inclusive, representing the minute of the hour.

Syntax

Minute(*time*)

The required *time* argument is any **Variant**, numeric expression, string expression, or any combination, that can represent a time. If *time* contains **Null**, **Null** is returned.

See Also

Day Function, **Hour** Function, **Now** Function, **Second** Function, **Time** Function, **Time** Statement

Example

This example uses the **Minute** function to obtain the minute of the hour from a specified time. In the development environment, the time literal is displayed in short time format using the locale settings of your code.

```
Dim MyTime, MyMinute
MyTime = #4:35:17 PM#       ' Assign a time.
MyMinute = Minute(MyTime)   ' MyMinute contains 35.
```

MIRR Function

Returns a **Double** specifying the modified internal rate of return for a series of periodic cash flows (payments and receipts).

Syntax

MIRR(*values*(), *finance_rate*, *reinvest_rate*)

The **MIRR** function has these named arguments:

Part	Description
values()	Required. Array of **Double** specifying cash flow values. The array must contain at least one negative value (a payment) and one positive value (a receipt).
finance_rate	Required. **Double** specifying interest rate paid as the cost of financing.
reinvest_rate	Required. **Double** specifying interest rate received on gains from cash reinvestment.

Remarks

The modified internal rate of return is the internal rate of return when payments and receipts are financed at different rates. The **MIRR** function takes into account both the cost of the investment (*finance_rate*) and the interest rate received on reinvestment of cash (*reinvest_rate*).

The *finance_rate* and *reinvest_rate* arguments are percentages expressed as decimal values. For example, 12 percent is expressed as 0.12.

The **MIRR** function uses the order of values within the array to interpret the order of payments and receipts. Be sure to enter your payment and receipt values in the correct sequence.

See Also

DDB Function, **FV** Function, **IPmt** Function, **IRR** Function, **NPer** Function, **NPV** Function, **Pmt** Function, **PPmt** Function, **PV** Function, **Rate** Function, **SLN** Function, **SYD** Function

Example

This example uses the **MIRR** function to return the modified internal rate of return for a series of cash flows contained in the array Values(). LoanAPR represents the financing interest, and InvAPR represents the interest rate received on reinvestment.

```
Dim LoanAPR, InvAPR, Fmt, RetRate, Msg
Static Values(5) As Double              ' Set up array.
LoanAPR = .1                            ' Loan rate.
InvAPR = .12                            ' Reinvestment rate.
Fmt = "#0.00"                           ' Define money format.
Values(0) = -70000                      ' Business start-up costs.
' Positive cash flows reflecting income for four successive years.
Values(1) = 22000 : Values(2) = 25000
Values(3) = 28000 : Values(4) = 31000
RetRate = MIRR(Values(), LoanAPR, InvAPR) ' Calculate internal rate.
Msg = "The modified internal rate of return for these five cash flows is"
Msg = Msg & Format(Abs(RetRate) * 100, Fmt) & "%."
MsgBox Msg                              ' Display internal return
                                        ' rate.
```

MiscFlags Property

Returns or sets a value that determines access to one or more additional features of the **OLE** container control.

Applies To

OLE Container Control

Syntax

object.**MiscFlags** [= *value*]

The **MiscFlags** property syntax has these parts:

Part	Description
object	An object expression that evaluates to an object in the **Applies To** list.
value	An integer or constant specifying access to an additional feature, as described in Settings.

Settings

The settings for *value* are:

Constant	Value	Description
vbOLEMiscFlagMemStorage	1	Causes the control to use memory to store the object while it's loaded.
VbOLEMiscFlagDisableInPlace	2	Overrides the control's default behavior of allowing in-place activation for objects that support it.

Remarks

The **vbOLEMiscFlagMemStorage** flag setting is faster than the object's default action, which is to store it on disk as a temporary file. This setting can, however, use a great deal of memory for objects whose data requires a lot of space, such as a bitmap for a paint program.

If an object supports in-place activation, you can use the **vbOLEMiscFlagDisableInPlace** setting to force the object to activate in a separate window.

To combine values, use the **Or** operator. For example, to combine both flags, you could use this code:

```
Ole1.MiscFlags = vbOLEMiscFlagMemStorage Or _
  vbOLEMiscFlagDisableInPlace
```

MkDir Statement

Creates a new directory or folder.

Syntax

MkDir *path*

The required *path* argument is a string expression that identifies the directory or folder to be created. The *path* may include the drive. If no drive is specified, **MkDir** creates the new directory or folder on the current drive.

See Also

ChDir Statement, **CurDir** Function, **RmDir** Statement

Example

This example uses the **MkDir** statement to create a directory or folder. If the drive is not specified, the new directory or folder is created on the current drive.

```
MkDir "MYDIR"   ' Make new directory or folder.
```

Mod Operator

Used to divide two numbers and return only the remainder.

Syntax

result = *number1* **Mod** *number2*

The **Mod** operator syntax has these parts:

Part	Description
result	Required; any numeric variable.
number1	Required; any numeric expression.
number2	Required; any numeric expression.

Remarks

The modulus, or remainder, operator divides *number1* by *number2* (rounding floating-point numbers to integers) and returns only the remainder as *result*. For example, in the following expression, A (*result*) equals 5.

```
A = 19 Mod 6.7
```

Usually, the data type of *result* is a **Byte**, **Byte** variant, **Integer**, **Integer** variant, **Long**, or **Variant** containing a **Long**, regardless of whether or not *result* is a whole number. Any fractional portion is truncated. However, if any expression is **Null**, *result* is **Null**. Any expression that is **Empty** is treated as 0.

See Also

Operator Summary, **Operator** Precedence, **Arithmetic** Operators

Example

This example uses the **Mod** operator to divide two numbers and return only the remainder. If either number is a floating-point number, it is first rounded to an integer.

```
Dim MyResult
MyResult = 10 Mod 5   ' Returns 0.
MyResult = 10 Mod 3   ' Returns 1.
MyResult = 12 Mod 4.3' Returns 0.
MyResult = 12.6 Mod 5' Returns 3.
```

Mode Property

Returns a value containing the mode of the specified project. Read-only.

Applies To

VBProject Object

Return Values

The **Mode** property return values are:

Constant	Description
vbext_vm_Run	The specified project is in run mode.
vbext_vm_Break	The specified project is in break mode.
vbext_vm_Design	The specified project is in design mode.

See Also

ActiveVBProject Property, **Protection** Property

Example

The following example uses the **Mode** property to return the mode of the active project. The value returned is a predefined constant representing the project's mode.

```
Debug.Print Application.VBE.ActiveVBProject.Mode
```

Month Function

Returns a **Variant** (**Integer**) specifying a whole number between 1 and 12, inclusive, representing the month of the year.

Syntax

Month(*date*)

The required *date* argument is any **Variant**, numeric expression, string expression, or any combination, that can represent a date. If *date* contains **Null**, **Null** is returned.

See Also

Date Function, **Date** Statement, **Day** Function, **Now** Function, **Weekday** Function, **Year** Function

Example

This example uses the **Month** function to obtain the month from a specified date. In the development environment, the date literal is displayed in short date format using the locale settings of your code.

```
Dim MyDate, MyMonth
MyDate = #February 12, 1969#   ' Assign a date.
MyMonth = Month(MyDate)        ' MyMonth contains 2.
```

MoreResults Method (Remote Data)

Clears the current result set of any pending rows and returns a **Boolean** value that indicates if one or more additional result sets are pending.

Applies To

rdoResultset Object

Syntax

variable = *object*.**MoreResults**

The **MoreResults** method syntax has these parts:

Part	Description
variable	A Boolean variable that indicates if additional result sets are found as described in Return Values.
object	An object expression that evaluates to an open **rdoResultset** object variable.

Return Values

The return values for *variable* are:

Value	Description
True	Additional result sets are ready to be processed.
False	All result sets in the **rdoResultset** have been processed.

Remarks

Calling this method will flush the current result set, call the ODBC API **SQLMoreResults** function to see if there is another result set on the same statement, and if there is, loads the new result set, positions the current row pointer at the first row and returns **True**. If there are no more result sets, this method will return **False**, and both the **EOF** and **BOF** properties will be **True**.

If the result set was created asynchronously (developer used **rdAsyncEnable** in the *Options* parameter), the **MoreResults** method will be executed asynchronously as well. You should use the **StillExecuting** property to determine when the next result set has been enabled. Asynchronous execution of the **MoreResults** method follows the same rules as asynchronously opening a result set.

When the query used to create an **rdoResultset** returns more than one result set, use the **MoreResults** method to end processing of the current result set and test for subsequent result sets. If there are no additional result sets to process, the **MoreResults** method returns **False** and both **BOF** and **EOF** are set to **True**. In any case, using the **MoreResults** method flushes the current **rdoResultset**.

You can also use the **Cancel** method to flush the contents of an **rdoResultset**. However, **Cancel** also flushes any additional result sets not yet processed.

Not all cursor libraries support multiple resultset queries. For example, the Server-side cursor library does not support this type of query unless you disable the cursor processor by requesting a forward-only, read-only cursor with a **RowsetSize** property of 1.

See Also

Cancel Method (Remote Data), **rdoResultset** Object, **BOF**, **EOF** Properties (Remote Data)

Example

The following example illustrates use of the **MoreResults** method. In this example, an SQL query containing three separate SELECT queries is executed. The first query simply returns the number of publishers in the *Publishers* table. The next two queries each return two columns resulting from more complex join operations. All of this information is displayed in a **ListBox** control.

```
Option Explicit
Dim Cn As New rdoConnection
Dim Rs As rdoResultset
Dim SQL As String

Private Sub Test_Click()
SQL = "Select Count(*) From Publishers" _
   & " Select Pub_Name, Title    " _
   & " From Publishers P, Titles T" _
   & " Where P.Pub_ID = T.Pub_ID" _
   & " Select Au_Lname, Title " _
   & " From Titles T, TitleAuthor Ta, Authors A" _
   & " Where T.title_ID = ta.Title_ID " _
   & " and Ta.Au_ID = A.Au_ID"
Set Rs = Cn.OpenResultset(SQL, rdOpenForwardOnly, _
   rdConcurReadOnly)
' From the first set of results
List1.AddItem "Publishers: " & Rs(0)
'
'   Loop through all of the remaining result sets
'
Do While Rs.MoreResults
   List1.AddItem Rs(0).Name & " - " & Rs(1).Name
   Do Until Rs.EOF
      List1.AddItem Rs(0) & "        -     " & Rs(1)
      Rs.MoveNext
   Loop
Loop
End Sub

Private Sub Form_Load()
On Error GoTo CnEh
With Cn
   .Connect = "UID=;PWD=;Database=Pubs;" _
   & "Server=SEQUEL;Driver={SQL Server}" _
   & "DSN='';"
   .LoginTimeout = 5
   .CursorDriver = rdUseOdbc
   .EstablishConnection rdDriverNoPrompt, True
End With
Exit Sub

CnEh:
Dim er As rdoError
Debug.Print Err, Error
For Each er In rdoErrors
   Debug.Print er.Description, er.Number
Next er
Resume Next
End Sub
```

MouseDown, MouseUp Events

Occur when the user presses (**MouseDown**) or releases (**MouseUp**) a mouse button.

Applies To

Animation Control, **Data** Control, **DBCombo** Control, **DBGrid** Control, **DBList** Control, **ListView** Control, **MSFlexGrid** Control, **ProgressBar** Control, **RemoteData** Control, **RichTextBox** Control, **Slider** Control, **StatusBar** Control, **TabStrip** Control, **Toolbar** Control, **TreeView** Control, **UpDown** Control, **PropertyPage** Object, **UserControl** Object, **UserDocument** Object, **CheckBox** Control, **CommandButton** Control, **DirListBox** Control, **FileListBox** Control, **Form** Object, **Forms** Collection, **Frame** Control, **Image** Control, **Label** Control, **ListBox** Control, **MDIForm** Object, **OptionButton** Control, **PictureBox** Control, **TextBox** Control, **OLE Container** Control

Syntax

Private Sub Form_MouseDown(*button* **As Integer**, *shift* **As Integer**, *x* **As Single**, *y* **As Single**)
Private Sub MDIForm_MouseDown(*button* **As Integer**, *shift* **As Integer**, *x* **As Single**, *y* **As Single**)
Private Sub *object*_**MouseDown**([*index* **As Integer**,]*button* **As Integer**, *shift* **As Integer**,
  ↪ *x* **As Single**, *y* **As Single**)
Private Sub Form_MouseUp(*button* **As Integer**, *shift* **As Integer**, *x* **As Single**, *y* **As Single**)
Private Sub MDIForm_MouseUp(*button* **As Integer**, *shift* **As Integer**, *x* **As Single**, *y* **As Single**)
Private Sub *object* _**MouseUp**([*index* **As Integer**,]*button* **As Integer**, *shift* **As Integer**,
  ↪ *x* **As Single**, *y* **As Single**)

The **MouseDown** and **MouseUp** event syntaxes have these parts:

Part	Description
object	Returns an object expression that evaluates to an object in the **Applies To** list.
Index	Returns an integer that uniquely identifies a control if it's in a control array.
Button	Returns an integer that identifies the button that was pressed (**MouseDown**) or released (**MouseUp**) to cause the event. The *button* argument is a bit field with bits corresponding to the left button (bit 0), right button (bit 1), and middle button (bit 2). These bits correspond to the values 1, 2, and 4, respectively. Only one of the bits is set, indicating the button that caused the event.
Shift	Returns an integer that corresponds to the state of the SHIFT, CTRL, and ALT keys when the button specified in the *button* argument is pressed or released. A bit is set if the key is down. The *shift* argument is a bit field with the least-significant bits corresponding to the SHIFT key (bit 0), the CTRL key (bit 1), and the ALT key (bit 2). These bits correspond to the values 1, 2, and 4, respectively. The *shift* argument indicates the state of these keys. Some, all, or none of the bits can be set, indicating that some, all, or none of the keys are pressed. For example, if both CTRL and ALT were pressed, the value of *shift* would be 6.
x, y	Returns a number that specifies the current location of the mouse pointer. The *x* and *y* values are always expressed in terms of the coordinate system set by the **ScaleHeight**, **ScaleWidth**, **ScaleLeft**, and **ScaleTop** properties of the object.

Remarks

Use a **MouseDown** or **MouseUp** event procedure to specify actions that will occur when a given mouse button is pressed or released. Unlike the **Click** and **DblClick** events, **MouseDown** and **MouseUp** events enable you to distinguish between the left, right, and middle mouse buttons. You can also write code for mouse-keyboard combinations that use the SHIFT, CTRL, and ALT keyboard modifiers.

The following applies to both **Click** and **DblClick** events:

- If a mouse button is pressed while the pointer is over a form or control, that object "captures" the mouse and receives all mouse events up to and including the last **MouseUp** event. This implies that the *x*, *y* mouse-pointer coordinates returned by a mouse event may not always be in the internal area of the object that receives them.

- If mouse buttons are pressed in succession, the object that captures the mouse after the first press receives all mouse events until all buttons are released.

If you need to test for the *button* or *shift* arguments, you can use constants listed in the Visual Basic (VB) object library in the Object Browser to define the bits within the argument:

Constant (Button)	Value	Description
vbLeftButton	1	Left button is pressed
vbRightButton	2	Right button is pressed
vbMiddleButton	4	Middle button is pressed

Constant (Shift)	Value	Description
vbShiftMask	1	SHIFT key is pressed.
VbCtrlMask	2	CTRL key is pressed.
VbAltMask	4	ALT key is pressed.

The constants then act as bit masks you can use to test for any combination of buttons without having to figure out the unique bit field value for each combination.

Note You can use a **MouseMove** event procedure to respond to an event caused by moving the mouse. The *button* argument for **MouseDown** and **MouseUp** differs from the *button* argument used for **MouseMove**. For **MouseDown** and **MouseUp**, the *button* argument indicates exactly one button per event, whereas for **MouseMove**, it indicates the current state of all buttons.

See Also

Click Event, **MouseMove** Event, **DblClick** Event, **MousePointer** Property

Example

This example demonstrates a simple paint application. The **MouseDown** event procedure works with a related **MouseMove** event procedure to enable painting when any mouse button is pressed. The **MouseUp** event procedure disables painting. To try this example, paste the code into the Declarations section of a form, and then press F5 and click the form and move the mouse while the mouse button is pressed.

```
Dim PaintNow As Boolean              ' Declare variable.
Private Sub Form_MouseDown (Button As Integer, Shift As Integer,
X As Single, Y As Single)
   PaintNow = True                   ' Brush on.
End Sub

Private Sub Form_MouseUp (Button As Integer, X As Single, Y As Single)
   PaintNow = False                  ' Turn off painting.
End Sub

Private Sub Form_MouseMove (Button As Integer, Shift As Integer,
X As Single, Y As Single)
   If PaintNow Then
      PSet (X, Y)                    ' Draw a point.
   End If
End Sub

Private Sub Form_Load ()
   DrawWidth = 10                    ' Use wider brush.
   ForeColor = RGB(0, 0, 255)        ' Set drawing color.
End Sub
```

MouseIcon Property

Returns or sets a custom mouse icon.

Applies To

PropertyPage Object, **Data** Control, **DBCombo** Control, **DBList** Control, **UserControl** Object, **UserDocument** Object, **Screen** Object, **CheckBox** Control, **ComboBox** Control, **CommandButton** Control, **DirListBox** Control, **DriveListBox** Control, **FileListBox** Control, **Form** Object, **Forms** Collection, **Frame** Control, **HScrollBar, VScrollBar** Controls, **MSFlexGrid** Control, **ProgressBar** Control, **RichTextBox** Control, **Screen** Object, **Slider** Control, **SSTab** Control, **StatusBar** Control, **TabStrip** Control, **Toolbar** Control, **TreeView** Control, **Image** Control, **Label** Control, **ListBox** Control, **MDIForm** Object, **OptionButton** Control, **PictureBox** Control, **TextBox** Control, **OLE Container** Control

Syntax

object.**MouseIcon** = **LoadPicture**(*pathname*)
object.**MouseIcon** [= *picture*]

The **MouseIcon** property syntax has these parts:

Part	Description
object	An object expression that evaluates to an object in the **Applies To** list.
Pathname	A string expression specifying the path and filename of the file containing the custom icon.
Picture	The **Picture** property of a **Form** object, **PictureBox** control, or **Image** control.

Remarks

The **MouseIcon** property provides a custom icon that is used when the **MousePointer** property is set to 99.

Although Visual Basic does not create or support color cursor (.cur) files (such as those that ship with Windows NT), you can use the **MouseIcon** property to load either cursor or icon files. Color cursor files such as those shipped with Windows NT 3.51, are displayed in black and white. To display a color cursor, use a color icon file (.ico). The **MouseIcon** property provides your program with easy access to custom cursors of any size, with any desired hot spot location. Visual Basic does not load animated cursor (.ani) files, even though 32-bit versions of Windows support these cursors.

See Also

LoadPicture Function, **SavePicture** Statement, **Icon** Property, **Picture** Property, **DragIcon** Property, **MousePointer** Property

Example

This example illustrates how the **MouseIcon** property sets a custom mouse icon. To try the example, create a **ListBox** control on a form, and then set the **MultiSelect** property to 1 or 2. At run time, select one or more items. Different icons will appear, depending on whether you selected a single item or multiple items.

```
Private Sub Form_Load ()
   ' Put some items in the ListBox.
   List1.AddItem "Selection 1"
   List1.AddItem "Selection 2"
   List1.AddItem "Selection 3"
   List1.AddItem "Selection 4"
   List1.AddItem "Selection 5"
End Sub

Private Sub List1_MouseDown (Button As Integer, Shift As Integer,
X As Single, Y As Single)
   ' Set the custom mouse icon for multiple items.
   If List1.SelCount > 1 Then
      List1.MouseIcon = LoadPicture("ICONS\COMPUTER\MOUSE04.ICO")
      List1.MousePointer = 99

Else   ' Set the custom mouse icon for a single item.
      List1.MouseIcon = LoadPicture("ICONS\COMPUTER\MOUSE02.ICO")
      List1.MousePointer = 99
   End If
End Sub
```

MouseMove Event

Occurs when the user moves the mouse.

Applies To

Animation Control, **Data** Control, **DBCombo** Control, **DBGrid** Control, **DBList** Control, **ListView** Control, **MSFlexGrid** Control, **ProgressBar** Control, **RemoteData** Control, **RichTextBox** Control, **Slider** Control, **StatusBar** Control, **TabStrip** Control, **Toolbar** Control, **TreeView** Control, **UpDown** Control, **PropertyPage** Object, **UserControl** Object, **UserDocument** Object, **CheckBox** Control, **CommandButton** Control, **DirListBox** Control, **FileListBox** Control, **Form** Object, **Forms** Collection, **Frame** Control, **Image** Control, **Label** Control, **ListBox** Control, **MDIForm** Object, **OptionButton** Control, **PictureBox** Control, **TextBox** Control, **OLE Container** Control

Syntax

Private Sub Form_MouseMove(*button* **As Integer,** *shift* **As Integer,**
↪ *x* **As Single,** *y* **As Single)**
Private Sub MDIForm_MouseMove(*button* **As Integer,** *shift* **As Integer,**
↪ *x* **As Single,** *y* **As Single)**
Private Sub *object*_**MouseMove([***index* **As Integer,]** *button* **As Integer,**
↪ *shift* **As Integer,** *x* **As Single,** *y* **As Single)**

The **MouseMove** event syntax has these parts:

Part	Description
object	An object expression that evaluates to an object in the **Applies To** list.
Index	An integer that uniquely identifies a control if it's in a control array.
Button	An integer that corresponds to the state of the mouse buttons in which a bit is set if the button is down. The *button* argument is a bit field with bits corresponding to the left button (bit 0), right button (bit 1), and middle button (bit 2). These bits correspond to the values 1, 2, and 4, respectively. It indicates the complete state of the mouse buttons; some, all, or none of these three bits can be set, indicating that some, all, or none of the buttons are pressed.
Shift	An integer that corresponds to the state of the SHIFT, CTRL, and ALT keys. A bit is set if the key is down. The *shift* argument is a bit field with the least-significant bits corresponding to the SHIFT key (bit 0), the CTRL key (bit 1), and the ALT key (bit 2). These bits correspond to the values 1, 2, and 4, respectively. The *shift* argument indicates the state of these keys. Some, all, or none of the bits can be set, indicating that some, all, or none of the keys are pressed. For example, if both CTRL and ALT were pressed, the value of *shift* would be 6.
x, y	A number that specifies the current location of the mouse pointer. The *x* and *y* values are always expressed in terms of the coordinate system set by the **ScaleHeight**, **ScaleWidth**, **ScaleLeft**, and **ScaleTop** properties of the object.

Remarks

The **MouseMove** event is generated continually as the mouse pointer moves across objects. Unless another object has captured the mouse, an object recognizes a **MouseMove** event whenever the mouse position is within its borders.

If you need to test for the *button* or *shift* arguments, you can use constants listed in the Visual Basic (VB) object library in the Object Browser to define the bits within the argument:

Constant (Button)	Value	Description
vbLeftButton	1	Left button is pressed.
VbRightButton	2	Right button is pressed.
VbMiddleButton	4	Middle button is pressed.

Constant (Shift)	Value	Description
vbShiftMask	1	SHIFT key is pressed.
VbCtrlMask	2	CTRL key is pressed.
VbAltMask	4	ALT key is pressed.

The constants then act as bit masks you can use to test for any combination of buttons without having to figure out the unique bit field value for each combination.

You test for a condition by first assigning each result to a temporary integer variable and then comparing the *button* or *shift* arguments to a bit mask. Use the **And** operator with each argument to test if the condition is greater than zero, indicating the key or button is pressed, as in this example:

```
LeftDown = (Button And vbLeftButton) > 0
CtrlDown = (Shift And vbCtrlMask) > 0
```

Then, in a procedure, you can test for any combination of conditions, as in this example:

```
If LeftDown And CtrlDown Then
```

Note You can use **MouseDown** and **MouseUp** event procedures to respond to events caused by pressing and releasing mouse buttons.

The *button* argument for **MouseMove** differs from the *button* argument for **MouseDown** and **MouseUp**. For **MouseMove**, the *button* argument indicates the current state of all buttons; a single **MouseMove** event can indicate that some, all, or no buttons are pressed. For **MouseDown** and **MouseUp**, the *button* argument indicates exactly one button per event.

Any time you move a window inside a **MouseMove** event, it can cause a cascading event. **MouseMove** events are generated when the window moves underneath the pointer. A **MouseMove** event can be generated even if the mouse is perfectly stationary.

See Also

Click Event, **MouseDown**, **MouseUp** Events, **DblClick** Event, **MousePointer** Property

Example

This example demonstrates a simple paint application. The **MouseDown** event procedure works with a related **MouseMove** event procedure to enable painting when any mouse button is pressed. The **MouseUp** event procedure disables painting. To try this example, paste the code into the Declarations section of a form, and then press F5 and click the form and move the mouse while the mouse button is pressed.

```
Dim PaintNow As Boolean ' Declare variable.
Private Sub Form_MouseDown (Button As Integer, Shift As Integer,
X As Single, Y As Single)
   PaintNow = True' Brush on.
End Sub

Private Sub Form_MouseUp (Button As Integer, X As Single, Y As Single)
   PaintNow = False  ' Turn off painting.
End Sub

Private Sub Form_MouseMove (Button As Integer, Shift As Integer,
X As Single, Y As Single)
   If PaintNow Then
      PSet (X, Y)    ' Draw a point.
   End If
End Sub

Private Sub Form_Load ()
   DrawWidth = 10    ' Use wider brush.
   ForeColor = RGB(0, 0, 255) ' Set drawing color.
End Sub
```

MousePointer Property

Returns or sets a value indicating the type of mouse pointer displayed when the mouse is over a particular part of an object at run time.

Applies To

CheckBox Control, **ComboBox** Control, **CommandButton** Control, **Data** Control, **DirListBox** Control, **DriveListBox** Control, **FileListBox** Control, **Form** Object, **Forms** Collection, **Frame** Control, **HScrollBar, VScrollBar** Control, **Image** Control, **Label** Control, **ListBox** Control, **MDIForm** Control, **OLE Container** Control, **OptionButton** Control, **PictureBox** Control, **Propertypage** Control, **Screen** Control, **TextBox** Control, **UserControl** Object, **UserDocument** Object

Syntax

object.**MousePointer** [= *value*]

The **MousePointer** property syntax has these parts:

Part	Description
object	An object expression that evaluates to an object in the **Applies To** list.
Value	An integer specifying the type of mouse pointer displayed, as described in Settings.

Settings

The settings for *value* are:

Constant	Value	Description
vbDefault	0	(Default) Shape determined by the object.
VbArrow	1	Arrow.
VbCrosshair	2	Cross (crosshair pointer).
VbIbeam	3	I beam.
VbIconPointer	4	Icon (small square within a square).
VbSizePointer	5	Size (four-pointed arrow pointing north, south, east, and west).
VbSizeNESW	6	Size NE SW (double arrow pointing northeast and southwest).
VbSizeNS	7	Size N S (double arrow pointing north and south).
VbSizeNWSE	8	Size NW SE (double arrow pointing northwest and southeast).
VbSizeWE	9	Size W E (double arrow pointing west and east).
VbUpArrow	10	Up Arrow.
VbHourglass	11	Hourglass (wait).
VbNoDrop	12	No Drop.
VbArrowHourglass	13	Arrow and hourglass.
vbArrowQuestion	14	Arrow and question mark.
vbSizeAll	15	Size all.
vbCustom	99	Custom icon specified by the **MouseIcon** property.

Remarks

You can use this property when you want to indicate changes in functionality as the mouse pointer passes over controls on a form or dialog box. The Hourglass setting (11) is useful for indicating that the user should wait for a process or operation to finish.

Note If your application calls DoEvents, the **MousePointer** property may temporarily change when over an ActiveX component.

See Also

MouseMove Event, **DragIcon** Property, **MouseIcon** Property, **Mouse Pointer** Constants, **RichTextBox Control** Constants

Example

This example changes the mouse pointer to an hourglass while circles are drawn across the screen and then changes the hourglass back to a pointer at the end of the procedure. To try this example, paste the code into the Declarations section of a form. Press F5 to run the program, and then click the form.

```
Private Sub Form_Click ()
   Dim I    ' Declare variable.
   ' Change mouse pointer to hourglass.
   Screen.MousePointer = vbHourglass
   ' Set random color and draw circles on form.
   For I = 0 To ScaleWidth Step 50
      ForeColor = RGB(Rnd * 255, Rnd * 255, Rnd * 255)
      Circle (I, ScaleHeight * Rnd), 400
   Next
   ' Return mouse pointer to normal.
   Screen.MousePointer = vbDefault
End Sub
```

Move Method

Moves an **MDIForm**, **Form**, or control. Doesn't support named arguments.

Applies To

Animation Control, **CheckBox** Control, **ComboBox** Control, **CommandButton** Control, **Data** Control, **DBCombo** Control, **DBGrid** Control, **DBList** Control, **DirListBox** Control, **DriveListBox** Control, **FileListBox** Control, **Form Object**, **Forms** Collection, **Frame** Control, **HScrollBar, VScrollBar** Controls, **Image** Control, **Label** Control, **Line** Control, **ListBox** Control, **ListView** Control, **Masked Edit** Control, **MDIForm** Object, **MSFlexGrid** Control, **OLE Container** Control, **OptionButton** Control, **PictureBox** Control, **ProgressBar** Control, **RemoteData** Control, **RichTextBox** Control, **Shape** Control, **Slider** Control, **StatusBar** Control, **TabStrip** Control, **TextBox** Control, **Toolbar** Control, **TreeView** Control, **UpDown** Control

Syntax

object.**Move** *left*, *top*, *width*, *height*

The **Move** method syntax has these parts:

Part	Description
object	Optional. An object expression that evaluates to an object in the **Applies To** list. If *object* is omitted, the form with the focus is assumed to be *object*.
left	Required. Single-precision value indicating the horizontal coordinate (x-axis) for the left edge of *object*.
top	Optional. Single-precision value indicating the vertical coordinate (y-axis) for the top edge of *object*.
width	Optional. Single-precision value indicating the new width of *object*.
height	Optional. Single-precision value indicating the new height of *object*.

Remarks

Only the *left* argument is required. However, to specify any other arguments, you must specify all arguments that appear in the syntax before the argument you want to specify. For example, you can't specify *width* without specifying *left* and *top*. Any trailing arguments that are unspecified remain unchanged.

For forms and controls in a **Frame** control, the coordinate system is always in twips. Moving a form on the screen or moving a control in a **Frame** is always relative to the origin (0,0), which is the upper-left corner. When moving a control on a **Form** object or in a **PictureBox** (or an MDI child form on an **MDIForm** object), the coordinate system of the container object is used. The coordinate system or unit of measure is set with the **ScaleMode** property at design time. You can change the coordinate system at run time with the **Scale** method.

See Also

Height, **Width** Properties, **Left**, **Top** Properties, **ScaleHeight**, **ScaleWidth** Properties, **ScaleLeft, ScaleTop** Properties, **ScaleMode** Property

Example

This example uses the **Move** method to move a form around on the screen. To try this example, paste the code into the Declarations section of a form, and then press F5 and click the form.

```
Private Sub Form_Click ()
    Dim Inch, Msg  ' Declare variables.
    Msg = "Choose OK to resize and move this form by "
    Msg = Msg & "changing the value of properties."
    MsgBox Msg  ' Display message.
    Inch = 1440 ' Set inch in twips.
    Width = 4 * Inch  ' Set width.
    Height = 2 * Inch ' Set height.
    Left = 0 ' Set left to origin.
    Top = 0  ' Set top to origin.
    Msg = "Now choose OK to resize and move this form "
    Msg = Msg & "using the Move method."
    MsgBox Msg  ' Display message.

    Move Screen.Width - 2 * Inch, Screen.Height - Inch, 2 * Inch, Inch
End Sub
```

Move Method (DAO)

Moves the position of the current record in a **Recordset** object.

Applies To

Dynaset-Type Recordset Object, **Recordset** Object, **Snapshot-Type Recordset** Object, **Table-Type Recordset** Object, **Forward-Only–Type Recordset** Object, **Dynamic-Type Recordset** Object

Syntax

recordset.**Move** *rows*, *start*

The **Move** method syntax has these parts.

Part	Description
recordset	An object variable that represents the **Recordset** object whose current record position is being moved.
rows	A signed **Long** value specifying the number of rows the position will move. If *rows* is greater than 0, the position is moved forward (toward the end of the file). If *rows* is less than 0, the position is moved backward (toward the beginning of the file).
startbookmark	Optional. A **Variant** (**String** subtype) value identifying a bookmark. If you specify *startbookmark,* the move begins relative to this bookmark. Otherwise, **Move** begins from the current record.

Remarks

If you use **Move** to position the current record pointer before the first record, the current record pointer moves to the beginning of the file. If the **Recordset** contains no records and its **BOF** property is **True**, using this method to move backward causes an error.

If you use **Move** to position the current record pointer after the last record, the current record pointer position moves to the end of the file. If the **Recordset** contains no records and its **EOF** property is **True**, then using this method to move forward causes an error.

If either the **BOF** or **EOF** property is **True** and you attempt to use the **Move** method without a valid bookmark, a run-time error occurs.

Notes

- When you use **Move** on a forward-only-type **Recordset** object, the *rows* argument must be a positive integer and bookmarks aren't allowed. This means you can only move forward.

- To make the first, last, next, or previous record in a **Recordset** the current record, use either the **MoveFirst, MoveLast, MoveNext, or MovePrevious** method.

- Using **Move** with *rows* equal to 0 is an easy way to retrieve the underlying data for the current record. This is useful if you want to make sure that the current record has the most recent data from the base tables. It will also cancel any pending **Edit** or **AddNew** calls.

See Also

MoveFirst, MoveLast, MoveNext, MovePrevious Methods, **BOF**, **EOF** Properties, **Bookmark** Property

Example

This example uses the **Move** method to position the record pointer based on user input.

```
Sub MoveX()

    Dim dbsNorthwind As Database
    Dim rstSuppliers As Recordset
    Dim varBookmark As Variant
```

```
    Dim strCommand As String
    Dim lngMove As Long

    Set dbsNorthwind = OpenDatabase("Northwind.mdb")
    Set rstSuppliers = _
        dbsNorthwind.OpenRecordset("SELECT CompanyName, " & _
        "City, Country FROM Suppliers ORDER BY CompanyName", _
        dbOpenDynaset)

    With rstSuppliers
        ' Populate recordset.
        .MoveLast
        .MoveFirst

        Do While True
            ' Display information about current record and ask
            ' how many records to move.
            strCommand = InputBox( _
                "Record " & (.AbsolutePosition + 1) & " of " & _
                .RecordCount & vbCr & "Company: " & _
                !CompanyName & vbCr & "Location: " & !City & _
                ", " & !Country & vbCr & vbCr & _
                "Enter number of records to Move " & _
                "(positive or negative).")

            If strCommand = "" Then Exit Do

            ' Store bookmark in case the Move doesn't work.
            varBookmark = .Bookmark

            ' Move method requires parameter of data type Long.
            lngMove = CLng(strCommand)
            .Move lngMove

            ' Trap for BOF or EOF.
            If .BOF Then
                MsgBox "Too far backward! " & _
                    "Returning to current record."
                .Bookmark = varBookmark
            End If
            If .EOF Then
                MsgBox "Too far forward! " & _
                    "Returning to current record."
                .Bookmark = varBookmark
            End If
        Loop
        .Close
    End With

    dbsNorthwind.Close

End Sub
```

Move Method (Remote Data)

Repositions the current row pointer in an **rdoResultset** object.

Applies To

rdoResultset Object

Syntax

object.**Move** *rows*[, *start*]

The **Move** method syntax has these parts:

Part	Description
object	An object expression that evaluates to an object in the **Applies To** list.
Rows	A signed **Long** value that specifies the number of rows the position will move as described in Settings.
Start	A **Variant** value that identifies a bookmark as described in Settings.

Settings

If *rows* is greater than 0, the position is moved forward (toward the end of the cursor). If *rows* is less than 0, the position is moved backward (toward the beginning of the cursor). If *rows* is equal to 0, any pending edits are discarded and the current row is refreshed from the data source. At a lower level, when you use 0 as the *rows* argument, RDO executes the ODBC **SQLExtendedFetch** function to re-fetch the current rowset (as determined by the **RowsetSize** property) from the database.

If *start* is specified, the move begins relative to this bookmark. If *start* is not specified, **Move** begins from the current row.

Remarks

If using **Move** repositions the current row to a position before the first row, the position is moved to the beginning-of-file (**BOF**) position. If the **rdoResultset** contains no rows and its **BOF** property is set to **True**, using this method to move backward triggers a trappable run-time error. If either the **BOF** or **EOF** property is **True** and you attempt to use the **Move** method without a valid bookmark, a trappable error is triggered.

If using **Move** repositions the current row to a position after the last row, the position is moved to the end-of-file (**EOF**) position. If the **rdoResultset** contains no rows and its **EOF** property is set to **True**, then using this method to move forward produces a trappable run-time error.

If you use **Move** on an **rdoResultset** object based on an SQL-specific query or **rdoQuery**, the query is forced to completion and the **rdoResultset** object is fully populated.

If you use any method that repositions the current row pointer after using the **Edit** or **AddNew** method but before using the **Update** method, any changes made to the copy buffer are lost.

To make the first, last, next, or previous row in an **rdoResultset** the current row, use the **MoveFirst**, **MoveLast**, **MoveNext**, or **MovePrevious** method. To position the current row pointer based on an absolute row number, use the **AbsolutePosition** property. To position the current row pointer based on a percentage of the accessed rows of a result set, use the **PercentPosition** property.

When you use the **Move** method or any other method to reposition the current row pointer, the **RowCurrencyChange** event is fired.

When using a forward-only **rdoResultset**, the you can reposition the current row *only* by using the **MoveNext** method. You cannot use the **MoveLast**, **MovePrevious**, **MoveFirst**, or **Move** method, or the **PercentPosition** or **AbsolutePosition** property, to reposition the current row pointer.

See Also

RowCurrencyChange Event, **MoveFirst**, **MoveLast**, **MoveNext**, **MovePrevious** Methods (Remote Data), **rdoResultset** Object, **AbsolutePosition** Property (Remote Data), **BOF**, **EOF** Properties (Remote Data), **Bookmark** Property (Remote Data), **PercentPosition** Property (Remote Data

---

Moveable Property

Returns or sets a value which specifies if the object can be moved.

Applies To

Form Object, **Forms** Collection, **MDIForm** Object

Syntax

object.**Moveable** = *boolean*

Part	Description
object	An object expression that evaluates to an object in the **Applies To** list.
boolean	A Boolean expression that specifies if the object can be moved.

Settings

The settings for *boolean* are:

Constant	Value	Description
True	-1	The object can be moved.
False	0	The object cannot be moved.

MoveFirst, MoveLast, MoveNext, MovePrevious Methods

Move to the first, last, next, or previous record in a specified **Recordset** object and make that record the current record.

Applies To

Dynaset-Type Recordset Object, **Recordset** Object, **Snapshot-Type Recordset** Object, **Table-Type Recordset** Object, **Forward-Only–Type Recordset** Object, **Dynamic-Type Recordset** Object

Syntax

recordset.{**MoveFirst** | **MoveLast** [**dbRunAsync**] | **MoveNext** | **MovePrevious**}

The *recordset* placeholder is an object variable that represents an open **Recordset** object.

Remarks

Use the **Move** methods to move from record to record without applying a condition.

Caution If you edit the current record, be sure you use the **Update** method to save the changes before you move to another record. If you move to another record without updating, your changes are lost without warning.

When you open a **Recordset**, the first record is current and the **BOF** property is **False**. If the **Recordset** contains no records, the **BOF** property is **True**, and there is no current record.

If the first or last record is already current when you use **MoveFirst** or **MoveLast**, the current record doesn't change.

If you use **MovePrevious** when the first record is current, the **BOF** property is **True**, and there is no current record. If you use **MovePrevious** again, an error occurs, and **BOF** remains **True**.

If you use **MoveNext** when the last record is current, the **EOF** property is **True**, and there is no current record. If you use **MoveNext** again, an error occurs, and **EOF** remains **True**.

If *recordset* refers to a table-type **Recordset** (Microsoft Jet workspaces only), movement follows the current index. You can set the current index by using the **Index** property. If you don't set the current index, the order of returned records is undefined.

Important You can use the **MoveLast** method to fully populate a dynaset- or snapshot-type **Recordset** to provide the current number of records in the **Recordset**. However, if you use **MoveLast** in this way, you can slow down your application's performance. You should only use

MoveLast to get a record count if it is absolutely necessary to obtain an accurate record count on a newly opened **Recordset**. If you use the **dbRunAsync** constant with **MoveLast**, the method call is asynchronous. You can use the **StillExecuting** property to determine when the **Recordset** is fully populated, and you can use the **Cancel** method to terminate execution of the asynchronous **MoveLast** method call.

You can't use the **MoveFirst**, **MoveLast**, and **MovePrevious** methods on a forward-only – type **Recordset** object.

To move the position of the current record in a **Recordset** object a specific number of records forward or backward, use the **Move** method.

See Also

FindFirst, **FindLast**, **FindNext**, **FindPrevious** Methods, **Move** Method, **Seek** Method, **Cancel** Method, **AbsolutePosition** Property, **BOF**, **EOF** Properties, **Index** Property, **RecordCount** Property, **StillExecuting** Property

Example

This example uses the **MoveFirst**, **MoveLast**, **MoveNext**, and **MovePrevious** methods to move the record pointer of a **Recordset** based on the supplied command. The MoveAny procedure is required for this procedure to run.

```
Sub MoveFirstX()

    Dim dbsNorthwind As Database
    Dim rstEmployees As Recordset
    Dim strMessage As String
    Dim intCommand As Integer

    Set dbsNorthwind = OpenDatabase("Northwind.mdb")
    Set rstEmployees = dbsNorthwind.OpenRecordset( _
        "SELECT FirstName, LastName FROM Employees " & _
        "ORDER BY LastName", dbOpenSnapshot)

    With rstEmployees
        ' Populate Recordset.
        .MoveLast
        .MoveFirst
        Do While True
            ' Show current record information and get user's
            ' method choice.
            strMessage = "Name: " & !FirstName & " " & _
                !LastName & vbCr & "Record " & _
                (.AbsolutePosition + 1) & " of " & _
                .RecordCount & vbCr & vbCr & _
                "[1 - MoveFirst, 2 - MoveLast, " & vbCr & _
                "3 - MoveNext, 4 - MovePrevious]"
            intCommand = Val(Left(InputBox(strMessage), 1))
            If intCommand < 1 Or intCommand > 4 Then Exit Do
```

```
            ' Call method based on user's input.
            MoveAny intCommand, rstEmployees
        Loop
        .Close
    End With

    dbsNorthwind.Close

End Sub

Sub MoveAny(intChoice As Integer, _
    rstTemp As Recordset)

    ' Use specified method, trapping for BOF and EOF.
    With rstTemp
        Select Case intChoice
            Case 1
                .MoveFirst
            Case 2
                .MoveLast
            Case 3
                .MoveNext
                If .EOF Then
                    MsgBox "Already at end of recordset!"
                    .MoveLast
                End If
            Case 4
                .MovePrevious
                If .BOF Then
                    MsgBox "Already at beginning of recordset!"
                    .MoveFirst
                End If
        End Select
    End With

End Sub
```

MoveFirst, MoveLast, MoveNext, MovePrevious Methods (Remote Data)

Repositions the current row pointer to the first, last, next, or previous row in a specified **rdoResultset** object and makes that row the current row.

The syntax for these methods have these parts:

object.{**MoveFirst** | **MoveNext** | **MovePrevious**}
object. **MoveLast** ([*Options* as Variant])

Part	Description
object	An object expression that evaluates to a **rdoResultset** object.
Options	A **Variant** or constant that determines how the operation is carried out, as specified in Settings.

Applies To

rdoResultset Object

Settings

You can use the following constant for the *options* argument:

Constant	Value	Description
rdAsyncEnable	32	Execute operation asynchronously.

Remarks

Use the *Move* methods to reposition the current row pointer from row to row without applying a condition.

If you specify the **rdAsyncEnable** option with the **MoveLast** method, the move operation is executed asynchronously. That is, control is returned to your application immediately—often before the operation has completed. This prevents your application from blocking until the operation is complete. To check for completion of the operation, you can either wait for the **QueryComplete** or **RowCurrencyChange** events, or periodically check the **StillExecuting** property which returns **False** when the move operation is complete.

Caution   If you edit the current row, be sure to save the changes using the **Update** method before you move to another row. If you move to another row without updating, your changes are lost without warning.

When you open the result set named by *object*, the first row is current and the **BOF** property is set to **False**. If the result set contains no rows, the **BOF** property is set to **True**, and there is no current row.

If the first or last row is already current when you use **MoveFirst** or **MoveLast**, the current row doesn't change.

If you use **MovePrevious** when the first row is current, the **BOF** property is set to **True**, and there is no current row. If you use **MovePrevious** again, an error occurs; **BOF** remains **True**.

If you use **MoveNext** when the last row is current, the **EOF** property is set to **True**, and there is no current row. If you use **MoveNext** again, an error occurs; **EOF** remains **True**.

If you use **MoveLast** on an **rdoResultset** object based on an SQL-specific query or **rdoQuery**, the query is forced to completion and the **rdoResultset** object is fully populated.

If you use any method that repositions the current row pointer after using the **Edit** or **AddNew** method but before using the **Update** method, any changes made to the copy buffer are lost.

To move the position of the current row in an **rdoResultset** object a specific number of rows forward or backward, use the **Move** method.

To position the current row pointer based on an absolute row number, use the **AbsolutePosition** property. To position the current row pointer based on a percentage of the accessed rows of a result set, use the **PercentPosition** property.

When you use the **Move** method or any other method to reposition the current row pointer, the **RowCurrencyChange** event is fired.

When using a forward-only **rdoResultset**, the you can reposition the current row *only* by using the **MoveNext** method. You cannot use the **MoveLast**, **MovePrevious**, **MoveFirst**, or **Move** method, or the **PercentPosition** or **AbsolutePosition** property, to reposition the current row pointer. If you use one of the prohibited Move methods on a forward-only result set, your code will trip an ODBC "Fetch type out of range" error.

See Also

Move Method (Remote Data), **Update** Method (Remote Data), **rdoPreparedStatement** Object, **rdoResultset** Object, **AbsolutePosition** Property (Remote Data), **BOF**, **EOF** Properties (Remote Data), **PercentPosition** Property (Remote Data), **RowCount** Property (Remote Data)

Example

This example illustrates use of the **rdAsyncEnable** option in conjunction with the **MoveLast** method. The *Phones* table is simply a table with over 15,000 rows which takes some time to process. While this is not a recommended technique, it provides a way to illustrate a query that takes a significant length of time to run and fully populate—as is done when you execute the **MoveLast** method. The application uses a status bar to indicate the degree of completion of the operations.

```
Option Explicit
Dim rdoCn As New rdoConnection
Dim rdoRs As rdoResultset
Dim SQL As String
Dim TimeExpected As Single
Dim Ts As Single, Tn As Single

Private Sub Command1_Click()
TimeExpected = 5        ' We expect this to take about 5 seconds
SQL = "Select Email, Name From Phones"
Set rdoRs = rdoCn.OpenResultset(Name:=SQL, _
   Type:=rdOpenStatic, _
   LockType:=rdConcurReadOnly, _
   Option:=rdAsyncEnable)
ShowProgress "Query"
'
'   Query Has completed... now move to the last row
'
rdoRs.MoveLast rdAsyncEnable
' We expect this to take about 15 seconds
TimeExpected = 15
ShowProgress "MoveLast"
rdoCn.Close
End Sub

Sub ShowProgress(Operation As String)
Ts = Timer
'  time to execute  query
ProgressBar1.Max = TimeExpected
While rdoRs.StillExecuting
   Tn = Int(Timer - Ts)
   If Tn < TimeExpected Then
      ProgressBar1 = Tn
   Else
      ProgressBar1.Max = ProgressBar1.Max + 10
      TimeExpected = ProgressBar1.Max
   End If
   DoEvents
Wend
Status = Operation & "Done. Duration:" _
   & Int(Timer - Ts)
End Sub
Private Sub Form_Load()
With rdoCn
   .Connect = "UID=;PWD=;Database=WorkDB;" _
   & "Server=BETAV486;Driver={SQL Server}" _
   & "DSN='';"
   .LoginTimeout = 5
   .EstablishConnection rdDriverNoPrompt, True
End With
Exit Sub
End Sub
```

MsgBox Function

Displays a message in a dialog box, waits for the user to click a button, and returns an **Integer** indicating which button the user clicked.

Syntax

MsgBox(*prompt*[, *buttons*] [, *title*] [, *helpfile*, *context*])

The **MsgBox** function syntax has these named arguments:

Part	Description
prompt	Required. String expression displayed as the message in the dialog box. The maximum length of *prompt* is approximately 1024 characters, depending on the width of the characters used. If *prompt* consists of more than one line, you can separate the lines using a carriage return character (**Chr**(13)), a linefeed character (**Chr**(10)), or carriage return–linefeed character combination (**Chr**(13) & **Chr**(10)) between each line.
buttons	Optional. Numeric expression that is the sum of values specifying the number and type of buttons to display, the icon style to use, the identity of the default button, and the modality of the message box. If omitted, the default value for *buttons* is 0.
title	Optional. String expression displayed in the title bar of the dialog box. If you omit *title*, the application name is placed in the title bar.
helpfile	Optional. String expression that identifies the Help file to use to provide context-sensitive Help for the dialog box. If *helpfile* is provided, *context* must also be provided.
context	Optional. Numeric expression that is the Help context number assigned to the appropriate Help topic by the Help author. If *context* is provided, *helpfile* must also be provided.

Settings

The *buttons* argument settings are:

Constant	Value	Description
vbOKOnly	0	Display **OK** button only.
vbOKCancel	1	Display **OK** and **Cancel** buttons.
vbAbortRetryIgnore	2	Display **Abort**, **Retry**, and **Ignore** buttons.

(continued)

Constant	Value	Description
vbYesNoCancel	3	Display **Yes**, **No**, and **Cancel** buttons.
vbYesNo	4	Display **Yes** and **No** buttons.
vbRetryCancel	5	Display **Retry** and **Cancel** buttons.
vbCritical	16	Display **Critical Message** icon.
vbQuestion	32	Display **Warning Query** icon.
vbExclamation	48	Display **Warning Message** icon.
vbInformation	64	Display **Information Message** icon.
vbDefaultButton1	0	First button is default.
vbDefaultButton2	256	Second button is default.
vbDefaultButton3	512	Third button is default.
vbDefaultButton4	768	Fourth button is default.
vbApplicationModal	0	Application modal; the user must respond to the message box before continuing work in the current application.
vbSystemModal	4096	System modal; all applications are suspended until the user responds to the message box.
vbMsgBoxHelpButton	16384	Adds Help button to the message box
VbMsgBoxSetForeground	65536	Specifies the message box window as the foreground window
vbMsgBoxRight	524288	Text is right aligned
vbMsgBoxRtlReading	1048576	Specifies text should appear as right-to-left reading on Hebrew and Arabic systems

The first group of values (0–5) describes the number and type of buttons displayed in the dialog box; the second group (16, 32, 48, 64) describes the icon style; the third group (0, 256, 512) determines which button is the default; and the fourth group (0, 4096) determines the modality of the message box. When adding numbers to create a final value for the *buttons* argument, use only one number from each group.

Note These constants are specified by Visual Basic for Applications. As a result, the names can be used anywhere in your code in place of the actual values.

Return Values

Constant	Value	Description
vbOK	1	**OK**
vbCancel	2	**Cancel**
vbAbort	3	**Abort**
vbRetry	4	**Retry**
vbIgnore	5	**Ignore**
vbYes	6	**Yes**
vbNo	7	**No**

Remarks

When both *helpfile* and *context* are provided, the user can press F1 to view the Help topic corresponding to the **context**. Some host applications, for example, Microsoft Excel, also automatically add a **Help** button to the dialog box.

If the dialog box displays a **Cancel** button, pressing the ESC key has the same effect as clicking **Cancel**. If the dialog box contains a **Help** button, context-sensitive Help is provided for the dialog box. However, no value is returned until one of the other buttons is clicked.

Note To specify more than the first named argument, you must use **MsgBox** in an expression. To omit some positional arguments, you must include the corresponding comma delimiter.

See Also

InputBox Function

Example

This example uses the **MsgBox** function to display a critical-error message in a dialog box with Yes and No buttons. The No button is specified as the default response. The value returned by the **MsgBox** function depends on the button chosen by the user. This example assumes that DEMO.HLP is a Help file that contains a topic with a Help context number equal to 1000.

```
Dim Msg, Style, Title, Help, Ctxt, Response, MyString
Msg = "Do you want to continue ?"              ' Define message.
Style = vbYesNo + vbCritical + vbDefaultButton2 ' Define buttons.
Title = "MsgBox Demonstration"                 ' Define title.
Help = "DEMO.HLP"                              ' Define Help file.
Ctxt = 1000                                    ' Define topic
                                               ' context.
                                               ' Display message.
Response = MsgBox(Msg, Style, Title, Help, Ctxt)
If Response = vbYes Then                       ' User chose Yes.
   MyString = "Yes"                            ' Perform some action.
Else                                           ' User chose No.
   MyString = "No"                             ' Perform some action.
End If
```

MultiLine Property

Returns or sets a value indicating whether a **TextBox** control can accept and display multiple lines of text. Read only at run time.

Applies To

TextBox Control

Syntax

object.**MultiLine**

The *object* placeholder represents an object expression that evaluates to an object in the **Applies To** list.

Settings

The **MultiLine** property settings are:

Setting	Description
True	Allows multiple lines of text.
False	(Default) Ignores carriage returns and restricts data to a single line.

Remarks

A multiple-line **TextBox** control wraps text as the user types text extending beyond the text box.

You can also add scroll bars to larger **TextBox** controls using the **ScrollBars** property. If no horizontal scroll bar is specified, the text in a multiple-line **TextBox** automatically wraps.

Note   On a form with no default button, pressing ENTER in a multiple-line **TextBox** control moves the focus to the next line. If a default button exists, you must press CTRL+ENTER to move to the next line.

See Also

Default Property, **ScrollBars** Property

MultiSelect Property

Returns or sets a value indicating whether a user can make multiple selections in a **FileListBox** or **ListBox** control and how the multiple selections can be made. Read only at run time.

Applies To

FileListBox Control, **ListBox** Control

Syntax

object.**MultiSelect**

The *object* placeholder represents an object expression that evaluates to an object in the **Applies To** list.

Settings

The **MultiSelect** property settings are:

Setting	Description
0	(Default) Multiple selection isn't allowed.
1	Simple multiple selection. A mouse click or pressing the SPACEBAR selects or deselects an item in the list. (Arrow keys move the focus.)
2	Extended multiple selection. Pressing SHIFT and clicking the mouse or pressing SHIFT and one of the arrow keys (UP ARROW, DOWN ARROW, LEFT ARROW, and RIGHT ARROW) extends the selection from the previously selected item to the current item. Pressing CTRL and clicking the mouse selects or deselects an item in the list.

See Also

AddItem Method, **Clear** Method (Clipboard, ComboBox, ListBox), **RemoveItem** Method, **List** Property, **ListCount** Property, **NewIndex** Property, **Selected** Property, **TopIndex** Property

Example

This example fills a **ListBox** control with the names of your screen fonts and illustrates how the **MultiSelect** property affects the behavior of a **ListBox**. To try this example, create two **ListBox** controls and a **CommandButton** control on a form. In the first **ListBox**, set the **MultiSelect** property to 1 or 2. At run time, select several items in the first **ListBox**, and then click the **CommandButton**. All selected items are displayed in the second **ListBox**. Run the example several times with different settings of the **MultiSelect** property. Paste the code into the Declarations section, and then press F5 to run the program.

```
Private Sub Form_Load ()
   Dim I            ' Declare variable.
   ' Fill the list box with screen font names.
   For I = 0 To Screen.FontCount - 1
      List1.AddItem Screen.Fonts(I)
   Next I
End Sub

Private Sub Command1_Click ()
   Dim I            ' Declare variable.
   ' Clear all items from the list.
   List2.Clear
   ' If an item is selected, add it to List2.
   For I = 0 To List1.ListCount - 1
      If List1.Selected(I) Then /
         List2.AddItem List1.List(I)
      End If
   Next I

End Sub
```

Name Property

Returns the name used in code to identify a form, control, or data access object. Read-only at run time.

Applies To

Animation Control, **CheckBox** Control, **ComboBox** Control, **CommandButton** Control, **CommonDialog** Control, **Data** Control, **DBCombo** Control, **DBGrid** Control, **DBList** Control, **DirListBox** Control, **DriveListBox** Control, **Extender** Object, **FileListBox** Control, **Font** Object, **Form** Object, **Forms** Collection, **Frame** Control, **HscrollBar**, **VscrollBar** Controls, **Image** Control, **ImageList** Control, **Label** Control, **Line** Control, **ListBox** Control, **ListView** Control, **MAPIMessages** Control, **MAPISession** Control, **Masked Edit** Control, **MDIForm** Object, **Menu** Control, **MSComm** Control, **OLE Container** Control, **OptionButton** Control, **PictureBox** Control, **PictureClip** Control, **ProgressBar** Control, **PropertyPage** Control, **RichTextBox** Control, **Shape** Control, **Slider** Control, **SSTab** Control, **StatusBar** Control, **TabStrip** Control, **TextBox** Control, **Timer** Control, **Toolbar** Control, **TreeView** Control, **UpDown** Control, **UserControl** Object, **UserDocument** Object

Syntax

object.**Name**

The *object* placeholder represents an object expression that evaluates to an object in the **Applies To** list. If *object* is omitted, the form associated with the active form module is assumed to be *object.*

Remarks

The default name for new objects is the kind of object plus a unique integer. For example, the first new **Form** object is Form1, a new **MDIForm** object is MDIForm1, and the third **TextBox** control you create on a form is Text3.

An object's **Name** property must start with a letter and can be a maximum of 40 characters. It can include numbers and underline (_) characters but can't include punctuation or spaces. Forms can't have the same name as another public object such as **Clipboard**, **Screen**, or **App**. Although the **Name** property setting can be a keyword, property name, or the name of another object, this can create conflicts in your code.

You can use a form's **Name** property with the **Dim** statement at run time to create other instances of the form. You can't have two forms with the same name at design time.

You can create an array of controls of the same type by setting the **Name** property to the same value. For example, when you set the name of all option buttons in a group to MyOpt, Visual Basic assigns unique values to the **Index** property of each control to distinguish it from others in the array. Two controls of different types can't share the same name.

Note Although Visual Basic often uses the **Name** property setting as the default value for the **Caption**, **LinkTopic**, and **Text** properties, changing one of these properties doesn't affect the others.

See Also

Text Property, **LinkTopic** Property, **ActiveForm** Property, **Caption** Property, **Index** Property (Control Array)

Name Property (Add-ins)

Returns or sets a **String** containing the name used in code to identify an object. For the **VBProject** object and the **VBComponent** object, read/write; for the **Property** object and the **Reference** object, read-only.

Applies To

VBComponent Object, **Property** Object, **Reference** Object, **VBProject** Object

Remarks

The following table describes how the **Name** property setting applies to different objects.

Object	Result of Using Name Property Setting
VBProject	Returns or sets the name of the active project.
VBComponent	Returns or sets the name of the component. An error occurs if you try to set the **Name** property to a name already being used or an invalid name.
Property	Returns the name of the property as it appears in the **Property Browser**. This is the value used to index the **Properties** collection. The name can't be set.
Reference	Returns the name of the reference in code. The name can't be set.

The default name for new objects is the type of object plus a unique integer. For example, the first new Form object is Form1, a new Form object is Form1, and the third TextBox control you create on a form is TextBox3.

An object's **Name** property must start with a letter and can be a maximum of 40 characters. It can include numbers and underline (_) characters but can't include punctuation or spaces. Forms and modules can't have the same name as another public object such as **Clipboard**, **Screen**, or **App**. Although the **Name** property setting can be a keyword, property name, or the name of another object, this can create conflicts in your code.

See Also

Description Property, **Type** Property

Example

The following example uses the **Name** property to return the name of the specified member of the **VBComponents** collection in a particular project.

```
Debug.Print Application.VBE.VBProjects(1).VBComponents(1).Name
```

Name Property (DAO)

Sets or returns a user-defined name for a DAO object. For an object not appended to a collection, this property is read/write.

Applies To

Container Object, **Database** Object, **Document** Object, **Dynaset-Type Recordset** Object, **Field** Object, **Group** Object, **Index** Object, **Parameter** Object, **Property** Object, **QueryDef** Object, **Recordset** Object, **Relation** Object, **Snapshot-Type Recordset** Object, **Table-Type Recordset** Object, **TableDef** Object, **User** Object, **Workspace** Object, **Connection** Object, **Forward-Only–Type Recordset** Object, **Dynamic-Type Recordset** Object

Settings and Return Values

The setting or return value is a **String** that specifies a name. The name must start with a letter. The maximum number of characters depends on the type of object **Name** applies to, as shown in Remarks. It can include numbers and underscore characters (_) but can't include punctuation or spaces.

Remarks

TableDef, **QueryDef**, **Field**, **Index**, **User**, and **Group** objects can't share the same name with any object in the same collection.

The **Name** property of a **Recordset** object opened by using an SQL statement is the first 256 characters of the SQL statement.

You can use an object's **Name** property with the Visual Basic for Applications **Dim** statement in code to create other instances of the object.

Note   For many of the DAO objects, the **Name** property reflects the name as known to the **Database** object, as in the name of a **TableDef**, **Field**, or **QueryDef** object. There is no direct link between the name of the DAO object and the object variable used to reference it.

The read/write usage of the **Name** property depends on the type of object it applies to, and whether or not the object has been appended to a collection. In an ODBCDirect workspace, the **Name** property of an appended object is always read-only. The following table indicates whether the **Name** property in a Microsoft Jet workspace is read/write or read-only for an object that is appended to a collection (unless otherwise noted), and also indicates its maximum length in cases where it is read/write.

Name Property (DAO)

Object	Usage	Maximum length
Container	Read-only	
Connection	Read-only	
Database	Read-only	
Document	Read-only	
Field		
Unappended	Read/write	64
Appended to **Index**	Read-only	
Appended to **QueryDef**	Read-only	
Appended to **Recordset**	Read-only	
Appended to **TableDef** (native)	Read/write	64
Appended to **TableDef** (linked)	Read-only	
Appended to **Relation**	Read-only	
Group		
Unappended	Read/write	20
Appended	Read-only	
Index		
Unappended	Read/write	64
Appended	Read-only	
Parameter	Read-only	
Property		
Unappended	Read/write	64
Appended	Read-only	
Built-in	Read-only	
QueryDef		
Unappended	Read/write	64
Temporary	Read-only	
Appended	Read/write	64
Recordset	Read-only	
Relation		
Unappended	Read/write	64
Appended	Read-only	
TableDef	Read/write	64
User		
Unappended	Read/write	20
Appended	Read-only	
Workspace		
Unappended	Read/write	20
Appended	Read-only	

See Also

      CreateDatabase Method, **CreateField** Method, **CreateIndex** Method,
      CreateQueryDef Method

Example

      This example uses the **Name** property to give a name to a newly created object, to
      show what objects are in a given collection, and to delete an object from a collection.

```
Sub NameX()

    Dim dbsNorthwind As Database
    Dim qdfNew As QueryDef
    Dim qdfLoop As QueryDef

    Set dbsNorthwind = OpenDatabase("Northwind.mdb")

    With dbsNorthwind
        ' Create a new permanent QueryDef object and append it
        ' to the QueryDefs collection.
        Set qdfNew = .CreateQueryDef()
        qdfNew.Name = "NewQueryDef"
        qdfNew.SQL = "SELECT * FROM Employees"
        .QueryDefs.Append qdfNew

        ' Enumerate the QueryDefs collection to display the
        ' names of the QueryDef objects.
        Debug.Print "Names of queries in " & .Name

        For Each qdfLoop In .QueryDefs
            Debug.Print "    " & qdfLoop.Name
        Next qdfLoop

        ' Delete new QueryDef object because this is a
        ' demonstration.
        .QueryDefs.Delete qdfNew.Name

        .Close
    End With
End Sub
```

Name Property (Remote Data)

      Returns the name of a **RemoteData** object.

Applies To

      rdoColumn Object, **rdoConnection** Object, **rdoEnvironment** Object, **rdoError**
      Object, **rdoParameter** Object, **rdoPreparedStatement** Object, **rdoQuery** Object,
      rdoResultset Object, **rdoTable** Object, **RemoteData** Control

Syntax

      object.**Name**

      The *object* placeholder represents an object expression that evaluates to an object in
      the **Applies To** list.

Return Values

The **Name** property returns a string expression that represents the name assigned to the object. The following table describes how each object is assigned its name.

Remote Data Object	Name property is determined by ...
rdoEnvironments(0)	**rdoEngine** — Set to "Default_Environment."
rdoEnvironments(1-*n*)	*name* argument of **rdoCreateEnvironment.**
rdoConnection	Data source name (DSN) used for connection.
rdoResultset	First 256 characters of the SQL query.
rdoQuery	*name* argument in **CreateQuery** method or set directly for stand-alone **rdoQuery** objects.
rdoTable	Database table name once the **rdoTables** collection is populated.
rdoParameter	"Param*n*" where "*n*" is the ordinal number.
rdoColumn	Database column name.
rdoError	Not applicable. **rdoErrors** collection members can only be referenced by their ordinal number.

Remarks

rdoTable and **rdoQuery** objects can't share the same name. In other words, you cannot create two **rdoQuery** objects that have the same name.

Use the **Name** property to reference members of a collection in code, but in most cases, it is easier to simply use the ordinal number. Generally, you can use the **Name** property to map database table and column names.

See Also

CreatePreparedStatement Method

Example

The following example illustrates use of the Name property to expose the names of all tables associated with a chosen database, the names of each column for the selected table, and specific type information about a selected column. This application uses three **Listbox** controls and a **Command** button control.

```
Option Explicit
Dim en As rdoEnvironment
Dim cn As rdoConnection
Dim rs As rdoResultset
Dim tb As rdoTable
Dim cl As rdoColumn
Dim er As rdoError

Private Sub Command1_Click()
Set en = rdoEngine.rdoEnvironments(0)

Set cn = en.OpenConnection(dsName:="WorkDB", _
    prompt:=rdDriverNoPrompt, _
    Connect:="Uid=;pwd=;database=Pubs")
```

```
For Each tb In cn.rdoTables
    List1.AddItem tb.Name
Next
List1.ListIndex = 1
End Sub

Private Sub List1_Click()
List3.Enabled = False
List2.Clear
For Each cl In cn.rdoTables((List1)).rdoColumns
    List2.AddItem cl.Name
Next
List3.Enabled = True
End Sub

Private Sub List2_Click()
List3.Clear
With cn.rdoTables((List1)).rdoColumns((List2))
    List3.AddItem "Source Column:" & .SourceColumn
    List3.AddItem "Source Table:" & .SourceTable
    List3.AddItem "Type:" & .Type
    List3.AddItem "Size:" & .Size
    List3.AddItem "Ordinal Position:" _
    & .OrdinalPosition
    List3.AddItem "Allow Zero Length ?" _
    & .AllowZeroLength
    List3.AddItem "Required:" & .Required
    List3.AddItem "Chunk Required?:" & .ChunkRequired
    List3.AddItem "Updatable?:" & .Updatable
End With
End Sub
```

Name Statement

Renames a disk file, directory, or folder.

Syntax

Name *oldpathname* **As** *newpathname*

The **Name** statement syntax has these parts:

Part	Description
oldpathname	Required. String expression that specifies the existing file name and location—may include directory or folder, and drive.
newpathname	Required. String expression that specifies the new file name and location—may include directory or folder, and drive. The file name specified by *newpathname* can't already exist.

Remarks

Both *newpathname* and *oldpathname* must be on the same drive. If the path in *newpathname* exists and is different from the path in *oldpathname*, the **Name** statement moves the file to the new directory or folder and renames the file, if necessary. If *newpathname* and *oldpathname* have different paths and the same file name, **Name** moves the file to the new location and leaves the file name unchanged. Using **Name**, you can move a file from one directory or folder to another, but you can't move a directory or folder.

Using **Name** on an open file produces an error. You must close an open file before renaming it. **Name** arguments cannot include multiple-character (*) and single-character (?) wildcards.

See Also

Kill Statement

Example

This example uses the **Name** statement to rename a file. For purposes of this example, assume that the directories or folders that are specified already exist.

```
Dim OldName, NewName
OldName = "OLDFILE": NewName = "NEWFILE"      ' Define filenames.
Name OldName As NewName                       ' Rename file.

OldName = "C:\MYDIR\OLDFILE": NewName = "C:\YOURDIR\NEWFILE"
Name OldName As NewName                       ' Move and rename file.
```

Named Date/Time Formats (Format Function)

The following table identifies the predefined date and time format names:

Format Name	Description
General Date	Display a date and/or time. For real numbers, display a date and time, for example, 4/3/93 05:34 PM. If there is no fractional part, display only a date, for example, 4/3/93. If there is no integer part, display time only, for example, 05:34 PM. Date display is determined by your system settings.
Long Date	Display a date according to your system's long date format.
Medium Date	Display a date using the medium date format appropriate for the language version of the host application.
Short Date	Display a date using your system's short date format.
Long Time	Display a time using your system's long time format; includes hours, minutes, seconds.
Medium Time	Display time in 12-hour format using hours and minutes and the AM/PM designator.
Short Time	Display a time using the 24-hour format, for example, 17:45.

See Also

Format Function, **Named Numeric** Formats (Format Function), **User-Defined Date/Time** Formats (Format Function)

Named Numeric Formats (Format Function)

The following table identifies the predefined numeric format names:

Format name	Description
General Number	Display number with no thousand separator.
Currency	Display number with thousand separator, if appropriate; display two digits to the right of the decimal separator. Output is based on system locale settings.
Fixed	Display at least one digit to the left and two digits to the right of the decimal separator.
Standard	Display number with thousand separator, at least one digit to the left and two digits to the right of the decimal separator.
Percent	Display number multiplied by 100 with a percent sign (%) appended to the right; always display two digits to the right of the decimal separator.
Scientific	Use standard scientific notation.
Yes/No	Display No if number is 0; otherwise, display Yes.
True/False	Display **False** if number is 0; otherwise, display **True**.
On/Off	Display Off if number is 0; otherwise, display On.

See Also

Format Function, **User-Defined Numeric** Formats (Format Function), **Named Date/Time** Formats (Format Function)

NavigateTo Method

Execute a hyperlink jump to the specified target.

Applies To

Hyperlink Object

Syntax

object.**NavigateTo** *Target* [, *Location* [, *FrameName*]]

The **NavigateTo** method syntax has these parts:

Part	Description
object	An object expression that evaluates to an object in the **Applies To** list.
Target	A string expression specifying the location to jump to. This can be a document or a URL.
Location	A string expression specifying the location within the URL specified in *Target* to jump to. If *Location* is not specified, the default document will be jumped to.
FrameName	A string expression specifying the frame within the URL specified in *Target* to jump to. If *FrameName* is not specified, the default frame will be jumped to.

Remarks

If the object is in a container that supports OLE hyperlinking, then the container will jump to the specified location. If the object is in a container that does not support OLE hyperlinking, then an application that is registered as supporting hyperlinking is started to handle the request.

If *Target* does not specify a valid location, an error is raised.

Negotiate Property

Sets a value that determines whether a control that can be aligned is displayed when an active object on the form displays one or more toolbars. Not available at run time.

Applies To

PictureBox Control

Settings

The **Negotiate** property has these settings:

Setting	Description
True	If the control is aligned within the form (the **Align** property is set to a nonzero value), the control remains visible when an active object on the form displays a toolbar.
False	(Default) The control isn't displayed when an active object on the form displays a toolbar. The toolbar of the active object is displayed in place of the control.

Remarks

The **Negotiate** property exists for all controls with an **Align** property. You use the **Align** property to align the control within a **Form** or **MDIForm** object; however, the toolbar negotiation occurs only on the **MDIForm**. The aligned control must be on the **MDIForm**.

If the **NegotiateToolbars** property is set to **False**, the setting of the **Negotiate** property has no effect.

See Also

NegotiateToolbars Property, **Align** Property

NegotiateMenus Property

Sets a value that determines whether or not a form incorporates the menus from an object on the form on the form's menu bar. Not available at run time.

Applies To

Form Object, Forms Collection

Settings

The **NegotiateMenus** property has these settings:

Setting	Description
True	(Default) When an object on the form is active for editing, the menus of that object are displayed on the form's menu bar.
False	Menus of objects on the form aren't displayed on the form's menu bar.

Remarks

Using the **NegotiateMenus** property, you determine if the menu bar of a form will share (or negotiate) space with the menus of an active object on the form. If you don't want to include the menus of the active object on the menu bar of your form, set **NegotiateMenus** to **False**.

You can't negotiate menus between an **MDIForm** object and an object on the **MDIForm**.

If **NegotiateMenus** is set to **True**, the form must have a menu bar defined, even if the menu bar isn't visible. If the **MDIChild** property of the form is set to **True**, the menus of the active object are displayed on the menu bar of the MDI parent window (**MDIForm** object).

When **NegotiateMenus** is set to **True**, you can use the **NegotiatePosition** property of individual **Menu** controls to determine the menus that your form displays along with the menus of the active object.

See Also

NegotiatePosition Property

NegotiatePosition Property

Sets a value that determines whether or not top-level **Menu** controls are displayed on the menu bar while a linked object or embedded object object on a form is active and displaying its menus. Not available at run time.

Applies To

Menu Control

Settings

The **NegotiatePosition** property has these settings:

Setting	Description
0	(Default) None. The menu isn't displayed on the menu bar when the object is active.
1	Left. The menu is displayed at the left end of the menu bar when the object is active.
2	Middle. The menu is displayed in the middle of the menu bar when the object is active.
3	Right. The menu is displayed at the right end of the menu bar when the object is active.

Remarks

Using the **NegotiatePosition** property, you determine the individual menus on the menu bar of your form that share (or negotiate) menu bar space with the menus of an active object on the form. Any menu with **NegotiatePosition** set to a nonzero value is displayed on the menu bar of the form along with menus from the active object.

If the **NegotiateMenus** property is set to **False**, the setting of the **NegotiatePosition** property has no effect.

See Also

NegotiateMenus Property

NegotiateToolbars Property

Sets a value that determines whether the toolbars of an object on an MDI child form are displayed on the **MDIForm** when the object on the MDI child form is active. Not available at run time.

Applies To

MDIForm Object

Settings

The **NegotiateToolbars** property has these settings:

Setting	Description
True	(Default) The **MDIForm** object displays the toolbars of the active object on the top or bottom of the **MDIForm**. The active object determines whether the toolbars are displayed at the top or bottom of the **MDIForm**.
False	The toolbars of the active object either aren't displayed at all or are displayed as floating tool palettes, as determined by the active object.

Remarks

Use the **NegotiateToolbars** property when creating a multiple-document interface (MDI) application that includes objects on MDI child forms. With this property, you determine how the active object displays its toolbars. By setting this property to **True**, the **MDIForm** shares (or negotiates) space at the top or bottom of the form to display the toolbars of the active object.

If the **MDIForm** also contains a toolbar, use the **Negotiate** property to determine how the various toolbars share the available space.

See Also

Negotiate Property

NewIndex Property

Returns the index of the item most recently added to a **ComboBox** or **ListBox** control. Read only at run time.

Applies To

ComboBox Control, **ListBox** Control

Syntax

object.**NewIndex**

The *object* placeholder represents an object expression that evaluates to an object in the **Applies To** list.

Remarks

You can use this property with sorted lists when you need a list of values that correspond to each item in the **ItemData** property array. As you add an item in a sorted list, Visual Basic inserts the item in the list in alphabetic order. This property tells you where the item was inserted so that you can insert a corresponding value in the **ItemData** property at the same index.

The **NewIndex** property returns –1 if there are no items in the list or if an item has been deleted since the last item was added.

See Also

AddItem Method, **Clear** Method (Clipboard, ComboBox, ListBox), **RemoveItem** Method, **List** Property, **ListCount** Property, **ItemData** Property, **MultiSelect** Property, **Selected** Property, **TopIndex** Property

NewPage Method

Ends the current page and advances to the next page on the **Printer** object.

Applies To

Printer Object**, Printers** Collection

Syntax

*object***.NewPage**

The *object* placeholder represents an object expression that evaluates to an object in the **Applies To** list.

Remarks

NewPage advances to the next printer page and resets the print position to the upper-left corner of the new page. When invoked, **NewPage** increments the **Printer** object's **Page** property by 1.

See Also

EndDoc Method, **KillDoc** Method, **Page** Property

Example

This example uses the **NewPage** method to begin a new printer page after printing a single, centered line of text on a page. To try this example, paste the code into the **Declarations** section of a form, and then press F5 and click the form.

```
Private Sub Form_Click ()
   Dim HWidth, HHeight, I, Msg        ' Declare variables.
   On Error GoTo ErrorHandler ' Set up error handler.
   Msg = "This is printed on page"
   For I = 1 To 2 ' Set up two iterations.
      HWidth = Printer.TextWidth(Msg) / 2     ' Get one-half width.
      HHeight = Printer.TextHeight(Msg) /2    ' Get one-half height.
      Printer.CurrentX = Printer.ScaleWidth / 2 - HWidth
      Printer.CurrentY = Printer.ScaleHeight / 2 - HHeight
      Printer.Print Msg & Printer.Page & "." ' Print.

Printer.NewPage    ' Send new page.
   Next I
   Printer.EndDoc ' Print done.
   Msg = "Two pages, each with a single, centered line of text, "
   Msg = Msg & "have been sent to your printer."
   MsgBox Msg      ' Display message.
   Exit Sub
ErrorHandler:
   MsgBox "There was a problem printing to your printer."
   Exit Sub
End Sub
```

NewPassword Method

Changes the password of an existing user account or Microsoft Jet database (Microsoft Jet workspaces only).

Applies To

Database Object, **User** Object

Syntax

object.**NewPassword** *oldpassword*, *newpassword*

The **NewPassword** method syntax has these parts.

Part	Description
object	An object variable that represents the **User** object or a Microsoft Jet 3.*x* **Database** object whose **Password** property you want to change.
oldpassword	A **String** that is the current setting of the **Password** property of the **User** or Jet 3.*x* **Database** object.
newpassword	A **String** that is the new setting of the **Password** property of the **User** or Jet 3.*x* **Database** object.

Remarks

The *oldpassword* and *newpassword* strings can be up to 14 characters long and can include any characters except the ASCII character 0 (null). To clear the password, use a zero-length string ("") for *newpassword*.

Passwords are case-sensitive.

If *object* refers to a **User** object that is not yet appended to a **Users** collection, an error occurs. To set a new password, you must either log on as the user whose account you're changing, or you must be a member of the Admins group. The **Password** property of a **User** object is write-only—users can't read the current value.

If *object* refers to a Microsoft Jet version 3.0 or later **Database** object, this method offers some security by means of password protection. When you create or open a Microsoft Jet 3.*x* .mdb file, part of the **Connect** connection string can describe the password.

If a database has no password, Microsoft Jet will automatically create one by passing a zero-length string ("") for the old password.

Caution   If you lose your password, you can never open the database again.

See Also

Name Property, **PID** Property

NewPassword Method

Example

This example asks the user for a new password for user Pat Smith. If the input is a string between 1 and 14 characters long, the example uses the **NewPassword** method to change the password. The user must be logged on as Pat Smith or as a member of the Admins group.

```
Sub NewPasswordX()

    Dim wrkDefault As Workspace
    Dim usrNew As User
    Dim grpNew As Group
    Dim grpMember As Group
    Dim strPassword As String

    ' Get default workspace.
    Set wrkDefault = DBEngine.Workspaces(0)

    With wrkDefault

        ' Create and append new user.
        Set usrNew = .CreateUser("Pat Smith", _
            "abc123DEF456", "Password1")
        .Users.Append usrNew

        ' Create and append new group.
        Set grpNew = .CreateGroup("Accounting", _
            "UVW987xyz654")
        .Groups.Append grpNew

        ' Make the new user a member of the new group.
        Set grpMember = usrNew.CreateGroup("Accounting")
        usrNew.Groups.Append grpMember

        ' Ask user for new password. If input is too long, ask
        ' again.
        Do While True
            strPassword = InputBox("Enter new password:")
            Select Case Len(strPassword)
                Case 1 To 14
                    usrNew.NewPassword "Password1", strPassword
                    MsgBox "Password changed!"
                    Exit Do
                Case Is > 14
                    MsgBox "Password too long!"
                Case 0
                    Exit Do
            End Select
        Loop

        ' Delete new User and Group objects because this
        ' is only a demonstration.
        .Users.Delete "Pat Smith"
        .Groups.Delete "Accounting"

    End With

End Sub
```

NextRecordset Method

Gets the next set of records, if any, returned by a multi-part select query in an **OpenRecordset** call, and returns a **Boolean** value indicating whether one or more additional records are pending (ODBCDirect workspaces only).

Applies To

Dynaset-Type Recordset Object, **Recordset** Object, **Snapshot-Type Recordset** Object, **Forward-Only–Type Recordset** Object, **Dynamic-Type Recordset** Object

Syntax

Set *boolean* = *recordset*.**NextRecordset**

The **NextRecordset** method syntax has these parts:

Part	Description
boolean	A **Boolean** variable. **True** indicates the next set of records is available in *recordset*; **False** indicates that no more records are pending and *recordset* is now empty.
recordset	An existing **Recordset** variable to which you want to return pending records.

Remarks

In an ODBCDirect workspace, you can open a **Recordset** containing more than one select query in the *source* argument of **OpenRecordset**, or the **SQL** property of a select query **QueryDef** object, as in the following example.

```
SELECT LastName, FirstName FROM Authors
WHERE LastName = 'Smith';
SELECT Title, ISBN FROM Titles
WHERE Pub_ID = 9999
```

The returned **Recordset** will open with the results of the first query. To obtain the result sets of records from subsequent queries, use the **NextRecordset** method.

If more records are available (that is, there was another select query in the **OpenRecordset** call or in the **SQL** property), the records returned from the next query will be loaded into the **Recordset**, and **NextRecordset** will return **True**, indicating that the records are available. When no more records are available (that is, results of the last select query have been loaded into the **Recordset**), then **NextRecordset** will return **False**, and the **Recordset** will be empty.

You can also use the **Cancel** method to flush the contents of a **Recordset**. However, **Cancel** also flushes any additional records not yet loaded.

Example

This example uses the **NextRecordset** method to view the data from a compound SELECT query. The **DefaultCursorDriver** property must be set to **dbUseODBCCursor** when executing such queries. The **NextRecordset** method will return **True** even if some or all of the SELECT statements return zero records — it will return **False** only after all the individual SQL clauses have been checked.

```
Sub NextRecordsetX()

    Dim wrkODBC As Workspace
    Dim conPubs As Connection
    Dim rstTemp As Recordset
    Dim intCount As Integer
    Dim booNext As Boolean

    ' Create ODBCDirect Workspace object and open Connection
    ' object. The DefaultCursorDriver setting is required
    ' when using compound SQL statements.
    Set wrkODBC = CreateWorkspace("", _
        "admin", "", dbUseODBC)
    wrkODBC.DefaultCursorDriver = dbUseODBCCursor
    Set conPubs = wrkODBC.OpenConnection("Publishers", , , _
        "ODBC;DATABASE=pubs;UID=sa;PWD=;DSN=Publishers")

    ' Construct compound SELECT statement.
    Set rstTemp = conPubs.OpenRecordset("SELECT * " & _
        "FROM authors; " & _
        "SELECT * FROM stores; " & _
        "SELECT * FROM jobs")

    ' Try printing results from each of the three SELECT
    ' statements.
    booNext = True
    intCount = 1
    With rstTemp
        Do While booNext
            Debug.Print "Contents of recordset #" & intCount
            Do While Not .EOF
                Debug.Print , .Fields(0), .Fields(1)
                .MoveNext
            Loop
            booNext = .NextRecordset
            Debug.Print "    rstTemp.NextRecordset = " & _
                booNext
            intCount = intCount + 1
        Loop
    End With

    rstTemp.Close
    conPubs.Close
    wrkODBC.Close

End Sub
```

Another way to accomplish the same task would be to create a prepared statement containing the compound SQL statement. The **CacheSize** property of the **QueryDef** object must be set to 1, and the **Recordset** object must be forward-only and read-only.

```
Sub NextRecordsetX2()

    Dim wrkODBC As Workspace
    Dim conPubs As Connection
    Dim qdfTemp As QueryDef
    Dim rstTemp As Recordset
    Dim intCount As Integer
    Dim booNext As Boolean

    ' Create ODBCDirect Workspace object and open Connection
    ' object. The DefaultCursorDriver setting is required
    ' when using compound SQL statements.
    Set wrkODBC = CreateWorkspace("", _
        "admin", "", dbUseODBC)
    wrkODBC.DefaultCursorDriver = dbUseODBCCursor
    Set conPubs = wrkODBC.OpenConnection("Publishers", , , _
        "ODBC;DATABASE=pubs;UID=sa;PWD=;DSN=Publishers")

    ' Create a temporary stored procedure with a compound
    ' SELECT statement.
    Set qdfTemp = conPubs.CreateQueryDef("", _
        "SELECT * FROM authors; " & _
        "SELECT * FROM stores; " & _
        "SELECT * FROM jobs")
    ' Set CacheSize and open Recordset object with arguments
    ' that will allow access to multiple recordsets.
    qdfTemp.CacheSize = 1
    Set rstTemp = qdfTemp.OpenRecordset(dbOpenForwardOnly, _
        dbReadOnly)

    ' Try printing results from each of the three SELECT statements.
    booNext = True
    intCount = 1
    With rstTemp
        Do While booNext
            Debug.Print "Contents of recordset #" & intCount
            Do While Not .EOF
                Debug.Print , .Fields(0), .Fields(1)
                .MoveNext
            Loop
            booNext = .NextRecordset
            Debug.Print "    rstTemp.NextRecordset = " & _
                booNext
            intCount = intCount + 1
        Loop
    End With

    rstTemp.Close
    qdfTemp.Close
    conPubs.Close
    wrkODBC.Close

End Sub
```

NoMatch Property

Indicates whether a particular record was found by using the **Seek** method or one of the **Find** methods (Microsoft Jet workspaces only).

Applies To

Dynaset-Type Recordset Object, **Recordset** Object, **Snapshot-Type Recordset** Object, **Table-Type Recordset** Object

Return Values

The return value is a **Boolean** that is **True** if the desired record was not found. When you open or create a **Recordset** object, its **NoMatch** property is set to **False**.

Remarks

To locate a record, use the **Seek** method on a table-type **Recordset** object or one of the **Find** methods on a dynaset- or snapshot-type **Recordset** object. Check the **NoMatch** property setting to see whether the record was found.

If the **Seek** or **Find** method is unsuccessful and the **NoMatch** property is **True**, the current record will no longer be valid. Be sure to obtain the current record's bookmark before using the **Seek** method or a **Find** method if you'll need to return to that record.

Note Using any of the **Move** methods on a **Recordset** object won't affect its **NoMatch** property setting.

See Also

FindFirst, **FindLast**, **FindNext**, **FindPrevious** Methods, **Seek** Method, **BOF**, **EOF** Properties

Example

This example uses the **NoMatch** property to determine whether a **Seek** and a **FindFirst** were successful, and if not, to give appropriate feedback. The **SeekMatch** and **FindMatch** procedures are required for this procedure to run.

```
Sub NoMatchX()

    Dim dbsNorthwind As Database
    Dim rstProducts As Recordset
    Dim rstCustomers As Recordset
    Dim strMessage As String
    Dim strSeek As String
    Dim strCountry As String
    Dim varBookmark As Variant

    Set dbsNorthwind = OpenDatabase("Northwind.mdb")
    ' Default is dbOpenTable; required if Index property will
    ' be used.
    Set rstProducts = dbsNorthwind.OpenRecordset("Products")

    With rstProducts
        .Index = "PrimaryKey"
```

```
        Do While True
            ' Show current record information; ask user for
            ' input.
            strMessage = "NoMatch with Seek method" & vbCr & _
                "Product ID: " & !ProductID & vbCr & _
                "Product Name: " & !ProductName & vbCr & _
                "NoMatch = " & .NoMatch & vbCr & vbCr & _
                "Enter a product ID."
            strSeek = InputBox(strMessage)
            If strSeek = "" Then Exit Do

            ' Call procedure that seeks for a record based on
            ' the ID number supplied by the user.
            SeekMatch rstProducts, Val(strSeek)
        Loop

        .Close
    End With

    Set rstCustomers = dbsNorthwind.OpenRecordset( _
        "SELECT CompanyName, Country FROM Customers " & _
        "ORDER BY CompanyName", dbOpenSnapshot)

    With rstCustomers

        Do While True
            ' Show current record information; ask user for
            ' input.
            strMessage = "NoMatch with FindFirst method" & _
                vbCr & "Customer Name: " & !CompanyName & _
                vbCr & "Country: " & !Country & vbCr & _
                "NoMatch = " & .NoMatch & vbCr & vbCr & _
                "Enter country on which to search."
            strCountry = Trim(InputBox(strMessage))
            If strCountry = "" Then Exit Do

            ' Call procedure that finds a record based on
            ' the country name supplied by the user.
            FindMatch rstCustomers, _
                "Country = '" & strCountry & "'"
        Loop

        .Close
    End With

    dbsNorthwind.Close

End Sub

Sub SeekMatch(rstTemp As Recordset, _
    intSeek As Integer)

    Dim varBookmark As Variant
    Dim strMessage As String

    With rstTemp
        ' Store current record location.
        varBookmark = .Bookmark
        .Seek "=", intSeek
```

```
           ' If Seek method fails, notify user and return to the
           ' last current record.
           If .NoMatch Then
              strMessage = _
                 "Not found! Returning to current record." & _
                 vbCr & vbCr & "NoMatch = " & .NoMatch
              MsgBox strMessage
              .Bookmark = varBookmark
           End If

        End With

     End Sub

     Sub FindMatch(rstTemp As Recordset, _
        strFind As String)

        Dim varBookmark As Variant
        Dim strMessage As String

        With rstTemp
           ' Store current record location.
           varBookmark = .Bookmark
           .FindFirst strFind

           ' If Find method fails, notify user and return to the
           ' last current record.
           If .NoMatch Then
              strMessage = _
                 "Not found! Returning to current record." & _
                 vbCr & vbCr & "NoMatch = " & .NoMatch
              MsgBox strMessage
              .Bookmark = varBookmark
           End If

        End With

     End Sub
```

NonModalAllowed Property

Returns a value which indicates if a form can be shown non-modally (modeless). Not available at design-time.

Applies To

App Object

Syntax

object.**nonModalAllowed**

The *object* placeholder represents an object expression that evaluates to an object in the **Applies To** list.

Return Type

Boolean

Not Operator

Used to perform logical negation on an expression.

Syntax

result = **Not** *expression*

The **Not** operator syntax has these parts:

Part	Description
result	Required; any numeric variable.
expression	Required; any expression.

Remarks

The following table illustrates how *result* is determined:

If *expression* is	Then *result* is
True	**False**
False	**True**
Null	**Null**

In addition, the **Not** operator inverts the bit values of any variable and sets the corresponding bit in *result* according to the following table:

If bit in *expression* is	Then bit in *result* is
0	1
1	0

See Also

Operator Summary, **Operator** Precedence, **Logical** Operators

Example

This example uses the **Not** operator to perform logical negation on an expression.

```
Dim A, B, C, D, MyCheck
A = 10: B = 8: C = 6: D = Null   ' Initialize variables.
MyCheck = Not(A > B)             ' Returns False.
MyCheck = Not(B > A)             ' Returns True.
MyCheck = Not(C > D)             ' Returns Null.
MyCheck = Not A                  ' Returns -11
                                 ' (bitwise comparison).
```

Nothing

The **Nothing** keyword is used to disassociate an object variable from an actual object. Use the **Set** statement to assign **Nothing** to an object variable. For example:

```
Set MyObject = Nothing
```

Several object variables can refer to the same actual object. When **Nothing** is assigned to an object variable, that variable no longer refers to an actual object. When several object variables refer to the same object, memory and system resources associated with the object to which the variables refer are released only after all of them have been set to **Nothing**, either explicitly using **Set**, or implicitly after the last object variable set to **Nothing** goes out of scope.

See Also

Dim Statement, **Private** Statement, **Public** Statement, **Set** Statement

Now Function

Returns a **Variant** (**Date**) specifying the current date and time according your computer's system date and time.

Syntax

Now

See Also

Date Function, **Date** Statement, **Day** Function, **Hour** Function, **Minute** Function, **Month** Function, **Second** Function, **Time** Function, **Time** Statement, **Weekday** Function, **Year** Function

Example

This example uses the **Now** function to return the current system date and time.

```
Dim Today
Today = Now ' Assign current system date and time.
```

NPer Function

Returns a **Double** specifying the number of periods for an annuity based on periodic, fixed payments and a fixed interest rate.

Syntax

NPer(*rate*, *pmt*, *pv*[, *fv*[, *type*]])

The **NPer** function has these named arguments:

Part	Description
rate	Required. **Double** specifying interest rate per period. For example, if you get a car loan at an annual percentage rate (APR) of 10 percent and make monthly payments, the rate per period is 0.1/12, or 0.0083.
pmt	Required. **Double** specifying payment to be made each period. Payments usually contain principal and interest that doesn't change over the life of the annuity.
pv	Required. **Double** specifying present value, or value today, of a series of future payments or receipts. For example, when you borrow money to buy a car, the loan amount is the present value to the lender of the monthly car payments you will make.
fv	Optional. **Variant** specifying future value or cash balance you want after you've made the final payment. For example, the future value of a loan is $0 because that's its value after the final payment. However, if you want to save $50,000 over 18 years for your child's education, then $50,000 is the future value. If omitted, 0 is assumed.
type	Optional. **Variant** specifying when payments are due. Use 0 if payments are due at the end of the payment period, or use 1 if payments are due at the beginning of the period. If omitted, 0 is assumed.

Remarks

An annuity is a series of fixed cash payments made over a period of time. An annuity can be a loan (such as a home mortgage) or an investment (such as a monthly savings plan).

For all arguments, cash paid out (such as deposits to savings) is represented by negative numbers; cash received (such as dividend checks) is represented by positive numbers.

See Also

DDB Function, **FV** Function, **IPmt** Function, **IRR** Function, **MIRR** Function, **NPV** Function, **Pmt** Function, **PPmt** Function, **PV** Function, **Rate** Function, **SLN** Function, **SYD** Function

Example

This example uses the **NPer** function to return the number of periods during which payments must be made to pay off a loan whose value is contained in PVal. Also provided are the interest percentage rate per period (APR / 12), the payment (Payment), the future value of the loan (FVal), and a number that indicates whether the payment is due at the beginning or end of the payment period (PayType).

```
Dim FVal, PVal, APR, Payment, PayType, TotPmts
Const ENDPERIOD = 0, BEGINPERIOD = 1  ' When payments are made.
FVal = 0                              ' Usually 0 for a loan.
PVal = InputBox("How much do you want to borrow?")
APR = InputBox("What is the annual percentage rate of your loan?")
If APR > 1 Then APR = APR / 100      ' Ensure proper form.
Payment = InputBox("How much do you want to pay each month?")
PayType = MsgBox("Do you make payments at the end of month?", vbYesNo)
If PayType = vbNo Then PayType = BEGINPERIOD Else PayType = ENDPERIOD
TotPmts = NPer(APR / 12, -Payment, PVal, FVal, PayType)
If Int(TotPmts) <> TotPmts Then TotPmts = Int(TotPmts) + 1
MsgBox "It will take you " & TotPmts & " months to pay off your loan."
```

NPV Function

Returns a **Double** specifying the net present value of an investment based on a series of periodic cash flows (payments and receipts) and a discount rate.

Syntax

NPV(*rate*, *values*())

The **NPV** function has these named arguments:

Part	Description
rate	Required. **Double** specifying discount rate over the length of the period, expressed as a decimal.
values()	Required. Array of **Double** specifying cash flow values. The array must contain at least one negative value (a payment) and one positive value (a receipt).

Remarks

The net present value of an investment is the current value of a future series of payments and receipts.

The **NPV** function uses the order of values within the array to interpret the order of payments and receipts. Be sure to enter your payment and receipt values in the correct sequence.

The **NPV** investment begins one period before the date of the first cash flow value and ends with the last cash flow value in the array.

The net present value calculation is based on future cash flows. If your first cash flow occurs at the beginning of the first period, the first value must be added to the value returned by **NPV** and must not be included in the cash flow values of *values*().

The **NPV** function is similar to the **PV** function (present value) except that the **PV** function allows cash flows to begin either at the end or the beginning of a period. Unlike the variable **NPV** cash flow values, **PV** cash flows must be fixed throughout the investment.

See Also

DDB Function, **FV** Function, **IPmt** Function, **IRR** Function, **MIRR** Function, **NPer** Function, **Pmt** Function, **PPmt** Function, **PV** Function, **Rate** Function, **SLN** Function, **SYD** Function

Example

This example uses the **NPV** function to return the net present value for a series of cash flows contained in the array Values(). RetRate represents the fixed internal rate of return.

```
Dim Fmt, Guess, RetRate, NetPVal, Msg
Static Values(5) As Double          ' Set up array.
Fmt = "###,##0.00"                  ' Define money format.
Guess = .1                          ' Guess starts at 10 percent.
RetRate = .0625                     ' Set fixed internal rate.
Values(0) = -70000                  ' Business start-up costs.
' Positive cash flows reflecting income for four successive years.
Values(1) = 22000 : Values(2) = 25000
Values(3) = 28000 : Values(4) = 31000
NetPVal = NPV(RetRate, Values())    ' Calculate net present value.
Msg = "The net present value of these cash flows is "
Msg = Msg & Format(NetPVal, Fmt) & "."
MsgBox Msg                          ' Display net present value.
```

Null

The **Null** keyword is used as a **Variant** subtype. It indicates that a variable contains no valid data.

See Also

Variant Data Type, **VarType** Function

Number Property

Returns or sets a numeric value specifying an error. **Number** is the **Err** object's default property. Read/write.

Applies To

Error Object

Remarks

When returning a user-defined error from an object, set **Err.Number** by adding the number you selected as an error code to the **vbObjectError** constant. For example, you use the following code to return the number 1051 as an error code:

```
Err.Raise Number := vbObjectError + 1051, Source:= "SomeClass"
```

See Also

Err Object, **Description** Property, **HelpContext** Property, **HelpFile** Property, **LastDLLError** Property, **Source** Property, **HelpContextID** Property

Example

The first example illustrates a typical use of the **Number** property in an error-handling routine. The second example examines the **Number** property of the **Err** object to determine whether an error returned by an Automation object was defined by the object, or whether it was mapped to an error defined by Visual Basic. Note that the constant **vbObjectError** is a very large negative number that an object adds to its own error code to indicate that the error is defined by the server. Therefore, subtracting it from **Err.Number** strips it out of the result. If the error is object-defined, the base number is left in MyError, which is displayed in a message box along with the original source of the error. If **Err.Number** represents a Visual Basic error, then the Visual Basic error number is displayed in the message box.

```
' Typical use of Number property
Sub test()
    On Error GoTo out

    Dim x, y
    x = 1 / y' Create division by zero error
    Exit Sub
    out:
    MsgBox Err.Number
    MsgBox Err.Description
    ' Check for division by zero error
    If Err.Number = 11 Then
        y = y + 1
    End If
    Resume
End Sub


' Using Number property with an error from an
' Automation object
Dim MyError, Msg
' First, strip off the constant added by the object to indicate one
' of its own errors.
MyError = Err.Number - vbObjectError
' If you subtract the vbObjectError constant, and the number is still
' in the range 0-65,535, it is an object-defined error code.
If MyError > 0 And MyError < 65535 Then
    Msg = "The object you accessed assigned this number to the error: " _
        & MyError & ". The originator of the error was: " _
        & Err.Source & ". Press F1 to see originator's Help topic."
' Otherwise it is a Visual Basic error number.
Else
    Msg = "This error (# " & Err.Number & ") is a Visual Basic error" & _
        " number. Press Help button or F1 for the Visual Basic Help" _
        & " topic for this error."
End If
    MsgBox Msg, , "Object Error", Err.HelpFile, Err.HelpContext
```

Number Property (Remote Data)

Returns a numeric value specifying a native error.

Applies To

rdoError Object

Syntax

object.**Number**

The *object* placeholder represents an object expression that evaluates to an object in the **Applies To** list.

Return Values

The return value is a **Long** integer representing an error number.

Remarks

Use the **Number** property to determine the nature of an error that occurred on the remote server or in the ODBC interface with the data source. The value of the property corresponds to a unique number that corresponds to an error condition generated by a stored procedure, a syntax or other procedural error, a permissions or rule violation or some other type of error. This native number can also be generated by a remote procedure executing a statement such as SQL Server's RAISERROR statement.

Note The SQL Server error severity level is *not* returned by the ODBC driver, and is therefore unavailable.

See Also

Description Property, **HelpContext**, **HelpFile** Properties, **rdoError** Object, **Source** Property, **SQLRetCode** Property, **SQLState** Property

Example

The following code opens a read-only ODBC cursor connection against the SQL Server "SEQUEL" and includes a simple error handler that displays the error description and number.

```
Sub MakeConnection()
Dim rdoCn As New rdoConnection
On Error GoTo CnEh
With rdoCn
    .Connect = "UID=;PWD=;Database=WorkDB;" _
        & "Server=SEQUEL;Driver={SQL Server}" _
        & "DSN='';"
    .LoginTimeout = 5
    .CursorDriver = rdUseODBC
    .EstablishConnection rdDriverNoPrompt, True
End With
AbandonCn:
Exit Sub
```

```
CnEh:
Dim er As rdoError
Dim msg as string
   Msg = "An error occured " _
   & "while opening the connection:" _
   & Err & " - " & Error & VbCr
   For Each er In rdoErrors
      Msg = Msg & er.Description _
          & ":" & er.Number & VbCr
   Next er
   Resume AbandonCn
End Sub
```

NumberFormat Property

Returns or sets a value indicating the format string for the **Column** object of a **DBGrid** control.

Applies To

Column Object

Syntax

object.**NumberFormat** [= *value*]

The **NumberFormat** property syntax has these parts:

Part	Description
object	An object expression that evaluates to an object in the **Applies To** list.
value	A string expression that defines how the expression in the **Value** property is formatted. The default value is a zero-length string ("").

Remarks

The **Text** property of the **Column** object is derived by applying this format to the **Value** property of the **Column** object. If **NumberFormat** is set to an invalid string, data in the cells are displayed as #ERR# and the value set in the **Value** property remains unchanged. See the **Format** function for information about valid format strings.

Example

This example formats the second column in a **DBGrid** control as a *long date*:

```
Private Sub Command1_Click ()
   DBGrid1.Columns(1).NumberFormat = "long date"
End Sub
```

NumIndices Property

Returns the number of indices on the property returned by the **Property** object, which is the number of indices required to access the value.

Applies To

Property Object

Syntax

object.**NumIndices**

The object placeholder represents an object expression that evaluates to an object in the **Applies To** list.

Remarks

The value of **NumIndices** can have a value from 0 to 4. For normal properties, as in the **ForeColor** property, **NumIndices** returns 0. Conventionally indexed properties, such as the **List** property of a **ListBox** control, return 1. Property arrays might return a 2.

See Also

IndexedValue Property

Object Data Type

Object variables are stored as 32-bit (4-byte) addresses that refer to objects. Using the **Set** statement, a variable declared as an **Object** can have any object reference assigned to it.

Note Although a variable declared with **Object** type is flexible enough to contain a reference to any object, binding to the object referenced by that variable is always late (run-time binding). To force early binding (compile-time binding), assign the object reference to a variable declared with a specific class name.

See Also

Data Type Summary, **Variant Data** Type, **Deftype** Statements, **IsObject** Function

---

Object Property

Returns a reference to a property or method of a control which has the same name as a property or method automatically extended to the control by Visual Basic.

Syntax

object.**Object**[.*property* | .*method*]

The **Object** property syntax has these parts:

Part	Description
object	An object expression that evaluates to an object in the **Applies To** list.
property	Property of the control that is identical to the name of a Visual Basic-supplied property.
Method	Method of the control that is identical to the name of a Visual Basic-supplied method.

Applies To

RemoteData Control

Remarks

Note The **Object** property returns the object which is the basis for the control without the properties or methods automatically extended to the control by Visual Basic. Therefore, you can also reference the controls' "custom" properties and methods through the **Object** property, such as `Print SSTab1.Object.Tabs`.

Visual Basic supplies some or all of a standard set of properties and methods to controls in a Visual Basic project. It is possible for a control or ActiveX component (such as Microsoft Excel or Microsoft Word) to define a property or method which has the same name as one of these standard properties or methods. When this occurs, Visual Basic automatically uses the property or method it supplies instead of the one with the same name defined in the control. The **Object** property allows you to bypass the Visual Basic-supplied property or method and use the identically named property or method defined in the control.

For example, the **Tag** property is a property supplied to all controls in a Visual Basic project. If a control in a project has the name `ctlDemo`, and you access the **Tag** property using this syntax:

```
ctlDemo.Tag
```

Visual Basic automatically uses the **Tag** property it supplies. However, if the control defines its own **Tag** property and you want to access that property, you use the **Object** property in this syntax:

```
ctlDemo.Object.Tag
```

Visual Basic automatically extends some or all of the following properties, methods, and events to controls in a Visual Basic project:

Properties

Align	**Height**	**Object**
Binding	**HelpContextID**	**Parent**
Bindings	**Index**	**TabIndex**
Cancel	**Left**	**TabStop**
Container	**LeftNoRun**	**TagParent**

(continued)

Properties

DataChanged	**LinkItem**	**ToolTipText**
DataField	**LinkMode**	**Top**
DataSource	**LinkTimeout**	**TopNoRun**
Default	**LinkTopic**	**VisibleTabStop**
DragIcon	**Name**	**WhatsThisHelpID**
DragMode	**NegotiateLinkItem**	**Width**

Methods

Drag	**LinkSend**	**ShowWhatsThis**
LinkExecute	**Move**	**ZOrder**
LinkPoke	**Refresh**	
LinkRequest	**SetFocus**	

Events

GotFocus	**LinkError**	**LinkOpen**
LinkClose	**LinkNotify**	**LostFocus**

If you use a property or method of a control and don't get the behavior you expect, check to see if the property or method has the same name as one of those shown in the preceding list. If the names match, check the documentation provided with the control to see if the behavior matches the Visual Basic-supplied property or method. If the behaviors aren't identical, you may need to use the **Object** property to access the feature of the control that you want.

See Also

Object Property (OLE Container)

Object Property (OLE Container)

Returns the object and/or a setting of an object's method or property in an **OLE** container control.

Applies To

DBCombo Control, **DBList** Control, **ImageList** Control, **ListView** Control, **Masked Edit** Control, **MSComm** Control, **MSFlexGrid** Control, **OLE Container** Control, **PictureClip** Control, **ProgressBar** Control, **RichTextBox** Control, **Slider** Control, **StatusBar** Control, **TabStrip** Control, **Toolbar** Control, **TreeView** Control

Syntax

object.**Object**[*.property* | *.method*]

The **Object** property syntax has these parts:

Part	Description
object	An object expression that evaluates to an object in the **Applies To** list.
property	Property that the object supports.
method	Method that the object supports.

Remarks

Use this property to specify an object you want to use in an Automation task.

You use the object returned by the **Object** property in an Automation task by using the properties and methods of that object. For information on which properties and methods an object supports, see the documentation for the application that created the object.

ObjectAcceptFormats Property

Returns the list of formats an object can accept.

Applies To

OLE Container Control

Syntax

object.**ObjectAcceptFormats**(*number*)

The **ObjectAcceptFormats** property syntax has these parts:

Part	Description
object	An object expression that evaluates to an object in the **Applies To** list.
number	A numeric expression that evaluates to an integer indicating the element in the array.

Remarks

The list is a zero-based string array. Elements of the array can be used to set the **Format** property when getting data from an object using the **Data** and **DataText** properties.

See Also

OLE Container Control, **Data** Property, **DataText** Property

ObjectAcceptFormatsCount Property

Returns the number of formats that can be accepted by an object.

Applies To

OLE Container Control

Syntax

object.**ObjectAcceptFormatsCount**

The *object* is an object expression that evaluates to an object in the **Applies To** list.

Remarks

Use this property to get the number of elements in the **ObjectAcceptFormats** property array.

See Also

Data Property, **DataText** Property, **ObjectGetFormats** Property, **ObjectGetFormatsCount** Property, **Format** Property

Example

To run this example, place an **OLE** container control and three **ListBox** controls on a form. Paste the example code into the Declarations section of the form and press F5. When the Insert Object dialog box is displayed, select an application in the New Object list box and choose OK to create an object.

```
Private Sub Form_Click ()
   Dim I ' Declare variable.
   ' Display the Insert Object dialog box.
   Ole1.InsertObjDlg
   ' Update the list of available verbs.
   Ole1.FetchVerbs' Fetch verbs.
   ' Clear the list boxes.
   List1.Clear
   List2.Clear
   List3.Clear
   ' Fill the verbs list box. Because ObjectVerbs(0) is
   ' the default verb and is repeated in the ObjectVerbs()
   ' array, start the count at 1.
   For I = 1 To Ole1.ObjectVerbsCount - 1
      List1.AddItem Ole1.ObjectVerbs(I)

   Next I
   'Fill the Accept Formats list box.
   For I = 0 To Ole1.ObjectAcceptFormatsCount - 1
      List2.AddItem Ole1.ObjectAcceptFormats(I)
   Next I
   ' Fill the Get Formats list box.
   For I = 0 To Ole1.ObjectGetFormatsCount - 1
      List3.AddItem Ole1.ObjectGetFormats(I)
   Next I
End Sub
```

ObjectGetFormats Property

Returns the list of formats an object can provide.

Applies To

OLE Container Control

Syntax

object.**ObjectGetFormats**(*number*)

The **ObjectGetFormats** property syntax has these parts:

Part	Description
object	An object expression that evaluates to an object in the **Applies To** list.
number	A numeric expression indicating the element in the array.

Remarks

The list is a zero-based string array. Elements of the array can be used to set the **Format** property when getting data from an object using the **Data** and **DataText** properties.

See Also

Data Property, **DataText** Property, **ObjectGetFormatsCount** Property, **Format** Property

Example

To run this example, place an **OLE** container control and three **ListBox** controls on a form. Paste the example code into the Declarations section of the form and press F5. When the Insert Object dialog box is displayed, select an application in the New Object list box and choose OK to create an object.

```
Private Sub Form_Click ()
   Dim I ' Declare variable.
   ' Display the Insert Object dialog box.
   Ole1.InsertObjDlg
   ' Update the list of available verbs.
   Ole1.FetchVerbs' Fetch verbs.
   ' Clear the list boxes.
   List1.Clear
   List2.Clear
   List3.Clear
   ' Fill the verbs list box. Because ObjectVerbs(0) is
   ' the default verb and is repeated in the ObjectVerbs()
   ' array, start the count at 1.
   For I = 1 To Ole1.ObjectVerbsCount - 1
      List1.AddItem Ole1.ObjectVerbs(I)
```

```
Next I
   'Fill the Accept Formats list box.
   For I = 0 To Ole1.ObjectAcceptFormatsCount - 1
      List2.AddItem Ole1.ObjectAcceptFormats(I)
   Next I
   ' Fill the Get Formats list box.
   For I = 0 To Ole1.ObjectGetFormatsCount - 1
      List3.AddItem Ole1.ObjectGetFormats(I)
   Next I
End Sub
```

ObjectGetFormatsCount Property

Returns the number of formats an object can provide.

Applies To

OLE Container Control

Syntax

object.**ObjectGetFormatsCount**

The *object* is an object expression that evaluates to an object in the **Applies To** list.

Remarks

Use this property to determine the number of elements in the **ObjectGetFormats** property array.

See Also

Data Property, **DataText** Property, **ObjectAcceptFormatsCount** Property, **Format** Property

Example

To run this example, place an **OLE** container control and three **ListBox** controls on a form. Paste the example code into the Declarations section of the form and press F5. When the Insert Object dialog box is displayed, select an application in the New Object list box and choose OK to create an object.

```
Private Sub Form_Click ()
   Dim I ' Declare variable.
   ' Display the Insert Object dialog box.
   Ole1.InsertObjDlg
   ' Update the list of available verbs.
   Ole1.FetchVerbs' Fetch verbs.
   ' Clear the list boxes.
   List1.Clear
   List2.Clear
   List3.Clear
   ' Fill the verbs list box. Because ObjectVerbs(0) is
   ' the default verb and is repeated in the ObjectVerbs()
   ' array, start the count at 1.
```

```
        For I = 1 To Ole1.ObjectVerbsCount - 1
            List1.AddItem Ole1.ObjectVerbs(I)

Next I
    'Fill the Accept Formats list box.
    For I = 0 To Ole1.ObjectAcceptFormatsCount - 1
        List2.AddItem Ole1.ObjectAcceptFormats(I)
    Next I
    ' Fill the Get Formats list box.
    For I = 0 To Ole1.ObjectGetFormatsCount - 1
        List3.AddItem Ole1.ObjectGetFormats(I)
    Next I
End Sub
```

ObjectMove Event

Occurs immediately after the object within an **OLE** container control is moved or resized while the object is active.

Applies To

OLE Container Control

Syntax

Private Sub *object*_**ObjectMove(***left* **As Single,** *top* **As Single,** *width* **As Single,**
↳ *height* **As Single)**

The **ObjectMove** event syntax has these parts:

Part	Description
object	An object expression that evaluates to an object in the **Applies To** list.
left	The coordinate of the left edge of the **OLE** container control immediately after it's moved or resized.
top	The coordinate of the top edge of the **OLE** container control immediately after it's moved or resized.
width	The width of the **OLE** container control immediately after it's moved or resized.
height	The height of the **OLE** container control immediately after it's moved or resized.

Remarks

When a user moves or resizes an **OLE** container control, your application can use the **ObjectMove** event to determine whether to actually change the size and position of the control. If the **ObjectMove** event procedure doesn't change the **OLE** container control's position or size, the object within the **OLE** container control returns to its original position and is informed of its new size. The coordinates passed as arguments to this event include the border of the **OLE** container control.

The **ObjectMove** and Resize events are triggered when the **OLE** container control receives information about the size of the object it contains. However, the Resize event doesn't receive any information about the position of the control. If the **OLE** container control is moved off the form, the arguments have negative or positive values that represent the position of the object relative to the top and left of the form.

See Also

Resize Event, **Move** Method, **SizeMode** Property, **DragMode** Property

ObjectVerbFlags Property

Returns the menu state (such as enabled or disabled, checked, and so on) for each verb in a given **ObjectVerbs** array.

Applies To

OLE Container Control, **OLEObject** Object

Syntax

object.**ObjectVerbFlags**(*number*)

The **ObjectVerbFlags** property syntax has these parts:

Part	Description
object	An object expression that evaluates to an object in the **Applies To** list.
number	A numeric expression indicating the element in the array.

Return Values

The **ObjectVerbFlags** property returns the following values:

Constant	Value	Description
vbOLEFlagChecked	&H0008	The menu item is checked.
vbOLEFlagDisabled	&H0002	The menu item is disabled (but not dimmed).
vbOLEFlagEnabled	&H0000	The menu item is enabled.
vbOLEFlagGrayed	&H0001	The menu item is dimmed.
vbOLEFlagSeparator	&H0800	The menu item is a separator bar.

Note These constants are also listed in the Visual Basic objects and procedures library in the Object Browser.

Remarks

The first verb in the **ObjectVerbs** array is the default verb. The **ObjectVerbFlags** array contains information about the menu state (such as dimmed, checked, and so on) for each verb in the **ObjectVerbs** array.

When displaying a menu containing an object's verbs, check the value of this property to see how the item is set to be displayed.

See Also

ObjectVerbs Property, **ObjectVerbsCount** Property, **Verb** Property, **AutoVerbMenu** Property

ObjectVerbs Property

Returns the list of verbs an object supports.

Applies To

OLE Container Control, **RichTextBox** Control

Syntax

object.**ObjectVerbs**(*number*)

The **ObjectVerbs** property syntax has these parts:

Part	Description
object	An object expression that evaluates to an object in the **Applies To** list.
number	A numeric expression indicating the element in the array.

Remarks

ObjectVerbs is a zero-based string array. Use this property along with the **ObjectVerbsCount** property to get the verbs supported by an object. These verbs are used to determine an action to perform when an object is activated with the **DoVerb** method. The list of verbs in the array varies from object to object and depends on the current conditions.

Each object can support its own set of verbs. The following values represent standard verbs supported by every object:

Constant	Value	Description
vbOLEPrimary	0	The default action for the object.
vbOLEShow	−1	Activates the object for editing. If the application that created the object supports in-place activation, the object is activated within the **OLE** container control.
vbOLEOpen	−2	Opens the object in a separate application window. If the application that created the object supports in-place activation, the object is activated in its own window.

(continued)

Constant	Value	Description
vbOLEHide	−3	For embedded objects, hides the application that created the object.
vbOLEUInPlaceUIActivate	−4	If the object supports in-place activation, activates the object for in-place activation and shows any user interface tools. If the object doesn't support in-place activation, the object doesn't activate, and an error occurs.
vbOLEInPlaceActivate	−5	If the user moves the focus to the **OLE** container control, creates a window for the object and prepares the object to be edited. An error occurs if the object doesn't support activation on a single mouse click.
vbOLEDiscardUndoState	−6	Used when the object is activated for editing to discard all record of changes that the object's application can undo.

Note   These verbs may not be listed in the **ObjectVerbs** property array.

The first verb in the **ObjectVerbs** array, **ObjectVerbs(0)**, is the default verb. Unless otherwise specified, this verb activates the object.

The remaining verbs in the array can be displayed on a menu. If it's appropriate to display the default verb in a menu, the default verb has two entries in the **ObjectVerbs** array.

Applications that display objects typically include an Object command on the Edit menu. When the user chooses Edit Object, a menu displays the object's verbs. Use the **ObjectVerbs**, **ObjectVerbsCount**, and **ObjectVerbFlags** properties to create such a menu at run time.

The list of verbs an object supports may vary, depending on the state of the object. To update the list of verbs an object supports, use the **FetchVerbs** method. Be sure to update the list of verbs before presenting it to the user.

To automatically display the verbs in the **ObjectVerbs** array in a pop-up menu when the user clicks an object with the right mouse button, set the **AutoVerbMenu** property to **True**.

See Also

ObjectVerbFlags Property, **ObjectVerbsCount** Property, **Verb** Property, **AutoVerbMenu** Property, **DoVerb** Method, **FetchVerbs** Method

Example

To run this example, place an **OLE** container control and three **ListBox** controls on a form. Paste the example code into the Declarations section of the form and press F5. When the Insert Object dialog box is displayed, select an application in the New Object list box and choose OK to create an object.

```
Private Sub Form_Click ()
    Dim I ' Declare variable.
    ' Display the Insert Object dialog box.
    Ole1.InsertObjDlg
    ' Update the list of available verbs.
    Ole1.FetchVerbs' Fetch verbs.
    ' Clear the list boxes.
    List1.Clear
    List2.Clear
    List3.Clear
    ' Fill the verbs list box. Because ObjectVerbs(0) is
    ' the default verb and is repeated in the ObjectVerbs()
    ' array, start the count at 1.
    For I = 1 To Ole1.ObjectVerbsCount - 1
        List1.AddItem Ole1.ObjectVerbs(I)

Next I
    'Fill the Accept Formats list box.
    For I = 0 To Ole1.ObjectAcceptFormatsCount - 1
        List2.AddItem Ole1.ObjectAcceptFormats(I)
    Next I
    ' Fill the Get Formats list box.
    For I = 0 To Ole1.ObjectGetFormatsCount - 1
        List3.AddItem Ole1.ObjectGetFormats(I)
    Next I
End Sub
```

ObjectVerbsCount Property

Returns the number of verbs supported by an object.

Applies To

OLE Container Control, **RichTextBox** Control

Syntax

object.**ObjectVerbsCount**

The *object* is an object expression that evaluates to an **OLE** container control.

Remarks

Use this property to determine the number of elements in the **ObjectVerbs** property array.

The list of verbs an object supports may vary, depending on the state of the object. To update the list of verbs an object supports, use the **FetchVerbs** method.

See Also

> **ObjectVerbFlags** Property, **ObjectVerbs** Property, **Verb** Property,
> **FetchVerbs** Method

Example

> To run this example, place an **OLE** container control and three **ListBox**
> controls on a form. Paste the example code into the Declarations section
> of the form and press F5. When the Insert Object dialog box is displayed,
> select an application in the New Object list box and choose OK to create
> an object.

```
Private Sub Form_Click ()
   Dim I ' Declare variable.
   ' Display the Insert Object dialog box.
   Ole1.InsertObjDlg
   ' Update the list of available verbs.
   Ole1.FetchVerbs' Fetch verbs.
   ' Clear the list boxes.
   List1.Clear
   List2.Clear
   List3.Clear
   ' Fill the verbs list box. Because ObjectVerbs(0) is
   ' the default verb and is repeated in the ObjectVerbs()
   ' array, start the count at 1.
   For I = 1 To Ole1.ObjectVerbsCount - 1
      List1.AddItem Ole1.ObjectVerbs(I)

Next I
   'Fill the Accept Formats list box.
   For I = 0 To Ole1.ObjectAcceptFormatsCount - 1
      List2.AddItem Ole1.ObjectAcceptFormats(I)
   Next I
   ' Fill the Get Formats list box.
   For I = 0 To Ole1.ObjectGetFormatsCount - 1
      List3.AddItem Ole1.ObjectGetFormats(I)
   Next I
End Sub
```

Oct Function

> Returns a **Variant** (**String**) representing the octal value of a number.

Syntax

> **Oct**(*number*)
>
> The required *number* argument is any valid numeric expression or
> string expression.

Remarks

If *number* is not already a whole number, it is rounded to the nearest whole number before being evaluated.

If *number* is	Oct returns
Null	**Null**
Empty	Zero (0)
Any other number	Up to 11 octal characters

You can represent octal numbers directly by preceding numbers in the proper range with &0. For example, &010 is the octal notation for decimal 8.

See Also

Hex Function

Example

This example uses the **Oct** function to return the octal value of a number.

```
Dim MyOct
MyOct = Oct(4)     ' Returns 4.
MyOct = Oct(8)     ' Returns 10.
MyOct = Oct(459)   ' Returns 713.
```

ODBCTimeout Property

Indicates the number of seconds to wait before a timeout error occurs when a **QueryDef** is executed on an ODBC database.

Applies To

QueryDef Object

Settings and Return Values

The setting or return value is an **Integer** representing the number of seconds to wait before a timeout error occurs.

When the **ODBCTimeout** property is set to −1, the timeout defaults to the current setting of the **QueryTimeout** property of the **Connection** or **Database** object that contains the **QueryDef**. When the **ODBCTimeout** property is set to 0, no timeout error occurs.

Remarks

When you're using an ODBC database, such as Microsoft SQL Server, delays can occur because of network traffic or heavy use of the ODBC server. Rather than waiting indefinitely, you can specify how long to wait before returning an error.

Setting the **ODBCTimeout** property of a **QueryDef** object overrides the value
specified by the **QueryTimeout** property of the **Connection** or **Database** object
containing the **QueryDef**, but only for that **QueryDef** object.

Note In an ODBCDirect workspace, after setting **ODBCTimeout** to an explicit value you can
reset it back to the default (i.e., −1) only once during the life of the **QueryDef** object.
Otherwise, an error will occur.

See Also

QueryTimeout Property

Example

This example uses the **ODBCTimeout** and **QueryTimeout** properties to show how
the **QueryTimeout** setting on a **Database** object sets the default **ODBCTimeout**
setting on any **QueryDef** objects created from the **Database** object.

```
Sub ODBCTimeoutX()

    Dim dbsCurrent As Database
    Dim qdfStores As QueryDef
    Dim rstStores As Recordset

    Set dbsCurrent = OpenDatabase("Northwind.mdb")

    ' Change the default QueryTimeout of the Northwind
    ' database.
    Debug.Print "Default QueryTimeout of Database: " & _
        dbsCurrent.QueryTimeout
    dbsCurrent.QueryTimeout = 30
    Debug.Print "New QueryTimeout of Database: " & _
        dbsCurrent.QueryTimeout

    ' Create a new QueryDef object.
    Set qdfStores = dbsCurrent.CreateQueryDef("Stores", _
        "SELECT * FROM stores")
    qdfStores.Connect = _
        "ODBC;DATABASE=pubs;UID=sa;PWD=;DSN=Publishers"

    ' Change the ODBCTimeout setting of the new QueryDef
    ' object from its default setting.
    Debug.Print "Default ODBCTimeout of QueryDef: " & _
        qdfStores.ODBCTimeout
    qdfStores.ODBCTimeout = 0
    Debug.Print "New ODBCTimeout of QueryDef: " & _
        qdfStores.ODBCTimeout

    ' Execute the query and display the results.
    Set rstStores = qdfStores.OpenRecordset()
```

```
            Debug.Print "Contents of recordset:"
            With rstStores
                Do While Not .EOF
                    Debug.Print , .Fields(0), .Fields(1)
                    .MoveNext
                Loop
                .Close
            End With

            ' Delete new QueryDef because this is a demonstration.
            dbsCurrent.QueryDefs.Delete qdfStores.Name
            dbsCurrent.Close

        End Sub
```

OLE Container Control

The **OLE** container control enables you to add insertable objects to the forms in your Visual Basic applications. With the **OLE** container control, you can:

- Create a placeholder in your application for an insertable object. At run time you can create the object that is displayed within the **OLE** container control or change an object you placed within the **OLE** container control at design time.

- Create a linked object in your application.

- Bind the **OLE** container control to a database using the **Data** control.

You either create the object at design time using the Insert Object dialog box (which contains the commands Insert Object, Paste Special, and so on), or at run time by setting the appropriate properties.

When you move an **OLE** container control on a form using the **ObjectMove** method, the **Height** and **Width** property values of the object may be slightly different after the move. This is because the parameters to the **ObjectMove** method are pixel values converted to the current form's scaling mode. The conversion from pixels to twips and back doesn't always result in identical values.

Using the OLE Container Control's Pop-up Menus

Each time you draw an **OLE** container control on a form, the Insert Object dialog box is displayed. Use this dialog box to create a linked or embedded object. If you choose Cancel, no object is created.

At design time, click the **OLE** container control with the right mouse button to display a pop-up menu. The commands displayed on this pop-up menu depend on the state of the **OLE** container control as shown in the following table:

Command	Enabled in pop-up menu when
Insert Object	Always enabled.
Paste Special	**Clipboard** object contains a valid object.
Delete Embedded Object	**OLE** container control contains an embedded object.
Delete Linked Object	**OLE** container control contains a linked object.
Create Link	**SourceDoc** property is set.
Create Embedded Object	**Class** or **SourceDoc** property is set.

An **OLE** container control can contain only one object at a time. You can create a linked or embedded object in several ways:

- Use the Insert Object or Paste Special dialog boxes (run time or design time).

- Set the **Class** property in the Properties window, click the **OLE** container control with the right mouse button, and then select the appropriate command (design time only).

- Use the appropriate method of the **OLE** container control.

Finding Class Names

You can get a list of the class names available to your application by selecting the **Class** property in the Properties window and clicking the Properties button.

Note The Insert Object dialog box doesn't display a list of class names. This dialog box displays user-friendly names for each class of object, which are generally longer and more easily understood.

Properties

Action Property, **Appearance** Property, **ApplsRunning** Property, **AutoActivate** Property, **AutoVerbMenu** Property, **BackColor, ForeColor** Properties, **BackStyle** Property, **BorderStyle** Property, **Class** Property, **Container** Property, **Data** Property, **DataChanged** Property, **DataField** Property, **DataText** Property, **DisplayType** Property, **DragIcon** Property, **DragMode** Property, **Enabled** Property, **FileNumber** Property, **Format** Property, **Format Height, Width** Properties, **HelpContextId** Property, **HostName** Property, **hWnd** Property, **Index** Property, **Left, Top** Properties, **IpOleObject** Property, **MiscFlags** Property, **MouseIcon** Property, **MousePointer** Property, **Name** Property, **Object** Property, **ObjectAcceptFormats** Property, **ObjectAcceptFormatsCount** Property, **ObjectGetFormats** Property, **ObjectGetFormatsCount** Property, **ObjectVerbFlags** Property, **ObjectVerbs**

Property, **ObjectVerbsCount** Property, **OLEDropAllowed** Property, **OLEType** Property, **OLETypeAllowed** Property, **Parent** Property, **PasteOK** Property, **Picture** Property, **SizeMode** Property, **SourceDoc** Property, **SourceItem** Property, **TabIndex** Property, **TabStop** Property, **Tag** Property, **UpdateOptions** Property, **Verb** Property, **Visible** Property, **WhatsThisHelpId** Property

Events

Click Event, **DblClick** Event, **DragDrop** Event, **DragOver** Event, **GotFocus** Event, **KeyDown**, **KeyUp** Events, **KeyPress** Event, **LostFocus** Event, **MouseDown**, **MouseUp** Events, **MouseMove** Event, **ObjectMove** Event, **Resize** Event, **Updated** Event

Methods

Close Method (OLE Container), **Copy** Method, **CreateEmbed** Method, **CreateLink** Method, **Delete** Method, **DoVerb** Method, **Drag** Method, **FetchVerbs** Method, **InsertObjDlg** Method, **Move** Method, **Paste** Method, **PasteSpecialDlg** Method, **ReadFromFile** Method, **Refresh** Method, **SaveToFile** Method, **SaveToOle1File** Method, **SetFocus** Method, **ShowWhatsThis** Method, **Update** Method, **ZOrder** Method

See Also

Object Property (OLE Container)

OLECompleteDrag Event

Occurs when a source component is dropped onto a target component, informing the source component that a drag action was either performed or canceled.

Applies To

CheckBox Control, **ComboBox** Control, **CommandButton** Control, **Data** Control, **DBCombo** Control, **DBList** Control, **DirListBox** Control, **DriveListBox** Control, **FileListBox** Control, **Form** Object **Forms** Collection, **Frame** Control, **Image** Control, **Label** Control, **ListBox** Control, **MDIForm** Object, **OptionButton** Control, **PictureBox** Control, **Propertypage** Object, **TextBox** Control, **UserControl** Object, **UserDocument** Object

Syntax

Private Sub *object*_**CompleteDrag**([*effect* **As Long**])

The **CompleteDrag** event syntax has these parts:

Part	Description
object	An object expression that evaluates to an object in the **Applies To** list.
effect	A long integer set by the source object identifying the action that has been performed, thus allowing the source to take appropriate action if the component was moved (such as the source deleting data if it is moved from one component to another). The possible values are listed in Settings.

Settings

The settings for *effect* are:

Constant	Value	Description
vbDropEffectNone	0	Drop target cannot accept the data, or the drop operation was cancelled.
vbDropEffectCopy	1	Drop results in a copy of data from the source to the target. The original data is unaltered by the drag operation.
vbDropEffectMove	2	Drop results in a link to the original data being created between drag source and drop target.

Remarks

The **OLECompleteDrag** event is the final event to be called in an OLE drag/drop operation. This event informs the source component of the action that was performed when the object was dropped onto the target component. The target sets this value through the *effect* parameter of the **OLEDragDrop** event. Based on this, the source can then determine the appropriate action it needs to take. For example, if the object was moved into the target (**vbDropEffectMove**), the source needs to delete the object from itself after the move.

If **OLEDragMode** is set to **Automatic**, then Visual Basic handles the default behavior. The event still occurs, however, allowing the user to add to or change the behavior.

Most components support manual OLE drag and drop events, and some support automatic OLE drag and drop events.

OLEDrag Method

Causes a component to initiate an OLE drag/drop operation.

Applies To

CheckBox Control, **ComboBox** Control, **CommandBox** Control, **Data** Control, **DBCombo** Control, **DBList** Control, **DirListBox** Control, **DriveListBox** Control, **FileListBox** Control, **Form** Object, **Forms** Collection, **Frame** Control, **Image** Control, **Label** Control, **ListBox** Control, **MDIForm** Object, **OptionButton** Control, **PictureBox** Control, **PropertyPage** Object, **TextBox** Control, **UserControl** Object, **UserDocument** Object

Syntax

object.**OLEDrag**

The *object* placeholder represents an object expression that evaluates to an object in the **Applies To** list.

Remarks

When the **OLEDrag** method is called, the component's OLEStartDrag event occurs, allowing it to supply data to a target component.

OLEDragDrop Event

Occurs when a source component is dropped onto a target component when the source component determines that a drop can occur.

Note This event occurs only if **OLEDropMode** is set to **1 (Manual)**.

Applies To

CheckBox Control, **ComboBox** Control, **CommandButton** Control, **Data** Control, **DBCombo** Control, **DBList** Control, **DirListBox** Control, **DriveListBox** Control, **FileListBox** Control, **Form** Object, **Forms** Collection, **Frame** Control, **Image** Control, **Label** Control, **ListBox** Control, **MDIForm** Object, **Object** Control, **OptionButton** Control, **PictureBox** Control, **PropertyPage** Object, **TextBox** Control, **UserControl** Object, **UserDocument** Object

Syntax

Private Sub *object*_**OLEDragDrop**(*data* **As DataObject**, *effect* **As Long**, *button* **As Integer**, *shift* **As Integer**, *x* **As Single**, *y* **As Single**)

The OLEDragDrop event syntax has these parts:

Part	Description
object	An object expression that evaluates to an object in the **Applies To** list.
data	A **DataObject** object containing formats that the source will provide and, in addition, possibly the data for those formats. If no data is contained in the **DataObject**, it is provided when the control calls the **GetData** method. The **SetData** and **Clear** methods cannot be used here.
effect	A long integer set by the target component identifying the action that has been performed (if any), thus allowing the source to take appropriate action if the component was moved (such as the source deleting the data). The possible values are listed in Settings.
button	An integer which acts as a bit field corresponding to the state of a mouse button when it is depressed. The left button is bit 0, the right button is bit 1, and the middle button is bit 2. These bits correspond to the values 1, 2, and 4, respectively. It indicates the state of the mouse buttons; some, all, or none of these three bits can be set, indicating that some, all, or none of the buttons are depressed.

(continued)

Part	Description
shift	An integer which acts as a bit field corresponding to the state of the SHIFT, CTRL, and ALT keys when they are depressed. The SHIFT key is bit 0, the CTRL key is bit 1, and the ALT key is bit 2. These bits correspond to the values 1, 2, and 4, respectively. The *shift* parameter indicates the state of these keys; some, all, or none of the bits can be set, indicating that some, all, or none of the keys are depressed. For example, if both the CTRL and ALT keys were depressed, the value of *shift* would be 6.
x,y	A number which specifies the current location of the mouse pointer. The *x* and *y* values are always expressed in terms of the coordinate system set by the **ScaleHeight**, **ScaleWidth**, **ScaleLeft**, and **ScaleTop** properties of the object.

Settings

The settings for *effect* are:

Constant	Value	Description
vbDropEffectNone	0	Drop target cannot accept the data.
vbDropEffectCopy	1	Drop results in a copy of data from the source to the target. The original data is unaltered by the drag operation.
vbDropEffectMove	2	Drop results in data being moved from drag source to drop source. The drag source should remove the data from itself after the move.

Remarks

The source ActiveX component should always mask values from the *effect* parameter to ensure compatibility with future implementations of ActiveX components. Presently, only three of the 32 bits in the *effect* parameter are used. In future versions of Visual Basic, however, these other bits may be used. Therefore, as a precaution against future problems, drag sources and drop targets should mask these values appropriately before performing any comparisons.

For example, a source component should not compare an *effect* against, say, **vbDropEffectCopy**, such as in this manner:

```
If Effect = vbDropEffectCopy...
```

Instead, the source component should mask for the value or values being sought, such as this:

```
If Effect And vbDropEffectCopy = vbDropEffectCopy...
```

-or-

```
If (Effect And vbDropEffectCopy)...
```

This allows for the definition of new drop effects in future versions of Visual Basic while preserving backwards compatibility with your existing code.

Most components support manual OLE drag and drop events, and some support automatic OLE drag and drop events.

See Also

OLECompleteDrag Event, **OLEDragOver** Event, **OLEGiveFeedback** Event, **OLESetData** Event, **OLEStartDrag** Event

---

OLEDragMode Property

Returns or sets whether the component or the programmer handles an OLE drag/drop operation.

Applies To

DBCombo Control, **DBList** Control, **ComboBox** Control, **DirListBox** Control, **FileListBox** Control, **Image** Control, **ListBox** Control, **PictureBox** Control, **TextBox** Control

Syntax

object.**OLEDragMode** = *mode*

The **OLEDragMode** property syntax has these parts:

Part	Description
object	An object expression that evaluates to an object in the **Applies To** list.
mode	An integer which specifies the method with which an component handles OLE drag/drop operations, as described in Settings.

Settings

The settings for *mode* are:

Constant	Value	Description
vbOLEDragManual	0	(Default) Manual. The programmer handles all OLE drag/drop operations.
vbOLEDragAutomatic	1	Automatic. The component handles all OLE drag/drop operations.

Remarks

When **OLEDragMode** is set to **Manual**, you must call the **OLEDrag** method to start dragging, which then triggers the **OLEStartDrag** event.

When **OLEDragMode** is set to **Automatic**, the source component fills the **DataObject** object with the data it contains and sets the *effects* parameter before initiating the **OLEStartDrag** event (as well as the **OLESetData** and other source-level OLE drag/drop events) when the user attempts to drag out of the control.

This gives you control over the drag/drop operation and allows you to intercede by adding other formats, or by overriding or disabling the automatic data and formats using the **Clear** or **SetData** methods.

If the source's **OLEDragMode** property is set to **Automatic**, and no data is loaded in the **OLEStartDrag** event, or *aftereffects* is set to **0**, then the OLE drag/drop operation does not occur.

Note If the **DragMode** property of a control is set to **Automatic**, the setting of **OLEDragMode** is ignored, because regular Visual Basic drag and drop events take precedence.

OLEDragOver Event

Occurs when one component is dragged over another.

Applies To

CheckBox Control, **ComboBox** Control, **CommandButton** Control, **Data** Control, **DBCombo** Control, **DBList** Control, **DirListBox** Control, **DriveListBox** Control, **FileListBox** Control, **Form** Object, **Forms** Collection, **Frame** Control, **Image** Control, **Label** Control, **ListBox** Control, **MDIForm** Object, **OptionButton** Control, **PictureBox** Control, **PropertyPage** Object, **TextBox** Control, **UserControl** Object, **UserDocument** Object

Syntax

Private Sub *object*_**OLEDragOver**(*data* **As DataObject**, *effect* **As Long**, *button* **As Integer**, *shift* **As Integer**, *x* **As Single**, *y* **As Single**, *state* **As Integer**)

The **OLEDragOver** event syntax has these parts:

Part	Description
object	An object expression that evaluates to an object in the **Applies To** list.
data	A **DataObject** object containing formats that the source will provide and, in addition, possibly the data for those formats. If no data is contained in the **DataObject**, it is provided when the control calls the **GetData** method. The **SetData** and **Clear** methods cannot be used here.
effect	A long integer initially set by the source object identifying all effects it supports. This parameter must be correctly set by the target component during this event. The value of *effect* is determined by logically **Or**'ing together all active effects (as listed in Settings). The target component should check these effects and other parameters to determine which actions are appropriate for it, and then set this parameter to one of the allowable effects (as specified by the source) to specify which actions will be performed if the user drops the selection on the component. The possible values are listed in Settings.

(continued)

907

(continued)

Part	Description
button	An integer which acts as a bit field corresponding to the state of a mouse button when it is depressed. The left button is bit 0, the right button is bit 1, and the middle button is bit 2. These bits correspond to the values 1, 2, and 4, respectively. It indicates the state of the mouse buttons; some, all, or none of these three bits can be set, indicating that some, all, or none of the buttons are depressed.
shift	An integer which acts as a bit field corresponding to the state of the SHIFT, CTRL, and ALT keys when they are depressed. The SHIFT key is bit 0, the CTRL key is bit 1, and the ALT key is bit 2. These bits correspond to the values 1, 2, and 4, respectively. The *shift* parameter indicates the state of these keys; some, all, or none of the bits can be set, indicating that some, all, or none of the keys are depressed. For example, if both the CTRL and ALT keys are depressed, the value of *shift* would be 6.
x,y	A number that specifies the current horizontal (x) and vertical (y) position of the mouse pointer within the target form or control. The x and y values are always expressed in terms of the coordinate system set by the **ScaleHeight**, **ScaleWidth**, **ScaleLeft**, and **ScaleTop** properties of the object.
state	An integer that corresponds to the transition state of the control being dragged in relation to a target form or control. The possible values are listed in Settings.

Settings

The settings for *effect* are:

Constant	Value	Description
vbDropEffectNone	0	Drop target cannot accept the data.
vbDropEffectCopy	1	Drop results in a copy of data from the source to the target. The original data is unaltered by the drag operation.
vbDropEffectMove	2	Drop results in data being moved from drag source to drop source. The drag source should remove the data from itself after the move.
vbDropEffectScroll	–2147483648 (&H80000000)	Scrolling is occuring or about to occur in the target component. This value is used in conjunction with the other values. **Note** Use only if you are performing your own scrolling in the target component.

The settings for *state* are:

Constant	Value	Description
vbEnter	0	Source component is being dragged within the range of a target.
vbLeave	1	Source component is being dragged out of the range of a target.
vbOver	2	Source component has moved from one position in the target to another.

Remarks

Note If the *state* parameter is **vbLeave**, indicating that the mouse pointer has left the target, then the *x* and *y* parameters will contain zeros.

The source component should always mask values from the *effect* parameter to ensure compatibility with future implementations of ActiveX components. Presently, only three of the 32 bits in the *effect* parameter are used. In future versions of Visual Basic, however, these other bits may be used. Therefore, as a precaution against future problems, drag sources and drop targets should mask these values appropriately before performing any comparisons.

For example, a source component should not compare an *effect* against, say, **vbDropEffectCopy**, such as in this manner:

```
If Effect = vbDropEffectCopy...
```

Instead, the source component should mask for the value or values being sought, such as this:

```
If Effect And vbDropEffectCopy = vbDropEffectCopy...
```

-or-

```
If (Effect And vbDropEffectCopy)...
```

This allows for the definition of new drop effects in future versions of Visual Basic while preserving backwards compatibility with your existing code.

Most components support manual OLE drag and drop events, and some support automatic OLE drag and drop events.

OLEDropAllowed Property

Returns or sets a value that determines whether an **OLE** container control can be a drop target for OLE drag-and-drop operations.

Applies To

UserControl Object, **OLE Container** Control

Syntax

object.**OLEDropAllowed** [= *boolean*]

The **OLEDropAllowed** property syntax has these parts:

Part	Description
object	An object expression that evaluates to an object in the **Applies To** list.
boolean	A Boolean expression specifying whether the **OLE** container control can be a drop target, as described in Settings.

Settings

The settings for *Boolean* are:

Setting	Description
True	When dragging an object that can be linked object or embedded object, a drop icon appears when the mouse pointer moves over the **OLE** container control. Dropping the object on the **OLE** container control has the same effect as pasting the object from the system Clipboard using the **Paste** method.
False	(Default) No drop icon appears over the **OLE** container control when dragging an object that can be linked or embedded. Dropping the object on the **OLE** container control has no effect on the control.

Remarks

The **MousePointer** property determines the shape of the mouse pointer when the **OLEDropAllowed** property is set to **True**. If the setting of the **MousePointer** property is 0 (Default), Visual Basic displays the standard drag-and-drop icon for the action taking place.

The setting of the **OLETypeAllowed** property must be 1 (**vbOLEEmbedded**) or 2 (**vbOLEEither**) to move or copy the object that can be linked or embedded, or 0 (**vbOLELinked**) or 2 to link the object. Dropping an object when **OLEDropAllowed** is set to **True** has the same effect on the **Class**, **SourceDoc**, and **SourceItem** property settings as using the **Paste** method of the **OLE** container control.

If the **OLEDropAllowed** property is set to **True**, the **OLE** container control doesn't receive **DragDrop** or **DragOver** events when dragging an object. Also, the setting of the **DragMode** property has no effect on the drag-and-drop behavior of the **OLE** container control when the **OLEDropAllowed** property is set to **True**.

See Also

Class Property, **SourceDoc** Property, **SourceItem** Property, **OLETypeAllowed** Property, **Paste** Method, **DragMode** Property

OLEDropMode Property

Returns or sets how a target component handles drop operations.

Applies To

CheckBox Control, **ComboBox** Control, **CommandButton** Control, **Data** Control, **DBCombo** Control, **DBList** Control, **DirListBox** Control, **DriveListBox** Control, **FileListBox** Control, **Form** Object, **Forms** Collection, **Frame** Control, **Image** Control, **Label** Control, **ListBox** Control, **MDIForm** Object, **OptionButton** Control, **PictureBox** Control, **PropertyPage** Object, **TextBox** Control, **UserControl** Object, **UserDocument** Object

Syntax

object.**OLEDropMode** [= *mode*]

The **OLEDropMode** property syntax has these parts:

Part	Description
object	An object expression that evaluates to an object in the **Applies To** list.
mode	An enumerated integer which specifies the method which a component handles OLE drag/drop operations, as described in Settings.

Settings

The settings for *mode* are:

Constant	Value	Description
vbOLEDropNone	0	(Default) None. The target component does not accept OLE drops and displays the No Drop cursor.
vbOLEDropManual	1	Manual. The target component triggers the OLE drop events, allowing the programmer to handle the OLE drop operation in code.
vbOLEDropAutomatic	2	Automatic. The target component automatically accepts OLE drops if the **DataObject** object contains data in a format it recognizes. No mouse or OLE drag/drop events on the target will occur when **OLEDropMode** is set to **vbOLEDropAutomatic**.

Remarks

Note The target component inspects what is being dragged over it in order to determine which events to trigger; the OLE drag/drop events, or the Visual Basic drag/drop events. There is no collision of components or confusion about which events are fired, since only one type of object can be dragged at a time.

OLEGiveFeedback Event

Occurs after every **OLEDragOver** event. **OLEGiveFeedback** allows the source component to provide visual feedback to the user, such as changing the mouse cursor to indicate what will happen if the user drops the object, or provide visual feedback on the selection (in the source component) to indicate what will happen.

Applies To

CheckBox Control, **ComboBox** Control, **CommandButton** Control, **Data** Control, **DBCombo** Control, **DBList** Control, **DirListBox** Control, **DriveListBox** Control, **FileListBox** Control, **Form** Object, **Forms** Collection, **Frame** Control, **Image** Control, **Label** Control, **ListBox** Control, **MDIForm** Object, **OptionButton** Control, **PictureBox** Control, **PropertyPage** Object, **TextBox** Control, **UserControl** Object, **UserDocument** Object

Syntax

Private Sub *object*_**OLEGiveFeedback**(*effect* **As Long**, defaultcursors **As Boolean**)

The **OLEGiveFeedback** event syntax has these parts:

Part	Description
object	An object expression that evaluates to an object in the **Applies To** list.
effect	A long integer set by the target component in the OLEDragOver event specifying the action to be performed if the user drops the selection on it. This allows the source to take the appropriate action (such as giving visual feedback). The possible values are listed in Settings.
defaultcursors	A Boolean value which determines whether Visual Basic uses the default mouse cursor proved by the component, or uses a user-defined mouse cursor.
	True (default) = use default mouse cursor.
	False = do not use default cursor. Mouse cursor must be set with the **MousePointer** property of the **Screen** object.

Settings

The settings for *effect* are:

Constant	Value	Description
vbDropEffectNone	0	Drop target cannot accept the data.
vbDropEffectCopy	1	Drop results in a copy of data from the source to the target. The original data is unaltered by the drag operation.

(continued)

Constant	Value	Description
vbDropEffectMove	2	Drop results in data being moved from drag source to drop source. The drag source should remove the data from itself after the move.
vbDropEffectScroll	–2147483648 (&H80000000)	Scrolling is occurring or about to occur in the target component. This value is used in conjunction with the other values.
		Note Use only if you are performing your own scrolling in the target component.

Remarks

If there is no code in the **OLEGiveFeedback** event, or if the *defaultcursors* parameter is set to **True**, then Visual Basic automatically sets the mouse cursor to the default cursor provided by the component.

The source component should always mask values from the *effect* parameter to ensure compatibility with future implementations of components. Presently, only three of the 32 bits in the *effect* parameter are used. In future versions of Visual Basic, however, these other bits may be used. Therefore, as a precaution against future problems, drag sources and drop targets should mask these values appropriately before performing any comparisons.

For example, a source component should not compare an *effect* against, say, **vbDropEffectCopy**, such as in this manner:

```
If Effect = vbDropEffectCopy...
```

Instead, the source component should mask for the value or values being sought, such as this:

```
If Effect And vbDropEffectCopy = vbDropEffectCopy...
```

-or-

```
If (Effect And vbDropEffectCopy)...
```

This allows for the definition of new drop effects in future versions of Visual Basic while preserving backwards compatibility with your existing code.

Most components support manual OLE drag and drop events, and some support automatic OLE drag and drop events.

OLERequestPendingMsgText Property

Returns or sets the text of the alternate "busy" message displayed when mouse or keyboard input is received while an automation request is pending. Not available at design time.

Applies To

App Object

Syntax

object.**OLERequestPendingMsgText** [= *string*]

The **OLERequestPendingMsgText** property syntax has these parts:

Part	Description
object	An object expression that evaluates to an object in the **Applies To** list.
string	A string expression that evaluates to the message text that will be displayed in the alternate message box for the ActiveX request pending condition.

Remarks

Visual Basic displays a default Component Request Pending dialog box when mouse or keyboard input is received while an automation request is pending. This dialog box includes text and a **Switch To** button which are intended for use with visible ActiveX components such as Microsoft Excel. There are situations in which the default dialog box may not meet your needs:

- Your program may call a method of an object provided by an ActiveX component that has no user interface. ActiveX components created using Visual Basic Professional edition, for example, may run in the background without any visible forms.

- The ActiveX component you call may have been created using the Remote Automation features of Visual Basic, Enterprise edition, and may be running on another computer located at some distance from the user.

- If your program has loaded a Microsoft Excel workbook using the **GetObject** function, the workbook will not be visible when the user switches to Microsoft Excel. In fact, Microsoft Excel itself may not be visible, in which case the Switch To button does nothing.

In these situations, the default text and **Switch To** button are inappropriate and may confuse the user of your program.

The **OLERequestPendingMsgText** property allows you to replace the default Component Request Pending dialog box with an alternate message box. Setting **OLERequestPendingMsgText** to your own message string causes the default

Component Request Pending dialog box to be replaced by a simple message box containing your message text and an OK button.

Note Once an automation request has been accepted by an ActiveX component, there is no way to cancel it.

If **OLERequestPendingMsgText** is equal to an empty string (""), the default Component Request Pending dialog is displayed.

Important When you know that an automation request may take more than a few seconds, and you are using a hidden or remote ActiveX component, you should set an alternate message. For remote ActiveX components, the alternate message is recommended for all requests. Network traffic may occasionally cause even a very short ActiveX request to take several seconds.

See Also

OLERequestPendingMsgTitle Property, **OLERequestPendingTimeout** Property, **OLEServerBusyMsgText** Property, **OLEServerBusyMsgTitle** Property, **OLEServerBusyRaiseError** Property, **OLEServerBusyTimeout** Property

---

OLERequestPendingMsgTitle Property

Returns or sets the caption of the alternate "busy" message displayed when mouse or keyboard input is received while an automation request is pending. Not available at design time.

Applies To

App Object

Syntax

object.**OLERequestPendingMsgTitle** [= *string*]

The **OLERequestPendingMsgTitle** property syntax has these parts:

Part	Description
object	An object expression that evaluates to an object in the **Applies To** list.
string	A string expression that evaluates to the caption of the alternate message box for the ActiveX request pending condition.

Remarks

If the **OLERequestPendingMsgText** property has been set, the value of the **OLERequestPendingMsgTitle** property is used as the caption of the alternate "busy" message box that replaces the default Component Request Pending dialog box. The default value of the **OLERequestPendingMsgTitle** property is the current value of the **Title** property of the **App** object. This is the recommended setting.

If the **OLERequestPendingMsgText** property is set to an empty string (""),
the **OLERequestPendingMsgTitle** property is ignored.

See Also

OLERequestPendingMsgText Property, **OLERequestPendingTimeout**
Property, **OLEServerBusyMsgText** Property, **OLEServerBusyMsgTitle**
Property, **OLEServerBusyRaiseError** Property, **OLEServerBusyTimeout**
Property

OLERequestPendingTimeout Property

Returns or sets the number of milliseconds that must elapse before the
Component Request Pending dialog box (or an alternate message) can be
triggered by mouse or keyboard input received while an automation request
is pending. Not available at design time.

Applies To

App Object

Syntax

object.**OLERequestPendingTimeout** [= *milliseconds*]

The **OLERequestPendingTimeout** property syntax has these parts:

Part	Description
object	An object expression that evaluates to an object in the **Applies To** list.
milliseconds	A **Long** integer representing the number of milliseconds that must elapse before a busy message can be triggered.

Remarks

The default value of this property is 5000 milliseconds (five seconds).

Important   This time-out value also affects documents you link or embed using
the **OLE Container** control or the Toolbox. If you are using linked or embedded
documents and you change this property before an automation request, it is a
good idea to reset the value afterward.

See Also

OLERequestPendingMsgText Property, **OLERequestPendingMsgTitle**
Property, **OLEServerBusyMsgText** Property, **OLEServerBusyMsgTitle**
Property, **OLEServerBusyRaiseError** Property, **OLEServerBusyTimeout**
Property

OLEServerBusyMsgText Property

Returns or sets the text of the alternate "busy" message which is displayed in place of the default Component Busy dialog if an ActiveX component rejects an automation request. Not available at design time.

Applies To

App Object

Syntax

object.**OLEServerBusyMsgText** [= *string*]

The **OLEServerBusyMsgText** property syntax has these parts:

Part	Description
object	An object expression that evaluates to an object in the **Applies To** list.
string	A string expression that evaluates to the message text that will be displayed in the alternate message box for the ActiveX component busy condition.

Remarks

Visual Basic continues to retry an automation request for the number of milliseconds specified by the **OLEServerBusyTimeout** property. If the ActiveX component has not accepted the request in that interval, Visual Basic displays a default Component Busy dialog box. This dialog box includes text and a Switch To button which are intended for use with visible ActiveX components such as Microsoft Excel. There are situations in which the default dialog box may not meet your needs:

- Your program may call a method of an object provided by an ActiveX component that has no user interface. ActiveX components created using Visual Basic Professional edition, for example, may run in the background without any visible forms.

- The ActiveX component you call may have been created using the Remote automation features of Visual Basic, Enterprise edition, and may be running on another computer located at some distance from the user.

- If your program has loaded a Microsoft Excel workbook using the **GetObject** function, the workbook will not be visible when the user switches to Microsoft Excel. In fact, Microsoft Excel itself may not be visible, in which case the Switch To button does nothing.

In these situations, the default text and **Switch To** button are inappropriate and may confuse the user of your program.

The **OLEServerBusyMsgText** property allows you to replace the default Component Busy dialog box with an alternate message box. Setting **OLEServerBusyMsgText** to your own message string causes the default Component Busy dialog box to be replaced by a simple message box containing your message text, an OK button, and a Cancel button.

If **OLERequestPendingMsgText** is equal to an empty string (""), the default Component Busy dialog is displayed.

If the user presses the Cancel button of the default Component Busy dialog box or the alternate message box, the ActiveX error -2147418111 (&H80010001) is raised in the procedure that made the automation request.

Important When you know that an automation request may take more than a few seconds and you are using a hidden or remote ActiveX component, you should set an alternate message. For remote ActiveX components, the alternate message is recommended for all requests. Network traffic may occasionally cause even a very short ActiveX request to take several seconds.

See Also

OLERequestPendingMsgText Property, **OLERequestPendingMsgTitle** Property, **OLERequestPendingTimeout** Property, **OLEServerBusyMsgTitle** Property, **OLEServerBusyRaiseError** Property, **OLEServerBusyTimeout** Property

---

OLEServerBusyMsgTitle Property

Returns or sets the caption of the alternate "busy" message which is displayed when an ActiveX component rejects an automation request. Not available at design time.

Applies To

App Object

Syntax

object.**OLEServerBusyMsgTitle** [= *string*]

The **OLEServerBusyMsgTitle** property syntax has these parts:

Part	Description
object	An object expression that evaluates to an object in the **Applies To** list.
string	A string expression that evaluates to the caption of the alternate message box for the ActiveX component busy condition.

Remarks

If the **OLEServerBusyMsgText** property has been set, the value of the **OLEServerBusyMsgTitle** property is used as the caption of the alternate busy message that replaces the default Component Busy dialog box. The default value of the **OLEServerBusyMsgTitle** property is the current value of the **Title** property of the **App** object. This is the recommended setting.

If the **OLEServerBusyMsgText** property is set to an empty string (""), the **OLEServerBusyMsgTitle** property is ignored.

See Also

OLERequestPendingMsgText Property, **OLERequestPendingMsgTitle** Property, **OLERequestPendingTimeout** Property, **OLEServerBusyMsgText** Property, **OLEServerBusyRaiseError** Property, **OLEServerBusyTimeout** Property

OLEServerBusyRaiseError Property

Determines whether a rejected automation request raises an error, instead of displaying the default Component Busy dialog box or an alternate message. Not available at design time.

Applies To

App Object

Syntax

object.**OLEServerBusyRaiseError** [= *boolean*]

The **OLEServerBusyRaiseError** property syntax has these parts:

Part	Description
object	An object expression that evaluates to an object in the **Applies To** list.
boolean	A Boolean expression that specifies whether an error is to be raised, as described in **Settings**.

Settings

The settings for *boolean* are:

Setting	Description
True	(Default) An error is raised when the number of milliseconds specified by the **OLEServerBusyTimeout** property have elapsed.
False	Depending on the setting of the **OLEServerBusyMsgText** property, either the default Server Busy dialog box or an alternate busy message will be displayed.

Remarks

Raising an error when an ActiveX component rejects an automation request returns control to your program, which allows you to provide your own custom dialog box in place of either the default Component Busy dialog box or the alternate busy message.

The automation error that will be raised is -2147418111 (&H80010001).

See Also

OLERequestPendingMsgText Property, **OLERequestPendingMsgTitle** Property, **OLERequestPendingTimeout** Property, **OLEServerBusyMsgText** Property, **OLEServerBusyMsgTitle** Property, **OLEServerBusyTimeout** Property

OLEServerBusyTimeout Property

Returns or sets the number of milliseconds during which an automation request will continue to be retried, before the default Component Busy dialog box (or an alternate message) is displayed. Not available at design time.

Applies To

App Object

Syntax

object.**OLEServerBusyTimeout** [= *milliseconds*]

The **OLEServerBusyTimeout** property syntax has these parts:

Part	Description
object	An object expression that evaluates to an object in the **Applies To** list.
milliseconds	A **Long** integer representing the number of milliseconds during which an automation request will be retried.

Remarks

The default value of this property is 10000 milliseconds (ten seconds).

Important   This time-out value also affects documents you link or embed using the **OLE Container** control or the Toolbox. If you are using linked or embedded documents and you change this property before an automation request, it is a good idea to reset the value afterward.

See Also

OLERequestPendingMsgText Property, **OLERequestPendingMsgTitle** Property, **OLERequestPendingTimeout** Property, **OLEServerBusyMsgText** Property, **OLEServerBusyMsgTitle** Property, **OLEServerBusyRaiseError** Property

OLESetData Event

Occurs on an source component when a target component performs the **GetData** method on the source's **DataObject** object, but the data for the specified format has not yet been loaded.

Applies To

CheckBox Control, **ComboBox** Control, **CommandButton** Control, **Data** Control, **DBCombo** Control, **DBList** Control, **DirListBox** Control, **DriveListBox** Control, **FileListBox** Control, **Form** Object**, Forms** Collection, **Frame** Control, **Image** Control, **Label** Control, **ListBox** Control, **MDIForm** Object, **OptionButton** Control, **PictureBox** Control, **PropertyPage** Object, **TextBox** Control, **UserControl** Object, **UserDocument** Object

Syntax

Private Sub *object*_**OLESetData**(*data* **As DataObject**, *dataformat* **As Integer**)

The **OLESetData** event syntax has these parts:

Part	Description
object	An object expression that evaluates to an object in the **Applies To** list.
data	A **DataObject** object in which to place the requested data. The component calls the **SetData** method to load the requested format.
dataformat	An integer specifying the format of the data that the target component is requesting. The source component uses this value to determine what to load into the **DataObject** object.

Remarks

In certain cases, you may wish to defer loading data into the **DataObject** object of a source component to save time, especially if the source component supports many formats. This event allows the source to respond to only one request for a given format of data. When this event is called, the source should check the *format* parameter to determine what needs to be loaded and then perform the **SetData** method on the **DataObject** object to load the data which is then passed back to the target component.

OLEStartDrag Event

Occurs when a component's **OLEDrag** method is performed, or when a component initiates an OLE drag/drop operation when the **OLEDragMode** property is set to **Automatic**.

This event specifies the data formats and drop effects that the source component supports. It can also be used to insert data into the **DataObject** object.

Applies To

CheckBox Control, **ComboBox** Control, **CommandButton** Control, **Data** Control, **DBCombo** Control, **DBList** Control, **DirListBox** Control, **DriveListBox** Control, **FileListBox** Control, **Form** Object**, Forms** Collection, **Frame** Control, **Image** Control, **Label** Control, **ListBox** Control, **MDIForm** Object, **OptionButton** Control, **PictureBox** Control, **PropertyPage** Object, **TextBox** Control, **UserControl** Object, **UserDocument** Object

Syntax

Private Sub *object*_**StartDrag**(*data* **As DataObject**, *allowedeffects* **As Long**)

The **StartDrag** event syntax has these parts:

Part	Description
object	An object expression that evaluates to an object in the **Applies To** list.
data	A **DataObject** object containing formats that the source will provide and, optionally, the data for those formats. If no data is contained in the **DataObject**, it is provided when the control calls the **GetData** method. The programmer should provide the values for this parameter in this event. The **SetData** and **Clear** methods cannot be used here.
allowedeffects	A long integer containing the effects that the source component supports. The possible values are listed in Settings. The programmer should provide the values for this parameter in this event.

Settings

The settings for *allowedeffects* are:

Constant	Value	Description
vbDropEffectNone	0	Drop target cannot accept the data.
vbDropEffectCopy	1	Drop results in a copy of data from the source to the target. The original data is unaltered by the drag operation.
vbDropEffectMove	2	Drop results in data being moved from drag source to drop source. The drag source should remove the data from itself after the move.

Remarks

The source component should logically **Or** together the supported values and places the result in the *allowedeffects* parameter. The target component can use this value to determine the appropriate action (and what the appropriate user feedback should be).

The **StartDrag** event also occurs if the component's **OLEDragMode** property is set to **Automatic**. This allows you to add formats and data to the **DataObject** object after the component has done so. You can also override the default behavior of the component by clearing the **DataObject** object (using the **Clear** method) and then adding your data and formats.

You may wish to defer putting data into the **DataObject** object until the target component requests it. This allows the source component to save time by not loading multiple data formats. When the target performs the **GetData** method on the **DataObject**, the source's **OLESetData** event will occur if the requested data is not contained in the **DataObject**. At this point, the data can be loaded into the **DataObject**, which will in turn provide the data to the target.

If the user does not load any formats into the **DataObject**, then the drag/drop operation is canceled.

OLEType Property

Returns the status of the object in an **OLE** container control.

Applies To

OLE Container Control

Syntax

object.**OLEType**

The *object* is an object expression that evaluates to an object in the **Applies To** list.

Return Values

The **OLEType** property returns the following values:

Constant	Value	Description
vbOLELinked	0	Linked. The **OLE** container control contains a linked object. All the object's data is managed by the application that created it. When the object is saved using the **SaveToFile** method, only link information such as **SourceDoc**, **SourceItem**, and so on is saved in the specified file by your Visual Basic application.
vbOLEEmbedded	1	Embedded. The **OLE** container control contains an embedded object. All the object's data is managed within the Visual Basic application. When the object is saved using the **SaveToFile** method, all data associated with the object is saved in the specified file.
vbOLENone	3	None. The **OLE** container control doesn't contain an object.

Remarks

Use this property to determine if the **OLE** container control contains an object or to determine the type of object the **OLE** container control contains.

Use the **AppIsRunning** property to determine if the application that created the object is running.

When creating an object, use the **OLETypeAllowed** property to determine the type of object that can be created.

See Also

FileNumber Property, **AppIsRunning** Property, **OLETypeAllowed** Property, **SaveToFile** Method

OLETypeAllowed Property

Returns or sets the type of object the **OLE** container control can contain.

Applies To

OLE Container Control

Syntax

*object***.OLETypeAllowed** [= *value*]

The **OLETypeAllowed** property syntax has these parts:

Part	Description
object	An object expression that evaluates to an object in the **Applies To** list.
value	An integer or constant that specifies the type of object, as described in Settings.

Settings

The settings for *value* are:

Constant	Value	Description
vbOLELinked	0	Linked. The **OLE** container control can contain only a linked object.
vbOLEEmbedded	1	Embedded. The **OLE** container control can contain only an embedded object.
vbOLEEither	2	(Default) Either. The **OLE** container control can contain either a linked or an embedded object.

Remarks

This property determines the type of object a user can create:

- When using the Insert Object dialog box, use the **InsertObjDlg** method to display this dialog box.
- When using the Paste Special dialog box, use the **PasteSpecialDlg** method to display this dialog box.
- When pasting an object from the system Clipboard, use the **Paste** method to paste objects from the system Clipboard.

Use the **OLEType** property to determine an object's type (linked, embedded, or none).

See Also

OLEType Property, **AppIsRunning** Property, **PasteSpecialDlg** Method, **InsertObjDlg** Method, **Paste** Method

On Error Statement

Enables an error-handling routine and specifies the location of the routine within a procedure; can also be used to disable an error-handling routine.

Syntax

On Error GoTo *line*
On Error Resume Next
On Error GoTo 0

The **On Error** statement syntax can have any of the following forms:

Statement	Description
On Error GoTo *line*	Enables the error-handling routine that starts at *line* specified in the required *line* argument. The *line* argument is any line label or line number. If a run-time error occurs, control branches to *line*, making the error handler active. The specified *line* must be in the same procedure as the **On Error** statement; otherwise, a compile-time error occurs.
On Error Resume Next	Specifies that when a run-time error occurs, control goes to the statement immediately following the statement where the error occurred where execution continues. Use this form rather than **On Error GoTo** when accessing objects.
On Error GoTo 0	Disables any enabled error handler in the current procedure.

Remarks

If you don't use an **On Error** statement, any run-time error that occurs is fatal; that is, an error message is displayed and execution stops.

An "enabled" error handler is one that is turned on by an **On Error** statement; an "active" error handler is an enabled handler that is in the process of handling an error. If an error occurs while an error handler is active (between the occurrence of the error and a **Resume**, **Exit Sub**, **Exit Function**, or **Exit Property** statement), the current procedure's error handler can't handle the error. Control returns to the calling procedure. If the calling procedure has an enabled error handler, it is activated to handle the error. If the calling procedure's error handler is also active, control passes back through previous calling procedures until an enabled, but inactive, error handler is found. If no inactive, enabled error handler is found, the error is fatal at the point at which it actually occurred. Each time the error handler passes control back to a calling procedure, that procedure becomes the current procedure. Once an error is handled by an error handler in any procedure, execution resumes in the current procedure at the point designated by the **Resume** statement.

Note An error-handling routine is not a **Sub** procedure or **Function** procedure. It is a section of code marked by a line label or line number.

Error-handling routines rely on the value in the **Number** property of the **Err** object to determine the cause of the error. The error-handling routine should test or save relevant property values in the **Err** object before any other error can occur or before a procedure that might cause an error is called. The property values in the **Err** object reflect only the most recent error. The error message associated with **Err.Number** is contained in **Err.Description**.

On Error Resume Next causes execution to continue with the statement immediately following the statement that caused the run-time error, or with the statement immediately following the most recent call out of the procedure containing the **On Error Resume Next** statement. This statement allows execution to continue despite a run-time error. You can place the error-handling routine where the error would occur, rather than transferring control to another location within the procedure. An **On Error Resume Next** statement becomes inactive when another procedure is called, so you should execute an **On Error Resume Next** statement in each called routine if you want inline error handling within that routine.

Note The **On Error Resume Next** construct may be preferable to **On Error GoTo** when handling errors generated during access to other objects. Checking **Err** after each interaction with an object removes ambiguity about which object was accessed by the code. You can be sure which object placed the error code in **Err.Number**, as well as which object originally generated the error (the object specified in **Err.Source**).

On Error GoTo 0 disables error handling in the current procedure. It doesn't specify line 0 as the start of the error-handling code, even if the procedure contains a line numbered 0. Without an **On Error GoTo 0** statement, an error handler is automatically disabled when a procedure is exited.

To prevent error-handling code from running when no error has occurred, place an **Exit Sub**, **Exit Function**, or **Exit Property** statement immediately before the error-handling routine, as in the following fragment:

```
Sub InitializeMatrix(Var1, Var2, Var3, Var4)
    On Error GoTo ErrorHandler
    . . .
    Exit Sub
ErrorHandler:
    . . .
    Resume Next
End Sub
```

Here, the error-handling code follows the **Exit Sub** statement and precedes the **End Sub** statement to separate it from the procedure flow. Error-handling code can be placed anywhere in a procedure.

Untrapped errors in objects are returned to the controlling application when the object is running as an executable file. Within the development environment, untrapped errors are only returned to the controlling application if the proper options are set. See your host application's documentation for a description of which options should be set during debugging, how to set them, and whether the host can create classes.

If you create an object that accesses other objects, you should try to handle errors passed back from them unhandled. If you cannot handle such errors, map the error code in **Err.Number** to one of your own errors, and then pass them back to the caller of your object. You should specify your error by adding your error code to the **vbObjectError** constant. For example, if your error code is 1052, assign it as follows:

```
Err.Number = vbObjectError + 1052
```

Note System errors during calls to dynamic-link libraries (DLL) do not raise exceptions and cannot be trapped with Visual Basic error trapping. When calling DLL functions, you should check each return value for success or failure (according to the API specifications), and in the event of a failure, check the value in the **Err** object's **LastDLLError** property.

See Also

End Statement, **Exit** Statement, **Resume** Statement, **Err** Object, **LastDLLError** Property, **Trappable Errors**

Example

This example first uses the **On Error GoTo** statement to specify the location of an error-handling routine within a procedure. In the example, an attempt to delete an open file generates error number 55. The error is handled in the error-handling routine, and control is then returned to the statement that caused the error. The **On Error GoTo 0** statement turns off error trapping. Then the **On Error Resume Next** statement is used to defer error trapping so that the context for the error generated by the next statement can be known for certain. Note that **Err.Clear** is used to clear the **Err** object's properties after the error is handled.

```
Sub OnErrorStatementDemo()
    On Error GoTo ErrorHandler        ' Enable error-handling routine.
    Open "TESTFILE" For Output As #1  ' Open file for output.
    Kill "TESTFILE"                   ' Attempt to delete open file.
    On Error Goto 0                   ' Turn off error trapping.
    On Error Resume Next              ' Defer error trapping.
    ObjectRef = GetObject("MyWord.Basic") ' Try to start nonexistent
                                      ' object, then test for
                                      ' likely Automation errors.
    If Err.Number = 440 Or Err.Number = 432 Then
        ' Tell user what happened. Then clear the Err object.
        Msg = "There was an error attempting to open the Automation object!"
        MsgBox Msg, , "Deferred Error Test"
        Err.Clear                     ' Clear Err object fields
    End If
Exit Sub                              ' Exit to avoid handler.
```

```
ErrorHandler:                           ' Error-handling routine.
    Select Case Err.Number              ' Evaluate error number.
        Case 55                         ' "File already open" error.
            Close #1                    ' Close open file.
        Case Else                       ' Handle other situations here...
    End Select
    Resume                              ' Resume execution at same line
                                        ' that caused the error.

End Sub
```

On...GoSub, On...GoTo Statements

Branch to one of several specified lines, depending on the value of an expression.

Syntax

On *expression* **GoSub** *destinationlist*
On *expression* **GoTo** *destinationlist*

The **On...GoSub** and **On...GoTo** statement syntax has these parts:

Part	Description
expression	Required. Any numeric expression that evaluates to a whole number between 0 and 255, inclusive. If *expression* is any number other than a whole number, it is rounded before it is evaluated.
destinationlist	Required. List of line numbers or line labels separated by commas.

Remarks

The value of *expression* determines which line is branched to in *destinationlist*. If the value of *expression* is less than 1 or greater than the number of items in the list, one of the following results occurs:

If *expression* is	Then
Equal to 0	Control drops to the statement following **On...GoSub** or **On...GoTo**.
Greater than number of items in list	Control drops to the statement following **On...GoSub** or **On...GoTo**.
Negative	An error occurs.
Greater than 255	An error occurs.

You can mix line numbers and line labels in the same list. You can use as many line labels and line numbers as you like with **On...GoSub** and **On...GoTo**. However, if you use more labels or numbers than fit on a single line, you must use the line-continuation character to continue the logical line onto the next physical line.

Tip **Select Case** provides a more structured and flexible way to perform multiple branching.

See Also

GoSub...Return Statement, **GoTo** Statement, **Select Case** Statement

Example

This example uses the **On...GoSub** and **On...GoTo** statements to branch to subroutines and line labels, respectively.

```
Sub OnGosubGotoDemo()
Dim Number, MyString
   Number = 2                          ' Initialize variable.
                                       ' Branch to Sub2.
   On Number GoSub Sub1, Sub2          ' Execution resumes here after
                                       ' On...GoSub.
   On Number GoTo Line1, Line2         ' Branch to Line2.
   ' Execution does not resume here after On...GoTo.
   Exit Sub
Sub1:
   MyString = "In Sub1" : Return
Sub2:
   MyString = "In Sub2" : Return
Line1:
   MyString = "In Line1"
Line2:
   MyString = "In Line2"
End Sub
```

OnAddinsUpdate Method

Occurs automatically when changes to the Vbaddin.Ini file are saved.

Applies To

IDTExtensibility Interface

Syntax

object.**IDTExtensibility_OnAddinsUpdate** (*custom()* **As Variant**)

The **OnAddinsUpdate** method syntax has these parts:

Part	Description
object	An object expression that evaluates to an object in the **Applies To** list.
custom()	An array of variant expressions to hold user-defined data.

Remarks

This method is part of the **IDTExtensibility** interface, which you should implement in the class that provides your connection object.

Important Don't directly enter the syntax given above. Instead, use the **Implements** statement to generate the appropriate method template for the interface. To do this, in the Declarations section of the Class module that provides your add-in's connection object, enter:

```
Implements IDTExtensibility
```

After adding this line, you can select **IDTExtensibility** from the module's **Object** drop down box. Select each method from the **Procedure** drop down to get the procedure template shown above in Syntax. Notice that the necessary code is automatically added to the Class module.

An interface's methods are exposed through the **Implements** statement. When the above syntax is entered in the Declarations section of the Class module that handles an add-in's events, the interface's methods become available for your use through the module's **Procedure** and **Object** drop down boxes. To add the code to the module, select the method from the **Procedure** drop down box.

Note While the **OnAddinsUpdate** method is a method to the **IDTExtensibility** interface, to you as a Visual Basic programmer it acts and behaves like an event. In other words, when changes made to the Vbaddin.Ini file are saved, any code in the **OnAddinsUpdate** method automatically occurs, just as if it were an event procedure.

Important Since an interface is a contract between an object and Visual Basic, you must be sure to implement *all* of the methods in the interface. This means that all four **IDTExtensibility** interface methods are present in your Class module, each containing at least one executable statement. This can consist of as little as a single remark statement, but they must each contain at least one executable statement to prevent the compiler from removing them as empty procedures.

OnAddNew Event

Occurs when a user action invokes an **AddNew** operation.

Applies To

DBGrid Control

Syntax

Private Sub *object*_**OnAddNew**([*index* **As Integer**])

The **OnAddNew** event syntax has these parts:

Part	Description
object	An object expression that evaluates to an object in the **Applies To** list.
index	An integer that identifies a control if it is in a control array.

Remarks

The **OnAddNew** event occurs when an **AddNew** operation has been initiated by either of the following:

- The user modifies a cell within the **AddNew** row. Typically, this occurs as soon as the user types a character, but may also occur as a result of a built-in radio button or combo box selection.

- The **Value** or **Text** property of a column is set in code when the current cell is within the **AddNew** row.

This event is fired in both bound and unbound modes. However, it will only be fired if the grid's **AllowAddNew** property is **True**.

When the **OnAddNew** event is fired, the value of the **AddNewMode** property is 2 - **AddNew** Pending.

See Also

Value Property (Column Object), **AddNewMode** Property, **Text** Property (Column Object Dummy Topic), **AllowAddNew** Property

---

OnConnection Method

Occurs when an add-in is connected to the Visual Basic IDE, either through the **Add-In Manager** dialog box or another add-in.

Applies To

IDTExtensibility Interface

Syntax

object. **IDTExtensibility_OnConnection** (*vbinst* **As Object**, *connectmode* **As vbext_ConnectMode**, *addininst* **As AddIn**, *custom( )* **As Variant**)

The **OnConnection** method syntax has these parts:

Part	Description
object	An object expression that evaluates to an object in the **Applies To** list.
vbinst	An object representing the instance of the current Visual Basic session.
connectmode	An enumerated value of type **vbext_ConnectMode**, as specified in Settings.
addininst	An **AddIn** object representing the instance of the add-in.
custom( )	An array of variant expressions to hold user-defined data.

Settings

The settings for *connectmode* (**vbext_ConnectMode**) are:

Constant	Value	Description
vbext_cm_AfterStartup	0	Add-in was started after the initial **Open Project** dialog box was shown.
vbext_cm_Startup	1	Add-in was started before the initial **Open Project** dialog box was shown.
vbext_cm_External	2	Add-in was started externally by another program or component.

Remarks

This method is part of the **IDTExtensibility** interface, which you should implement in the class that provides your connection object.

Important Don't directly enter the syntax given above. Instead, use the **Implements** statement to generate the appropriate method template for the interface. To do this, in the Declarations section of the Class module that provides your add-in's connection object, enter:

```
Implements IDTExtensibility
```

After adding this line, you can then select **IDTExtensibility** from the module's **Object** drop down box. Select each method from the **Procedure** drop down to get the procedure template shown above in Syntax. Notice that the necessary code is automatically added to the Class module.

An interface's methods are exposed through the **Implements** statement. When the above syntax is entered in the Declarations section of the Class module that handles an add-in's events, the interface's methods become available for your use through the module's **Procedure** and **Object** drop down boxes. To add the code to the module, select the method from the **Procedure** drop down box.

Note While the **OnConnection** method is a method to the **IDTExtensibility** interface, to you as a Visual Basic programmer it acts and behaves like an event. In other words, when an add-in is connected to the Visual Basic IDE, either through the **Add-In Manager** dialog box or another add-in, any code in the **OnConnection** method automatically occurs, just as if it were an event procedure.

Important Since an interface is a contract between an object and Visual Basic, you must be sure to implement *all* of the methods in the interface. This means that all four **IDTExtensibility** interface methods are present in your Class module, each containing at least one executable statement. This can consist of as little as a single remark statement, but they must each contain at least one executable statement to prevent the compiler from removing them as empty procedures.

OnDisconnection Method

Occurs when an add-in is disconnected from the Visual Basic IDE, either programmatically or through the **Add-In Manager** dialog box.

Applies To

IDTExtensibility Interface

Syntax

object. **IDTExtensibility_OnDisconnection** (*removemode* **As vbext_DisconnectMode**, *custom()* **As Variant**)

The **OnDisconnection** method syntax has these parts:

Part	Description
object	An object expression that evaluates to an object in the **Applies To** list.
removemode	An enumerated value of type **vbext_DisconnectMode**, as specified in Settings.
custom( )	An array of variant expressions to hold user-defined data.

Settings

The settings for *removemode* (**vbext_ConnectMode**) are:

Constant	Value	Description
vbext_dm_HostShutdown	0	Add-in was removed by the add-in's host being closed.
vbext_dm_UserClosed	1	Add-in was removed by the user closing it.

Remarks

This method is part of the **IDTExtensibility** interface, which you should implement in the class that provides your connection object.

Important Don't directly enter the syntax given above. Instead, use the **Implements** statement to generate the appropriate method template for the interface. To do this, in the Declarations section of the Class module that provides your add-in's connection object, enter:

```
Implements IDTExtensibility
```

After adding this line, you can then select **IDTExtensibility** from the module's **Object** drop down box. Select each method from the **Procedure** drop down to get the procedure template shown above in Syntax. Notice that the necessary code is automatically added to the Class module.

An interface's methods are exposed through the **Implements** statement. When the above syntax is entered in the Declarations section of the Class module that handles an add-in's events, the interface's methods become available for your use through the module's **Procedure** and **Object** drop down boxes. To add the code to the module, select the method from the **Procedure** drop down box.

Note While the **OnDisconnection** method is a method to the **IDTExtensibility** interface, to you as a Visual Basic programmer it acts and behaves like an event. In other words, when an add-in is disconnected from the Visual Basic IDE, either programmatically or through the **Add-In Manager** dialog box, any code in the **OnDisconnection** method automatically occurs, just as if it were an event procedure.

Important Since an interface is a contract between an object and Visual Basic, you must be sure to implement *all* of the methods in the interface. This means that all four **IDTExtensibility** interface methods are present in your Class module, each containing at least one executable statement. This can consist of as little as a single remark statement, but they must each contain at least one executable statement to prevent the compiler from removing them as empty procedures.

OnStartupComplete Method

Occurs when the startup of the Visual Basic IDE is complete.

Applies To

IDTExtensibility Interface

Syntax

object. **IDTExtensibility_OnStartupComplete** (*custom()* **As Variant**)

The **OnStartupComplete** method syntax has these parts:

Part	Description
object	An object expression that evaluates to an object in the **Applies To** list.
custom()	An array of variant expressions to hold user-defined data.

Remarks

This method is part of the IDTExtensibility interface, which you should implement in the class that provides your connection object.

Important Don't directly enter the syntax given above. Instead, use the **Implements** statement to generate the appropriate method template for the interface. To do this, in the Declarations section of the Class module that provides your add-in's connection object, enter:

```
Implements IDTExtensibility
```

After adding this line, you can then select **IDTExtensibility** from the module's **Object** drop down box. Select each method from the **Procedure** drop down to get the procedure template shown above in Syntax. Notice that the necessary code is automatically added to the Class module.

An interface's methods are exposed through the **Implements** statement. When the above syntax is entered in the Declarations section of the Class module that handles an add-in's events, the interface's methods become available for your use through the module's **Procedure** and **Object** drop down boxes. To add the code to the module, select the method from the **Procedure** drop down box.

Note While the **OnStartupComplete** method is a method to the **IDTExtensibility** interface, to you as a Visual Basic programmer it acts and behaves like an event. In other words, when the startup of the Visual Basic IDE is complete, any code in the **OnStartupComplete** method automatically occurs, just as if it were an event procedure.

Important Since an interface is a contract between an object and Visual Basic, you must be sure to implement *all* of the methods in the interface. This means that all four **IDTExtensibility** interface methods are present in your Class module, each containing at least one executable statement. This can consist of as little as a single remark statement, but they must each contain at least one executable statement to prevent the compiler from removing them as empty procedures.

Open Statement

Enables input/output (I/O) to a file.

Open *pathname* **For** *mode* [**Access** *access*] [*lock*] **As** [**#**]*filenumber* [**Len**=*reclength*]

The **Open** statement syntax has these parts:

Part	Description
pathname	Required. **String expression** that specifies a file name —may include directory or folder, and drive.
mode	Required. Keyword specifying the file mode: **Append**, **Binary**, **Input**, **Output**, or **Random**. If unspecified, the file is opened for **Random** access.
access	Optional. Keyword specifying the operations permitted on the open file: **Read**, **Write**, or **Read Write**.
lock	Optional. Keyword specifying the operations permitted on the open file by other processes: **Shared**, **Lock Read**, **Lock Write**, and **Lock Read Write**.
filenumber	Required. A valid file number in the range 1 to 511, inclusive. Use the **FreeFile** function to obtain the next available file number.
reclength	Optional. Number less than or equal to 32,767 (bytes). For files opened for random access, this value is the record length. For sequential files, this value is the number of characters buffered.

You must open a file before any I/O operation can be performed on it. **Open** allocates a buffer for I/O to the file and determines the mode of access to use with the buffer.

If the file specified by *pathname* doesn't exist, it is created when a file is opened for **Append**, **Binary**, **Output**, or **Random** modes.

If the file is already opened by another process and the specified type of access is not allowed, the **Open** operation fails and an error occurs.

The **Len** clause is ignored if *mode* is **Binary**.

Important In **Binary**, **Input**, and **Random** modes, you can open a file using a different file number without first closing the file. In **Append** and **Output** modes, you must close a file before opening it with a different file number.

Close Statement, **FreeFile** Function

Example

This example illustrates various uses of the **Open** statement to enable input and output to a file.

The following code opens the file TESTFILE in sequential-input mode.

```
Open "TESTFILE" For Input As #1
' Close before reopening in another mode.
Close #1
```

This example opens the file in Binary mode for writing operations only.

```
Open "TESTFILE" For Binary Access Write As #1
' Close before reopening in another mode.
Close #1
```

The following example opens the file in Random mode. The file contains records of the user-defined type Record.

```
Type Record                  ' Define user-defined type.
    ID As Integer
    Name As String * 20
End Type

Dim MyRecord As Record   ' Declare variable.
Open "TESTFILE" For Random As #1 Len = Len(MyRecord)
' Close before reopening in another mode.
Close #1
```

This code example opens the file for sequential output; any process can read or write to file.

```
Open "TESTFILE" For Output Shared As #1
' Close before reopening in another mode.
Close #1
```

This code example opens the file in Binary mode for reading; other processes can't read file.

```
Open "TESTFILE" For Binary Access Read Lock Read As #1
```

OpenConnection Method

Opens a **Connection** object on an ODBC data source (ODBCDirect workspaces only).

Applies To

DBEngine Object, **Workspace** Object

Syntax

Set *connection* = *workspace*.**OpenConnection** (*name, options, readonly, connect*)

The **OpenConnection** method syntax has these parts.

Part	Description
connection	A **Connection** object variable to which the new connection will be assigned.
workspace	Optional. A variable of a **Workspace** object data type that references the existing **Workspace** object that will contain the new connection.
name	A string expression. See the discussion under Remarks.
options	Optional. A **Variant** that sets various options for the connection, as specified in Settings. Based on this value, the ODBC driver manager prompts the user for connection information such as data source name (DSN), user name, and password.
readonly	Optional. A **Boolean** value that is **True** if the connection is to be opened for read-only access and **False** if the connection is to be opened for read/write access (default).
connect	Optional. An ODBC connect string. See the **Connect** property for the specific elements and syntax of this string. A prepended "ODBC;" is required. If connect is omitted, the UID and/or PWD will be taken from the **UserName** and **Password** properties of the **Workspace**.

Settings

The *options* argument determines if and when to prompt the user to establish the connection, and whether or not to open the connection asynchronously. You can use one of the following constants.

Constant	Description
dbDriverNoPrompt	The ODBC Driver Manager uses the connection string provided in *dbname* and *connect*. If you don't provide sufficient information, a run-time error occurs.
dbDriverPrompt	The ODBC Driver Manager displays the **ODBC Data Sources** dialog box, which displays any relevant information supplied in *dbname* or *connect*. The connection string is made up of the DSN that the user selects via the dialog boxes, or, if the user doesn't specify a DSN, the default DSN is used.

(continued)

(continued)

Constant	Description
dbDriverComplete	Default. If the *connect* argument includes all the necessary information to complete a connection, the ODBC Driver Manager uses the string in *connect*. Otherwise it behaves as it does when you specify **dbDriverPrompt**.
dbDriverCompleteRequired	This option behaves like **dbDriverComplete** except the ODBC driver disables the prompts for any information not required to complete the connection.
dbRunAsync	Execute the method asynchronously. This constant may be used with any of the other *options* constants.

Remarks

Use the **OpenConnection** method to establish a connection to an ODBC data source from an ODBCDirect workspace. The **OpenConnection** method is similar but not equivalent to **OpenDatabase**. The main difference is that **OpenConnection** is available only in an ODBCDirect workspace.

If you specify a registered ODBC data source name (DSN) in the *connect* argument, then the *name* argument can be any valid string, and will also provide the **Name** property for the **Connection** object. If a valid DSN is not included in the *connect* argument, then *name* must refer to a valid ODBC DSN, which will also be the **Name** property. If neither *name* nor *connect* contains a valid DSN, the ODBC driver manager can be set (via the *options* argument) to prompt the user for the required connection information. The DSN supplied through the prompt then provides the **Name** property.

OpenConnection returns a **Connection** object which contains information about the connection. The **Connection** object is similar to a **Database** object. The principal difference is that a **Database** object usually represents a database, although it can be used to represent a connection to an ODBC data source from a Microsoft Jet workspace.

See Also

Connection Object, **Cancel** Method, **StillExecuting** Property

Example

This example uses the **OpenConnection** method with different parameters to open three different **Connection** objects.

```
Sub OpenConnectionX()

    Dim wrkODBC As Workspace
    Dim conPubs As Connection
    Dim conPubs2 As Connection
    Dim conPubs3 As Connection
    Dim conLoop As Connection
```

```
' Create ODBCDirect Workspace object.
Set wrkODBC = CreateWorkspace("NewODBCWorkspace", _
    "admin", "", dbUseODBC)

' Open Connection object using supplied information in
' the connect string. If this information were
' insufficient, you could trap for an error rather than
' go to an ODBC Driver Manager dialog box.
MsgBox "Opening Connection1..."
Set conPubs = wrkODBC.OpenConnection("Connection1", _
    dbDriverNoPrompt, , _
    "ODBC;DATABASE=pubs;UID=sa;PWD=;DSN=Publishers")

' Open read-only Connection object based on information
' you enter in the ODBC Driver Manager dialog box.
MsgBox "Opening Connection2..."
Set conPubs2 = wrkODBC.OpenConnection("Connection2", _
    dbDriverPrompt, True, "ODBC;DSN=Publishers;")

' Open read-only Connection object by entering only the
' missing information in the ODBC Driver Manager dialog
' box.
MsgBox "Opening Connection3..."
Set conPubs3 = wrkODBC.OpenConnection("Connection3", _
    dbDriverCompleteRequired, True, _
    "ODBC;DATABASE=pubs;DSN=Publishers;")

' Enumerate the Connections collection.
For Each conLoop In wrkODBC.Connections
    Debug.Print "Connection properties for " & _
        conLoop.Name & ":"

    With conLoop
        ' Print property values by explicitly calling each
        ' Property object; the Connection object does not
        ' support a Properties collection.
        Debug.Print "    Connect = " & .Connect
        ' Property actually returns a Database object.
        Debug.Print "    Database[.Name] = " & _
            .Database.Name
        Debug.Print "    Name = " & .Name
        Debug.Print "    QueryTimeout = " & .QueryTimeout
        Debug.Print "    RecordsAffected = " & _
            .RecordsAffected
        Debug.Print "    StillExecuting = " & _
            .StillExecuting
        Debug.Print "    Transactions = " & .Transactions
        Debug.Print "    Updatable = " & .Updatable
    End With

Next conLoop

conPubs.Close
conPubs2.Close
conPubs3.Close
wrkODBC.Close

End Sub
```

OpenConnection Method (Remote Data)

Opens a connection to an ODBC data source and returns a reference to the **rdoConnection** object that represents a specific database.

Applies To

rdoEnvironment Object

Syntax

Set *connection* = *environment*.**OpenConnection**(*dsName*[, *prompt*[, *readonly*[, *connect*[, *options*]]]])

The **OpenConnection** method syntax has these parts:

Part	Description
connection	An object expression that evaluates to an **rdoConnection** object that you're opening.
Environment	An object expression that evaluates to an existing **rdoEnvironment** object. You must provide an **rdoEnvironment** object.
DsName	A string expression that is the name of a registered ODBC data source name or a zero-length string ("") as described in Settings.
Prompt	A **Variant** or constant that determines how the operation is carried out, as specified in Settings.
Readonly	A **Boolean** value that is **True** if the connection is to be opened for read-only access, and **False** if the connection is to be opened for read/write access. If you omit this argument, the connection is opened for read/write access.
Connect	A string expression used to pass arguments to the ODBC driver manager for opening the database—the *connect string* as described in Settings.
Options	A **Variant** or constant that determines how the operation is carried out, as specified in Settings.

Settings

The *connect* argument constitutes the ODBC connect arguments, and is dependent on the ODBC driver. See the **Connect** property for syntax and typical settings. If the *connect* argument is an empty string (""), the user name and password are taken from the **rdoEnvironment** object's **UserName** and **Password** properties, and a *dsName* argument *must* be provided.

If the provided *dsName* doesn't refer to a valid ODBC data source name, and the Data Source Name (DSN) parameter does not appear in the *connect* argument an error occurs if *prompt* is **rdDriverNoPrompt**; otherwise, the user is prompted to select from a list of registered data source names. If *dsName* is a zero-length string, the connect string must indicate the driver and server names.

Based on the *prompt* value, the ODBC driver manager exposes a dialog which prompts the user for connection information such as DSN, user name, and password. Use one of the following constants that defines how the user should be prompted:

prompt Constant	Value	Description
rdDriverPrompt	0	The driver manager displays the ODBC Data Sources dialog box. The connection string used to establish the connection is constructed from the DSN selected and completed by the user via the dialog boxes, or, if no DSN is chosen and the **DataSourceName** property is empty (in the case of the **RemoteData control**), the default DSN is used.
RdDriverNoPrompt	1	The driver manager uses the connection string provided in *dsName* and *connect*. If sufficient information is not provided, the **OpenConnection** method returns a trappable error.
RdDriverComplete	2	(Default) If the connection string provided includes the DSN keyword, the driver manager uses the string as provided in *connect*. Otherwise it behaves as it does when **rdDriverPrompt** is specified.
RdDriverCompleteRequired	3	Behaves like **rdDriverComplete** except the driver disables the controls for any information not required to complete the connection. If the controls are disabled, users cannot select or specify missing arguments.

You can use the following constant for the *options* argument:

options Constant	Value	Description
rdAsyncEnable	32	Execute operation asynchronously.

Remarks

When you successfully execute the **OpenConnection** method, a new **rdoConnection** object is instantiated and added to the **rdoConnections** collection, and a network connection is established to the remote server. If the connection cannot be established, no object is created and a trappable error is fired.

Note RDO 2.0 behaves differently than RDO 1.0 in how it handles orphaned references to **rdoConnection** objects. When you Set a variable already assigned to an **rdoConnection** object with another **rdoConnection** object using the **OpenConnection** method, the existing **rdoConnection** object is closed and dropped from the **rdoConnections** collection. In RDO 1.0, the existing object remained open and was left in the **rdoConnections** collection.

If you set the *options* argument to **rdAsyncEnable**, the connection operation is executed asynchronously. That is, control returns to your application before the connection has been established to prevent your application from blocking while the connection is being made. You can check for completion of the connection by polling the **rdoConnection** object's **StillConnecting** property, which returns **False** when the connection operation is complete. You can also code an event procedure for the Connect event which is fired when the connect operation is complete. If you use the **Cancel** method while waiting for an asynchronous connection to be established, the connection attempt is abandoned.

Before the process of establishing a connection is started, the **BeforeConnect** event is fired. This event procedure permits you to examine and modify the connect string and prompt levels as needed.

There are a variety of reasons why a connection might not be made. These include but are not limited to the following:

- Lack of proper user ID and password.

- Incorrect driver or options configuration.

- Lack of correct network or server permissions.

- The remote server could not be found on the network, or is not operating.

- The remote server did not have sufficient resources or connections to permit another user to connect.

DSN-Less Connections

In some cases, it might not be necessary to create and register a Data Source Name (DSN) before attempting to open a connection to a data source. If your remote server uses the named pipes LAN protocol and the default OEMTOANSI settings, you can simply provide the name of the server and ODBC driver in the connect string. You must provide an empty DSN entry in the connect string, or in the **dsName** parameter as the *last* argument. If the ODBC driver manager finds a null DSN entry, it attempts to locate it unless it has already determined the driver and server values. The connect string shown below is used to establish a DSN-less connection to a SQL Server named "BETAV486":

```
Connect = "UID=;PWD=;Database=WorkDB;" _
& "Server=BETAV486;Driver={SQL Server}" _
& "DSN='';"
```

Other Connect String Options

Establishing an **rdoConnection** may require that the user specified by the **UserName** property, or UID connect string argument have permission to access the network, the specific data source server, and the chosen database on that server. Failure to meet these qualifications might result in failure to connect.

If you do not specify a database either through the DATABASE parameter of the *connect* argument or through the data source entry, the database opened when you establish a connection is determined by the default database assigned to the user by the database administrator. In some cases, you can change the default database by executing an action query containing an SQL command such as the Transact SQL USE *database* statement.

Note The *connect* part of the **OpenConnection** method is coded differently than the *source* part of the **OpenDatabase** method as used with DAO. The *connect* part neither requires nor supports use of the "ODBC;" keyword at the beginning of the connect string. In addition, the *connect* part does not support use of the LOGINTIMEOUT argument—use the **LoginTimeout** property of the **rdoEnvironment** object instead.

Use the **Close** method on the object to close a database associated with an **rdoConnection**, remove the connection from the **rdoConnections** collection, and disconnect from the data source.

You can also declare a new **rdoConnection** object using the **Dim** statement as follows:

```
Dim myCn as New rdoConnection
```

Once instantiated in this manner, you can set the **rdoConnection** properties as required, and use the **EstablishConnection** method to open the connection.

For more information about ODBC drivers and the specific connect string arguments they require, see the Help file provided with the driver.

See Also

Connect Event, **Close** Method (Remote Data), **rdoConnection** Object, **rdoEnvironment** Object, **Connect** Property (Remote Data), **UserName** Property (Remote Data)

Examples

The following example establishes an ODBC connection using the **OpenConnection** method but requires the user to provide all connection information. In this case the example prints the resulting **Connect** property to the Immediate window.

```
Dim cn As rdoConnection
Dim en As rdoEnvironment

Set en = rdoEnvironments(0)
Set cn = en.OpenConnection(dsName:="WorkDB", _
    Prompt:=rdDriverCompleteRequired)
debug.print cn.Connect
```

The following example establishes a DSN-less ODBC connection using the **OpenConnection** method against the default **rdoEnvironment**. In this case the example prints the resulting **Connect** property to the Immediate window.

```
Dim en as rdoEnvironment
Dim cn as rdoConnection

Set en = rdoEnvironments(0)
Set cn = en.OpenConnection(dsName:="", _
    Prompt:=rdDriverNoPrompt, _
    Connect:="uid=;pwd=;driver={SQL Server};" _
        & "server=SEQUEL;database=pubs;")
debug.print cn.Connect
```

OpenDatabase Method

Opens a specified database in a **Workspace** object and returns a reference to the **Database** object that represents it.

Applies To

DBEngine Object, **Workspace** Object

Syntax

Set *database* = *workspace*.**OpenDatabase** (*dbname, options, read-only, connect*)

The **OpenDatabase** method syntax has these parts.

Part	Description
database	An object variable that represents the **Database** object that you want to open.
workspace	Optional. An object variable that represents the existing **Workspace** object that will contain the database. If you don't include a value for *workspace*, **OpenDatabase** uses the default workspace.
dbname	A **String** that is the name of an existing Microsoft Jet database file, or the data source name (DSN) of an ODBC data source. See the **Name** property for more information about setting this value.
options	Optional. A **Variant** that sets various options for the database, as specified in Settings.
read-only	Optional. A **Variant** (**Boolean** subtype) value that is **True** if you want to open the database with read-only access, or **False** (default) if you want to open the database with read/write access.
connect	Optional. A **Variant** (**String** subtype) that specifies various connection information, including passwords.

Settings

For Microsoft Jet workspaces, you can use the following values for the *options* argument.

Setting	Description
True	Opens the database in exclusive mode.
False	(Default) Opens the database in shared mode.

For ODBCDirect workspaces, the *options* argument determines if and when to prompt the user to establish the connection. You can use one of the following constants.

Constant	Description
dbDriverNoPrompt	The ODBC Driver Manager uses the connection string provided in *dbname* and *connect*. If you don't provide sufficient information, a run-time error occurs.

(continued)

Constant	Description
dbDriverPrompt	The ODBC Driver Manager displays the **ODBC Data Sources** dialog box, which displays any relevant information supplied in *dbname* or *connect*. The connection string is made up of the DSN that the user selects via the dialog boxes, or, if the user doesn't specify a DSN, the default DSN is used.
dbDriverComplete	(Default) If the *connect* and *dbname* arguments include all the necessary information to complete a connection, the ODBC Driver Manager uses the string in *connect*. Otherwise it behaves as it does when you specify **dbDriverPrompt**.
dbDriverCompleteRequired	This option behaves like **dbDriverComplete** except the ODBC driver disables the prompts for any information not required to complete the connection.

Remarks

When you open a database, it is automatically added to the **Databases** collection. Further, in an ODBCDirect workspace, the **Connection** object corresponding to the new **Database** object is also created and appended to the **Connections** collection of the same **Workspace** object.

Some considerations apply when you use *dbname*:

- If it refers to a database that is already open for exclusive access by another user, an error occurs.

- If it doesn't refer to an existing database or valid ODBC data source name, an error occurs.

- If it's a zero-length string ("") and *connect* is "ODBC;", a dialog box listing all registered ODBC data source names is displayed so the user can select a database.

- If you're opening a database through an ODBCDirect workspace and you provide the DSN in *connect*, you can set *dbname* to a string of your choice that you can use to reference this database in subsequent code.

The *connect* argument is expressed in two parts: the database type, followed by a semicolon (;) and the optional arguments. You must first provide the database type, such as "ODBC;" or "FoxPro 2.5;". The optional arguments follow in no particular order, separated by semicolons. One of the parameters may be the password (if one is assigned). For example:

```
"FoxPro 2.5; pwd=mypassword"
```

Using the **NewPassword** method on a **Database** object other than an ODBCDirect database changes the password parameter that appears in the `";pwd=..."` part of this argument. You must supply the *options* and *read-only* arguments to supply a source string. See the **Connect** property for syntax.

To close a database, and thus remove the **Database** object from the **Databases** collection, use the **Close** method on the object.

Note   When you access a Microsoft Jet-connected ODBC data source, you can improve your application's performance by opening a **Database** object connected to the ODBC data source, rather than by linking individual **TableDef** objects to specific tables in the ODBC data source.

See Also

Close Method, **Connect** Property

Example

This example uses the **OpenDatabase** method to open one Microsoft Jet database and two Microsoft Jet-connected ODBC databases.

```
Sub OpenDatabaseX()

    Dim wrkJet As Workspace
    Dim dbsNorthwind As Database
    Dim dbsPubs As Database
    Dim dbsPubs2 As Database
    Dim dbsLoop As Database
    Dim prpLoop As Property

    ' Create Microsoft Jet Workspace object.
    Set wrkJet = CreateWorkspace("", "admin", "", dbUseJet)

    ' Open Database object from saved Microsoft Jet database
    ' for exclusive use.
    MsgBox "Opening Northwind..."
    Set dbsNorthwind = wrkJet.OpenDatabase("Northwind.mdb", _
        True)

    ' Open read-only Database object based on information in
    ' the connect string.
    MsgBox "Opening pubs..."
    Set dbsPubs = wrkJet.OpenDatabase("Publishers", _
        dbDriverNoPrompt, True, _
        "ODBC;DATABASE=pubs;UID=sa;PWD=;DSN=Publishers")

    ' Open read-only Database object by entering only the
    ' missing information in the ODBC Driver Manager dialog
    ' box.
    MsgBox "Opening second copy of pubs..."
    Set dbsPubs2 = wrkJet.OpenDatabase("Publishers", _
        dbDriverCompleteRequired, True, _
        "ODBC;DATABASE=pubs;DSN=Publishers;")

    ' Enumerate the Databases collection.
    For Each dbsLoop In wrkJet.Databases
        Debug.Print "Database properties for " & _
            dbsLoop.Name & ":"
```

```
      On Error Resume Next
      ' Enumerate the Properties collection of each Database
      ' object.
      For Each prpLoop In dbsLoop.Properties
         If prpLoop.Name = "Connection" Then
            ' Property actually returns a Connection object.
            Debug.Print "    Connection[.Name] = " & _
               dbsLoop.Connection.Name
         Else
            Debug.Print "    " & prpLoop.Name & " = " & _
               prpLoop
         End If
      Next prpLoop
      On Error GoTo 0

   Next dbsLoop

   dbsNorthwind.Close
   dbsPubs.Close
   dbsPubs2.Close
   wrkJet.Close

End Sub
```

OpenRecordset Method

Creates a new **Recordset** object and appends it to the **Recordsets** collection.

Applies To

Database Object, **Dynaset-Type Recordset** Object, **QueryDef** Object, **Recordset** Object, **Snapshot-Type Recordset** Object, **Table-Type Recordset** Object, **TableDef** Object, **Connection** Object

Syntax

For **Connection** and **Database** objects:

Set *recordset* = *object*.**OpenRecordset** (*source*, *type*, *options*, *lockedits*)

For **QueryDef**, **Recordset**, and **TableDef** objects:

Set *recordset* = *object*.**OpenRecordset** (*type*, *options*, *lockedits*)

The **OpenRecordset** method syntax has these parts.

Part	Description
recordset	An object variable that represents the **Recordset** object you want to open.
object	An object variable that represents an existing object from which you want to create the new **Recordset**.
source	A **String** specifying the source of the records for the new **Recordset**. The source can be a table name, a query name, or an SQL statement that returns records. For table-type **Recordset** objects in Microsoft Jet databases, the source can only be a table name.

(continued)

(continued)

Part	Description
type	Optional. A constant that indicates the type of **Recordset** to open, as specified in Settings.
options	Optional. A combination of constants that specify characteristics of the new **Recordset**, as listed in Settings.
lockedits	Optional. A constant that determines the locking for the **Recordset**, as specified in Settings.

Settings

You can use one of the following constants for the *type* argument.

Constant	Description
dbOpenTable	Opens a table-type **Recordset** object (Microsoft Jet workspaces only).
DbOpenDynamic	Opens a dynamic-type **Recordset** object, which is similar to an ODBC dynamic cursor. (ODBCDirect workspaces only)
dbOpenDynaset	Opens a dynaset-type **Recordset** object, which is similar to an ODBC keyset cursor.
DbOpenSnapshot	Opens a snapshot-type **Recordset** object, which is similar to an ODBC static cursor.
dbOpenForwardOnly	Opens a forward-only–type **Recordset** object.

Note If you open a **Recordset** in a Microsoft Jet workspace and you don't specify a type, **OpenRecordset** creates a table-type **Recordset**, if possible. If you specify a linked table or query, **OpenRecordset** creates a dynaset-type **Recordset**. In an ODBCDirect workspace, the default setting is **dbOpenForwardOnly**.

You can use a combination of the following constants for the *options* argument.

Constant	Description
dbAppendOnly	Allows users to append new records to the **Recordset**, but prevents them from editing or deleting existing records (Microsoft Jet dynaset-type **Recordset** only).
dbSQLPassThrough	Passes an SQL statement to a Microsoft Jet-connected ODBC data source for processing (Microsoft Jet snapshot-type **Recordset** only).
DbSeeChanges	Generates a run-time error if one user is changing data that another user is editing (Microsoft Jet dynaset-type **Recordset** only). This is useful in applications where multiple users have simultaneous read/write access to the same data.
dbDenyWrite	Prevents other users from modifying or adding records (Microsoft Jet **Recordset** objects only).

(continued)

Constant	Description
dbDenyRead	Prevents other users from reading data in a table (Microsoft Jet table-type **Recordset** only).
dbForwardOnly	Creates a forward-only **Recordset** (Microsoft Jet snapshot-type **Recordset** only). It is provided only for backward compatibility, and you should use the **dbOpenForwardOnly** constant in the *type* argument instead of using this option.
dbReadOnly	Prevents users from making changes to the **Recordset** (Microsoft Jet only). The **dbReadOnly** constant in the *lockedits* argument replaces this option, which is provided only for backward compatibility.
DbRunAsync	Runs an asynchronous query (ODBCDirect workspaces only).
dbExecDirect	Runs a query by skipping **SQLPrepare** and directly calling **SQLExecDirect** (ODBCDirect workspaces only). Use this option only when you're not opening a **Recordset** based on a parameter query. For more information, see the "Microsoft ODBC 3.0 Programmer's Reference."
dbInconsistent	Allows inconsistent updates (Microsoft Jet dynaset-type and snapshot-type **Recordset** objects only).
dbConsistent	Allows only consistent updates (Microsoft Jet dynaset-type and snapshot-type **Recordset** objects only).

Note The constants **dbConsistent** and **dbInconsistent** are mutually exclusive, and using both causes an error. Supplying a *lockedits* argument when *options* uses the **dbReadOnly** constant also causes an error.

You can use the following constants for the *lockedits* argument.

Constant	Description
dbReadOnly	Prevents users from making changes to the **Recordset** (default for ODBCDirect workspaces). You can use **dbReadOnly** in either the *options* argument or the *lockedits* argument, but not both. If you use it for both arguments, a run-time error occurs.
dbPessimistic	Uses pessimistic locking to determine how changes are made to the **Recordset** in a multiuser environment. The page containing the record you're editing is locked as soon as you use the **Edit** method (default for Microsoft Jet workspaces).

(continued)

(continued)

Constant	Description
dbOptimistic	Uses optimistic locking to determine how changes are made to the **Recordset** in a multiuser environment. The page containing the record is not locked until the **Update** method is executed.
dbOptimisticValue	Uses optimistic concurrency based on row values (ODBCDirect workspaces only).
dbOptimisticBatch	Enables batch optimistic updating (ODBCDirect workspaces only).

Remarks

In a Microsoft Jet workspace, if *object* refers to a **QueryDef** object, or a dynaset- or snapshot-type **Recordset**, or if *source* refers to an SQL statement or a **TableDef** that represents a linked table, you can't use **dbOpenTable** for the *type* argument; if you do, a run-time error occurs. If you want to use an SQL pass-through query on a linked table in a Microsoft Jet-connected ODBC data source, you must first set the **Connect** property of the linked table's database to a valid ODBC connection string. If you only need to make a single pass through a **Recordset** opened from a Microsoft Jet-connected ODBC data source, you can improve performance by using **dbOpenForwardOnly** for the *type* argument.

If *object* refers to a dynaset- or snapshot-type **Recordset**, the new **Recordset** is of the same type *object*. If *object* refers to a table-type **Recordset** object, the type of the new object is a dynaset-type **Recordset**. You can't open new **Recordset** objects from forward-only–type or ODBCDirect **Recordset** objects.

In an ODBCDirect workspace, you can open a **Recordset** containing more than one select query in the *source* argument, such as

```
"SELECT LastName, FirstName FROM Authors
WHERE LastName = 'Smith';
SELECT Title, ISBN FROM Titles
WHERE ISBN Like '1-55615-*'"
```

The returned **Recordset** will open with the results of the first query. To obtain the result sets of records from subsequent queries, use the **NextRecordset** method.

Note You can send DAO queries to a variety of different database servers with ODBCDirect, and different servers will recognize slightly different dialects of SQL. Therefore, context-sensitive Help is no longer provided for Microsoft Jet SQL, although online Help for Microsoft Jet SQL is still included through the Help menu. Be sure to check the appropriate reference documentation for the SQL dialect of your database server when using either ODBCDirect connections or pass-through queries in Microsoft Jet-connected client/server applications.

Use the **dbSeeChanges** constant in a Microsoft Jet workspace if you want to trap changes while two or more users are editing or deleting the same record. For example, if two users start editing the same record, the first user to execute the **Update** method succeeds. When the second user invokes the **Update** method, a run-time error occurs. Similarly, if the second user tries to use the **Delete** method to delete the record, and the first user has already changed it, a run-time error occurs.

Typically, if the user gets this error while updating a record, your code should refresh the contents of the fields and retrieve the newly modified values. If the error occurs while deleting a record, your code could display the new record data to the user and a message indicating that the data has recently changed. At this point, your code can request a confirmation that the user still wants to delete the record.

You should also use the **dbSeeChanges** constant if you open a **Recordset** in a Microsoft Jet-connected ODBC workspace against a Microsoft SQL Server 6.0 (or later) table that has an IDENTITY column, otherwise an error may result.

In an ODBCDirect workspace, you can execute asynchronous queries by setting the **dbRunAsync** constant in the *options* argument. This allows your application to continue processing other statements while the query runs in the background. But, you cannot access the **Recordset** data until the query has completed. To determine whether the query has finished executing, check the **StillExecuting** property of the new **Recordset**. If the query takes longer to complete than you anticipated, you can terminate execution of the query with the **Cancel** method.

Opening more than one **Recordset** on an ODBC data source may fail because the connection is busy with a prior **OpenRecordset** call. One way around this is to use a server-side cursor and ODBCDirect, if the server supports this. Another solution is to fully populate the **Recordset** by using the **MoveLast** method as soon as the **Recordset** is opened.

If you open a **Connection** object with **DefaultCursorDriver** set to **dbUseClientBatchCursor**, you can open a **Recordset** to cache changes to the data (known as batch updating) in an ODBCDirect workspace. Include **dbOptimisticBatch** in the *lockedits* argument to enable update caching. See the **Update** method topic for details about how to write changes to disk immediately, or to cache changes and write them to disk as a batch.

Closing a **Recordset** with the **Close** method automatically deletes it from the **Recordsets** collection.

Note If *source* refers to an SQL statement composed of a string concatenated with a non-integer value, and the system parameters specify a non-U.S. decimal character such as a comma (for example, strSQL = "PRICE > " & lngPrice, and lngPrice = 125,50), an error occurs when you try to open the **Recordset**. This is because during concatenation, the number will be converted to a string using your system's default decimal character, and SQL only accepts U.S. decimal characters.

See Also

> **Cancel** Method, **Connect** Property, **Type** Property, **StillExecuting** Property

Example

> This example uses the **OpenRecordset** method to open five different **Recordset** objects and display their contents. The **OpenRecordsetOutput** procedure is required for this procedure to run.

```
Sub OpenRecordsetX()

    Dim wrkJet As Workspace
    Dim wrkODBC As Workspace
    Dim dbsNorthwind As Database
    Dim conPubs As Connection
    Dim rstTemp As Recordset
    Dim rstTemp2 As Recordset

    ' Open Microsoft Jet and ODBCDirect workspaces, Microsoft
    ' Jet database, and ODBCDirect connection.
    Set wrkJet = CreateWorkspace("", "admin", "", dbUseJet)
    Set wrkODBC = CreateWorkspace("", "admin", "", dbUseODBC)
    Set dbsNorthwind = wrkJet.OpenDatabase("Northwind.mdb")
    Set conPubs = wrkODBC.OpenConnection("", , , _
        "ODBC;DATABASE=pubs;UID=sa;PWD=;DSN=Publishers")

    ' Open five different Recordset objects and display the
    ' contents of each.

    Debug.Print "Opening forward-only-type recordset " & _
        "where the source is a QueryDef object..."
    Set rstTemp = dbsNorthwind.OpenRecordset( _
        "Ten Most Expensive Products", dbOpenForwardOnly)
    OpenRecordsetOutput rstTemp

    Debug.Print "Opening read-only dynaset-type " & _
        "recordset where the source is an SQL statement..."
    Set rstTemp = dbsNorthwind.OpenRecordset( _
        "SELECT * FROM Employees", dbOpenDynaset, dbReadOnly)
    OpenRecordsetOutput rstTemp

    ' Use the Filter property to retrieve only certain
    ' records with the next OpenRecordset call.
    Debug.Print "Opening recordset from existing " & _
        "Recordset object to filter records..."
    rstTemp.Filter = "LastName >= 'M'"
    Set rstTemp2 = rstTemp.OpenRecordset()
    OpenRecordsetOutput rstTemp2

    Debug.Print "Opening dynamic-type recordset from " & _
        "an ODBC connection..."
    Set rstTemp = conPubs.OpenRecordset( _
        "SELECT * FROM stores", dbOpenDynamic)
    OpenRecordsetOutput rstTemp
```

```
' Use the StillExecuting property to determine when the
' Recordset is ready for manipulation.
Debug.Print "Opening snapshot-type recordset based " & _
    "on asynchronous query to ODBC connection..."
Set rstTemp = conPubs.OpenRecordset("publishers", _
    dbOpenSnapshot, dbRunAsync)
Do While rstTemp.StillExecuting
    Debug.Print "    [still executing...]"
Loop
OpenRecordsetOutput rstTemp

rstTemp.Close
dbsNorthwind.Close
conPubs.Close
wrkJet.Close
wrkODBC.Close

End Sub

Sub OpenRecordsetOutput(rstOutput As Recordset)

' Enumerate the specified Recordset object.
With rstOutput
    Do While Not .EOF
        Debug.Print , .Fields(0), .Fields(1)
        .MoveNext
    Loop
End With

End Sub
```

OpenResultset Method (Remote Data)

Creates a new **rdoResultset** object.

Applies To

rdoConnection Object, **rdoPreparedStatement** Object, **rdoTable** Object

Syntax

Set *variable* = *connection*.**OpenResultset**(*name* [,*type* [,*locktype* [,*option*]]])
Set *variable* = *object*.**OpenResultset**([*type* [,*locktype* [, *option*]]])

The **OpenResultset** method syntax has these parts:

Part	Description
variable	An object expression that evaluates to an **rdoResultset** object.
Connection	An object expression that evaluates to an existing **rdoConnection** object you want to use to create the new **rdoResultset**.
Object	An object expression that evaluates to an existing **rdoQuery** or **rdoTable** object you want to use to create the new **rdoResultset**.

(continued)

(continued)	
Part	**Description**
Name	A **String** that specifies the source of the rows for the new **rdoResultset**. This argument can specify the name of an **rdoTable** object, the name of an **rdoQuery**, or an SQL statement that might return rows.
Type	A **Variant** or constant that specifies the type of cursor to create as indicated in Settings.
Locktype	A **Variant** or constant that specifies the type of concurrency control. If you don't specify a *locktype*, **rdConcurReadOnly** is assumed.
Option	A **Variant** or constant that specifies characteristics of the new **rdoResultset**.

Settings

- *name*

  The ***name*** argument is used when the **OpenResultset** method is used against the **rdoConnection** object, and no query has been pre-defined. In this case, name typically contains a row-returning SQL query. The query can contain more than one SELECT statement, or a combination of action queries and SELECT statements, but not just action queries, or a trappable error will result. See the **SQL** property for additional details.

- Cursor *type*

  Note   Not all types of cursors and concurrency are supported by every ODBC data source driver. See **rdoResultset** for more information. In addition, not all types of cursor drivers support SQL statements that return more than one set of results. For example, server-side cursors do not support queries that contain more than one SELECT statement.

  The ***type*** argument specifies the type of cursor used to manage the result set. If you don't specify a type, **OpenResultset** creates a forward-only **rdoResultset**. Not all ODBC data sources or drivers can implement all of the cursor types. If your driver cannot implement the type chosen, a warning message is generated and placed in the **rdoErrors** collection. Use one of the following result set type constants that defines the cursor type of the new **rdoResultset** object. For additional details on types of cursors, see the **CursorType** property.

type Constant	Value	Description
rdOpenForwardOnly	0	(Default) Opens a forward-only-type **rdoResultset** object.
RdOpenKeyset	1	Opens a keyset-type **rdoResultset** object.
RdOpenDynamic	2	Opens a dynamic-type **rdoResultset** object.
RdOpenStatic	3	Opens a static-type **rdoResultset** object.

- Concurrency *LockType*

  In order to maintain adequate control over the data being updated, RDO provides a number of concurrency options that control how other users are granted, or refused access to the data being updated. In many cases, when you lock a particular row using one of the **LockType** settings, the remote engine might also lock the entire page containing the row. If too many pages are locked, the remote engine might also escalate the page lock to a table lock to improve overall system performance.

  Not all lock types are supported on all data sources. For example, for SQL Server and Oracle servers, static-type **rdoResultset** objects can only support **rdConcurValues** or **rdConcurReadOnly**. For additional details on the types of concurrency, see the **LockType** property.

locktype Constant	Value	Description
rdConcurReadOnly	1	(Default) Read-only .
rdConcurLock	2	Pessimistic concurrency.
RdConcurRowVer	3	Optimistic concurrency based on row ID.
RdConcurValues	4	Optimistic concurrency based on row values.
RdConcurBatch	5	Optimistic concurrency using batch mode updates. **Status** values returned for each row successfully updated.

- Other *options*

  If you use the **rdAsyncEnable** option, control returns to your application as soon as the query is begun, but before a result set is available. To test for completion of the query, use the **StillExecuting** property. The **rdoResultset** object is not valid until **StillExecuting** returns **False**. You can also use the QueryComplete event to determine when the query is ready to process. Until the **StillExecuting** property returns **True**, you cannot reference any other property of the uninitialized **rdoResultset** object and only the **Cancel** and **Close** methods are valid.

  If you use the **rdExecDirect** option, RDO uses the *SQLExecDirect* ODBC API function to execute the query. In this case, no temporary stored procedure is created to execute the query. This option can save time if you don't expect to execute the query more than a few times in the course of your application. In addition, when working with queries that should not be run as stored procedures but executed directly, this option is mandatory. For example, in queries that create temporary tables for use by subsequent queries, you must use the **rdExecDirect** option.

  You can use the following constants for the *options* argument:

Constant	Value	Description
rdAsyncEnable	32	Execute operation asynchronously.
RdExecDirect	64	Bypass creation of a stored procedure to execute the query. Uses SQLExecDirect instead of SQLPrepare and SQLExecute.

Remarks

If the **OpenResultset** method succeeds, RDO instantiates a new **rdoResultset** object and appends it to the **rdoResultsets** collection – even if no rows are returned by the query. If the query fails to compile or execute due to a syntax error, permissions problem or other error, the **rdoResultset** is not created and a trappable error is fired. The **rdoResultset** topic contains additional details on **rdoResultset** behavior and managing the **rdoResultsets** collection.

Note RDO 2.0 behaves differently than RDO 1.0 in how it handles orphaned references to **rdoResultset** objects. When you Set a variable already assigned to an **rdoResultset** object with another **rdoResultset** object using the **OpenResultset** method, the existing **rdoResultset** object is closed and dropped from the **rdoResultsets** collection. In RDO 1.0, the existing object remained open and was left in the **rdoResultsets** collection.

Note Before you can use the name of a base table in the *name* argument, you must first use the **Refresh** method against the **rdoTables** collection to populate it. You can also populate the **rdoTables** collection by referencing one of its members by its ordinal number. For example, referencing **rdoTables**(0) will populate the entire collection.

Executing Multiple Operations on a Connection

If there is an unpopulated **rdoResultset** pending on a data source that can only support a single operation on an **rdoConnection** object, you cannot create additional **rdoQuery** or **rdoResultset** objects using the **OpenResultset** method, or use the **Refresh** method on the **rdoTable** object until the **rdoResultset** is flushed, closed, or fully populated. For example, when using SQL Server 4.2 as a data source, you cannot create an additional **rdoResultset** object until you move to the last row of the last result set of the current **rdoResultset** object. To populate the result set, use the **MoreResults** method to move through all pending result sets, or use the **Cancel** or **Close** method on the **rdoResultset** to flush all pending result sets.

See Also

Cancel Method (Remote Data), **Close** Method (Remote Data), **MoreResults** Method (Remote Data), **rdoResultset** Object, **AbsolutePosition** Property (Remote Data), **BOF**, **EOF** Properties (Remote Data), **Connect** Property (Remote Data), **LockType** Property (Remote Data), **PercentPosition** Property (Remote Data), **ResultsetType** Property, **StillExecuting** Property (Remote Data), **Type** Property (Remote Data)

Example

The following example illustrates execution of a multiple result set query. While this query uses three SELECT statements, only two return rows to your application. The subquery used instead of a join does not pass rows outside the scope of the query itself. This is also an example of a simple parameter query that concatenates the arguments instead of using an **rdoQuery** to manage the query. The **OpenResultset** also runs asynchronously – the code checks for completion of the operation by polling the **StillExecuting** property.

```
Private Sub ShowResultset_Click()
Dim rs As rdoResultset
Dim cn As New rdoConnection
Dim cl As rdoColumn
Dim SQL As String
Const None As String = ""

cn.Connect = "uid=;pwd=;server=SEQUEL;" _
   & "driver={SQL Server};database=pubs;" _
   & "DSN='';"

cn.CursorDriver = rdUseOdbc
cn.EstablishConnection rdDriverNoPrompt

SQL = "Select Au_Lname, Au_Fname" _
   & " From Authors A" _
   & " Where Au_ID in " _
   & " (Select Au_ID" _
   & "     from TitleAuthor TA, Titles T" _

   & "     Where TA.Au_ID = A.Au_ID" _
   & "     And TA.Title_ID = T.Title_ID " _
   & "     And T.Title Like '" _
   & InputBox("Enter search string", , "C") & "%')" _
   & "Select * From Titles Where price > 10"

Set rs = cn.OpenResultset(SQL, rdOpenKeyset, _
   rdConcurReadOnly, rdAsyncEnable + rdExecDirect)

Debug.Print "Executing ";
While rs.StillExecuting
   Debug.Print ".";
   DoEvents
Wend

Do
   Debug.Print String(50, "-") _
   & "Processing Result Set " & String(50, "-")

   For Each cl In rs.rdoColumns
      Debug.Print cl.Name,
   Next
   Debug.Print

   Do Until rs.EOF
      For Each cl In rs.rdoColumns
         Debug.Print cl.Value,
      Next
      rs.MoveNext
   Debug.Print
   Loop
   Debug.Print "Row count="; rs.RowCount

Loop Until rs.MoreResults = False
End Sub
```

Operator Precedence

When several operations occur in an expression, each part is evaluated and resolved in a predetermined order called operator precedence.

When expressions contain operators from more than one category, arithmetic operators are evaluated first, comparison operators are evaluated next, and logical operators are evaluated last. Comparison operators all have equal precedence; that is, they are evaluated in the left-to-right order in which they appear. Arithmetic and logical operators are evaluated in the following order of precedence:

Arithmetic	Comparison	Logical
Exponentiation (^)	Equality (=)	**Not**
Negation (–)	Inequality (<>)	**And**
Multiplication and division (*, /)	Less than (<)	**Or**
Integer division (\)	Greater than (>)	**Xor**
Modulus arithmetic (**Mod**)	Less than or equal to (<=)	**Eqv**
Addition and subtraction (+, –)	Greater than or equal to (>=)	**Imp**
String concatenation (**&**)	**Like** **Is**	

When multiplication and division occur together in an expression, each operation is evaluated as it occurs from left to right. When addition and subtraction occur together in an expression, each operation is evaluated in order of appearance from left to right. Parentheses can be used to override the order of precedence and force some parts of an expression to be evaluated before others. Operations within parentheses are always performed before those outside. Within parentheses, however, operator precedence is maintained.

The string concatenation operator (**&**) is not an arithmetic operator, but in precedence, it does follow all arithmetic operators and precede all comparison operators.

The **Like** operator is equal in precedence to all comparison operators, but is actually a pattern-matching operator.

The **Is** operator is an object reference comparison operator. It does not compare objects or their values; it checks only to determine if two object references refer to the same object.

See Also

Operator Summary, **Is** Operator, **Like** Operator

Operator Summary

Operators	Description
Arithmetic Operators	Operators used to perform mathematical calculations.
Comparison Operators	Operators used to perform comparisons.
Concatenation Operators	Operators used to combine strings.
Logical Operators	Operators used to perform logical operations.

See Also

Operator Precedence

Option Base Statement

Used at module level to declare the default lower bound for array subscripts.

Syntax

Option Base {0 | 1}

Remarks

Because the default base is **0**, the **Option Base** statement is never required. If used, the statement must appear in a module before any procedures. **Option Base** can appear only once in a module and must precede array declarations that include dimensions.

Note The **To** clause in the **Dim**, **Private**, **Public**, **ReDim**, and **Static** statements provides a more flexible way to control the range of an array's subscripts. However, if you don't explicitly set the lower bound with a **To** clause, you can use **Option Base** to change the default lower bound to 1. The base of an array created with the **ParamArray** keyword is zero; **Option Base** does not affect **ParamArray** (or the **Array** function, when qualified with the name of its type library, for example **VBA.Array**).

The **Option Base** statement only affects the lower bound of arrays in the module where the statement is located.

See Also

Dim Statement, **LBound** Function, **Option Compare** Statement, **Option Explicit** Statement, **Option Private** Statement, **Private** Statement, **Public** Statement, **ReDim** Statement, **Static** Statement

Example

This example uses the **Option Base** statement to override the default base array subscript value of 0. The **LBound** function returns the smallest available subscript for the indicated dimension of an array. The **Option Base** statement is used at the module level only.

```
Option base 1                    ' Set default array subscripts to 1.

Dim Lower
Dim MyArray(20), TwoDArray(3, 4) ' Declare array variables.
Dim ZeroArray(0 To 5)            ' Override default base subscript.
' Use LBound function to test lower bounds of arrays.
Lower = LBound(MyArray)          ' Returns 1.
Lower = LBound(TwoDArray, 2)     ' Returns 1.
Lower = LBound(ZeroArray)        ' Returns 0.
```

Option Compare Statement

Used at module level to declare the default comparison method to use when string data is compared.

Syntax

Option Compare {Binary | Text | Database}

Remarks

If used, the **Option Compare** statement must appear in a module before any procedures.

The **Option Compare** statement specifies the string comparison method (**Binary**, **Text**, or **Database**) for a module. If a module doesn't include an **Option Compare** statement, the default text comparison method is **Binary**.

Option Compare Binary results in string comparisons based on a sort order derived from the internal binary representations of the characters. In Microsoft Windows, sort order is determined by the code page. A typical binary sort order is shown in the following example:

A < B < E < Z < a < b < e < z < À < Ê < Ø < à < ê < ø

Option Compare Text results in string comparisons based on a case-insensitive text sort order determined by your system's locale. When the same characters are sorted using **Option Compare Text**, the following text sort order is produced:

(A=a) < (À=à) < (B=b) < (E=e) < (Ê=ê) < (Z=z) < (Ø=ø)

Option Compare Database can only be used within Microsoft Access. This results in string comparisons based on the sort order determined by the locale ID of the database where the string comparisons occur.

See Also

Option Base Statement, **Option Explicit** Statement, **Option Private** Statement, **Comparison** Operators, **InStr** Function, **StrComp** Function

Example

This example uses the **Option Compare** statement to set the default string comparison method. The **Option Compare** statement is used at the module level only.

```
' Set the string comparison method to Binary.
Option compare Binary    ' That is, "AAA" is less than "aaa".
' Set the string comparison method to Text.
Option compare Text      ' That is, "AAA" is equal to "aaa".
```

Option Explicit Statement

Used at module level to force explicit declaration of all variables in that module.

Syntax

Option Explicit

Remarks

If used, the **Option Explicit** statement must appear in a module before any procedures.

When **Option Explicit** appears in a module, you must explicitly declare all variables using the **Dim**, **Private**, **Public**, **ReDim**, or **Static** statements. If you attempt to use an undeclared variable name, an error occurs at compile time.

If you don't use the **Option Explicit** statement, all undeclared variables are of **Variant** type unless the default type is otherwise specified with a **Def***type* statement.

Note   Use **Option Explicit** to avoid incorrectly typing the name of an existing variable or to avoid confusion in code where the scope of the variable is not clear.

See Also

Const Statement, **Deftype** Statements, **Dim** Statement, **Function** Statement, **Option Base** Statement, **Option Compare** Statement, **Option Private** Statement, **Private** Statement, **Public** Statement, **ReDim** Statement, **Static** Statement, **Sub** Statement

Example

This example uses the **Option Explicit** statement to force explicit declaration of all variables. Attempting to use an undeclared variable causes an error at compile time. The **Option Explicit** statement is used at the module level only.

```
Option explicit    ' Force explicit variable declaration.
Dim MyVar          ' Declare variable.
MyInt = 10         ' Undeclared variable generates error.
MyVar = 10         ' Declared variable does not generate error.
```

Option Private Statement

When used in host applications that allow references across multiple projects, **Option Private Module** prevents a module's contents from being referenced outside its project. In host applications that don't permit such references, for example, standalone versions of Visual Basic, **Option Private** has no effect.

Syntax

Option Private Module

Remarks

If used, the **Option Private** statement must appear at module level, before any procedures.

When a module contains **Option Private Module**, the public parts, for example, variables, objects, and user-defined types declared at module level, are still available within the project containing the module, but they are not available to other applications or projects.

Note **Option Private** is only useful for host applications that support simultaneous loading of multiple projects and permit references between the loaded projects. For example, Microsoft Excel permits loading of multiple projects and **Option Private Module** can be used to restrict cross-project visibility. Although Visual Basic permits loading of multiple projects, references between projects are never permitted in Visual Basic.

See Also

Option Base Statement, **Option Compare** Statement, **Option Explicit** Statement, **Private** Statement, **Public** Statement

Example

This example demonstrates the **Option Private** statement, which is used at module level to indicate that the entire module is private. With **Option Private Module**, module-level parts not declared **Private** are available to other modules in the project, but not to other projects or applications.

```
Option private Module    ' Indicates that module is private.
```

OptionButton Control

An **OptionButton** control displays an option that can be turned on or off.

Syntax

OptionButton

Remarks

Usually, **OptionButton** controls are used in an option group to display options from which the user selects only one. You group **OptionButton** controls by drawing them inside a container such as a **Frame** control, a **PictureBox** control, or a form. To group **OptionButton** controls in a **Frame** or **PictureBox**, draw the **Frame** or **PictureBox** first, and then draw the **OptionButton** controls inside. All **OptionButton** controls within the same container act as a single group.

While **OptionButton** controls and **CheckBox** controls may appear to function similarly, there is an important difference: When a user selects an **OptionButton**, the other **OptionButton** controls in the same group are automatically unavailable. In contrast, any number of **CheckBox** controls can be selected.

Properties

Alignment Property, **Appearance** Property, **BackColor, ForeColor** Properties, **Caption** Property, **Container** Property, **DisabledPicture** Property, **DownPicture** Property, **DragIcon** Property, **DragMode** Property, **Enabled** Property, **Font** Property, **FontBold, FontItalic, FontStrikeThru, FontUnderline** Properties, **Fontname** Property, **FontSize** Property, **Height, Width** Properties, **HelpContextID** Property, **hWnd** Property, **Index** Property, **Left, Top** Properties, **MaskColor** Property, **MouseIcon** Property, **MousePointer** Property, **Name** Property, **OLEDropMode** Property, **Parent** Property, **Picture** Property, **Style** Property, **TabIndex** Property, **TabStop** Property, **Tag** Property, **ToolTipText** Property, **UseMaskColor** Property, **Value** Property, **Visible** Property, **WhatsThisHelpID** Property

Events

Click Event, **DblClick** Event, **DragDrop** Event, **DragOver** Event, **GotFocus** Event, **KeyDown, KeyUp** Events, **KeyPress** Event, **LostFocus** Event, **MouseDown, MouseUp** Events, **MouseMove** Event, **OLECompleteDrag** Event, **OLEDragDrop** Event, **OLEDragOver** Event, **OLEGiveFeedback** Event, **OLESetData** Event, **OLEStartDrag** Event

Methods

Refresh Method, **SetFocus** Method, **Drag** Method, **Move** Method, **ZOrder** Method, **OLEDrag** Method, **ShowWhatsThis** Method

See Also

CheckBox Control, **Form** Object, **Forms** Collection, **Frame** Control, **PictureBox** Control

Options Property

Returns or sets a value that specifies one or more characteristics of the **Recordset** object in the control's **Recordset** property.

Applies To

Data Control

Syntax

*object***.Options** [= *value*]

The **Options** property syntax has these parts:

Part	Description
object	An object expression that evaluates to an object in the Applies To list.
value	A constant or value that specifies a characteristic of a **Recordset**, as described in Settings.

Settings

Use one or more of the following values to set the **Options** property. If you use more than one option, you must add their values:

Constant	Value	Description
dbDenyWrite	1	In a multi-user environment, other users can't make changes to records in the **Recordset**.
dbDenyRead	2	In a multi-user environment, other users can't read records (table-type **Recordset** only).
dbReadOnly	4	You can't make changes to records in the **Recordset**.
dbAppendOnly	8	You can add new records to the **Recordset**, but you can't read existing records.
dbInconsistent	16	Updates can apply to all fields of the **Recordset**, even if they violate the join condition.
dbConsistent	32	(Default) Updates apply only to those fields that don't violate the join condition.
dbSQLPassThrough	64	When using **Data** controls with an SQL statement in the **RecordSource** property, sends the SQL statement to an ODBC database, such as a SQL Server or Oracle database, for processing.
dbForwardOnly	256	The **Recordset** object supports forward-only scrolling. The only move method allowed is **MoveNext**. This option cannot be used on **Recordset** objects manipulated with the **Data** control.
dbSeeChanges	512	Generate a trappable error if another user is changing data you are editing.

Remarks

These constants are listed in the Visual Basic (VB) object library in the Object Browser.

If you change the **Options** property at run time, you must use the **Refresh** method for the change to have any effect.

In the Professional and Enterprise Editions, this property corresponds to the *options* argument in the **OpenRecordset** method.

To set more than one value for this property, you can combine options by adding values together. For example, to set both **dbAppendOnly** and **dbInconsistent** you can use this code:

```
Data1.Options = dbAppendOnly + dbInconsistent
```

To determine if the property contains a specific value, you can use the **And** operator. For example, to find out if the **Recordset** is open for read-only access, you could use this code:

```
If Data1.Options And dbReadOnly Then...
```

Using both **dbInconsistent** and **dbConsistent** results in consistent updates, the default for **Recordset** objects.

Note The **dbSQLPassThrough** option can only be used when creating dynaset- or snapshot-type **Recordset** objects and is supported only to provide compatibility with previous versions. For better performance and functionality, you should use a previously created SQL **PassThrough QueryDef** object and set the **Data** control's **Recordset** property to a **Recordset** object created with the **QueryDef**.

Note If you attempt to access a SQL Server 6.0 table that includes an identity column, you can trigger an erroneous 3622 error. To prevent this problem, use the **dbSeeChanges** option with the **Options** property or **OpenRecordset** method.

Data Type
Integer

See Also
OpenRecordset Method, **Recordset** Property, **RecordSource** Property

---

Options Property (Remote Data)

Returns or sets a value that specifies one or more operational characteristics of the **RemoteData** control.

Applies To
RemoteData Control

Syntax

object.**Options** [= *value*]

The **Options** property syntax has these parts:

Part	Description
object	An object expression that evaluates to an object in the **Applies To** list.
value	A constant or **Integer** as described in Settings.

Settings

Use the following values to set the **Options** property for the **RemoteData** control:

Constant	Value	Description
rdAsyncEnable	32	Execute the query asynchronously.
rdExecDirect	64	Use the ODBC **SQLExecDirect** API function to execute query.

Remarks

This property corresponds to the *options* argument in the **OpenResultset** and **Execute** methods. If you change the **Options** property at run time, you must use the **Refresh** method for the change to have any effect.

Enable Asynchronous Operations

Asynchronous operations permit **RemoteData** objects to work in the background on operations like creating result sets or executing procedures while your foreground code continues to work.

Whenever you use the **OpenResultset**, **Execute**, **Move** or **MoreResults** methods with the **rdAsyncEnable** option, control returns immediately to your application—before the operation is completed by RDO. If required, RDO periodically checks the data source to see if the operation is complete. You can adjust the frequency of this polling by setting the **AsyncCheckInterval** property. To see if your operation has completed, check the **StillExecuting** property which remains **True** until RDO completes the operation. To cancel the operation, use the **rdoResultset** object's **Cancel** method. In addition, when queries are complete, RDO fires the **QueryComplete** event to indicate that the **rdoResultset** is ready to access.

Enable Use of SQLExecDirect

If you use the **rdExecDirect** option, RDO uses the **SQLExecDirect** ODBC API function to execute the query. In this case, no temporary stored procedure is created to execute the query. This option can save time if you don't expect to execute the query more than a few times in the course of your application. In addition, when working with queries that should not be run as stored procedures but executed directly, this option is mandatory. For example, in queries that create temporary tables for use by subsequent queries, you must use the **rdExecDirect** option.

See Also

CreatePreparedStatement Method, **Execute** Method, **MoreResults** Method, **OpenResultset** Method, **QueryCompleted** Event, **ResultsetType** Property

Or Operator

Used to perform a logical disjunction on two expressions.

Syntax

result = *expression1* **Or** *expression2*

The **Or** operator syntax has these parts:

Part	Description
result	Required; any numeric variable.
expression1	Required; any expression.
expression2	Required; any expression.

Remarks

If either or both expressions evaluate to **True**, *result* is **True**. The following table illustrates how *result* is determined:

If *expression1* is	And *expression2* is	Then *result* is
True	True	True
True	False	True
True	Null	True
False	True	True
False	False	False
False	Null	Null
Null	True	True
Null	False	Null
Null	Null	Null

The **Or** operator also performs a bitwise comparison of identically positioned bits in two numeric expressions and sets the corresponding bit in *result* according to the following table:

If bit in *expression1* is	And bit in *expression2* is	Then *result* is
0	0	0
0	1	1
1	0	1
1	1	1

See Also

Operator Summary, **Operator** Precedence, **Logical** Operators

Example

This example uses the **Or** operator to perform logical disjunction on two expressions.

```
Dim A, B, C, D, MyCheck
A = 10: B = 8: C = 6: D = Null          ' Initialize variables.
MyCheck = A > B Or B > C                 ' Returns True.
MyCheck = B > A Or B > C                 ' Returns True.
MyCheck = A > B Or B > D                 ' Returns True.
MyCheck = B > D Or B > A                 ' Returns Null.
MyCheck = A Or B                         ' Returns 10 (bitwise comparison).
```

OrdinalPosition Property

Sets or returns the relative position of a **Field** object within a **Fields** collection. For an object not yet appended to the **Fields** collection, this property is read/write.

Applies To

Field Object

Settings and Return Values

The setting or return value is an **Integer** that specifies the numeric order of fields. The default is 0.

Remarks

The availability of the **OrdinalPosition** property depends on the object that contains the **Fields** collection, as shown in the following table.

If the Fields collection belongs to a

	Then OrdinalPosition is
Index object	Not supported
QueryDef object	Read-only
Recordset object	Read-only
Relation object	Not supported
TableDef object	Read/write

Generally, the ordinal position of an object that you append to a collection depends on the order in which you append the object. The first appended object is in the first position (0), the second appended object is in the second position (1), and so on. The last appended object is in ordinal position *count* −1, where *count* is the number of objects in the collection as specified by the **Count** property setting.

You can use the **OrdinalPosition** property to specify an ordinal position for new **Field** objects that differs from the order in which you append those objects to a collection. This enables you to specify a field order for your tables, queries, and recordsets when you use them in an application. For example, the order in which fields are returned in a SELECT * query is determined by the current **OrdinalPosition** property values.

You can permanently reset the order in which fields are returned in recordsets by setting the **OrdinalPosition** property to any positive integer.

Two or more **Field** objects in the same collection can have the same **OrdinalPosition** property value, in which case they will be ordered alphabetically. For example, if you have a field named Age set to 4 and you set a second field named Weight to 4, Weight is returned after Age.

You can specify a number that is greater than the number of fields minus 1. The field will be returned in an order relative to the largest number. For example, if you set a field's **OrdinalPosition** property to 20 (and there are only 5 fields) and you've set the **OrdinalPosition** property for two other fields to 10 and 30, respectively, the field set to 20 is returned between the fields set to 10 and 30.

Note Even if the **Fields** collection of a **TableDef** has not been refreshed, the field order in a **Recordset** opened from the **TableDef** will reflect the **OrdinalPosition** data of the **TableDef** object. A table-type **Recordset** will have the same **OrdinalPosition** data as the underlying table, but any other type of **Recordset** will have new **OrdinalPosition** data (starting with 0) that follow the order determined by the **OrdinalPosition** data of the **TableDef**.

See Also

Refresh Method, **Count** Property

Example

This example changes the **OrdinalPosition** property values in the Employees **TableDef** in order to control the **Field** order in a resulting **Recordset**. By setting the **OrdinalPosition** of all the **Fields** to 1, any resulting **Recordset** will order the **Fields** alphabetically. Note that the **OrdinalPosition** values in the **Recordset** don't match the values in the **TableDef**, but simply reflect the end result of the **TableDef** changes.

```
Sub OrdinalPositionX()

    Dim dbsNorthwind As Database
    Dim tdfEmployees As TableDef
    Dim aintPosition() As Integer
    Dim astrFieldName() As String
    Dim intTemp As Integer
    Dim fldTemp As Field
    Dim rstEmployees As Recordset

    Set dbsNorthwind = OpenDatabase("Northwind.mdb")
    Set tdfEmployees = dbsNorthwind.TableDefs("Employees")

    With tdfEmployees
        ' Display and store original OrdinalPosition data.
        Debug.Print _
            "Original OrdinalPosition data in TableDef."
        ReDim aintPosition(0 To .Fields.Count - 1) As Integer
        ReDim astrFieldName(0 To .Fields.Count - 1) As String
        For intTemp = 0 To .Fields.Count - 1
            aintPosition(intTemp) = _
```

```
                .Fields(intTemp).OrdinalPosition
            astrFieldName(intTemp) = .Fields(intTemp).Name
            Debug.Print , aintPosition(intTemp), _
                astrFieldName(intTemp)
        Next intTemp

        ' Change OrdinalPosition data.
        For Each fldTemp In .Fields
            fldTemp.OrdinalPosition = 1
        Next fldTemp

        ' Open new Recordset object to show how the
        ' OrdinalPosition data has affected the record order.
        Debug.Print _
            "OrdinalPosition data from resulting Recordset."
        Set rstEmployees = dbsNorthwind.OpenRecordset( _
            "SELECT * FROM Employees")
        For Each fldTemp In rstEmployees.Fields
            Debug.Print , fldTemp.OrdinalPosition, fldTemp.Name
        Next fldTemp
        rstEmployees.Close

        ' Restore original OrdinalPosition data because this is
        ' a demonstration.
        For intTemp = 0 To .Fields.Count - 1
            .Fields(astrFieldName(intTemp)).OrdinalPosition = _
                aintPosition(intTemp)
        Next intTemp

    End With

    dbsNorthwind.Close

End Sub
```

OrdinalPosition Property (Remote Data)

Returns the relative position of an **rdoColumn** object within the **rdoColumns** collection.

Applies To

rdoColumn Object

Syntax

object.**OrdinalPosition**

The *object* placeholder represents an object expression that evaluates to an object in the **Applies To** list.

Return Values

The **OrdinalPosition** property return value is an **Integer** expression as described in Remarks.

Remarks

Each of these data columns in an **rdoResultset** is returned in the order specified by the query and are numbered starting at one. Because of this numbering scheme, the first column of an **rdoResultset** (`rdoResultset(0)`) has an **OrdinalPosition** of 1.

See Also

rdoColumn Object, **rdoPreparedStatement** Object, **rdoResults** Object, **rdoTable** Object, **Refresh** Method

Orientation Property

Returns or sets a value indicating whether documents are printed in portrait or landscape mode. Not available at design time.

Applies To

Printer Object, **Printers** Collection

Syntax

object.**Orientation** [= *value*]

The **Orientation** property syntax has these parts:

Part	Description
object	An object expression that evaluates to an object in the **Applies To** list.
value	A value or constant that determines the page orientation, as described in Settings.

Settings

The settings for *value* are:

Constant	Value	Description
vbPRORPortrait	1	Documents are printed with the top at the narrow side of the paper.
vbPRORLandscape	2	Documents are printed with the top at the wide side of the paper.

Remarks

These constants are listed in the Visual Basic (VB) object library in the Object Browser.

Note The effect of the properties of the **Printer** object depends on the driver supplied by the printer manufacturer. Some property settings may have no effect, or several different property settings may all have the same effect. Settings outside the accepted range may or may not produce an error. For more information, see the manufacturer's documentation for the specific driver.

See Also

Printer Object, **Printers** Collection

Example

This example toggles the orientation of a **Slider** control on a form. To try the example, place a **Slider** control onto a form and paste the code into the form's Declarations section, and then run the example. Click the form to toggle the **Slider** control's orientation.

```
Private Sub Form_Click()
    If Slider1.Orientation = 0 Then
        Slider1.Orientation = 1
    Else
        Slider1.Orientation = 0
    End If
End Sub
```

OriginalValue Property (DAO)

Returns the value of a **Field** in the database that existed when the last batch update began (**ODBCDirect** workspaces only).

Applies To

Field Object

Return Values

The return value is a variant expression.

Remarks

During an optimistic batch update, a collision may occur where a second client modifies the same field and record in between the time the first client retrieves the data and the first client's update attempt. The **OriginalValue** property contains the value of the field at the time the last batch **Update** began. If this value does not match the value actually in the database when the batch **Update** attempts to write to the database, a collision occurs. When this happens, the new value in the database will be accessible through the **VisibleValue** property.

OriginalValue Property (Remote Data)

Returns the value of the column as first fetched from the database.

Applies To

rdoColumn Object

Syntax

object.**OriginalValue**

The *object* placeholder represents an object expression that evaluates to an object in the **Applies To** list.

Return Values

The **OriginalValue** property return value is a **Variant** value whose datatype is determined by the datatype of the **rdoColumn** specified.

Remarks

When working with optimistic batch update operations, you might need to resolve update conflicts by comparing the column values as originally returned by RDO with the value as supplied by the user. The **OriginalValue** property provides this value as first fetched from the database.

See Also

BatchUpdate Method (Remote Data), **Edit** Method (Remote Data), **OpenResultset** Method (Remote Data), **rdoColumn** Object, **rdoResultset** Object, **U0pdate** Method (Remote Data)

Owner Property

Sets or returns a value that specifies the owner of the object (Microsoft Jet workspaces only).

Applies To

Container Object, **Document** Object

Settings and Return Values

The setting or return value is a **String** that evaluates to either the name of a **User** object in the **Users** collection or the name of a **Group** object in the **Groups** collection.

Remarks

The owner of an object has certain access privileges denied to other users. Any individual user account (represented by a **User** object) or group of user accounts (represented by a **Group** object) can change the **Owner** property setting at any time if it has the appropriate permissions.

See Also

User Object, **Permissions** Property

Example

This example uses the **Owner** and **SystemDB** properties to show the owners of a variety of **Document** objects.

```
Sub OwnerX()

    ' Ensure that the Microsoft Jet workgroup file is
    ' available.
    DBEngine.SystemDB = "system.mdw"

    Dim dbsNorthwind As Database
    Dim ctrLoop As Container

    Set dbsNorthwind = OpenDatabase("Northwind.mdb")
```

```
With dbsNorthwind
    Debug.Print "Document owners:"
    ' Enumerate Containers collection and show the owner
    ' of the first Document in each container's Documents
    ' collection.
    For Each ctrLoop In .Containers
        With ctrLoop
            Debug.Print "    [" & .Documents(0).Name & _
                "] in [" & .Name & _
                "] container owned by [" & _
                .Documents(0).Owner & "]"
        End With
    Next ctrLoop

    .Close
End With

End Sub
```

Page Property

Returns the current page number.

Applies To

Printer Object, **Printers** Collection

Syntax

object.**Page**

The *object* placeholder represents an object expression that evaluates to an object in the **Applies To** list.

Remarks

Visual Basic keeps a count of pages that have been printed since your application started or since the last time the **EndDoc** statement was used on the **Printer** object. This count starts at one and increases by one if:

- You use the **NewPage** method.
- You use the **Print** method and the text you want to print doesn't fit on the current page.

Note Graphics methods output that doesn't fit on the page doesn't generate a new page. The output is clipped to fit the page's printable area.

See Also

EndDoc Method, **NewPage** Method

Example

This example prints three pages of text with the current page number at the top of each page. To try this example, paste the code into the **Declarations** section of a form, and then press F5 and click the form.

```
Private Sub Form_Click ()
    Dim Header, I, Y                          ' Declare variables.
    Print "Now printing..."                   ' Put notice on form.
    Header = "Printing Demo - Page "          ' Set header string.
    For I = 1 To 3
        Printer.Print Header;                 ' Print header.
        Printer.Print Printer.Page            ' Print page number.
        Y = Printer.CurrentY + 10             ' Set position for line.
        ' Draw a line across page.
        Printer.Line (0, Y) - (Printer.ScaleWidth, Y) ' Draw line.
        For K = 1 To 50
            Printer.Print String(K, " ");     ' Print string of spaces.

Printer.Print "Visual Basic ";               ' Print text.
        Printer.Print Printer.Page            ' Print page number.
        Next
        Printer.NewPage
    Next I
    Printer.EndDoc
    End
End Sub
```

Paint Event

Occurs when part or all of an object is exposed after being moved or enlarged, or after a window that was covering the object has been moved.

Applies To

PropertyPage Object, **UserControl** Object, **UserDocument** Object, **Form** Object, **Forms** Collection, **PictureBox** Control

Syntax

Private Sub Form_Paint( )
Private Sub *object*_**Paint**([*index* **As Integer**])

The Paint event syntax has these parts:

Part	Description
object	An object expression that evaluates to an object in the **Applies To** list.
index	An integer that uniquely identifies a control if it's in a control array.

Remarks

A **Paint** event procedure is useful if you have output from graphics methods in your code. With a **Paint** procedure, you can ensure that such output is repainted when necessary.

The **Paint** event is invoked when the **Refresh** method is used. If the **AutoRedraw** property is set to **True**, repainting or redrawing is automatic, so no **Paint** events are necessary.

If the **ClipControls** property is set to **False**, graphics methods in the Paint event procedure affect only newly exposed areas of the form; otherwise, the graphics methods repaint all areas of the form not covered by controls (except **Image**, **Label**, **Line**, and **Shape** controls).

Using a **Refresh** method in a Resize event procedure forces repainting of the entire object every time a user resizes the form.

Note Using a Paint event procedure for certain tasks can cause a cascading event. In general, avoid using a Paint event procedure to do the following:

- Move or size a form or control.
- Change any variables that affect size or appearance, such as setting an object's **BackColor** property.
- Invoke a **Refresh** method.

A **Resize** event procedure may be more appropriate for some of these tasks.

See Also

Resize Event, **Refresh** Method, **AutoRedraw** Property, **ClipControls** Property

Example

This example draws a diamond that intersects the midpoint of each side of a form and adjusts automatically as the form is resized. To try this example, paste the code into the **Declarations** section of a form, and then press F5 and resize the form.

```
Private Sub Form_Paint ()
   Dim HalfX, HalfY                    ' Declare variables.
   HalfX = ScaleLeft + ScaleWidth / 2  ' Set to one-half of width.
   HalfY = ScaleTop + ScaleHeight / 2  ' Set to one-half of height.
   ' Draw a diamond.
   Line (ScaleLeft, HalfY) - (HalfX, ScaleTop)
   Line -(ScaleWidth + ScaleLeft, HalfY)
   Line -(HalfX, ScaleHeight + ScaleTop)
   Line -(ScaleLeft, HalfY)
End Sub

Private Sub Form_Resize
   Refresh
End Sub
```

PaintPicture Method

Draws the contents of a graphics file (.bmp, .wmf, .emf, .ico, or .dib) on a **Form**, **PictureBox**, or **Printer**. Doesn't support named arguments.

Applies To

PropertyPage Object, **UserControl** Object, **UserDocument** Object, **Printer** Object, **Printers** Collection, **Form** Object, **Forms** Collection, **PictureBox** Control

Syntax

object.**PaintPicture** *picture*, *x1*, *y1*, *width1*, *height1*, *x2*, *y2*, *width2*, *height2*, *opcode*

The **PaintPicture** method syntax has these parts:

Part	Description
object	Optional. An object expression that evaluates to an object in the Applies To list. If *object* is omitted, the **Form** object with the focus is assumed to be *object*.
Picture	Required. The source of the graphic to be drawn onto *object*. Must be the **Picture** property of a **Form** or **PictureBox**.
x1, y1	Required. Single-precision values indicating the destination coordinates (x-axis and y-axis) on *object* for *picture* to be drawn. The **ScaleMode** property of *object* determines the unit of measure used.
Width1	Optional. Single-precision value indicating the destination width of *picture*. The **ScaleMode** property of *object* determines the unit of measure used. If the destination width is larger or smaller than the source width (*width2*), *picture* is stretched or compressed to fit. If omitted, the source width is used.
Height1	Optional. Single-precision value indicating the destination height of *picture*. The **ScaleMode** property of *object* determines the unit of measure used. If the destination height is larger or smaller than the source height (*height2*), *picture* is stretched or compressed to fit. If omitted, the source height is used.
x2, y2	Optional. Single-precision values indicating the coordinates (x-axis and y-axis) of a clipping region within *picture*. The **ScaleMode** property of *object* determines the unit of measure used. If omitted, 0 is assumed.
Width2	Optional. Single-precision value indicating the source width of a clipping region within *picture*. The **ScaleMode** property of *object* determines the unit of measure used. If omitted, the entire source width is used.
Height2	Optional. Single-precision value indicating the source height of a clipping region within *picture*. The **ScaleMode** property of *object* determines the unit of measure used. If omitted, the entire source height is used.
Opcode	Optional. Long value or code that is used only with bitmaps. It defines a bit-wise operation (such as **vbMergeCopy** or **vbSrcAnd**) that is performed on *picture* as it's drawn on *object*. For a complete list of bit-wise operator constants, see the "RasterOp Constants" topic in Visual Basic Help.

Remarks

You can flip a bitmap horizontally or vertically by using negative values for the destination height (*height1*) and/or the destination width (*width1*).

You can omit as many optional trailing arguments as you want. If you omit an optional trailing argument or arguments, don't use any commas following the last argument you specify. If you want to specify an optional argument, you must specify all optional arguments that appear in the syntax before it.

See Also

Scale Method, **ScaleX**, **ScaleY** Methods, **ScaleMode** Property, **RasterOp** Constants

Palette Property

Returns or sets an image that contains the palette to use for the control.

Applies To

AmbientProperties Object, **PropertyPage** Object, **UserControl** Object, **UserDocument** Object, **Form** Object, **Forms** Collection, **PictureBox** Control

Syntax

object.**Palette** = *path*

Part	Description
object	An object expression that evaluates to an object in the **Applies To** list.
path	The path of the bitmap image containing the palette to be used.

Remarks

You can use a .dib, .gif, or .pal file to set the palette as well as .bmp files.

PaletteMode Property

Returns or sets a value that determines which palette to use for the controls on a object.

Applies To

PropertyPage Object, **UserControl** Object, **UserDocument** Object, **Form** Object, **Forms** Collection

Syntax

object.**PaletteMode** = *integer*

Part	Description
object	An object expression that evaluates to an object in the **Applies To** list.
integer	Determines the palette mode to be used, as described in Settings, below.

Settings

The settings for *integer* are:

Constant	Value	Description
vbPaletteModeHalfTone	0	(Default) Use the Halftone palette.
vbPaletteModeUseZOrder	1	Use the palette from the topmost control that has a palette.
vbPaletteModeCustom	2	Use the palette specified in the **Palette** property.
vbPaletteModeContainer	3	Use the container's palette for containers that support ambient **Palette** property. Applies to **UserControls** only.
vbPaletteModeNone	4	Do not use any palette. Applies to **UserControls** only.
vbPaletteModeObject	5	Use the ActiveX designer's palette. (Applies only to ActiveX designers which contain a palette.)

Remarks

If no palette is available, the halftone palette becomes the default palette.

Note For previous versions of Visual Basic, **PaletteMode** corresponded to **UseZOrder**.

PaperBin Property

Returns or sets a value indicating the default paper bin on the printer from which paper is fed when printing. Not available at design time.

Applies To

Printer Object**, Printers** Collection

Syntax

object.**PaperBin** [= *value*]

The **PaperBin** property syntax has these parts:

Part	Description
object	An object expression that evaluates to an object in the **Applies To** list.
value	A value or constant specifying the default paper bin, as described in Settings.

Settings

The settings for *value* are:

Constant	Value	Description
vbPRBNUpper	1	Use paper from the upper bin.
VbPRBNLower	2	Use paper from the lower bin.

(continued)

(continued)

Constant	Value	Description
VbPRBNMiddle	3	Use paper from the middle bin.
VbPRBNManual	4	Wait for manual insertion of each sheet of paper.
VbPRBNEnvelope	5	Use envelopes from the envelope feeder.
VbPRBNEnvManual	6	Use envelopes from the envelope feeder, but wait for manual insertion.
VbPRBNAuto	7	(Default) Use paper from the current default bin.
VbPRBNTractor	8	Use paper fed from the tractor feeder.
VbPRBNSmallFmt	9	Use paper from the small paper feeder.
VbPRBNLargeFmt	10	Use paper from the large paper bin.
VbPRBNLargeCapacity	11	Use paper from the large capacity feeder.
VbPRBNCassette	14	Use paper from the attached cassette cartridge.

Remarks

These constants are listed in the Visual Basic (VB) object library in the Object Browser.

Not all of the bin options are available on every printer. Check the printer documentation for more specific descriptions of these options.

Note The effect of the properties of the **Printer** object depends on the driver supplied by the printer manufacturer. Some property settings may have no effect, or several different property settings may all have the same effect. Settings outside the accepted range may or may not produce an error. For more information, see the manufacturer's documentation for the specific driver.

See Also

Printer Object, **Printers** Collection

PaperSize Property

Returns or sets a value indicating the paper size for the current printer. Not available at design time.

Applies To

Printer Object, **Printers** Collection

Syntax

object.**PaperSize** [= *value*]

The **PaperSize** property syntax has these parts:

Part	Description
object	An object expression that evaluates to an object in the **Applies To** list.
value	A value or constant specifying the paper size, as described in Settings.

Settings

The settings for *value* are:

Constant	Value	Description
vbPRPSLetter	1	Letter, 8 1/2 x 11 in.
vbPRPSLetterSmall	2	Letter Small, 8 1/2 x 11 in.
vbPRPSTabloid	3	Tabloid, 11 x 17 in.
vbPRPSLedger	4	Ledger, 17 x 11 in.
vbPRPSLegal	5	Legal, 8 1/2 x 14 in.
vbPRPSStatement	6	Statement, 5 1/2 x 8 1/2 in.
vbPRPSExecutive	7	Executive, 7 1/2 x 10 1/2 in.
vbPRPSA3	8	A3, 297 x 420 mm
vbPRPSA4	9	A4, 210 x 297 mm
vbPRPSA4Small	10	A4 Small, 210 x 297 mm
vbPRPSA5	11	A5, 148 x 210 mm
vbPRPSB4	12	B4, 250 x 354 mm
vbPRPSB5	13	B5, 182 x 257 mm
vbPRPSFolio	14	Folio, 8 1/2 x 13 in.
vbPRPSQuarto	15	Quarto, 215 x 275 mm
vbPRPS10x14	16	10 x 14 in.
vbPRPS11x17	17	11 x 17 in.
vbPRPSNote	18	Note, 8 1/2 x 11 in.
vbPRPSEnv9	19	Envelope #9, 3 7/8 x 8 7/8 in.
vbPRPSEnv10	20	Envelope #10, 4 1/8 x 9 1/2 in.
vbPRPSEnv11	21	Envelope #11, 4 1/2 x 10 3/8 in.
vbPRPSEnv12	22	Envelope #12, 4 1/2 x 11 in.
vbPRPSEnv14	23	Envelope #14, 5 x 11 1/2 in.
vbPRPSCSheet	24	C size sheet
vbPRPSDSheet	25	D size sheet

(continued)

(continued)

Constant	Value	Description
vbPRPSESheet	26	E size sheet
vbPRPSEnvDL	27	Envelope DL, 110 x 220 mm
vbPRPSEnvC3	29	Envelope C3, 324 x 458 mm
vbPRPSEnvC4	30	Envelope C4, 229 x 324 mm
vbPRPSEnvC5	28	Envelope C5, 162 x 229 mm
vbPRPSEnvC6	31	Envelope C6, 114 x 162 mm
vbPRPSEnvC65	32	Envelope C65, 114 x 229 mm
vbPRPSEnvB4	33	Envelope B4, 250 x 353 mm
vbPRPSEnvB5	34	Envelope B5, 176 x 250 mm
vbPRPSEnvB6	35	Envelope B6, 176 x 125 mm
vbPRPSEnvItaly	36	Envelope, 110 x 230 mm
vbPRPSEnvMonarch	37	Envelope Monarch, 3 7/8 x 7 1/2 in.
vbPRPSEnvPersonal	38	Envelope, 3 5/8 x 6 1/2 in.
vbPRPSFanfoldUS	39	U.S. Standard Fanfold, 14 7/8 x 11 in.
vbPRPSFanfoldStdGerman	40	German Standard Fanfold, 8 1/2 x 12 in.
vbPRPSFanfoldLglGerman	41	German Legal Fanfold, 8 1/2 x 13 in.
vbPRPSUser	256	User-defined

Remarks

These constants are listed in the Visual Basic (VB) object library in the Object Browser.

Setting a printer's **Height** or **Width** property automatically sets **PaperSize** to **vbPRPSUser**.

Note The effect of the properties of the **Printer** object depends on the driver supplied by the printer manufacturer. Some property settings may have no effect, or several different property settings may all have the same effect. Settings outside the accepted range may or may not produce an error. For more information, see the manufacturer's documentation for the specific driver.

See Also

Printer Object, **Printers** Collection

Parameter Object

A **Parameter** object represents a value supplied to a query. The parameter is associated with a **QueryDef** object created from a parameter query.

Remarks

Parameter objects allow you to change the arguments in a frequently run **QueryDef** object without having to recompile the query.

Using the properties of a **Parameter** object, you can set a query parameter that can be changed before the query is run. You can:

- Use the **Name** property to return the name of a parameter.
- Use the **Value** property to set or return the parameter values to be used in the query.
- Use the **Type** property to return the data type of the **Parameter** object.
- Use the **Direction** property to set or return whether the parameter is an input parameter, an output parameter, or both.

In an ODBCDirect workspace, you can also:

- Change the setting of the **Type** property. Doing so will also clear the Value property.
- Use the **Direction** property to set or return whether the parameter is an input parameter, an output parameter, or both.

Properties

Name Property, **Type** Property, **Value** Property, **Direction** Property

See Also

Property Object, **Properties Collection** Summary

Example

This example demonstrates **Parameter** objects and the **Parameters** collection by creating a temporary **QueryDef** and retrieving data based on changes made to the **QueryDef** object's **Parameters**. The **ParametersChange** procedure is required for this procedure to run.

```
Sub ParameterX()

    Dim dbsNorthwind As Database
    Dim qdfReport As QueryDef
    Dim prmBegin As Parameter
    Dim prmEnd As Parameter
```

```
        Set dbsNorthwind = OpenDatabase("Northwind.mdb")

        ' Create temporary QueryDef object with two
        ' parameters.
        Set qdfReport = dbsNorthwind.CreateQueryDef("", _
            "PARAMETERS dteBegin DateTime, dteEnd DateTime; " & _
            "SELECT EmployeeID, COUNT(OrderID) AS NumOrders " & _
            "FROM Orders WHERE ShippedDate BETWEEN " & _
            "[dteBegin] AND [dteEnd] GROUP BY EmployeeID " & _
            "ORDER BY EmployeeID")
        Set prmBegin = qdfReport.Parameters!dteBegin
        Set prmEnd = qdfReport.Parameters!dteEnd

        ' Print report using specified parameter values.
        ParametersChange qdfReport, prmBegin, #1/1/95#, _
            prmEnd, #6/30/95#
        ParametersChange qdfReport, prmBegin, #7/1/95#, _
            prmEnd, #12/31/95#

        dbsNorthwind.Close

End Sub

Sub ParametersChange(qdfTemp As QueryDef, _
    prmFirst As Parameter, dteFirst As Date, _
    prmLast As Parameter, dteLast As Date)
    ' Report function for ParameterX.

    Dim rstTemp As Recordset
    Dim fldLoop As Field

    ' Set parameter values and open recordset from
    ' temporary QueryDef object.
    prmFirst = dteFirst
    prmLast = dteLast
    Set rstTemp = _
        qdfTemp.OpenRecordset(dbOpenForwardOnly)
    Debug.Print "Period " & dteFirst & " to " & dteLast

    ' Enumerate recordset.
    Do While Not rstTemp.EOF

        ' Enumerate Fields collection of recordset.
        For Each fldLoop In rstTemp.Fields
            Debug.Print " - " & fldLoop.Name & " = " & fldLoop;
        Next fldLoop

        Debug.Print
        rstTemp.MoveNext
    Loop

    rstTemp.Close

End Sub
```

Parameters Collection

A **Parameters** collection contains all the **Parameter** objects of a **QueryDef** object.

Remarks

The **Parameters** collection provides information only about existing parameters. You can't append objects to or delete objects from the **Parameters** collection.

Properties

Count Property

Methods

Refresh Method

Example

This example demonstrates **Parameter** objects and the **Parameters** collection by creating a temporary **QueryDef** and retrieving data based on changes made to the **QueryDef** object's **Parameters**. The **ParametersChange** procedure is required for this procedure to run.

```
Sub ParameterX()

    Dim dbsNorthwind As Database
    Dim qdfReport As QueryDef
    Dim prmBegin As Parameter
    Dim prmEnd As Parameter

    Set dbsNorthwind = OpenDatabase("Northwind.mdb")

    ' Create temporary QueryDef object with two
    ' parameters.
    Set qdfReport = dbsNorthwind.CreateQueryDef("", _
        "PARAMETERS dteBegin DateTime, dteEnd DateTime; " & _
        "SELECT EmployeeID, COUNT(OrderID) AS NumOrders " & _
        "FROM Orders WHERE ShippedDate BETWEEN " & _
        "[dteBegin] AND [dteEnd] GROUP BY EmployeeID " & _
        "ORDER BY EmployeeID")
    Set prmBegin = qdfReport.Parameters!dteBegin
    Set prmEnd = qdfReport.Parameters!dteEnd

    ' Print report using specified parameter values.
    ParametersChange qdfReport, prmBegin, #1/1/95#, _
        prmEnd, #6/30/95#
    ParametersChange qdfReport, prmBegin, #7/1/95#, _
        prmEnd, #12/31/95#

    dbsNorthwind.Close

End Sub
```

```
Sub ParametersChange(qdfTemp As QueryDef, _
   prmFirst As Parameter, dteFirst As Date, _
   prmLast As Parameter, dteLast As Date)
   ' Report function for ParameterX.

   Dim rstTemp As Recordset
   Dim fldLoop As Field

   ' Set parameter values and open recordset from
   ' temporary QueryDef object.
   prmFirst = dteFirst
   prmLast = dteLast
   Set rstTemp = _
      qdfTemp.OpenRecordset(dbOpenForwardOnly)
   Debug.Print "Period " & dteFirst & " to " & dteLast

   ' Enumerate recordset.
   Do While Not rstTemp.EOF

      ' Enumerate Fields collection of recordset.
      For Each fldLoop In rstTemp.Fields
         Debug.Print " - " & fldLoop.Name & " = " & fldLoop;
      Next fldLoop

      Debug.Print
      rstTemp.MoveNext
   Loop

   rstTemp.Close

End Sub
```

Parent Property

Returns the form, object, or collection that contains a control or another object or collection.

Applies To

Animation Control, **CheckBox** Control, **ComboBox** Control, **CommandButton** Control, **CommonDialog** Control, **Data** Control, **DBCombo** Control, **DBGrid** Control, **DBList** Control, **DirListBox** Control, **DriveListBox** Control, **Extender** Control, **FileListBox** Control, **Frame** Control, **HScrollBar**, **VScrollBar** Controls, **Image** Control, **ImageList** Control, **Label** Control, **Line** Control, **ListBox** Control, **ListView** Control, **MAPIMessages** Control, **MAPISession** Control, **Masked** Edit Control, **Menu** Control, **MSComm** Control, **MSFlexGrid** Control, **OLE Container** Control, **OptionButton** Control, **PictureBox** Control, **PictureClip** Control, **ProgressBar** Control, **RemoteData** Control, **RichTextBox** Control, **Shape** Control, **Slider** Control, **SSTab** Control, **StatusBar** Control, **TabStrip** Control, **TextBox** Control, **Timer** Control, **Toolbar** Control, **TreeView** Control, **UpDown** Control, **UserDocument** Object

Syntax

object.**Parent**

The *object* placeholder represents an object expression that evaluates to an object in the **Applies To** list.

Remarks

Use the **Parent** property to access the properties, methods, or controls of an object's parent. For example:

```
MyButton.Parent.MousePointer = 4
```

The **Parent** property is useful in an application in which you pass objects as arguments. For example, you could pass a control variable to a general procedure in a module, and use the **Parent** property to access its parent form.

There is no relationship between the **Parent** property and the **MDIChild** property. There is, however, a parent-child relationship between an **MDIForm** object and any **Form** object that has its **MDIChild** property set to **True**.

See Also

MDIChild Property, **ActiveControl** Property, **ActiveForm** Property

Example

This example passes a control from a form that doesn't have the focus to a procedure in a module, and then displays the state of the control on the parent form. To try this example, create three forms: Form1, containing a **CommandButton** control, and Form2 and Form3, each containing a **CheckBox** control. You must also create a new module (click Add Module in the Project menu). Paste the code into the **Declarations** sections of the respective forms or module, and then press F5 to run the program.

```
' Enter this code into Form1.
Private Sub Form_Load ()
   Form2.Show   ' Display all forms.
   Form3.Show
   Form2.AutoRedraw = True
   Form3.AutoRedraw = True
End Sub

Private Sub Command1_Click ()
   ReadCheckBox Form2.Check1   ' Call procedure in other module
   ReadCheckBox Form3.Check1   ' and send control as argument.
End Sub

' Enter this code into Module1.
Sub ReadCheckBox (Source As Control)
   If Source.Value Then
      Source.Parent.Cls ' Clear parent form.

Source.Parent.Print "CheckBox is ON." ' Display on parent form.
   Else
      Source.Parent.Cls ' Clear parent form.
      Source.Parent.Print "CheckBox is OFF." ' Display on parent form.
   End If
End Sub
```

ParentControls Property

Returns a collection of the other controls in the control's container. The **ParentControls** property is not available at the control's authoring time, and read-only at the control's run time.

Applies To

UserControl Object

Syntax

object.**ParentControls**

The **ParentControls** property syntax has this part:

Part	Description
object	An object expression that evaluates to an object in the **Applies To** list.

Remarks

In most cases, the container of the control will be a form; this collection functions in a similar manner to the **Controls** collection on the form, but will also contain the form itself.

This collection is useful if the control wants to perform some action on the controls on the form; the control can iterate through the collection.

Controls cannot be added or removed by the developer who uses the control through this collection; the controls must be changed in whatever manner the container allows.

The contents of this collection is determined entirely by the container.

See Also

Controls Collection

PartialReplica Property

Sets or returns a value on a **Relation** object indicating whether that relation should be considered when populating a partial replica from a full replica. (Microsoft Jet databases only.)

Applies To

Relation Object

Settings and Return Values

The setting or return value is a **Boolean** data type that is **True** when the relation should be enforced during synchronization.

Remarks

This property enables you to replicate data from the full replica to the partial replica based on relationships between tables. You can use the **PartialReplica** property when setting the **ReplicaFilter** property alone can't adequately specify what data should be replicated to the partial. For example, suppose you have a database in which the Customers table has a one-to-many relationship with the Orders table, and you want to configure a partial replica that only replicates orders from customers in the California region (instead of all orders). It is not possible to set the **ReplicaFilter** property on the Orders table to `Region = 'CA'` because the Region field is in the Customers table, not the Orders table.

To replicate all orders from the California region, you must indicate that the relation between the Orders and Customers tables will be active during replication. Once you've created a partial replica, the following steps will populate it with all orders from the California region:

1 Set the **ReplicaFilter** property on the Customers **TableDef** object to `"Region = 'CA'"`.

2 Set the value of the **PartialReplica** property to **True** on the **Relation** object corresponding to the relationship between Orders and Customers.

3 Invoke the **PopulatePartial** method.

Caution When you set a replica filter or replica relation, be aware that records in the partial replica that don't satisfy the restriction criteria will be removed from the partial replica, but not from the full replica. For example, suppose you set the **ReplicaFilter** property on the Customers **TableDef** in the partial replica to `"Region = 'CA'"` and you then repopulate the database. This will insert or update all records for California-based customers. If you then reset the **ReplicaFilter** property to `"Region = 'FL'"` and repopulate the database, all California region records in the partial replica will be removed, and all records from Florida-based customers will be inserted from the full replica. No records in the full replica will be deleted.

Before setting either the **ReplicaFilter** or **PartialReplica** property, it's a good idea to synchronize the partial replica in which you are setting these properties with the full replica. This will ensure that pending changes in the partial replica will be merged into the full replica before any records are removed in the partial replica.

Example

The following code example uses the **PartialReplica** property to replicate all records representing orders from customers in California:

```
Sub PartialReplicaX()

    ' Assumptions: dbsTemp is the partial replica and
    ' appropriate relationships already exist between
    ' the tables.
```

```
        Dim tdfOrders As TableDef
        Dim relCustOrd As Relation
        Dim dbsTemp As Database
        Dim relLoop As Relation

        Set dbsTemp = OpenDatabase("Northwind.mdb")
        Set tdfOrders = dbsTemp.TableDefs("Orders")

        ' Find the "Customers to Orders" Relation object.
        For Each relLoop In dbsTemp.Relations
           If relLoop.Table = "Customers" And _
               relLoop.ForeignTable = "Orders" Then
              ' Set the Relation object's PartialReplica
              ' property to True.
              relLoop.PartialReplica = True
              Exit For
           End If
        Next relLoop

     End Sub
```

Note If you have set a replica filter and a replica relation on the same table, the two act in combination as a logical OR operation, not a logical AND operation. For instance, in the preceding example, the records exchanged during synchronization are all orders greater than $1000 OR all orders from the California region, not all orders from the California region that are over $1000.

Partition Function

Returns a **Variant** (**String**) indicating where a number occurs within a calculated series of ranges.

Syntax

Partition(*number, start, stop, interval*)

The **Partition** function syntax has these named arguments:

Part	Description
number	Required. Whole number that you want to evaluate against the ranges.
start	Required. Whole number that is the start of the overall range of numbers. The number can't be less than 0.
stop	Required. Whole number that is the end of the overall range of numbers. The number can't be equal to or less than *start*.
interval	Required. Whole number that is the interval spanned by each range in the series from *start* to *stop*. The number can't be less than 1.

Remarks

The **Partition** function identifies the particular range in which *number* falls and returns a **Variant** (**String**) describing that range. The **Partition** function is most useful in queries. You can create a select query that shows how many orders fall within various ranges, for example, order values from 1 to 1000, 1001 to 2000, and so on.

The following table shows how the ranges are determined using three sets of *start*, *stop*, and *interval* parts. The First Range and Last Range columns show what **Partition** returns. The ranges are represented by *lowervalue:uppervalue*, where the low end (*lowervalue*) of the range is separated from the high end (*uppervalue*) of the range with a colon (**:**).

start	stop	interval	Before First	First Range	Last Range	After Last
0	99	5	" :-1"	" 0: 4"	" 95: 99"	" 100: "
20	199	10	" : 19"	" 20: 29"	" 190: 199"	" 200: "
100	1010	20	" : 99"	" 100: 119"	" 1000: 1010"	" 1011: "

In the table shown above, the third line shows the result when *start* and *stop* define a set of numbers that can't be evenly divided by *interval*. The last range extends to *stop* (11 numbers) even though *interval* is 20.

If necessary, **Partition** returns a range with enough leading spaces so that there are the same number of characters to the left and right of the colon as there are characters in *stop*, plus one. This ensures that if you use **Partition** with other numbers, the resulting text will be handled properly during any subsequent sort operation.

If *interval* is 1, the range is *number:number*, regardless of the *start* and *stop* arguments. For example, if *interval* is 1, *number* is 100 and *stop* is 1000, **Partition** returns " 100: 100".

If any of the parts is **Null**, **Partition** returns a **Null**.

Example

This example assumes you have an Orders table that contains a Freight field. It creates a select procedure that counts the number of orders for which freight cost falls into each of several ranges. The **Partition** function is used first to establish these ranges, then the SQL Count function counts the number of orders in each range. In this example, the arguments to the **Partition** function are *start* = 0, *stop* = 500, *interval* = 50. The first range would therefore be 0:49, and so on up to 500.

```
SELECT DISTINCTROW Partition([freight],0, 500, 50) AS Range,
Count(Orders.Freight) AS Count
FROM Orders
GROUP BY Partition([freight],0,500,50);
```

Password Property

Sets the password for a user account (Microsoft Jet workspaces only).

Applies To

User Object

Settings

The setting is a **String** that can be up to 14 characters long and can include any characters except the ASCII character 0 (null). This property setting is write-only for new objects not yet appended to a collection, and is not available for existing objects.

Remarks

Set the **Password** property along with the **PID** property when you create a new **User** object.

Use the **NewPassword** method to change the **Password** property setting for an existing **User** object. To clear a password, set the *newpassword* argument of the **NewPassword** method to a zero-length string ("").

Passwords are case-sensitive.

Note If you don't have access permission, you can't change the password of any other user.

See Also

NewPassword Method, **Permissions** Property, **PID** Property, **UserName** Property

Example

This example uses the **CreateUser** method and **Password** and **PID** properties to create a new **User** object; it then makes the new **User** object a member of different **Group** objects and lists its properties and groups.

```
Sub CreateUserX()

    Dim wrkDefault As Workspace
    Dim usrNew As User
    Dim grpNew As Group
    Dim usrTemp As User
    Dim prpLoop As Property
    Dim grpLoop As Group

    Set wrkDefault = DBEngine.Workspaces(0)

    With wrkDefault

        ' Create and append new User.
        Set usrNew = .CreateUser("NewUser")
        usrNew.PID = "AAA123456789"
        usrNew.Password = "NewPassword"
        .Users.Append usrNew
```

```
' Create and append new Group.
Set grpNew = .CreateGroup("NewGroup", _
   "AAA123456789")
.Groups.Append grpNew

' Make the user "NewUser" a member of the
' group "NewGroup" by creating and adding the
' appropriate User object to the group's Users
' collection.
Set usrTemp = _
   .Groups("NewGroup").CreateUser("NewUser")
.Groups("NewGroup").Users.Append usrTemp

Debug.Print "Properties of " & usrNew.Name

' Enumerate the Properties collection of NewUser. The
' PID property is not readable.
For Each prpLoop In usrNew.Properties
   On Error Resume Next
   If prpLoop <> "" Then Debug.Print "    " & _
      prpLoop.Name & " = " & prpLoop
   On Error GoTo 0
Next prpLoop

Debug.Print "Groups collection of " & usrNew.Name

' Enumerate the Groups collection of NewUser.
For Each grpLoop In usrNew.Groups
   Debug.Print "    " & _
      grpLoop.Name
Next grpLoop

' Delete the new User and Group objects because this
' is a demonstration.
.Users.Delete "NewUser"
.Groups.Delete "NewGroup"

   End With

End Sub
```

Password Property (Remote Data)

Represents the password used during creation of an **rdoEnvironment** object.

Applies To

rdoEnvironment Object, **RemoteData** Control

Syntax

object.**Password**

The *object* placeholder represents an object expression that evaluates to an object in the **Applies To** list.

Remarks

The **rdoDefaultPassword** property of the **rdoEngine** object is used as a default if no password is provided. The initial default password is "".

This property setting is write-only—it may only be provided in code, it cannot be read back from the **Password** property.

The password is set:

- When the **rdoEnvironment** is created automatically by the **RemoteData** control.
- By the first reference to a **RemoteData** object.
- When the **rdoCreateEnvironment** method is executed.
- In the connect string via the **Connect** property or the **Connect** argument of the **OpenConnection** method.

See Also

rdoCreateEnvironment Method, **rdoDefaultUser**, **rdoDefaultPassword** Properties, **rdoEngine** Object, **rdoEnvironment** Object, **UserName** Property

PasswordChar Property

Returns or sets a value indicating whether the characters typed by a user or placeholder characters are displayed in a **TextBox** control; returns or sets the character used as a placeholder.

Applies To

TextBox Control

Syntax

object.**PasswordChar** [= *value*]

The **PasswordChar** property syntax has these parts:

Part	Description
object	An object expression that evaluates to an object in the **Applies To** list.
value	A string expression specifying the placeholder character.

Remarks

Use this property to create a password field in a dialog box. Although you can use any character, most Windows-based applications use the asterisk (*) (**Chr**(42)).

This property doesn't affect the **Text** property; **Text** contains exactly what the user types or what was set from code. Set **PasswordChar** to a zero-length string (""), which is the default, to display the actual text.

You can assign any string to this property, but only the first character is significant; all others are ignored.

Note If the **MultiLine** Property is set to **True**, setting the **PasswordChar** property will have no effect.

See Also

Text Property

Example

This example illustrates how the **PasswordChar** property affects the way a **TextBox** control displays text. To try this example, paste the code into the Declarations section of a form that contains a **TextBox**, and then press F5 and click the form. Each time you click the form, the text toggles between an asterisk (*) password character and plain text.

```
Private Sub Form_Click ()
   If Text1.PasswordChar = "" Then
      Text1.PasswordChar = "*"
   Else
      Text1.PasswordChar = ""
   End If
End Sub
```

Paste Method

Copies data from the system Clipboard to an **OLE** container control.

Applies To

OLE Container Control

Syntax

object.**Paste**

The *object* is an object expression that evaluates to an object in the **Applies To** list

Remarks

To use this method, set the **OLETypeAllowed** property, and then check the value of the **PasteOK** property. You can't paste successfully unless **PasteOK** returns a value of **True**.

If the **Paste** method was carried out, the **OLEType** property is set to **vbOLELinked** (0) or **vbOLEEmbedded** (1). If the **Paste** method wasn't carried out, the **OLEType** property is set to **vbOLENone** (3).

You can use this method to support an Edit Paste command on a menu.

If the **PasteOK** property setting is **True** and Visual Basic can't paste the object, the **OLE** container control deletes any object already in the control.

See Also

OLEType Property, **OLETypeAllowed** Property, **PasteOK** Property

PasteOK Property

Returns a value that determines whether the contents of the system Clipboard can be pasted into the **OLE** container control.

Applies To

OLE Container Control

Syntax

object.**PasteOK**

The *object* is an object expression that evaluates to an object in the **Applies To** list.

Remarks

When this property setting is **True**, you can paste the contents of the system Clipboard into the **OLE** container control.

Use the **OLETypeAllowed** property to specify the type of object (linked or embedded) you want to paste into the **OLE** container control. Once you successfully paste an object into the **OLE** container control, you can check the **OLEType** property setting to determine the type of object that was created.

You can use this property if your application supports a Paste command on an Edit menu. If **PasteOK** is **False**, disable the menu command; otherwise, it can be enabled. Enable and disable menu commands by setting their **Enabled** property to **True** or **False**, respectively.

You paste an object into the **OLE** container control with the **Paste** method.

To provide more flexibility to the user, display a Paste Special dialog box when the user chooses the Edit Paste command. (Set **OLETypeAllowed** = 2, and then use the **PasteSpecialDlg** method.) When this dialog box is displayed, an object is pasted onto the system Clipboard based on the user's selections in the dialog box.

See Also

OLEType Property, **OLETypeAllowed** Property, **PasteSpecialDlg** Method, **Paste** Method, **Enabled** Property

Example

This example pastes an object in the OLE container control if the **PasteOK** property setting is True. Otherwise, the example displays a message box.

```
Private Sub mnuEditPaste_Click ()
   ' Check value of PasteOK.
   If Ole1.PasteOK Then
      Ole1.Paste          ' Enable Paste command if True.
   Else          ' Otherwise, disable Paste
      mnuEditPaste.Enabled = False    ' menu command and give
      MsgBox "Can't paste."' appropriate message.
   End If
End Sub
```

PasteSpecialDlg Method

Displays the Paste Special dialog box.

Applies To

OLE Container Control

Syntax

object.**PasteSpecialDlg**

The *object* is an object expression that evaluates to an object in the **Applies To** list.

Remarks

At run time, you display this dialog box to enable the user to paste an object from the system Clipboard. This dialog box displays several options to the user, including pasting either a linked or embedded object.

Use the **OLETypeAllowed** property to determine the type of object that can be created (linked, embedded, or either) using this dialog box.

If the **PasteOK** property setting is **True** and Visual Basic can't paste the object, the **OLE** container control deletes any object already in the control.

See Also

OLETypeAllowed Property

Path Property

Returns or sets the current path. Not available at design time. For the **App** object, read-only at run time.

Applies To

App Object, **DirListBox** Control, **FileListBox** Control

Syntax

object.**Path** [= *pathname*]

The **Path** property syntax has these parts:

Part	Description
object	An object expression that evaluates to an object in the **Applies To** list.
pathname	A string expression that evaluates to the path name.

Remarks

The value of the **Path** property is a string indicating a path, such as C:\Ob or C:\Windows\System. For a **DirListBox** or **FileListBox** control, the default is the current path when the control is created at run time. For the **App** object, **Path** specifies the path of the project .VBP file when running the application from the development environment or the path of the .exe file when running the application as an executable file.

Use this property when building an application's file-browsing and manipulation capabilities. Setting the **Path** property has effects on a control similar to the MS-DOS **chdir** command—relative paths are allowed with or without a drive specification. Specifying only a drive with a colon (:) selects the current directory on that drive.

The **Path** property can also be set to a qualified network path without a drive connection using the following syntax:

*servername**sharename**path*

The preceding syntax changes the **Drive** property to a zero-length string ("").

Changing the value of **Path** has these effects:

- For a **DirListBox** control, generates a **Change** event.
- For a **FileListBox** control, generates a **PathChange** event.

Note   For **DirListBox**, the return value of **Path** is different from that of List(ListIndex), which returns only the selection.

See Also

Change Event, **PathChange** Event, **PatternChange** Event, **List** Property, **ListCount** Property, **ListIndex** Property, **Archive**, **Hidden**, **Normal**, **System** Properties, **Drive** Property, **FileName** Property, **Locked** Property, **Pattern** Property

Example

This example displays a list of files for the selected drive and directory. To try this example, paste the code into the Declarations section of a form that contains **DriveListBox**, **DirListBox**, and **FileListBox** controls. Press F5. Use the mouse to change the drive or directory.

```
Private Sub Drive1_Change ()
   Dir1.Path = Drive1.Drive' Set directory path.
End Sub

Private Sub Dir1_Change ()
   File1.Path = Dir1.Path   ' Set file path.
End Sub
```

PathChange Event

Occurs when the path is changed by setting the **FileName** or **Path** property in code.

Applies To

FileListBox Control

Syntax

Private Sub *object_**PathChange**([*index* **As Integer**])

The **PathChange** event syntax has these parts:

Part	Description
object	An object expression that evaluates to an object in the **Applies To** list.
index	An integer that uniquely identifies a control if it's in a control array.

Remarks

You can use a **PathChange** event procedure to respond to path changes in a **FileListBox** control. When you assign a string containing a new path to the **FileName** property, the **FileListBox** control invokes the **PathChange** event.

See Also

PatternChange Event, **FileName** Property, **Pattern** Property, **Path** Property

Example

This example demonstrates how to update a Label control to reflect the current path for a **FileListBox** control. Double-clicking a directory name displays a list of that directory's files in the **FileListBox**; it also displays the directory's complete path in the Label control. To try this example, paste the code into the Declarations section of a form that contains a Label control, a **DirListBox** control, and a **FileListBox** control, and then press F5. Double-click a directory to change the path.

```
Private Sub File1_PathChange ()
    Label1.Caption = "Path: " & Dir1.Path      ' Show path in Label.
End Sub

Private Sub Dir1_Change ()
    File1.Path = Dir1.Path                      ' Set file path.
End Sub

Private Sub Form_Load ()
    Label1.Caption = "Path: " & Dir1.Path      ' Show path in Label.
End Sub
```

Pattern Property

Returns or sets a value indicating the filenames displayed in a **FileListBox** control at run time.

Applies To

FileListBox Control

Syntax

object.**Pattern** [= *value*]

The **Pattern** property syntax has these parts:

Part	Description
object	An object expression that evaluates to an object in the **Applies To** list.
value	A string expression indicating a file specification, such as "*.*" or "*.FRM". The default is "*.*", which returns a list of all files. In addition to using wildcard characters, you can also use multiple patterns separated by semicolons (;). For example, "*.exe; *.bat" would return a list of all executable files and all MS-DOS batch files.

Remarks

The **Pattern** property plays a key role in designing an application's file-browsing and manipulation capabilities. Use **Pattern** in combination with other file-control properties to provide the user with ways to explore files or groups of similar files. For example, in an application dedicated to launching other programs, you could designate that only .exe files be displayed in the file list box (*.exe). Other key file-control properties include **Drive**, **FileName**, and **Path**.

Changing the value of the **Pattern** property generates a **PatternChange** event.

See Also

PathChange Event, **PatternChange** Event, **Archive**, **Hidden**, **Normal**, **System** Properties, **Drive** Property, **FileName** Property, **Path** Property

Example

This example updates a **TextBox** control with the new pattern selected in a **FileListBox** control. The controls are set up so that when the user enters a pattern in the **TextBox**, such as *.txt, it's reflected in the **FileListBox**, much like the interaction you see in a typical File Open dialog box in a Windows-based application. If a full path such as C:\Bin*.exe is entered into the **TextBox** control, the text is automatically parsed into path and pattern components by the **FileListBox** control. To try this example, paste the code into the Declarations section of a form that contains the following controls: a **DirListBox**, a **FileListBox**, a **TextBox**, and a **CommandButton**. Press F5 and type a valid file pattern into the **TextBox**.

```
Private Sub Form_Load ()
    Command1.Default = True ' Set Default property.
End Sub

Private Sub Command1_Click ()
    ' Text is parsed into path and pattern components.
    File1.Filename = Text1.Text
    Dir1.Path = File1.Path  ' Set directory path.
End Sub

Private Sub File1_PatternChange ()
    Text1.Text = File1.Pattern ' Set text to new pattern.
End Sub

Private Sub Dir1_Change
    File1.Path = Dir1.Path  ' Set file list box path.
End Sub
```

PatternChange Event

Occurs when the file listing pattern, such as "*.*", is changed by setting the **FileName** or **Pattern** property in code.

Applies To

FileListBox Control

Syntax

Private Sub *object*_**PatternChange(**[*index* **As Integer**]**)**

The **PatternChange** event syntax has these parts:

Part	Description
object	An object expression that evaluates to an object in the **Applies To** list.
index	An integer that uniquely identifies a control if it's in a control array.

Remarks

You can use a **PatternChange** event procedure to respond to pattern changes in a **FileListBox** control. When you assign a string containing a new pattern to the **FileName** property, the **FileListBox** invokes the **PathChange** event.

See Also

PathChange Event, **FileName** Property, **Pattern** Property, **Path** Property

Example

This example updates a **FileListBox** control with files matching the pattern entered in a **TextBox** control. If a full path is entered into the **TextBox**, such as C:\BIN*.EXE, the text is automatically parsed into path and pattern components. To try this example, paste the code into the Declarations section of a form that contains a **TextBox** control, a Label control, a **FileListBox** control, and a **CommandButton** control, and then press F5 and enter a valid file pattern in the **TextBox**.

```
Private Sub Form_Load ()
   Command1.Default = True          ' Set Default property.
   Command1.Caption = "OK"          ' Set Caption.
End Sub

Private Sub Command1_Click () ' OK button clicked.
   ' Text is parsed into path and pattern components.
   File1.FileName = Text1.Text
   Label1.Caption = "Path: " & File1.Path
End Sub

Private Sub File1_PatternChange ()
   Text1.Text = File1.Pattern ' Set text to new pattern.
End Sub
```

PercentPosition Property

Sets or returns a value indicating the approximate location of the current record in the **Recordset** object based on a percentage of the records in the **Recordset**.

Applies To

Recordset Object, **Snapshot-Type Recordset** Object, **Table-Type Recordset** Object, **Dynamic-Type Recordset** Object

Settings and Return Values

The setting or return value is a **Single** that is a number between 0.0 and 100.00.

Remarks

To indicate or change the approximate position of the current record in a **Recordset** object, you can check or set the **PercentPosition** property. When working with a dynaset- or snapshot-type **Recordset** object opened directly from a base table, first populate the **Recordset** object by moving to the last record before you set or check the **PercentPosition** property. If you use the **PercentPosition** property before fully populating the **Recordset** object, the amount of movement is relative to the number of records accessed as indicated by the **RecordCount** property setting. You can move to the last record by using the **MoveLast** method.

Note Using the **PercentPosition** property to move the current record to a specific record in a **Recordset** object isn't recommended—the **Bookmark** property is better suited for this task.

Once you set the **PercentPosition** property to a value, the record at the approximate position corresponding to that value becomes current, and the **PercentPosition** property is reset to a value that reflects the approximate position of the current record. For example, if your **Recordset** object contains only five records, and you set its **PercentPosition** property value to 77, the value returned from the **PercentPosition** property may be 80, not 77.

The **PercentPosition** property applies to all types of **Recordset** objects except for forward-only–type **Recordset** objects or **Recordset** objects opened from pass-through queries against remote databases.

You can use the **PercentPosition** property with a scroll bar on a form or text box to indicate the location of the current record in a **Recordset** object.

See Also

Move Method, **MoveFirst**, **MoveLast**, **MoveNext**, **MovePrevious** Methods, **Bookmark** Property, **Index** Property

Example

This example uses the **PercentPosition** property to show the position of the current record pointer relative to the beginning of the **Recordset**.

```
Sub PercentPositionX()

    Dim dbsNorthwind As Database
    Dim rstProducts As Recordset
    Dim strFind As String
    Dim strMessage As String

    Set dbsNorthwind = OpenDatabase("Northwind.mdb")
    ' PercentPosition only works with dynasets or snapshots.
    Set rstProducts = dbsNorthwind.OpenRecordset( _
        "SELECT ProductName FROM Products " & _
        "ORDER BY ProductName", dbOpenSnapshot)

    With rstProducts
        ' Populate the Recordset.
        .MoveLast
        .MoveFirst

        Do While True
            ' Show current record information and ask user
            ' for input.
            strMessage = "Product: " & !ProductName & vbCr & _
                "The record pointer is " & _
                Format(.PercentPosition, "##0.0") & _
                "% from the " & vbCr & _
                "beginning of the Recordset." & vbCr & _
                "Please enter a character search string " & _
                "for a product name."
            strFind = Trim(InputBox(strMessage))
            If strFind = "" Then Exit Do
```

```
            ' Try to find a record matching the search string.
            .FindFirst "ProductName >= '" & strFind & "'"
            If .NoMatch Then .MoveLast
        Loop

        .Close
    End With

    dbsNorthwind.Close

End Sub
```

PercentPosition Property (Remote Data)

Returns or sets a value that indicates or changes the approximate location of the current row in the **rdoResultset** object based on a percentage of the rows in the **rdoResultset**.

Applies To

rdoResultset Object

Syntax

object.**PercentPosition** [= *value*]

The **PercentPosition** property syntax has these parts:

Part	Description
object	An object expression that evaluates to an object in the **Applies To** list.
value	A number between 0.0 and 100.00. (Data type is Single)

Remarks

To indicate or change the approximate position of the current row in an **rdoResultset**, you can check or set the **PercentPosition** property. Before you set or check the **PercentPosition** property, populate the **rdoResultset** by moving to the last row. If you use the **PercentPosition** property *before* fully populating the **rdoResultset**, the amount of movement is relative to the number of rows accessed—as indicated by the **RowCount** property. You can move to the last row and populate the **rdoResultset** using the **MoveLast** method.

Note Using the **PercentPosition** property to move the current row to a specific row in an **rdoResultset** isn't recommended—the **Bookmark** property or **AbsolutePosition** property is better suited for this task.

Once you set the **PercentPosition** property to a value, the row at the approximate position corresponding to that value becomes current, and the **PercentPosition** property is reset to a value that reflects the approximate position of the current row. For example, if your **rdoResultset** contains only five rows, and you set its **PercentPosition** value to 77, the value returned from the **PercentPosition** property might be 80, not 77.

You can use the **PercentPosition** property with a scroll bar on a **Form** or **TextBox** to indicate the location of the current row in an **rdoResultset**.

The **PercentPosition** property is not supported by all cursor types and driver combinations. For example, this property applies only to keyset-type and dynamic-type **rdoResultset** objects. If the setting is not supported, the **PercentPosition** property returns 50. If the position cannot be set, no movement occurs.

See Also

AbsolutePosition Property, **Bookmark** Property, **MoveFirst**, **MoveLast**, **MoveNext**, **MovePrevious** Methods, **rdoResultset** Object

Example

This example illustrates use of the **PercentPosition** property. In this example a list of publishers is generated and when one of these is chosen, a list of associated titles is displayed in a **DBGrid** control. When the scroll bar associated with the grid is manipulated, the relative location of the selected row is determined by examining the **PercentPosition** property and displayed. See the **AbsolutePosition** property example for further details on this example.

```
Dim rs As rdoResultset

Private Sub Form_Load()
Dim Li As Integer
'
'   Fill Sections list combo box.
'
Set en = rdoEnvironments(0)
Set cn = en.OpenConnection(dsName:="", _
   Prompt:=rdDriverNoPrompt, _
   Connect:="uid=;pwd=;driver={SQL Server};" _
      & "server=BETAV486;database=pubs;")

MsRdc1.Connect = cn.Connect

Set rs = cn.OpenResultset _
   ("Select distinct Pub_Name, Pub_ID from Publishers",
   rdOpenStatic, rdConcurReadOnly)
Do Until rs.EOF
   If rs(0) = Null Then
   Else
      PubList.AddItem " " & rs!Pub_ID & ":" & rs!Pub_Name
   End If
```

```
        rs.MoveNext
Loop
PubList.ListIndex = 1
rs.Close

Publist_Click

End Sub

Private Sub MoveCRow_Change()
MoveCRow_Scroll
End Sub

Private Sub MoveCRow_Scroll()
PercentPoint = MoveCRow.Value & "%"
MsRdc1.Resultset.PercentPosition = MoveCRow.Value
End Sub

Private Sub Publist_Click()
SetSQL
If MsRdc1.Resultset.EOF Then
    MoveCRow.Enabled = False
Else
    MoveCRow.Enabled = True
    MsRdc1.Resultset.MoveFirst
End If
End Sub

Sub SetSQL()
Dim PubWanted As String
PubWanted = Trim(Left(PubList, InStr(PubList, ":") - 1))
Screen.MousePointer = vbHourglass

MsRdc1.SQL = "select * from Titles" _
    & " where Pub_ID = '" _
    & PubWanted & "'" _
    & " order by Title"
MsRdc1.Refresh
Screen.MousePointer = vbDefault
End Sub
```

Permissions Property

Sets or returns a value that establishes the permissions for the user or group identified by the **UserName** property of a **Container** or **Document** object (Microsoft Jet workspaces only).

Applies To

Container Object, **Document** Object

Settings and Return Values

The setting or return value is a **Long** constant that establishes permissions. The following tables list the valid constants for the **Permissions** property of various DAO objects. Unless otherwise noted, all constants shown in all tables are valid for **Document** objects.

The following table lists possible values for **Container** objects other than Tables and Databases containers.

Constant	Description
dbSecNoAccess	The user doesn't have access to the object (not valid for **Document** objects).
dbSecFullAccess	The user has full access to the object.
dbSecDelete	The user can delete the object.
dbSecReadSec	The user can read the object's security-related information.
dbSecWriteSec	The user can alter access permissions.
dbSecWriteOwner	The user can change the **Owner** property setting.

The following tables lists the possible settings and return values for the Tables container.

Constant	Description
dbSecCreate	The user can create new documents (not valid for **Document** objects).
dbSecReadDef	The user can read the table definition, including column and index information.
dbSecWriteDef	The user can modify or delete the table definition, including column and index information.
dbSecRetrieveData	The user can retrieve data from the **Document** object.
dbSecInsertData	The user can add records.
dbSecReplaceData	The user can modify records.
dbSecDeleteData	The user can delete records.

The following tables lists the possible settings and return values for the Databases container.

Constant	Description
dbSecDBAdmin	The user can replicate a database and change the database password (not valid for **Document** objects).
dbSecDBCreate	The user can create new databases. This option is valid only on the Databases container in the workgroup information file (Systen.mdw). This constant isn't valid for **Document** objects.
dbSecDBExclusive	The user has exclusive access to the database.
dbSecDBOpen	The user can open the database.

Remarks

Use this property to establish or determine the type of read/write permissions the user has for a **Container** or **Document** object.

A **Document** object inherits the permissions for users from its **Container** object, provided the **Inherit** property of the **Container** object is set for those users or for a group to which the users belong. By setting a **Document** object's **Permissions** and **UserName** properties later, you can further refine the access control behavior of your object.

If you want to set or return permissions for a user that includes permissions inherited from any groups to which the user belongs, use the **AllPermissions** property.

See Also

Inherited Property, **UserName** Property

Example

This example uses the **SystemDB**, **AllPermissions**, and **Permissions** properties to show how users can have different levels of permissions depending on the permissions of the group to which they belong.

```
Sub AllPermissionsX()

    ' Ensure that the Microsoft Jet workgroup information
    ' file is available.
    DBEngine.SystemDB = "system.mdw"

    Dim dbsNorthwind As Database
    Dim ctrLoop As Container

    Set dbsNorthwind = OpenDatabase("Northwind.mdb")

    ' Enumerate Containers collection and display the current
    ' user and the permissions set for that user.
    For Each ctrLoop In dbsNorthwind.Containers
        With ctrLoop
            Debug.Print "Container: " & .Name
            Debug.Print "User: " & .UserName
            Debug.Print "    Permissions: " & .Permissions
            Debug.Print "    AllPermissions: " & _
                .AllPermissions
        End With
    Next ctrLoop

    dbsNorthwind.Close

End Sub
```

Picture Object

The **Picture** object enables you to manipulate bitmaps, icons, metafiles enhanced metafiles, GIF, and JPEG images assigned to objects having a **Picture** property.

Syntax

Picture

Remarks

You frequently identify a **Picture** object using the **Picture** property of an object that displays graphics (such as a **Form** object or a **PictureBox** control). If you have a **PictureBox** control named Picture1, you can set one **Picture** object equal to another using the **Set** statement, as in the following example:

```
Dim X As Picture
Set X = LoadPicture("PARTY.BMP")
Set Picture1.Picture = X
```

You can use an array of **Picture** objects to keep a series of graphics in memory without needing a form that contains multiple **PictureBox** or **Image** controls.

You can not create a **Picture** object using code like `Dim X As New Picture`. If you want to create a **Picture** object, you must use the **StdPicture** object like this:

```
Dim X As New StdPicture
```

Properties

Handle Property, **Height, Width** Properties, **hPal** Property, **Type** Property

Methods

Render Method

See Also

LoadPicture Function, **PictureBox** Control, **Picture** Property

Picture Property

Returns or sets a graphic to be displayed in a control. For the **OLE** container control, not available at design time and read-only at run time.

Applies To

PropertyPage Object, **UserControl** Object, **UserDocument** Object, **CheckBox** Control, **CommandButton** Control, **Form** Object, **Forms** Collection, **Image** Control, **MDIForm** Object, **OptionButton** Control, **PictureBox** Control, **OLE Container** Control

Syntax

object.**Picture** [= *picture*]

The **Picture** property syntax has these parts:

Part	Description
object	An object expression that evaluates to an object in the **Applies To** list.
picture	A string expression specifying a file containing a graphic, as described in Settings.

Settings

The settings for *picture* are:

Setting	Description
(None)	(Default) No picture.
(Bitmap, icon, metafile, GIF, JPEG)	Specifies a graphic. You can load the graphic from the Properties window at design time. At run time, you can also set this property using the **LoadPicture** function on a bitmap, icon, or metafile.

Remarks

At design time, you can transfer a graphic with the Clipboard using the Copy, Cut, and Paste commands on the Edit menu. At run time, you can use Clipboard methods such as **GetData**, **SetData**, and **GetFormat** with the nontext Clipboard constants **vbCFBitmap**, **vbCFMetafile**, and **vbCFDIB**, which are listed in the Visual Basic (VB) object library in the Object Browser.

When setting the **Picture** property at design time, the graphic is saved and loaded with the form. If you create an executable file, the file contains the image. When you load a graphic at run time, the graphic isn't saved with the application. Use the **SavePicture** statement to save a graphic from a form or picture box into a file.

Note   At run time, the **Picture** property can be set to any other object's **DragIcon**, **Icon**, **Image**, or **Picture** property, or you can assign it the graphic returned by the **LoadPicture** function.

See Also

LoadPicture Function

Example

This example loads icons from the Visual Basic icon library into two of three **PictureBox** controls. When you click the form, the third **PictureBox** is used to switch the icons. You can use any two icons. Paste the code into the Declarations section of a form that has three small **PictureBox** controls (for Picture3, set Visible = False). Press F5 to run the program, and then click the form.

```
Private Sub Form_Load ()
   ' Load the icons.
   Picture1.Picture = LoadPicture("ICONS\COMPUTER\TRASH02A.ICO")
   Picture2.Picture = LoadPicture("ICONS\COMPUTER\TRASH02B.ICO")
End Sub
```

```
Private Sub Form_Click ()
   ' Switch the icons.
   Picture3.Picture = Picture1.Picture
   Picture1.Picture = Picture2.Picture
   Picture2.Picture = Picture3.Picture
   ' Clear the third picture (not necessary if not visible).

Picture3.Picture = LoadPicture()
End Sub
```

This example pastes a bitmap from the Clipboard into a PictureBox control. To find the value of Clipboard format constants (starting with vbCF), see the Visual Basic (VB) object library in the Object Browser. To try this example, paste the code into the Declarations section of a form that has a PictureBox control. Press F5, and then in another application, copy an icon onto the Clipboard, switch to Visual Basic, and click the form.

```
Private Sub Form_Click ()
   Picture1.Picture = Clipboard.GetData(vbCFDIB)
End Sub
```

PictureBox Control

A **PictureBox** control can display a graphic from a bitmap, icon, or metafile, as well as enhanced metafile, JPEG, or GIF files. It clips the graphic if the control isn't large enough to display the entire image.

Syntax

PictureBox

Remarks

You can also use a **PictureBox** control to group **OptionButton** controls and to display output from graphics methods and text written with the **Print** method.

To make a **PictureBox** control automatically resize to display an entire graphic, set its **AutoSize** property to **True**.

To create animation or simulation, you can manipulate graphics properties and methods in code. Graphics properties and events are useful for run-time print operations, such as modifying the format of a screen form for printing.

A **PictureBox** control can also act as a destination link in a DDE conversation.

The PictureBox and **Data** controls are the only standard Visual Basic controls that you can place in the internal area of an MDI form. You can use it to group controls at the top or bottom of the internal area to create a toolbar or status bar.

Properties

Align Property, **Appearance** Property, **AutoRedraw** Property, **AutoSize** Property, **BackColor, ForeColor** Properties, **Borderstyle** Property, **ClipControls** Property, **Container** Property, **CurrentX, CurrentY** Properties, **DataChanged** Property, **DataField** Property, **DataSource** Property, **DragIcon** Property, **DragMode** Property, **DrawMode** Property, **DrawStyle** Property, **DrawWidth** Property, **Enabled** Property, **FillColor** Property, **FillStyle** Property, **Font** Property, **FontBold, FontItalic, FontStrikethru, FontUnderline** Properties, **FontName** Property, **FontSize** Property, **FontTransparent** Property, **hDC** Property, **Height, Width** Properties, **HelpContextID** Property, **hWnd** Property, **Image** Property, **Index** Property, **Left, top** Properties, **LinkItem** Property, **LinkMode** Property, **LinkTimeout** Property, **LinkTopic** Property, **MouseIcon** Property, **MousePointer** Property, **Name** Property, **Negotiate** Property, **OLEDragMode** Property, **OLEDropMode** Property, **Palette** Property, **Parent** Property, **Picture** Property, **ScaleHeight, ScaleWidth** Properties, **ScaleLeft, ScaleTop** Properties, **ScaleMode** Property, **TabIndex** Property, **TabStop** Property, **Tag** Property, **ToolTipText** Property, **Visible** Property, **WhatsThisHelpID** Property

Methods

Circle Method, **Cls** Method, **Drag** Method, **Line** Method, **LinkExecute** Method, **LinkPoke** Method, **LinkRequest** Method, **LinkSend** Method, **Move** Method, **OLEDrag** Method, **PaintPicture** Method, **Point** Method, **Pset** Method, **Refresh** Method, **Scale ScaleX, ScaleY** Methods **SetFocus** Method, **ShowWhatsThis** Method, **TextHeight** Method, **TextWidth** Method, **Zorder** Method

See Also

Image Control, **MDIForm** Object, **AutoSize** Property

PID Property

Sets the personal identifier (PID) for either a group or a user account (Microsoft Jet workspaces only).

Applies To

Group Object, **User** Object

Settings

The setting is a **String** containing 4-20 alphanumeric characters. This property setting is write-only for new objects not yet appended to a collection, and is not available for existing objects.

Remarks

Set the **PID** property along with the **Name** property when you create a new **Group** object. Set the **PID** property along with the **Name** and **Password** properties when you create a new **User** object.

See Also

Name Property, **Password** Property

Example

This example uses the **CreateUser** method and **Password** and **PID** properties to create a new **User** object; it then makes the new **User** object a member of different **Group** objects and lists its properties and groups.

```
Sub CreateUserX()

    Dim wrkDefault As Workspace
    Dim usrNew As User
    Dim grpNew As Group
    Dim usrTemp As User
    Dim prpLoop As Property
    Dim grpLoop As Group

    Set wrkDefault = DBEngine.Workspaces(0)

    With wrkDefault

        ' Create and append new User.
        Set usrNew = .CreateUser("NewUser")
        usrNew.PID = "AAA123456789"
        usrNew.Password = "NewPassword"
        .Users.Append usrNew

        ' Create and append new Group.
        Set grpNew = .CreateGroup("NewGroup", _
            "AAA123456789")
        .Groups.Append grpNew

        ' Make the user "NewUser" a member of the
        ' group "NewGroup" by creating and adding the
        ' appropriate User object to the group's Users
        ' collection.
        Set usrTemp = _
            .Groups("NewGroup").CreateUser("NewUser")
        .Groups("NewGroup").Users.Append usrTemp

        Debug.Print "Properties of " & usrNew.Name

        ' Enumerate the Properties collection of NewUser. The
        ' PID property is not readable.
        For Each prpLoop In usrNew.Properties
            On Error Resume Next
            If prpLoop <> "" Then Debug.Print "    " & _
                prpLoop.Name & " = " & prpLoop
            On Error GoTo 0
        Next prpLoop

        Debug.Print "Groups collection of " & usrNew.Name
```

```
' Enumerate the Groups collection of NewUser.
For Each grpLoop In usrNew.Groups
   Debug.Print "    " & _
        grpLoop.Name
Next grpLoop

' Delete the new User and Group objects because this
' is a demonstration.
.Users.Delete "NewUser"
.Groups.Delete "NewGroup"

   End With

End Sub
```

Pmt Function

Returns a **Double** specifying the payment for an annuity based on periodic, fixed payments and a fixed interest rate.

Syntax

Pmt(*rate*, *nper*, *pv*[, *fv*[, *type*]])

The **Pmt** function has these named arguments:

Part	Description
rate	Required. **Double** specifying interest rate per period. For example, if you get a car loan at an annual percentage rate (APR) of 10 percent and make monthly payments, the rate per period is 0.1/12, or 0.0083.
nper	Required. **Integer** specifying total number of payment periods in the annuity. For example, if you make monthly payments on a four-year car loan, your loan has a total of 4 * 12 (or 48) payment periods.
pv	Required. **Double** specifying present value (or lump sum) that a series of payments to be paid in the future is worth now. For example, when you borrow money to buy a car, the loan amount is the present value to the lender of the monthly car payments you will make.
fv	Optional. **Variant** specifying future value or cash balance you want after you've made the final payment. For example, the future value of a loan is $0 because that's its value after the final payment. However, if you want to save $50,000 over 18 years for your child's education, then $50,000 is the future value. If omitted, 0 is assumed.
type	Optional. **Variant** specifying when payments are due. Use 0 if payments are due at the end of the payment period, or use 1 if payments are due at the beginning of the period. If omitted, 0 is assumed.

Remarks

An annuity is a series of fixed cash payments made over a period of time. An annuity can be a loan (such as a home mortgage) or an investment (such as a monthly savings plan).

The *rate* and *nper* arguments must be calculated using payment periods expressed in the same units. For example, if *rate* is calculated using months, *nper* must also be calculated using months.

For all arguments, cash paid out (such as deposits to savings) is represented by negative numbers; cash received (such as dividend checks) is represented by positive numbers.

See Also

DDB Function, **FV** Function, **IPmt** Function, **IRR** Function, **MIRR** Function, **NPer** Function, **NPV** Function, **PPmt** Function, **PV** Function, **Rate** Function, **SLN** Function, **SYD** Function

Example

This example uses the **Pmt** function to return the monthly payment for a loan over a fixed period. Given are the interest percentage rate per period (APR / 12), the total number of payments (TotPmts), the present value or principal of the loan (PVal), the future value of the loan (FVal), and a number that indicates whether the payment is due at the beginning or end of the payment period (PayType).

```
Dim Fmt, FVal, PVal, APR, TotPmts, PayType, Payment
Const ENDPERIOD = 0, BEGINPERIOD = 1          ' When payments are made.
Fmt = "###,###,##0.00"                        ' Define money format.
FVal = 0                                      ' Usually 0 for a loan.
PVal = InputBox("How much do you want to borrow?")
APR = InputBox("What is the annual percentage rate of your loan?")
If APR > 1 Then APR = APR / 100               ' Ensure proper form.
TotPmts = InputBox("How many monthly payments will you make?")
PayType = MsgBox("Do you make payments at the end of month?", vbYesNo)

If PayType = vbNo Then PayType = BEGINPERIOD Else PayType = ENDPERIOD
Payment = Pmt(APR / 12, TotPmts, -PVal, FVal, PayType)
MsgBox "Your payment will be " & Format(Payment, Fmt) & " per month."
```

Point Method

Returns, as a long integer, the red-green-blue (RGB) color of the specified point on a **Form** or **PictureBox**. Doesn't support named arguments.

Applies To

PropertyPage Object, **UserControl** Object, **UserDocument** Object, **Form** Object, **Forms** Collection, **PictureBox** Control

Syntax

object.**Point**(*x*, *y*)

The **Point** method syntax has these parts:

Part	Description
object	Optional. An object expression that evaluates to an object in the **Applies To** list. If *object* is omitted, the **Form** object with the focus is assumed to be *object*.
x, y	Required. Single-precision values indicating the horizontal (x-axis) and vertical (y-axis) coordinates of the point in the **ScaleMode** property of the **Form** or **PictureBox**. Parentheses must enclose the values.

Remarks

If the point referred to by the *x* and *y* coordinates is outside *object*, the **Point** method returns -1.

Example

This example uses the **Point** method to determine the color of a specific point on a form. To try this example, paste the code into the Declarations section of a form, and then press F5 and click the form.

```
Private Sub Form_Click ()
    Dim LeftColor, MidColor, Msg, RightColor   ' Declare variables.
    AutoRedraw = -1                            ' Turn on AutoRedraw.
    Height = 3 * 1440                          ' Set height to 3 inches.
    Width = 5 * 1440                           ' Set width to 5 inches.
    BackColor = QBColor(1)                     ' Set background to blue.
    ForeColor = QBColor(4)                     ' Set foreground to red.
    Line (0, 0)-(Width / 3, Height), , BF      ' Red box.
    ForeColor = QBColor(15)                    ' Set foreground to white.
    Line (Width / 3, 0)-((Width / 3) * 2, Height), , BF

    LeftColor = Point(0, 0)                       ' Find color of left box,
    MidColor = Point(Width / 2, Height / 2)   ' middle box, and
    RightColor = Point(Width, Height) ' right box.
    Msg = "The color number for the red box on the left side of "
    Msg = Msg & "the form is " & LeftColor & ". The "
    Msg = Msg & "color of the white box in the center is "
    Msg = Msg & MidColor & ". The color of the blue "
    Msg = Msg & "box on the right is " & RightColor & "."

    MsgBox Msg                                 ' Display message.
End Sub
```

PopulatePartial Method

Synchronizes any changes in a partial replica with the full replica, clears all records in the partial replica, and then repopulates the partial replica based on the current replica filters. (Microsoft Jet databases only.)

Applies To

Database Object

Syntax

database.**PopulatePartial** *dbname*

The **PopulatePartial** method syntax has the following parts.

Part	Description
database	An object variable that references the partial replica **Database** object that you want to populate.
dbname	A **string** specifying the path and name of the full replica from which to populate records.

Remarks

When you synchronize a partial replica with a full replica, it is possible to create "orphaned" records in the partial replica. For example, suppose you have a Customers table with its **ReplicaFilter** set to `"Region = 'CA'"`. If a user changes a customer's region from CA to NY in the partial replica, and then a synchronization occurs via the **Synchronize** method, the change is propagated to the full replica but the record containing NY in the partial replica is orphaned because it now doesn't meet the replica filter criteria.

To solve the problem of orphaned records, you can use the **PopulatePartial** method. The **PopulatePartial** method is similar to the **Synchronize** method, but it synchronizes any changes with the full replica, removes all records in the partial replica, and then repopulates the partial replica based on the current replica filters. Even if your replica filters have not changed, **PopulatePartial** will always clear all records in the partial replica and repopulate it based on the current filters.

Generally, you should use the **PopulatePartial** method when you create a partial replica and whenever you change your replica filters. If your application changes replica filters, you should follow these steps:

1 Synchronize your full replica with the partial replica in which the filters are being changed.

2 Use the **ReplicaFilter** and **PartialReplica** properties to make the desired changes to the replica filter.

3 Call the **PopulatePartial** method to remove all records from the partial replica and transfer all records from the full replica that meet the new replica filter criteria.

If a replica filter has changed, and the **Synchronize** method is invoked without first invoking **PopulatePartial**, a trappable error occurs.

The **PopulatePartial** method can only be invoked on a partial replica that has been opened for exclusive access. Furthermore, you can't call the **PopulatePartial** method from code running within the partial replica itself. Instead, open the partial replica exclusively from the full replica or another database, then call **PopulatePartial**.

Note   Although **PopulatePartial** performs a one-way synchronization before clearing and repopulating the partial replica, it is still a good idea to call **Synchronize** before calling **PopulatePartial**. This is because if the call to **Synchronize** fails, a trappable error occurs. You can use this error to decide whether or not to proceed with the **PopulatePartial** method (which removes all records in the partial replica). If **PopulatePartial** is called by itself and an error occurs while records are being synchronized, records in the partial replica will still be cleared, which may not be the desired result.

See Also

Synchronize Method

Example

The following example uses the **PopulatePartial** method after changing a replica filter.

```
Sub PopulatePartialX()

    Dim tdfCustomers As TableDef
    Dim strFilter As String
    Dim dbsTemp As Database

    ' Open the partial replica in exclusive mode.
    Set dbsTemp = OpenDatabase("F:\SALES\FY96CA.MDB", True)

    With dbsTemp
        Set tdfCustomers = .TableDefs("Customers")

        ' Synchronize with full replica
        ' before setting replica filter.
        .Synchronize "C:\SALES\FY96.MDB"

        strFilter = "Region = 'CA'"
        tdfCustomers.ReplicaFilter = strFilter

        ' Populate records from the full replica.
        .PopulatePartial "C:\SALES\FY96.MDB"

        .Close
    End With

End Sub
```

PopupMenu Method

Displays a pop-up menu on an **MDIForm** or **Form** object at the current mouse location or at specified coordinates. Doesn't support named arguments.

Applies To

PropertyPage Object, **UserControl** Object, **UserDocument** Object, **Form** Object, **Forms** Collection, **MDIForm** Object

Syntax

object.**PopupMenu** *menuname*, *flags*, *x*, *y*, *boldcommand*

The **PopupMenu** method syntax has these parts:

Part	Description
object	Optional. An object expression that evaluates to an object in the **Applies To** list. If *object* is omitted, the form with the focus is assumed to be *object*.
Menuname	Required. The name of the pop-up menu to be displayed. The specified menu must have at least one submenu.
Flags	Optional. A value or constant that specifies the location and behavior of a pop-up menu, as described in Settings.
X	Optional. Specifies the x-coordinate where the pop-up menu is displayed. If omitted, the mouse coordinate is used.
Y	Optional. Specifies the y-coordinate where the pop-up menu is displayed. If omitted, the mouse coordinate is used.
boldcommand	Optional. Specifies the name of a menu control in the pop-up menu to display its caption in bold text. If omitted, no controls in the pop-up menu appear in bold.

Settings

The settings for *flags* are:

Constant (location)	Value	Description
vbPopupMenuLeftAlign	0	(Default) The left side of the pop-up menu is located at *x*.
vbPopupMenuCenterAlign	4	The pop-up menu is centered at *x*.
vbPopupMenuRightAlign	8	The right side of the pop-up menu is located at *x*.

Constant (behavior)	Value	Description
vbPopupMenuLeftButton	0	(Default) An item on the pop-up menu reacts to a mouse click only when you use the left mouse button.
vbPopupMenuRightButton	2	An item on the pop-up menu reacts to a mouse click when you use either the right or the left mouse button.

Note The *flags* parameter has no effect on applications running under Microsoft Windows version 3.0 or earlier. To specify two *flags*, combine one constant from each group using the **Or** operator.

Remarks

These constants are listed in the Visual Basic (VB) object library in the Object Browser.

You specify the unit of measure for the x and y coordinates using the **ScaleMode** property. The x and y coordinates define where the pop-up is displayed relative to the specified form. If the x and y coordinates aren't included, the pop-up menu is displayed at the current location of the mouse pointer.

When you display a pop-up menu, the code following the call to the **PopupMenu** method isn't executed until the user either chooses a command from the menu (in which case the code for that command's **Click** event is executed before the code following the **PopupMenu** statement) or cancels the menu. In addition, only one pop-up menu can be displayed at a time; therefore, calls to this method are ignored if a pop-up menu is already displayed or if a pull-down menu is open.

See Also

MouseDown, MouseUp Events, **Visible** Property, **ScaleMode** Property

Example

This example displays a pop-up menu at the cursor location when the user clicks the right mouse button over a form. To try this example, create a form that includes a **Menu** control named mnuFile (mnuFile must have at least one submenu). Copy the code into the **Declarations** section of the form, and press F5.

```
Private Sub Form_MouseDown (Button As Integer, Shift As Integer,
X As Single, Y As Single)
   If Button = 2 Then
      PopupMenu mnuFile
   End If
End Sub
```

Port Property

Returns the name of the port through which a document is sent to a printer.

Applies To

Printer Object**, Printers** Collection

Syntax

*object***.Port**

The *object* placeholder represents an object expression that evaluates to an object in the **Applies To** list.

Remarks

The operating system determines the name of the port, such as LPT1: or LPT2:.

Note The effect of the properties of the **Printer** object depends on the driver supplied by the printer manufacturer. Some property settings may have no effect, or several different property settings may all have the same effect. Settings outside the accepted range may or may not produce an error. For more information, see the manufacturer's documentation for the specific driver.

See Also

Printer Object, **Printers** Collection

Example

This example examines each **Printer** object in the **Printers** collection to find one connected to a specific port and makes it the default printer.

```
Dim P As Object
For Each P In Printers
    If P.Port = "LPT2:" Or P.DeviceName Like "*LaserJet*" Then
        Set Printer = P
        Exit For
    End If
Next P
```

PPmt Function

Returns a **Double** specifying the principal payment for a given period of an annuity based on periodic, fixed payments and a fixed interest rate.

Syntax

PPmt(*rate*, *per*, *nper*, *pv*[, *fv*[, *type*]])

The **PPmt** function has these named arguments:

Part	Description
rate	Required. **Double** specifying interest rate per period. For example, if you get a car loan at an annual percentage rate (APR) of 10 percent and make monthly payments, the rate per period is 0.1/12, or 0.0083.
per	Required. **Integer** specifying payment period in the range 1 through *nper*.
nper	Required. **Integer** specifying total number of payment periods in the annuity. For example, if you make monthly payments on a four-year car loan, your loan has a total of 4 * 12 (or 48) payment periods.
pv	Required. **Double** specifying present value, or value today, of a series of future payments or receipts. For example, when you borrow money to buy a car, the loan amount is the present value to the lender of the monthly car payments you will make.

(continued)

(continued)

Part	Description
fv	Optional. **Variant** specifying future value or cash balance you want after you've made the final payment. For example, the future value of a loan is $0 because that's its value after the final payment. However, if you want to save $50,000 over 18 years for your child's education, then $50,000 is the future value. If omitted, 0 is assumed.
type	Optional. **Variant** specifying when payments are due. Use 0 if payments are due at the end of the payment period, or use 1 if payments are due at the beginning of the period. If omitted, 0 is assumed.

Remarks

An annuity is a series of fixed cash payments made over a period of time. An annuity can be a loan (such as a home mortgage) or an investment (such as a monthly savings plan).

The *rate* and *nper* arguments must be calculated using payment periods expressed in the same units. For example, if *rate* is calculated using months, *nper* must also be calculated using months.

For all arguments, cash paid out (such as deposits to savings) is represented by negative numbers; cash received (such as dividend checks) is represented by positive numbers.

See Also

DDB Function, **FV** Function, **IPmt** Function, **IRR** Function, **MIRR** Function, **NPer** Function, **NPV** Function, **Pmt** Function, **PV** Function, **Rate** Function, **SLN** Function, **SYD** Function

Example

This example uses the **PPmt** function to calculate how much of a payment for a specific period is principal when all the payments are of equal value. Given are the interest percentage rate per period (APR / 12), the payment period for which the principal portion is desired (Period), the total number of payments (TotPmts), the present value or principal of the loan (PVal), the future value of the loan (FVal), and a number that indicates whether the payment is due at the beginning or end of the payment period (PayType).

```
Dim NL, TB, Fmt, FVal, PVal, APR, TotPmts, PayType, Payment,
↵ Msg, MakeChart, Period, P, I
Const ENDPERIOD = 0, BEGINPERIOD = 1      ' When payments are made.
NL = Chr(13) & Chr(10)                    ' Define newline.
TB = Chr(9)                               ' Define tab.
Fmt = "###,###,##0.00"                    ' Define money format.
FVal = 0                                  ' Usually 0 for a loan.
PVal = InputBox("How much do you want to borrow?")
APR = InputBox("What is the annual percentage rate of your loan?")
If APR > 1 Then APR = APR / 100           ' Ensure proper form.
TotPmts = InputBox("How many monthly payments do you have to make?")
PayType = MsgBox("Do you make payments at the end of month?", vbYesNo)
```

```
If PayType = vbNo Then PayType = BEGINPERIOD Else PayType = ENDPERIOD
Payment = Abs(-Pmt(APR / 12, TotPmts, PVal, FVal, PayType))
Msg = "Your monthly payment is " & Format(Payment, Fmt) & ". "
Msg = Msg & "Would you like a breakdown of your principal and "
Msg = Msg & "interest per period?"
MakeChart = MsgBox(Msg, vbYesNo)          ' See if chart is desired.
If MakeChart <> vbNo Then
    If TotPmts > 12 Then MsgBox "Only first year will be shown."
    Msg = "Month  Payment  Principal  Interest" & NL
    For Period = 1 To TotPmts
        If Period > 12 Then Exit For      ' Show only first 12.
        P = PPmt(APR / 12, Period, TotPmts, -PVal, FVal, PayType)
        P = (Int((P + .005) * 100) / 100) ' Round principal.
        I = Payment - P
        I = (Int((I + .005) * 100) / 100) ' Round interest.
        Msg = Msg & Period & TB & Format(Payment, Fmt)
        Msg = Msg & TB & Format(P, Fmt) & TB & Format(I, Fmt) & NL
    Next Period
    MsgBox Msg                                ' Display amortization table.
End If
```

Prepare Property

Sets or returns a value that indicates whether the query should be prepared on the server as a temporary stored procedure, using the ODBC **SQLPrepare** API function, prior to execution, or just executed using the ODBC **SQLExecDirect** API function (**ODBCDirect** workspaces only).

Applies To

QueryDef Object

Settings and Return Values

The setting or return value is a **Long** value that can be one of the following constants:

Constant	Description
dbQPrepare	(Default) The statement is prepared (that is, the ODBC **SQLPrepare** API is called).
dbQUnprepare	The statement is not prepared (that is, the ODBC **SQLExecDirect** API is called).

Remarks

You can use the **Prepare** property to either have the server create a temporary stored procedure from your query and then execute it, or just have the query executed directly. By default the **Prepare** property is set to **dbQPrepare**. However, you can set this property to **dbQUnprepare** to prohibit preparing of the query. In this case, the query is executed using the **SQLExecDirect** API.

Creating a stored procedure can slow down the initial operation, but increases performance of all subsequent references to the query. However, some queries cannot be executed in the form of stored procedures. In these cases, you must set the **Prepare** property to **dbQUnprepare**.

If **Prepare** is set to **dbQPrepare**, this can be overridden when the query is executed by setting the **Execute** method's *options* argument to **dbExecDirect**.

Note The ODBC **SQLPrepare** API is called as soon as the DAO **SQL** property is set. Therefore, if you want to improve performance using the **dbQUnprepare** option, you must set the **Prepare** property before setting the **SQL** property.

Example

This example uses the **Prepare** property to specify that a query should be executed directly rather than first creating a temporary stored procedure on the server.

```
Sub PrepareX()

    Dim wrkODBC As Workspace
    Dim conPubs As Connection
    Dim qdfTemp As QueryDef
    Dim rstTemp As Recordset

    ' Create ODBCDirect Workspace object and open Connection
    ' object.
    Set wrkODBC = CreateWorkspace("", _
        "admin", "", dbUseODBC)
    Set conPubs = wrkODBC.OpenConnection("Publishers", , , _
        "ODBC;DATABASE=pubs;UID=sa;PWD=;DSN=Publishers")

    Set qdfTemp = conPubs.CreateQueryDef("")

    With qdfTemp
        ' Because you will only run this query once, specify
        ' the ODBC SQLExecDirect API function. If you do
        ' not set this property before you set the SQL
        ' property, the ODBC SQLPrepare API function will
        ' be called anyway which will nullify any
        ' performance gain.
        .Prepare = dbQUnprepare
        .SQL = "UPDATE roysched " & _
            "SET royalty = royalty * 2 " & _
            "WHERE title_id LIKE 'BU____' OR " & _
            "title_id LIKE 'PC____'"
        .Execute
    End With

    Debug.Print "Query results:"
```

```
' Open recordset containing modified records.
Set rstTemp = conPubs.OpenRecordset( _
   "SELECT * FROM roysched " & _
   "WHERE title_id LIKE 'BU____' OR " & _
   "title_id LIKE 'PC____'")

' Enumerate recordset.
With rstTemp
   Do While Not .EOF
      Debug.Print , !title_id, !lorange, _
         !hirange, !royalty
      .MoveNext
   Loop
   .Close
End With

conPubs.Close
wrkODBC.Close

End Sub
```

Prepared Property

Returns or sets a value that determines if the query should be prepared using the **SQLPrepare** or **SQLExecDirect** ODBC API function.

Applies To

rdoQuery Object

Syntax

object.**Prepared** [= *value*]

The **Prepared** property syntax has these parts:

Part	Description
object	An object expression that evaluates to an object in the **Applies To** list.
value	A **Boolean** expression as described in Settings.

Settings

The **Prepared** property has these settings:

Setting	Description
True	The statement is prepared. (Default)
False	The statement is not prepared.

Remarks

By default the **Prepared** property is **True**. However, you can set this property to **False** to prohibit "preparation" of the query. In this case, the query is executed using the **SQLExecDirect** API.

When the ODBC interface submits a query to the remote server, it either submits the query directly to the server, or creates a stored procedure to perform the operation. Creating a stored procedure can slow down the initial operation, but increases performance of all subsequent references to the query. However, some queries cannot be executed in the form of stored procedures. In these cases, you must set the **Prepare** property to **False**.

See Also

Execute Method, **rdoQuery** Object, **rdoResultset** Object

PrevInstance Property

Returns a value indicating whether a previous instance of an application is already running.

Applies To

App Object

Syntax

object.**PrevInstance**

The *object* placeholder represents an object expression that evaluates to an object in the **Applies To** list.

Remarks

You can use this property in a Load event procedure to specify whether a user is already running an instance of an application. Depending on the application, you might want only one instance running in the Microsoft Windows operating environment at a time.

Primary Property

Sets or returns a value that indicates whether an **Index** object represents a primary index for a table (Microsoft Jet workspaces only).

Applies To

Index Object

Settings and Return Values

The setting or return value is a **Boolean** that is **True** if the **Index** object represents a primary index.

The **Primary** property setting is read/write for a new **Index** object not yet appended to a collection and read-only for an existing **Index** object in an **Indexes** collection. If the **Index** object is appended to the **TableDef** object but the **TableDef** object isn't appended to the **TableDefs** collection, the **Index** property is read/write.

Remarks

A primary index consists of one or more fields that uniquely identify all records in a table in a predefined order. Because the index field must be unique, the **Unique** property of the **Index** object is set to **True**. If the primary index consists of more than one field, each field can contain duplicate values, but each combination of values from all the indexed fields must be unique. A primary index consists of a key for the table and usually contains the same fields as the primary key.

Note You don't have to create indexes for tables, but in large, unindexed tables, accessing a specific record can take a long time. The **Attributes** property of each **Field** object in the **Index** object determines the order of records and consequently determines the access techniques to use for that index. When you create a new table in your database, it's a good idea to create an index on one or more fields that uniquely identify each record, and then set the **Primary** property of the **Index** object to **True**.

When you set a primary key for a table, the primary key is automatically defined as the primary index for the table.

See Also

Attributes Property, **Clustered** Property, **Unique** Property

Example

This example uses the **Primary** property to designate a new **Index** in a new **TableDef** as the primary **Index** for that table. Note that setting the **Primary** property to **True** automatically sets **Unique** and **Required** properties to **True** as well.

```
Sub PrimaryX()

    Dim dbsNorthwind As Database
    Dim tdfNew As TableDef
    Dim idxNew As Index
    Dim idxLoop As Index
    Dim fldLoop As Field
    Dim prpLoop As Property

    Set dbsNorthwind = OpenDatabase("Northwind.mdb")

    ' Create and append a new TableDef object to the
    ' TableDefs collection of the Northwind database.
    Set tdfNew = dbsNorthwind.CreateTableDef("NewTable")
    tdfNew.Fields.Append tdfNew.CreateField("NumField", _
        dbLong, 20)
    tdfNew.Fields.Append tdfNew.CreateField("TextField", _
        dbText, 20)
    dbsNorthwind.TableDefs.Append tdfNew
```

```
With tdfNew
   ' Create and append a new Index object to the
   ' Indexes collection of the new TableDef object.
   Set idxNew = .CreateIndex("NumIndex")
   idxNew.Fields.Append idxNew.CreateField("NumField")
   idxNew.Primary = True
   .Indexes.Append idxNew
   Set idxNew = .CreateIndex("TextIndex")
   idxNew.Fields.Append idxNew.CreateField("TextField")
   .Indexes.Append idxNew

   Debug.Print .Indexes.Count & " Indexes in " & _
      .Name & " TableDef"

   ' Enumerate Indexes collection.
   For Each idxLoop In .Indexes

      With idxLoop
         Debug.Print "    " & .Name

         ' Enumerate Fields collection of each Index
         ' object.
         Debug.Print "      Fields"
         For Each fldLoop In .Fields
            Debug.Print "         " & fldLoop.Name
         Next fldLoop

         ' Enumerate Properties collection of each
         ' Index object.
         Debug.Print "      Properties"
         For Each prpLoop In .Properties
            Debug.Print "         " & prpLoop.Name & _
               " = " & IIf(prpLoop = "", "[empty]", _
               prpLoop)
         Next prpLoop
      End With

   Next idxLoop

End With

dbsNorthwind.TableDefs.Delete tdfNew.Name
dbsNorthwind.Close

End Sub
```

Print # Statement

Writes display-formatted data to a sequential file.

Syntax

Print #*filenumber*, [*outputlist*]

The **Print #** statement syntax has these parts:

Part	Description
filenumber	Required. Any valid file number.
outputlist	Optional. Expression or list of expressions to print.

Settings

The *outputlist* argument settings are:

[{**Spc**(*n*) | **Tab**[(*n*)]}] [*expression*] [*charpos*]

Setting	Description
Spc(*n*)	Used to insert space characters in the output, where *n* is the number of space characters to insert.
Tab(*n*)	Used to position the insertion point to an absolute column number, where *n* is the column number. Use **Tab** with no argument to position the insertion point at the beginning of the next print zone.
expression	Numeric expressions or string expressions to print.
charpos	Specifies the insertion point for the next character. Use a semicolon to position the insertion point immediately after the last character displayed. Use **Tab**(*n*) to position the insertion point to an absolute column number. Use **Tab** with no argument to position the insertion point at the beginning of the next print zone. If *charpos* is omitted, the next character is printed on the next line.

Remarks

Data written with **Print #** is usually read from a file with **Line Input #** or **Input**.

If you omit *outputlist* and include only a list separator after *filenumber*, a blank line is printed to the file. Multiple expressions can be separated with either a space or a semicolon. A space has the same effect as a semicolon.

For **Boolean** data, either `True` or `False` is printed. The **True** and **False** keywords are not translated, regardless of the locale.

Date data is written to the file using the standard short date format recognized by your system. When either the date or the time component is missing or zero, only the part provided gets written to the file.

Nothing is written to the file if *outputlist* data is **Empty**. However, if *outputlist* data is **Null**, **Null** is written to the file.

For **Error** data, the output appears as Error errorcode. The **Error** keyword is not translated regardless of the locale.

All data written to the file using **Print #** is internationally aware; that is, the data is properly formatted using the appropriate decimal separator.

Because **Print #** writes an image of the data to the file, you must delimit the data so it prints correctly. If you use **Tab** with no arguments to move the print position to the next print zone, **Print #** also writes the spaces between print fields to the file.

Note If, at some future time, you want to read the data from a file using the **Input #** statement, use the **Write #** statement instead of the **Print #** statement to write the data to the file. Using **Write #** ensures the integrity of each separate data field by properly delimiting it, so it can be read back in using **Input #**. Using **Write #** also ensures it can be correctly read in any locale.

See Also

Open Statement, **Spc** Function, **Tab** Function, **Write #** Statement, **Print** Method

Example

This example uses the **Print #** statement to write data to a file.

```
Open "TESTFILE" For Output As #1        ' Open file for output.
Print #1, "This is a test"              ' Print text to file.
Print #1,                               ' Print blank line to file.
Print #1, "Zone 1"; Tab ; "Zone 2"      ' Print in two print zones.
Print #1, "Hello" ; " " ; "World"       ' Separate strings with space.
Print #1, Spc(5) ; "5 leading spaces "  ' Print five leading spaces.
Print #1, Tab(10) ; "Hello"             ' Print word at column 10.

' Assign Boolean, Date, Null and Error values.
Dim MyBool, MyDate, MyNull, MyError
MyBool = False : MyDate = #February 12, 1969# : MyNull = Null
MyError = CVErr(32767)
' True, False, Null, and Error are translated using locale settings of
' your system. Date literals are written using standard short date
' format.
Print #1, MyBool ; " is a Boolean value"
Print #1, MyDate ; " is a date"
Print #1, MyNull ; " is a null value"
Print #1, MyError ; " is an error value"
Close #1                                ' Close file.
```

Print Method

Prints text in the **Immediate** pane of the **Debug** window.

Applies to

Debug Object

Syntax

object.**Print** [*outputlist*]

The **Print** method syntax has the following object qualifier and part:

Part	Description
object	Optional. An object expression that evaluates to an object in the **Applies To** list.
outputlist	Optional. Expression or list of expressions to print. If omitted, a blank line is printed.

The *outputlist* argument has the following syntax and parts:

{**Spc**(*n*) | **Tab**(*n*)} *expression charpos*

Part	Description
Spc(*n*)	Optional. Used to insert space characters in the output, where *n* is the number of space characters to insert.
Tab(*n*)	Optional. Used to position the insertion point at an absolute column number where *n* is the column number. Use **Tab** with no argument to position the insertion point at the beginning of the next print zone.
expression	Optional. Numeric expression or string expression to print.
charpos	Optional. Specifies the insertion point for the next character. Use a semicolon (;) to position the insertion point immediately following the last character displayed. Use **Tab**(*n*) to position the insertion point at an absolute column number. Use **Tab** with no argument to position the insertion point at the beginning of the next print zone. If *charpos* is omitted, the next character is printed on the next line.

Remarks

Multiple expressions can be separated with either a space or a semicolon.

All data printed to the **Immediate** window is properly formatted using the decimal separator for the locale settings specified for your system. The keywords are output in the appropriate language for the host application.

For **Boolean** data, either True or False is printed. The **True** and **False** keywords are translated according to the locale setting for the host application.

Date data is written using the standard short date format recognized by your system. When either the date or the time component is missing or zero, only the data provided is written.

Nothing is written if *outputlist* data is **Empty**. However, if *outputlist* data is **Null**, Null is output. The **Null** keyword is appropriately translated when it is output.

For error data, the output is written as Error errorcode. The **Error** keyword is appropriately translated when it is output.

The *object* is required if the method is used outside a module having a default display space. For example an error occurs if the method is called in a standard module without specifying an *object*, but if called in a form module, *outputlist* is displayed on the form.

Note Because the **Print** method typically prints with proportionally-spaced characters, there is no correlation between the number of characters printed and the number of fixed-width columns those characters occupy. For example, a wide letter, such as a "W", occupies more than one fixed-width column, and a narrow letter, such as an "i", occupies less. To allow for cases where wider than average characters are used, your tabular columns must be positioned far enough apart. Alternatively, you can print using a fixed-pitch font (such as Courier) to ensure that each character uses only one column.

See Also

Print # Statement, **Spc** Function, **Tab** Function, **Assert** Method

Example

Using the **Print** method, this example displays the value of the variable MyVar in the **Immediate** pane of the **Debug** window. Note that the **Print** method only applies to objects that can display text.

```
Dim MyVar
MyVar = "Come see me in the Immediate pane."
Debug.Print MyVar
```

Printer Object, Printers Collection

The **Printer** object enables you to communicate with a system printer (initially the default system printer).

The **Printers** collection enables you to gather information about all the available printers on the system.

Syntax

Printer
Printers(*index*)

The *index* placeholder represents an integer with a range from 0 to Printers.Count-1.

Remarks

Use graphics methods to draw text and graphics on the **Printer** object. Once the **Printer** object contains the output you want to print, you can use the **EndDoc** method to send the output directly to the default printer for the application.

You should check and possibly revise the layout of your forms if you print them. If you use the **PrintForm** method to print a form, for example, graphical images may be clipped at the bottom of the page and text carried over to the next page.

The **Printers** collection enables you to query the available printers so you can specify a default printer for your application. For example, you may want to find out which of the available printers uses a specific printer driver. The following code searches all available printers to locate the first printer with its page orientation set to portrait, then sets it as the default printer:

```
Dim X As Printer
For Each X In Printers
    If X.Orientation = vbPRORPortrait Then
        ' Set printer as system default.
        Set Printer = X
        ' Stop looking for a printer.
        Exit For
    End If
Next
```

You designate one of the printers in the **Printers** collection as the default printer by using the **Set** statement. The preceding example designates the printer identified by the object variable X, the default printer for the application.

Note If you use the **Printers** collection to specify a particular printer, as in `Printers(3)`, you can only access properties on a read-only basis. To both read and write the properties of an individual printer, you must first make that printer the default printer for the application.

Properties

ColorMode Property, **Copies** Property, **Count** Property, **CurrentX, CurrentY** Properties, **DeviceName** Property, **DrawMode** Property, **DrawStyle** Property, **DrawWidth** Property, **DriverName** Property, **Duplex** Property, **FillColor** Property, **FillStyle** Property, **Font** Property, **FontBold, FontItalic, FontStrikethru, FontUnderline** Properties, **FontCount** Property, **FontName** Property, **Fonts** Property, **FontSize** Property, **FontTransparent** Property, **hDC** Property, **Height, Width** Properties, **Orientation** Property, **Page** Property, **PaperBin** Property, **PaperSize** Property, **Port** Property, **PrintQuality** Property, **ScaleHeight, ScaleWidth** Properties, **ScaleLeft, ScaleTop** Properties, **ScaleMode** Property, **TrackDefault** Property, **TwipsPerPixelX, TwipsPerPixelY** Properties, **Zoom** Property

Methods

Circle Method, **Line** Method, **PSet** Method, **EndDoc** Method, **KillDoc** Method, **NewPage** Method, **PaintPicture** Method, **Scale** Method, **ScaleX, ScaleY** Methods, **TextHeight** Method, **TextWidth** Method

Printer Property

Returns a **Printer** object, which enables you to communicate with a system printer (initially the default system printer).

Applies To

Global Object

Syntax

Printer

Remarks

Use graphics methods to draw text and graphics on the **Printer** object. Once the **Printer** object contains the output you want to print, you can use the **EndDoc** method to send the output directly to the default printer for the application.

You should check and possibly revise the layout of your forms if you print them. If you use the **PrintForm** method to print a form, for example, graphical images may be clipped at the bottom of the page and text carried over to the next page.

See Also

Global Object, **Printer** Object, **Printers** Collection

Printers Property

Returns a **Printers** collection, which enables you to gather information about all the available printers on the system.

Applies To

Global Object

Syntax

Printers(*index*)

The *index* placeholder represents an integer with a range from 0 to `Printers.Count-1`.

Remarks

The **Printers** collection enables you to query the available printers so you can specify a default printer for your application. For example, you may want to find out which of the available printers uses a specific printer driver. The following code searches all available printers to locate the first printer with its page orientation set to portrait, then sets it as the default printer:

```
Dim X As Printer
For Each X In Printers
    If X.Orientation = vbPRORPortrait Then
        ' Set printer as system default.
```

```
        Set Printer = X
        ' Stop looking for a printer.
        Exit For
    End If
Next
```

You designate one of the printers in the **Printers** collection as the default printer by using the **Set** statement. The preceding example designates the printer identified by the object variable X, the default printer for the application.

Note If you use the **Printers** collection to specify a particular printer, as in `Printers(3)`, you can only access properties on a read-only basis. To both read and write the properties of an individual printer, you must first make that printer the default printer for the application.

See Also

Global Object, **Printer** Object, **Printers** Collection

PrintForm Method

Sends a bit-by-bit image of a **Form** object to the printer.

Applies To

UserDocument Object, **Form** Object, **Forms** Collection

Syntax

object.**PrintForm**

The *object* placeholder represents an object expression that evaluates to an object in the **Applies To** list. If *object* is omitted, the **Form** with the focus is assumed to be *object*.

Remarks

PrintForm prints all visible objects and bitmaps of the **Form** object. **PrintForm** also prints graphics added to a **Form** object or **PictureBox** control at run time if the **AutoRedraw** property is **True** when the graphics are drawn.

The printer used by **PrintForm** is determined by the operating system's Control Panel settings.

See Also

Printer Object**, Printers** Collection, **EndDoc** Method, **AutoRedraw** Property, **TrackDefault** Property

Example

This example uses the **PrintForm** method to print the current form. To try this example, paste the code into the **Declarations** section of a form. Place on the form any controls you want to see on the printed form, and then press F5 and click the form.

```
Private Sub Form_Click ()
   Dim Msg                    ' Declare variable.
   On Error GoTo ErrorHandler ' Set up error handler.
   PrintForm                  ' Print form.
   Exit Sub
ErrorHandler:
   Msg = "The form can't be printed."
   MsgBox Msg                 ' Display message.
   Resume Next
End Sub
```

PrintQuality Property

Returns or sets a value indicating the printer resolution. Not available at design time.

Applies To

Printer Object, **Printers** Collection

Syntax

object.**PrintQuality** [= *value*]

The **PrintQuality** property syntax has these parts:

Part	Description
object	An object expression that evaluates to an object in the **Applies To** list.
value	A value or constant specifying printer resolution, as described in Settings.

Settings

The settings for *value* are:

Constant	Value	Description
vbPRPQDraft	−1	Draft resolution
vbPRPQLow	−2	Low resolution
vbPRPQMedium	−3	Medium resolution
vbPRPQHigh	−4	High resolution

In addition to the predefined negative values, you can also set *value* to a positive dots per inch (dpi) value, such as 300.

Remarks

These constants are listed in the Visual Basic (VB) object library in the Object Browser.

The default value depends on the printer driver and the current settings of the printer. The effect of these settings varies among printers and printer drivers. On some printers, some or all of the settings may produce the same result.

Note The effect of the properties of the **Printer** object depends on the driver supplied by the printer manufacturer. Some property settings may have no effect, or several different property settings may all have the same effect. Settings outside the accepted range may or may not produce an error. For more information, see the manufacturer's documentation for the specific driver.

See Also

Printer Object, **Printers** Collection

Private Statement

Used at module level to declare private variables and allocate storage space.

Syntax

Private [**WithEvents**] *varname*[([*subscripts*])] [**As** [**New**] *type*] [,[**WithEvents**]
→ *varname*[([*subscripts*])] [**As** [**New**] *type*]] . . .

The **Private** statement syntax has these parts:

Part	Description
WithEvents	Optional. Keyword that specifies that *varname* is an object variable used to respond to events triggered by an **ActiveX** object. **WithEvents** is valid only in class modules. You can declare as many individual variables as you like using **WithEvents**, but you can't create arrays with **WithEvents**. You can't use **New** with **WithEvents**.
varname	Required. Name of the variable; follows standard variable naming conventions.
subscripts	Optional. Dimensions of an array variable; up to 60 multiple dimensions may be declared. The *subscripts* argument uses the following syntax:
	[*lower* **To**] *upper* [,[*lower* **To**] *upper*] . . .
	When not explicitly stated in *lower*, the lower bound of an array is controlled by the **Option Base** statement. The lower bound is zero if no **Option Base** statement is present.
New	Optional. Keyword that enables implicit creation of an object. If you use **New** when declaring the object variable, a new instance of the object is created on first reference to it, so you don't have to use the **Set** statement to assign the object reference. The **New** keyword can't be used to declare variables of any intrinsic data type, can't be used to declare instances of dependent objects, and can't be used with **WithEvents**.
type	Optional. Data type of the variable; may be **Byte**, **Boolean**, **Integer**, **Long**, **Currency**, **Single**, **Double**, **Decimal** (not currently supported), **Date**, **String** (for variable-length strings), **String** * *length* (for fixed-length strings), **Object**, **Variant**, a user-defined type, or an object type. Use a separate **As** *type* clause for each variable being defined.

Remarks

Private variables are available only to the module in which they are declared.

Use the **Private** statement to declare the data type of a variable. For example, the following statement declares a variable as an **Integer**:

```
Private NumberOfEmployees As Integer
```

You can also use a **Private** statement to declare the object type of a variable. The following statement declares a variable for a new instance of a worksheet.

```
Private X As New Worksheet
```

If the **New** keyword isn't used when declaring an object variable, the variable that refers to the object must be assigned an existing object using the **Set** statement before it can be used. Until it's assigned an object, the declared object variable has the special value **Nothing**, which indicates that it doesn't refer to any particular instance of an object.

If you don't specify a data type or object type, and there is no **Def**_type_ statement in the module, the variable is **Variant** by default.

You can also use the **Private** statement with empty parentheses to declare a dynamic array. After declaring a dynamic array, use the **ReDim** statement within a procedure to define the number of dimensions and elements in the array. If you try to redeclare a dimension for an array variable whose size was explicitly specified in a **Private**, **Public**, or **Dim** statement, an error occurs.

When variables are initialized, a numeric variable is initialized to 0, a variable-length string is initialized to a zero-length string (""), and a fixed-length string is filled with zeros. **Variant** variables are initialized to **Empty**. Each element of a user-defined type variable is initialized as if it were a separate variable.

Note When you use the **Private** statement in a procedure, you generally put the **Private** statement at the beginning of the procedure.

See Also

Array Function, **Const** Statement, **Dim** Statement, **Function** Statement, **Option Base** Statement, **Option Private** Statement, **Property Get** Statement, **Property Let** Statement, **Property Set** Statement, **Public** Statement, **ReDim** Statement, **Set** Statement, **Static** Statement, **Sub** Statement, **Type** Statemen

Example

This example shows the Private statement being used at the module level to declare variables as private; that is, they are available only to the module in which they are declared.

```
Private Number As Integer          ' Private Integer variable.
Private NameArray(1 To 5) As String  ' Private array variable.
' Multiple declarations, two Variants and one Integer, all Private.
Private MyVar, YourVar, ThisVar As Integer
```

ProcBodyLine Method

Returns the first line of a procedure.

Applies To

CodeModule Object

Syntax

object.**ProcBodyLine**(*procname*, *prockind*) **As Long**

ProcBodyLine syntax has these parts:

Part	Description
object	Required. An object expression that evaluates to an object in the **Applies To** list.
procname	Required. A **String** containing the name of the procedure.
prockind	Required. Specifies the kind of procedure to locate. Because property procedures can have multiple representations in the module, you must specify the kind of procedure you want to locate. All procedures other than property procedures (that is, **Sub** and **Function** procedures) use **vbext_pk_Proc**.

You can use one of the following constants for the *prockind* argument:

Constant	Description
vbext_pk_Get	Specifies a procedure that returns the value of a property.
vbext_pk_Let	Specifies a procedure that assigns a value to a property.
vbext_pk_Set	Specifies a procedure that sets a reference to an object.
vbext_pk_Proc	Specifies all procedures other than property procedures.

Remarks

The first line of a procedure is the line on which the **Sub**, **Function**, or **Property** statement appears.

See Also

DeleteLines Method, **Find** Method, **GetSelection** Method, **InsertLines** Method, **ProcCountLines** Method, **ProcOfLine** Method, **ProcStartLine** Method, **CodePane** Object

Example

The following example uses the **ProcBodyLine** method to return the line number of the first line of code in the specified procedure, SetupTabs, in a particular code pane.

```
Debug.Print Application.VBE.CodePanes(3).CodeModule.
➥ ProcBodyLine ("SetupTabs", vbext_pk_Proc)
```

ProcCountLines Method

Returns the number of lines in the specified procedure.

Applies To

CodeModule Object

Syntax

object.**ProcCountLines**(*procname*, *prockind*) **As Long**

ProcCountLines syntax has these parts:

Part	Description
object	Required. An object expression that evaluates to an object in the **Applies To** list.
procname	Required. A **String** containing the name of the procedure.
prockind	Required. Specifies the kind of procedure to locate. Because property procedures can have multiple representations in the module, you must specify the kind of procedure you want to locate. All procedures other than property procedures (that is, **Sub** and **Function** procedures) use **vbext_pk_Proc**.

You can use one of the following constants for the *prockind* argument:

Constant	Description
vbext_pk_Get	Specifies a procedure that returns the value of a property.
vbext_pk_Let	Specifies a procedure that assigns a value to a property.
vbext_pk_Set	Specifies a procedure that sets a reference to an object.
vbext_pk_Proc	Specifies all procedures other than property procedures.

Remarks

The **ProcCountLines** method returns the count of all blank or comment lines preceding the procedure declaration and, if the procedure is the last procedure in a code module, any blank lines following the procedure.

See Also

DeleteLines Method, **Find** Method, **GetSelection** Method, **InsertLines** Method, **ProcBodyLine** Method, **ProcOfLine** Method, **ProcStartLine** Method, **CodePane** Object

Example

The following example uses the **ProcCountLines** method to return the number of lines of code in the specified procedure, SetupTabs, in a particular code pane.

```
Debug.Print Application.VBE.CodePanes(3).CodeModule.
→ ProcCountLines ("SetupTabs", vbext_pk_Proc)
```

ProcOfLine Method

Returns the name of the procedure that the specified line is in.

Applies To

CodeModule Object

Syntax

object.**ProcOfLine**(*line*, *prockind*) **As String**

ProcOfLine syntax has these parts:

Part	Description
object	Required. An object expression that evaluates to an object in the **Applies To** list.
line	Required. A **Long** specifying the line to check.
prockind	Required. Specifies the kind of procedure to locate. Because property procedures can have multiple representations in the module, you must specify the kind of procedure you want to locate. All procedures other than property procedures (that is, **Sub** and **Function** procedures) use **vbext_pk_Proc**.

You can use one of the following constants for the *prockind* argument:

Constant	Description
vbext_pk_Get	Specifies a procedure that returns the value of a property.
vbext_pk_Let	Specifies a procedure that assigns a value to a property.
vbext_pk_Set	Specifies a procedure that sets a reference to an object.
vbext_pk_Proc	Specifies all procedures other than property procedures.

Remarks

A line is within a procedure if it's a blank line or comment line preceding the procedure declaration and, if the procedure is the last procedure in a code module, a blank line or lines following the procedure.

See Also

DeleteLines Method, **Find** Method, **GetSelection** Method, **InsertLines** Method, **ProcBodyLine** Method, **ProcCountLines** Method, **ProcStartLine** Method, **CodePane** Object

Example

The following example uses the **ProcOfLine** method to return the name of the procedure containing the specified line number in a particular code pane.

```
Debug.Print Application.VBE.CodePanes(3).CodeModule.ProcOfLine
↪ (1270, vbext_pk_Proc)
```

ProcStartLine Method

Returns the line at which the specified procedure begins.

Applies To

CodeModule Object

Syntax

object.**ProcStartLine**(*procname*, *prockind*) **As Long**

ProcStartLine syntax has these parts:

Part	Description
object	Required. An object expression that evaluates to an object in the **Applies To** list.
procname	Required. A **String** containing the name of the procedure.
prockind	Required. Specifies the kind of procedure to locate. Because property procedures can have multiple representations in the module, you must specify the kind of procedure you want to locate. All procedures other than property procedures (that is, **Sub** and **Function** procedures) use **vbext_pk_Proc**.

You can use one of the following constants for the *prockind* argument:

Constant	Description
vbext_pk_Get	Specifies a procedure that returns the value of a property.
vbext_pk_Let	Specifies a procedure that assigns a value to a property.
vbext_pk_Set	Specifies a procedure that sets a reference to an object.
vbext_pk_Proc	Specifies all procedures other than property procedures.

Remarks

A procedure starts at the first line below the **End Sub** statement of the preceding procedure. If the procedure is the first procedure, it starts at the end of the general Declarations section.

See Also

DeleteLines Method, **Find** Method, **GetSelection** Method, **InsertLines** Method, **ProcBodyLine** Method, **ProcCountLines** Method, **ProcOfLine** Method, **CodePane** Object

Example

The following example uses the **ProcStartLine** method to return the line at which the specified procedure begins in a particular code pane.

```
Debug.Print Application.VBE.CodePanes(3).CodeModule.
↳ ProcStartLine ("SetupTabs", vbext_pk_Proc)
```

ProductName Property

Returns or sets a string value containing the product name of the running application. Read-only at run time.

Applies To

App Object

Syntax

object.**ProductName**

The *object* placeholder represents an object expression that evaluates to an object in the **Applies To** list.

Remarks

You can set this property at design time in the **Type** box in the **Make** tab of the **Project Properties** dialog box.

See Also

Comments Property, **CompanyName** Property, **FileDescription** Property, **LegalCopyright** Property, **LegalTrademarks** Property

---

ProgID Property

Returns the **ProgID** (programmatic ID) for the control represented by the **VBControl** object.

Applies To

AddIn Object, **VBControl** Object

Syntax

object.**ProgID**

The *object* placeholder represents an object expression that evaluates to an object in the **Applies To** list.

Prompt Property (Remote Data)

Returns or sets a value that specifies if the ODBC driver manager should prompt for missing connect string arguments.

Applies To

RemoteData Control

Syntax

object.**Prompt** [= *value*]

The **Prompt** property syntax has these parts:

Part	Description
object	An object expression that evaluates to an object in the **Applies To** list.
value	A constant or **Integer** as described in Settings.

Settings

The settings for the **Prompt** property are:

Constant	Value	Description
rdDriverPrompt	0	The driver manager displays the ODBC Data Sources dialog box. The connection string used to establish the connection is constructed from the data source name (DSN) selected and completed by the user via the dialog boxes. Or, if no DSN is chosen and the **DataSourceName** property is empty, the default DSN is used.
rdDriverNoPrompt	1	The driver manager uses the connection string provided in *connect*. If sufficient information is not provided, the **OpenConnection** method returns a trappable error.
rdDriverComplete	2	If the connection string provided includes the DSN keyword, the driver manager uses the string as provided in *connect*, otherwise it behaves as it does when **rdDriverPrompt** is specified.
rdDriverCompleteRequired	3	(Default) Behaves like **rdDriverComplete** except the driver disables the controls for any information not required to complete the connection.

Remarks

When RDO opens a connection based on the parameters of the **RemoteData control**, the **Connect** property is expected to contain sufficient information to establish the connection. If information like the data source name, user name, or password are not provided, the ODBC driver manager exposes one or more dialog boxes to gather this information from the user. If you do not want these dialog boxes to appear, set the **Prompt** property accordingly to disable this feature.

The constants shown above are also used to set the ODBC prompt behavior for the **EstablishConnection** method.

See Also

OpenConnection Method

Properties Collection

Returns the available properties of a control or component.

Syntax

Properties

Remarks

This object or collection includes all the properties that can normally be accessed at design time.

The default value for the **Properties** collection is determined by the **Item** method.

Use the **Properties** collection to access the properties displayed in the **Properties** window. For every property listed in the **Properties** window, there is an object in the **Properties** collection.

Properties

VBE Property

Methods

Item Method

Properties Collection (DAO)

A **Properties** collection contains all the **Property** objects for a specific instance of an object.

Remarks

Every DAO object except the **Connection** and **Error** objects contains a **Properties** collection, which has certain built-in **Property** objects. These **Property** objects (which are often just called properties) uniquely characterize that instance of the object.

In addition to the built-in properties, you can also create and add your own user-defined properties. To add a user-defined property to an existing instance of an object, first define its characteristics with the **CreateProperty** method, then add it to the collection with the **Append** method. Referencing a user-defined **Property** object that has not yet been appended to a **Properties** collection will cause an error, as will appending a user-defined **Property** object to a **Properties** collection containing a **Property** object of the same name.

You can use the **Delete** method to remove user-defined properties from the **Properties** collection, but you can't remove built-in properties.

Note A user-defined **Property** object is associated only with the specific instance of an object. The property isn't defined for all instances of objects of the selected type.

You can use the **Properties** collection of an object to enumerate the object's built-in and user-defined properties. You don't need to know beforehand exactly which properties exist or what their characteristics (**Name** and **Type** properties) are to manipulate them. However, if you try to read a write-only property, such as the **Password** property of a **Workspace** object, or try to read or write a property in an inappropriate context, such as the **Value** property setting of a **Field** object in the **Fields** collection of a **TableDef** object, an error occurs.

To refer to a built-in **Property** object in a collection by its ordinal number or by its **Name** property setting, use any of the following syntax forms:

object.**Properties**(0)
object.**Properties**("*name*")
object.**Properties**![*name*]

For a built-in property, you can also use this syntax:

object.name

Note For a user-defined property, you must use the full *object*.**Properties**("*name*") syntax.

With the same syntax forms, you can also refer to the **Value** property of a **Property** object. The context of the reference will determine whether you are referring to the **Property** object itself or the **Value** property of the **Property** object.

Properties

Count Property

Methods

Append Method, **Delete** Method, **Refresh** Method

Example

This example creates a user-defined property for the current database, sets its **Type** and **Value** properties, and appends it to the **Properties** collection of the database. Then the example enumerates all properties in the database. See the properties listed in the **Property** summary topic for additional examples.

```
Sub PropertyX()

    Dim dbsNorthwind As Database
    Dim prpNew As Property
    Dim prpLoop As Property

    Set dbsNorthwind = OpenDatabase("Northwind.mdb")
```

```
    With dbsNorthwind
        ' Create and append user-defined property.
        Set prpNew = .CreateProperty()
        prpNew.Name = "UserDefined"
        prpNew.Type = dbText
        prpNew.Value = "This is a user-defined property."
        .Properties.Append prpNew

        ' Enumerate all properties of current database.
        Debug.Print "Properties of " & .Name
        For Each prpLoop In .Properties
            With prpLoop
                Debug.Print "    " & .Name
                Debug.Print "        Type: " & .Type
                Debug.Print "        Value: " & .Value
                Debug.Print "        Inherited: " & _
                    .Inherited
            End With
        Next prpLoop

        ' Delete new property because this is a
        ' demonstration.
        .Properties.Delete "UserDefined"
    End With

End Sub
```

Property Get Statement

Declares the name, arguments, and code that form the body of a **Property** procedure, which gets the value of a property.

Syntax

[**Public** | **Private** | **Friend**] [**Static**] **Property Get** *name* [(*arglist*)] [**As** *type*]
  [*statements*]
  [*name* = *expression*]
  [**Exit Property**]
  [*statements*]
  [*name* = *expression*]
End Property

The **Property Get** statement syntax has these parts:

Part	Description
Public	Optional. Indicates that the **Property Get** procedure is accessible to all other procedures in all modules. If used in a module that contains an **Option Private** statement, the procedure is not available outside the project.
Private	Optional. Indicates that the **Property Get** procedure is accessible only to other procedures in the module where it is declared.

(continued)

(continued)

Part	Description
Friend	Optional. Used only in a class module. Indicates that the **Property Get** procedure is visible throughout the project, but not visible to a controller of an instance of an object.
Static	Optional. Indicates that the **Property Get** procedure's local variables are preserved between calls. The **Static** attribute doesn't affect variables that are declared outside the **Property Get** procedure, even if they are used in the procedure.
name	Required. Name of the **Property Get** procedure; follows standard variable naming conventions, except that the name can be the same as a **Property Let** or **Property Set** procedure in the same module.
arglist	Optional. List of variables representing arguments that are passed to the **Property Get** procedure when it is called. Multiple arguments are separated by commas. The name and data type of each argument in a **Property Get** procedure must be the same as the corresponding argument in a **Property Let** procedure (if one exists).
type	Optional. Data type of the value returned by the **Property Get** procedure; may be **Byte**, **Boolean**, **Integer**, **Long**, **Currency**, **Single**, **Double**, **Decimal** (not currently supported), **Date**, **String** (except fixed length), **Object**, **Variant**, or user-defined type. Arrays of any type can't be returned, but a **Variant** containing an array can.
	The return *type* of a **Property Get** procedure must be the same data type as the last (or sometimes the only) argument in a corresponding **Property Let** procedure (if one exists) that defines the value assigned to the property on the right side of an expression.
statements	Optional. Any group of statements to be executed within the body of the **Property Get** procedure.
expression	Optional. Value of the property returned by the procedure defined by the **Property Get** statement.

The *arglist* argument has the following syntax and parts:

[**Optional**] [**ByVal** | **ByRef**] [**ParamArray**] *varname*[( )] [**As** *type*] [= *defaultvalue*]

Part	Description
Optional	Optional. Indicates that an argument is not required. If used, all subsequent arguments in *arglist* must also be optional and declared using the **Optional** keyword.
ByVal	Optional. Indicates that the argument is passed by value.
ByRef	Optional. Indicates that the argument is passed by reference. **ByRef** is the default in Visual Basic.

(continued)

Part	Description
ParamArray	Optional. Used only as the last argument in *arglist* to indicate that the final argument is an **Optional** array of **Variant** elements. The **ParamArray** keyword allows you to provide an arbitrary number of arguments. It may not be used with **ByVal**, **ByRef**, or **Optional**.
varname	Required. Name of the variable representing the argument; follows standard variable naming conventions.
type	Optional. Data type of the argument passed to the procedure; may be **Byte**, **Boolean**, **Integer**, **Long**, **Currency**, **Single**, **Double**, **Decimal** (not currently supported), **Date**, **String** (variable length only), **Object**, **Variant**. If the parameter is not **Optional**, a user-defined type or an object type may also be specified.
defaultvalue	Optional. Any constant or constant expression. Valid for **Optional** parameters only. If the type is an **Object**, an explicit default value can only be **Nothing**.

Remarks

If not explicitly specified using **Public**, **Private**, or **Friend**, **Property** procedures are public by default. If **Static** is not used, the value of local variables is not preserved between calls. The **Friend** keyword can only be used in class modules. However, **Friend** procedures can be accessed by procedures in any module of a project. A **Friend** procedure doesn't appear in the type library of its parent class, nor can a **Friend** procedure be late bound.

All executable code must be in procedures. You can't define a **Property Get** procedure inside another **Property**, **Sub**, or **Function** procedure.

The **Exit Property** statement causes an immediate exit from a **Property Get** procedure. Program execution continues with the statement following the statement that called the **Property Get** procedure. Any number of **Exit Property** statements can appear anywhere in a **Property Get** procedure.

Like a **Sub** and **Property Let** procedure, a **Property Get** procedure is a separate procedure that can take arguments, perform a series of statements, and change the values of its arguments. However, unlike a **Sub** or **Property Let** procedure, you can use a **Property Get** procedure on the right side of an expression in the same way you use a **Function** or a property name when you want to return the value of a property.

See Also

Function Statement, **Property Let** Statement, **Property Set** Statement, **Sub** Statement, **AddressOf** Operator, **Friend**

Example

This example uses the **Property Get** statement to define a property procedure that gets the value of a property. The property identifies the current color of a pen as a string.

```
Dim CurrentColor As Integer
Const BLACK = 0, RED = 1, GREEN = 2, BLUE = 3

' Returns the current color of the pen as a string.
Property Get PenColor() As String
    Select Case CurrentColor
        Case RED
            PenColor = "Red"
        Case GREEN
            PenColor = "Green"
        Case BLUE
            PenColor = "Blue"
    End Select
End Property

' The following code gets the color of the pen
' calling the Property Get procedure.
ColorName = PenColor
```

Property Let Statement

Declares the name, arguments, and code that form the body of a **Property Let** procedure, which assigns a value to a property.

Syntax

[**Public** | **Private** | **Friend**] [**Static**] **Property Let** *name* ([*arglist*,] *value*)
    [*statements*]
    [**Exit Property**]
    [*statements*]
End Property

The **Property Let** statement syntax has these parts:

Part	Description
Public	Optional. Indicates that the **Property Let** procedure is accessible to all other procedures in all modules. If used in a module that contains an **Option Private** statement, the procedure is not available outside the project.
Private	Optional. Indicates that the **Property Let** procedure is accessible only to other procedures in the module where it is declared.
Friend	Optional. Used only in a class module. Indicates that the **Property Let** procedure is visible throughout the project, but not visible to a controller of an instance of an object.

Part	Description
Static	Optional. Indicates that the **Property Let** procedure's local variables are preserved between calls. The **Static** attribute doesn't affect variables that are declared outside the **Property Let** procedure, even if they are used in the procedure.
name	Required. Name of the **Property Let** procedure; follows standard variable naming conventions, except that the name can be the same as a **Property Get** or **Property Set** procedure in the same module.
arglist	Required. List of variables representing arguments that are passed to the **Property Let** procedure when it is called. Multiple arguments are separated by commas. The name and data type of each argument in a **Property Let** procedure must be the same as the corresponding argument in a **Property Get** procedure.
value	Required. Variable to contain the value to be assigned to the property. When the procedure is called, this argument appears on the right side of the calling expression. The data type of *value* must be the same as the return type of the corresponding **Property Get** procedure.
statements	Optional. Any group of statements to be executed within the **Property Let** procedure.

The *arglist* argument has the following syntax and parts:

[**Optional**] [**ByVal** | **ByRef**] [**ParamArray**] *varname*[( )] [**As** *type*] [= *defaultvalue*]

Part	Description
Optional	Optional. Indicates that an argument is not required. If used, all subsequent arguments in *arglist* must also be optional and declared using the **Optional** keyword. Note that it is not possible for the right side of a **Property Let** expression to be **Optional**.
ByVal	Optional. Indicates that the argument is passed by value.
ByRef	Optional. Indicates that the argument is passed by reference. **ByRef** is the default in Visual Basic.
ParamArray	Optional. Used only as the last argument in *arglist* to indicate that the final argument is an **Optional** array of **Variant** elements. The **ParamArray** keyword allows you to provide an arbitrary number of arguments. It may not be used with **ByVal**, **ByRef**, or **Optional**.
varname	Required. Name of the variable representing the argument; follows standard variable naming conventions.

(continued)

(continued)

Part	Description
type	Optional. Data type of the argument passed to the procedure; may be **Byte**, **Boolean**, **Integer**, **Long**, **Currency**, **Single**, **Double**, **Decimal** (not currently supported), **Date**, **String** (variable length only), **Object**, **Variant**. If the parameter is not **Optional**, a user-defined type, or an object type may also be specified.
defaultvalue	Optional. Any constant or constant expression. Valid for **Optional** parameters only. If the type is an **Object**, an explicit default value can only be **Nothing**.

Note Every **Property Let** statement must define at least one argument for the procedure it defines. That argument (or the last argument if there is more than one) contains the actual value to be assigned to the property when the procedure defined by the **Property Let** statement is invoked. That argument is referred to as *value* in the preceding syntax.

Remarks

If not explicitly specified using **Public**, **Private**, or **Friend**, **Property** procedures are public by default. If **Static** isn't used, the value of local variables is not preserved between calls. The **Friend** keyword can only be used in class modules. However, **Friend** procedures can be accessed by procedures in any module of a project. A **Friend** procedure doesn't appear in the type library of its parent class, nor can a **Friend** procedure be late bound.

All executable code must be in procedures. You can't define a **Property Let** procedure inside another **Property**, **Sub**, or **Function** procedure.

The **Exit Property** statement causes an immediate exit from a **Property Let** procedure. Program execution continues with the statement following the statement that called the **Property Let** procedure. Any number of **Exit Property** statements can appear anywhere in a **Property Let** procedure.

Like a **Function** and **Property Get** procedure, a **Property Let** procedure is a separate procedure that can take arguments, perform a series of statements, and change the value of its arguments. However, unlike a **Function** and **Property Get** procedure, both of which return a value, you can only use a **Property Let** procedure on the left side of a property assignment expression or **Let** statement.

See Also

Function Statement, **Let** Statement, **Property Get** Statement, **Property Set** Statement, **Sub** Statement, **AddressOf** Operator, **Friend**

Example

This example uses the **Property Let** statement to define a procedure that assigns a value to a property. The property identifies the pen color for a drawing package.

```
Dim CurrentColor As Integer
Const BLACK = 0, RED = 1, GREEN = 2, BLUE = 3
```

```
' Set the pen color property for a Drawing package.
' The module-level variable CurrentColor is set to
' a numeric value that identifies the color used for drawing.
Property Let PenColor(ColorName As String)
    Select Case ColorName         ' Check color name string.
        Case "Red"
            CurrentColor = RED     ' Assign value for Red.
        Case "Green"
            CurrentColor = GREEN   ' Assign value for Green.
        Case "Blue"
            CurrentColor = BLUE    ' Assign value for Blue.
        Case Else
            CurrentColor = BLACK   ' Assign default value.
    End Select
End Property


' The following code sets the PenColor property for a drawing package
' by calling the Property let procedure.

PenColor = "Red"
```

Property Object

Represents the properties of an object that are visible in the **Properties** window for any given component.

PropertiesCollection
PropertyObject

Remarks

Use **Value** property of the **Property** object to return or set the value of a property of a component.

At a minimum, all components have a **Name** property. Use the **Value** property of the **Property** object to return or set the value of a property. The **Value** property returns a **Variant** of the appropriate type. If the value returned is an object, the **Value** property returns the **Properties** collection that contains **Property** objects representing the individual properties of the object. You can access each of the **Property** objects by using the **Item** method on the returned **Properties** collection.

If the value returned by the **Property** object is an object, you can use the **Object** property to set the **Property** object to a new object.

Properties

Collection Property, **IndexedValue** Property, **Name** Property, **NumIndices** Property, **Object** Property, **Value** Property, **VBE** Property

See Also

Item Method, **Properties** Collection

Property Object (DAO)

A **Property** object represents a built-in or user-defined characteristic of a DAO object.

Remarks

Every DAO object except the **Connection** and **Error** objects contains a **Properties** collection which has **Property** objects corresponding to built-in properties of that DAO object. The user can also define **Property** objects and append them to the **Properties** collection of some DAO objects. These **Property** objects (which are often just called properties) uniquely characterize that instance of the object.

You can create user-defined properties for the following objects:

- **Database**, **Index**, **QueryDef**, and **TableDef** objects
- **Field** objects in **Fields** collections of **QueryDef** and **TableDef** objects

To add a user-defined property, use the **CreateProperty** method to create a **Property** object with a unique **Name** property setting. Set the **Type** and **Value** properties of the new **Property** object, and then append it to the **Properties** collection of the appropriate object. The object to which you are adding the user-defined property must already be appended to a collection. Referencing a user-defined **Property** object that has not yet been appended to a **Properties** collection will cause an error, as will appending a user-defined **Property** object to a **Properties** collection containing a **Property** object of the same name.

You can delete user-defined properties from the **Properties** collection, but you can't delete built-in properties.

Note A user-defined **Property** object is associated only with the specific instance of an object. The property isn't defined for all instances of objects of the selected type.

You can use the **Properties** collection of an object to enumerate the object's built-in and user-defined properties. You don't need to know beforehand exactly which properties exist or what their characteristics (**Name** and **Type** properties) are to manipulate them. However, if you try to read a write-only property, such as the **Password** property of a **Workspace** object, or try to read or write a property in an inappropriate context, such as the **Value** property setting of a **Field** object in the **Fields** collection of a **TableDef** object, an error occurs.

The **Property** object also has four built-in properties:

- The **Name** property, a **String** that uniquely identifies the property.

- The **Type** property, an **Integer** that specifies the property data type.

- The **Value** property, a **Variant** that contains the property setting.

- The **Inherited** property, a **Boolean** that indicates whether the property is inherited from another object. For example, a **Field** object in a **Fields** collection of a **Recordset** object can inherit properties from the underlying **TableDef** or **QueryDef** object.

To refer to a built-in **Property** object in a collection by its ordinal number or by its **Name** property setting, use any of the following syntax forms:

object.**Properties**(0)
object.**Properties**("*name*")
object.**Properties**![*name*]

For a built-in property, you can also use this syntax:

object.name

Note For a user-defined property, you must use the full *object*.**Properties**("*name*") syntax.

With the same syntax forms, you can also refer to the **Value** property of a **Property** object. The context of the reference will determine whether you are referring to the **Property** object itself or the **Value** property of the **Property** object.

Properties

    Inherited Property, **Name** Property, **Type** Property, **Value** Property

See Also

    Database Object, **CreateProperty** Method

Example

    This example creates a user-defined property for the current database, sets its **Type** and **Value** properties, and appends it to the **Properties** collection of the database. Then the example enumerates all properties in the database. See the properties listed in the **Property** summary topic for additional examples.

```
Sub PropertyX()

    Dim dbsNorthwind As Database
    Dim prpNew As Property
    Dim prpLoop As Property

    Set dbsNorthwind = OpenDatabase("Northwind.mdb")
```

```
With dbsNorthwind
    ' Create and append user-defined property.
    Set prpNew = .CreateProperty()
    prpNew.Name = "UserDefined"
    prpNew.Type = dbText
    prpNew.Value = "This is a user-defined property."
    .Properties.Append prpNew

    ' Enumerate all properties of current database.
    Debug.Print "Properties of " & .Name
    For Each prpLoop In .Properties
        With prpLoop
            Debug.Print "    " & .Name
            Debug.Print "        Type: " & .Type
            Debug.Print "        Value: " & .Value
            Debug.Print "        Inherited: " & _
                .Inherited
        End With
    Next prpLoop

    ' Delete new property because this is a
    ' demonstration.
    .Properties.Delete "UserDefined"
End With

End Sub
```

Property Set Statement

Declares the name, arguments, and code that form the body of a **Property** procedure, which sets a reference to an object.

Syntax

[**Public** | **Private** | **Friend**] [**Static**] **Property Set** *name* ([*arglist*,] *reference*)
    [*statements*]
    [**Exit Property**]
    [*statements*]
End Property

The **Property Set** statement syntax has these parts:

Part	Description
Optional	Optional. Indicates that the argument may or may not be supplied by the caller.
Public	Optional. Indicates that the **Property Set** procedure is accessible to all other procedures in all modules. If used in a module that contains an **Option Private** statement, the procedure is not available outside the project.
Private	Optional. Indicates that the **Property Set** procedure is accessible only to other procedures in the module where it is declared.

(continued)

Part	Description
Friend	Optional. Used only in a class module. Indicates that the **Property Set** procedure is visible throughout the project, but not visible to a controller of an instance of an object.
Static	Optional. Indicates that the **Property Set** procedure's local variables are preserved between calls. The **Static** attribute doesn't affect variables that are declared outside the **Property Set** procedure, even if they are used in the procedure.
name	Required. Name of the **Property Set** procedure; follows standard variable naming conventions, except that the name can be the same as a **Property Get** or **Property Let** procedure in the same module.
arglist	Required. List of variables representing arguments that are passed to the **Property Set** procedure when it is called. Multiple arguments are separated by commas.
reference	Required. Variable containing the object reference used on the right side of the object reference assignment.
statements	Optional. Any group of statements to be executed within the body of the **Property** procedure.

The *arglist* argument has the following syntax and parts:

[**Optional**] [**ByVal** I **ByRef**] [**ParamArray**] *varname*[( )] [**As** *type*] [= *defaultvalue*]

Part	Description
Optional	Optional. Indicates that an argument is not required. If used, all subsequent arguments in *arglist* must also be optional and declared using the **Optional** keyword. Note that it is not possible for the right side of a **Property Set** expression to be **Optional**.
ByVal	Optional. Indicates that the argument is passed by value.
ByRef	Optional. Indicates that the argument is passed by reference. **ByRef** is the default in Visual Basic.
ParamArray	Optional. Used only as the last argument in *arglist* to indicate that the final argument is an **Optional** array of **Variant** elements. The **ParamArray** keyword allows you to provide an arbitrary number of arguments. It may not be used with **ByVal**, **ByRef**, or **Optional**.
varname	Required. Name of the variable representing the argument; follows standard variable naming conventions.

(continued)

(continued)

Part	Description
type	Optional. Data type of the argument passed to the procedure; may be **Byte**, **Boolean**, **Integer**, **Long**, **Currency**, **Single**, **Double**, **Decimal** (not currently supported), **Date**, **String** (variable length only), **Object**, **Variant**. If the parameter is not **Optional**, a user-defined type, or an object type may also be specified.
defaultvalue	Optional. Any constant or constant expression. Valid for **Optional** parameters only. If the type is an **Object**, an explicit default value can only be **Nothing**.

Note Every **Property Set** statement must define at least one argument for the procedure it defines. That argument (or the last argument if there is more than one) contains the actual object reference for the property when the procedure defined by the **Property Set** statement is invoked. It is referred to as *reference* in the preceding syntax. It can't be **Optional**.

Remarks

If not explicitly specified using **Public**, **Private**, or **Friend**, **Property** procedures are public by default. If **Static** isn't used, the value of local variables is not preserved between calls. The **Friend** keyword can only be used in class modules. However, **Friend** procedures can be accessed by procedures in any module of a project. A **Friend** procedure doesn't appear in the type library of its parent class, nor can a **Friend** procedure be late bound.

All executable code must be in procedures. You can't define a **Property Set** procedure inside another **Property**, **Sub**, or **Function** procedure.

The **Exit Property** statement causes an immediate exit from a **Property Set** procedure. Program execution continues with the statement following the statement that called the **Property Set** procedure. Any number of **Exit Property** statements can appear anywhere in a **Property Set** procedure.

Like a **Function** and **Property Get** procedure, a **Property Set** procedure is a separate procedure that can take arguments, perform a series of statements, and change the value of its arguments. However, unlike a **Function** and **Property Get** procedure, both of which return a value, you can only use a **Property Set** procedure on the left side of an object reference assignment (**Set** statement).

See Also

Function Statement, **Property Get** Statement, **Property Let** Statement, **Set** Statement, **Sub** Statement, **AddressOf** Operator, **Friend**

Example

This example uses the **Property Set** statement to define a property procedure that sets a reference to an object.

```
' The Pen property may be set to different Pen implementations.
Property Set Pen(P As Object)
    Set CurrentPen = P      ' Assign Pen to object.
End Property
```

PropertyBag Object

A **PropertyBag** object holds information that is to be saved and restored across invocations of an object.

Remarks

A **PropertyBag** object is passed into an object through the **ReadProperties** event and the **WriteProperties** event in order to save and restore the state of the object. Using the methods of the **PropertyBag** object, the object can read or write properties of itself. The **ReadProperty** method of the **PropertyBag** object is used to read a value for a property, while the **WriteProperty** method of the **PropertyBag** object is used to write a value of a property. The value of a property can itself be an object; in that case the **PropertyBag** object will attempt to save it.

See Also

ReadProperties Event, **WriteProperties** Event

Methods

ReadProperty Method, **WriteProperty** Method

PropertyChanged Method

Notifies the container that a property's value has been changed.

Applies To

UserControl Object, **UserDocument** Object

Syntax

object.**PropertyChanged** *PropertyName*

The **PropertyChanged** method syntax has these parts:

Part	Description
object	An object expression that evaluates to an object in the **Applies To** list.
PropertyName	A string expression that represents a name of the property that the control has changed the value of.

Remarks

By notifying the container that a property's value has changed, the container can synchronize its property window with the new values of the object's properties. Also, the container would not know if an instance of the object needed to be saved (through raising a **WriteProperties** event) unless the container was notified that a property's value had changed.

This method needs to be called, for example, when a user changes a property value on a property page, or the object itself changes a property value. This method should also be called when a databound property is modified; otherwise the data source will not be updated.

Properties that are available only at run time do not need to call the **PropertyChanged** method, unless they can be data-bound.

As an example, the following code shows how the **PropertyChanged** method is used:

```
Public Property Let Address(ByVal cValue As String)
   m_Address = cValue
   PropertyChanged "Address"
End Property
```

See Also

WriteProperties Event

PropertyName Property

The behavior of the **PropertyName** property depends upon the context in which it is being used.

- **AsyncRead** method—Sets the name of the property that will be associated with the **AsyncProperty** object's **Value** property.

- AsyncReadComplete event—Specifies the name of the property currently being read. This should correspond to a name assigned to the **AsyncProperty** object when invoking the **AsyncRead** method.

- **DataBinding Object**— Read-only. Returns the name of the property that the **DataBinding** object refers to.

Applies To

AsyncProperty Object

Syntax

object.**PropertyName** = *string*

Part	Description
object	An object expression that evaluates to an object in the **Applies To** list.
string	The name of a property to be saved or retrieved.

See Also

AsyncRead Method, **AsyncReadComplete** Event

Example

The example assigns a value to the **PropertyName** property in the **AsyncRead** method. The same value will be used to assign the result of the method to a **PictureBox** control. To try the example, place a **PictureBox** control on a

UserDocument object. Paste the code into the General section, and press F5 to run. Start Internet Explorer 3.0 (or later), and type the path and file name of the UserDocument.vbd file into the **Address** box.

```
Private Sub UserDocument_InitProperties()
    Dim strPath As String
    ' Set the variable to a valid path for a bitmap
    ' on your computer.
    strPath = "C:\Program Files\DevStudio\VB\" & _
        "Samples\PGuide\VCR\Bfly1.bmp"
    AsyncRead strPath, vbAsyncTypeFile, _
        PropertyName:= "butterfly"
End Sub

Private Sub UserDocument_AsyncReadComplete (AsyncProp _
    As AsyncProperty)
    ' Use the Select statement to determine which
    ' Property is being returned.
    Select Case AsyncProp.PropertyName
        Case "butterfly"
            Picture1.Picture = _
            LoadPicture(AsyncProp.Value)
    End Select
End Sub
```

PropertyPage Object

The base object used to create an ActiveX Property Page.

Remarks

Property pages provide an alternative to the Properties window for viewing properties. You can group several related properties on a page, or use a page to provide a dialog-like interface for a property that's too complex for the Properties window. A **PropertyPage** object represents one page, which is to say one tab in the **Property Pages** dialog box.

Properties

ActiveControl Property, **Appearance** Property, **AutoRedraw** Property, **BackColor**, **ForeColor** Properties, **Caption** Property, **Changed** Property, **ClipControls** Property, **Controls** Property, **Count** Property, **CurrentX, CurrentY** Properties, **DrawMode** Property, **DrawStyle** Property, **DrawWidth** Property, **FillColor** Property, **FillStyle** Property, **Font** Property, **FontBold, FontItalic, FontStrikethru, FontUnderline** Properties, **FontName** Property, **FontSize** Property, **FontTransparent** Property, **hDC** Property, **Height, Width** Properties, **HelpContextID** Property, **hWnd** Property, **Image** Property, **KeyPreview** Property, **MouseIcon** Property, **MousePointer** Property, **Name** Property, **OLEDropMode** Property, **Palette** Property, **PaletteMode** Property, **Picture** Property, **ScaleHeight, ScaleWidth** Properties, **ScaleLeft, ScaleTop** Properties, **ScaleMode** Property, **SelectedControls** Property, **StandardSize** Property, **Tag** Property

Events

Activate, Deactivate Events, ApplyChanges Event, Click Event, DblClick Event, DragDrop Event, DragOver Event, EditProperty Event, GotFocus Event, Initialize Event, KeyDown, KeyUp Events, KeyPress Event, Load Event, LostFocus Event, MouseDown, MouseUp Events, MouseMove Event, OLECompleteDrag Event, OLEDragDrop Event, OLEDragOver Event, OLEGiveFeedback Event, OLESetData Event, OLEStartDrag Event, Paint Event, SelectionChanged Event, Terminate Event, Unload Event

Methods

Circle Method, Cls Method, Line Method, OLEDrag Method, PaintPicture Method, Point Method, PopupMenu Method, Pset Method, Refresh Method, Scale Method, ScaleX, ScaleY Methods, SetFocus Method, TextHeight Method, TextWidth Method

PropertyPage Property

Returns or sets the **PropertyPage** attribute of a **Member** object.

Applies To

Member Object

Syntax

object.**PropertyPage**

The *object* placeholder represents an object expression that evaluates to an object in the **Applies To** list.

PropertyPages Property

Returns or sets a string that is the name of a property page that is associated with a control.

Applies To

UserControl Object

Syntax

object.**PropertyPages**(*index*) [= *PropPageName*]

The **PropertyPages** property syntax has these parts:

Part	Description
object	An object expression that evaluates to an object in the **Applies To** list.
index	Index into the string array.
PropPageName	A string containing the name of a property page in the project.

Remarks

PropertyPages property is a string array containing the names of the property pages in the project that are associated with this control. A property page may be added to the array by setting the last item in the array (which is always empty). A property page may be deleted from the array by setting that element in the array to an empty string.

The order of the names of property pages in the array determine the order in which pages appear in the property page's dialog box for the control.

Protection Property

Returns a value indicating the state of protection of a project. Read-only.

Applies to

VBProject Object

Return Values

The **Protection** property return values are:

Constant	Description
vbext_pp_locked	The specified project is locked.
vbext_pp_none	The specified project isn't protected.

See Also

Saved Property, **Mode** Property

Example

The following example uses the **Protection** property to return a value indicating whether or not a project is protected. The value returned is a number that corresponds to a predefined constant representing the project's status.

```
Debug.Print Application.VBE.ActiveVBProject.Protection
```

PSet Method

Sets a point on an object to a specified color.

Applies To

PropertyPage Object, **UserControl** Object, **UserDocument** Object, **Printer** Object, **Printers** Collection, **Form** Object, **Forms** Collection, **PictureBox** Control

Syntax

object.**PSet** [**Step**] (*x, y*)**,** [*color*]

The **PSet** method syntax has the following object qualifier and parts:

Part	Description
object	Optional. Object expression that evaluates to an object in the Applies To list. If *object* is omitted, the **Form** with the focus is assumed to be *object*.
Step	Optional. Keyword specifying that the coordinates are relative to the current graphics position given by the **CurrentX** and **CurrentY** properties.
(x, y)	Required. **Single** values indicating the horizontal (x-axis) and vertical (y-axis) coordinates of the point to set.
color	Optional. **Long** integer value indicating the RGB color specified for point. If omitted, the current **ForeColor** property setting is used. You can use the **RGB** function or **QBColor** function to specify the color.

Remarks

The size of the point drawn depends on the setting of the **DrawWidth** property. When **DrawWidth** is 1, **PSet** sets a single pixel to the specified color. When **DrawWidth** is greater than 1, the point is centered on the specified coordinates.

The way the point is drawn depends on the setting of the **DrawMode** and **DrawStyle** properties.

When **PSet** executes, the **CurrentX** and **CurrentY** properties are set to the point specified by the arguments.

To clear a single pixel with the **PSet** method, specify the coordinates of the pixel and use the **BackColor** property setting as the *color* argument.

This method cannot be used in an **With**…**End With** block.

Example

This example uses the **PSet** method to draw confetti on a form. To try this example, paste the code into the General section of a form. Then press F5 and click the form.

```
Sub Form_Click ()
    Dim CX, CY, Msg, XPos, YPos    ' Declare variables.
    ScaleMode = 3                  ' Set ScaleMode to
                                   ' pixels.
    DrawWidth = 5                  ' Set DrawWidth.
    ForeColor = QBColor(4)         ' Set foreground to red.
    FontSize = 24                  ' Set point size.
    CX = ScaleWidth / 2            ' Get horizontal center.
    CY = ScaleHeight / 2           ' Get vertical center.
    Cls                            ' Clear form.
    Msg = "Happy New Year!"
    CurrentX = CX - TextWidth(Msg) / 2 ' Horizontal position.
    CurrentY = CY - TextHeight(Msg)    ' Vertical position.
    Print Msg                      ' Print message.
```

```
    Do
        XPos = Rnd * ScaleWidth        ' Get horizontal position.
        YPos = Rnd * ScaleHeight       ' Get vertical position.
        PSet (XPos, YPos), QBColor(Rnd * 15)   ' Draw confetti.
        DoEvents                       ' Yield to other
    Loop                               ' processing.
End Sub
```

Public Property

Returns or sets a value determining if a control can be shared with other applications. The **Public** property is read/write at the control's authoring time, and not available at the control's run time.

Applies To

UserControl Object

Settings

The settings for **Public** are:

Setting	Description
True	The control can be shared with other applications. This is the default for ActiveX Control project types.
False	The control cannot be shared with other applications. When the control is contained in an ActiveX Control project, the control cannot be seen outside of the ActiveX Control project. This means that other controls or other forms in the project can use the control, but outside applications cannot. This is the only valid value for project types other than ActiveX Control.

Public Statement

Used at module level to declare public variables and allocate storage space.

Syntax

Public [**WithEvents**] *varname*[([*subscripts*])] [**As** [**New**] *type*] [,[**WithEvents**]
→ *varname*[([*subscripts*])] [**As** [**New**] *type*]] . . .

The **Public** statement syntax has these parts:

Part	Description
WithEvents	Optional. Keyword specifying that *varname* is an object variable used to respond to events triggered by an **ActiveX** object. **WithEvents** is valid only in class modules. You can declare as many individual variables as you like using **WithEvents**, but you can't create arrays with **WithEvents**. You can't use **New** with **WithEvents**.

(continued)

Part	Description
varname	Required. Name of the variable; follows standard variable naming conventions.
subscripts	Optional. Dimensions of an array variable; up to 60 multiple dimensions may be declared. The *subscripts* argument uses the following syntax: [*lower* **To**] *upper* [,[*lower* **To**] *upper*] **. . .** When not explicitly stated in *lower*, the lower bound of an array is controlled by the **Option Base** statement. The lower bound is zero if no **Option Base** statement is present.
New	Optional. Keyword that enables implicit creation of an object. If you use **New** when declaring the object variable, a new instance of the object is created on first reference to it, so you don't have to use the **Set** statement to assign the object reference. The **New** keyword can't be used to declare variables of any intrinsic data type, can't be used to declare instances of dependent objects, and can't be used with **WithEvents**.
type	Optional. Data type of the variable; may be **Byte**, **Boolean**, **Integer**, **Long**, **Currency**, **Single**, **Double**, **Decimal** (not currently supported), **Date**, **String**, (for variable-length strings), **String** * *length* (for fixed-length strings), **Object**, **Variant**, a user-defined type, or an object type. Use a separate **As** *type* clause for each variable being defined.

Remarks

Variables declared using the **Public** statement are available to all procedures in all modules in all applications unless **Option Private Module** is in effect; in which case, the variables are public only within the project in which they reside.

Caution The **Public** statement can't be used in a class module to declare a fixed-length string variable.

Use the **Public** statement to declare the data type of a variable. For example, the following statement declares a variable as an **Integer**:

```
Public NumberOfEmployees As Integer
```

Also use a **Public** statement to declare the object type of a variable. The following statement declares a variable for a new instance of a worksheet.

```
Public X As New Worksheet
```

If the **New** keyword is not used when declaring an object variable, the variable that refers to the object must be assigned an existing object using the **Set** statement before it can be used. Until it is assigned an object, the declared object variable has the special value **Nothing**, which indicates that it doesn't refer to any particular instance of an object.

You can also use the **Public** statement with empty parentheses to declare a dynamic array. After declaring a dynamic array, use the **ReDim** statement within a procedure to define the number of dimensions and elements in the array. If you try to redeclare a dimension for an array variable whose size was explicitly specified in a **Private**, **Public**, or **Dim** statement, an error occurs.

If you don't specify a data type or object type and there is no **Def***type* statement in the module, the variable is **Variant** by default.

When variables are initialized, a numeric variable is initialized to 0, a variable-length string is initialized to a zero-length string (""), and a fixed-length string is filled with zeros. **Variant** variables are initialized to **Empty**. Each element of a user-defined type variable is initialized as if it were a separate variable.

See Also

Array Function, **Const** Statement, **Dim** Statement, **Option Base** Statement, **Option Private** Statement, **Private** Statement, **Property Get** Statement, **Property Let** Statement, **Property Set** Statement, **ReDim** Statement, **Set** Statement, **Static** Statement, **Type** Statement

Example

This example uses the **Public** statement at the module level (General section) of a standard module to explicitly declare variables as public; that is, they are available to all procedures in all modules in all applications unless **Option Private Module** is in effect.

```
Public Number As Integer              ' Public Integer variable.
Public NameArray(1 To 5) As String    ' Public array variable.
' Multiple declarations, two Variants and one Integer, all Public.
Public MyVar, YourVar, ThisVar As Integer
```

Put Statement

Writes data from a variable to a disk file.

Syntax

Put [#]*filenumber*, [*recnumber*], *varname*

The **Put** statement syntax has these parts:

Part	Description
filenumber	Required. Any valid file number.
recnumber	Optional. **Variant** (**Long**). Record number (**Random** mode files) or byte number (**Binary** mode files) at which writing begins.
varname	Required. Name of variable containing data to be written to disk.

Remarks

Data written with **Put** is usually read from a file with **Get**.

The first record or byte in a file is at position 1, the second record or byte is at position 2, and so on. If you omit *recnumber*, the next record or byte after the last **Get** or **Put** statement or pointed to by the last **Seek** function is written. You must include delimiting commas, for example:

```
Put #4,,FileBuffer
```

For files opened in **Random** mode, the following rules apply:

- If the length of the data being written is less than the length specified in the **Len** clause of the **Open** statement, **Put** writes subsequent records on record-length boundaries. The space between the end of one record and the beginning of the next record is padded with the existing contents of the file buffer. Because the amount of padding data can't be determined with any certainty, it is generally a good idea to have the record length match the length of the data being written. If the length of the data being written is greater than the length specified in the **Len** clause of the **Open** statement, an error occurs.

- If the variable being written is a variable-length string, **Put** writes a 2-byte descriptor containing the string length and then the variable. The record length specified by the **Len** clause in the **Open** statement must be at least 2 bytes greater than the actual length of the string.

- If the variable being written is a **Variant** of a numeric type, **Put** writes 2 bytes identifying the **VarType** of the **Variant** and then writes the variable. For example, when writing a **Variant** of **VarType** 3, **Put** writes 6 bytes: 2 bytes identifying the **Variant** as **VarType** 3 (**Long**) and 4 bytes containing the **Long** data. The record length specified by the **Len** clause in the **Open** statement must be at least 2 bytes greater than the actual number of bytes required to store the variable.

Note You can use the **Put** statement to write a **Variant** array to disk, but you can't use **Put** to write a scalar **Variant** containing an array to disk. You also can't use **Put** to write objects to disk.

- If the variable being written is a **Variant** of **VarType** 8 (**String**), **Put** writes 2 bytes identifying the **VarType**, 2 bytes indicating the length of the string, and then writes the string data. The record length specified by the **Len** clause in the **Open** statement must be at least 4 bytes greater than the actual length of the string.

- If the variable being written is a dynamic array, **Put** writes a descriptor whose length equals 2 plus 8 times the number of dimensions, that is, $2 + 8 *$ *NumberOfDimensions*. The record length specified by the **Len** clause in the **Open** statement must be greater than or equal to the sum of all the bytes required to write the array data and the array descriptor. For example, the following array declaration requires 118 bytes when the array is written to disk.

```
Dim MyArray(1 To 5,1 To 10) As Integer
```

- The 118 bytes are distributed as follows: 18 bytes for the descriptor (2 + 8 * 2), and 100 bytes for the data (5 * 10 * 2).
- If the variable being written is a fixed-size array, **Put** writes only the data. No descriptor is written to disk.
- If the variable being written is any other type of variable (not a variable-length string or a **Variant**), **Put** writes only the variable data. The record length specified by the **Len** clause in the **Open** statement must be greater than or equal to the length of the data being written.
- **Put** writes elements of user-defined types as if each were written individually, except there is no padding between elements. On disk, a dynamic array in a user-defined type written with **Put** is prefixed by a descriptor whose length equals 2 plus 8 times the number of dimensions, that is, 2 + 8 * *NumberOfDimensions*. The record length specified by the **Len** clause in the **Open** statement must be greater than or equal to the sum of all the bytes required to write the individual elements, including any arrays and their descriptors.

For files opened in **Binary** mode, all of the **Random** rules apply, except:

- The **Len** clause in the **Open** statement has no effect. **Put** writes all variables to disk contiguously; that is, with no padding between records.
- For any array other than an array in a user-defined type, **Put** writes only the data. No descriptor is written.
- **Put** writes variable-length strings that are not elements of user-defined types without the 2-byte length descriptor. The number of bytes written equals the number of characters in the string. For example, the following statements write 10 bytes to file number 1:

```
VarString$ = String$(10," ")
Put #1,,VarString$
```

See Also

Type Statement, **Get** Statement, **Open** Statement, **Seek** Function, **VarType** Function

Example

This example uses the **Put** statement to write data to a file. Five records of the user-defined type Record are written to the file.

```
Type Record                        ' Define user-defined type.
   ID As Integer
   Name As String * 20
End Type

Dim MyRecord As Record, RecordNumber        ' Declare variables.
' Open file for random access.
Open "TESTFILE" For Random As #1 Len = Len(MyRecord)
For RecordNumber = 1 To 5                    ' Loop 5 times.
   MyRecord.ID = RecordNumber                ' Define ID.
   MyRecord.Name = "My Name" & RecordNumber  ' Create a string.
   Put #1, RecordNumber, MyRecord            ' Write record to file.
Next RecordNumber
Close #1                                      ' Close file.
```

PV Function

Returns a **Double** specifying the present value of an annuity based on periodic, fixed payments to be paid in the future and a fixed interest rate.

Syntax

PV(*rate*, *nper*, *pmt*[, *fv*[, *type*]])

The **PV** function has these named arguments:

Part	Description
rate	Required. **Double** specifying interest rate per period. For example, if you get a car loan at an annual percentage rate (APR) of 10 percent and make monthly payments, the rate per period is 0.1/12, or 0.0083.
nper	Required. **Integer** specifying total number of payment periods in the annuity. For example, if you make monthly payments on a four-year car loan, your loan has a total of 4 * 12 (or 48) payment periods.
pmt	Required. **Double** specifying payment to be made each period. Payments usually contain principal and interest that doesn't change over the life of the annuity.
fv	Optional. **Variant** specifying future value or cash balance you want after you've made the final payment. For example, the future value of a loan is $0 because that's its value after the final payment. However, if you want to save $50,000 over 18 years for your child's education, then $50,000 is the future value. If omitted, 0 is assumed.
type	Optional. **Variant** specifying when payments are due. Use 0 if payments are due at the end of the payment period, or use 1 if payments are due at the beginning of the period. If omitted, 0 is assumed.

Remarks

An annuity is a series of fixed cash payments made over a period of time. An annuity can be a loan (such as a home mortgage) or an investment (such as a monthly savings plan).

The *rate* and *nper* arguments must be calculated using payment periods expressed in the same units. For example, if *rate* is calculated using months, *nper* must also be calculated using months.

For all arguments, cash paid out (such as deposits to savings) is represented by negative numbers; cash received (such as dividend checks) is represented by positive numbers.

See Also

DDB Function, **FV** Function, **IPmt** Function, **IRR** Function, **MIRR** Function, **NPer** Function, **NPV** Function, **Pmt** Function, **PPmt** Function, **Rate** Function, **SLN** Function, **SYD** Function

Example

In this example, the **PV** function returns the present value of an $1,000,000 annuity that will provide $50,000 a year for the next 20 years. Provided are the expected annual percentage rate (APR), the total number of payments (TotPmts), the amount of each payment (YrIncome), the total future value of the investment (FVal), and a number that indicates whether each payment is made at the beginning or end of the payment period (PayType). Note that YrIncome is a negative number because it represents cash paid out from the annuity each year.

```
Dim Fmt, APR, TotPmts, YrIncome, FVal, PayType, PVal
Const ENDPERIOD = 0, BEGINPERIOD = 1 ' When payments are made.
Fmt = "###,##0.00"' Define money format.
APR = .0825 ' Annual percentage rate.
TotPmts = 20' Total number of payments.
YrIncome = 50000   ' Yearly income.
FVal = 1000000 ' Future value.
PayType = BEGINPERIOD' Payment at beginning of month.
PVal = PV(APR, TotPmts, -YrIncome, FVal, PayType)
MsgBox "The present value is " & Format(PVal, Fmt) & "."
```

QBColor Function

Returns a **Long** representing the RGB color code corresponding to the specified color number.

Syntax

QBColor(*color*)

The required *color* argument is a whole number in the range 0–15.

Settings

The *color* argument has these settings:

Number	Color	Number	Color
0	Black	8	Gray
1	Blue	9	Light Blue
2	Green	10	Light Green
3	Cyan	11	Light Cyan
4	Red	12	Light Red
5	Magenta	13	Light Magenta
6	Yellow	14	Light Yellow
7	White	15	Bright White

Remarks

The *color* argument represents color values used by earlier versions of Basic (such as Microsoft Visual Basic for MS-DOS and the Basic Compiler). Starting with the least-significant byte, the returned value specifies the red, green, and blue values used to set the appropriate color in the RGB system used by Visual Basic for Applications.

See Also

RGB Function

Example

This example uses the **QBColor** function to change the **BackColor** property of the form passed in as MyForm to the color indicated by ColorCode. **QBColor** accepts integer values between 0 and 15.

```
Sub ChangeBackColor (ColorCode As Integer, MyForm As Form)
   MyForm.BackColor = QBColor(ColorCode)
End Sub
```

QueryClose Event

Occurs before a **UserForm** closes.

Applies To

UserForm Object, **UserForms** Collection

Syntax

Private Sub UserForm_QueryClose(*cancel* **As Integer,** *closemode* **As Integer)**

The **QueryClose** event syntax has these parts:

Part	Description
cancel	An integer. Setting this argument to any value other than 0 stops the **QueryClose** event in all loaded user forms and prevents the **UserForm** and application from closing.
Closemode	A value or constant indicating the cause of the **QueryClose** event.

Return Values

The *closemode* argument returns the following values:

Constant	Value	Description
vbFormControlMenu	0	The user has chosen the **Close** command from the **Control** menu on the **UserForm**.
vbFormCode	1	The **Unload** statement is invoked from code.
vbAppWindows	2	The current Windows operating environment session is ending.
vbAppTaskManager	3	The Windows **Task Manager** is closing the application.

These constants are listed in the Visual Basic for Applications object library in the **Object Browser**. Note that **vbFormMDIForm** is also specified in the **Object Browser**, but is not yet supported.

Remarks

This event is typically used to make sure there are no unfinished tasks in the user forms included in an application before that application closes. For example, if a user hasn't saved new data in any **UserForm**, the application can prompt the user to save the data.

When an application closes, you can use the **QueryClose** event procedure to set the **Cancel** property to **True**, stopping the closing process.

Example

The following code forces the user to click the **UserForm's** client area to close it. If the user tries to use the **Close** box in the title bar, the Cancel parameter is set to a nonzero value, preventing termination. However, if the user has clicked the client area, `CloseMode` has the value 1 and the Unload Me is completed.

```
Private Sub UserForm_Activate()
   UserForm1.Caption = "You must Click me to kill me!"
End Sub

Private Sub UserForm_Click()
  Unload Me
End Sub

Private Sub UserForm_QueryClose(Cancel As Integer, CloseMode As Integer)
   'Prevent user from closing with the Close box in the title bar.
   If CloseMode <> 1 Then Cancel = 1
   UserForm1.Caption = "The Close box won't work! Click me!"
End Sub
```

QueryComplete Event

Occurs after the query of an **rdoResultset** returns the first result set

Applies To

rdoConnection Object

Syntax

Private Sub *object*.**QueryComplete**(*Query* as **rdoQuery**, *ErrorOccured* as **Boolean**)

The **QueryComplete** event syntax has these parts:

Part	Description
object	An object expression that evaluates to an object in the **Applies To** list.
Query	An object expression that evaluates to an **rdoQuery** object whose query has just completed.
ErrorOccured	A **Boolean** expression indicating if an error occurred while processing the query.

The settings for *ErrorOccurred* are:

Setting	Description
True	An error occurred during query processing.
False	An error did not occur during query processing.

Fired when a query has completed. You can use this event as a notification that the result set is now ready for processing.

The *ErrorOccured* parameter indicates if there was an error while the query was executing. If this flag is **True**, you should check the **rdoErrors** collection for more information.

The **QueryComplete** event fires for all queries execute on this **rdoConnection**. This includes those queries executed via the **OpenResultset** or **Execute** methods, as well as those executed from an associated **rdoQuery** object. The *Query* argument is an object reference indicating which query just finished executing. Using this argument, you can write a single event handler for all queries on the connection, but still customize the handler for specific queries. When executing queries against the **rdoConnection** object itself, RDO creates an **rdoQuery** object internally, and a reference to this internal **rdoQuery** is passed as the *Query* argument.

This event should be used instead of polling the **StillExecuting** property to test for completion of **OpenResultset** or **Execute** method queries.

See Also

QueryCompleted Event (Remote Data), **Execute** Method (Remote Data), **GetRows** Method (Remote Data), **OpenResultset** Method (Remote Data), **Requery** Method (Remote Data), **CreateQuery** Method (Remote Data), **rdoQuery** Object, **rdoResultset** Object

QueryCompleted Event (Remote Data)

Occurs after the query of an **rdoResultset** generated by a **RemoteData** Control returns the first result set.

Applies To

RemoteData Control

Syntax

Private Sub *object*.**QueryCompleted** ([*index* **As Integer**])

The **QueryCompleted** event syntax has these parts:

Part	Description
object	An object expression that evaluates to an object in the **Applies To** list.
index	Identifies the control if it's in a control array.

Remarks

When a **RemoteData control** completes the creation of an **rdoResultset**, the **QueryCompleted** event is fired. This event is not triggered if you execute the **Cancel** method which terminates processing of the query before the query has been completed.

This event fires for both asynchronous and synchronous query operations.

See Also

InfoMessage Event, **QueryComplete** Event, **Cancel** Method (Remote Data), **rdoResultset** Object, **AsyncCheckInterval** Property (Remote Data), **StillExecuting** Property (Remote Data)

Example

This example illustrates several of the Remote Data Object (RDO) event handlers. The code establishes event variables and handlers to trap connection and query events. To help illustrate use of the **BeforeConnect** event, the code concatenates a workstation ID value and the current time to the end of the connect string. This permits identification of the specific connection at the server. After establishing the connection, the code executes a query that takes an fairly long time to execute—the query is designed to run for about a minute. Because a five second **QueryTimeout** value is set, the **QueryTimeout** event should fire unless the query returns before 5 seconds has elapsed. Notice that the query itself is run asynchronously and the code does not poll for completion of the query. In this case the code simply waits for the **QueryComplete** or **QueryTimeout** events to fire—indicating that the query is finished. The code also permits you to request another five seconds of waiting time.

```
Option Explicit
Private WithEvents cn As rdoConnection
Private WithEvents EngEv As rdoEngine
Dim er As rdoError
Dim strConnect As String
Dim rs As rdoResultset
Dim TimeStart As Single
Dim clock As Integer

Private Sub EngEv_InfoMessage()
   InfoMsg = "For your information..." _
   & " the following message" _
      & " was returned by the server." & vbCrLf
   For Each er In rdoErrors
      InfoMsg = InfoMsg & er.Number _
   & " - " & er.Description & vbCrLf
   Next

End Sub
Private Sub cn_BeforeConnect( _
   ConnectString As String, Prompt As Variant)
   InfoMsg = "About to connect to:" & ConnectString _
   & " - " & Prompt
   ConnectString = ConnectString & ";WSID=" _
   & "EventTest" & Time$ & ";"
End Sub
```

```
Private Sub cn_Connect()    'Fires once connected.
  Connected = True
End Sub

Private Sub cn_Disconnect()'Fires when disconnected
  Connected = False
End Sub

Private Sub cn_QueryComplete( _
    ByVal ErrorOccured As Boolean)
    Timer1.Enabled = False
    QueryComplete = vbChecked
    RunButton.Enabled = True
    Beep

    MsgBox "Query Done"
End Sub

Private Sub cn_QueryTimeout(Cancel As Boolean)
    ans = MsgBox("The query did not complete "
    & "in the time allocated. " _
    & "Press Cancel to abandon the query " _
    & "or Retry to keep working.", _
        vbRetryCancel + vbQuestion, "Query Timed Out")
    If ans = vbRetry Then
        Cancel = False
        QueryComplete = vbGrayed
    Else
        Timer1.Enabled = False
        QueryComplete = vbChecked
    End If
End Sub

Private Sub MenufileExit_Click()
cn.Close
Unload Form1
End Sub

Private Sub RunButton_Click()
    RunButton.Enabled = False
    On Error GoTo C1EH
    QueryComplete = vbGrayed
    Timer1.Enabled = True
    Set rs = cn.OpenResultset( _
        "execute VeryLongProcedure", _
        rdOpenKeyset, rdConcurValues, rdAsyncEnable)
    TimeStart = Timer
QuitRun:
Exit Sub
```

```
C1EH:
    Debug.Print Err, Error
        InfoMsg = "Error:.. the following error" _
        & " was returned by the server." & vbCrLf
    For Each er In rdoErrors
        InfoMsg = InfoMsg & er.Number _
        & " - " & er.Description & vbCrLf
    Next
    MsgBox "Query Failed to run"
    Timer1.Enabled = False
    Resume QuitRun

End Sub

Private Sub Form_Load()
On Error GoTo FLeh
Set EngEv = rdoEngine
Set cn = New rdoConnection
Show
    With cn
        .Connect = "UID=;PWD=;database=Workdb;" _
            & "Server=SEQUEL;" _
            & "driver={SQL Server};DSN='';"
        .QueryTimeout = 5
        .CursorDriver = rdUseClientBatch
        .EstablishConnection rdDriverNoPrompt
    End With
Exit Sub

FLeh:
    Debug.Print Err, Error
    For Each er In rdoErrors
        Debug.Print er.Description
    Next
    Stop
    Resume

End Sub

Private Sub Timer1_Timer()
Static ot As Integer
' Display number of seconds
ShowClock = Int(Timer - TimeStart)
If ShowClock = ot Then ShowClock.Refresh
End Sub
```

QueryDef Object

A **QueryDef** object is a stored definition of a query in a Microsoft Jet database, or a temporary definition of a query in an ODBCDirect workspace.

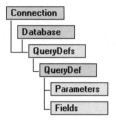

Remarks

You can use the **QueryDef** object to define a query. For example, you can:

- Use the **SQL** property to set or return the query definition.

- Use the **QueryDef** object's **Parameters** collection to set or return query parameters.

- Use the **Type** property to return a value indicating whether the query selects records from an existing table, makes a new table, inserts records from one table into another table, deletes records, or updates records.

- Use the **MaxRecords** property to limit the number of records returned from a query.

- Use the **ODBCTimeout** property to indicate how long to wait before the query returns records. The **ODBCTimeout** property applies to any query that accesses ODBC data.

In a Microsoft Jet workspace, you can also:

- Use the **ReturnsRecords** property to indicate that the query returns records. The **ReturnsRecords** property is only valid on SQL pass-through queries.

- Use the **Connect** property to make an SQL pass-through query to an ODC database.

In an ODBCDirect workspace, you can also:

- Use the **Prepare** property to determine whether to invoke the ODBC **SQLPrepare** API when the query is executed.

- Use the **CacheSize** property to cache records returned from a query.

You can also create temporary **QueryDef** objects. Unlike permanent **QueryDef** objects, temporary **QueryDef** objects are not saved to disk or appended to the **QueryDefs** collection. Temporary **QueryDef** objects are useful for queries that you must run repeatedly during run time but do not not need to save to disk, particularly if you create their SQL statements during run time.

You can think of a permanent **QueryDef** object in a Microsoft Jet workspaces as a compiled SQL statement. If you execute a query from a permanent **QueryDef** object, the query will run faster than if you run the equivalent SQL statement from the **OpenRecordset** method. This is because the Microsoft Jet database engine doesn't need to compile the query before executing it.

The preferred way to use the native SQL dialect of an external database engine accessed through the Microsoft Jet database engine is through **QueryDef** objects. For example, you can create a Microsoft SQL Server query and store it in a **QueryDef** object. When you need to use a non-Microsoft Jet database engine SQL query, you must provide a **Connect** property string that points to the external data source. Queries with valid **Connect** properties bypass the Microsoft Jet database engine and pass the query directly to the external database server for processing.

To create a new **QueryDef** object, use the **CreateQueryDef** method. In a Microsoft Jet workspace, if you supply a string for the *name* argument or if you explicitly set the **Name** property of the new **QueryDef** object to a non–zero-length string, you will create a permanent **QueryDef** that will automatically be appended to the **QueryDefs** collection and saved to disk. Supplying a zero-length string as the *name* argument or explicitly setting the **Name** property to a zero-length string will result in a temporary **QueryDef** object.

In an ODBCDirect workspace, a **QueryDef** is always temporary. The **QueryDefs** collection contains all open **QueryDef** objects. When a **QueryDef** is closed, it is automatically removed from the **QueryDefs** collection.

To refer to a **QueryDef** object in a collection by its ordinal number or by its **Name** property setting, use any of the following syntax forms:

QueryDefs(0)
QueryDefs("*name*")
QueryDefs![*name*]

You can refer to temporary **QueryDef** objects only by the object variables that you have assigned to them.

Properties

CacheSize Property, **Connect** Property, **DateCreated, LastUpdated** Properties, **LogMessages** Property, **Name** Property, **ODBCTimeout** Property, **RecordsAffected** Property, **ReturnsRecords** Property, **SQL** Property, **Type** Property, **Updatable** Property, **KeepLocal** Property, **Replicable** Property, **MaxRecords** Property, **Prepare** Property, **StillExecuting** Property

Methods

Close Method, **CreateProperty** Method, **Execute** Method, **OpenRecordset** Method, **Cancel** Method

QueryDef Object

See Also

Parameter Object, **Parameters Collection** Summary, **Property** Object, **Properties Collection** Summary, **CreateQueryDef** Method

Example

This example creates a new **QueryDef** object and appends it to the **QueryDefs** collection of the Northwind **Database** object. It then enumerates the **QueryDefs** collection and the **Properties** collection of the new **QueryDef**.

```
Sub QueryDefX()

    Dim dbsNorthwind As Database
    Dim qdfNew As QueryDef
    Dim qdfLoop As QueryDef
    Dim prpLoop As Property

    Set dbsNorthwind = OpenDatabase("Northwind.mdb")

    ' Create new QueryDef object. Because it has a
    ' name, it is automatically appended to the
    ' QueryDefs collection.
    Set qdfNew = dbsNorthwind.CreateQueryDef("NewQueryDef", _
        "SELECT * FROM Categories")

    With dbsNorthwind
        Debug.Print .QueryDefs.Count & _
            " QueryDefs in " & .Name

        ' Enumerate QueryDefs collection.
        For Each qdfLoop In .QueryDefs
            Debug.Print "    " & qdfLoop.Name
        Next qdfLoop

        With qdfNew
            Debug.Print "Properties of " & .Name

            ' Enumerate Properties collection of new
            ' QueryDef object.
            For Each prpLoop In .Properties
                On Error Resume Next
                Debug.Print "    " & prpLoop.Name & " - " & _
                    IIf(prpLoop = "", "[empty]", prpLoop)
                On Error Goto 0
            Next prpLoop
        End With

        ' Delete new QueryDef because this is a
        ' demonstration.
        .QueryDefs.Delete qdfNew.Name
        .Close
    End With

End Sub
```

QueryDefs Collection

A **QueryDefs** collection contains all **QueryDef** objects of a **Database** object in a Microsoft Jet database, and all **QueryDef** objects of a **Connection** object in an ODBCDirect workspace.

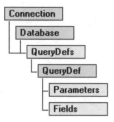

Remarks

To create a new **QueryDef** object, use the **CreateQueryDef** method. In a Microsoft Jet workspace, if you supply a string for the *name* argument or if you explicitly set the **Name** property of the new **QueryDef** object to a non–zero-length string, you will create a permanent **QueryDef** that will automatically be appended to the **QueryDefs** collection and saved to disk. Supplying a zero-length string as the *name* argument or explicitly setting the **Name** property to a zero-length string will result in a temporary **QueryDef** object.

In an ODBCDirect workspace, a **QueryDef** is always temporary. The **QueryDefs** collection contains all open **QueryDef** objects. When a **QueryDef** is closed, it is automatically removed from the **QueryDefs** collection.

To refer to a **QueryDef** object in a collection by its ordinal number or by its **Name** property setting, use any of the following syntax forms:

QueryDefs(0)
QueryDefs("*name*")
QueryDefs![*name*]

You can refer to temporary **QueryDef** objects only by the object variables that you have assigned to them.

Properties

Count Property

Methods

Append Method, **Delete** Method, **Refresh** Method

Example

This example creates a new **QueryDef** object and appends it to the **QueryDefs** collection of the Northwind **Database** object. It then enumerates the **QueryDefs** collection and the **Properties** collection of the new **QueryDef**.

```
Sub QueryDefX()

    Dim dbsNorthwind As Database
    Dim qdfNew As QueryDef
    Dim qdfLoop As QueryDef
    Dim prpLoop As Property

    Set dbsNorthwind = OpenDatabase("Northwind.mdb")

    ' Create new QueryDef object. Because it has a
    ' name, it is automatically appended to the
    ' QueryDefs collection.
    Set qdfNew = dbsNorthwind.CreateQueryDef("NewQueryDef", _
        "SELECT * FROM Categories")

    With dbsNorthwind
        Debug.Print .QueryDefs.Count & _
            " QueryDefs in " & .Name

        ' Enumerate QueryDefs collection.
        For Each qdfLoop In .QueryDefs
            Debug.Print "    " & qdfLoop.Name
        Next qdfLoop

        With qdfNew
            Debug.Print "Properties of " & .Name

            ' Enumerate Properties collection of new
            ' QueryDef object.
            For Each prpLoop In .Properties
                On Error Resume Next
                Debug.Print "    " & prpLoop.Name & " - " & _
                    IIf(prpLoop = "", "[empty]", prpLoop)
                On Error Goto 0
            Next prpLoop
        End With

        ' Delete new QueryDef because this is a
        ' demonstration.
        .QueryDefs.Delete qdfNew.Name
        .Close
    End With

End Sub
```

QueryTimeout Event

Occurs when the query execution time has exceeded the value set in the **QueryTimeout** property.

Applies To

rdoConnection Object

Syntax

Private Sub *object*.**QueryTimeout**(*Query* as **rdoQuery**, *Cancel* as **Boolean**)

The **BeforeConnect** event syntax has these parts:

Part	Description
object	An object expression that evaluates to an object in the **Applies To** list.
Query	An object expression that evaluates to an **rdoQuery** object whose query has just completed.
Cancel	A **Boolean** expression indicating if an error occurred while processing the query.

The settings for *Cancel* are:

Setting	Description
True	RDO should cancel further query processing.
False	RDO should continue processing the query for another query timeout period.

Remarks

Fired when a running query has exceeded the time specified by the **QueryTimeout** property. This event is fired each time the **QueryTimeout** time has been reached. This event is fired on both asynchronous and synchronous queries.

The *Cancel* parameter indicates if RDO should cancel the query or continue processing the query and wait for the number of seconds specified in the **QueryTimeout** property. The default value of this parameter is **True**, so if your code not respond to this event, the query is canceled after the **QueryTimeout** time has been reached. If the value of the parameter is set to **False**, RDO continues to wait for the query to complete for another **QueryTimeout** period.

You can use this method to display a message box to the user asking them if they wanted to cancel the query, or continue to wait another *N* seconds.

The **QueryTimeout** event fires for all queries execute on this **rdoConnection**. This includes those queries executed via the **OpenResultset** or **Execute** methods, as well as those executed from an associated **rdoQuery** object. The *Query* argument is an object reference indicating which query just timed out. Using this argument, you can write a single event handler for all queries on the connection, but still customize the handler for specific queries. When executing queries against the **rdoConnection** object itself, RDO creates an **rdoQuery** object internally, and a reference to this internal **rdoQuery** is passed as the *Query* argument.

See Also

Execute Method (Remote Data), **GetRows** Method (Remote Data), **OpenResultset** Method (Remote Data), **Requery** Method (Remote Data), **CreateQuery** Method (Remote Data), **rdoConnection** Object, **rdoEnvironment** Object, **rdoQuery** Object, **rdoResultset** Object, **QueryTimeout** Property (Remote Data)

QueryTimeout Property

Sets or returns a value that specifies the number of seconds to wait before a timeout error occurs when a query is executed on an ODBC data source.

Applies To

Database Object, **Connection** Object

Settings and Return Values

The setting or return value is an **Integer** representing the number of seconds to wait. The default value is 60.

Remarks

When you're using an ODBC database, such as Microsoft SQL Server, there may be delays due to network traffic or heavy use of the ODBC server. Rather than waiting indefinitely, you can specify how long to wait.

When you use **QueryTimeout** with a **Connection** or **Database** object, it specifies a global value for all queries associated with the database. You can override this value for a specific query by setting the **ODBCTimeout** property of the particular **QueryDef** object.

In a Microsoft Jet workspace, you can override the default value by creating a new "ODBC" key in the Registry path **\HKEY_LOCAL_MACHINE\SOFTWARE\Jet\3.5**, creating a **QueryTimeout** parameter in this key, and setting the value as desired.

See Also

ODBCTimeout Property

Example

This example uses the **ODBCTimeout** and **QueryTimeout** properties to show how the **QueryTimeout** setting on a **Database** object sets the default **ODBCTimeout** setting on any **QueryDef** objects created from the **Database** object.

```
Sub ODBCTimeoutX()

    Dim dbsCurrent As Database
    Dim qdfStores As QueryDef
    Dim rstStores As Recordset
```

```
Set dbsCurrent = OpenDatabase("Northwind.mdb")

' Change the default QueryTimeout of the Northwind
' database.
Debug.Print "Default QueryTimeout of Database: " & _
    dbsCurrent.QueryTimeout
dbsCurrent.QueryTimeout = 30
Debug.Print "New QueryTimeout of Database: " & _
    dbsCurrent.QueryTimeout

' Create a new QueryDef object.
Set qdfStores = dbsCurrent.CreateQueryDef("Stores", _
    "SELECT * FROM stores")
qdfStores.Connect = _
    "ODBC;DATABASE=pubs;UID=sa;PWD=;DSN=Publishers"

' Change the ODBCTimeout setting of the new QueryDef
' object from its default setting.
Debug.Print "Default ODBCTimeout of QueryDef: " & _
    qdfStores.ODBCTimeout
qdfStores.ODBCTimeout = 0
Debug.Print "New ODBCTimeout of QueryDef: " & _
    qdfStores.ODBCTimeout

' Execute the query and display the results.
Set rstStores = qdfStores.OpenRecordset()

Debug.Print "Contents of recordset:"
With rstStores
    Do While Not .EOF
        Debug.Print , .Fields(0), .Fields(1)
        .MoveNext
    Loop
    .Close
End With

' Delete new QueryDef because this is a demonstration.
dbsCurrent.QueryDefs.Delete qdfStores.Name
dbsCurrent.Close

End Sub
```

QueryTimeout Property (Remote Data)

Returns or sets a value that specifies the number of seconds the ODBC driver manager waits before a timeout error occurs when a query is executed.

Applies To

rdoConnection Object, **rdoPreparedStatement** Object, **rdoQuery** Object, **RemoteData** Control

Syntax

object.**QueryTimeout** [= *value*]

The **QueryTimeout** property syntax has these parts:

Part	Description
object	An object expression that evaluates to an object in the **Applies To** list.
value	A **Long** integer representing the number of seconds the driver manager waits before timing out and returning an error.

Remarks

The default **QueryTimeout** property setting is 30 seconds. When you're accessing an ODBC data source using the **OpenResultset** or **Execute** methods, there may be delays due to network traffic or heavy use of the remote server—perhaps caused by your query. Rather than waiting indefinitely, use the **QueryTimeout** property to determine how long your application should wait before the **QueryTimeout** event is fired and your application trips a trappable error. At this point you have the option to continue waiting for another 'n' seconds as determined by the **QueryTimeout** property, or cancel the query in progress by using the **Cancel** argument in the QueryTimeout event procedure.

Setting this property to 0 disables the timer so your query will run indefinitely. Setting **QueryTimeout** to 0 is *not* recommended for synchronous operations as your application can be blocked for the entire duration of the query.

When used with an **rdoConnection** object, the **QueryTimeout** property specifies a global value for all queries associated with the data source.

When you use an **rdoQuery** object, the **rdoConnection** object's **QueryTimeout** property is used as a default value unless you specify a new value in the **rdoQuery** object's **QueryTimeout** property.

When working with asynchronous queries, the **StillExecuting** property remains **True** until the query completes, or the query timeout period is exhausted.

If the specified timeout exceeds the maximum timeout permitted by the data source, or is smaller than the minimum timeout, the driver substitutes that value and the following error is logged to the **rdoErrors** collection: SQLState 01S02: "Option value changed."

See Also

Execute Method, **LoginTimeout** Property, **OpenResultset** Method, **QueryTimeout** Event, **rdoConnection** Object, **rdoDefaultLoginTimeout** Property

Example

The following example sets up the query event handlers to deal with query timeout contingencies. Notice that the **QueryTimeout** event procedure displays a message box that permits the user to decide if they want to wait for an additional timeout period for the query. The **ShowRows** procedure simply dumps the rows returned.

```
Option Explicit
Dim en As rdoEnvironment
Dim cn As New rdoConnection
Dim rs As rdoResultset
```

```
Dim SQL As String
Dim col As rdoColumn
Dim er As rdoError
Public WithEvents Qd As rdoQuery

Private Sub cn_QueryTimeout( _
    ByVal Query As RDO.rdoQuery, Cancel As Boolean)
Dim ans As Integer
ans = MsgBox("Query Timed out... Press Retry to continue waiting", _
    vbRetryCancel + vbCritical, "Query Took Too Long")
If ans = vbRetry Then
    Cancel = False
Else
    Cancel = True
End If
End Sub

Private Sub RunQuery_Click()

On Error GoTo RunQueryEH

    Qd(0) = Param1
    Qd.QueryTimeout = 5
    Set rs = Qd.OpenResultset(rdOpenKeyset, _
        rdConcurReadOnly)

    If rs Is Nothing Then Else ShowRows

Exit Sub

RunQueryEH:
Debug.Print Err, Error$
    For Each er In rdoErrors
        Debug.Print er.Description, er.Number
    Next
    rdoErrors.Clear
    Resume Next

End Sub

Private Sub Form_Load()
Set en = rdoEngine.rdoEnvironments(0)
With cn
    .Connect = "uid=;pwd=;database=workdb;dsn=WorkDB;"
    .CursorDriver = rdUseClientBatch
    .EstablishConnection Prompt:=rdDriverNoPrompt
End With

Set Qd = cn.CreateQuery("LongQuery", "")
With Qd
    .SQL = "{call VeryLongStoredProcedure (?,?)}"
    .rdoParameters(1).Direction = rdParamOutput
    .rdoParameters(0).Type = rdTypeVARCHAR
End With

End Sub
```

QueryUnload Event

Occurs before a form or application closes. When an **MDIForm** object closes, the **QueryUnload** event occurs first for the MDI form and then in all MDI child forms. If no form cancels the **QueryUnload** event, the Unload event occurs first in all other forms and then in an MDI form. When a child form or a **Form** object closes, the **QueryUnload** event in that form occurs before the form's Unload event.

Applies To

Form Object, **Forms** Collection, **MDIForm** Object

Syntax

Private Sub Form_QueryUnload(*cancel* **As Integer**, *unloadmode* **As Integer**)
Private Sub MDIForm_QueryUnload(*cancel* **As Integer**, *unloadmode* **As Integer**)

The **QueryUnload** event syntax has these parts:

Part	Description
cancel	An integer. Setting this argument to any value other than 0 stops the **QueryUnload** event in all loaded forms and stops the form and application from closing.
unloadmode	A value or constant indicating the cause of the **QueryUnload** event, as described in Return Values.

Return Values

The *unloadmode* argument returns the following values:

Constant	Value	Description
vbFormControlMenu	0	The user chose the Close command from the Control menu on the form.
vbFormCode	1	The **Unload** statement is invoked from code.
vbAppWindows	2	The current Microsoft Windows operating environment session is ending.
vbAppTaskManager	3	The Microsoft Windows Task Manager is closing the application.
vbFormMDIForm	4	An MDI child form is closing because the MDI form is closing.

These constants are listed in the Visual Basic (VB) object library in the Object Browser.

Remarks

This event is typically used to make sure there are no unfinished tasks in the forms included in an application before that application closes. For example, if a user has not yet saved some new data in any form, your application can prompt the user to save the data.

When an application closes, you can use either the **QueryUnload** or **Unload** event procedure to set the **Cancel** property to **True**, stopping the closing process. However, the **QueryUnload** event occurs in all forms before any are unloaded, and the Unload event occurs as each form is unloaded.

See Also

Unload Event, **Unload** Statement

Example

This example uses an **MDIForm** object containing two MDI child forms. When you choose the Close command from the Control menu to close a form, a different message is displayed than if you choose the Exit command from the File menu. To try this example, create an **MDIForm**, and then use the Menu Editor to create a File menu containing an Exit command named FileExit. Make sure that this menu item is enabled. On Form1, set the **MDIChild** property to **True**. Paste the code into the Declarations sections of the respective forms, and then press F5 to run the program.

```
' Paste into Declarations section of MDIForm1.
Private Sub MDIForm_Load ()
   Dim NewForm As New Form1   ' New instance of Form1.
   NewForm.Caption = "Form2"  ' Set caption and show.
End Sub

Private Sub FileExit_Click ()
   Unload MDIForm1            ' Exit the application.
End Sub

Private Sub MDIForm_QueryUnload (Cancel As Integer, UnloadMode As Integer)
   Dim Msg                    ' Declare variable.
   ' Set the message text.
   Msg = "Do you really want to exit the application?"
   ' If user clicks the No button, stop QueryUnload.
   If MsgBox(Msg, vbQuestion + vbYesNo, Me.Caption) = vbNo Then Cancel = True
End Sub

' Paste into Declarations section of Form1.
Private Sub Form_QueryUnload (Cancel As Integer, UnloadMode As Integer)
   Dim Msg                    ' Declare variable.

If UnloadMode > 0 Then
     ' If exiting the application.
     Msg = "Do you really want to exit the application?"
   Else
     ' If just closing the form.
     Msg = "Do you really want to close the form?"
   End If
   ' If user clicks the No button, stop QueryUnload.
   If MsgBox(Msg, vbQuestion + vbYesNo, Me.Caption) = vbNo Then Cancel = True
End Sub
```

Quit Method (Add-Ins)

Attempts to exit Visual Basic.

Applies To

VBE Object

Syntax

object.**Quit**

The *object* placeholder represents an object expression that evaluates to an object in the **Applies To** list.

Raise Method

Generates a run-time error.

Applies to

Err Object

Syntax

object.**Raise** *number, source, description, helpfile, helpcontext*

The **Raise** method has the following object qualifier and named arguments:

Argument	Description
object	Required. Always the **Err** object.
number	Required. **Long** integer that identifies the nature of the error. Visual Basic errors (both Visual Basic-defined and user-defined errors) are in the range 0–65535. When setting the **Number** property to your own error code in a class module, you add your error code number to the **vbObjectError** constant. For example, to generate the error number 1050, assign **vbObjectError** + 1050 to the **Number** property.
source	Optional. String expression naming the object or application that generated the error. When setting this property for an object, use the form *project.class*. If *source* is not specified, the programmatic ID of the current Visual Basic project is used.
description	Optional. String expression describing the error. If unspecified, the value in **Number** is examined. If it can be mapped to a Visual Basic run-time error code, the string that would be returned by the **Error** function is used as **Description**. If there is no Visual Basic error corresponding to **Number**, the "Application-defined or object-defined error" message is used.
helpfile	Optional. The fully qualified path to the Microsoft Windows Help file in which help on this error can be found. If unspecified, Visual Basic uses the fully qualified drive, path, and file name of the Visual Basic Help file.

Argument	Description
helpcontext	Optional. The context ID identifying a topic within *helpfile* that provides help for the error. If omitted, the Visual Basic Help file context ID for the error corresponding to the **Number** property is used, if it exists.

Remarks

All of the arguments are optional except *number*. If you use **Raise** without specifying some arguments, and the property settings of the **Err** object contain values that have not been cleared, those values serve as the values for your error.

Raise is used for generating run-time errors and can be used instead of the **Error** statement. **Raise** is useful for generating errors when writing class modules, because the **Err** object gives richer information than is possible if you generate errors with the **Error** statement. For example, with the **Raise** method, the source that generated the error can be specified in the **Source** property, online Help for the error can be referenced, and so on.

See Also

Error Statement, **Clear** Method, **Err** Object, **Description** Property, **HelpContext** Property, **HelpFile** Property, **LastDLLError** Property, **Number** Property, **Source** Property, **HelpContextID** Property

Example

This example uses the **Err** object's **Raise** method to generate an error within an Automation object written in Visual Basic. It has the programmatic ID `MyProj.MyObject`.

```
Const MyContextID = 1010407          ' Define a constant for contextID.
Function TestName(CurrentName, NewName)
    If Instr(NewName, "bob") Then    ' Test the validity of NewName.
                                     ' Raise the exception
        Err.Raise vbObjectError + 27, "MyProj.MyObject", _
        "No ""bob"" allowed in your name", "c:\MyProj\MyHelp.Hlp", _
        MyContextID
    End If
End Function
```

RaiseEvent Statement

Fires an event declared at module level within a class, form, or document.

Syntax

RaiseEvent *eventname* [(*argumentlist*)]

The required *eventname* is the name of an event declared within the module and follows Basic variable naming conventions.

The **RaiseEvent** statement syntax has these parts:

Part	Description
eventname	Required. Name of the event to fire.
argumentlist	Optional. Comma-delimited list of variables, arrays, or expressions The *argumentlist* must be enclosed by parentheses. If there are no arguments, the parentheses must be omitted.

Remarks

If the event has not been declared within the module in which it is raised, an error occurs. The following fragment illustrates an event declaration and a procedure in which the event is raised.

```
' Declare an event at module level of a class module
Event LogonCompleted (UserName as String)

Sub
    ' Raise the event.
    RaiseEvent LogonCompleted ("AntoineJan")
End Sub
```

If the event has no arguments, including empty parentheses, in the **RaiseEvent**, invocation of the event causes an error. You can't use **RaiseEvent** to fire events that are not explicitly declared in the module. For example, if a form has a Click event, you can't fire its Click event using **RaiseEvent**. If you declare a Click event in the form module, it shadows the form's own Click event. You can still invoke the form's Click event using normal syntax for calling the event, but not using the **RaiseEvent** statement.

Event firing is done in the order that the connections are established. Since events can have **ByRef** parameters, a process that connects late may receive parameters that have been changed by an earlier event handler.

See Also

Event Statement

Example

The following example uses events to count off seconds during a demonstration of the fastest 100 meter race. The code illustrates all of the event-related methods, properties, and statements, including the **RaiseEvent** statement.

The class that raises an event is the event source, and the classes that implement the event are the sinks. An event source can have multiple sinks for the events it generates. When the class raises the event, that event is fired on every class that has elected to sink events for that instance of the object.

The example also uses a form (Form1) with a button (Command1), a label (Label1), and two text boxes (Text1 and Text2). When you click the button, the first text box displays "From Now" and the second starts to count seconds. When the full time (9.84 seconds) has elapsed, the first text box displays "Until Now" and the second displays "9.84"

The code for `Form1` specifies the initial and terminal states of the form. It also contains the code executed when events are raised.

```
Option Explicit

Private WithEvents mText As TimerState

Private Sub Command1_Click()
    Text1.Text = "From Now"
    Text1.Refresh
    Text2.Text = "0"
    Text2.Refresh
    Call mText.TimerTask(9.84)
End Sub

Private Sub Form_Load()
    Command1.Caption = "Click to Start Timer"
    Text1.Text = ""
    Text2.Text = ""
    Label1.Caption = "The fastest 100 meters ever run took this long:"
    Set mText = New TimerState
    End Sub

Private Sub mText_ChangeText()
    Text1.Text = "Until Now"
    Text2.Text = "9.84"
End Sub

Private Sub mText_UpdateTime(ByVal dblJump As Double)
    Text2.Text = Str(Format(dblJump, "0"))
    DoEvents
End Sub
```

The remaining code is in a class module named **TimerState**. Included among the commands in this module are the **Raise Event** statements.

```
Option Explicit
Public Event UpdateTime(ByVal dblJump As Double)
Public Event ChangeText()

Public Sub TimerTask(ByVal Duration As Double)
    Dim dblStart As Double
    Dim dblSecond As Double
    Dim dblSoFar As Double
    dblStart = Timer
    dblSoFar = dblStart

    Do While Timer < dblStart + Duration
        If Timer - dblSoFar >= 1 Then
            dblSoFar = dblSoFar + 1
            RaiseEvent UpdateTime(Timer - dblStart)
        End If
    Loop

    RaiseEvent ChangeText

End Sub
```

Randomize Statement

Initializes the random-number generator.

Syntax

Randomize [*number*]

The optional *number* argument is a **Variant** or any valid numeric expression.

Remarks

Randomize uses *number* to initialize the **Rnd** function's random-number generator, giving it a new seed value. If you omit *number,* the value returned by the system timer is used as the new seed value.

If **Randomize** is not used, the **Rnd** function (with no arguments) uses the same number as a seed the first time it is called, and thereafter uses the last generated number as a seed value.

Note To repeat sequences of random numbers, call **Rnd** with a negative argument immediately before using **Randomize** with a numeric argument. Using **Randomize** with the same value for *number* does not repeat the previous sequence.

See Also

Timer Function, **Rnd** Function

Example

This example uses the **Randomize** statement to initialize the random-number generator. Because the number argument has been omitted, **Randomize** uses the return value from the **Timer** function as the new seed value.

```
Dim MyValue
Randomize                      ' Initialize random-number generator.
MyValue = Int((6 * Rnd) + 1)   ' Generate random value between 1 and 6.
```

Rate Function

Returns a **Double** specifying the interest rate per period for an annuity.

Syntax

Rate(*nper*, *pmt*, *pv*[, *fv*[, *type*[, *guess*]]])

The **Rate** function has these named arguments:

Part	Description
nper	Required. **Double** specifying total number of payment periods in the annuity. For example, if you make monthly payments on a four-year car loan, your loan has a total of 4 * 12 (or 48) payment periods.

(continued)

Part	Description
pmt	Required. **Double** specifying payment to be made each period. Payments usually contain principal and interest that doesn't change over the life of the annuity.
pv	Required. **Double** specifying present value, or value today, of a series of future payments or receipts. For example, when you borrow money to buy a car, the loan amount is the present value to the lender of the monthly car payments you will make.
fv	Optional. **Variant** specifying future value or cash balance you want after you make the final payment. For example, the future value of a loan is $0 because that's its value after the final payment. However, if you want to save $50,000 over 18 years for your child's education, then $50,000 is the future value. If omitted, 0 is assumed.
type	Optional. **Variant** specifying a number indicating when payments are due. Use 0 if payments are due at the end of the payment period, or use 1 if payments are due at the beginning of the period. If omitted, 0 is assumed.
guess	Optional. **Variant** specifying value you estimate will be returned by **Rate**. If omitted, *guess* is 0.1 (10 percent).

Remarks

An annuity is a series of fixed cash payments made over a period of time. An annuity can be a loan (such as a home mortgage) or an investment (such as a monthly savings plan).

For all arguments, cash paid out (such as deposits to savings) is represented by negative numbers; cash received (such as dividend checks) is represented by positive numbers.

Rate is calculated by iteration. Starting with the value of *guess*, **Rate** cycles through the calculation until the result is accurate to within 0.00001 percent. If **Rate** can't find a result after 20 tries, it fails. If your guess is 10 percent and **Rate** fails, try a different value for *guess*.

See Also

DDB Function, **FV** Function, **IPmt** Function, **IRR** Function, **MIRR** Function, **NPer** Function, **NPV** Function, **Pmt** Function, **PPmt** Function, **PV** Function, **SLN** Function, **SYD** Function

Example

This example uses the **Rate** function to calculate the interest rate of a loan given the total number of payments (TotPmts), the amount of the loan payment (Payment), the present value or principal of the loan (PVal), the future value of the loan (FVal), a number that indicates whether the payment is due at the beginning or end of the payment period (PayType), and an approximation of the expected interest rate (Guess).

```
Dim Fmt, FVal, Guess, PVal, Payment, TotPmts, PayType, APR
Const ENDPERIOD = 0, BEGINPERIOD = 1  ' When payments are made.
Fmt = "##0.00"                        ' Define percentage format.
FVal = 0                              ' Usually 0 for a loan.
Guess = .1                            ' Guess of 10 percent.
PVal = InputBox("How much did you borrow?")
Payment = InputBox("What's your monthly payment?")
TotPmts = InputBox("How many monthly payments do you have to make?")
PayType = MsgBox("Do you make payments at the end of the month?", _
vbYesNo)
If PayType = vbNo Then PayType = BEGINPERIOD Else PayType = ENDPERIOD
APR = (Rate(TotPmts, -Payment, PVal, FVal, PayType, Guess) * 12) * 100
MsgBox "Your interest rate is " & Format(CInt(APR), Fmt) & " percent."
```

rdoColumn Object

An **rdoColumn** object represents a column of data with a common data type and a common set of properties.

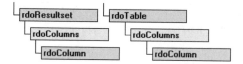

Remarks

The **rdoTable**, or **rdoResultset** object's **rdoColumns** collection represents the **rdoColumn** object in a row of data. You can use the **rdoColumn** object in an **rdoResultset** to read and set values for the data columns in the current row of the object. However, in most cases, references to the **rdoColumn** object is only implied because the **rdoColumns** collection is the **rdoResultset** object's default collection.

An **rdoColumn** object's name is determined by the name used to define the column in the data source table or by the name assigned to it in an SQL query. For example, if an SQL query aliases the column, this name is assigned to the **Name** property; otherwise, the column's name is used.

You manipulate database columns using an **rdoColumn** object and its methods and properties. For example, you can:

- Use the **Value** property of an **rdoColumn** to extract data from a specified column.
- Use the **Type** and **Size** property settings to determine the data type and size of the data.
- Use the **Updatable** property to see if the column can be changed.

- Use the **SourceColumn** and **SourceTable** property settings to locate the original source of the data.

- Use the **OrdinalPosition** property to get presentation order of the **rdoColumn** objects in an **rdoColumns** collection.

- Use the **Attributes** and **Required** property settings to determine optional characteristics and if Nulls are permitted in the column.

- Use the **AllowZeroLength** property to determine how zero-length strings are handled.

- Use the **BatchConflictValue,** and **OriginalValue** properties to resolve optimistic batch update conflicts.

- Use the **KeyColumn** to determine if this column is part of the primary key.

- Use the **Status** property to determine if the column has been modified.

- Use the **AppendChunk, ColumnSize**, and **GetChunk** methods to manipulate columns that require the use of these methods, as determined by the **ChunkRequired** property.

When you need to reference data from an **rdoResultset** column, you can refer to the **Value** property of an **rdoColumn** object by:

- Referencing the **Name** property setting using this syntax:

```
' Refers to the Au_Fname column rdoColumns("Au_Fname")
rs.rdoColumns("Au_Fname")
```

-Or-

```
' Refers to the Au_Fname column
rs.rdoColumns!Au_Lname
```

- Referencing its ordinal position in the **rdoColumns** collection using this syntax:

```
rs.rdoColumns(0)
```

The **rdoTable** object's **rdoColumns** collection contains specifications for the data columns. You can use the **rdoColumn** object of an **rdoTable** object to map a base table's column structure. However, you cannot directly alter the structure of a database table using RDO properties and methods. You can, however, use data definition language (DDL) action queries to modify database schema.

When the **rdoColumn** object is accessed as part of an **rdoResultset** object, data from the current row is visible in the **rdoColumn** object's **Value** property. To manipulate data in the **rdoResultset**, you don't usually reference the **rdoColumns** collection directly. Instead, use syntax that references the **rdoColumns** collection as the default collection of the **rdoResultset**.

```
dim rs As rdoResultset
Set rs = cn.OpenResultset("Select * from Authors" _
    & "Where Au_Lname = 'White'",rdOpenForwardOnly)
debug.print rs!Au_Fname
    'Refers to rdoRecordset object's rdoColumns collection.
```

Properties

AllowZeroLength Property (Remote Data), **Attributes** Property (Remote Data), **ChunkRequired** Property (Remote Data), **Name** Property (Remote Data), **OrdinalPosition** Property (Remote Data), **BatchConflictValue** Property, **KeyColumn** Property, **Status** Property, **OriginalValue** Property, **Required Property**, **Size** Property (Remote Data), **SourceColumn** Property (Remote Data), **SourceTable** Property, **Type** Property (Remote Data), **Updatable** Property (Remote Data), **Value** Property (Remote Data)

Events

DataChanged Event, **WillChangeData** Event

Methods

AppendChunk Method (Remote Data), **ColumnSize** Method (Remote Data), **GetChunk** Method (Remote Data)

See Also

rdoPreparedStatement Object, **rdoQuery** Object, **rdoResultset** Object, **rdoTable** Object

Example

The following example opens a connection against an SQL Server database and creates an **rdoResultset** that returns two columns: one normal column, and one derived from an expression. Next, the example maps the **rdoColumn** objects returned from the result set.

```
Private Sub rdoColumnButton_Click()
Dim cl As rdoColumn
Dim rs As rdoResultset
Dim sSQL As String
Dim cn As rdoConnection
Dim connect As String

connect = "uid=;pwd=;database=pubs;"

Set cn = rdoEnvironments(0).OpenConnection(workdb, _
            rdDriverNoPrompt, False, connect)

sSQL = "Select Pub_ID, Max(Price) BestPrice " _
    & " from Titles Group by Pub_ID"

Set rs = cn.OpenResultset(sSQL, rdOpenForwardOnly, _
    rdConcurReadOnly)

With rs
    For Each cl In .rdoColumns
```

```
        Print cl.Name; "-"; cl.Type; ":"; cl.Size, _
           cl.SourceTable, cl.SourceColumn
     Next cl
     Print
     Do Until .EOF
        For Each cl In .rdoColumns
           Print cl.Value,
        Next cl
        Print
        .MoveNext
     Loop
  End With
  End Sub
```

rdoColumns Collection

An **rdoColumns** collection contains all **rdoColumn** objects of an **rdoResultset**, or **rdoTable** object.

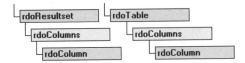

Remarks

The **rdoTable**, or **rdoResultset** object's **rdoColumns** collection r epresents the **rdoColumn** objects in a row of data. You use the **rdoColumn** object in an **rdoResultset** to read and set values for the data columns in the current row of the object.

The **rdoColumn** object is either created automatically by RDO when

- An **rdoTable**, or **rdoResultset** object is created.
- An **rdoTable** object is referenced.
- An **rdoResultset** is created via **OpenResultset**.

Properties

Item Property (RDO), **Count** Property (VB Collections)

Methods

Refresh Method (Remote Data)

See Also

rdoColumn Object, **rdoResultset** Object, **rdoTable** Object

Example

The following example opens a connection against an SQL Server database and creates an **rdoResultset** that returns two columns: one normal column, and one derived from an expression. Next, the example maps the **rdoColumn** objects returned from the result set.

```
Private Sub rdoColumnButton_Click()
Dim cl As rdoColumn
Dim rs As rdoResultset
Dim sSQL As String
Dim cn As rdoConnection
Dim connect As String

connect = "uid=;pwd=;database=pubs;"

Set cn = rdoEnvironments(0).OpenConnection(workdb, _
            rdDriverNoPrompt, False, connect)

sSQL = "Select Pub_ID, Max(Price) BestPrice " _
    & " from Titles Group by Pub_ID"

Set rs = cn.OpenResultset(sSQL, rdOpenForwardOnly, _
    rdConcurReadOnly)

With rs
    For Each cl In .rdoColumns
        Print cl.Name; "-"; cl.Type; ":"; cl.Size, _
            cl.SourceTable, cl.SourceColumn
    Next cl
    Print
    Do Until .EOF
        For Each cl In .rdoColumns
            Print cl.Value,
        Next cl
        Print
        .MoveNext
    Loop
End With
End Sub
```

rdoConnection Object

An **rdoConnection** object represents an open connection to a remote data source and a specific database on that data source, or an allocated but as yet unconnected object, which can be used to subsequently establish a connection.

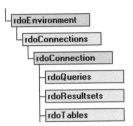

Remarks

Generally, an **rdoConnection** object represents a physical connection to the remote data source and corresponds to a single ODBC **hDbc** handle. A connection to a remote data source is required before you can access its data. You can open connections to remote ODBC data sources and create **rdoConnection** objects with either the **RemoteData** control or the **OpenConnection** method of an **rdoEnvironment** object.

To establish a connection to a remote server using the **rdoConnection** object, you can use the **OpenConnection** method to gather the *connect*, *dsname*, *readonly* and *prompt* arguments and open the connection. These arguments are then applied to the newly created **rdoConnection** object. You can also establish connections using the **RemoteData** control.

Creating Stand Alone rdoConnection Objects

You can also create a new **rdoConnection** object that is *not* immediately linked with a specific physical connection to a data source. For example, the following code creates a new stand-alone **rdoConnection** object:

```
Dim X as new rdoConnection.
```

Once created, you can set the properties of a stand-alone **rdoConnection** object and subsequently use the **EstablishConnection** method. This method determines how users are prompted—based on the *prompt* argument, and sets the read-only status of the connection based on the *readonly* argument.

When using this technique, RDO sets the following properties based on **rdoEngine** default values: **CursorDriver**, **LoginTimeout**, **UserName**, **Password** and **ErrorThreshold**. The **CursorDriver** and **LoginTimeout** properties can be set in the **rdoConnection** object itself and the **UserName** and **Password** can be set through arguments in the connect string. Once the connection is open, all of these properties are read-only.

When you declare a stand-alone **rdoConnection** object or use the **EstablishConnection** method, the object is not automatically appended to the **rdoConnections** collection. Use the **Add** or **Remove** methods to add or delete stand-alone **rdoConnection** objects to or from the **rdoConnections** collection. It is not necessary, however to add an **rdoConnection** object to the **rdoConnections** collection before it can be used to establish a connection.

Note RDO 1.0 collections behave differently than Data Access Object (DAO) collections. When you **Set** a variable containing a reference to a RDO object like **rdoResultset**, the existing **rdoResultset** is *not* closed and removed from the **rdoResultsets** collection. The existing object remains open and a member of its respective collection.

In contrast, RDO 2.0 collections do not behave in this manner. When you use the Set statement to assign a variable containing a reference to an RDO object, the existing object *is* closed and removed from the associated collection. This change is designed to make RDO more compatible with DAO.

Asynchronous Operations

Both the **EstablishConnection** and **OpenConnection** methods support synchronous, asynchronous, and event-managed operations. By setting the **rdAsyncEnable** option, control returns to your application *before* the connection is established. Once the **StillConnecting** property returns **False**, and the **Connect** event fires, the connection has either been made or failed to complete. You can check the success or failure of this operation by examining errors returned through the **rdoErrors** collection.

Opening Connections without Data Source Names

In many situations, it is difficult to ensure that a registered Data Source Name (DSN) exists on the target system, and in some cases it is not advisable to create one. Actually, a DSN is not needed to establish a connection if you are using the default network protocol (named pipes) and you know the name of the server and ODBC driver. If this is the case, you can establish a *DSN-less* connection by following these steps:

1 Set the *DSN* argument of the connect string to an empty string (DSN=").

2 Include the server name in the connect string.

3 Include the ODBC driver name in the connect string. Since many driver names have more than one word, enclose the name in curly braces { }.

Note This option is not available if you need to use other than the named pipes network protocol or one of the other DSN-set options such as OEMTOANSI conversion.

For example, the following code opens a read-only ODBC cursor connection against the SQL Server "SEQUEL" and includes a simple error handler:

```
Sub MakeConnection()
Dim rdoCn As New rdoConnection
On Error GoTo CnEh
```

```
With rdoCn
   .Connect = "UID=;PWD=;Database=WorkDB;" _
      & "Server=SEQUEL;Driver={SQL Server}" _
      & "DSN='';"
   .LoginTimeout = 5
   .CursorDriver = rdUseODBC
   .EstablishConnection rdDriverNoPrompt, True
End With
Exit Sub
CnEh:
Dim er As rdoError
   Debug.Print Err, Error
   For Each er In rdoErrors
      Debug.Print er.Description, er.Number
   Next er
   Resume Next
End Sub
```

Choosing a Specific Database

Once a connection is established, you can manipulate a database associated with the **rdoConnection** using the **rdoConnection** object and its methods and properties. For servers that support more than one database per connection, the default database is:

- Assigned to the user name by the database system administrator

- Specified with the DATABASE connect argument used when the **rdoConnection** is created.

- Specified in the registered ODBC data source entry.

- Selected by using an SQL statement such as USE <database> submitted with an action query.

All queries executed against the server assume this default database unless another database is specifically referenced in your SQL query.

Preparing for Errors when Connecting

There are a variety of reasons why you might be unable to connect to your remote database. Consider the following conditions that can typically prevent connections from completing:

- Your server might not have sufficient connection resources due to administrative settings or licensing restrictions.

- Your user might not have permission to access the network, server, or database with the password provided.

- The server, network or WAN bridges might be down or simply running slower than expected.

Closing the rdoConnection

When you use the **Close** method against an **rdoConnection** object, any open **rdoResultset,** or **rdoQuery** objects are closed. However, if the **rdoConnection** object simply loses scope, these objects remain open until the **rdoConnection** or the objects are explicitly closed. Closing a connection is not recommended when there are incomplete queries or uncommitted transactions pending.

Closing a connection also removes it from the **rdoConnections** collection. However, the **rdoConnection** object itself is not destroyed. If needed, you can use the **EstablishConnection** method to re-connect to the same server using the same settings, or change the **rdoConnection** object's properties and then use **EstablishConnection** to connect to another server.

Closing a connection also instructs the remote server to discard any instance-specific objects associated with the connection. For example, server-side cursors, temporary tables or any other objects created in the *TempDB* database on SQL Server are all dropped.

Working with rdoConnection Methods and Properties

You can manipulate the connection, databases, and queries associated with them using the methods and properties of the **rdoConnection** object. For example, you can:

- Use the **CursorDriver** property to determine the type of cursor requested by result sets created against the connection.

- Use the **OpenResultset** method to create a new **rdoResultset** object.

- Use the **LastQueryResults** to reference the last **rdoResultset** created against this connection.

- Use the **QueryTimeout** or **LoginTimeout** properties to specify how long the ODBC driver manager should wait before abandoning a query or connection attempt.

- Use the **RowsAffected** property to determine how many rows were affected by the last action query.

- Use the **Execute** method to run an action query or pass an SQL statement to a database for execution.

- Use the **CreateQuery** method to create a new **rdoQuery** object.

- Use the **Close** method to close an open connection, remove the **rdoConnection** object from the **rdoConnections** collection, deallocate the connection handle, and terminate the connection.

- Use the **Transactions** property to determine if the connection supports transactions, which you can implement using the **BeginTrans**, **CommitTrans**, and **RollbackTrans** methods.

- Use the **AsyncCheckInterval** property to determine how often RDO should poll for a completed asynchronous operation.

- Use the ODBC API with the **hDbc** property to set connection options.

- Use the **Connect** property to determine the *connect* argument used in the **OpenConnection** method, or the **Connect** property of the **RemoteData** control.

rdoConnection Events

The following events are fired as the **rdoConnection** object is manipulated. These can be used to micro-manage the process of connecting and disconnecting and provide additional retry handling in query timeout situations.

Event Name	Description
BeforeConnect	Fired before ODBC is called to establish the connection.
Connect	Fired after a connection is established.
Disconnect	Fired after a connection has been closed
QueryComplete	Fired after a query run against this connection is complete
QueryTimeout	Fired after the QueryTimeout period is exhausted.

Addressing the rdoConnection Object

The **Name** property setting of an **rdoConnection** specifies the data source name (DSN) parameter used to open the connection. This property is often empty as it is not used when making a DSN-less connection. In cases where you specify a different DSN to open each connection, you can refer to any **rdoConnection** object by its **Name** property setting using the following syntax. This code refers to the connection opened against the *Accounting* DSN:

```
rdoConnections("Accounting")
```

You can also refer to the object by its ordinal number using this syntax (which refers to the first member of the **rdoConnections** collection):

```
rdoConnections(0)
```

Properties

AsyncCheckInterval Property (Remote Data), **Connect** Property (Remote Data), **CursorDriver** Property (Remote Data), **hDbc** Property (Remote Data), **LoginTimeout** Property (Remote Data), **LogMessages** Property (Remote Data), **Name** Property (Remote Data), **QueryTimeout** Property (Remote Data), **LastQueryResults** Property, **UpdateOperation** Property, **RowsAffected** Property, **StillExecuting** Property (Remote Data), **Transactions** Property (Remote Data), **Version** Property (Remote Data), **StillConnecting** Property

Events

BeforeConnect Event, **Connect** Event, **Disconnect** Event, **QueryComplete** Event, **QueryTimeout** Event, **WillExecute** Event

Methods

BeginTrans, CommitTrans, RollbackTrans Methods , **Cancel** Method (Remote Data), **Close** Method (Remote Data), **Execute** Method (Remote Data), **OpenResultset** Method (Remote Data), **CreateQuery** Method (Remote Data), **EstablishConnection** Method (Remote Data)

See Also

Close Method (Remote Data), **OpenConnection** Method (Remote Data),
rdoEnvironment Object, **rdoPreparedStatement** Object, **rdoResultset** Object,
rdoTable Object, **RemoteData** Control, **Name** Property (Remote Data),
QueryTimeout Property (Remote Data)

rdoConnections Collection

An **rdoConnections** collection contains all **rdoConnection** objects opened or created
in an **rdoEnvironment** object of the remote database engine, or allocated and
appended to the **rdoConnections** collection using the **Add** method.

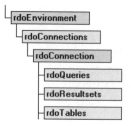

Remarks

The **rdoConnections** collection is used to manage your **rdoConnection** objects.
However, only **rdoConnection** objects created using the **OpenConnection** method,
or using the **RemoteData** control are automatically appended to the collection. When
you allocate a stand-alone **rdoConnection** object, it is not appended to the
rdoConnections collection until you use the **Add** method.

Note   RDO 1.0 collections behave differently than Data Access Object (DAO) collections.
When you **Set** a variable containing a reference to a RDO object like **rdoResultset**, the existing
rdoResultset is *not* closed and removed from the **rdoResultsets** collection. The existing object
remains open and a member of its respective collection.

In contrast, RDO 2.0 collections do not behave in this manner. When you use the Set statement
to assign a variable containing a reference to an RDO object, the existing object *is* closed and
removed from the associated collection. This change is designed to make RDO more
compatible with DAO.

Closing rdoConnection Objects

When you use the **Close** method against an **rdoConnection** object, any open
rdoResultset, or **rdoQuery** objects are closed and the **rdoConnection** object is
removed from the **rdoConnections** collection. However, if the **rdoConnection** object
simply loses scope, these objects remain open until the **rdoConnection** or the objects
are explicitly closed.

Properties

Item Property (RDO), **Count** Property (VB Collections)

Methods

Add Method, **Remove** Method

See Also

BeginTrans, **CommitTrans**, **RollbackTrans** Methods, **OpenConnection** Method
(Remote Data), **EstablishConnection** Method (Remote Data), **rdoConnection**
Object, **rdoEnvironment** Object, **rdoError** Object, **rdoErrors Collection** Example,
rdoResultset Object, **RemoteData** Control

Example

This example establishes a stand-alone **rdoConnection** object, sets its properties and
uses the **EstablishConnection** method to open the connection.

```
Option Explicit
Dim cn As New rdoConnection

Private Sub rdoConnectionButton_Click()
WorkingLight.Caption = "Connecting"
With cn
   .Connect = "DSN=BadServerName;" _
   & "UID=;PWD=;DATABASE=WorkDB;"
   .LoginTimeout = 20
   .CursorDriver = rdUseOdbc
   .EstablishConnection _
      prompt:=rdDriverNoPrompt, _
      Option:=rdAsyncEnable
End With
While .StillConnecting
   ToggleLight     ' Flash status indicator
   DoEvents
Wend
WorkingLight = True     ' Show status indicator
WorkingLight.Caption = "Connected"
End Sub

Sub ToggleLight() 'Flashes "Opening" light
WorkingLight = Not WorkingLight
End Sub
```

rdoCreateEnvironment Method

Creates a new **rdoEnvironment** object.

Applies To

rdoEngine Object

Syntax

Set *variable* = **rdoCreateEnvironment**(*name*, *user*, *password*)

The **rdoCreateEnvironment** method syntax has these parts:

Part	Description
variable	An object expression that evaluates to an **rdoEnvironment** object.
Name	A **String** variable that uniquely names the new **rdoEnvironment** object. See the **Name** property for details on valid **rdoEnvironment** names.
User	A **String** variable that identifies the owner of the new **rdoEnvironment** object. See the **UserName** property for more information.
Password	A **String** variable that contains the password for the new **rdoEnvironment** object. The password can be up to 14 characters long and can include any characters except ASCII character 0 (null).

Remarks

The **rdoEnvironment** object defines a transaction, user, and password context. When the **rdoEngine** is initialized, a default **rdoEnvironments**(0) is created automatically with the **rdoDefaultUser** and **rdoDefaultPassword** user name and password. If you need to define alternate transaction scopes that contain specific **rdoConnection** objects, or specific users, use the **rdoCreateEnvironment** method and specify the specific users for the environment. You can then open connections against this new environment.

Unlike the other methods you use to create Remote Data Objects, **rdoCreateEnvironment** requires that you provide all of its parts. If you don't provide all of the parts, the object won't be added to the collection. In addition, **rdoEnvironment** objects aren't permanent and can't be saved. Once you create an **rdoEnvironment** object, you can only modify the **UserName** and **Timeout** property settings.

You don't have to append the new **rdoEnvironment** object to a collection before you can use it — it is automatically appended to the **rdoEnvironments** collection.

If *name* refers to an object that is already a member of the **rdoEnvironments** collection, a trappable error occurs.

Once you use **rdoCreateEnvironment** to create a new **rdoEnvironment** object, an **rdoEnvironment** session is started, and you can refer to the **rdoEnvironment** object in your application.

To remove an **rdoEnvironment** object from the **rdoEnvironments** collection, use the **Close** method on the **rdoEnvironment** object. You cannot remove **rdoEnvironments**(0).

See Also

Close Method (Remote Data), **rdoEngine** Object, **rdoEnvironment** Object, **Name** Property (Remote Data), **Password** Property (Remote Data), **rdoDefaultUser**, **rdoDefaultPassword** Properties, **UserName** Property (Remote Data)

rdoDefaultCursorDriver Property

Returns or sets the cursor library used by the ODBC driver manager.

Applies To

rdoEngine Object

Syntax

object.**rdoDefaultCursorDriver** [= *value*]

The **rdoDefaultCursorDriver** property syntax has these parts:

Part	Description
object	An object expression that evaluates to an object in the **Applies To** list.
value	An **Integer** constant or value that specifies a type of ODBC cursor as described in Settings.

Settings

The settings for *value* are:

Constant	Value	Description
rdUseIfNeeded	0	(Default)RDO chooses the style of cursors most appropriate for the driver. Server-side cursors are used if they are available.
rdUseODBC	1	RDO uses the ODBC cursor library. This option gives better performance for small result sets, but degrades quickly for larger result sets.
rdUseServer	2	RDO uses server-side cursors. For most large operations this gives better performance, but might cause more network traffic.
rdUseClientBatch	3	RDO uses the optimistic batch cursor library as required by all batch mode operations and dissociate **rdoResultset** objects.
rdUseNone	4	RDO does not create a scrollable cursor. Basically, this is a forward-only, read-only resultset with a **RowsetSize** set to 1. This type of resultset performs faster than those that require creation of a cursor.

Remarks

When server-side cursors are used, the database engine uses its own resources to store keyset values. Data values are still transmitted over the network as with client-side cursors, but the impact on local workstation memory and disk space is reduced.

For SQL Server, server-side cursors are not used if the cursor is read-only and forward-only.

See Also

CursorDriver Property (Remote Data), **Type** Property (Remote Data)

rdoDefaultErrorThreshold Property

Returns or sets a value that indicates the default value for the **ErrorThreshold** property for **rdoQuery objects**.

Note   This property is provided for backward compatibility with RDO version 1.0 code. It should be replaced with code that implements the **rdoEngine** object's InfoMessage event which provides equivalent functionality.

Applies To

rdoEngine Object

Remarks

In version 4.x of Microsoft SQL Server, it is not possible to set the severity of errors using the RAISERROR statement. As a result, the **ErrorThreshold** property was needed to permit your code to filter those messages beyond a threshold of severity.

Version 6.x of Microsoft SQL Server now supports the inclusion of a severity level in the RAISERROR statement so it is no longer necessary to use the **ErrorThreshold** property.

All errors that are returned with a severity of less than 10 are trapped by the ODBC layers and set the SQL_SUCCESS_WITH_INFO result code. This causes RDO to raise the **InfoMessage** event but not stop query processing.

See Also

rdoError Object, **ErrorThreshold** Property (Remote Data), **Number** Property (Remote Data), **SQLRetCode** Property (Remote Data)

---

rdoDefaultLoginTimeout Property

Returns or sets a default value that determines the number of seconds the ODBC driver waits before abandoning an attempt to connect to a data source.

Applies To

rdoEngine Object

Syntax

object.**rdoDefaultLoginTimeout** [= *value*]

The **rdoDefaultLoginTimeout** property syntax has these parts:

Part	Description
object	An object expression that evaluates to an object in the **Applies To** list.
value	A **Long** expression that specifies the number of seconds as described in Settings.

Settings

The setting for *value* is the number of seconds to wait for a login request to complete before returning a trappable error or firing a **QueryTimeout** event. A setting of 0 indicates the timeout is disabled, and a connection attempt will wait indefinitely—or until the connection is complete.

Remarks

The **rdoDefaultLoginTimeout** property is used as an application-wide default unless the **LoginTimeout** property of the **rdoEnvironment** object is used to override this value.

Login requests are made when the **RemoteData control** creates an **rdoConnection object**, or when you use the **OpenConnection** or **EstablishConnection** methods of the **rdoEnvironment** object. The maximum value is dependent on the data source driver. The ODBC driver determines the maximum permissible LoginTimeout value—any attempt to set a value higher than this value is reset to this driver-dependent maximum value.

The default timeout value, if not specified, is 15 seconds.

When the timeout period is exhausted, the **ConnectionTimeout** event on the parent **rdoEnvironment** object fires.

Note When you use Data Access Objects (DAO), the LOGINTIMEOUT argument is used in the **Connect** property, this is not a valid argument for ODBC connect strings. Use the **rdoDefaultLoginTimeout** property instead.

See Also

OpenConnection Method (Remote Data), **EstablishConnection** Method (Remote Data), **rdoEnvironment** Object, **RemoteData** Control, **Connect** Property (Remote Data), **QueryTimeout** Property (Remote Data)

rdoDefaultUser, rdoDefaultPassword Properties

- **rdoDefaultUser**—returns or sets the default user name assigned to any new **rdoEnvironment**.
- **rdoDefaultPassword**—returns or sets the default password assigned to any new **rdoEnvironment**.

Applies To

rdoEngine Object

Syntax

object.**rdoDefaultUser** [= *value*]
object.**rdoDefaultPassword** [= *value*]

The syntax for the **rdoDefaultUser** and **rdoDefaultPassword** properties have these parts:

Part	Description
object	An object expression that evaluates to an object in the **Applies To** list.
value	A string expression that specifies either a user name or password.

Remarks

Unless other values are supplied in the **rdoCreateEnvironment** method, the **rdoDefaultUser** and **rdoDefaultPassword** properties determine the user name and password used when the **rdoEnvironment** object is created. These properties can also return the name used when an **rdoEnvironment** is created.

By default, the *value* for **rdoDefaultUser** and **rdoDefaultPassword** is "" (a zero-length string).

See Also

rdoCreateEnvironment Method (Remote Data), **rdoEnvironment** Object, **Password** Property (Remote Data), **UserName** Property (Remote Data)

---

rdoEngine Object

The **rdoEngine** object represents the remote data source. As the top-level object, it contains all other objects in the hierarchy of Remote Data Objects (RDO).

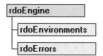

Remarks

The **rdoEngine** object can represent a remote database engine or another data source managed by the ODBC driver manager as a database. The **rdoEngine** object is a predefined object, therefore you can't create additional **rdoEngine** objects and it isn't a member of any collection.

The **rdoEngine** object is used to reference the **rdoEnvironments** collection, or establish default values for newly created **rdoEnvironment** objects. When an **rdoEnvironment** object is created, its properties are initialized based on the default values set in the **rdoEngine**. A default **rdoEnvironments**(0) object is created automatically when it is first referenced.

The **rdoEngine** object fires the **InfoMessage** event when an informational message is returned from the remote data source. Informational messages are indicated by an ODBC SQL_SUCCESS_WITH_INFO return code. These messages are placed in the **rdoErrors** collection. In cases where several messages arrive at once, only a single **InfoMessage** event is fired—after the last message arrives and has been added to the **rdoErrors** collection.

Setting Default rdoEnvironment Properties

The following properties establish default settings for all newly-created **rdoEnvironment** objects. They are also used when instantiating stand-alone **rdoConnection** objects.

- Use the **rdoDefaultLoginTimeout** property to determine the **rdoEnvironment** object's default **LoginTimeout** property used in connection timeout management.

- Use the **rdoDefaultCursorDriver** property to determine the **rdoEnvironment** object's default **CursorDriver** value. This property determines if the ODBC driver manager creates client batch, local, server-side, or no cursors.

- Use the **rdoDefaultUser** and **rdoDefaultPassword** properties to determine the default **rdoEnvironment** object's **UserName** and **Password** properties. These determine the user name and password when opening connections if no specific values are supplied.

Working with other rdoEngine Properties and Methods

You can establish the default configuration of new **rdoEnvironment** objects and create new ODBC data source entries using the properties and methods of the **rdoEngine** object. For example, you can:

- Use the **rdoEnvironments** collection to examine **rdoEnvironment** objects that have been appended to the collection. Note that **rdoEnvironment** objects can be allocated as stand-alone objects.

- Use the **rdoLocaleID** property to determine which language-localized DLLs are loaded.

- Use the **Version** property to examine the version of RDO in use.

- Use the **rdoErrors** collection to examine information about errors generated by the ODBC interface. Errors generated by Visual Basic are maintained in a separate **Errors** collection.

- Use the **rdoRegisterDataSource** method to create a new data source entry in the Windows System Registry.

- Use the **rdoCreateEnvironment** method to create a new **rdoEnvironment** object. You can also allocate a new **rdoEnvironment** object by coding

```
Dim MyEnv as New rdoEnvironment
```

Properties

AbsolutePosition Property (Remote Data), **rdoDefaultCursorDriver** Property, **rdoDefaultUser, rdoDefaultPassword** Properties, **rdoDefaultErrorThreshold** Property, **rdoDefaultLoginTimeout** Property, **rdoLocaleID** Property, **rdoVersion** Property (Remote Data)

Events

InfoMessage Event

Methods

rdoCreateEnvironment Method (Remote Data), **rdoRegisterDataSource** Method (Remote Data)

See Also

rdoCreateEnvironment Method (Remote Data), **rdoRegisterDataSource** Method (Remote Data), **rdoConnection** Object, **rdoError** Object, Remote Data Objects and Collections, **rdoDefaultUser, rdoDefaultPassword** Properties, **rdoDefaultErrorThreshold** Property, **rdoDefaultLoginTimeout** Property, Remote Data Objects and Collections

Example

This example sets a number of **rdoEngine** properties and creates a customized **rdoEnvironment** object based on these new default settings. Note that while your code can *set* a password in an **rdoEnvironment** object, it cannot be read once it is set.

```
Dim en As rdoEnvironment
Private Sub Form_Load()
With rdoEngine
    .rdoDefaultLoginTimeout = 20
    .rdoDefaultCursorDriver = rdUseOdbc
    .rdoDefaultUser = "Fred"
    .rdoDefaultPassword = ""
End With
Set en = rdoEnvironments(0)
'
'   Dump current rdoEnvironments collection
'   and display current properties where
'   possible.
'
For Each en In rdoEnvironments
    Debug.Print "LoginTimeout:" & en.LoginTimeout
    Debug.Print "CursorDriver:" & en.CursorDriver
    Debug.Print "User:" & en.UserName
    ' (Write-only) Debug.Print "Password:" & en.Password
Next
End Sub
```

rdoEnvironment Object

An **rdoEnvironment** object defines a logical set of connections and transaction scope for a particular user name. It contains both open and allocated but unopened connections, provides mechanisms for simultaneous transactions, and provides a security context for data manipulation language (DML) operations on the database.

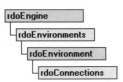

Remarks

Generally, an **rdoEnvironment** object corresponds to an ODBC environment that can be referred to by the **rdoEnvironment** object's **hEnv** property. However, if the *Name* argument is *not* provided when the **rdoEnvironment** object is created by the **rdoCreateEnvironment** method, a stand-alone **rdoEnvironment** is created that is not added to the **rdoEnvironments** collection. Stand-alone **rdoEnvironment** objects are not exposed to other in-process DLLs unless specifically designated as public. If the reference count for any private **rdoEnvironment** is reduced to zero, all **rdoConnections** associated with the **rdoEnvironment** are closed.

Once you set the properties of an **rdoEnvironment** object, you can use the **Add** method to append it to the **rdoEnvironments** collection or the **Remove** method to detach and deallocate the object. The **Name** property is read-only and is determined by the specific remote data object.

The default **rdoEnvironment** is created automatically when the **RemoteData** control is initialized, or the first remote data object is referenced in code. The **Name** property of **rdoEnvironments**(0) is "Default_Environment". The user name and password for **rdoEnvironments**(0) are both "".

rdoEnvironment objects can be created with the **rdoCreateEnvironment** method of the **rdoEngine** object which automatically appends the new object to the **rdoEnvironments** collection. All **rdoEnvironment** objects created in this manner are assigned properties based on the default properties set in the **rdoEngine** object.

The user name and password information from the **rdoEnvironment** is used to establish the connection if these values are not supplied in the *connect* argument of the **OpenConnection** method, or in the **Connect** property of the **RemoteData** control.

All **rdoEnvironment** objects share a common **hEnv** value that is created on an application basis. Use the **rdoEnvironment** object to manage the current ODBC environment, or to start an additional connection. In an **rdoEnvironment**, you can open multiple connections, manage transactions, and establish security based on user names and passwords. For example, you can:

- Create an **rdoEnvironment** object using the **Name**, **Password**, and **UserName** properties to establish a named, password-protected environment. The environment creates a scope in which you can open multiple connections and conduct one instance of coordinated transactions.

- Use the **CursorDriver** property to determine which cursor driver library is used to build **rdoResultset** objects. You can choose one of four types of cursors, or set the **CursorDriver** property to **rdUseNone** to indicate that no cursor is to be used to manage result sets.

- Use the **OpenConnection** method to open one or more existing connections in that **rdoEnvironment**.

- Use the **LoginTimeout** property to determine how long the ODBC drivers should wait before abandoning the connection attempt.

- Use the **BeginTrans**, **CommitTrans**, and **RollbackTrans** methods to manage transaction processing within an **rdoEnvironment** across several connections.

- Use several **rdoEnvironment** objects to conduct multiple, simultaneous, independent, and overlapping transactions.

- Use the **Close** method to terminate an environment and the connection and remove the **rdoEnvironment** object from the **rdoEnvironments** collection. This also closes all connections associated with the object.

Managing Transactions

The **rdoEnvironment** also determines transaction scope. Committing an **rdoEnvironment** transaction commits all open **rdoConnection** databases and their corresponding open **rdoResultset** objects. This does not imply a two-phase commit operation—simply that individual **rdoConnection** objects are instructed to commit any pending operations—one at a time.

For Microsoft SQL Server databases, the Distributed Transaction Coordinator (DTC) can be used to manage blocks of transactions simply by introducing the SQL query with the BEGIN DISTRIBUTED TRANSACTION statement. DTC facilitates the creation of network-wide database updates through its own two-phase commit protocol. Whenever SQL Server commits a transaction, the DTC ensures all related resources also commit the transaction. If any part of the transaction fails, the DTC ensures that the entire transaction is rolled back across all enlisted servers.

When you use transactions, all databases in the specified **rdoEnvironment** are affected – even if multiple **rdoConnection** objects are opened in the **rdoEnvironment**. For example, suppose you use a **BeginTrans** method against one of the databases visible from the connection, update several rows in the database, and then delete rows in another **rdoConnection** object's database. When you use the **RollbackTrans** method, both the update and delete operations are rolled back. To avoid this problem, you can create additional **rdoEnvironment** objects to manage transactions independently across **rdoConnection** objects. Note that transactions executed by multiple **rdoEnvironment** objects are serialized and are not atomic operations. Because of this, their success or failure is not interdependent. This is an example of batched transactions.

You can execute nested transactions *only* if your data source supports them. For example, on a single connection, you can execute a BEGIN TRANS SQL statement, execute several UPDATE queries, and another BEGIN TRANS statement. Any operations executed after the second BEGIN TRANS SQL statement can be rolled back independently of the statements executed after the first BEGIN TRANS. This is an example of nested transactions. To commit the first set of UPDATE statements, you must execute a COMMIT TRANS statement, or a ROLLBACK TRANS statement for each BEGIN TRANS executed.

rdoEnvironment Events

The following events are fired as the **rdoEnvironment** object is manipulated. These can be used to micro-manage RDO transactions associated with the **rdoEnvironment** or to synchronize some other process with the transaction.

Event Name	Description
BeginTrans	Fired after the **BeginTrans** method has completed.
CommitTrans	Fired after the **CommitTrans** method has completed.
RollbackTrans	Fired after the **RollbackTrans** method has completed.

Addressing rdoEnvironment Objects

The **Name** property of **rdoEnvironment** objects is set from the *name* argument passed to the **rdoCreateEnvironment** method. You can refer to any other **rdoEnvironment** object by specifying its **Name** property setting using this syntax:

rdoEnvironments("MyEnvName")

or simply:

rdoEnvironments!*MyEnvName*

You can also refer to **rdoEnvironment** objects by their position in the **rdoEnvironments** collection using this syntax (where *n* is the *n*th member of the zero-based **rdoEnvironments** collection):

rdoEngine.rdoEnvironments(*n*)

or simply:

rdoEnvironments(*n*)

Properties

Item Property (RDO), **Count** Property (VB Collections)

Methods

Add Method, **Remove** Method

See Also

rdoCreateEnvironment Method (Remote Data), **rdoConnection** Object, **rdoEngine** Object, **RemoteData** Control, **Connect** Property (Remote Data), **hEnv** Property (Remote Data)

Example

The following example illustrates creation of the **rdoEnvironment** object and its subsequent use to open an **rdoConnection** object.

```
Private Sub rdoEnvironmentButton_Click()
Dim en As rdoEnvironment
Dim cn As rdoConnection
Set en = rdoEngine.rdoEvironments(0)
With en
    en.CursorDriver = rdUseOdbc
    en.LoginTimeout = 5
    en.Name = "TransOp1"
    Set cn = en.OpenConnection(dsname:="", _
        prompt:=rdDriverNoPrompt, _
        Connect:="UID=;PWD=;" _
        driver={SQL Server};Server=SEQUEL;", _
        Options:=rdAsyncEnable)
End With
Print "Connecting ";
While cn.StillConnecting

    Print ".";
    DoEvents
Wend
Print "done."

End Sub
```

rdoEnvironments Collection

The **rdoEnvironments** collection contains all active **rdoEnvironment** objects of the **rdoEngine** object.

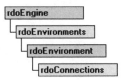

Remarks

rdoEnvironment objects are created with the **rdoCreateEnvironment** method of the **rdoEngine** object. Newly created **rdoEnvironment** objects are automatically appended to the **rdoEnvironments** collection unless you do not provide a name for the new object when using the **rdoCreateEnvironment** method or simply declare a new **rdoEnvironment** object in code.

The **rdoEnvironments** collection is automatically initialized with a default **rdoEnvironment** object based on the default properties set in the **rdoEngine** object.

If you use the **Close** method against an **rdoEnvironment** object, all **rdoConnections** it contains are closed and the object is removed from the **rdoEnvironments** collection.

Properties

Item Property (RDO), **Count** Property (VB Collections)

Methods

Add Method, **Remove** Method

See Also

rdoConnection Object, **rdoEnvironment** Object

Example

The following example illustrates creation of the **rdoEnvironment** object and its subsequent use to open an **rdoConnection** object.

```
Private Sub rdoEnvironmentButton_Click()
Dim en As rdoEnvironment
Dim cn As rdoConnection
Set en = rdoEngine.rdoEvironments(0)
With en
    en.CursorDriver = rdUseOdbc
    en.LoginTimeout = 5
    en.Name = "TransOp1"
    Set cn = en.OpenConnection(dsname:="", _
        prompt:=rdDriverNoPrompt, _
        Connect:="UID=;PWD=;" _
```

```
          driver={SQL Server};Server=SEQUEL;", _
          Options:=rdAsyncEnable)
   End With
   Print "Connecting ";
   While cn.StillConnecting
       Print ".";
       DoEvents
   Wend
   Print "done."

   End Sub
```

rdoError Object

Contains details about remote data access errors.

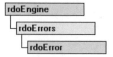

Remarks

Any operation involving remote data objects can potentially generate one or more ODBC errors or informational messages. As each error occurs or as messages are generated, one or more **rdoError** objects are placed in the **rdoErrors** collection of the **rdoEngine** object. When a subsequent RDO operation generates an error, the **rdoErrors** collection is cleared, and the new set of **rdoError** objects is placed in the **rdoErrors** collection. RDO operations that don't generate an error have no effect on the **rdoErrors** collection. To make error handling easier. you can use the **Clear** method to purge the **rdoErrors** collection between operations.

Generally, all ODBC errors generate a trappable Visual Basic error of some kind. This is your cue to check the contents of the **rdoErrors** collection for any and all errors resulting from the last operation which provide specific details on the cause of the error.

Not all errors generated by ODBC are fatal. In the normal course of working with connections, default databases, stored procedure print statements and other operations, the remote server often returns warnings or messages that are usually safe to ignore. When an informational message arrives, the **rdoEngine InfoMessage** event is fired. You should examine the **rdoErrors** collection in this event procedure.

If the severity of the error number is below the error threshold as specified in either the **rdoDefaultErrorThreshold** or **ErrorThreshold** property, then a trappable error is triggered when the error is detected. Otherwise, an **rdoError** object is simply appended to the **rdoErrors** collection. To control trappable errors in Microsoft SQL

Server, you should use the Transact SQL RAISERROR statement coupled with an appropriate *Severity* argument to indicate the error or other information.

Use the **rdoError** object to determine the type and severity of any errors generated by the **RemoteData** control or RDO operations. For example, you can:

- Use the **Description** property to display a text message describing the error.
- Use the **Number** property to determine the native data source error number.
- Use the **Source** property to determine the source of the error and the object class causing the error.
- Use the **SQLRetCode** and **SQLState** properties to determine the ODBC return code and **SQLState** flags.
- Use the **Clear** method on the **rdoErrors** collection to remove all **rdoError** objects. In most cases, it is not necessary to use the **Clear** method because the **rdoErrors** collection is cleared automatically when a new error occurs.

Members of the **rdoErrors** collection aren't appended as is typical with other collections. The most general errors are placed at the end of the collection (**Count** -1), and the most detailed errors are placed at index 0. Because of this implementation, you can often determine the root cause of the failure by examining **rdoErrors**(0).

The set of **rdoError** objects in the **rdoErrors** collection describes one error. The first **rdoError** object is the lowest level error, the second is the next higher level, and so forth. For example, if an ODBC error occurs while the **RemoteData** control tries to create an **rdoResultset** object, the last **rdoError** object contains the RDO error indicating the object couldn't be opened. The first error object contains the lowest level ODBC error. Subsequent errors contain the ODBC errors returned by the various layers of ODBC. In this case, the driver manager, and possibly the driver itself, returns separate errors which generate **rdoError** objects.

The **rdoErrors** collection is also used to manage informational messages returned by the data source. For example, messages returned back from PRINT statements, showplan requests, or DBCC operations in SQL Server are returned as **rdoError** objects in the **rdoErrors** collection. This type of message causes the **InfoMessage** event to fire, but does not trip a trappable error. Because of this, you must check the **rdoErrors** collection's **Count** property to see if any new errors have arrived.

Properties

Description Property (Remote Data), **HelpContext**, **HelpFile** Properties (Remote Data), **Number** Property (Remote Data), **Source** Property (Remote Data), **SQLRetCode** Property (Remote Data), **SQLState** Property (Remote Data)

See Also

rdoEngine Object, rdoResultset Object, RemoteData Control

Example

The following code illustrates a simple design-time RDO error handler. Note that the handler simply displays the errors in the **rdoErrors** collection in the Immediate window.

```
Dim er as rdoError
On Error GoTo CnEh
    .
    .
    .

CnEh:
Dim er As rdoError
    Debug.Print Err, Error
    For Each er In rdoErrors
        Debug.Print er.Description, er.Number
    Next er
    Resume Next
```

rdoErrors Collection

Contains all stored **rdoError** objects which pertain to a single operation involving Remote Data Objects (RDO).

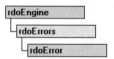

Remarks

Any operation involving remote data objects can generate one or more errors. As each error occurs, one or more **rdoError** objects are placed in the **rdoErrors** collection of the **rdoEngine** object. When another RDO operation generates an error, the **rdoErrors** collection is cleared, and the new set of **rdoError** objects is placed in the **rdoErrors** collection. RDO operations that don't generate an error have no effect on the **rdoErrors** collection.

- Use the **Clear** method on the **rdoErrors** collection to remove all **rdoError** objects. In most cases, it is not necessary to use the **Clear** method because the **rdoErrors** collection is cleared automatically when a new error occurs.

Members of the **rdoErrors** collection aren't appended as is typical with other collections. The most general errors are placed at the end of the collection (Count -1), and the most detailed errors are placed at index 0. Because of this implementation, you can determine the root cause of the failure by examining **rdoErrors**(0).

The set of **rdoError** objects in the **rdoErrors** collection describes one error. The first **rdoError** object is the lowest level error, the second is the next higher level, and so forth. For example, if an ODBC error occurs while the **RemoteData** control tries to create an **rdoResultset** object, the last **rdoError** object contains the RDO error indicating the object couldn't be opened. The first error object contains the lowest level ODBC error. Subsequent errors contain the ODBC errors returned by the various layers of ODBC. In this case, the driver manager, and possibly the driver itself, returns separate errors which generate **rdoError** objects.

Properties

Item Property (RDO), **Count** Property (VB Collections)

Methods

Clear Method (Remote Data)

See Also

rdoError Object

Example

The following code illustrates a simple design-time RDO error handler. Note that the handler simply displays the errors in the **rdoErrors** collection in the Immediate window.

```
Dim er as rdoError
On Error GoTo CnEh
.
.
.

CnEh:
Dim er As rdoError
   Debug.Print Err, Error
   For Each er In rdoErrors
      Debug.Print er.Description, er.Number
   Next er
   Resume Next
```

rdoLocaleID Property

Returns or sets a value indicating the locale of the RDO library.

Applies To

rdoEngine Object

Syntax

object.**rdoLocaleID** [= *value*]

The **rdoLocaleID** property syntax has these parts:

Part	Description
object	An object expression that evaluates to an object in the **Applies To** list.
value	A constant or value that specifies a locale as described in Settings.

Settings

The settings for *value* are:

Constant	Value	Description
rdLocaleSystem	0	System
rdLocaleEnglish	1	English
rdLocaleFrench	2	French
rdLocaleGerman	3	German
rdLocaleItalian	4	Italian
rdLocaleJapanese	5	Japanese
rdLocaleSpanish	6	Spanish
rdLocaleChinese	7	Chinese
rdLocaleSimplifiedChinese	8	Simplified Chinese
rdLocaleKorean	9	Korean

Remarks

The locale determines which language is used when generating RDO error messages. The **rdoLocaleID** defaults to the Windows system locale when the **rdoEngine** is initialized.

You can override the current locale at any time by setting the **rdoLocaleID** to any of the supported values. If you use an unsupported value, a trappable error occurs.

When the **rdoLocaleID** property is set or changed, RDO loads the appropriate language dynamic-link library (DLL) to show error messages in the correct language.

If the specified language DLL is not present on the user's machine, RDO is set to **rdLocaleEnglish**, which does not require a separate DLL. When this happens, an informational message is placed in the **rdoErrors** collection indicating that RDO was unable to load the resource DLL for the specified locale.

When you distribute your application, be sure to include the appropriate language DLL.

See Also

rdoEngine Object, **rdoError** Object

rdoParameter Object

An **rdoParameter** object represents a parameter associated with an **rdoQuery** object.

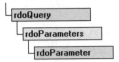

rdoQuery
rdoParameters
rdoParameter

Remarks

When working with stored procedures or SQL queries that require use of arguments that change from execution to execution, you should create an **rdoQuery** object to manage the query and its parameters. For example, if you submit a query that includes information provided by the user such as a date range, or part number, RDO and the ODBC interface can insert these values automatically into the SQL statement at specific positions in the query.

Providing Parameters

Your query's parameters can be provided in a number of ways:

- As hard-coded arguments in the SQL query string.

  ```
  "Select Name from Animals Where ID = 'Cat'"
  ```

- As concatenated text or numeric values extracted from **TextBox**, **Label** or other controls.

  ```
  "Select Name from Animals Where ID = '"  _
        & IDWanted.Text & "'"
  ```

- As the question mark (?) parameter placeholders.

  ```
  "Select Name from Animals Where ID = ?"
  ```

- As the question mark (?) parameter placeholders in a stored procedure call that accepts input, output and/or return status arguments.

  ```
  "{ ? = Call MySP (?, ?, ?) }"
  ```

Note   Stored procedure invocations that use the Call syntax (as shown above) are executed in their "native" format so they do not require parsing and data conversion by the ODBC Driver Manager. Because of this the Call syntax can be executed somewhat faster than other syntaxes.

Using Parameter Markers

The only time you *must* use parameter markers is when executing stored procedures that require input, output or return status arguments. If the stored procedure only requires input arguments, these can be provided in-line as imbedded values concatenated into the query (as shown below).

When the **rdoParameter** collection is first referenced (but not before) RDO and the ODBC interface pre-processes the query, and creates an **rdoParameter** object for each *marked* parameter. You can also create queries with multiple parameters, and in this case you can mark some parameters and provide the others by hard-coding or concatenation—in any combination. However, all marked parameters must appear to the left of all other parameters. If you don't, a trappable error occurs indicating "Wrong number of parameters".

Note Due to the extra overhead involved in creating and managing **rdoQuery** objects and their **rdoParameters** collection, you should not use parameter queries for SQL statements that do not change from execution to execution—especially those that are executed only once or infrequently.

Marking Parameters

Each query parameter that you want to have RDO manage must be indicated by a question mark (?) in the text of the SQL statement, and correspond to an **rdoParameter** object referenced by its ordinal number counting from zero—left to right. For example, to execute a query that takes a single input parameter, your SQL statement would look something like this:

```
SQL$ = "Select Au_Lname, Au_Fname where Au_ID Like ? "
Dim qd as rdoQuery, rd as rdoResultset
Set qd = CreateQuery ("SeekAUID", SQL$)
qd(0) = "236-66-%"
set rd = qd.OpenResultset(rdOpenForwardOnly)
```

Note You can also create an **rdoQuery** object using the Query Connection designer and name and set the data type and direction of individual parameters.

Acceptable Parameters

Not all types of data are passable as parameters. For example you cannot always use a TEXT or IMAGE data type as an OUTPUT parameter. In addition, if your query does not require parameters or has no parameters in a specific invocation of the query, you cannot use parenthesis in the query. For example, for a stored procedure that does not require parameters could be coded as follows:

```
"{ ? = Call MySP }"
```

When submitting queries that return output parameters, these parameters must be submitted at the end of the list of your query's parameters. While it is possible to provide both marked and unmarked (in-line) parameters, your output parameters must still appear at the end of the list of parameters.

All in-line parameters must be provided to the right of marked parameters. If this is not the case, RDO returns an error indicating "Wrong number of parameters".

RDO 2.0 supports BLOB data types as parameters and you also can use the **AppendChunk** method against the **rdoParameter** object to pass TEXT or IMAGE data types as parameters into a procedure.

Identifying the Parameter's Data Type

When your parameter query is processed by ODBC, it attempts to identify the data type of each parameter by executing ODBC functions that query the remote server for specific information about the query. In some cases, the data type cannot be correctly determined. In these cases, use the **Type** property to set the correct data type or create a custom query using the User Connection Designer.

For example, in the following query, the parameter passed to the TSQL **Charindex** function is typed as an integer. While this is correct for the function itself, the parameter is referencing a string argument of the TSQL function, so it must be set to an ODBC character type to work properly.

```
Dim SQL as string, qd as rdoQuery
SQL = "Select * From Titles " _
    & "Where Charindex( ?,  Title) > 0
Set qd = cn.CreateQuery("FindTitle", SQL)
qd(0).Type = rdTypeChar
```

Note You do not have to surround text parameters with quotes as this is handled automatically by the ODBC API interface.

Handling Output and Return Status Arguments

In some cases, a stored procedure returns an output or return status argument instead of or in addition to any rows returned by a SELECT statement. Each of these parameters must also be marked in the SQL statement with a question mark. Using this technique, you can mark the position of any number of parameters in your SQL query—including input, output or input/output.

Whenever your query returns output or return status arguments, you *must* use the ODBC CALL syntax when setting the SQL property of the **rdoQuery** object. In this case, a typical stored procedure call would look like this:

```
Dim qd as rdoQuery, rd as rdoResultset, SQL as String
SQL = "{ ? = Call master..sp_password (?, ?) }"
Set qd = CreateQuery ("SetPassword", SQL)
qd.rdoParameters(0).Direction = rdParamReturnValue
qd(1) = "Fred"     ' the old password
qd(2) = "George"   ' the new password
set rd = qd.Execute
if qd(0) <> 0 then _
    MsgBox "Operation failed"
```

Tip Be sure to specifically address stored procedures that do not reside in the current (default) database. In this example, the default database is *not* Master where the **sp_password** procedure is maintained, so this procedure is specifically addressed.

When control returns to your application after the procedure is executed, the **rdoParameter** objects designated as **rdParamReturnValue**, **rdParamOutput** or **rdParamInputOutput** contain the returned argument values. In the example shown above, the return status is available by examining qd(0) after the query is executed.

Using Other Properties

Using the properties of an **rdoParameter** object, you can set a query parameter that can be changed before the query is run. You can:

- Use the **Direction** property setting to determine if the parameter is an input, output, or input/output parameter, or a return value. In RDO 2.0, the **Direction** property is usually set automatically, so it is unnecessary to set this value. It is also unnecessary to set it for input parameters—which is the default value.

- Use the **Type** property setting to determine the data type of the **rdoParameter**. Data types are identical to those specified by the **rdoColumn.Type** property. In some cases, RDO might not be able to determine the correct parameter data type. In these cases, you can force a specific data type by setting the **Type** property.

- Use the **Value** property (the default property of an **rdoParameter**) to pass values to the SQL queries containing parameter markers used in **rdoQuery.Execute** or **rdoQuery.OpenResultset** methods. For example:

```
MyQuery(0) = 5
```

Note RDO requires that your ODBC driver support a number of Level II compliant options and support the **SQLNumParams, SQLProcedureColumns** and **SQLDescribeParam** ODBC API functions in order to be able to create the **rdoParameters** collection and parse parameter markers in SQL statements. While some drivers can be used to create and execute queries, if your driver does not support creation of the **rdoParameters** collection, RDO fails quietly and simply does not create the collection. As a result, any reference to the collection results in a trappable error.

Addressing the Parameters

By default, members of the **rdoParameters** collection are named "Param*n*" where *n* is the **rdoParameter** object's ordinal number. For example, if an **rdoParameters** collection has two members, they are named "Param0" and "Param1". However, if you use the User Connection Designer, you can specify names for specific parameters.

Because the **rdoParameters** collection is the default collection for the **rdoQuery** object, addressing parameters is easy. Assuming you have created an **rdoQuery** object referenced by rdoQo, you can refer to the **Value** property of its **rdoParameter** objects by:

- Referencing the **Name** property setting using this syntax:

```
' Refers to PubDate parameter
rdoQo("PubDate")
```

-Or-

```
' Refers to PubDate parameter
rdoQo!PubDate
```

- Referencing its ordinal position in the **rdoParameters** collection using this syntax:

```
' Refers to the first parameter marker
rdoQo(0)
```

Properties

Direction Property (Remote Data), **Name** Property (Remote Data), **Type** Property (Remote Data), **Value** Property (Remote Data)

Methods

AppendChunk Method (Remote Data)

See Also

Execute Method (Remote Data), **OpenResultset** Method (Remote Data), **rdoPreparedStatement** Object, **rdoQuery** Object, **rdoResultset** Object, **Direction** Property (Remote Data), **Type** Property (Remote Data)

Example

This example executes a stored procedure against the SQL Server 'Pubs' database. The procedure text is also included here so you can setup this example on your own machine. The stored procedure expects your code to provide three input arguments: A string to use in an expression to choose the title, and two numbers used to choose a price range for the books. The procedure returns the number of books that fall in the range, and the maximum price of the books. It also returns a set of rows containing detailed information about the books.

To establish the connection, we assume the name of the server is "SEQUEL" and it is a Microsoft SQL Server—this is a DSN-less connection. Next, we use the ODBC CALL syntax to prepare the query. Notice that each parameter is marked with a question mark. Once, marked, the **rdoParameters** collection is used to set the direction for the output and return value parameters and the initial values for the input parameters. While you don't see the **rdoParameters** collection called out specifically, understand that it is the default collection of the **rdoQuery** object so references are made simpler by *not* including a reference to the **rdoParameters** collection itself.

```
Sub RunQuery_Click()
Dim rs As rdoResultset
Dim cn As New rdoConnection
Dim qd As New rdoQuery
Dim cl As rdoColumn
Const None As String = ""

cn.Connect = "uid=;pwd=;server=SEQUEL;" _
    & "driver={SQL Server};database=pubs;" _
    & "DSN='';"
cn.CursorDriver = rdUseOdbc
cn.EstablishConnection rdDriverNoPrompt

Set qd.ActiveConnection = cn
qd.SQL = "{ ? = Call ShowOutputRS (?,?,?,?,?) }"
qd(0).Direction = rdParamReturnValue
qd(4).Direction = rdParamOutput
```

1129

```
    qd(5).Direction = rdParamOutput
    qd(1) = "c"
    qd(2) = 5
    qd(3) = 50

    Set rs = qd.OpenResultset(rdOpenForwardOnly, _
        rdConcurReadOnly)

    For Each cl In rs.rdoColumns
        Debug.Print cl.Name,
    Next
    Debug.Print

    Do Until rs.EOF
        For Each cl In rs.rdoColumns
            Debug.Print cl.Value,
        Next
        rs.MoveNext
    Debug.Print
    Loop

    Debug.Print "Output from SP="; qd(3)
    Debug.Print "Return Status from SP="; qd(0)

    rs.Close
    qd.Close
    cn.Close

End Sub
```

This is the stored procedure that is executed by the example shown above.

```
CREATE PROCEDURE ShowOutputRS
(
    @Ser varChar(128),
    @PriceLow Integer,
    @PriceHigh Integer,
    @Hits Integer OUTPUT,
    @MaxPrice integer OUTPUT
)
AS
Select @MaxPrice = Max(Price) from Titles
where Charindex(@Ser, title) > 0
and price between @priceLow and @priceHigh

Select * from Titles
where Charindex(@Ser, title) > 0
and price between @priceLow and @PriceHigh

Select @Hits = @@RowCount

return @@ROWCOUNT
```

rdoParameters Collection

An **rdoParameters** collection contains all the **rdoParameter** objects of an **rdoQuery** object.

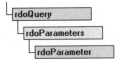

Remarks

The **rdoParameters** collection provides information only about *marked* parameters in an **rdoQuery** object or stored procedure. You can't append objects to or delete objects from the **rdoParameters** collection.

When the **rdoParameters** collection is first referenced, RDO and the ODBC interface parse the query searching for parameter markers—the question mark (?). For each marker found, RDO creates an **rdoParameter** object and places it in the **rdoParameters** collection. However, if the query cannot be compiled or otherwise processed, the **rdoParameters** collection is *not* created and your code will trigger a trappable error indicating that the object does not exist. In this case, check the query for improper syntax, permissions on underlying objects, and proper placement of parameter markers.

Properties

Item Property (RDO), **C**ount Property (VB Collections)

See Also

rdoParameter Object, **rdoPreparedStatement** Object, **rdoQuery** Object, **rdoResultset** Object, **rdoTable** Object

Example

This example executes a stored procedure against the SQL Server 'Pubs' database. The procedure text is also included here so you can setup this example on your own machine. The stored procedure expects your code to provide three input arguments: A string to use in an expression to choose the title, and two numbers used to choose a price range for the books. The procedure returns the number of books that fall in the range, and the maximum price of the books. It also returns a set of rows containing detailed information about the books.

To establish the connection, we assume the name of the server is "SEQUEL" and it is a Microsoft SQL Server—this is a DSN-less connection. Next, we use the ODBC CALL syntax to prepare the query. Notice that each parameter is marked with a question mark. Once, marked, the **rdoParameters** collection is used to set the direction for the output and return value parameters and the initial values for the input parameters. While you don't see the **rdoParameters** collection called out specifically, understand that it is the default collection of the **rdoQuery** object so references are made simpler by *not* including a reference to the **rdoParameters** collection itself.

```
Sub RunQuery_Click()
Dim rs As rdoResultset
Dim cn As New rdoConnection
Dim qd As New rdoQuery
Dim cl As rdoColumn
Const None As String = ""

cn.Connect = "uid=;pwd=;server=SEQUEL;" _
    & "driver={SQL Server};database=pubs;" _
    & "DSN='';"
cn.CursorDriver = rdUseOdbc
cn.EstablishConnection rdDriverNoPrompt

Set qd.ActiveConnection = cn
qd.SQL = "{ ? = Call ShowOutputRS (?,?,?,?,?) }"
qd(0).Direction = rdParamReturnValue
qd(4).Direction = rdParamOutput
qd(5).Direction = rdParamOutput
qd(1) = "c"
qd(2) = 5
qd(3) = 50

Set rs = qd.OpenResultset(rdOpenForwardOnly, _
    rdConcurReadOnly)

For Each cl In rs.rdoColumns
    Debug.Print cl.Name,
Next
Debug.Print

Do Until rs.EOF
    For Each cl In rs.rdoColumns
        Debug.Print cl.Value,
    Next
    rs.MoveNext
Debug.Print
Loop

Debug.Print "Output from SP="; qd(3)
Debug.Print "Return Status from SP="; qd(0)

rs.Close
qd.Close
cn.Close

End Sub
```

This is the stored procedure that is executed by the example shown above.

```
CREATE PROCEDURE ShowOutputRS
(
    @Ser varChar(128),
    @PriceLow Integer,
    @PriceHigh Integer,
    @Hits Integer OUTPUT,
    @MaxPrice integer OUTPUT
)
AS
Select @MaxPrice = Max(Price) from Titles
where Charindex(@Ser, title) > 0
and price between @priceLow and @priceHigh

Select * from Titles
where Charindex(@Ser, title) > 0
and price between @priceLow and @PriceHigh

Select @Hits = @@RowCount

return @@ROWCOUNT
```

rdoPreparedStatement Object

An **rdoPreparedStatement** object is a prepared query definition.

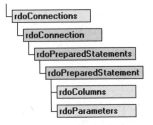

Remarks

Note The **rdoPreparedStatement** object is outdated and only maintained for backward compatibility. It should be replaced with the **rdoQuery** object. The **rdoQuery** object supports all of the **rdoPreparedStatement** object's properties and methods. In contrast, the **rdoPreparedStatement** only a subset of the **rdoQuery** object's properties and methods and none of its events.

Properties

BindThreshold Property, **Connect** Property (Remote Data), **ErrorThreshold** Property (Remote Data), **hStmt** Property (Remote Data), **KeysetSize** Property

(Remote Data), **LockType** Property (Remote Data), **LogMessages** Property
(Remote Data), **MaxRows** Property (Remote Data), **Name** Property (Remote Data),
QueryTimeout Property (Remote Data), **RowsAffected** Property, **RowsetSize**
Property, **SQL** Property, **StillExecuting** Property (Remote Data), **Type** Property
(Remote Data), **Updatable** Property (Remote Data)

Methods

Cancel Method (Remote Data), **Close** Method (Remote Data), **Execute** Method
(Remote Data), **OpenResultset** Method (Remote Data)

See Also

CreatePreparedStatement Method (Remote Data), **OpenResultset** Method
(Remote Data), **CreateQuery** Method (Remote Data), **rdoColumn** Object,
rdoConnection Object, **rdoParameter** Object, **rdoQuery** Object

rdoPreparedStatements Collection

An **rdoPreparedStatements** collection contains all **rdoPreparedStatement**
objects in an **rdoConnection**.

Remarks

Note   The **rdoPreparedStatements** collection is outdated and maintained for compatibility.
It should be replaced with the **rdoQueries** collection. The **rdoQuery** object and **rdoQueries**
collection supports all of the **rdoPreparedStatement** object's properties and methods. In
contrast, the **rdoPreparedStatement** supports only a subset of the **rdoQuery** object's
properties and methods and none of its events.

Note   RDO requires that your ODBC driver support a number of Level II options and support
the **SQLNumParams, SQLProcedureColumns** and **SQLDescribeParam** ODBC API functions
in order to be able to create the **rdoParameters** collection and parse SQL statement parameter
markers. While some drivers can be used to create and execute queries, if your driver does not
support creation of the **rdoParameters** collection, RDO fails quietly and simply does not create
the collection.

Properties

    Item Property (RDO), **Count** Property (VB Collections)

See Also

    rdoPreparedStatement Object, **rdoQuery** Object

rdoQueries Collection

Contains **rdoQuery** objects that have been added to the **rdoQueries** collection either automatically via the **CreateQuery** method, or with the **Add** method.

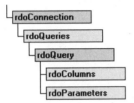

Remarks

An **rdoQuery** object is automatically appended to the **rdoQueries** collection when you use the **CreateQuery** method of the **rdoConnection** object. You can also use the **Add** method against the **rdoQueries** collection supplying a stand-alone **rdoQuery** object as the argument.

When you use the **Close** method against and **rdoQuery** object, it is removed from the **rdoQueries** collection, but the object remains instantiated. By resetting the **ActiveConnection** property, you can associate the **rdoQuery** object with another connection and use the **Add** method to append it to the **rdoQueries** collection.

An **rdoQuery** object need not be a member of the **rdoQueries** collection before it can be associated with an **rdoConnection** object and used with the **Execute** or **OpenResultset** methods.

Properties

    Item Property (RDO), **Count** Property (VB Collections)

See Also

    CreateQuery Method (Remote Data), **rdoConnection** Object, **rdoQuery** Object

rdoQuery Object

An **rdoQuery** object is a query definition that can include zero or more parameters.

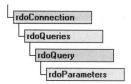

Remarks

The **rdoQuery** object is used to manage SQL queries requiring the use of input, output or input/output parameters. Basically, an **rdoQuery** functions as a compiled SQL statement. When working with stored procedures or queries that require use of arguments that change from execution to execution, you can create an **rdoQuery** object to manage the query parameters. If your stored procedure returns output parameters or a return value, or you wish to use **rdoParameter** objects to handle the parameters, you *must* use an **rdoQuery** object to manage it. For example, if you submit a query that includes information provided by the user such as a date range or part number, RDO can substitute these values automatically into the SQL statement when the query is executed.

Note The **rdoQuery** object replaces the outdated **rdoPreparedStatement** object. The **rdoQuery** object remains similar to the **rdoPreparedStatement** in its interface, but adds the ability to be persisted into a Visual Basic project, allowing you to create and manipulate it at design time. Additionally, the **rdoQuery** objects can be prepared or not, allowing the you to choose the most appropriate use of the query.

Creating rdoQuery Objects

To create an **rdoQuery** object, use the **CreateQuery** method which associates the **rdoQuery** with a specific **rdoConnection** object and adds it to the **rdoQueries** collection. Once created, you must fill in required parameters using the **rdoParameters** collection, and then use the **OpenResultset** method to create resultsets from the query, or the **Execute** method to simply run the query if it does not return rows.

You can also use the User Connection Designer (CQD) to create **rdoQuery** objects in your project. The CQD takes your SQL query and permits you to specify the data types for each parameter. It then inserts appropriate code in your application to expose these procedures very much like methods off of the **rdoQuery** object.

Note Due to the extra overhead involved in creating and managing **rdoQuery** objects and the **rdoParameters** collection, you should not use parameter queries for SQL statements that do not change from execution to execution—especially those that are executed only once or infrequently.

Stand Alone rdoQuery Objects

You can declare a stand-alone **rdoQuery** object using the **Dim** statement as follows:

```
Dim MyQuery as New rdoQuery
```

Stand-alone **rdoQuery** objects are not assigned to a specific **rdoConnection** object, so you must set the **ActiveConnection** property before attempting to execute the query, or to use the **OpenResultset** object against it. The **CursorType** and **ErrorThreshold** properties are set from default values established by the **rdoEngine** default settings. In addition, new **rdoQuery** objects are not automatically appended to the **rdoQueries** collection until you use the **Add** method.

For example, the code shown below creates an **rdoQuery** object, associates it with a connection, and executes it. Next, the **rdoQuery** object is associated with a different connection and executed again. The query object becomes more of an encapsulation of any kind of query, and thus can be executed against any kind of connection, provided the SQL statement would be appropriate for the connection.

```
Dim MyQuery As rdoQuery '
MyQuery.SQL = "Update customers " _
    & " Set LastTouched = GetDate()"
MyQuery.Prepared = False    'don't prepare it,
                            'just SQLExecDirect
'assume that cnSomeConnection
'is an rdoConnection or stand-alone object
MyQuery.ActiveConnection = cnSomeConnection
MyQuery.Execute

MyQuery.ActiveConnection = cnOtherConnection
'the cnOtherConnection is over a WAN, so I can increase
'my query timeout to compensate
MYQuery.QueryTimeout = 120
MyQuery.Execute
```

Choosing the right SQL Syntax

When coding the SQL property of an **rdoQuery** object, you can choose between one of three syntax styles to code your parameter query:

- Concatenated Strings: Your code builds up the SQL statement and its parameters using the Visual Basic concatenation (&) operator. This statement can be passed to the *SQL* argument of the **OpenResultset** method or the **rdoQuery** object's **SQL** property. In this case, a parameter query might look like this:

    ```
    sSQL = "Select Name, Age From Animals " _
        & " Where Weight > " & WeightWanted.Text _
        & " and Type = ' & TypeWanted.Text & "'"
    ```

- Native SQL syntax: The SQL syntax used by the remote server. In this case you can execute your own query or stored procedure, and pass in parameters by concatenation, or using placeholders, or both. The parameters marked with placeholders are managed by RDO as **rdoParameter** objects. A parameter query might look like this:

```
sSQL = "Select Au_LName from Authors" _
    & " Where Au_Fname = ?"
```

–Or–

```
sSQL = "Execute MyStoredProc 'Arg1', 450, '" _ & Text1
```

–Or–

```
sSQL = "Execute MyStoredProc ?, ?, ?"
```

- ODBC CALL syntax: Designed to call stored procedures that return a return status or output parameters. In this case, a placeholder can be defined for each input, output, or input/output parameter which is automatically mapped to **rdoParameter** objects. You can also mix in concatenated operators as needed. In this case, a parameter query might look like this:

```
sSQL = "{call ParameterTest (?,?,?) }"
```

–Or–

```
sSQL = "{? = call ParameterTest (?,?,?) }"
```

–Or–

```
sSQL = "{? = call CountAnimals (?, ?, 14, 'Pig')}"
```

The **rdoQuery** object is managed by setting the following properties and methods.

- Use the **SQL** property to specify a parameterized SQL statement to execute. The *name* argument of the **CreateQuery** method can also be used to provide the SQL query string.

- Set query parameters by using the **rdoQuery** object's **rdoParameters** collection.

- Use the **Prepared** property to indicate if the **rdoQuery** object should be prepared by the ODBC **SQLPrepare** function. If **False**, the query is executed using the **SQLExecDirect** function.

- Use the **Type** property to determine whether the query selects rows from an existing table (select query), performs an action (an action query), contains both action and select operations, or represents a stored procedure.

- Use the **RowsetSize** property setting to determine how many rows are buffered internally when building a cursor and locked when using pessimistic locking.

- Use the **KeysetSize** property to indicate the size of the keyset buffer when creating cursors.

- Use the **MaxRows** property to indicate the maximum number of rows to be returned by a query.

- Use the **RowsAffected** property to indicate how many rows are affected by an action query.

- Use the **QueryTimeout** property to indicate how long the driver manager waits before pausing a query and firing the **QueryTimeout** event.

- Use the **BindThreshold** property to indicate the largest column to be automatically bound.

- Use the **ErrorThreshold** property to indicate the error level that constitutes a trappable error.

- Use the **Updatable** property to see if the result set generated by an **rdoQuery** can be updated.

- Use the **OpenResultset** method to create an **rdoResultset** based on the **OpenResultset** arguments and properties of the **rdoQuery**.

- Use the **Execute** method to run an action query using **SQL** and other **rdoQuery** properties, including any values specified in the **rdoParameters** collection.

- Use the **LogMessages** property to activate ODBC tracing.

rdoQuery Object Events

The following events are fired as the **rdoQuery** object is manipulated. These can be used to micro-manage queries associated with the **rdoQuery** or coordinate other processes in your application.

Event Name	Description
QueryComplete	Fired when a query has completed.
QueryTimeout	Fired when the **QueryTimeout** period has elapsed and the query has not begun to return rows.
WillExecute	Fired before the query is executed permitting last-minute changes to the SQL, or to prevent the query from executing.

Closing the rdoQuery Object

Use the **Close** method to close an **rdoQuery** object, set its **ActiveConnection** property to **Nothing**, and remove it from the **rdoQueries** collection. However, you can still re-associate the **rdoQuery** object with another **rdoConnection** object by setting its **ActiveConnection** property to another **rdoConnection** object. Using the **Execute** method or **OpenResultset** method against an **rdoQuery** object that has its **ActiveConnection** property set to **Nothing** or an invalid **rdoConnection** causes a trappable error.

Addressing rdoQuery Objects

rdoQuery objects are the preferred way to submit parameter queries to the external server. For example, you can create a parameterized Transact SQL query (as used on Microsoft SQL Server) and store it in an **rdoQuery** object.

You refer to an **rdoQuery** object by its **Name** property setting using the following syntax. Since the **rdoQuery** object's default collection is the **rdoParameters** collection, all unqualified references to the **rdoQuery** object refer to the **rdoParameters** collection. In these examples, assume we have created an **rdoQuery** object named `rdoQo`. The first two examples refer to the **rdoQuery** object named "MyQuery".

rdoQo("MyQuery")

–Or–

rdoQo!*MyQuery*

You can also refer to **rdoQuery** objects (and the **rdoPreparedStatements** collection) by their position in the **rdoQueries** collection using this syntax (where *n* is the *n*th member of the zero-based **rdoQueries** collection):

rdoQo(*n***)**

Properties

BindThreshold Property, **hStmt** Property (Remote Data), **KeysetSize** Property (Remote Data), **LockType** Property (Remote Data), **MaxRows** Property (Remote Data), **Name** Property (Remote Data), **QueryTimeout** Property (Remote Data), **CursorType** Property, **Prepared** Property, **RowsAffected** Property, **RowsetSize** Property, **SQL** Property, **StillExecuting** Property (Remote Data), **Type** Property (Remote Data), **ActiveConnection** Property

Methods

Cancel Method (Remote Data), **Close** Method (Remote Data), **Execute** Method (Remote Data), **OpenResultset** Method (Remote Data)

See Also

BeginTrans, **CommitTrans**, **RollbackTrans** Methods, **CreatePreparedStatement** Method (Remote Data), **Execute** Method (Remote Data), **OpenResultset** Method (Remote Data), **BatchUpdate** Method (Remote Data), **CreateQuery** Method (Remote Data), **rdoPreparedStatement** Object, **rdoQueries** Collection, **rdoResultset** Object

Example

This example leverages RDO's ability to set the data type of individual arguments of a query. In this case, a CHARINDEX function argument is passed as a parameter. Since the ODBC driver does not recognize this data type correctly, we simply change it to CHAR before assigning a value to the parameter. The query itself uses TSQL syntax—it does not need to use the ODBC CALL syntax as it does not execute a parameter-based stored procedure. This example also creates a DSN-less connection to a Microsoft SQL Server and uses the sample Pubs database.

```
Private Sub Query1_Click()
Dim rs As rdoResultset
Dim cn As New rdoConnection
Dim qd As New rdoQuery
Dim cl As rdoColumn
Const None As String = ""
```

```
cn.Connect = "uid=;pwd=;server=SEQUEL;" _
   & "driver={SQL Server};database=pubs;" _
   & "DSN='';"
cn.CursorDriver = rdUseOdbc
cn.EstablishConnection rdDriverNoPrompt

Set qd.ActiveConnection = cn
qd.SQL = "Select * From Titles" _
   & " Where CharIndex( ?, Title) > 0"

qd(0).Type = rdTypeCHAR
qd(0) = InputBox("Enter search string", , "C")

Set rs = qd.OpenResultset(rdOpenForwardOnly, rdConcurReadOnly)

For Each cl In rs.rdoColumns
   Debug.Print cl.Name,
Next
Debug.Print

Do Until rs.EOF
   For Each cl In rs.rdoColumns
      Debug.Print cl.Value,
   Next
   rs.MoveNext
Debug.Print
Loop
End Sub
```

rdoRegisterDataSource Method

Enters connection information for an ODBC data source into the Windows Registry.

Applies To

rdoEngine Object

Syntax

rdoRegisterDataSource *DSN*, *driver*, *silent*, *attributes*

The **rdoRegisterDataSource** method syntax has these parts:

Part	Description
DSN	A string expression that is the name used in the **OpenConnection** method that refers to a block of descriptive information about the data source. For example, if the data source is an ODBC remote database, it could be the name of the server.
Driver	A string expression that is the name of the ODBC driver. This isn't the name of the ODBC driver dynamic link library (DLL) file. For example, *SQL Server* is a driver name, but *SQLSRVR.DLL* is the name of a DLL file. You must have ODBC and the appropriate driver already installed.

(continued)

Part	Description
Silent	A **Boolean** value that is **True** if you don't want to display the ODBC driver dialog boxes that prompt for driver-specific information, or **False** if you do want to display the ODBC driver dialog boxes. If *silent* is **True**, *attributes* must contain all the necessary driver-specific information or the dialog boxes are displayed anyway.
Attributes	A string expression that is a list of keywords to be added to the ODBC.INI file. The keywords are in a carriage-return-delimited string.

Remarks

When you use the **OpenConnection** or **EstablishConnection** method, you can use a registered data source entry to provide connection information.

If the data source is already registered in the Windows Registry when you use the **rdoRegisterDataSource** method, the connection information is updated. If the **rdoRegisterDataSource** method fails for any reason, no changes are made to the Windows Registry, and an error occurs.

For more information about ODBC drivers such as SQL Server, see the Help file provided with the driver.

Note You are encouraged to use the Windows Control Panel 32-bit ODBC Data Sources dialog box to add new data sources, or to make changes to existing entries.

Microsoft SQL Server Attributes

The following attributes are used when setting up DSN entries for Microsoft SQL Server drivers as extracted from the Drvssrvr.Hlp file. Other vendor's drivers expose their own set of attributes that might or might not conform to this set. See the documentation provided with your driver for additional details.

Keyword	Description
ADDRESS	The network address of the SQL Server database management system from which the driver retrieves data.
DATABASE	The name of the SQL Server database.
DESCRIPTION	A description of the data in the data source.
LANGUAGE	The national language to be used by SQL Server.
NETWORK	The network library connecting the platforms on which SQL Server and the SQL Server driver reside.
OEMTOANSI	Enables conversion of the OEM character set to the ANSI character set if the SQL Server client machine and SQL Server are using the same non-ANSI character set. Valid values are YES for on (conversion is enabled) and NO for off.

(continued)

Keyword	Description
SERVER	The name of the network computer on which the data source resides.
TRANSLATIONDLL	The name of the DLL that translates data passing between an application and a data source.
TRANSLATIONNAME	The name of the translator that translates data passing between an application and a data source.
TRANSLATIONOPTION	Enables translation of data passing between an application and a data source.
USEPROCFORPREPARE	Disables generation of stored procedures for SQLPrepare. Valid values are NO for off (generation is disabled) and YES for on. The default value (set in the setup dialog box) is YES.

Setting the OEMTOANSI Option

If the SQL Server client computer and SQL Server are using the same non-ANSI character set, select this option. For example, if SQL Server uses code page 850 and this client computer uses code page 850 for the OEM code page, selecting this option will ensure that extended characters stored in the database are property converted to ANSI for use by Windows-based applications.

When this option is set to YES and the SQL Server client machine and SQL Server are using different character sets, you must specify a character set translator.

Setting the Server Option

The Server option sets the name of the server. "(local)" can be entered as the server on a Microsoft Windows NT computer if the DSN is intended to reference a server on the local system. The user can then use a local copy of SQL Server (that listens on named pipes), even when running a non-networked version of SQL Server. Note that when the 16-bit SQL Server driver is using "(local)" without a network, the MS Loopback Adapter must be installed.

For more information about server names for different types of networks, see Microsoft SQL Server Setup.

Setting the Address Option

The Address option sets the network pathname address of the SQL Server database management system (DBMS) from which the driver retrieves data. For Microsoft SQL Server you can usually omit this argument when sets it to (Default).

Setting the Network Option

The Network attribute sets the name of the 32-bit SQL Server Net-Library
DLL that the SQL Server driver uses to communicate with the network software.
If this option is not provided, the SQL Server driver uses the client computer's
default Net-Library, which is specified in the Default Network box in the
Net-Library tab of the SQL Server Client Configuration Utility.

If you create a data source using a Network Library and optionally a Network
Address, ODBC SQL Server Setup will create a server name entry that you
can see in the Advanced tab in the SQL Server Client Configuration Utility.
These server name entries can also be used by DB-Library applications.

See Also

OpenConnection Method (Remote Data), **rdoConnection** Object, **rdoEngine**
Object

Example

The following example illustrates use of the **rdoRegisterDataSource** method
to create a new ODBC data source entry.

```
Private Sub RegisterDataSource()
Dim en As rdoEnvironment
Dim cnTest As rdoConnection
Dim strAttribs As String
' Build keywords string.
strAttribs = "Description=" _
        & "SQL Server on server SEQUEL" _
    & Chr$(13) & "OemToAnsi=No" _
    & Chr$(13) & "SERVER=SEQUEL" _
    & Chr$(13) & "Network=DBNMPNTW" _
    & Chr$(13) & "Database=WorkDB" _
    & Chr$(13) & "Address=\\SEQUEL\PIPE\SQL\QUERY"

' Create new registered DSN.
rdoEngine.rdoRegisterDataSource "Example", _
        "SQL Server", True, strAttribs
' Open the database.
Set en = rdoEngine.rdoEnvironments(0)
Set cnTest = en.OpenConnection( _
    dsname:="Example", _
    Prompt:=rdDriverNoPrompt, _
    Connect:="UID=;PWD=;")


End Sub
```

rdoResultset Object

An **rdoResultset** object represents the rows that result from running a query

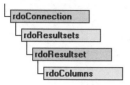

Remarks

When you use remote data objects, you interact with data almost entirely using **rdoResultset** objects. **rdoResultset** objects are created using the **RemoteData** control, or the **OpenResultset** method of the **rdoQuery**, **rdoTable,** or **rdoConnection** object.

When you execute a query that contains one or more SQL SELECT statements, the data source returns zero or more rows in an **rdoResultset** object. All **rdoResultset** objects are constructed using rows and columns.

A single **rdoResultset** can contain zero or any number of result sets—so-called "multiple" result sets. Once you have completed processing the first result set in an **rdoResultset** object, use the **MoreResults** method to discard the current **rdoResultset** rows and activate the next **rdoResultset**. You can process individual rows of the new result set just as you processed the first **rdoResultset**. You can repeat this until the **MoreResults** method returns **False**.

A new **rdoResultset** is automatically added to the **rdoResultsets** collection when you open the object, and it's automatically removed when you close it.

Note RDO 1.0 collections behave differently than Data Access Object (DAO) collections. When you **Set** a variable containing a reference to a RDO object like **rdoResultset**, the existing **rdoResultset** is *not* closed and removed from the **rdoResultsets** collection. The existing object remains open and a member of its respective collection.

In contrast, RDO 2.0 collections do not behave in this manner. When you use the **Set** statement to assign a variable containing a reference to an RDO object, the existing object *is* closed and removed from the associated collection. This change is designed to make RDO more compatible with DAO.

Processing Multiple Result Sets

When you execute a query that contains more than one SELECT statement, you must use the **MoreResults** method to discard the current **rdoResultset** rows and activate each subsequent **rdoResultset**. Each of the **rdoResultset** rows *must* be processed or discarded before you can process subsequent result sets. To process result set rows, use the *Move* methods to position to individual rows, or the **MoveLast** method to position to the last row of the **rdoResultset**. You can use the **Cancel** or **Close** methods against **rdoResultset** objects that have not been fully processed.

Choosing a Cursor Type

You can choose the type of **rdoResultset** object you want to create using the *type* argument of the **OpenResultset** method—the default **Type** is **rdOpenForwardOnly** for RDO and **rdOpenKeyset** for the **RemoteData** control. If you specify **rdUseNone** as the **CursorDriver** property, a forward-only, read-only result set is created. Each type of **rdoResultset** can contain columns from one or more tables in a database.

There are four types of **rdoResultset** objects based on the type of cursor that is created to access the data:

- Forward-only—type **rdoResultset**—individual rows in the result set can be accessed and can be updatable (when using server-side cursors), but the current row pointer can only be moved toward the end of the **rdoResultset** using the **MoveNext** method—no other method is supported.

- Static-type **rdoResultset**—a static copy of a set of rows that you can use to find data or generate reports. Static cursors might be updatable when using either the ODBC cursor library or server-side cursors, depending on which drivers are supported and whether the source data can be updated.

- Keyset-type **rdoResultset**—the result of a query that can have updatable rows. Movement within the keyset is unrestricted. A keyset-type **rdoResultset** is a dynamic set of rows that you can use to add, change, or delete rows from an underlying database table or tables. Membership of a keyset **rdoResultset** is fixed.

- Dynamic-type **rdoResultset**—the result of a query that can have updatable rows. A dynamic-type **rdoResultset** is a dynamic set of rows that you can use to add, change, or delete rows from an underlying database table or tables. Membership of a dynamic-type **rdoResultset** is not fixed.

Dissociate rdoResultset objects

When using the client batch cursor library, RDO permits you to disconnect an **rdoResultset** object from the **rdoConnection** object used to populate its rows by setting the **ActiveConnection** property to **Nothing**. While dissociated, the **rdoResultset** object becomes a temporary static snapshot of a local cursor. It can be updated, new rows can be added and rows can be removed from this **rdoResultset**. You can re-associate the **rdoResultset** by setting the **ActiveConnection** property to another (or the same) **rdoConnection** object. Once reconnected, you can use the **BatchUpdate** method to synchronize the **rdoResultset** with a remote database.

To perform this type of dissociated update operation, you should open the **rdoResultset** using an **rdOpenStatic** cursor, and use the **rdConcurBatch** as the concurrency option.

Managing rdoResultset Object Properties and Methods

You can use the methods and properties of the **rdoResultset** object to manipulate data and navigate the rows of a result set. For example, you can:

- Use the **Type** property to indicate the type of **rdoResultset** created, and the **Updatable** property indicates whether or not you can change the object's rows.

- Use the **BOF** and **EOF** properties to see if the current row pointer is positioned beyond either end of the **rdoResultset** or it contains no rows.

- Use the **MoveNext** method to reposition the current row in forward-only type **rdoResultset** objects.

- Use the **Bookmarkable, Transactions**, and **Restartable** properties to determine if the **rdoResultset** supports bookmarks or transactions, or can be restarted.

- Use the **LockEdits** property to determine the type of locking used to update the **rdoResultset**.

- Use the **RowCount** property to determine how many rows in the **rdoResultset** are available. If the **RowCount** property returns -1, RDO cannot determine how many rows have been processed. Only when you move to **EOF** does the **RowCount** property reflect the number of rows returned by the query. Not all cursor types support this functionality. The **RowCount** property returns -1 if it is not available.

- Use the **AddNew**, **Edit**, **Update**, and **Delete** methods to add new rows or otherwise modify updatable **rdoResultset** objects. Use the **CancelUpdate** method to cancel pending edits.

- Use the **Requery** method to restart the query used to create an **rdoResultset** object. This method can be used to re-execute a parameterized query.

- Use the **MoreResults** method to complete processing of the current **rdoResultset** and begin processing the next result set generated from a query. Use the **Cancel** method to terminate processing of all pending queries when the query contains more than one SQL operation. When you use the **Close** method against an **rdoResultset**, all pending queries are flushed and the **rdoResultset** is automatically dropped from the **rdoResultsets** collection.

- Use the **Close** method to terminate and deallocate the **rdoResultset** object and remove it from the **rdoResultsets** collection.

rdoResultset Events

The following events are fired as the **rdoResultset** object is manipulated. These can be used to micro-manage result sets or to synchronize other processes with the operations performed on the **rdoResultset** object.

Event Name	Description
Associate	Fired after a new connection is associated with the object.
ResultsChange	Fired after current rowset is changed (multiple result sets).
Dissociate	Fired after the connection is set to nothing.

(continued)

(continued)

Event Name	Description
QueryComplete	Fired after a query has completed.
RowStatusChange	Fired after the state of the current row has changed (edit, delete, insert).
RowCurrencyChange	Fired after the current row pointer is repositioned.
WillAssociate	Fired before a new connection is associated with the object.
WillDissociate	Fired before the connection is set to nothing.
WillUpdateRows	Fired before an update to the server occurs.

Executing Multiple Operations on a Connection

If there is an unpopulated **rdoResultset** pending on a data source that can only support a single operation on an **rdoConnection** object, you cannot create additional **rdoQuery** or **rdoResultset** objects**,** or use the **Refresh** method on the **rdoTable** object until the **rdoResultset** is flushed, closed, or fully populated. For example, when using SQL Server 4.2 as a data source, you cannot create an additional **rdoResultset** object until you move to the last row of the last result set of the current **rdoResultset** object. To populate the result set, use the **MoreResults** method to move through all pending result sets, or use the **Cancel** or **Close** method on the **rdoResultset** to flush all pending result sets.

Handing Beginning and End of File Conditions

When you create an **rdoResultset**, the current row is positioned to the first row if there are any rows. If there are no rows, the **RowCount** property setting is 0, and the **BOF** and **EOF** property settings are both **True**.

Note An **rdoResultset** may not be updatable even if you request an updatable **rdoResultset**. If the underlying database, table, or column isn't updatable, or if your user does not have update permission, all or portions of your **rdoResultset** may be read-only. Examine the **rdoConnection**, **rdoResultset,** and **rdoColumn** objects' **Updatable** property to determine if your code can change the rows.

Closing rdoResultset objects

Use the **Close** method to remove an **rdoResultset** object from the **rdoResultsets** collection, disassociate it from its connection, and free all associated resources. No events are fired when you use the **Close** method.

Setting the **ActiveConnection** property to **Nothing** removes the **rdoResultset** object from the **rdoResultsets** collection and fires events, but does not deallocate the object resources. Setting the **rdoResultset** object's **ActiveConnection** property to a valid **rdoConnection** object causes the **rdoResultset** object to be re-appended to the **rdoResultsets** collection of the **rdoConnection** object.

Addressing rdoResultset Objects

The default collection of an **rdoResultset** is the **rdoColumns** collection, and the default property of an **rdoColumn** object is the **Value** property. You can simplify your code by taking advantage of these defaults. For example, the following lines of code all set the value of the PubID column in the current row of an **rdoResultset**:

```
MyRs.rdoColumns("PubID").Value = 99
MyRs("PubID") = 99
MyRs!PubID = 99
' This is the first column
' returned by the SELECT statement...
MyRs(0) = 99
```

The **Name** property of an **rdoResultset** object contains the first 255 characters of the query used to create the resultset, so it is often unsuitable as an index into the **rdoResultsets** collection—especially since several queries might be created with the same SQL query.

You can refer to **rdoResultset** objects by their position in the **rdoResultsets** collection using this syntax (where *n* is the *n*th member of the zero-based **rdoResultsets** collection):

```
rdoResultsets(n)
```

Properties

AbsolutePosition Property (Remote Data), **BOF, EOF** Properties (Remote Data), **Bookmark** Property (Remote Data), **Bookmarkable** Property (Remote Data), **EditMode** Property (Remote Data), **hStmt** Property (Remote Data), **LastModified** Property (Remote Data), **LockType** Property (Remote Data), **LockEdits** Property (Remote Data), **Name** Property (Remote Data), **PercentPosition** Property (Remote Data), **BatchCollisionCount** Property, **BatchCollisionRows** Property, **BatchSize** Property, **Status** Property, **UpdateCriteria** Property, **UpdateOperation** Property, **Restartable** Property, **RowCount** Property (Remote Data), **StillExecuting** Property (Remote Data), **Transactions** Property (Remote Data), **Type** Property (Remote Data), **Updatable** Property (Remote Data), **ActiveConnection** Property

Events

Associate Event, **Dissociate** Event, **ResultsChanged** Event, **RowCurrencyChange** Event, **RowStatusChanged** Event, **WillAssociate** Event, **WillDissociate** Event, **WillUpdateRows** Event

Methods

AddNew Method (Remote Data), **Cancel** Method (Remote Data), **CancelUpdate** Method (Remote Data), **Close** Method (Remote Data), **Delete** Method (Remote Data), **Edit** Method (Remote Data), **GetRows** Method (Remote Data), **MoreResults** Method (Remote Data), **Move** Method (Remote Data), **MoveFirst, MoveLast, MoveNext, MovePrevious** Method, **Requery** Method (Remote Data), **Update** Method (Remote Data), **BatchUpdate** Method (Remote Data), **CancelBatch** Method (Remote Data), **GetClipString** Method

See Also

Move Method (Remote Data), **MoveFirst**, **MoveLast**, **MoveNext**, **MovePrevious** Methods (Remote Data), **OpenResultset** Method (Remote Data), **rdoColumn** Object, **rdoConnection** Object, **rdoPreparedStatement** Object, **rdoQuery** Object, **rdoTable** Object, **RemoteData** Control, **BOF**, **EOF** Properties (Remote Data), **Resultset** Property, **Type** Property (Remote Data)

Example

The following example illustrates execution of a multiple result set query. While this query uses three SELECT statements, only two return rows to your application. The subquery used instead of a join does not pass rows outside the scope of the query itself. This is also an example of a simple parameter query that concatenates the arguments instead of using an **rdoQuery** to manage the query. The **OpenResultset** also runs asynchronously—the code checks for completion of the operation by polling the **StillExecuting** property.

```
Private Sub ShowResultset_Click()
Dim rs As rdoResultset
Dim cn As New rdoConnection
Dim cl As rdoColumn
Dim SQL As String
Const None As String = ""

cn.Connect = "uid=;pwd=;server=SEQUEL;" _
    & "driver={SQL Server};database=pubs;" _
    & "DSN='';"

cn.CursorDriver = rdUseOdbc
cn.EstablishConnection rdDriverNoPrompt

SQL = "Select Au_Lname, Au_Fname" _
    & " From Authors A" _
    & " Where Au_ID in " _
    & " (Select Au_ID" _
    & "     from TitleAuthor TA, Titles T" _
    & "     Where TA.Au_ID = A.Au_ID" _
    & "     And TA.Title_ID = T.Title_ID " _
    & "     And T.Title Like '" _
    & InputBox("Enter search string", , "C") & "%')" _
    & "Select * From Titles Where price > 10"

Set rs = cn.OpenResultset(SQL, rdOpenKeyset, _
    rdConcurReadOnly, rdAsyncEnable + rdExecDirect)

Debug.Print "Executing ";
While rs.StillExecuting
    Debug.Print ".";
    DoEvents
Wend

Do
    Debug.Print String(50, "-") _
```

```
        & "Processing Result Set " & String(50, "-")
        For Each cl In rs.rdoColumns
            Debug.Print cl.Name,
        Next
        Debug.Print

        Do Until rs.EOF
            For Each cl In rs.rdoColumns
                Debug.Print cl.Value,
            Next
            rs.MoveNext
        Debug.Print
        Loop
        Debug.Print "Row count="; rs.RowCount

Loop Until rs.MoreResults = False
End Sub
```

rdoResultsets Collection

The **rdoResultsets** collection contains all open **rdoResultset** objects in an **rdoConnection**.

Remarks

A new **rdoResultset** is automatically added to the **rdoResultsets** collection when you open the object, and it's automatically removed when you close it. Several **rdoResultset** objects might be active at any one time.

Use the **Close** method to remove an **rdoResultset** object from the **rdoResultsets** collection, disassociate it from its connection, and free all associated resources. No events are fired when you use the **Close** method.

Setting the **ActiveConnection** property to **Nothing** removes the **rdoResultset** object from the **rdoResultsets** collection and fires events, but does not deallocate the object resources. Setting the **rdoResultset** object's **ActiveConnection** property to a valid **rdoConnection** object causes the **rdoResultset** object to be re-appended to the **rdoResultsets** collection.

Note RDO 1.0 collections behave differently than Data Access Object (DAO) collections. When you **Set** a variable containing a reference to a RDO object like **rdoResultset**, the existing **rdoResultset** is *not* closed and removed from the **rdoResultsets** collection. The existing object remains open and a member of its respective collection.

In contrast, RDO 2.0 collections do not behave in this manner. When you use the Set statement to assign a variable containing a reference to an RDO object, the existing object *is* closed and removed from the associated collection. This change is designed to make RDO more compatible with DAO.

Managing the rdoResultsets Collection

When you use the **OpenResultset** method against an **rdoConnection** or **rdoQuery**, and assign the result to an existing **rdoResultset** object, the existing object is maintained and a new **rdoResultset** object is appended to the **rdoResultsets** collection. When performing similar operations using the Microsoft Jet database engine and Data Access Objects (DAO), existing recordset objects are automatically closed when the variable is assigned, and no two **Recordsets** collection members can have the same name. For example, using RDO:

```
Dim rs as rdoResultset
Dim cn as rdoConnection
Set cn = OpenConnection....
Set rs = cn.OpenResultset("Select * from Authors", _
    rdOpenStatic)
Set rs = cn.OpenResultset("Select * from Titles", _
    rdOpenDynamic)
```

This code opens two separate **rdoResultset** objects; both are stored in the **rdoResultsets** collection. After this code runs, the second query, which is stored in **rdoResultsets**(1), is assigned to the **rdoResultset** variable `rs`. The first query is available and its cursor is still available by referencing **rdoResultsets**(0). Because of this implementation, more than one member of the **rdoResultsets** collection can have the same name.

This behavior permits you to maintain existing **rdoResultset** objects, which are maintained in the **rdoResultsets** collection, or close them as needed. In other words, you must explicitly close any **rdoResultset** objects that are no longer needed. Simply assigning another **rdoResultset** to a **rdoResultset**-type variable has no affect on the existing **rdoResultset** formerly referenced by the variable. Note that the procedures and other temporary objects created to manage the **rdoResultset** are maintained on the remote server as long as the **rdoResultset** remains open.

If you write an application that does not close each **rdoResultset** before opening additional **rdoResultset** objects, the number of procedures maintained in *TempDB* or elsewhere on the server increases each time another **rdoResultset** object is opened. In addition those resultsets might require significant client or server resources to store keysets or row values. Over time, this behavior can overflow the capacity of the server or workstation resources.

Properties

Item Property (RDO), **Count** Property (VB Collections)

See Also

Close Method (Remote Data), **OpenResultset** Method (Remote Data), **rdoConnection** Object, **rdoResultset** Object

rdoTable Object

An **rdoTable** object represents the stored definition of a base table or an SQL view.

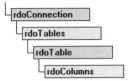

Remarks

Note You are discouraged from using the **rdoTable** object and **rdoTables** collection to manage or inspect the structure of your database tables. This object is maintained for backward compatibility and might not be supported in future versions of Visual Basic or RDO.

You can map a table definition using an **rdoTable** object and determine the characteristics of an **rdoTable** object by using its methods and properties. For example, you can:

- Examine the column properties of any table in an ODBC database. (Note that all **rdoTable** object properties are read-only.)

- Use the **OpenResultset** method to create an **rdoResultset** object based on all of the rows of the base table.

- Use the **Name** property to determine the name of the table or view.

- Use the **RowCount** property to determine the number of rows in the table or view. Referencing the **RowCount** property causes the query to be completed—just as if you had used the **MoveLast** method.

- Use the **Type** property to determine the type of table. The ODBC data source driver determines the supported table types.

- Use the **Updatable** property to determine if the table supports changes to its data.

You cannot reference the **rdoTable** objects until you have populated the **rdoTables** collection because it is not automatically populated when you connect to a data source. To populate the **rdoTables** collection, use the **Refresh** method or reference individual members of the collection by their ordinal number.

When you use the **OpenResultset** method against an **rdoTable** object, RDO executes a "SELECT * FROM *table*" query that returns *all* rows of the table using the cursor type specified. By default, a forward-only cursor is created.

You cannot define new tables or change the structure of existing tables using RDO or the RemoteData control. To change the structure of a database or perform other administrative functions, use SQL queries or the administrative tools that are provided with the database.

The default collection of an **rdoTable** object is the **rdoColumns** collection. The default property of an **rdoTable** is the **Name** property. You can simplify your code by using these defaults. For example, the following statements are identical in that they both print the number corresponding to the column data type of a column in an **rdoTable** using a **RemoteData** control:

```
Print RemoteData1.Connection.rdoTables _
    ("Publishers").rdoColumns("PubID").Type
Print RemoteData1.Connection("Publishers"). _
    ("PubID").Type
```

The **Name** property of an **rdoTable** object isn't the same as the name of an object variable to which it's assigned—it is derived from the name of the base table in the database.

You refer to an **rdoTable** object by its **Name** property setting using this syntax:

```
rdoTables("Authors")   'Refers to the Authors table
```

–Or–

```
rdoTables!Authors      'Refers to the Authors table
```

You can also refer to **rdoTable** objects by their position in the **rdoTables** collection using this syntax (where *n* is the *n*th member of the zero-based **rdoTables** collection):

```
rdoTables(n)
```

Properties

Name Property (Remote Data), **RowCount** Property (Remote Data), **Type** Property (Remote Data), **Updatable** Property (Remote Data)

Methods

OpenResultset Method (Remote Data)

See Also

OpenResultset Method (Remote Data), **rdoColumn** Object, **rdoConnection** Object, **rdoQuery** Object, **rdoResultset** Object, **Name** Property (Remote Data), **RowCount** Property (Remote Data), **Type** Property (Remote Data), **Updatable** Property (Remote Data)

rdoTables Collection

The **rdoTables** collection contains all stored **rdoTable** objects in a database.

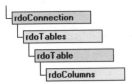

Remarks

Note You are discouraged from using the **rdoTable** object and **rdoTables** collection to manage or inspect the structure of your database tables. This object is maintained for backward compatibility and might not be supported in future versions of Visual Basic.

For performance reasons, you cannot reference an **rdoTable** object until you have first populated the **rdoTables** collection because it is not automatically populated when you connect to a data source. To populate the **rdoTables** collection, use the **Refresh** method or reference individual members of the collection by their ordinal number. Depending on the number of tables in your database, this can take quite some time.

Properties

Item Property (RDO), **Count** Property (VB Collections)

Methods

Refresh Method (Remote Data)

See Also

rdoColumn Object, **rdoQuery** Object, **rdoResultset** Object

---

rdoVersion Property

Returns a value that indicates the version of the RDO library associated with the object.

Applies To

rdoEngine Object

Syntax

object.**rdoVersion**

The *object* placeholder represents an object expression that evaluates to an object in the **Applies To** list.

Return Values

The **rdoVersion** property return value is a 5-character string expression.

Remarks

This property identifies the version of the database engine that created the connection. The version is in the form #.#.####, where the first two digits are the major version number and the last two digits are the minor version. For example, RDO version 2.0 returns 2.0.0000.

See Also

OpenConnection Method (Remote Data), **rdoConnection** Object, **Version** Property (Remote Data)

ReadFromFile Method

Loads an object from a data file created using the **SaveToFile** method. Doesn't support named arguments.

Applies To

OLE Container Control

Syntax

object.**ReadFromFile** *filenumber*

The **ReadFromFile** method syntax has these parts:

Part	Description
object	An object expression that evaluates to an object in the **Applies To** list.
filenumber	Required. A numeric expression specifying the file number used when loading an object. This number must correspond to an open, binary file.

Remarks

You can save an object to a data file using the **SaveToFile** or **SaveToOle1File** methods.

See Also

SaveToFile Method, **SaveToOle1File** Method

ReadOnly Property

Returns or sets a value that determines whether a **FileListBox** control contains files with read-only attributes.

Applies To

FileListBox Control

Syntax

object.**ReadOnly** [= *boolean*]

The **ReadOnly** property syntax has these parts:

Part	Description
object	An object expression that evaluates to an object in the **Applies To** list.
boolean	A Boolean expression that specifies whether the control displays files with read-only attributes, as described in Settings.

Settings

The settings for *boolean* are:

Setting	Description
True	The control includes read-only files in the list.
False	No read-only files are listed in the control.

Remarks

Use the **ReadOnly** property with a **FileListBox** control to specify whether files with read-only attributes are displayed in the file list or not.

See Also

Locked Property

ReadOnly Property (DAO)

Returns or sets a value that determines whether the control's Database is opened for read-only access.

Applies To

Data Control

Syntax

object.**ReadOnly** [= *boolean*]

The **ReadOnly** property syntax has these parts:

Part	Description
object	An object expression that evaluates to an object in the **Applies To** list.
boolean	A Boolean expression that determines read/write access, as described in Settings.

Settings

The settings for *value* are:

Setting	Description
True	The control's **Database** object is opened with read-only access. Changes to data aren't allowed.
False	(Default) The control's **Database** is opened with read/write access to data.

Remarks

Use the **ReadOnly** property with a **Data** control to specify whether data in the underlying **Database** can be changed. For example, you might create an application that only displays data. Accessing a **Database** using read-only result sets is also faster.

For a **Data** control, this property is used only the first time a database is opened by your application. If your application subsequently opens other instances of the database, the property is ignored. For a change in this property to take effect, you must close all instances of the database and then use the **Refresh** method.

In the Professional and Enterprise Editions, this property corresponds to the *readonly* argument in the **OpenDatabase** method.

Data Type

Boolean

See Also

Database Property, **OpenDatabase** Method

ReadOnly Property (Remote Data)

Returns or sets a value that determines whether the control's **rdoConnection** is opened for read-only access.

Applies To

RemoteData Control

Syntax

object.**ReadOnly** [= *value*]

The **ReadOnly** property syntax has these parts:

Part	Description
object	An object expression that evaluates to an object in the **Applies To** list.
value	A Boolean expression that determines read/write access, as described in Settings.

Settings

The settings for *value* are:

Setting	Description
True	The **RemoteData** control's **rdoConnection** object is opened with read-only access. Changes to data aren't allowed.
False	(Default) The **RemoteData** control's **rdoConnection** is opened with read/write access to data.

Remarks

Use the **ReadOnly** property with a **RemoteData** control to specify whether data in the underlying **rdoConnection** can be changed. For example, you might create an application that only displays data. Accessing a read-only **rdoConnection** might be faster.

Even if the **ReadOnly** property is **False**, a user might not have write access to a database because the user does not have permission or the type of **rdoResultset** in use does not support updates.

This property corresponds to the **OpenConnection** method's *readonly* argument.

See Also

OpenConnection Method (Remote Data), **Refresh** Method (Remote Data), **rdoConnection** Object, **RemoteData** Control, **Connection** Property (Remote Data)

ReadOnlyMode Property

Returns or sets a value that determines how the Visual Basic development environment interacts with read-only files.

Applies To

VBE Object

Syntax

object.**ReadOnlyMode** [= *value*]

The **ReadOnlyMode** property syntax has these parts:

Part	Description
object	An object expression that evaluates to an object in the **Applies To** list.
value	A long integer or constant that determines the project status, as described in Settings.

Settings

The settings for *value* are:

Value	Description
1	Strict. **Remove File** and **Add File** commands are not available if the project file is read-only on the disk. Windows and forms can be moved, but changes will not be saved. For files which are also read-only on disk, the Code Window is read-only; controls cannot be added or removed, control positions are locked, and custom **Properties** dialog boxes are disabled.
0	Lenient. Modifications can be made to code, forms, and the project if files are read-only, but changes can't be saved back to the files.

See Also

IconState Property

ReadProperties Event

Occurs when loading an old instance of an object that has a saved state.

Applies To

UserControl Object, **UserDocument** Object

Syntax

Sub *object*_**ReadProperties**(*pb* **As PropertyBag**)

The **ReadProperties** event syntax has these parts:

Part	Description
object	An object expression that evaluates to an object in the **Applies To** list.
pb	An object of the type **PropertyBag** class that contains the saved data to load.

Remarks

When this event occurs, the object author can load in the saved state from *pb*, by calling the **ReadProperty** method of the **PropertyBag** object for each value that is to be loaded. This event occurs after the **Initialize** event.

Always include error trapping when handling the **ReadProperties** event, to protect the control from invalid property values that may have been entered by users editing the file containing the saved data with text editors. However, you should not raise an error in an event, since doing so may be fatal to the container, so any error trapping in the **ReadProperties** event procedure should not include raising errors.

See Also

Initialize Event

ReadProperty Method

Returns a saved value from a **PropertyBag** class object.

Applies To

PropertyBag Object

Syntax

object.**ReadProperty**(*DataName*[, *DefaultValue*])

The **ReadProperty** method syntax has these parts:

Part	Description
object	An object expression that evaluates to an object in the **Applies To** list.
DataName	A string expression that represents a data value in the property bag.
DefaultValue	The value to be returned if no value is present in the property bag.

Remarks

The **ReadProperty** method will return the value of the saved data that is represented by the string expression *DataName*, or *DefaultValue* if there is no saved value. *DataName* should match the string expression that was used to store the saved data value in the property bag.

Note Specifying a default value reduces the size of the file belonging to the container of the control. A line for the property is written to the file only if the value to be written is different from the default. Wherever possible, you should specify default values for the properties of the control when initializing, saving, and retrieving property values.

ReadProperty Method (Add-Ins)

Returns a string from the specified user-defined section and key in the project's .Vbp or component file.

- **VBComponent** object:
- **VBProject** object:

Applies To

PropertyBag Object

Syntax

object.**ReadProperty** (*key* **As String**) **As String**
object.**ReadProperty** (*section* **As String**, *key* **As String**) **As String**

The **ReadProperty** function syntax has these parts:

Part	Description
object	An object expression that evaluates to an object in the **Applies To** list.
section	A string expression containing the name of the section where the key is found.
key	A string expression containing the name of the key to return.

Remarks

If the *section* or *key* area in the file is empty or doesn't exist, you'll get run-time error 5: "Illegal function call."

Rebind Method

Re-creates the **DBGrid** control properties and columns. Doesn't support named arguments.

Applies To

DBGrid Control

Syntax

object.**Rebind**

Remarks

The **Rebind** method causes the **DBGrid** control to perform the same operations that occur when you set the **DataSource** property. The **DBGrid** control resets the columns, headings and other properties based on the current **Data** control properties.

If you have not modified the grid columns at design time, then executing the **ReBind** method will reset the columns, headings, and other properties based on the current data source.

However, if you have altered the columns in any way at design time (even if you leave the **DataField** properties blank), then the grid will assume that you wish to maintain the modified grid layout and will not automatically reset the columns.

For an unbound grid (one with its **DataMode** property set to 1), this method is similar to the **Refresh** method except that the grid attempts to restore the current and topmost rows.

Note To force the grid to reset the column bindings even if the columns were modified at design time, invoke the **ClearFields** method immediately before **ReBind**. Conversely, to cancel the grid's automatic layout response and force the grid to use the current column/field layout, invoke the **HoldFields** method immediately before **ReBind**.

See Also

Data Control, **DBGrid** Control

Example

This example checks a global variable to see if the user changed the table layout and reconfigures using the original table information.

```
Sub CheckForRebind_Click ()
    If UserChangedLayout Then
        DBGrid1.Rebind
    End If
End Sub
```

RecordCount Property

Returns the number of records accessed in a **Recordset** object, or the total number of records in a table-type **Recordset** or **TableDef** object.

Applies To

Dynaset-Type Recordset Object, **Recordset** Object, **Snapshot-Type Recordset** Object, **Table-Type Recordset** Object, **TableDef** Object, **Forward-Only–Type Recordset** Object, **Dynamic-Type Recordset** Object

Return Values

The return value is a **Long** data type.

Remarks

Use the **RecordCount** property to find out how many records in a **Recordset** or **TableDef** object have been accessed. The **RecordCount** property doesn't indicate how many records are contained in a dynaset-, snapshot-, or forward-only–type **Recordset** object until all records have been accessed. Once the last record has been accessed, the **RecordCount** property indicates the total number of undeleted records in the **Recordset** or **TableDef** object. To force the last record to be accessed, use the **MoveLast** method on the **Recordset** object. You can also use an SQL **Count** function to determine the approximate number of records your query will return.

Note Using the **MoveLast** method to populate a newly opened **Recordset** negatively impacts performance. Unless it is necessary to have an accurate **RecordCount** as soon as you open a **Recordset**, it's better to wait until you populate the **Recordset** with other portions of code before checking the **RecordCount** property.

As your application deletes records in a dynaset-type **Recordset** object, the value of the **RecordCount** property decreases. However, records deleted by other users aren't reflected by the **RecordCount** property until the current record is positioned to a deleted record. If you execute a transaction that affects the **RecordCount** property setting and you subsequently roll back the transaction, the **RecordCount** property won't reflect the actual number of remaining records.

The **RecordCount** property of a snapshot- or forward-only–type **Recordset** object isn't affected by changes in the underlying tables.

A **Recordset** or **TableDef** object with no records has a **RecordCount** property setting of 0.

When you work with linked **TableDef** objects, the **RecordCount** property setting is always −1.

Using the **Requery** method on a **Recordset** object resets the **RecordCount** property just as if the query were re-executed.

See Also

MoveFirst, MoveLast, MoveNext, MovePrevious Methods, **Requery** Method

Example

This example demonstrates the **RecordCount** property with different types of **Recordsets** before and after they're populated.

```
Sub RecordCountX()

    Dim dbsNorthwind As Database
    Dim rstEmployees As Recordset

    Set dbsNorthwind = OpenDatabase("Northwind.mdb")
```

```
With dbsNorthwind
   ' Open table-type Recordset and show RecordCount
   ' property.
   Set rstEmployees = .OpenRecordset("Employees")
   Debug.Print _
      "Table-type recordset from Employees table"
   Debug.Print "    RecordCount = " & _
      rstEmployees.RecordCount
   rstEmployees.Close

   ' Open dynaset-type Recordset and show RecordCount
   ' property before populating the Recordset.
   Set rstEmployees = .OpenRecordset("Employees", _
      dbOpenDynaset)
   Debug.Print "Dynaset-type recordset " & _
      "from Employees table before MoveLast"
   Debug.Print "    RecordCount = " & _
      rstEmployees.RecordCount

   ' Show the RecordCount property after populating the
   ' Recordset.
   rstEmployees.MoveLast
   Debug.Print "Dynaset-type recordset " & _
      "from Employees table after MoveLast"
   Debug.Print "    RecordCount = " & _
      rstEmployees.RecordCount
   rstEmployees.Close

   ' Open snapshot-type Recordset and show RecordCount
   ' property before populating the Recordset.
   Set rstEmployees = .OpenRecordset("Employees", _
      dbOpenSnapshot)
   Debug.Print "Snapshot-type recordset " & _
      "from Employees table before MoveLast"
   Debug.Print "    RecordCount = " & _
      rstEmployees.RecordCount

   ' Show the RecordCount property after populating the
   ' Recordset.
   rstEmployees.MoveLast
   Debug.Print "Snapshot-type recordset " & _
      "from Employees table after MoveLast"
   Debug.Print "    RecordCount = " & _
      rstEmployees.RecordCount
   rstEmployees.Close

   ' Open forward-only-type Recordset and show
   ' RecordCount property before populating the
   ' Recordset.
   Set rstEmployees = .OpenRecordset("Employees", _
      dbOpenForwardOnly)
   Debug.Print "Forward-only-type recordset " & _
      "from Employees table before MoveLast"
   Debug.Print "    RecordCount = " & _
      rstEmployees.RecordCount
```

```
    ' Show the RecordCount property after calling the
    ' MoveNext method.
    rstEmployees.MoveNext
    Debug.Print "Forward-only-type recordset " & _
        "from Employees table after MoveNext"
    Debug.Print "    RecordCount = " & _
        rstEmployees.RecordCount
    rstEmployees.Close

        .Close
    End With

End Sub
```

RecordsAffected Property

Returns the number of records affected by the most recently invoked **Execute** method.

Applies To

Database Object, **QueryDef** Object, **Connection** Object

Return Values

The return value is a **Long** from 0 to the number of records affected by the most recently invoked **Execute** method on either a **Database** or **QueryDef** object.

Remarks

When you use the **Execute** method to run an action query from a **QueryDef** object, the **RecordsAffected** property will contain the number of records deleted, updated, or inserted.

When you use **RecordsAffected** in an ODBCDirect workspace, it will not return a useful value from an SQL DROP TABLE action query.

Example

This example uses the **RecordsAffected** property with action queries executed from a **Database** object and from a **QueryDef** object. The **RecordsAffectedOutput** function is required for this procedure to run.

```
Sub RecordsAffectedX()

    Dim dbsNorthwind As Database
    Dim qdfTemp As QueryDef
    Dim strSQLChange As String
    Dim strSQLRestore As String

    Set dbsNorthwind = OpenDatabase("Northwind.mdb")
```

```
    With dbsNorthwind
        ' Print report of contents of the Employees
        ' table.
        Debug.Print _
            "Number of records in Employees table: " & _
            .TableDefs!Employees.RecordCount
        RecordsAffectedOutput dbsNorthwind

        ' Define and execute an action query.
        strSQLChange = "UPDATE Employees " & _
            "SET Country = 'United States' " & _
            "WHERE Country = 'USA'"
        .Execute strSQLChange

        ' Print report of contents of the Employees
        ' table.
        Debug.Print _
            "RecordsAffected after executing query " & _
            "from Database: " & .RecordsAffected
        RecordsAffectedOutput dbsNorthwind

        ' Define and run another action query.
        strSQLRestore = "UPDATE Employees " & _
            "SET Country = 'USA' " & _
            "WHERE Country = 'United States'"
        Set qdfTemp = .CreateQueryDef("", strSQLRestore)
        qdfTemp.Execute

        ' Print report of contents of the Employees
        ' table.
        Debug.Print _
            "RecordsAffected after executing query " & _
            "from QueryDef: " & qdfTemp.RecordsAffected
        RecordsAffectedOutput dbsNorthwind

        .Close

    End With

End Sub

Function RecordsAffectedOutput(dbsNorthwind As Database)

    Dim rstEmployees As Recordset

    ' Open a Recordset object from the Employees table.
    Set rstEmployees = _
        dbsNorthwind.OpenRecordset("Employees")

    With rstEmployees
        ' Enumerate Recordset.
        .MoveFirst
        Do While Not .EOF
            Debug.Print "    " & !LastName & ", " & !Country
```

```
      .MoveNext
   Loop
      .Close
   End With

End Function
```

RecordSelectors Property

Returns or sets a value indicating if record selectors are displayed in the **DBGrid** control or **Split** object.

Applies To

Split Object, **DBGrid** Control

Syntax

object.**RecordSelectors** [= *value*]

The **RecordSelectors** property syntax has these parts:

Part	Description
object	An object expression that evaluates to an object in the **Applies To** list.
value	A Boolean expression that determines if record selectors are displayed, as described in Settings.

Settings

The settings for *value* are:

Setting	Description
True	Record selectors are displayed.
False	Record selectors aren't displayed.

Remarks

Record selectors, when displayed, appear to the left of the rows in the grid or split.

If a grid contains multiple splits, then setting its **RecordSelectors** property has the same effect as setting the **RecordSelectors** property of each split individually.

Note When the user selects a row by clicking its record selector, the bookmark of the selected row is added to the **SelBookmarks** collection.

See Also

Data Control, **Column** Object, **SelBookmarks** Property

Recordset Object

A **Recordset** object represents the records in a base table or the records that result from running a query.

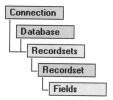

Remarks

You use **Recordset** objects to manipulate data in a database at the record level. When you use DAO objects, you manipulate data almost entirely using **Recordset** objects. All **Recordset** objects are constructed using records (rows) and fields (columns). There are five types of **Recordset** objects:

- **Table-type Recordset**—representation in code of a base table that you can use to add, change, or delete records from a single database table (Microsoft Jet workspaces only).

- **Dynaset-type Recordset**—the result of a query that can have updatable records. A dynaset-type **Recordset** object is a dynamic set of records that you can use to add, change, or delete records from an underlying database table or tables. A dynaset-type **Recordset** object can contain fields from one or more tables in a database. This type corresponds to an ODBC keyset cursor.

- **Snapshot-type Recordset**—a static copy of a set of records that you can use to find data or generate reports. A snapshot-type **Recordset** object can contain fields from one or more tables in a database but can't be updated. This type corresponds to an ODBC static cursor.

- **Forward-only-type Recordset**—identical to a snapshot except that no cursor is provided. You can only scroll forward through records. This improves performance in situations where you only need to make a single pass through a result set. This type corresponds to an ODBC forward-only cursor.

- **Dynamic-type Recordset**—a query result set from one or more base tables in which you can add, change, or delete records from a row-returning query. Further, records other users add, delete, or edit in the base tables also appear in your **Recordset**. This type corresponds to an ODBC dynamic cursor (ODBCDirect workspaces only).

You can choose the type of **Recordset** object you want to create using the *type* argument of the **OpenRecordset** method.

In a Microsoft Jet workspace, if you don't specify a *type*, DAO attempts to create the type of **Recordset** with the most functionality available, starting with table. If this type isn't available, DAO attempts a dynaset, then a snapshot, and finally a forward-only type **Recordset** object.

In an ODBCDirect workspace, if you don't specify a *type*, DAO attempts to create the type of **Recordset** with the fastest query response, starting with forward-only. If this type isn't available, DAO attempts a snapshot, then a dynaset, and finally a dynamic-type **Recordset** object.

When creating a **Recordset** object using a non-linked **TableDef** object in a Microsoft Jet workspace, table-type **Recordset** objects are created. Only dynaset-type or snapshot-type **Recordset** objects can be created with linked tables or tables in Microsoft Jet-connected ODBC databases.

A new **Recordset** object is automatically added to the **Recordsets** collection when you open the object, and is automatically removed when you close it.

Note If you use variables to represent a **Recordset** object and the **Database** object that contains the **Recordset**, make sure the variables have the same scope, or lifetime. For example, if you declare a public variable that represents a **Recordset** object, make sure the variable that represents the **Database** containing the **Recordset** is also public, or is declared in a **Sub** or **Function** procedure using the **Static** keyword.

You can create as many **Recordset** object variables as needed. Different **Recordset** objects can access the same tables, queries, and fields without conflicting.

Dynaset-, snapshot-, and forward-only–type **Recordset** objects are stored in local memory. If there isn't enough space in local memory to store the data, the Microsoft Jet database engine saves the additional data to TEMP disk space. If this space is exhausted, a trappable error occurs.

The default collection of a **Recordset** object is the **Fields** collection, and the default property of a **Field** object is the **Value** property. Use these defaults to simplify your code.

When you create a **Recordset** object, the current record is positioned to the first record if there are any records. If there are no records, the **RecordCount** property setting is 0, and the **BOF** and **EOF** property settings are **True**.

You can use the **MoveNext**, **MovePrevious**, **MoveFirst**, and **MoveLast** methods to reposition the current record. Forward-only–type **Recordset** objects support only the **MoveNext** method. When using the Move methods to visit each record (or "walk" through the **Recordset**), you can use the **BOF** and **EOF** properties to check for the beginning or end of the **Recordset** object.

With dynaset-and snapshot-type **Recordset** objects in a Microsoft Jet workspace, you can also use the Find methods, such as **FindFirst**, to locate a specific record based on criteria. If the record isn't found, the **NoMatch** property is set to **True**. For table-type **Recordset** objects, you can scan records using the **Seek** method.

The **Type** property indicates the type of **Recordset** object created, and the **Updatable** property indicates whether you can change the object's records.

Information about the structure of a base table, such as the names and data types of each **Field** object and any **Index** objects, is stored in a **TableDef** object.

To refer to a **Recordset** object in a collection by its ordinal number or by its **Name** property setting, use any of the following syntax forms:

Recordsets(0)
Recordsets("*name*")
Recordsets![*name*]

Note You can open a **Recordset** object from the same data source or database more than once, creating duplicate names in the **Recordsets** collection. You should assign **Recordset** objects to object variables and refer to them by variable name.

Properties

AbsolutePosition Property, **BOF, EOF** Properties, **Bookmark** Property, **Bookmarkable** Property, **CacheSize** Property, **DateCreated, LastUpdated** Properties, **EditMode** Property, **Filter** Property, **Index** Property, **LastModified** Property, **LockEdits** Property, **Name** Property, **NoMatch** Property, **PercentPosition** Property, **RecordCount** Property, **Restartable** Property, **Sort** Property, **Transactions** Property, **Type** Property, **Updatable** Property, **ValidationRule** Property, **ValidationText** Property, **BatchCollisionCount** Property, **BatchCollisions** Property, **BatchSize** Property, **CacheStart** Property, **Connection** Property, **RecordStatus** Property, **StillExecuting** Property, **UpdateOptions** Property

Methods

AddNew Method, **CancelUpdate** Method, **Clone** Method, **Close** Method, **CopyQueryDef** Method, **Delete** Method, **Edit** Method, **FillCache** Method, **FindFirst, FindLast, FindNext, FindPrevious** Methods, **GetRows** Method, **Move** Method, **MoveFirst, MoveLast, MoveNext, MovePrevious** Methods, **OpenRecordset** Method, **Requery** Method, **Seek** Method, **Update** Method, **Cancel** Method, **NextRecordset** Method

See Also

Dynaset-Type Recordset Object, **Index** Object, **Snapshot-Type Recordset** Object, **Table-Type Recordset** Object, **Forward-Only–Type Recordset** Object, **Dynamic-Type Recordset** Object

Example

This example demonstrates **Recordset** objects and the **Recordsets** collection by opening four different types of **Recordsets**, enumerating the **Recordsets** collection of the current **Database**, and enumerating the **Properties** collection of each **Recordset**.

```
Sub RecordsetX()

    Dim dbsNorthwind As Database
    Dim rstTable As Recordset
```

```
Dim rstDynaset As Recordset
Dim rstSnapshot As Recordset
Dim rstForwardOnly As Recordset
Dim rstLoop As Recordset
Dim prpLoop As Property

Set dbsNorthwind = OpenDatabase("Northwind.mdb")

With dbsNorthwind

    ' Open one of each type of Recordset object.
    Set rstTable = .OpenRecordset("Categories", _
        dbOpenTable)
    Set rstDynaset = .OpenRecordset("Employees", _
        dbOpenDynaset)
    Set rstSnapshot = .OpenRecordset("Shippers", _
        dbOpenSnapshot)
    Set rstForwardOnly = .OpenRecordset _
        ("Employees", dbOpenForwardOnly)

    Debug.Print "Recordsets in Recordsets " & _
        "collection of dbsNorthwind"

    ' Enumerate Recordsets collection.
    For Each rstLoop In .Recordsets

        With rstLoop
            Debug.Print "    " & .Name

            ' Enumerate Properties collection of each
            ' Recordset object. Trap for any
            ' properties whose values are invalid in
            ' this context.
            For Each prpLoop In .Properties
                On Error Resume Next
                If prpLoop <> "" Then Debug.Print _
                    "        " & prpLoop.Name & _
                    " = " & prpLoop
                On Error GoTo 0
            Next prpLoop

        End With

    Next rstLoop

    rstTable.Close
    rstDynaset.Close
    rstSnapshot.Close
    rstForwardOnly.Close

    .Close
End With

End Sub
```

Recordset Property

Returns or sets a **Recordset** object defined by a **Data** control's properties or by an existing **Recordset** object.

Applies To

Data Control

Syntax

Set *object*.**Recordset** [= *value*]

The **Recordset** property syntax has these parts:

Part	Description
object	An object expression that evaluates to an object in the **Applies To** list.
value	An object variable containing a **Recordset** object.

Remarks

The **Data** control is automatically initialized when your application starts before the initial **Form_Load** procedure. If the **Connect**, **DatabaseName**, **Options**, **RecordSource**, **Exclusive**, **ReadOnly** and **RecordsetType** properties are valid, or if you set these **Data** control properties at run time and use the **Refresh** method, the Microsoft Jet database engine attempts to create a new **Recordset** object based on those properties. This **Recordset** is accessible through the **Data** control's **Recordset** property. If, however, one or more of these properties is set incorrectly at design time, an untrappable error occurs when Visual Basic attempts to use the **properties** to open the specified database and create the **Recordset** object.

You can use the **Recordset** property as you would any other **Recordset** object. For example, you can use any of the **Recordset** methods or properties and examine the structure of the **Recordset** object's underlying schema.

You can also request the type of **Recordset** to be created by setting the **Data** control's **RecordsetType** property. If you don't request a specific type, a dynaset-type **Recordset** is created. Using the **RecordsetType** property, you can request to create either a table-, snapshot- or dynaset-type **Recordset**. However, if the Jet engine can't create the type requested, a trappable error occurs.

In many cases, the default type and configuration of the **Recordset** object created is extremely inefficient. That is, you might not need an updatable, fully-scrollable, keyset-type cursor to access your data. For example, a read-only, snapshot-type **Recordset** might be far faster to create than the default **Recordset**. Be sure to choose the most efficient Type, **Exclusive**, **Options** and **ReadOnly** properties possible for your situation.

The type of **Recordset** created can be determined at run time by examining the **Recordset** property's **Type** property or the **Data** control's **RecordsetType** property.

Note, however, that the constants used for the type of **Recordset** created are different. For example:

```
If Data1.Recordset.Type = dbOpenDynaset Then ...
If Data1.RecordsetType = dbDynasetType Then ...
```

A **Recordset** might not be updatable even if you request a dynaset- or table-type **Recordset**. If the underlying database, table, or field isn't updatable, all or portions of your **Recordset** may be read-only. Examine the **Database** and **Recordset** objects' **Updatable** property or the **Field** object's **DataUpdatable** property to determine if your code can change the records. Even when the **DataUpdatable** property returns **True**, there are situations where the underlying data fields might *not* be updatable if, for example, you do not have sufficient permissions to make changes. Other factors can also prevent fields from being updatable.

The number of records returned by the **Recordset** can be determined by moving to the last record in the **Recordset** and examining the **Recordset** object's **RecordCount** property. Before you move to the last record, the value returned by the **RecordCount** property only reflects the number of rows processed by the Jet engine. The following example shows how you can combine the **RecordCount** property of a **Recordset** with the **Recordset** property to display the number of records in a **Data** control's recordset:

```
Data1.Recordset.MoveLast
MsgBox "Records: " & Data1.Recordset.RecordCount
```

Professional and Enterprise Editions

If you create a **Recordset** object using either code or another **Data** control, you can set the **Recordset** property of the **Data** control to this new **Recordset**. Any existing **Recordset** in the **Data** control, and the **Database** object associated with it are released when a new **Recordset** is assigned to the **Recordset** property.

Note When the **Recordset** property is set, the **Data** control doesn't close the current **Recordset** or **Database,** but it does release it. If there are no other users, the database is closed automatically. You may wish to consider closing the **Recordset** and **Database** associated with the **Data** control prior to setting the **Recordset** property using the **Close** method.

Make sure the **DataField** properties of the bound controls connected to the **Data** control are set to match the new **Recordset** object's field names.

For example, to create a **Recordset** in code and pass it to an existing **Data** control:

```
Dim Db As Database, Rs As Recordset   ' Defined as public variables.
Sub ApplyRecordset()
    Set Db = Workspaces(0).OpenDatabase("BIBLIO.MDB")
    Set Rs = Db.OpenRecordset("AUTHORS") ' Defaults to Table object.
    Set Data1.Recordset = Rs' Assign Recordset.
    Data1.Recordset.Index = "PrimaryKey"
    Debug.print Rs.Type   ' Show type created.
End Sub
```

You can use this technique to create an MDI parent and child data connection with a single hidden **Data** control on the MDI parent form and another visible **Data** control on the MDI child. In the MDI child's **Form_Load** event, set the child's **Data** control **Recordset** property to the parent's **Data** control **Recordset** property. Using this technique synchronizes all the child forms and their bound controls with the parent.

Note   The **Data** control doesn't support forward-only **Recordset** objects. If you try to assign a forward-only **Recordset** object to the **Recordset** property of the **Data** control, a trappable error results.

All **Recordset** objects created by the **Data** control are created in **Workspaces**(0) except ODBCDirect (**DefaultType** = **dbUseODBC**) **Recordset** objects. If you need to use the **Data** control to manipulate a database in another **Workspace**, use the technique shown above to open the database in the desired **Workspace**, create a new **Recordset** and set the **Data** control's **Recordset** property to this new **Recordset**.

Important   You can always reference the properties of the **Data** control's **Recordset** by using the **Recordset** property. By directly referencing the **Recordset**, you can determine the **Index** to use with **Table** objects, the **Parameters** collection of a **QueryDef,** or the **Recordset** type.

Data Type

Recordset

See Also

DatabaseName Property, **DataField** Property, **DataUpdatable** Property, **Exclusive** Property, **Options** Property, **QueryDef** Object, **ReadOnly** Property, **RecordCount** Property, **RecordsetType** Property, **RecordSource** Property, **Updatable** Property

---

Recordsets Collection

A **Recordsets** collection contains all open **Recordset** objects in a **Database** object.

Remarks

When you use DAO objects, you manipulate data almost entirely using **Recordset** objects.

A new **Recordset** object is automatically added to the **Recordsets** collection when you open the **Recordset** object, and is automatically removed when you close it.

You can create as many **Recordset** object variables as needed. Different **Recordset** objects can access the same tables, queries, and fields without conflicting.

To refer to a **Recordset** object in a collection by its ordinal number or by its **Name** property setting, use any of the following syntax forms:

Recordsets(0)
Recordsets("*name*")
Recordsets![*name*]

Note   You can open a **Recordset** object from the same data source or database more than once, creating duplicate names in the **Recordsets** collection. You should assign **Recordset** objects to object variables and refer to them by variable name.

Properties

Count Property

Methods

Refresh Method

Example

This example demonstrates **Recordset** objects and the **Recordsets** collection by opening four different types of **Recordsets**, enumerating the **Recordsets** collection of the current **Database**, and enumerating the **Properties** collection of each **Recordset**.

```
Sub RecordsetX()

    Dim dbsNorthwind As Database
    Dim rstTable As Recordset
    Dim rstDynaset As Recordset
    Dim rstSnapshot As Recordset
    Dim rstForwardOnly As Recordset
    Dim rstLoop As Recordset
    Dim prpLoop As Property

    Set dbsNorthwind = OpenDatabase("Northwind.mdb")

    With dbsNorthwind

        ' Open one of each type of Recordset object.
        Set rstTable = .OpenRecordset("Categories", _
            dbOpenTable)
        Set rstDynaset = .OpenRecordset("Employees", _
            dbOpenDynaset)
        Set rstSnapshot = .OpenRecordset("Shippers", _
            dbOpenSnapshot)
        Set rstForwardOnly = .OpenRecordset _
            ("Employees", dbOpenForwardOnly)

        Debug.Print "Recordsets in Recordsets " & _
            "collection of dbsNorthwind"
```

```
            ' Enumerate Recordsets collection.
            For Each rstLoop In .Recordsets

                With rstLoop
                    Debug.Print "      " & .Name

                        ' Enumerate Properties collection of each
                        ' Recordset object. Trap for any
                        ' properties whose values are invalid in
                        ' this context.
                        For Each prpLoop In .Properties
                            On Error Resume Next
                            If prpLoop <> "" Then Debug.Print _
                                "           " & prpLoop.Name & _
                                " = " & prpLoop
                            On Error GoTo 0
                        Next prpLoop

                End With

            Next rstLoop

            rstTable.Close
            rstDynaset.Close
            rstSnapshot.Close
            rstForwardOnly.Close

            .Close
        End With

    End Sub
```

RecordsetType Property

Returns or sets a value indicating the type of **Recordset** object you want the **Data**
control to create.

Applies To

Data Control

Syntax

object.**RecordsetType** [= *value*]

The **RecordsetType** property syntax has these parts:

Part	Description
object	An object expression that evaluates to an object in the **Applies To** list.
value	A constant or value that specifies a type of **Recordset**, as described in Settings.

Settings

The settings for *value* are:

Setting	Value	Description
vbRSTypeTable	0	A table-type **Recordset**
vbRSTypeDynaset	1	(Default) A dynaset-type **Recordset**
vbRSTypeSnapshot	2	A snapshot-type **Recordset**

Remarks

If the Microsoft Jet database engine can't create the type of **Recordset** you requested, a trappable error occurs.

If you don't specify a **RecordsetType** before the **Data** control creates the **Recordset**, a dynaset-type **Recordset** is created (if possible).

If you create a **Recordset** without using the **Data** control (even with another **Data** control) and set the **Recordset** property with this new **Recordset** object, the **RecordsetType** property of the **Data** control is set to the **Recordset.Type** property of the new **Recordset**.

Important The **RecordsetType** property *value* doesn't correspond to the value used to identify **Recordset** object types. See the **OpenRecordset** method or the **Type** property for details.

In many cases, the default type and configuration of the **Recordset** object created is extremely inefficient. That is, you might not need an updatable, fully-scrollable, keyset-type cursor to access your data. For example, a read-only, forward-only, snapshot-type **Recordset** might be far faster to create than the default cursor. Be sure to choose the most efficient settings for the **RecordsetType**, **Exclusive**, **Options** and **ReadOnly** properties for your situation.

Data Type

Integer

RecordSource Property

Returns or sets the underlying table, SQL statement, or **QueryDef** object for a **Data** control.

Applies To

Data Control

Syntax

object.**RecordSource** [= *value*]

The **RecordSource** property syntax has these parts:

Part	Description
object	An object expression that evaluates to an object in the **Applies To** list.
value	A string expression specifying a name, as described in Settings.

Settings

The settings for *value* are:

Setting	Description
A table name	The name of one of the tables defined in the **Database** object's **TableDefs** collection.
An SQL query	A valid SQL string using syntax appropriate for the data source.
A **QueryDef**	The name of one of the **QueryDef** objects in the **Database** object's **QueryDefs** collection when accessing a Jet database.

Remarks

The **RecordSource** property specifies the source of the records accessible through bound controls on your form.

If you set the **RecordSource** property to the name of an existing table in the database, all of the fields in that table are visible to the bound controls attached to the **Data** control. For table-type recordsets (**RecordsetType = vbRSTypeTable**), the order of the records retrieved is set by the **Index** object that you select using the **Index** property of the **Recordset**. For dynaset-type and snapshot-type **Recordset** objects, you can order the records by using a SQL statement with an Order By clause in the **RecordSource** property of the **Data** control. Otherwise, the data is returned in no particular order.

If you set the **RecordSource** property to the name of an existing **QueryDef** in the database, all fields returned by the **QueryDef** are visible to the bound controls attached to the **Data** control. The order of the records retrieved is set by the **QueryDef** object's query. For example, the **QueryDef** may include an ORDER BY clause to change the order of the records returned by the **Recordset** created by the **Data** control or a WHERE clause to filter the records. If the **QueryDef** doesn't specify an order, the data is returned in no particular order.

Note At design-time, the **QueryDef** objects displayed in the Properties window for the **RecordSource** property are filtered out to display only **QueryDef** objects that are usable with the **Data** control. **QueryDef** objects which have parameters, and **QueryDef** objects which have the following types are not displayed: **dbQAction**, **dbQCrosstab**, **dbQSQLPassThrough** and **dbQSetOperation**.

If you set the **RecordSource** property to an SQL statement that returns records, all fields returned by the SQL query are visible to the bound controls attached to the **Data** control. This statement may include an ORDER BY clause to change the order of the records returned by the **Recordset** created by the **Data** control or a WHERE clause to filter the records. If the database you specify in the **Database** and **Connect** property isn't a Microsoft Jet engine database, and if the **dbSQLPassThrough** option is set in the **Options** property, your SQL query must use the syntax required by that database engine.

Note Whenever your **QueryDef** or SQL statement returns a value from an expression, the field name of the expression is created automatically by the Microsoft Jet database engine. Generally, the name is Expr1 followed by a three-character number beginning with 000. For example, the first expression would be named: Expr1000.

In most cases you'll want to alias expressions so you know the name of the column to bind to the bound control. See the SQL SELECT statement AS clause for more information.

After changing the value of the **RecordSource** property at run time, you must use the **Refresh** method to enable the change and rebuild the **Recordset**.

At run time, if the **Recordset** specifies an invalid **Table** name, **QueryDef** name, or contains invalid SQL syntax, a trappable error will result. If this error occurs during the initial **Form_Load** procedure, the error is not trappable.

Note Make sure each bound control has a valid setting for its **DataField** property. If you change the setting of a **Data** control's **RecordSource** property and then use **Refresh**, the **Recordset** identifies the new object. This may invalidate the **DataField** settings of bound controls and cause a trappable error.

Data Type
> **String**

RecordStatus Property

ReDynamic-Type Recordset Object, turns a value indicating the update status of the current record if it is part of a batch update (**ODBCDirect** workspaces only).

Applies To
> **Dynaset-Type Recordset** Object, **Recordset** Object, **Snapshot-Type Recordset** Object, **Forward-Only–Type Recordset** Object, **Dynamic-Type Recordset** Object

Return Values
> The return value is a **Long** that can be any of the following constants:

Constant	Description
dbRecordUnmodified	(Default) The record has not been modified or has been updated successfully.
dbRecordModified	The record has been modified and not updated in the database.
dbRecordNew	The record has been inserted with the **AddNew** method, but not yet inserted into the database.
dbRecordDeleted	The record has been deleted, but not yet deleted in the database.
dbRecordDBDeleted	The record has been deleted locally *and* in the database.

Remarks

The value of the **RecordStatus** property indicates whether and how the current record will be involved in the next optimistic batch update.

When a user changes a record, the **RecordStatus** for that record automatically changes to **dbRecordModified**. Similarly, if a record is added or deleted, **RecordStatus** reflects the appropriate constant. When you then use a batch-mode **Update** method, DAO will submit an appropriate operation to the remote server for each record, based on the record's **RecordStatus** property.

Example

This example uses the **RecordStatus** and **DefaultCursorDriver** properties to show how changes to a local **Recordset** are tracked during batch updating. The **RecordStatusOutput** function is required for this procedure to run.

```
Sub RecordStatusX()

    Dim wrkMain As Workspace
    Dim conMain As Connection
    Dim rstTemp As Recordset

    Set wrkMain = CreateWorkspace("ODBCWorkspace", _
        "admin", "", dbUseODBC)
    ' This DefaultCursorDriver setting is required for
    ' batch updating.
    wrkMain.DefaultCursorDriver = dbUseClientBatchCursor

    Set conMain = wrkMain.OpenConnection("Publishers", _
        dbDriverNoPrompt, False, _
        "ODBC;DATABASE=pubs;UID=sa;PWD=;DSN=Publishers")
    ' The following locking argument is required for
    ' batch updating.
    Set rstTemp = conMain.OpenRecordset( _
        "SELECT * FROM authors", dbOpenDynaset, 0, _
        dbOptimisticBatch)

    With rstTemp
        .MoveFirst
        Debug.Print "Original record: " & !au_lname
        Debug.Print , RecordStatusOutput2(.RecordStatus)

        .Edit
        !au_lname = "Bowen"
        .Update
        Debug.Print "Edited record: " & !au_lname
        Debug.Print , RecordStatusOutput2(.RecordStatus)

        .AddNew
        !au_lname = "NewName"
        .Update
        Debug.Print "New record: " & !au_lname
        Debug.Print , RecordStatusOutput2(.RecordStatus)
```

```
        .Delete
        Debug.Print "Deleted record: " & !au_lname
        Debug.Print , RecordStatusOutput2(.RecordStatus)

        ' Close the local recordset without updating the
        ' data on the server.
        .Close
    End With

    conMain.Close
    wrkMain.Close

End Sub

Function RecordStatusOutput(lngTemp As Long) As String

    Dim strTemp As String

    strTemp = ""

    ' Construct an output string based on the RecordStatus
    ' value.
If lngTemp = dbRecordUnmodified Then _
        strTemp = "[dbRecordUnmodified]"
    If lngTemp = dbRecordModified Then _
        strTemp = "[dbRecordModified]"
    If lngTemp = dbRecordNew Then _
        strTemp = "[dbRecordNew]"
    If lngTemp = dbRecordDeleted Then _
        strTemp = "[dbRecordDeleted]"
    If lngTemp = dbRecordDBDeleted Then _
        strTemp = "[dbRecordDBDeleted]"

    RecordStatusOutput = strTemp

End Function
```

ReDim Statement

Used at procedure level to reallocate storage space for dynamic array variables.

Syntax

ReDim [**Preserve**] *varname*(*subscripts*) [**As** *type*] [, *varname*(*subscripts*) [**As** *type*]] . . .

The **ReDim** statement syntax has these parts:

Part	Description
Preserve	Optional. Keyword used to preserve the data in an existing array when you change the size of the last dimension.
varname	Required. Name of the variable; follows standard variable naming conventions.

(continued)

Part	Description
subscripts	Required. Dimensions of an array variable; up to 60 multiple dimensions may be declared. The *subscripts* argument uses the following syntax: [*lower* **To**] *upper* [,[*lower* **To**] *upper*] . . . When not explicitly stated in *lower*, the lower bound of an array is controlled by the **Option Base** statement. The lower bound is zero if no **Option Base** statement is present.
type	Optional. Data type of the variable; may be **Byte**, **Boolean**, **Integer**, **Long**, **Currency**, **Single**, **Double**, **Decimal** (not currently supported), **Date**, **String** (for variable-length strings), **String** * *length* (for fixed-length strings), **Object**, **Variant**, a user-defined type, or an object type. Use a separate **As** *type* clause for each variable being defined. For a **Variant** containing an array, *type* describes the type of each element of the array, but doesn't change the **Variant** to some other type.

Remarks

The **ReDim** statement is used to size or resize a dynamic array that has already been formally declared using a **Private**, **Public**, or **Dim** statement with empty parentheses (without dimension subscripts).

You can use the **ReDim** statement repeatedly to change the number of elements and dimensions in an array. However, you can't declare an array of one data type and later use **ReDim** to change the array to another data type, unless the array is contained in a **Variant**. If the array is contained in a **Variant**, the type of the elements can be changed using an **As** *type* clause, unless you're using the **Preserve** keyword, in which case, no changes of data type are permitted.

If you use the **Preserve** keyword, you can resize only the last array dimension and you can't change the number of dimensions at all. For example, if your array has only one dimension, you can resize that dimension because it is the last and only dimension. However, if your array has two or more dimensions, you can change the size of only the last dimension and still preserve the contents of the array. The following example shows how you can increase the size of the last dimension of a dynamic array without erasing any existing data contained in the array.

```
ReDim X(10, 10, 10)
. . .
ReDim Preserve X(10, 10, 15)
```

Similarly, when you use **Preserve**, you can change the size of the array only by changing the upper bound; changing the lower bound causes an error.

Caution   If you make an array smaller than it was, data in the eliminated elements will be lost. If you pass an array to a procedure by reference, you can't redimension the array within the procedure.

When variables are initialized, a numeric variable is initialized to 0, a variable-length string is initialized to a zero-length string (""), and a fixed-length string is filled with zeros. **Variant** variables are initialized to **Empty**. Each element of a user-defined type variable is initialized as if it were a separate variable. A variable that refers to an object must be assigned an existing object using the **Set** statement before it can be used. Until it is assigned an object, the declared object variable has the special value **Nothing**, which indicates that it doesn't refer to any particular instance of an object.

Caution The **ReDim** statement acts as a declarative statement if the variable it declares doesn't exist at module level or procedure level. If another variable with the same name is created later, even in a wider scope, **ReDim** will refer to the later variable and won't necessarily cause a compilation error, even if **Option Explicit** is in effect. To avoid such conflicts, **ReDim** should not be used as a declarative statement, but simply for redimensioning arrays.

Note To resize an array contained in a **Variant**, you must explicitly declare the **Variant** variable before attempting to resize its array.

See Also

Array Function, **Dim** Statement, **Option Base** Statement, **Private** Statement, **Public** Statement, **Set** Statement, **Static** Statement

Example

This example uses the **ReDim** statement to allocate and reallocate storage space for dynamic-array variables. It assumes the **Option Base** is **1**.

```
Dim MyArray() As Integer     ' Declare dynamic array.
Redim MyArray(5)             ' Allocate 5 elements.
For I = 1 To 5               ' Loop 5 times.
   MyArray(I) = I            ' Initialize array.
Next I
```

The next statement resizes the array and erases the elements.

```
Redim MyArray(10)            ' Resize to 10 elements.
For I = 1 To 10              ' Loop 10 times.
   MyArray(I) = I            ' Initialize array.
Next I
```

The following statement resizes the array but does not erase elements.

```
Redim Preserve MyArray(15) ' Resize to 15 elements.
```

Reference Object

Represents a reference to a type library or a project.

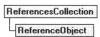

Remarks

Use the **Reference** object to verify whether a reference is still valid.

The **IsBroken** property returns **True** if the reference no longer points to a valid reference. The **BuiltIn** property returns **True** if the reference is a default reference that can't be moved or removed. Use the **Name** property to determine if the reference you want to add or remove is the correct one.

Specifics

References Collection

Properties

Collection Property, **Description** Property, **GUID** Property, **IsBroken** Property, **BuiltIn** Property, **FullPath** Property, **Major** Property, **Minor** Property, **Name** Property, **Type** Property, **VBE** Property

See Also

AddFromFile Method (Add-Ins), **AddFromGuid** Method, **References** Collection

---

References Collection

Represents the set of references in the project.

Applies To

ItemAdded Event, **ItemRemoved** Event

Remarks

Use the **References** collection to add or remove references. The **References** collection is the same as the set of references selected in the **References** dialog box.

Properties

Count Property, **Parent** Property, **VBE** Property

Methods

AddFromFile Method, **AddFromGuid** Method, **Item** Method, **Remove** Method

AddFromFile Method (Add-Ins), **AddFromGuid** Method, **Item** Method, **Remove** Method, **Reference** Object, **ReferencesEvents** Object, **VBProject** Object

---

ReferencesEvents Object

Returned by the **ReferencesEvents** property.

Applies To

ItemAdded Event, **ItemRemoved** Event

Remarks

The **ReferencesEvents** object is the source of events that occur when a reference is added to or removed from a project. The **ItemAdded** event is triggered after a reference is added to a project. The **ItemRemoved** event is triggered after a reference is removed from a project.

Properties

ItemAdded Event, **ItemRemoved** Event

See Also

Events Object, **References** Collection, **ReferencesEvents** Property

---

ReferencesEvents Property

Returns the **ReferencesEvents** object. Read-only.

Applies to

Events Object

Settings

The setting for the argument you pass to the **ReferencesEvents** property is:

Argument	Description
vbproject	If *vbproject* points to **Nothing**, the object that is returned will supply events for the **References** collections of all **VBProject** objects in the **VBProjects** collection. If *vbproject* points to a valid **VBProject** object, the object that is returned will supply events for only the **References** collection for that project.

Remarks

The **ReferencesEvents** property takes an argument and returns an event source object. The **ReferencesEvents** object is the source for events that are triggered when references are added or removed.

See Also

See Also

Add Method, **Remove** Method, **ReferencesEvents** Object, **VBProject** Object, **VBProjects** Collection, **CommandBarEvents** Property

Example

The following example uses code including the **ReferencesEvents** property to support event-handling code for adding or removing references.

```
Private WithEvents X As ReferencesEvents

Sub Test()
   Set X = Application.VBE.Events.ReferencesEvents
End Sub

Private Sub X_ItemAdded(ByVal Reference As VBIDE.Reference)
   ' Put code to support item addition here
End Sub

Private Sub X_ItemRemoved(ByVal Reference As VBIDE.Reference)
   ' Put code to support item removal here
End Sub
```

ReFill Method

Re-creates the list of a **DBList** or **DBCombo** control and forces a repaint.

Applies To

DBCombo Control, **DBList** Control

Syntax

object.**ReFill**

The *object* placeholder represents an object expression that evaluates to an object in the Applies To list.

Remarks

The **ReFill** method is different than the standard **Refresh** method, which just forces a Repaint event.

Refresh Method

Forces a complete repaint of a form or control.

Applies To

CheckBox Control, **ComboBox** Control, **CommandButton** Control, **Data** Control, **DirListBox** Control, **FriveListBox** Control, **FileListBox** Control, **Form Object,** **Forms** Collection, **Frame** Control, **HScrollBar, VScrollBar** Controls, **Image** Control, **Label** Control, **Line** Control, **ListBox** Control, **OLE Container** Control, **OptionButton** Control, **PictureBox** Control, **PropertyPage** Object, **Shape** Control, **TextBox** Control, **UserControl** Object, **UserDocument** Object

Syntax

object.**Refresh**

The *object* placeholder represents an object expression that evaluates to an object in the **Applies To** list.

Remarks

Use the **Refresh** method when you want to:

- Completely display one form while another form loads.
- Update the contents of a file-system list box, such as a **FileListBox** control.
- Update the data structures of a **Data** control.

Refresh can't be used on MDI forms , but can be used on MDI child forms. You can't use **Refresh** on **Menu** or **Timer** controls.

Generally, painting a form or control is handled automatically while no events are occurring. However, there may be situations where you want the form or control updated immediately. For example, if you use a file list box, a directory list box, or a drive list box to show the current status of the directory structure, you can use **Refresh** to update the list whenever a change is made to the directory structure.

You can use the **Refresh** method on a **Data** control to open or reopen the database (if the **DatabaseName**, **ReadOnly**, **Exclusive**, or **Connect** property settings have changed) and rebuild the dynaset in the control's **Recordset** property.

See Also

Paint Event, **MDIForm** Object, **MDIChild** Property

Example

This example uses the **Refresh** method to update a **FileListBox** control as test files are created. To try this example, paste the code into the Declarations section of a form with a **FileListBox** control named File1, and then run the example and click the form.

```
Private Sub Form_Click ()
    ' Declare variables.
    Dim FilName, Msg as String, I as Integer
    File1.Pattern = "TestFile.*"      ' Set file pattern.
    For I = 1 To 8 ' Do eight times.
        FilName = "TESTFILE." & I
        ' Create empty file.
        Open FilName For Output As FreeFile
        File1.Refresh ' Refresh file list box.
        Close ' Close file.
    Next I
    Msg = "Choose OK to remove the created test files."
    MsgBox Msg   ' Display message.
    Kill "TESTFILE.*" ' Remove test files.
    File1.Refresh   ' Update file list box.
End Sub
```

Refresh Method (DAO)

Updates the objects in a collection to reflect the current database's schema.

Applies To

Databases Collection, **Documents** Collection, **Errors** Collection, **Fields** Collection, **Groups** Collection, **Indexes** Collection, **Parameters** Collection, **Properties** Collection, **QueryDefs** Collection, **Recordsets** Collection, **Relations** Collection, **TableDefs** Collection, **Users** Collection, **Workspaces** Collection, **Connections** Collection

Syntax

collection.**Refresh**

The *collection* placeholder is an object variable that represents a persistent collection.

Remarks

You can't use the **Refresh** method with collections that aren't persistent, such as **Connections**, **Databases**, **Recordsets**, **Workspaces**, or the **QueryDefs** collection of a **Connection** object.

To determine the position that the Microsoft Jet database engine uses for **Field** objects in the **Fields** collection of a **QueryDef**, **Recordset**, or **TableDef** object, use the **OrdinalPosition** property of each **Field** object. Changing the **OrdinalPosition** property of a **Field** object may not change the order of the **Field** objects in the collection until you use the **Refresh** method.

Use the **Refresh** method in multiuser environments in which other users may change the database. You may also need to use it on any collections that are indirectly affected by changes to the database. For example, if you change a **Users** collection, you may need to refresh a **Groups** collection before using the **Groups** collection.

A collection is filled with objects the first time it's referred to and won't automatically reflect subsequent changes other users make. If it's likely that another user has changed a collection, use the **Refresh** method on the collection immediately before carrying out any task in your application that assumes the presence or absence of a particular object in the collection. This will ensure that the collection is as up-to-date as possible. On the other hand, using **Refresh** can unnecessarily slow performance.

See Also

Append Method, **Close** Method, **Delete** Method, **Requery** Method, **OrdinalPosition** Property

Example

This example uses the **Refresh** method to update the **Fields** collection of the Categories table based on changes to the **OrdinalPosition** data. The order of the **Fields** in the collection changes only after the **Refresh** method is used.

```
Sub RefreshX()
```

```
   Dim dbsNorthwind As Database
   Dim tdfEmployees As TableDef
   Dim aintPosition() As Integer
   Dim astrFieldName() As String
   Dim intTemp As Integer
   Dim fldLoop As Field

   Set dbsNorthwind = OpenDatabase("Northwind.mdb")
   Set tdfEmployees = dbsNorthwind.TableDefs("Categories")

   With tdfEmployees
      ' Display original OrdinalPosition data and store it
      ' in an array.
      Debug.Print _
         "Original OrdinalPosition data in TableDef."
      ReDim aintPosition(0 To .Fields.Count - 1) As Integer
      ReDim astrFieldName(0 To .Fields.Count - 1) As String
      For intTemp = 0 To .Fields.Count - 1
         aintPosition(intTemp) = _
            .Fields(intTemp).OrdinalPosition
         astrFieldName(intTemp) = .Fields(intTemp).Name
         Debug.Print , aintPosition(intTemp), _
            astrFieldName(intTemp)
      Next intTemp

      ' Change OrdinalPosition data.
      For Each fldLoop In .Fields
         fldLoop.OrdinalPosition = _
            100 - fldLoop.OrdinalPosition
      Next fldLoop
      Set fldLoop = Nothing

      ' Print new data.
      Debug.Print "New OrdinalPosition data before Refresh."
      For Each fldLoop In .Fields
         Debug.Print , fldLoop.OrdinalPosition, fldLoop.Name
      Next fldLoop

      .Fields.Refresh

      ' Print new data, showing how the field order has been
      ' changed.
      Debug.Print "New OrdinalPosition data after Refresh."
      For Each fldLoop In .Fields
         Debug.Print , fldLoop.OrdinalPosition, fldLoop.Name
      Next fldLoop

      ' Restore original OrdinalPosition data.
      For intTemp = 0 To .Fields.Count - 1
         .Fields(astrFieldName(intTemp)).OrdinalPosition = _
            aintPosition(intTemp)
      Next intTemp
   End With

   dbsNorthwind.Close

End Sub
```

Refresh Method (Remote Data)

Closes and rebuilds the **rdoResultset** object created by a **RemoteData control** or refreshes the members of the collections in the **Applies To** list.

Applies To

rdoColumns Collection, **rdoTables** Collection, **RemoteData** Control

Syntax

object.**Refresh**

The *object* placeholder represents an object expression that evaluates to an object in the **Applies To** list.

Remarks

You can use the **Refresh** method on a **RemoteData** control to close and reopen the **rdoResultset** if the properties that describe the result set have changed. When you use the **Refresh** method, the properties and current row position is reset to the state set when the query was first run.

Once the **Refresh** method has been executed against the **RemoteData** control, all stored **rdoResultset** bookmarks are invalid.

If both the **BOF** and **EOF** property settings of the **rdoResultset** object are **True**, or the **RowCount** property is set to 0 after you use the **Refresh** method, the query didn't return any rows and the new **rdoResultset** contains no data.

Use the **Refresh** method in multi-user environments in which the database schema is subject to change to retrieve current table definitions. Using the **Refresh** method on an **rdoTables** collection fetches table names from the base tables in the database. Using **Refresh** on a specific **rdoTable** object's **rdoColumns** collection fetches the table structures including column names and data types from the base tables.

Note Before you can use the name of a base table in the *name* argument of the **OpenResultset** method, you must first use the **Refresh** method against the **rdoTables** collection to populate it. You can also populate the **rdoTables** collection by referencing one of its members by its ordinal number. For example, referencing **rdoTables**(0) will populate the entire collection.

See Also

Close Method (Remote Data), **Execute** Method (Remote Data), **Requery** Method (Remote Data), **rdoTable** Object, **RemoteData** Control, **BOF**, **EOF** Properties (Remote Data), **RowCount** Property (Remote Data)

Example

The following example illustrates use of the **Refresh** method to rebuild an **rdoResultset** on the **RemoteData** control. The example resets the SQL property with a new query built using the concatenation technique. When the **Refresh** method is executed, the query is re-executed. Since the **Connect** property is not changed for each invocation of the Search procedure, the connection is not re-established each time – it is opened only on the first invocation. When the **Refresh** method is complete, the bound controls reflect data from the columns returned by the query.

```
Option Explicit
Private Sub Search_Click()
On Error GoTo eh
With MSRDC1
    .Connect = "UID=;PWD=;Database=Pubs;"
    .DataSourceName = "WorkDB"
    .SQL = "Select Au_Fname " _
        & " From Authors " _
        & " Where Au_Lname like '%" _
        & AuthorWanted & "%'"
    Debug.Print .SQL
    .Refresh

    If .Resultset.EOF Then
        MsgBox "No authors on file with that last name"
    End If
End With
Exit Sub

eh:
Dim er As rdoError
For Each er In rdoErrors
Debug.Print er
Next
Resume Next
End Sub
```

RefreshLink Method

Updates the connection information for a linked table (Microsoft Jet workspaces only).

Applies To

TableDef Object

Syntax

tabledef.**RefreshLink**

The *tabledef* placeholder specifies the **TableDef** object representing the linked table whose connection information you want to update.

Remarks

To change the connection information for a linked table, reset the **Connect** property of the corresponding **TableDef** object and then use the **RefreshLink** method to update the information. Using **RefreshLink** method doesn't change the linked table's properties and **Relation** objects.

For this connection information to exist in all collections associated with the **TableDef** object that represents the linked table, you must use the **Refresh** method on each collection.

See Also

Refresh Method, **Connect** Property

Example

This example uses the **RefreshLink** method to refresh the data in a linked table after its connection has been changed from one data source to another. The **RefreshLinkOutput** procedure is required for this procedure to run.

```
Sub RefreshLinkX()

    Dim dbsCurrent As Database
    Dim tdfLinked As TableDef

    ' Open a database to which a linked table can be
    ' appended.
    Set dbsCurrent = OpenDatabase("DB1.mdb")

    ' Create a linked table that points to a Microsoft
    ' SQL Server database.
    Set tdfLinked = _
        dbsCurrent.CreateTableDef("AuthorsTable")
    tdfLinked.Connect = _
        "ODBC;DATABASE=pubs;UID=sa;PWD=;DSN=Publishers"
    tdfLinked.SourceTableName = "authors"
    dbsCurrent.TableDefs.Append tdfLinked

    ' Display contents of linked table.
    Debug.Print _
        "Data from linked table connected to first source:"
    RefreshLinkOutput dbsCurrent

    ' Change connection information for linked table and
    ' refresh the connection in order to make the new data
    ' available.
    tdfLinked.Connect = _
        "ODBC;DATABASE=pubs;UID=sa;PWD=;DSN=NewPublishers"
    tdfLinked.RefreshLink

    ' Display contents of linked table.
    Debug.Print _
        "Data from linked table connected to second source:"
    RefreshLinkOutput dbsCurrent

    ' Delete linked table because this is a demonstration.
    dbsCurrent.TableDefs.Delete tdfLinked.Name

    dbsCurrent.Close

End Sub

Sub RefreshLinkOutput(dbsTemp As Database)

    Dim rstRemote As Recordset
    Dim intCount As Integer
```

```
' Open linked table.
Set rstRemote = _
    dbsTemp.OpenRecordset("AuthorsTable")

intCount = 0

' Enumerate Recordset object, but stop at 50 records.
With rstRemote
    Do While Not .EOF And intCount < 50
        Debug.Print , .Fields(0), .Fields(1)
        intCount = intCount + 1
        .MoveNext
    Loop
    If Not .EOF Then Debug.Print , "[more records]"
    .Close
End With

End Sub
```

RegisterDatabase Method

Enters connection information for an ODBC data source in the Windows Registry. The ODBC driver needs connection information when the ODBC data source is opened during a session.

Applies To

DBEngine Object

Syntax

DBEngine.RegisterDatabase *dbname*, *driver*, *silent*, *attributes*

The **RegisterDatabase** method syntax has these parts.

Part	Description
dbname	A **String** that is the name used in the **OpenDatabase** method. It refers to a block of descriptive information about the data source. For example, if the data source is an ODBC remote database, it could be the name of the server.
Driver	A **String** that is the name of the ODBC driver. This isn't the name of the ODBC driver DLL file. For example, SQL Server is a driver name, but SQLSRVR.dll is the name of a DLL file. You must have ODBC and the appropriate driver already installed.
Silent	A **Boolean** that is **True** if you don't want to display the ODBC driver dialog boxes that prompt for driver-specific information; or **False** if you want to display the ODBC driver dialog boxes. If *silent* is **True**, *attributes* must contain all the necessary driver-specific information or the dialog boxes are displayed anyway.
Attributes	A **String** that is a list of keywords to be added to the Windows Registry. The keywords are in a carriage-return–delimited string.

Remarks

If the database is already registered (connection information is already entered) in the Windows Registry when you use the **RegisterDatabase** method, the connection information is updated.

If the **RegisterDatabase** method fails for any reason, no changes are made to the Windows Registry, and an error occurs.

For more information about ODBC drivers such as SQL Server, see the Help file provided with the driver.

You should use the **ODBC Data Sources** dialog box in the Control Panel to add new data sources, or to make changes to existing entries. However, if you use the **RegisterDatabase** method, you should set the *silent* option to **True**.

See Also

Database Object, **OpenDatabase** Method

Example

This example uses the **RegisterDatabase** method to register a Microsoft SQL Server data source named Publishers in the Windows Registry.

Using the Windows ODBC Control Panel icon is the preferred way to create, modify, or delete data source names.

```
Sub RegisterDatabaseX()

    Dim dbsRegister As Database
    Dim strDescription As String
    Dim strAttributes As String
    Dim errLoop As Error

    ' Build keywords string.
    strDescription = InputBox( "Enter a description " & _
        "for the database to be registered.")
    strAttributes = "Database=pubs" & _
        vbCr & "Description=" & strDescription & _
        vbCr & "OemToAnsi=No" & _
        vbCr & "Server=Server1"

    ' Update Windows Registry.
    On Error GoTo Err_Register
    DBEngine.RegisterDatabase "Publishers", "SQL Server", _
        True, strAttributes
    On Error GoTo 0

    MsgBox "Use regedit.exe to view changes: " & _
        "HKEY_CURRENT_USER\" & _
        "Software\ODBC\ODBC.INI"

    Exit Sub

Err_Register:

    ' Notify user of any errors that result from
    ' the invalid data.
```

```
    If DBEngine.Errors.Count > 0 Then
       For Each errLoop In DBEngine.Errors
          MsgBox "Error number: " & errLoop.Number & _
             vbCr & errLoop.Description
       Next errLoop
    End If

    Resume Next

End Sub
```

Relation Object

A **Relation** object represents a relationship between fields in tables or queries
(Microsoft Jet databases only).

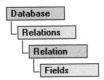

Remarks

You can use the **Relation** object to create new relationships and examine existing
relationships in your database.

Using a **Relation** object and its properties, you can:

- Specify an enforced relationship between fields in base tables (but not a
  relationship that involves a query or a linked table).

- Establish unenforced relationships between any type of table or query—native or
  linked.

- Use the **Name** property to refer to the relationship between the fields in the
  referenced primary table and the referencing foreign table.

- Use the **Attributes** property to determine whether the relationship between fields
  in the table is one-to-one or one-to-many and how to enforce referential integrity.

- Use the **Attributes** property to determine whether the Microsoft Jet database
  engine can perform cascading update and cascading delete operations on primary
  and foreign tables.

- Use the **Attributes** property to determine whether the relationship between fields
  in the table is left join or right join.

- Use the **Name** property of all **Field** objects in the **Fields** collection of a **Relation**
  object to set or return the names of the fields in the primary key of the referenced
  table, or the **ForeignName** property settings of the **Field** objects to set or return the
  names of the fields in the foreign key of the referencing table.

If you make changes that violate the relationships established for the database, a trappable error occurs. If you request cascading update or cascading delete operations, the Microsoft Jet database engine also modifies the primary or foreign key tables to enforce the relationships you establish.

For example, the Northwind database contains a relationship between an Orders table and a Customers table. The **CustomerID** field of the Customers table is the primary key, and the **CustomerID** field of the Orders table is the foreign key. For Microsoft Jet to accept a new record in the Orders table, it searches the Customers table for a match on the **CustomerID** field of the Orders table. If Microsoft Jet doesn't find a match, it doesn't accept the new record, and a trappable error occurs.

When you enforce referential integrity, a unique index must already exist for the key field of the referenced table. The Microsoft Jet database engine automatically creates an index with the **Foreign** property set to act as the foreign key in the referencing table.

To create a new **Relation** object, use the **CreateRelation** method. To refer to a **Relation** object in a collection by its ordinal number or by its **Name** property setting, use any of the following syntax forms:

Relations(0)
Relations("*name*")
Relations![*name*]

See Also

Property Object, **Properties Collection** Summary, **CreateRelation** Method, **Foreign** Property

Properties

Attributes Property, **ForeignTable** Property, **Name** Property, **Table** Property, **PartialReplica** Property

Methods

CreateField Method

Example

This example shows how an existing **Relation** object can control data entry. The procedure attempts to add a record with a deliberately incorrect **CategoryID**; this triggers the error-handling routine.

```
Sub RelationX()

    Dim dbsNorthwind As Database
    Dim rstProducts As Recordset
    Dim prpLoop As Property
    Dim fldLoop As Field
    Dim errLoop As Error
```

```
    Set dbsNorthwind = OpenDatabase("Northwind.mdb")
    Set rstProducts = dbsNorthwind.OpenRecordset("Products")

    ' Print a report showing all the different parts of
    ' the relation and where each part is stored.
    With dbsNorthwind.Relations!CategoriesProducts
        Debug.Print "Properties of " & .Name & " Relation"
        Debug.Print "    Table = " & .Table
        Debug.Print "    ForeignTable = " & .ForeignTable
        Debug.Print "Fields of " & .Name & " Relation"
        With .Fields!CategoryID
            Debug.Print "    " & .Name
            Debug.Print "        Name = " & .Name
            Debug.Print "            ForeignName = " & .ForeignName
        End With
    End With

    ' Attempt to add a record that violates the relation.
    With rstProducts
        .AddNew
        !ProductName = "Trygve's Lutefisk"
        !CategoryID = 10
        On Error GoTo Err_Relation
        .Update
        On Error GoTo 0
        .Close
    End With

    dbsNorthwind.Close

    Exit Sub

Err_Relation:

    ' Notify user of any errors that result from
    ' the invalid data.
    If DBEngine.Errors.Count > 0 Then
        For Each errLoop In DBEngine.Errors
            MsgBox "Error number: " & errLoop.Number & _
                vbCr & errLoop.Description
        Next errLoop
    End If

    Resume Next

End Sub
```

Relations Collection

A **Relations** collection contains stored **Relation** objects of a **Database** object (Microsoft Jet databases only).

Remarks

You can use the **Relation** object to create new relationships and examine existing relationships in your database. To add a **Relation** object to the **Relations** collection, first create it with the **CreateRelation** method, and then append it to the **Relations** collection with the **Append** method. This will save the **Relation** object when you close the **Database** object. To remove a **Relation** object from the collection, use the **Delete** method.

To refer to a **Relation** object in a collection by its ordinal number or by its **Name** property setting, use any of the following syntax forms:

Relations(0)
Relations("*name*")
Relations![*name*]

Properties

Count Property

Methods

Append Method, **Delete** Method, **Refresh** Method

Reload Method

Reloads the specified component from disk, discarding any unsaved changes.

Applies To

VBComponent Object

Syntax

object.**Reload**

The *object* placeholder represents an object expression that evaluates to an object in the **Applies To** list.

Remarks

Cursor position, code window and form visibility are not affected by the **Reload** method. **Reload** doesn't change the setting which indicates whether the project was edited since the last time it was saved.

See Also

FileCount Property, **FileNames** Property

Rem Statement

Used to include explanatory remarks in a program.

Syntax

Rem *comment*

You can also use the following syntax:

' *comment*

The optional *comment* argument is the text of any comment you want to include. A space is required between the **Rem** keyword and *comment*.

Remarks

If you use line numbers or line labels, you can branch from a **GoTo** or **GoSub** statement to a line containing a **Rem** statement. Execution continues with the first executable statement following the **Rem** statement. If the **Rem** keyword follows other statements on a line, it must be separated from the statements by a colon (:).

You can use an apostrophe (') instead of the **Rem** keyword. When you use an apostrophe, the colon is not required after other statements.

Example

This example illustrates the various forms of the **Rem** statement, which is used to include explanatory remarks in a program.

```
Dim MyStr1, MyStr2
MyStr1 = "Hello": Rem Comment after a statement separated by a colon.
MyStr2 = "Goodbye"  ' This is also a comment; no colon is needed.
```

Remote Data Objects and Collections

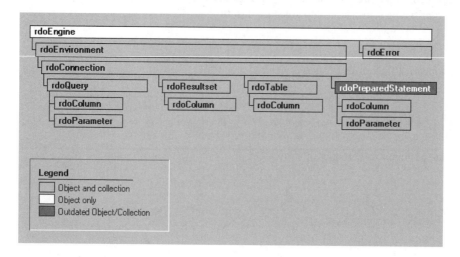

Remote Data objects and collections provide a framework for using code to create and manipulate components of a remote ODBC database system. Objects and collections have properties that describe the characteristics of database components and methods that you use to manipulate them. Using the containment framework, you create relationships among objects and collections, and these relationships represent the logical structure of your database system.

Objects and collections provide different types of containment relationships: Objects contain zero or more collections, all of different types; and collections contain zero or more objects, all of the same type. Although objects and collections are similar entities, the distinction differentiates the two types of relationships.

Note The RDO is only supported on 32-bit operating systems such as Windows 95 and Windows NT. To use the Remote Data Objects, you must set a reference to the Microsoft Remote Data Object 2.0 object library in the Visual Basic References dialog box.

In the following table, the type of collection in the first column contains the type of object in the second column. The third column describes what each type of object represents.

Collection	Object	Description
rdoConnections	**rdoConnection**	An open or allocated connection
None	**rdoEngine**	The remote database engine
rdoErrors	**rdoError**	Information about ODBC errors

(continued)

Collection	Object	Description
rdoEnvironments	**rdoEnvironment**	A logical set of **rdoConnection** objects with a common user name and password
rdoColumns	**rdoColumn**	A column that is part of an **rdoResultset**
rdoParameters	**rdoParameter**	A parameter for an **rdoQuery** or an **rdoPreparedStatement**
rdoPreparedStatements	**rdoPreparedStatements**	A saved query definition (outdated)
rdoQueries	**rdoQuery**	A saved query definition
rdoResultsets	**rdoResultset**	The rows resulting from a query
rdoTables	**rdoTable**	A table definition

RemoteData Control

Provides access to data stored in a remote ODBC data source through bound controls. The **RemoteData** control enables you to move from row to row in a result set and to display and manipulate data from the rows in bound controls.

Syntax

RemoteData

Remarks

The **RemoteData** control provides an interface between Remote Data Objects (RDO) and data-aware bound controls. With the **RemoteData** control, you can:

- Establish a connection to a data source based on its properties.

- Create an **rdoResultset**.

- Pass the current row's data to corresponding bound controls.

- Permit the user to position the current row pointer.

- Pass any changes made to the bound controls back to the data source.

Overview

Without a **RemoteData** control, a **Data** control or its equivalent, data-aware (bound) controls on a form can't automatically access data. The **RemoteData** and **Data** controls are examples of *DataSource Controls*. You can perform most remote data access operations using the **DataSource** controls without writing any code at all. Data-aware controls bound to a **DataSource** control automatically display data from one or more columns for the current row or, in some cases, for a set of rows on either side of the current row. **DataSource** controls perform all operations on the current row.

The RemoteData DataSource Control

If the **RemoteData** control is instructed to move to a different row, all bound controls automatically pass any changes to the **RemoteData** control to be saved to the ODBC data source. The **RemoteData** control then moves to the requested row and passes back data from the current row to the bound controls where it's displayed.

The **RemoteData** control automatically handles a number of contingencies including empty result sets, adding new rows, editing and updating existing rows, converting and displaying complex data types, and handling some types of errors. However, in more sophisticated applications, you must trap some error conditions that the **RemoteData** control can't handle. For example, if the remote server has a problem accessing the data source, the user doesn't have permission, or the query can't be executed as coded, a trappable error results. If the error occurs *before* your application procedures start, or as a result of some internal errors, the Error event is triggered.

Operation

Use the **RemoteData** control properties to describe the data source, establish a connection, and specify the type of cursor to create. If you alter these properties once the result set is created, use the **Refresh** method to rebuild the underlying **rdoResultset** based on the new property settings.

The **RemoteData** control behaves like the Jet-driven **Data** control in most respects. The following guidelines illustrate a few differences that apply when setting the **SQL** property.

You can treat the **RemoteData** control's **SQL** property like the **Data** control's **RecordSource** property except that it cannot accept the name of a table by itself, unless you populate the **rdoTables** collection first. Generally, the **SQL** property specifies an SQL query. For example, instead of just "Authors", you would code "SELECT * FROM AUTHORS" which provides the same functionality. However, specifying a table in this manner is not a good programming practice as it tends to return too many rows and can easily exhaust workstation resources or lock large segments of the database.

The result set created by the **RemoteData** control might not be in the same order as the **Recordset** created by the **Data** control. For example, if the **Data** control's **RecordSource** property is set to "Authors" and the **RemoteData** control's **SQL** property is set to "SELECT * FROM AUTHORS", the first record returned by Jet to the **Data** control is based on the first available index on the Authors table. The **RemoteData** control, however, returns the first row returned by the remote database engine based on the physical sequence of the rows in the database, regardless of any indexes. In some cases, the order of the records could be identical, but not always.

This difference in behavior can affect how bound controls handle the resulting rows—especially multiple-row bound controls like the **DBGrid** control. You can manipulate the **RemoteData** control with the mouse—to move the current row pointer from row to row, or to the beginning or end of the **rdoResultset** by clicking the control. As you manipulate the **RemoteData** control buttons, the current row pointer is repositioned in the **rdoResultset**. You cannot move off either end of the **rdoResultset** using the mouse. You also can't set focus to the **RemoteData** control.

Other Features

You can use the objects created by the **RemoteData** control to create additional **rdoConnection, rdoResultset**, or **rdoQuery**objects.

You can set the **RemoteData** control **Resultset** property to an **rdoResultset** created independently of the control. If this is done, the **RemoteData** control properties are reset based on the new **rdoResultset** and **rdoConnection**.

You can set the **Options** property to enable asynchronous creation of the **rdoResultset** (**rdAsyncEnable**) or to execute the query without creating a temporary stored procedure (**rdExecDirect**).

The Validate event is triggered before each reposition of the current row pointer. You can choose to accept the changes made to bound controls or cancel the operation using the Validate event's *action* argument.

The **RemoteData** control can also manage what happens when you encounter an **rdoResultset** with no rows. By changing the **EOFAction** property, you can program the **RemoteData** control to enter **AddNew** mode automatically.

Programmatic Operation

To create an **rdoResultset** programmatically with the **RemoteData** control:

- Set the **RemoteData** control properties to describe the desired characteristics of the **rdoResultset**.

- Use the **Refresh** method to begin the automated process or to create the new **rdoResultset**. Any existing **rdoResultset** is discarded.

All of the **RemoteData** control properties and the new **rdoResultset** object may be manipulated independently of the **RemoteData** control—with or without bound controls. The **rdoConnection** and **rdoResultset** objects each have properties and methods of their own that can be used with procedures that you write.

For example, the **MoveNext** method of an **rdoResultset** object moves the current row to the next row in the **rdoResultset**. To invoke this method with an **rdoResultset** created by a **RemoteData** control, you could use this code:

```
RemoteData1.Resultset.MoveNext
```

Properties

Align Property, **Appearance** Property, **BackColor, ForeColor** Properties, **Caption** Property, **Container** Property, **BOFAction, EOFAction** Properties (Remote Data), **Connect** Property (Remote Data), **Connection** Property (Remote Data), **CursorDriver** Property (Remote Data), **DataSourceName** Property (Remote Data), **DragIcon** Property, **DragMode** Property, **Container** Property, **Enabled** Property, **Font** Property, **Height, Width** Properties, **Index** Property, **Left, Top** Properties, **Negotiate** Property, **Object** Property, **Parent** Property, **Tag** Property, **ToolTipText** Property, **WhatsThisHelpID** Property, Visible Property, **EditMode** Property (Remote Data), **Environment** Property (Remote Data), **ErrorThreshold** Property (Remote Data), **KeysetSize** Property (Remote Data), **LockType** Property (Remote Data), **LoginTimeout** Property (Remote Data), **LogMessages** Property (Remote Data), **MaxRows** Property (Remote Data), **Name** Property (Remote Data), **Options** Property (Remote Data), **Password** Property (Remote Data), **Prompt** Property (Remote Data), **QueryTimeout** Property (Remote Data), **BatchCollisionCount** Property, **BatchCollisionRows** Property, **BatchSize** Property, **UpdateCriteria** Property, **UpdateOperation** Property, **Resultset** Property, **ResultsetType** Property, **ReadOnly** Property (Remote Data), **RowsetSize** Property, **SQL** Property, **UserName** Property (Remote Data), **Version** Property (Remote Data)

Methods

BeginTrans, CommitTrans, RollbackTrans Methods (Remote Data), **Cancel** Method (Remote Data), **Refresh** Method (Remote Data), **UpdateControls** Method (Remote Data), **UpdateRow** Method (Remote Data), **Zorder** Method, **ShowWhatsThis** Method, **Move** Method, **Drag** Method

Events

DragDrop Event, **DragOver** Event, **Error** Event, **MouseDown**, **MouseUp** Event, **MouseMove** Event, **QueryCompleted** Event, **Reposition** Event, **Validate** Event

---

Remove Method

Removes a member from a **Collection** object.

Syntax

object.**Remove** *index*

The **Remove** method syntax has the following object qualifier and part:

Part	Description
object	Required. An object expression that evaluates to an object in the **Applies To** list.
index	Required. An expression that specifies the position of a member of the collection. If a numeric expression, *index* must be a number from 1 to the value of the collection's **Count** property. If a string expression, *index* must correspond to the *key* argument specified when the member referred to was added to the collection.

Remarks

If the value provided as *index* doesn't match an existing member of the collection, an error occurs.

Remove Method (Add-Ins)

Removes an item from a collection.

Applies To

VBComponents Collection, **LinkedWindows** Collection, **References** Collection

Syntax

object.**Remove**(*component*)

Remove syntax has these parts:

Part	Description
object	Required. An object expression that evaluates to an object in the **Applies To** list.
component	Required. For the **LinkedWindows** collection, an object. For the **References** collection, a reference to a type library or a project. For the **VBComponents** collection, an enumerated constant representing a class module, a form, or a standard module.

Remarks

When used on the **LinkedWindows** collection, the **Remove** method removes a window from the collection of currently linked windows. The removed window becomes a floating window that has its own linked window frame.

Example

The example verifies that a particular member of the **VBComponents** collection is a module, and then it uses the **Remove** method to remove the module.

```
Debug.Print Application.VBE.ActiveVBProject.VBComponents(4).Name
Application.VBE.ActiveVBProject.VBComponents.Remove
Application.VBE.ActiveVBProject.VBComponents(4)
```

ExampleThis example illustrates the use of the **Remove** method to remove objects from a **Collection** object, MyClasses. This code removes the object whose index is 1 on each iteration of the loop.

```
Dim Num, MyClasses
For Num = 1 To MyClasses.Count
    MyClasses.Remove 1       ' Remove the first object each time
                             ' through the loop until there are
                             ' no objects left in the collection.
Next Num
```

Remove Method (DBGrid)

Removes the specified row from the **SelBookmarks** collection, or the specified **Column** object from the **Columns** collection of a **DBGrid** control.

Applies To

Columns Collection, **SelBookmarks** Collection

Syntax

*object***.Remove** *index*

The **Remove** method syntax has these parts:

Part	Description
object	An object expression that evaluates to an object in the **Applies To** list.
index	Required. An integer in the range of 0 to the **Count** property setting of the collection–1.

Remarks

For the **SelBookmarks** collection, the **Remove** method removes the row specified by the *index* argument, then decrements the **SelBookmarks.Count** property by 1. If the row removed from the **SelBookmarks** collection is visible, it will be deselected in the **DBGrid** control.

For the **Columns** collection, the **Remove** method removes the column specified by the *index* argument, then decrements the **Columns.Count** property by 1.

If you specify a row that isn't in the **SelBookmarks** collection or a **Column** object that isn't in the **Columns** collection, a trappable error occurs.

See Also

Data Control, **DBGrid** Control, **Add** Method (Columns, SelBookmarks, Splits Collections), **ColIndex** Property

---

Remove Method (Add-Ins)

Removes an item from a collection.

Applies To

LinkedWindows Collection, **VBControls** Collection, **VBProjects** Collection

Syntax

*object***.Remove** (*index*)

Part	Description
object	An object expression that evaluates to an object in the **Applies To** list.
index	Required. A variant expression specifying the name or index in the collection of the object to be accessed.

Remarks

For the **LinkedWindows** collection, removes a window from the collection of currently linked windows. The removed window becomes a floating window that has its own **LinkedWindowFrame**. This is the point at which **LinkedWindowFrame** windows are created.

For the **VBProjects** collection, removes the specified project from the collection.

For the **References** collection, removes the specified reference from the collection.

RemoveAddInFromToolbar Method

Removes a button from the Add-In toolbar which references an add-in or Wizard.

Applies To

Add-In Toolbar

Syntax

object.**RemoveAddInFromToolbar** (*saddinname* **As String**)

Part	Description
object	An object expression that evaluates to an object in the **Applies To** list.
saddinname	Required. A string expression specifying the name of the add-in or Wizard to remove from the Add-In toolbar (as specified by the *saddinname* parameter from the **AddToAddInToolbar** method).

See Also

Add-In Toolbar, **AddToAddInToolbar** Method, **AddToAddInToolbar Method** Example, **RemoveAddInFromToolbar Method** Example

Example

This example removes an existing button from the Add-In toolbar that references a fictitious add-in called **MyAddIn** Title:

```
Sub Main()
   dim x as Object
   Set x=CreateObject("AddInToolbar.Manager")
   x.RemoveAddInFromToolbar sAddInName:="MyAddIn Title"
End Sub
```

RemoveItem Method

Removes an item from a **ListBox** or **ComboBox** control or a row from a **MS Flex Grid** control. Doesn't support named arguments.

Applies To

ComboBox Control, **ListBox** Control

Syntax

object.**RemoveItem** *index*

The **RemoveItem** method syntax has these parts:

Part	Description
object	Required. An object expression that evaluates to an object in the **Applies To** list.
index	Required. Integer representing the position within the object of the item or row to remove. For the first item in a **ListBox** or **ComboBox** or for the first row in a **MS Flex Grid** control, *index* = 0.

Remarks

A **ListBox** or **ComboBox** that is bound to a **Data** control doesn't support the **RemoveItem** method.

See Also

AddItem Method, **Clear** Method (Clipboard, ComboBox, ListBox)

Example

This example uses the **RemoveItem** method to remove entries from a list box. To try this example, paste the code into the Declarations section of a form with a **ListBox** control named List1, and then press F5 and click the form.

```
Private Sub Form_Click ()
   Dim Entry, I, Msg ' Declare variables.
   Msg = "Choose OK to add 100 items to your list box."
   MsgBox Msg  ' Display message.
   For I = 1 To 100   ' Count from 1 to 100.
      Entry = "Entry " & I ' Create entry.
      List1.AddItem Entry  ' Add the entry.
   Next I
   Msg = "Choose OK to remove every other entry."
   MsgBox Msg  ' Display message.
   For I = 1 To 50' Determine how to
      List1.RemoveItem I' remove every other

Next I' item.
   Msg = "Choose OK to remove all items from the list box."
   MsgBox Msg  ' Display message.
   List1.Clear ' Clear list box.
End Sub
```

Render Method

Draws all or part of a source image to a destination object.

Applies To

Picture Object

Syntax

object.**Render**(*hdc, xdest, ydest, destwid, desthgt, xsrc, ysrc, srcwid, srchgt, wbounds*)

The **Render** method syntax has these parts:

Part	Description
object	Required. An object expression that evaluates to an object in the **Applies To** list.
hdc	Required. The handle to the destination object's device context.
xdest	Required. The x-coordinate of upper left corner of the drawing region in the destination object. This coordinate is in the scale units of the destination object.
ydest	Required. The y-coordinate of upper left corner of the drawing region in the destination object. This coordinate is in the scale units of the destination object.
destwid	Required. The width of drawing region in the destination object, expressed in the scale units of the destination object.
desthgt	Required. The height of drawing region in the destination object, expressed in the scale units of the destination object.
xsrc	Required. The x-coordinate of upper left corner of the drawing region in the source object. This coordinate is in HIMETRIC units.
ysrc	Required. The y-coordinate of upper left corner of the drawing region in the source object. This coordinate is in HIMETRIC units.
srcwid	Required. The width of drawing region in the source object, expressed in HIMETRIC units.
srchgt	Required. The height of drawing region in the source object, expressed in HIMETRIC units.
wbounds	Required. The world bounds of a metafile. This argument should be passed a value of Null unless drawing to a metafile, in which case the argument is passed a user-defined type corresponding to a RECTL structure.

Remarks

The recommended way to paint part of a graphic into a destination is through the **PaintPicture** method.

See Also

PaintPicture Method

RepairDatabase Method

Attempts to repair a corrupted Microsoft Jet database (Microsoft Jet databases only).

Applies To

DBEngine Object

Syntax

DBEngine.RepairDatabase *dbname*

The *dbname* argument is a **String** that is the path and file name for an existing Microsoft Jet database file. If you omit the path, only the current directory is searched. If your system supports the uniform naming convention (UNC), you can also specify a network path, such as `"\\server1\share1\dir1\db1.mdb"`.

Remarks

You must close the database specified by *dbname* before you repair it. In a multiuser environment, other users can't have *dbname* open while you're repairing it. If *dbname* isn't closed or isn't available for exclusive use, an error occurs.

This method attempts to repair a database that was marked as possibly corrupt by an incomplete write operation. This can occur if an application using the Microsoft Jet database engine is closed unexpectedly because of a power outage or computer hardware problem. The database won't be marked as possibly corrupt if you use the **Close** method or if you quit your application in a usual way.

The **RepairDatabase** method also attempts to validate all system tables and all indexes. Any data that can't be repaired is discarded. If the database can't be repaired, a run-time error occurs.

When you attempt to open or compact a corrupted database, a run-time error usually occurs. In some situations, however, a corrupted database may not be detected, and no error occurs. It's a good idea to provide your users with a way to use the **RepairDatabase** method in your application if their database behaves unpredictably.

Some types of databases can become corrupted if a user ends an application without closing **Database** or **Recordset** objects and the Microsoft Jet database engine; Microsoft Windows doesn't have a chance to write data caches to disk. To avoid corrupt databases, establish procedures for closing applications and shutting down systems that ensure that all cached pages are saved to the database. In some cases, power supplies that can't be interrupted may be necessary to prevent accidental data loss during power fluctuations.

Note After repairing a database, it's also a good idea to compact it using the **CompactDatabase** method to defragment the file and to recover disk space.

See Also

Database Object, **Close** Method, **CompactDatabase** Method

Example

This example attempts to repair the database named Northwind.mdb. You cannot run this procedure from a module within Northwind.mdb.

```
Sub RepairDatabaseX()

    Dim errLoop As Error

    If MsgBox("Repair the Northwind database?", _
        vbYesNo) = vbYes Then
        On Error GoTo Err_Repair
        DBEngine.RepairDatabase "Northwind.mdb"
        On Error GoTo 0
        MsgBox "End of repair procedure!"
    End If

    Exit Sub

Err_Repair:

    For Each errLoop In DBEngine.Errors
        MsgBox "Repair unsuccessful!" & vbCr & _
            "Error number: " & errLoop.Number & _
            vbCr & errLoop.Description
    Next errLoop

End Sub
```

ReplaceLine Method

Replaces an existing line of code with a specified line of code.

Applies To

CodeModule Object

Syntax

object.**ReplaceLine**(*line*, *code*)

ReplaceLine syntax has these parts:

Part	Description
object	Required. An object expression that evaluates to an object in the **Applies To** list.
line	Required. A **Long** specifying the location of the line you want to replace.
code	Required. A **String** containing the code you want to insert.

See Also

CreateEventProc Method, **DeleteLines** Method, **InsertLines** Method, **CountOfLines** Property, **CountOfDeclarationLines** Property, **CountOfVisibleLines** Property

Example

The following example has two steps. The first **For...Next** loop uses the **InsertLines** method to insert into `CodePanes(1)` 26 ever-longer initial segments of the alphabet, starting with "a." The last line inserted is the entire alphabet.

The second **For...Next** loop uses the **ReplaceLine** method to replace each even-numbered line with the last letter in the string that previously occupied that line. Odd-numbered lines are unchanged.

```
For I = 1 to 26
    Application.VBE.CodePanes(1).CodeModule.InsertLines I,
↪ Mid$("abcdefghijklmnopqrstuvwxyz", 1, I)
Next I
For I = 1 to 13
    Application.VBE.CodePanes(1).CodeModule.ReplaceLine 2*I,
↪ Mid$("abcdefghijklmnopqrstuvwxyz", 1, I)
Next I
```

Replicable Property

Sets or returns a value that determines whether a database or object in a database can be replicated (Microsoft Jet workspaces only).

Note   Before getting or setting the **Replicable** property on a **Database**, **TableDef**, or **QueryDef** object, you must create it by using the **CreateProperty** method and append it to the **Properties** collection for the object.

Applies To

Database Object, **Document** Object, **QueryDef** Object, **TableDef** Object

Setting and Return Values

The setting or return value is a **Text** data type.

On a **Database** object, setting this property to `"T"` makes the database replicable. Once you set the property to `"T"`, you can't change it; setting the property to `"F"` (or any value other than `"T"`) causes an error.

On an object in a database, setting this property to `"T"` replicates the object (and subsequent changes to the object) at all replicas in the replica set. You can also set this property in the object's property sheet in Microsoft Access.

Note   Microsoft Jet 3.5 also supports the **Boolean ReplicableBool** property. Its functionality is identical to the **Replicable** property, except that it takes a **Boolean** value. Setting **ReplicableBool** to **True** makes the object replicable.

Remarks

Before setting the **Replicable** property on a database, make a backup copy of the database. If setting the **Replicable** property fails, you should delete the partially replicated database, make a new copy from the backup, and try again.

When you set this property on a **Database** object, Microsoft Jet adds fields, tables, and properties to objects within the database. Microsoft Jet uses these fields, tables, and properties to synchronize database objects. For example, all existing tables have three new fields added to them that help identify which records have changed. The addition of these fields and other objects increase the size of your database.

On forms, reports, macros, and modules defined by a host application (such as Microsoft Access), you set this property on the host-defined object through the host user interface. Once set, the **Replicable** property will appear in the **Properties** collection for the **Document** object representing the host object.

If the **Replicable** property has already been set on an object using the **Replicated** check box in the property sheet for the object, you cannot set the **Replicable** property in code.

When you create a new table, query, form, report, macro, or module at a replica, the object is considered local and is stored only at that replica. If you want users at other replicas to be able to use the object, you must change it from local to replicable. Either create the object at or import it into the Design Master and then set the **Replicable** property to "T".

The object on which you are setting the **Replicable** property might have already inherited that property from another object. However, the value set by the other object has no effect on the behavior of the object you want to make replicable. You must explicitly set the property for each object.

See Also

CreateProperty Method, **MakeReplica** Method, **KeepLocal** Property

Example

These examples illustrate two situations for using the **Replicable** Property—on a database and on an object in the database.

This example makes Northwind.mdb a replicable database. It's recommended that you make a back-up copy of Northwind before running this code, and that you adjust the path to Northwind as appropriate to its location on your computer.

```
Sub MakeDesignMasterX()

    Dim dbsNorthwind As Database
    Dim prpNew As Property

    ' Open database for exclusive access.
    Set dbsNorthwind = OpenDatabase("Northwind.mdb", _
        True)

    With dbsNorthwind

        ' If Replicable property doesn't exist, create it.
        ' Turn off error handling in case property exists.
        On Error Resume Next
```

```
            Set prpNew = .CreateProperty("Replicable", _
                dbText, "T")
            .Properties.Append prpNew

            ' Set database Replicable property to True.
            .Properties("Replicable") = "T"

            .Close

    End With

End Sub
```

This example creates a new **TableDef** and then makes it replicable. The database must first be replicable for this procedure to work.

```
Sub CreateReplLocalTableX()

    Dim dbsNorthwind As Database
    Dim tdfNew As TableDef
    Dim fldNew As Field
    Dim prpNew As Property

    Set dbsNorthwind = OpenDatabase("Northwind.mdb")
    ' Create a new TableDef named "Taxes".
    Set tdfNew = dbsNorthwind.CreateTableDef("Taxes")
    ' Define a text field named "Grade".
    Set fldNew = tdfNew.CreateField("Grade", dbText, 3)
    ' Append new field to the TableDef.
    tdfNew.Fields.Append fldNew

    ' Add the new TableDef to the database.
    dbsNorthwind.TableDefs.Append tdfNew

    ' Create a new Replicable property for new TableDef.
    Set prpNew = tdfNew.CreateProperty("Replicable", _
        dbText, "T")
    ' Append the Replicable property to the new
    ' TableDef.
    tdfNew.Properties.Append prpNew
    dbsNorthwind.Close

End Sub
```

The following code sets the **Replicable** property on the specified **TableDef** object to "T". If the property does not exist, it is created and appended to the table's **Properties** collection, and given a value of "T".

```
Sub SetReplicable(tdfTemp As TableDef)

    On Error GoTo ErrHandler

    tdfTemp.Properties("Replicable") = "T"
```

```
    On Error GoTo 0

    Exit Sub

ErrHandler:

    Dim prpNew As Property

    If Err.Number = 3270 Then
        Set prpNew = tdfTemp.CreateProperty("Replicable", _
            dbText, "T")
        tdfTemp.Properties.Append prpNew
    Else
        MsgBox "Error " & Err & ": " & Error
    End If

End Sub
```

ReplicaFilter Property

Sets or returns a value on a **TableDef** object within a partial replica that indicates
which subset of records is replicated to that table from a full replica. (Microsoft Jet
databases only.)

Applies To
TableDef Object

Settings And Return Values
The setting or return value is a **String** or **Boolean** that indicates which subset of
records is replicated, as specified in the following table:

Value	Description
A string	A criteria that a record in the partial replica table must satisfy in order to be replicated from the full replica.
True	Replicates all records.
False	(Default) Doesn't replicate any records.

Remarks
This property is similar to an SQL WHERE clause (without the word WHERE), but
you cannot specify subqueries, aggregate functions (such as **Count**), or user-defined
functions within the criteria.

You can only synchronize data between a full replica and a partial replica. You can't
synchronize data between two partial replicas. Also, with partial replication you can
set restrictions on which records are replicated, but you can't indicate which fields are
replicated.

Usually, you reset a replica filter when you want to replicate a different set of records.
For example, when a sales representative temporarily takes over another sales

representative's region, the database application can temporarily replicate data for both regions and then return to the previous filter. In this scenario, the application resets the **ReplicaFilter** property and then repopulates the partial replica.

If your application changes replica filters, you should follow these steps:

1   Use the **Synchronize** method to synchronize your full replica with the partial replica in which the filters are being changed.

2   Use the **ReplicaFilter** property to make the desired changes to the replica filter.

3   Use the **PopulatePartial** method to remove all records from the partial replica and transfer all records from the full replica that meet the new replica filter criteria.

To remove a filter, set the **ReplicaFilter** property to **False**. If you remove all filters and invoke the **PopulatePartial** method, no records will appear in any replicated tables in the partial replica.

Note   If a replica filter has changed, and the **Synchronize** method is invoked without first invoking **PopulatePartial**, a trappable error occurs.

Example

The following example uses the **ReplicaFilter** property to replicate only customer records from the California region.

```
Sub ReplicaFilterX()

   ' This example assumes the current open database
   ' is the replica.
   Dim tdfCustomers As TableDef
   Dim strFilter As String
   Dim dbsTemp As Database

   Set dbsTemp = OpenDatabase("Northwind.mdb")
   Set tdfCustomers = dbsTemp.TableDefs("Customers")

   ' Synchronize with full replica
   ' before setting replica filter.
   dbsTemp.Synchronize "C:\SALES\FY96.MDB"

   strFilter = "Region = 'CA'"
   tdfCustomers.ReplicaFilter = strFilter
   dbsTemp.PopulatePartial "C:\SALES\FY96.MDB"

   ' Now remove the replica filter (for example purposes
   ' only).
   tdfCustomers.ReplicaFilter = False
   ' Repopulate the database.
   dbsTemp.PopulatePartial "C:\SALES\DATA96.MDB"

End Sub
```

ReplicaID Property

Returns a 16-byte value that uniquely identifies a database replica (Microsoft Jet workspaces only).

Applies To

Database Object

Return Values

The return value is a **GUID** value that uniquely identifies the replica or Design Master.

Remarks

The Microsoft Jet database engine automatically generates this value when you create a new replica.

The **ReplicaID** property of each replica (and the Design Master) is stored in the MSysReplicas system table.

See Also

DesignMasterID Property

Example

This example makes a replica from the Design Master of Northwind.mdb, and then returns the replica's **ReplicaID**, which is automatically created by the Microsoft Jet database engine. (If you have not yet created a Design Master of Northwind, refer to the **Replicable** property, or change the name of the database in the code to an existing Design Master.)

```
Sub MakeReplicaReplicaIDX()

    Dim dbsNorthwind As Database
    Dim prpReplicaID As Property
    Dim dbsReplica As Database

    Set dbsNorthwind = OpenDatabase("Northwind.mdb")

    ' Makes a new replica.
    dbsNorthwind.MakeReplica "Nwreplica2.mdb", _
        "second replica"
    dbsNorthwind.Close

    ' Opens the new replica to read its ReplicaID.
    Set dbsReplica = OpenDatabase("Nwreplica2.mdb")

    Debug.Print dbsReplica.ReplicaID
    dbsReplica.Close

End Sub
```

Reposition Event

Occurs after a record becomes the current record.

Applies To

Data Control

Syntax

Private Sub *object*.**Reposition** ([*index* **As Integer**])

The **Reposition** event syntax has these parts:

Part	Description
object	An object expression that evaluates to an object in the **Applies To** list.
index	Identifies the control if it's in a control array.

Remarks

When a **Data** control is loaded, the first record in the **Recordset** object becomes the current record, causing the **Reposition** event. Whenever a user clicks any button on the **Data** control, moving from record to record, or if you use one of the **Move** methods, such as **MoveNext**, the **Find** methods, such as **FindFirst**, or any other property or method that changes the current record, the **Reposition** event occurs after each record becomes current.

In contrast, the **Validate** event occurs before moving to a different record.

You can use this event to perform calculations based on data in the current record or to change the form in response to data in the current record.

Example

This example uses the Reposition event to update a list of Titles from the selected Publisher in the Biblio.mdb sample database. First place a **DBGrid**, **TextBox**, and two **Data** controls on a form. Set the **DatabaseName** properties of both **Data** controls to the Biblio.mdb sample database. Set the **RecordSource** property of Data1 to **Publishers**. Set the **DataSource** property of Text1 to **Data1** and the **DataField** property to **Name**. Set the **DataSource** property of DBGrid1 to **Data2**. Add the following code:

```
Private Sub Data1_Reposition()
   ' Select all Titles that are published by
   ' the current record in Data1
   Data2.RecordSource = "Select * from Titles where PubID = " &
Data1.Recordset("PubID")
   Data2.Refresh ' Rebuild the recordset
End Sub
```

The list of Titles in the **DBGrid** control will automatically be updated as you move through the Publishers recordset with Data1.

Reposition Event (Remote Data)

Occurs after a row becomes the current row.

Applies To

RemoteData Control

Syntax

Private Sub *object*.**Reposition** ([*index* **As Integer**])

The **Reposition** event syntax has these parts:

Part	Description
object	An object expression that evaluates to an object in the **Applies To** list.
index	Identifies the control if it's in a control array.

Remarks

When a **RemoteData control** is loaded, the first row in the **rdoResultset** object becomes the current row, causing the Reposition event to fire. The Reposition event fires after each row becomes current:

Whenever a user clicks any button on the **RemoteData** control to move from row to row.

- You use one of the *Move* methods, such as **MoveNext**.

- You use any other property or method that changes the current row

In contrast, the Validate event occurs before moving to a different row. The **RowCurrencyChange** event associated with the **rdoResultset** also fires when the current result set row changes.

You can use the Reposition event to perform calculations based on data in the current row or to change the form in response to data in the current row.

See Also

Error Event (Remote Data), **Validate** Event (Remote Data), **MoveFirst**, **MoveLast**, **MoveNext**, **MovePrevious** Methods (Remote Data), **rdoResultset** Object, **AbsolutePosition** Property (Remote Data), **PercentPosition** Property (Remote Data)

Requery Method

Updates the data in a **Recordset** object by re-executing the query on which the object is based.

Applies To

Dynaset-Type Recordset Object, **Recordset** Object, **Snapshot-Type Recordset** Object, **Forward-Only–Type Recordset** Object, **Dynamic-Type Recordset** Object

Syntax

recordset.**Requery** *newquerydef*

The **Requery** method syntax has the following parts.

Part	Description
recordset	An object variable that represents an existing Microsoft Jet dynaset-, snapshot-, or forward-only–type **Recordset** object, or an ODBCDirect **Recordset** object.
Newquerydef	Optional. A **Variant** that represents the **Name** property value of a **QueryDef** object (Microsoft Jet workspaces only).

Remarks

Use this method to make sure that a **Recordset** contains the most recent data. This method re-populates the current **Recordset** by using either the current query parameters or (in a Microsoft Jet workspace) the new ones supplied by the *newquerydef* argument.

In an ODBCDirect workspace, if the original query was asynchronous, then **Requery** will also execute an asynchronous query.

If you don't specify a *newquerydef* argument, the **Recordset** is re-populated based on the same query definition and parameters used to originally populate the **Recordset**. Any changes to the underlying data will be reflected during this re-population. If you didn't use a **QueryDef** to create the **Recordset**, the **Recordset** is re-created from scratch.

If you specify the original **QueryDef** in the *newquerydef* argument, then the **Recordset** is requeried using the parameters specified by the **QueryDef**. Any changes to the underlying data will be reflected during this re-population. To reflect any changes to the query parameter values in the **Recordset**, you must supply the *newquerydef* argument.

If you specify a different **QueryDef** than what was originally used to create the **Recordset**, the **Recordset** is re-created from scratch.

When you use **Requery**, the first record in the **Recordset** becomes the current record.

You can't use the **Requery** method on dynaset- or snapshot-type **Recordset** objects whose **Restartable** property is set to **False**. However, if you supply the optional *newquerydef* argument, the **Restartable** property is ignored.

If both the **BOF** and **EOF** property settings of the **Recordset** object are **True** after you use the **Requery** method, the query didn't return any records and the **Recordset** contains no data.

See Also

QueryDef Object, **BOF**, **EOF** Properties, **Restartable** Property

Example

This example shows how the **Requery** method can be used to refresh a query after underlying data has been changed.

```
Sub RequeryX()

    Dim dbsNorthwind As Database
    Dim qdfTemp As QueryDef
    Dim rstView As Recordset
    Dim rstChange As Recordset

    Set dbsNorthwind = OpenDatabase("Northwind.mdb")
    Set qdfTemp = dbsNorthwind.CreateQueryDef("", _
        "PARAMETERS ViewCountry Text; " & _
        "SELECT FirstName, LastName, Country FROM " & _
        "Employees WHERE Country = [ViewCountry] " & _
        "ORDER BY LastName")

    qdfTemp.Parameters!ViewCountry = "USA"
    Debug.Print "Data after initial query, " & _
        [ViewCountry] = USA"
    Set rstView = qdfTemp.OpenRecordset
    Do While Not rstView.EOF
        Debug.Print "    " & rstView!FirstName & " " & _
            rstView!LastName & ", " & rstView!Country
        rstView.MoveNext
    Loop

    ' Change underlying data.
    Set rstChange = dbsNorthwind.OpenRecordset("Employees")
    rstChange.AddNew
    rstChange!FirstName = "Nina"
    rstChange!LastName = "Roberts"
    rstChange!Country = "USA"
    rstChange.Update

    rstView.Requery
    Debug.Print "Requery after changing underlying data"
    Set rstView = qdfTemp.OpenRecordset
    Do While Not rstView.EOF
        Debug.Print "    " & rstView!FirstName & " " & _
            rstView!LastName & ", " & rstView!Country
        rstView.MoveNext
    Loop

    ' Restore original data because this is only a
    ' demonstration.
    rstChange.Bookmark = rstChange.LastModified
    rstChange.Delete
    rstChange.Close

    rstView.Close
    dbsNorthwind.Close

End Sub
```

Requery Method (Remote Data)

Updates the data in an **rdoResultset** object by re-executing the query on which the object is based.

Applies To

rdoResultset Object

Syntax

object.**Requery** [*options*]

The **Requery** method syntax has these parts:

Part	Description
object	The *object* placeholder represents an object expression that evaluates to an object in the **Applies To** list.
options	A **Variant** or constant that determines how the query is run, as specified in Settings.

Settings

You can use the following constant for the *options* part:

Constant	Value	Description
rdAsyncEnable	32	Execute operation asynchronously.

Remarks

Use this method to ensure an **rdoResultset** contains the most recent data. When you use **Requery**, all changes made to the data in the underlying table(s) by you and other users is displayed in the **rdoResultset**, and the first row in the **rdoResultset** becomes the current row.

If you use the **rdAsyncEnable** option, control returns to your application as soon as the query is begun, often before a result set is available. To test for completion of the query, use the **StillExecuting** property. The **rdoResultset** object is not valid until **StillExecuting** returns **False**. You can also use the **QueryCompleted** event to indicate when the query is completed.

If the **rdoParameter** objects have changed, their new values are used in the query used to generate the new **rdoResultset**.

Once the **Requery** method has been executed, all previously stored **rdoResultset** bookmarks are invalid.

If both the **BOF** and **EOF** property settings of the **rdoResultset** object are **True**, or the **RowCount** property is set to 0 after you use the **Requery** method, the query didn't return any rows and the **rdoResultset** contains no data.

You can't use the **Requery** method on **rdoResultset** objects whose **Restartable** property is set to **False**.

See Also

Execute Method (Remote Data), **rdoParameter** Object, **rdoPreparedStatement** Object, **rdoResultset** Object, **BOF**, **EOF** Properties (Remote Data), **Restartable** Property, **RowCount** Property (Remote Data)

Example

The following example illustrates use of the **Requery** method to re-execute an **rdoQuery**. Note that the **rdoResultset** is created only at form load and only re-executed on each invocation of the **Requery** method.

```
Option Explicit
Dim Cn As New rdoConnection
Dim Rs As rdoResultset
Dim Col As rdoColumn
Dim Qy As rdoQuery
Dim SQL As String
Dim TimeExpected As Single
Dim Ts As Single, Tn As Single

Private Sub SpWho_Click()
Rs.Cancel
With Rs
   .Requery
   While .StillExecuting
      SpinGlobe
      DoEvents
   Wend
   ShowRS
End With

End Sub
Sub ShowRS()
With Rs
   Form1.Cls
   For Each Col In .rdoColumns
      Print Col.Name,
   Next
   Print
   Do Until .EOF
      For Each Col In .rdoColumns
         Print Col,
      Next
      Print
      .MoveNext
   Loop
End With
End Sub
Sub SpinGlobe()
' Animate a globe here to show query is in progress.
Print ".";
End Sub

Private Sub Form_Load()
```

```
With Cn
    .Connect = "UID=;PWD=;Database=WorkDB;" _
    & "Server=sequel;Driver={SQL Server}" _
    & "DSN='';"
    .LoginTimeout = 5
    .EstablishConnection rdDriverNoPrompt, True
    Set Qy = .CreateQuery("SpWho", _
    "{ call master..sp_who (?) }")
    Qy.RowsetSize = 1
    Set Rs = Qy.OpenResultset(rdOpenForwardOnly, _
    rdConcurReadOnly, rdAsyncEnable)
    Show
    ShowRS
End With
End Sub
```

RequestChangeFileName Event

Occurs after specifying a new filename for a component or project, and the name change is completed.

Applies To

FileControlEvents Object

Syntax

Sub RequestChangeFileName(*vbproject* **As VBProject,** *filetype* **As vbext_FileType,** *newname* **As String,** *oldname* **As String,** *cancel* **As Boolean)**

The RequestChangeFileName event syntax has these parts:

Part	Description
vbproject	A **VBProject** object specifying the name of the project the new file will be added to.
filetype	An enumerated value (**vbext_FileType**) specifying the type of file that was written, as listed in Settings.
newname	A string expression specifying the name given to the renamed file.
oldname	A string expression specifying containing the name of the file before it was renamed.
cancel	A Boolean expression that determines the default Visual Basic action, as described in Settings.

Settings

The settings for *filetype* are:

Constant	Value	Description
vbext_ft_Form	0	File type is a form.
vbext_ft_Module	1	File type is a basic module.

(continued)

Constant	Value	Description
vbext_ft_Class	2	File type is a class module.
vbext_ft_Project	3	File type is a project.
vbext_ft_Exe	4	File type is an executable file.
vbext_ft_Res	6	File type is a resource file.
vbext_ft_UserControl	7	File type is a **User** control.
vbext_ft_PropertyPage	8	File type is a **Property Page**.
vbext_ft_DocObject	9	File type is a **User Document**.
vbext_ft_Binary	10	File type is a binary file.
vbext_ft_GroupProject	11	File type is a group project.
vbext_ft_Designer	12	File type is a designer object.

The settings for *cancel* are:

Setting	Description
True	Cancel the renaming of the file. This event won't be triggered for any subsequent add-ins connected to the **FileControl** object.
False	Continue triggering this event for subsequent add-ins connected to the **FileControl** object.

Remarks

This event allows all the add-ins to examine the new filename that is proposed to be added to the project, and decide whether to accept or cancel the name change.

This event occurs in all add-ins that are connected to the **FileControl** object. The add-in cannot prevent the file from being written to disk because the operation is complete. However, you can use this event to perform other tasks, such as:

- Log information about the event.
- Update information about the file.
- Back up the file.

RequestEdit Property

Returns or sets the **RequestEdit** attribute of a **Member** object.

Applies To

Member Object

Syntax

object.**RequestEdit**

The *object* placeholder represents an object expression that evaluates to an object in the **Applies To** list.

RequestWriteFile Event

Occurs prior to saving any project component with unsaved changes.

Applies To

FileControlEvents Object

Syntax

Sub RequestWriteFile(*vbproject* **As VBProject**, *filename* **As String**,
↪ *cancel* **As Boolean**)

The **RequestWriteFile** event syntax has these parts:

Part	Description
vbproject	A **VBProject** object specifying the name of the project containing the component.
filename	A string expression containing the name of the file to be saved.
cancel	A Boolean expression used as a flag to cancel the action, as described in Settings.

Settings

The settings for *cancel* are:

Setting	Description
True	Does not write the file to disk. This event is not triggered for any subsequent add-ins connected to the **FileControl** object.
False	Continues triggering this event for subsequent add-ins connected to the **FileControl** object.

Remarks

The **RequestWriteFile** event occurs once for each saved component, and once for each associated binary data file (such as .Frx or .Pgx files).

This event allows add-ins to prepare the specified file for writing. For example, you could use it to enable an add-in to check out a file from a source code control project prior to writing to it.

This event occurs in all add-ins that are connected to the **FileControl** object. The add-in cannot prevent the file from being written to disk because the operation is complete. However, you can use this event to perform other tasks, such as:

- Log information about the event.
- Update information about the file.
- Back up the file.

Required Property (DAO)

Sets or returns a value that indicates whether a **Field** object requires a non-**Null** value or whether all the fields in an **Index** object must have a value.

Applies To

Field Object, **Index** Object

Settings and Return Values

The setting or return value is a **Boolean** that is **True** if a field can't contain a **Null** value.

For an object not yet appended to a collection, this property is read/write. For an **Index** object, this property setting is read-only for objects appended to **Indexes** collections in **Recordset** and **TableDef** objects.

Remarks

The availability of the **Required** property depends on the object that contains the **Fields** collection, as shown in the following table.

If the Fields collection belongs to a	Then Required is
Index object	Not supported
QueryDef object	Read-only
Recordset object	Read-only
Relation object	Not supported
TableDef object	Read/write

For a **Field** object, you can use the **Required** property along with the **AllowZeroLength**, **ValidateOnSet**, or **ValidationRule** property to determine the validity of the **Value** property setting for that **Field** object. If the **Required** property is set to **False**, the field can contain **Null** values as well as values that meet the conditions specified by the **AllowZeroLength** and **ValidationRule** property settings.

Note When you can set this property for either an **Index** object or a **Field** object, set it for the **Field** object. The validity of the property setting for a **Field** object is checked before that of an **Index** object.

See Also

AllowZeroLength Property, **ValidateOnSet** Property, **ValidationRule** Property, **ValidationText** Property, **Value** Property

Example

This example uses the **Required** property to report which fields in three different tables must contain data in order for a new record to be added. The **RequiredOutput** procedure is required for this procedure to run.

```
Sub RequiredX()
```

```
          Dim dbsNorthwind As Database
          Dim tdfloop As TableDef

          Set dbsNorthwind = OpenDatabase("Northwind.mdb")

          With dbsNorthwind
             ' Show which fields are required in the Fields
             ' collections of three different TableDef objects.
             RequiredOutput .TableDefs("Categories")
             RequiredOutput .TableDefs("Customers")
             RequiredOutput .TableDefs("Employees")
             .Close
          End With

       End Sub

       Sub RequiredOutput(tdfTemp As TableDef)

          Dim fldLoop As Field

          ' Enumerate Fields collection of the specified TableDef
          ' and show the Required property.
          Debug.Print "Fields in " & tdfTemp.Name & ":"
          For Each fldLoop In tdfTemp.Fields
             Debug.Print , fldLoop.Name & ", Required = " & _
                fldLoop.Required
          Next fldLoop

       End Sub
```

Required Property (Remote Data)

Returns a value that indicates whether an **rdoColumn** requires a non-**Null** value.

Applies To

rdoColumn Object

Syntax

object.**Required**

The *object* placeholder represents an object expression that evaluates to an object in the **Applies To** list.

Return Values

The return values for the **Required** property are:

Value	Description
True	A **Null** value isn't allowed.
False	A **Null** value is allowed.

Remarks

For an **rdoColumn** object, you can use the **Required** property along with the **AllowZeroLength** property to determine the validity of the **Value** property setting for that **rdoColumn** object. If **Required** is set to **False**, the column can contain **Null** values as well as values that meet the conditions specified by the **AllowZeroLength** property setting.

See Also

rdoColumn Object, **rdoPreparedStatement** Object, **AllowZeroLength** Property (Remote Data), **Value** Property (Remote Data)

Reset Statement

Closes all disk files opened using the **Open** statement.

Syntax

Reset

Remarks

The **Reset** statement closes all active files opened by the **Open** statement and writes the contents of all file buffers to disk.

See Also

End Statement, **Close** Statement, **Open** Statement

Example

This example uses the **Reset** statement to close all open files and write the contents of all file buffers to disk. Note the use of the **Variant** variable FileNumber as both a string and a number.

```
Dim FileNumber
For FileNumber = 1 To 5                ' Loop 5 times.
    ' Open file for output. FileNumber is concatenated into the string
    ' TEST for the filename, but is a number following a #.
    Open "TEST" & FileNumber For Output As #FileNumber
    Write #FileNumber, "Hello World"   ' Write data to file.
Next FileNumber
Reset                                  ' Close files and write contents
                                       ' to disk.
```

Resize Event

Occurs when an object is first displayed or when the window state of an object changes. (For example, a form is maximized, minimized, or restored.)

Applies To

Data Control, **UserControl** Object, **UserDocument** Object, **Form** Object, **Forms** Collection, **MDIForm** Object, **PictureBox** Control, **OLE Container** Control

Syntax

Private Sub Form_Resize( )
Private Sub *object*_**Resize**(*height* **As Single**, *width* **As Single**)

The **Resize** event syntax has these parts:

Part	Description
object	An object expression that evaluates to an object in the **Applies To** list.
height	Number specifying the new height of the control.
width	Number specifying the new width of the control.

Remarks

Use a Resize event procedure to move or resize controls when the parent form is resized. You can also use this event procedure to recalculate variables or properties, such as **ScaleHeight** and **ScaleWidth**, that may depend on the size of the form. If you want graphics to maintain sizes proportional to the form when it's resized, invoke the Paint event by using the **Refresh** method in a Resize event procedure.

Whenever the **AutoRedraw** property is set to **False** and the form is resized, Visual Basic also calls the related events, Resize and Paint, in that order. When you attach procedures for these related events, be sure their actions don't conflict.

When an **OLE** container control's **SizeMode** property is set to 2 (Autosize), the control is automatically sized according to the display size of the object contained in the control. If the display size of the object changes, the control is automatically resized to fit the object. When this occurs, the Resize event is invoked for the object before the **OLE** container control is resized. The *height* and *width* parts indicate the optimal size for displaying the object (this size is determined by the application that created the object). You can size the control differently by changing the values of the *height* and *width* parts in the Resize event.

See Also

Paint Event, **Refresh** Method, **Load** Statement, **Show** Method, **AutoRedraw** Property

Example

This example changes the size of a **Shape** control to correspond to the value of a horizontal scroll bar (**HScrollBar**) as you drag the scroll box on the scroll bar. To try this example, paste the code into the Declarations section of a form that contains a

Shape control, a **Label** control, and an **HScrollBar** control. Set the **Index** property for the **Shape** control to 0 to create a control array. Then press F5 and move the scroll bar.

```
Private Sub Form_Load ()
    ' Move and size the first Shape control.
    Shape1(0).Move HScroll.Left, HScroll1.Top * 1.5, HScroll1.Width,
    ↳ HScroll.Height
    Label1.Caption = ""                 ' Set the Label caption.
    Load Shape1(1)                      ' Create the second Shape.
    ' Move and size the second Shape control.
    Shape1(1).Move Shape1(0).Left, Shape1(0).Top, 1, Shape1(0).Height
    Shape1(1).BackStyle = 1             ' Set BackStyle to Opaque.
    Shape1(1).Visible = True            ' Display the second Shape.
    HScroll.Min = 1                     ' Set values of the scroll bar.
    HScroll.Max = HScroll.Width
End Sub

Private Sub HScroll1_Change ()
    Label1.Caption = "Changed"          ' Display message after change.
End Sub

Private Sub HScroll1_Scroll ()
    Shape1(1).BackColor = &HFF0000      ' Set Shape color to Blue.
    Label1.Caption = "Changing"         ' Display message while scrolling.
    Shape1(1).Width = HScroll1.Value    ' Size Shape to Scroll Value.
End Sub
```

Restartable Property (DAO)

Returns a value that indicates whether a **Recordset** object supports the **Requery** method, which re-executes the query on which the **Recordset** object is based.

Applies To

Dynaset-Type Recordset Object, **Recordset** Object, **Snapshot-Type Recordset** Object, **Table-Type Recordset** Object, **Forward-Only–Type Recordset** Object, **Dynamic-Type Recordset** Object

Return Values

The return value is a **Boolean** data type that is **True** if the **Recordset** object supports the **Requery** method. Table-type **Recordset** objects always return **False**.

Remarks

Check the **Restartable** property before using the **Requery** method on a **Recordset** object. If the object's **Restartable** property is set to **False**, use the **OpenRecordset** method on the underlying **QueryDef** object to re-execute the query.

See Also

QueryDef Object, **OpenRecordset** Method, **Requery** Method

Example

This example demonstrates the **Restartable** property with different **Recordset** objects.

```
Sub RestartableX()

    Dim dbsNorthwind As Database
    Dim rstTemp As Recordset

    Set dbsNorthwind = OpenDatabase("Northwind.mdb")

    With dbsNorthwind
        ' Open a table-type Recordset and print its
        ' Restartable property.
        Set rstTemp = .OpenRecordset("Employees", dbOpenTable)
        Debug.Print _
            "Table-type recordset from Employees table"
        Debug.Print "    Restartable = " & rstTemp.Restartable
        rstTemp.Close

        ' Open a Recordset from an SQL statement and print its
        ' Restartable property.
        Set rstTemp = _
            .OpenRecordset("SELECT * FROM Employees")
        Debug.Print "Recordset based on SQL statement"
        Debug.Print "    Restartable = " & rstTemp.Restartable
        rstTemp.Close

        ' Open a Recordset from a saved QueryDef object and
        ' print its Restartable property.
        Set rstTemp = .OpenRecordset("Current Product List")
        Debug.Print _
            "Recordset based on permanent QueryDef (" & _
            rstTemp.Name & ")"
        Debug.Print "    Restartable = " & rstTemp.Restartable
        rstTemp.Close

        .Close
    End With

End Sub
```

Restartable Property (Remote Data)

Returns a value that indicates whether an **rdoResultset** object supports the **Requery** method, which re-executes the query the **rdoResultset** is based on.

Applies To

rdoResultset Object

Syntax

object.**Restartable**

The *object* placeholder represents an object expression that evaluates to an object in the **Applies To** list.

Return Values

The **Restartable** property return values are:

Value	Description
True	The **rdoResultset** object supports the **Requery** method.
False	The **rdoResultset** object doesn't support the **Requery** method.

Remarks

Check the **Restartable** property before using the **Requery** method on an **rdoResultset**. If the object's **Restartable** property is set to **False**, use the **OpenResultset** method on the underlying **rdoQuery** to re-execute the query.

You can use the **Requery** method to update an **rdoResultset** object's underlying parameter query after the parameter values have been changed.

If the **rdoQuery** does not contain parameters, the **Restartable** property is always **True**.

See Also

OpenResultset Method (Remote Data), **Requery** Method (Remote Data), **rdoPreparedStatement** Object, **rdoResultset** Object

ResultsChanged Event

Occurs when a new result set is made available after the **MoreResults** method is executed.

Applies To

rdoResultset Object

Syntax

Private Sub *object*.**ResultsChanged**( )

The *object* placeholder represents an object expression that evaluates to an object in the Applies To list.

Remarks

This event is raised after the **MoreResults** method completes and a new set of rows is loaded into the result set. This event is fired even if there are no more sets and the **MoreResults** method returns **False**. In this case, both the EOF and BOF properties will be **True**, indicating that the result set is empty.

See Also

MoreResults Method (Remote Data), **OpenResultset** Method (Remote Data), **rdoResultset** Object

Resultset Property

Returns or sets an **rdoResultset** object defined by a **RemoteData control** or as returned by the **OpenResultset** method.

Applies To

RemoteData Control

Syntax

Set *object*.**Resultset** [= *value*]

The **Resultset** property syntax has these parts:

Part	Description
object	An object expression that evaluates to an object in the **Applies To** list.
value	An object expression that evaluates to an **rdoResultset** object as described in Settings.

Settings

The setting for *value* is an **rdoResultset** object.

Remarks

The **RemoteData** control is automatically initialized when your application starts. If the **SQL** property is valid, or if you set the **SQL** property at run time and use the **Refresh** method, the **RemoteData** control attempts to create a new **rdoResultset** object. This **rdoResultset** is accessible through the **RemoteData** control's **Resultset** property.

If you create an **rdoResultset** object using either RDO code or another **RemoteData** control, you can set the **Resultset** property of the **RemoteData** control to this new **rdoResultset**. Any existing **rdoResultset** in the **RemoteData** control, and the **rdoConnection** object associated with it, are released when a new **rdoResultset** is assigned to the **Resultset** property.

You can also create an **rdoResultset** object using the **OpenResultset** method and setting the **Resultset** property to the resulting **rdoResultset** object. However, the bound controls using the **RemoteData** control must correctly specify the columns of the new **rdoResultset**. To do so, make sure the **DataField** properties of the bound controls connected to the **RemoteData** control are set to match the new **rdoResultset** object's column names.

Type of Result Set

You can also determine the type of **rdoResultset** cursor by examining or setting the **RemoteData** control's **ResultsetType** property. If you don't request a specific type when using the **RemoteData** control, a keyset-type **rdoResultset** is created. You can determine the type of **rdoResultset** at run time by examining the **rdoResultset** object's **Type** property or the **RemoteData** control's **ResultsetType** property.

The **RemoteData** control can create either keyset- or static-type **rdoResultset** objects when accessing SQL Server 6. However, if the ODBC driver does not support keyset cursors, they cannot be created—all drivers support static cursors. A trappable error is triggered if you set the **RemoteData** control's **Resultset** property to an unsupported type of **rdoResultset**.

Note When the **Resultset** property is set, the **RemoteData** control doesn't close the current **rdoResultset** or **rdoConnection,** but it does release it. If there are no other users, the **rdoConnection** is closed automatically. You may want to consider closing the **rdoResultset** and **rdoConnection** associated with the **RemoteData** control before setting the **Resultset** property.

All **rdoResultset** objects created by the **RemoteData** control are built in **rdoEnvironments**(0). If you need to use the **RemoteData** control to manipulate a database in another **rdoEnvironment**, use the technique demonstrated in the example to open the **rdoConnection** in the desired **rdoEnvironment**, create a new **rdoResultset**, and set the **RemoteData** control's **Resultset** property to this new **rdoResultset**.

See Also

MoveFirst, **MoveLast**, **MoveNext**, **MovePrevious** Methods (Remote Data), **OpenResultset** Method (Remote Data), **rdoConnection** Object, **rdoEnvironment** Object, **rdoResultset** Object, **RemoteData** Control, **ResultsetType** Property, **RowCount** Property (Remote Data), **SQL** Property, **Type** Property (Remote Data), **Updatable** Property (Remote Data)

Example

The following example shows how to create an **rdoResultset** in code and pass it to an existing **RemoteData** control:

```
Option Explicit
Dim qy As rdoQuery
Dim rs As rdoResultset
Dim cn As rdoConnection

Private Sub Form_Load()
Dim SQL As String
Set cn = MSRDC1.Connection

SQL = "{ call ChooseAuthor (?) }"
Set qy = cn.CreateQuery("GetAuthor", SQL)
End Sub

Private Sub Search_Click()
qy(0) = NameWanted.Text
Set MSRDC1.Resultset = qy.OpenResultset( _
    rdOpenStatic, rdConcurReadOnly)

End Sub
```

The stored procedure executed by the query example is shown below:

```
CREATE PROCEDURE ChooseAuthor (@authorwanted char(20)) as
select t.title from titles t, titleauthor ta, authors a
where t.title_id = ta.title_id
and ta.au_id = a.au_id
and a.au_lname = @authorWanted
```

ResultsetType Property

Returns or sets a value indicating the type of **rdoResultset** cursor created or to create.

Applies To

RemoteData Control

Syntax

object.**ResultsetType** [= *value*]

The **ResultsetType** property syntax has these parts:

Part	Description
object	An object expression that evaluates to an object in the **Applies To** list.
value	A constant or value that specifies a type of **rdoResultset**, as described in Settings.

Settings

The settings for *value* are:

Constant	Value	Description
rdOpenStatic	3	A static-type **rdoResultset**.
rdOpenKeyset	1	(Default)A keyset-type **rdoResultset**.

Remarks

Not all drivers support all types of cursors. For example, SQL Server 6 supports both static and keyset cursors, but SQL Server 4.2 only supports static cursors. If the ODBC driver does not support keyset cursors, they cannot be created by RDO or the **RemoteData control**. If the **RemoteData** control can't create the type of **rdoResultset** cursor requested, RDO builds one of the types that can be created and returns the cursor type in the **ResultsetType** property.

If you don't specify a **ResultsetType** before the **RemoteData** control creates the **rdoResultset**, a keyset type **rdoResultset** is created.

If you create an **rdoResultset** and set the **Resultset** property with this new object, the **ResultsetType** property of the **RemoteData** control is set to the **Type** property of the new **rdoResultset**.

OpenResultset Method (Remote Data), **Refresh** Method (Remote Data), **Requery** Method (Remote Data), **rdoResultset** Object, **RemoteData** Control, **Type** Property (Remote Data)

Resume Statement

Resumes execution after an error-handling routine is finished.

Syntax

Resume [0]
Resume Next
Resume *line*

The **Resume** statement syntax can have any of the following forms:

Statement	Description
Resume	If the error occurred in the same procedure as the error handler, execution resumes with the statement that caused the error. If the error occurred in a called procedure, execution resumes at the statement that last called out of the procedure containing the error-handling routine.
Resume Next	If the error occurred in the same procedure as the error handler, execution resumes with the statement immediately following the statement that caused the error. If the error occurred in a called procedure, execution resumes with the statement immediately following the statement that last called out of the procedure containing the error-handling routine (or **On Error Resume Next** statement).
Resume *line*	Execution resumes at *line* specified in the required *line* argument. The *line* argument is a line label or line number and must be in the same procedure as the error handler.

Remarks

If you use a **Resume** statement anywhere except in an error-handling routine, an error occurs.

See Also

End Statement, **Exit** Statement, **On Error** Statement, **Err** Object

Example

This example uses the **Resume** statement to end error handling in a procedure, and then resume execution with the statement that caused the error. Error number 55 is generated to illustrate using the **Resume** statement.

```
Sub ResumeStatementDemo()
    On Error GoTo ErrorHandler      ' Enable error-handling routine.
    Open "TESTFILE" For Output As #1 ' Open file for output.
    Kill "TESTFILE"                 ' Attempt to delete open file.
    Exit Sub                        ' Exit Sub to avoid error handler.
```

```
ErrorHandler:                          ' Error-handling routine.
   Select Case Err.Number              ' Evaluate error number.
      Case 55                          ' "File already open" error.
         Close #1                      ' Close open file.
      Case Else

                                       ' Handle other situations here....

   End Select
   Resume                              ' Resume execution at same line
                                       ' that caused the error.

End Sub
```

Resync Method (Remote Data)

Fetches the batch conflict values for the current row.

Applies To

rdoResultset Object

Syntax

object.**Resync**

The *object* placeholder represents an object expression that evaluates to an object in the **Applies To** list.

Remarks

The **Resync** method is valid only when using Client-Batch Cursors.

Resync resynchronizes the columns in the current row in the cursor library with the current data on the server (visible to your transaction). If you have not modified the row, this method changes the **Value** and **OriginalValue** properties to match what is currently on the server.

If you have modified the row, this method will only adjust the **OriginalValue** property so as not to loose your edits. This second case is useful when you want to avoid an optimistic concurrency conflict.

The last case where this is used is when you're dealing with a row that you attempted to update using **BatchUpdate**, but a conflict occurred because the concurrency check failed. In this case, this method will adjust the **BatchConflictValue** to reflect the most recent version of the column on the server.

ReturnsRecords Property

Sets or returns a value that indicates whether an SQL pass-through query to an external database returns records.

Applies To

QueryDef Object

Settings and Return Values

The setting or return value is a **Boolean** that is **True** (default) if a pass-through query returns records.

Remarks

Not all SQL pass-through queries to external databases return records. For example, an SQL UPDATE statement updates records without returning records, while an SQL SELECT statement does return records. If the query returns records, set the **ReturnsRecords** property to **True**; if the query doesn't return records, set the **ReturnsRecords** property to **False**.

Note You must set the **Connect** property before you set the **ReturnsRecords** property.

See Also

Connect Property, **QueryTimeout** Property, **SQL** Property

Example

This example uses the **Connect** and **ReturnsRecords** properties to select the top five book titles from a Microsoft SQL Server database based on year-to-date sales amounts. In the event of an exact match in sales amounts, the example increases the size of the list displaying the results of the query and prints a message explaining why this occurred.

```
Sub ClientServerX1()

    Dim dbsCurrent As Database
    Dim qdfPassThrough As QueryDef
    Dim qdfLocal As QueryDef
    Dim rstTopFive As Recordset
    Dim strMessage As String

    ' Open a database from which QueryDef objects can be
    ' created.
    Set dbsCurrent = OpenDatabase("DB1.mdb")

    ' Create a pass-through query to retrieve data from
    ' a Microsoft SQL Server database.
    Set qdfPassThrough = _
        dbsCurrent.CreateQueryDef("AllTitles")
    qdfPassThrough.Connect = _
        "ODBC;DATABASE=pubs;UID=sa;PWD=;DSN=Publishers"
    qdfPassThrough.SQL = "SELECT * FROM titles " & _
        "ORDER BY ytd_sales DESC"
    qdfPassThrough.ReturnsRecords = True

    ' Create a temporary QueryDef object to retrieve
    ' data from the pass-through query.
    Set qdfLocal = dbsCurrent.CreateQueryDef("")
    qdfLocal.SQL = "SELECT TOP 5 title FROM AllTitles"

    Set rstTopFive = qdfLocal.OpenRecordset()
```

```
        ' Display results of queries.
        With rstTopFive
           strMessage = _
              "Our top 5 best-selling books are:" & vbCr

           Do While Not .EOF
              strMessage = strMessage & "     " & !Title & _
                 vbCr
              .MoveNext
           Loop

           If .RecordCount > 5 Then
              strMessage = strMessage & _
                 "(There was a tie, resulting in " & _
                 vbCr & .RecordCount & _
                 " books in the list.)"
           End If

           MsgBox strMessage
           .Close
        End With

        ' Delete new pass-through query because this is a
        ' demonstration.
        dbsCurrent.QueryDefs.Delete "AllTitles"
        dbsCurrent.Close

     End Sub
```

Example

This example uses the **LogMessages** and **ReturnsRecords** properties to create a pass-through query that will return data and any messages generated by the remote server.

```
Sub LogMessagesX()

     Dim wrkJet As Workspace
     Dim dbsCurrent As Database
     Dim qdfTemp As QueryDef
     Dim prpNew As Property
     Dim rstTemp As Recordset

     ' Create Microsoft Jet Workspace object.
     Set wrkJet = CreateWorkspace("", "admin", "", dbUseJet)

     Set dbsCurrent = wrkJet.OpenDatabase("DB1.mdb")

     ' Create a QueryDef that will log any messages from the
     ' server in temporary tables.
     Set qdfTemp = dbsCurrent.CreateQueryDef("NewQueryDef")
     qdfTemp.Connect = _
        "ODBC;DATABASE=pubs;UID=sa;PWD=;DSN=Publishers"
     qdfTemp.SQL = "SELECT * FROM stores"
     qdfTemp.ReturnsRecords = True
```

```
    Set prpNew = qdfTemp.CreateProperty("LogMessages", _
        dbBoolean, True)
    qdfTemp.Properties.Append prpNew

    ' Execute query and display results.
    Set rstTemp = qdfTemp.OpenRecordset()

    Debug.Print "Contents of recordset:"
    With rstTemp
        Do While Not .EOF
            Debug.Print , .Fields(0), .Fields(1)
            .MoveNext
        Loop
        .Close
    End With

    ' Delete new QueryDef because this is a demonstration.
    dbsCurrent.QueryDefs.Delete qdfTemp.Name
    dbsCurrent.Close
    wrkJet.Close

End Sub
```

Revision Property

Returns or sets the revision version number of the project. Read-only at run time.

See Also

Major Property, **Minor** Property

Applies To

App Object

Syntax

object.**Revision**

The *object* placeholder represents an object expression that evaluates to an object in the **Applies To** list.

Remarks

The value of the **Revision** property is in the range from 0 to 9999.

This property provides version information about the running application.

You can set this property at design time in the **Revision** box in the **Make** tab of the **Project Properties** dialog box.

RGB Function

Returns a **Long** whole number representing an RGB color value.

RGB(*red, green, blue*)

The **RGB** function syntax has these named arguments:

Part	Description
red	Required; **Variant** (**Integer**). Number in the range 0–255, inclusive, that represents the red component of the color.
green	Required; **Variant** (**Integer**). Number in the range 0–255, inclusive, that represents the green component of the color.
blue	Required; **Variant** (**Integer**). Number in the range 0–255, inclusive, that represents the blue component of the color.

Application methods and properties that accept a color specification expect that specification to be a number representing an RGB color value. An RGB color value specifies the relative intensity of red, green, and blue to cause a specific color to be displayed.

The value for any argument to **RGB** that exceeds 255 is assumed to be 255.

The following table lists some standard colors and the red, green, and blue values they include:

Color	Red Value	Green Value	Blue Value
Black	0	0	0
Blue	0	0	255
Green	0	255	0
Cyan	0	255	255
Red	255	0	0
Magenta	255	0	255
Yellow	255	255	0
White	255	255	255

QBColor Function

This example shows how the **RGB** function is used to return a whole number representing an **RGB** color value. It is used for those application methods and properties that accept a color specification. The object MyObject and its property are used for illustration purposes only. If `MyObject` does not exist, or if it does not have a Color property, an error occurs.

```
Dim RED, I, RGBValue, MyObject
Red = RGB(255, 0, 0)              ' Return the value for Red.
I = 75                           ' Initialize offset.
RGBValue = RGB(I, 64 + I, 128 + I)  ' Same as RGB(75, 139, 203).
MyObject.Color = RGB(255, 0, 0)   ' Set the Color property of
                                 ' MyObject to Red.
```

Right Function

Returns a **Variant** (**String**) containing a specified number of characters from the right side of a string.

Syntax

Right(*string*, *length*)

The **Right** function syntax has these named arguments:

Part	Description
string	Required. String expression from which the rightmost characters are returned. If *string* contains **Null**, **Null** is returned.
length	Required; **Variant** (**Long**). Numeric expression indicating how many characters to return. If 0, a zero-length string ("") is returned. If greater than or equal to the number of characters in *string*, the entire string is returned.

Remarks

To determine the number of characters in *string*, use the **Len** function.

Note Use the **RightB** function with byte data contained in a string. Instead of specifying the number of characters to return, *length* specifies the number of bytes.

See Also

Left Function, **Len** Function, **Mid** Function

Example

This example uses the **Right** function to return a specified number of characters from the right side of a string.

```
Dim AnyString, MyStr
AnyString = "Hello World"    ' Define string.
MyStr = Right(AnyString, 1)  ' Returns "d".
MyStr = Right(AnyString, 6)  ' Returns " World".
MyStr = Right(AnyString, 20) ' Returns "Hello World".
```

RightToLeft Property

Returns a Boolean value that indicates the text display direction and controls the visual appearance on a bi-directional system.

Applies To

AmbientProperties Object

Syntax

object.**RightToLeft**

The **RightToLeft** property syntax has this part:

Part	Description
object	An object expression that evaluates to an object in the **Applies To** list.

Settings

The possible boolean return values from the **RightToLeft** property are:

Setting	Description
True	The control is running on a bi-directional platform, such as Arabic Windows 95 or Hebrew Windows 95, and text is running from right to left. The control should modify its behavior, such as putting vertical scroll bars at the left side of a text or list box, putting labels to the right of text boxes, etc.
False	The control should act as though it was running on a non-bidirectional platform, such as English Windows 95, and text is running from left to right. If the container does not implement this ambient property, this will be the default value.

RmDir Statement

Removes an existing directory or folder.

Syntax

RmDir *path*

The required *path* argument is a string expression that identifies the directory or folder to be removed. The *path* may include the drive. If no drive is specified, **RmDir** removes the directory or folder on the current drive.

Remarks

An error occurs if you try to use **RmDir** on a directory or folder containing files. Use the **Kill** statement to delete all files before attempting to remove a directory or folder.

See Also

ChDir Statement, **CurDir** Function, **Kill** Statement, **MkDir** Statement

Example

This example uses the **RmDir** statement to remove an existing directory or folder.

```
' Assume that MYDIR is an empty directory or folder.
RmDir "MYDIR"   ' Remove MYDIR.
```

Rnd Function

Returns a **Single** containing a random number.

Syntax

Rnd[(*number*)]

The optional *number* argument is a **Single** or any valid numeric expression.

Return Values

If *number* is	Rnd generates
Less than zero	The same number every time, using *number* as the seed.
Greater than zero	The next random number in the sequence.
Equal to zero	The most recently generated number.
Not supplied	The next random number in the sequence.

Remarks

The **Rnd** function returns a value less than 1 but greater than or equal to zero.

The value of *number* determines how **Rnd** generates a random number:

For any given initial seed, the same number sequence is generated because each successive call to the **Rnd** function uses the previous number as a seed for the next number in the sequence.

Before calling **Rnd**, use the **Randomize** statement without an argument to initialize the random-number generator with a seed based on the system timer.

To produce random integers in a given range, use this formula:

```
Int((upperbound - lowerbound + 1) * Rnd + lowerbound)
```

Here, *upperbound* is the highest number in the range, and *lowerbound* is the lowest number in the range.

Note To repeat sequences of random numbers, call **Rnd** with a negative argument immediately before using **Randomize** with a numeric argument. Using **Randomize** with the same value for *number* does not repeat the previous sequence.

See Also

Timer Function, **Math** Functions, **Randomize** Statement

Example

This example uses the **Rnd** function to generate a random integer value from 1 to 6.

```
Dim MyValue
MyValue = Int((6 * Rnd) + 1)   ' Generate random value between 1 and 6.
```

RollbackTrans Event

Occurs after the **RollbackTrans** method has completed.

Applies To

rdoEnvironment Object

Syntax

Private Sub *object*.**RollbackTrans**( )

The *object* placeholder represents an object expression that evaluates to an object in the Applies To list.

Remarks

You can respond to this event to synchronize some other process with the transaction.

See Also

BeginTrans Event, **CommitTrans** Event, **BeginTrans**, **CommitTrans**, **RollbackTrans** Methods

---

RowBookmark Method

Returns a value containing a bookmark for a visible row in the **DBGrid** control. Doesn't support named arguments.

Applies To

DBGrid Control

Syntax

object.**RowBookmark** *value*

The **RowBookmark** method syntax has these parts:

Part	Description
object	An object expression that evaluates to an object in the **Applies To** list.
value	Required. An integer in the range of 0 to the setting of the **DBGrid** control's **VisibleRows** property minus 1.

Remarks

RowBookmark(0) returns the same bookmark as the **FirstRow** property of the **DBGrid** control. The current row, as determined by the **DBGrid** control's **Bookmark** property, may not be returned by this method if the current row isn't visible.

Note   The bookmarks returned by **RowBookmark** should not be saved because their values change as soon as rows visible in the **DBGrid** control change.

See Also

> **SelBookmarks** Collection, **GetBookmark** Method, **FirstRow** Property,
> **SelBookmarks** Property, **VisibleRows** Property

Example

> This example selects all the rows that are currently visible on the grid.

```
Sub SelectAllVisible_Click ()
   Dim I
   For I = 0 To DBGrid1.VisibleRows - 1
      DBGrid1.SelBookmarks.Add DBGrid1.RowBookmark(I)
   Next I
End Sub
```

RowBuffer Object

> The **RowBuffer** object is used to contain one or more rows of retrieved data and
> transfer it between your application and an unbound **DBGrid** control.

> **Note** The **RowBuffer** object is not a derivable object which can be used by other applications.
> It is an internal class usable only by unbound **DBGrid** controls.

Syntax

> **DBGrid.RowBuffer**

Remarks

> A **RowBuffer** is used in the following circumstances:

> - The **RowBuffer** object is passed as an argument to the **UnboundReadData** event,
>   where one or more rows of data are placed in the **RowBuffer** object, which the
>   **DBGrid** uses to fill its cache with data.

> - When data is updated in the **DBGrid**, the **RowBuffer** object is passed to the
>   **UnboundWriteData** event. Only one row of data is updated at a time, and the row
>   updated is supplied with the original bookmark provided when the row was
>   retrieved.

> - When a new row is added, the newly-added data is placed in the **RowBuffer** object
>   and passed to the **UnboundAddData** event.

> In all of the these cases, the **RowBuffer** object is passed to you by the unbound
> **DBGrid** control. It is incumbent upon you and your application to add this data to
> your data set (when passed by the **UnboundReadData** event) or update existing data
> in your dataset (when passed by the **UnboundWriteData**, **UnboundAddData**, or
> **UnboundDeleteRow** events).

UnboundAddData Event, **UnboundDeleteRow** Event, **UnboundReadData** Event, **UnboundWriteData** Event, **RowCount** Property, **DBGrid** Control

Properties

Bookmark Property (DBGrid, ColumnName Property, ColumnCount Property, RowCount Property, Value Property (RowBuffer)

RowColChange Event

Occurs when the current cell changes to a different cell.

Applies To

DBGrid Control

Syntax

Private Sub *object*_**RowColChange** ([*index* **As Integer**, *lastrow* **As String**, *lastcol* **As Integer**])

The **RowColChange** event syntax has these parts:

Part	Description
object	An object expression that evaluates to an object in the **Applies To** list.
index	An integer that uniquely identifies a control if it is in a control array.
lastrow	(For **DBGrid** control) A string expression specifying the previous row position.
lastcol	(For **DBGrid** control) An integer specifying the previous column position.

Remarks

This event occurs whenever the user clicks a cell other than the current cell or when you programmatically change the current cell within a selection using the **Col** and **Row** properties.

The **SelChange** event also occurs when a user clicks a new cell, but doesn't occur when you programmatically change the selected range without changing the current cell.

For the **DBGrid** control, the position of the current cell is provided by the **Bookmark** and **ColIndex** properties. The previous cell position is specified by *lastrow* and *lastcol*. If you edit data and then move the current cell position to a new row, the update events for the original row are completed before another cell becomes the current cell.

See Also

SelChange Event, **Col**, **Row** Properties

RowContaining Method

Returns a value corresponding to the row number of the specified vertical (Y) coordinate of the **DBGrid** control. Doesn't support named arguments.

Applies To

DBGrid Control

Syntax

object.**RowContaining** *coordinate*

The **RowContaining** method syntax has these parts:

Part	Description
object	An object expression that evaluates to an object in the **Applies To** list.
coordinate	Required. A single numeric expression that specifies a vertical coordinate (Y value) based on the coordinate system of the container.

Remarks

The **RowContaining** method returns a value that corresponds to one of the column indexes of the control specified by *object*. This value ranges from 0 to the setting of the **VisibleRows** property -1. This method is useful when working with mouse and drag events when you are trying to determine where the user clicked or dropped another control in terms of a row of the **DBGrid** control.

If *coordinate* is outside of the coordinate system of the container, a trappable error occurs.

See Also

Data Control, **Column** Object, **ColContaining** Method, **ColIndex** Property

Example

This example saves the value of the cell where the user began a drag method.

```
Dim SaveValue
Sub DBGrid1_MouseDown (Button As Integer, Shift As Integer, _
 X As Single, Y As Single)
   Dim RowValue, ColValue
   ' Get the value of the row and column that the mouse is over
   RowValue = DBGrid1.RowContaining(Y)
   ColValue = DBGrid1.ColContaining(X)
   ' If the values are both valid, save the text of the cell and
   ' begin dragging.
   If RowValue > 0 And RowValue < DBGrid1.VisibleRows And _
    ColValue > 0 And ColValue < DBGrid1.VisibleCols Then
      SaveValue = DBGrid1.Columns(ColValue). _
      CellValue(DBGrid1.RowBookmark(RowValue))
      DBGrid1.Drag 1
   End If
End Sub
```

RowCount Property

Returns or sets the number of rows contained in the **RowBuffer** object in an unbound **DBGrid** control.

Applies To

RowBuffer Object

Syntax

object.**RowCount** [= *number*]

The **RowCount** property syntax has these parts:

Part	Description
object	An object expression that evaluates to an object in the **Applies To** list.
number	A long integer indicating the number of rows.

Remarks

In the **UnboundWriteData** event, this property specifies how many rows will be written, and is always set to a value of 1, since you can write only one row of data at a time. You can set this property to a value of 0, however, to indicate that the write operation failed.

In the **UnboundAddData** event, this property is always set to a value of 1, since only a single row can be added at a time. You can set this property to a value of 0, however, to indicate that the add operation failed.

In the **UnboundReadData** event, this property indicates how many rows have been requested to be filled. After filling those rows, you should set **RowCount** to the number of rows actually stored in the **RowBuffer** object.

See Also

MoveFirst, **MoveLast**, **MoveNext**, **MovePrevious** Methods (Remote Data), **Requery** Method (Remote Data), **rdoResultset** Object, **rdoTable** Object

Example

In this example, the **RowCount** property is used to process the correct amount of rows in the **RowBuffer** object.

```
For Row% = 0 To RowBuf.RowCount - 1
' Process RowCount number of rows
Next Row%
```

RowCount Property (Remote Data)

Returns the number of rows accessed in an **rdoResultset** object.

Applies To

rdoResultset Object, **rdoTable** Object

Syntax

object.**RowCount**

The *object* placeholder represents an object expression that evaluates to an object in the **Applies To** list.

Return Values

The **RowCount** property return value is a **Long** integer as discussed in Remarks.

Remarks

Use the **RowCount** property to find out how many rows in an **rdoResultset** object have been accessed, or if the **rdoResultset** returned any rows at all. **RowCount** doesn't indicate how many rows will be returned by an **rdoResultset** query until all rows have been accessed. *After* all rows have been accessed, the **RowCount** property reflects the total number of rows in the **rdoResultset**.

Referencing the **RowCount** property causes RDO to fully-populate the result set— just as if you had executed a **MoveLast** method.

Depending on the driver and data source, the **RowCount** property might return either -1 to indicate that the number of rows is not available, or 0 to indicate that no rows were returned by the **rdoResultset**. If the driver is capable of returning a row count, the **RowCount** property returns the number of rows in the **rdoResultset**.

Using the **Requery** method on an **rdoResultset** resets the **RowCount** property, just as it does when a query is run for the first time.

See Also

MoveFirst, **MoveLast**, **MoveNext**, **MovePrevious** Methods (Remote Data), **Requery** Method (Remote Data), **rdoResultset** Object, **rdoTable** Object

Example

This example illustrates use of the **RowCount** property to determine if any rows resulted from the query and how many rows have been processed after each **MoveNext** method is executed and how many rows are in the result set once all rows are processed.

```
Option Explicit
Dim ps As rdoPreparedStatement
Dim rs As rdoResultset
Dim cn As rdoConnection
```

```
        Private Sub Form_Load()
        Dim SQL As String
        Set cn = MSRDC1.Connection

        SQL = "{call ChooseAuthor (?)}"
        Set ps = cn.CreatePreparedStatement("GetAuthor", SQL)
        End Sub

        Private Sub Search_Click()
        ps(0) = NameWanted.Text
        Set MSRDC1.Resultset = ps.OpenResultset( _
           rdOpenKeyset, rdConcurReadOnly)
        With MSRDC1.Resultset
           If .RowCount = 0 Then
              MsgBox "No titles by that author were found."
              NameWanted.SetFocus
           Else
              Do Until .EOF
              .MoveNext
              TitlesFound = .RowCount          ' How many so far
           Loop
              TitlesFound = .RowCount          ' Total rows found
           End If
           .MoveFirst
        End With
        End Sub
```

RowCurrencyChange Event

Occurs after the result set has repositioned to a new row, BOF or EOF.

Applies To

rdoResultset Object

Syntax

Private Sub *object*.**RowCurrencyChange( )**

The *object* placeholder represents an object expression that evaluates to an object in the **Applies To** list.

Remarks

This event is raised after the result set has repositioned to a new row, or has moved to either BOF or EOF. Any of the *Move* methods, the **AbsolutePosition**, **PercentPosition**, or **Bookmark** properties, or the **Requery**, **MoreResults**, or **Update** (after an **AddNew**) methods can also cause a the current row pointer to be repositioned and cause the **RowCurrencyChange** event to fire. The current position can be determined by accessing the **AbsolutePosition**, **PercentPosition**, or **Bookmark** properties of the object.

The **RowCurrencyChange** event can be used to execute a detail query when an associated master row currency changes. For example, if you setup a form containing a master customer record, and a set of rows corresponding to customer orders, you can use the **RowCurrencyChange** event to launch a query that returns all associated order information each time the user chooses another master customer record.

Note The order in which the **RowCurrencyChange** and **Reposition** events fire cannot be predicted.

See Also

AddNew Method (Remote Data), **GetRows** Method (Remote Data), **MoreResults** Method (Remote Data), **Move** Method (Remote Data), **MoveFirst**, **MoveLast**, **MoveNext**, **MovePrevious** Methods (Remote Data), **Update** Method (Remote Data), **BatchUpdate** Method (Remote Data), **AbsolutePosition** Property (Remote Data), **Bookmark** Property (Remote Data), **PercentPosition** Property (Remote Data)

RowDividerStyle Property

Returns or sets a value that specifies the style of border drawn between the rows of the selected **DBGrid** control.

Applies To

DBGrid Control

Syntax

object.**RowDividerStyle** [= *value*]

The **RowDividerStyle** property syntax has these parts:

Part	Description
object	An object expression that evaluates to an object in the **Applies To** list.
value	An integer that specifies the border style, as described in Settings.

Settings

The settings for *value* are:

Setting	Description
0	No divider
1	Black line
2	(Default) Dark gray line
3	Raised
4	Inset
5	Divider is drawn using the **ForeColor** property setting color

Remarks

The **RowDividerStyle** property doesn't affect whether the border can be dragged or not. When the border is raised or inset, Microsoft Windows sets the colors.

See Also

Data Control, **Column** Object, **DividerStyle** Property, **BackColor**, **ForeColor** Properties

Example

This example toggles through the different row line styles when you click a command button.

```
Private Sub ChangeStyle_Click ()
   If DBGrid1.RowDividerStyle < 5 Then
      DBGrid1.RowDividerStyle = DBGrid1.RowDividerStyle + 1
   Else
      DBGrid1.RowDividerStyle = 0
   End If
End Sub
```

RowHeight Property

Returns or sets the height of all rows in the **DBGrid** control. **RowHeight** is always in the same unit of measure as the container for the **DBGrid** control.

Applies To

DBGrid Control

Syntax

object.**RowHeight**[= *value*]

The **RowHeight** property syntax has these parts:

Part	Description
object	An object expression that evaluates to an object in the **Applies To** list.
value	A numeric expression specifying height.

Remarks

Users can change the **RowHeight** of any row at run time by placing the mouse pointer on a gridline between rows and dragging.

Remarks

Col, **Row** Properties

Example

his example sets the height of the current row to 500 twips when you click the form. To try this example, create a new project, use the Components dialog box to add a **DBGrid** control to the toolbox (from the Project menu, choose Components, and then select Microsoft Data Bound Grid Control), and then draw a **DBGrid** control on the form. Paste the code into the Declarations section of the form, press F5 to run the program, and then select a cell and click the form.

```
Private Sub Form_Load ()
    DBGrid1.Rows = 5  ' Set columns and rows.
    DBGrid1.Cols = 7
End Sub

Private Sub Form_Click ()
    DBGrid1.RowHeight(DBGrid1.Row) = 500
End Sub
```

RowResize Event

Occurs when a user resizes a row in a **DBGrid** control.

Applies To
DBGrid Control

Syntax

Private Sub *object*_**RowResize** ([*index* **As Integer**,] *cancel* **As Integer**)

The **RowResize** event syntax has these parts:

Part	Description
object	An object expression that evaluates to an object in the **Applies To** list.
index	An integer that identifies a control if it is in a control array.
cancel	A Boolean expression that determines if a change is canceled, as described in Settings.

Settings

The settings for *cancel* are:

Setting	Description
True	Cancels the change and restores row to its original height.
False	(Default) Continues with change of row height.

Remarks

The user can resize the **DBGrid** control rows using the mouse. When the user changes the height, the **RowResize** event is triggered. Your event procedure can accept the change, alter the degree of change, or cancel the change completely.

The **DBGrid** control's **RowHeight** property determines the height for all rows in the control.

If you set the *cancel* argument to **True**, the row height is restored. To alter the degree of change, set the **RowHeight** property to the desired value.

Executing the **Refresh** method within the procedure causes the control to be repainted even if the *cancel* argument is **True**.

Example

This example ensures that there are at least five visible rows in the grid.

```
Private Sub DataGrid1_RowResize (Cancel As Integer)
   If DataGrid1.VisibleRows < 5 Then Cancel = True
End Sub
```

RowsAffected Property

Returns the number of rows affected by the most recently invoked **Execute** method.

Applies To

rdoConnection Object, **rdoPreparedStatement** Object, **rdoQuery** Object

Syntax

object.**RowsAffected**

The *object* placeholder represents an object expression that evaluates to an object in the **Applies To** list.

Return Values

The **RowsAffected** property return value is a **Long** value ranging from 0 to the number of rows affected by the most recently invoked **Execute** method on either an **rdoConnection** or **rdoQuery** object.

Remarks

RowsAffected contains the number of rows deleted, updated, or inserted when running an action query. When you use the **Execute** method to run an **rdoQuery**, the **RowsAffected** property setting is the number of rows affected. For example, when you execute a query that deletes 50 rows from a table, the **RowsAffected** property returns 50.

This property is especially useful when you need to determine how many rows were affected in an action query with an ambiguous WHERE clause. For example, in a query that deletes all rows where the *Price* column is greater than 10, the **RowsAffected** property would indicate how many rows actually qualified and were deleted.

See Also

Execute Method (Remote Data), **rdoQuery** Object, **rdoResultset** Object

Example

This example illustrates use of the **RowsAffected** property to determine the number of rows changed by an ambiguous update statement. In this case we do not know how many authors live in Salt Lake City, but once the update takes place, we can determine how many rows were updated by checking the **RowsAffected** property of the **rdoQuery** object.

```
Option Explicit
Dim SQL As String
Dim cn as rdoConnection
Dim qd as rdoQuery

Private Sub Form_Load()
Set cn = rdoEnvironments(0).OpenConnection( _
    dsname:="WorkDB", _
    Prompt:=rdDriverNoPrompt, _
    Connect:="uid=;pwd=;database=pubs")

SQL = "Update Authors Set Zip = ?" _
    & " Where City = ?"
Set qd = cn.CreateQuery("FixZip", SQL)
End Sub

Private Sub UpdateButton_Click()
qd(0) = NewZip          ' From a TextBox
qd(1) = CityToFind      ' From a TextBox
ps.Execute
NumberChanged = qd.RowsAffected
End Sub
```

RowsetSize Property

Returns or sets a value that determines the number of rows in an **rdoResultset cursor**.

Applies To

rdoPreparedStatement Object, **RemoteData** Control

Syntax

object.**RowsetSize** [= *value*]

The **RowsetSize** property syntax has these parts:

Part	Description
object	An object expression that evaluates to an object in the **Applies To** list.
value	A value that specifies the size of the rowset as described in Settings. (Data type is a **Long** expression.)

Settings

The upper limit of the **RowsetSize** is determined by the data source driver. The lower limit for *value* is 1, and the default value is 100.

Remarks

The **RowsetSize** property determines how many rows of the keyset are buffered by the application. RDO uses the **RowsetSize** property to determine how many rows are read into memory with the ODBC **SQLExtendedFetch** function. Tuning the size of **RowsetSize** can affect performance and the amount of memory required to maintain the keyset buffer.

This property must be set before creating an **rdoResultset** object.

Impact on Pessimistic Cursors

In addition, the **RowsetSize** property determines how many rows (and data pages) are locked when using Pessimistic (**rdConcurLock**) concurrency. For example, if you set the **RowsetSize** property to 100 and execute an **rdoQuery** object with the **rdConcurLock** option, the first 100 rows of the result set and every page associated with each row is locked until the cursor is closed or you move the current row pointer toward the end of the result set. In any case, at least **RowsetSize** rows are locked.

See Also

KeysetSize Property (Remote Data), **MaxRows** Property (Remote Data)

RowSource Property

Sets a value that specifies the **Data** control from which the **DBList** and **DBCombo** controls' list is filled. Not available at run time.

Applies To

DBCombo Control, **DBList** Control

Syntax

object.**RowSource** [= *value*]

The **RowSource** property syntax has these parts:

Part	Description
object	An object expression that evaluates to an object in the **Applies To** list.
value	A string expression that specifies the name of a **Data** control.

Remarks

To fill the list in a **DBCombo** or **DBList** control, you must specify a **Data** control in the **RowSource** property at design time using the **Properties** window.

To complete the connection with a field in the **Recordset** object managed by the **Data** control, you must also provide the name of a **Field** object in the **ListField** property.

Data Type

String

RowStatusChanged Event

Occurs after the data state of the current row changes due to an edit, delete or insert.

Applies To

rdoResultset Object

Syntax

Private Sub *object*.**RowStatusChange**( )

The *object* placeholder represents an object expression that evaluates to an object in the **Applies To** list.

Remarks

This event is raised after the status of the current row data changes. The status of a row can change due to an **Delete**, or **Update** operation. The current status for the row can be determined using the **Status** property of the object.

See Also

AddNew Method (Remote Data), **Edit** Method (Remote Data), **Update** Method (Remote Data), **BatchUpdate** Method (Remote Data), **Status** Property

---

RowTop Method

Returns a value containing the Y coordinate of the top of a specified row of a **DBGrid** control. Doesn't support named arguments.

Applies To

DBGrid Control

Syntax

object.**RowTop** *value*

The **RowTop** method syntax has these parts:

Part	Description
object	An object expression that evaluates to an object in the **Applies To** list.
value	Required. An integer that specifies a row in the range of 0 to the setting of the **VisibleRows** property -1.

Remarks

The **RowTop** method returns a value that corresponds to the Y coordinate of the top of the row specified by *value*. The return value is based on the **ScaleMode** property of the container.

You can use the **RowTop** method with the **RowHeight**, **Left**, and **Width** properties of the **Column** object to determine the exact location and dimension of a chosen cell in the **DBGrid** control.

See Also

Data Control, **Column** Object, **ColContaining** Method, **VisibleRows** Property

Example

This example begins a drag operation in the grid. Using the grid cell location and size properties, a **Label** control the size of the cell is used as the drag object.

```
Sub DBGrid1_MouseDown (Button As Integer, _
Shift As Integer, X As Single, Y As Single)
    ' Declare variables.
    Dim DY, DX, RowValue, ColValue, CellLeft, CellTop
    ColValue = DBGrid1.ColContaining(X)
    RowValue = DBGrid1.RowContaining(Y)
    ' Get the height of the cell.
    DY = DBGrid1.RowHeight
    ' Get the width of the cell.
    DX = DBGrid1.Columns(ColValue).Width
    CellLeft = DBGrid1.Columns(ColValue).Left
    CellTop = DBGrid1.RowTop(RowValue)
    Label1.Caption = DBGrid1.Columns(ColValue). _
        CellValue(DBGrid1.RowBookmark(RowValue))
    Label1.Move CellLeft, CellTop, DX, DY
    Label1.Drag ' Drag label outline.
End Sub
```

RSet Statement

Right aligns a string within a string variable.

Syntax

RSet *stringvar* = *string*

The **RSet** statement syntax has these parts:

Part	Description
stringvar	Required. Name of string variable.
string	Required. String expression to be right-aligned within *stringvar*.

Remarks

If *stringvar* is longer than *string*, **RSet** replaces any leftover characters in *stringvar* with spaces, back to its beginning.

Note **RSet** can't be used with user-defined types.

See Also

Data Type Summary, **LSet** Statement

Example

This example uses the **RSet** statement to right align a string within a string variable.

```
Dim MyString
MyString = "0123456789"    ' Initialize string.
Rset MyString = "Right->"  ' MyString contains "    Right->".
```

SaveAs Method

Saves a component or project to a given location using a new filename.

Applies To
VBComponent Object, **VBProject** Object, **VBProjects** Collection

Syntax

object.**SaveAs** (*newfilename* **As String**)

The **SaveAs** method syntax has these parts:

Part	Description
object	An object expression that evaluates to an object in the **Applies To** list.
newfilename	Required. A string expression specifying the new filename for the component to be saved.

Remarks

If a new path name is given, it is used. Otherwise, the old path name is used. If the new filename is invalid or refers to a read-only file, an error occurs.

When a form is saved, *newfilename* specifies the new name of the form file itself. The .Frx file, if applicable, is saved automatically with an .Frx extension.

Note Successfully invoking this method causes the associated events from the **FileControl** object to be invoked.

Saved Property

Returns a **Boolean** value indicating whether or not the object was edited since the last time it was saved. Read/write.

Applies to
VBProject Object

Return Values

The **Saved** property returns these values:

Value	Description
True	The object has not been edited since the last time it was saved.
False	The object has been edited since the last time it was saved.

Remarks

The **SaveAs** method sets the **Saved** property to **True**.

Note If you set the **Saved** property to **False** in code, it returns **False**, and the object is marked as if it were edited since the last time it was saved.

See Also

Protection Property

Example

The following example uses the **Saved** property to return a **Boolean** value indicating whether or not the specified project has been saved in its current state.

```
Debug.Print Application.VBE.VBProjects(1).Saved
```

SavePicture Statement

Saves a graphic from the **Picture** or **Image** property of an object or control (if one is associated with it) to a file.

Syntax

SavePicture *picture*, *stringexpression*

The **SavePicture** statement syntax has these parts:

Part	Description
picture	**Picture** or **Image** control from which the graphics file is to be created.
stringexpression	Filename of the graphics file to save.

Remarks

If a graphic was loaded from a file to the **Picture** property of an object, either at design time or at run time, and it's a bitmap, icon, metafile, or enhanced metafile, it's saved using the same format as the original file. If it is a GIF or JPEG file, it is saved as a bitmap file.

Graphics in an **Image** property are always saved as bitmap (.bmp) files regardless of their original format.

See Also

LoadPicture Function, **Picture** Property, **Image** Property

Example

This example uses the **SavePicture** statement to save a graphic drawn into a **Form** object's **Picture** property. To try this example, paste the code into the Declarations section of a **Form** object, and then run the example and click the **Form** object.

```
Private Sub Form_Click ()
                                   ' Declare variables.
    Dim CX, CY, Limit, Radius  as Integer, Msg as String
    ScaleMode = vbPixels              ' Set scale to pixels.
    AutoRedraw = True                 ' Turn on AutoRedraw.
    Width = Height                    ' Change width to match height.
```

```
            CX = ScaleWidth / 2                ' Set X position.
            CY = ScaleHeight / 2               ' Set Y position.
            Limit = CX                         ' Limit size of circles.
            For Radius = 0 To Limit            ' Set radius.
                Circle (CX, CY), Radius, RGB(Rnd * 255, Rnd * 255, Rnd * 255)
                DoEvents                       ' Yield for other processing.
            Next Radius
            Msg = "Choose OK to save the graphics from this form "
            Msg = Msg & "to a bitmap file."
            MsgBox Msg
            SavePicture Image, "TEST.BMP"      ' Save picture to file.
        End Sub
```

SaveSetting Statement

Saves or creates an application entry in the Windows registry.

Syntax

SaveSetting *appname, section, key, setting*

The **SaveSetting** statement syntax has these named arguments:

Part	Description
appname	Required. String expression containing the name of the application or project to which the setting applies.
section	Required. String expression containing the name of the section where the key setting is being saved.
key	Required. String expression containing the name of the key setting being saved.
setting	Required. Expression containing the value that *key* is being set to.

Remarks

An error occurs if the key setting can't be saved for any reason.

See Also

DeleteSetting Statement, **GetAllSettings** Function, **GetSetting** Function

Example

The following example first uses the **SaveSetting** statement to make entries in the Windows registry (or .ini file on 16-bit Windows platforms) for the MyApp application, and then uses the **DeleteSetting** statement to remove them.

```
' Place some settings in the registry.
SaveSetting appname := "MyApp", section := "Startup", _
            key := "Top", setting := 75
SaveSetting "MyApp","Startup", "Left", 50
' Remove section and all its settings from registry.
DeleteSetting "MyApp", "Startup"
```

SaveToFile Method

Saves an object to a data file. Doesn't support named arguments.

Applies To

OLE Container Control

Syntax

*object.***SaveToFile** *filenumber*

The **SaveToFile** method syntax has these parts:

Part	Description
object	An object expression that evaluates to an object in the **Applies To** list.
filenumber	Required. A numeric expression specifying the file number used when saving an object. This number must correspond to an open, binary file.

Remarks

Use this method to save ActiveX components. To save an ActiveX component in the OLE version 1.0 format, use the **SaveToOle1File** method instead.

If the object is linked (**OLEType = vbOLELinked**, 0), only the link information and an image of the data is saved to the specified file. The object's data is maintained by the application that created the object. If the object is embedded (**OLEType = vbOLEEmbedded**, 1), the object's data is maintained by the **OLE** container control and can be saved by your Visual Basic application.

You can load an object saved to a data file with the **ReadFromFile** method.

See Also

OLEType Property, **ReadFromFile** Method, **SaveToOle1File** Method

SaveToOle1File Method

Saves an object in the OLE version 1.0 file format. Doesn't support named arguments.

Applies To

OLE Container Control

Syntax

*object.***SaveToOle1File** *filenumber*

The **SaveToOle1File** method syntax has these parts:

Part	Description
object	An object expression that evaluates to an object in the **Applies To** list.
filenumber	Required. A numeric expression specifying the file number used when saving or loading an object. This number must correspond to an open, binary file.

Remarks

If the object is linked (**OLEType = vbOLELinked**, 0), only the link information and an image of the data is saved to the specified file. The object's data is maintained by the application that created the object. If the object is embedded (**OLEType = vbOLEEmbedded**, 1), the object's data is maintained by the **OLE** container control and can be saved by your Visual Basic application.

If you want to save the object in the current ActiveX component format, use the **SaveToFile** method instead.

See Also

ReadFromFile Method, **SaveToFile** Method

Scale Method

Defines the coordinate system for a **Form**, **PictureBox**, or **Printer**. Doesn't support named arguments.

Applies To

PropertyPage Object, **UserControl** Object, **UserDocument** Object, **Printer** Object, **Printers** Collection, **Form** Object, **Forms** Collection, **PictureBox** Control

Syntax

object.**Scale** (*x1*, *y1*) **-** (*x2*, *y2*)

The **Scale** method syntax has these parts:

Part	Description
object	Optional. An object expression that evaluates to an object in the **Applies To** list. If *object* is omitted, the **Form** object with the focus is assumed to be *object*.
x1, y1	Optional. Single-precision values indicating the horizontal (x-axis) and vertical (y-axis) coordinates that define the upper-left corner of *object*. Parentheses must enclose the values. If omitted, the second set of coordinates must also be omitted.
x2, y2	Optional. Single-precision values indicating the horizontal and vertical coordinates that define the lower-right corner of *object*. Parentheses must enclose the values. If omitted, the first set of coordinates must also be omitted.

Remarks

The **Scale** method enables you to reset the coordinate system to any scale you choose. **Scale** affects the coordinate system for both run-time graphics statements and the placement of controls.

If you use **Scale** with no arguments (both sets of coordinates omitted), it resets the coordinate system to twips.

See Also

TextHeight Method, **TextWidth** Method, **ScaleHeight**, **ScaleWidth** Properties, **ScaleLeft, ScaleTop** Properties,**ScaleMode** Property

Example

This example uses the **Scale** method to set up a custom coordinate system so that a bar chart can be drawn on a form. To try this example, paste the code into the Declarations section of a form, and then press F5 and click the form.

```
Private Sub Form_Click ()
    Dim I, OldFontSize                  ' Declare variables.
    Width = 8640: Height = 5760         ' Set form size in twips.
    Move 100,100                        ' Move form origin.
    AutoRedraw = -1                     ' Turn on AutoRedraw.
    OldFontSize = FontSize              ' Save old font size.
    BackColor = QBColor(7)              ' Set background to gray.
    Scale (0, 110)-(130, 0)             ' Set custom coordinate system.
    For I = 100 To 10 Step -10
        Line (0, I)-(2, I)              ' Draw scale marks every 10 units.
        CurrentY = CurrentY + 1.5       ' Move cursor position.
        Print I                         ' Print scale mark value on left.
        Line (ScaleWidth - 2, I)-(ScaleWidth, I)
        CurrentY = CurrentY + 1.5       ' Move cursor position.
        CurrentX = ScaleWidth - 9
        Print I                         ' Print scale mark value on right.
    Next I
                                        ' Draw bar chart.
    Line (10, 0)-(20, 45), RGB(0, 0, 255), BF    ' First blue bar.
    Line (20, 0)-(30, 55), RGB(255, 0, 0), BF    ' First red bar.
    Line (40, 0)-(50, 40), RGB(0, 0, 255), BF
    Line (50, 0)-(60, 25), RGB(255, 0, 0), BF
    Line (70, 0)-(80, 35), RGB(0, 0, 255), BF
    Line (80, 0)-(90, 60), RGB(255, 0, 0), BF
    Line (100, 0)-(110, 75), RGB(0, 0, 255), BF
    Line (110, 0)-(120, 90), RGB(255, 0, 0), BF
    CurrentX = 18: CurrentY = 100       ' Move cursor position.
    FontSize = 14                       ' Enlarge font for title.
    Print "Widget Quarterly Sales"      ' Print title.
    FontSize = OldFontSize              ' Restore font size.
    CurrentX = 27: CurrentY = 93        ' Move cursor position.
    Print "Planned Vs. Actual"          ' Print subtitle.
    Line (29, 86)-(34, 88), RGB(0, 0, 255), BF      ' Print legend.
    Line (43, 86)-(49, 88), RGB(255, 0, 0), BF
End Sub
```

ScaleHeight, ScaleWidth Properties

Return or set the number of units for the horizontal (**ScaleWidth**) and vertical (**ScaleHeight**) measurement of the interior of an object when using graphics methods or when positioning controls. For **MDIForm** objects, not available at design time and read-only at run time.

Applies To

PropertyPage Object, **UserControl** Object, **UserDocument** Object, **Printer** Object, **Printers** Collection, **Form** Object, **Forms** Collection, **MDIForm** Object, **PictureBox** Control

Syntax

object.**ScaleHeight** [= *value*]
object.**ScaleWidth** [= *value*]

The **ScaleHeight** and **ScaleWidth** property syntaxes have these parts:

Part	Description
object	An object expression that evaluates to an object in the **Applies To** list.
value	A numeric expression specifying the horizontal or vertical measurement.

Remarks

You can use these properties to create a custom coordinate scale for drawing or printing. For example, the statement `ScaleHeight = 100` changes the units of measure of the actual interior height of the form. Instead of the height being *n* current units (twips, pixels, ...), the height will be 100 user-defined units. Therefore, a distance of 50 units is half the height/width of the object, and a distance of 101 units will be off the object by 1 unit.

Use the **ScaleMode** property to define a scale based on a standard unit of measurement, such as twips, points, pixels, characters, inches, millimeters, or centimeters.

Setting these properties to positive values makes coordinates increase from top to bottom and left to right. Setting them to negative values makes coordinates increase from bottom to top and right to left.

Using these properties and the related **ScaleLeft** and **ScaleTop** properties, you can set up a full coordinate system with both positive and negative coordinates. All four of these Scale properties interact with the **ScaleMode** property in the following ways:

- Setting any other Scale property to any value automatically sets **ScaleMode** to 0. A **ScaleMode** of 0 is user-defined.

- Setting **ScaleMode** to a number greater than 0 changes **ScaleHeight** and **ScaleWidth** to the new unit of measurement and sets **ScaleLeft** and **ScaleTop** to 0. In addition, the **CurrentX** and **CurrentY** settings change to reflect the new coordinates of the current point.

You can also use the **Scale** method to set the **ScaleHeight**, **ScaleWidth**, **ScaleLeft**, and **ScaleTop** properties in one statement.

Note The **ScaleHeight** and **ScaleWidth** properties aren't the same as the **Height** and **Width** properties.

For **MDIForm** objects, **ScaleHeight** and **ScaleWidth** refer only to the area not covered by **PictureBox** controls in the form. Avoid using these properties to size a **PictureBox** in the Resize event of an **MDIForm**.

See Also

Scale Method, **BackColor**, **ForeColor** Properties, **Height**, **Width** Properties, **CurrentX**, **CurrentY** Properties, **DrawMode** Property, **DrawStyle** Property, **FillColor** Property, **ScaleLeft**, **ScaleTop** Properties, **ScaleMode** Property

Example

This example creates a grid in a **PictureBox** control and sets coordinates for the upper-left corner to –1, –1 instead of 0, 0. Every 0.25 second, dots are randomly plotted from the upper-left corner to the lower-right corner. To try this example, paste the code into the Declarations section of a form that contains a large **PictureBox** and a **Timer** control, and then press F5.

```
Private Sub Form_Load ()
    Timer1.Interval = 250' Set Timer interval.
    Picture1.ScaleTop = -1  ' Set scale for top of grid.
    Picture1.ScaleLeft = -1 ' Set scale for left of grid.
    Picture1.ScaleWidth = 2 ' Set scale (-1 to 1).
    Picture1.ScaleHeight = 2
    Picture1.Line (-1, 0)-(1, 0)        ' Draw horizontal line.
    Picture1.Line (0, -1)-(0, 1)        ' Draw vertical line.
End Sub

Private Sub Timer1_Timer ()
    Dim I ' Declare variable.
    ' Plot dots randomly within a range.
    For I = -1 To 1 Step .05
        Picture1.PSet (I * Rnd, I * Rnd)        ' Draw a point.
    Next I
End Sub
```

ScaleLeft, ScaleTop Properties

Return or set the horizontal (**ScaleLeft**) and vertical (**ScaleTop**) coordinates for the left and top edges of an object when using graphics methods or when positioning controls.

Applies To

PropertyPage Object, **UserControl** Object, **UserDocument** Object, **Printer** Object, **Printers** Collection, **Form** Object, **Forms** Collection, **PictureBox** Control

Syntax

object.**ScaleLeft** [= *value*]
object.**ScaleTop** [= *value*]

The **ScaleLeft** and **ScaleTop** property syntaxes have these parts:

Part	Description
object	An object expression that evaluates to an object in the **Applies To** list.
value	A numeric expression specifying the horizontal or vertical coordinate. The default is 0.

Remarks

Using these properties and the related **ScaleHeight** and **ScaleWidth** properties, you can set up a full coordinate system with both positive and negative coordinates. These four Scale properties interact with the **ScaleMode** property in the following ways:

- Setting any other Scale property to any value automatically sets **ScaleMode** to 0. A **ScaleMode** of 0 is user-defined.

- Setting the **ScaleMode** property to a number greater than 0 changes **ScaleHeight** and **ScaleWidth** to the new unit of measurement and sets **ScaleLeft** and **ScaleTop** to 0. The **CurrentX** and **CurrentY** property settings change to reflect the new coordinates of the current point.

You can also use the **Scale** method to set the **ScaleHeight**, **ScaleWidth**, **ScaleLeft**, and **ScaleTop** properties in one statement.

Note The **ScaleLeft** and **ScaleTop** properties aren't the same as the **Left** and **Top** properties.

See Also

Scale Method, **BackColor**, **ForeColor** Properties, **Left**, **Top** Properties, **DrawMode** Property, **DrawStyle** Property, **FillColor** Property, **ScaleHeight**, **ScaleWidth** Properties, **ScaleMode** Property

Example

This example shows how different **ScaleMode** property settings change the size of a circle. To try this example, paste the code into the Declarations section of a form, and then press F5 and click the form. When you click the form, the unit of measurement changes to the next **ScaleMode** setting and a circle is drawn on the form.

```
Private Sub Form_Click ()
   ' Cycle through each of the seven ScaleMode settings.
   ScaleMode = ((ScaleMode + 1) Mod 7) + 1
   ' Draw a circle with radius of 2 in center of form.
   Circle (ScaleWidth / 2, ScaleHeight / 2), 2
End Sub
```

ScaleMode Property

Returns or sets a value indicating the unit of measurement for coordinates of an object when using graphics methods or when positioning controls.

Applies To

PropertyPage Object, **UserControl** Object, **UserDocument** Object, **Printer** Object, **Printers** Collection, **Form** Object, **Forms** Collection, **PictureBox** Control

Syntax

object.**ScaleMode** [= *value*]

The **ScaleMode** property syntax has these parts:

Part	Description
object	An object expression that evaluates to an object in the **Applies To** list.
value	An integer specifying the unit of measurement, as described in Settings.

Settings

The settings for *value* are:

Constant	Setting	Description
vbUser	0	Indicates that one or more of the **ScaleHeight**, **ScaleWidth**, **ScaleLeft**, and **ScaleTop** properties are set to custom values.
VbTwips	1	(Default) Twip (1440 twips per logical inch; 567 twips per logical centimeter).
VbPoints	2	Point (72 points per logical inch).
VbPixels	3	Pixel (smallest unit of monitor or printer resolution).
vbCharacters	4	Character (horizontal = 120 twips per unit; vertical = 240 twips per unit).
VbInches	5	Inch.
VbMillimeters	6	Millimeter.
VbCentimeters	7	Centimeter.

Remarks

Using the related **ScaleHeight**, **ScaleWidth**, **ScaleLeft**, and **ScaleTop** properties, you can create a custom coordinate system with both positive and negative coordinates. These four Scale properties interact with the **ScaleMode** property in the following ways:

- Setting the value of any other Scale property to any value automatically sets **ScaleMode** to 0. A **ScaleMode** of 0 is user-defined.

- Setting the **ScaleMode** property to a number greater than 0 changes **ScaleHeight** and **ScaleWidth** to the new unit of measurement and sets **ScaleLeft** and **ScaleTop** to 0. The **CurrentX** and **CurrentY** property settings change to reflect the new coordinates of the current point.

See Also

Scale Method, **BackColor**, **ForeColor** Properties, **DrawMode** Property, **DrawStyle** Property, **FillColor** Property, **ScaleHeight**, **ScaleWidth** Properties, **ScaleLeft**, **ScaleTop** Properties

Example

This example shows how different **ScaleMode** property settings change the size of a circle. To try this example, paste the code into the Declarations section of a form, and then press F5 and click the form. When you click the form, the unit of measurement changes to the next **ScaleMode** setting and a circle is drawn on the form.

```
Private Sub Form_Click ()
   ' Cycle through each of the seven ScaleMode settings.
   ScaleMode = ((ScaleMode + 1) Mod 7) + 1
   ' Draw a circle with radius of 2 in center of form.
   Circle (ScaleWidth / 2, ScaleHeight / 2), 2
End Sub
```

ScaleUnits Property

Returns a string value that is the name of the coordinate units being used by the container.

Applies To

AmbientProperties Object

Syntax

object.**ScaleUnits**

The **ScaleUnits** property syntax has this part:

Part	Description
object	An object expression that evaluates to an object in the **Applies To** list.

Remarks

This string represents the coordinates used by the container of the control, such as "twips". This string can be used by the control as a units indicator when displaying coordinate values.

If the container does not implement this ambient property, the default value will be an empty string.

ScaleX, ScaleY Methods

Converts the value for the width or height of a **Form**, **PictureBox**, or **Printer** from one of the **ScaleMode** property's unit of measure to another. Doesn't support named arguments.

Applies To

PropertyPage Object, **UserControl** Object, **UserDocument** Object, **Printer Object, Printers** Collection, **Form Object, Forms** Collection, **PictureBox** Control

Syntax

object.**ScaleX** (*width, fromscale, toscale*)
object.**ScaleY** (*height, fromscale, toscale*)

The **ScaleX** and **ScaleY** method syntaxes have these parts:

Part	Description
object	Optional. An object expression that evaluates to an object in the **Applies To** list. If *object* is omitted, the **Form** object with the focus is assumed to be *object*.
width	Required. Specifies, for *object*, the number of units of measure to be converted.
height	Required. Specifies, for *object*, the number of units of measure to be converted.
fromscale	Optional. A constant or value specifying the coordinate system from which *width* or *height* of *object* is to be converted, as described in Settings. The possible values of *fromscale* are the same as for the **ScaleMode** property, plus the new value of HiMetric.
toscale	Optional. A constant or value specifying the coordinate system to which *width* or *height* of *object* is to be converted, as described in Settings. The possible values of *toscale* are the same as for the **ScaleMode** property, plus the new value of HiMetric.

Settings

The settings for *fromscale* and *toscale* are:

Constant	Value	Description
vbUser	0	User-defined: indicates that the width or height of *object* is set to a custom value.
vbTwips	1	Twip (1440 twips per logical inch; 567 twips per logical centimeter).
vbPoints	2	Point (72 points per logical inch).
vbPixels	3	Pixel (smallest unit of monitor or printer resolution).
vbCharacters	4	Character (horizontal = 120 twips per unit; vertical = 240 twips per unit).

(continued)

Constant	Value	Description
vbInches	5	Inch.
vbMillimeters	6	Millimeter.
vbCentimeters	7	Centimeter.
vbHimetric	8	HiMetric. If *fromscale* is omitted, HiMetric is assumed as the default.
vbContainerPosition	9	Determines control's position.
vbContainerSize	10	Determines control's size.

Remarks

The **ScaleX** and **ScaleY** methods take a value (*width* or *height*), with its unit of measure specified by *fromscale*, and convert it to the corresponding value for the unit of measure specified by *toscale*.

You can also use **ScaleX** and **ScaleY** with the **PaintPicture** method.

See Also

ScaleHeight, **ScaleWidth** Properties, **ScaleLeft, ScaleTop** Properties, **ScaleMode** Property

Scope Property

Returns whether a member is public, private, or friend.

Applies To

Member Object

Syntax

object.**Scope**

The *object* placeholder represents an object expression that evaluates to an object in the **Applies To** list.

Screen Object

Manipulates forms according to their placement on the screen and controls the mouse pointer outside your application's forms at run time. The **Screen** object is accessed with the keyword **Screen**.

Syntax

Screen

Remarks

The **Screen** object is the entire Windows desktop. Using the **Screen** object, you can set the **MousePointer** property of the **Screen** object to the hourglass pointer while a modal form is displayed.

Properties

Height, Width Properties, **FontCount** Property, **Fonts** Property, **MouseIcon** Property, **MousePointer** Property, **TwipsPerPixelX, TwipsPerPixelY** Properties, **ActiveControl** Property, **ActiveForm** Property

---

Screen Property

Returns a **Screen** object, which enables you to manipulate forms according to their placement on the screen and control the mouse pointer outside your application's forms at run time. The **Screen** object is accessed with the keyword **Screen**.

Applies To

Global Object

Syntax

Screen

Remarks

The **Screen** object is the entire Windows desktop. Using the **Screen** object, you can set the **MousePointer** property of the **Screen** object to the hourglass pointer while a modal form is displayed.

See Also

Global Object, **Screen** Object

Scroll Event

Occurs when the scroll box on a **ScrollBar** control, or an object which contains a scrollbar, is repositioned or scrolled horizontally or vertically.

Applies To

ComboBox Control, **DBGrid** Control, **DirListBox** Control, **DriveListBox** Control, **FileListBox** Control, **HScrollBar, Vscrollbar** Controls, **ListBox** Control, **Slider** Control, **UserDocument** Object

Syntax

Private Sub *dbgrid*_**Scroll**([*cancel* **As Integer**])
Private Sub *object*_**Scroll**( )

The **Scroll** event syntax has these parts:

Part	Description
object	An object expression that evaluates to an object in the **Applies To** list.
cancel	Determines whether the scroll operation succeeds and the **ScrollBar** or **DBGrid** are repainted, as described in Remarks.

Remarks

For a **DBGrid** control, this event occurs when the user scrolls the grid horizontally or vertically but before the grid is repainted to display the results of the scroll operation.

For a **ComboBox** control, this event occurs only when the scrollbars in the dropdown portion of the control are manipulated.

Setting *cancel* to **True** causes the **DBGrid** scroll operation to fail, and no repaint operation occurs. If the **Refresh** method is invoked within this event, the grid is repainted in its new (scrolled) arrangement even if *cancel* is set to **True**. However, in this case, the grid is repainted again because the scroll operation fails and it snaps back to its previous position.

You can use this event to perform calculations or to manipulate controls that must be coordinated with ongoing changes in scroll bars. In contrast, use the Change event when you want an update to occur only once, after a **ScrollBar** control changes.

Note Avoid using a **MsgBox** statement or function in this event.

See Also

Change Event, **Slider** Control

Example

This example changes the size of a **Shape** control to correspond to the value of a horizontal scroll bar (**HScrollBar**) as you drag the scroll box on the scroll bar. To try this example, paste the code into the Declarations section of a form that contains a **Shape** control, a **Label** control, and an **HScrollBar** control. Set the **Index** property for the **Shape** control to 0 to create a control array. Then press F5 and move the scroll bar.

```
Private Sub Form_Load ()
   ' Move and size the first Shape control.
   Shape1(0).Move HScroll1.Left, HScroll1.Top * 1.5, HScroll1.Width,
   ↪ HScroll1.Height
   Label1.Caption = ""                ' Set the Label caption.
   Load Shape1(1)                     ' Create the second Shape.
   ' Move and size the second Shape control.
   Shape1(1).Move Shape1(0).Left, Shape1(0).Top, 1, Shape1(0).Height
   Shape1(1).BackStyle = 1            ' Set BackStyle to Opaque.
   Shape1(1).Visible = True           ' Display the second Shape.
   HScroll1.Min = 1                   ' Set values of the scroll bar.

HScroll1.Max = HScroll1.Width
End Sub
```

```
Private Sub HScroll1_Change ()
   Label1.Caption = "Changed"          ' Display message after change.
End Sub

Private Sub HScroll1_Scroll ()
   Shape1(1).BackColor = &HFF0000      ' Set Shape color to Blue.
   Label1.Caption = "Changing"         ' Display message while scrolling.
   Shape1(1).Width = HScroll1.Value    ' Size Shape to Scroll Value.
End Sub
```

Scroll Method

Scrolls the **DBGrid** control horizontally and vertically in a single operation. Doesn't support named arguments.

Applies To

DBGrid Control

Syntax

object.**Scroll** *colvalue, rowvalue*

The **Scroll** method syntax has these parts:

Part	Description
object	An object expression that evaluates to an object in the **Applies To** list.
colvalue	Required. A long numeric expression that specifies a column in the control.
rowvalue	Required. A long numeric expression that specifies a row in the control.

Remarks

Positive values scroll right and down. Negative values scroll left and up. Values that are out of range don't cause an error—the **DBGrid** control scrolls to the maximum degree possible. The same effect can be achieved by setting the **FirstRow** and **LeftCol** properties, but these must be set independently, causing two separate **Paint** events.

See Also

FirstRow Property

Example

This example creates two buttons that enable you to scroll diagonally, one to move down and to the right and the other to move up and to the left.

```
Sub ScrollDownRight_Click
   ' Scroll down and to the right.
   DBGrid1.Scroll DBGrid1.VisibleCols, DBGrid1.VisibleRows
End Sub

Sub ScrollUpLeft_Click
   ' Scroll up and to the left.
   DBGrid1.Scroll -DBGrid1.VisibleCols, -DBGrid1.VisibleRows
End Sub
```

ScrollBars Property

Returns or sets a value indicating whether an object has horizontal or vertical scroll bars. Read only at run time.

Applies To

DBGrid Control, **Split** Object, **UserDocument** Object, **MDIForm** Object, **TextBox** Control

Syntax

object.**ScrollBars**

The *object* placeholder represents an object expression that evaluates to an object in the **Applies To** list.

Settings

For an **MDIForm** object, the **ScrollBars** property settings are:

Setting	Description
True	(Default) The form has a horizontal or vertical scroll bar, or both.
False	The form has no scroll bars.

For a **TextBox** control, the **ScrollBars** property settings are:

Constant	Setting	Description
vbSBNone	0	(Default) None
vbHorizontal	1	Horizontal
vbVertical	2	Vertical
vbBoth	3	Both

Remarks

For a **TextBox** control with setting 1 (Horizontal), 2 (Vertical), or 3 (Both), you must set the **MultiLine** property to **True**.

At run time, the Microsoft Windows operating environment automatically implements a standard keyboard interface to allow navigation in **TextBox** controls with the arrow keys (UP ARROW, DOWN ARROW, LEFT ARROW, and RIGHT ARROW), the HOME and END keys, and so on.

Scroll bars are displayed on an object only if its contents extend beyond the object's borders. For example, in an **MDIForm** object, if part of a child form is hidden behind the border of the parent MDI form, a horizontal scroll bar (**HScrollBar** control) is displayed. Similarly, a vertical scroll bar appears on a **TextBox** control when it can't display all of its lines of text. If **ScrollBars** is set to **False**, the object won't have scroll bars, regardless of its contents.

See Also

WordWrap Property

ScrollGroup Property

Used to synchronize vertical scrolling between splits.

Applies To

Split Object

Syntax

object.**ScrollGroup** [= *value*]

The **ScrollGroup** property syntax has these parts:

Part	Description
object	An object expression that evaluates to an object in the **Applies To** list.
value	An integer expression that determines the scroll group that a split belongs to.

Remarks

This property is used to synchronize vertical scrolling between splits. All splits with the same **ScrollGroup** setting will be synchronized when vertical scrolling occurs within any one of them. Splits belonging to different groups can scroll independently, allowing different splits to display different parts of the database.

If the **ScrollBars** property for a split is set to 4 - Automatic, only the rightmost split of the group will have a vertical scroll bar. If there is only one split, setting this property has no effect.

Setting the **FirstRow** property for one split affects all other splits in the same group, keeping the group synchronized.

Newly created splits have a **ScrollGroup** value of 1.

See Also

FirstRow Property, **ScrollBars** Property

Second Function

Returns a **Variant** (**Integer**) specifying a whole number between 0 and 59, inclusive, representing the second of the minute.

Syntax

Second(*time*)

The required *time* argument is any **Variant**, numeric expression, string expression, or any combination, that can represent a time. If *time* contains **Null**, **Null** is returned.

See Also

Day Function, **Hour** Function, **Minute** Function, **Now** Function, **Time** Function, **Time** Statement

Example

This example uses the **Second** function to obtain the second of the minute from a specified time. In the development environment, the time literal is displayed in short time format using the locale settings of your code.

```
Dim MyTime, MySecond
MyTime = #4:35:17 PM#       ' Assign a time.
MySecond = Second(MyTime)   ' MySecond contains 17.
```

Seek Function

Returns a **Long** specifying the current read/write position within a file opened using the **Open** statement.

Syntax

Seek(*filenumber*)

The required *filenumber* argument is an **Integer** containing a valid file number.

Remarks

Seek returns a value between 1 and 2,147,483,647 (equivalent to $2^{31} - 1$), inclusive.

The following describes the return values for each file access mode.

Mode	Return Value
Random	Number of the next record read or written
Binary, **Output**, **Append**, **Input**	Byte position at which the next operation takes place. The first byte in a file is at position 1, the second byte is at position 2, and so on.

See Also

Get Statement, **Loc** Function, **Open** Statement, **Put** Statement, **Seek** Statement

Example

This example uses the **Seek** function to return the current file position. The example assumes TESTFILE is a file containing records of the user-defined type Record.

```
Type Record                          ' Define user-defined type.
   ID As Integer
   Name As String * 20
End Type
```

For files opened in Random mode, **Seek** returns number of next record.

```
Dim MyRecord As Record              ' Declare variable.
Open "TESTFILE" For Random As #1 Len = Len(MyRecord)
Do While Not EOF(1)                 ' Loop until end of file.
   Get #1, , MyRecord               ' Read next record.
   Debug.Print Seek(1)              ' Print record number to Debug
                                    ' window.
Loop
Close #1                            ' Close file.
```

For files opened in modes other than Random mode, **Seek** returns the byte position at which the next operation takes place. Assume TESTFILE is a file containing a few lines of text.

```
Dim MyChar
Open "TESTFILE" For Input As #1     ' Open file for reading.
Do While Not EOF(1)                 ' Loop until end of file.
   MyChar = Input(1, #1)            ' Read next character of data.
   Debug.Print Seek(1)             ' Print byte position to Debug
                                    ' window.
Loop
Close #1                            ' Close file.
```

Seek Method

Locates the record in an indexed table-type **Recordset** object that satisfies the specified criteria for the current index and makes that record the current record (Microsoft Jet workspaces only).

Applies To

Recordset Object, **Table-Type Recordset** Object

Syntax

recordset.**Seek** *comparison, key1, key2...key13*

The **Seek** method syntax has the following parts.

Part	Description
recordset	An object variable that represents an existing table-type **Recordset** object that has a defined index as specified by the **Recordset** object's **Index** property.
comparison	One of the following string expressions: <, <=, =, >=, or >.
key1, key2...key13	One or more values corresponding to fields in the **Recordset** object's current index, as specified by its **Index** property setting. You can use up to 13 *key* arguments.

Remarks

You must set the current index with the **Index** property before you use **Seek**. If the index identifies a nonunique key field, **Seek** locates the first record that satisfies the criteria.

The **Seek** method searches through the specified key fields and locates the first record that satisfies the criteria specified by *comparison* and *key1*. Once found, it makes that record current and sets the **NoMatch** property to **False**. If the **Seek** method fails to locate a match, the **NoMatch** property is set to **True**, and the current record is undefined.

If *comparison* is equal (=), greater than or equal (>=), or greater than (>), **Seek** starts at the beginning of the index and searches forward.

If *comparison* is less than (<) or less than or equal (<=), **Seek** starts at the end of the index and searches backward. However, if there are duplicate index entries at the end of the index, **Seek** starts at an arbitrary entry among the duplicates and then searches backward.

You must specify values for all fields defined in the index. If you use **Seek** with a multiple-column index, and you don't specify a comparison value for every field in the index, then you cannot use the equal (=) operator in the comparison. That's because some of the criteria fields (*key2*, *key3*, and so on) will default to **Null**, which will probably not match. Therefore, the equal operator will work correctly only if you have a record which is all **Null** except the key you're looking for. It's recommended that you use the greater than or equal (>=) operator instead.

The *key1* argument must be of the same field data type as the corresponding field in the current index. For example, if the current index refers to a number field (such as Employee ID), *key1* must be numeric. Similarly, if the current index refers to a Text field (such as Last Name), *key1* must be a string.

There doesn't have to be a current record when you use **Seek**.

You can use the **Indexes** collection to enumerate the existing indexes.

To locate a record in a dynaset- or snapshot-type **Recordset** that satisfies a specific condition that is not covered by existing indexes, use the **Find** methods. To include all records, not just those that satisfy a specific condition, use the **Move** methods to move from record to record.

You can't use the **Seek** method on a linked table because you can't open linked tables as table-type **Recordset** objects. However, if you use the **OpenDatabase** method to directly open an installable ISAM (non-ODBC) database, you can use **Seek** on tables in that database.

In an ODBCDirect workspace, the **Find** and **Seek** methods are not available on any type of **Recordset** object, because executing a **Find** or **Seek** through an ODBC connection is not very efficient over the network. Instead, you should design the query (that is, using the *source* argument to the **OpenRecordset** method) with an appropriate WHERE clause that restricts the returned records to only those that meet the criteria you would otherwise use in a **Find** or **Seek**.

Seek Method

See Also

Index Object, **FindFirst**, **FindLast**, **FindNext**, **FindPrevious** Methods, **Move** Method, **MoveFirst**, **MoveLast**, **MoveNext**, **MovePrevious** Methods, **OpenDatabase** Method, **AbsolutePosition** Property, **BOF**, **EOF** Properties, **Index** Property, **NoMatch** Property

Example

This example demonstrates the **Seek** method by allowing the user to search for a product based on an ID number.

```
Sub SeekX()

    Dim dbsNorthwind As Database
    Dim rstProducts As Recordset
    Dim intFirst As Integer
    Dim intLast As Integer
    Dim strMessage As String
    Dim strSeek As String
    Dim varBookmark As Variant

    Set dbsNorthwind = OpenDatabase("Northwind.mdb")
    ' You must open a table-type Recordset to use an index,
    ' and hence the Seek method.
    Set rstProducts = _
        dbsNorthwind.OpenRecordset("Products", dbOpenTable)

    With rstProducts
        ' Set the index.
        .Index = "PrimaryKey"

        ' Get the lowest and highest product IDs.
        .MoveLast
        intLast = !ProductID
        .MoveFirst
        intFirst = !ProductID

        Do While True
            ' Display current record information and ask user
            ' for ID number.
            strMessage = "Product ID: " & !ProductID & vbCr & _
                "Name: " & !ProductName & vbCr & vbCr & _
                "Enter a product ID between " & intFirst & _
                " and " & intLast & "."
            strSeek = InputBox(strMessage)

            If strSeek = "" Then Exit Do

            ' Store current bookmark in case the Seek fails.
            varBookmark = .Bookmark

            .Seek "=", Val(strSeek)
```

```
      ' Return to the current record if the Seek fails.
      If .NoMatch Then
         MsgBox "ID not found!"
         .Bookmark = varBookmark
      End If
   Loop

   .Close
End With

dbsNorthwind.Close

End Sub
```

Seek Statement

Sets the position for the next read/write operation within a file opened using the **Open** statement.

Syntax

Seek [#]*filenumber, position*

The **Seek** statement syntax has these parts:

Part	Description
filenumber	Required. Any valid file number.
position	Required. Number in the range 1–2,147,483,647, inclusive, that indicates where the next read/write operation should occur.

Remarks

Record numbers specified in **Get** and **Put** statements override file positioning performed by **Seek**.

Performing a file-write operation after a **Seek** operation beyond the end of a file extends the file. If you attempt a **Seek** operation to a negative or zero position, an error occurs.

See Also

Get Statement, **Loc** Function, **Open** Statement, **Put** Statement, **Seek** Function

Example

This example uses the **Seek** statement to set the position for the next read or write within a file. This example assumes TESTFILE is a file containing records of the user-defined type Record.

```
Type Record                          ' Define user-defined type.
   ID As Integer
   Name As String * 20
End Type
```

For files opened in Random mode, **Seek** sets the next record.

```
Dim MyRecord As Record, MaxSize, RecordNumber   ' Declare variables.
' Open file in random-file mode.
Open "TESTFILE" For Random As #1 Len = Len(MyRecord)
MaxSize = LOF(1) \ Len(MyRecord)      ' Get number of records in file.
' The loop reads all records starting from the last.
For RecordNumber = MaxSize To 1 Step - 1
    Seek #1, RecordNumber             ' Set position.
    Get #1, , MyRecor                 ' Read record.
Next RecordNumber
Close #1                              ' Close file.
```

For files opened in modes other than Random mode, **Seek** sets the byte position at which the next operation takes place. Assume TESTFILE is a file containing a few lines of text.

```
Dim MaxSize, NextChar, MyChar
Open "TESTFILE" For Input As #1       ' Open file for input.
MaxSize = LOF(1)                      ' Get size of file in bytes.
' The loop reads all characters starting from the last.
For NextChar = MaxSize To 1 Step -1
    Seek #1, NextChar                 ' Set position.
    MyChar = Input(1, #1)             ' Read character.
Next NextChar
Close #1                              ' Close file.
```

SelBookmarks Collection

A **SelBookmarks** collection contains a bookmark for each row selected in a **DBGrid** control.

Syntax

SelBookmarks

Remarks

Use the **SelBookmarks** property of the **DBGrid** control to return the **SelBookmarks** collection. Bookmarks are added to the **SelBookmarks** collection in the order they're selected. You can reposition the **DBGrid** control's current record pointer by setting the **Bookmark** property to one of the selected bookmarks in the **SelBookmarks** collection.

Use the **Add** method to add bookmarks to the **SelBookmarks** collection. Once a bookmark is appended to the **SelBookmarks** collection, it appears selected in the **DBGrid** control.

To remove a bookmark from the **SelBookmarks** collection, use the **Remove** method. Once a bookmark is removed from the **SelBookmarks** collection, it no longer appears selected in the **DBGrid** control.

The **SelBookmarks** collection supports the **Add** and **Remove** methods as well as the **Count** property. Using these methods and properties, you can manipulate the list of selected items in the **DBGrid** control. For example, you can programmatically select additional items by using the **Add** method, or determine the total number of selected items using the **Count** property.

Properties

Count Property (VB Collections)

Methods

Add Method (Columns, SelBookmarks, Splits Collection), **Item** Method, **Remove** Method (DB Grid)

See Also

Column Object, **DBGrid** Control, **GetBookmark** Method, **RowBookmark** Method, **SelBookmarks** Property

---

SelBookmarks Property

Returns a collection of bookmarks for all selected records in the **DBGrid** control.

Applies To

DBGrid Control

Syntax

object.**SelBookmarks**

The *object* placeholder represents an object expression that evaluates to an object in the **Applies To** list.

Remarks

When a record is selected in the **DBGrid** control, its bookmark is appended to the collection returned by the **SelBookmarks** property. For example, if you create a clone of the **Recordset** object created by the **DBGrid** control, you can process individual data records by repositioning the cloned **Recordset** with bookmarks taken from the **SelBookmarks** collection.

See Also

Data Control, **Add** Method (Columns, **SelBookmarks,** Splits Collections), **Remove** Method (DBGrid), **Recordset** Property, **SelBookmarks** Collection

Example

This example loops through the rows the user has selected and deletes them from the database.

```
Sub DeleteRows()
    Do While DBGrid1.SelBookmarks.Count <> 0
        Data1.Recordset.Bookmark = DBGrid1.SelBookmarks(0)
        Data1.Recordset.Delete
        Data1.Refresh
    Loop
End Sub
```

SelChange Event

Occurs when the current range changes to a different cell or range of cells.

Syntax

Private Sub DBGrid_SelChange ([*cancel* **As Integer**])
Private Sub *object*_**SelChange( )**

The **SelChange** event syntax has these parts:

Part	Description
object	An object expression that evaluates to an object in the **Applies To** list.
cancel	Determines whether the selection reverts to its position before the event occurred.

Remarks

The **SelChange** event occurs whenever a user clicks a cell other than the current cell and as a user drags to select a new range of cells. A user can also select a range of cells by pressing the SHIFT key and using the arrow keys.

You can trigger this event in code for a **DBGrid** control by changing the selected region using the **SelStartCol** and **SelEndCol** properties.

The **RowColChange** event also occurs when a user clicks a new cell but doesn't occur while a user drags the selection across the **DBGrid** control or when you programmatically change the selection without moving the current cell.

Setting *cancel* to **True** in the **DBGrid** control causes the selection to revert to the cell or range active before the event occurred.

See Also

RowColChange Event, **SelEndCol, SelStartCol, SelEndRow, SelStartRow**
Properties

SelChange Event (DBGrid Control)

Occurs when the user selects a different range of rows or columns.

Applies To

DBGrid Control

Syntax

Private Sub *object*_**SelChange**([*index* **As Integer**,] *cancel* **As Integer**)

The **SelChange** event syntax has these parts:

Part	Description
object	An object expression that evaluates to an object in the **Applies To** list.
index	An integer that identifies a control if it is in a control array.
cancel	A Boolean expression that determines if a change is canceled, as described in Settings.

Settings

The settings for *cancel* are:

Setting	Description
True	If your event procedure sets the Cancel argument to **True**, the previous row and column selections (if any) are restored, and the **SelStartCol**, **SelEndCol**, and **SelBookmarks** properties revert to their previous values
False	(Default) Continues with change.

Remarks

This event is triggered under several circumstances:

- When the user selects a single row by clicking its record selector.

- When the user adds a row to the list of selected rows by clicking its record selector while holding down the CTRL key.

- When the user selects a single column by clicking its header.

- When the user changes the range of selected columns by dragging to an adjacent column within the header row.

- When the user extends the range of selected columns by holding down the SHIFT key and clicking on an unselected column header.

- When the user clears the current row or column selection by clicking an individual cell, this event will fire before the **RowColChange** event.

The current range of selected columns is provided by the **SelStartCol** and **SelEndCol** properties. The bookmarks of the selected rows are available in the collection provided by the **SelBookmarks** property. Within this event procedure, these properties reflect the user's pending selection(s).

This event is only triggered by user interaction with the grid. It cannot be triggered by code.

Note When the user selects a column, any row selections are cleared. Similarly, when the user selects a row, any column selections are cleared.

SelBookmarks Property, **RowColChange** Event, **SelEndCol, SelStartCol, SelEndRow, SelStartRow** Properties

---

SelCount Property

Returns the number of selected items in a **ListBox** control.

Applies To

ListBox Control

Syntax

object.**SelCount**

The *object* placeholder represents an object expression that evaluates to an object in the **Applies To** list.

Remarks

The **SelCount** property returns 0 if no items are selected. Otherwise, it returns the number of list items currently selected. This property is particularly useful when users can make multiple selections.

See Also

AddItem Method, **RemoveItem** Method, **List** Property, **ListIndex** Property, **MultiSelect** Property, **NewIndex** Property, **Selected** Property, **TopIndex** Property

---

Select Case Statement

Executes one of several groups of statements, depending on the value of an expression.

Syntax

Select Case *testexpression*
   [**Case** *expressionlist-n*
    [*statements-n*]] . . .
   [**Case Else**
    [*elsestatements*]]
End Select

The **Select Case** statement syntax has these parts:

Part	Description
testexpression	Required. Any numeric expression or string expression.
expressionlist-n	Required if a **Case** appears. Delimited list of one or more of the following forms: *expression*, *expression* **To** *expression*, **Is** *comparisonoperator expression*. The **To** keyword specifies a range of values. If you use the **To** keyword, the smaller value must appear before **To**. Use the **Is** keyword with comparison operators (except **Is** and **Like**) to specify a range of values. If not supplied, the **Is** keyword is automatically inserted.
statements-n	Optional. One or more statements executed if *testexpression* matches any part of *expressionlist-n*.
elsestatements	Optional. One or more statements executed if *testexpression* doesn't match any of the **Case** clause.

Remarks

If *testexpression* matches any **Case** *expressionlist* expression, the *statements* following that **Case** clause are executed up to the next **Case** clause, or, for the last clause, up to **End Select**. Control then passes to the statement following **End Select**. If *testexpression* matches an *expressionlist* expression in more than one **Case** clause, only the statements following the first match are executed.

The **Case Else** clause is used to indicate the *elsestatements* to be executed if no match is found between the *testexpression* and an *expressionlist* in any of the other **Case** selections. Although not required, it is a good idea to have a **Case Else** statement in your **Select Case** block to handle unforeseen *testexpression* values. If no **Case** *expressionlist* matches *testexpression* and there is no **Case Else** statement, execution continues at the statement following **End Select**.

You can use multiple expressions or ranges in each **Case** clause. For example, the following line is valid:

```
Case 1 To 4, 7 To 9, 11, 13, Is > MaxNumber
```

Note The **Is** comparison operator is not the same as the **Is** keyword used in the **Select Case** statement.

You also can specify ranges and multiple expressions for character strings. In the following example, **Case** matches strings that are exactly equal to `everything`, strings that fall between `nuts` and `soup` in alphabetic order, and the current value of `TestItem`:

```
Case "everything", "nuts" To "soup", TestItem
```

Select Case statements can be nested. Each nested **Select Case** statement must have a matching **End Select** statement.

See Also

Choose Function, **End** Statement, **If...Then...Else** Statement, **On...GoSub**, **On...GoTo** Statements

Example

This example uses the **Select Case** statement to evaluate the value of a variable. The second **Case** clause contains the value of the variable being evaluated, and therefore only the statement associated with it is executed.

```
Dim Number
Number = 8                       ' Initialize variable.
Select Case Number               ' Evaluate Number.
Case 1 To 5                      ' Number between 1 and 5.
   Debug.Print "Between 1 and 5"
' The following is the only Case clause that evaluates to True.
Case 6, 7, 8                     ' Number between 6 and 8.
   Debug.Print "Between 6 and 8"
Case Is > 8 And Number < 11      ' Number is 9 or 10.
Debug.Print "Greater than 8"
Case Else                        ' Other values.
   Debug.Print "Not between 1 and 10"
End Select
```

SelectAll Method

Selects all of the controls contained on a form.

Applies To

VBForm Object

Syntax

object.**SelectAll**

The *object* placeholder represents an object expression that evaluates to an object in the **Applies To** list.

Selected Property

Returns or sets the selection status of an item in a **FileListBox** or **ListBox** control. This property is an array of Boolean values with the same number of items as the **List** property. Not available at design time.

Applies To

FileListBox Control, **ListBox** Control

Syntax

object.**Selected**(*index*) [= *boolean*]

The **Selected** property syntax has these parts:

Part	Description
object	An object expression that evaluates to an object in the **Applies To** list.
index	The index number of the item in the control.
boolean	A Boolean expression specifying whether the item is selected, as described in Settings.

Settings

The settings for *boolean* are:

Setting	Description
True	The item is selected.
False	(Default) The item isn't selected.

Remarks

This property is particularly useful when users can make multiple selections. You can quickly check which items in a list are selected. You can also use this property to select or deselect items in a list from code.

If the **MultiSelect** property is set to 0, you can use the **ListIndex** property to get the index of the selected item. However, in a multiple selection, the **ListIndex** property returns the index of the item contained within the focus rectangle, whether or not the item is actually selected.

If a **ListBox** control's **Style** property is set to 1 (check boxes), the **Selected** property returns **True** only for those items whose check boxes are selected. The **Selected** property will not return **True** for those items which are only highlighted.

See Also

SelectedControls Property, **PropertyPage** Object, **AddItem** Method, **Clear** Method (Clipboard, ComboBox, ListBox), **RemoveItem** Method, **Controls** Collection, **List** Property, **ListCount** Property, **ListIndex** Property, **MultiSelect** Property, **NewIndex** Property, **TopIndex** Property

---

SelectedControls Property

Returns a collection that contains all the currently selected controls on the form. The **SelectedControls** property is not available at the property page's authoring time, and read-only at the property page's run time.

Applies To

PropertyPage Object

Syntax

object.**SelectedControls**

The **SelectedControls** property syntax has this part:

Part	Description
object	An object expression that evaluates to an object in the **Applies To** list.

Remarks

This collection is useful to a property page in determining which controls are currently selected, and therefore which controls might need properties changed. Some containers only allow one control to be selected at once; in that case **SelectedControls** will only contain one control. Other containers allow more than one control to be selected at once; in that case there may be more than one control selected, and the property page must iterate through the controls in the **SelectedControls** collection and attempt to set the changed properties. Suitable error handling should be written to take care of the cases when a particular control in the collection does not have the changed property, or when the control raises an error when the property is set.

See Also

Controls Collection

SelectedItem Property

Returns a value containing a bookmark for the selected record in a **DBCombo** or **DBList** control.

Applies To

DBCombo Control, **DBList** Control

Syntax

object.**SelectedItem**

The *object* placeholder represents an object expression that evaluates to an object in the **Applies To** list.

Remarks

When you select an item in the list portion of the control, the **SelectedItem** property contains a bookmark that you can use to reposition to the selected record in the **Recordset** of the **Data** control specified by the **RowSource** property.

Data Type

Variant

SelectedVBComponent Property

Returns the selected component. Read-only.

Applies to

VBE Object

Remarks

The **SelectedVBComponent** property returns the selected component in the **Project** window. If the selected item in the **Project** window isn't a component, **SelectedVBComponent** returns **Nothing**.

See Also

VBComponent Object, **ActiveVBProject** Property

Example

The following example uses the **SelectedVBComponent** property to return the selected component.

```
Debug.Print Application.VBE.SelectedVBComponent.Name
```

SelectedVBControls Collection

Returns a collection of currently selected controls on a component.

Syntax

SelectedVBControls

Remarks

You can use this collection to access all currently selected controls on a form. The code can step through the collection of controls or request a specific control.

This collection has the same specifications as the **VBControls** collection, except this collection doesn't implement the **Add** method. The default method for the **SelectedVBControls** collection is the **Item** method and is indexed with integers.

This collection replaces the **SelectedControlTemplates** collection from Visual Basic version 4.0.

Properties

VBE Property

Methods

Clear Method, **Copy** Method, **Item** Method

Events

ItemAdded Event, **ItemRemoved** Event

SelectedVBControlsEvents Object

Represents a source of events supported by all currently selected controls.

Syntax

SelectedVBControlsEvents

Events

ItemAdded Event, **Item Removed** Event

SelectedVBControlsEvents Property

Returns all events supported by the controls currently selected on a form.

Applies To

Events Object

Syntax

object.**SelectedVBControlsEvents** (*vbproject* **As Variant**)

The **SelectedVBControlsEvents** property syntax has these parts:

Part	Description
object	An object expression that evaluates to an object in the **Applies To** list.
vbproject	A variant expression specifying the project which contains the form and controls.

Remarks

Returns an event object of type **SelectedVBControlsEvents**. This event is sourced from a **VBForm**.

SelectionChanged Event

Occurs when the selection of controls on the form has changed.

Applies To

PropertyPage Object

Syntax

Sub *object*_**SelectionChanged**()

The **SelectionChanged** event syntax has these parts:

Part	Description
object	An object expression that evaluates to an object in the **Applies To** list.

Remarks

The firing of this event notifies the property page that the selection of controls has changed, and therefore the display of current property values may need to be updated. The **SelectedControls** property should be read to find out the new set of selected controls.

The **SelectionChanged** event is also raised when the property page is first brought up for a control.

See Also

SelectedControls Property

SelEndCol, SelStartCol, SelEndRow, SelStartRow Properties

Return or set the first or last row or column for a range of cells. Not available at design time.

- **SelEndCol**—the last selected column on the right.
- **SelStartCol**—the first selected column on the left.
- **SelEndRow**—the last selected row.
- **SelStartRow**—the first selected row.

Applies To

DBGrid Control, **Split** Object

Syntax

object.**SelEndCol** [= *value*]
object.**SelStartCol** [= *value*]
object.**SelEndRow** [= *value*]
object.**SelStartRow** [= *value*]

The **SelEndCol**, **SelStartCol**, **SelEndRow**, and **SelStartRow** property syntaxes have these parts:

Part	Description
object	An object expression that evaluates to an object in the **Applies To** list.
value	A numeric expression specifying the first or last column or row.

Remarks

You can use these properties to select a specific region of a **DBGrid** control from code or to return in code the dimensions of an area that the user selects.

SelStartCol and **SelStartRow** together specify the cell in the upper-left corner of a selected range. **SelEndCol** and **SelEndRow** specify the cell in the lower-right corner of a selected range.

To specify a cell without moving the current selection, use the **Col** and **Row** properties.

The default value for **SelStartCol** and **SelEndCol** is –1.

Remarks

Col, **Row** Properties

SelLength, SelStart, SelText Properties

- **SelLength**—returns or sets the number of characters selected.
- **SelStart**—returns or sets the starting point of text selected; indicates the position of the insertion point if no text is selected.
- **SelText**—returns or sets the string containing the currently selected text; consists of a zero-length string ("") if no characters are selected.

These properties aren't available at design time.

Applies To

Masked Edit Control, **RichTextBox** Control, **Slider** Control

Syntax

object.**SelLength** [= *number*]
object.**SelStart** [= *index*]
object.**SelText** [= *value*]

The **SelLength**, **SelStart**, and **SelText** property syntaxes have these parts:

Part	Description
object	An object expression that evaluates to an object in the **Applies To** list.
number	A numeric expression specifying the number of characters selected. For **SelLength** and **SelStart**, the valid range of settings is 0 to text length—the total number of characters in the edit area of a **ComboBox** or **TextBox** control.
index	A numeric expression specifying the starting point of the selected text, as described in Settings.
value	A string expression containing the selected text.

Remarks

Use these properties for tasks such as setting the insertion point, establishing an insertion range, selecting substrings in a control, or clearing text. Used in conjunction with the **Clipboard** object, these properties are useful for copy, cut, and paste operations.

When working with these properties:

- Setting **SelLength** less than 0 causes a run-time error.

- Setting **SelStart** greater than the text length sets the property to the existing text length; changing **SelStart** changes the selection to an insertion point and sets **SelLength** to 0.

- Setting **SelText** to a new value sets **SelLength** to 0 and replaces the selected text with the new string.

See Also

Text Property, **ActiveControl** Property, **ActiveForm** Property

Example

This example enables the user to specify some text to search for and then searches for the text and selects it, if found. To try this example, paste the code into the Declarations section of a form that contains a wide **TextBox** control, and then press F5 and click the form.

```
Private Sub Form_Load ()
    Text1.Text = "Two of the peak human experiences"
    Text1.Text = Text1.Text & " are good food and classical music."
End Sub
Private Sub Form_Click ()
    Dim Search, Where ' Declare variables.
    ' Get search string from user.
    Search = InputBox("Enter text to be found:")
    Where = InStr(Text1.Text, Search) ' Find string in text.
    If Where Then  ' If found,
        Text1.SelStart = Where - 1     ' set selection start and
        Text1.SelLength = Len(Search)  ' set selection length.

Else
        MsgBox "String not found."     ' Notify user.
    End If
End Sub
```

This example shows how the **Clipboard** object is used in cut, copy, paste, and delete operations. To try this example, create a form with a **TextBox** control and use the Menu Editor to create an Edit menu (for each of the commands, set the **Caption** property = Cut, Copy, Paste, and Delete, respectively; set the **Name** property = EditCut, EditCopy, EditPaste, and EditDelete, respectively).

```
Private Sub EditCut_Click ()
   ' Clear the contents of the Clipboard.
   Clipboard.Clear
   ' Copy selected text to Clipboard.
   ClipBoard.SetText Screen.ActiveControl.SelText
   ' Delete selected text.
   Screen.ActiveControl.SelText = ""
End Sub

Private Sub EditCopy_Click ()
   ' Clear the contents of the Clipboard.
   Clipboard.Clear
   ' Copy selected text to Clipboard.
   ClipBoard.SetText Screen.ActiveControl.SelText
End Sub

Private Sub EditPaste_Click ()
   ' Place text from Clipboard into active control.
   Screen.ActiveControl.SelText = ClipBoard.GetText ()
End Sub

Private Sub EditDelete_Click ()
' Delete selected text.
Screen.ActiveControl.SelText = ""
End Sub
```

SendKeys Statement

Sends one or more keystrokes to the active window as if typed at the keyboard.

Syntax

SendKeys *string*[, *wait*]

The **SendKeys** statement syntax has these named arguments:

Part	Description
string	Required. String expression specifying the keystrokes to send.
Wait	Optional. **Boolean** value specifying the wait mode. If **False** (default), control is returned to the procedure immediately after the keys are sent. If **True**, keystrokes must be processed before control is returned to the procedure.

Remarks

Each key is represented by one or more characters. To specify a single keyboard character, use the character itself. For example, to represent the letter A, use "A" for *string*. To represent more than one character, append each additional character to the one preceding it. To represent the letters A, B, and C, use "ABC" for *string*.

The plus sign (+), caret (^), percent sign (%), tilde (~), and parentheses ( ) have special meanings to **SendKeys**. To specify one of these characters, enclose it within braces ({ }). For example, to specify the plus sign, use {+}. Brackets ([ ]) have no special meaning to **SendKeys**, but you must enclose them in braces. In other applications, brackets do have a special meaning that may be significant when dynamic data exchange (DDE) occurs. To specify brace characters, use {{} and {}}.

To specify characters that aren't displayed when you press a key, such as ENTER or TAB, and keys that represent actions rather than characters, use the codes shown below:

Key	Code
BACKSPACE	{BACKSPACE}, {BS}, or {BKSP}
BREAK	{BREAK}
CAPS LOCK	{CAPSLOCK}
DEL or DELETE	{DELETE} or {DEL}
DOWN ARROW	{DOWN}
END	{END}
ENTER	{ENTER} or ~
ESC	{ESC}
HELP	{HELP}
HOME	{HOME}
INS or INSERT	{INSERT} or {INS}
LEFT ARROW	{LEFT}
NUM LOCK	{NUMLOCK}
PAGE DOWN	{PGDN}
PAGE UP	{PGUP}
PRINT SCREEN	{PRTSC}
RIGHT ARROW	{RIGHT}
SCROLL LOCK	{SCROLLLOCK}
TAB	{TAB}
UP ARROW	{UP}
F1	{F1}
F2	{F2}
F3	{F3}
F4	{F4}
F5	{F5}
F6	{F6}
F7	{F7}

(continued)

(continued)

Key	Code
F8	{F8}
F9	{F9}
F10	{F10}
F11	{F11}
F12	{F12}
F13	{F13}
F14	{F14}
F15	{F15}
F16	{F16}

To specify keys combined with any combination of the SHIFT, CTRL, and ALT keys, precede the key code with one or more of the following codes:

Key	Code
SHIFT	+
CTRL	^
ALT	%

To specify that any combination of SHIFT, CTRL, and ALT should be held down while several other keys are pressed, enclose the code for those keys in parentheses. For example, to specify to hold down SHIFT while E and C are pressed, use "+(EC)". To specify to hold down SHIFT while E is pressed, followed by C without SHIFT, use "+EC".

To specify repeating keys, use the form {key number}. You must put a space between key and number. For example, {LEFT 42} means press the LEFT ARROW key 42 times; {h 10} means press H 10 times.

Note You can't use **SendKeys** to send keystrokes to an application that is not designed to run in Microsoft Windows. **Sendkeys** also can't send the PRINT SCREEN key {PRTSC} to any application.

See Also

DoEvents Function, **AppActivate** Statement

Example

This example uses the **Shell** function to run the Calculator application included with Microsoft Windows. It uses the **SendKeys** statement to send keystrokes to add some numbers, and then quit the Calculator. (To see the example, paste it into a procedure, then run the procedure. Because **AppActivate** changes the focus to the Calculator application, you can't single step through the code.)

```
Dim ReturnValue, I
ReturnValue = Shell("CALC.EXE", 1)        ' Run Calculator.
AppActivate ReturnValue                   ' Activate the Calculator.
For I = 1 To 100                          ' Set up counting loop.
    SendKeys I & "{+}", True              ' Send keystrokes to Calculator
Next I                                    ' to add each value of I.
SendKeys "=", True                        ' Get grand total.
SendKeys "%{F4}", True                    ' Send ALT+F4 to close Calculator.
```

Set Statement

Assigns an object reference to a variable or property.

Syntax

Set *objectvar* = {[**New**] *objectexpression* | **Nothing**}

The **Set** statement syntax has these parts:

Part	Description
objectvar	Required. Name of the variable or property; follows standard variable naming conventions.
New	Optional. **New** is usually used during declaration to enable implicit object creation. When **New** is used with **Set**, it creates a new instance of the class. If *objectvar* contained a reference to an object, that reference is released when the new one is assigned. The **New** keyword can't be used to create new instances of any intrinsic data type and can't be used to create dependent objects.
objectexpression	Required. Expression consisting of the name of an object, another declared variable of the same object type, or a function or method that returns an object of the same object type.
Nothing	Optional. Discontinues association of *objectvar* with any specific object. Assigning **Nothing** to *objectvar* releases all the system and memory resources associated with the previously referenced object when no other variable refers to it.

Remarks

To be valid, *objectvar* must be an object type consistent with the object being assigned to it.

The **Dim**, **Private**, **Public**, **ReDim**, and **Static** statements only declare a variable that refers to an object. No actual object is referred to until you use the **Set** statement to assign a specific object.

The following example illustrates how **Dim** is used to declare an array with the type Form1. No instance of Form1 actually exists. **Set** then assigns references to new instances of Form1 to the myChildForms variable. Such code might be used to create child forms in an MDI application.

```
Dim myChildForms(1 to 4) As Form1
Set myChildForms(1) = New Form1
Set myChildForms(2) = New Form1
Set myChildForms(3) = New Form1
Set myChildForms(4) = New Form1
```

Generally, when you use **Set** to assign an object reference to a variable, no copy of the object is created for that variable. Instead, a reference to the object is created. More than one object variable can refer to the same object. Because such variables are references to the object rather than copies of the object, any change in the object is reflected in all variables that refer to it. However, when you use the **New** keyword in the **Set** statement, you are actually creating an instance of the object.

See Also

Dim Statement, **Let** Statement, **Private** Statement, **Public** Statement, **ReDim** Statement, **Static** Statement

Example

This example uses the **Set** statement to assign object references to variables. YourObject is assumed to be a valid object with a Text property.

```
Dim YourObject, MyObject, MyStr
Set MyObject = YourObject   ' Assign object reference.
' MyObject and YourObject refer to the same object.
YourObject.Text = "Hello World"        ' Initialize property.
MyStr = MyObject.Text' Returns "Hello World".

' Discontinue association. MyObject no longer refers to YourObject.
Set MyObject = Nothing   ' Release the object.
```

SetAttr Statement

Sets attribute information for a file.

Syntax

SetAttr *pathname, attributes*

The **SetAttr** statement syntax has these named arguments:

Part	Description
pathname	Required. String expression that specifies a file name—may include directory or folder, and drive.
attributes	Required. Constant or numeric expression, whose sum specifies file attributes.

Settings

The *attributes* argument settings are:

Constant	Value	Description
vbNormal	0	Normal (default)
vbReadOnly	1	Read-only
vbHidden	2	Hidden
vbSystem	4	System file
vbArchive	32	File has changed since last backup

Note These constants are specified by Visual Basic for Applications. The names can be used anywhere in your code in place of the actual values.

Remarks

A run-time error occurs if you try to set the attributes of an open file.

See Also

GetAttr Function, **FileAttr** Function

Example

This example uses the **SetAttr** statement to set attributes for a file.

```
SetAttr "TESTFILE", vbHidden             ' Set hidden attribute.
SetAttr "TESTFILE", vbHidden + vbReadOnly  ' Set hidden and read-only
                                         ' attributes.
```

SetAutoServerSettings Method

Sets the Remote Automation registry values to meet ActiveX and Remote Automation requirements, including configuration settings for remote server access.

Syntax

object. **SetAutoServerSettings**(*remote*, [*progid*], [*clsid*], [*servername*],
↳ [*protocol*], [*authentication*])

The **SetAutoServerSettings** method syntax has these parts:

Part	Description
object	Required. An object expression that evaluates to an object in the **Applies To** list.
remote	Required. Boolean. **True** if the server is remote, **False** if local.
progid	Optional. A variant expression specifying the ProgID for the server.
clsid	Optional. A variant expression specifying the CLSID for the server.
servername	Optional. A variant expression specifying the name of the server machine.
protocol	Optional. A variant expression specifying the RPC name of the protocol to be used.
authentication	Optional. A variant expression specifying the RPC authentication level.

Return Values

The **SetAutoServerSettings** method returns the following error codes:

Value	Description
0	No error.
1	Unknown run time error occurred.
2	No protocol was specified.
3	No server machine name was specified.
4	An error occurred reading from the registry.
5	An error occurred writing to the registry.
6	Both the ProgID and CLSID parameters were missing.
7	There is no local server (either in-process or cross-process, 16-bit or 32-bit).
8	There was an error looking for the Proxy DLLs, check that they were installed properly.

Remarks

The **SetAutoServerSettings** method takes either a CLSID or a ProgID and sets the registry information to local or remote depending on the value of the *remote* parameter. If both a CLSID and a **ProgID** are passed to the method, the CLSID takes precedence.

Example

This example switches a server named "Hello" from local registration to remote, and then back again:

```
Sub SwitchHello()
   Dim oRegClass As New RegClass
   ' Register Hello to run remotely on a machine
   ' called Server1.
   oRegClass.SetAutoServerSettings True, _
   "HelloProj.HelloClass",1 _
   ServerName:="Server1", Protocol:="ncacn_ip_tcp"
   ' Register Hello to run locally again.
   oRegClass.SetAutoServerSettings False, _
   "HelloProj.HelloClass"
End Sub
```

SetData Method

Puts a picture on the **Clipboard** object using the specified graphic format. Doesn't support named arguments.

Applies To

Clipboard Object, **DataObject** Object

Syntax

object.**SetData** *data*, *format*

The **SetData** method syntax has these parts:

Part	Description
object	Required. An object expression that evaluates to an object in the **Applies To** list.
data	Required. A graphic to be placed on the **Clipboard** object.
format	Optional. A constant or value that specifies one of the **Clipboard** object formats recognized by Visual Basic, as described in Settings. If *format* is omitted, **SetData** automatically determines the graphic format.

Settings

The settings for *format* are:

Constant	Value	Description
vbCFBitmap	2	Bitmap (.bmp files)
vbCFMetafile	3	Metafile (.wmf files)
vbCFDIB	8	Device-independent bitmap (DIB)
vbCFPalette	9	Color palette

Remarks

These constants are listed in the Visual Basic (VB) object library in the Object Browser.

You set the graphic that is to be placed onto the **Clipboard** object with either the **LoadPicture** function or the **Picture** property of a **Form**, **Image**, or **PictureBox**.

See Also

GetData Method, **GetFormat** Method, **GetText** Method, **SetText** Method

---

SetData Method (DataObject Object)

Inserts data into a **DataObject** object using the specified data format.

Applies To

DataObject Object

Syntax

object.**SetData** [*data*], [*format*]

The **SetData** method syntax has these parts:

Part	Description
object	Required. An object expression that evaluates to an object in the **Applies To** list.
data	Optional A variant containing the data to be passed to the **DataObject** object.
format	Optional. A constant or value that specifies the format of the data being passed, as described in Settings.

Settings

The settings for *format* are:

Constant	Value	Description
vbCFText	1	Text (.txt files)
vbCFBitmap	2	Bitmap (.bmp files)
vbCFMetafile	3	Metafile (.wmf files)
vbCFEMetafile	14	Enhanced metafile (.emf files)
vbCFDIB	8	Device-independent bitmap (DIB)
vbCFPalette	9	Color palette
vbCFFiles	15	List of files
vbCFRTF	−16639	Rich text format (.rtf files)

Remarks

These constants are listed in the Visual Basic (VB) object library in the Object Browser.

The *data* argument is optional. This allows you to set several different formats that the source component can support without having to load the data separately for each format. Multiple formats are set by calling **SetData** several times, each time using a different format. If you wish to start fresh, use the **Clear** method to clear all data and format information from the **DataObject**.

The *format* argument is also optional, but either the *data* or *format* argument must be specified. If *data* is specified, but not *format*, then Visual Basic will try to determine the format of the data. If it is unsuccessful, then an error is generated. When the target requests the data, and a format was specified, but no data was provided, the source's **OLESetData** event occurs, and the source can then provide the requested data type.

It's possible for the **GetData** and **SetData** methods to use data formats other than those listed in Settings, including user-defined formats registered with Windows via the RegisterClipboardFormat() API function. However, there are a few caveats:

- The **SetData** method requires the data to be in the form of a byte array when it does not recognize the data format specified.

- The **GetData** method always returns data in a byte array when it is in a format that it doesn't recognize, although Visual Basic can transparently convert this returned byte array into other data types, such as strings.

- The byte array returned by **GetData** will be larger than the actual data when running on some operating systems, with arbitrary bytes at the end of the array. The reason for this is that Visual Basic does not know the data's format, and knows only the amount of memory that the operating system has allocated for the data. This allocation of memory is often larger than is actually required for the data. Therefore, there may be extraneous bytes near the end of the allocated memory segment. As a result, you must use appropriate functions to interpret the returned data in a meaningful way (such as truncating a string at a particular length with the **Left** function if the data is in a text format).

SetFocus Method

Moves the focus to the specified control or form.

Applies To

Animation Control, **CheckBox** Control, **ComboBox** Control, **CommandButton** Control, **DBCombo** Control, **DBGrid** Control, **DBList** Control, **DirListBox** Control, **DriveListBox** Control, **FileListBox** Control, **Form Object, Forms** Collection, **HScrollBar, VScrollBar** Controls, **ListBox** Control, **ListView** Control, **Masked Edit** Control, **MDIForm** Object, **MSFlexGrid** Control, **OLE Container** Control, **OptionButton** Control, **PictureBox** Control, **PropertyPage** Object, **RichTextBox** Control, **Slider** Control, **TabStrip** Control, **TextBox** Control, **TreeView** Control, **UpDown** Control, **UserControl** Object, **UserDocument** Object

Syntax

object.**SetFocus**

The *object* placeholder represents an object expression that evaluates to an object in the **Applies To** list.

Remarks

The object must be a **Form** object, **MDIForm** object, or control that can receive the focus. After invoking the **SetFocus** method, any user input is directed to the specified form or control.

You can only move the focus to a visible form or control. Because a form and controls on a form aren't visible until the form's **Load** event has finished, you can't use the **SetFocus** method to move the focus to the form being loaded in its own **Load** event unless you first use the **Show** method to show the form before the **Form_Load** event procedure is finished.

You also can't move the focus to a form or control if the **Enabled** property is set to **False**. If the **Enabled** property has been set to **False** at design time, you must first set it to **True** before it can receive the focus using the **SetFocus** method.

See Also

Load Statement, **Show** Method, **Enabled** Property

SetOption Method

Temporarily overrides values for the Microsoft Jet database engine keys in the Windows Registry (Microsoft Jet workspaces only).

Applies To

DBEngine Object

Syntax

DBEngine.SetOption *parameter*, *newvalue*

The **SetOption** method syntax has these parts.

Part	Description
parameter	A **Long** constant as described in Settings.
Newvalue	A **Variant** value that you want to set *parameter* to.

Settings

Each constant refers to the corresponding registry key in the path Jet\3.5\Engines\Jet 3.5\ (that is, **dbSharedAsyncDelay** corresponds to the key Jet\3.5\Engines\Jet 3.5\SharedAsyncDelay, and so on.).

Constant	Description
dbPageTimeout	The PageTimeout key
dbSharedAsyncDelay	The SharedAsyncDelay key
dbExclusiveAsyncDelay	The ExclusiveAsyncDelay key
dbLockRetry	The LockRetry key
dbUserCommitSync	The UserCommitSync key
dbImplicitCommitSync	The ImplicitCommitSync key
dbMaxBufferSize	The MaxBufferSize key
dbMaxLocksPerFile	The MaxLocksPerFile key
dbLockDelay	The LockDelay key
dbRecycleLVs	The RecycleLVs key
dbFlushTransactionTimeout	The FlushTransactionTimeout key

Remarks

Use the **SetOption** method to override registry values at run-time. New values established with the **SetOption** method remain in effect until changed again by another **SetOption** call, or until the **DBEngine** object is closed.

For further details on what the registry keys do, and appropriate values to set them to, see Initializing the Microsoft Jet 3.5 Database Engine.

Example

This example uses the **SetOption** method to change the value of two registry keys based on input from the user. The **SetOption** method only overrides the stored registry values for the current application. The stored settings will remain unchanged and will be the only values visible to the user through REGEDIT.EXE.

```
Sub SetOptionX()

    Dim intExclusiveDelay As Integer
    Dim intSharedDelay As Integer

    ' Get user input for new values of ExclusiveAsyncDelay
    ' and SharedAsyncDelay registry keys.
    intExclusiveDelay = Val(InputBox("Enter a new value " & _
        " for the ExclusiveAsyncDelay registry key " & _
        "(in milliseconds):"))
    intSharedDelay = Val(InputBox("Enter a new value " & _
        "for the SharedAsyncDelay registry key " & _
        "(in milliseconds):"))

    If intExclusiveDelay > 0 And intSharedDelay > 0 Then
        ' Change values of registry keys.
        SetOption dbExclusiveAsyncDelay, intExclusiveDelay
        SetOption dbSharedAsyncDelay, intSharedDelay
        MsgBox "Registry keys changed to new values " & _
            "for duration of program."
    Else
        MsgBox "Registry keys left unchanged."
    End If

End Sub
```

SetSelection Method

Sets the selection in the code pane.

Applies To

CodePane Object

Syntax

object.**SetSelection**(*startline*, *startcol*, *endline*, *endcol*)

SetSelection syntax has these parts:

Part	Description
object	Required. An object expression that evaluates to an object in the **Applies To** list.
startline	Required. A **Long** specifying the first line of the selection.
startcol	Required. A **Long** specifying the first column of the selection.
endline	Required. A **Long** specifying the last line of the selection.
endcol	Required. A **Long** specifying the last column of the selection.

See Also

GetSelection Method, **SetFocus** Method, **Window** Object

Example

The following example uses the **SetSelection** method to select the text whose first character is the one immediately after the fourth character on the second line of CodePanes(1) and whose last character is the fifteenth character on the third line.

```
Application.VBE.CodePanes(1).SetSelection 2,4,3,15
```

SetText Method

Puts a text string on the **Clipboard** object using the specified **Clipboard** object format. Doesn't support named arguments.

Applies To

Clipboard Object

Syntax

object.**SetText** *data*, *format*

The **SetText** method syntax has these parts:

Part	Description
object	Required. An object expression that evaluates to an object in the **Applies To** list.
data	Required. String data to be placed onto the Clipboard.
Format	Optional. A constant or value that specifies one of the Clipboard formats recognized by Visual Basic, as described in Settings.

Settings

The settings for *format* are:

Constant	Value	Description
vbCFLink	&HBF00	DDE conversation information
vbCFRTF	&HBF01	RichText Format
vbCFText	1	(Default) Text

Remarks

These constants are listed in the Visual Basic (VB) object library in the Object Browser.

See Also

GetData Method, **GetFormat** Method, **GetText** Method, **SetData** Method

Example

This example uses the **SetText** method to copy text from a text box to the Clipboard. To try this example, paste the code into the Declarations section of a form with a text box named Text1, and then press F5 and click the form.

```
Private Sub Form_Click ()
   Const CF_TEXT = 1 ' Define bitmap format.
   Dim I, Msg, Temp  ' Declare variables.
   On Error Resume Next ' Set up error handling.
   Msg = "Type anything you like into the text box below."
   Text1.Text = InputBox(Msg) ' Get text from user.
   Msg = "Choose OK to copy the contents of the text box "
   Msg = Msg & "to the Clipboard."
   MsgBox Msg  ' Display message.
   ClipBoard.Clear' Clear Clipboard.
   Clipboard.SetText Text1.Text        ' Put text on Clipboard.

If Clipboard.GetFormat(CF_TEXT) Then
      Text1.Text = ""' Clear the text box.
      Msg = "The text is now on the Clipboard. Choose OK "
      Msg = Msg & "to copy the text from the Clipboard back "
      Msg = Msg & "to the text box."
      MsgBox Msg  ' Display message.
      Temp = Clipboard.GetText(CF_TEXT)        ' Get Clipboard text.
      For I = Len(Temp) To 1 Step -1 ' Reverse the text.
         Text1.Text = Text1.Text & Mid(Temp, I, 1)
      Next I
   Else
      Msg = "There is no text on the Clipboard."

MsgBox Msg  ' Display error message.
   End If
End Sub
```

SetViewport Method

Sets the left and top coordinates of the **UserDocument** that will be visible in the **Viewport**.

Applies To

UserDocument Object

Syntax

object.**SetViewPort** *left, top*

Part	Description
object	An object expression that evaluates to an object in the **Applies To** list.
left	Required. A value of type Single that specifies the left coordinate of the **UserDocument**.
top	Required. A value of type Single that specifies the top coordinate of the **UserDocument**.

See Also

MinHeight, **MinWidth** Properties, **ViewportHeight**, **ViewportLeft**, **ViewportTop**, **ViewportWidth** Properties

Example

The example uses **SetViewport** method to automatically place the **TextBox** control with focus into the top left corner of the Viewport of container. To try the example, place an array of three or more **TextBox** controls onto a **UserDocument** object. Paste the code below into the General section. Press F5 to run the project, then run Internet Explorer (3.0 or later). In Internet Explorer, type the path and file name of the ActiveX document (UserDocument1.vbd) into the **Address** box (the file will be in the same directory as the Visual Basic executable). When the ActiveX document is displayed, type any distinctive text into the first **TextBox** control. Press TAB to move to the next control to see the effect of the **SetViewPort** method.

```
Private Sub Text1_GotFocus(Index As Integer)
   UserDocument.SetViewport Text1(Index).Left, _
      Text1(Index).Top
End Sub

Private Sub UserDocument_Initialize()
   ' The container must be small enough for scrollbars
   ' to appear. To assure this, set the MinHeight and
   ' MinWidth properties to be larger than the container.
   UserDocument.MinHeight = 10000
   UserDocument.MinWidth = 10000
End Sub
```

Sgn Function

Returns a **Variant** (**Integer**) indicating the sign of a number.

Syntax

Sgn(*number*)

The required *number* argument can be any valid numeric expression.

Return Values

If *number* is	Sgn returns
Greater than zero	1
Equal to zero	0
Less than zero	-1

Remarks

The sign of the *number* argument determines the return value of the **Sgn** function.

See Also

Math Functions, **Abs** Function

Example

This example uses the **Sgn** function to determine the sign of a number.

```
Dim MyVar1, MyVar2, MyVar3, MySign
MyVar1 = 12: MyVar2 = -2.4: MyVar3 = 0
MySign = Sgn(MyVar1) ' Returns 1.
MySign = Sgn(MyVar2) ' Returns -1.
MySign = Sgn(MyVar3) ' Returns 0.
```

Shape Control

The **Shape** control is a graphical control displayed as a rectangle, square, oval, circle, rounded rectangle, or rounded square.

Syntax

Shape

Remarks

Use **Shape** controls at design time instead of, or in addition to, invoking **Circle** and **Line** methods at run time. You can draw a **Shape** control in a container, but it can't act as a container. The effect of setting the **BorderStyle** property depends on the setting of the **BorderWidth** property. If **BorderWidth** isn't 1 and **BorderStyle** isn't 0 or 6, **BorderStyle** is set to 1.

Properties

BackColor, ForeColor Properties, **BackStyle** Property, **BorderColor** Property, **BorderStyle** Property, **BorderWidth** Property, **Height, Width** Properties, **Left, Top** Properties, **Tag** Property, **Visible** Property, **DrawMode** Property, **FillColor** Property, **FillStyle** Property, **Shape** Property, **Index** Property (Control Array), **Name** Property, **Parent** Property, **Container** Property

Methods

Refresh Method**, Move** Method**, ZOrder** Method

See Also

Frame Control, **PictureBox** Control

Shape Property

Returns or sets a value indicating the appearance of a **Shape** control.

Applies To

Shape Control

Syntax

object.**Shape** [= *value*]

The **Shape** property syntax has these parts:

Part	Description
object	An object expression that evaluates to an object in the **Applies To** list.
value	An integer specifying the control's appearance, as described in Settings.

Settings

The settings for *value* are:

Constant	Setting	Description
vbShapeRectangle	0	(Default) Rectangle
vbShapeSquare	1	Square
vbShapeOval	2	Oval
vbShapeCircle	3	Circle
VbShapeRoundedRectangle	4	Rounded Rectangle
VbShapeRoundedSquare	5	Rounded Square

See Also

BorderStyle Property

Example

This example illustrates the six possible shapes of the **Shape** control. To try this example, paste the code into the Declarations section of a form that contains an **OptionButton** control and a **Shape** control. For the **OptionButton**, set the **Index** property to 0 to create a control array of one element, and then press F5. Click each **OptionButton** to see each different shape.

```
Private Sub Form_Load ()
   ' Load an icon into the Image control.
   Image1.Picture = LoadPicture("ICONS\ARROWS\ARW02RT.ICO")
   Image1.Left = 0' Move image to left edge.
   ImgW = Image1.Width   ' Save width of image.
   Timer1.Interval = 300
   Timer1.Enabled = False   ' Turn off timer.
   Check1.Caption = "Stretch Property"
End Sub
```

```
Private Sub Form_Click ()
   Timer1.Enabled = True' Turn on the timer.
End Sub

Private Sub Timer1_Timer ()
   Static MoveIcon As Integer ' Flag for moving the icon.
   If Not MoveIcon Then
      Image1.Move Image1.Left + ImgW, Image1.Top, ImgW * 2
   Else
      ' Move the image and return it to original width.
      Image1.Move Image1.Left + ImgW, Image1.Top, ImgW
   End If
   ' If image is off edge of form, start over.
   If Image1.Left > ScaleWidth Then
      Image1.Left = 0
      Timer1.Enabled = False
   End If
   MoveIcon = Not MoveIcon ' Reset flag.
End Sub

Private Sub Check1_Click ()
   Image1.Stretch = Check1.Value
End Sub
```

Shell Function

Runs an executable program and returns a **Variant** (**Double**) representing the program's task ID if successful, otherwise it returns zero.

Syntax

Shell(*pathname*[,*windowstyle*])

The **Shell** function syntax has these named arguments:

Part	Description
pathname	Required; **Variant** (**String**). Name of the program to execute and any required arguments or command-line switches; may include directory or folder and drive.
windowstyle	Optional. **Variant** (**Integer**) corresponding to the style of the window in which the program is to be run. If *windowstyle* is omitted, the program is started minimized with focus.

The *windowstyle* named argument has these values:

Constant	Value	Description
vbHide	0	Window is hidden and focus is passed to the hidden window.

(continued)

(continued)

Constant	Value	Description
vbNormalFocus	1	Window has focus and is restored to its original size and position.
vbMinimizedFocus	2	Window is displayed as an icon with focus.
vbMaximizedFocus	3	Window is maximized with focus.
vbNormalNoFocus	4	Window is restored to its most recent size and position. The currently active window remains active.
vbMinimizedNoFocus	6	Window is displayed as an icon. The currently active window remains active.

Remarks

If the **Shell** function successfully executes the named file, it returns the task ID of the started program. The task ID is a unique number that identifies the running program. If the **Shell** function can't start the named program, an error occurs.

Note The **Shell** function runs other programs asynchronously. This means that a program started with **Shell** might not finish executing before the statements following the **Shell** function are executed.

See Also

AppActivate Statement

Example

This example uses the **Shell** function to run an application specified by the user.

```
' Specifying 1 as the second argument opens the application in
' normal size and gives it the focus.
Dim RetVal
RetVal = Shell("C:\WINDOWS\CALC.EXE", 1)      ' Run Calculator.
```

Shortcut Property

Sets a value that specifies a shortcut key for a **Menu** object. Not available at run time.

Applies To

Menu Control

Remarks

Use this property to provide keyboard shortcuts for menu commands. You can set this property using the Menu Editor. For a list of shortcut keys you can use, see the Shortcut list in the Menu Editor.

Note In addition to shortcut keys, you can also assign access keys to commands, menus, and controls by using an ampersand (&) in the **Caption** property setting.

See Also

Caption Property, **Menu Editor Dialog Box**

Show Event (UserControl Object)

Occurs when the object's **Visible** property changes to **True**.

Applies To

UserControl Object

Syntax

Sub *object*_**Show**()

The **Show** event syntax has these parts:

Part	Description
object	An object expression that evaluates to an object in the **Applies To** list.

Remarks

In order to draw to the screen in Windows, any object must have a window, temporarily or permanently. Visual Basic ActiveX controls have permanent windows. Before a control has been sited on a form, its window is not on the container. The control receives Show events when the window is added.

While the control's window is on the form, the control receives a Show event when the control's **Visible** property changes to **True**.

The control does *not* receive Show events if the form is hidden and then shown again, or if the form is minimized and then restored. The control's window remains on the form during these operations, and its **Visible** property doesn't change.

If the control is being shown in an Internet browser, a Show event occurs if the user returns to the page containing the control.

Note If the control is used with earlier versions of Visual Basic than 5.0, the control will not receive Show events at design time. This is because earlier versions of Visual Basic did not put any visible windows on a form at design time.

See Also

Visible Property

Show Event (UserDocument Object)

Occurs when the object's **Visible** property changes to **True**.

Applies To

UserDocument Object

Syntax

Sub *object*_**Show**()

The Show event syntax has these parts:

Part	Description
object	An object expression that evaluates to an object in the **Applies To** list.

Remarks

In order to draw to the screen in Windows, any object must have a window, temporarily or permanently; Visual Basic ActiveX documents have permanent windows. Before *object* has been sited on a form, its window is not on the container. The **UserDocument** object receives Show events when the window is added.

While *object's* window is on the container, *object* receives a Show event when *object's* **Visible** property changes to **True**.

Object does *not* receive Show events if the container is hidden and then shown again, or if the container is minimized and then restored. *Object's* window remains on the container during these operations, and its **Visible** property doesn't change.

If *object* is being shown in an Internet browser, a Show event occurs when the user navigates to the page.

Note If *object* is used with earlier versions of Visual Basic than 5.0, *object* will not receive Show events at design time. This is because earlier versions of Visual Basic did not put any visible windows on a form at design time.

See Also

Visible Property

Show Method

Displays an **MDIForm** or **Form** object. Doesn't support named arguments.

Applies To

Form Object, **Forms** Collection, **MDIForm** Object

Syntax

object.**Show** *style, ownerform*

The **Show** method syntax has these parts:

Part	Description
object	Optional. An object expression that evaluates to an object in the **Applies To** list. If *object* is omitted, the form associated with the active form module is assumed to be *object*.
style	Optional. Integer that determines if the form is modal or modeless. If *style* is 0, the form is modeless; if *style* is 1, the form is modal.
ownerform	Optional. A string expression that specifies the component which "owns" the form being shown. For standard Visual Basic forms, use the keyword **Me**

Remarks

If the specified form isn't loaded when the **Show** method is invoked, Visual Basic automatically loads it.

When **Show** displays a modeless form, subsequent code is executed as it's encountered. When **Show** displays a modal form, no subsequent code is executed until the form is hidden or unloaded.

When **Show** displays a modal form, no input (keyboard or mouse click) can occur except to objects on the modal form. The program must hide or unload a modal form (usually in response to some user action) before input to another form can occur. An **MDIForm** can't be modal.

Although other forms in your application are disabled when a modal form is displayed, other applications aren't.

The startup form of an application is automatically shown after its Load event is invoked.

Here is an example of how the *ownerform* argument is used with the **Show** method:

```
Private Sub cmdShowResults_Click()
    ' Show a modal form named frmResults.
    frmResults.Show vbModal, Me
End Sub
```

See Also

Activate, Deactivate Events, **Load** Statement, **Unload** Statement, **Hide** Method, **Visible** Property

Example

This example uses the Show method to show a hidden form. To try this example, paste the code into the Declarations section of a non-MDI form, and then press F5 and click the form.

```
Private Sub Form_Click ()
    Dim Msg  ' Declare variable.
    Hide  ' Hide form.
    Msg = "Choose OK to make the form reappear."
    MsgBox Msg  ' Display message.
    Show  ' Show form again.
End Sub
```

Show Method (Add-Ins)

Makes the specified code pane the visible code pane in its window.

Applies To

CodePane Object

Syntax

object.**Show**

The *object* placeholder is an object expression that evaluates to an object in the **Applies To** list.

Remarks

The **Show** method makes the specified code pane the pane with the focus in its window.

Example

The following example uses the **Show** method to move the specified code pane to the foreground.

```
Application.VBE.CodePanes(2).Show
```

Show Method (Microsoft Forms 2.0)

Displays a **UserForm** object.

Applies To

CodePane Object,

Syntax

[*object.*]**Show**

The optional *object* is an object expression that evaluates to an object in the **Applies To** list. If *object* is omitted, the **UserForm** associated with the active **UserForm** module is assumed to be *object*.

Remarks

If the specified object isn't loaded when the **Show** method is invoked, Visual Basic automatically loads it.

A **UserForm** is always modal; therefore, the user must respond before using any other part of the application. No subsequent code is executed until the **UserForm** is hidden or unloaded.

Although other forms in the application are disabled when a **UserForm** is displayed, other applications are not.

See Also

Activate, **Deactivate** Events, **Load** Statement, **Unload** Statement, **Hide** Method, **Visible** Property

Example

The following example assumes two **UserForms** in a program. In UserForm1's **Initialize** event, UserForm2 is loaded and shown. When the user clicks UserForm2, it is hidden and UserForm1 appears. When UserForm1 is clicked, UserForm2 is shown again.

```
' This is the Initialize event procedure for UserForm1
Private Sub UserForm_Initialize()
    Load UserForm2
    UserForm2.Show
End Sub
' This is the Click event for UserForm2
Private Sub UserForm_Click()
    UserForm2.Hide
End Sub

' This is the click event for UserForm1
Private Sub UserForm_Click()
    UserForm2.Show
End Sub
```

ShowGrabHandles Property

Returns a Boolean value stating whether the control should show grab handles.

Applies To

AmbientProperties Object

Syntax

object.**ShowGrabHandles**

The **ShowGrabHandles** property syntax has this part:

Part	Description
object	An object expression that evaluates to an object in the **Applies To** list.

Settings

The possible Boolean return values from the **ShowGrabHandles** property are:

Setting	Description
True	The control should show grab handles, if needed. If the container does not implement this ambient property, this will be the default value.
False	The control should not show grab handles.

Remarks

The default behavior for a control is to automatically show grab handles when the control is in a container that is in design mode (the control's run mode.) However, many containers do not want the control to show grab handles, preferring to handle the indication of control sizing in another way. The **ShowGrabHandles** property is how the container notifies the control of who is to display the sizing indications.

Note All known containers prefer to handle the indication of control sizing themselves, and therefore set the **ShowGrabHandles** property to **False**. It is probably not necessary to actually handle the case when **ShowGrabHandles** is **True**.

ShowHatching Property

Returns a Boolean value stating whether the control should show hatching around the control.

Applies To

AmbientProperties Object

Syntax

object.**ShowHatching**

The **ShowHatching** property syntax has this part:

Part	Description
object	An object expression that evaluates to an object in the **Applies To** list.

Settings

The possible boolean return values from the **ShowHatching** property are:

Setting	Description
True	The control should show hatch marks, if needed. If the container does not implement this ambient property, this will be the default value.
False	The control should not show hatch marks.

Remarks

The default behavior for a control is to automatically show hatching when the control is in a container that is in design mode (the control's run mode) and the control is the one that has focus. However, many containers do not want the control to show hatching, preferring to handle the indication of control focus in another way. The **ShowHatching** property is how the container notifies the control of who is to display the control focus indications.

Note Visual Basic forms do not implement this ambient property, and therefore the **ShowHatching** property is set to the default value of **True** when the control is placed in a Visual Basic form. However, Visual Basic does not expect the control to actually do anything in response to a **ShowHatching** value of **True**, therefore it is probably not necessary to actually handle the case when **ShowHatching** is **True**.

ShowInTaskbar Property

Returns or sets a value that determines whether a **Form** object appears in the Windows 95 taskbar. Read-only at run time.

See Also

BorderStyle Property

Applies To

Form Object, **Forms** Collection

Syntax

object.**ShowInTaskbar**

The *object* placeholder represents an object expression that evaluates to an object in the **Applies To** list.

Settings

The settings for the **ShowInTaskbar** property are:

Setting	Description
True	(Default) The **Form** object appears in the taskbar.
False	The **Form** object does not appear in the taskbar.

Remarks

Use the **ShowInTaskbar** property to keep dialog boxes in your application from appearing in the taskbar.

The default value for the **ShowInTaskbar** property assumes the default setting for the **BorderStyle** property of the **Form** object (Sizable). Changing the **BorderStyle** property may change the setting of the **ShowInTaskbar** property.

WhatsThisHelpID Property, **WhatsThisButton** Property, **ShowWhatsThis** Method, **WhatsThisMode** Method

---

ShowWhatsThis Method

Displays a selected topic in a Help file using the What's This pop-up provided by Windows 95 Help.

Applies To

Animation Control, **CheckBox** Control, **ComboBox** Control, **CommandButton** Control, **Data** Control, **DBCombo** Control, **DBGrid** Control, **DBList** Control, **DirListBox** Control, **DriveListBox** Control, **FileListBox** Control, **Frame** Control, **HScrollBar**, **VScrollBar** Controls, **Image** Control, **Label** Control, **ListBox** Control, **ListView** Control, **Masked Edit** Control, **MSChart** Control, **MSFlexGrid** Control, **OLE Container** Control, **OptionButton** Control, **PictureBox** Control, **ProgressBar** Control, **RemoteData** Control, **RichTextBox** Control, **Slider** Control, **StatusBar** Control, **TabStrip** Control, **TextBox** Control, **Toolbar** Control, **TreeView** Control, **UpDown** Control

Syntax

object.**ShowWhatsThis**

The *object* placeholder represents an object expression that evaluates to an object in the **Applies To** list.

Remarks

The **ShowWhatsThis** method is very useful for providing context-sensitive Help from a context menu in your application. The method displays the topic identified by the **WhatsThisHelpID** property of the object specified in the syntax.

See Also

WhatsThisHelpID Property, **WhatsThisButton** Property, **WhatsThisHelp** Property, **WhatsThisMode** Method

Example

This example displays the What's This Help topic for a **CommandButton** control by selecting a menu command from a context menu created for the button. Set the **WhatsThisHelp** property of the form to **True**. Place a **CommandButton** control on a form, create a menu using the Menu Editor with a top-level invisible item named mnuBtnContextMenu, and a sub-menu named mnuBtnWhatsThis with a caption of "What's This?".

```
Private ThisControl As Control

Private Sub Command1_MouseUp(Button As Integer, Shift As Integer, X As Single, Y As Single)
      If Button = vbRightButton Then
          Set ThisControl = Command1
          Pop-upMenu mnuBtnContextMenu
      End If
    Set ThisControl = Nothing
End Sub

Private Sub mnuBtnWhatsThis_Click()
    ThisControl.ShowWhatsThis
End Sub
```

Sin Function

Returns a **Double** specifying the sine of an angle.

Syntax

Sin(*number*)

The required *number* argument is a **Double** or any valid numeric expression that expresses an angle in radians.

Remarks

The **Sin** function takes an angle and returns the ratio of two sides of a right triangle. The ratio is the length of the side opposite the angle divided by the length of the hypotenuse.

The result lies in the range -1 to 1.

To convert degrees to radians, multiply degrees by pi/180. To convert radians to degrees, multiply radians by 180/pi.

See Also

Math Functions, **Atn** Function, **Cos** Function, **Tan** Function, **Derived Math** Functions

Example

This example uses the **Sin** function to return the sine of an angle.

```
Dim MyAngle, MyCosecant
MyAngle = 1.3                    ' Define angle in radians.
MyCosecant = 1 / Sin(MyAngle) ' Calculate cosecant.
```

Single Data Type

Single (single-precision floating-point) variables are stored as IEEE 32-bit (4-byte) floating-point numbers, ranging in value from -3.402823E38 to -1.401298E-45 for negative values and from 1.401298E-45 to 3.402823E38 for positive values. The type-declaration character for **Single** is the exclamation point (!).

See Also

Data Type Summary, **Double Data** Type, **Variant Data** Type, **Deftype** Statements

Size Method

Changes the width and height of a **UserControl** object.

Applies To

UserControl Object

Syntax

object.**Size** *width, height*

Part	Description
object	An object expression that evaluates to an object in the **Applies To** list.
width	Required. The width in twips of the object.
height	Required. The height in twips of the object.

Remarks

The **Width** and **Height** properties of a **UserControl** object are always given in twips, regardless of **ScaleMode**.

See Also

Height, **Width** Properties

Size Property

Sets or returns a value that indicates the maximum size, in bytes, of a **Field** object.

Applies To

Field Object

Settings and Return Values

The setting or return value is a constant that indicates the maximum size of a **Field** object. For an object not yet appended to the **Fields** collection, this property is read/write. The setting depends on the **Type** property setting of the **Field** object, as discussed under Remarks.

Remarks

For fields (other than Memo type fields) that contain character data, the **Size** property indicates the maximum number of characters that the field can hold. For numeric fields, the **Size** property indicates how many bytes of storage are required.

Use of the **Size** property depends on the object that contains the **Fields** collection to which the **Field** object is appended, as shown in the following table.

Object appended to	Usage
Index	Not supported
QueryDef	Read-only
Recordset	Read-only
Relation	Not supported
TableDef	Read-only

When you create a **Field** object with a data type other than Text, the **Type** property setting automatically determines the **Size** property setting; you don't need to set it. For a **Field** object with the Text data type, however, you can set **Size** to any integer up to the maximum text size (255 for Microsoft Jet databases). If you do not set the size, the field will be as large as the database allows.

For Long Binary and Memo **Field** objects, **Size** is always set to 0. Use the **FieldSize** property of the **Field** object to determine the size of the data in a specific record. The maximum size of a Long Binary or Memo field is limited only by your system resources or the maximum size that the database allows.

See Also

Index Object, **Attributes** Property, **Type** Property

Example

This example demonstrates the **Size** property by enumerating the names and sizes of the **Field** objects in the Employees table.

```
Sub SizeX()

    Dim dbsNorthwind As Database
    Dim tdfEmployees As TableDef
    Dim fldNew As Field
    Dim fldLoop As Field

    Set dbsNorthwind = OpenDatabase("Northwind.mdb")
    Set tdfEmployees = dbsNorthwind.TableDefs!Employees

    With tdfEmployees
```

```
                 ' Create and append a new Field object to the
                 ' Employees table.
                 Set fldNew = .CreateField("FaxPhone")
                 fldNew.Type = dbText
                 fldNew.Size = 20
                 .Fields.Append fldNew

                 Debug.Print "TableDef: " & .Name
                 Debug.Print "    Field.Name - Field.Type - Field.Size"

                 ' Enumerate Fields collection; print field names,
                 ' types, and sizes.
                 For Each fldLoop In .Fields
                    Debug.Print "        " & fldLoop.Name & " - " & _
                       fldLoop.Type & " - " & fldLoop.Size
                 Next fldLoop

                 ' Delete new field because this is a demonstration.
                 .Fields.Delete fldNew.Name

              End With

              dbsNorthwind.Close

           End Sub
```

Size Property (Font)

Returns or sets the font size used in the **Font** object.

Applies To

Font Object

Syntax

object.**Size** [= *number*]

The **Size** property syntax has these parts:

Part	Description
object	An object expression that evaluates to an object in the **Applies To** list.
number	A numeric expression specifying the size of the font in points.

Remarks

Use this property to format text in the font size you want. The default font size is determined by the operating system. To change the default, specify the size of the font in points. The maximum value for the **Size** property is 2048 points.

The **Font** object isn't directly available at design time. Instead you set the **Size** property by selecting a control's **Font** property in the Properties window and clicking the Properties button. In the Size box of the Font dialog box, select the size you want. At run time, however, set **Size** directly by specifying its setting for the **Font** object.

See Also

Bold Property, **FontTransparent** Property, **Italic** Property, **StrikeThrough** Property, **Underline** Property, **Weight** Property, **Name** Property

Example

This example prints text on a form with each mouse click. To try this example, paste the code into the Declarations section of a form, and then press F5 and click the form twice.

```
Private Sub Form_Click ()
    Font.Bold = Not Font.Bold  ' Toggle bold.
    Font.StrikeThrough = Not Font.StrikeThrough ' Toggle strikethrough.
    Font.Italic = Not Font.Italic     ' Toggle italic.
    Font.Underline = Not Font.Underline       ' Toggle underline.
    Font.Size = 16 ' Set Size property.
    If Font.Bold Then
        Print "Font weight is " & Font.Weight & " (bold)."
    Else
        Print "Font weight is " & Font.Weight & " (not bold)."

    End If
End Sub
```

Size Property (Remote Data)

Returns a value that indicates the maximum size, in bytes, of the underlying data of an **rdoColumn** object that contains text or the fixed size of an **rdoColumn** object that contains text or numeric values.

Applies To

rdoColumn Object

Syntax

object.**Size**

The *object* placeholder is an object expression that evaluates to an object in the **Applies To** list.

Return Values

The **Size** property return value is a **Long** value. The value depends on the **Type** property setting of the **rdoColumn** object, as discussed in Remarks.

Remarks

For columns that return character values, the **Size** property indicates the maximum number of characters that the data source column can hold. For numeric columns, the **Size** property indicates how many bytes of data source storage are required for the column data. This value depends on the data source implementation.

For data source columns that require the use of **GetChunk** and **AppendChunk** methods, the **Size** property is always 0—you can use the **ColumnSize** method to return correct size information. The maximum size of a *chunk*-type column is limited only by your system resources or the maximum size of the database.

See Also

ColumnSize Method (Remote Data), **rdoColumn** Object, **rdoPreparedStatement** Object, **rdoResultset** Object, **Attributes** Property (Remote Data), **Type** Property (Remote Data)

Size Property (Split Object)

Sets or returns the size of a split.

Applies To

Split Object

Syntax

object.**Size** [= *value*]

The **Size** property syntax has these parts:

Part	Description
object	An object expression that evaluates to an object in the **Applies To** list.
value	An integer expression that specifies the size of the split.

Remarks

The meaning of the value returned by this property is determined by the split's **SizeMode** property setting.

If **SizeMode** is set to the default value of 0 - Scalable, the value returned by the **Size** property is an integer indicating the relative size of the split with respect to other scalable splits.

If **SizeMode** is set to 1 - Exact, the value returned by the **Size** property is a floating point number indicating the exact size of the split in terms of the coordinate system of the grid's container.

If **SizeMode** is set to 2 - Number of Columns, the value returned by the **Size** property is an integer indicating the number of columns displayed in the split.

Note When there is only one split (the grid's default behavior), the split spans the entire width of the grid, the **SizeMode** property is always 0 - **dbgScalable**, and the **Size** property is always 1. Setting either of these properties has no effect when there is only one split. If there are multiple splits, and you then remove all but one, the **SizeMode** and **Size** properties of the remaining split automatically revert to 0 and 1, respectively.

See Also

SizeMode Property (Split Object)

SizeMode Property

Returns or sets a value specifying how the **OLE** container control is sized or how its image is displayed when it contains an object.

Applies To

OLE Container Control

Syntax

object.**SizeMode** [= *value*]

The **SizeMode** property syntax has these parts:

Part	Description
object	An object expression that evaluates to an object in the **Applies To** list.
value	An integer or constant specifying how the control is sized or how its image is displayed, as described in Settings.

Settings

The settings for *value* are:

Constant	Value	Description
vbOLESizeClip	0	(Default) Clip. The object is displayed in actual size. If the object is larger than the **OLE** container control, its image is clipped by the control's borders.
vbOLESizeStretch	1	Stretch. The object's image is sized to fill the **OLE** container control. The image may not maintain the original proportions of the object.
vbOLESizeAutoSize	2	Autosize. The **OLE** container control is resized to display the entire object.
vbOLESizeZoom	3	Zoom. The object is resized to fill the **OLE** container control as much as possible while still maintaining the original proportions of the object.

Remarks

When **SizeMode** is set to 2 (Autosize), the **OLE** container control is automatically resized when the display size of an object changes. When this occurs, the Resize event is invoked before the **OLE** container control is automatically resized. The *heightnew* and *widthnew* arguments in the Resize event procedure indicate the optimal size for displaying the object (this size is determined by the application that created the object). You can size the control by changing the values of the *heightnew* and *widthnew* arguments in the Resize event procedure.

See Also

Resize Event, **Updated** Event

SizeMode Property (Split Object)

Sets or returns a value that determines how the **Size** property is used to determine the actual size of a split.

Applies To

Split Object

Syntax

object.**SizeMode** [= *value*]

The **SizeMode** property syntax has these parts:

Part	Description
object	An object expression that evaluates to an object in the **Applies To** list.
value	A number or constant that determines how the **Size** property is used, as described in Settings.

Settings

The settings for *value* are:

Constant	Value	Description
dbgScalable	0	(default) The value returned by the **Size** property is an integer indicating the relative size of the split with respect to other scalable splits. For example, if a grid contains 3 scalable splits with **Size** properties equal to 1, 2, and 3, the size of each split would be 1/6, 1/3, and 1/2 of the total grid width, respectively.
dbgExact	1	The value returned by the **Size** property is a floating point number indicating the exact size of the split in terms of the coordinate system of the grid's container. This setting allows you to fix the size of the split so that it always has the same width, even if new splits are added or existing splits are removed.

(continued)

Constant	Value	Description
dbgNumberOfColumns	2	The value returned by the **Size** property is an integer indicating the number of columns displayed in the split, and the split will adjust its width to display the number of full columns specified by the **Size** property. For example, if **Size** is set to 2, and the user scrolls the split horizontally, the width of the split will change so that 2 full columns are displayed, regardless of how wide the columns are.

Remarks

When there is only one split (the grid's default behavior), the split spans the entire width of the grid, the **SizeMode** property is always 0-**dbgScalable**, and the **Size** property is always 1. Setting either of these properties has no effect when there is only one split. If there are multiple splits, and you then remove all but one, the **SizeMode** and **Size** properties of the remaining split automatically revert to 0 and 1, respectively.

Consider a grid containing both scalable splits and splits with a fixed number of columns. If a split with a fixed number of columns is scrolled horizontally, the total width remaining for the scalable splits may change because grid columns are generally of different widths. However, the ratios of the sizes of the scalable splits remain the same as specified by their **Size** properties.

See Also

MarqueeStyle Property, **Split** Property, **Size** Property (Split Object)

SLN Function

Returns a **Double** specifying the straight-line depreciation of an asset for a single period.

Syntax

SLN(*cost*, *salvage*, *life*)

The **SLN** function has these named arguments:

Part	Description
cost	Required. **Double** specifying initial cost of the asset.
salvage	Required. **Double** specifying value of the asset at the end of its useful life.
life	Required. **Double** specifying length of the useful life of the asset.

Remarks

The depreciation period must be expressed in the same unit as the *life* argument. All arguments must be positive numbers.

See Also

DDB Function, **FV** Function, **IPmt** Function, **IRR** Function, **MIRR** Function, **NPer** Function, **NPV** Function, **Pmt** Function, **PPmt** Function, **PV** Function, **Rate** Function, **SYD** Function

Example

This example uses the **SLN** function to return the straight-line depreciation of an asset for a single period given the asset's initial cost (InitCost), the salvage value at the end of the asset's useful life (SalvageVal), and the total life of the asset in years (LifeTime).

```
Dim Fmt, InitCost, SalvageVal, MonthLife, LifeTime, PDepr
Const YEARMONTHS = 12                ' Number of months in a year.
Fmt = "###,##0.00"                   ' Define money format.
InitCost = InputBox("What's the initial cost of the asset?")
SalvageVal = InputBox("What's the asset's value at the end of its
↳ useful life?")
MonthLife = InputBox("What's the asset's useful life in months?")
Do While MonthLife < YEARMONTHS      ' Ensure period is >= 1 year.
   MsgBox "Asset life must be a year or more."
   MonthLife = InputBox("What's the asset's useful life in months?")
Loop
LifeTime = MonthLife / YEARMONTHS    ' Convert months to years.
If LifeTime <> Int(MonthLife / YEARMONTHS) Then
   LifeTime = Int(LifeTime + 1)      ' Round up to nearest year.
End If
PDepr = SLN(InitCost, SalvageVal, LifeTime)
MsgBox "The depreciation is " & Format(PDepr, Fmt) & " per year."
```

Snapshot-Type Recordset Object

A snapshot-type **Recordset** object is a static set of records that you can use to examine data in an underlying table or tables. In an ODBCDirect database, a snapshot-type **Recordset** object corresponds to a static cursor.

Remarks

To create a snapshot-type **Recordset** object, use the **OpenRecordset** method on an open database, on another dynaset- or snapshot-type **Recordset** object, or on a **QueryDef** object.

A snapshot-type **Recordset** object can contain fields from one or more tables in a database. In a Microsoft Jet workspace, a snapshot can't be updated. In an ODBCDirect workspace, a snapshot may be updatable, depending on the ODBC driver.

When you create a snapshot-type **Recordset** object, data values for all fields (except Memo and OLE Object (Long Binary) field data types in .mdb files) are brought into memory. Once loaded, changes made to base table data aren't reflected in the snapshot-type **Recordset** object data. To reload the snapshot-type **Recordset** object with current data, use the **Requery** method, or re-execute the **OpenRecordset** method.

The order of snapshot-type **Recordset** object data doesn't necessarily follow any specific sequence. To order your data, use an SQL statement with an ORDER BY clause to create the **Recordset** object. You can also use this technique to filter the records so that only certain records are added to the **Recordset** object. Using this technique instead of using the **Filter** or **Sort** properties or testing each record individually generally results in faster access to your data.

Snapshot-type **Recordset** objects are generally faster to create and access than dynaset-type **Recordset** objects because their records are either in memory or stored in TEMP disk space, and the Microsoft Jet database engine doesn't need to lock pages or handle multiuser issues. However, snapshot-type **Recordset** objects use more resources than dynaset-type **Recordset** objects because the entire record is downloaded to local memory.

Properties

AbsolutePosition Property, **BOF, EOF** Properties, **Bookmark** Property, **Bookmarkable** Property, **EditMode** Property, **Filter** Property, **LastModified** Property, **LockEdits** Property, **Name** Property, **NoMatch** Property, **PercentPosition** Property, **RecordCount** Property, **Restartable** Property, **Sort** Property, **Transactions** Property, **Type** Property, **Updatable** Property, **ValidationRule** Property, **ValidationText** Property, **BatchCollisionCount** Property, **BatchCollisions** Property, **BatchSize** Property, **Connection** Property, **RecordStatus** Property, **StillExecuting** Property, **UpdateOptions** Property

Methods

AddNew Method, **CancelUpdate** Method, **Clone** Method, **Close** Method, **CopyQueryDef** Method, **Delete** Method, **Edit** Method, **FindFirst**, **FindLast**, **FindNext**, **FindPrevious** Method, **GetRows** Method, **Move** Method, **MoveFirst, MoveLast, MoveNext, MovePrevious** Methods, **OpenRecordset** Method, **Requery** Method, **Update** Method, **Cancel** Method, **NextRecordset** Method

See Also

Dynaset-Type Recordset Object, **Recordset** Object, **Table-Type Recordset** Object, **Forward-Only – Type Recordset** Object

Example

This example opens a snapshot-type **Recordset** and demonstrates its read-only characteristics.

```
Sub dbOpenSnapshotX()

    Dim dbsNorthwind As Database
    Dim rstEmployees As Recordset
    Dim prpLoop As Property

    Set dbsNorthwind = OpenDatabase("Northwind.mdb")
    Set rstEmployees = _
        dbsNorthwind.OpenRecordset("Employees", _
        dbOpenSnapshot)

    With rstEmployees
        Debug.Print "Snapshot-type recordset: " & _
            .Name

        ' Enumerate the Properties collection of the
        ' snapshot-type Recordset object, trapping for
        ' any properties whose values are invalid in
        ' this context.
        For Each prpLoop In .Properties
            On Error Resume Next
            Debug.Print "    " & _
                prpLoop.Name & " = " & prpLoop
            On Error Goto 0
        Next prpLoop

        .Close
    End With

    dbsNorthwind.Close

End Sub
```

Sort Property

Sets or returns the sort order for records in a **Recordset** object (Microsoft Jet workspaces only).

Applies To

Dynaset-Type Recordset Object, **Recordset** Object, **Snapshot-Type Recordset** Object

Settings and Return Values

The setting or return value is a **String** that contains the ORDER BY clause of an SQL statement without the reserved words ORDER BY.

Remarks

You can use the **Sort** property with dynaset- and snapshot-type **Recordset** objects.

When you set this property for an object, sorting occurs when a subsequent **Recordset** object is created from that object. The **Sort** property setting overrides any sort order specified for a **QueryDef** object.

The default sort order is ascending (A to Z or 0 to 100).

The **Sort** property doesn't apply to table- or forward-only–type **Recordset** objects. To sort a table-type **Recordset** object, use the **Index** property.

Note In many cases, it's faster to open a new **Recordset** object by using an SQL statement that includes the sorting criteria.

See Also

QueryDef Object, **Filter** Property, **Index** Property, **SQL** Property

Example

This example demonstrates the **Sort** property by changing its value and creating a new **Recordset**. The **SortOutput** function is required for this procedure to run.

```
Sub SortX()

    Dim dbsNorthwind As Database
    Dim rstEmployees As Recordset
    Dim rstSortEmployees As Recordset

    Set dbsNorthwind = OpenDatabase("Northwind.mdb")
    Set rstEmployees = _
        dbsNorthwind.OpenRecordset("Employees", _
        dbOpenDynaset)

    With rstEmployees
        SortOutput "Original Recordset:", rstEmployees
        .Sort = "LastName, FirstName"
        ' Print report showing Sort property and record order.
        SortOutput _
            "Recordset after changing Sort property:", _
            rstEmployees
        ' Open new Recordset from current one.
        Set rstSortEmployees = .OpenRecordset
        ' Print report showing Sort property and record order.
        SortOutput "New Recordset:", rstSortEmployees
        rstSortEmployees.Close
        .Close
    End With

    dbsNorthwind.Close
```

```
End Sub

Function SortOutput(strTemp As String, _
    rstTemp As Recordset)

    With rstTemp
        Debug.Print strTemp
        Debug.Print "    Sort = " & _
            IIf(.Sort <> "", .Sort, "[Empty]")
        .MoveFirst

        ' Enumerate Recordset.
        Do While Not .EOF
            Debug.Print "        " & !LastName & _
                ", " & !FirstName
            .MoveNext
        Loop

    End With

End Function
```

Note   When you know the data you want to select, it's usually more efficient to create a **Recordset** with an SQL statement. This example shows how you can create just one **Recordset** and obtain the same results as in the preceding example.

```
Sub SortX2()

    Dim dbsNorthwind As Database
    Dim rstEmployees As Recordset

    Set dbsNorthwind = OpenDatabase("Northwind.mdb")
    ' Open a Recordset from an SQL statement that specifies a
    ' sort order.
    Set rstEmployees = _
        dbsNorthwind.OpenRecordset("SELECT * " & _
        "FROM Employees ORDER BY LastName, FirstName", _
        dbOpenDynaset)

    dbsNorthwind.Close

End Sub
```

Sorted Property

Returns a value indicating whether the elements of a control are automatically sorted alphabetically.

Applies To
ComboBox Control, **ListBox** Control

Syntax

object.**Sorted**

The *object* placeholder represents an object expression that evaluates to an object in the **Applies To** list.

Return Values

The **Sorted** property return values are:

Setting	Description
True	List items are sorted by character code order.
False	(Default) List items aren't sorted alphabetically.

Remarks

When this property is **True**, Visual Basic handles almost all necessary string processing to maintain alphabetic order, including changing the index numbers for items as required by the addition or removal of items.

Note Using the **AddItem** method to add an element to a specific location in the list may violate the sort order, and subsequent additions may not be correctly sorted.

See Also

AddItem Method, **RemoveItem** Method, **List** Property, **ListCount** Property, **ListIndex** Property

Source Property

Returns or sets a string expression specifying the name of the object or application that originally generated the error. Read/write.

Applies To

Err Object

Remarks

The **Source** property specifies a string expression representing the object that generated the error; the expression is usually the object's class name or programmatic ID. Use **Source** to provide information when your code is unable to handle an error generated in an accessed object. For example, if you access Microsoft Excel and it generates a Division by zero error, Microsoft Excel sets **Err.Number** to its error code for that error and sets **Source** to Excel.Application.

When generating an error from code, **Source** is your application's programmatic ID. For class modules, **Source** should contain a name having the form *project.class*. When an unexpected error occurs in your code, the **Source** property is automatically filled in. For errors in a standard module, **Source** contains the project name. For errors in a class module, **Source** contains a name with the *project.class* form.

See Also

GetObject Function, **On Error** Statement, **Err** Object, **Description** Property, **HelpContext** Property, **HelpFile** Property, **LastDLLError** Property, **Number** Property, **HelpContextID** Property

Example

This example assigns the Programmatic ID of an Automation object created in Visual Basic to the variable MyObjectID, and then assigns that to the **Source** property of the **Err** object when it generates an error with the **Raise** method. When handling errors, you should not use the **Source** property (or any **Err** properties other than **Number**) programatically. The only valid use of properties other than **Number** is for displaying rich information to an end user in cases where you can't handle an error. The example assumes that App and MyClass are valid references.

```
Dim MyClass, MyObjectID, MyHelpFile, MyHelpContext
' An object of type MyClass generates an error and fills all Err object
' properties, including Source, which receives MyObjectID, which is a
' combination of the Title property of the App object and the Name
' property of the MyClass object.
MyObjectID = App.Title & "." & MyClass.Name
Err.RaiseNumber := vbObjectError + 894, Source := MyObjectID, _
        Description := "Was not able to complete your task", _
        HelpFile := MyHelpFile, HelpContext := MyHelpContext
```

Source Property (Remote Data)

Returns a value that indicates the source of a remote data access error.

Applies To

rdoError Object

Syntax

object.**Source**

The *object* placeholder represents an object expression that evaluates to an object in the **Applies To** list.

Return Values

The **Source** property return value is a string expression as described in Remarks.

Remarks

When an error occurs during an ODBC operation, an **rdoError** object is appended to the **rdoErrors** collection. If the error occurred within RDO, the return value begins with "MSRDO20". The object class that caused the error might also be appended to the value of the **Source** property.

rdoError Object, **Description** Property (Remote Data), **HelpContext**, **HelpFile** Properties (Remote Data), **Number** Property (Remote Data), **SQLRetCode** Property (Remote Data), **SQLState** Property (Remote Data)

SourceColumnProperty (Remote Data)

The **SourceColumn** property returns a value that indicates the name of the column that is the original source of the data for an **rdoColumn** object.

This property is not available at design time and is read-only at run time.

Applies To

rdoColumn Object

Syntax

object.**SourceColumn**

The *object* placeholder is an object expression that evaluates to an object in the **Applies To** list.

Return Values

The **SourceColumn** property returns a string expression that specifies the name of the column that is the source of data.

Remarks

This property indicates the original column name associated with an **rdoColumn** object. For example, you could use this property to determine the original source of the data in a query column whose name is unrelated to the name of the column in the underlying table.

For columns in **rdoResultset** objects, the **SourceColumn** and **SourceTable** properties return the column name and table name of the base table or the columns and table(s) used to define the query.

See Also

rdoColumn Object, **rdoPreparedStatement** Object, **rdoResultset** Object, **rdoTable** Object

SourceDoc Property

Returns or sets the filename to use when you create an object.

Note You set the **SourceDoc** property for compatibility with the **Action** property in earlier versions. For current functionality, use the **CreateEmbed** and **CreateLink** methods.

Applies To

OLE Container Control

Syntax

object.**SourceDoc** [= *name*]

The **SourceDoc** property syntax has these parts:

Part	Description
object	An object expression that evaluates to an object in the **Applies To** list.
name	A string expression specifying a filename.

Remarks

Use the **SourceDoc** property to specify the file to be linked when creating a linked object using the **Action** property. Use the **SourceItem** property to specify data within the file to be linked.

When creating an embedded object using the **Action** property, if the **SourceDoc** property is set to a valid filename, an embedded object is created using the specified file as a template.

When a linked object is created, the **SourceItem** property is concatenated to the **SourceDoc** property. At run time, the **SourceItem** property returns a zero-length string (""), and the **SourceDoc** property returns the entire path to the linked file, followed by an exclamation point (!) or a backslash (\), followed by the **SourceItem**. For example:

```
"C:\WORK\QTR1\REVENUE.XLS!R1C1:R30C15"
```

See Also

Class Property, **OLEType** Property, **SourceItem** Property, **OLETypeAllowed** Property, **CreateEmbed** Method, **CreateLink** Method, **Action** Property (OLE Container)

SourceField, SourceTable Properties

- **SourceField**—returns a value that indicates the name of the field that is the original source of the data for a **Field** object.

- **SourceTable**—returns a value that indicates the name of the table that is the original source of the data for a **Field** object.

Applies To

Field Object

Return Values

The return value is a **String** specifying the name of the field or table that is the source of data.

Remarks

For a **Field** object, use of the **SourceField** and **SourceTable** properties depends on the object that contains the **Fields** collection that the **Field** object is appended to, as shown in the following table.

Object appended to	Usage
Index	Not supported
QueryDef	Read-only
Recordset	Read-only
Relation	Not supported
TableDef	Read-only

These properties indicate the original field and table names associated with a **Field** object. For example, you could use these properties to determine the original source of the data in a query field whose name is unrelated to the name of the field in the underlying table.

Note The **SourceTable** property will not return a meaningful table name if used on a **Field** object in the **Fields** collection of a table-type **Recordset** object.

See Also

SourceTableName Property

Example

This example demonstrates the **SourceField** and **SourceTable** properties by opening a **Recordset** made up of fields from two tables.

```
Sub SourceFieldX()

    Dim dbsNorthwind As Database
    Dim rstProductCategory As Recordset
    Dim fldLoop As Field
    Dim strSQL As String

    Set dbsNorthwind = OpenDatabase("Northwind.mdb")
    ' Open a Recordset from an SQL statement that uses fields
    ' from two different tables.
    strSQL = "SELECT ProductID AS ProdID, " & _
        "ProductName AS ProdName, " & _
        "Categories.CategoryID AS CatID, " & _
        "CategoryName AS CatName " & _
        "FROM Categories INNER JOIN Products ON " & _
        "Categories.CategoryID = Products.CategoryID " & _
        "ORDER BY ProductName"
    Set rstProductCategory = _
        dbsNorthwind.OpenRecordset(strSQL)
```

```
    Debug.Print "Field - SourceTable - SourceField"
    ' Enumerate Fields collection of Recordset, printing
    ' name, original table, and original name.
    For Each fldLoop In rstProductCategory.Fields
        Debug.Print "    " & fldLoop.Name & " - " & _
            fldLoop.SourceTable & " - " & fldLoop.SourceField
    Next fldLoop

    rstProductCategory.Close
    dbsNorthwind.Close

End Sub
```

SourceItem Property

Returns or sets the data within the file to be linked when you create a linked object.

Applies To

OLE Container Control

Syntax

object.**SourceItem** [= *string*]

The **SourceItem** property syntax has these parts:

Part	Description
object	An object expression that evaluates to an object in the **Applies To** list.
string	A string expression specifying the data to be linked.

Remarks

OLETypeAllowed must be set to 0 (Linked) or 2 (Either) when using this property. Use the **SourceDoc** property to specify the file to link.

Each object uses its own syntax to describe units of data. To set this property, specify a unit of data recognized by the object. For example, when you link to Microsoft Excel, specify the **SourceItem** using a cell or cell-range reference such as R1C1 or R3C4:R9C22, or a named range such as Revenues.

To determine the syntax to describe a unit of data for an object, see the documentation for the application that created the object.

Note You may be able to determine this syntax by creating a linked object at design timeusing the Paste Special command (click the **OLE** container control with the right mouse button). Once the object is created, select the **SourceDoc** property in the Properties window and look at the string in the Settings box. For most objects, this string contains a path to the linked file, followed by an exclamation point (!) or a backslash (\) and the syntax for the linked data.

When a linked object is created, the **SourceItem** property is concatenated to the **SourceDoc** property. At run time, the **SourceItem** property returns a zero-length string (""), and the **SourceDoc** property returns the entire path to the linked file, followed by an exclamation point (!) or a backslash (\), followed by the **SourceItem**. For example:

```
"C:\WORK\QTR1\REVENUE.XLS!R1C1:R30C15"
```

See Also

Class Property, **OLEType** Property, **SourceDoc** Property, **OLETypeAllowed** Property

SourceTable Property

SourceTable returns a value that indicates the name of the table that is the original source of the data for an **rdoColumn** object.

This property is not available at design time and is read-only at run time.

Applies To

rdoColumn Object

Syntax

object.**SourceTable**

The *object* placeholder is an object expression that evaluates to an object in the **Applies To** list.

Return Values

The **SourceTable** property returns a string expression that specifies the name of the table that is the source of data.

Remarks

This property indicates the original table name associated with an **rdoColumn** object. For example, you could use these properties to determine the original source of the data in a query column whose name is unrelated to the name of the column in the underlying table.

For columns in **rdoResultset** objects, the **SourceColumn** and **SourceTable** properties return the column name and table name of the base table or the columns and table(s) used to define the query.

See Also

rdoColumn Object, **rdoResultset** Object

SourceTableName Property

Sets or returns a value that specifies the name of a linked table or the name of a base table (Microsoft Jet workspaces only).

Applies To

TableDef Object

Settings and Return Values

The setting or return value is a **String** that specifies a table name. For a base table, the setting is a zero-length string (""). This property setting is read-only for a base table and read/write for a linked table or an object not appended to a collection.

See Also

OpenDatabase Method, **RefreshLink** Method, **Connect** Property, **SourceField**, **SourceTable** Properties

Example

This example uses the **Connect** and **SourceTableName** properties to link various external tables to a Microsoft Jet database. The **ConnectOutput** procedure is required for this procedure to run.

```
Sub ConnectX()

    Dim dbsTemp As Database
    Dim strMenu As String
    Dim strInput As String

    ' Open a Microsoft Jet database to which you will link
    ' a table.
    Set dbsTemp = OpenDatabase("DB1.mdb")

    ' Build menu text.
    strMenu = "Enter number for data source:" & vbCr
    strMenu = strMenu & _
        "    1. Microsoft Jet database" & vbCr
    strMenu = strMenu & _
        "    2. Microsoft FoxPro 3.0 table" & vbCr
    strMenu = strMenu & _
        "    3. dBASE table" & vbCr
    strMenu = strMenu & _
        "    4. Paradox table" & vbCr
    strMenu = strMenu & _
        "    M. (see choices 5-9)"

    ' Get user's choice.
    strInput = InputBox(strMenu)

    If UCase(strInput) = "M" Then
```

```
   ' Build menu text.
   strMenu = "Enter number for data source:" & vbCr
   strMenu = strMenu & _
      "   5. Microsoft Excel spreadsheet" & vbCr
   strMenu = strMenu & _
      "   6. Lotus spreadsheet" & vbCr
   strMenu = strMenu & _
      "   7. Comma-delimited text (CSV)" & vbCr
   strMenu = strMenu & _
      "   8. HTML table" & vbCr
   strMenu = strMenu & _
      "   9. Microsoft Exchange folder"

   ' Get user's choice.
   strInput = InputBox(strMenu)

End If

' Call the ConnectOutput procedure. The third argument
' will be used as the Connect string, and the fourth
' argument will be used as the SourceTableName.
Select Case Val(strInput)
   Case 1
      ConnectOutput dbsTemp, _
         "JetTable", _
         ";DATABASE=C:\My Documents\Northwind.mdb", _
         "Employees"
   Case 2
      ConnectOutput dbsTemp, _
         "FoxProTable", _
         "FoxPro 3.0;DATABASE=C:\FoxPro30\Samples", _
         "Q1Sales"
   Case 3
      ConnectOutput dbsTemp, _
         "dBASETable", _
         "dBase IV;DATABASE=C:\dBASE\Samples", _
         "Accounts"
   Case 4
      ConnectOutput dbsTemp, _
         "ParadoxTable", _
         "Paradox 3.X;DATABASE=C:\Paradox\Samples", _
         "Accounts"
   Case 5
      ConnectOutput dbsTemp, _
         "ExcelTable", _
         "Excel 5.0;" & _
            "DATABASE=C:\Excel\Samples\Q1Sales.xls", _
         "January Sales"
   Case 6
      ConnectOutput dbsTemp, _
         "LotusTable", _
         "Lotus WK3;" & _
            "DATABASE=C:\Lotus\Samples\Sales.xls", _
         "THIRDQTR"
```

```
        Case 7
          ConnectOutput dbsTemp, _
            "CSVTable", _
            "Text;DATABASE=C:\Samples", _
            "Sample.txt"
        Case 8
          ConnectOutput dbsTemp, _
            "HTMLTable", _
            "HTML Import;DATABASE=http://" & _
              "www.server1.com/samples/page1.html", _
            "Q1SalesData"
        Case 9
          ConnectOutput dbsTemp, _
            "ExchangeTable", _
            "Exchange 4.0;MAPILEVEL=" & _
              "Mailbox - Michelle Wortman (Exchange)" & _
              "|People\Important;", _
            "Jerry Wheeler"
    End Select

    dbsTemp.Close

End Sub

Sub ConnectOutput(dbsTemp As Database, _
    strTable As String, strConnect As String, _
    strSourceTable As String)

    Dim tdfLinked As TableDef
    Dim rstLinked As Recordset
    Dim intTemp As Integer

    ' Create a new TableDef, set its Connect and
    ' SourceTableName properties based on the passed
    ' arguments, and append it to the TableDefs collection.
    Set tdfLinked = dbsTemp.CreateTableDef(strTable)

    tdfLinked.Connect = strConnect
    tdfLinked.SourceTableName = strSourceTable
    dbsTemp.TableDefs.Append tdfLinked

    Set rstLinked = dbsTemp.OpenRecordset(strTable)

    Debug.Print "Data from linked table:"

    ' Display the first three records of the linked table.
    intTemp = 1
    With rstLinked
        Do While Not .EOF And intTemp <= 3
            Debug.Print , .Fields(0), .Fields(1)
            intTemp = intTemp + 1
            .MoveNext
        Loop
        If Not .EOF Then Debug.Print , "[additional records]"
        .Close
    End With
```

```
' Delete the linked table because this is a demonstration.
dbsTemp.TableDefs.Delete strTable

End Sub
```

Space Function

Returns a **Variant** (**String**) consisting of the specified number of spaces.

Syntax

Space(*number*)

The required *number* argument is the number of spaces you want in the string.

Remarks

The **Space** function is useful for formatting output and clearing data in fixed-length strings.

See Also

Spc Function, **String** Function

Example

This example uses the **Space** function to return a string consisting of a specified number of spaces.

```
Dim MyString
' Returns a string with 10 spaces.
MyString = Space(10)

' Insert 10 spaces between two strings.
MyString = "Hello" & Space(10) & "World"
```

Spc Function

Used with the **Print #** statement or the **Print** method to position output.

Syntax

Spc(*n*)

The required *n* argument is the number of spaces to insert before displaying or printing the next expression in a list.

Remarks

If *n* is less than the output line width, the next print position immediately follows the number of spaces printed. If *n* is greater than the output line width, **Spc** calculates the next print position using the formula:

currentprintposition + (*n* **Mod** *width*)

For example, if the current print position is 24, the output line width is 80, and you specify **Spc**(90), the next print will start at position 34 (current print position + the remainder of 90/80). If the difference between the current print position and the output line width is less than *n* (or *n* **Mod** *width*), the **Spc** function skips to the beginning of the next line and generates spaces equal to *n* – (*width* – *currentprintposition*).

Note   Make sure your tabular columns are wide enough to accommodate wide letters.

When you use the **Print** method with a proportionally spaced font, the width of space characters printed using the **Spc** function is always an average of the width of all characters in the point size for the chosen font. However, there is no correlation between the number of characters printed and the number of fixed-width columns those characters occupy. For example, the uppercase letter W occupies more than one fixed-width column and the lowercase letter i occupies less than one fixed-width column.

See Also

Print # Statement, **Tab** Function, **Width #** Statement, **Print** Method, **Mod** Operator, **Space** Function

Example

This example uses the **Spc** function to position output in a file and in the **Debug** window.

```
' The Spc function can be used with the Print # statement.
Open "TESTFILE" For Output As #1      ' Open file for output.
Print #1, "10 spaces between here"; Spc(10); "and here."
Close #1                              ' Close file.
```

The following statement causes the text to be printed in the **Debug** window (using the **Print** method), preceded by 30 spaces.

```
Debug.Print Spc(30); "Thirty spaces later..."
```

Split Object

A **Split** object represents a split within a **DBGrid** control.

Remarks

DBGrid supports Excel-like splits that divide the grid into vertical panes to provide users with different views of a database. Each split is represented by a **Split** object and contains a group of adjacent columns that scroll as a unit. When a **DBGrid** object is created, it contains one **Split** object by default.

You can use splits to present your data in multiple vertical panes. The data panes (or splits) can display data in different colors and fonts. They can scroll (vertically) together or independently of each other, and they can display the same or different columns. You can also use splits to fix one or more columns from scrolling. Unlike other grid products, the fixed columns do not have to be at the left edge of the grid, but can be at the right edge or anywhere in the middle. You can even have multiple groups of fixed columns within a grid.

Each **Split** object maintains its own Columns collection. These independent splits and columns provide you with very powerful and flexible data presentation capabilities.

As mentioned above, a grid (a **DBGrid** object) initially contains a single split. If additional splits are created, you can determine or set the current split (i.e., the split that has received focus) using the grid's **Split** property as follows:

```
' Read the zero-based index of the current split
Variable% = DBGrid1.Split

' Set focus to the split with an index equal to
' Variable%
DBGrid1.Split = Variable%
```

Each split in a grid is a different view of the same data source, and each split behaves just like an independent grid. If you create additional **Split** objects without customizing any of the split properties, all splits will be identical and each will behave very much like the original grid with one split.

Some of the properties of the **DBGrid** control are the same as the properties of a **Split** object and are considered common. Changes made to a **DBGrid** control common property also change the same property of the current **Split** object and vice versa. For example, consider a grid with two splits, and assume that the current split index is 1 (i.e., the grid's **Split** property is set to 1). If you want to determine the marquee style in use, the following statements are identical:

```
marquee% = DBGrid1.MarqueeStyle
marquee% = DBGrid1.Splits(1).MarqueeStyle
```

If the current split index is set to 1, then the following code is equivalent for setting the **MarqeeStyle** property to **dbgSolidCellBorder**:

```
DBGrid1.MarqueeStyle = dbgSolidCellBorder
DBGrid1.Splits(1).MarqueeStyle = dbgSolidCellBorder
```

Note Common properties are unique to **DBGrid** objects and their associated **Split** objects. No other object pairs possess similar relationships.

Properties

CurrentCellVisible Property, MarqueeStyle Property, AllowFocus Property, ScrollGroup Property, Size Property (Split Object), SizeMode Property (Split Object), AllowSizing Property, AllowRowSizing Property, Columns Property (DBGrid), FirstRow Property, RecordSelectors Property, Index Property (Control Array), Locked Property, ScrollBars Property, SelEndCol, SelStartCol, SelEndRow, SelStartRow Properties

Methods

ClearSelCols Method

See Also

Splits Collection, DBGrid Control

Split Property

Sets or returns the index of the current split. Not available at design time.

Applies To

DBGrid Control

Syntax

object.**Split** [= *value*]

The **Split** property syntax has these parts:

Part	Description
object	An object expression that evaluates to an object in the **Applies To** list.
value	An integer that specifies the index of the current split, as described in Remarks.

Remarks

The **Split** property specifies a zero-based index of the current split.

See Also

Split Object

SplitChange Event

Occurs when the current cell changes to a different cell in another split.

Applies To

DBGrid Control

Private Sub *object*_**SplitChange**([*index* **As Integer**])

The **SplitChange** event syntax has these parts:

Part	Description
object	An object expression that evaluates to an object in the **Applies To** list.
index	An integer that identifies a control if it is in a control array.

Remarks

This event is triggered under several circumstances:

- When the grid is first displayed.
- When the user clicks a cell in another split (subject to the setting of the **AllowFocus** property).
- When the user presses a navigation key to cross a split boundary (subject to the setting of the **TabAcrossSplits** property).
- When the **Split** property is changed in code to a different value.
- When a new split is inserted before the current split via code or user interaction.
- When the current split is removed via code or user interaction.

If the user edits data and then moves the current cell position to a new row in another split, the update events for the original row are completed before the **SplitChange** event is executed.

If a split change also results in a change to the current row or column, then the **SplitChange** event will always precede the **RowColChange** event.

See Also

Split Property, **TabAcrossSplits** Property, **AllowFocus** Property, **RowColChange** Event

SplitContaining Method

Returns the **Index** value of the split containing the specified coordinate pair.

Applies To

DBGrid Control

Syntax

object.**SplitContaining** *x, y*

The **SplitContaining** method syntax has these parts:

Part	Description
object	An object expression that evaluates to an object in the **Applies To** list.
x	Required. A single precision value that defines the horizontal coordinate, based on the coordinate system of the grid's container.
y	Required. A single precision value that defines the vertical coordinate, based on the coordinate system of the grid's container.

Remarks

This value ranges from 0 to 1 less than the setting of the **Count** property of the **Splits** collection (0 to **Splits.Count** - 1).

This method is useful when working with mouse and drag events when you are trying to determine where the user clicked or dropped another control in terms of a grid column.

If either argument is outside of the grid's data area, this method returns -1.

See Also

Splits Collection, **Splits** PropertySplit

Similar to the "split window" capabilities available with Microsoft Excel where a window is divided into separate vertical panes to provide users with different views of data. Each split is represented by a **Split** object and contains a group of adjacent columns that scroll as a unit.

Splits Collection

The Splits collection contains all stored **Split** objects in a **DBGrid** control.

Syntax

Splits(*index*)
Splits.Item(*index*)

Remarks

You can create splits at design time using the grid's UI-active context menu. At run time, you can create and remove splits using the Splits collection's **Add** and **Remove** methods. Each method takes a zero-based split index. The following code demonstrates adding and removing splits at run time:

```
' Create a Split object with index 0
DBGrid1.Splits.Add 0
' Remove the Split object with index 1
DBGrid1.Splits.Remove 1
```

You can determine the number of splits in a grid using the Splits collection's **Count** property.

Properties

    Index Property (ControlArray)

Methods

    Add Method (Columns, SelBookmarks, Splits Collection), **Item** Method, **Remove** Method (DB Grid)

See Also

    DBGrid Control

Splits Property

Returns a collection of **Split** objects. Not available at design time.

Applies To

    DBGrid Control

Syntax

object.**Splits**

The **Splits** property syntax has these parts:

Part	Description
object	An object expression that evaluates to an object in the **Applies To** list.

See Also

    Split Object

SQL Property (DAO)

Sets or returns the SQL statement that defines the query executed by a **QueryDef** object.

Applies To

    QueryDef Object

Settings and Return Values

The setting or return value is a **String** that contains an SQL statement.

Remarks

The **SQL** property contains the SQL statement that determines how records are selected, grouped, and ordered when you execute the query. You can use the query to select records to include in a **Recordset** object. You can also define action queries to modify data without returning records.

The SQL syntax used in a query must conform to the SQL dialect of the query engine, which is determined by the type of workspace. In a Microsoft Jet workspace, use the Microsoft Jet SQL dialect, unless you create an SQL pass-through query, in which case you should use the dialect of the server. In an **ODBCDirect** workspace, use the SQL dialect of the server.

Note You can send DAO queries to a variety of different database servers with ODBCDirect, and different servers will recognize slightly different dialects of SQL. Therefore, context-sensitive Help is no longer provided for Microsoft Jet SQL, although online Help for Microsoft Jet SQL is still included through the Help menu. Be sure to check the appropriate reference documentation for the SQL dialect of your database server when using either ODBCDirect connections or pass-through queries in Microsoft Jet-connected client/server applications.

If the SQL statement includes parameters for the query, you must set these before execution. Until you reset the parameters, the same parameter values are applied each time you execute the query.

In an **ODBCDirect** workspace, you can also use the **SQL** property to execute a prepared statement on the server. For example, setting the **SQL** property to the following string will execute a prepared statement named "GetData" with one parameter on a Microsoft SQL Server back-end.

```
"{call GetData (?)}"
```

In a Microsoft Jet workspace, using a **QueryDef** object is the preferred way to perform SQL pass-through operations on Microsoft Jet-connected ODBC data sources. By setting the **QueryDef** object's **Connect** property to an ODBC data source, you can use non–Microsoft-Jet-database SQL in the query to be passed to the external server. For example, you can use TRANSACT SQL statements (with Microsoft SQL Server or Sybase SQL Server databases), which the Microsoft Jet database engine would otherwise not process.

Note If you set the property to a string concatenated with a non-integer value, and the system parameters specify a non-U.S. decimal character such as a comma (for example, `strSQL = "PRICE > " & lngPrice`, and `lngPrice = 125,50`), an error will result when you try to execute the **QueryDef** object in a Microsoft Jet database. This is because during concatenation, the number will be converted to a string using your system's default decimal character, and Microsoft Jet SQL only accepts U.S. decimal characters.

See Also

Parameter Object, **Recordset** Object, **CreateQueryDef** Method, **OpenRecordset** Method, **Filter** Property, **Sort** Property

Example

This example demonstrates the **SQL** property by setting and changing the **SQL** property of a temporary **QueryDef** and comparing the results. The SQLOutput function is required for this procedure to run.

```
Sub SQLX()

    Dim dbsNorthwind As Database
    Dim qdfTemp As QueryDef
    Dim rstEmployees As Recordset

    Set dbsNorthwind = OpenDatabase("Northwind.mdb")
    Set qdfTemp = dbsNorthwind.CreateQueryDef("")

    ' Open Recordset using temporary QueryDef object and
    ' print report.
    SQLOutput "SELECT * FROM Employees " & _
        "WHERE Country = 'USA' " & _
        "ORDER BY LastName", qdfTemp

    ' Open Recordset using temporary QueryDef object and
    ' print report.
    SQLOutput "SELECT * FROM Employees " & _
        "WHERE Country = 'UK' " & _
        "ORDER BY LastName", qdfTemp

    dbsNorthwind.Close

End Sub

Function SQLOutput(strSQL As String, qdfTemp As QueryDef)

    Dim rstEmployees As Recordset

    ' Set SQL property of temporary QueryDef object and open
    ' a Recordset.
    qdfTemp.SQL = strSQL
    Set rstEmployees = qdfTemp.OpenRecordset

    Debug.Print strSQL

    With rstEmployees
        ' Enumerate Recordset.
        Do While Not .EOF
            Debug.Print "     " & !FirstName & " " & _
                !LastName & ", " & !Country
            .MoveNext
        Loop
        .Close
    End With

End Function
```

SQL Property (Remote Data)

Returns or sets the SQL statement that defines the query executed by an **rdoQuery object** or a **RemoteData** control.

Applies To

rdoPreparedStatement Object, **rdoQuery** Object, **RemoteData** Control

Syntax

object.**SQL** [= *value*]

The **SQL** property syntax has these parts:

Part	Description
object	An object expression that evaluates to an object in the **Applies To** list.
value	A string expression that contains a value as described in Settings. (Data type is **String**.)

Settings

The settings for *value* are:

Setting	Description
A valid SQL statement	An SQL query using syntax appropriate for the data source.
A stored procedure	The name of a stored procedure supported by the data source preceded with the keyword "Execute".
An **rdoQuery**	The name of one of the **rdoQuery** objects in the **rdoConnection** object's **rdoQueries** collection.
An **rdoResultset**	The name of one of the **rdoResultset** objects in the **rdoConnection** object's **rdoResultsets** collection.
A table name	The name of one of the populated **rdoTable** objects defined in the **rdoConnection** object's **rdoTables** collection.

Remarks

The **SQL** property contains the structured query language statement that determines how rows are selected, grouped, and ordered when you execute a query. You can use a query to select rows to include in an **rdoResultset** object. You can also define action queries to modify data without returning rows.

You cannot provide a table name at design time for the **SQL** property. However, you can either use a simple query like SELECT * FROM <table>, or at runtime, populate the **rdoTables** collection and use one of the table names returned in the collection. The **rdoTables** collection is populated as soon as it is associated with an active connection and referenced.

The SQL syntax used in a query must conform to the SQL dialect as defined by the data source query processor. The SQL dialect supported by the ODBC interface is defined by the X/Open standard. Generally, a driver scans an SQL statement looking for specific escape sequences that are used to identify non-standard operands like timestamp literals and functions.

When you need to return rows from a query, you generally provide a SELECT statement in the **SQL** property. The SELECT statement specifies:

- The name of each column to return or "*" to indicate all columns of the specified tables are to be returned. Ambiguous column names must be addressed to include the table name as needed. You can also specify aggregate expressions to perform arithmetic or other functions on the columns selected.

- The name of each table that is to be searched for the information requested. If you specify more than one table, you must provide a WHERE clause to indicate which column(s) are used to cross-reference the information in the tables. Generally, these columns have the same name and meaning. For example the **CustomerID** column in the Customers table and the Orders table might be referenced.

- (Optionally) a WHERE clause to specify how to join the tables specified and how to limit or filter the number and types of rows returned. You can use parameters in the WHERE clause to specify different sets of information from query to query.

- (Optionally) other clauses such as ORDER BY to set a particular order for the rows or GROUP BY to structure the rows in related sets.

Each SQL dialect supports different syntax and different ancillary clauses. See the documentation provided with your remote server for more details.

Specifying Parameters

If the SQL statement includes question mark parameter markers (?) for the query, you must provide these parameters before you execute the query. Until you reset the parameters, the same parameter values are applied each time you execute the query. To use the **rdoParameters** collection to manage SQL query parameters, you must include the "?" parameter marker in the SQL statement. Input, output, input/output and return value parameters must all be identified in this manner. In some cases, you must use the **Direction** property to indicate how the parameter will be used.

Note When executing stored procedures that do *not* require parameters, do not include the parenthesis in the SQL statement. For example, to execute the "MySP" procedure use the following syntax: `{Call MySP }`.

Note When using Microsoft SQL Server 6 as a data source, the ODBC driver automatically sets the **Direction** property. You also do not need to set the **Direction** property for input parameters, as this is the default setting.

If the user changes the parameter value, you can re-apply the parameter value and re-execute the query by using the **Requery** method against the **rdoResultset** (MyRs).

```
Cpw(0) = Text1.Text
MyRs.Requery
```

You can also specify parameters in any SQL statement by concatenating the parameters to the SQL statement string. For example, to submit a query using this technique, you can use the following code:

```
QSQL$ = "SELECT * FROM Authors WHERE Au_Lname = '" _
 & Text.Text & "'"
Set CPw = cn.CreateQuery("",QSQL$)
Set MyRs = Cpw.OpenResultSet()
```

In this case, the **rdoParameters** collection is *not* created and cannot be referenced. To change the query parameter, you must rebuild the SQL statement with the new parameter value each time the query is executed, or before you use the **Requery** method.

The SQL statement may include an ORDER BY clause to change the order of the rows returned by the **rdoResultset** or a WHERE clause to filter the rows.

Note You can't use the **rdoTable** object names until the **rdoTables** collection is referenced. When your code references the **rdoTables** collection by enumerating one or more of its members, RDO queries the data source for table meta data. This results in population of the **rdoTables** collection. This means that you cannot simply provide a table name for the *value* argument without first enumerating the **rdoTables** collection.

RemoteData Control

When used with the **RemoteData** control, the **SQL** property specifies the source of the data rows accessible through bound controls on your form.

If you set the **SQL** property to an SQL statement that returns rows or to the name of an existing **rdoQuery**, all columns returned by the **rdoResultset** are visible to the bound controls associated with the **RemoteData** control.

After changing the value of the **SQL** property at run time, you must use the **Refresh** method to activate the change.

Note Whenever your **rdoQuery** or SQL statement returns a value from an expression, the column name of the expression is determined by the wording of the SQL query. In most cases you'll want to alias expressions so you know the name of the column to bind to the bound control.

Make sure each bound control has a valid setting for its **DataField** property. If you change the setting of a **RemoteData** control's **SQL** property and then use **Refresh**, the **rdoResultset** identifies the new object. This may invalidate the **DataField** settings of bound controls and cause a trappable error.

See Also

CreatePreparedStatement Method (Remote Data), **Execute** Method (Remote Data),
OpenResultset Method (Remote Data), **rdoParameter** Object,
rdoPreparedStatement Object, **rdoResultset** Object, **rdoTable** Object

Example

For example, to execute a procedure that accepts two input parameters and returns a
return value and an output parameter, you can use the following code. The example
creates an **rdoQuery** object whose SQL property is set to the string specified by
QSQL$. This query calls a stored procedure that returns a return status, and an output
argument as well as accepting two input arguments.

```
Dim Cqy as new rdoQuery
Dim MyRs as rdoResultset
Cqy.SQL = "{ ? = call sp_MyProc (?, ?, ?) }"
Cqy(0).Direction = rdReturnValue
Cqy(1).Direction = rdParamInput
Cqy(2).Direction = rdParamInput
Cqy(3).Direction = rdParamOutput
Cqy(1) = "Victoria"
Cqy(0) = 21
Set MyRs = Cqy.OpenResultSet(rdOpenForwardOnly)
```

SQLRetCode Property (Remote Data)

Returns the ODBC error return code from the most recent RDO operation.

Applies To

rdoError Object

Syntax

object.**SQLRetCode**

The *object* placeholder represents an object expression that evaluates to an object in
the **Applies To** list.

Return Values

The **SQLRetCode** property return value is a **Long** value that corresponds to one of
the following constants:

Constant	Value	Description
rdSQLSuccess	0	The operation is successful.
rdSQLSuccessWithInfo	1	The operation is successful, and additional information is available.
rdSQLNoDataFound	100	No additional data is available.
rdSQLError	-1	An error occurred performing the operation.
rdSQLInvalidHandle	-2	The handle supplied is invalid.

rdoError Object, **Description** Property (Remote Data), **HelpContext**, **HelpFile**
Properties (Remote Data), **Number** Property (Remote Data), **Source** Property
(Remote Data), **SQLState** Property (Remote Data)

SQLState Property (Remote Data)

Returns a value corresponding to the type of error as defined by the X/Open and SQL
Access Group SQL.

Applies To

rdoError Object

Syntax

object.**SQLState**

The *object* placeholder represents an object expression that evaluates to an object in
the **Applies To** list.

Return Values

The **SQLState** return value is a five-character string expression, as described in
Remarks.

Remarks

When an RDO operation returns an error, or completes an operation, the
SQLState property of the **rdoError** object is set. If the error is not caused
by ODBC or if no **SQLState** is available, the **SQLState** property returns
an empty string.

The character string value returned by the **SQLState** property consists of a
two-character class value followed by a three-character subclass value. A class
value of "01" indicates a warning and is accompanied by a return code of
rdSQLSuccessWithInfo.

Class values other than "01", except for the class "IM", indicate an error
and are accompanied by a return code of **rdSQLError**. The class "IM" is
specific to warnings and errors that derive from the implementation of ODBC
itself. The subclass "000" in any class is for implementation-defined conditions
within the given class. The assignment of class and subclass values is defined by
ANSI SQL-92.

See Also

rdoError Object, **Description** Property (Remote Data), **HelpContext**, **HelpFile**
Properties (Remote Data), **Number** Property (Remote Data), **Source** Property
(Remote Data), **SQLRetCode** Property (Remote Data)

Sqr Function

Returns a **Double** specifying the square root of a number.

Syntax

Sqr(*number*)

The required *number* argument is a **Double** or any valid numeric expression greater than or equal to zero.

See Also

Math Functions, **Derived Math** Functions

Example

This example uses the **Sqr** function to calculate the square root of a number.

```
Dim MySqr
MySqr = Sqr(4) ' Returns 2.
MySqr = Sqr(23)' Returns 4.79583152331272.
MySqr = Sqr(0) ' Returns 0.
MySqr = Sqr(-4)' Generates a run-time error.
```

StandardMethod Property

Returns or sets the **StandardMethod** attribute of a **Member** object.

Applies To

Member Object

Syntax

object.**StandardMethod**

The *object* placeholder represents an object expression that evaluates to an object in the **Applies To** list.

StandardSize Property

Sets the property page to a standard size.

Applies To

PropertyPage Object

Syntax

object.**StandardSize** [= *value*]

The **StandardSize** property syntax has these parts:

Part	Description
object	An object expression that evaluates to an object in the **Applies To** list.
value	An integer expression specifying the type of mouse pointer displayed, as described in **Settings**.

Settings

The settings for *value* are:

Constant	Value	Description
Custom	0	(Default) Size determined by the object.
Small	1	Sets the **PropertyPage StandardSize** to 101 pixels high by 375 pixels wide.
Large	2	Sets the **PropertyPage StandardSize** to 179 pixels high by 375 pixels wide.

See Also

PropertyPage Object

StartLogging Method

Sets the log target and log mode of an operation.

Applies To

App Object

Syntax

object.**StartLogging** *logTarget, logMode*

Part	Description
object	An object expression that evaluates to an object in the **Applies To** list.
logTarget	Path and filename of the file used to capture output from the **LogEvent** method.
logMode	A value which determines how logging (through the **LogEvent** method) will be carried out. See **Settings** below.

Settings

The settings for *logMode* are:

Constant	Value	Description
vbLogAuto	0	If running on Windows 95, this option logs messages to the file specified in the **LogFile** property. If running on Windows NT, messages are logged to the NT Application Event Log, with the App.Title string used as the application source.

(continued)

Constant	Value	Description
VbLogOff	1	Turns all logging off. Messages from UI shunts as well as from the **LogEvent** method are ignored and discarded.
VbLogToFile	2	Forces logging to a file. If no valid filename is present in **LogPath**, logging is ignored, and the property is set to **vbLogOff**.
VbLogToNT	3	Forces logging to the NT Event log. If not running on Windows NT, or the event log is unavailable, logging is ignored and the property is set to **vbLogOff**.
VbLogOverwrite	0x10	Indicates that the logfile should be recreated each time the application starts. This value can be combined with other mode options using the **OR** operator. The default action for logging is to append to the existing file. In the case of NT event logging, this flag has no meaning.
VbLogThreadID	0x20	Indicates that the current thread ID be prepended to the message, in the form "[T:0nnn]". This value can be combined with other mode options using the **OR** operator. The default action is to show the thread ID only when the application is multi-threaded (either explicitly marked as thread-safe, or implemented as an implicit multithreaded app, such as a local server with the instancing property set to Single-Use, multithreaded).

StartMode Property

Returns or sets a value that determines whether an application starts as a stand-alone project or as an ActiveX component. Read-only at run time.

Applies To

App Object

Syntax

object.**StartMode**

The *object* placeholder represents an object expression that evaluates to an object in the **Applies To** list.

Settings

The **StartMode** property settings are:

Constant	Value	Description
vbSModeStandalone	0	(Default) Application starts as a stand-alone project.
VbSModeAutomation	1	Application starts as an ActiveX component.

Remarks

These constants are listed in the Visual Basic (VB) object library in the Object Browser.

At design time, you can set **StartMode** in the Project Options dialog box to 1 (**vbSModeAutomation**) to debug an application as if it were started as an ActiveX component.

Once a project is compiled, the value of the **StartMode** property is determined by how that application is started, not by its nominal setting in the Project Options dialog box.

When **StartMode** is set to 1 and there are no public classes in the project, you must use the **End** statement or choose End from the Run menu or toolbar to end the application. If you choose Close from the System menu, the form closes but the project is still running.

See Also

HelpFile Property (App, CommonDialog, MenuLine), **PrevInstance** Property, **Title** Property, **Path** Property, **EXEName** Property

Example

This example shows one possible effect of setting the **StartMode** property to 1 (**vbSModeAutomation**) at design time. Create an ActiveX EXE project. Create a new form. From the Project menu, choose the Project Properties command. Select the Component tab, then select the ActiveX component option button in the Start Mode group. Choose OK to close the Project Properties dialog box. To try this example, paste the code into the Declarations section of the form, and then press F5 and double-click the Control menu at the left of the form's title bar. If the form doesn't display, enter Form1.Show in the Immediate window.

```
Private Sub Form_QueryUnload(Cancel As Integer, UnloadMode As Integer)
    If UnloadMode = vbFormControlMenu And App.StartMode = vbSModeAutomation Then
        Msg = "Form will close but application will still be running." & Chr(10)
        Msg = Msg + "To terminate application without a public class," & Chr(10)
        Msg = Msg + "you must use an End statement."
        MsgBox Msg
    End If
End Sub
```

StartProject Property

Returns or sets the project that will start when the user selects **Start** from the **Run** menu, or presses the F5 key.

Applies To

VBProjects Collection

Syntax

object.**StartProject**

The *object* placeholder represents an object expression that evaluates to an object in the **Applies To** list.

StartUpObject Property

Returns or sets the startup component for the project.

Applies To

VBComponents Collection

Syntax

object.**StartUpObject**

The *object* placeholder represents an object expression that evaluates to an object in the **Applies To** list.

Return Values

The value that is returned is a variant that contains either an enumerated value of type **vbext_StartupObject**, or a **VBComponent** object that represents the startup object.

The **StartUpObject** property settings for **vbext_StartUpObject** are:

Constant	Value	Description
vbext_so_SubMain	0	Startup object is the sub Main.
vbext_so_None	1	There is no startup object.

Remarks

Only visual at run-time project items can be the startup object.

StartUpPosition Property

Returns or sets a value specifying the position of a **UserForm** when it first appears.

You can use one of four settings for **StartUpPosition**:

Setting	Value	Description
Manual	0	No initial setting specified.
CenterOwner	1	Center on the item to which the **UserForm** belongs.
CenterScreen	2	Center on the whole screen.
Windows Default	3	Position in upper-left corner of screen.

Applies To

Form Object, **Forms** Collection, **MDIForm** Object

Remarks

You can set the **StartUpPosition** property programmatically or from the **Properties** window.

See Also

Load Statement

Example

The following example uses the **Load** statement and the **Show** method in UserForm1's Click event to load UserForm2 with the **StartUpPosition** property set to 3 (the Windows default position). The **Show** method then makes UserForm2 visible.

```
Private Sub UserForm_Click()
    Load UserForm2
    UserForm2.StartUpPosition = 3
    UserForm2.Show
End Sub
```

Static Property

Returns whether the referenced variable or method is declared as **Static**.

Applies To

Member Object

Syntax

object.**Static**

The *object* placeholder represents an object expression that evaluates to an object in the **Applies To** list.

Static Statement

Used at procedure level to declare variables and allocate storage space. Variables declared with the **Static** statement retain their values as long as the code is running.

Syntax

Static *varname*[([*subscripts*])] [**As** [**New**] *type*] [**,** *varname*[([*subscripts*])]
    ↳ [**As** [**New**] *type*]] ...

The **Static** statement syntax has these parts:

Part	Description
varname	Required. Name of the variable; follows standard variable naming conventions.
subscripts	Optional. Dimensions of an array variable; up to 60 multiple dimensions may be declared. The *subscripts* argument uses the following syntax:
	[*lower* **To**] *upper* [,[*lower* **To**] *upper*] ...
	When not explicitly stated in *lower*, the lower bound of an array is controlled by the **Option Base** statement. The lower bound is zero if no **Option Base** statement is present.
New	Optional. Keyword that enables implicit creation of an object. If you use **New** when declaring the object variable, a new instance of the object is created on first reference to it, so you don't have to use the **Set** statement to assign the object reference. The **New** keyword can't be used to declare variables of any intrinsic data type and can't be used to declare instances of dependent objects.
type	Optional. Data type of the variable; may be **Byte**, **Boolean**, **Integer**, **Long**, **Currency**, **Single**, **Double**, **Decimal** (not currently supported), **Date**, **String**, (for variable-length strings), **String** * *length* (for fixed-length strings), **Object**, **Variant**, a user-defined type, or an object type. Use a separate **As** *type* clause for each variable being defined.

Remarks

Once module code is running, variables declared with the **Static** statement retain their value until the module is reset or restarted. Use the **Static** statement in nonstatic procedures to explicitly declare variables that are visible only within the procedure, but whose lifetime is the same as the module in which the procedure is defined.

Use a **Static** statement within a procedure to declare the data type of a variable that retains its value between procedure calls. For example, the following statement declares a fixed-size array of integers:

```
Static EmployeeNumber(200) As Integer
```

The following statement declares a variable for a new instance of a worksheet:

```
Static X As New Worksheet
```

If the **New** keyword isn't used when declaring an object variable, the variable that refers to the object must be assigned an existing object using the **Set** statement before it can be used. Until it is assigned an object, the declared object variable has the special value **Nothing**, which indicates that it doesn't refer to any particular instance of an object. When you use the **New** keyword in the declaration, an instance of the object is created on the first reference to the object.

If you don't specify a data type or object type, and there is no **Def***type* statement in the module, the variable is **Variant** by default.

Note The **Static** statement and the **Static** keyword are similar, but used for different effects. If you declare a procedure using the **Static** keyword (as in `Static Sub CountSales ()`), the storage space for all local variables within the procedure is allocated once, and the value of the variables is preserved for the entire time the program is running. For nonstatic procedures, storage space for variables is allocated each time the procedure is called and released when the procedure is exited. The **Static** statement is used to declare specific variables within nonstatic procedures to preserve their value for as long as the program is running.

When variables are initialized, a numeric variable is initialized to 0, a variable-length string is initialized to a zero-length string (""), and a fixed-length string is filled with zeros. **Variant** variables are initialized to **Empty**. Each element of a user-defined type variable is initialized as if it were a separate variable.

Note When you use **Static** statements within a procedure, put them at the beginning of the procedure with other declarative statements such as **Dim**.

See Also

Array Function, **Dim** Statement, **Function** Statement, **Option Base** Statement, **Private** Statement, **Public** Statement, **ReDim** Statement, **Sub** Statement

Example

This example uses the **Static** statement to retain the value of a variable for as long as module code is running.

```
' Function definition.
Function KeepTotal(Number)
   ' Only the variable Accumulate preserves its value between calls.
   Static Accumulate
   Accumulate = Accumulate + Number
   KeepTotal = Accumulate
End Function

' Static function definition.
Static Function MyFunction(Arg1, Arg2, Arg3)
   ' All local variables preserve value between function calls.
   Accumulate = Arg1 + Arg2 + Arg3
   Half = Accumulate / 2
   MyFunction = Half
End Function
```

Status Property

Returns or sets the status of a row.

This property indicates or sets the status of the current row.

Applies To

rdoColumn Object, **rdoResultset** Object

Syntax

object.**Status** [= *value*]

The **Status** property syntax has these parts:

Part	Description
object	An object expression that evaluates to an object in the **Applies To** list.
value	A **Long** integer representing the type of cursor as described in Settings:

Settings

The **Status** property has these settings:

Constant	Value	Prepared **Property Setting**
rdRowUnmodified	0	(Default) The row has not been modified or has been updated successfully.
rdRowModified	1	The row has been modified and not updated in the database.
rdRowNew	2	The row has been inserted with the **AddNew** method, but not yet inserted into the database.
rdRowDeleted	3	The row has been deleted, but not yet deleted in the database.
rdRowDBDeleted	4	The row has been deleted locally *and* in the database.

Remarks

The value of this property indicates if and how this row will be involved in the next optimistic batch update.

When you use the optimistic batch update cursor library and need to specify which rows are to be updated in the next batch operation, you set the **rdoResultset** object's **Status** property. For example, suppose you are working with an unbound Grid control filled with rows from a query. The user selects one of the rows and you detect that a change has been made in the row. At this point you can mark this row for updating by setting the **Status** property to **rdRowModified**. Similarly, if a row is added or deleted, you can use the appropriate **Status** property setting to so indicate. When you use the **BatchUpdate** method, RDO will submit an appropriate operation to the remote server for each row based on its **Status** property.

Once the **BatchUpdate** operation is complete, you can examine the **Status** property of each row to determine if the update is successful. If the **Status** value does not return rdRowUnmodified after the **BatchUpdate**, the operation to update the row could not be completed. In this case you should check the **rdoErrors** collection and the **BatchCollisionRows** property for rows.

See Also

BatchCollisionCount Property, **BatchCollisionRows** Property, **BatchConflictValue** Property, **BatchSize** Property, **BatchUpdate** Method, **CancelBatch** Method

StillConnecting Property

Returns a value that indicates if the connection has been established.

Applies To

rdoConnection Object

Syntax

object.**StillConnecting**

The *object* placeholder represents an object expression that evaluates to an object in the **Applies To** list.

Return Values

The **StillConnecting** property return values are:

Value	Description
True	The connection is being made asynchronously but has not been established.
False	The connection has been established.

Remarks

This property works very similarly to the **StillExecuting** property, except that it is **True** while an asynchronous connection to the server is being performed. This property is set to **False** again after the connection has been established.

All method and property access of the connection object (with the exception of this property and the **Cancel** method) will result in trappable errors while an asynchronous connection is in progress.

See Also

BeforeConnect Event, **Connect** Event, **Disconnect** Event, **OpenConnection** Method (Remote Data)

Example

This example illustrates use of the **StillConnecting** property when establishing a connection using the **rdAsyncEnable** option.

```
Dim rdoCn As New rdoConnection
Dim TimeExpected As Single
Dim Ts As Single, Tn As Single
```

```
TimeExpected = 15
With rdoCn
   .Connect = "UID=;PWD=;Database=WorkDB;" _
      & "Server=FarAway;Driver={SQL Server}" _
      & "DSN='';"
   .LoginTimeout = 45
   .EstablishConnection rdDriverNoPrompt, _
      True, rdAsyncEnable
   Ts = Timer
   ProgressBar1.Max = TimeExpected   ' time to Open
   While .StillConnecting
      Tn = Int(Timer - Ts)
      If Tn < TimeExpected Then
         ProgressBar1 = Tn
      Else
         ProgressBar1.Max = ProgressBar1.Max + 10
         TimeExpected = ProgressBar1.Max
      End If
      DoEvents
   Wend
   Status = "Duration:" & Int(Timer - Ts)

End With
rdoCn.Close
Exit Sub
```

StillExecuting Property

Indicates whether or not an asynchronous operation (that is, a method called with the **dbRunAsync** option) has finished executing (**ODBCDirect** workspaces only).

Applies To

Dynaset-Type Recordset Object, **QueryDef** Object, **Recordset** Object, **Snapshot-Type Recordset** Object, **Connection** Object, **Forward-Only–Type Recordset** Object, **Dynamic-Type Recordset** Object

Settings And Return Values

The return value is a **Boolean** that is **True** if the query is still executing, and **False** if the query has completed.

Remarks

Use the **StillExecuting** property to determine if the most recently called asynchronous **Execute**, **MoveLast**, **OpenConnection,** or **OpenRecordset** method (that is, a method executed with the **dbRunAsync** option) is complete. While the **StillExecuting** property is **True**, any returned object cannot be accessed.

The following table shows what method is evaluated when you use **StillExecuting** on a particular type of object.

If StillExecuting is used on	This asynchronous method is evaluated
Connection	**Execute** or **OpenConnection**
QueryDef	**Execute**
Recordset	**MoveLast** or **OpenRecordset**

Once the **StillExecuting** property on a **Connection** or **Recordset** object returns **False**, follwing the **OpenConnection** or **OpenRecordset** call that returns the associated **Recordset** or **Connection** object, the object can be referenced. So long as **StillExecuting** remains **True**, the object may not be referenced, other than to read the **StillExecuting** property. When you use the **NextRecordset** method to complete processing of a **Recordset**, the **StillExecuting** property is reset to **True** while subsequent result sets are retrieved.

Use the **Cancel** method to terminate execution of a task in progress.

See Also

Execute Method, **MoveFirst, MoveLast, MoveNext, MovePrevious** Methods, **OpenRecordset** Method, **Cancel** Method, **OpenConnection** Method

Example

This example uses the **StillExecuting** property and the **Cancel** method to asynchronously open a **Connection** object.

```
Sub CancelConnectionX()

    Dim wrkMain As Workspace
    Dim conMain As Connection
    Dim sngTime As Single

    Set wrkMain = CreateWorkspace("ODBCWorkspace", _
        "admin", "", dbUseODBC)
    ' Open the connection asynchronously.
    Set conMain = wrkMain.OpenConnection("Publishers", _
        dbDriverNoPrompt + dbRunAsync, False, _
        "ODBC;DATABASE=pubs;UID=sa;PWD=;DSN=Publishers")

    sngTime = Timer

    ' Wait five seconds.
    Do While Timer - sngTime < 5
    Loop

    ' If the connection has not been made, ask the user
    ' if she wants to keep waiting. If she does not, cancel
    ' the connection and exit the procedure.
    Do While conMain.StillExecuting
```

```
        If MsgBox("No connection yet--keep waiting?", _
            vbYesNo) = vbNo Then
           conMain.Cancel
           MsgBox "Connection cancelled!"
           wrkMain.Close
           Exit Sub
        End If

   Loop

   With conMain
      ' Use the Connection object conMain.
      .Close
   End With

   wrkMain.Close

End Sub
```

This example uses the **StillExecuting** property and the **Cancel** method to asynchronously execute a **QueryDef** object.

```
Sub CancelQueryDefX()

   Dim wrkMain As Workspace
   Dim conMain As Connection
   Dim qdfTemp As QueryDef
   Dim sngTime As Single

   Set wrkMain = CreateWorkspace("ODBCWorkspace", _
      "admin", "", dbUseODBC)
   Set conMain = wrkMain.OpenConnection("Publishers", _
      dbDriverNoPrompt, False, _
      "ODBC;DATABASE=pubs;UID=sa;PWD=;DSN=Publishers")

   Set qdfTemp = conMain.CreateQueryDef("")

   With qdfTemp
      .SQL = "UPDATE roysched " & _
         "SET royalty = royalty * 2 " & _
         "WHERE title_id LIKE 'BU____' OR " & _
         "title_id LIKE 'PC____'"

      ' Execute the query asynchronously.
      .Execute dbRunAsync

      sngTime = Timer

      ' Wait five seconds.
      Do While Timer - sngTime < 5
      Loop
```

```
                 ' If the query has not completed, ask the user if
                 ' she wants to keep waiting. If she does not, cancel
                 ' the query and exit the procedure.
                 Do While .StillExecuting

                     If MsgBox( _
                             "Query still running--keep waiting?", _
                             vbYesNo) = vbNo Then
                         .Cancel
                         MsgBox "Query cancelled!"
                         Exit Do
                     End If

                 Loop

             End With

             conMain.Close
             wrkMain.Close

         End Sub
```

This example uses the **StillExecuting** property and the **Cancel** method to asynchronously move to the last record of a **Recordset** object.

```
Sub CancelRecordsetX()

    Dim wrkMain As Workspace
    Dim conMain As Connection
    Dim rstTemp As Recordset
    Dim sngTime As Single

    Set wrkMain = CreateWorkspace("ODBCWorkspace", _
        "admin", "", dbUseODBC)
    Set conMain = wrkMain.OpenConnection("Publishers", _
        dbDriverNoPrompt, False, _
        "ODBC;DATABASE=pubs;UID=sa;PWD=;DSN=Publishers")
    Set rstTemp = conMain.OpenRecordset( _
        "SELECT * FROM roysched", dbOpenDynaset)

    With rstTemp

        ' Call the MoveLast method asynchronously.
        .MoveLast dbRunAsync

        sngTime = Timer

        ' Wait five seconds.
        Do While Timer - sngTime < 5
        Loop
```

```
' If the MoveLast has not completed, ask the user if
' she wants to keep waiting. If she does not, cancel
' the MoveLast and exit the procedure.
Do While .StillExecuting

    If MsgBox( _
        "Not at last record yet--keep waiting?", _
        vbYesNo) = vbNo Then
      .Cancel
      MsgBox "MoveLast cancelled!"
      conMain.Close
      wrkMain.Close
      Exit Sub
    End If

Loop

' Use recordset.

.Close

End With

conMain.Close
wrkMain.Close

End Sub
```

StillExecuting Property (Remote Data)

Returns a Boolean value that indicates whether a query is still executing.

Applies To

rdoConnection Object, **rdoPreparedStatement** Object, **rdoQuery** Object, **rdoResultset** Object

Syntax

object.**StillExecuting**

The *object* placeholder represents an object expression that evaluates to an object in the **Applies To** list.

Return Values

The **StillExecuting** property return values are:

Value	Description
True	The query is still executing.
False	The query is ready to return the result set.

Remarks

Use the **StillExecuting** property to determine if a query is ready to return the first result set. Until the **StillExecuting** property is **False**, the associated object cannot be accessed. However, unless you use the **rdAsyncEnable** option, your application will block until the query is completed and ready to process the result set.

Once the **StillExecuting** property returns **False**, the first or next result set is ready for processing. When you use the **MoreResults** method to complete processing of a result set, the **StillExecuting** property is reset to **True** while the next result sets is retrieved.

The **StillExecuting** property also changes to **True** when you execute a Move method. For example executing **MoveLast** against an **rdoResultset** resets the **StillExecuting** property to **True** as long as RDO continues to fetch rows from the remote server.

You can also use the **QueryComplete** event to indicate when a query has completed and the associated **rdoResultset** object is ready to process.

Use the **Cancel** method to terminate processing of an executing query, including all statements in a batch query.

See Also

Cancel Method (Remote Data), **Execute** Method (Remote Data), **MoreResults** Method (Remote Data), **OpenResultset** Method (Remote Data)

Example

This example illustrates use of the **StillExecuting** property to monitor the progress of a query that is expected to take more than a few seconds. By enabling RDO's asynchronous mode, control returns to the application long before the query is complete. While waiting for the **StillExecuting** property to return **False**, we display a progress bar that has been programmed to reflect the length of time that the query is expected to take. Note that if this time is exceeded, the progress bar is re-calibrated to reflect the longer duration.

```
Dim rdoCn As New rdoConnection
Dim rdoRs As rdoResultset
Dim SQL As String
Dim TimeExpected As Single
Dim Ts As Single, Tn As Single

With rdoCn
    .Connect = "UID=;PWD=;Database=WorkDB;" _
        & "Server=SEQUEL;Driver={SQL Server}" _
        & "DSN='';"
    .LoginTimeout = 5
    .EstablishConnection rdDriverNoPrompt, True

    SQL = "Execute VeryLongProcedure"
    TimeExpected = 20 ' We expect this to take 60 sec.
```

```
            Set rdoRs = .OpenResultset(Name:=SQL, _
                Type:=rdOpenForwardOnly, _
                LockType:=rdConcurReadOnly, _
                Option:=rdAsyncEnable)
        Ts = Timer
        ProgressBar1.Max = TimeExpected
        While rdoRs.StillExecuting
            Tn = Int(Timer - Ts)
            If Tn < TimeExpected Then
                ProgressBar1 = Tn
            Else
                ProgressBar1.Max = ProgressBar1.Max + 10
                TimeExpected = ProgressBar1.Max
            End If
            DoEvents
        Wend
        Status = "Query done. Duration:" & Int(Timer - Ts)

    End With
    rdoRs.Close
    rdoCn.Close
```

Stop Statement

Suspends execution.

Syntax

Stop

Remarks

You can place **Stop** statements anywhere in procedures to suspend execution. Using the **Stop** statement is similar to setting a breakpoint in the code.

The **Stop** statement suspends execution, but unlike **End**, it doesn't close any files or clear variables, unless it is in a compiled executable (.exe) file.

See Also

End Statement

Example

This example uses the **Stop** statement to suspend execution for each iteration through the **For...Next** loop.

```
Dim I
For I = 1 To 10    ' Start For...Next loop.
   Debug.Print I   ' Print I to Debug window.
   Stop            ' Stop during each iteration.
Next I
```

Str Function

Returns a **Variant** (**String**) representation of a number.

Syntax

Str(*number*)

The required *number* argument is a **Long** containing any valid numeric expression.

Remarks

When numbers are converted to strings, a leading space is always reserved for the sign of *number*. If *number* is positive, the returned string contains a leading space and the plus sign is implied.

Use the **Format** function to convert numeric values you want formatted as dates, times, or currency or in other user-defined formats. Unlike **Str**, the **Format** function doesn't include a leading space for the sign of *number*.

Note The **Str** function recognizes only the period (**.**) as a valid decimal separator. When different decimal separators may be used (for example, in international applications), use **CStr** to convert a number to a string.

See Also

Val Function, **Format** Function

Example

This example uses the **Str** function to return a string representation of a number. When a number is converted to a string, a leading space is always reserved for its sign.

```
Dim MyString
MyString = Str(459)     ' Returns " 459".
MyString = Str(-459.65) ' Returns "-459.65".
MyString = Str(459.001) ' Returns " 459.001".
```

StrComp Function

Returns a **Variant** (**Integer**) indicating the result of a string comparison.

Syntax

StrComp(*string1*, *string2*[, *compare*])

The **StrComp** function syntax has these named arguments:

Part	Description
string1	Required. Any valid string expression.
string2	Required. Any valid string expression.

(continued)

Part	Description
compare	Optional. Specifies the type of string comparison. The *compare* argument can be omitted, or it can be 0, 1 or 2. Specify **0** (default) to perform a binary comparison. Specify **1** to perform a textual comparison. For Microsoft Access only, specify **2** to perform a comparison based on information contained in your database. If *compare* is **Null**, an error occurs. If *compare* is omitted, the **Option Compare** setting determines the type of comparison.

Return Values

The **StrComp** function has the following return values:

If	StrComp returns
string1 is less than *string2*	-1
string1 is equal to *string2*	0
string1 is greater than *string2*	1
string1 or *string2* is **Null**	**Null**

See Also

Option Compare Statement, **InStr** Function

Example

This example uses the **StrComp** function to return the results of a string comparison. If the third argument is 1, a textual comparison is performed; if the third argument is 0 or omitted, a binary comparison is performed.

```
Dim MyStr1, MyStr2, MyComp
MyStr1 = "ABCD": MyStr2 = "abcd"      ' Define variables.
MyComp = StrComp(MyStr1, MyStr2, 1)   ' Returns 0.
MyComp = StrComp(MyStr1, MyStr2, 0)   ' Returns -1.
MyComp = StrComp(MyStr2, MyStr1)      ' Returns 1.
```

StrConv Function

Returns a **Variant** (**String**) converted as specified.

Syntax

StrConv(*string, conversion*)

The **StrConv** function syntax has these named arguments:

Part	Description
string	Required. String expression to be converted.
conversion	Required; **Integer**. The sum of values specifying the type of conversion to perform.

Settings

The *conversion* argument settings are:

Constant	Value	Description
vbUpperCase	1	Converts the string to uppercase characters.
vbLowerCase	2	Converts the string to lowercase characters.
vbProperCase	3	Converts the first letter of every word in string to uppercase.
vbWide*	4*	Converts narrow (single-byte) characters in string to wide (double-byte) characters.
vbNarrow*	8*	Converts wide (double-byte) characters in string to narrow (single-byte) characters.
vbKatakana**	16**	Converts Hiragana characters in string to Katakana characters.
vbHiragana**	32**	Converts Katakana characters in string to Hiragana characters.
vbUnicode	64	Converts the string to Unicode using the default code page of the system.
vbFromUnicode	128	Converts the string from Unicode to the default code page of the system.

*   Applies to Far East locales.

** Applies to Japan only.

Note These constants are specified by Visual Basic for Applications. As a result, they may be used anywhere in your code in place of the actual values. Most can be combined, for example, **vbUpperCase + vbWide**, except when they are mutually exclusive, for example, **vbUnicode + vbFromUnicode**. The constants **vbWide**, **vbNarrow**, **vbKatakana**, and **vbHiragana** cause run-time errors when used in locales where they do not apply.

The following are valid word separators for proper casing: **Null** (**Chr\$**(0)), horizontal tab (**Chr\$**(9)), linefeed (**Chr\$**(10)), vertical tab (**Chr\$**(11)), form feed (**Chr\$**(12)), carriage return (**Chr\$**(13)), space (SBCS) (**Chr\$**(32)). The actual value for a space varies by country for DBCS.

See Also

String Data Type, **Chr** Function

Stretch Property

Returns or sets a value indicating whether a graphic resizes to fit the size of an **Image** control.

Applies To

Image Control

Syntax

object.**Stretch** [= *boolean*]

The **Stretch** property syntax has these parts:

Part	Description
object	An object expression that evaluates to an object in the **Applies To** list.
boolean	A Boolean expression specifying whether the graphic resizes, as described in Settings.

Settings

The settings for *boolean* are:

Setting	Description
True	The graphic resizes to fit the control.
False	(Default) The control resizes to fit the graphic.

Remarks

If **Stretch** is set to **True**, resizing the control also resizes the graphic it contains.

See Also

Picture Property, **Image** Property

Example

This example loads an arrow icon from an icons directory into an **Image** control. The arrow crawls across the form when the **Stretch** property is set to **True** and hops across the form when **Stretch** is set to **False**. To try this example, paste the code into the Declarations section of a form that contains an Image control, a **CheckBox** control, and a **Timer** control, and then press F5 and click the form. Be sure to check the path to your icons directory and change it if necessary. To see the effects of the **Stretch** property, click the **CheckBox**, and then click the form again.

```
Dim ImgW ' Declare variable.
Private Sub Form_Load ()
    ' Load an icon into the Image control.
    Image1.Picture = LoadPicture("ICONS\ARROWS\ARW02RT.ICO")
    Image1.Left = 0' Move image to left edge.
    ImgW = Image1.Width   ' Save width of image.
    Timer1.Interval = 300
    Timer1.Enabled = False   ' Turn off timer.
    Check1.Caption = "Stretch Property"
End Sub
```

```
Private Sub Form_Click ()
   Timer1.Enabled = True' Turn on the timer.
End Sub

Private Sub Timer1_Timer ()

Static MoveIcon As Integer ' Flag for moving the icon.
   If Not MoveIcon Then
      Image1.Move Image1.Left + ImgW, Image1.Top, ImgW * 2
   Else
      ' Move the image and return it to original width.
      Image1.Move Image1.Left + ImgW, Image1.Top, ImgW
   End If
   ' If image is off edge of form, start over.
   If Image1.Left > ScaleWidth Then
      Image1.Left = 0
      Timer1.Enabled = False
   End If
   MoveIcon = Not MoveIcon ' Reset flag.
End Sub

Private Sub Check1_Click ()

Image1.Stretch = Check1.Value
End Sub
```

StrikeThrough Property

Returns or sets the font style of the **Font** object to either strikethrough or nonstrikethrough.

Applies To

Font Object

Syntax

object.**StrikeThrough** [= *boolean*]

The **StrikeThrough** property syntax has these parts:

Part	Description
object	An object expression that evaluates to an object in the **Applies To** list.
boolean	A Boolean expression specifying the font style, as described in **Settings**.

Settings

The settings for *boolean* are:

Setting	Description
True	Turns on strikethrough formatting.
False	(Default) Turns off strikethrough formatting.

Remarks

The **Font** object isn't directly available at design time. Instead you set the **StrikeThrough** property by choosing a control's **Font** property in the Properties window and clicking the Properties button. In the Font dialog box, select the Strikeout check box. At run time, however, you set **StrikeThrough** directly by specifying its setting for the **Font** object.

See Also

Bold Property, **FontTransparent** Property, **Italic** Property, **Size** Property (Font), **Underline** Property, **Weight** Property, **Name** Property

Example

This example prints text on a form with each mouse click. To try this example, paste the code into the Declarations section of a form, and then press F5 and click the form twice.

```
Private Sub Form_Click ()
   Font.Bold = Not Font.Bold  ' Toggle bold.
   Font.StrikeThrough = Not Font.StrikeThrough ' Toggle strikethrough.
   Font.Italic = Not Font.Italic      ' Toggle italic.
   Font.Underline = Not Font.Underline       ' Toggle underline.
   Font.Size = 16 ' Set Size property.
   If Font.Bold Then
      Print "Font weight is " & Font.Weight & " (bold)."
   Else
      Print "Font weight is " & Font.Weight & " (not bold)."
   End If
End Sub
```

String Data Type

There are two kinds of strings: variable-length and fixed-length strings.

- A variable-length string can contain up to approximately 2 billion (2^{31}) characters.

- A fixed-length string can contain 1 to approximately 64K (2^{16}) characters.

Note A **Public** fixed-length string can't be used in a class module.

The codes for **String** characters range from 0–255. The first 128 characters (0–127) of the character set correspond to the letters and symbols on a standard U.S. keyboard. These first 128 characters are the same as those defined by the ASCII character set. The second 128 characters (128–255) represent special characters, such as letters in international alphabets, accents, currency symbols, and fractions. The type-declaration character for **String** is the dollar sign ($).

See Also

Data Type Summary, **Variant Data** Type, **Deftype** Statements, **String** Function

String Function

Returns a **Variant** (**String**) containing a repeating character string of the length specified.

Syntax

String(*number*, *character*)

The **String** function syntax has these named arguments:

Part	Description
number	Required; **Long**. Length of the returned string. If *number* contains **Null**, **Null** is returned.
character	Required; **Variant**. Character code specifying the character or string expression whose first character is used to build the return string. If *character* contains **Null**, **Null** is returned.

Remarks

If you specify a number for *character* greater than 255, **String** converts the number to a valid character code using the formula:

character **Mod** 256

See Also

String Data Type, **Mod** Operator, **Space** Function

Example

This example uses the **String** function to return repeating character strings of the length specified.

```
Dim MyString
MyString = String(5, "*")      ' Returns "*****".
MyString = String(5, 42)       ' Returns "*****".
MyString = String(10, "ABC")   ' Returns "AAAAAAAAAA".
```

Style Property

Returns or sets a value indicating the display type and behavior of the control. Read only at run time.

Applies To

DBCombo Control, **CheckBox** Control, **ComboBox** Control, **CommandButton** Control, **ListBox** Control, **OptionButton** Control

Syntax

object.**Style**

The *object* placeholder represents an object expression that evaluates to an object in the **Applies To** list.

Settings

The **Style** property settings for the **Checkbox**, **CommandButton**, and **OptionButton** controls are:

Constant	Value	Description
vbButtonStandard	0	(Default) Standard. The control displays as it did in previous versions of Visual Basic. That is, a **Checkbox** control displays as a checkbox with a label next to it, an **OptionButton** as an option button with a label next to it, and a **CommandButton** as standard **CommandButton** without an associated graphic.
vbButtonGraphical	1	Graphical. The control displays in a graphical style. That is, a **Checkbox** control displays as a **CommandButton**-like button which can be toggled either up or down, an **OptionButton** displays as a **CommandButton**-like button which remains toggled up or down until another **OptionButton** in its option group is selected, and a **CommandButton** displays as a standard **CommandButton** that can also display an associated graphic.

The **Style** property settings for the **ComboBox** control are:

Constant	Value	Description
vbComboDropDown	0	(Default) Dropdown Combo. Includes a drop-down list and a text box. The user can select from the list or type in the text box.
vbComboSimple	1	Simple Combo. Includes a text box and a list, which doesn't drop down. The user can select from the list or type in the text box. The size of a Simple combo box includes both the edit and list portions. By default, a Simple combo box is sized so that none of the list is displayed. Increase the **Height** property to display more of the list.
vbComboDrop-DownList	2	Dropdown List. This style allows selection only from the drop-down list.

The **Style** property settings for the **ListBox** control are:

Constant	Value	Description
vbListBoxStandard	0	(Default) Standard. The **ListBox** control displays as it did in previous versions of Visual Basic; That is, as a list of text items.
vbListBoxCheckbox	1	CheckBox. The **ListBox** control displays with a checkbox next to each text item. Multiple items in the **ListBox** can be selected by selecting the checkbox beside them.

Remarks

For the **ComboBox** control, follow these guidelines in deciding which setting to choose:

- Use setting 0 (Dropdown Combo) or setting 1 (Simple Combo) to give the user a list of choices. Either style enables the user to enter a choice in the text box. Setting 0 saves space on the form because the list portion closes when the user selects an item.

- Use setting 2 (Dropdown List) to display a fixed list of choices from which the user can select one. The list portion closes when the user selects an item.

See Also

Change Event, **Click** Event, **DropDown** Event, **DblClick** Event

---

Sub Statement

Declares the name, arguments, and code that form the body of a **Sub** procedure.

Syntax

[**Private** | **Public** | **Friend**] [**Static**] **Sub** *name* [(*arglist*)]
    [*statements*]
    [**Exit Sub**]
    [*statements*]
End Sub

The **Sub** statement syntax has these parts:

Part	Description
Public	Optional. Indicates that the **Sub** procedure is accessible to all other procedures in all modules. If used in a module that contains an **Option Private** statement, the procedure is not available outside the project.
Private	Optional. Indicates that the **Sub** procedure is accessible only to other procedures in the module where it is declared.

(continued)

Part	Description
Friend	Optional. Used only in a class module. Indicates that the **Sub** procedure is visible throughout the project, but not visible to a controller of an instance of an object.
Static	Optional. Indicates that the **Sub** procedure's local variables are preserved between calls. The **Static** attribute doesn't affect variables that are declared outside the **Sub**, even if they are used in the procedure.
name	Required. Name of the **Sub**; follows standard variable naming conventions.
arglist	Optional. List of variables representing arguments that are passed to the **Sub** procedure when it is called. Multiple variables are separated by commas.
statements	Optional. Any group of statements to be executed within the **Sub** procedure.

The *arglist* argument has the following syntax and parts:

[Optional] [ByVal | ByRef] [ParamArray] *varname*[( )] **[As** *type*] **[=** *defaultvalue*]

Part	Description
Optional	Optional. Keyword indicating that an argument is not required. If used, all subsequent arguments in *arglist* must also be optional and declared using the **Optional** keyword. **Optional** can't be used for any argument if **ParamArray** is used.
ByVal	Optional. Indicates that the argument is passed by value.
ByRef	Optional. Indicates that the argument is passed by reference. **ByRef** is the default in Visual Basic.
ParamArray	Optional. Used only as the last argument in *arglist* to indicate that the final argument is an **Optional** array of **Variant** elements. The **ParamArray** keyword allows you to provide an arbitrary number of arguments. **ParamArray** can't be used with **ByVal**, **ByRef**, or **Optional**.
varname	Required. Name of the variable representing the argument; follows standard variable naming conventions.
type	Optional. Data type of the argument passed to the procedure; may be **Byte**, **Boolean**, **Integer**, **Long**, **Currency**, **Single**, **Double**, **Decimal** (not currently supported), **Date**, **String** (variable-length only), **Object**, **Variant**. If the parameter is not **Optional**, a user-defined type, or an object type may also be specified.
defaultvalue	Optional. Any constant or constant expression. Valid for **Optional** parameters only. If the type is an **Object**, an explicit default value can only be **Nothing**.

Remarks

If not explicitly specified using **Public**, **Private**, or **Friend**, **Sub** procedures are public by default. If **Static** isn't used, the value of local variables is not preserved between calls. The **Friend** keyword can only be used in class modules. However, **Friend** procedures can be accessed by procedures in any module of a project. A **Friend** procedure doesn't appear in the type library of its parent class, nor can a **Friend** procedure be late bound.

Caution **Sub** procedures can be recursive; that is, they can call themselves to perform a given task. However, recursion can lead to stack overflow. The **Static** keyword usually is not used with recursive **Sub** procedures.

All executable code must be in procedures. You can't define a **Sub** procedure inside another **Sub**, **Function**, or **Property** procedure.

The **Exit Sub** keywords cause an immediate exit from a **Sub** procedure. Program execution continues with the statement following the statement that called the **Sub** procedure. Any number of **Exit Sub** statements can appear anywhere in a **Sub** procedure.

Like a **Function** procedure, a **Sub** procedure is a separate procedure that can take arguments, perform a series of statements, and change the value of its arguments. However, unlike a **Function** procedure, which returns a value, a **Sub** procedure can't be used in an expression.

You call a **Sub** procedure using the procedure name followed by the argument list. See the **Call** statement for specific information on how to call **Sub** procedures.

Variables used in **Sub** procedures fall into two categories: those that are explicitly declared within the procedure and those that are not. Variables that are explicitly declared in a procedure (using **Dim** or the equivalent) are always local to the procedure. Variables that are used but not explicitly declared in a procedure are also local unless they are explicitly declared at some higher level outside the procedure.

Caution A procedure can use a variable that is not explicitly declared in the procedure, but a naming conflict can occur if anything you defined at the module level has the same name. If your procedure refers to an undeclared variable that has the same name as another procedure, constant or variable, it is assumed that your procedure is referring to that module-level name. To avoid this kind of conflict, explicitly declare variables. You can use an **Option Explicit** statement to force explicit declaration of variables.

Note You can't use **GoSub**, **GoTo**, or **Return** to enter or exit a **Sub** procedure.

See Also

Call Statement, **Dim** Statement, **Function** Statement, **Option Explicit** Statement, **Property Get** Statement, **Property Let** Statement, **Property Set** Statement, **AddressOf** Operator, **Friend**

Example

This example uses the **Sub** statement to define the name, arguments, and code that form the body of a **Sub** procedure.

```
' Sub procedure definition.
' Sub procedure with two arguments.
Sub SubComputeArea(Length, TheWidth)
    Dim Area As Double                  ' Declare local variable.
    If Length = 0 Or TheWidth = 0 Then
                                        ' If either argument = 0.
        Exit Sub                        ' Exit Sub immediately.
    End If
    Area = Length * TheWidth            ' Calculate area of rectangle.
    Debug.Print Area                    ' Print Area to Debug window.
End Sub
```

SupportsMnemonics Property

Returns a boolean value stating whether the control's container handles access keys for the control.

Applies To

AmbientProperties Object

Syntax

object.**SupportsMnemonics**

The **SupportsMnemonics** property syntax has this part:

Part	Description
object	An object expression that evaluates to an object in the Applies To list.

Settings

The possible Boolean return values from the **SupportsMnemonics** property are:

Setting	Description
True	The container for the control does handle access keys.
False	The container for the control does not handle access keys. If the container does not implement this ambient property, this will be the default value.

Remarks

Most containers of controls are capable of handling all the processing of access keys for the controls contained within the container. This includes figuring out which control is to be given a particular access key. If a container is not capable of processing access keys, it is indicated with this **SupportsMnemonics** property, and the control can take action, such as not displaying the underlined character as an indication of keyboard accelerators.

Switch Function

Evaluates a list of expressions and returns a **Variant** value or an expression associated with the first expression in the list that is **True**.

Syntax

Switch(*expr-1*, *value-1*[, *expr-2*, *value-2* ... [, *expr-n*,*value-n*]])

The **Switch** function syntax has these parts:

Part	Description
expr	Required. **Variant** expression you want to evaluate.
value	Required. Value or expression to be returned if the corresponding expression is **True**.

Remarks

The **Switch** function argument list consists of pairs of expressions and values. The expressions are evaluated from left to right, and the value associated with the first expression to evaluate to **True** is returned. If the parts aren't properly paired, a run-time error occurs. For example, if *expr-1* is **True**, **Switch** returns *value-1*. If *expr-1* is **False**, but *expr-2* is **True**, **Switch** returns *value-2*, and so on.

Switch returns a **Null** value if:

- None of the expressions is **True**.

- The first **True** expression has a corresponding value that is **Null**.

Switch evaluates all of the expressions, even though it returns only one of them. For this reason, you should watch for undesirable side effects. For example, if the evaluation of any expression results in a division by zero error, an error occurs.

See Also

Choose Function, **IIf** Function, **Select Case** Statement

Example

This example uses the **Switch** function to return the name of a language that matches the name of a city.

```
Function MatchUp (CityName As String)
    Matchup = Switch(CityName = "London", "English", CityName _
              = "Rome", "Italian", CityName = "Paris", "French")
End Function
```

SYD Function

Returns a **Double** specifying the sum-of-years' digits depreciation of an asset for a specified period.

Syntax

SYD(*cost*, *salvage*, *life*, *period*)

The **SYD** function has these named arguments:

Part	Description
cost	Required. **Double** specifying initial cost of the asset.
salvage	Required. **Double** specifying value of the asset at the end of its useful life.
life	Required. **Double** specifying length of the useful life of the asset.
period	Required. **Double** specifying period for which asset depreciation is calculated.

Remarks

The *life* and *period* arguments must be expressed in the same units. For example, if *life* is given in months, *period* must also be given in months. All arguments must be positive numbers.

See Also

DDB Function, **FV** Function, **IPmt** Function, **IRR** Function, **MIRR** Function, **NPer** Function, **NPV** Function, **Pmt** Function, **PPmt** Function, **PV** Function, **Rate** Function, **SLN** Function

Example

This example uses the **SYD** function to return the depreciation of an asset for a specified period given the asset's initial cost (InitCost), the salvage value at the end of the asset's useful life (SalvageVal), and the total life of the asset in years (LifeTime). The period in years for which the depreciation is calculated is PDepr.

```
Dim Fmt, InitCost, SalvageVal, MonthLife, LifeTime, DepYear, PDepr
Const YEARMONTHS = 12                  ' Number of months in a year.
Fmt = "###,##0.00"                     ' Define money format.
InitCost = InputBox("What's the initial cost of the asset?")
SalvageVal = InputBox("What's the asset's value at the end of its life?")
MonthLife = InputBox("What's the asset's useful life in months?")
Do While MonthLife < YEARMONTHS        ' Ensure period is >= 1 year.
   MsgBox "Asset life must be a year or more."
   MonthLife = InputBox("What's the asset's useful life in months?")
Loop
LifeTime = MonthLife / YEARMONTHS      ' Convert months to years.
If LifeTime <> Int(MonthLife / YEARMONTHS) Then
   LifeTime = Int(LifeTime + 1)        ' Round up to nearest year.
End If
```

```
DepYear = CInt(InputBox("For which year do you want depreciation?"))
Do While DepYear < 1 Or DepYear > LifeTime
    MsgBox "You must enter at least 1 but not more than " & LifeTime
    DepYear = CInt(InputBox("For what year do you want depreciation?"))
Loop
PDepr = SYD(InitCost, SalvageVal, LifeTime, DepYear)
MsgBox "The depreciation for year " & DepYear & " is "
↪ & Format(PDepr, Fmt) & "."
```

Synchronize Method

Synchronizes two replicas. (Microsoft Jet databases only).

Applies To

Database Object

Syntax

database.**Synchronize** *pathname*, *exchange*

The **Synchronize** method syntax has the following parts.

Part	Description
database	An object variable that represents a **Database** object that is a replica.
Pathname	A **String** that contains the path to the target replica with which *database* will be synchronized. The .mdb file name extension is optional.
Exchange	Optional. A constant indicating which direction to synchronize changes between the two databases, as specified in Settings.

Settings

You can use the following constants in the *exchange* argument. You can use one of the first three constants with or without the fourth constant.

Constant	Description
dbRepExportChanges	Sends changes from *database* to *pathname*.
DbRepImportChanges	Sends changes from *pathname* to *database*.
DbRepImpExpChanges	(Default) Sends changes from *database* to *pathname*, and vice-versa, also known as bidirectional exchange.
dbRepSyncInternet	Exchanges data between files connected by an Internet pathway.

Remarks

You use **Synchronize** to exchange data and design changes between two databases. Design changes always happen first. Both databases must be at the same design level before they can exchange data. For example, an exchange of type **dbRepExportChanges** might cause design changes at a replica even though data changes flow only from the *database* to *pathname*.

The replica identified in *pathname* must be part of the same replica set. If both replicas have the same **ReplicaID** property setting or are Design Masters for two different replica sets, the synchronization fails.

When you synchronize two replicas over the Internet, you must use the **dbRepSyncInternet** constant. In this case, you specify a Uniform Resource Locator (URL) address for the *pathname* argument instead of specifying a local area network path.

Note You can't synchronize partial replicas with other partial replicas. See the **PopulatePartial** method for more information.

Synchronization over the Internet requires the Replication Manager, which is only available in the Microsoft Office 97, Developer Edition.

Example

These four examples use the **Synchronize** method to demonstrate one-way and bi-directional exchanges of information between two members of a replica set. They will work if you have converted Northwind.mdb to a Design Master (see the **Replicable** Property), and created a replica from it. The replica name specified is Nwreplica.mdb. Change the name of the replica to fit your situation, or use the **MakeReplica** method to create a replica if you need one.

This example sends the changes from the Northwind Design Master to Nwreplica. Adjust the paths to the locations of the files on your computer.

```
Sub SendChangeToReplicaX()

    Dim dbsNorthwind As Database

    ' Opens the replicable database Northwind.mdb.
    Set dbsNorthwind = OpenDatabase("Northwind.mdb")

    ' Sends data or structural changes to the replica.
    dbsNorthwind.Synchronize "Nwreplica.mdb", _
        dbRepExportChanges

    dbsNorthwind.Close

End Sub
```

In this example, the replicable database Northwind.mdb receives changes from the replica in the path—Nwreplica. You must run this procedure from the database receiving the changes.

```
Sub ReceiveChangeX()

    Dim dbsNorthwind As Database

    Set dbsNorthwind = OpenDatabase("Northwind.mdb")

    ' Sends changes from replica to Design Master.
    dbsNorthwind.Synchronize "Nwreplica.mdb", _
        dbRepImportChanges

    dbsNorthwind.Close

End Sub
```

In this example, changes from both the replicable database Northwind and a replica are exchanged. This is the default argument for this method.

```
Sub TwoWayExchangeX()

    Dim dbsNorthwind As Database

    Set dbsNorthwind = OpenDatabase("Northwind.mdb")

    ' Sends changes made in each replica to the other.
    dbsNorthwind.Synchronize "Nwreplica.mdb", _
        dbRepImpExpChanges

    dbsNorthwind.Close

End Sub
```

The following code sample synchronizes two databases over the Internet.

```
Sub InternetSynchronizeX()

    Dim dbsTemp As Database

    Set dbsTemp = OpenDatabase("C:\Data\OrdEntry.mdb")

    ' Synchronize the local database with the replica on
    ' the Internet server.
    dbsTemp.Synchronize _
        "www.mycompany.myserver.com" _
        & "/files/Orders.mdb", _
        dbRepImpExpChanges + dbRepSyncInternet

    dbsTemp.Close

End Sub
```

SystemDB Property

Sets or returns the path for the current location of the workgroup information file (Microsoft Jet workspaces only).

Applies To

DBEngine Object

Settings and Return Values

The setting or return value is a **String** describing the fully resolved path to the workgroup information file.

Remarks

The Microsoft Jet database engine allows you to define a workgroup and set different access permissions to each object in the database for each user in the workgroup. The workgroup is defined by the workgroup information file, typically called "system.mda". For users to gain access to the secured objects in your database, DAO must have the location of this workgroup information file. The location can be identified to DAO either by specifying it in the Windows Registry or by setting the **SystemDB** property. On setup, the default setting is simply "system.mda" with no path.

For this option to have any effect, you must set the **SystemDB** property before your application initializes the **DBEngine** object (that is, before creating an instance of any other DAO object). The scope of this setting is limited to your application and can't be changed without restarting your application.

See Also

IniPath Property

Example

This example uses the **SystemDB**, **AllPermissions**, and **Permissions** properties to show how users can have different levels of permissions depending on the permissions of the group to which they belong.

```
Sub AllPermissionsX()

    ' Ensure that the Microsoft Jet workgroup information
    ' file is available.
    DBEngine.SystemDB = "system.mdw"

    Dim dbsNorthwind As Database
    Dim ctrLoop As Container

    Set dbsNorthwind = OpenDatabase("Northwind.mdb")

    ' Enumerate Containers collection and display the current
    ' user and the permissions set for that user.
    For Each ctrLoop In dbsNorthwind.Containers
        With ctrLoop
            Debug.Print "Container: " & .Name
            Debug.Print "User: " & .UserName
            Debug.Print "    Permissions: " & .Permissions
            Debug.Print "    AllPermissions: " & _
                .AllPermissions
        End With
    Next ctrLoop

    dbsNorthwind.Close

End Sub
```

Tab Function

Used with the **Print #** statement or the **Print** method to position output.

Syntax

Tab[(*n*)]

The optional *n* argument is the column number moved to before displaying or printing the next expression in a list. If omitted, **Tab** moves the insertion point to the beginning of the next print zone. This allows **Tab** to be used instead of a comma in locales where the comma is used as a decimal separator.

Remarks

If the current print position on the current line is greater than *n*, **Tab** skips to the *n*th column on the next output line. If *n* is less than 1, **Tab** moves the print position to column 1. If *n* is greater than the output line width, **Tab** calculates the next print position using the formula:

n **Mod** *width*

For example, if *width* is 80 and you specify **Tab**(90), the next print will start at column 10 (the remainder of 90/80). If *n* is less than the current print position, printing begins on the next line at the calculated print position. If the calculated print position is greater than the current print position, printing begins at the calculated print position on the same line.

The leftmost print position on an output line is always 1. When you use the **Print #** statement to print to files, the rightmost print position is the current width of the output file, which you can set using the **Width #** statement.

Note Make sure your tabular columns are wide enough to accommodate wide letters.

When you use the **Tab** function with the **Print** method, the print surface is divided into uniform, fixed-width columns. The width of each column is an average of the width of all characters in the point size for the chosen font. However, there is no correlation between the number of characters printed and the number of fixed-width columns those characters occupy. For example, the uppercase letter W occupies more than one fixed-width column and the lowercase letter i occupies less than one fixed-width column.

See Also

Print # Statement, **Spc** Function, **Width #** Statement, **Print** Method, **Mod** Operator, **Space** Function

Example

This example uses the **Tab** function to position output in a file and in the **Debug** window.

```
' The Tab function can be used with the Print # statement.
Open "TESTFILE" For Output As #1      ' Open file for output.
' The second word prints at column 20.
Print #1, "Hello"; Tab(20); "World."
' If the argument is omitted, cursor is moved to the next print zone.
Print #1, "Hello"; Tab; "World"
Close #1                              ' Close file.
```

The **Tab** function can also be used with the **Print** method. The following statement prints text starting at column 10.

```
Debug.Print Tab(10); "10 columns from start."
```

TabAcrossSplits Property

Sets or returns the behavior of the tab and arrow keys at split borders.

Applies To

DBGrid Control

Syntax

object.**TabAcrossSplits** [= *value*]

The **TabAcrossSplits** property syntax has these parts:

Part	Description
object	An object expression that evaluates to an object in the **Applies To** list.
value	A Boolean expression that determines the behavior of the tab and arrow keys at split borders, as described in Settings.

Settings

The settings for *value* are:

Setting	Description
True	Tab and arrow keys will move the current cell across split boundaries. When at the last column of the rightmost split (or the first column of the leftmost split), they will either wrap to the next row, stop, or move to other controls depending on the values of the **WrapCellPointer** and **TabAction** properties.
False	(Default) The tab and arrow keys will not move the current cell across split boundaries. They will either wrap to the next row, stop, or move to other controls depending on the values of the **WrapCellPointer** and **TabAction** properties.

Remarks

The **TabAcrossSplits** property does not determine if the tab and arrow keys will move from cell to cell, or from control to control, or wrap to the next row. Use the **AllowArrows**, **WrapCellPointer**, and **TabAction** properties to control this behavior. If the tab and arrow keys are able to move from cell to cell, this property determines whether they will move across split boundaries to adjacent splits.

See Also

AllowArrows Property, **TabAction** Property, **WrapCellPointer** Property

---

TabAction Property

Sets or returns a value that defines the behavior of the tab key.

Applies To

DBGrid Control

Syntax

object.**TabAction** [= *value*]

The **TabAction** property syntax has these parts:

Part	Description
object	An object expression that evaluates to an object in the **Applies To** list.
value	A number or constant that defines the behavior of the tab key, as described in Settings.

Settings

The settings for *value* are:

Constant	Value	Description
dbgControlNavigation	0	(Default) The tab key moves to the next or previous control on the form.
dbgColumnNavigation	1	The tab key moves the current cell to the next or previous column. However, if this action would cause the current row to change, then the next or previous control on the form receives focus.
dbgGridNavigation	2	The tab key moves the current cell to the next or previous column. The behavior of the tab key at row boundaries is determined by the **WrapCellPointer** property. When this setting is used, the tab key never results in movement to another control.

Remarks

The **TabAction** property does not determine if the tab key will cross split boundaries. Use the **TabAcrossSplits** property to control this behavior.

See Also

TabAcrossSplits Property, **WrapCellPointer** Property

TabIndex Property

Returns or sets the tab order of most objects within their parent form.

Applies To

Animation Control, **CheckBox** Control, **ComboBox** Control, **CommandButton** Control, **DBCombo** Control, **DBGrid** Control, **DBList** Control, **DirListBox** Control, **DriveListBox** Control, **FileListBox** Control, **Frame** Control, **HScrollBar, VScrollBar** Controls, **Label** Control, **ListBox** Control, **ListView** Control, **Masked Edit** Control, **MSChart** Control, **MSFlexGrid** Control, **OLE Container** Control, **OptionButton** Control, **PictureBox** Control, **ProgressBar** Control, **RichTextBox** Control, **Slider** Control, **SSTab** Control, **StatusBar** Control, **TabStrip** Control, **TextBox** Control, **Toolbar** Control, **TreeView** Control, **UpDown**Control

Syntax

object.**TabIndex** [= *index*]

The **TabIndex** property syntax has these parts:

Part	Description
object	An object expression that evaluates to an object in the **Applies To** list.
index	An integer from 0 to (*n*–1), where *n* is the number of controls on the form that have a **TabIndex** property. Assigning a **TabIndex** value of less than 0 generates an error.

Remarks

By default, Visual Basic assigns a tab order to controls as you draw them on a form, with the exception of the **Menu**, **Timer**, **Data**, **Image**, **Line** and **Shape** controls, which are not included in the tab order. At run time, invisible or disabled controls and controls that can't receive the focus (**Frame** and **Label** controls) remain in the tab order but are skipped during tabbing.

Each new control is placed last in the tab order. If you change the value of a control's **TabIndex** property to adjust the default tab order, Visual Basic automatically renumbers the **TabIndex** of other controls to reflect insertions and deletions. You can make changes at design time using the Properties window or at run time in code.

The **TabIndex** property isn't affected by the **ZOrder** method.

Note A control's tab order doesn't affect its associated access key. If you press the access key for a **Frame** or **Label** control, the focus moves to the next control in the tab order that can receive the focus.

When loading forms saved as ASCII text, controls with a **TabIndex** property that aren't listed in the form description are automatically assigned a **TabIndex** value. In subsequently loaded controls, if existing **TabIndex** values conflict with earlier assigned values, the controls are automatically assigned new values.

When you delete one or more controls, you can use the **Undo** command to restore the controls and all their properties except for the **TabIndex** property, which can't be restored. **TabIndex** is reset to the end of the tab order when you use Undo.

See Also

ZOrder Method, **TabStop** Property

Example

This example reverses the tab order of a group of buttons by changing the **TabIndex** property of a command button array. To try this example, paste the code into the Declarations section of a form that contains four **CommandButton** controls. Set the **Name** property to CommandX for each button to create the control array, and then press F5 and click the form to reverse the tab order of the buttons.

```
Private Sub Form_Click ()
    Dim I, X ' Declare variables.
    ' Reverse tab order by setting start value of X.
    If CommandX(0).TabIndex = 0 Then X = 4 Else X = 1
        For I = 0 To 3
            CommandX(I).Caption = X      ' Set caption.
            CommandX(I).TabIndex = X - 1' Set tab order.
            If CommandX(0).TabIndex = 3 Then
                X = X - 1' Decrement X.
            Else
                X = X + 1' Increment X.
            End If
        Next I
End Sub
```

Table-Type Recordset Object

A table-type **Recordset** object represents a base table you can use to add, change, or delete records from a table. Only the current record is loaded into memory. A predefined index determines the order of the records in the **Recordset** object (Microsoft Jet workspaces only).

Remarks

To create a table-type **Recordset** object, use the **OpenRecordset** method on an open **Database** object.

You can create a table-type **Recordset** object from a base table of a Microsoft Jet database, but not from an ODBC or linked table. You can use the table-type **Recordset** object with ISAM databases (like FoxPro, dBASE, or Paradox) when you open them directly.

Unlike dynaset- or snapshot-type **Recordset** objects, the table-type **Recordset** object can't refer to more than one base table, and you can't create it with an SQL statement that filters or sorts the data. Generally, when you access a table-type **Recordset** object, you specify one of the predefined indexes for the table, which orders the data returned to your application. If the table doesn't have an index, the data won't necessarily be in a particular order. If necessary, your application can create an index that returns records in a specific order. To choose a specific order for your table-type **Recordset** object, set the **Index** property to a valid index.

Also unlike dynaset- or snapshot-type **Recordset** objects, you don't need to explicitly populate table-type **Recordset** objects to obtain an accurate value for the **RecordCount** property.

To maintain data integrity, table-type **Recordset** objects are locked during the **Edit** and **Update** methods operations so that only one user can update a particular record at a time. When the Microsoft Jet database engine locks a record, it locks the entire 2K page containing the record.

Two kinds of locking are used with non-ODBC tables—pessimistic and optimistic. ODBC-accessed tables always use optimistic locking. The **LockEdits** property determines the locking conditions in effect during editing.

Properties

BOF, EOF Properties, **Bookmark** Property, **Bookmarkable** Property, **DateCreated, LastUpdated** Properties, **EditMode** Property, **Index** Property, **LastModified** Property, **LockEdits** Property, **Name** Property, **NoMatch** Property, **PercentPosition** Property, **RecordCount** Property, **Restartable** Property, **Transactions** Property, **Type** Property, **Updatable** Property, **ValidationRule** Property, **ValidationText** Property

Methods

AddNew Method, **Clone** Method, **Close** Method, **Delete** Method, **Edit** Method, **GetRows** Method, **Move** Method, **MoveFirst, MoveLast, MoveNext, MovePrevious** Methods, **OpenRecordset** Method, **Seek** Method, **Update** Method d

See Also

Dynaset-Type Recordset Object, **Index** Object, **Recordset** Object, **Snapshot-Type Recordset** Object, **Forward-Only – Type Recordset** Object

Example

This example opens a table-type **Recordset**, sets its **Index** property, and enumerates its records.

```
Sub dbOpenTableX()

    Dim dbsNorthwind As Database
    Dim rstEmployees As Recordset

    Set dbsNorthwind = OpenDatabase("Northwind.mdb")
    ' dbOpenTable is default.
    Set rstEmployees = _
        dbsNorthwind.OpenRecordset("Employees")

    With rstEmployees
        Debug.Print "Table-type recordset: " & .Name

        ' Use predefined index.
        .Index = "LastName"
        Debug.Print "   Index = " & .Index

        ' Enumerate records.
        Do While Not .EOF
            Debug.Print "        " & !LastName & ", " & _
                !FirstName
            .MoveNext
        Loop

        .Close
    End With

    dbsNorthwind.Close

End Sub
```

Table Property

Indicates the name of a **Relation** object's primary table. This should be equal to the **Name** property setting of a **TableDef** or **QueryDef** object (Microsoft Jet workspaces only).

Applies To

Relation Object

Settings and Return Values

The setting or return value is a **String** that evaluates to the name of a table in the **TableDefs** collection or query in the **QueryDefs** collection. The **Table** property setting is read/write for a new **Relation** object not yet appended to a collection and read-only for an existing **Relation** object in a **Relations** collection.

Remarks

Use the **Table** property with the **ForeignTable** property to define a **Relation** object, which represents the relationship between fields in two tables or queries. Set the **Table** property to the **Name** property setting of the primary **TableDef** or **QueryDef** object, and set the **ForeignTable** property to the **Name** property setting of the foreign (referencing) **TableDef** or **QueryDef** object. The **Attributes** property determines the type of relationship between the two objects.

For example, if you had a list of valid part codes (in a field named PartNo) stored in a ValidParts table, you could establish a one-to-many relationship with an OrderItem table such that if a part code were entered into the OrderItem table, it would have to already be in the ValidParts table. If the part code didn't exist in the ValidParts table and you had not set the **Attributes** property of the **Relation** object to **dbRelationDontEnforce**, a trappable error would occur.

In this case, the ValidParts table is the primary table, so the **Table** property of the **Relation** object would be set to ValidParts and the **ForeignTable** property of the **Relation** object would be set to OrderItem. The **Name** and **ForeignName** properties of the **Field** object in the **Relation** object's **Fields** collection would be set to PartNo.

The following illustration depicts this relation.

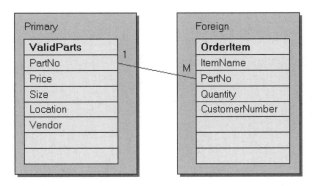

See Also

Field Object, **Attributes** Property, **ForeignTable** Property, **Name** Property

Example

This example shows how the **Table**, **ForeignTable**, and **ForeignName** properties define the terms of a **Relation** between two tables.

```
Sub ForeignNameX()

    Dim dbsNorthwind As Database
    Dim relLoop As Relation

    Set dbsNorthwind = OpenDatabase("Northwind.mdb")

    Debug.Print "Relation"
    Debug.Print "                    Table - Field"
    Debug.Print "    Primary (One)    ";
    Debug.Print ".Table - .Fields(0).Name"
    Debug.Print "    Foreign (Many)   ";
    Debug.Print ".ForeignTable - .Fields(0).ForeignName"

    ' Enumerate the Relations collection of the Northwind
    ' database to report on the property values of
    ' the Relation objects and their Field objects.
    For Each relLoop In dbsNorthwind.Relations
        With relLoop
            Debug.Print
            Debug.Print .Name & " Relation"
            Debug.Print "                    Table - Field"
            Debug.Print "    Primary (One)    ";
            Debug.Print .Table & " - " & .Fields(0).Name
            Debug.Print "    Foreign (Many)   ";
            Debug.Print .ForeignTable & " - " & _
                .Fields(0).ForeignName
        End With
    Next relLoop

    dbsNorthwind.Close

End Sub
```

TableDef Object

A **TableDef** object represents the stored definition of a base table or a linked table (Microsoft Jet workspaces only).

Remarks

You manipulate a table definition using a **TableDef** object and its methods and properties. For example, you can:

- Examine the field and index structure of any local, linked, or external table in a database.

- Use the **Connect** and **SourceTableName** properties to set or return information about linked tables, and use the **RefreshLink** method to update connections to linked tables.

- Use the **ValidationRule** and **ValidationText** properties to set or return validation conditions.

- Use the **OpenRecordset** method to create a table-, dynaset-, dynamic-, snapshot-, or forward-only–type **Recordset** object, based on the table definition.

For base tables, the **RecordCount** property contains the number of records in the specified database table. For linked tables, the **RecordCount** property setting is always -1.

To create a new **TableDef** object, use the **CreateTableDef** method.

▶ To add a field to a table

1 Make sure any **Recordset** objects based on the table are all closed.

2 Use the **CreateField** method to create a **Field** object variable and set its properties.

3 Use the **Append** method to add the **Field** object to the **Fields** collection of the **TableDef** object.

You can delete a **Field** object from a **TableDefs** collection if it doesn't have any indexes assigned to it, but you will lose the field's data.

▶ **To create a table that is ready for new records in a database**

1 Use the **CreateTableDef** method to create a **TableDef** object.

2 Set its properties.

3 For each field in the table, use the **CreateField** method to create a **Field** object variable and set its properties.

4 Use the **Append** method to add the fields to the **Fields** collection of the **TableDef** object.

5 Use the **Append** method to add the new **TableDef** object to the **TableDefs** collection of the **Database** object.

A linked table is connected to the database by the **SourceTableName** and **Connect** properties of the **TableDef** object.

▶ **To link a table to a database**

1 Use the **CreateTableDef** method to create a **TableDef** object.

2 Set its **Connect** and **SourceTableName** properties (and optionally, its **Attributes** property).

3 Use the **Append** method to add it to the **TableDefs** collection of a **Database**.

To refer to a **TableDef** object in a collection by its ordinal number or by its **Name** property setting, use any of the following syntax forms:

TableDefs(0)
TableDefs("*name*")
TableDefs![*name*]

Properties

Attributes Property, **ConflictTable** Property, **Connect** Property, **DateCreated, LastUpdated** Properties, **Name** Property, **RecordCount** Property, **SourceTableName** Property, **Updatable** Property, **ValidationRule** Property, **ValidationText** Property, **KeepLocal** Property, **Replicable** Property, **ReplicaFilter** Property

Methods

CreateField Method, **CreateIndex** Method, **CreateProperty** Method, **OpenRecordset** Method, **RefreshLink** Method

See Also

Index Object, **Indexes Collection** Summary, **Property** Object, **Properties Collection** Summary, **CreateTableDef** Method

Example

This example creates a new **TableDef** object and appends it to the **TableDefs** collection of the Northwind **Database** object. It then enumerates the **TableDefs** collection and the **Properties** collection of the new **TableDef**.

```
Sub TableDefX()

    Dim dbsNorthwind As Database
    Dim tdfNew As TableDef
    Dim tdfLoop As TableDef
    Dim prpLoop As Property

    Set dbsNorthwind = OpenDatabase("Northwind.mdb")

    ' Create new TableDef object, append Field objects
    ' to its Fields collection, and append TableDef
    ' object to the TableDefs collection of the
    ' Database object.
    Set tdfNew = dbsNorthwind.CreateTableDef("NewTableDef")
    tdfNew.Fields.Append tdfNew.CreateField("Date", dbDate)
    dbsNorthwind.TableDefs.Append tdfNew

    With dbsNorthwind
        Debug.Print .TableDefs.Count & _
            " TableDefs in " & .Name

        ' Enumerate TableDefs collection.
        For Each tdfLoop In .TableDefs
            Debug.Print "      " & tdfLoop.Name
        Next tdfLoop

        With tdfNew
            Debug.Print "Properties of " & .Name

            ' Enumerate Properties collection of new
            ' TableDef object, only printing properties
            ' with non-empty values.
            For Each prpLoop In .Properties
                Debug.Print "    " & prpLoop.Name & " - " & _
                    IIf(prpLoop = "", "[empty]", prpLoop)
            Next prpLoop

        End With

        ' Delete new TableDef since this is a
        ' demonstration.
        .TableDefs.Delete tdfNew.Name
        .Close
    End With

End Sub
```

TableDefs Collection

A **TableDefs** collection contains all stored **TableDef** objects in a database (Microsoft Jet workspaces only).

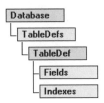

Remarks

You manipulate a table definition using a **TableDef** object and its methods and properties.

The default collection of a **Database** object is the **TableDefs** collection.

To refer to a **TableDef** object in a collection by its ordinal number or by its **Name** property setting, use any of the following syntax forms:

TableDefs(0)
TableDefs("*name*")
TableDefs![*name*]

Properties

Count Property

Methods

Append Method, **Delete** Method, **Refresh** Method

Example

This example creates a new **TableDef** object and appends it to the **TableDefs** collection of the Northwind **Database** object. It then enumerates the **TableDefs** collection and the **Properties** collection of the new **TableDef**.

```
Sub TableDefX()

    Dim dbsNorthwind As Database
    Dim tdfNew As TableDef
    Dim tdfLoop As TableDef
    Dim prpLoop As Property

    Set dbsNorthwind = OpenDatabase("Northwind.mdb")
```

```
' Create new TableDef object, append Field objects
' to its Fields collection, and append TableDef
' object to the TableDefs collection of the
' Database object.
Set tdfNew = dbsNorthwind.CreateTableDef("NewTableDef")
tdfNew.Fields.Append tdfNew.CreateField("Date", dbDate)
dbsNorthwind.TableDefs.Append tdfNew

With dbsNorthwind
    Debug.Print .TableDefs.Count & _
       " TableDefs in " & .Name

    ' Enumerate TableDefs collection.
    For Each tdfLoop In .TableDefs
        Debug.Print "    " & tdfLoop.Name
    Next tdfLoop

    With tdfNew
        Debug.Print "Properties of " & .Name

        ' Enumerate Properties collection of new
        ' TableDef object, only printing properties
        ' with non-empty values.
        For Each prpLoop In .Properties
            Debug.Print "    " & prpLoop.Name & " - " & _
                IIf(prpLoop = "", "[empty]", prpLoop)
        Next prpLoop

    End With

    ' Delete new TableDef since this is a
    ' demonstration.
    .TableDefs.Delete tdfNew.Name
    .Close
End With

End Sub
```

TabStop Property

Returns or sets a value indicating whether a user can use the TAB key to give the focus to an object.

Applies To

Animation Control, **CheckBox** Control, **ComboBox** Control, **CommandButton** Control, **DBCombo** Control, **DBGrid** Control, **DBList** Control, **DirListBox** Control, **DriveListBox** Control, **FileListBox** Control, **Frame** Control, **HScrollBar,** **VScrollBar** Controls, **ListBox** Control, **ListView** Control, **Masked Edit** Control, **MSChart** Control, **MSFlexGrid** Control, **OLE Container** Control, **OptionButton**

Control, **PictureBox** Control, **ProgressBar** Control, **RichTextBox** Control, **Slider** Control, **SSTab** Control, **StatusBar** Control, **TabStrip** Control, **TextBox** Control, **Toolbar** Control, **TreeView** Control, **UpDown**Control

Syntax

object.**TabStop** [= *boolean*]

The **TabStop** property syntax has these parts:

Part	Description
object	An object expression that evaluates to an object in the **Applies To** list.
boolean	A Boolean expression specifying whether the object is a tab stop, as described in Settings.

Settings

The settings for *boolean* are:

Setting	Description
True	(Default) Designates the object as a tab stop.
False	Bypasses the object when the user is tabbing, although the object still holds its place in the actual tab order, as determined by the **TabIndex** property.

Remarks

This property enables you to add or remove a control from the tab order on a form. For example, if you're using a **PictureBox** control to draw a graphic, set its **TabStop** property to **False**, so the user can't tab to the **PictureBox**.

See Also

TabIndex Property

Tag Property

Returns or sets an expression that stores any extra data needed for your program. Unlike other properties, the value of the **Tag** property isn't used by Visual Basic; you can use this property to identify objects.

Applies To

CheckBox Control, **ComboBox** Control, **CommandButton** Control, **CommonDialog** Control, **Data** Control, **DBCombo** Control, **DBGrid** Control, **DBList** Control, **DirListBox** Control, **DriveListBox** Control, **FileListBox** Control, **Form** Object, **Forms** Collection, **Frame** Control, **HScrollBar, VScrollBar** Controls, **Image** Control, **Label** Control, **Line** Control, **ListBox** Control, **MDIForm** Object, **Menu** Control, **MSChart** Control, **OLE Container** Control, **OLEObject** Object, **OptionButton** Control, **PictureBox** Control, **PropertyPage** Object, **RemoteData** Control, **Shape** Control, **TextBox** Control, **Timer** Control, **UserControl** Object, **UserDocument** Object

Syntax

object.**Tag** [= *expression*]

The **Tag** property syntax has these parts:

Part	Description
object	An object expression that evaluates to an object in the **Applies To** list.
expression	A string expression identifying the object. The default is a zero-length string ("").

Remarks

You can use this property to assign an identification string to an object without affecting any of its other property settings or causing side effects. The **Tag** property is useful when you need to check the identity of a control or **MDIForm** object that is passed as a variable to a procedure.

Tip When you create a new instance of a form, assign a unique value to the **Tag** property.

See Also

Name Property

Example

This example displays a unique icon for each control being dragged. To try this example, paste the code into the Declarations section of a form that contains three **PictureBox** controls. Set the **DragMode** property to 1 for Picture1 and Picture2, and then press F5. Use the mouse to drag Picture1 or Picture2 over Picture3 controls.

```
Private Sub Form_Load ()
    Picture1.Tag = "ICONS\ARROWS\POINT03.ICO"
    Picture2.Tag = "ICONS\ARROWS\POINT04.ICO"
End Sub
Private Sub Picture3_DragOver (Source As Control, X As Single, Y As Single, State As
Integer)
    If State = vbEnter Then
        ' Select based on each PictureBox's Name property.
        Select Case Source.Name
        Case "Picture1"
            ' Load icon for Picture1.
            Source.DragIcon = LoadPicture(Picture1.Tag)          Case "Picture2"
            ' Load icon for Picture2.

Source.DragIcon = LoadPicture(Picture2.Tag)
        End Select
    ElseIf State = vbLeave Then
        ' When source isn't over Picture3, unload icon.
        Source.DragIcon = LoadPicture ()
    End If
End Sub
```

Tan Function

Returns a **Double** specifying the tangent of an angle.

Syntax

Tan(*number*)

The required *number* argument is a **Double** or any valid numeric expression that expresses an angle in radians.

Remarks

Tan takes an angle and returns the ratio of two sides of a right triangle. The ratio is the length of the side opposite the angle divided by the length of the side adjacent to the angle.

To convert degrees to radians, multiply degrees by pi/180. To convert radians to degrees, multiply radians by 180/pi.

See Also

Math Functions, **Atn** Function, **Cos** Function, **Sin** Function, **Derived Math** Functions

Example

This example uses the **Tan** function to return the tangent of an angle.

```
Dim MyAngle, MyCotangent
MyAngle = 1.3                         ' Define angle in radians.
MyCotangent = 1 / Tan(MyAngle)        ' Calculate cotangent.
```

TaskVisible Property

Returns or sets a value that determines if the application appears in the Windows task list.

Applies To

App Object

Syntax

object.**TaskVisible** [= *boolean*]

The **TaskVisible** property syntax has these parts:

Part	Description
object	An object expression that evaluates to an object in the **Applies To** list.
boolean	A Boolean expression that determines if the application appears in the task list, as described in **Settings**.

Settings

The settings for *boolean* are:

Setting	Description
True	(Default) The application appears in the Windows task list.
False	The application does not appear in the Windows task list.

Remarks

The **TaskVisible** property can only be set to **False** in applications that do not display an interface, such as ActiveX components that do not contain or display **Form** objects. While the application displays an interface, the **TaskVisible** property is automatically set to **True**.

See Also

ShowInTaskbar Property

TemplatePath Property

Returns the full pathname where Visual Basic stores template files.

Applies To

VBE Object

Syntax

object.**TemplatePath**

The *object* placeholder represents an object expression that evaluates to an object in the **Applies To** list.

Terminate Event

Occurs when all references to an instance of a **Form**, **MDIForm**, **User** control, **Property Page**, or class are removed from memory by setting all the variables that refer to the object to **Nothing** or when the last reference to the object falls out of scope.

Applies To

PropertyPage Object, **UserControl** Object, **UserDocument** Object, **Form** Object, **Forms** Collection, **MDIForm Object** Syntax

Private Sub *object*_**Terminate( )**

The *object* placeholder represents an object expression that evaluates to an object in the **Applies To** list.

Remarks

For all objects except classes, the Terminate event occurs after the Unload event.

The Terminate event isn't triggered if the instances of the form or class were removed from memory because the application terminated abnormally. For example, if your application invokes the **End** statement before removing all existing instances of the class or form from memory, the Terminate event isn't triggered for that class or form.

See Also

QueryUnload Event, **Unload** Event, **Initialize** Event

Text Property

- **ComboBox** control (**Style** property set to 0 [**Dropdown** Combo] or to 1 [Simple Combo]) and **TextBox** control—returns or sets the text contained in the edit area.

- **ComboBox** control (**Style** property set to 2 [**Dropdown** List]) and **ListBox** control—returns the selected item in the list box; the value returned is always equivalent to the value returned by the expression `List(ListIndex)`. Read-only at design time; read-only at run time.

Applies To

ComboBox Control, **ListBox** Control, **TextBox** Control

Syntax

*object.***Text** [= *string*]

The **Text** property syntax has these parts:

Part	Description
object	An object expression that evaluates to an object in the **Applies To** list.
string	A string expression specifying text.

Remarks

At design time only, the defaults for the **Text** property are:

- **ComboBox** and **TextBox** controls—the control's **Name** property.

- **ListBox** control—a zero-length string ("").

For a **ComboBox** with the **Style** property set to 0 (**Dropdown** Combo) or to 1 (Simple Combo) or for a **TextBox**, this property is useful for reading the actual string contained in the edit area of the control. For a **ComboBox** or **ListBox** control with the **Style** property set to 2 (**Dropdown** List), you can use the **Text** property to determine the currently selected item.

The **Text** setting for a **TextBox** control is limited to 2048 characters unless the **MultiLine** property is **True**, in which case the limit is about 32K.

Value Property, **SelLength**, **SelStart**, **SelText** Properties

Example

This example illustrates the **Text** property. To try this example, paste the code into the Declarations section of a form that contains three **TextBox** controls and a **CommandButton** control, and then press F5 and enter text in Text1.

```
Private Sub Text1_Change ()
    Text2.Text = LCase(Text1.Text)     ' Display text as lowercase.
    Text3.Text = UCase(Text1.Text)     ' Display text as uppercase.
End Sub

Private Sub Command1_Click ()          ' Delete text.
    Text1.Text = ""
End Sub
```

TextAlign Property

Returns an enumerated value of type **TextAlignChoices** stating what kind of text alignment the container would like the control to do.

Applies To

AmbientProperties Object

Syntax

object.**TextAlign**

The **TextAlign** property syntax has this part:

Part	Description
object	An object expression that evaluates to an object in the **Applies To** list.

Settings

The possible enumerated return values from the **TextAlign** property are:

Setting	Description
0-General	General alignment: text to the left, numbers to the right. If the container does not implement this ambient property, this will be the default value.
1-Left	Align to the left.
2-Center	Align in the center.
3-Right	Align to the right.
4-FillJustify	Fill justify.

Remarks

This ambient property is the way that a container communicates to a contained control how to perform justification; this is a hint from the container that the control may or may not choose to follow.

TextBox Control

A **TextBox** control, sometimes called an edit field or edit control, displays information entered at design time, entered by the user, or assigned to the control in code at run time.

Syntax

TextBox

Remarks

To display multiple lines of text in a **TextBox** control, set the **MultiLine** property to **True**. If a multiple-line **TextBox** doesn't have a horizontal scroll bar, text wraps automatically even when the **TextBox** is resized. To customize the scroll bar combination on a **TextBox**, set the **ScrollBars** property.

Scroll bars will always appear on the **TextBox** when its **MultiLine** property is set to **True**, and its **ScrollBars** property is set to anything except **None** (0).

If you set the **MultiLine** property to **True**, you can use the **Alignment** property to set the alignment of text within the **TextBox**. The text is left-justified by default. If the **MultiLine** property is **False**, setting the **Alignment** property has no effect.

A **TextBox** control can also act as a destination link in a DDE conversation.

Properties

Alignment Property, **Appearance** Property, **BackColor, ForeColor** Properties, **BorderStyle** Property, **Container** Property, **DataChanged** Property, **DataField** Property, **DataSource** Property, **DragIcon** Property, **DragMode** Property, **Enabled** Property, **Font** Property, **FontBold, FontItalic, FontStrikethru, FontUnderline** Properties, **FontName** Property, **FontSize** Property, **Height, Width** Properties, **HelpContextID** Property, **Hides Selection** Property, **hWnd** Property, **Index** Property, **Left, Top** Properties, **LinkItem** Property, **LinkMode** Property, **LinkTimeout** Property, **LinkTopic** Property, **Locked** Property, **MaxLength** Property, **MouseIcon** Property, **MousePointer** Property, **MultiLine** Property, **Name** Property, **OLEDragMode** Property, **OLEDropMode** Property, **Parent** Property, **PasswordChar** Property, **ScrollBars** Property, **SelLength, SelStart, SelText** Properties, **TabIndex** Property, **TabStop** Property, **Tag** Property, **Text** Property, **ToolTipText** Property, **Visible** Property, **WhatsThisHelpID** Property

Methods

Refresh Method, **SetFocus** Method, **Drag** Method, **LinkExecute** Method, **LinkPoke** Method, **LinkRequest** Method, **LinkSend** Method, **Move** Method, **ZOrder** Method, **OLEDrag** Method, **ShowWhatsThis** Method

See Also

Alignment Property, **MultiLine** Property, **ScrollBars** Property

TextHeight Method

Returns the height of a text string as it would be printed in the current font of a **Form**, **PictureBox**, or **Printer**. Doesn't support named arguments.

Applies To

PropertyPage Object, **UserControl** Object, **UserDocument** Object, **Printer Object**, **Printers** Collection, **Form Object**, **Forms** Collection, **PictureBox** Control

Syntax

object.**TextHeight**(*string*)

The **TextHeight** method syntax has these parts:

Part	Description
object	Optional. An object expression that evaluates to an object in the Applies To list. If *object* is omitted, the **Form** object with the focus is assumed to be *object*.
String	Required. A string expression that evaluates to a string for which the text height is determined. Parentheses must enclose the string expression.

Remarks

The height is expressed in terms of the **ScaleMode** property setting or **Scale** method coordinate system in effect for *object*. Use **TextHeight** to determine the amount of vertical space required to display the text. The height returned includes the normal leading space above and below the text, so you can use the height to calculate and position multiple lines of text within *object*.

If *string* contains embedded carriage returns, **TextHeight** returns the cumulative height of the lines, including the leading space above and below each line.

See Also

Scale Method, **TextWidth** Method, **FontSize** Property, **ScaleMode** Property

Example

The **TextWidth** method is used to center a line of text horizontally on a form. To try this example, paste the code into the Declarations section of a form, and then press F5 and click the form.

```
Private Sub Form_Click ()
    Dim HalfHeight, HalfWidth, Msg        ' Declare variables.
    AutoRedraw = -1                       ' Turn on AutoRedraw.
    BackColor = QBColor(4)                ' Set background color.
    ForeColor = QBColor(15)               ' Set foreground color.
    Msg = "Visual Basic"                  ' Create message.
    FontSize = 48                         ' Set font size.
    HalfWidth = TextWidth(Msg) / 2        ' Calculate one-half width.
    HalfHeight = TextHeight(Msg) / 2      ' Calculate one-half height.
    CurrentX = ScaleWidth / 2 - HalfWidth     ' Set X.
    CurrentY = ScaleHeight / 2 - HalfHeight   ' Set Y.
    Print Msg                             ' Print message.
End Sub
```

TextWidth Method

Returns the width of a text string as it would be printed in the current font of a **Form**, **PictureBox**, or **Printer**. Doesn't support named arguments.

Applies To

PropertyPage Object, **UserControl** Object, **UserDocument** Object, **Printer** Object, **Printers** Collection, **Form** Object, **Forms** Collection, **PictureBox** Control

Syntax

object.**TextWidth**(*string*)

The **TextWidth** method syntax has these parts:

Part	Description
object	Optional. An object expression that evaluates to an object in the **Applies To** list. If *object* is omitted, the **Form** with the focus is assumed to be *object*.
String	Required. A string expression that evaluates to a string for which the text width is determined. Parentheses must surround the string expression.

Remarks

The width is expressed in terms of the **ScaleMode** property setting or **Scale** method coordinate system in effect for *object*. Use **TextWidth** to determine the amount of horizontal space required to display the text. If *string* contains embedded carriage returns, **TextWidth** returns the width of the longest line.

See Also

Scale Method, **TextHeight** Method, **FontSize** Property, **ScaleMode** Property

Example

The **TextWidth** method is used to center a line of text horizontally on a form. To try this example, paste the code into the Declarations section of a form, and then press F5 and click the form.

```
Private Sub Form_Click ()
    Dim HalfHeight, HalfWidth, Msg    ' Declare variables.
    AutoRedraw = -1' Turn on AutoRedraw.
    BackColor = QBColor(4)                ' Set background color.
    ForeColor = QBColor(15)               ' Set foreground color.
    Msg = "Visual Basic"                  ' Create message.
    FontSize = 48                         ' Set font size.
    HalfWidth = TextWidth(Msg) / 2      ' Calculate one-half width.
    HalfHeight = TextHeight(Msg) / 2    ' Calculate one-half height.
    CurrentX = ScaleWidth / 2 - HalfWidth      ' Set X.
    CurrentY = ScaleHeight / 2 - HalfHeight    ' Set Y.
    Print Msg                             ' Print message.
End Sub
```

ThreadID Property

Returns the Win32 ID of the executing thread. (Used for Win32 API calls.)

Applies To

App Object

Syntax

object.**ThreadID**

The *object* placeholder represents an object expression that evaluates to an object in the **Applies To** list.

Return Type

Long

Time Function

Returns a **Variant** (**Date**) indicating the current system time.

Syntax

Time

Remarks

To set the system time, use the **Time** statement.

See Also

Date Function, **Date** Statement, **Time** Statement, **Timer** Function

Example

This example uses the **Time** function to return the current system time.

```
Dim MyTime
MyTime = Time    ' Return current system time.
```

Time Statement

Sets the system time.

Syntax

Time = *time*

The required *time* argument is any numeric expression, string expression, or any combination, that can represent a time.

Remarks

If *time* is a string, **Time** attempts to convert it to a time using the time separators you specified for your system. If it can't be converted to a valid time, an error occurs.

See Also

Date Function, **Date** Statement, **Time** Function

Example

This example uses the **Time** statement to set the computer system time to a user-defined time.

```
Dim MyTime
MyTime = #4:35:17 PM#    ' Assign a time.
Time = MyTime            ' Set system time to MyTime.
```

Timer Control

A **Timer** control can execute code at regular intervals by causing a Timer event to occur.

Syntax

Timer

Remarks

The **Timer** control, invisible to the user, is useful for background processing.

You can't set the **Enabled** property of a **Timer** for a multiple selection of controls other than **Timer** controls.

There is no practical limit on the number of active timer controls you can have in Visual Basic 5.0 running under Windows 95 or Windows NT.

Properties

Interval Property, **Left, Top** Properties, **Tag** Property, **Enabled** Property, **Index** Property (Control Array), **Name** Property, **Parent** Property

See Also

Timer Event, **Enabled** Property

Timer Event

Occurs when a preset interval for a **Timer** control has elapsed. The interval's frequency is stored in the control's **Interval** property, which specifies the length of time in milliseconds.

Applies To

Timer Control

Syntax

Private Sub *object*_**Timer**([*index* **As Integer**])

The **Timer** event syntax has these parts:

Part	Description
object	An object expression that evaluates to an object in the **Applies To** list.
index	An integer that uniquely identifies a control if it's in a control array.

Remarks

Use this event procedure to tell Visual Basic what to do after each **Timer** control interval has elapsed. When you're working with the Timer event:

- The **Interval** property specifies the interval between Timer events in milliseconds.

- Whenever the **Timer** control's **Enabled** property is set to **True** and the **Interval** property is greater than 0, the Timer event waits for the period specified in the **Interval** property.

See Also

Interval Property, **Enabled** Property

Example

This example demonstrates a digital clock. To try this example, paste the code into the Declarations section of a form that contains a **Label** control and a **Timer** control, and then press F5.

```
Private Sub Form_Load ()
   Timer1.Interval = 1000   ' Set Timer interval.
End Sub

Private Sub Timer1_Timer ()
   Label1.Caption = Time' Update time display.
End Sub
```

This example moves a **PictureBox** control across a form. To try this example, paste the code into the Declarations section of a form that contains a **Timer** control and a **PictureBox** control, and then press F5. For a better visual effect you can assign a bitmap to the **PictureBox** using the **Picture** property.

```
Dim DeltaX, DeltaY As Integer ' Declare variables.
Private Sub Timer1_Timer ()
   Picture1.Move Picture1.Left + DeltaX, Picture1.Top + DeltaY
   If Picture1.Left < ScaleLeft Then DeltaX = 100
   If Picture1.Left + Picture1.Width > ScaleWidth + ScaleLeft Then
      DeltaX = -100
   End If
   If Picture1.Top < ScaleTop Then DeltaY = 100
   If Picture1.Top + Picture1.Height > ScaleHeight + ScaleTop Then
      DeltaY = -100
   End If
End Sub

Private Sub Form_Load ()

Timer1.Interval = 1000   ' Set Interval.
   DeltaX = 100' Initialize variables.
   DeltaY = 100
End Sub
```

Timer Function

Returns a **Single** representing the number of seconds elapsed since midnight.

Syntax

Timer

See Also

Time Function, **Randomize** Statement

Example

This example uses the **Timer** function to pause the application. The example also uses **DoEvents** to yield to other processes during the pause.

```
Dim PauseTime, Start, Finish, TotalTime
If (MsgBox("Press Yes to pause for 5 seconds", 4)) = vbYes Then
    PauseTime = 5               ' Set duration.
    Start = Timer               ' Set start time.
    Do While Timer < Start + PauseTime
        DoEvents                ' Yield to other processes.
    Loop
    Finish = Timer              ' Set end time.
    TotalTime = Finish - Start  ' Calculate total time.
    MsgBox "Paused for " & TotalTime & " seconds"
Else
    End
End If
```

TimeSerial Function

Returns a **Variant** (**Date**) containing the time for a specific hour, minute, and second.

Syntax

TimeSerial(*hour, minute, second*)

The **TimeSerial** function syntax has these named arguments:

Part	Description
hour	Required; **Variant** (**Integer**). Number between 0 (12:00 A.M.) and 23 (11:00 P.M.), inclusive, or a numeric expression.
minute	Required; **Variant** (**Integer**). Any numeric expression.
second	Required; **Variant** (**Integer**). Any numeric expression.

Remarks

To specify a time, such as 11:59:59, the range of numbers for each **TimeSerial** argument should be in the normal range for the unit; that is, 0–23 for hours and 0–59 for minutes and seconds. However, you can also specify relative times for each argument using any numeric expression that represents some number of hours, minutes, or seconds before or after a certain time. The following example uses expressions instead of absolute time numbers. The **TimeSerial** function returns a time for 15 minutes before (-15) six hours before noon (12 - 6), or 5:45:00 A.M.

```
TimeSerial(12 - 6, -15, 0)
```

When any argument exceeds the normal range for that argument, it increments to the next larger unit as appropriate. For example, if you specify 75 minutes, it is evaluated as one hour and 15 minutes. If any single argument is outside the range -32,768 to 32,767, an error occurs. If the time specified by the three arguments causes the date to fall outside the acceptable range of dates, an error occurs.

See Also

DateSerial Function, **DateValue** Function, **Hour** Function, **Minute** Function, **Now** Function, **Second** Function, **TimeValue** Function

Example

This example uses the **TimeSerial** function to return a time for the specified hour, minute, and second.

```
Dim MyTime
MyTime = TimeSerial(16, 35, 17)     ' MyTime contains serial
                                    ' representation of 4:35:17 PM.
```

TimeValue Function

Returns a **Variant** (**Date**) containing the time.

Syntax

TimeValue(*time*)

The required *time* argument is normally a string expression representing a time from 0:00:00 (12:00:00 A.M.) to 23:59:59 (11:59:59 P.M.), inclusive. However, *time* can also be any expression that represents a time in that range. If *time* contains **Null**, **Null** is returned.

Remarks

You can enter valid times using a 12-hour or 24-hour clock. For example, "2:24PM" and "14:24" are both valid *time* arguments.

If the *time* argument contains date information, **TimeValue** doesn't return it. However, if *time* includes invalid date information, an error occurs.

DateSerial Function, **DateValue** Function, **Hour** Function, **Minute** Function, **Now** Function, **Second** Function, **TimeSerial** Function

Example

This example uses the **TimeValue** function to convert a string to a time. You can also use date literals to directly assign a time to a **Variant** or **Date** variable, for example, MyTime = #4:35:17 PM#.

```
Dim MyTime
MyTime = TimeValue("4:35:17 PM")        ' Return a time.
```

Title Property

Returns or sets the title of the application that is displayed in the Microsoft Windows Task List. If changed at run time, changes aren't saved with the application.

Applies To

App Object

Syntax

object.**Title** [= *value*]

The **Title** property syntax has these parts:

Part	Description
object	An object expression that evaluates to an object in the **Applies To** list.
value	A string expression specifying the title of the application. The maximum length of *value* is 40 characters. In DBCS (double-byte character set) systems, this means the maximum length is 40 bytes.

Remarks

This property is available at design time in the dialog box for the Project Properties command on the Project menu.

See Also

Caption Property

ToolboxBitmap Property

Returns or sets a bitmap that will be used as the picture representation of the control in the toolbox. The size of the space for the bitmap in the toolbox is 16x15 pixels; the bitmap specified by this property will be scaled to these **dimensions** if necessary. The **ToolboxBitmap** property is read/write at the control's authoring time, and not available at the control's run time.

Applies To

UserControl Object

Remarks

Important   Do not assign an icon to the **ToolboxBitmap** property. Icons do not scale well to Toolbox bitmap size.

Visual Basic automatically uses the class name of the control as the tool tip text when users hover the mouse pointer over the icon in the Toolbox.

Tip   When creating bitmaps, remember that for many forms of color-blindness, colors with the same overall level of brightness will appear to be the same. You can avoid this by restricting the bitmap to white, black, and shades of gray, or by careful color selection.

ToolTipText Property

Returns or sets a **ToolTip**.

Applies To

Animation Control, **Button** Object, **CheckBox** Control, **ComboBox** Control, **CommandButton** Control, **Data** Control, **DBCombo** Control, **DBGrid** Control, **DBList** Control, **DirListBox** Control, **DriveListBox** Control, **FileListBox** Control, **Frame** Control, **Image** Control, **Label** Control, **ListBox** Control, **ListView** Control, **MaskedEdit** Control, **MSChart** Control, **MSFlexGrid** Control, **Multimedia MCI** Control, **OptionButton** Control, **Panel** Control, **PictureBox** Control, **ProgressBar** Control, **RemoteData** Control, **RichTextBox** Control, **Slider** Control, **SSTab** Control, **StatusBar** Control, **Tab** Control, **Object** Control, **TabStrip** Control, **TextBox** Control, **Toolbar** Control, **TreeView** Control, **UpDown** Control

Syntax

object.**ToolTipText** [= *string*]

The **ToolTipText** property syntax has these parts:

Part	Description
object	An object expression that evaluates to an object in the **Applies To** list.
string	A string associated with an object in the **Applies To** list. that appears in a small rectangle below the object when the user's cursor hovers over the object at run time for about one second.

Remarks

If you use only an image to label an object, you can use this property to explain each object with a few words.

At design time you can set the **ToolTipText** property string in the control's properties dialog box.

For the **Toolbar** and **TabStrip** controls, you must set the **ShowTips** property to True to display **ToolTips**.

Specifics

ToolTipText Property

Top Property

Returns or sets a **Single** specifying the location of the top of the window on the screen in twips. Read/write.

Applies to

Window Object

Remarks

The value returned by the **Top** property depends on whether or not the window is docked, linked, or in docking view.

Note Changing the **Top** property setting of a linked or docked window has no effect as long as the window remains linked or docked.

See Also

Height Property, **Left** Property, **Width** Property

TopIndex Property

Returns or sets a value that specifies which item in a **ComboBox, DirListBox, DriveListBox, FileListBox,** or **ListBox** control is displayed in the topmost position. Not available at design time.

Applies To

ComboBox Control, **DirListBox** Control, **DriveListBox** Control, **FileListBox** Control, **ListBox** Control

Syntax

object.**TopIndex** [= *value*]

The **TopIndex** property syntax has these parts:

Part	Description
object	An object expression that evaluates to an object in the **Applies To** list.
value	The number of the list item that is displayed in the topmost position. The default is 0, or the first item in the list.

Remarks

Use this property to scroll through a control without selecting an item.

If the **Columns** property is set to 0 for the **ListBox** control, the item is displayed at the topmost position if there are enough items below it to fill the visible portion of the list.

If the **Columns** property setting is greater than 0 for the **ListBox** control, the item's column moves to the leftmost position without changing its position within the column.

See Also

AddItem Method, **Clear** Method (Clipboard, ComboBox, ListBox), **RemoveItem** Method, **List** Property, **ListCount** Property, **Columns** Property (ListBox), **MultiSelect** Property, **NewIndex** Property, **Selected** Property

Example

This example fills a **ListBox** control with names of screen fonts and then scrolls through the **ListBox** when you click the form. To try this example, paste the code into the Declarations section of a form that contains a **ListBox** control, and then press F5 and click the form.

```
Private Sub Form_Load ()
   Dim I ' Declare variable.
   For I = 0 To Screen.FontCount -1   ' Fill list box with
      List1.AddItem Screen.Fonts(I)   ' screen font names.
   Next I
End Sub

Private Sub Form_Click ()
   Dim X ' Declare variable.
   X = List1.TopIndex' Get current index.
   List1.TopIndex = List1.TopIndex + 5        ' Reset topmost item.
   If List1.TopIndex = X Then List1.TopIndex = 0
End Sub
```

TopLine Property

Returns a **Long** specifying the line number of the line at the top of the code pane or sets the line showing at the top of the code pane. Read/write.

Applies to

CodePane Object

Remarks

Use the **TopLine** property to return or set the line showing at the top of the code pane. For example, if you want line 25 to be the first line showing in a code pane, set the **TopLine** property to 25.

The **TopLine** property setting must be a positive number. If the **TopLine** property setting is greater than the actual number of lines in the code pane, the setting will be the last line in the code pane.

See Also

GetSelection Method, **SetSelection** Method, **CountOfVisibleLines** Property

Example

The following example uses the **TopLine** property to return the line number of the top line in the specified code pane.

```
Debug.Print Application.VBE.CodePanes(3).TopLine
```

TrackDefault Property

Returns or sets a value that determines whether the **Printer** object always points to the same printer or changes the printer it points to if you change the default printer setting in the operating system's Control Panel. Not available at design time.

Applies To

Printer Object**, Printers** Collection

Syntax

object.**TrackDefault** [= *boolean*]

The **TrackDefault** property syntax has these parts:

Part	Description
object	An object expression that evaluates to an object in the **Applies To** list.
boolean	A Boolean expression specifying the printer *object* points to, as described in Settings.

Settings

The settings for *boolean* are:

Setting	Description
True	(Default) The **Printer** object changes the printer it points to when you change the default printer settings in the operating system's Control Panel.
False	The **Printer** object continues to point to the same printer even though you change the default printer settings in the operating system's Control Panel.

Remarks

Changing the **TrackDefault** property setting while a print job is in progress sends an implicit **EndPage** statement to the **Printer** object.

See Also

EndDoc Method, **Height, Width** Properties, **ColorMode** Property, **Copies** Property, **PaperBin** Property, **PrintQuality** Property

---

Transactions Property

Returns a value that indicates whether an object supports transactions.

Applies To

Database Object, **Dynaset-Type Recordset** Object, **Recordset** Object, **Snapshot-Type Recordset** Object, **Table-Type Recordset** Object, **Connection** Object, **Forward-Only–Type Recordset** Object

Return Values

The return value is a **Boolean** data type that is **True** if the object supports transactions.

Remarks

In an **ODBCDirect** workspace, the **Transactions** property is available on Connection and Database objects, and indicates whether or not the ODBC driver you are using supports transactions.

In a Microsoft Jet workspace, you can also use the **Transactions** property with dynaset- or table-type **Recordset** objects. Snapshot- and forward-only–type **Recordset** objects always return **False**.

If a dynaset- or table-type **Recordset** is based on a Microsoft Jet database engine table, the **Transactions** property is **True** and you can use transactions. Other database engines may not support transactions. For example, you can't use transactions in a dynaset-type **Recordset** object based on a Paradox table.

Check the **Transactions** property before using the **BeginTrans** method on the **Recordset** object's **Workspace** object to make sure that transactions are supported. Using the **BeginTrans**, **CommitTrans**, or **Rollback** methods on an unsupported object has no effect.

See Also

BeginTrans, CommitTrans, Rollback Methods

Example

This example demonstrates the **Transactions** property in Microsoft Jet and **ODBCDirect** workspaces.

```
Sub TransactionsX()

    Dim wrkJet As Workspace
    Dim wrkODBC As Workspace
    Dim dbsNorthwind As Database
    Dim conPubs As Connection
    Dim rstTemp As Recordset

    ' Open Microsoft Jet and ODBCDirect workspaces, a Microsoft
    ' Jet database, and an ODBCDirect connection.
    Set wrkJet = CreateWorkspace("", "admin", "", dbUseJet)
    Set wrkODBC = CreateWorkspace("", "admin", "", dbUseODBC)
    Set dbsNorthwind = wrkJet.OpenDatabase("Northwind.mdb")
    Set conPubs = wrkODBC.OpenConnection("", , , _
        "ODBC;DATABASE=pubs;UID=sa;PWD=;DSN=Publishers")

    ' Open two different Recordset objects and display the
    ' Transactions property of each.

    Debug.Print "Opening Microsoft Jet table-type " & _
        "recordset..."
    Set rstTemp = dbsNorthwind.OpenRecordset( _
        "Employees", dbOpenTable)
    Debug.Print "    Transactions = " & rstTemp.Transactions

    Debug.Print "Opening forward-only-type " & _
        "recordset where the source is an SQL statement..."
    Set rstTemp = dbsNorthwind.OpenRecordset( _
        "SELECT * FROM Employees", dbOpenForwardOnly)
    Debug.Print "    Transactions = " & rstTemp.Transactions

    ' Display Transactions property of a Connection object in
    ' an ODBCDirect workspace.
    Debug.Print "Testing Transaction property of " & _
        "an ODBC connection..."
    Debug.Print "    Transactions = " & conPubs.Transactions

    rstTemp.Close
    dbsNorthwind.Close
    conPubs.Close
    wrkJet.Close
    wrkODBC.Close

End Sub
```

Transactions Property (Remote Data)

Returns a value that indicates whether an object supports the recording of a series of changes that can later be rolled back (undone) or committed (saved).

Applies To

rdoConnection Object, **rdoResultset** Object

Syntax

object.**Transactions**

The *object* placeholder represents an object expression that evaluates to an object in the **Applies To** list.

Return Values

The **Transactions** property return values are:

Value	Description
True	The object supports transactions.
False	The object doesn't support transactions.

Remarks

Check the **Transactions** property before using the **BeginTrans** method to make sure that transactions are supported. When **Transactions** is **False,** using the **BeginTrans, CommitTrans,** or **RollbackTrans** method has no effect.

The **Transactions** property calls the ODBC **SQLGetInfo** function to determine if the ODBC driver is *capable* of supporting transactions, not if the current result set is updatable. You can always call the **BeginTrans** method on the **rdoConnection** object if the **Transactions** property is **True**—even for read-only **rdoResultset** objects.

See Also

BeginTrans, CommitTrans, RollbackTrans Methods (Remote Data), **rdoConnection** Object, **rdoEnvironment** Object, **rdoResultset** Object, **rdoTable** Object

---

True

The **True** keyword has a value equal to -1.

See Also

Boolean Data Type, **False**

TwipsPerPixelX, TwipsPerPixelY Properties

Return the number of twips per pixel for an object measured horizontally (**TwipsPerPixelX**) or vertically (**TwipsPerPixelY**).

Applies To

Screen Object, **Printer** Object, **Printers** Collection

Syntax

object.**TwipsPerPixelX**
object.**TwipsPerPixelY**

The *object* placeholder represents an object expression that evaluates to an object in the **Applies To** list.

Remarks

Windows API routines generally require measurements in pixels. You can use these properties to convert measurements quickly without changing an object's **ScaleMode** property setting.

See Also

ScaleHeight, **ScaleWidth** Properties, **ScaleLeft**, **ScaleTop** Properties, **ScaleMode** Property

---

Type Conversion Functions

Each function coerces an expression to a specific data type.

Syntax

CBool(*expression*)

CByte(*expression*)

CCur(*expression*)

CDate(*expression*)

CDbl(*expression*)

CDec(*expression*)

CInt(*expression*)

CLng(*expression*)

CSng(*expression*)

CVar(*expression*)

CStr(*expression*)

The required *expression* argument is any string expression or numeric expression.

Return Types

The function name determines the return type as shown in the following:

Function	Return Type	Range for *expression* argument
CBool	**Boolean**	Any valid string or numeric expression.
CByte	**Byte**	0 to 255.
CCur	**Currency**	-922,337,203,685,477.5808 to 922,337,203,685,477.5807.
CDate	**Date**	Any valid date expression.
CDbl	**Double**	-1.79769313486232E308 to -4.94065645841247E-324 for negative values; 4.94065645841247E-324 to 1.79769313486232E308 for positive values.
CDec	**Decimal**	+/-79,228,162,514,264,337,593,543,950,335 for zero-scaled numbers, that is, numbers with no decimal places. For numbers with 28 decimal places, the range is +/-7.9228162514264337593543950335. The smallest possible non-zero number is 0.0000000000000000000000000001.
CInt	**Integer**	-32,768 to 32,767; fractions are rounded.
CLng	**Long**	-2,147,483,648 to 2,147,483,647; fractions are rounded.
CSng	**Single**	-3.402823E38 to -1.401298E-45 for negative values; 1.401298E-45 to 3.402823E38 for positive values.
CVar	**Variant**	Same range as **Double** for numerics. Same range as **String** for non-numerics.
CStr	**String**	Returns for CStr depend on the *expression* argument.

Remarks

If the *expression* passed to the function is outside the range of the data type being converted to, an error occurs.

In general, you can document your code using the data-type conversion functions to show that the result of some operation should be expressed as a particular data type rather than the default data type. For example, use **CCur** to force currency arithmetic in cases where single-precision, double-precision, or integer arithmetic normally would occur.

You should use the data-type conversion functions instead of **Val** to provide internationally aware conversions from one data type to another. For example, when you use **CCur**, different decimal separators, different thousand separators, and various currency options are properly recognized depending on the locale setting of your computer.

When the fractional part is exactly 0.5, **CInt** and **CLng** always round it to the nearest even number. For example, 0.5 rounds to 0, and 1.5 rounds to 2. **CInt** and **CLng** differ from the **Fix** and **Int** functions, which truncate, rather than round, the fractional part of a number. Also, **Fix** and **Int** always return a value of the same type as is passed in.

Use the **IsDate** function to determine if *date* can be converted to a date or time. **CDate** recognizes date literals and time literals as well as some numbers that fall within the range of acceptable dates. When converting a number to a date, the whole number portion is converted to a date. Any fractional part of the number is converted to a time of day, starting at midnight.

CDate recognizes date formats according to the locale setting of your system. The correct order of day, month, and year may not be determined if it is provided in a format other than one of the recognized date settings. In addition, a long date format is not recognized if it also contains the day-of-the-week string.

A **CVDate** function is also provided for compatibility with previous versions of Visual Basic. The syntax of the **CVDate** function is identical to the **CDate** function, however, **CVDate** returns a **Variant** whose subtype is **Date** instead of an actual **Date** type. Since there is now an intrinsic **Date** type, there is no further need for **CVDate**. The same effect can be achieved by converting an expression to a **Date**, and then assigning it to a **Variant**. This technique is consistent with the conversion of all other intrinsic types to their equivalent **Variant** subtypes.

Note The **CDec** function does not return a discrete data type; instead, it always returns a **Variant** whose value has been converted to a **Decimal** subtype.

Examples

This example uses the **CBool** function to convert an expression to a **Boolean**. If the expression evaluates to a nonzero value, **CBool** returns **True**; otherwise, it returns **False**.

```
Dim A, B, Check
A = 5: B = 5          ' Initialize variables.
Check = CBool(A = B) ' Check contains True.

A = 0 ' Define variable.
Check = CBool(A)     ' Check contains False.
```

This example uses the **CByte** function to convert an expression to a **Byte**.

```
Dim MyDouble, MyByte
MyDouble = 125.5678     ' MyDouble is a Double.
MyByte = CByte(MyDouble)' MyByte contains 126.
```

This example uses the **CCur** function to convert an expression to a **Currency**.

```
Dim MyDouble, MyCurr
MyDouble = 543.214588' MyDouble is a Double.
MyCurr = CCur(MyDouble * 2)' Convert result of MyDouble * 2
                    ' (1086.429176) to a
                    ' Currency (1086.4292).
```

This example uses the **CDate** function to convert a string to a **Date**. In general, hard-coding dates and times as strings (as shown in this example) is not recommended. Use date literals and time literals, such as #2/12/1969# and #4:45:23 PM#, instead.

```
Dim MyDate, MyShortDate, MyTime, MyShortTime
MyDate = "February 12, 1969"  ' Define date.
MyShortDate = CDate(MyDate)   ' Convert to Date data type.

MyTime = "4:35:47 PM"         ' Define time.
MyShortTime = CDate(MyTime)   ' Convert to Date data type.
```

This example uses the **CDbl** function to convert an expression to a **Double**.

```
Dim MyCurr, MyDouble
MyCurr = CCur(234.456784)              ' MyCurr is a Currency.
MyDouble = CDbl(MyCurr * 8.2 * 0.01)   ' Convert result to a Double.
```

This example uses the **CInt** function to convert a value to an **Integer**.

```
Dim MyDouble, MyInt
MyDouble = 2345.5678    ' MyDouble is a Double.
MyInt = CInt(MyDouble)  ' MyInt contains 2346.
```

This example uses the **CLng** function to convert a value to a **Long**.

```
Dim MyVal1, MyVal2, MyLong1, MyLong2
MyVal1 = 25427.45: MyVal2 = 25427.55  ' MyVal1, MyVal2 are Doubles.
MyLong1 = CLng(MyVal1)                ' MyLong1 contains 25427.
MyLong2 = CLng(MyVal2)                ' MyLong2 contains 25428.
```

This example uses the **CSng** function to convert a value to a **Single**.

```
Dim MyDouble1, MyDouble2, MySingle1, MySingle2
' MyDouble1, MyDouble2 are Doubles.
MyDouble1 = 75.3421115: MyDouble2 = 75.3421555
MySingle1 = CSng(MyDouble1)' MySingle1 contains 75.34211.
MySingle2 = CSng(MyDouble2)' MySingle2 contains 75.34216.
```

This example uses the **CStr** function to convert a numeric value to a **String**.

```
Dim MyDouble, MyString
MyDouble = 437.324' MyDouble is a Double.
MyString = CStr(MyDouble)  ' MyString contains "437.324".
```

This example uses the **CVar** function to convert an expression to a **Variant**.

```
Dim MyInt, MyVar
MyInt = 4534                 ' MyInt is an Integer.
MyVar = CVar(MyInt & "000")' MyVar contains the string
                             ' 4534000.
```

Returns for CStr

If *expression* is	CStr returns
Boolean	A string containing **True** or **False**
Date	A string containing a date in the short date format of your system

(continued)

(*continued*)

If *expression* is	CStr returns
Null	A run-time error
Empty	A zero-length string ("")
Error	A string containing the word **Error** followed by the error number
Other numeric	A string containing the number

Type Property (DAO)

Set**Dynamic-Type Recordset** Object, sets or returns a value that indicates the operational type or data type of an object

Applies To

Dynaset-Type Recordset Object, **Field** Object, **Parameter** Object, **Property** Object, **QueryDef** Object, **Recordset** Object, **Snapshot-Type Recordset** Object, **Table-Type Recordset** Object, **Workspace** Object, **Forward-Only–Type Recordset** Object, **Dynamic-Type Recordset** Object

Settings and Return Values

The setting or return value is a constant that indicates an operational or data type. For a **Field** or **Property** object, this property is read/write until the object is appended to a collection or to another object, after which it's read-only. For a **QueryDef**, **Recordset**, or **Workspace** object, the property setting is read-only. For a **Parameter** object in a Microsoft Jet workspace the property is read-only, while in an **ODBCDirect** workspace the property is always read/write.

For a **Field**, **Parameter**, or **Property** object, the possible settings and return values are described in the following table.

Constant	Description
dbBigInt	Big Integer
dbBinary	Binary
dbBoolean	Boolean
dbByte	Byte
dbChar	Char
dbCurrency	Currency
dbDate	Date/Time
dbDecimal	Decimal
dbDouble	Double
dbFloat	Float
dbGUID	GUID
dbInteger	Integer

(*continued*)

Constant	Description
dbLong	Long
dbLongBinary	Long Binary (OLE Object)
dbMemo	Memo
dbNumeric	Numeric
dbSingle	Single
dbText	Text
dbTime	Time
dbTimeStamp	Time Stamp
dbVarBinary	VarBinary

For a **QueryDef** object, the possible settings and return values are shown in the following table.

Constant	Query type
dbQAction	Action
dbQAppend	Append
dbQCompound	Compound
dbQCrosstab	Crosstab
dbQDDL	Data-definition
dbQDelete	Delete
dbQMakeTable	Make-table
dbQProcedure	Procedure (ODBCDirect workspaces only)
dbQSelect	Select
dbQSetOperation	Union
dbQSPTBulk	Used with **dbQSQLPassThrough** to specify a query that doesn't return records (Microsoft Jet workspaces only).
DbQSQLPassThrough	Pass-through (Microsoft Jet workspaces only)
dbQUpdate	Update

Note   To create an SQL pass-through query in a Microsoft Jet workspace, you don't need to explicitly set the **Type** property to **dbQSQLPassThrough**. The Microsoft Jet database engine automatically sets this when you create a **QueryDef** object and set the **Connect** property.

For a **Recordset** object, the possible settings and return values are as follows.

Constant	Recordset type
dbOpenTable	Table (Microsoft Jet workspaces only)
dbOpenDynamic	Dynamic (ODBCDirect workspaces only)
dbOpenDynaset	Dynaset
dbOpenSnapshot	Snapshot
dbOpenForwardOnly	Forward-only

For a **Workspace** object, the possible settings and return values are as follows.

Constant	Workspace type
dbUseJet	The **Workspace** is connected to the Microsoft Jet database engine.
DbUseODBC	The **Workspace** is connected to an ODBC data source.

Remarks

When you append a new **Field**, **Parameter**, or **Property** object to the collection of an **Index**, **QueryDef**, **Recordset**, or **TableDef** object, an error occurs if the underlying database doesn't support the data type specified for the new object.

Example

This example demonstrates the **Type** property by returning the name of the constant corresponding to the value of the **Type** property of four different **Recordsets**. The **RecordsetType** function is required for this procedure to run.

```
Sub TypeX()

    Dim dbsNorthwind As Database
    Dim rstEmployees As Recordset

    Set dbsNorthwind = OpenDatabase("Northwind.mdb")

    ' Default is dbOpenTable.
    Set rstEmployees = _
        dbsNorthwind.OpenRecordset("Employees")
    Debug.Print _
        "Table-type recordset (Employees table): " & _
        RecordsetType(rstEmployees.Type)
    rstEmployees.Close

    Set rstEmployees = _
        dbsNorthwind.OpenRecordset("Employees", _
        dbOpenDynaset)
    Debug.Print _
        "Dynaset-type recordset (Employees table): " & _
        RecordsetType(rstEmployees.Type)
    rstEmployees.Close

    Set rstEmployees = _
        dbsNorthwind.OpenRecordset("Employees", _
        dbOpenSnapshot)
    Debug.Print _
        "Snapshot-type recordset (Employees table): " & _
        RecordsetType(rstEmployees.Type)
    rstEmployees.Close

    Set rstEmployees = _
        dbsNorthwind.OpenRecordset("Employees", _
        dbOpenForwardOnly)
    Debug.Print _
```

```
            "Forward-only-type recordset (Employees table): " & _
            RecordsetType(rstEmployees.Type)
    rstEmployees.Close

    dbsNorthwind.Close

End Sub

Function RecordsetType(intType As Integer) As String

    Select Case intType
        Case dbOpenTable
            RecordsetType = "dbOpenTable"
        Case dbOpenDynaset
            RecordsetType = "dbOpenDynaset"
        Case dbOpenSnapshot
            RecordsetType = "dbOpenSnapshot"
        Case dbOpenForwardOnly
            RecordsetType = "dbOpenForwardOnly"
    End Select

End Function
```

This example demonstrates the **Type** property by returning the name of the constant corresponding to the value of the **Type** property of all the **Field** objects in the Employees table. The **FieldType** function is required for this procedure to run.

```
Sub TypeX2()

    Dim dbsNorthwind As Database
    Dim fldLoop As Field

    Set dbsNorthwind = OpenDatabase("Northwind.mdb")

    Debug.Print "Fields in Employees TableDef:"
    Debug.Print "    Type - Name"

    ' Enumerate Fields collection of Employees table.
    For Each fldLoop In _
        dbsNorthwind.TableDefs!Employees.Fields
        Debug.Print "        " & FieldType(fldLoop.Type) & _
            " - " & fldLoop.Name
    Next fldLoop

    dbsNorthwind.Close

End Sub

Function FieldType(intType As Integer) As String
```

```
      Select Case intType
         Case dbBoolean
            FieldType = "dbBoolean"
         Case dbByte
            FieldType = "dbByte"
         Case dbInteger
            FieldType = "dbInteger"
         Case dbLong
            FieldType = "dbLong"
         Case dbCurrency
            FieldType = "dbCurrency"
         Case dbSingle
            FieldType = "dbSingle"
         Case dbDouble
            FieldType = "dbDouble"
         Case dbDate
            FieldType = "dbDate"
         Case dbText
            FieldType = "dbText"
         Case dbLongBinary
            FieldType = "dbLongBinary"
         Case dbMemo
            FieldType = "dbMemo"
         Case dbGUID
            FieldType = "dbGUID"
      End Select

End Function
```

This example demonstrates the **Type** property by returning the name of the constant corresponding to the value of the **Type** property of all the **QueryDef** objects in Northwind. The **QueryDefType** function is required for this procedure to run.

```
Sub TypeX3()

    Dim dbsNorthwind As Database
    Dim qdfLoop As QueryDef

    Set dbsNorthwind = OpenDatabase("Northwind.mdb")

    Debug.Print "QueryDefs in Northwind Database:"
    Debug.Print "    Type - Name"

    ' Enumerate QueryDefs collection of Northwind database.
    For Each qdfLoop In dbsNorthwind.QueryDefs
        Debug.Print "        " & _
            QueryDefType(qdfLoop.Type) & " - " & qdfLoop.Name
    Next qdfLoop

    dbsNorthwind.Close

End Sub
```

```
        Function QueryDefType(intType As Integer) As String

        Select Case intType
            Case dbQSelect
                QueryDefType = "dbQSelect"
            Case dbQAction
                QueryDefType = "dbQAction"
            Case dbQCrosstab
                QueryDefType = "dbQCrosstab"
            Case dbQDelete
                QueryDefType = "dbQDelete"
            Case dbQUpdate
                QueryDefType = "dbQUpdate"
            Case dbQAppend
                QueryDefType = "dbQAppend"
            Case dbQMakeTable
                QueryDefType = "dbQMakeTable"
            Case dbQDDL
                QueryDefType = "dbQDDL"
            Case dbQSQLPassThrough
                QueryDefType = "dbQSQLPassThrough"
            Case dbQSetOperation
                QueryDefType = "dbQSetOperation"
            Case dbQSPTBulk
                QueryDefType = "dbQSPTBulk"
        End Select

        End Function
```

Type Property (Member or Project Object)

Returns the type of the currently selected member or project.

Applies To

Member Object, **Reference** Object, **VBComponent** Object, **VBProject** Object, **Window** Object

Syntax

object.**Type**

The *object* placeholder represents an object expression that evaluates to an object in the **Applies To** list.

Return Values

The **Type** property settings for the **Member** object (**vbext_MemberType**) are:

Constant	Value	Description
vbext_mt_Method	1	Member is a method.
vbext_mt_Property	2	Member is a property.
vbext_mt_Variable	3	Member is a variable.

(continued)

Constant	Value	Description
vbext_mt_Event	4	Member is an event.
vbext_mt_Enum	5	Member is an enumerated value.
vbext_mt_Const	6	Member is a constant.
vbext_mt_EventSink	7	Member is an event sink.

The **Type** property settings for the **Project** object (**vbext_ProjectType**) are:

Constant	Value	Description
vbext_pt_StandardExe	1	Project type is Standard Exe.
vbext_pt_ActiveXExe	2	Project type is ActiveX Exe.
vbext_pt_ActiveXDll	3	Project type is ActiveX Dll.
vbext_pt_ActiveXControl	4	Project type is ActiveX control.

Type Property (Picture)

Returns the graphic format of a **Picture** object. Not available at design time; read-only at run time.

Applies To

Picture Object, **AxisScale** Object

Syntax

object.**Type**

The *object* placeholder represents an object expression that evaluates to an object in the **Applies To** list.

Return Values

The return values for the **Type** property are:

Constant	Value	Description
vbPicTypeNone	0	Picture is empty
vbPicTypeBitmap	1	Bitmap (.bmpBMP files)
vbPicTypeMetafile	2	Metafile (.wmfWMF files)
vbPicTypeIcon	3	Icon (.icoICO files)
vbPicTypeEMetafile	4	Enhanced Metafile (.emfEMF files)

Remarks

These constants are listed in the Visual Basic (VB) object library in the Object Browser.

See Also

Height, **Width** Properties, **PercentBasis** Property

Example

This example reads the setting of the **Type** and **Width** properties of a **Picture** object in a **PictureBox** control. To try this example, paste the code into the Declarations section of a form that contains a **PictureBox** whose **Picture** property is set to an icon, and then press F5 and click the form.

```
Private Sub Form_Click()
    If Picture1.Picture.Type = vbPicTypeIcon Then
        Print "The graphic in the picture box is an icon."
    Else
        Print "The Picture property isn't set to an icon."
    End If
    Print "Width of the graphic in HiMetrics is " & Picture1.Picture.Width
    Print "Width of picture box itself in twips is " & Picture1.Width
End Sub
```

Type Property (Remote Data)

Returns or sets a value that indicates the type or data type of an object.

Applies To

rdoColumn Object, **rdoParameter** Object, **rdoPreparedStatement** Object, **rdoQuery** Object, **rdoResultset** Object, **rdoTable** Object

Syntax

object.**Type** [= *value*]

The **Type** property syntax has these parts:

Part	Description
object	An object expression that evaluates to an object in the **Applies To** list.
value	A constant or **Integer** value that specifies a datatype, as described in Return Values.

The *object* placeholder represents an object expression that evaluates to an object in the **Applies To** list.

Return Values

For an **rdoColumn** or **rdoParameter** object, the **Type** property returns an **Integer**. You can also set the **Type** property on the **rdoParameter** object to indicate the datatype of a specific procedure argument. The valid values are:

Constant	Value	Description
rdTypeCHAR	1	Fixed-length character string. Length set by **Size** property.
rdTypeNUMERIC	2	Signed, exact, numeric value with precision p and scale s ($1 \leq p \leq 15$; $0 \leq s \leq p$).
rdTypeDECIMAL	3	Signed, exact, numeric value with precision p and scale s ($1 \leq p \leq 15$; $0 \leq s \leq p$).

(*continued*)

Constant	Value	Description
rdTypeINTEGER	4	Signed, exact numeric value with precision 10, scale 0 (signed: $-2^{31} \leq n \leq 2^{31}$-1; unsigned: $0 \leq n \leq 2^{32}$-1).
rdTypeSMALLINT	5	Signed, exact numeric value with precision 5, scale 0 (signed: $-32,768 \leq n \leq 32,767$, unsigned: $0 \leq n \leq 65,535$).
rdTypeFLOAT	6	Signed, approximate numeric value with mantissa precision 15 (zero or absolute value 10^{-308} to 10^{308}).
rdTypeREAL	7	Signed, approximate numeric value with mantissa precision 7 (zero or absolute value 10^{-38} to 10^{38}).
rdTypeDOUBLE	8	Signed, approximate numeric value with mantissa precision 15 (zero or absolute value 10^{-308} to 10^{308}).
rdTypeDATE	9	Date—data source dependent.
rdTypeTIME	10	Time—data source dependent.
rdTypeTIMESTAMP	11	TimeStamp—data source dependent.
rdTypeVARCHAR	12	Variable-length character string. Maximum length 255.
rdTypeLONGVARCHAR	-1	Variable-length character string. Maximum length determined by data source.
rdTypeBINARY	-2	Fixed-length binary data. Maximum length 255.
rdTypeVARBINARY	-3	Variable-length binary data. Maximum length 255.
rdTypeLONGVARBINARY	-4	Variable-length binary data. Maximum data source dependent.
rdTypeBIGINT	-5	Signed, exact numeric value with precision 19 (signed) or 20 (unsigned), scale 0; (signed: $-2^{63} \leq n \leq 2^{63}$-1; unsigned: $0 \leq n \leq 2^{64}$-1).
rdTypeTINYINT	-6	Signed, exact numeric value with precision 3, scale 0; (signed: $-128 \leq n \leq 127$, unsigned: $0 \leq n \leq 255$).
rdTypeBIT	-7	Single binary digit.

For an **rdoQuery** object, the **Type** property returns an **Integer**. The return values are:

Constant	Value	Query type
rdQSelect	0	Select
rdQAction	1	Action
rdQProcedures	2	Procedural
rdQCompound	3	The query contains both action and select statements

For an **rdoResultset** object, the **Type** property returns an **Integer** that determines the type of **rdoResultset**. The return values are:

Constant	Value	rdoResultset type
rdOpenForwardOnly	0	Fixed set, non-scrolling.
rdOpenKeyset	1	Updatable, fixed set, scrollable query result set cursor.
rdOpenDynamic	2	Updatable, dynamic set, scrollable query result set cursor.
rdOpenStatic	3	Read-only, fixed set.

Note Not all ODBC drivers or data sources support every type of **rdoResultset** cursor type. If you choose a cursor that is not supported, the ODBC driver attempts to revert to a supported type. If no supported type is available, a trappable error is fired.

For an **rdoTable** object, the **Type** property returns a **String**. The settings for *value* are determined by the data source driver.

Typically, this string value is "TABLE", "VIEW", "SYSTEM TABLE", "GLOBAL TEMPORARY". "LOCAL TEMPORARY", "ALIAS", "SYNONYM" or some other data source-specific type identifier.

Remarks

Depending on the object, the **Type** property indicates:

Object	Type indicates
rdoColumn, rdoParameter	Object data type
rdoQuery	Type of query
rdoResultset	Type of **rdoResultset**
rdoTable	Type of table on data source

In some cases, you must override the **Type** property assignment made by RDO when creating some types of parameter queries. For example, if a parameter is passed to an expression inside of an SQL statement, the ODBC driver might not be able to determine the correct type. In these cases, you can force a specific parameter to be handled as the correct type by simply setting the **rdoParameter** object's **Type** property. This is the only situation that permits you to change the **Type** property. In all other cases, this property is read-only.

See Also

rdoColumn Object, **rdoParameter** Object, **rdoPreparedStatement** Object, **rdoResultset** Object, **rdoTable** Object

Type Property (Window Object)

Returns a numeric or string value containing the type of object. Read-only.

Applies to

VBComponent Object, **Reference** Object, **Window** Object

Return Values

The **Type** property settings for the **Window** object are described in the following table:

Constant	Value	Description
vbext_wt_CodeWindow	0	**Code** window
vbext_wt_Designer	1	Designer
vbext_wt_Browser	2	**Object Browser**
vbext_wt_Watch	3	Watch pane
vbext_wt_Locals	4	Locals
vbext_wt_Immediate	5	**Immediate** window
vbext_wt_ProjectWindow	6	**Project** window
vbext_wt_PropertyWindow	7	**Properties** window
vbext_wt_Find	8	**Find** dialog box
vbext_wt_FindReplace	9	**Search and Replace** dialog box
vbext_wt_LinkedWindowFrame	11	Linked window frame
vbext_wt_MainWindow	12	Main window

The **Type** property settings for the **VBComponent** object are described in the following table:

Constant	Description
vbext_ct_ClassModule	Class module
vbext_ct_MSForm	Microsoft Form
vbext_ct_StdModule	Standard module
vbext_ct_Document	Document module

The **Type** property settings for the **Reference** object are described in the following table:

Constant	Description
vbext_rk_TypeLib	Type library
vbext_rk_Project	Project

See Also

IndexedValue Property, **Name** Property, **Value** Property

Example

The following example uses the **Type** property to return a value indicating the type of the specified member of the **VBComponents** collection in a particular project. The value returned is a number that corresponds to a predefined constant for one of the component object types.

```
Debug.Print Application.VBE.VBProjects(1).VBComponents(1).Type
```

Type Statement

Used at module level to define a user-defined data type containing one or more elements.

Syntax

[**Private** | **Public**] **Type** *varname*
   elementname [([*subscripts*])] **As** *type*
   [*elementname* [([*subscripts*])] **As** *type*]
   . . .
End Type

The **Type** statement syntax has these parts:

Part	Description
Public	Optional. Used to declare user-defined types that are available to all procedures in all modules in all projects.
Private	Optional. Used to declare user-defined types that are available only within the module where the declaration is made.
varname	Required. Name of the user-defined type; follows standard variable naming conventions.
elementname	Required. Name of an element of the user-defined type. Element names also follow standard variable naming conventions, except that keywords can be used.
subscripts	Optional. Dimensions of an array element. Use only parentheses when declaring an array whose size can change. The *subscripts* argument uses the following syntax: [*lower* **To**] *upper* [,[*lower* **To**] *upper*] **. . .** When not explicitly stated in *lower*, the lower bound of an array is controlled by the **Option Base** statement. The lower bound is zero if no **Option Base** statement is present.
type	Required. Data type of the element; may be **Byte**, **Boolean**, **Integer**, **Long**, **Currency**, **Single**, **Double**, **Decimal** (not currently supported), **Date**, **String** (for variable-length strings), **String** * *length* (for fixed-length strings), **Object**, **Variant**, another user-defined type, or an object type.

Remarks

The **Type** statement can be used only at module level. Once you have declared a user-defined type using the **Type** statement, you can declare a variable of that type anywhere within the scope of the declaration. Use **Dim**, **Private**, **Public**, **ReDim**, or **Static** to declare a variable of a user-defined type.

In standard modules, user-defined types are public by default. This visibility can be changed using the **Private** keyword. In class modules, however, user-defined types can only be private and the visibility can't be changed using the **Public** keyword.

Line numbers and line labels aren't allowed in **Type...End Type** blocks.

User-defined types are often used with data records, which frequently consist of a number of related elements of different data types.

The following example shows the use of fixed-size arrays in a user-defined type:

```
Type StateData
    CityCode (1 To 100) As Integer      ' Declare a static array.
    County As String * 30
End Type

Dim Washington(1 To 100) As StateData
```

In the preceding example, `StateData` includes the `CityCode` static array, and the record `Washington` has the same structure as `StateData`.

When you declare a fixed-size array within a user-defined type, its dimensions must be declared with numeric literals or constants rather than variables.

The setting of the **Option Base** statement determines the lower bound for arrays within user-defined types.

See Also

Data Type Summary, **Dim** Statement, **Enum** Statement, **Option Base** Statement, **Private** Statement, **Public** Statement, **ReDim** Statement, **Static** Statement

Example

This example uses the **Type** statement to define a user-defined data type. The **Type** statement is used at the module level only. If it appears in a class module, a **Type** statement must be preceded by the keyword **Private**.

```
Type EmployeeRecord                     ' Create user-defined type.
    ID As Integer                       ' Define elements of data type.
    Name As String * 20
    Address As String * 30
    Phone As Long
    HireDate As Date
End Type
Sub CreateRecord()
    Dim MyRecord As EmployeeRecord      ' Declare variable.

    ' Assignment to EmployeeRecord variable must occur in a procedure.
    MyRecord.ID = 12003                 ' Assign a value to an element.
End Sub
```

TypeName Function

Returns a **String** that provides information about a variable.

Syntax

TypeName(*varname*)

The required *varname* argument is a **Variant** containing any variable except a variable of a user-defined type.

Remarks

The string returned by **TypeName** can be any one of the following:

String returned	Variable
object type	An object whose type is *objecttype*
Byte	Byte value
Integer	Integer
Long	Long integer
Single	Single-precision floating-point number
Double	Double-precision floating-point number
Currency	Currency value
Decimal	Decimal value
Date	Date value
String	String
Boolean	Boolean value
Error	An error value
Empty	Uninitialized
Null	No valid data
Object	An object
Unknown	An object whose type is unknown
Nothing	Object variable that doesn't refer to an object

If *varname* is an array, the returned string can be any one of the possible returned strings (or **Variant**) with empty parentheses appended. For example, if *varname* is an array of integers, **TypeName** returns "Integer()".

See Also

Data Type Summary, **IsArray** Function, **IsDate** Function, **IsEmpty** Function, **IsError** Function, **IsMissing** Function, **IsNull** Function, **IsNumeric** Function, **IsObject** Function, **Variant Data** Type, **VarType** Function

Example

This example uses the **TypeName** function to return information about a variable.

```
' Declare variables.
Dim NullVar, MyType, StrVar As String, IntVar As Integer, CurVar As Currency
Dim ArrayVar (1 To 5) As Integer
NullVar = Null                  ' Assign Null value.
MyType = TypeName(StrVar)       ' Returns "String".
MyType = TypeName(IntVar)       ' Returns "Integer".
MyType = TypeName(CurVar)       ' Returns "Currency".
MyType = TypeName(NullVar)      ' Returns "Null".
MyType = TypeName(ArrayVar)     ' Returns "Integer()".
```

UBound Function

Returns a **Long** containing the largest available subscript for the indicated dimension of an array.

Syntax

UBound(arrayname[, dimension])

The **UBound** function syntax has these parts:

Part	Description
arrayname	Required. Name of the array variable; follows standard variable naming conventions.
dimension	Optional; **Variant** (**Long**). Whole number indicating which dimension's upper bound is returned. Use 1 for the first dimension, 2 for the second, and so on. If dimension is omitted, 1 is assumed.

Remarks

The **UBound** function is used with the **LBound** function to determine the size of an array. Use the **LBound** function to find the lower limit of an array dimension.

UBound returns the following values for an array with these dimensions:

```
Dim A(1 To 100, 0 To 3, -3 To 4)
```

Statement	Return Value
UBound(A, 1)	100
UBound(A, 2)	3
UBound(A, 3)	4

See Also

Dim Statement, **LBound** Function, **Option Base** Statement, **Public** Statement, **ReDim** Statement

Example

This example uses the **UBound** function to determine the largest available subscript for the indicated dimension of an array.

```
Dim Upper
Dim MyArray(1 To 10, 5 To 15, 10 To 20)      ' Declare array variables.
Dim AnyArray(10)
Upper = UBound(MyArray, 1)                    ' Returns 10.
Upper = UBound(MyArray, 3)                    ' Returns 20.
Upper = UBound(AnyArray)                      ' Returns 10.
```

UBound Property

Returns the highest ordinal value of a control in a control array.

Syntax

object.**UBound**

The *object* placeholder represents an object expression that evaluates to an object in the **Applies To** list.

Remarks

UBound is equal to the **Index** property value of the last control in the array.

See Also

LBound Property, **Index** Property (Control Array)

Example

This example prints the values of these two properties for a control array. Put an **OptionButton** control on a form, and set its **Index** property to 0 (to create a control array). To try this example, paste the code into the Declarations section of a form, and then press F5 and click the form.

```
Private Sub Form_Paint ()
   Static FlagFormPainted As Integer
   If FlagFormPainted <> True Then  ' When form is painting for first time.
      For i = 1 To 3
         Load Option1(i)' add three option buttons to array.
         Option1(i).Top = Option1(i - 1).Top + 350
         Option1(i).Visible = True
      Next I
      For I =  0 to 3  ' Put captions on the option buttons.
         Option1(i).Caption = "Option #" & CStr(i)
      Next I
      Option1(0).Value = True  ' Select first option button.

FlagFormPainted = True  ' Form is done painting.
   End If
End Sub
Private Sub Form_Click ()
   Print "Control array's Count property is " & Option1().Count
   Print "Control array's LBound property is " & Option1().LBound
   Print "Control array's UBound property is " & Option1().UBound
End Sub
```

UCase Function

Returns a **Variant** (**String**) containing the specified string, converted to uppercase.

Syntax

UCase(*string*)

The required *string* argument is any valid string expression. If *string* contains **Null**, **Null** is returned.

Remarks

Only lowercase letters are converted to uppercase; all uppercase letters and non-letter characters remain unchanged.

See Also

LCase Function

Example

This example uses the **UCase** function to return an uppercase version of a string.

```
Dim LowerCase, UpperCase
LowerCase = "Hello World 1234"        ' String to convert.
UpperCase = UCase(LowerCase)          ' Returns "HELLO WORLD 1234".
```

UIDead Property

Returns a boolean value indicating whether the control should be responsive to the user or not.

Applies To

AmbientProperties Object

Syntax

object.**UIDead**

The **UIDead** property syntax has this part:

Part	Description
object	An object expression that evaluates to an object in the **Applies To** list.

Settings

The possible Boolean return values from the **UIDead** property are:

Setting	Description
True	The control should not respond to the user.
False	The control should respond to the user. If the container does not implement this ambient property, this will be the default value.

Remarks

This property is typically used to indicate that the container is in break mode: during this mode, the control should not respond to any user input. That is, the control should ignore mouse clicks and keystrokes, and not change the mouse cursor even when the mouse is over the control window. A container such as a Visual Basic form would set this flag to TRUE when the programmer stops the program during execution—the container is not in design mode, yet not in run mode either; Visual Basic simply wants the controls to be inoperative.

UIDefault Property

Returns or sets the **UIDefault** attribute of a **Member** object.

Applies To

Member Object

Syntax

object.**UIDefault**

The *object* placeholder represents an object expression that evaluates to an object in the **Applies To** list.

UnattendedApp Property

Returns a value that determines if an application will run without any user interface.

Applies To

App Object

Syntax

object.**UnattendedApp=** *boolean*

The **UnattendedApp** property syntax has these parts:

Part	Description
object	An object expression that evaluates to an object in the **Applies To** list.
boolean	A Boolean expression that specifies if the application will run without any user interface.

Settings

The settings for *boolean* are:

Constant	Value	Description
True	-1	The application has no user interface.
False	0	The application has a user interface.

UnboundAddData Event

Occurs in an unbound **DBGrid** control when a new row is added to it. This event alerts your application that it must add a new row of data to its data set.

Applies To

DBGrid Control

Syntax

Private Sub *object*_**UnboundAddData**(*rowbuf* **As RowBuffer,**
  ➥ *newrowbookmark* **As Variant)**

The **UnboundAddData** event syntax has these parts:

Part	Description
object	An object expression that evaluates to an object in the **Applies To** list.
rowbuf	The **RowBuffer** object which contains the retrieved row of data.
newrowbookmark	A bookmark which acts as a unique identifier for each row of data.

Remarks

The number of rows to be retrieved is determined by the **RowCount** property, which is always set to a value of 1 in this event, because you can add only one row at a time.

A new row of data can be added to the data set only if the **AllowAddNew** property is **True**.

The **RowBuffer** object may not be fully populated, but contains entries only for those cells that were modified. Therefore check the **Value** property of the **RowBuffer** object for **Null** for each column. For **Null** valued columns, you can assign the **DefaultValue** property of the **Column** object to your data set.

To cancel the **UnboundAddData** event, set the **RowCount** property of the **RowBuffer** object to 0. This signals the **DBGrid** that the add attempt failed. By doing this, you can gracefully handle data conversion and insufficient permission errors.

The *rowbuf* argument contains a single row of data to be written to the data set. Before returning from this event, *newrowbookmark* must be set to the bookmark of the newly added row.

See Also

UnboundDeleteRow Event, **UnboundReadData** Event, **UnboundWriteData** Event, **RowBuffer** Object, **Bookmark** Property (DBGrid), **RowCount** Property, **Value** Property (RowBuffer), **AllowAddNew** Property

Example

This example illustrates the use of the **UnboundAddData** event to add a row of data to a database, in this case, a simple array.

```
Private Sub DBGrid1_UnboundAddData(ByVal RowBuf As RowBuffer,
NewRowBookmark As Variant)
Dim Col%

mTotalRows = mTotalRows + 1
ReDim Preserve UserData(MAXCOLS - 1, mTotalRows - 1)
' Sets the bookmark to the last row.
NewRowBookmark = mTotalRows - 1

' The following loop adds a new record to the database.
For Col% = 0 To UBound(UserData, 1)
   If Not IsNull(RowBuf.Value(0, Col%)) Then
      UserData(Col%, mTotalRows - 1) = RowBuf.Value(0, Col%)
   Else
      ' If no value set for column, then use the
      ' DefaultValue
      UserData(Col%, mTotalRows - 1) = DBGrid1.Columns(Col%).DefaultValue
   End If
Next Col%
End Sub
```

UnboundDeleteRow Event

Occurs whenever a row of data is deleted from the unbound **DBGrid**. This event alerts your application that it must delete a row of data from its data set.

Applies To

DBGrid Control

Syntax

Private Sub *object*_**UnboundDeleteRow**(*bookmark* **As Variant**)

The **UnboundDeleteRow** event syntax has these parts:

Part	Description
object	An object expression that evaluates to an object in the **Applies To** list.
bookmark	A value representing the bookmark of the row to be deleted.

Remarks

The *bookmark* argument must be set to the bookmark value provided when the row was retrieved with the **UnboundReadData** event or added by the **UnboundAddData** event.

To cancel the **UnboundDeleteRow** event, set the *bookmark* parameter to **Null** which will prevent the row from being deleted.

See Also

UnboundAddData Event, **UnboundReadData** Event, **UnboundWriteData** Event, **Bookmark** Property (DBGrid)

Example

This example illustrates the use of the **UnboundDeleteRow** event to delete a row of data from a database, in this case, a simple array.

```
Private Sub DBGrid1_UnboundDeleteRow(Bookmark As Variant)
Dim Col%, Row%

' Move all rows above the deleted row down in the
' array.
For Row% = Bookmark + 1 To mTotalRows - 1
    For Col% = 0 To MAXCOLS - 1
        UserData(Col%, Row% - 1) = UserData(Col%, Row%)
    Next Col%
Next Row%

mTotalRows = mTotalRows - 1
End Sub
```

UnboundGetRelativeBookmark Event

Occurs whenever the grid requires data for display.

Applies To

DBGrid Control

Syntax

Private Sub *object*_**UnboundGetRelativeBookmark([** *index* **As Integer,]**
→ *startlocation* **As Variant, ByVal** *offset* **As Long,** *newlocation* **As Variant,**
→ *approximateposition* **As Long)**

The **UnboundGetRelativeBookmark** event syntax has these parts:

Part	Description
object	An object expression that evaluates to an object in the **Applies To** list.
index	An integer that identifies a control if it is in a control array.
startlocation	A bookmark which, together with *offset*, specifies the row to be returned in *newlocation*. A *startlocation* of **Null** indicates a request for a row from BOF or EOF.
offset	Specifies the relative position (from *startlocation*) of the row to be returned in *newlocation*. A positive number indicates a forward relative position while a negative number indicates a backward relative position.
newlocation	The bookmark of the row which is specified by *startlocation* plus *offset*. If the row specified is beyond the first or the last row (or beyond BOF or EOF), then *newlocation* should be set to **Null**.
approximateposition	A value which indicates the ordinal position of *newlocation*. Setting this variable will enhance the ability of the grid to display its vertical scroll bar accurately. If the exact ordinal position of *newlocation* is not known, user can set it to a reasonable, approximate value, or just ignore this parameter.

Remarks

This optional event is to be used in conjunction with the **UnboundReadData** event (when the **DataMode** property is set to 1 - Unbound). It is fired by the grid whenever it requires data for display. You can add code to this event to improve your project performance (often quite dramatically), otherwise, you can ignore this event and your project will function properly.

Before returning from this event, the user is expected to set *newlocation* and (optionally) *approximateposition*. For example:

If *offset* is 1 (or -1), then the user returns in *newlocation*, the bookmark of the next (or previous) row from *startlocation*.

If *startlocation* is **NULL** and *offset* is 2 (or -2), then the user returns in *newlocation*, the bookmark of the second (or second to last) row.

If the requested row is beyond the first or last row (or beyond BOF or EOF), then the user returns **Null** in *newlocation*.

See Also

DataMode Property, **UnboundReadData** Event

UnboundReadData Event

Occurs whenever an unbound **DBGrid** control requires data for display, such as when you scroll the **DBGrid** display.

Applies To

DBGrid Control

Syntax

Private Sub *object*_**UnboundReadData**(*rowbuf* **As RowBuffer,** *startlocation* **As Variant,** *readpriorrows* **As Boolean**)

The **UnboundReadData** event syntax has these parts:

Part	Description
object	An object expression that evaluates to an object in the **Applies To** list.
rowbuf	The **RowBuffer** object that will contain the retrieved data. When entering this event, the **RowCount** property contains the number of rows to be retrieved.
startlocation	A variant bookmark which specifies the row to position to before fetching the next or previous set of records. If *readpriorrows* is **False** then *startlocation* specifies the bookmark before the first record to be read. If *readpriorrows* is **True** then *startlocation* specifies the bookmark after the first record to be read. If *startlocation* is null, then fetching occurs at the first record or the last record, depending on the *readpriorrows* argument.
readpriorrows	**True** if the grid is requesting rows before the *startlocation*. **False** if the grid is requesting rows after the *startlocation*.

Remarks

Once the data is retrieved, it is stored in the **DBGrid** control's cache.

It is not necessary to fill the row buffer completely, and it is in fact acceptable to return no rows at all. The value of the **RowCount** property of the **RowBuffer** object can be set to indicate that fewer rows were returned than requested. The **DBGrid** interprets this to mean that there are no more rows to retrieve in the indicated direction. Thus, it is only necessary to fill the row buffer completely if there are more valid rows to be retrieved. You can inform **DBGrid** of BOF/EOF and error conditions by setting the **RowBuffer** object's **RowCount** property to 0.

For each row retrieved, you must provide a bookmark, which can later be used to refer to that row. This bookmark is specified by setting the **Bookmark** property of the **RowBuffer** object for each row returned. The data itself is specified by setting the **Value** property of the **RowBuffer** object for each column of data in each row returned.

See Also

UnboundAddData Event, **UnboundDeleteRow** Event, **UnboundWriteData** Event, **RowBuffer** Object, **Bookmark** Property (DBGrid), **RowCount** Property, **Value** Property (RowBuffer)

Example

This example illustrates the use of the **UnboundReadData** event to read a row of data from a database, in this case, a simple array.

```
Private Sub DBGrid1_UnboundReadData(ByVal RowBuf As RowBuffer,
StartLocation As Variant, ByVal ReadPriorRows As Boolean)
Dim CurRow&, Row%, Col%, RowsFetched%, Incr%

If ReadPriorRows Then
   Incr% = -1
Else
   Incr% = 1
End If

' If StartLocation is Null then start reading at the
' end or beginning of the data set.
If IsNull(StartLocation) Then
   If ReadPriorRows Then
      CurRow& = RowBuf.RowCount - 1
   Else
      CurRow& = 0
   End If
Else
   ' Find the position to start reading based on the
   ' StartLocation bookmark and the lngIncr% variable
   CurRow& = CLng(StartLocation) + Incr%
End If
```

```
' Transfer data from our data set array to the RowBuf
' object which DBGrid uses to display the data
For Row% = 0 To RowBuf.RowCount - 1
   If CurRow& < 0 Or CurRow& >= mTotalRows& Then Exit For
   For Col% = 0 To UBound(UserData, 1)
      RowBuf.Value(Row%, Col%) = UserData(Col%, CurRow&)
   Next Col%
   ' Set bookmark using CurRow& which is also our
   ' array index
   RowBuf.Bookmark(Row%) = CStr(CurRow&)
   CurRow& = CurRow& + Incr%
   RowsFetched% = RowsFetched% + 1
Next Row%
RowBuf.RowCount = RowsFetched%
End Sub
```

UnboundWriteData Event

Occurs when an unbound **DBGrid** control has an entire row of modified data to write to the data set. It alerts your application that it must update an edited existing row of data to its dataset.

Applies To

DBGrid Control

Syntax

Private Sub *object_***UnboundWriteData**(*rowbuf* **As RowBuffer**,
  ↦ *writelocation* **As Variant**)

The **UnboundWriteData** event syntax has these parts:

Part	Description
object	An object expression that evaluates to an object in the **Applies To** list.
rowbuf	The **RowBuffer** object that contains the modified row of data.
writelocation	A value that identifies the unique bookmark of the row of data as specified in the **UnboundReadData** and **UnboundWriteData** events.

Remarks

The value of the **RowCount** property of the **RowBuffer** object will always be 1, because you can update only one row of data at a time.

The **RowBuffer** object may not be fully populated, but contains entries only for those cells that were modified. Therefore, check the **Value** property of the **RowBuffer** object for **Null** for each column.

To cancel the **UnboundWriteData** event, set the **RowCount** property of the **RowBuffer** object to 0. This signals the **DBGrid** that the write attempt failed. By doing this, you can gracefully handle data conversion and insufficient permission errors.

See Also

UnboundAddData Event, **UnboundDeleteRow** Event, **UnboundReadData** Event, **RowBuffer** Object, **Bookmark** Property (DBGrid), **RowCount** Property

Example

This example illustrates the use of the **UnboundReadData** event to read a row of data from a database, in this case, a simple array.

```
Private Sub DBGrid1_UnboundWriteData(ByVal RowBuf As RowBuffer,
WriteLocation As Variant)
Dim Col%

' Update each column in the data set array
For Col% = 0 To MAXCOLS - 1
    ' Only columns that have been changed will be
    ' updated. Otherwise, the value will be set to NULL
    If Not IsNull(RowBuf.Value(0, Col%)) Then
        UserData(Col%, WriteLocation) = RowBuf.Value(0, Col%)
    End If
Next Col%
End Sub
```

Underline Property

Returns or sets the font style of the **Font** object to either underlined or nonunderlined.

Applies To

Font Object

Syntax

object.**Underline** [= *boolean*]

The **Underline** property syntax has these parts:

Part	Description
object	An object expression that evaluates to an object in the **Applies To** list.
boolean	A Boolean expression specifying the font style, as described in Settings.

Settings

The settings for *boolean* are:

Setting	Description
True	Turns on underline formatting.
False	(Default) Turns off underline formatting.

Remarks

The **Font** object isn't directly available at design time. Instead you set the **Underline** property by selecting a control's **Font** property in the Properties window and clicking the Properties button. In the Font dialog box, select the Underline check box. At run time, however, you set **Underline** directly by specifying its setting for the **Font** object.

See Also

Bold Property, **FontTransparent** Property, **Italic** Property, **Size** Property (Font), **StrikeThrough** Property, **Weight** Property, **Name** Property

Example

This example prints text on a form with each mouse click. To try this example, paste the code into the Declarations section of a form, and then press F5 and click the form twice.

```
Private Sub Form_Click ()
    Font.Bold = Not Font.Bold   ' Toggle bold.
    Font.StrikeThrough = Not Font.StrikeThrough ' Toggle strikethrough.
    Font.Italic = Not Font.Italic     ' Toggle italic.
    Font.Underline = Not Font.Underline      ' Toggle underline.
    Font.Size = 16 ' Set Size property.
    If Font.Bold Then
        Print "Font weight is " & Font.Weight & " (bold)."
    Else
        Print "Font weight is " & Font.Weight & " (not bold)."

    End If
End Sub
```

Unique Property

Sets or returns a value that indicates whether an **Index** object represents a unique (key) index for a table (Microsoft Jet workspaces only).

Applies To

Index Object

Settings and Return Values

The setting or return value is a **Boolean** that is **True** if the **Index** object represents a unique index. For an **Index** object, this property setting is read/write until the object is appended to a collection, after which it's read-only.

Remarks

A unique index consists of one or more fields that logically arrange all records in a table in a unique, predefined order. If the index consists of one field, values in that field must be unique for the entire table. If the index consists of more than one field, each field can contain duplicate values, but each combination of values from all the indexed fields must be unique.

If both the **Unique** and **Primary** properties of an **Index** object are set to **True**, the index is unique and primary: It uniquely identifies all records in the table in a predefined, logical order. If the **Primary** property is set to **False**, the index is a secondary index. Secondary indexes (both key and nonkey) logically arrange records in a predefined order without serving as an identifier for records in the table.

Notes

- You don't have to create indexes for tables, but in large, unindexed tables, accessing a specific record can take a long time.

- Records retrieved from tables without indexes are returned in no particular sequence.

- The **Attributes** property of each **Field** object in the **Index** object determines the order of records and consequently determines the access techniques to use for that **Index** object.

- A unique index helps optimize finding records.

- Indexes don't affect the physical order of a base table—indexes affect only how the records are accessed by the table-type **Recordset** object when a particular index is chosen or when the Microsoft Jet database engine creates **Recordset** objects.

See Also

Attributes Property, **Clustered** Property, **Primary** Property

Example

This example sets the **Unique** property of a new **Index** object to **True**, and appends the **Index** to the **Indexes** collection of the Employees table. It then enumerates the **Indexes** collection of the **TableDef** and the **Properties** collection of each **Index**. The new **Index** will only allow one record with a particular combination of **Country**, **LastName**, and **FirstName** in the **TableDef**.

```
Sub UniqueX()

    Dim dbsNorthwind As Database
    Dim tdfEmployees As TableDef
    Dim idxNew As Index
    Dim idxLoop As Index
    Dim prpLoop As Property

    Set dbsNorthwind = OpenDatabase("Northwind.mdb")
    Set tdfEmployees = dbsNorthwind!Employees

    With tdfEmployees
        ' Create and append new Index object to the Indexes
        ' collection of the Employees table.
        Set idxNew = .CreateIndex("NewIndex")

        With idxNew
            .Fields.Append .CreateField("Country")
            .Fields.Append .CreateField("LastName")
            .Fields.Append .CreateField("FirstName")
            .Unique = True
        End With
```

```
            .Indexes.Append idxNew
            .Indexes.Refresh

            Debug.Print .Indexes.Count & " Indexes in " & _
               .Name & " TableDef"

            ' Enumerate Indexes collection of Employees table.
            For Each idxLoop In .Indexes
               Debug.Print "    " & idxLoop.Name

               ' Enumerate Properties collection of each Index
               ' object.
               For Each prpLoop In idxLoop.Properties
                  Debug.Print "        " & prpLoop.Name & _
                     " = " & IIf(prpLoop = "", "[empty]", prpLoop)
               Next prpLoop

            Next idxLoop

            ' Delete new Index because this is a demonstration.
            .Indexes.Delete idxNew.Name
         End With

         dbsNorthwind.Close

      End Sub
```

Unload Event

Occurs when a form is about to be removed from the screen. When that form is reloaded, the contents of all its controls are reinitialized. This event is triggered by a user closing the form using the Close command on the Control menu or an **Unload** statement.

Applies To

PropertyPage Object, **Form** Object, **Forms** Collection, **MDIForm** Object

Syntax

Private Sub *object*_**Unload**(*cancel* **As Integer**)

The **Unload** event syntax has these parts:

Part	Description
object	An object expression that evaluates to an object in the **Applies To** list.
cancel	Integer that determines whether the form is removed from the screen. If *cancel* is 0, the form is removed. Setting *cancel* to any nonzero value prevents the form from being removed.

Remarks

Setting *cancel* to any nonzero value prevents the form from being removed, but doesn't stop other events, such as exiting from the Microsoft Windows operating environment. Use the **QueryUnload** event to stop exiting from Windows.

Use an Unload event procedure to verify that the form should be unloaded or to specify actions that you want to take place when the form is unloaded. You can also include any form-level validation code you may need for closing the form or saving the data in it to a file.

The **QueryUnload** event occurs before the **Unload** event. The **Unload** event occurs before the **Terminate** event.

The **Unload** event can be caused by using the **Unload** statement, or by the user choosing the Close command on a form's Control menu, exiting the application with the End Task button on the Windows Task List, closing the MDI form for which the current form is a child form, or exiting the Microsoft Windows operating environment while the application is running.

See Also

Load Event, **QueryUnload** Event, **Load** Statement, **Unload** Statement

Example

This example demonstrates a simple procedure to close a form while prompting the user with various message boxes. In an actual application, you can add calls to general purpose **Sub** procedures that emulate the processing of the Exit, Save, and Save As commands on the File menu in Visual Basic. To try this example, paste the code into the Declarations section of a form, and then press F5. Once the form is displayed, press ALT+F4 to close the form.

```
Private Sub Form_Unload (Cancel As Integer)
    Dim Msg, Response ' Declare variables.
    Msg = "Save Data before closing?"
    Response = MsgBox(Msg, vbQuestion + vbYesNoCancel, "Save Dialog")
    Select Case Response
        Case vbCancel  ' Don't allow close.
            Cancel = -1
            Msg = "Command has been canceled."
        Case vbYes
        ' Enter code to save data here.
            Msg = "Data saved."'
        Case vbNo
            Msg = "Data not saved."
    End Select
    MsgBox Msg, vbOKOnly, "Confirm"   ' Display message.

End Sub
```

Unload Statement (Forms and Controls)

Unloads a form or control from memory.

Syntax

Unload *object*

The *object* placeholder is the name of a **Form** object or control array element to unload.

Remarks

Unloading a form or control may be necessary or expedient in some cases where the memory used is needed for something else, or when you need to reset properties to their original values.

Before a form is unloaded, the **Query_Unload** event procedure occurs, followed by the **Form_Unload** event procedure. Setting the *cancel* argument to **True** in either of these events prevents the form from being unloaded. For **MDIForm** objects, the **MDIForm** object's **Query_Unload** event procedure occurs, followed by the **Query_Unload** event procedure and **Form_Unload** event procedure for each MDI child form, and finally the **MDIForm** object's **Form_Unload** event procedure.

When a form is unloaded, all controls placed on the form at run time are no longer accessible. Controls placed on the form at design time remain intact; however, any run-time changes to those controls and their properties are lost when the form is reloaded. All changes to form properties are also lost. Accessing any controls on the form causes it to be reloaded.

Note When a form is unloaded, only the displayed component is unloaded. The code associated with the form module remains in memory.

Only control array elements added to a form at run time can be unloaded with the **Unload** statement. The properties of unloaded controls are reinitialized when the controls are reloaded.

See Also

QueryUnload Event, **Load** Statement, **Hide** Method, **Show** Method

Example

This example uses the **Unload** statement to unload a **Form** object. To try this example, paste the code into the Declarations section of a **Form** object, and then run the example and click the **Form** object.

```
Private Sub Form_Click ()
    Dim Answer, Msg                    ' Declare variable.
    Unload Form1                       ' Unload form.
    Msg = "Form1 has been unloaded. Choose Yes to load and "
    Msg = Msg & "display the form. Choose No to load the form "
    Msg = Msg & "and leave it invisible."
    Answer = MsgBox(Msg, vbYesNo)      ' Get user response.
```

```
      If Answer = vbYes Then          ' Evaluate answer.
         Show                         ' If Yes, show form.
      Else
         Load Form1                   ' If No, just load it.
         Msg = "Form1 is now loaded. Choose OK to display it."
         MsgBox Msg                   ' Display message.
         Show                         ' Show form.
      End If
End Sub
```

Unload Statement (VBA)

Removes an object from memory.

Syntax

Unload *object*

The required *object* placeholder represents an object expression that evaluates to an object in the **Applies To** list.

Remarks

When an object is unloaded, it's removed from memory and all memory associated with the object is reclaimed. Until it is placed in memory again using the **Load** statement, a user can't interact with an object, and the object can't be manipulated programmatically.

See Also

QueryUnload Event, **Hide** Method, **Show** Method, **Load** Statement

Example

The following example assumes two **UserForms** in a program. In UserForm1's **Initialize** event, UserForm2 is loaded and shown. When the user clicks UserForm2, it is unloaded and UserForm1 appears. When UserForm1 is clicked, it is unloaded in turn.

```
' This is the Initialize event procedure for UserForm1
Private Sub UserForm_Initialize()
   Load UserForm2
   UserForm2.Show
End Sub
' This is the Click event for UserForm2
Private Sub UserForm_Click()
   Unload UserForm2
End Sub

' This is the click event for UserForm1
Private Sub UserForm_Click()
   Unload UserForm1
End Sub
```

Updatable Property

Returns a value that indicates whether you can change a DAO object.

Applies To

Database Object, **Dynaset-Type Recordset** Object, **QueryDef** Object, **Recordset** Object, **Snapshot-Type Recordset** Object, **Table-Type Recordset** Object, **TableDef** Object, **Connection** Object, **Forward-Only–Type Recordset** Object, **Dynamic-Type Recordset** Object

Return Values

The return value is a **Boolean** data type that is **True** if the object can be changed or updated. (Snapshot- and forward-only–type **Recordset** objects always return **False**.)

Remarks

Depending on the object, if the **Updatable** property setting is **True**, the associated statement in the following table is true.

Object	Type indicates
Database	The object can be changed
QueryDef	The query definition can be changed
Recordset	The records can be updated
TableDef	The table definition can be changed

The **Updatable** property setting is always **True** for a newly created **TableDef** object and **False** for a linked **TableDef** object. A new **TableDef** object can be appended only to a database for which the current user has write permission.

Many types of objects can contain fields that can't be updated. For example, you can create a dynaset-type **Recordset** object in which only some fields can be changed. These fields can be fixed or contain data that increments automatically, or the dynaset can result from a query that combines updatable and nonupdatable tables.

If the object contains only read-only fields, the value of the **Updatable** property is **False**. When one or more fields are updatable, the property's value is **True**. You can edit only the updatable fields. A trappable error occurs if you try to assign a new value to a read-only field.

The **Updatable** property of a **QueryDef** object is set to **True** if the query definition can be updated, even if the resulting **Recordset** object isn't updatable.

Because an updatable object can contain read-only fields, check the **DataUpdatable** property of each field in the **Fields** collection of a **Recordset** object before you edit a record.

See Also

Field Object

Example

This example demonstrates the **Updatable** property for a **Database**, four types of **Recordset** objects, a **TableDef**, and a **QueryDef**.

```
Sub UpdatableX()

    Dim dbsNorthwind As Database
    Dim rstEmployees As Recordset

    Set dbsNorthwind = OpenDatabase("Northwind.mdb")

    With dbsNorthwind
        Debug.Print .Name
        Debug.Print "    Updatable = " & .Updatable

        ' Default is dbOpenTable.
        Set rstEmployees = .OpenRecordset("Employees")
        Debug.Print _
            "Table-type recordset from Employees table"
        Debug.Print "    Updatable = " & _
            rstEmployees.Updatable
        rstEmployees.Close

        Set rstEmployees = .OpenRecordset("Employees", _
            dbOpenDynaset)
        Debug.Print _
            "Dynaset-type recordset from Employees table"
        Debug.Print "    Updatable = " & _
            rstEmployees.Updatable
        rstEmployees.Close

        Set rstEmployees = .OpenRecordset("Employees", _
            dbOpenSnapshot)
        Debug.Print _
            "Snapshot-type recordset from Employees table"
        Debug.Print "    Updatable = " & _
            rstEmployees.Updatable
        rstEmployees.Close

        Set rstEmployees = .OpenRecordset("Employees", _
            dbOpenForwardOnly)
        Debug.Print _
            "Forward-only-type recordset from Employees table"
        Debug.Print "    Updatable = " & _
            rstEmployees.Updatable
        rstEmployees.Close

        Debug.Print "'" & .TableDefs(0).Name & "' TableDef"
        Debug.Print "    Updatable = " & _
            .TableDefs(0).Updatable

        Debug.Print "'" & .QueryDefs(0).Name & "' QueryDef"
        Debug.Print "    Updatable = " & _
            .QueryDefs(0).Updatable

        .Close
    End With

End Sub
```

Updatable Property (Remote Data)

Returns a Boolean value that indicates whether changes can be made to a remote data object.

Applies To

rdoColumn Object, **rdoConnection** Object, **rdoPreparedStatement** Object, **rdoQuery** Object, **rdoResultset** Object, **rdoTable** Object

Syntax

object.**Updatable**

The *object* placeholder represents an object expression that evaluates to an object in the **Applies To** list.

Return Values

The **Updatable** property return values are:

Value	Description
True	The object can be changed or updated.
False	The object can't be changed or updated. This is the only setting for static-type **rdoResultset** objects.

Remarks

If the **Updatable** property setting is **True**, the specified:

- **rdoConnection** object refers to an updatable data source.

- **rdoQuery** object refers to an updatable result set.

- **rdoResultset** contains updatable rows.

- **rdoTable** object refers to a table whose data can be changed through use of a query.

- **rdoColumn** object refers to data that can be changed. Only **rdoColumn** objects which are part of an **rdoResultset** object can be changed.

You can use the **Updatable** property with all types of **rdoResultset** objects.

Many types of **rdoResultset** objects can contain columns that can't be updated. For example, you can create a forward-only **rdoResultset** that is derived from nonupdatable sources or that contains computed or derived columns.

If the object contains only nonupdatable columns, the value of the **Updatable** property is **False**. When one or more columns are updatable, the property's value is **True**. You can edit only the updatable columns. A trappable error occurs if you try to assign a new value to a nonupdatable column.

Because an updatable object can contain columns that cannot be updated, check the **Updatable** property of each **rdoColumn** before editing a row in the **rdoResultset**.

Even when a cursor cannot be updated, it might still be possible to update the data through use of an action query. In many cases, database tables are protected and not updatable by design—as they are protected from direct access by the system administrator and the remote system's permission scheme. If this is the case, check with your system administrator for the availability of stored procedures or special login accounts that permit you to perform your changes.

See Also

Update Method (Remote Data), **rdoColumn** Object, **rdoPreparedStatement** Object, **rdoResultset** Object, **rdoTable** Object

Update Method (Add-Ins)

Refreshes the contents of the **AddIns** collection from the add-ins listed in the Vbaddin.ini file in the same manner as if the user had opened the Add-In Manager dialog box.

Applies To

AddIns Collection

Syntax

object.**Update**

The *object* placeholder represents an object expression that evaluates to an object in the **Applies To** list.

Remarks

All add-ins listed in the Vbaddin.ini file must be registered ActiveX components in the Registry before they can be used in Visual Basic.

Update Method (DAO)

Saves the contents of the copy buffer to an updatable **Recordset** object.

Applies To

Dynaset-Type Recordset Object, **Recordset** Object, **Snapshot-Type Recordset** Object, **Table-Type Recordset** Object, **Forward-Only–Type Recordset** Object, **Dynamic-Type Recordset** Object

Syntax

recordset.**Update** (*type*, *force*)

The **Update** method syntax has the following parts.

Part	Description
recordset	An object variable that represents an open, updatable **Recordset** object.
type	Optional. A constant indicating the type of update, as specified in Settings (ODBCDirect workspaces only).
force	Optional. A **Boolean** value indicating whether or not to force the changes into the database, regardless of whether the underlying data has been changed by another user since the **AddNew**, **Delete**, or **Edit** call. If **True**, the changes are forced and changes made by other users are simply overwritten. If **False** (default), changes made by another user while the update is pending will cause the update to fail for those changes that are in conflict. No error occurs, but the **BatchCollisionCount** and **BatchCollisions** properties will indicate the number of conflicts and the rows affected by conflicts, respectively (ODBCDirect workspaces only).

Settings

You can use the following values for the *type* argument. You can use the non-default values only if batch updating is enabled.

Constant	Description
dbUpdateRegular	Default. Pending changes aren't cached and are written to disk immediately.
dbUpdateBatch	All pending changes in the update cache are written to disk.
dbUpdateCurrentRecord	Only the current record's pending changes are written to disk.

Remarks

Use **Update** to save the current record and any changes you've made to it.

Caution Changes to the current record are lost if:

- You use the **Edit** or **AddNew** method, and then move to another record without first using **Update**.

- You use **Edit** or **AddNew**, and then use **Edit** or **AddNew** again without first using **Update**.

- You set the **Bookmark** property to another record.

- You close *recordset* without first using **Update**.

- You cancel the **Edit** operation by using **CancelUpdate**.

To edit a record, use the **Edit** method to copy the contents of the current record to the copy buffer. If you don't use **Edit** first, an error occurs when you use **Update** or attempt to change a field's value.

In an ODBCDirect workspace, you can do batch updates, provided the cursor library supports batch updates, and the **Recordset** was opened with the optimistic batch locking option.

In a Microsoft Jet workspace, when the **Recordset** object's **LockEdits** property setting is **True** (pessimistically locked) in a multiuser environment, the record remains locked from the time **Edit** is used until the **Update** method is executed or the edit is canceled. If the **LockEdits** property setting is **False** (optimistically locked), the record is locked and compared with the pre-edited record just before it is updated in the database. If the record has changed since you used the **Edit** method, the **Update** operation fails. Microsoft Jet-connected ODBC and installable ISAM databases always use optimistic locking. To continue the **Update** operation with your changes, use the **Update** method again. To revert to the record as the other user changed it, refresh the current record by using Move 0.

Note To add, edit, or delete a record, there must be a unique index on the record in the underlying data source. If not, a "Permission denied" error will occur on the **AddNew, Delete,** or **Edit** method call in a Microsoft Jet workspace, or an "Invalid argument" error will occur on the **Update** call in an ODBCDirect workspace.

See Also

AddNew Method, **OpenRecordset** Method, **LockEdits** Property

Example

This example demonstrates the **Update** method in conjunction with **Edit** method.

```
Sub UpdateX()

    Dim dbsNorthwind As Database
    Dim rstEmployees As Recordset
    Dim strOldFirst As String
    Dim strOldLast As String
    Dim strMessage As String

    Set dbsNorthwind = OpenDatabase("Northwind.mdb")
    Set rstEmployees = _
        dbsNorthwind.OpenRecordset("Employees")

    With rstEmployees
        .Edit
        ' Store original data.
        strOldFirst = !FirstName
        strOldLast = !LastName
        ' Change data in edit buffer.
        !FirstName = "Linda"
        !LastName = "Kobara"

        ' Show contents of buffer and get user input.
        strMessage = "Edit in progress:" & vbCr & _
            "    Original data = " & strOldFirst & " " & _
            strOldLast & vbCr & "    Data in buffer = " & _
            !FirstName & " " & !LastName & vbCr & vbCr & _
            "Use Update to replace the original data with " & _
            "the buffered data in the Recordset?"
```

```
            If MsgBox(strMessage, vbYesNo) = vbYes Then
               .Update
            Else
               .CancelUpdate
            End If

            ' Show the resulting data.
            MsgBox "Data in recordset = " & !FirstName & " " & _
               !LastName

            ' Restore original data because this is a demonstration.
            If Not (strOldFirst = !FirstName And _
                  strOldLast = !LastName) Then
               .Edit
               !FirstName = strOldFirst
               !LastName = strOldLast
               .Update
            End If

            .Close
      End With

      dbsNorthwind.Close

End Sub
```

This example demonstrates the **Update** method in conjunction with the **AddNew** method.

```
Sub UpdateX2()

   Dim dbsNorthwind As Database
   Dim rstEmployees As Recordset
   Dim strOldFirst As String
   Dim strOldLast As String
   Dim strMessage As String

   Set dbsNorthwind = OpenDatabase("Northwind.mdb")
   Set rstEmployees = _
      dbsNorthwind.OpenRecordset("Employees")

   With rstEmployees
      .AddNew
      !FirstName = "Bill"
      !LastName = "Sornsin"

      ' Show contents of buffer and get user input.
      strMessage = "AddNew in progress:" & vbCr & _
         "    Data in buffer = " & !FirstName & " " & _
         !LastName & vbCr & vbCr & _
         "Use Update to save buffer to recordset?"

      If MsgBox(strMessage, vbYesNoCancel) = vbYes Then
         .Update
         ' Go to the new record and show the resulting data.
         .Bookmark = .LastModified
         MsgBox "Data in recordset = " & !FirstName & _
            " " & !LastName
```

```
        ' Delete new data because this is a demonstration.
        .Delete
    Else
        .CancelUpdate
        MsgBox "No new record added."
    End If

    .Close
End With

dbsNorthwind.Close

End Sub
```

Update Method (OLE Container)

Retrieves the current data from the application that supplied the object and displays that data as a graphic in the **OLE** container control.

Applies To

 OLE Container Control

Syntax

 object.**Update**

 The *object* is an object expression that evaluates to an object in the **Applies To** list.

Update Method (Remote Data)

Saves the contents of the copy buffer row to a specified updatable **rdoResultset** object and discards the copy buffer.

Applies To

 rdoResultset Object

Syntax

 object.**Update**

 The *object* placeholder represents an object expression that evaluates to an object in the **Applies To** list.

Remarks

 Use **Update** to save the current row and any changes you've made to it to the underlying database table(s). Changes you make to the **rdoResultset** after using the **AddNew** or **Edit** methods can be lost if you do not use the **Update** method before the application ends.

Note When you use the ClientBatch cursor library, all updates to the base tables are deferred until you use the **BatchUpdate** method. In this case, the **Update** method updates the local **rdoResultset**, but does not update the base tables. These changes can be lost if the application ends before the **BatchUpdate** method has been completed.

Changes to the current row are lost if:

- You use the **Edit** or **AddNew** method, and then reposition the current row pointer to another row without first using **Update**.

- You use **Edit** or **AddNew**, and then use **Edit** or **AddNew** again without first using **Update**.

- You cancel the update with the **CancelUpdate** method.

- You set the **Bookmark** property to another row.

- You close the result set referred to by *object* without first using **Update**.

- The application ends before the **Update** method is executed, as when system power is interrupted.

To edit a row, use the **Edit** method to copy the contents of the current row to the copy buffer. If you don't use **AddNew** or **Edit** first, an error occurs when you use **Update** or attempt to add a new row.

To add a new row, use the **AddNew** method to initialize and activate the copy buffer.

Using **Update** produces an error under any of the following conditions:

- There is no current row.

- The connection or **rdoResultset** is read-only.

- No columns in the row are updatable.

- You do not have an **Edit** or **AddNew** operation pending.

- Another user has locked the row or data page containing your row.

- The user does not have permission to perform the operation.

- Depending on the driver and type of cursor being used, you might not be able to use the cursor to update the primary key.

See Also

AddNew Method (Remote Data), **BeginTrans**, **CommitTrans**, **RollbackTrans** Methods, **Edit** Method (Remote Data), **OpenResultset** Method (Remote Data), **Update** Method (Remote Data), **UpdateControls** Method (Remote Data), **UpdateRow** Method (Remote Data), **rdoResultset** Object, **RemoteData** Control, **Bookmark** Property (Remote Data), **LockEdits** Property (Remote Data)

Example

The following example illustrates use of the **AddNew** method to add new rows to a base table. This example assumes that you have read-write access to the table, that the column data provided meets the rules and other constraints associated with the table, and there is a unique index on the table. The data values for the operation are taken from three **TextBox** controls on the form. Note that the unique key for this table is not provided here as it is provided automatically—it is an identity column.

```
Option Explicit
Dim er As rdoError
Dim cn As New rdoConnection
Dim qy As New rdoQuery
Dim rs As rdoResultset
Dim col As rdoColumn

Private Sub AddNewJob_Click()
On Error GoTo ANEH

With rs
    .AddNew
    !job_desc = JobDescription
    !min_lvl = MinLevel
    !max_lvl = MaxLevel
    .Update
End With
Exit Sub

UpdateFailed:
MsgBox "Update did not suceed."
rs.CancelUpdate
Exit Sub
A
NEH:
Debug.Print Err, Error
For Each er In rdoErrors

Debug.Print er
Next
Resume UpdateFailed

End Sub

Private Sub Form_Load()

cn.CursorDriver = rdUseOdbc
cn.Connect = "uid=;pwd=;server=sequel;" _
    & "driver={SQL Server};database=pubs;dsn='';"
cn.EstablishConnection
With qy
    .Name = "JobsQuery"
    .SQL = "Select * from Jobs"
    .RowsetSize = 1
    Set .ActiveConnection = cn
    Set rs = .OpenResultset(rdOpenKeyset, _
        rdConcurRowver)
    Debug.Print rs.Updatable
End With

Exit Sub
End Sub
```

UpdateControls Method

Gets the current record from a **Data** control's **Recordset** object and displays the appropriate data in controls bound to a **Data** control. Doesn't support named arguments.

Applies To

Data Control

Syntax

object.**UpdateControls**

The *object* placeholder represents an object expression that evaluates to an object in the **Applies To** list.

Remarks

Use this method to restore the contents of bound controls to their original values, as when a user makes changes to data and then decides to cancel the changes.

This method creates the same effect as making the current record current again, except that no events occur.

The **UpdateControls** method terminates any pending **Edit** or **AddNew** operation.

See Also

Recordset Object, **UpdateRecord** Method, **ValidationRule** Property

---

UpdateControls Method (Remote Data)

Gets the current row from a **RemoteData** control's **rdoResultset** object and displays the appropriate data in controls bound to a **RemoteData** control.

Applies To

RemoteData Control

Syntax

object.**UpdateControls**

The *object* placeholder represents an object expression that evaluates to an object in the **Applies To** list.

Remarks

Use this method to restore the contents of bound controls to their original values, as when a user makes changes to data and then decides to cancel the changes.

This method creates the same effect as making the current row current again, except that no events occur. By not invoking any events, this method can be used to simplify an update operation because no additional validation or change event procedures are triggered.

See Also

Edit Method (Remote Data), **Update** Method (Remote Data), **UpdateRow** Method (Remote Data)

UpdateCriteria Property

Returns or sets a value that specifies how the WHERE clause is constructed for each row during an optimistic batch update operation.

Applies To

rdoResultset Object, **RemoteData** Control

Syntax

object.**UpdateCriteria** [= *value*]

The **UpdateCriteria** property syntax has these parts:

Part	Description
object	An object expression that evaluates to an object in the **Applies To** list.
value	A **Long** integer representing the type of cursor as described in Settings

Settings

The **UpdateCriteria** property has these settings:

Constant	Value	rdoResultset type
rdCriteriaKey	0	(Default). Uses just the key column(s) in the where clause.
rdCriteriaAllCols	1	Uses the key column(s) and all updated columns in the where clause.
rdCriteriaUpdCols	2	Uses the key column(s) and all the columns in the where clause.
rdCriteriaTimeStamp	3	Uses just the timestamp column if available (will generate a runtime error if no timestamp column is in the result set).

Remarks

When a batch mode operation is executed, RDO and the **ClientBatch** cursor library create a series of UPDATE statements to make the needed changes. An SQL WHERE clause is created for each update to isolate the rows that are marked as changed (by the **Status** property). Because some remote servers use triggers or other ways to enforce referential integrity, is it often important to limit the columns being updated to just those affected by the change. This way, only the absolute minimum amount of trigger code is executed. As a result, the update operation is executed more quickly, and with fewer potential errors.

You should set the **UpdateCriteria** property to **rdCriteriaKey** when BLOB columns are included in the result set.

Setting this property to a value other than the ones listed here results in a runtime error.

See Also

AddNew Method, **BatchCollisionCount** Property, **BatchCollisionRows** Property, **BatchConflictValue** Property, **BatchSize** Property, **Update** Method

---

Updated Event

Occurs when an object's data has been modified.

Applies To

OLE Container Control

Syntax

Sub *object*_**Updated** (*code* **As Integer**)

The **Updated** event syntax has these parts:

Part	Description
object	An object expression that evaluates to an object in the **Applies To** list.
code	An integer that specifies how the object was updated, as described in Settings.

Settings

The settings for *code* are:

Constant	Value	Description
vbOLEChanged	0	The object's data has changed.
vbOLESaved	1	The object's data has been saved by the application that created the object.
vbOLEClosed	2	The file containing the linked object's data has been closed by the application that created the object.
vbOLERenamed	3	The file containing the linked object's data has been renamed by the application that created the object.

Remarks

These constants are listed in the Visual Basic (VB) object library in the Object Browser. You can use this event to determine if an object's data has been changed since it was last saved. To do this, set a global variable in the Updated event indicating that the object needs to be saved. After you save the object, reset the variable.

See Also

Class Property, **OLEType** Property, **UpdateOptions** Property, **OLETypeAllowed** Property

---

UpdateOperation Property

Returns or sets a value that specifies if the optimistic batch update should use an Update statement or a Delete followed by an Insert.

Applies To

rdoResultset Object, **RemoteData** Control

Syntax

object.**UpdateOperation** [= *value*]

The **UpdateOperation** property syntax has these parts:

Part	Description
object	An object expression that evaluates to an object in the **Applies To** list.
value	A **Long** integer representing the type of cursor as described in Settings:

Settings

The **UpdateOperation** property has these settings:

Constant	Value	UpdateOperation type
rdOperationUpdate	0	(Default) Uses an Update statement for each modified row.
rdOperationDelIns	1	Uses a pair of Delete and Insert statements for each modified row.

Remarks

Setting the **UpdateOperation** property to a value other than the ones listed here results in a runtime error.

This property determines whether the optimistic batch update cursor library uses an update statement, or a pair of delete and insert statements when sending modifications back to the database server. In the latter case, two separate operations are required to update the row. In some cases, especially where the remote system implements Delete, Insert and Update triggers, choosing the correct **UpdateOperation** property can significantly impact performance.

Newly added rows will always generate Insert statements and deleted rows will always generate Delete statements, so this property only **Applies To** how the cursor library updates modified rows.

See Also

BatchCollisionCount Property, **BatchCollisionRows** Property, **BatchConflictValue** Property, **BatchSize** Property, **BatchUpdate** Method, **CancelBatch** Method

UpdateOptions Property

Returns or sets a value specifying how an object is updated when linked data is modified.

Applies To

OLE Container Control

Syntax

object.**UpdateOptions** [= *number*]

The **UpdateOptions** property syntax has these parts:

Part	Description
object	An object expression that evaluates to an object in the **Applies To** list.
number	A integer specifying how an object is updated, as described in Settings.

Settings

The settings for *number* are:

Constant	Value	Description
vbOLEAutomatic	0	(Default) Automatic. The object is updated each time the linked data changes.
vbOLEFrozen	1	Frozen. The object is updated whenever the user saves the linked data from within the application in which it was created.
vbOLEManual	2	Manual. The object is updated only by using the **Update** method.

Remarks

This property is useful for linked objects where other users or applications can access and modify the linked data.

When an object's data is changed, the **Updated** event is invoked.

See Also

Class Property, **OLEType** Property, **Updated** Event, **OLETypeAllowed** Property, **Update** Method (OLE Container)

UpdateOptions Property (DAO)

Sets or returns a value that indicates how the WHERE clause is constructed for each record during a batch update, and whether the batch update should use an UPDATE statement or a DELETE followed by an INSERT (**ODBCDirect** workspaces only).

Applies To

Dynaset-Type Recordset Object, **Recordset** Object, **Snapshot-Type Recordset** Object, **Forward-Only–Type Recordset** Object, **Dynamic-Type Recordset** Object

Settings And Return Values

The setting or return value is a **Long** that can be any of the following constants:

Constant	Description
dbCriteriaKey	(Default) Uses just the key column(s) in the where clause.
dbCriteriaModValues	Uses the key column(s) and all updated columns in the where clause.
dbCriteriaAllCols	Uses the key column(s) and all the columns in the where clause.
dbCriteriaTimeStamp	Uses just the timestamp column if available (will generate a run-time error if no timestamp column is in the result set).
dbCriteriaDeleteInsert	Uses a set of DELETE and INSERT statements for each modified row.
dbCriteriaUpdate	(Default) Uses an UPDATE statement for each modified row.

Remarks

When a batch-mode **Update** is executed, DAO and the client batch cursor library create a series of SQL UPDATE statements to make the needed changes. An SQL WHERE clause is created for each update to isolate the records that are marked as changed by the **RecordStatus** property. Because some remote servers use triggers or other ways to enforce referential integrity, is it often important to limit the fields being updated to just those affected by the change. To do this, set the **UpdateOptions** property to one of the constants **dbCriteriaKey**, **dbCriteriaModValues**, **dbCriteriaAllCols**, or **dbCriteriaTimeStamp**. This way, only the absolute minimum amount of trigger code is executed. As a result, the update operation is executed more quickly, and with fewer potential errors.

You can also concatenate either of the constants **dbCriteriaDeleteInsert** or **dbCriteriaUpdate** to determine whether to use a set of SQL DELETE and INSERT statements or an SQL UPDATE statement for each update when sending batched modifications back to the server. In the former case, two separate operations are required to update the record. In some cases, especially where the remote system implements DELETE, INSERT, and UPDATE triggers, choosing the correct **UpdateOptions** property setting can significantly impact performance.

If you don't specify any constants, **dbCriteriaUpdate** and **dbCriteriaKey** will be used.

Newly added records will always generate INSERT statements and deleted records will always generate DELETE statements, so this property only Applies To how the cursor library updates modified records.

Example

This example uses the **BatchSize** and **UpdateOptions** properties to control aspects of any batch updating for the specified **Recordset** object.

```
Sub BatchSizeX()

    Dim wrkMain As Workspace
    Dim conMain As Connection
    Dim rstTemp As Recordset

    Set wrkMain = CreateWorkspace("ODBCWorkspace", _
        "admin", "", dbUseODBC)
    ' This DefaultCursorDriver setting is required for
    ' batch updating.
    wrkMain.DefaultCursorDriver = dbUseClientBatchCursor

    Set conMain = wrkMain.OpenConnection("Publishers", _
        dbDriverNoPrompt, False, _
        "ODBC;DATABASE=pubs;UID=sa;PWD=;DSN=Publishers")
    ' The following locking argument is required for
    ' batch updating.
    Set rstTemp = conMain.OpenRecordset( _
        "SELECT * FROM roysched", dbOpenDynaset, 0, _
        dbOptimisticBatch)

    With rstTemp
        ' Increase the number of statements sent to the server
        ' during a single batch update, thereby reducing the
        ' number of times an update would have to access the
        ' server.
        .BatchSize = 25

        ' Change the UpdateOptions property so that the WHERE
        ' clause of any batched statements going to the server
        ' will include any updated columns in addition to the
        ' key column(s). Also, any modifications to records
        ' will be made by deleting the original record
        ' and adding a modified version rather than just
        ' modifying the original record.
        .UpdateOptions = dbCriteriaModValues + _
            dbCriteriaDeleteInsert

        ' Engage in batch updating using the new settings
        ' above.
        ' ...

        .Close
    End With

    conMain.Close
    wrkMain.Close

End Sub
```

UpdateRecord Method

Saves the current values of bound controls. Doesn't support named arguments.

Applies To

Data Control

Syntax

object.**UpdateRecord**

The *object* placeholder represents an object expression that evaluates to an object in the **Applies To** list.

Remarks

Use this method to save the current contents of bound controls to the database during the **Validate** event without triggering the **Validate** event again. Using this method avoids creating a cascading event.

The **UpdateRecord** method has the same effect as executing the **Edit** method, changing a field, and then executing the **Update** method, except that no events occur.

You can use this method to avoid triggering the **Validate** event.

Whenever you attempt to update a record in the database, any validation rules must be satisfied before the record is written to the database. These rules are established by setting the **ValidationRule** property or, in the case of Microsoft SQL Server, by Transact SQL defaults, rules, and triggers written to enforce referential and data integrity.

In some cases, the update may not occur because the operation violates referential integrity constraints, the page containing the record is locked, the database or **Recordset** object isn't updatable, or the user doesn't have permission to perform the operation. Any of these conditions generates a trappable error.

UpdateRow Method (Remote Data)

Saves the current values of bound controls to the database.

Applies To

RemoteData Control

Syntax

object.**UpdateRow**

The *object* placeholder represents an object expression that evaluates to an object in the **Applies To** list.

Remarks

Use this method to save the current contents of bound controls to the database during the **Validate** event, but without triggering the Validate event again. You can use this method to avoid triggering the **Validate** event. Using this method avoids a cascading event.

The **UpdateRow** method has the same effect as executing the **Edit** method, changing a column, and then executing the **Update** method, except that no events occur.

Note When you use the **ClientBatch** cursor library, all updates to the base tables are deferred until you use the **BatchUpdate** method. In this case, the **UpdateRow** method updates the local **rdoResultset**, but does not update the base tables. These changes can be lost if the application ends before the **BatchUpdate** method has been completed.

Whenever you attempt to update a row in the database, any validation rules must be satisfied before the row is written to the database. In the case of Microsoft SQL Server, these rules are established by Transact SQL defaults, rules, and triggers written to enforce referential and data integrity.

An update may not occur because of any of the following reasons, which can also trigger a trappable error:

- The page containing the row or the row itself is locked.
- The database or **rdoResultset** object isn't updatable.
- The user doesn't have permission to perform the operation.

See Also

AddNew Method (Remote Data), **BeginTrans**, **CommitTrans**, **RollbackTrans** Methods, **Edit** Method (Remote Data), **OpenResultset** Method (Remote Data), **UpdateControls** Method (Remote Data), **rdoResultset** Object, **RemoteData** Control, **Bookmark** Property (Remote Data), **LockEdits** Property (Remote Data)

UseMaskColor Property

Returns or sets a value that determines whether the color assigned in the **MaskColor** property is used as a "mask". (That is, used to create transparent regions.)

Applies To

CheckBox Control, **CommandButton** Control, **OptionButton** Control

Syntax

object.**UseMask** [= *boolean*]

The **UseMask** property syntax has these parts:

Part	Description
object	An object expression that evaluates to an object in the **Applies To** list.
boolean	A Boolean expression that specifies whether the color assigned to the **MaskColor** property is used as a mask.

Settings

The settings for *boolean* are:

Setting	Description
True	The color assigned to the **MaskColor** property is used as a mask, creating a transparent region wherever that color is.
False	(Default) The color assigned to the **MaskColor** property is ignored, and the color remains opaque.

UseMnemonic Property

Returns or sets a value that specifies whether an ampersand (&) included in the text of the **Caption** property of the **Label** control defines an access key.

Applies To

Label Control

Syntax

object.**UseMnemonic** [= *boolean*]

The **UseMnemonic** property syntax has these parts:

Part	Description
object	An object expression that evaluates to an object in the **Applies To** list.
boolean	A Boolean expression specifying whether the **Label** control enables an access key, as described in Settings.

Settings

The settings for *boolean* are:

Setting	Description
True	(Default) Any ampersand appearing in the text of the **Caption** property causes the character following the ampersand to become an access key. The ampersand itself isn't displayed in the interface of the **Label** control.
False	Any ampersand appearing in the text of the **Caption** property is displayed as an ampersand in the interface of the **Label** control.

Remarks

At run time, pressing ALT+ the access key defined in the **Label** control's **Caption** property moves focus to the control that follows the **Label** control in the tab order.

See Also

  Caption Property

Example

  This example reads the setting of the **UseMnemonic** property of a **Label** control. To
  try this example, paste the code into the Declarations section of a form that contains a
  Label, and then press F5 and click the form.

```
Private Sub Form_Click()
    If Label1.UseMnemonic And InStr(Label1, "&") Then
        MsgBox "The label has an access key character."
    ElseIf Label1.UseMnemonic And Not InStr(Label1, "&") Then
        MsgBox "The label supports an access key character but
        doesn't have an ampersand."
    Else
        MsgBox "The label doesn't support an access key character."
    End If
End Sub
```

User Object

  A **User** object represents a user account that has access permissions when a
  Workspace object operates as a secure workgroup (Microsoft Jet workspaces only).

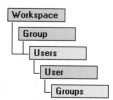

Remarks

  You use **User** objects to establish and enforce access permissions for the **Document**
  objects that represent databases, tables, and queries. Also, if you know the properties
  of a specific **User** object, you can create a new **Workspace** object that has the same
  access permissions as the **User** object.

  You can append an existing **User** object to the **Users** collection of a **Group** object to
  give a user account the access permissions for that **Group** object. Alternatively, you
  can append the **Group** object to the **Groups** collection in a **User** object to establish
  membership of the user account in that group. If you use a **Users** or **Groups**
  collection other than the one to which you just appended an object, you may need to
  use the **Refresh** method.

  With the properties of a **User** object, you can:

  • Use the **Name** property to return the name of an existing user. You can't return the
   PID and **Password** properties of an existing **User** object.

- Use the **Name**, **PID**, and **Password** properties of a newly created, unappended **User** object to establish the identity of that **User** object. If you don't set the **Password** property, it's set to a zero-length string ("").

The Microsoft Jet database engine predefines two **User** objects named Admin and Guest. The user Admin is a member of both of the **Group** objects named Admins and Users; the user Guest is a member only of the **Group** object named Guests.

To create a new **User** object, use the **CreateUser** method.

To refer to a **User** object in a collection by its ordinal number or by its **Name** property setting, use any of the following syntax forms:

[*workspace* | *group*].**Users**(0)
[*workspace* | *group*].**Users**("*name*")
[*workspace* | *group*].**Users**![*name*]

Properties

Name Property, **Password** Property, **PID** Property

Methods

CreateGroup Method, **NewPassword** Method

See Also

CreateUser Method

Example

This example illustrates the use of the **Group** and **User** objects and the **Groups** and **Users** collections. First, it creates a new **User** object and appends the object to the **Users** collection of the default **Workspace** object. Next, it creates a new **Group** object and appends the object to the **Groups** collection of the default **Workspace** object. Then the example adds user Pat Smith to the Accounting group. Finally, it enumerates the **Users** and **Groups** collections of the default **Workspace** object. See the methods and properties listed in the **Group** and **User** summary topics for additional examples.

```
Sub GroupX()

    Dim wrkDefault As Workspace
    Dim usrNew As User
    Dim usrLoop As User
    Dim grpNew As Group
    Dim grpLoop As Group
    Dim grpMember As Group

    Set wrkDefault = DBEngine.Workspaces(0)

    With wrkDefault
```

```
' Create and append new user.
Set usrNew = .CreateUser("Pat Smith", _
    "abc123DEF456", "Password1")
.Users.Append usrNew

' Create and append new group.
Set grpNew = .CreateGroup("Accounting", _
    "UVW987xyz654")
.Groups.Append grpNew

' Make the user Pat Smith a member of the
' Accounting group by creating and adding the
' appropriate Group object to the user's Groups
' collection. The same is accomplished if a User
' object representing Pat Smith is created and
' appended to the Accounting group's Users
' collection.
Set grpMember = usrNew.CreateGroup("Accounting")
usrNew.Groups.Append grpMember

Debug.Print "Users collection:"

' Enumerate all User objects in the default
' workspace's Users collection.
For Each usrLoop In .Users
    Debug.Print "    " & usrLoop.Name
    Debug.Print "        Belongs to these groups:"

    ' Enumerate all Group objects in each User
    ' object's Groups collection.
    If usrLoop.Groups.Count <> 0 Then
        For Each grpLoop In usrLoop.Groups
            Debug.Print "            " & _
                grpLoop.Name
        Next grpLoop
    Else
        Debug.Print "            [None]"
    End If

Next usrLoop

Debug.Print "Groups collection:"

' Enumerate all Group objects in the default
' workspace's Groups collection.
For Each grpLoop In .Groups
    Debug.Print "    " & grpLoop.Name
    Debug.Print "        Has as its members:"

    ' Enumerate all User objects in each Group
    ' object's Users collection.
    If grpLoop.Users.Count <> 0 Then
        For Each usrLoop In grpLoop.Users
            Debug.Print "            " & _
```

```
            usrLoop.Name
        Next usrLoop
    Else
        Debug.Print "              [None]"
    End If

    Next grpLoop

    ' Delete new User and Group objects because this
    ' is only a demonstration.
    .Users.Delete "Pat Smith"
    .Groups.Delete "Accounting"

    End With

End Sub
```

UserControl Object

The **UserControl** object is the base object used to create an
ActiveX control.

Remarks

An ActiveX control created with Visual Basic is always composed
of a **UserControl** object, plus any controls—referred to as constituent
controls—that you choose to place on the **UserControl**.

Like Visual Basic forms, **UserControl** objects have code modules
and visual designers. Place constituent controls on the **UserControl**
object's designer, just as you would place controls on a form.

Properties

AccessKeys Property, **ActiveControl** Property, **Ambient** Property,
Appearance Property, **AutoRedraw** Property, **BackColor, ForeColor**
Properties, **BackStyle** Property, **BorderStyle** Property, **ClipControls**
Property, **Controls** Property, **Count** Property, **CurrextX, CurrentY**
Properties, **DrawMode** Property, **DrawStyle** Property, **DrawWidth**
Property, **Enabled** Property, **EventsFrozen** Property, **Extender**
Property, **FillColor** Property, **FillStyle** Property, **Font** Property,
FontBold, FontItalic, FontStrikethru, FontUnderline Properties,
FontName Property, **FontSize** Property, **FontTransparent** Property,
hDC Property, **Height, Width** Properties, **hWnd** Property, **Hyperlink**
Property, **Image** Property, **KeyPreview** Property, **MouseIcon** Property,
MousePointer Property, **Name** Property, **OLEDragMode** Property,
Palette Property, **PaletteMode** Property, **ParentControls** Property,
Picture Property, **PropertyPages** Property, **ScaleHeight, ScaleWidth**
Properties, **ScaleLeft, ScaleTop** Properties, **ScaleMode** Property, **Tag**
Property

Events

> **AccessKeyPress** Event, **AmbientChanged** Event, **AsyncReadComplete** Event, **Click** Event, **DblClick** Event, **DragDrop** Event, **DragOver** Event, **EnterFocus** Event, **ExitFocus** Event, **GotFocus** Event, **Hide** Event, **Initialize** Event, **InitProperties** Event, **KeyDown, KeyUp** Events, **KeyPress** Event, **LostFocus** Event, **MouseDown, MouseUp** Events, **MouseMove** Event, **OLECompleteDrag** Event, **OLEDragDrop** Event, **OLEDragOver** Event, **OLEGiveFeedback** Event, **OLESetData** Event, **OLEStartDrag Paint** Event, **ReadProperties** Event, **Resize** Event, **Show** Event, **Terminate** Event, **WriteProperties** Event

Methods

> **AsyncRead** Method, **CancelAsyncRead** Method, **CanPropertyChange** Method, **Circle** Method, **Cls** Method, **Line** Method, **OLEDrag** Method, **PaintPicture** Method, **Point** Method, **PopupMenu** Method, **PropertyChanged** Method, **Pset** Method, **Refresh** Method, **Scale** Method, **ScaleX, ScaleY** Methods, **SetFocus** Method, **Size** Method, **TextHeight,** Method, **TextWidth** Method

See Also

> **Hyperlink** Object, **UserDocument** Object

UserDocument Object

> The base object of an ActiveX document, the **UserDocument** object resembles a standard Visual Basic **Form** object with some exceptions.

Remarks

> The **UserDocument** object has most, but not all, of the events that are found on a **Form** object. The events present on a **Form** that are not found on the **UserDocument** include: **Activate**, **Deactivate**, **LinkClose**, **LinkError**, **LinkExecute**, **LinkOpen**, **Load**, **QueryUnload**, and **Unload** events.
>
> Events present on the **UserDocument**, but not found on a **Form** object include: **AsycReadComplete**, **EnterFocus**, **ExitFocus**, **Hide**, **InitProperties**, **ReadProperties**, **Scroll**, **Show**, and **WriteProperties** events.
>
> You cannot place embedded objects (such as an Excel or Word document) or an **OLE Container** control on a **UserDocument**.

Properties

> **ActiveControl** Property, **Appearance** Property, **AutoRedraw** Property, **BackColor, ForeColor** Properties, **ClipControls** Property, **ContainedControls** Property, **ContinuousScroll** Property, **Controls** Property, **Count** Property, **CurrentX, CurrentY** Properties, **DrawMode** Property, **DrawStyle** Property, **DrawWidth** Property, **FillColor** Property, **FillStyle** Property, **Font** Property, **FontBold, FontItalic, FontStrikethru Font Underline** Properties, **FontName** Property, **FontSize** Property, **FontTransparent** Property, **hDC** Property, **Height, Width** Properties, **HScrollSmallChange, VScrollSmallChange** Properties, **hWnd** Property, **Hyperlink**

Property, **Image** Property, **KeyPreview** Property, **MinHeight, MinWidth** Properties, **MouseIcon** Property, **MousePointer** Property, **Name** Property, **OLEDropMode** Property, **Palette** Property, **PaletteMode** Property, **Parent** Property, **Picture ScaleHeight, ScaleWidth** Properties Example, **ScaleLeft, ScaleTop** Properties, **ScaleMode** Property, **ScrollBars** Property, **Tag** Property, **ViewPortHeight, ViewportLeft, ViewportTop, ViewportWidth** Properties

Events

AsyncReadComplete Event, **Click** Event, **DblClick** Event, **DragDrop** Event, **DragOver** Event, **EnterFocus** Event, **ExitFocus** Event, **GotFocus** Event, **Hide** Event, **Initialize** Event, **InitProperties** Event, **KeyDown, KeyUp** Events, **KeyPress** Event, **LostFocus** Event, **MouseDown, MouseUp** Events, **MouseMove** Event, **OLECompleteDrag** Event, **OLEDragDrop** Event, **OLEDragOver** Event, **OLEGiveFeedback** Event, **OLESetDate** Event, **OLEStartDrag** Event, **Paint** Event, **ReadProperties** Event, **Resize** Event, **Scroll** Event, **Show** Event, **Terminate** Event, **WriteProperties** Event

Methods

AsyncRead Method, **CancelAsyncRead** Method, **Circle** Method, **Cls** Method, **Line** Method, **OLEDrag** Method, **PaintPicture** Method, **Point** Method, **PopupMenu** Method, **PrintForm** Method, **PropertyChange** Method, **Pset** Method, **Refresh** Method, **Scale ScaleX, ScaleY** Methods, **SetFocus** Method, **SetViewport** Method, **TextHeight** Method, **TextWidth** Method

See Also

Hyperlink Object, **UserControl** Object, **Form** Object, **Forms** Collection

---

UserForm Object, UserForms Collection

A **UserForm** object is a window or dialog box that makes up part of an application's user interface.

The **UserForms** collection is a collection whose elements represent each loaded **UserForm** in an application. The **UserForms** collection has a **Count** property, an **Item** property, and an **Add** method. **Count** specifies the number of elements in the collection; **Item** (the default member) specifies a specific collection member; and **Add** places a new **UserForm** element in the collection.

Syntax

UserForm
UserForms[.Item](*index*)

The placeholder *index* represents an integer with a range from 0 to **UserForms.Count** − 1. **Item** is the default member of the **UserForms** collection and need not be specified.

Remarks

You can use the **UserForms** collection to iterate through all loaded user forms in an application. It identifies an intrinsic global variable named **UserForms**. You can pass **UserForms**(*index*) to a function whose argument is specified as a **UserForm** class.

User forms have properties that determine appearance such as position, size, and color; and aspects of their behavior.

User forms can also respond to events initiated by a user or triggered by the system. For example, you can write code in the **Initialize** event procedure of the **UserForm** to initialize module-level variables before the **UserForm** is displayed.

In addition to properties and events, you can use methods to manipulate user forms using code. For example, you can use the **Move** method to change the location and size of a **UserForm**.

When designing user forms, set the **BorderStyle** property to define borders, and set the **Caption** property to put text in the title bar. In code, you can use the **Hide** and **Show** methods to make a **UserForm** invisible or visible at run time.

UserForm is an **Object** data type. You can declare variables as type **UserForm** before setting them to an instance of a type of **UserForm** declared at design time. Similarly, you can pass an argument to a procedure as type **UserForm**. You can create multiple instances of user forms in code by using the **New** keyword in **Dim**, **Set**, and **Static** statements.

You can access the collection of controls on a **UserForm** using the **Controls** collection. For example, to hide all the controls on a **UserForm**, use code similar to the following:

```
For Each Control in UserForm1.Controls
    Control.Visible = False
Next Control
```

Properties

StartUpPosition Property, **WhatsThisButton** Property, **WhatsThisHelp** Property

Methods

Hide Method, **Load** Statement, **PrintForm** Method, **Show** Method, **Unload** Statement, **WhatsThisMode** Method

See Also

Unload Statement

UserMode Property

Returns a Boolean value indicating whether the control is being used by a form designer or a form user.

Applies To

AmbientProperties Object

Syntax

object.**UserMode**

The **UserMode** property syntax has this part:

Part	Description
object	An object expression that evaluates to an object in the **Applies To** list.

Settings

The possible Boolean return values from the **UserMode** property are:

Setting	Description
True	The control is currently being used by a form user. If the container does not implement this ambient property, this will be the default value. In Visual Basic, this is Run Mode.
False	The control is currently being used by a form designer (the developer). In Visual Basic, this is Design Mode.

UserName Property

Sets or returns a value that represents a user, a group of users, or the owner of a **Workspace** object.

Applies To

Container Object, **Document** Object, **Workspace** Object

Settings and Return Values

The setting or return value is a **String** that evaluates to the name of a user. In a Microsoft Jet workspace, this represents a **User** object in the **Users** collection or a **Group** object in the **Groups** collection. For Microsoft Jet **Container** and **Document** objects, this property setting is read/write. For all **Workspace** objects, this property setting is read-only.

Remarks

Depending on the type of object, the **UserName** property represents the following.

- The owner of a **Workspace** object.

- A user or group of users when you manipulate the access permissions of a **Container** object or a **Document** object (Microsoft Jet workspaces only).

To find or set the permissions for a particular user or group of users, first set the **UserName** property to the user or group name that you want to examine. Then check the **Permissions** property setting to determine what permissions that user or group of users has, or set the **Permissions** property to change the permissions.

For a **Workspace** object, check the **UserName** property setting to determine the owner of the **Workspace** object. Set the **UserName** property to establish the owner of the **Workspace** object before you append the object to the **Workspaces** collection.

See Also

Append Method, **Inherited** Property, **Password** Property, **Permissions** Property

Example

This example uses the **UserName** property to change a particular user's permissions on an object and to verify that user's ability to append new data to the same object.

```
Sub UserNameX()

    ' Ensure that the Microsoft Jet workgroup information
    ' file is available.
    DBEngine.SystemDB = "system.mdw"

    Dim dbsNorthwind As Database
    Dim docTemp As Document

    Set dbsNorthwind = OpenDatabase("Northwind.mdb")

    Set docTemp = _
        dbsNorthwind.Containers("Tables").Documents(0)

    ' Change the permissions of NewUser on the first Document
    ' object in the Tables container.
    With docTemp
        .UserName = "NewUser"
        .Permissions = dbSecRetrieveData
        If (.Permissions And dbSecInsertData) = _
                dbSecInsertData Then
            Debug.Print .UserName & " can insert data."
        Else
            Debug.Print .UserName & " can't insert data."
        End If
    End With

    dbsNorthwind.Close

End Sub
```

UserName Property (Remote Data)

Returns or sets a value that represents a user of an **rdoEnvironment** object. Use the **UserName** property with the **Password** property to connect to an ODBC data source.

Applies To

rdoEnvironment Object, **RemoteData** Control

Syntax

object.**UserName** [= *value*]

The **UserName** property syntax has these parts:

Part	Description
object	An object expression that evaluates to an object in the **Applies To** list.
value	A string expression that contains a user name as described in Settings. (Data type is **String**.)

Settings

The user name syntax depends on the ODBC data source.

Return Values

The **UserName** property represents the user of an **rdoEnvironment** object. The user name is set when the **rdoEnvironment** is either created automatically by the **RemoteData** control, by the first reference to a remote data object, or when the **rdoCreateEnvironment** method is executed.

You can determine the default user name with the **rdoDefaultUser** property of the **rdoEngine** object. If no specific user name is supplied in **UserName**, the value of the **rdoDefaultUser** property is used.

See Also

rdoCreateEnvironment Method (Remote Data), **rdoEnvironment** Object, **RemoteData** Control, **Password** Property (Remote Data), **rdoDefaultUser**, **rdoDefaultPassword** Properties

---

Users Collection

A **Users** collection contains all stored **User** objects of a **Workspace** or **Group** object (Microsoft Jet workspaces only).

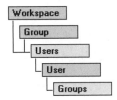

Remarks

You can append an existing **User** object to the **Users** collection of a **Group** object to give a user account the access permissions for that **Group** object. Alternatively, you can append the **Group** object to the **Groups** collection in a **User** object to establish membership of the user account in that group. If you use a **Users** or **Groups** collection other than the one to which you just appended an object, you may need to use the **Refresh** method.

The Microsoft Jet database engine predefines two **User** objects named Admin and Guest. The user Admin is a member of both of the **Group** objects named Admins and Users; the user Guest is a member only of the **Group** object named Guests.

To refer to a **User** object in a collection by its ordinal number or by its **Name** property setting, use any of the following syntax forms:

[*workspace* | *group*].**Users**(0)
[*workspace* | *group*].**Users**("*name*")
[*workspace* | *group*].**Users**![*name*]

Properties

Count Property

Methods

Append Method, **Delete** Method, **Refresh** Method

Example

This example illustrates the use of the **Group** and **User** objects and the **Groups** and **Users** collections. First, it creates a new **User** object and appends the object to the **Users** collection of the default **Workspace** object. Next, it creates a new **Group** object and appends the object to the **Groups** collection of the default **Workspace** object. Then the example adds user Pat Smith to the Accounting group. Finally, it enumerates the **Users** and **Groups** collections of the default **Workspace** object. See the methods and properties listed in the **Group** and **User** summary topics for additional examples.

```
Sub GroupX()

    Dim wrkDefault As Workspace
    Dim usrNew As User
    Dim usrLoop As User
    Dim grpNew As Group
    Dim grpLoop As Group
    Dim grpMember As Group

    Set wrkDefault = DBEngine.Workspaces(0)

    With wrkDefault

        ' Create and append new user.
        Set usrNew = .CreateUser("Pat Smith", _
            "abc123DEF456", "Password1")
        .Users.Append usrNew

        ' Create and append new group.
        Set grpNew = .CreateGroup("Accounting", _
```

```
        "UVW987xyz654")
    .Groups.Append grpNew

    ' Make the user Pat Smith a member of the
    ' Accounting group by creating and adding the
    ' appropriate Group object to the user's Groups
    ' collection. The same is accomplished if a User
    ' object representing Pat Smith is created and
    ' appended to the Accounting group's Users
    ' collection.
    Set grpMember = usrNew.CreateGroup("Accounting")
    usrNew.Groups.Append grpMember

    Debug.Print "Users collection:"

    ' Enumerate all User objects in the default
    ' workspace's Users collection.
    For Each usrLoop In .Users
        Debug.Print "    " & usrLoop.Name
        Debug.Print "        Belongs to these groups:"

        ' Enumerate all Group objects in each User
        ' object's Groups collection.
        If usrLoop.Groups.Count <> 0 Then
            For Each grpLoop In usrLoop.Groups
                Debug.Print "            " & _
                    grpLoop.Name
            Next grpLoop
        Else
            Debug.Print "            [None]"
        End If

    Next usrLoop

    Debug.Print "Groups collection:"

    ' Enumerate all Group objects in the default
    ' workspace's Groups collection.
    For Each grpLoop In .Groups
        Debug.Print "    " & grpLoop.Name
        Debug.Print "        Has as its members:"

        ' Enumerate all User objects in each Group
        ' object's Users collection.
        If grpLoop.Users.Count <> 0 Then
            For Each usrLoop In grpLoop.Users
                Debug.Print "            " & _
                    usrLoop.Name
            Next usrLoop
        Else
            Debug.Print "            [None]"
        End If

    Next grpLoop

    ' Delete new User and Group objects because this
    ' is only a demonstration.
    .Users.Delete "Pat Smith"
    .Groups.Delete "Accounting"

End With

End Sub
```

V1xNullBehavior Property

Indicates whether zero-length strings ("") used in code to fill Text or Memo fields are converted to **Null**.

Applies To

Database Object

Settings and Return Values

The setting or return value is a **Boolean** that is **True** if zero-length strings are converted to **Null**.

Remarks

This property applies to Microsoft Jet database engine version 1.x databases that have been converted to Microsoft Jet database engine version 2.0 or 3.0 databases.

Note The Microsoft Jet database engine automatically creates this property when it converts a version 1.x database to a version 2.0 or 3.x database. A 2.0 database will retain this property when it is converted to a 3.x database.

If you change this property setting, you must close and then reopen the database for your change to take effect.

For fastest performance, modify code that sets any Text or Memo fields to zero-length strings so that the fields are set to **Null** instead, and remove the **V1xNullBehavior** property from the **Properties** collection.

See Also

Index Property

Example

This example converts a Microsoft Jet version 1.1 database file to a Microsoft Jet version 3.0 database file. During conversion, the **V1xNullBehavior** property is created and added to the **Properties** collection of the new database. The **Properties** collections of both database files are enumerated to show the change. Finally, the **V1xNullBehavior** property is deleted. This assumes that any applications will be modified to store **Null** values in empty Text and Memo fields rather than empty strings.

Note Unless you can obtain a Microsoft Jet version 1.1 file called "Nwind11.mdb," this procedure will not run.

```
Sub V1xNullBehaviorX()

    Dim dbsNorthwind As Database
    Dim prpLoop As Property

    Set dbsNorthwind = OpenDatabase("Nwind11.mdb")
```

```
   With dbsNorthwind
      Debug.Print .Name & ", version " & .Version
      ' Enumerate Properties collection of Northwind
      ' database.
      For Each prpLoop In .Properties
         On Error Resume Next
         If prpLoop <> "" Then Debug.Print "    " & _
            prpLoop.Name & " = " & prpLoop
         On Error GoTo 0
      Next prpLoop

      .Close
   End With

   DBEngine.CompactDatabase "Nwind11.mdb", _
      "Nwind30.mdb", , dbVersion30

   Set dbsNorthwind = OpenDatabase("Nwind30.mdb")

   With dbsNorthwind
      Debug.Print .Name & ", version " & .Version

      ' Enumerate Properties collection of compacted
      ' database. The V1xNullBehavior property cannot be
      ' referred to explicitly, that is,
      ' dbsNorthwind.V1xNullBehavior, but it can be accessed
      ' in loops or by string reference, that is,
      ' dbsNorthwind.Properties("V1xNullBehavior").
      For Each prpLoop In .Properties
         On Error Resume Next
         If prpLoop <> "" Then Debug.Print "    " & _
            prpLoop.Name & " = " & prpLoop
         On Error GoTo 0
      Next prpLoop

      .Properties.Delete "V1xNullBehavior"
      .Close
   End With

End Sub
```

Val Function

Returns the numbers contained in a string as a numeric value of appropriate type.

Syntax

Val(*string*)

The required *string* argument is any valid string expression.

Remarks

The **Val** function stops reading the string at the first character it can't recognize as part of a number. Symbols and characters that are often considered parts of numeric values, such as dollar signs and commas, are not recognized. However, the function recognizes the radix prefixes &0 (for octal) and &H (for hexadecimal). Blanks, tabs, and linefeed characters are stripped from the argument.

The following returns the value 1615198:

```
Val("    1615 198th Street N.E.")
```

In the code below, **Val** returns the decimal value -1 for the hexadecimal value shown:

```
Val("&HFFFF")
```

Note The **Val** function recognizes only the period (.) as a valid decimal separator. When different decimal separators can be used, for example, in international applications, use **CDbl** instead to convert a string to a number.

See Also

Str Function

Example

This example uses the **Val** function to return the numbers contained in a string.

```
Dim MyValue
MyValue = Val("2457")        ' Returns 2457.
MyValue = Val(" 2 45 7")     ' Returns 2457.
MyValue = Val("24 and 57")   ' Returns 24.
```

Validate Event

Occurs before a different record becomes the current record; before the **Update** method (except when data is saved with the **UpdateRecord** method); and before a **Delete**, **Unload**, or **Close** operation.

Applies To

Data Control

Syntax

Private Sub *object_***Validate** ([*index* **As Integer**,] *action* **As Integer**, *save* **As Integer**)

The **Validate** event syntax has these parts:

Part	Description
object	An object expression that evaluates to an object in the **Applies To** list.
index	Identifies the control if it's in a control array.
action	An integer that indicates the operation causing this event to occur, as described in Settings.
save	A Boolean expression specifying whether bound data has changed, as described in Settings.

Settings

The settings for *action* are:

Constant	Value	Description
vbDataActionCancel	0	Cancel the operation when the **Sub** exits
vbDataActionMoveFirst	1	**MoveFirst** method
vbDataActionMovePrevious	2	**MovePrevious** method
vbDataActionMoveNext	3	**MoveNext** method
vbDataActionMoveLast	4	**MoveLast** method
vbDataActionAddNew	5	**AddNew** method
vbDataActionUpdate	6	**Update** operation (not **UpdateRecord**)
vbDataActionDelete	7	**Delete** method
vbDataActionFind	8	**Find** method
vbDataActionBookmark	9	The **Bookmark** property has been set
vbDataActionClose	10	The **Close** method
vbDataActionUnload	11	The form is being unloaded

The settings for *save* are:

Setting	Description
True	Bound data has changed
False	Bound data has not changed

Remarks

These constants are listed in the Visual Basic (VB) object library in the Object Browser.

The *save* argument initially indicates whether bound data has changed. This argument can still be **False** if data in the copy buffer is changed. If *save* is **True** when this event exits, the **Edit** and **UpdateRecord** methods are invoked. Only data from bound controls or from the copy buffer where the **DataChanged** property is set to **True** are saved by the **UpdateRecord** method.

This event occurs even if no changes have been made to data in bound controls and even if no bound controls exist. You can use this event to change values and update data. You can also choose to save data or stop whatever action is causing the event to occur and substitute a different action.

You can change the *action* argument to convert one action into another. You can change the various Move methods and the **AddNew** method, which can be freely exchanged (any Move into **AddNew**, any Move into any other Move, or **AddNew** into any Move). When using **AddNew**, you can use **MoveNext** and then execute another **AddNew** to examine the **EditMode** property to determine if an **Edit** or **AddNew** operation is in progress. Attempting to change **AddNew** or one of the Moves into any of the other actions is either ignored or produces a trappable error. Any action can be stopped by setting *action* to 0.

In your code for this event, you can check the data in each bound control where **DataChanged** is **True**. You can then set **DataChanged** to **False** to avoid saving that data in the database.

You can't use any methods (such as **MoveNext**) on the underlying **Recordset** object during this event.

Validate Event (Remote Data)

Occurs before a different row becomes the current row; before the **Update** method (except when data is saved with the **UpdateRow** method); and before a **Delete**, **Unload**, or **Close** operation.

Applies To

RemoteData Control

Syntax

Private Sub *object*_**Validate** ([*index* **As Integer**,] *action* **As Integer**, *save* **As Integer**)

The **Validate** event syntax has these parts:

Part	Description
object	An object expression that evaluates to an object in the Applies To list.
index	Identifies the control if it's in a control array.
action	An **Integer** or constant that indicates the operation causing this event to occur, as described in Settings.
save	A **Boolean** expression that specifies whether bound data has changed, as described in Settings.

Settings

The settings for *action* are:

Constant	Value	Description
rdActionCancel	0	Cancel the operation when the **Sub** exits.
rdActionMoveFirst	1	**MoveFirst** method.
rdActionMovePrevious	2	**MovePrevious** method.
rdActionMoveNext	3	**MoveNext** method.
rdActionMoveLast	4	**MoveLast** method.
rdActionAddNew	5	**AddNew** method.
rdActionUpdate	6	**Update** operation (not **UpdateRow**).
rdActionDelete	7	**Delete** method.
rdActionFind	8	**Find** method (not implemented).

(continued)

(*continued*)

Constant	Value	Description
rdActionBookmark	9	The **Bookmark** property has been set.
rdActionClose	10	The **Close** method.
rdActionUnload	11	The form is being unloaded.
rdActionUpdateAddNew	12	A new row was inserted into the result set.
rdActionUpdateModified	13	The current row changed.
rdActionRefresh	14	**Refresh** method executed.
rdActionCancelUpdate	15	Update canceled.
rdActionBeginTransact	16	**BeginTrans** method.
rdActionCommitTransact	17	**CommitTrans** Method.
rdActionRollbackTransact	18	**RollbackTrans** Method
rdActionNewParameters	19	Change in parameters, or order of columns or rows.
rdActionNewSQL	20	SQL statement changed.

The settings for *save* are:

Setting	Description
True	A **Boolean** expression indicating bound data has changed.
False	A **Boolean** expression indicating bound data has not changed.

Remarks

The *save* argument initially indicates whether bound data has changed. This argument can still be **False** if data in the copy buffer is changed. If *save* is **True** when this event exits, the **Edit** and **UpdateRow** methods are invoked.

This event can occur regardless of whether data in bound controls changes, or whether bound controls exist. You can use this event to change values and update data. You can also choose to save data or stop whatever action is causing the event to occur and substitute a different action.

You can change the various *Move* methods and the **AddNew** method, which can be freely exchanged (any *Move* into **AddNew**, any *Move* into any other *Move*, or **AddNew** into any *Move*). Attempting to change **AddNew** or one of the *Moves* into any of the other actions is either ignored or produces a trappable error. Any action can be stopped by setting *action* to **rdActionCancel**. If you change the *action* argument, the current action will also be canceled.

In your code for this event, you can check the data in each bound control where **DataChanged** is **True**. You can then set **DataChanged** to **False** to avoid saving that data in the database.

Note Because a data-aware control can have more than one bound property, the **DataChanged** property must be examined for each of the bound properties as enumerated in the **Bindings** collection.

You can't use any methods (such as **MoveNext**) on the underlying **rdoResultset** object during this event.

See Also

AddNew Method (Remote Data), **Close** Method (Remote Data), **Delete** Method (Remote Data), **Edit** Method (Remote Data), **MoveFirst**, **MoveLast**, **MoveNext**, **MovePrevious** Methods (Remote Data), **Update** Method (Remote Data), **UpdateRow** Method (Remote Data), **rdoResultset** Object, **RemoteData** Control, **Bookmark** Property (Remote Data), **EditMode** Property (Remote Data)

ValidateOnSet Property

Sets or returns a value that specifies whether or not the value of a **Field** object is immediately validated when the object's **Value** property is set (Microsoft Jet workspaces only).

Applies To

Field Object

Settings and Return Values

The setting or return value is a **Boolean** that can be one of the following values.

Value	Description
True	The validation rule specified by the **ValidationRule** property setting of the **Field** object is checked when you set the object's **Value** property.
False	(Default) Validate when the record is updated.

Only **Field** objects in **Recordset** objects support the **ValidateOnSet** property as read/write.

Remarks

Setting the **ValidateOnSet** property to **True** can be useful in a situation when a user is entering records that include substantial Memo data. Waiting until the **Update** call to validate the data can result in unnecessary time spent writing the lengthy Memo data to the database if it turns out that the data was invalid anyway because a validation rule was broken in another field.

See Also

AllowZeroLength Property, **Required** Property, **ValidationRule** Property, **ValidationText** Property, **Value** Property

Example

This example uses the **ValidateOnSet** property to demonstrate how one might trap for errors during data entry. The **ValidateData** function is required for this procedure to run.

```
Sub ValidateOnSetX()

    Dim dbsNorthwind As Database
    Dim fldDays As Field
    Dim rstEmployees As Recordset

    Set dbsNorthwind = OpenDatabase("Northwind.mdb")

    ' Create and append a new Field object to the Fields
    ' collection of the Employees table.
    Set fldDays = _
        dbsNorthwind.TableDefs!Employees.CreateField( _
        "DaysOfVacation", dbInteger, 2)
    fldDays.ValidationRule = "BETWEEN 1 AND 20"
    fldDays.ValidationText = _
        "Number must be between 1 and 20!"
    dbsNorthwind.TableDefs!Employees.Fields.Append fldDays

    Set rstEmployees = _
        dbsNorthwind.OpenRecordset("Employees")

    With rstEmployees

        Do While True
            ' Add new record.
            .AddNew

            ' Get user input for three fields. Verify that the
            ' data do not violate the validation rules for any
            ' of the fields.
            If ValidateData(!FirstName, _
                "Enter first name.") = False Then Exit Do
            If ValidateData(!LastName, _
                "Enter last name.") = False Then Exit Do
            If ValidateData(!DaysOfVacation, _
                "Enter days of vacation.") = False Then Exit Do

            .Update
            .Bookmark = .LastModified
            Debug.Print !FirstName & " " & !LastName & _
                " - " & "DaysOfVacation = " & !DaysOfVacation

            ' Delete new record because this is a demonstration.
            .Delete
            Exit Do
        Loop
```

```
               ' Cancel AddNew method if any of the validation rules
               ' were broken.
               If .EditMode <> dbEditNone Then .CancelUpdate
               .Close
         End With

         ' Delete new field because this is a demonstration.
         dbsNorthwind.TableDefs!Employees.Fields.Delete _
            fldDays.Name
         dbsNorthwind.Close

   End Sub

   Function ValidateData(fldTemp As Field, _
      strMessage As String) As Boolean

      Dim strInput As String
      Dim errLoop As Error

      ValidateData = True
      ' ValidateOnSet is only read/write for Field objects in
      ' Recordset objects.
      fldTemp.ValidateOnSet = True

      Do While True
         strInput = InputBox(strMessage)
         If strInput = "" Then Exit Do
         ' Trap for errors when setting the Field value.
         On Error GoTo Err_Data
         If fldTemp.Type = dbInteger Then
            fldTemp = Val(strInput)
         Else
            fldTemp = strInput
         End If
         On Error GoTo 0
         If Not IsNull(fldTemp) Then Exit Do
      Loop

      If strInput = "" Then ValidateData = False

      Exit Function

   Err_Data:

      If DBEngine.Errors.Count > 0 Then
         ' Enumerate the Errors collection. The description
         ' property of the last Error object will be set to
         ' the ValidationText property of the relevant
         ' field.
         For Each errLoop In DBEngine.Errors
            MsgBox "Error number: " & errLoop.Number & _
               vbCr & errLoop.Description
         Next errLoop
      End If

      Resume Next

   End Function
```

ValidationRule Property

Sets or returns a value that validates the data in a field as it's changed or added to a table (Microsoft Jet workspaces only).

Applies To

Dynaset-Type Recordset Object, **Field** Object, **Recordset** Object, **Snapshot-Type Recordset** Object, **Table-Type Recordset** Object, **TableDef** Object, **Forward-Only–Type Recordset** Object

Settings and Return Values

The settings or return values is a **String** that describes a comparison in the form of an SQL WHERE clause without the WHERE reserved word. For an object not yet appended to the **Fields** collection, this property is read/write. See Remarks for the more specific read/write characteristics of this property.

Remarks

The **ValidationRule** property determines whether or not a field contains valid data. If the data is not valid, a trappable run-time error occurs. The returned error message is the text of the **ValidationText** property, if specified, or the text of the expression specified by **ValidationRule**.

For a **Field** object, use of the **ValidationRule** property depends on the object that contains the **Fields** collection to which the **Field** object is appended.

Object appended to	Usage
Index	Not supported
QueryDef	Read-only
Recordset	Read-only
Relation	Not supported
TableDef	Read/write

For a **Recordset** object, use of the **ValidationRule** property is read-only. For a **TableDef** object, use of the **ValidationRule** property depends on the status of the **TableDef** object, as the following table shows.

TableDef	Usage
Base table	Read/write
Linked table	Read-only

Validation is supported only for databases that use the Microsoft Jet database engine.

The string expression specified by the **ValidationRule** property of a **Field** object can refer only to that **Field**. The expression can't refer to user-defined functions, SQL aggregate functions, or queries. To set a **Field** object's **ValidationRule** property when its **ValidateOnSet** property setting is **True**, the expression must successfully parse (with the field name as an implied operand) and evaluate to **True**. If its **ValidateOnSet** property setting is **False**, the **ValidationRule** property setting is ignored.

The **ValidationRule** property of a **Recordset** or **TableDef** object can refer to multiple fields in that object. The restrictions noted earlier in this topic for the **Field** object apply.

For a table-type **Recordset** object, the **ValidationRule** property inherits the **ValidationRule** property setting of the **TableDef** object that you use to create the table-type **Recordset** object.

For a **TableDef** object based on an linked table, the **ValidationRule** property inherits the **ValidationRule** property setting of the underlying base table. If the underlying base table doesn't support validation, the value of this property is a zero-length string ("").

Note If you set the property to a string concatenated with a non-integer value, and the system parameters specify a non-U.S. decimal character such as a comma (for example, `strRule = "PRICE > " & lngPrice`, and `lngPrice = 125,50`), an error will result when your code attempts to validate any data. This is because during concatenation, the number will be converted to a string using your system's default decimal character, and Microsoft Jet SQL only accepts U.S. decimal characters.

See Also

ValidateOnSet Property, **ValidationText** Property

Example

This example creates a new **Field** object in the specified **TableDef** object and sets the **ValidationRule** and **ValidationText** properties based on the passed data. It also shows how the **ValidationRule** and **ValidationText** properties are used during actual data entry. The SetValidation function is required for this procedure to run.

```
Sub ValidationRuleX()

    Dim dbsNorthwind As Database
    Dim fldDays As Field
    Dim rstEmployees As Recordset
    Dim strMessage As String
    Dim strDays As String
    Dim errLoop As Error
```

```
Set dbsNorthwind = OpenDatabase("Northwind.mdb")
' Create a new field for the Employees TableDef object
' using the specified property settings.
Set fldDays = _
    SetValidation(dbsNorthwind.TableDefs!Employees, _
    "DaysOfVacation", dbInteger, 2, "BETWEEN 1 AND 20", _
    "Number must be between 1 and 20!")
Set rstEmployees = _
    dbsNorthwind.OpenRecordset("Employees")

With rstEmployees

    ' Enumerate Recordset. With each record, fill the new
    ' field with data supplied by the user.
    Do While Not .EOF
        .Edit
        strMessage = "Enter days of vacation for " & _
            !FirstName & " " & !LastName & vbCr & _
            "[" & !DaysOfVacation.ValidationRule & "]"

        Do While True
            ' Get user input.
            strDays = InputBox(strMessage)
            If strDays = "" Then
                .CancelUpdate
                Exit Do
            End If
            !DaysOfVacation = Val(strDays)

            ' Because ValidateOnSet defaults to False, the
            ' data in the buffer will be checked against the
            ' ValidationRule during Update.
            On Error GoTo Err_Rule
            .Update
            On Error GoTo 0

            ' If the Update method was successful, print the
            ' results of the data change.
            If .EditMode = dbEditNone Then
                Debug.Print !FirstName & " " & !LastName & _
                    " - " & "DaysOfVacation = " & _
                    !DaysOfVacation
                Exit Do
            End If

        Loop

        If strDays = "" Then Exit Do
        .MoveNext
    Loop

    .Close
End With
```

```
                  ' Delete new field because this is a demonstration.
                  dbsNorthwind.TableDefs!Employees.Fields.Delete _
                     fldDays.Name
                  dbsNorthwind.Close

                  Exit Sub

            Err_Rule:

                  If DBEngine.Errors.Count > 0 Then
                     ' Enumerate the Errors collection.
                     For Each errLoop In DBEngine.Errors
                        MsgBox "Error number: " & _
                           errLoop.Number & vbCr & _
                           errLoop.Description
                     Next errLoop
                  End If

                  Resume Next

            End Sub

            Function SetValidation(tdfTemp As TableDef, _
               strFieldName As String, intType As Integer, _
               intLength As Integer, strRule As String, _
               strText As String) As Field

                  ' Create and append a new Field object to the Fields
                  ' collection of the specified TableDef object.
                  Set SetValidation = tdfTemp.CreateField(strFieldName, _
                     intType, intLength)

                  SetValidation.ValidationRule = strRule
                  SetValidation.ValidationText = strText
                  tdfTemp.Fields.Append SetValidation

            End Function
```

ValidationText Property

Sets or returns a value that specifies the text of the message that your application displays if the value of a **Field** object doesn't satisfy the validation rule specified by the **ValidationRule** property setting (Microsoft Jet workspaces only).

Applies To

Dynaset-Type Recordset Object, **Field** Object, **Recordset** Object, **Snapshot-Type Recordset** Object, **Table-Type Recordset** Object, **TableDef** Object, **Forward-Only– Type Recordset** Object

Settings and Return Values

The setting or return value is a **String** that specifies the text displayed if a user tries to enter an invalid value for a field. For an object not yet appended to a collection, this property is read/write. For a **Recordset** object, this property setting is read-only. For a **TableDef** object, this property setting is read-only for a linked table and read/write for a base table.

Remarks

For a **Field** object, use of the **ValidationText** property depends on the object that contains the **Fields** collection to which the **Field** object is appended, as the following table shows.

Object appended to	Usage
Index	Not supported
QueryDef	Read-only
Recordset	Read-only
Relation	Not supported
TableDef	Read/write

See Also

AllowZeroLength Property, **Required** Property, **ValidateOnSet** Property, **ValidationRule** Property, **Value** Property

Example

This example creates a new **Field** object in the specified **TableDef** object and sets the **ValidationRule** and **ValidationText** properties based on the passed data. It also shows how the **ValidationRule** and **ValidationText** properties are used during actual data entry. The **SetValidation** function is required for this procedure to run.

```
Sub ValidationRuleX()

    Dim dbsNorthwind As Database
    Dim fldDays As Field
    Dim rstEmployees As Recordset
    Dim strMessage As String
    Dim strDays As String
    Dim errLoop As Error

    Set dbsNorthwind = OpenDatabase("Northwind.mdb")
    ' Create a new field for the Employees TableDef object
    ' using the specified property settings.
    Set fldDays = _
        SetValidation(dbsNorthwind.TableDefs!Employees, _
        "DaysOfVacation", dbInteger, 2, "BETWEEN 1 AND 20", _
        "Number must be between 1 and 20!")
    Set rstEmployees = _
        dbsNorthwind.OpenRecordset("Employees")

    With rstEmployees
```

```
        ' Enumerate Recordset. With each record, fill the new
        ' field with data supplied by the user.
        Do While Not .EOF
            .Edit
            strMessage = "Enter days of vacation for " & _
                !FirstName & " " & !LastName & vbCr & _
                "[" & !DaysOfVacation.ValidationRule & "]"

            Do While True
                ' Get user input.
                strDays = InputBox(strMessage)
                If strDays = "" Then
                    .CancelUpdate
                    Exit Do
                End If
                !DaysOfVacation = Val(strDays)

                ' Because ValidateOnSet defaults to False, the
                ' data in the buffer will be checked against the
                ' ValidationRule during Update.
                On Error GoTo Err_Rule
                .Update
                On Error GoTo 0

                ' If the Update method was successful, print the
                ' results of the data change.
                If .EditMode = dbEditNone Then
                    Debug.Print !FirstName & " " & !LastName & _
                        " - " & "DaysOfVacation = " & _
                        !DaysOfVacation
                    Exit Do
                End If

            Loop

            If strDays = "" Then Exit Do
            .MoveNext
        Loop

        .Close
    End With

    ' Delete new field because this is a demonstration.
    dbsNorthwind.TableDefs!Employees.Fields.Delete _
        fldDays.Name
    dbsNorthwind.Close

    Exit Sub

Err_Rule:
```

```
    If DBEngine.Errors.Count > 0 Then
       ' Enumerate the Errors collection.
       For Each errLoop In DBEngine.Errors
          MsgBox "Error number: " & _
              errLoop.Number & vbCr & _
              errLoop.Description
       Next errLoop
    End If

    Resume Next

End Sub

Function SetValidation(tdfTemp As TableDef, _
    strFieldName As String, intType As Integer, _
    intLength As Integer, strRule As String, _
    strText As String) As Field

    ' Create and append a new Field object to the Fields
    ' collection of the specified TableDef object.
    Set SetValidation = tdfTemp.CreateField(strFieldName, _
       intType, intLength)

    SetValidation.ValidationRule = strRule
    SetValidation.ValidationText = strText
    tdfTemp.Fields.Append SetValidation

End Function
```

Value Property

- **CheckBox** and **OptionButton** controls—returns or sets the state of the control.
- **CommandButton** control—returns or sets a value indicating whether the button is chosen; not available at design time.
- **Field** object—returns or sets the content of a field; not available at design time.
- **HScrollBar** and **VScrollBar** controls (horizontal and vertical scroll bars)—returns or sets the current position of the scroll bar, whose return value is always between the values for the **Max** and **Min** properties, inclusive.

Applies To

AsyncProperty Object, **Column** Object, **CheckBox** Control, **CommandButton** Control, **HScrollBar, VScrollBar** Controls, **OptionButton** Control

Syntax

object.**Value** [= *value*]

The **Value** property syntax has these parts:

Part	Description
object	An object expression that evaluates to an object in the **Applies To** list.
value	Value specifying the state, content, or position of a control, as described in Settings.

Settings

The settings for *value* are:

- **CheckBox** control—0 is Unchecked (default), 1 is Checked, and 2 is Grayed (dimmed).

- **CommandButton** control—**True** indicates the button is chosen; **False** (default) indicates the button isn't chosen. Setting the **Value** property to **True** in code invokes the button's **Click** event.

- **Field** object—restricted only by the Field data types.

- **HScrollBar** and **VScrollBar** controls—set values between –32,768 and 32,767 to position the scroll box.

- **OptionButton** control—**True** indicates the button is selected; **False** (default) indicates the button isn't selected.

Remarks

A default property of an object is assumed, and doesn't need to be specified in code. For example, **Field** is the default property of any **Recordset**, and **Value** is the default property of a **Field** object. This makes the two statements below equivalent:

```
Dn.Fields("PubID").Value = X
Dn.("PubID") = X
```

The first statement *specifies* the default properties; the second statement *assumes* them.

Applies To

CheckBox Control, **Column** Control, **ComboBox** Control, **CommandButton** Control, **Data** Control, **DirListBox** Control, **DriveListBox** Control, **Extender** Control, **FileListBox** Control, **Form** Object, **Forms** Collection, **Frame** Control, **HScrollBar, VScrollBar** Controls, **Image** Control, **Label** Control, **Line** Control, **ListBox** Control, **MDIForm** Control, **Menu** Control, **OLE Container** Control, **OptionButton** Control, **PictureBox** Control, **RemoteData** Control, **Shape** Control, **TextBox** Control

See Also

Max, Min Properties (Scroll Bar)

Example

This example displays an **HScrollBar** (horizontal scroll bar) control's numeric value in a **TextBox** control. To try this example, paste the code into the Declarations section of a form that has a **TextBox** control and an **HScrollBar** control. Press F5 to run the program, and then click the scroll bar.

```
Private Sub Form_Load ()
    HScroll1.Min = 0  ' Initialize scroll bar.
    HScroll1.Max = 1000
    HScroll1.LargeChange = 100
    HScroll1.SmallChange = 1
End Sub

Private Sub HScroll1_Change ()
    Text1.Text = Format (HScroll1.Value)
End Sub
```

Value Property (Add-Ins)

Returns or sets a **Variant** specifying the value of the property.
Read/write.

Applies To

Property Object

Remarks

Because the **Value** property returns a **Variant**, you can access any property. To access a list, use the **IndexedValue** property.

If the property that the **Property** object represents is read/write, the **Value** property is read/write. If the property is read-only, attempting to set the **Value** property causes an error. If the property is write-only, attempting to return the **Value** property causes an error.

The **Value** property is the default property for the **Property** object.

See Also

IndexedValue Property, **Name** Property, **Object** Property, **Type** Property

Example

The following example uses the **Value** property to return the value of the specified property of a member of the **VBComponents** collection.

```
Debug.Print Application.VBE.
ActiveVBProject.VBComponents(1).Properties("AcceptLabelsInFormulas").Value
```

Value Property (Column Object)

Sets or returns the underlying data value in a column for the current row. Not available at design time.

Applies To

Column Object

Syntax

object.**Value** [= *value*]

The **Value** property syntax has these parts:

Part	Description
object	An object expression that evaluates to an object in the **Applies To** list.
value	A string expression that represents the underlying data value in a column for the current row.

Remarks

The **Value** property is useful for simulating data entry within a cell. When this property is set, the value displayed in the cell respects the setting of the column's **NumberFormat** property.

This property always returns a string variant, even if the data type of the underlying field is numeric.

Use the **Text** property to access the formatted data value in a column for the current row.

See Also

Text Property (Column Object Dummy Topic), **NumberFormat** Property

Value Property (DAO)

Sets or returns the value of an object.

Applies To

Field Object, **Parameter** Object, **Property** Object

Settings and Return Values

The setting or return value is a **Variant** data type that evaluates to a value appropriate for the data type, as specified by the **Type** property of an object.

Remarks

Generally, the **Value** property is used to retrieve and alter data in **Recordset** objects.

The **Value** property is the default property of the **Field**, **Parameter**, and **Property** objects. Therefore, you can set or return the value of one of these objects by referring to them directly instead of specifying the **Value** property.

Trying to set or return the **Value** property in an inappropriate context (for example, the **Value** property of a **Field** object in the **Fields** collection of a **TableDef** object) will cause a trappable error.

Notes

- In an **ODBCDirect** workspace, you cannot read or set the **Value** property of a **Recordset** field more than once without refreshing the current record. For example, to read and then set the **Value** property, first read the property, then use the **Move** 0 method to refresh the current record, then write the new value.

- When reading decimal values from a Microsoft SQL Server database, they will be formatted using scientific notation through a Microsoft Jet workspace, but will appear as normal decimal values through an **ODBCDirect** workspace.

See Also

Name Property, **Updatable** Property

Example

This example demonstrates the **Value** property with **Field** and **Property** objects.

```
Sub ValueX()

    Dim dbsNorthwind As Database
    Dim rstEmployees As Recordset
    Dim fldLoop As Field
    Dim prpLoop As Property

    Set dbsNorthwind = OpenDatabase("Northwind.mdb")
    Set rstEmployees = _
        dbsNorthwind.OpenRecordset("Employees")

    With rstEmployees
        Debug.Print "Field values in rstEmployees"
        ' Enumerate the Fields collection of the Employees
        ' table.
        For Each fldLoop In .Fields
            Debug.Print "    " & fldLoop.Name & " = ";
            Select Case fldLoop.Type
                Case dbLongBinary
                    Debug.Print "[LongBinary]"
                Case dbMemo
                    Debug.Print "[Memo]"
                Case Else
                    ' Because Value is the default property of a
                    ' Field object, the use of the actual keyword
                    ' here is optional.
                    Debug.Print fldLoop.Value
            End Select
        Next fldLoop
```

```
            Debug.Print "Property values in rstEmployees"
            ' Enumerate the Properties collection of the
            ' Recordset object.
            For Each prpLoop In .Properties
               On Error Resume Next
               ' Because Value is the default property of a
               ' Property object, the use of the actual keyword
               ' here is optional.
               If prpLoop <> "" Then Debug.Print "     " & _
                  prpLoop.Name & " = " & prpLoop.Value
               On Error GoTo 0
            Next prpLoop

            .Close
         End With

         dbsNorthwind.Close

      End Sub
```

Value Property (Remote Data)

Returns or sets the value of an object.

Applies To

rdoColumn Object, **rdoParameter** Object

Syntax

object.**Value** [= *value*]

The **Value** property syntax has these parts:

Part	Description
object	An object expression that evaluates to an object in the **Applies To** list.
value	An expression that evaluates to a value appropriate for the data type, as specified by the **Type** property of an object. (Data type is **Variant**.)

Remarks

Use the **Value** property to retrieve and alter data in **rdoResultset** objects. The data type of the data returned is indicated by the **Type** property of the object.

The **Value** property is the default property of the **rdoColumn** and **rdoParameter** objects. Therefore, the following lines of code are equivalent (assuming Column1 is at the first ordinal position):

```
Dim MyResultset As rdoResultset
X = MyResultset!Column1
X = MyResultset!Column1.Value
X = MyResultset(0)
X = MyResultset(0).Value
X = MyResultset("Column1").Value
X = MyResultset("Column1")
X = RemoteData1.Resultset("Column1")
X = RemoteData1.Resultset(0)
F$ = "Column1" : X = MyResultset(F$).Value
X = MyResultset(F$)
Set X = MyResultset(0): X.Value : X
```

See Also

Execute Method (Remote Data), **OpenResultset** Method (Remote Data), **rdoColumn** Object, **rdoParameter** Object, **Name** Property (Remote Data), **Type** Property (Remote Data), **Updatable** Property (Remote Data)

Value Property (RowBuffer)

Returns or sets the value of an item of data within the **RowBuffer** object in an unbound **DBGrid** control.

Applies To

RowBuffer Object

Syntax

object.**Value** (*row, column*) [= *value*]

The **Value** property syntax has these parts:

Part	Description
object	An object expression that evaluates to an object in the Applies To list.
row	An integer from 0 to **RowCount**–1 indicating the row number of the item.
column	An integer from 0 to **ColumnCount**–1 indicating the column number of the item.
value	A variant value entered or displayed in the cell specified by *row* and *column*.

Remarks

The **RowBuffer** object can contain several columns and several rows of data.

In the **UnboundWriteData** and **UnboundAddData** events, the user enters the setting of the **Value** property into the unbound **DBGrid** control. You then use this value to update your database.

In the **UnboundReadData** event, you supply the values of the *row* and *column* arguments requested by the unbound **DBGrid** control.

See Also

> **UnboundAddData** Event, **UnboundReadData** Event, **UnboundWriteData** Event, **DBGrid** Control

Example

> This example illustrates how a previously read row, contained in the **Value** property, is added to a database; in this case, a simple array. In the following code fragment, if the **RowBuffer** object contains a row (**Not IsNull**), the row is written to the array.

```
For i% = 0 To MAXCOLS - 1
    If Not IsNull(RowBuf.Value(0, i%)) Then
        UserData(i%, RowCount - 1) = RowBuf.Value(0, i%)
    End If
Next i%
```

Variant Data Type

The **Variant** data type is the data type for all variables that are not explicitly declared as some other type (using statements such as **Dim**, **Private**, **Public**, or **Static**). The **Variant** data type has no type-declaration character.

A **Variant** is a special data type that can contain any kind of data except fixed-length **String** data and user-defined types. A **Variant** can also contain the special values **Empty**, **Error**, **Nothing**, and **Null**. You can determine how the data in a **Variant** is treated using the **VarType** function or **TypeName** function.

Numeric data can be any integer or real number value ranging from -1.797693134862315E308 to -4.94066E-324 for negative values and from 4.94066E-324 to 1.797693134862315E308 for positive values. Generally, numeric **Variant** data is maintained in its original data type within the **Variant**. For example, if you assign an **Integer** to a **Variant**, subsequent operations treat the **Variant** as an **Integer**. However, if an arithmetic operation is performed on a **Variant** containing a **Byte**, an **Integer**, a **Long**, or a **Single**, and the result exceeds the normal range for the original data type, the result is promoted within the **Variant** to the next larger data type. A **Byte** is promoted to an **Integer**, an **Integer** is promoted to a **Long**, and a **Long** and a **Single** are promoted to a **Double**. An error occurs when **Variant** variables containing **Currency**, **Decimal**, and **Double** values exceed their respective ranges.

You can use the **Variant** data type in place of any data type to work with data in a more flexible way. If the contents of a **Variant** variable are digits, they may be either the string representation of the digits or their actual value, depending on the context. For example:

```
Dim MyVar As Variant
MyVar = 98052
```

In the preceding example, MyVar contains a numeric representation—the actual value 98052. Arithmetic operators work as expected on **Variant** variables that contain numeric values or string data that can be interpreted as numbers. If you use the **+** operator to add MyVar to another **Variant** containing a number or to a variable of a numeric type, the result is an arithmetic sum.

The value **Empty** denotes a **Variant** variable that hasn't been initialized (assigned an initial value). A **Variant** containing **Empty** is 0 if it is used in a numeric context and a zero-length string ("") if it is used in a string context.

Don't confuse **Empty** with **Null**. **Null** indicates that the **Variant** variable intentionally contains no valid data.

In a **Variant**, **Error** is a special value used to indicate that an error condition has occurred in a procedure. However, unlike for other kinds of errors, normal application-level error handling does not occur. This allows you, or the application itself, to take some alternative action based on the error value. **Error** values are created by converting real numbers to error values using the **CVErr** function.

See Also

CVErr Function, **Data Type** Summary, **Deftype** Statements, **Dim** Statement, **Private** Statement, **Public** Statement, **Static** Statement, **TypeName** Function, **Operator** Summary

VarType Function

Returns an **Integer** indicating the subtype of a variable.

Syntax

VarType(*varname*)

The required *varname* argument is a **Variant** containing any variable except a variable of a user-defined type.

Return Values

Constant	Value	Description
vbEmpty	0	**Empty** (uninitialized)
vbNull	1	**Null** (no valid data)
vbInteger	2	Integer
vbLong	3	Long integer
vbSingle	4	Single-precision floating-point number
vbDouble	5	Double-precision floating-point number
vbCurrency	6	Currency value
vbDate	7	Date value
vbString	8	String

(continued)

Constant	Value	Description
vbObject	9	Object
vbError	10	Error value
vbBoolean	11	Boolean value
vbVariant	12	**Variant** (used only with arrays of variants)
vbDataObject	13	A data access object
vbDecimal	14	Decimal value
vbByte	17	Byte value
vbArray	8192	Array

Note These constants are specified by Visual Basic for Applications. The names can be used anywhere in your code in place of the actual values.

Remarks

The **VarType** function never returns the value for **vbArray** by itself. It is always added to some other value to indicate an array of a particular type. The constant **vbVariant** is only returned in conjunction with **vbArray** to indicate that the argument to the **VarType** function is an array of type **Variant**. For example, the value returned for an array of integers is calculated as **vbInteger + vbArray**, or 8194. If an object has a default property, **VarType** (*object*) returns the type of the object's default property.

See Also

Data Type Summary, **IsArray** Function, **IsDate** Function, **IsEmpty** Function, **IsError** Function, **IsMissing** Function, **IsNull** Function, **IsNumeric** Function, **IsObject** Function, **TypeName** Function, **Variant Data** Type

Example

This example uses the **VarType** function to determine the subtype of a variable.

```
Dim IntVar, StrVar, DateVar, MyCheck
' Initialize variables.
IntVar = 459: StrVar = "Hello World": DateVar = #2/12/69#
MyCheck = VarType(IntVar)    ' Returns 2.
MyCheck = VarType(DateVar)   ' Returns 7.
MyCheck = VarType(StrVar)    ' Returns 8.
```

VBComponent Object

Represents a component, such as a class module or standard module, contained in a project.

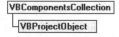

Remarks

Use the **VBComponent** object to access the code module associated with a component or to change a component's property settings.

You can use the **Type** property to find out what type of component the **VBComponent** object refers to. Use the **Collection** property to find out what collection the component is in.

Specifics

VBComponents Collection

Properties

CodeModule Property, **Collection** Property, **Designer** Property, **DesignerWindow** Property, **FileCount** Property, **Filenames** Property, **HasOpenDesigner** Property, **IconState** Property, **IsDirty** Property, **Saved** Property, **Name** Property, **Type** Property, **VBE** Property

Methods

Export Method, **Activate** Method, **ReadProperty** Method, **Reload** Method, **SaveAs** Method, **WriteProperty** Method

See Also

CodeModule Object, **VBComponents** Collection, **VBProject** Object

---

VBComponents Collection

Represents the components contained in a project.

Applies To

ItemActivated Event, **ItemAdded** Event, **ItemReloaded** Event, **ItemRemoved** Event, **ItemRenamed** Event, **ItemSelected** Event

Remarks

Use the **VBComponents** collection to access, add, or remove components in a project. A component can be a form, module, or class. The **VBComponents** collection is a standard collection that can be used in a **For Each** block.

You can use the **Parent** property to return the project the **VBComponents** collection is in.

In Visual Basic for Applications, you can use **Import** method to add a component to a project from a file.

Properties

Count Property, **Parent** Property, **VBE** Property, **StartUpObject** Property

Methods

Add Method, **AddCustom** Method, **AddFile** Method, **AddFromTemplate** Method, **Import** Method, **Item** Method, **Remove** Method

See Also

CodeModule Object, **VBComponent** Object, **VBProject** Object

---

VBComponentsEvents Object

Represents a source of events that occur when an object is added, removed, selected, renamed, or activated in a Visual Basic project.

Syntax

VBComponentsEvents

Events

ItemActivated Event, **ItemAdded** Event, **ItemReloaded** Event, **ItemRemoved** Event, **ItemRenamed** Event, **ItemSelected**Event

---

VBComponentsEvents Property

Returns an event object of type **VBComponentsEvents**.

Applies To

Events Object

Syntax

object.**VBComponentsEvents** (*vbproject* **As vbProject**)

The **VBComponentsEvents** property syntax has these parts:

Part	Description
object	An object expression that evaluates to an object in the **Applies To** list.
vbproject	An object of type **vbProject** which specifies the project which contains the components.

VBControl Object

Represents a control on a component in a project.

Syntax

VBControl

Remarks

A program can access a control through the **VBForm** object. Using the **VBForm** object, you can:

- Access all the design time properties of a control.
- Identify the container of the control.
- Change the Z-order of the control.

The **VBControl** object replaces the **ControlTemplate** object from Visual Basic version 4.0.

Properties

Collection Property, **ControlObject** Property, **ControlType** Property, **InSelection** Property, **ProgID** Property, **Properties** Collection, **VBE** Property

Methods

ZOrder Method

VBControls Collection

Returns a collection all components on a form.

Syntax

VBControls

Remarks

A program can access controls through the **VBControls** collection. Using the **VBControls** collection, you can:

- Access all the controls on a component.
- Step through the collection of controls.
- Return a specific control.
- Add controls to a component.

The **Item** method determines the default value of the **VBControls** collection.

The **VBControls** collection replaces the **ControlTemplates** collection from Visual Basic version 4.0.

Properties

VBE Property

Methods

Add Method**, Item** Method**, Remove** Method (**Visual Basic Extensibility**)

Events

ItemAdded Event, **ItemRemoved** Event, **ItemRenamed** Event

VBControlsEvents Object

Represents a source of events that occur when a control is added, removed, selected, renamed, or activated in a Visual Basic project.

Syntax

VBControlsEvents

Events

ItemAdded Event, **ItemRemoved** Event, **ItemRenamed** Event

---

VBControlsEvents Property

Returns all events supported by the controls on a form.

Applies To

Events Object

Syntax

object.**VBControlsEvents**(*vbproject* **As Variant**, *vbform* **As VBForm**)

The **VBControlsEvents** property syntax has these parts:

Part	Description
object	An object expression that evaluates to an object in the **Applies To** list.
vbproject	A variant expression specifying the project which contains the controls.
vbform	The form containing the controls.

Remarks

Returns an event object of type **VBControlsEvents**. This event is sourced from a **VBForm** or a control on a **VBForm** that can contain controls.

VBE Object

The root object that contains all other objects and collections represented in Visual Basic for Applications.

Remarks

You can use the following collections to access the objects contained in the **VBE** object:

- Use the **VBProjects** collection to access the collection of projects.
- Use the **Windows** collection to access the collection of windows.
- Use the **CodePanes** collection to access the collection of code panes.
- Use the **CommandBars** collection to access the collection of command bars.

Use the **Events** object to access properties that enable add-ins to connect to all events in Visual Basic for Applications. The properties of the **Events** object return objects of the same type as the property name. For example, the **CommandBarEvents** property returns the **CommandBarEvents** object.

You can use the **SelectedVBComponent** property to return the active component. The active component is the component that is being tracked in the **Project** window. If the selected item in the **Project** window isn't a component, **SelectedVBComponent** returns **Nothing**.

Note All objects in this object model have a **VBE** property that points to the **VBE** object.

Properties

SelectedVBComponent Property, **ActiveVBProject** Property, **ActiveWindow** Property, **ActiveCodePane** Property, **MainWindow** Property, **Parent** Property, **Version** Property

Methods

Quit Method

See Also

CommandBars Collection, **CodePanes** Collection, **Events** Object, **VBProjects** Collection, **Windows** Collection, **VBE** Property

VBE Property

Returns the root of the **VBE** object. Read-only.

Applies To

CodeModule Object, **VBComponent** Object, **VBComponents** Collection, **CodePane** Object, **CodePanes** Collection, **LinkedWindows** Collection, **Property** Object, **Properties** Collection, **Reference** Object, **References** Collection, **VBProject** Object, **VBProjects** Collection, **Window** Object, **Windows** Collection

Remarks

All objects have a **VBE** property that points to the root of the **VBE** object.

See Also

Collection Property, **Parent** Property

Example

The following example uses the **VBE** and **Name** properties to return the name of the active project.

```
Debug.Print Application.VBE.ActiveVBProject.Name
```

VBForm Object

Returns a component in a project.

Syntax

VBForm

Remarks

The **ClassName** property determines the default value of the **VBForm** object.

The **VBForm** object replaces the **ControlTemplate** object from Visual Basic version 4.0.

Properties

CanPaste Property, **ContainedVBControls** Collection, **SelectedVBControls** Collection, **VBE** Property

Methods

SelectAll Method, **Paste** Method

VBProject Object

Represents a project.

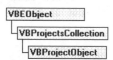

Remarks

Use the **VBProject** object to set properties for the project, to access the **VBComponents** collection, and to access the **References** collection.

Specifics

VBProjects Collection

Properties

Collection Property, **Description** Property, **HelpContextID** Property, **HelpFile** Property, **Saved** Property, **Mode** Property, **Name** Property, **Protection** Property, **VBE** Property

Methods

>   **AddToolBoxProgID** Method, **MakeCompiledFile** Method, **ReadProperty** Method, **SaveAs** Method, **WriteProperty** Method

See Also

>   **VBComponents** Collection, **References** Collection

VBProjects Collection

>   Represents all the projects that are open in the development environment.

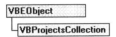

Applies To

>   **ItemActivated** Event, **ItemAdded** Event, **ItemRemoved** Event, **ItemRenamed** Event

Remarks

>   Use the **VBProjects** collection to access specific projects in an instance of the development environment. **VBProjects** is a standard collection that can be used in a **For Each** block.

Properties

>   **Count** Property, **Parent** Property, **VBE** Property, **IconState** Property, **StartProject** Property

Methods

>   **Item** Method, **Add** Method, **AddFromFile** Method, **AddFromTemplate** Method, **FileName** Property, **Remove** Method, **SaveAs** Method

See Also

>   **VBProject** Object

VBProjects Property

>   Returns the **VBProjects** collection, which represents all of the projects currently open in the Visual Basic IDE.

Syntax

>   *object*.**VBProjects**

>   The *object* placeholder represents an object expression that evaluates to an object in the **Applies To** list.

VBProjectsEvents Object

Represents a source of events that occur when projects are added, removed, renamed, or activated in a Visual Basic project.

Syntax

VBProjectsEvents

Events

ItemActivated Event, **ItemAdded** Event, **ItemRemoved** Event, **ItemRenamed** Event

---

VBProjectsEvents Property

Returns an event object of type **VBProjectsEvents**.

Applies To

Events Object

Syntax

object.**VBProjectsEvents**

The *object* placeholder represents an object expression that evaluates to an object in the **Applies To** list.

Remarks

This is identical to using the **VBProjects** collection events.

Verb Property

Returns or sets a value specifying an operation to perform when an object is activated using the **Action** property.

Note The **Verb** property is included for compatibility with the **Action** property in earlier versions. For current functionality, use the **DoVerb** method.

Applies To

OLE Container Control

Syntax

object.**Verb** [= *number*]

The **Verb** property syntax has these parts:

Part	Description
object	An object expression that evaluates to an object in the **Applies To** list.
number	A value that specifies the operation to perform.

Remarks

Each object can support its own set of verbs. Use the **ObjectVerbs** and **ObjectVerbsCount** properties to access the list of verbs supported by an object. Set **Verb** = 1 to specify the first verb in the list, set **Verb** = 2 to specify the second verb in the list, and so on.

Set **AutoActivate** to 2 (**Double-Click**) to automatically activate an object when it's double-clicked by the user.

Set **AutoVerbMenu = True** to display a pop-up menu containing the object's verbs when the user clicks the object with the right mouse button.

See Also

OLEType Property, **ObjectVerbs** Property, **ObjectVerbsCount** Property, **AutoActivate** Property, **AutoVerbMenu** Property, **OLETypeAllowed** Property, **DoVerb** Method, **Action** Property (OLE Container)

Version Property

Returns a **String** containing the version of Visual Basic for Applications that the application is using. Read-only.

Applies To

VBE Object

Remarks

The **Version** property value is a string beginning with one or two digits, a period, and two digits; the rest of the string is undefined and may contain text or numbers.

See Also

Major Property, **Minor** Property

Example

The following example uses the **Version** property to return the version number of the host application.

```
Debug.Print Application.VBE.Version
```

Version Property (DAO)

- Microsoft Jet workspace—On the **DBEngine** object, returns the version of DAO currently in use. On the **Database** object, returns the version of Jet that created the .mdb file.

- **ODBCDirect** workspace—On the **DBEngine** object, returns the version of DAO currently in use. On the **Database** object, returns the version of the ODBC driver currently in use.

Applies To

Database Object, **DBEngine** Object

Return Values

The return value is a **String** that evaluates to a version number, formatted as follows.

- Microsoft Jet workspace—represents the version number in the form "*major.minor*". For example, "3.0". The product version number consists of the version number (3), a period, and the release number (0).

- **ODBCDirect** workspace—represents the DAO version number in the form "*major.minor*", or represents the ODBC driver version number in the form "*major.minor.build*". For example, the **DBEngine.Version** value of "3.5" indicated DAO version 3.5. A **Database** object's **Version** value of 2.50.1032 indicates that the current instance of DAO is connected to ODBC version 2.5, build 1032.

Remarks

In a Microsoft Jet workspace, the **Version** property of a **Database** object corresponds to a version of the Microsoft Jet database engine, and doesn't necessarily match the version number of the Microsoft product with which the database engine was included. For example, the **Version** property of a **Database** object created with Microsoft Visual Basic 3.0 will be 1.1, not 3.0.

The following table shows which version of the database engine was included with various versions of Microsoft products.

Microsoft Jet Version (year released)	Microsoft Access	Microsoft Visual Basic	Microsoft Excel	Microsoft Visual C++
1.0 (1992)	1.0	N/A	N/A	N/A
1.1 (1993)	1.1	3.0	N/A	N/A
2.0 (1994)	2.0	N/A	N/A	N/A
2.5 (1995)	N/A	4.0 (16-bit)	N/A	N/A
3.0 (1995)	'95 (7.0)	4.0 (32-bit)	'95 (7.0)	4.x
3.5 (1996)	'97 (8.0)	5.0	'97 (8.0)	5.0

See Also

CreateDatabase Method

Example

This example uses the **Version** property to report on the Microsoft Jet database engine in memory, a Microsoft Jet database, and an ODBC connection.

```
Sub VersionX()

    Dim wrkJet As Workspace
    Dim dbsNorthwind As Database
    Dim wrkODBC As Workspace
    Dim conPubs As Connection

    ' Open Microsoft Jet Database object.
    Set wrkJet = CreateWorkspace("NewJetWorkspace", _
        "admin", "", dbUseJet)
    Set dbsNorthwind = wrkJet.OpenDatabase("Northwind.mdb")

    ' Create ODBCDirect Workspace object and open Connection
    ' objects.
    Set wrkODBC = CreateWorkspace("NewODBCWorkspace", _
        "admin", "", dbUseODBC)
    Set conPubs = wrkODBC.OpenConnection("Connection1", , , _
        "ODBC;DATABASE=pubs;UID=sa;PWD=;DSN=Publishers")

    ' Show three different uses for the Version property.
    Debug.Print "Version of DBEngine (Microsoft Jet " & _
        "in memory) = " & DBEngine.Version
    Debug.Print "Version of the Microsoft Jet engine " & _
        "with which " & dbsNorthwind.Name & _
        " was created = " & dbsNorthwind.Version
    Debug.Print "Version of ODBCDirect connection " & _
        "(using Database property) = " & _
        conPubs.Database.Version

    dbsNorthwind.Close
    conPubs.Close
    wrkJet.Close
    wrkODBC.Close

End Sub
```

Version Property (Remote Data)

Returns a value that indicates the version of the data source associated with the object.

Applies To

rdoConnection Object, **RemoteData** Control

Syntax

object.**Version**

The *object* placeholder represents an object expression that evaluates to an object in the **Applies To** list.

Return Values

The **Version** property return value is a 10-character string expression.

Remarks

For an **rdoConnection** object, this property identifies the version of the data source used when the connection was created. This value is the version of ODBC to which the driver manager conforms. The version is in the form ##.##.####, where the first two digits are the major version number, the next two digits are the minor version, and the last four digits are the build number.

See Also

OpenConnection Method (Remote Data), **rdoConnection** Object, **rdoVersion** Property (Remote Data)

ViewportHeight, ViewportLeft, ViewportTop, ViewportWidth Properties

Returns the current height, left, top, or width value of the **Viewport**.

Applies To

UserDocument Object

Syntax

object.**ViewportHeight**
object.**ViewportLeft**
object.**ViewportTop**
object.**ViewportWidth**

The *object* placeholder represents an object expression that evaluates to an object in the **Applies To** list.

Return Type

Single

Remarks

The application used to view the ActiveX document controls the size of the Viewport. However, you can use the **MinHeight** and **MinWidth** properties to resize the **UserDocument**. For example, the code below resizes a **PictureBox** control according to the size of the Viewport left height and width properties.

```
Private Sub UserDocument_Resize()
   Picture1.Width = UserDocument.ViewportWidth - _
      Picture1.Left
   Picture1.Height = UserDocument.ViewportHeight - _
      Picture1.Top
End Sub
```

See Also

MinHeight, **MinWidth** Properties, **SetViewport** Method

Visible Property

Returns or sets a value indicating whether an object is visible or hidden.

Syntax

object.**Visible** [= *boolean*]

The **Visible** property syntax has these parts:

Part	Description
object	An object expression that evaluates to an object in the **Applies To** list.
Boolean	A Boolean expression specifying whether the object is visible or hidden..

Settings

The settings for *boolean* are:

Setting	Description
True	(Default) Object is visible.
False	Object is hidden.

Remarks

To hide an object at startup, set the **Visible** property to **False** at design time. Setting this property in code enables you to hide and later redisplay a control run time in response to a particular event.

Note   Using the **Show** or **Hide** method on a form is the same as setting the form's Visible property in code to **True** or **False**, respectively.

See Also

Load Statement, **Hide** Method, **Show** Method

VisibleCols Property

Returns a value indicating the number of visible columns in the **DBGrid** control. Not available at design time and read-only at run time.

Applies To

DBGrid Control

Syntax

object.**VisibleCols**

The **VisibleCols** property syntax has these parts:

Part	Description
object	An object expression that evaluates to an object in the **Applies To** list.

Remarks

The **VisibleCols** property is an integer ranging from 0 to the total number of columns available, as determined by the **Count** property of the **Columns** collection.

This property returns the number of visible columns in the current split. The value returned includes both fully and partially displayed columns.

Use the **Split** property to determine the index of the current split.

See Also

Data Control, **SelBookmarks** Collection, **Add** Method (Columns, SelBookmarks, Splits Collections), **Remove** Method (DBGrid), **Recordset** Property

Example

This example defines buttons to move the grid a whole page left or right.

```
Private Sub PageRight_Click ()
   'Page grid to the right.
   If DBGrid1.LeftCol + DBGrid1.VisibleCols < _
      DBGrid1.Columns.Count Then
      DBGrid1.LeftCol = DBGrid1.LeftCol + _
      DBGrid1.VisibleCols
   End If
End Sub

Private Sub PageLeft_Click ()
   'Page grid to the left.
   If DBGrid1.LeftCol - DBGrid1.VisibleCols >= 0 Then
      DBGrid1.LeftCol = DBGrid1.LeftCol - _
      DBGrid1.VisibleCols
   End If
End Sub
```

VisibleCount Property

Returns a value indicating the number of visible items in the list portion of the **DBCombo** or **DBList** control.

Applies To
DBCombo Control, **DBList** Control

Syntax

object.**VisibleCount**

The *object* placeholder represents an object expression that evaluates to an object in the **Applies To** list.

Remarks

The **VisibleCount** property returns an integer from 0 to the number of items visible in the control. An item is considered visible even if only a portion of the text is visible, as when the **IntegralHeight** property setting is **False**.

Note   **VisibleCount** may be set to 0 before the first time the list portion of the **DBCombo** control is displayed.

Data Type
Integer

See Also

Data Control, **IntegralHeight** Property, **VisibleItems** Property

---

VisibleItems Property

Returns an array of bookmarks, one for each visible item in the **DBCombo** or **DBList** control's list.

Applies To
DBCombo Control, **DBList** Control

Syntax

object.**VisibleItems**(*Index*)

The **VisibleItems** property syntax has these parts:

Part	Description
object	An object expression that evaluates to an object in the **Applies To** list.
Index	An Integer expression that specifies the element in the array. This value can be 0 to **VisibleCount** - 1.

Remarks

> These bookmarks may be used to fetch individual records from the recordset used to fill the list.

Data Type

> **Variant**

See Also

> **Bookmark** Property (DBGrid), **Data** Control, **VisibleCount** Property

---

VisibleCount, VisibleItems Properties Example

The following sample code uses the **VisibleCount** and **VisibleItems** properties to display the fields in all the visible records of a **DBList** control:

```
Private Sub Command1_Click()
Dim I As Integer, fld As Field, msg As Variant

For I = 0 To DBList1.VisibleCount - 1
   Data1.Recordset.Bookmark = DBList1.VisibleItems(I)
   msg = ""
   For Each fld In Data1.Recordset.Fields
      msg = msg & fld.Value & "-"
   Next
   MsgBox msg
Next I

End Sub
```

VisibleRows Property

Returns a value indicating the number of visible rows in the **DBGrid** control. This property is read-only at run time.

Applies To

> **DBGrid** Control

Syntax

> *object*.**VisibleRows**

The *object* placeholder represents an object expression that evaluates to an object in the Applies To list.

Remarks

The **VisibleRows** property returns an integer ranging from 0 to the number of rows in the **DBGrid** control. The **VisibleRows** property includes either fully or partially visible **DBGrid** control rows.

See Also

Data Control, **VisibleCols** Property

Example

This example selects all the rows that are currently visible on the grid.

```
Private Sub SelectVisible_Click ()
    Dim I
      For I = 0 To DBGrid1.VisibleRows - 1
        DBGrid1.SelBookmarks.Add DBGrid1.RowBookmark(I)
    Next I
End Sub
```

VisibleValue Property

Returns a value currently in the database that is newer than the **OriginalValue** property as determined by a batch update conflict (**ODBCDirect** workspaces only).

Applies To

Field Object

Return Values

The return value is a variant expression.

Remarks

This property contains the value of the field that is currently in the database on the server. During an optimistic batch update, a collision may occur where a second client modified the same field and record in between the time the first client retrieved the data and the first client's update attempt. When this happens, the value that the second client set will be accessible through this property..

Weekday Function

Returns a **Variant** (**Integer**) containing a whole number representing the day of the week.

Syntax

Weekday(*date*, [*firstdayofweek*])

The **Weekday** function syntax has these named arguments:

Part	Description
date	Required. **Variant**, numeric expression, string expression, or any combination, that can represent a date. If *date* contains **Null**, **Null** is returned.
firstdayofweek	Optional. A constant that specifies the first day of the week. If not specified, **vbSunday** is assumed.

Settings

The *firstdayofweek* argument has these settings:

Constant	Value	Description
vbUseSystem	0	Use the NLS API setting.
vbSunday	1	Sunday (default)
vbMonday	2	Monday
vbTuesday	3	Tuesday
vbWednesday	4	Wednesday
vbThursday	5	Thursday
vbFriday	6	Friday
vbSaturday	7	Saturday

Return Values

The **Weekday** function can return any of these values:

Constant	Value	Description
vbSunday	1	Sunday
vbMonday	2	Monday
vbTuesday	3	Tuesday
vbWednesday	4	Wednesday
vbThursday	5	Thursday
vbFriday	6	Friday
vbSaturday	7	Saturday

See Also

Date Function, **Date** Statement, **Day** Function, **Month** Function, **Now** Function, **Year** Function

Example

This example uses the **Weekday** function to obtain the day of the week from a specified date.

```
Dim MyDate, MyWeekDay
MyDate = #February 12, 1969#   ' Assign a date.
MyWeekDay = Weekday(MyDate)    ' MyWeekDay contains 4 because
                               ' MyDate represents a Wednesday.
```

Weight Property

Returns or sets the weight of the characters that make up a **Font** object. The weight refers to the thickness of the characters, or the "boldness factor". The higher the value, the bolder the character.

Applies To

Font Object

Syntax

object.**Weight** [= *number*]

The **Weight** property syntax has these parts:

Part	Description
object	An object expression that evaluates to an object in the **Applies To** list.
number	A numeric expression specifying the weight of the font.

Remarks

The **Font** object isn't directly available at design time. You set the **Weight** property of the **Font** object by selecting a control's **Font** property in the Properties window and clicking the Properties button. You implicitly set the **Weight** property by selecting an item from the Font Style box in the Font dialog box. The Regular and Italic settings have a **Weight** value of 400 (the default), and the Bold and Bold Italic settings have a **Weight** value of 700. At run time, however, you set **Weight** directly by specifying its setting for the **Font** object.

If you set a **Font** object's **Weight** to a value other than 400 or 700 at run time, Visual Basic converts your value to either 400 or 700, depending on which value is closest to the value you set. The precise ranges are: **Weight** > 400 and < 551 converts to 400; **Weight** > 550 converts to 700.

See Also

Bold Property, **FontTransparent** Property, **Italic** Property, **Size** Property (Font), **StrikeThrough** Property, **Underline** Property, **Name** Property

Example

This example prints text on a form with each mouse click. To try this example, paste the code into the Declarations section of a form, and then press F5 and click the form twice.

```
Private Sub Form_Click ()
   Font.Bold = Not Font.Bold  ' Toggle bold.
   Font.StrikeThrough = Not Font.StrikeThrough ' Toggle strikethrough.
   Font.Italic = Not Font.Italic     ' Toggle italic.
   Font.Underline = Not Font.Underline       ' Toggle underline.
   Font.Size = 16 ' Set Size property.
   If Font.Bold Then
      Print "Font weight is " & Font.Weight & " (bold)."
   Else
      Print "Font weight is " & Font.Weight & " (not bold)."

   End If
End Sub
```

WhatsThisButton Property

Returns or sets a value that determines whether the What's This button appears in the title bar of a **Form** object. Read-only at run time.

Applies To

Form Object, **Forms** Collection

Syntax

object.**WhatsThisButton**

The *object* placeholder represents an object expression that evaluates to an object in the **Applies To** list.

Settings

The settings for the **WhatsThisButton** property are:

Setting	Description
True	Turns display of the What's This Help button on.
False	(Default) Turns display of the What's This Help button off.

Remarks

The **WhatsThisHelp** property must be **True** for the **WhatsThisButton** property to be **True**. In addition, the following properties must also be set as shown:

- **ControlBox** property = **True**
- **BorderStyle** property = Fixed Single or Sizable
- **MinButton** and **MaxButton** = **False**

  –Or–

- **BorderStyle** property = Fixed Dialog

See Also

BorderStyle Property, **WhatsThisHelpID** Property, **WhatsThisHelp** Property, **ShowWhatsThis** Method, **WhatsThisMode** Method

---

WhatsThisHelp Property

Returns or sets a value that determines whether context-sensitive Help uses the What's This pop-up provided by Windows 95 Help or the main Help window. Read-only at run time.

Applies To

Animation Control, **Form** Object, **Forms** Collection, **MDIForm** Object

Syntax

object.**WhatsThisHelp** [= *boolean*]

The **WhatsThisHelp** property syntax has these parts:

Part	Description
object	An object expression that evaluates to an object in the **Applies To** list.
boolean	A value that determines if Help uses the What's This pop-up, as described in **Settings**.

Settings

The settings for *boolean* are:

Setting	Description
True	The application uses one of the What's This access techniques to start Windows Help and load a topic identified by the **WhatsThisHelpID** property.
False	(Default) The application uses the F1 key to start Windows Help and load the topic identified by the **HelpContextID** property.

Remarks

There are three access techniques for providing What's This Help in an application. The **WhatsThisHelp** property must be set to **True** for any of these techniques to work.

- Providing a What's This button in the title bar of the form using the **WhatsThisButton** property. The mouse pointer changes into the What's This state (arrow with question mark). The topic displayed is identified by the **WhatsThisHelpID** property of the control clicked by the user.

- Invoking the **WhatsThisMode** method of a form. This produces the same behavior as clicking the What's This button without using a button. For example, you can invoke this method from a command on a menu in the menu bar of your application.

- Invoking the **ShowWhatsThis** method for a particular control. The topic displayed is identified by the **WhatsThisHelpID** property of the control.

See Also

WhatsThisHelpID Property, **WhatsThisButton** Property, **ShowWhatsThis** Method, **WhatsThisMode** Method

WhatsThisHelpID Property

Returns or sets an associated context number for an object. Use to provide context-sensitive Help for your application using the What's This pop-up in Windows 95 Help.

Applies To

CheckBox Control, **ComboBox** Control, **CommandButton** Control, **Data** Control, **DBCombo** Control, **DBGrid** Control, **DBList** Control, **DriveListBox** Control, **FileListBox** Control, **Frame** Control, **HScrollBar**, **VScrollBar** Controls, Image Control, **Label** Control, **ListBox** Control, **ListView** Control, **Masked Edit** Control, **MSChart** Control, **MSFlexGrid** Control, **OLE Container** Control, **OptionButton** Control, **PictureBox** Control, **ProgressBar** Control, **RemoteData** Control, **RichTextBox** Control, **Slider** Control, **SSTab** Control, **StatusBar** Control, **TabStrip** Control, **TextBox** Control, **Toolbar** Control, **TreeView** Control, **UpDown** Control

Syntax

object.**WhatsThisHelpID** [= *number*]

The **WhatsThisHelpID** property syntax has these parts:

Part	Description
object	An object expression that evaluates to an object in the **Applies To** list.
number	A numeric expression specifying a Help context number, as described in **Settings**.

Settings

The settings for *number* are:

Setting	Description
0	(Default) No context number specified.
>0	An integer specifying the valid context number for the What's This topic associated with the object.

Remarks

Windows 95 uses the What's This button in the upper-right corner of the window to start Windows Help and load a topic identified by the **WhatsThisHelpID** property.

See Also

HelpContextID Property, **WhatsThisButton** Property, **WhatsThisHelp** Property, **ShowWhatsThis** Method, **WhatsThisMode** Method

WhatsThisMode Method

Causes the mouse pointer to change into the What's This pointer and prepares the application to display What's This Help on the selected object.

Applies To

Form Object, **Forms** Collection, **MDIForm** Object

Syntax

object.**WhatsThisMode**

The *object* placeholder represents an object expression that evaluates to an object in the **Applies To** list.

Remarks

Executing the **WhatsThisMode** method places the application in the same state you get by clicking the What's This button in the title bar. The mouse pointer changes to the What's This pointer. When the user clicks an object, the **WhatsThisHelpID** property of the clicked object is used to invoke context-sensitive Help. This method is especially useful when invoking Help from a menu in the menu bar of your application.

See Also

WhatsThisHelpID Property, **WhatsThisButton** Property, **WhatsThisHelp** Property, **ShowWhatsThis** Method

Example

This example uses a command in a menu to change the mouse pointer to the What's This pointer and enable context-sensitive Help. To try the example, create a menu, and paste the code into the Click event of one of the **Menu** controls. Press F5, and click the menu command to toggle the application into the What's This state.

```
Private Sub mnuContextHelp_Click ()
    Form1.WhatsThisMode
End Sub
```

While...Wend Statement

Executes a series of statements as long as a given condition is **True**.

Syntax

While *condition*
    [*statements*]
Wend

The **While...Wend** statement syntax has these parts:

Part	Description
condition	Required. Numeric expression or string expression that evaluates to **True** or **False**. If *condition* is **Null**, *condition* is treated as **False**.
statements	Optional. One or more statements executed while condition is **True**.

Remarks

If *condition* is **True**, all *statements* are executed until the **Wend** statement is encountered. Control then returns to the **While** statement and *condition* is again checked. If *condition* is still **True**, the process is repeated. If it is not **True**, execution resumes with the statement following the **Wend** statement.

While...Wend loops can be nested to any level. Each **Wend** matches the most recent **While**.

Tip The **Do...Loop** statement provides a more structured and flexible way to perform looping.

See Also

Do...Loop Statement, **With** Statement

Example

This example uses the **While...Wend** statement to increment a counter variable. The statements in the loop are executed as long as the condition evaluates to **True**.

```
Dim Counter
Counter = 0              ' Initialize variable.
While Counter < 20       ' Test value of Counter.
    Counter = Counter + 1  ' Increment Counter.
Wend                     ' End While loop when Counter > 19.
Debug.Print Counter      ' Prints 20 in Debug window.
```

Width # Statement

Assigns an output line width to a file opened using the **Open** statement.

Syntax

Width #*filenumber, width*

The **Width #** statement syntax has these parts:

Part	Description
filenumber	Required. Any valid file number.
width	Required. Numeric expression in the range 0–255, inclusive, that indicates how many characters appear on a line before a new line is started. If *width* equals 0, there is no limit to the length of a line. The default value for *width* is 0.

See Also

Open Statement, **Print #** Statement

Example

This example uses the **Width #** statement to set the output line width for a file.

```
Dim I
Open "TESTFILE" For Output As #1    ' Open file for output.
Width #1, 5                          ' Set output line width to 5.
For I = 0 To 9                       ' Loop 10 times.
   Print #1, Chr(48 + I);           ' Prints five characters per line.
Next I
Close #1                             ' Close file.
```

Width Property

Returns or sets a **Single** containing the width of the window in twips. Read/write.

Applies to

Window Object

Remarks

Changing the **Width** property setting of a linked window or docked window has no effect as long as the window remains linked or docked.

See Also

Height Property, **Left** Property, **Top** Property

WillAssociate Event

Occurs before a new connection is associated with the object.

Applies To

rdoResultset Object

Syntax

Private Sub *object*.**WillAssociate**(*Connection* as **rdoConnection**, *Cancel* as **Boolean**)

The **WillAssociate** event syntax has these parts:

Part	Description
object	An object expression that evaluates to an object in the **Applies To** list.
Connection	An object expression that evaluates to the **rdoConnection** object that is to be associated.
Cancel	A **Boolean** expression indicating if RDO should prohibit the association.

The settings for *Cancel* are:

Setting	Description
True	RDO will prohibit the association.
False	(Default) RDO will not prohibit the association.

Remarks

This event is raised after you set the **ActiveConnection** property to a valid **rdoConnection** object, but before the actual associate is made.

The *Connection* argument is a reference to the **rdoConnection** object that you are attempting to associate with the **rdoResultset** object. When the **WillAssociate** event is raised, the **ActiveConnection** property remains set to the value *before* the attempted association. You can use this property to determine the current **rdoResultset** connection association.

You can prohibit the association by setting the *Cancel* argument to **True**, causing RDO to not associate the result set with the new connection and produce a runtime error. If you do not prohibit the association using the *Cancel* argument, the **ActiveConnection** property is set to the reference contained in the *Connection* parameter after this event procedure completes.

See Also

BeforeConnect Event, **Associate** Event, **Disconnect** Event, **Dissociate** Event, **WillDissociate** Event, **OpenConnection** Method (Remote Data), **EstablishConnection** Method (Remote Data), **rdoConnection** Object, **ActiveConnection** Property

WillChangeData Event

Occurs before data is changed in the column.

Applies To

rdoColumn Object

Syntax

Private Sub *object*.**WillChangeData**(*NewValue* as **Variant,** *Cancel* as **Boolean**)

The **WillChangeData** event syntax has these parts:

Part	Description
object	An object expression that evaluates to an object in the **Applies To** list.
NewValue	A **Variant** expression containing the data to be applied to the column.
Cancel	A **Boolean** expression indicating if RDO should prohibit the change.

The settings for *Cancel* are:

Setting	Description
True	RDO will prohibit the change.
False	(Default) RDO will not prohibit the change.

Remarks

This event is raised just before RDO commits any change to the data in a column. By trapping this event, you can either modify the new value, or prohibit the change by modifying the *Cancel* argument.

If you modify the *NewValue* parameter, the modified value is assigned to the column's **Value** property. This allows you translate or substitute data.

By default, the *Cancel* argument is **False**, but if you set it to **True**, the change to the column's data is canceled, and RDO generates a trappable error.

See Also

Edit Method (Remote Data), **Update** Method (Remote Data), **Value** Property (Remote Data)

WillDissociate Event

Occurs before the connection is set to nothing.

Applies To

rdoResultset Object

Syntax

Private Sub *object***.WillDissociate**(*Cancel* as **Boolean**)

The **WillDissociate** event syntax has these parts:

Part	Description
object	An object expression that evaluates to an object in the **Applies To** list.
Cancel	A **Boolean** expression indicating whether RDO should prohibit the disassociation.

The settings for *Cancel* are:

Setting	Description
True	RDO will prohibit the change.
False	(Default) RDO will not prohibit the change.

Remarks

This event is raised when the developer attempts to set the **ActiveConnection** property to **Nothing** but *before* the result set is dissociated from the connection.

If you wish to prohibit the dissociation, set the *Cancel* parameter to **True**, causing RDO to cancel the operation and trigger a trappable error.

The default value for the *Cancel* parameter is **False**, so if the event is not trapped, the dissociation is completed.

See Also

rdoConnection Object, **ActiveConnection** Property

WillExecute Event

Occurs before the execution of a query.

Applies To

rdoConnection Object

Syntax

Private Sub *object*.**WillExecute**(*Query* as **rdoQuery**, *Cancel* as **Boolean**)

The **WillExecute** event syntax has these parts:

Part	Description
object	An object expression that evaluates to an object in the **Applies To** list.
Query	An object expression that evaluates to an **rdoQuery** object whose query has just completed.
Cancel	A **Boolean** expression indicating if RDO should prohibit the change.

The settings for *Cancel* are:

Setting	Description
True	RDO will prohibit the change.
False	(Default) RDO will not prohibit the change.

Remarks

This event is fired before the execution of a query, regardless if it is an action or row-returning query. You can trap this event to disallow the execution of certain queries, or to make last-minute adjustments to the **rdoQuery** object's SQL string.

The *Cancel* argument allows you to disallow the query. The *Cancel* parameter will default to **False**, but if you set it to **True**, the query will not execute, and RDO generates a trappable error indicating that the query was canceled.

For example, you can pre-screen the query to make sure the WHERE clause will not cause a table-scan operation. Thus, by setting the *Cancel* argument to **True**, you can prohibit users from searching for customers with the last name of "Smith" without also providing a first name or street address.

The **WillExecute** event fires for all queries execute on this **rdoConnection**. This includes those queries executed via the **OpenResultset** or **Execute** methods, as well as those executed from an associated **rdoQuery** object. The *Query* argument is an object reference indicating which query is about to execute. Using this argument, you can write a single event handler for all queries on the connection, but still customize the handler for specific queries. When executing queries against the **rdoConnection** object itself, RDO creates an **rdoQuery** object internally, and a reference to this internal **rdoQuery** is passed as the *Query* argument.

See Also

Execute Method (Remote Data), **OpenResultset** Method (Remote Data), **Refresh** Method (Remote Data), **Requery** Method (Remote Data), **SQL** Property

---

WillUpdateRows Event

Occurs before an update to the database occurs.

Applies To

rdoResultset Object

Syntax

Private Sub *object***.WillUpdateRows**(*ReturnCode* as **Long**)

The **WillUpdateRows** event syntax has these parts:

Part	Description
object	An object expression that evaluates to an object in the **Applies To** list.
RetrunCode	An **Long** integer expression or constant indicating whether the developer handled the update or not as described in Settings.

The *Value* argument is used to notify RDO about what your code did during the event handling. The possible values for this argument are as follows:

Setting	Description
rdUpdateSuccessful	Your code handled the update and was successful in doing so.
rdUpdateWithCollisions	Your code handled the update successfully, but some rows produced collisions (batch mode only).
rdUpdateFailed	Your code attempted to handle the update, but encountered an error when doing so.
rdUpdateNotHandled	Your code did not handle the update. RDO should continue notifying and if no one handles the update, RDO should update the data itself.

Remarks

The **WillUpdateRows** event is raised before updated, new and deleted rows are committed to the server. You can override the update behavior of the cursor by responding to this event and perform your own updates using stored procedures or any other mechanism you choose.

If the result set is using batch optimistic concurrency, this event is only raised when the **BatchUpdate** method is called. In this case, the entire set of changes is about to be transmitted to the server.

If the result set is not in a batch mode, the **WillUpdateRows** event is raised for each call to the **Update** method, since the changes for that row are immediately sent to the server.

To summarize, no matter what mode the result set is in, this event is only raised before data is actually sent to the server.

If you set the *ReturnCode* argument to **rdUpdateSuccessful**, RDO assumes that your code successfully handled the update. RDO will not send this event to any additional clients (if there is more than one handler of this event) and the status for the row(s) and their columns is set to **rdRowUnmodified** and **rdColUnmodified** respectively.

If you set the *ReturnCode* parameter to **rdUpdateWithCollisions**, RDO assumes that you have successfully handled the update, but some rows caused collisions. RDO will not send this event to any additional clients (if there was more than one handler of this event) and the status for the rows and their columns is not changed. It is your code's responsibility to set the column status flags during the handling of this event. The **rdUpdateWithCollisions** would only be used if you are using batch optimistic concurrency and you wanted to check for and handle collisions in code.

If the developer sets the *ReturnCode* parameter to **rdUpdateFailed**, RDO assumes that your code attempted to handle the update, but encountered an error while doing so. RDO will not send this event to any additional clients (if there was more than one handler of this event) and the status for the row(s) and their columns remains unchanged. Finally, RDO generates a runtime error to be trapped by the **Update** method causing the WillUpdate event to fire.

If you set the *ReturnCode* parameter to **rdUpdateNotHandled**, RDO will assume that the developer did not handle the update, and RDO will continue to raise this event to all remaining clients (if there was more than one handler of this event). If all clients return **rdUpdateNotHandled**, RDO will perform the update itself, according the normal rules.

The default value for the *ReturnCode* parameter is **rdUpdateNotHandled**, so if no client sinks the event, or no client changes the value of *ReturnCode*, RDO will perform the update.

Update Method (Remote Data), **UpdateRow** Method (Remote Data), **BatchUpdate** Method (Remote Data)

Window Object

Represents a window in the development environment.

Remarks

Use the **Window** object to show, hide, or position windows.

You can use the **Close** method to close a window in the **Windows** collection. The **Close** method affects different types of windows as follows:

Window	Result of using Close method
Code window	Removes the window from the **Windows** collection.
Designer	Removes the window from the **Windows** collection.
Window objects of type linked window frame	Windows become unlinked separate windows.

Note   Using the **Close** method with code windows and designers actually closes the window. Setting the **Visible** property to **False** hides the window but doesn't close the window. Using the **Close** method with development environment windows, such as the **Project** window or **Properties** window, is the same as setting the **Visible** property to **False**.

You can use the **SetFocus** method to move the focus to a window.

You can use the **Visible** property to return or set the visibility of a window.

To find out what type of window you are working with, you can use the **Type** property. If you have more than one window of a type, for example, multiple designers, you can use the **Caption** property to determine the window you're working with. You can also find the window you want to work with using the **DesignerWindow** property of the **VBComponent** object or the **Window** property of the **CodePane** object.

Properties

Caption Property, **Collection** Property, **Height** Property, **Left** Property, **LinkedWindowFrame** Property, **Top** Property, **Type** Property, **VBE** Property, **Visible** Property, **Width** Property, **WindowState** Property

Methods

>   **Close** Method, **SetFocus** Method

See Also

>   **VBComponent** Object, **CodePane** Object, **Windows** Collection, **DesignerWindow** Property, **Window** Property

---

Window Property

Returns the window in which the code pane is displayed.
Read-only.

Applies to

>   **CodePane** Object

See Also

>   **SetFocus** Method, **SetSelection** Method, **Show** Method, **CodePaneView** Property, **LinkedWindowFrame** Property, **TopLine** Property, **Visible** Property

Specifics

>   **SetFocus** Method, **Window** Object, **ActiveWindow** Property, **MainWindow** Property, **Visible** Property, **WindowState** Property

Example

>   The following example uses the **Window** and **Caption** properties to return the caption of the specified code pane.

```
Debug.Print Application.VBE.CodePanes(1).Window.Caption
```

WindowList Property

Returns or sets a value that determines whether a **Menu** object maintains a list of the current MDI child windows in an **MDIForm** object. Read only at run time.

Applies To

>   **Menu** Control

Syntax

>   *object*.**WindowList**

>   The *object* placeholder represents an object expression that evaluates to an object in the **Applies To** list.

Settings

The **WindowList** property settings are:

Setting	Description
True	The **Menu** object maintains a list of open windows and displays a check mark next to the active window. Users can click a window name to activate that window.
False	(Default) The **Menu** doesn't maintain a list of open windows.

Remarks

Many multiple-document interface (MDI) applications, such as Microsoft Excel and Microsoft Word for Windows, have a Window menu containing a list of open MDI child windows. This property enables you to add this functionality to your application.

Only one **Menu** object on a form can have its **WindowList** property set to **True**.

When you select the **WindowList** check box in the Menu Editor for a **Menu** object, the list of open MDI child windows for the menu you're creating is displayed.

See Also

MDIForm Object, **Caption** Property

Example

This example creates some menu commands, illustrates the **WindowList** menu functionality, and shows how to enable your users to add new forms to a multiple-document interface (MDI) application. To try this example, create an **MDIForm** object with the Add MDI Form command on the Project menu. On Form1, set the **MDIChild** property to **True**, and create a menu named File. Select the **WindowList** box for the File menu. On your **File** menu, create a New command, set its Name property to FileMenu, and set its **Index** property to 0 to create a control array. Paste the code into the Declarations section of the form, and then press F5 to run the program. Choosing the New command on the File menu creates new MDI child forms. Their names are listed at the bottom of the File menu.

```
Private Sub Form_Load ()
    FileMenu(0).Caption = "&New"        ' Set access key in caption.
    Load FileMenu(1)   ' Create new menu item.
    FileMenu(1).Caption = "-"  ' Set separator.
    Load FileMenu(2)   ' Create new menu item.
    FileMenu(2).Caption = "E&xit"       ' Set caption and access key.
End Sub

Private Sub FileMenu_Click (Index As Integer)
    Select Case Index
        Case 0' Select New command.
            Dim NewForm As New Form1      ' Create a duplicate of Form1.
            ' Load NewForm and set a unique caption.

NewForm.Caption = "Untitled" & Forms.Count
        Case 2' Select Exit command.
            End' End the program.
    End Select
End Sub
```

Windows Collection

Contains all open or permanent windows.

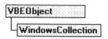

Remarks

Use the **Windows** collection to access **Window** objects.

The **Windows** collection has a fixed set of windows that are always available in the collection, such as the **Project** window, the **Properties** window, and a set of windows that represent all open code windows and designer windows. Opening a code or designer window adds a new member to the **Windows** collection. Closing a code or designer window removes a member from the **Windows** collection. Closing a permanent development environment window doesn't remove the corresponding object from this collection, but results in the window not being visible.

Properties

Count Property, **Parent** Property, **VBE** Property

Methods

Item Method

See Also

CodePane Object, **CodePanes** Collection, **Window** Object

Windows Property

Returns the **Window** object, which represents a window in the Visual Basic IDE.

Syntax

object.**Window**

The *object* placeholder represents an object expression that evaluates to an object in the **Applies To** list.

WindowState Property

Returns or sets a value indicating the visual state of a form window at run time.

Applies To

Form Object, **Forms** Collection, **MDIForm** Object

Syntax

object.**WindowState** [= *value*]

The **WindowState** property syntax has these parts:

Part	Description
object	An object expression that evaluates to an object in the **Applies To** list.
value	An integer specifying the state of the object, as described in Settings.

Settings

The settings for *value* are:

Constant	Value	Description
vbNormal	0	(Default) Normal.
VbMinimized	1	Minimized (minimized to an icon)
VbMaximized	2	Maximized (enlarged to maximum size)

Remarks

Before a form is displayed, the **WindowState** property is always set to Normal (0), regardless of its initial setting. This is reflected in the **Height**, **Left**, **ScaleHeight**, **ScaleWidth**, **Top**, and **Width** property settings. If a form is hidden after it's been shown, these properties reflect the previous state until the form is shown again, regardless of any changes made to the **WindowState** property in the meantime.

See Also

Load Event, **Paint** Event, **Resize** Event

Example

This example hides a dialog box (Form2) when the parent form (Form1) is minimized and redisplays the dialog box when the parent form is returned to either an original or maximized state. To try this example, paste the code into the Declarations section of Form1 of an application that contains two forms. Press F5 to start the example. Move Form1 so you can see both forms, and then minimize or maximize the form and observe the behavior of Form2.

```
Private Sub Form_Load ()
   Form2.Show  ' Show Form2.
End Sub

Private Sub Form_Resize ()
   ' If parent form is minimized...
   If Form1.WindowState = vbMinimized Then
   ' ...hide Form2.
     Form2.Visible = False
   ' If parent form isn't minimized...
   Else
      ' ...restore Form2.
     Form2.Visible = True
   End If
End Sub
```

WindowState Property (Add-Ins)

Returns or sets a numeric value specifying the visual state of the window. Read/write.

Applies to

Window Object

Settings

The **WindowState** property returns or sets the following values:

Constant	Value	Description
vbext_ws_Normal	0	(Default) Normal
vbext_ws_Minimize	1	Minimized (minimized to an icon)
vbext_ws_Maximize	2	Maximized (enlarged to maximum size)

See Also

SetFocus Method, **ActiveWindow** Property, **MainWindow** Property, **Visible** Property

Example

The following example uses the **WindowState** property to return the visual state of the specified window. The value returned is a number that corresponds to a predefined constant that specifies the visual state of a window.

```
Debug.Print Application.VBE.Windows(9).WindowState
```

With Statement

Executes a series of statements on a single object or a user-defined type.

Syntax

With *object*
    [*statements*]
End With

The **With** statement syntax has these parts:

Part	Description
object	Required. Name of an object or a user-defined type.
statements	Optional. One or more statements to be executed on *object*.

Remarks

The **With** statement allows you to perform a series of statements on a specified object without requalifying the name of the object. For example, to change a number of different properties on a single object, place the property assignment statements within the **With** control structure, referring to the object once instead of referring to it with each property assignment. The following example illustrates use of the **With** statement to assign values to several properties of the same object.

```
With MyLabel
    .Height = 2000
    .Width = 2000
    .Caption = "This is MyLabel"
End With
```

Note Once a **With** block is entered, *object* can't be changed. As a result, you can't use a single **With** statement to affect a number of different objects.

You can nest **With** statements by placing one **With** block within another. However, because members of outer **With** blocks are masked within the inner **With** blocks, you must provide a fully qualified object reference in an inner **With** block to any member of an object in an outer **With** block.

Important Do not jump into or out of **With** blocks. If statements in a **With** block are executed, but either the **With** or **End With** statement is not executed, you may get errors or unpredictable behavior.

See Also

> **Do...Loop** Statement

Example

This example uses the **With** statement to execute a series of statements on a single object. The object `MyObject` and its properties are generic names used for illustration purposes only.

```
With MyObject
    .Height = 100              ' Same as MyObject.Height = 100.
    .Caption = "Hello World"   ' Same as MyObject.Caption = "Hello World".
    With .Font
        .Color = Red           ' Same as MyObject.Font.Color = Red.
        .Bold = True           ' Same as MyObject.Font.Bold = True.
    End With
End With
```

WordWrap Property

Returns or sets a value indicating whether a **Label** control with its **AutoSize** property set to **True** expands vertically or horizontally to fit the text specified in its **Caption** property.

Applies To

> **Label** Control

Syntax

object.**WordWrap** [= *boolean*]

The **WordWrap** property syntax has these parts:

Part	Description
object	An object expression that evaluates to an object in the **Applies To** list.
boolean	A Boolean expression specifying whether the **Label** expands to fit the text, as described in Settings.

Settings

The settings for *boolean* are:

Setting	Description
True	The text wraps; the **Label** control expands or contracts vertically to fit the text and the size of the font. The horizontal size doesn't change.
False	(Default) The text doesn't wrap; the **Label** expands or contracts horizontally to fit the length of the text and vertically to fit the size of the font and the number of lines.

Remarks

Use this property to determine how a **Label** control displays its contents. For example, a graph that changes dynamically might have a **Label** containing text that also changes. To maintain a constant horizontal size for the **Label** and allow for increasing or decreasing text, set the **WordWrap** and **AutoSize** properties to **True**.

If you want a **Label** control to expand only horizontally, set **WordWrap** to **False**. If you don't want the **Label** to change size, set **AutoSize** to **False**.

Note If **AutoSize** is set to **False**, the text always wraps, regardless of the size of the **Label** control or the setting of the **WordWrap** property. This may obscure some text because the **Label** doesn't expand in any direction.

See Also

AutoSize Property, **Caption** Property

Example

This example puts text into two **Label** controls and uses the **WordWrap** property to illustrate their different behavior. To try this example, paste the code into the Declarations section of a form that contains two **Label** controls, and then press F5 and click the form to toggle the **WordWrap** property setting.

```
Private Sub Form_Load ()
   Dim Author1, Author2, Quote1, Quote2      ' Declare variables.
   Label1.AutoSize = True   ' Set AutoSize.
   Label2.AutoSize = True
   Label1.WordWrap = True   ' Set WordWrap.
   Quote1 = "I couldn't wait for success, so I went on without it."
   Author1 = "  - Jonathan Winters"
   Quote2 = "Logic is a system whereby one may go wrong with confidence."
```

```
    Author2 = "  - Charles Kettering"
    Label1.Caption = Quote1 & Chr(10) & Author1
    Label2.Caption = Quote2 & Chr(10) & Author2
End Sub

Private Sub Form_Click ()
    Label1.Width = 1440   ' Set width to 1 inch in twips.
    Label2.Width = 1440
    Label1.WordWrap = Not Label1.WordWrap ' Toggle WordWrap property.
    Label2.WordWrap = Not Label2.WordWrap
End Sub
```

Workspace Object

A **Workspace** object defines a named session for a user. It contains open databases
and provides mechanisms for simultaneous transactions and, in Microsoft Jet
workspaces, secure workgroup support. It also controls whether you are going
through the Microsoft Jet database engine or ODBCDirect to access external data.

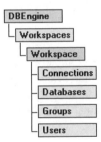

Remarks

A **Workspace** is a non-persistent object that defines how your application interacts
with data—either by using the Microsoft Jet database engine, or ODBCDirect. Use
the **Workspace** object to manage the current session or to start an additional session.
In a session, you can open multiple databases or connections, and manage
transactions. For example, you can:

- Use the **Name**, **UserName**, and **Type** properties to establish a named session. The
  session creates a scope in which you can open multiple databases and conduct one
  instance of nested transactions.

- Use the **Close** method to terminate a session.

- Use the **OpenDatabase** method to open one or more existing databases on a
  Workspace.

- Use the **BeginTrans**, **CommitTrans**, and **Rollback** methods to manage nested
  transaction processing within a **Workspace** and use several **Workspace** objects to
  conduct multiple, simultaneous, and overlapping transactions.

Further, using a Microsoft Jet database, you can establish security based on user names and passwords:

- Use the **Groups** and **Users** collections to establish group and user access permissions to objects in the **Workspace**.

- Use the **IsolateODBCTrans** property to isolate multiple transactions that involve the same Microsoft Jet-connected ODBC database.

Note For a complete list of all methods, properties, and collections available on a **Workspace** object in either a Microsoft Jet database or an ODBCDirect database, see the Summary topic.

When you first refer to or use a **Workspace** object, you automatically create the default workspace, `DBEngine.Workspaces(0)`. The settings of the **Name** and **UserName** properties of the default workspace are "#Default Workspace#" and "Admin," respectively. If security is enabled, the **UserName** property setting is the name of the user who logged on.

To establish an ODBCDirect **Workspace** object, and thereby avoid loading the Microsoft Jet database engine into memory, set the **DBEngine** object's **DefaultType** property to **dbUseODBC**, or set the *type* argument of the **CreateWorkspace** method to **dbUseODBC**.

When you use transactions, all databases in the specified **Workspace** are affected— even if multiple **Database** objects are opened in the **Workspace**. For example, you use a **BeginTrans** method, update several records in a database, and then delete records in another database. If you then use the **Rollback** method, both the update and delete operations are canceled and rolled back. You can create additional **Workspace** objects to manage transactions independently across **Database** objects.

You can create **Workspace** objects with the **CreateWorkspace** method. After you create a new **Workspace** object, you must append it to the **Workspaces** collection if you need to refer to it from the **Workspaces** collection.

You can use a newly created **Workspace** object without appending it to the **Workspaces** collection. However, you must refer to it by the object variable to which you have assigned it.

To refer to a **Workspace** object in a collection by its ordinal number or by its **Name** property setting, use any of the following syntax forms:

DBEngine.Workspaces(0)
DBEngine.Workspaces("*name*")
DBEngine.Workspaces![*name*]

Properties

IsolateODBCTrans Property, **LoginTimeout** Property, **Name** Property, **Type** Property, **UserName** Property, **DefaultCursorDriver** Property

Methods

BeginTrans, CommitTrans, Rollback Methods, **Close** Method, **CreateDatabase** Method, **CreateGroup** Method, **CreateUser** Method, **OpenDatabase** Method, **OpenConnection** Method

See Also

Transactions Property

Example

This example creates a new Microsoft Jet **Workspace** object and a new ODBCDirect **Workspace** object and appends them to the **Workspaces** collection. It then enumerates the **Workspaces** collections and the **Properties** collection of each **Workspace** object. See the methods and properties of the **Workspace** object or **Workspaces** collection for additional examples.

```
Sub WorkspaceX()

    Dim wrkNewJet As Workspace
    Dim wrkNewODBC As Workspace
    Dim wrkLoop As Workspace
    Dim prpLoop As Property

    ' Create a new Microsoft Jet workspace.
    Set wrkNewJet = CreateWorkspace("NewJetWorkspace", _
        "admin", "", dbUseJet)
    Workspaces.Append wrkNewJet

    ' Create a new ODBCDirect workspace.
    Set wrkNewODBC = CreateWorkspace("NewODBCWorkspace", _
        "admin", "", dbUseODBC)
    Workspaces.Append wrkNewODBC

    ' Enumerate the Workspaces collection.
    For Each wrkLoop In Workspaces
        With wrkLoop
            Debug.Print "Properties of " & .Name
            ' Enumerate the Properties collection of the new
            ' Workspace object.
            For Each prpLoop In .Properties
                On Error Resume Next
                If prpLoop <> "" Then Debug.Print "    " & _
                    prpLoop.Name & " = " & prpLoop
                On Error GoTo 0
            Next prpLoop
        End With
    Next wrkLoop

    wrkNewJet.Close
    wrkNewODBC.Close

End Sub
```

Workspaces Collection

A **Workspaces** collection contains all active, unhidden **Workspace** objects of the **DBEngine** object. (Hidden **Workspace** objects are not appended to the collection and referenced by the variable to which they are assigned.)

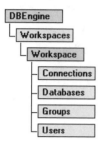

Remarks

Use the **Workspace** object to manage the current session or to start an additional session.

When you first refer to or use a **Workspace** object, you automatically create the default workspace, `DBEngine.Workspaces(0)`. The settings of the **Name** and **UserName** properties of the default workspace are "#Default Workspace#" and "Admin," respectively. If security is enabled, the **UserName** property setting is the name of the user who logged on.

You can create new **Workspace** objects with the **CreateWorkspace** method. After you create a new **Workspace** object, you must append it to the **Workspaces** collection if you need to refer to it from the **Workspaces** collection. You can, however, use a newly created **Workspace** object without appending it to the **Workspaces** collection.

To refer to a **Workspace** object in a collection by its ordinal number or by its **Name** property setting, use any of the following syntax forms:

DBEngine.Workspaces(0)
DBEngine.Workspaces("*name*")
DBEngine.Workspaces![*name*]

Properties

Count Property

Methods

Append Method, **Delete** Method, **Refresh** Method

Example

This example creates a new Microsoft Jet **Workspace** object and a new ODBCDirect **Workspace** object and appends them to the **Workspaces** collection. It then enumerates the **Workspaces** collections and the **Properties** collection of each **Workspace** object. See the methods and properties of the **Workspace** object or **Workspaces** collection for additional examples.

```
Sub WorkspaceX()

    Dim wrkNewJet As Workspace
    Dim wrkNewODBC As Workspace
    Dim wrkLoop As Workspace
    Dim prpLoop As Property

    ' Create a new Microsoft Jet workspace.
    Set wrkNewJet = CreateWorkspace("NewJetWorkspace", _
        "admin", "", dbUseJet)
    Workspaces.Append wrkNewJet

    ' Create a new ODBCDirect workspace.
    Set wrkNewODBC = CreateWorkspace("NewODBCWorkspace", _
        "admin", "", dbUseODBC)
    Workspaces.Append wrkNewODBC

    ' Enumerate the Workspaces collection.
    For Each wrkLoop In Workspaces
        With wrkLoop
            Debug.Print "Properties of " & .Name
            ' Enumerate the Properties collection of the new
            ' Workspace object.
            For Each prpLoop In .Properties
                On Error Resume Next
                If prpLoop <> "" Then Debug.Print "    " & _
                    prpLoop.Name & " = " & prpLoop
                On Error GoTo 0
            Next prpLoop
        End With
    Next wrkLoop

    wrkNewJet.Close
    wrkNewODBC.Close

    End Sub
```

WrapCellPointer Property

Sets or returns a value that determines the behavior of the arrow keys.

Applies To

DBGrid Control

Syntax

object.**WrapCellPointer** [= *value*]

The **WrapCellPointer** property syntax has these parts:

Part	Description
object	An object expression that evaluates to an object in the **Applies To** list.
value	A Boolean expression that determines the behavior of arrow keys, as described in Settings.

Settings

The settings for *value* are:

Setting	Description
True	The cell pointer will wrap from the last column to the first in the next row (or from the first column to the last in the previous row).
False	(Default) The cell pointer will not wrap to the next (or previous) row, but will stop at the last (or first) column of the current row.

Remarks

If **TabAcrossSplits** is **False**, the cell pointer will wrap only within the current split. If **TabAcrossSplits** is **True**, the cell pointer will move from one split to the next before wrapping occurs.

If **TabAction** is set to 2 - Grid Navigation, the tab key will behave like the arrow keys, and will automatically wrap to the next or previous cell.

See Also

AllowArrows Property, **TabAcrossSplits** Property, **TabAction** Property

---

WrapText Property (Column Object)

Sets or returns a value indicating whether an object word wraps text at cell boundaries.

Applies To

Column Object

Syntax

object.**WrapText** [= *value*]

The **WrapText** property syntax has these parts:

Part	Description
object	An object expression that evaluates to an object in the **Applies To** list.
value	A Boolean expression that determines whether an object word wraps, as described in Settings.

Settings

The settings for *value* are:

Setting	Description
True	A line break occurs before words that would otherwise be partially displayed.
False	(Default) No line break occurs and text is clipped at the cell's right edge.

Remarks

Use this property in conjunction with the **RowHeight** property to produce multi-line displays.

See Also

AllowArrows Property, **TabAcrossSplits** Property, **TabAction** Property

Write # Statement

Writes data to a sequential file.

Syntax

Write #*filenumber*, [*outputlist*]

The **Write #** statement syntax has these parts:

Part	Description
filenumber	Required. Any valid file number.
outputlist	Optional. One or more comma-delimited numeric expressions or string expressions to write to a file.

Remarks

Data written with **Write #** is usually read from a file with **Input #**.

If you omit *outputlist* and include a comma after *filenumber*, a blank line is printed to the file. Multiple expressions can be separated with a space, a semicolon, or a comma. A space has the same effect as a semicolon.

When **Write #** is used to write data to a file, several universal assumptions are followed so the data can always be read and correctly interpreted using **Input #**, regardless of locale:

- Numeric data is always written using the period as the decimal separator.
- For **Boolean** data, either #TRUE# or #FALSE# is printed. The **True** and **False** keywords are not translated, regardless of locale.
- **Date** data is written to the file using the universal date format. When either the date or the time component is missing or zero, only the part provided gets written to the file.

- Nothing is written to the file if *outputlist* data is **Empty**. However, for **Null** data, #NULL# is written.

- If *outputlist* data is **Null** data, #NULL# is written to the file.

- For **Error** data, the output appears as #ERROR errorcode#. The **Error** keyword is not translated, regardless of locale.

Unlike the **Print #** statement, the **Write #** statement inserts commas between items and quotation marks around strings as they are written to the file. You don't have to put explicit delimiters in the list. **Write #** inserts a newline character, that is, a carriage return–linefeed (**Chr**(13) + **Chr**(10)), after it has written the final character in *outputlist* to the file.

See Also

Input # Statement, **Open** Statement, **Print #** Statement

Example

This example uses the **Write #** statement to write raw data to a sequential file.

```
Open "TESTFILE" For Output As #1     ' Open file for output.
Write #1, "Hello World", 234         ' Write comma-delimited data.
Write #1,                            ' Write blank line.

Dim MyBool, MyDate, MyNull, MyError
' Assign Boolean, Date, Null, and Error values.
MyBool = False : MyDate = #February 12, 1969# : MyNull = Null
MyError = CVErr(32767)
' Boolean data is written as #TRUE# or #FALSE#. Date literals are
' written in universal date format, for example, #1994-07-13#
' represents July 13, 1994. Null data is written as #NULL#.
' Error data is written as #ERROR errorcode#.
Write #1, MyBool ; " is a Boolean value"
Write #1, MyDate ; " is a date"
Write #1, MyNull ; " is a null value"
Write #1, MyError ; " is an error value"
Close #1                             ' Close file.
```

WriteProperties Event

Occurs when an instance of an object is to be saved. This event signals to the object that the state of the object needs to be saved, so that the state can be restored later. In most cases, the state of the object consists only of property values.

Applies To

UserControl Object, **UserDocument** Object

Syntax

Sub *object*_**WriteProperties**(*pb* **As PropertyBag**)

The **WriteProperties** event syntax has these parts:

Part	Description
object	An object expression that evaluates to an object in the **Applies To** list.
pb	An object of the type **PropertyBag** class to write the data to.

Remarks

The author of *object* can have *object* save the state when the **WriteProperties** event occurs, by calling the **WriteProperty** method of the **PropertyBag** object for each value that is to be saved.

Note The *pb* property bag may be different from the *pb* that was passed to the most recent ReadProperties event.

The **WriteProperties** event may occur multiple times during the life of an instance of *object*.

See Also

ReadProperties Event

WriteProperty Method

Writes a value to be saved to a **PropertyBag** class object.

See Also

ReadProperty Method

Applies To

PropertyBag Object

Syntax

object.**WriteProperty**(*DataName*, *Value*[, *DefaultValue*])

The **WriteProperty** method syntax has these parts:

Part	Description
object	An object expression that evaluates to an object in the **Applies To** list.
DataName	A string expression to represents the data value to be placed in the property bag.
Value	The data value to save in the property bag.
DefaultValue	The default value for the data.

Remarks

The **WriteProperty** method will write a data value in the property bag, and associate it with the string value in *DataName*. This string value will be used to access the data value when the **ReadProperty** method is called to retrieve a saved data value from the property bag.

Note Specifying a default value reduces the size of the file belonging to the container of the control. A line for the property is written to the file only if the value to be written is different from the default. Wherever possible, you should specify default values for the properties of the control when initializing, saving, and retrieving property values.

X1, Y1, X2, Y2 Properties

Return or set the coordinates of the starting point (X1, Y1) and ending point (X2, Y2) of a **Line** control. The horizontal coordinates are X1 and X2; the vertical coordinates are Y1 and Y2.

Applies To

Line Control

Syntax

object.**X1** [= *value*]
object.**Y1** [= *value*]
object.**X2** [= *value*]
object.**Y2** [= *value*]

The **X1**, **Y1**, **X2**, and **Y2** property syntaxes have these parts:

Part	Description
object	An object expression that evaluates to an object in the **Applies To** list.
value	A numeric expression specifying a coordinate.

Remarks

Use these properties to dynamically extend a **Line** control from one point to another at run time. For example, you can show the relationships of items in one list to items in another list or connect points on a map.

Remarks

Left, **Top** Properties

Example

This example displays an animated line that walks down the form when you click the form. To try this example, paste the code into the Declarations section of a form that contains a **Timer** control and a **Line** control, and then press F5 and click the form.

```
Private Sub Form_Load ()
    Timer1.Interval = 100' Set Timer interval.
    ' Position the line near the upper-left corner.
    ' Set Line1's properties.
    With Line1
        .X1 = 100
        .Y1 = 100
        .X2 = 500
        .Y2 = 300
    End With
    Timer1.Enabled = False
End Sub
```

```
Private Sub Form_Click ()
    Timer1.Enabled = True' Start the timer.
End Sub

Private Sub Timer1_Timer ()
    Static Odd   ' Declare variable.
    If Odd Then

Line1.X2 = Line1.X2 + 250
        Line1.Y2 = Line1.Y2 + 600
    Else
        Line1.X1 = Line1.X1 + 250
        Line1.Y1 = Line1.Y1 + 600
    End If
    Odd = Not Odd   ' Toggle the value.
    ' If the line is off the form, start over.
    If Line1.Y1 > ScaleHeight Then
        Timer1.Enabled = False   ' Wait for another click.
        With Line1
           .X1 = 100
           .Y1 = 100
           .X2 = 500
           .Y2 = 300
        End With

Odd = False
    End If
End Sub
```

Xor Operator

Used to perform a logical exclusion on two expressions.

Syntax

[*result* =] *expression1* **Xor** *expression2*

The **Xor** operator syntax has these parts:

Part	Description
result	Optional; any numeric variable.
expression1	Required; any expression.
expression2	Required; any expression.

Remarks

If one, and only one, of the expressions evaluates to **True**, *result* is **True**. However, if either expression is **Null**, *result* is also **Null**. When neither expression is **Null**, *result* is determined according to the following table:

If *expression1* is	And *expression2* is	Then *result* is
True	True	False
True	False	True
False	True	True
False	False	False

The **Xor** operator performs as both a logical and bitwise operator. A bit-wise comparison of two expressions using exclusive-or logic to form the result, as shown in the following table:

If bit in *expression1* is	And bit in *expression2* is	Then *result* is
0	0	0
0	1	1
1	0	1
1	1	0

See Also

Operator Summary, **Operator** Precedence, **Logical** Operators

Example

This example uses the **Xor** operator to perform logical exclusion on two expressions.

```
Dim A, B, C, D, MyCheck
A = 10: B = 8: C = 6: D = Null          ' Initialize variables.
MyCheck = A > B Xor B > C               ' Returns False.
MyCheck = B > A Xor B > C               ' Returns True.
MyCheck = B > A Xor C > B               ' Returns False.
MyCheck = B > D Xor A > B               ' Returns Null.
MyCheck = A Xor B                       ' Returns 2 (bitwise comparison).
```

Year Function

Returns a **Variant** (**Integer**) containing a whole number representing the year.

Syntax

Year(*date*)

The required *date* argument is any **Variant**, numeric expression, string expression, or any combination, that can represent a date. If *date* contains **Null**, **Null** is returned.

See Also

Date Function, **Date** Statement, **Day** Function, **Month** Function, **Now** Function, **Weekday** Function

Example

This example uses the **Year** function to obtain the year from a specified date. In the development environment, the date literal is displayed in short date format using the locale settings of your code.

```
Dim MyDate, MyYear
MyDate = #February 12, 1969#  ' Assign a date.
MyYear = Year(MyDate)         ' MyYear contains 1969.
```

Zoom Property

Returns or sets the percentage by which printed output is to be scaled up or down. Not available at design time.

Applies To

Printer Object, **Printers** Collection

Syntax

object.**Zoom** [= *number*]

The **Zoom** property syntax has these parts:

Part	Description
object	An object expression that evaluates to an object in the **Applies To** list.
number	A numeric expression that evaluates to the percentage by which printed output is to be scaled. The default is 0, which specifies that the printed page appears at its normal size.

Remarks

The **Zoom** property setting scales the size of the physical page up or down, by a factor of Zoom/100, to the apparent size of the printed output. For example, a letter-size page printed with **Zoom** set to 50 contains as much data as a page of the size 17 by 22 inches because the printed text and graphics are scaled to one-half their original height and width.

Note The effect of the properties of the **Printer** object depends on the driver supplied by the printer manufacturer. Some property settings may have no effect, or several different property settings may all have the same effect. Settings outside the accepted range may or may not produce an error. For more information, see the manufacturer's documentation for the specific driver.

See Also

Printer Object, **Printers** Collection

ZOrder Method

Places a specified **MDIForm**, **Form**, or control at the front or back of the z-order within its graphical level. Doesn't support named arguments.

Applies To

Animation Control, **CheckBox** Control, **ComboBox** Control, **CommandButton** Control, **Data** Control, **DBCombo** Control, **DBGrid** Control, **DBList** Control, **DirListBox** Control, **DriveListBox** Control, **FileListBox** Control, **Form Object, Forms** Collection, **Frame** Control, **HScrollBar, VScrollBar** Controls, **Image** Control, **Label** Control, **Line** Control, **ListBox** Control, **ListView** Control, **Masked Edit** Control, **MDIForm** Object **MSFlexGrid** Control, **OLE Container** Control, **OptionButton** Control, **PictureBox** Control, **ProgressBar** Control, **RemoteData** Control, **RichTextBox** Control, **Shape** Control, **Slider** Control, **StatusBar** Control, **TabStrip** Control, **TextBox** Control, **Toolbar** Control, **TreeView** Control, **UpDown** Control

Syntax

object.**ZOrder** *position*

The **ZOrder** method syntax has these parts:

Part	Description
object	Optional. An object expression that evaluates to an object in the **Applies To** list. If *object* is omitted, the form with the focus is assumed to be *object*.
Position	Optional. Integer indicating the position of *object* relative to other instances of the same *object*. If position is 0 or omitted, *object* is positioned at the front of the z-order. If position is 1, *object* is positioned at the back of the z-order.

Remarks

The z-order of objects can be set at design time by choosing the Bring To Front or Send To Back menu command from the Edit menu.

Within an **MDIForm** object, **ZOrder** sends MDI child forms to either the front or the back of the MDI client area, depending on the value of *position*. For an **MDIForm** or **Form** object, **ZOrder** sends the form to either the front or the back of the screen, depending on the value of *position*. As a result, forms can be displayed in front of or behind other running applications.

Three graphical layers are associated with forms and containers. The back layer is the drawing space where the results of the graphics methods are displayed. Next is the middle layer where graphical objects and **Label** controls are displayed. The front layer is where all nongraphical controls like **CommandButton**, **CheckBox**, or **ListBox** are displayed. Anything contained in a layer closer to the front covers anything contained in the layer(s) behind it. **ZOrder** arranges objects only within the layer where the object is displayed.

See Also

Arrange Method

ANSI Character Set

Table A.1 ANSI Character Set

0	•	27	•	54	**6**	81	**Q**	108	**l**	135	•	162	¢	189	½
1	•	28	•	55	**7**	82	**R**	109	**m**	136	•	163	£	190	¾
2	•	29	•	56	**8**	83	**S**	110	**n**	137	•	164	¤	191	¿
3	•	30	•	57	**9**	84	**T**	111	**o**	138	•	165	¥	192	À
4	•	31	•	58	:	85	**U**	112	**p**	139	•	166	¦	193	Á
5	•	32		59	;	86	**V**	113	**q**	140	•	167	§	194	Â
6	•	33	!	60	<	87	**W**	114	**r**	141	•	168	¨	195	Ã
7	•	34	"	61	=	88	**X**	115	**s**	142	•	169	©	196	Ä
8	* *	35	#	62	>	89	**Y**	116	**t**	143	•	170	ª	197	Å
9	* *	36	$	63	?	90	**Z**	117	**u**	144	•	171	«	198	Æ
10	* *	37	%	64	@	91	[	118	**v**	145	'	172	¬	199	Ç
11	•	38	&	65	**A**	92	\	119	**w**	146	'	173	-	200	È
12	•	39	'	66	**B**	93	]	120	**x**	147	•	174	®	201	É
13	* *	40	(	67	**C**	94	^	121	**y**	148	•	175	¯	202	Ê
14	•	41	)	68	**D**	95	_	122	**z**	149	•	176	°	203	Ë
15	•	42	*	69	**E**	96	`	123	{	150	•	177	±	204	Ì
16	•	43	+	70	**F**	97	a	124			151	•	178	²	205	Í
17	•	44	,	71	**G**	98	b	125	}	152	•	179	³	206	Î
18	•	45	-	72	**H**	99	c	126	~	153	•	180	´	207	Ï
19	•	46	.	73	**I**	100	d	127	•	154	•	181	µ	208	Ð
20	•	47	/	74	**J**	101	e	128	•	155	•	182	¶	209	Ñ
21	•	48	**0**	75	**K**	102	f	129	•	156	•	183	·	210	Ò
22	•	49	**1**	76	**L**	103	g	130	•	157	•	184	¸	211	Ó
23	•	50	**2**	77	**M**	104	h	131	•	158	•	185	¹	212	Ô
24	•	51	**3**	78	**N**	105	i	132	•	159	•	186	º	213	Õ
25	•	52	**4**	79	**O**	106	j	133	•	160		187	»	214	Ö
26	•	53	**5**	80	**P**	107	k	134	•	161	¡	188	¼	215	×

Table A.1   ANSI Character Set *(continued)*

216	Ø	221	Ý	226	â	231	ç	236	ì	241	ñ	246	ö	251	û
217	Ù	222	Þ	227	ã	232	è	237	í	242	ò	247	÷	252	ü
218	Ú	223	ß	228	ä	233	é	238	î	243	ó	248	ø	253	ý
219	Û	224	à	229	å	234	ê	239	ï	244	ô	249	ù	254	þ
220	Ü	225	á	230	æ	235	ë	240	ð	245	õ	250	ú	255	ÿ

* * Values 8, 9, 10, and 13 convert to backspace, tab, linefeed, and carriage return characters, respectively. They have no graphical representation but, depending on the application, may affect the visual display of text.

• These characters aren't supported by the Microsoft Windows operating system.

Data Types

The following table shows the supported data types, including their storage sizes and ranges.

Data type	Storage size	Range
Byte	1 byte	0 to 255
Boolean	2 bytes	**True** or **False**.
Decimal (within a variant)	12 bytes	-79,228,162,514,264,337,543,950,335 to 79,228,162,514,264,337,543,950,335
Integer	2 bytes	-32,768 to 32,767.
Long (long integer)	4 bytes	-2,147,483,648 to 2,147,483,647.
Single (single-precision floating-point)	4 bytes	-3.402823E38 to -1.401298E-45 for negative values; 1.401298E-45 to 3.402823E38 for positive values.
Double (double-precision floating-point)	8 bytes	-1.79769313486232E308 to -4.94065645841247E-324 for negative values; 4.94065645841247E-324 to 1.79769313486232E308 for positive values.
Currency (scaled integer)	8 bytes	-922,337,203,685,477.5808 to 922,337,203,685,477.5807.
Date	8 bytes	January 1, 100 to December 31, 9999.
Object	4 bytes	Any **Object** reference.
String (variable-length)	10 bytes + string length	0 to approximately 2 billion (approximately 65,400 for Microsoft Windows version 3.1 and earlier).
String (fixed-length)	Length of string	1 to approximately 65,400.
Variant (with numbers)	16 bytes	Any numeric value up to the range of a **Double**.
Variant (with characters)	22 bytes + string length	Same range as for variable-length **String.**

(continued)

(continued)

Data type	Storage size	Range
User-defined (using **Type**)	Number required by elements	The range of each element is the same as the range of its data type.

Note Arrays of any data type require 20 bytes of memory plus four bytes for each array dimension plus the number of bytes occupied by the data itself. The memory occupied by the data can be calculated by multiplying the number of data elements by the size of each element. For example, the data in a single-dimension array consisting of four **Integer** data elements of two bytes each occupies eight bytes. The eight bytes the data requires plus the 24 bytes of overhead brings the total memory requirement for the array to 32 bytes.

A **Variant** containing an array requires 12 bytes more than the array alone.

See Also

Boolean Data Type, **Byte** Data Type, **Currency** Data Type, **Date** Data Type, **Def***type* Statements, **Double** Data Type, **Integer** Data Type, **Long** Data Type, **Object** Data Type, **Single** Data Type, **String** Data Type, **Type** Statement, User-Defined Data Type, **Variant** Data Type.

Comparison of Data Types

The Microsoft Jet database engine recognizes several overlapping sets of data types; which data type you use depends on whether or not you're writing code in Visual Basic or in one of the Microsoft Access development contexts. In Microsoft Access, there are four different contexts, each with its own set of data types—a table's Design view, the Query Parameters dialog box, Access Basic, and a query's SQL view. See online Help in Microsoft Access for more information on these contexts.

The following table compares the four sets of data types that correspond to each context. The first column lists the **Type** property settings available in a table's Design view and the five **FieldSize** property settings for the Number data type. The second column lists the data types for designing parameter queries that are available in the Query Parameters dialog box. The third column lists the Visual Basic data types. The fourth column lists the Microsoft Access SQL data types defined by the Jet engine along with their valid synonyms.

Table fields	Query parameters	Visual Basic	Microsoft Access SQL and synonyms
Not supported	Binary	Not supported	BINARY (See Notes) VARBINARY
Yes/No	Yes/No	Integer	BIT BOOLEAN, LOGICAL, LOGICAL1, YESNO

(continued)

Table fields	Query parameters	Visual Basic	Microsoft Access SQL and synonyms
Number; Size = Byte	Byte	Integer	BYTE INTEGER1
Counter	Not supported	Long	COUNTER AUTOINCREMENT
Currency	Currency	Currency	CURRENCY MONEY
Date/Time	Date/Time	Variant (See Notes)	DATETIME DATE, TIME, TIMESTAMP
Number; Size = Single	Single	Single	SINGLE, FLOAT4, IEEESINGLE, REAL
Number; Size = Double	Double	Double	DOUBLE FLOAT, FLOAT8, IEEEDOUBLE, NUMBER, NUMERIC
Number; Size = Integer	Integer (See Notes)	Integer (See Notes)	SHORT, INTEGER2, SMALLINT
Number; Size = Long Integer	Long Integer	Long	LONG (See Notes) INT, INTEGER, INTEGER4
OLE Object	OLE Object	String	LONGBINARY GENERAL, OLEOBJECT
Memo	Memo	String	LONGTEXT LONGCHAR, MEMO, NOTE
Text	Text	String	TEXT ALPHANUMERIC, CHAR, CHARACTER, STRING, VARCHAR
Not supported	Value	Variant	VALUE (See Notes)

Notes The Jet engine itself doesn't use the BINARY data type. It's recognized only for use in queries on attached tables from other database products that support the BINARY data type.

If you want to declare a Visual Basic variable that contains date/time information, declare it as a **Variant**. If you create a Date/Time table field in SQL view or in a table's Design view using Microsoft Access, check the field's **Type** property in Visual Basic; the returned integer constant corresponds to the constant **dbDate** (defined by the Jet engine) instead of the

Variant date constant **vbDate**. The variable types represented by these two constants are fully compatible, however, and no type mismatch error will occur if a **Variant** variable contains data from a Date/Time field in a Jet engine table or query.

The **Integer** data type in Jet engine SQL doesn't correspond to the **Integer** data type for table fields, query parameters, or Visual Basic. Instead, in Jet engine SQL, **Integer** corresponds to a Long Integer for table fields and query parameters and to a **Long** data type in Visual Basic.

The VALUE reserved word doesn't represent a data type defined by the Jet database engine. However, in Microsoft Access or SQL queries, VALUE can be considered a valid synonym for the Visual Basic **Variant** data type.

See Also

Equivalent ANSI SQL Data Types, Microsoft Jet Database Engine SQL Data Types, Microsoft Jet Database Engine SQL Reserved Words, **Type** Property, Visual Basic Data Types.

Note   Arrays of any data type require 20 bytes of memory plus four bytes for each array dimension plus the number of bytes occupied by the data itself. The memory occupied by the data can be calculated by multiplying the number of data elements by the size of each element. For example, the data in a single-dimension array consisting of four **Integer** data elements of two bytes each occupies eight bytes. The eight bytes the data requires plus the 24 bytes of overhead brings the total memory requirement for the array to 32 bytes.

A **Variant** containing an array requires 12 bytes more than the array alone.

See Also

Boolean Data Type, **Byte** Data Type, **Currency** Data Type, **Date** Data Type, **Def***type* Statements, **Double** Data Type, **Integer** Data Type, **Long** Data Type, **Object** Data Type, **Single** Data Type, **String** Data Type, **Type** Statement, **User-Defined Data Type**, **Variant** Data Type.

Equivalent ANSI SQL Data Types

The following table lists ANSI SQL data types and the equivalent Microsoft Jet database engine SQL data types and their valid synonyms.

ANSI SQL data type	Jet engine SQL data type	Synonym
BIT, BIT VARYING	BINARY (See Notes)	VARBINARY
Not supported	BIT (See Notes)	BOOLEAN, LOGICAL, LOGICAL1, YESNO
Not supported	BYTE	INTEGER1

(continued)

ANSI SQL data type	Jet engine SQL data type	Synonym
Not supported	COUNTER	AUTOINCREMENT
Not supported	CURRENCY	MONEY
DATE, TIME, TIMESTAMP	DATETIME	DATE, TIME, TIMESTAMP
DECIMAL	Not supported	
REAL	SINGLE	FLOAT4, IEEESINGLE, REAL
DOUBLE PRECISION, FLOAT	DOUBLE	FLOAT, FLOAT8, IEEEDOUBLE, NUMBER, NUMERIC
SMALLINT	SHORT	INTEGER2, SMALLINT
INTEGER	LONG	INT, INTEGER, INTEGER4
INTERVAL	Not supported	
Not supported	LONGBINARY	GENERAL, OLEOBJECT
Not supported	LONGTEXT	LONGCHAR, MEMO, NOTE
CHARACTER, CHARACTER VARYING	TEXT	ALPHANUMERIC, CHAR, CHARACTER, STRING, VARCHAR
Not supported	VALUE (See Notes)	

Notes The ANSI SQL BIT data type doesn't correspond to the Jet engine SQL BIT data type, but it corresponds to the BINARY data type instead. There is no ANSI SQL equivalent for the Jet engine SQL BIT data type.

The BINARY data type is recognized only for use in queries on attached tables from other database products that support the BINARY data type.

The VALUE reserved word doesn't represent a data type defined by the Jet engine. However, in Microsoft Access or SQL queries, VALUE can be considered a valid synonym for the Visual Basic **Variant** data type.

See Also

Comparison of Data Types, Microsoft Jet Database Engine SQL Data Types.

Microsoft Jet Database Engine SQL Data Types

The Microsoft Jet engine SQL data types consist of 13 primary data types defined by the Microsoft Jet database engine and several valid synonyms recognized for these data types.

The following table lists the primary data types. The synonyms are identified in the Comparison of Data Types and Jet Database Engine SQL Reserved Words topics.

Data type	Storage size	Description
BINARY	1 byte	For queries on attached tables from database products that define a Binary data type.
BIT	1 byte	Yes and No values and fields that contain only one of two values.
BYTE	1 byte	An integer value between 0 and 255.
COUNTER	4 bytes	A number automatically incremented by the Jet engine whenever a new record is added to a table. In the Jet engine, the data type for this value is a **Long**.
CURRENCY	8 bytes	A scaled integer between -922,337,203,685,477.5808 and 922,337,203,685,477.5807.
DATETIME (See DOUBLE)	8 bytes	A date or time value between the years 100 and 9999.
SINGLE	4 bytes	A single-precision floating-point value with a range of -3.402823E38 to -1.401298E-45 for negative values, 1.401298E-45 to 3.402823E38 for positive values, and 0.
DOUBLE	8 bytes	A single-precision floating-point value with a range of -1.79769313486232E308 to -4.94065645841247E-324 for negative values, 4.94065645841247E-324 to 1.79769313486232E308 for positive values, and 0.
SHORT	2 bytes	A short integer between -32,768 and 32,767.
LONG	4 bytes	A long integer between -2,147,483,648 and 2,147,483,647.
LONGTEXT	1 byte per character	Zero to a maximum of 1.2 gigabytes.

(continued)

Data type	Storage size	Description
LONGBINARY	As required	Zero to a maximum of approximately 1 gigabyte. Used for OLE objects.
TEXT	1 byte per character	Zero to 255 characters.

Note You can also use the VALUE reserved word in SQL statements. Although it doesn't represent a data type defined by the Jet database engine, VALUE can be considered a valid synonym for the Microsoft Visual Basic **Variant** data type.

See Also

Comparison of Data Types, **DataType** Property, Equivalent ANSI SQL Data Types, **FieldSize** Property, Microsoft Jet Database Engine SQL Reserved Words, Visual Basic Data Types.

Boolean Data Type

Boolean variables are stored as 16-bit (2-byte) numbers, but they can only be **True** or **False**. **Boolean** variables display as either True or False (when **Print** is used) or #TRUE# or #FALSE# (when **Write #** is used). Use the keywords **True** and **False** to assign one of the two states to **Boolean** variables.

When other numeric data types are converted to **Boolean** values, 0 becomes **False** while all other values become **True**. When **Boolean** values are converted to other data types, **False** becomes 0 while **True** becomes -1.

See Also

CBool Function, Data Type Summary, **Def***type* Statements, **Integer** Data Type.

Byte Data Type

Byte variables are stored as single, unsigned, 8-bit (1-byte) ranging in value from 0 to 255.

The **Byte** data type is useful for containing binary data that can be passed to and from dynamic link libraries (DLL) and OLE Automation objects.

See Also

CByte Function, Data Type Summary, **Def***type* Statements, **Integer** Data Type.

Currency Data Type

Currency variables are stored as 64-bit (8-byte) numbers in an integer format, scaled by 10,000 to give a fixed-point number with 15 digits to the left of the decimal point and 4 digits to the right. This representation provides a range of -922,337,203,685,477.5808 to 922,337,203,685,477.5807. The type-declaration character for **Currency** is @.

The **Currency** data type is useful for calculations involving money and for fixed-point calculations in which accuracy is particularly important.

See Also

    CCur Function, Data Type Summary, **Def**_type_ Statements, **Long** Data Type.

Date Data Type

Date variables are stored as IEEE 64-bit (8-byte) floating-point numbers that represent dates ranging from 1 January 100 to 31 December 9999 and times from 0:00:00 to 23:59:59. Any recognizable literal date values can be assigned to **Date** variables. Literal dates must be enclosed within number sign characters (#), for example, #January 1, 1993# or #1 Jan 93#.

Date variables display dates according to the short date format recognized by your computer. Times display according to the time format (either 12- or 24-hour) recognized by your computer.

When other numeric data types are converted to **Date**, values to the left of the decimal represent date information while values to the right of the decimal represent time. Midnight is 0 and midday is .5. Negative whole numbers represent dates before 30 December 1899.

See Also

    CDate Function, Data Type Summary, **Def**_type_ Statements, **Double** Data Type, **Variant** Data Type.

Decimal Data Type

Decimal variables are stored as 96-bit (12-byte) unsigned integers scaled by a variable power of 10. The power of 10 scaling factor specifies the number of digits to the right of the decimal point, and ranges from 0 to 28. With a scale of 0 (no decimal places), the largest possible value is +/-79,228,162,514,264,337,593,543,950,335. With 28 decimal places, the largest value is +/-7.9228162514264337593543950335 and the smallest, non-zero value is +/-0.0000000000000000000000000001.

At this time the **Decimal** data type can only be used within a **Variant**, that is, you cannot declare a variable to be of type **Decimal**. You can, however, create a **Variant** whose subtype is **Decimal** using the **CDec** function.

See Also

Data Type Summary.

Double Data Type

Double(double-precision floating-point) variables are stored as IEEE 64-bit (8-byte) floating-point numbers ranging in value from -1.79769313486232E308 to -4.94065645841247E-324 for negative values and from 4.94065645841247E-324 to 1.79769313486232E308 for positive values. The type-declaration character for **Double** is #.

See Also

CDbl Function, Data Type Summary, **Def***type* Statements, **Single** Data Type.

Integer Data Type

Integer variables are stored as 16-bit (2-byte) numbers ranging in value from -32,768 to 32,767. The type-declaration character for **Integer** is %.

You can also use **Integer** variables to represent enumerated values. An enumerated value can contain a finite set of unique whole numbers, each of which has special meaning in the context in which it is used. Enumerated values provide a convenient way to select among a known number of choices. For example, when asking the user to select a color from a list, you could have black = 0, white = 1, and so on. It is good programming practice to define constants using the **Const** statement for each enumerated value.

See Also

CInt Function, Data Type Summary, **Def***type* Statements, **Long** Data Type, **Variant** Data Type.

Long Data Type

Long (long integer) variables are stored as signed 32-bit (4-byte) numbers ranging in value from -2,147,483,648 to 2,147,483,647. The type-declaration character for **Long** is &.

See Also

CLng Function, Data Type Summary, **Def***type* Statements, **Integer** Data Type.

Object Data Type

Object variables are stored as 32-bit (4-byte) addresses that refer to OLE Automation objects within an application. A variable declared as an **Object** is one that can subsequently be assigned (using the **Set** statement) to refer to any object produced by the application.

See Also

Data Type Summary, **Def***type* Statements, **IsObject** Function, **Variant** Data Type.

Single Data Type

Single (single-precision floating-point) variables are stored as IEEE 32-bit (4-byte) floating-point numbers, ranging in value from -3.402823E38 to -1.401298E-45 for negative values and from 1.401298E-45 to 3.402823E38 for positive values. The type-declaration character for **Single** is **!**.

See Also

CSng Function, Data Type Summary, **Def***type* Statements, **Double** Data Type, **Variant** Data Type.

String Data Type

There are two kinds of strings:

- Variable-length strings, which can contain up to approximately 2 billion (2^{31}) characters (approximately 64K (2^{16}) characters for Microsoft Windows version 3.1 and earlier).

- Fixed-length strings, which can contain 1 to approximately 64K (2^{16}) characters.

Note **Public** fixed-length strings can't be used in class modules.

The type-declaration character for **String** is **$**. The codes for **String** characters range from 0 to 255. The first 128 characters (0–127) of the character set correspond to the letters and symbols on a standard U.S. keyboard. These first 128 characters are the same as those defined by the ASCII character set. The second 128 characters (128–255) represent special characters, such as letters in international alphabets, accents, currency symbols, and fractions.

See Also

CStr Function, Data Type Summary, **Def***type* Statements, **String** Function, **Variant** Data Type.

User-Defined Data Type

Any data type you define using the **Type** statement. User-defined data types can contain one or more elements of any data type, array, or a previously defined user-defined type. For example:

```
Type MyType
    MyName As String'' 180.' String variable stores a name.
    MyBirthDate As Date ' Date variable stores a birthdate.
    MySex As Integer' Integer variable stores sex (0 for
End Type' female, 1 for male).
```

See Also

Data Type Summary, **Type** Statement.

Variant Data Type

The **Variant** data type is the data type that all variables become if not explicitly declared as some other type (using statements such as **Dim**, **Private**, **Public**, or **Static**). The **Variant** data type has no type-declaration character.

The **Variant** is a special data type that can contain any kind of data except fixed-length **String** data and user-defined types. A **Variant** can also contain the special values **Empty**, **Error**, **Nothing**, and **Null**. You can determine how the data in a **Variant** is treated using the **VarType** or **TypeName** function.

Numeric data can be any integer or real number value ranging from -1.797693134862315E308 to -4.94066E-324 for negative values and from 4.94066E-324 to 1.797693134862315E308 for positive values. Generally, numeric **Variant** data is maintained in its original data type within the **Variant**. For example, if you assign an **Integer** to a **Variant**, subsequent operations treat the **Variant** as if it were an **Integer**. However, if an arithmetic operation is performed on a **Variant** containing a **Byte**, an **Integer**, a **Long**, or a **Single**, and the result exceeds the normal range for the original data type, the result is promoted within the **Variant** to the next larger data type. A **Byte** is promoted to an **Integer**, an **Integer** is promoted to a **Long**, and a **Long** and a **Single** are promoted to a **Double**. An error occurs when **Variant** variables containing **Currency** and **Double** values exceed their respective ranges.

You can use the **Variant** data type in place of any data type to work with data in a more flexible way. If the contents of a **Variant** variable are digits, they may be either the string representation of the digits or their actual value, depending on the context. For example:

```
Dim MyVar As Variant
MyVar = 98052
```

In the example shown above, MyVar contains a numeric representation—the actual value 98052. Arithmetic operators work as expected on **Variant** variables that contain numeric values or string data that can be interpreted as numbers. If you use the + operator to add MyVar to another **Variant** containing a number or to a variable of a numeric data type, the result is an arithmetic sum. See the information about addition and concatenation operators for complete information on how to use them with **Variant** data.

The value **Empty** denotes a **Variant** variable that hasn't been initialized (assigned an initial value). A **Variant** containing **Empty** is 0 if it is used in a numeric context and a zero-length string ("") if it is used in a string context.

Don't confuse **Empty** with **Null**. **Null** indicates that the **Variant** variable intentionally contains no valid data.

In a **Variant**, **Error** is a special value used to indicate that an error condition has occurred in a procedure. However, unlike for other kinds of errors, normal application-level error handling does not occur. This allows you, or the application itself, to take some alternative based on the error value. **Error** values are created by converting real numbers to error values using the **CVErr** function.

See Also

CVar Function, **CVErr** Function, Data Type Summary, **Def***type* Statements, **Dim** Statement, **Nothing** Keyword, Operator Summary, **Private** Statement, **Public** Statement, **Static** Statement, **TypeName** Function, **VarType** Function.

Operators

When several operations occur in an expression, each part is evaluated and resolved in a predetermined order. That order is known as operator precedence. Parentheses can be used to override the order of precedence and force some parts of an expression to be evaluated before others. Operations within parentheses are always performed before those outside. Within parentheses, however, normal operator precedence is maintained.

When expressions contain operators from more than one category, arithmetic operators are evaluated first, comparison operators are evaluated next, and logical operators are evaluated last. Comparison operators all have equal precedence; that is, they are evaluated in the left to right order in which they appear. Arithmetic and logical operators are evaluated in the following order of precedence:

Arithmetic	Comparison	Logical
Exponentiation (^)	Equality (=)	**Not**
Negation (-)'	Inequality (<>)	**And**
Multiplication and division (*,/)	Less than (<)	**Or**
Integer division (\)	Greater than (>)	**Xor**
Modulo arithmetic (**Mod**)	Less than or Equal to (<=)	**Eqv**
Addition and subtraction (+,-)	Greater than or Equal to (>=)	**Imp**
String concatenation (**&**)	**Like**	
	Is	

When multiplication and division occur together in an expression, each operation is evaluated as it occurs from left to right. Likewise, when addition and subtraction occur together in an expression, each operation is evaluated in order of appearance from left to right.

The string concatenation operator (**&**) is not an arithmetic operator, but in precedence it does fall after all arithmetic operators and before all comparison operators. Similarly, the **Like** operator, while equal in precedence to all comparison operators, is actually a pattern-matching operator. The **Is** operator is an object reference comparison operator. It does not compare objects or their values; it checks only to determine if two object references refer to the same object.

Information on specific operators is ncluded in the A-Z reference. The following table summarizes the oerators available in Visual Basic.

Operator	Description
^	Used to raise a number to the power of an exponent.
+	Used to sum two numbers.
-	Used to find the difference between two numbers or to indicate the negative value of a numeric expression.
*	Used to multiply two numbers.
/	Used to divide two numbers and return a floating-point result.
\	Used to divide two numbers and return an integer result.
&	Used to force string concatenation of two expressions.
<	Less than (comparison operator).
<=	Less than or equal to (comparison operator).
>	Greater than.
>=	Greater than or equal to (comparison operator).
=	Equal to (comparison operator).
<>	Not equal to (comparison operator).
And	Used to perform a logical conjunction on two expressions.
Eqv	Used to perform a logical equivalence on two expressions.
Imp	Used to perform a logical equivalence on two expressions.
Is	Used to compare two object reference variables.
Like	Used to compare two strings.
Mod	Used to divide two numbers and return only the remainder.
Not	Used to perform logical negation on an expression.
Or	Used to perform a logical disjunction on two expressions.
Xor	Used to perform a logical exclusion on two expressions.

See Also

Is Operator, **Like** Operator.

Arithmetic Operators

^ Operator	* Operator	/ Operator
\ Operator	**Mod** Operator	+ Operator
- Operator		

Concatenation Operators

& Operator	+ Operator

Logical Operators

And Operator	**Eqv** Operator	**Imp** Operator
Not Operator	**Or** Operator	**Xor** Operator

Derived Math Functions

The following is a list of non-intrinsic mathematical functions that can be derived from the intrinsic math functions provided with Visual Basic.

Table D.1   Derived Math Functions

Function	Derived equivalents
Secant	$Sec(X) = 1 / Cos(X)$
Cosecant	$Cosec(X) = 1 / Sin(X)$
Cotangent	$Cotan(X) = 1 / Tan(X)$
Inverse Sine	$Arcsin(X) = Atn(X / Sqr(-X * X + 1))$
Inverse Cosine	$Arccos(X) = Atn(-X / Sqr(-X * X + 1)) + 2 * Atn(1)$
Inverse Secant	$Arcsec(X) = Atn(X / Sqr(X * X - 1)) + Sgn((X) -1) * (2 * Atn(1))$
Inverse Cosecant	$Arccosec(X) = Atn(X / Sqr(X * X - 1)) + (Sgn(X) - 1) * (2 * Atn(1))$
Inverse Cotangent	$Arccotan(X) = Atn(X) + 2 * Atn(1)$
Hyperbolic Sine	$HSin(X) = (Exp(X) - Exp(-X)) / 2$
Hyperbolic Cosine	$HCos(X) = (Exp(X) + Exp(-X)) / 2$
Hyperbolic Tangent	$HTan(X) = (Exp(X) - Exp(-X)) / (Exp(X) + Exp(-X))$
Hyperbolic Secant	$HSec(X) = 2 / (Exp(X) + Exp(-X))$
Hyperbolic Cosecant	$HCosec(X) = 2 / (Exp(X) - Exp(-X))$
Hyperbolic Cotangent	$HCotan(X) = (Exp(X) + Exp(-X)) / (Exp(X) - Exp(-X))$
Inverse Hyperbolic Sine	$HArcsin(X) = Log(X + Sqr(X * X + 1))$
Inverse Hyperbolic Cosine	$HArccos(X) = Log(X + Sqr(X * X - 1))$
Inverse Hyperbolic Tangent	$HArctan(X) = Log((1 + X) / (1 - X)) / 2$
Inverse Hyperbolic Secant	$HArcsec(X) = Log((Sqr(-X * X + 1) + 1) / X)$
Inverse Hyperbolic Cosecant	$HArccosec(X) = Log((Sgn(X) * Sqr(X * X + 1) +1) / X)$
Inverse Hyperbolic Cotangent	$HArccotan(X) = Log((X + 1) / (X - 1)) / 2$
Logarithm to base N	$LogN(X) = Log(X) / Log(N)$

See Also

Atn Function, **Cos** Function, **Exp** Function, **Log** Function, **Sin** Function, **Sqr** Function, **Tan** Function.

Register Today!

Return this
Microsoft® Visual Basic® 5.0 Language Reference
registration card for
a Microsoft Press® catalog

U.S. and Canada addresses only. Fill in information below and mail postage-free. Please mail only the bottom half of this page.

1-57231-507-5A   ***MICROSOFT® VISUAL BASIC® 5.0***   *Owner Registration Card*
                        LANGUAGE REFERENCE

NAME

INSTITUTION OR COMPANY NAME

ADDRESS

CITY   STATE   ZIP

Microsoft *Press*
Quality Computer Books

**For a free catalog of
Microsoft Press® products, call
1-800-MSPRESS**